ARCHITECTURAL DRAWING

ARCHITECTURAL DRAWING

A Visual Compendium of Types and Methods

Third Edition

Rendow Yee

JOHN WILEY & SONS, INC.

This book is printed on acid-free paper. ♾

Published by John Wiley & Sons, Inc., Hoboken, New Jersey
Published simultaneously in Canada

For general information about our other products and services, please contact our Customer Care Department within the United States at (800) 762-2974, outside the United States at (317) 572-3993 or fax (317) 572-4002.

Wiley also publishes its books in a variety of electronic formats. Some content that appears in print may not be available in electronic books. For more information about Wiley products, visit our Web site at www.wiley.com.

Library of Congress Cataloging-in-Publication Data:

Yee, Rendow.
Architectural drawing : a visual compendium of types and methods / RendowYee.— 3rd ed.
p. cm.
Includes bibliographical references and index.
SBN 978-0-471-79366-3 (pbk.)
1. Architectural drawing—Technique. I. Title.
NA2708.Y439 2007
720.28'4— dc22

2007001695

Printed in the United States of America

10 9 8 7 6 5 4 3 2 1

Dedicated to each student studying this book

past and present —

Always a source of insightful and innovative ideas.

To my parents —

Always a source for inspiration.

Contents

PREFACE TO THE THIRD EDITION ix

PREFACE TO THE SECOND EDITION x

PREFACE TO THE FIRST EDITION xii

1 TOOL FUNDAMENTALS 1

2 LETTERING, TYPOGRAPHY, AND LINE TYPES 23

3 REPRESENTATIONAL SKETCHING 39
- Basics 41
- Basics Applied 56

4 CONVENTIONAL ORTHOGONAL TERMINOLOGY 85
- Basics 87
- Basics Applied 90

5 ORTHOGRAPHIC AND PARALINE DRAWING 113
- Basics 115
- Basics Applied 136

6 LINEAR PERSPECTIVE DRAWING 181
- Basics 183
- Basics Applied 212

7 LIGHT, SHADE, AND SHADOW 305
- Basics 307
- Basics Applied 334

8 DELINEATING AND RENDERING ENTOURAGE 367
Basics 369
Basics Applied 380

9 DIAGRAMMING AND CONCEPTUAL SKETCHING 427
Basics 429
Basics Applied 444

10 PRESENTATION FORMATS 489
Basics 491
Basics Applied 502

EPILOGUE 571

DRAWING EXERCISES 573
Level One 575
Level Two 624

BIBLIOGRAPHY 655

ABOUT THE AUTHOR 657

SUBJECT INDEX 659

CONTRIBUTOR INDEX 668

WEB SITE CONTRIBUTOR INDEX 672

CONTENTS OF COMPANION WEB SITE (www.wiley.com/go/yee)

11 CONVENTIONAL AND COMPUTERIZED REPRESENTATION IN COLOR

12 INTERFACING MANUAL WITH DIGITAL MEDIA:
Professional Office Example: Case Study of Architect Antoine Predock

13 INTERFACING MANUAL WITH DIGITAL MEDIA:
Academic Studio Examples

APPENDIX
Basic Geometric Definitions
Descriptive Geometry Principles Summarized
Notes on the Perspective Measuring Point System

SOLUTIONS FOR INSTRUCTORS (password protected)

Preface to the Third Edition

The third edition introduces hierarchy to make the book easier to use and its information more accessible. The hierarchical table of contents, for example, allows readers to reference the most salient topics quickly. Structural hierarchy within each chapter is based on two stages: **BASICS** and **BASICS APPLIED.** *Basics* incorporates fundamental elements such as theory, definitions, principles, and concepts. *Basics applied* provides step-by-step how-to applications, along with student and professional examples.

The third edition has also expanded the content in the companion Web site. In addition to the initial second-edition Web site chapter titled "Conventional and Computerized Representation in Color," two new chapters—and an appendix—have been added. The chapters are titled "Interfacing Manual with Digital: Professional Office Example" and "Interfacing Manual with Digital: Academic Studio Examples." The interfacing chapters show projects that integrate manual with digital methods. The appendix offers a brief review of geometric definitions and some important principles of descriptive geometry.

I would especially like to thank Professor William Chan of Morgan State University, who was so gracious in donating his time to review most of the chapters as well as the companion Web site in the second edition. I also appreciate the comments on specific pages by Professors Dick Davison of Texas A&M and Arpad Daniel Ronaszegi of the Savannah College of Art and Design. Finally, I would like to acknowledge the assistance of Tina Chau, Chalina Chen, and Susan Wu.

Acknowledgments

Professor William W. P. Chan, Morgan State University (Baltimore, Maryland)
Professor Mariana Donoso, University of Chile (Santiago)
Yu Jordy Fu, architecture graduate, Royal Academy of Art (London)
Professor Michael Hagge, University of Memphis (Tennessee)
Susan Hedges, CAS, Support Manager, University of Auckland (New Zealand)
Professor Andreas Luescher, Bowling Green State University (Ohio)
Dr. Yasser Mahgoub, Kuwait University
Professor LaRaine Papa Montgomery, Savannah College of Art and Design (Georgia)
Professor Marcela Pizzi, University of Chile (Santiago)
Professor Arpad Daniel Ronaszegi, Savannah College of Art and Design (Georgia)
Professor Richard H. Shiga, Portland State University (Oregon)
Professor Andrew Tripp, The Cooper Union (New York City)
Professor Joan Waltemath, The Cooper Union

Preface to the Second Edition

There are two important new features in the second edition. The first feature is the addition of a drawing and drafting exercises section at the end of the book. This will allow professors of architectural graphics and design communications to glean ideas for formulating fundamental drawing/drafting exercises to suit their own classes.

The second feature is a supplementary Web site chapter, "Conventional and Computerized Representation in Color," which can be found at www.wiley.com/go/yee. This overview chapter covers traditional color media such as watercolor, gouache, pastels, colored pencil, markers, airbrush, and mixed media. Various aspects of the potential of digital media are also discussed. In addition, typical student and professional solutions for the many drawing exercises in the textbook are shown on the Web site. These solutions are available to course instructors upon request at www.wiley.com/go/yee or by contacting your local Wiley college representative for details.

Finally, the topics of diagramming and conceptual sketching have been condensed into a single chapter with more explanatory text, and the chapter on presentation formats has been expanded to include professional competition drawings from notable offices.

Acknowledgments

I am very grateful for three insightful critiques of the first edition. All chapters were reviewed by Professors Dick Davison and Stephen Temple; and Professor Owen Cappleman reviewed the chapter on diagramming and conceptual sketching, as well as the Web site chapter. I would also like to express my gratitude to all of the office professionals who contributed work in a very timely manner. In addition, I am deeply indebted to the strong support team from educational institutions that supplied me with exceptional examples of drawing exercises. A warm thanks to the following architecture schools and professors who contributed projects:

Dr. Samer Akkach, Adelaide University (South Australia)
Professor Jonathan Brandt, Texas A&M University
Professor Owen Cappleman, University of Texas at Austin
Professor Rich Correa, Yuba College (California)
Professor Dick Davison, Texas A&M University
Professors Hank Dunlop and Mark Jensen, California College of Arts and Crafts
Professor Jane Grealy, Queensland University of Technology (Australia)
Professor Bob Hansman, Washington University in St. Louis (Missouri)
Professor Patrick Houlihan, California College of Arts and Crafts
Professor Chang-Shan Huang, Texas A&M University
Professor Karen Kensek, University of Southern California
Professor George S. Loli, University of Louisiana–Lafayette
Professor Fernando Magallanes, North Carolina State University
Professor David Matthews, Ohio University
Professor Valerian Miranda, Texas A&M University

Professor Dan Mullin, University of Idaho
Professor Douglas Noble, University of Southern California
Professor Arpad D. Ronaszegi, Andrews University (Michigan)
Professor M. Beth Tauke, State University of New York at Buffalo
Professor Stephen Temple, University of Texas at San Antonio
Professor Thomas L. Turman, Laney College (California)
Professor Mohammed Saleh Uddin, University of Missouri–Columbia

A special thanks to the following people who assisted me: Justin Ip, Brian W. Quan, Felix Ma, Lawrence Mak, Corvin Matei, and Hedy Hing Yee. I am very grateful for my superb editorial production team at John Wiley and Sons. Especially notable is the hard work and help I got from my editor, Margaret Cummins. She was always there to answer any questions I had. I also appreciate the coordination work of her editorial assistants, Kim Aleski and Rosanne Koneval. Finally, I would like to commend the fine work of the managing editor, David Sassian, and the copy editor, Lisa Story.

Preface to the First Edition

In the visual world of design education and the design professions, message (design) and language (graphics) are so interrelated that they cannot be separated. The design process always includes graphic skills to clarify and communicate the issues in question. This book's goal is to communicate a broad range of design-drawing methods; it is not intended to be a handbook on acquiring design skills.

People learn to communicate through language at an early age. They learn to speak, read, and write. The primary type of communication in any kind of design work, whether fashion or building, is drawing. To communicate our design ideas to others, we must learn how to draw. We must draw with enough facility to make our ideas clear. Furthermore, we need to be able to communicate graphic ideas to ourselves because, as we work on any design, our ideas are constantly changing and evolving.

The language of graphics requires the use of all aspects of the brain — analytical, intuitive, synthetic, and even emotional. The intent of this primer is to provide students and practitioners with graphic tools essential to visual communication methods in the design process. It will reinforce methods of perceiving existing reality in order to create an awareness of the visual world. It will also develop and build confidence in one's analytical and intuitive graphic skills and abilities.

It is quite common to find students with a wide range of backgrounds in drawing upon entering a beginning course in architectural drawing/graphics; some students may have had numerous courses in middle school and high school mechanical drawing and art; other students have never used or been exposed to drafting or sketching equipment. There are also students who show a strong potential on aptitude tests related to spatial visualization; but, for one reason or another, they have never had an opportunity to develop this potential. This book can be used by those who have little knowledge of geometry or basic mathematics. However, it is also designed for intermediate and advanced students in architectural drawing. Students and practitioners with a prior knowledge of pictorial drawing or perspective will find this book to be a convenient reference guide for presentation work.

The first four chapters, including "Representational Sketching," are basic to the study of architectural graphics and provide the necessary framework to pursue the major areas of two- and three-dimensional pictorial drawings. The chapters on paralines, perspectives, and shadows illustrate the most common manual methods in current practice with detailed but simple explanations on the theory behind their use. The use of these procedures will help both the student and the professional in communicating and presenting design ideas. The remainder of the book is devoted to a brief introduction to the topics described by chapter titles "Delineating and Rendering Entourage," "Diagramming and Conceptual Sketching," and "Presentation Formats." The variety of drawings illustrates a large number of diverse styles; and the medium used, the original size, and the scale used (if applicable) are given for each drawing where this information was available. In this sense, the book acts as a springboard to stimulate readers to explore each topic in more detail by investigating the extensive bibliography. Many of the images included are residential building types, but a large variety of other building types are shown as well. In view of today's global culture, many drawing exhibits from outside the United States are also included.

This comprehensive guide attempts to elaborate equally on each of the architectural design-drawing methods in current use. However, the last quarter of the twentieth century has seen an upsurge in the use of paraline drawings. This is due to their ease of construction and their impressive ability to allow the viewer to see and to comprehend the total composition of a design. For this reason, a large number of professional paraline examples are included. Architecture and other design professions have been expanding their expressive vocabulary to include the emerging methods of three-dimensional computer imaging, animation, film, and video. This visual compendium of diverse graphic images done in a variety of both traditional and avant-garde media is rich in its content. Many illustrations are supported by personal commentary from their originators to help shed light on why each type of drawing was chosen to express the design.

Both students and design professionals are continually striving to come up with new ways to represent and express their designs. The graphic image examples that I have chosen are by no means exhaustive. These examples are meant to extend basic techniques that the students learn to a more advanced level as well as to provoke their imagination. They are not meant to dogmatically lead students onto a narrow path of particular styles or "isms"; instead, their goal is to encourage students to start their own journey of discovery and exploration.

As a reference for precise graphic constructions the book is laid out in a simple, easy-to-follow, step-by-step format. Although mechanically constructed pictorials are emphasized, freehand visualization techniques are encouraged. Most architectural schools have courses covering architectural design-drawing in a time frame from one to three semesters. In many cases the material is covered as an adjunct to the design-drawing studio. This book can be used under any kind of flexible time schedule as a student text or a studio reference, or as an office reference for practitioners. The encyclopedic nature of the book encourages browsing and wandering. For ease of reference, design-drawing types have been categorized in such a way that both students and design professionals will find them handy for reviewing design-drawing methods or for obtaining and extrapolating ideas for their own creative presentation compositions.

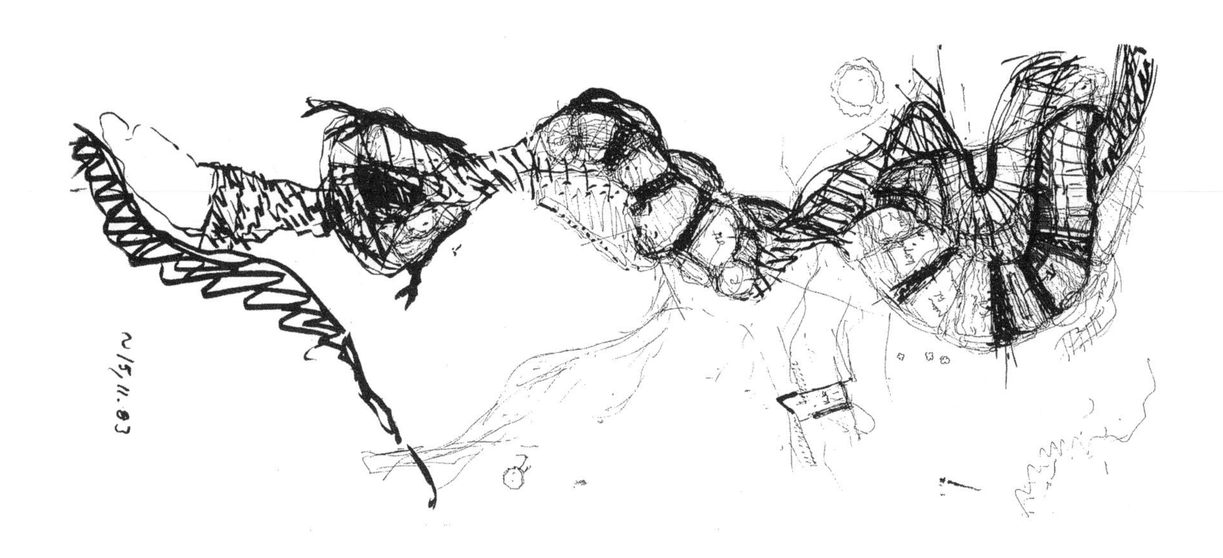

Plan sketch diagrams: Mica Moriane, Official residence of the President of Finland
Mäntyniemi, Helsinki, Finland
Medium: Color felt pens
Courtesy of Raili and Reima Pietilä, Architects

Acknowledgments

This book on architectural drawing developed from an expression of need over many semesters by the architecture faculty and the students enrolled in the basic architectural drawing course at the City College of San Francisco.

I would like to express my gratitude to my fellow staff members in architecture, Lawrence J. Franceschina, Ernest E. Lee, Enrique Limosner, and the late Gordon Phillips, without whose help and advice the realization of this textbook would not have been possible. Gordon gave me the necessary encouragement during the early stages of this book. In particular, I would like to recognize Ernest E. Lee, who along with Julian D. Munoz reviewed the book in its preliminary format. The latest edition is a result of continual revisions derived from frequent consultations with colleagues:

Robin Chiang	Norman C. Hall	Harry Leong	Curtis Poon
Alexander Diefenbach	Robert L. Hamilton	Pershing C. Lin	Nestor Regino
Jim Dierkes	Patrick Houlihan	Jerry W. Lum	Will S. Revilock
Olallo L. Fernandez	Spencer Jue	Ryszard Pochron	Russell Wong

A word of special thanks to Bernard Kuan for endless hours of typing the preliminary manuscript, and to Tony Ho and Winnie Chun for endless hours of pasteup work. I have always appreciated ideas and feedback from my students. A note of special appreciation goes to the following group of students who assisted me in small but significant ways:

Henry Beltran	Randy Furuta	Wilson Lee	Ann-Marie Ratkovits
Ed Broas	Randa Fushimi	Clarissa Leong	Suheil Shatara
Woo Sok Cha	Dennis Hodges	Hedy Mak	Lily Shen
Jason Chan	James Ke	Amos Malkin	Carl Stensel
Keng Chung	Andrew Kong	Amy Man	Nguyen N. Trong
Ken Cozine	Kenneth Lau	Corvin Matei	Kwok Gorran Tsui
Fred Dea	Albert Lee	Henry Ng	Kam Wong

I am deeply grateful to *Architectural Record* and *Progressive Architecture* magazines for giving me permission to reprint many drawings that were originally published in these magazines. Other magazines that I used as rich sources for graphic images were *GA Houses, GA Document International,* and *World Architecture.* Numerous illustrations are from student work contributed by various schools of architecture. Those contributing included Washington University in St. Louis, the University of Texas at Arlington, the University of Texas at Austin, Savannah College of Art and Design, Southern University, Columbia University, the University of Virginia, Cal Poly San Luis Obispo, the Catholic University of America, the University of Maryland, Texas A&M University, Andrews University, and the City College of San Francisco.

Initial exposure to drawing and drafting came from my father, the late Rodney Shue Yee. Kindled interest in the field of architectural drawing techniques came from two former professors of mine, the late Professor Emeritus Alexander S. Levens of the University of California at Berkeley and the late Professor Emeritus Roland W. Bockhorst of Washington University. Also, I would like to thank Dr. Wayne D. Barton of the City College of Sacramento for sharing his teaching experiences with me in basic drafting and drawing courses, and I would like to acknowledge Professor Zenryu Shirakawa of Boston University for improving my writing skills during my high school and college years. A special note of gratitude goes to all those who contributed illustrations to this book. The process of contacting everyone was both an arduous and an enjoyable task.

I am deeply indebted to the exceptional architectural teaching professionals who have reviewed my book. Their suggestions have been constructive and positive in helping me to sharpen my focus on elements that may need improvement. I want to give my heartfelt thanks to Dick Davison for his most significant, extensive page-by-page review. Other major review contributors included Owen Cappleman and Thomas L. Turman. William Benedict shared his excellent syllabus with me, and excerpts from it have particularly strengthened the chapters on linear perspective drawing and delineating and rendering entourage.

William R. Benedict, Assistant Professor, California Polytechnic State University–San Luis Obispo
Donald J. Bergsma, Professor, St. Petersburg Junior College (Florida)
Derek Bradford, Professor, Rhode Island School of Design
Owen Cappleman, Assistant Dean and Associate Professor, University of Texas at Austin
Ann Cederna, Assistant Professor, Catholic University of America (Washington, D.C.)
Rich Correa, Professor, Yuba College (California)
Dick Davison, Associate Professor, Texas A&M University
Phillip R. Dixon, Professor, College of San Mateo (California)
Jonathan B. Friedman, Dean and Professor, New York Institute of Technology
Robert Funk, Professor, Bakersfield College (California)
Todd Hamilton, Assistant Dean and Associate Professor, University of Texas at Arlington
Hiro Hata, Associate Professor, State University of New York at Buffalo
Steven House, AIA
Paul Laseau, Professor, Ball State University (Indiana)
Harold Linton, Assistant Dean, Lawrence Technological University (Michigan)
George Martin, Professor, Catholic University of America (Washington, D.C.)
Valerian Miranda, Associate Professor, Texas A&M University
David Pollak, Adjunct Professor of Design, Roger Williams University (Rhode Island)
Arpad Daniel Ronaszegi, Assistant Professor, Andrews University (Michigan)
James Shay, AIA Architect
Michael Stallings, Chair and Professor, El Camino College (California)
Paul Stevenson Oles, FAIA, American Society of Architectural Perspectivists–President Emeritus
Martha Sutherland, Assistant Professor, University of Arkansas
Stephen Temple, Lecturer and Architect, University of North Carolina–Greensboro
Thomas L. Turman, Professor, Laney College (California)
Mohammed S. Uddin, Associate Professor, Southern University (Louisiana)
Dr. Osamu A. Wakita, Chair and Professor, Los Angeles Harbor College
Lee Wright, Associate Professor, University of Texas at Arlington
Lindy Zichichi, Professor, Glendale Community College (California)

Acknowledgments would not be complete without paying tribute to the fine staff at John Wiley & Sons, notably editor Amanda L. Miller, associate managing editor Jennifer Mazurkie, and editorial assistant Mary Alice Yates, who transformed the preliminary manuscript into the final product.

The following illustrations were reprinted with the permission of *Progressive Architecture,* Penton Publishing:

Anti-Villa, Batey & Mack, Architects
Armacost Duplex, Rebecca L. Binder, FAIA
Casa Canovelles, MBM Arquitectos
Central Chiller Plant, Holt Hinshaw Pfau Jones Architecture
Church of Light, Tadao Ando, Architect
Clybourne Lofts, Pappageorge Haymes Ltd., Architects
Franklin/La Brea Family Housing, Adèle Naudé Santos and Associates, Architects
J. B. Speed Art Museum addition, GBQC Architects
Kress Residence, Robert W. Peters FAIA, Architect
Louisiana Department of Health and Hospitals, R-2 ARCH Designers/Researchers
Museum of Modern Art, Hans Hollein, Architect
Private Studio, William Adams, Architect
Springwood Drive Residence, David Lee Van Hoy and George Patrick Elian, Architects
The Stainless Steel Apartment, Krueck & Sexton, Architects
Waterfront Development Plan, Koetter, Kim & Associates Inc., Architects and Urban Designers

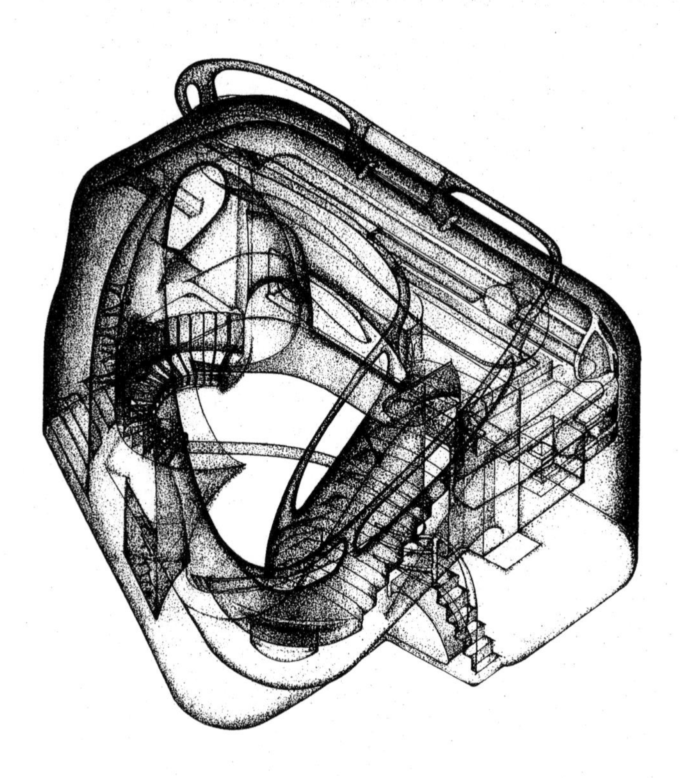

Drawing: Truss-Wall House, Machida, Tokyo, Japan
Transparent Isometric
Courtesy of Eisaku Ushida & Katheryn Findlay
of the Ushida-Findlay Partnership

1

Tool Fundamentals

Drafting tools should be treated with meticulous care, with the goal of making them last a lifetime. Always purchase the best quality that you can afford. These tools are a necessity for clarity of graphical expression.

The intent of this chapter is to show the variety of instruments that are available and how to use them properly.

The following are some of the important skills, terms, and concepts you will learn:

How to use a drafting pencil
How to use drafting instruments
How to use different kinds of scales
How to set up a workstation

Contour lines
Contour intervals

Tool Fundamentals

TOPIC: SCALES

Orr 1995.

Adler 2000.

Chapter Overview

By studying this chapter and doing the related exercises in the book's final section, you will learn how to use drafting equipment; how to measure with architects', engineers', and metric scales; and the meaning of contour lines.

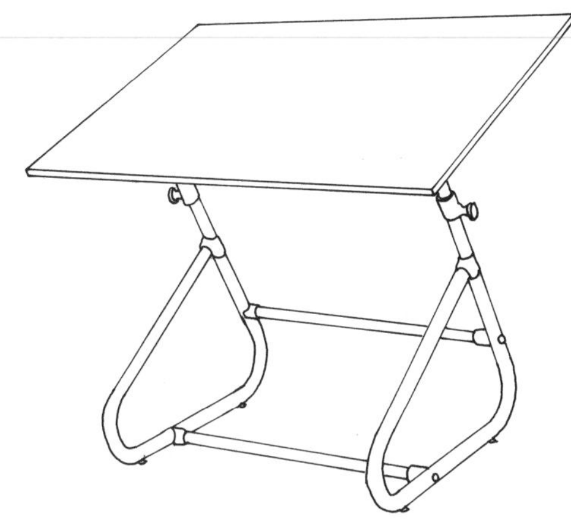

A **metal drafting stand** is characterized by an adjustable tabletop, which can be fitted with a parallel straightedge (see p. 14).

A **four-post table** has an adjustable whiteboard surface that can be moved to any comfortable work angle. It can function as a drafting table, computer workstation, or a reference table.

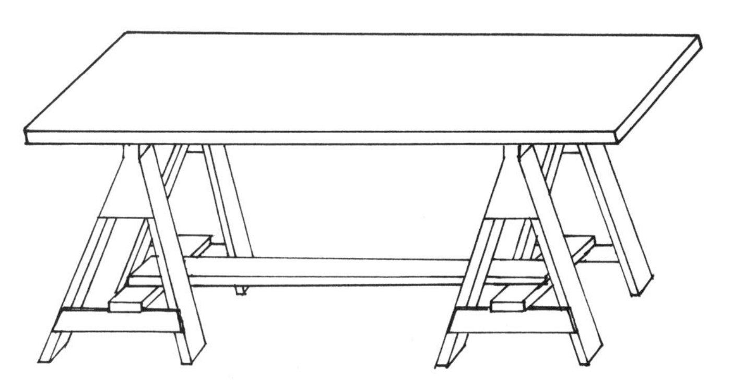

An economical **homemade table** can be made using a flush hollow core door placed on top of two metal or wooden sawhorses.

Types of Drawing Table or Drawing Board Covers

Vyco is a five-ply vinyl **drawing table or board cover** that counteracts eye strain and self-heals when dented, scratched, or punctured. The cover softens the lead when you draw. The two sides are either green and cream, gray and white, or translucent. Another option for a cover is an illustration board that is hot press, white, heavy, and dense. Board covers can be kept like new with special board cleaners that can do double duty as drafting-instrument cleaners. Remember never to draw on hard surfaces such as glass, wood, or hard plastic.

There are many different types of **drawing boards.** They can have a metal edge with a laminate surface and solid-core construction; a hard, smooth surface that resists chemicals, stains, and scratches; or a basswood surface on both sides with an ultralight weight core.

The technology for producing drawing tables, drawing boards, and table and board covers is continually changing—check art and drafting supply catalogs for the latest materials. Use the catalogs as a guide for important accessories, such as chairs, lamps, plan files, and Spiroll (a product that attaches to the front edge of the table or board, allowing drawings to be rolled for protection and providing more work room).

In an office setting, the preferred (and most common) arrangement is a large, flat surface (approximately 3' × 6'8") not more than 30" above the floor, although it can be higher in some offices. Pencils and pens tend to roll down a tilted work surface if you set them down while you're working.

GRAPHITE DRAFTING PENCILS

Cylindrical pencil leads range from the smallest diameter (hardest: 9H) to the largest diameter (softest: 6B). Architectural drawings (drafted or sketched) are produced by using leads in the grade range from 4H to 4B. Shown below are three equally good types of pencils that are commonly used. Try each one to determine which is most suitable for you.

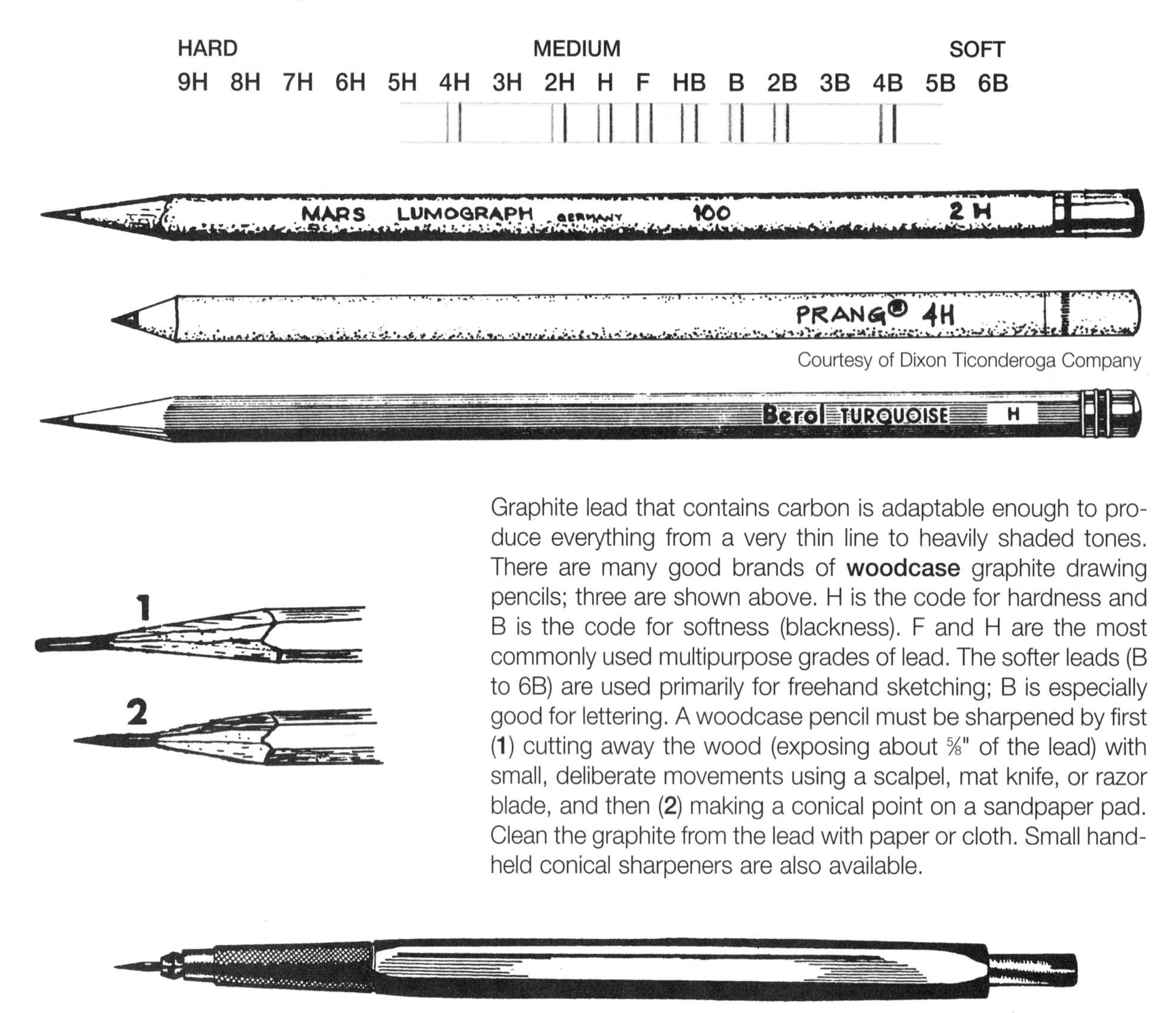

Courtesy of Dixon Ticonderoga Company

Graphite lead that contains carbon is adaptable enough to produce everything from a very thin line to heavily shaded tones. There are many good brands of **woodcase** graphite drawing pencils; three are shown above. H is the code for hardness and B is the code for softness (blackness). F and H are the most commonly used multipurpose grades of lead. The softer leads (B to 6B) are used primarily for freehand sketching; B is especially good for lettering. A woodcase pencil must be sharpened by first (**1**) cutting away the wood (exposing about ⅝" of the lead) with small, deliberate movements using a scalpel, mat knife, or razor blade, and then (**2**) making a conical point on a sandpaper pad. Clean the graphite from the lead with paper or cloth. Small handheld conical sharpeners are also available.

A mechanical leadholder or **clutch pencil** is shown above. It uses a standard-size 2-mm lead that can be drawn out or pulled back by the push-button on the end. Some variations include pocket clips and double-end holders. Leads in most tone qualities can be interchanged to suit drawing conditions. Use a pencil pointer to sharpen the leads to a taper similar to that on a common wood pencil.

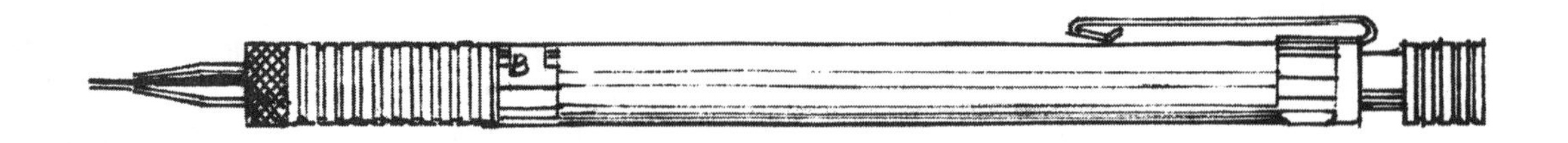

A **fine-line leadholder** with a push-button (propelling) lead advance is shown above. It uses a 0.3-mm to 0.9-mm lead (0.5 mm is a popular size). The lead is protected by a sliding sleeve. This type of pencil does not need to be sharpened. Lead sizes 0.7 mm and 0.9 mm can be used for sketching as well as drafting.

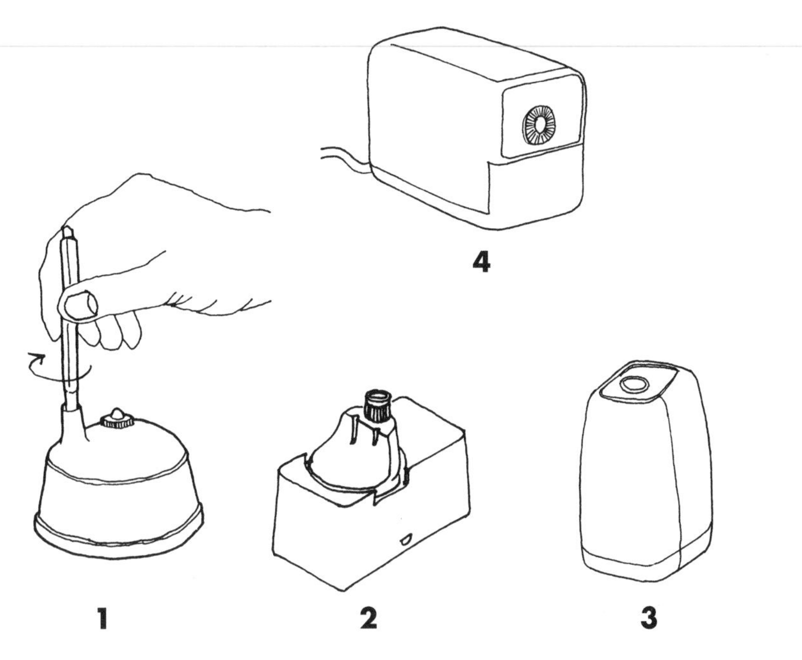

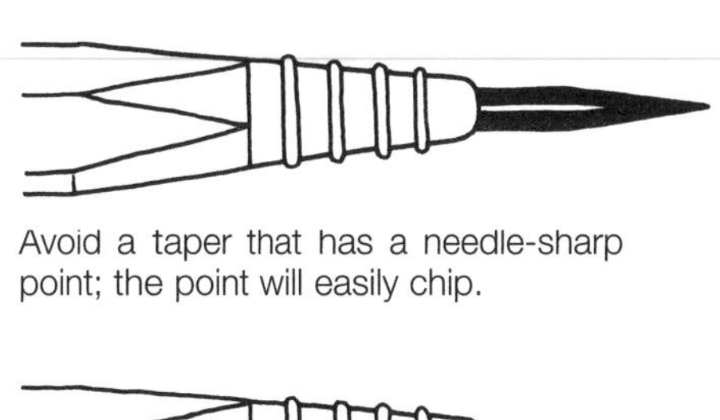

Avoid a taper that has a needle-sharp point; the point will easily chip.

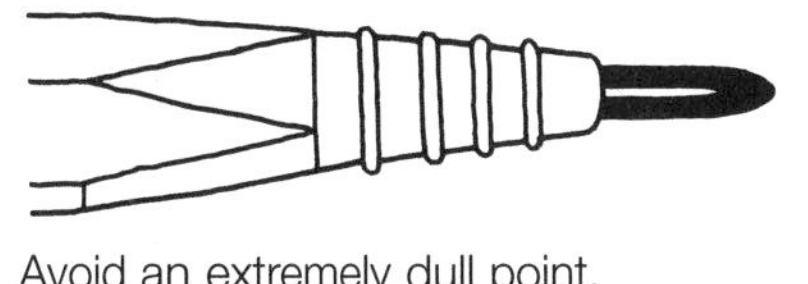

Avoid an extremely dull point.

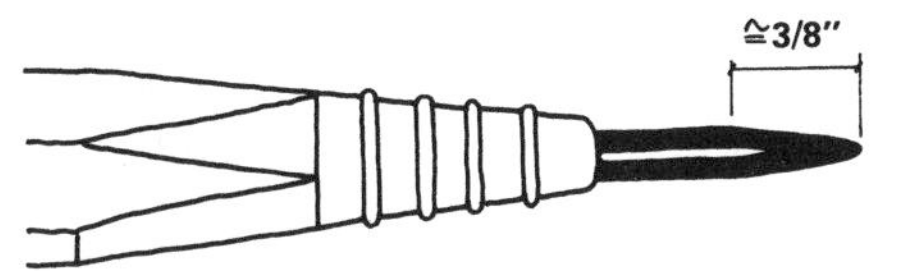

Strive to produce a **conical** point that is very slightly rounded at the tip. Achieve this by **rotating** the pencil when drawing lines.

To sharpen your lead to a conical point, use either (**1**) a sandpaper desktop pointer; (**2**) a cutting-wheel lead pointer; (**3**) a vertical electric pencil sharpener (a good brand is Panasonic); or (**4**) a Boston electric pencil sharpener. The more costly electric sharpeners are much faster. The sandpaper pointer works well with graphite lead but not with polyester lead. Use the sandpaper pointer by rotating your pencil-holding hand clockwise. The cutting-wheel pointer has one slot that creates a sharp point and one that creates a slightly dull point (for lettering). Very small handheld conical sharpeners are also available.

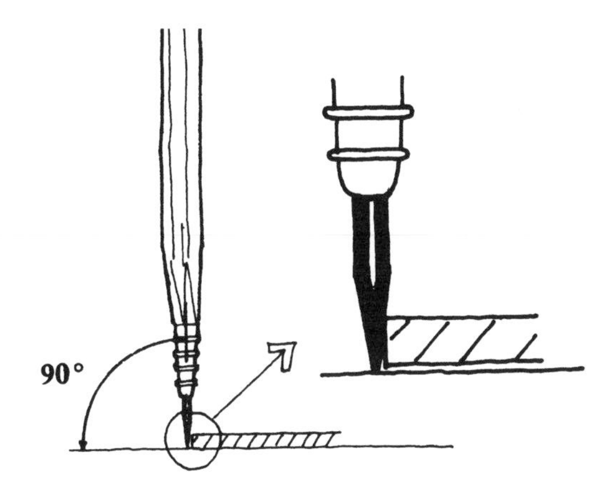

Always draw with a small space between the conical lead point and the straightedge (T-square, parallel bar, or triangle). This is best achieved by either keeping the pencil in a 90° vertical position or tilting the pencil toward you at a slight angle from the vertical. Never tilt it away from the straightedge. Horizontal, vertical, or oblique (slanted or angled) lines are best achieved by leaning the pencil at approximately 60° from the drawing surface. The pressure should be adequate to give a dark and crisp line.

A typical sandpaper block is shown above. It is a piece of wood with sandpaper sheets stapled to one end. Rotate the pencil and move it side-to-side to obtain a tapered, conical point. Apply minimal pressure to avoid snapping the lead. Also use this block to produce a tapered compass lead point (see p. 10).

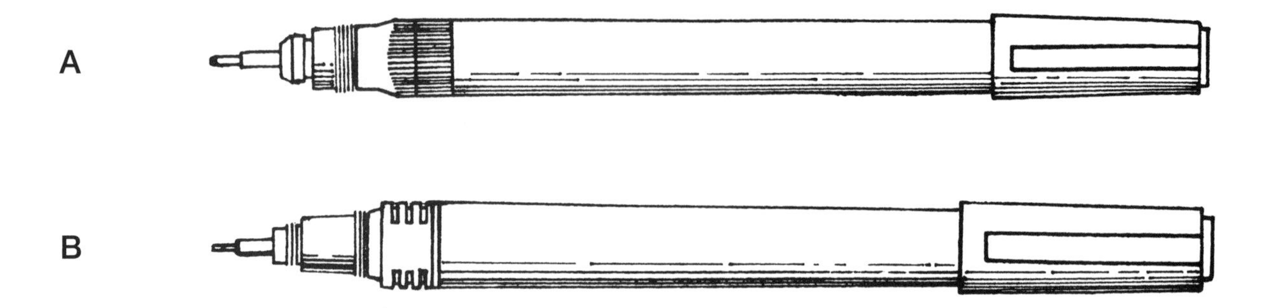

Technical pens are designed with a tubular point within which is a fine wire that controls the ink flow. The tubular point is long enough to clear the thicknesses of T-squares, parallel rules, and triangles. They provide excellent control, producing clear, even lines of constant width without requiring applied pressure. Koh-I-Noor's Rapidograph pens (**A**) are widely used. Koh-I-Noor's Rotring Rapidograph pens (**B**), with their prefilled ink cartridge, are virtually maintenance free. Pens are labeled by their point diameters. The most commonly used pen points are 000 through 4. A four-point set is a good, economical start (**C**); buy a larger set if it is affordable.

Use clog-free, waterproof drawing inks (**D**) that will not fade if exposed to light. Use Koh-I-Noor Liquid Eraser (**E**) for removing ink from drafting film (see p. 16). When not in use, store pens vertically, with the point tips up and the cap on.

Some metric width equivalents:

6 × 0	0.13 mm
4 × 0	0.18 mm
00	0.30 mm
0	0.35 mm
1	0.50 mm

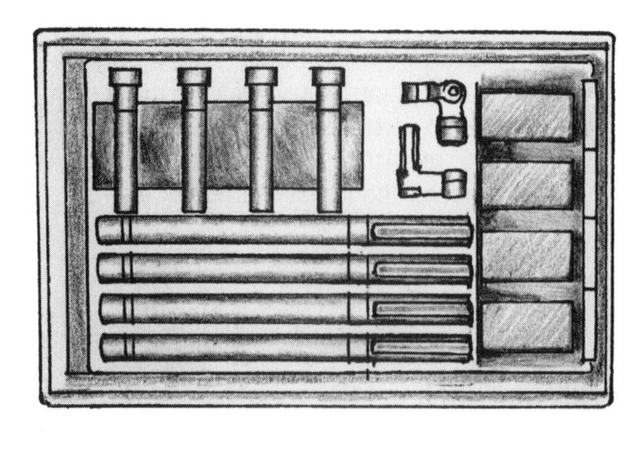

C

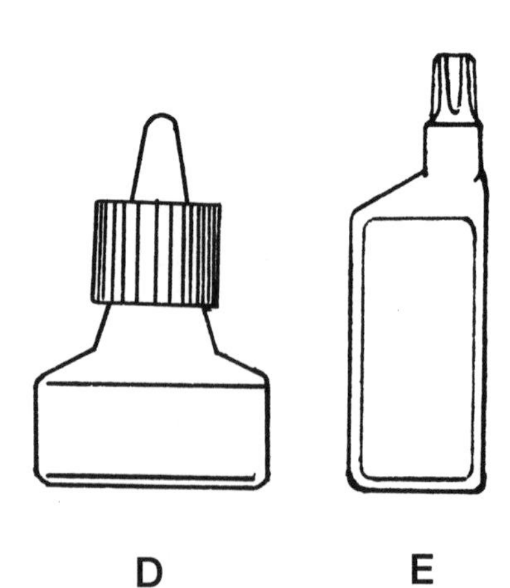

D E

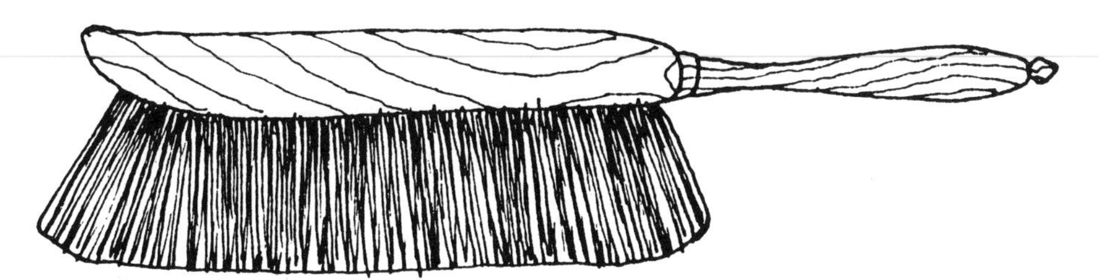

A drafting **duster** with horsehair or natural bristle is used to keep the drawing surface clean of graphite and eraser residue. Quic-Kleen is a finely ground white powder that keeps a drafting surface free of smudges, dirt, and dust. Similarly, Pounce cleaning powder can be used to prepare a surface for inking.

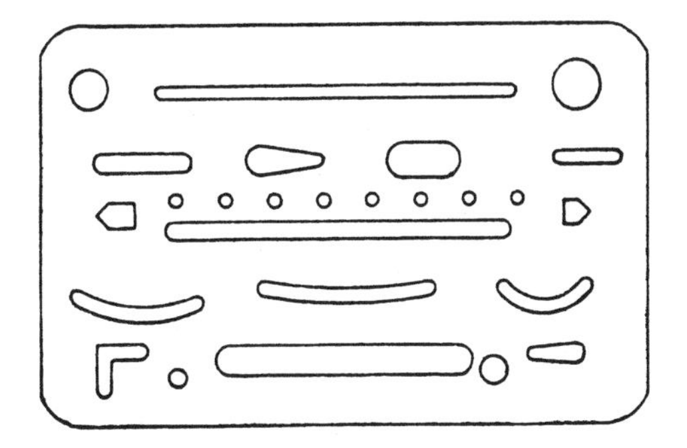

An **erasing shield** is a thin metal cover that protects drawn lines while erasing unwanted lines and areas with handheld or electric erasers. Not common—but more efficient—are those with rectilinear-cut openings.

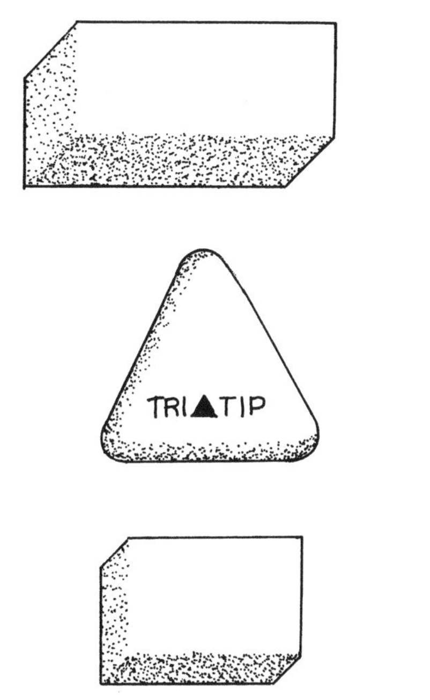

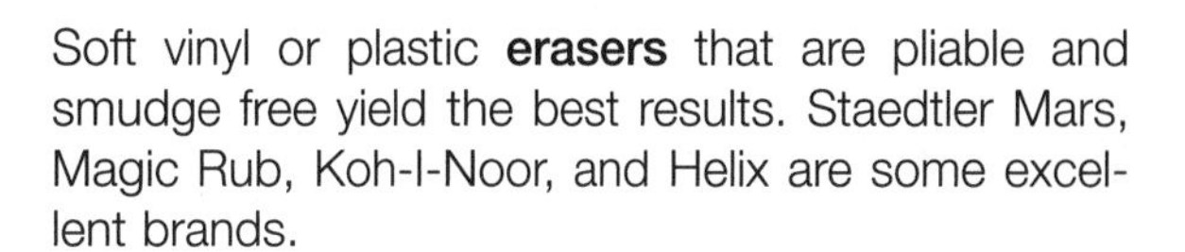

Soft vinyl or plastic **erasers** that are pliable and smudge free yield the best results. Staedtler Mars, Magic Rub, Koh-I-Noor, and Helix are some excellent brands.

General's Tri-Tip eraser is nonabrasive and an excellent tool when sketching with pastels or charcoal. Kneaded erasers are great for charcoal and are quite malleable. Radett's pencil-style stick/click eraser is most suitable for use with an erasing shield, as are electric erasers, which are sold both with cords and in cordless—or portable—varieties. Electric erasers are very effective for ink drawings. The portable ones are about 5½" long and use AA or AAA batteries.

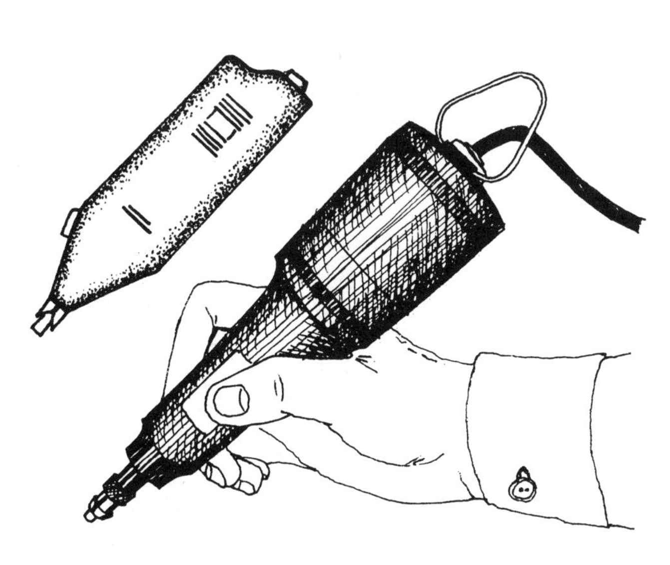

All of the small equipment mentioned in this chapter can be stored and transported efficiently in an art box or a fishing tackle box. Drawings (especially those on large sheets) should be transported using protective tubes, which can be purchased commercially.

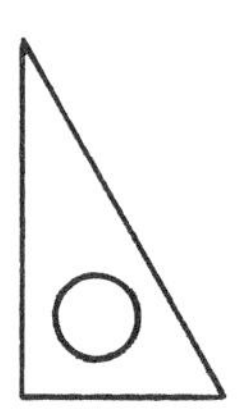

Small triangles (4") are ideal for producing vertical strokes for hand lettering and for producing cross-hatching.

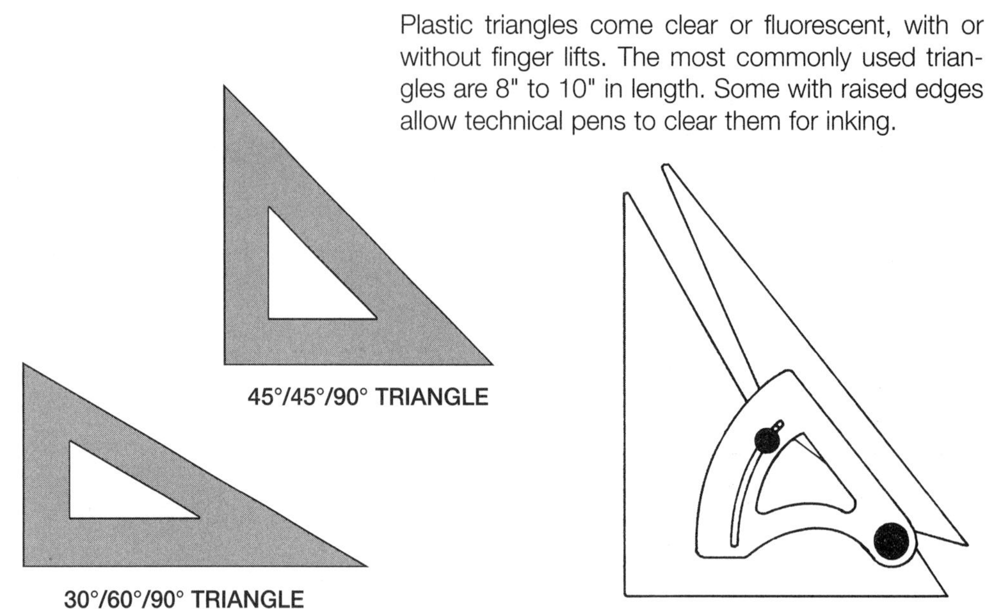

45°/45°/90° TRIANGLE

30°/60°/90° TRIANGLE

Plastic triangles come clear or fluorescent, with or without finger lifts. The most commonly used triangles are 8" to 10" in length. Some with raised edges allow technical pens to clear them for inking.

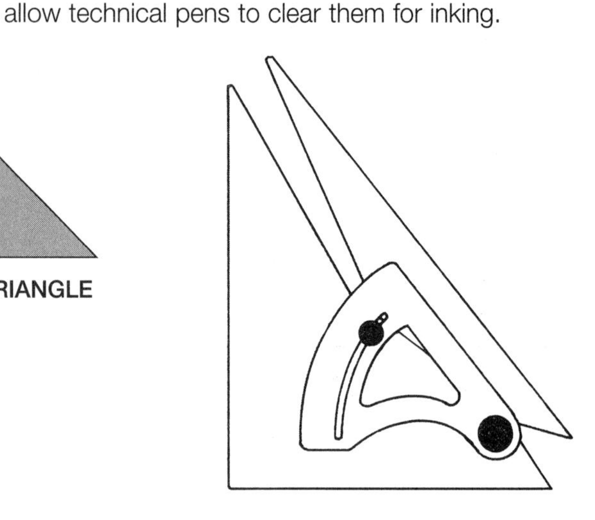

Triangles are used to draw vertical lines or lines at a specific angle (30°, 45°, or 60°) when used with a T-square or parallel bar. An adjustable triangle is used to draw a variety of inclined lines at any angle; some are graduated for slope and rise. A minimum 12" size is best.

T-squares for drawing horizontal lines come in lengths of 18", 24", 30", 36", 42", and 48"; 42" is an all-purpose length. Good blades are rigid and are made of aluminum, stainless steel, or wood. Metal blades can serve as a guide for cutting; the transparent acrylic edges on some T-squares make it easier to see what you are working on.

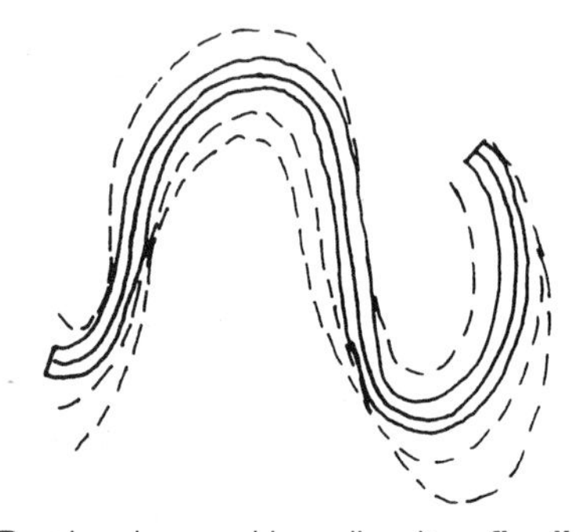

By shaping and bending it, a **flexible curve rule** can be used to draw almost any curve. The curve rule is made of plastic with a flexible core.

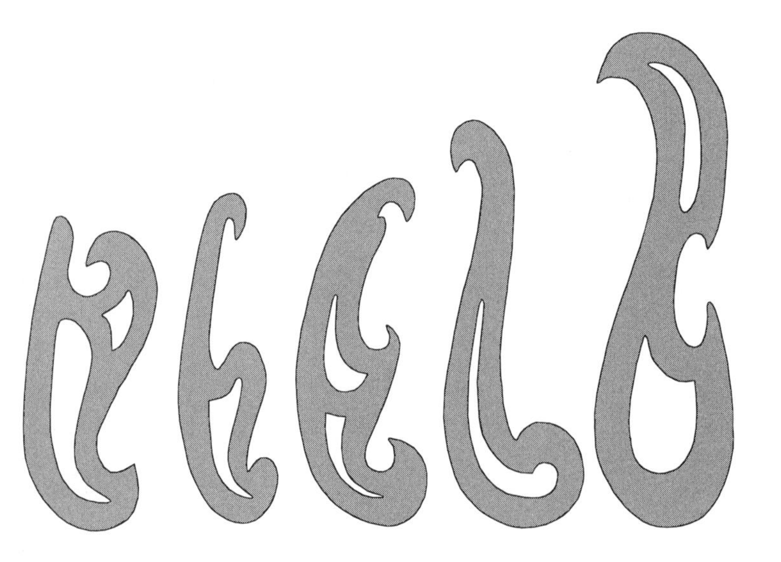

French curves are irregular curves that have no constant radii. Those made of clear, polished acrylic are best.

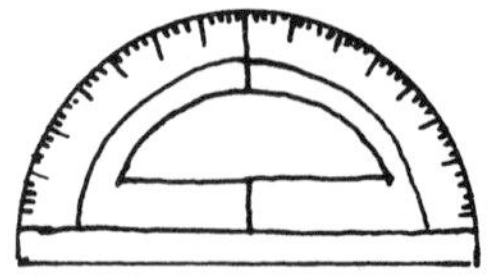

Protractors measure angles and can be either circular or semicircular.

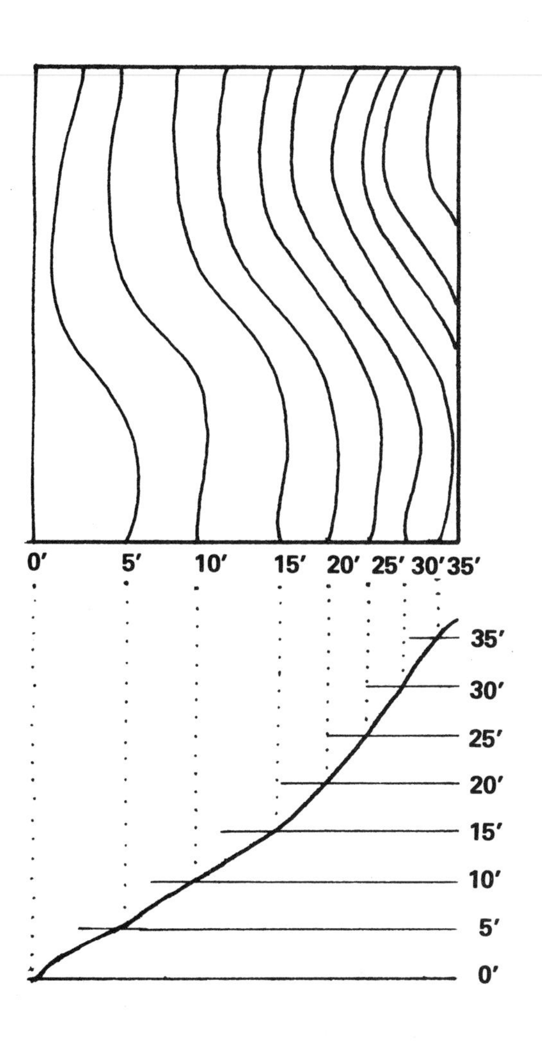

Contour lines are lines of constant elevation. Every point passes through the same elevation on the surface of the ground.

Contour intervals can be 1', 2', 5', or 10', depending on the conditions of the terrain and the size of the area being studied.

In the drawing on the left, note how the slope steepens when the contours become more closely spaced. It is less steep at the bottom since the spacing here is greater than at the top. Remember that contour lines should never cross one another.

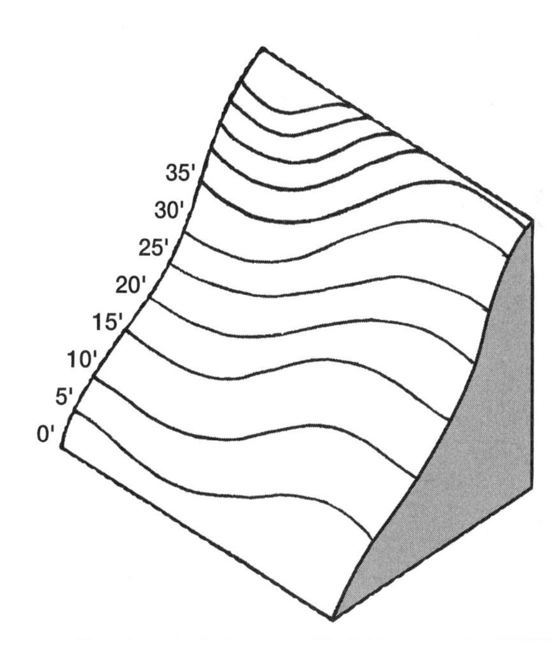

Contour lines can be drawn accurately by using a french curve. The **french curve** is used for noncircular curves. When fitting the curve through a series of points, be sure that the direction in which its curvature increases is the direction in which the curvature of the line increases. Tangents at each conjunction should coincide to avoid breaks and to provide continuity. At sharp turns, a combination of circle arcs and french curves may be used.

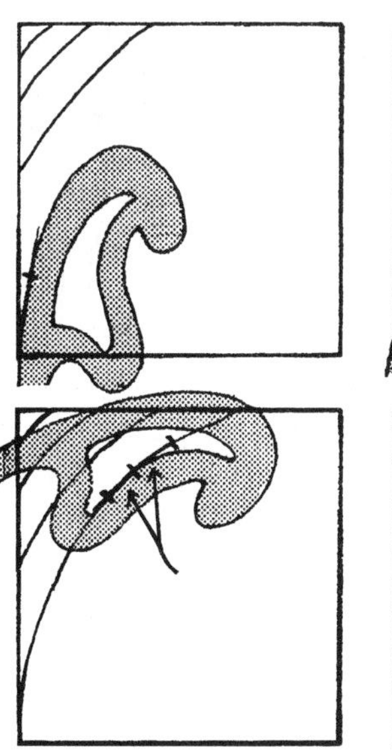

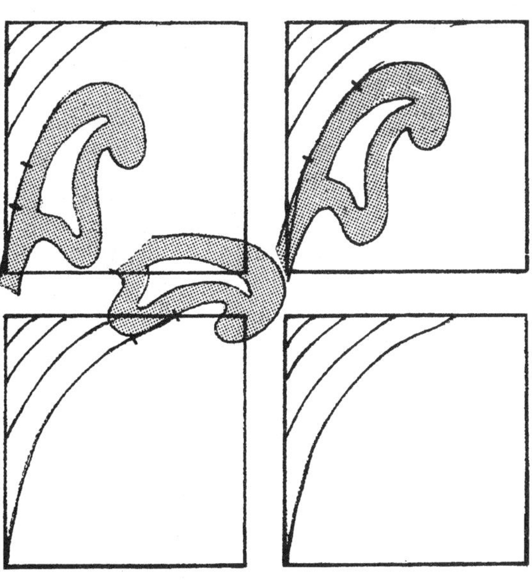

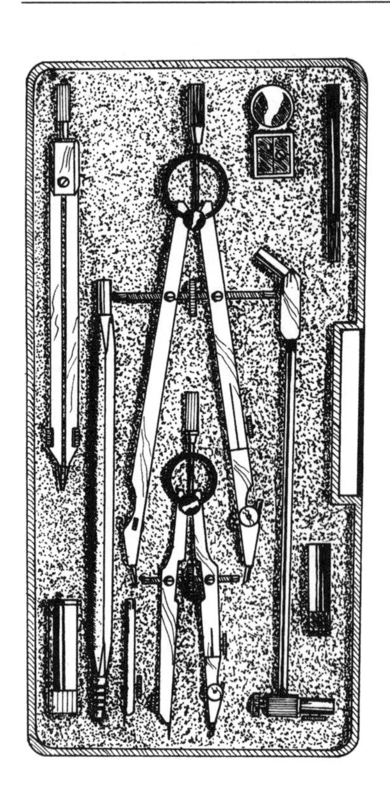

The primary instruments in a typical large drafting set include a large and a small pen/pencil compass, a divider, a 6" extension arm (for very large circles), a lead pencil pointer, and spare leads. A **divider** divides lines and transfers lengths. A **compass** is used for drawing small- and intermediate-size circles. The instruments are enclosed in a protective case. Alvin and Chartpak are excellent brands.

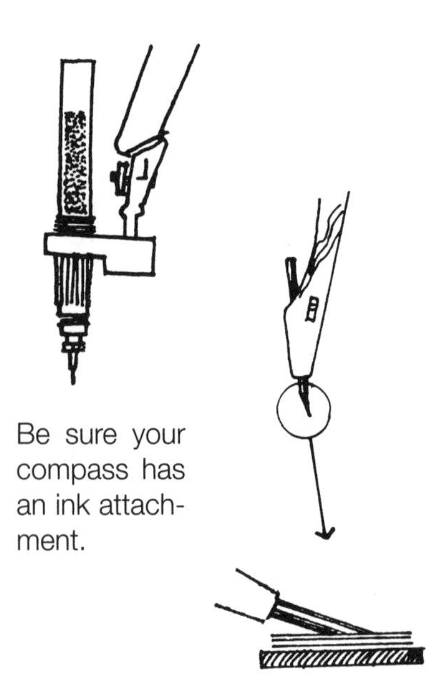

Be sure your compass has an ink attachment.

Keep a low angle when tapering the compass lead.

A chisel point is used to obtain a sharp line; a conical point's nonuniform point does not create as sharp a line when drawing a circle.

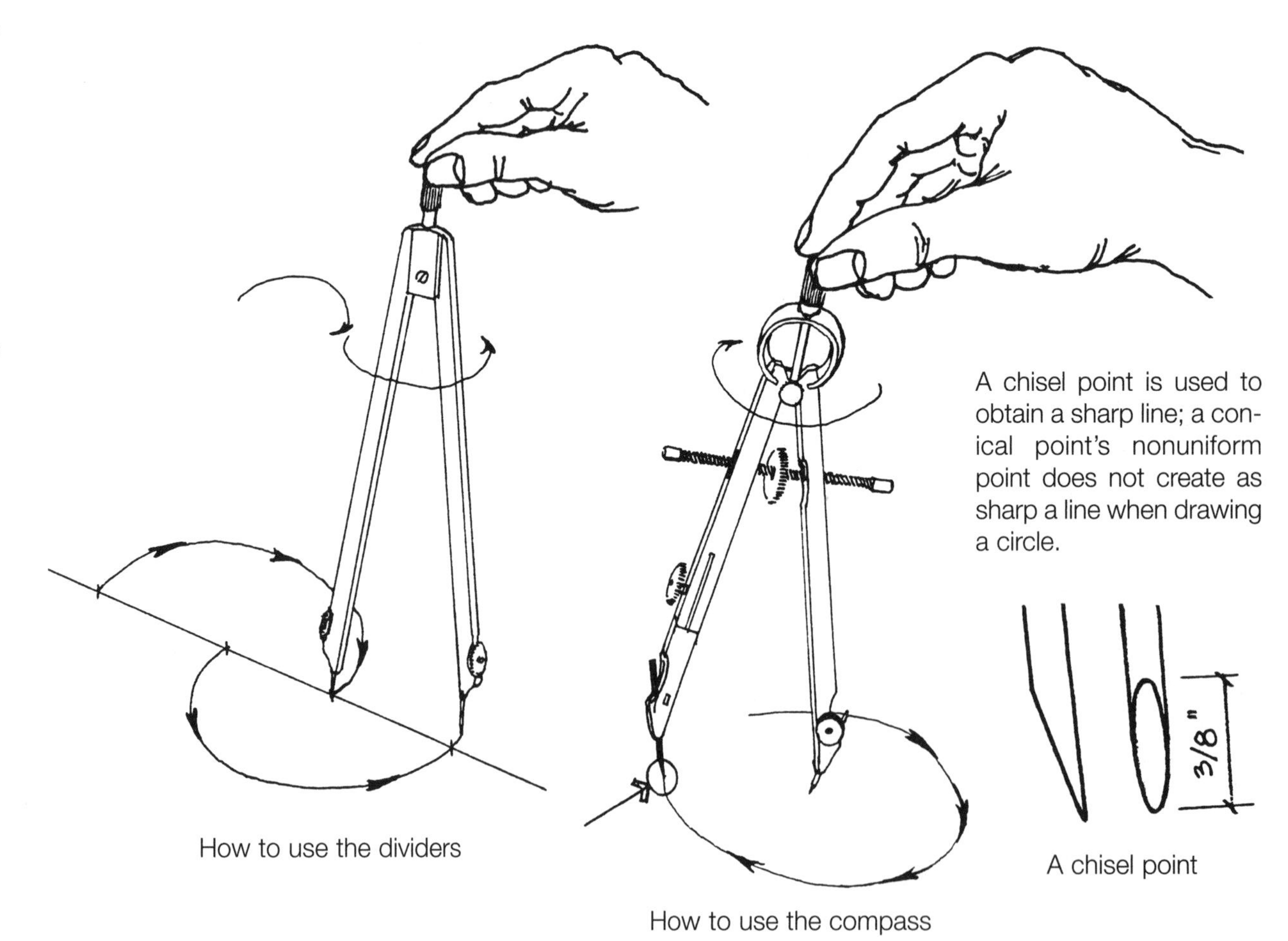

How to use the dividers

How to use the compass

A chisel point

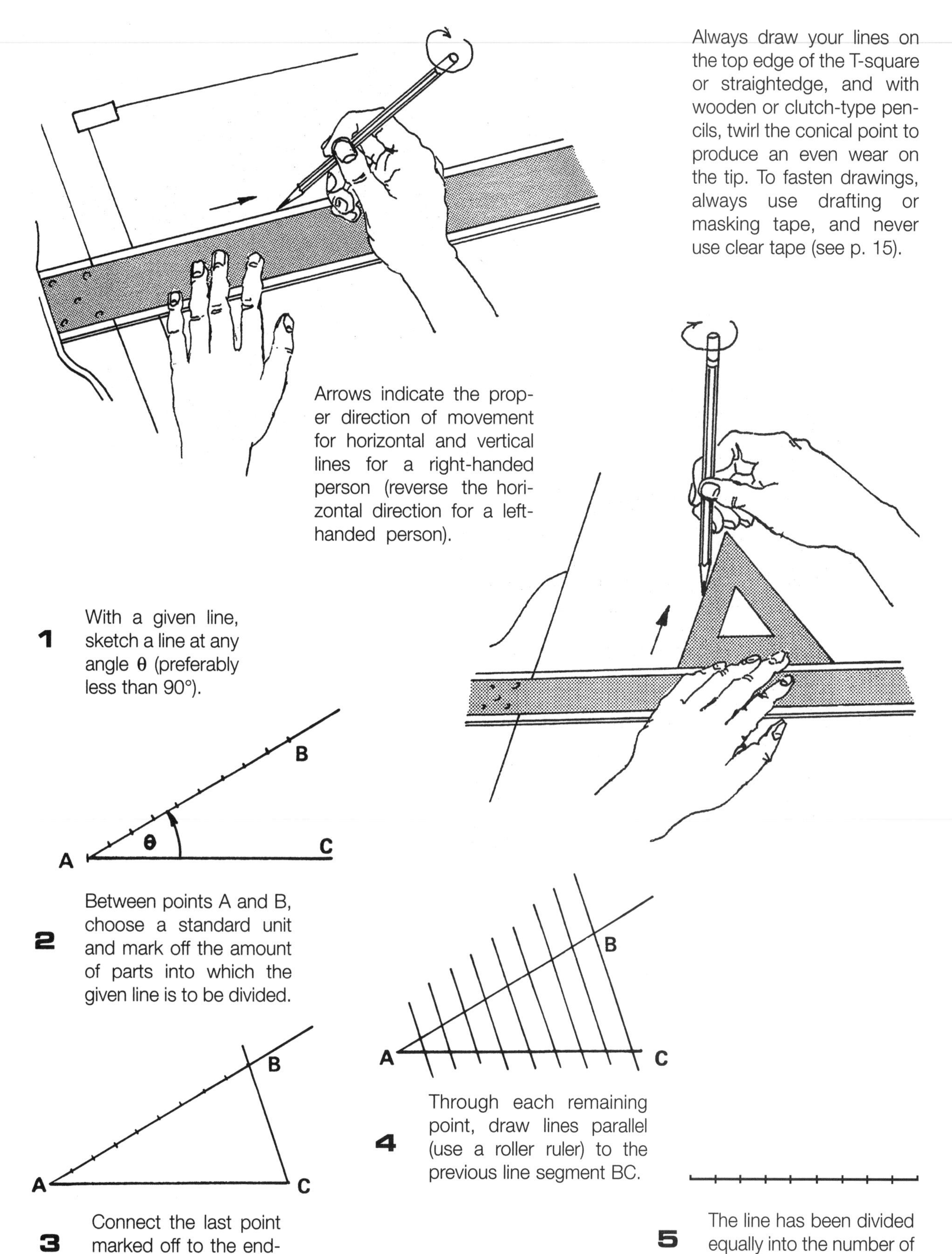

Always draw your lines on the top edge of the T-square or straightedge, and with wooden or clutch-type pencils, twirl the conical point to produce an even wear on the tip. To fasten drawings, always use drafting or masking tape, and never use clear tape (see p. 15).

Arrows indicate the proper direction of movement for horizontal and vertical lines for a right-handed person (reverse the horizontal direction for a left-handed person).

1 With a given line, sketch a line at any angle θ (preferably less than 90°).

2 Between points A and B, choose a standard unit and mark off the amount of parts into which the given line is to be divided.

3 Connect the last point marked off to the endpoint of the given line.

4 Through each remaining point, draw lines parallel (use a roller ruler) to the previous line segment BC.

5 The line has been divided equally into the number of parts desired.

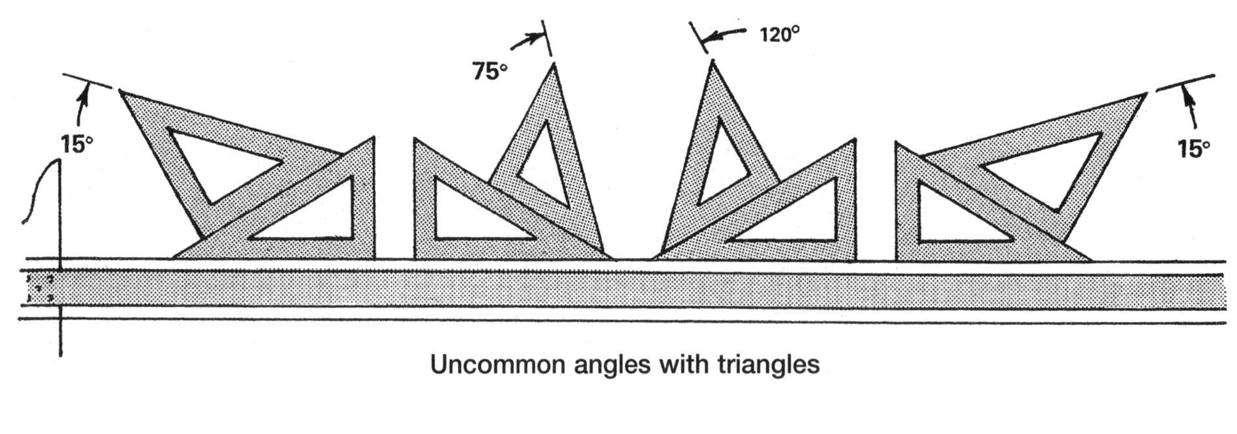

Uncommon angles with triangles

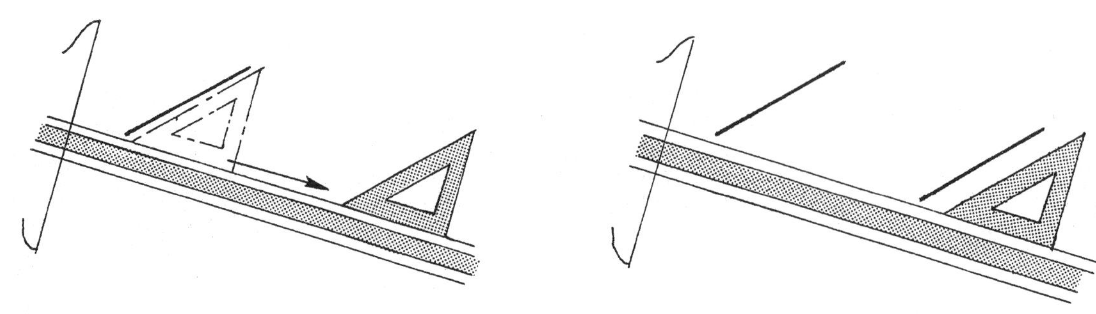

How to draw a line parallel to a given line

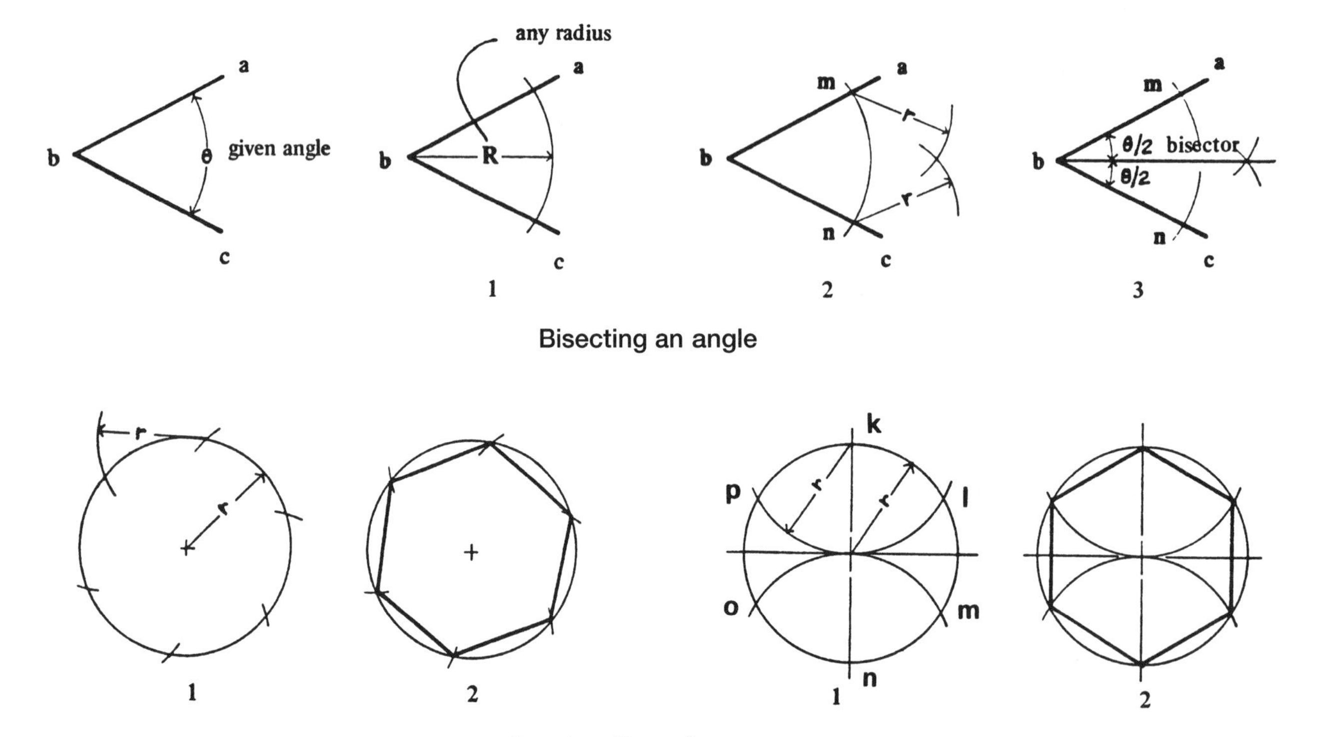

Bisecting an angle

Constructing a hexagon

Familiarity with drafting tools can be achieved by doing simple geometric operations and constructing various geometric shapes.

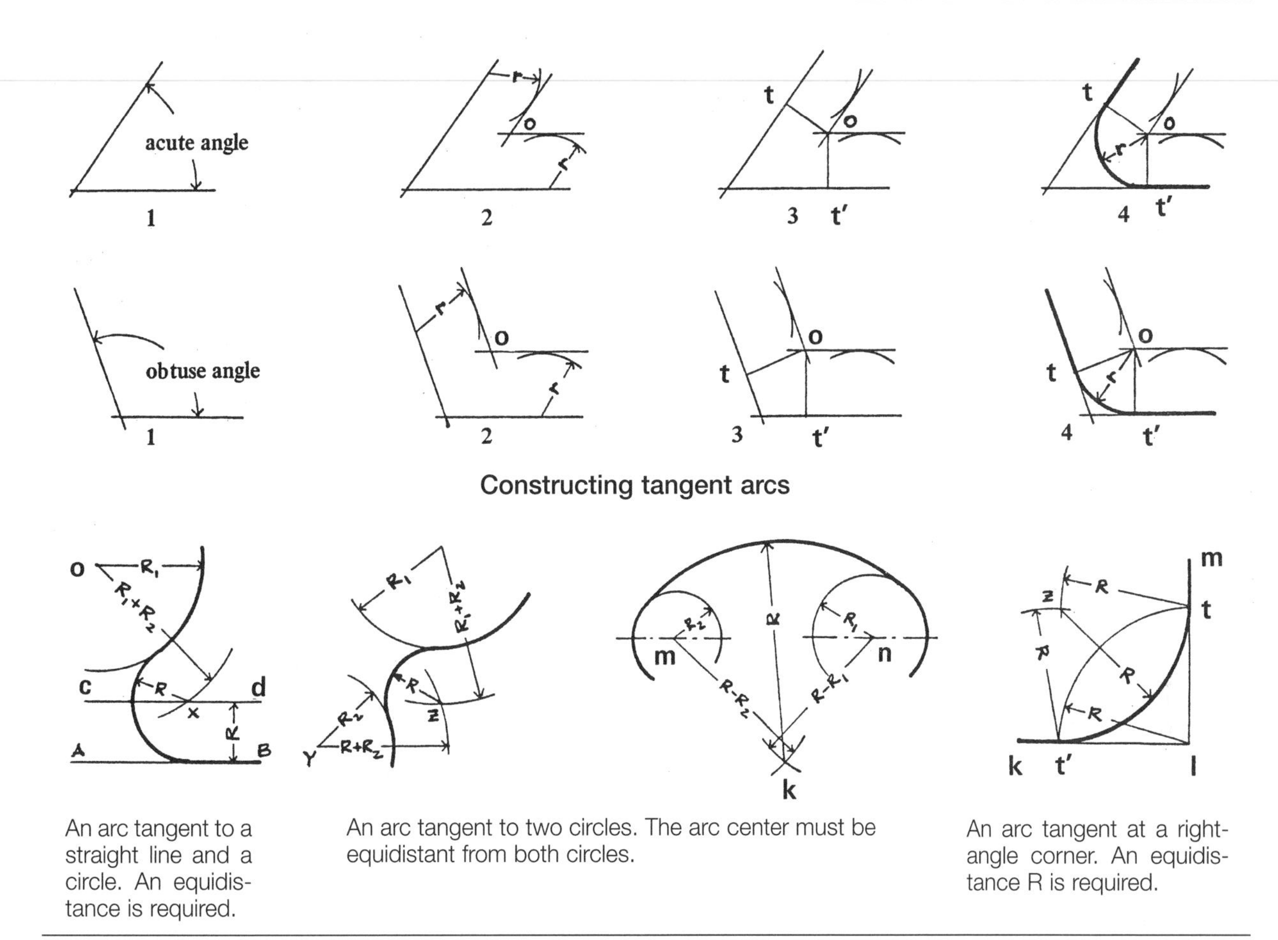

An arc tangent to a straight line and a circle. An equidistance is required.

An arc tangent to two circles. The arc center must be equidistant from both circles.

An arc tangent at a right-angle corner. An equidistance R is required.

Architectural **templates** have many standard plumbing and furniture symbols cut through them for tracing. This floor plan template includes door swings, sinks, and bathroom fixtures (see bathroom plan at right). It also has useful geometric forms, such as circles. Templates come in a variety of scales to suit any drawing requirement. Always keep your pen or pencil perpendicular (vertical) to the drawing surface when using an architectural template. This ensures a uniform line and an overall good result. **Underlays** and **overlays** are similar to templates. These time-savers have symbols printed or drawn on a sheet that can be traced or transferred onto an original drawing.

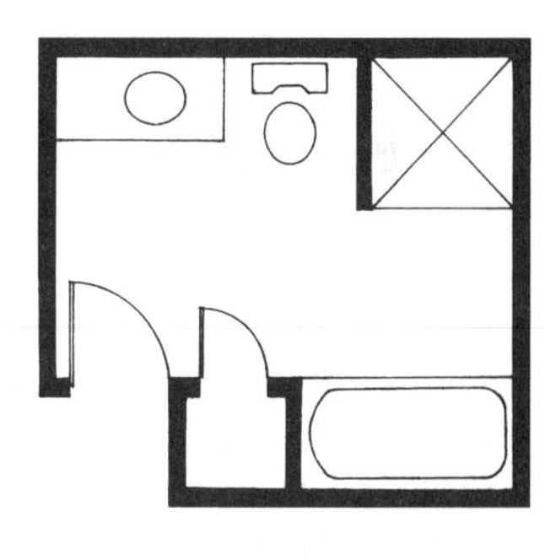

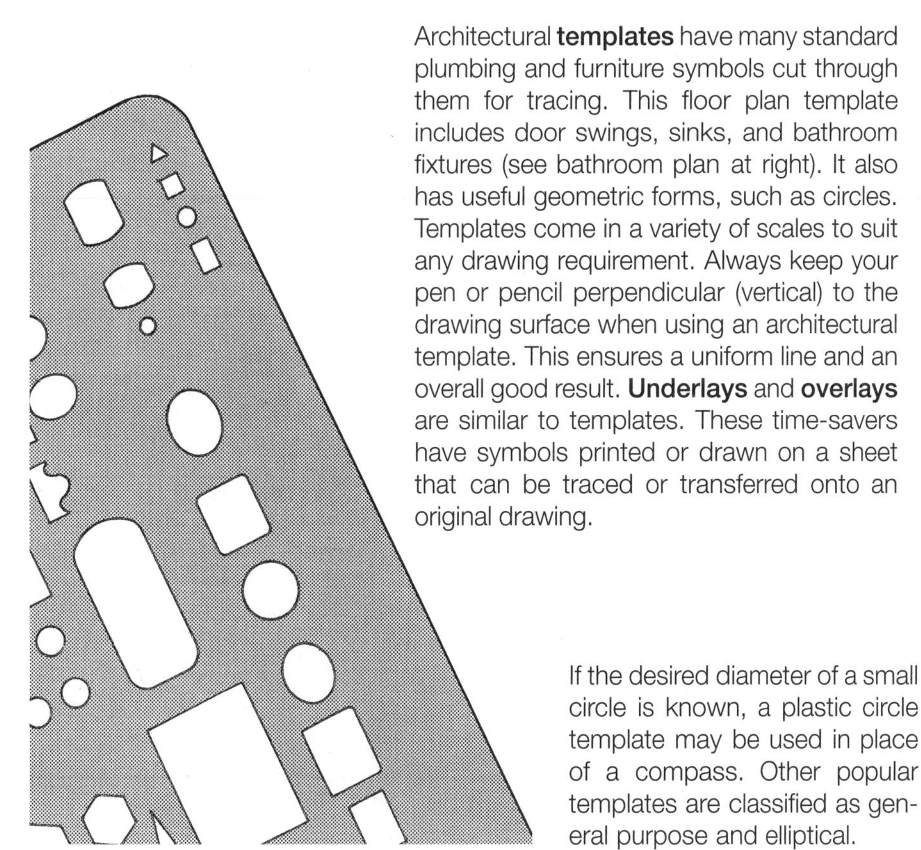

If the desired diameter of a small circle is known, a plastic circle template may be used in place of a compass. Other popular templates are classified as general purpose and elliptical.

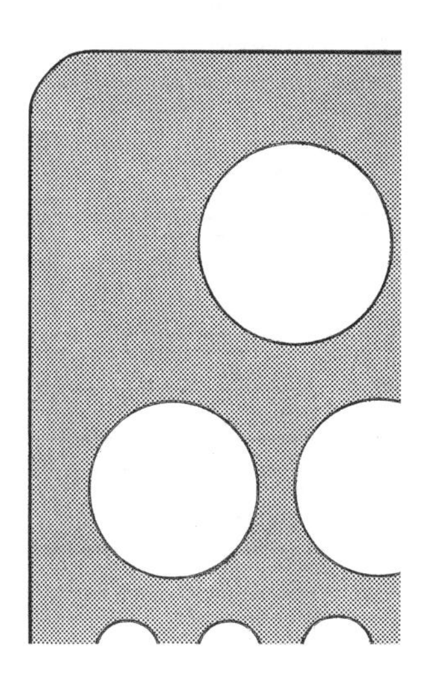

The **parallel roller rule,** with its effortless movement, has made the T-square relatively obsolete. A slight push with either hand glides the parallel rule into any desired position on the drawing board. Since it rolls on ball bearings, smudges on drawings commonly created by the use of a T-square are avoided. In addition, both ends are fixed; thus, a drawn horizontal line cannot deviate from its correct position. Special types of rules can have a built-in cutting edge.

When installing the parallel rule (also termed bar or straightedge), be sure that:

1. Corner plates A and B are firmly attached with ½"-long screws.
2. The cable wire is parallel to the edge of the drawing board on both sides.
3. The cable wire passes between the clamping washer and the plate.
4. The spring is centered between A and B.
5. The cable wire is moved in the directions indicated below.

Keep abreast of new technology. Alvin's 6" and 12" rolling parallel rules combine the functions of a straightedge, compass, protractor, and angle template in one. These multipurpose drawing instruments allow you to measure in inches or centimeters.

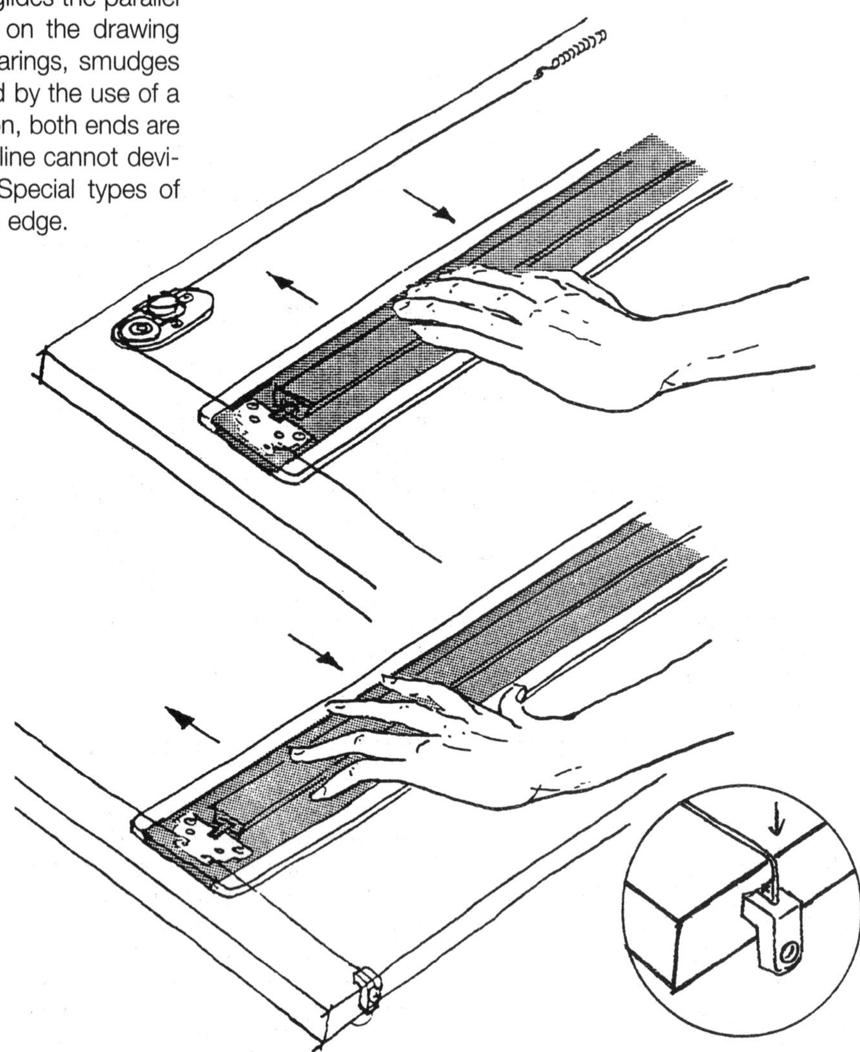

The cable wire is inserted through the hole on top of the stop and aligned with the slot on the rear of the stop. Trim excess cable, but leave enough for future adjustments.

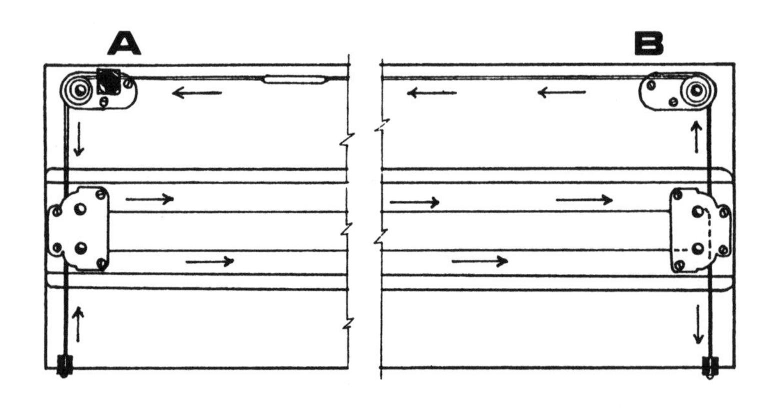

Long, continuous, parallel horizontal lines frequently occur on architectural drawings. The rule can also be adjusted to many inclined positions slightly away from the horizontal. Rules come in lengths of 36", 42", 48", 54", and 60". Highly recommended is the 42" rule, which permits you to work on a 30" × 40" sheet.

Provide yourself with a comfortable **work space** with adequate tack surface to pin up your work for reference. Architectural drawing is normally done in a sitting position, but it can also be done standing. Avoid slouching; don't arch your back and collapse your abdominal regions. Sit erect and maintain good posture. Designing and drawing require long hours of sitting in one position. Poor posture will lead to a tired feeling, reduced drawing capacity, and a deteriorated physical state.

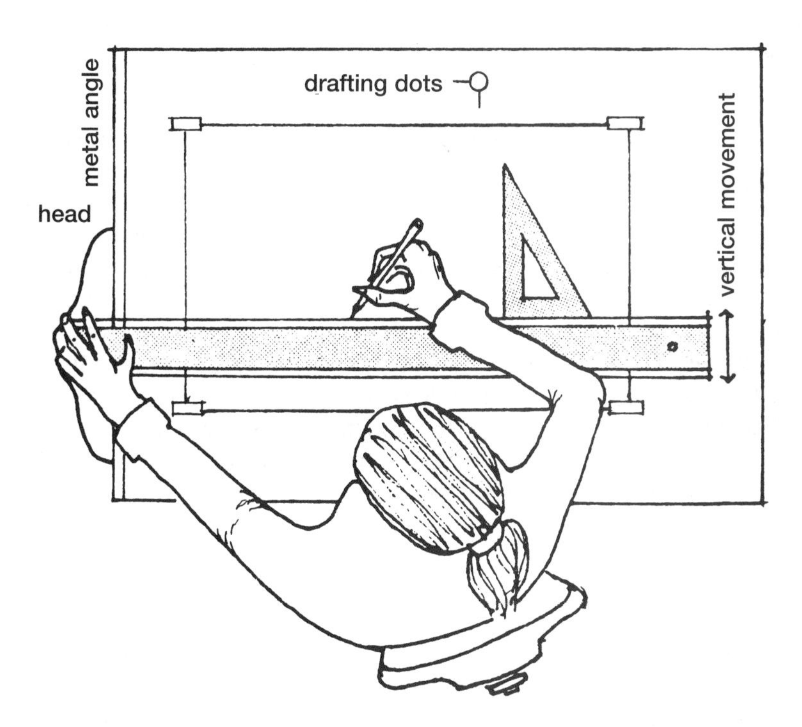

Most practitioners like a low-level, flat table surface; however, some prefer a tilted tabletop that reduces the need to lean over the work surface. A large surface gives you room for additional equipment like a laptop computer (see photo). An adjustable stool is ideal for varying the seat height and the backrest. If possible, place one foot on a pile bar or footrest in order to raise one knee above the hips. Elevating one leg at a time helps to keep the pelvic region tilted forward. It also preserves the natural curvature of the lower lumbar region, preventing undue physical stress and fatigue. Strive for ergonomic efficiency.

Purchase the best quality table light source that you can afford in order to prevent eyestrain. Anincandescent/fluorescent combination light is excellent. The light should have an adjustable counterpoise to give it the flexibility to be positioned over your work.

Line up the drawing sheet horizontally and vertically using a T-square or parallel straightedge and triangle. It is best to apply the drafting tape broadside (on the diagonal is also OK) to prevent the sheet from slipping. Drafting dots can also be used to secure drawings to a board or table. The head of the T-square should always slide firmly up against the edge of the drawing board or table. If the head is not firm, there will be vertical movement (play) at the end of the T-square. Use a metal angle with a T-square to keep a true edge. A clean, thin rag or towel can be used as a forearm rest and sheet protector for long drawing stints.

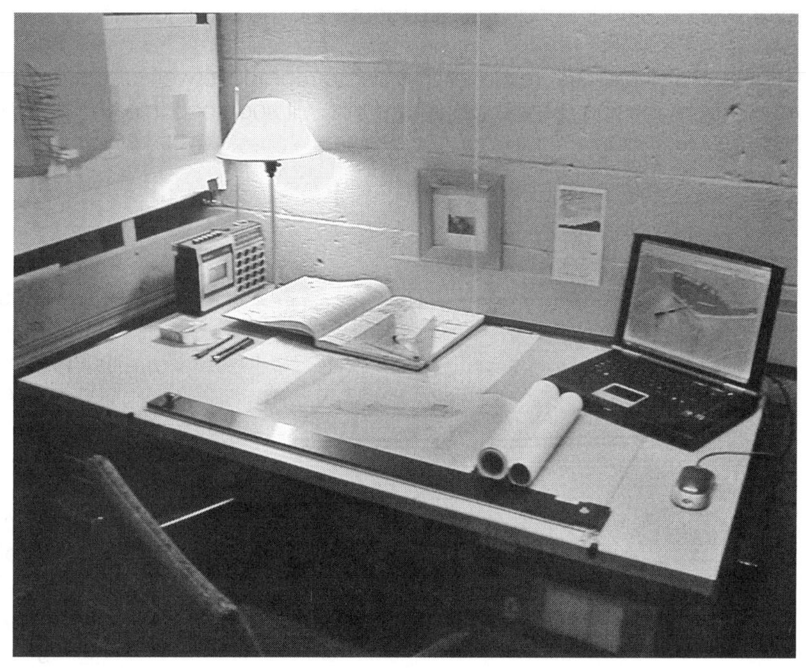

© Charles Roberts

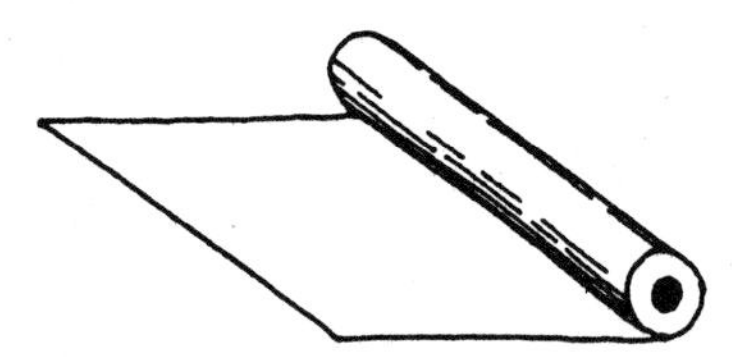

Transparent, lightweight **tracing paper** (commonly yellow or white and termed "flimsy" or "talking paper") is excellent for use with soft leads or markers. It is used for rough sketches, overlays, and preliminary drawings. Rolls range in size from 12" to 36".

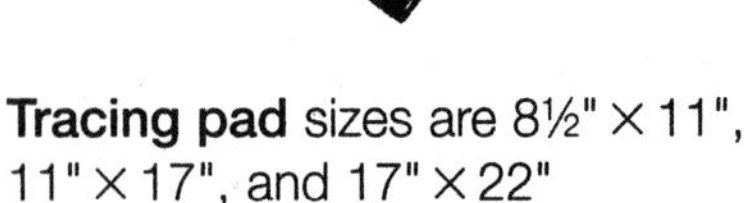

Tracing pad sizes are 8½" × 11", 11" × 17", and 17" × 22"

With a fade-out grid

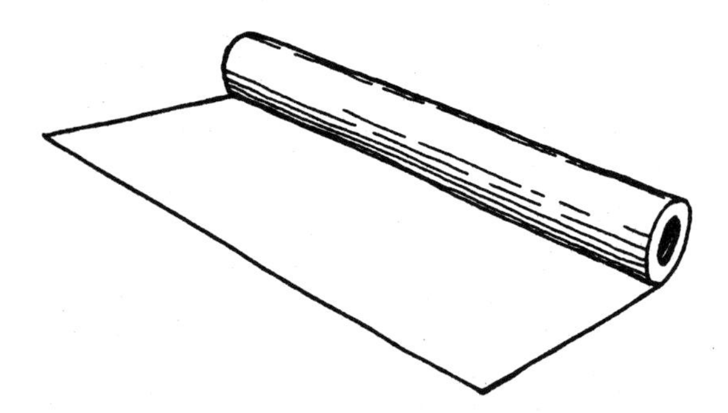

Vellums are 100% rag tracing papers with excellent erasability. They are available in either rolls, pads, or single sheets. Clearprint 1000H is widely used. Vellum papers are classified by weight, color, and rag content. Heavyweight (20 lb) white vellum is normally used for finished drawings. Medium-weight (16 lb) is used for rough layouts. **Plastic film** from polyester (Mylar) yields the highest quality reproductions. It is highly appropriate for ink and some pencil leads. Use erasing fluid to remove ink lines.

Rag is the cotton fiber in the paper. The higher the percentage of rag content, the better the quality. The peaks and valleys (fiber arrangement) on a tracing paper's surface are its tooth quality. Graphite and ink are used on both translucent and transparent tracing papers. Slick paper with less tooth is better for ink work, whereas paper with more tooth is better for pencil work. Gridded tracing paper is used to make the drawing of horizontals and verticals much easier. Drawings on quality papers are not harsh on the eyes and show no "ghosts" (grooves) even after pencil lines are redrawn in the same location.

Original drawings must read well in order to reproduce well for the use of others. Keep in mind that traditional reprographics using diazo papers for prints will soon become obsolete with the advent of digital reprographic technology.

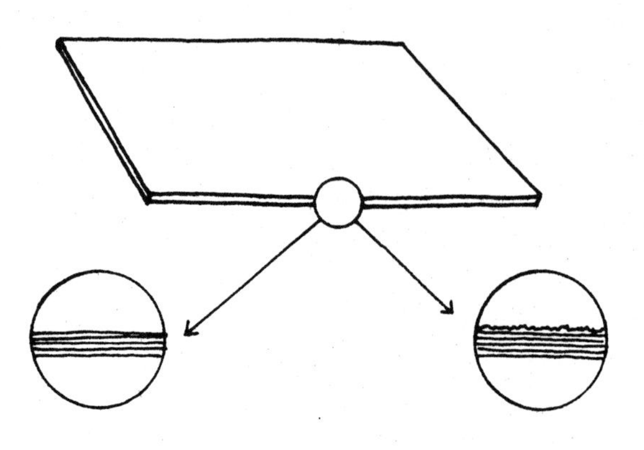

Hot press (less tooth)

Cold press (more tooth)

White **illustration board** comes at $\frac{1}{16}$" and $\frac{3}{32}$" in thickness. This makes it suitable for both finished drawing presentations and fine presentation models. Cold-press boards have a more textured surface and take to pencil, whereas hot-press boards are smoother and take to ink.

Preliminary study models are usually made of gray **chipboard**. Chipboard also comes in a variety of thicknesses. **Foam-core board** is a strong, lightweight board, excellent for model making.

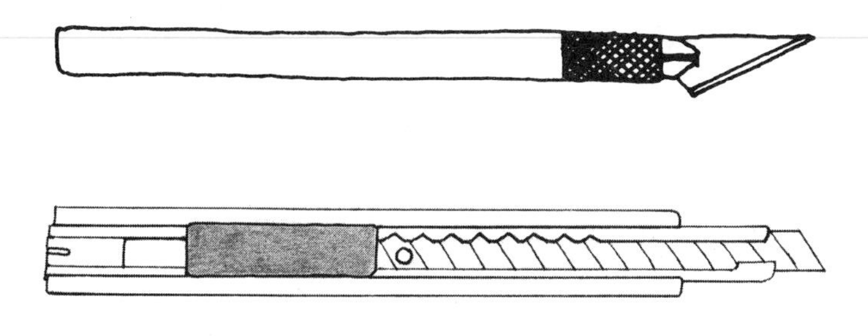

An **X-Acto knife** uses blades of several different shapes. The illustration shows the one most commonly used. It is excellent for small, detailed cuts (small apertures). A pack of #11-size blades for refills is strongly recommended. Another alternative, especially for cutting cardboard or foam-core board, is an **Olfa knife.**

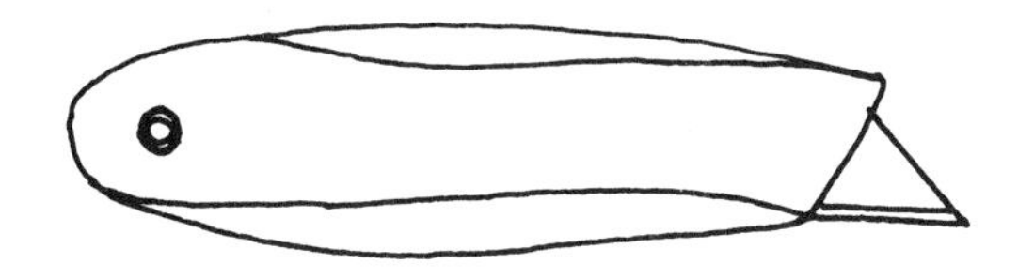

Utility knives are used primarily for long cuts on heavy materials such as thick illustration board, mat board, or cardboard. They are excellent for scoring. Stanley is a highly recommended brand. X-Acto's SurGrip utility knife is contoured to conform to your grip.

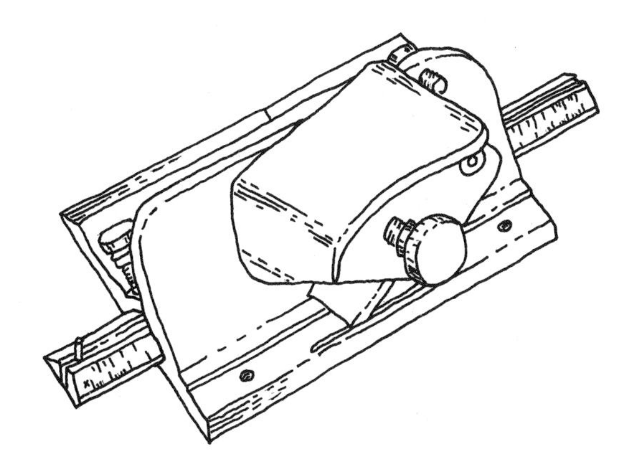

Good-quality **cutters** can make a clean, crisp 45° bevel. Highly recommended is the Logan Series 4000 mat cutter, which has a built-in marking system. With a pivoting blade holder, it can be used against any suitable straightedge. The less expensive series Logan Series 2000 push-style cutter has a start-and-stop indicator for precise corners. A **razor saw** with a thin blade and fine teeth is used for extrafine cuts on small pieces of wood, such as balsa. Zona Universal razor saws are highly recommended.

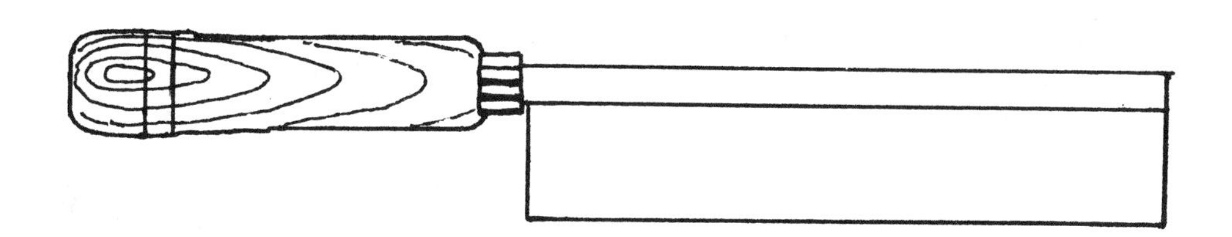

Adhesives, glues, and glue guns are used to fasten materials together for model making. A water-soluble glue is commonly used for cardboard. Rubber cement is excellent for collage work. Spray adhesives are most efficient for mounting drawings or photographs on cardboard, as well as for laminating smooth, porous sheets together. For a cutting guide, use an 18" stainless steel straightedge with a cork backing. A basic cutting rule of model making is to never make only one pass when cutting materials (especially thick cardboard). Make a series of light cuts. This will give you better control and accuracy. Cutting on a self-healing translucent plastic or rubber cutting surface (18" × 24" is a good mat size) will extend the life of your cutting blades.

The following are architect's scales:

12"=1'0"	1"=1'0"	¼"=1'0"
6"=1'0"	¾"=1'0"	3/16"=1'0"
3"=1'0"	½"=1'0"	⅛"=1'0"
1½"=1'0"	⅜"=1'0"	3/32"=1'0"

For architectural work, all of the above scales are used. Least used are the scales of 12"=1'0" and 6"=1'0". The scale is usually notated within the title block of an architectural drawing. It can also appear underneath the view of a particular detail. The choice of the proper scale size is dependent on the building size, the amount of detail to be drawn, and the size of paper used. Sometimes common practice dictates the size; for example, floor plans for residential buildings are normally drawn at ¼"=1'0". Construction details can use scales ranging from ½"=1'0" to 3"=1'0".

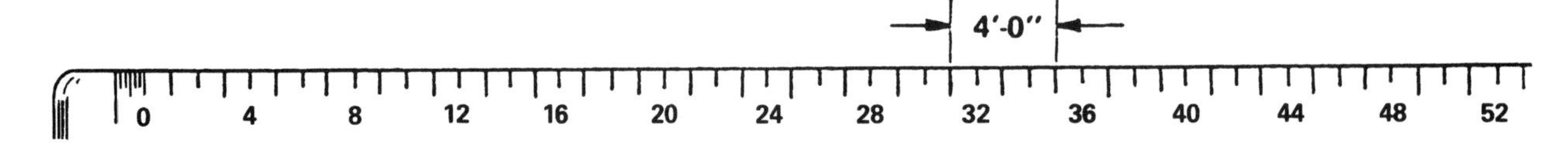

The actual size of the architect's scale. This scale is ⅛"=1'0"

The **architect's scale** is used primarily for drawing buildings, architectural details, structural details, and mechanical systems in buildings. The purpose is to represent large objects at a reduced scale to fit on drafting paper–size sheets. The best quality scale is unbreakable plastic with color-coded, engraved, calibrated graduations. Scales come in three beveled types, one triangular type, and one rapid rule type (see below). Choose the one most suited to your needs.

The **civil engineer's** or **engineer's scale** is used primarily for site plans, location plans, and land measurements in map drawing.

The following are civil engineer's scales:
10, 20, 30, 40, 50, 60, or 80 divisions to the inch, representing feet, 10 feet, 100 feet, rods, or miles.

Be careful not to confuse "scale" and "size."
¼"=1'0" is referred to as "quarter scale" in the architect's language, whereas ¼"=1" is referred to as "quarter size."

OPPOSITE BEVEL
Easy to pick up and handle

DOUBLE BEVEL
A good pocket scale

FLAT BEVEL
Easy to keep flat to a board

TRIANGULAR
Has many scales on the same stick.

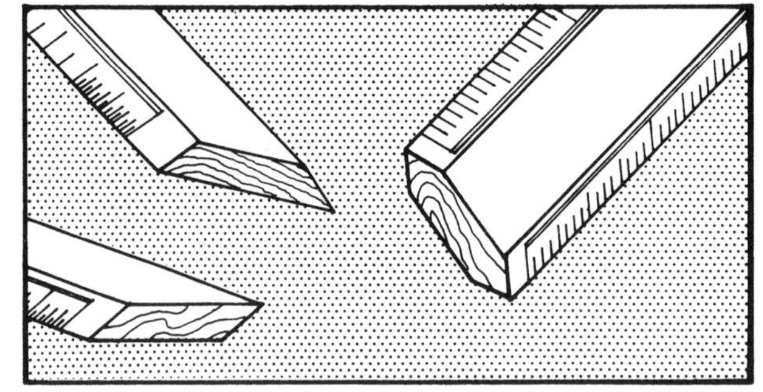

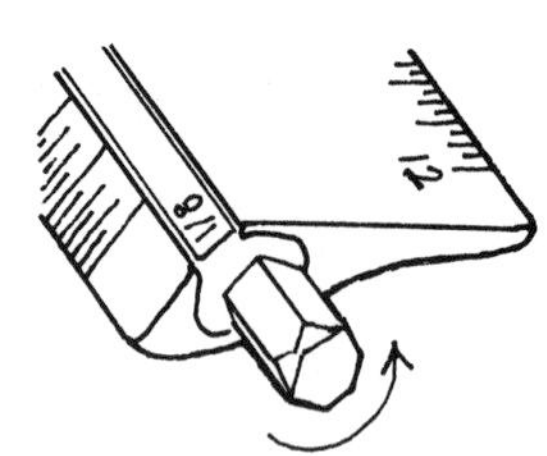

Rapid rule

Always observe a scale from directly above.

RAPID RULE
Made of lightweight, solid aluminum, you rotate a rapid rule's scale rod to see the desired scale. There's no need to search for the needed edge or read backward.

Remember to keep the scale clean; don't mark on it, and never use it as a straightedge!

Determining How Much Each Subdivision Represents

The best procedure is to ask yourself the following question: Each subdivision represents what part of one foot?

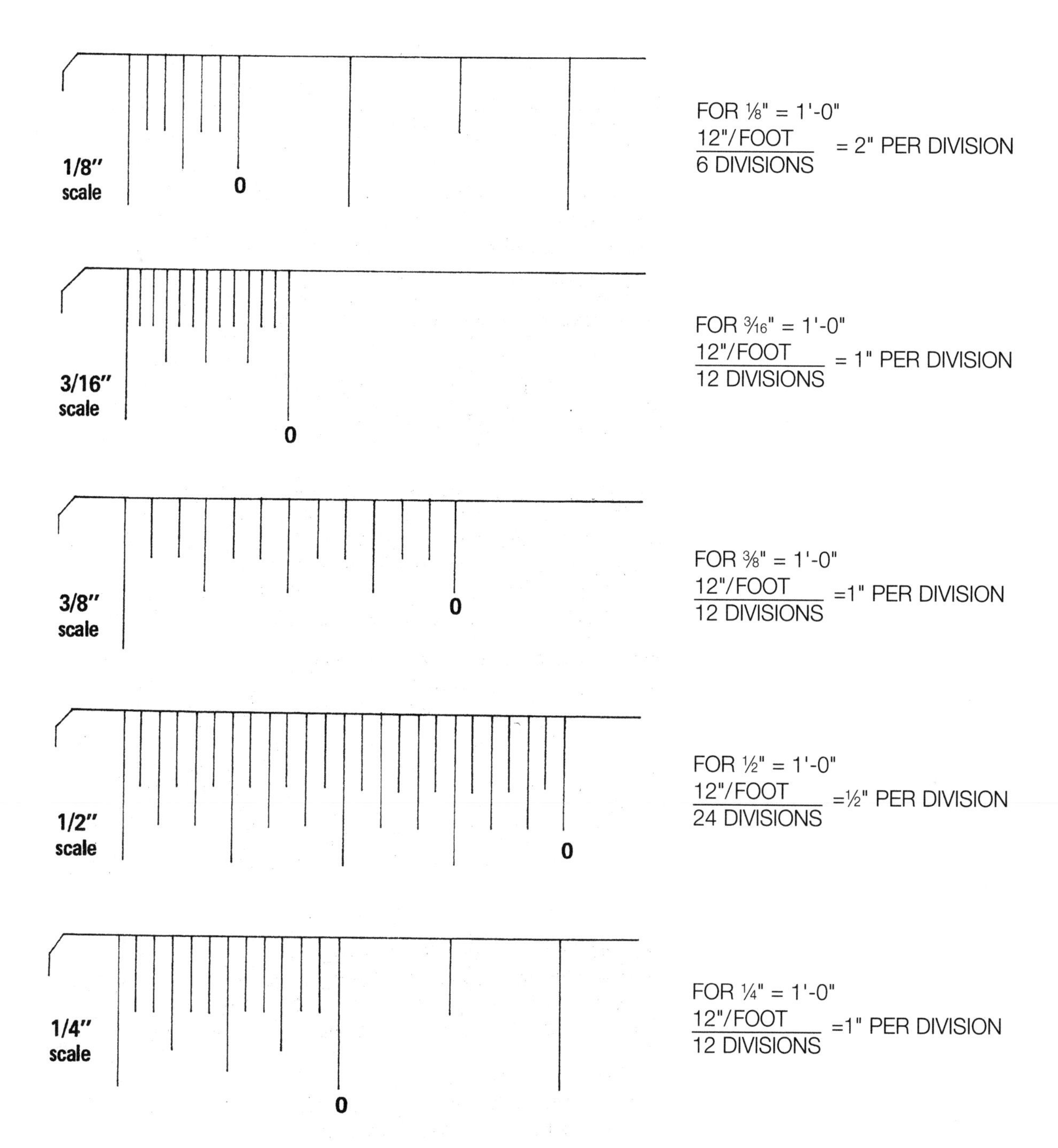

Note that in all of the reduced scales, the major divisions represent feet and their subdivisions represent inches and fractions thereof. Therefore, ½ means ½ inch = 1 foot, not ½ inch = 1 inch.

To facilitate the counting of subdivisions, the above scales have been enlarged from their actual size.

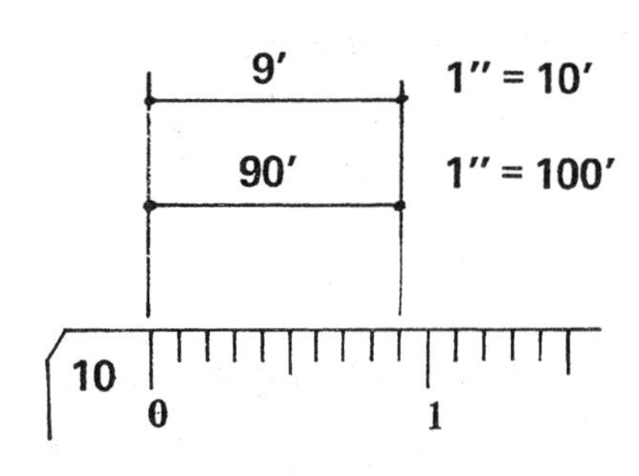

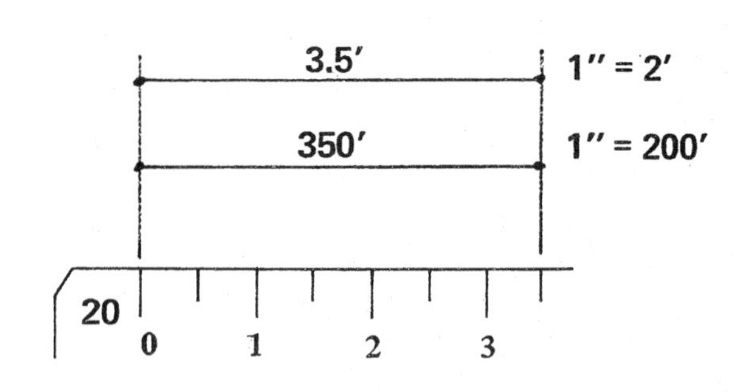

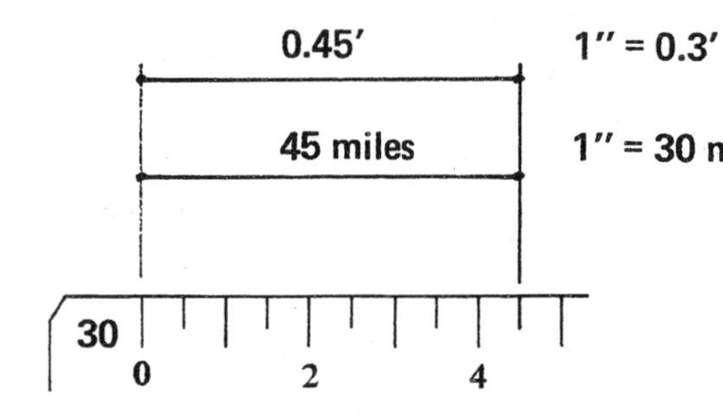

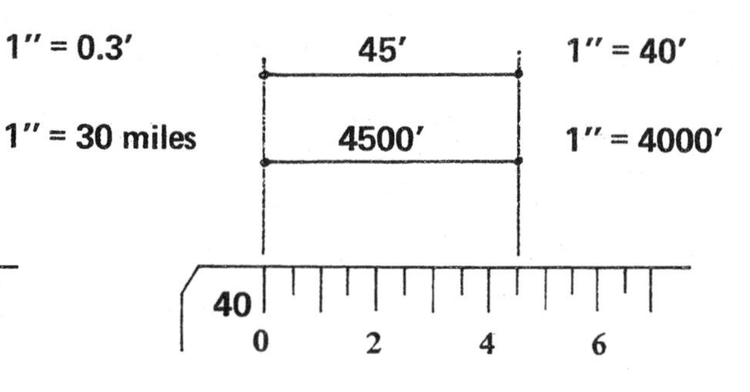

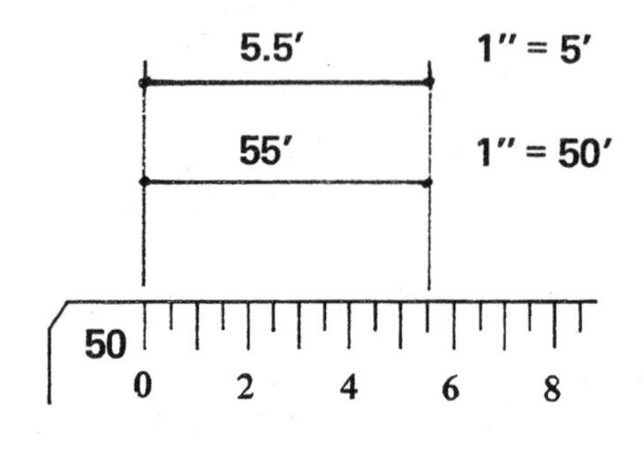

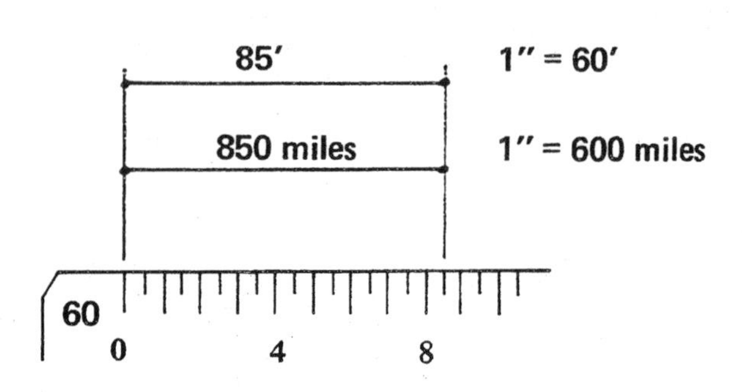

Shown above are the six standard scale units found on the **engineer's scale.** There are many possibilities for each scale unit since different lengths can be indicated for the scale unit. For example, in the case of a 10 scale, 1" can equal any one of the following: 0.1', 1', 10', 100', or 1,000 (feet or miles). Two possibilities are shown above for each of the six standard scale units. Divisions to the inch represent feet, rods, or miles.

Think of the scale number, such as 10, as the number of divisions per inch. Thus, 40 would indicate 40 increments or parts per inch. A 1" = 40' scale would have 40 increments, each increment being one foot. These incremental divisions are then continued along the full length of the scale. The engineer's scale is used primarily for site plans and location plans.

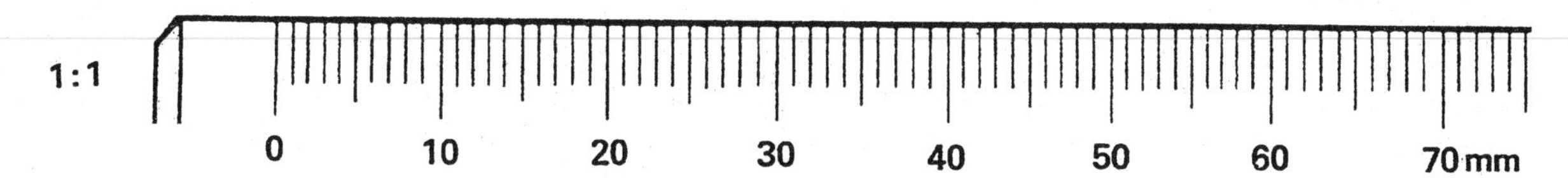

This metric scale has a 1:1 ratio and should be used for **full-size** drawings. For example, 10 mm on the drawing equals 10mm on the object or building.

This metric scale has a 1:5 ratio and should be used for drawings **one-fifth full size**. For example, 100 mm on the drawing equals 500 mm on the object or building.

As with the architect's scale, the **metric** scales above have been enlarged for easier reading. Metric scales are expressed as ratios (examples: 1:20 or 1:200). All countries except the United States (which uses inch-pound units) use the SI (International System of Units), a modern version of the metric system. A meter is 3.281 feet in length. It is easy to work with because converting from unit to unit merely requires multiplying or dividing by powers of ten. For example, 1,000 millimeters (mm) equals 1.0 meter (m)—(i.e., 1,000 divided by 1,000). A metric scale is 150 mm long (about 6"). Architects use various metric scales for various types of drawings. For example, 1:500 is a common scale reduction ratio for site plans, whereas 1:100 is used for floor plans and elevations. Ratio reductions of 1:1 and 1:5 are frequently seen for architectural details. These examples show architectural drawings that each require a different metric scale.

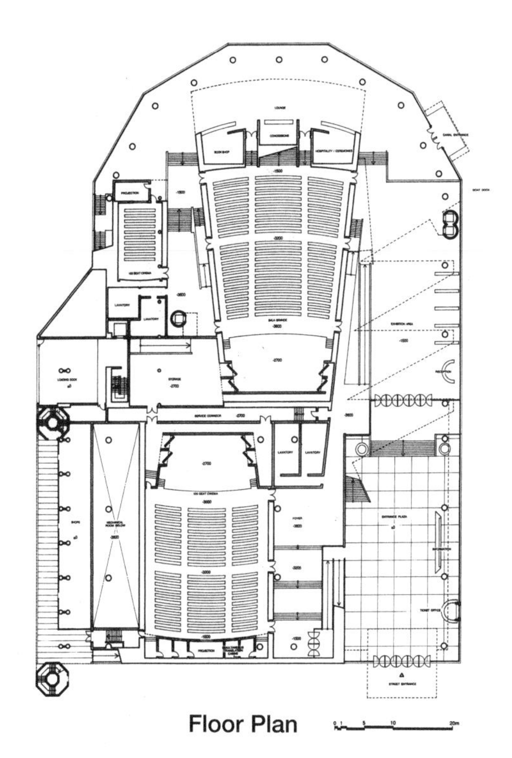

Floor Plan

Palazzo del Cinema, Venice, Italy
38 × 53 cm (15" × 20.9")
Medium: Ink on Mylar
Courtesy of Maki and Associates

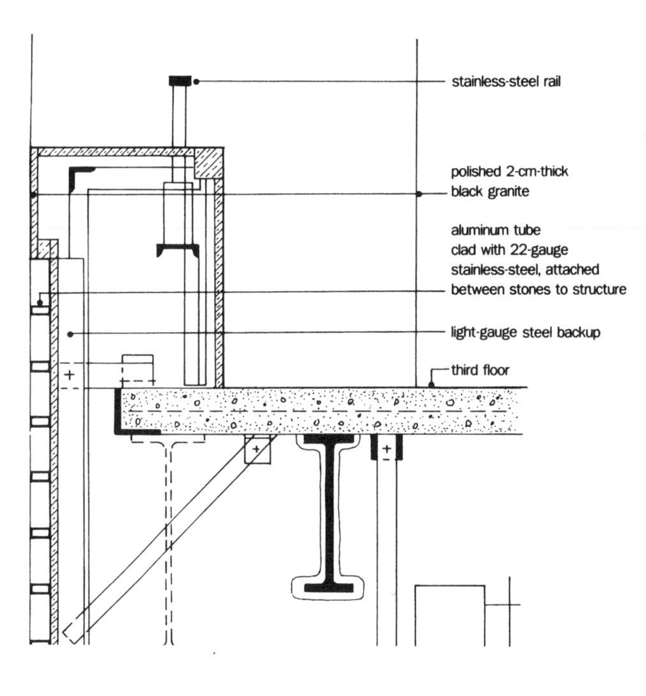

Partial section detail
One O'Hare Center
Rosemont, Illinois

Courtesy of Kohn Pedersen Fox Associates, Architects

2

Lettering, Typography, and Line Types

In drafting as well as in the design-drawing process, knowledge of line types, control of line quality, typography, and lettering are important. Well-executed hand lettering and proper line quality are needed for clear working drawings as well as for design drawings.

The intent of this chapter is to develop your ability first to recognize and ultimately to execute proficient lettering, typography, and line quality.

The following are some of the important skills, terms, and concepts you will learn:

How to hand letter efficiently and properly
How to recognize line types

Presentation typography

Line weights
Line quality

Lettering, Typography, and Line Types

TOPIC: LETTERING

Ching 2003,179–81.

Lin 1993, 75–76.

Sutherland 1989.

TOPIC: TYPOGRAPHY

Carter, Day, and Meggs 2007.

Craig 1990.

Chapter Overview

By studying this chapter and doing the related exercises in the book's final section, you will learn how to execute good architectural hand lettering and good line quality. For continued study, refer to Sutherland's *Lettering for Architects and Designers.*

Precise architectural **hand lettering** will always be needed despite the growing use of computer type in professional practice. When hand lettering, work from top to bottom; this prevents smudging. If it is not possible to move downward, then cover the previously lettered lower parts of the sheet with some clean paper to prevent hand-graphite contact. The example below shows the lettering of a partial wall detail from a set of working drawings. Working drawings are those from which a contractor erects a structure.

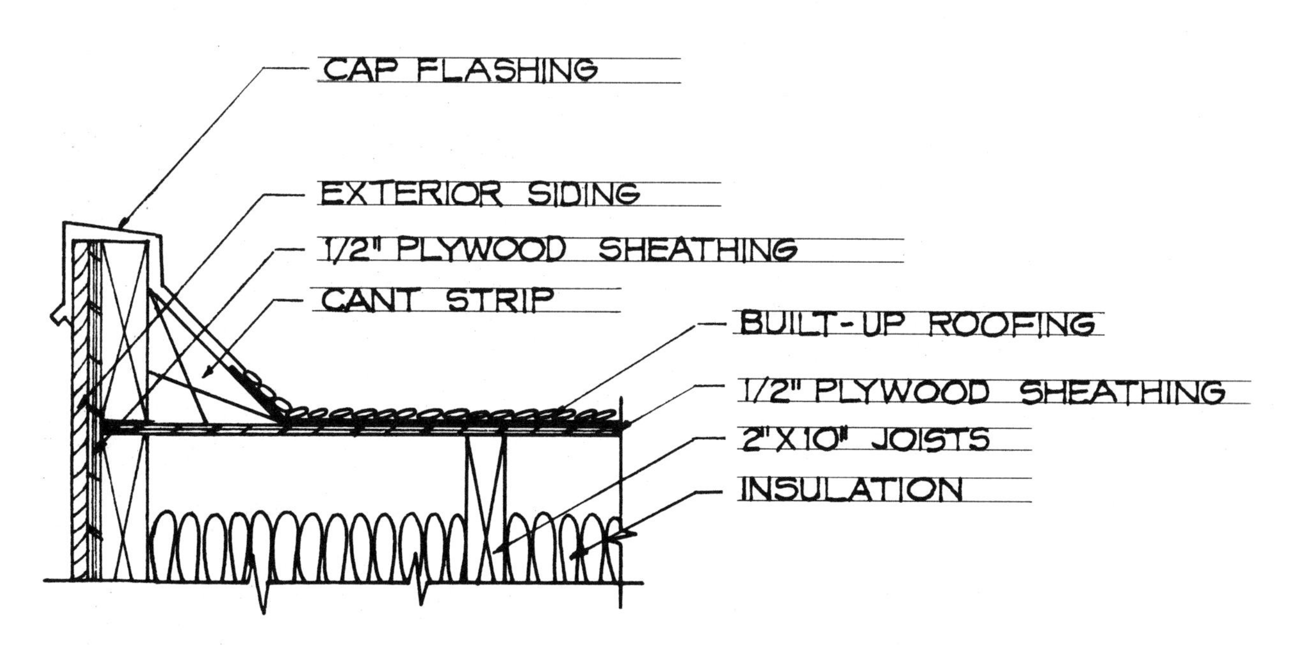

Evanston Public Library
Design Competition

P E N I N S U L A R E G E N T
BACKEN ARRIGONI & ROSS, INC.

Evanston Public Library Design Competition
Courtesy of Michael Blakemore/Sandy & Babcock, Inc.
Architecture & Planning

The Peninsula Regent, San Mateo, California
Courtesy of Backen Arrigoni & Ross, Inc.
Architecture, Planning & Interior Design

Since the primary purpose of an architectural drawing is the graphic representation of an object, any lettering should be small enough so that it does not compete with the graphics. It should be legible, orderly, and convey information in the most comprehensible manner possible. An appropriate visual hierarchy of **typography** should be used for architectural presentations. Titles, heads, subheads, and text material must be arranged in descending order of visual importance; different type styles, sizes, and weights are used to convey the relative importance of these chunks of information. Mechanical lettering methods such as stencils in the form of templates, pressure-transfer lettering sheets, traceable sheets in a variety of scales, and computer-based traceable typefaces can all be used to create presentation drawings. **Stenciled lettering** (made by Helix, Pickett, etc.) can create a handsome uniformity for a series of drawings and is commonly used for titles. Stencils are cut in clear plastic templates so that the guidelines are visible. Opaque color can be applied with brushes, flair pens, or ink pens.

When architectural lettering exceeds a height of ½", use larger block typefaces. **Pressure transfer** lettering catalogs like those from Chartpak come in sheets, provide a variety of excellent typefaces, and add a professional quality to drawings. Use a burnisher to apply (rub on). They are divided into two major groups: **serif** and **sans** (without) **serif**. Serifs were originally the terminations of parts of a letter that were chiseled by the Romans. Markers (see p. 44) are excellent for executing larger freehand titles quickly.

Serif and sans serif type is further divided into **light, medium,** and **heavy** weights, as shown in the three samples below. Always use serif or sans serif consistently for any set of drawings.

60 pt. l.c. 60 pt. CAPS Helvetica Light

bath ELEVATION

54 pt. l.c. 66 pt. CAPS Folio Medium Extended

A RESIDENCE

36 pt. CAPS Microgramma Bold Extended

When choosing a typeface, ask yourself if it is legible and appropriate for the audience. Some nicely proportioned lettering typefaces in both upper- and lowercase (which is usually easier to read) are Imperial Roman (serif), Bauhaus Demi (sans serif), and Katrina Heavy (serif).

kitchen DETAIL

48 pt. l.c. 72 pt. CAPS Imperial Roman

Preliminary PLAN

48 pt. l.c. 60 pt. CAPS Bauhaus Demi

storage NORTH

60 pt. l.c. 48 pt. CAPS Katrina Heavy

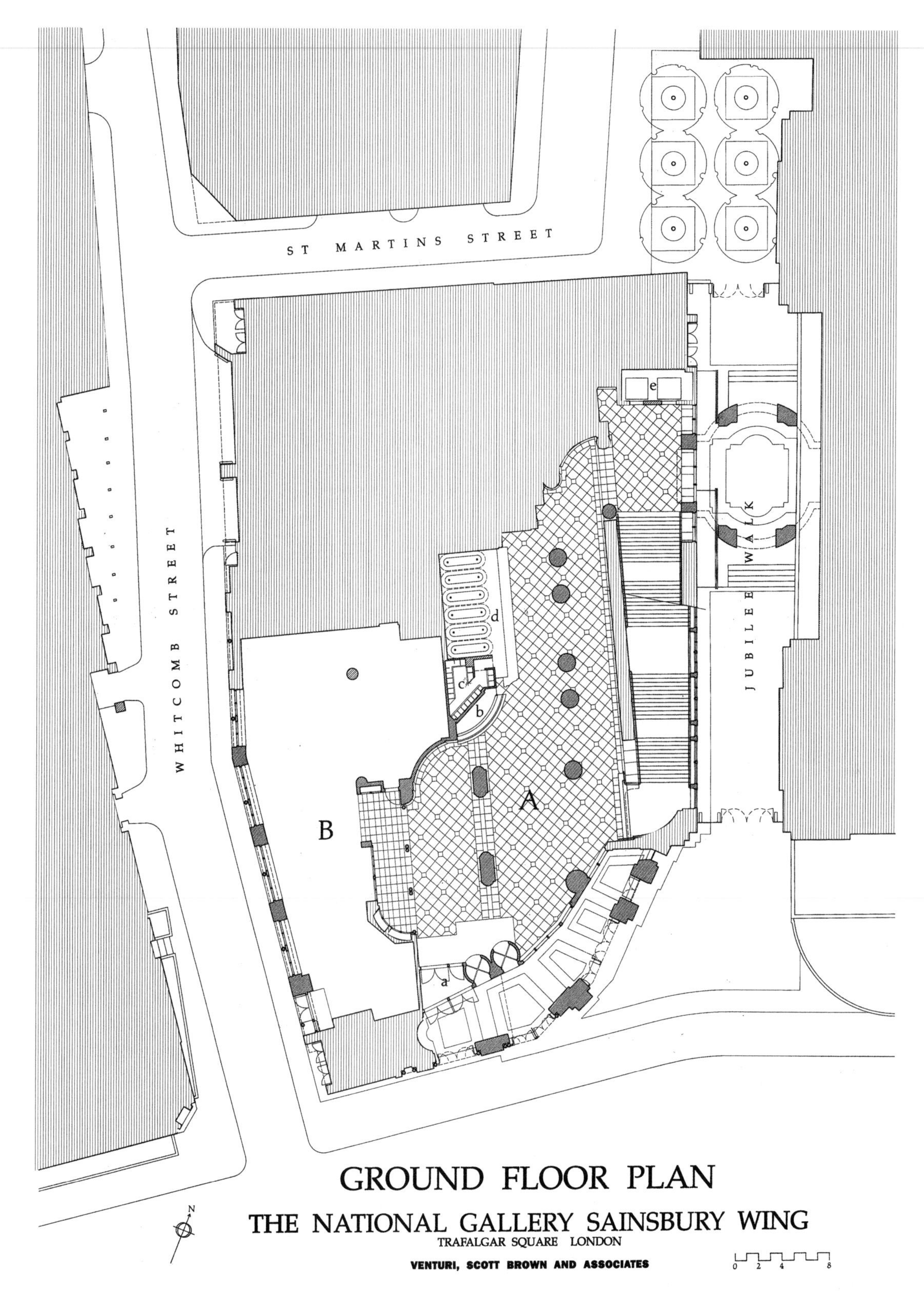

Drawing: Ground Floor Plan, The National Gallery, Sainsbury Wing. Trafalgar Square, London, England
Medium: Ink on vellum (CAD) 30.25" × 43.5" (76.8 × 110.5 cm)
Courtesy of Venturi, Scott Brown and Associates, Inc., Architects

Title typefaces should be adjacent to the drawings they refer to. The lettering size and thickness (darkness) reflects the importance of the title. Note the clear hierarchy of titles on this presentation drawing.

Architectural lettering is derived from uppercase Gothic letters; the relative proportions of each letter are easily seen using a gridded background. In actual practice a grid system is not used; try to eyeball the correct proportions for each letter. The suggested stroke order need not be followed; individuals differ in hand–eye coordination and may differ in the number of strokes needed to complete a letter. It is important to be consistent in forming an equally proportioned letter each time. For a left-handed person, the direction of the vertical strokes and curvilinear strokes remains the same, but the direction of horizontal strokes reverses.

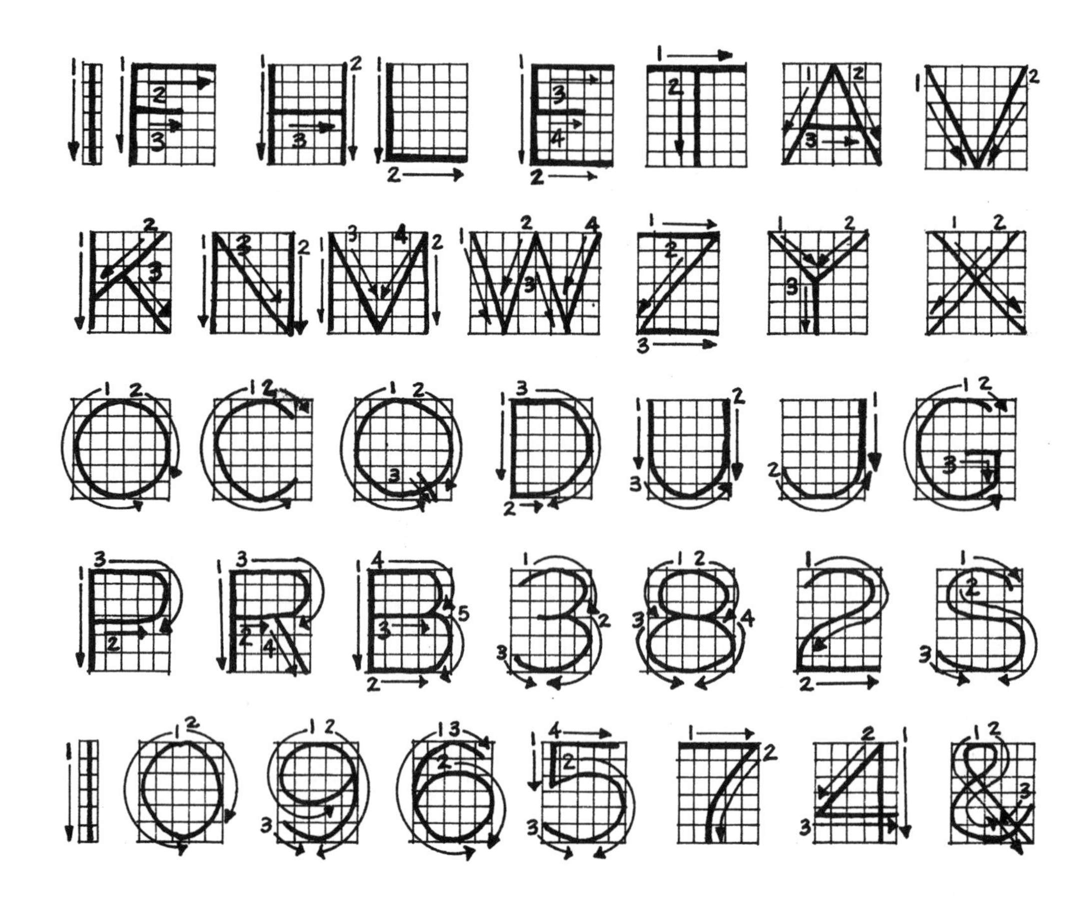

Notice that letters and numerals can be grouped in similar family types: the horizontal and vertical family (I through T); the horizontal, vertical, and angular family (A through X); and the curvilinear family (O through S). The numeral family has all the strokes. With time and practice, you should be able to make controlled, quick, even strokes. This is especially relevant to the rounded letters and numerals. Be sure the strokes are dark and crisp for good reproducibility. Good architectural hand lettering is the art of mastering basic motions: horizontal, vertical, angular, and curvilinear.

Lettering exercise: Become accustomed to the relative proportions shown for each letter by tracing or copying the letters and numerals on vellum. Repeat this exercise at two more heights: ¼" and ⅛".

The block lettering above is illustrated to help you develop your basic strokes. However, this type of lettering has the shortcoming of using too much space because it is very wide. In architectural work, a more narrowly proportioned alphabet, shown on the subsequent pages, is more suitable.

Lettering Examples

"I LIKE COMPLEXITY AND CONTRADICTION IN ARCHITECTURE. I LIKE ELEMENTS WHICH ARE HYBRID RATHER THAN "PURE," COMPROMISING RATHER THAN "CLEAN," DISTORTED RATHER THAN "STRAIGHTFORWARD," AMBIGUOUS RATHER THAN "ARTICULATED," PERVERSE AS WELL AS IMPERSONAL, BORING AS WELL AS "INTERESTING," CONVENTIONAL RATHER THAN "DESIGNED," ACCOMMODATING RATHER THAN EXCLUDING, REDUNDANT RATHER THAN SIMPLE, VESTIGIAL AS WELL AS INNOVATING, INCONSISTENT AND EQUIVOCAL RATHER THAN DIRECT AND CLEAR. . . . "

I LIKE COMPLEXITY AND CONTRADICTION IN ARCHITECTURE. I LIKE ELEMENTS WHICH ARE HYBRID RATHER THAN "PURE," COMPROMISING RATHER THAN "CLEAN," DISTORTED RATHER THAN "STRAIGHTFORWARD," AMBIGUOUS RATHER THAN "ARTICULATED," PERVERSE AS WELL AS IMPERSONAL, BORING AS WELL AS "INTERESTING," CONVENTIONAL RATHER THAN "DESIGNED," ACCOMMODATING RATHER THAN EXCLUDING, REDUNDANT RATHER THAN SIMPLE, VESTIGIAL AS WELL AS INNOVATING, INCONSISTENT AND EQUIVOCAL RATHER THAN DIRECT AND CLEAR. I AM FOR MESSY VITALITY OVER OBVIOUS UNITY. I INCLUDE THE NON SEQUITUR AND PROCLAIM THE DUALITY.

(VENTURI 1966, 16)

COMPUTER-GENERATED LETTERING

Robert Venturi, *Complexity and Contradiction in Architecture,* 2nd ed. (New York: The Museum of Modern Art, 1997).

Computer-generated lettering: Tekton
Used with express permission. Adobe® and Image Club Graphics™ are trademarks of Adobe Systems Incorporated.
Additional software from Handy by Epiphany Design Studio

BASIC GUIDES TO ARCHITECTURAL LETTERING

(1) ALWAYS USE LIGHTLY DRAWN GUIDELINES THAT ARE THE UPPER AND LOWER LIMITS OF THE AREA BEING LETTERED.

(2) LETTERING SHOULD BE SIMPLE BLOCK VERTICAL CAPITALS.

(3) MINIMUM HEIGHT FOR ANY LETTERING IS 1/8".

MAJOR TITLES SHOULD BE 1/4" HIGH.
3/16" HEIGHT CAN BE USED FOR MINOR TITLES.

(4) MANY INDIVIDUALS ARE INVOLVED WITH THE PRODUCTION OF WORKING DRAWINGS. THERE IS A TREND TOWARD THE ISSUING OF REDUCED DRAWINGS. THUS, A CLEAR, UNIFORM TYPE OF LETTERING IS NEEDED, USE AN HB, H, OR F PENCIL LEAD WEIGHT WITH A ROUNDED CONICAL POINT FOR YOUR LETTERING.

(5) THE AREA BETWEEN VARIOUS ADJACENT LETTER COMBINATIONS IN ANY WORD IS BASED ON GOOD JUDGMENT. GOOD SPACING DECISIONS BETWEEN LETTERS IS AN ART.

AREA IS ~ EQUAL

DETAIL SCALE PLAN BRICK

EQUAL SPACING IS BASED ON GOOD VISUAL JUDGMENT.

1/8"
1/16" OR 1/8"
1/8"
1/16" OR 1/8"
1/8"
1/16" OR 1/8"
1/8"
1/16" OR 1/8"
1/8"
3/16"
1/4"
3/16"
1/8"
1/16" OR 1/8"
1/8"

(6) EXAMPLE: ALPHABETS & NUMERALS

ABCDEFGHIJKLMNOPQRSTUVWXYZ

1 2 3 4 5 6 7 8 9 0

HAND LETTERING

IT IS ACCEPTABLE TO USE A SMALL TRIANGLE TO KEEP THE VERTICAL STROKES OF LETTERS VERTICAL. THIS IS COMMONLY DONE IN PROFESSIONAL PRACTICE AS A QUICK TECHNIQUE; HOWEVER, IT IS BEST TO EXECUTE FREEHAND VERTICALS IF YOU HAVE THE ABILITY TO KEEP LINES VERTICAL.

SLIGHT STYLIZATION OF LETTERS IS OFTEN DONE IN PROFESSIONAL PRACTICE; ANY DEVELOPMENT OF STYLE SHOULD ALWAYS EXHIBIT CONSISTENCY IN SPACING, PROPORTION, AND OVERALL APPEARANCE. FOR EXAMPLE, THE LETTERS ON THE PREVIOUS PAGE CAN BE STRETCHED HORIZONTALLY, AND HORIZONTAL STROKES CAN BE MADE AT A SLIGHT ANGLE TO THE HORIZONTAL. "I" AND "J" ARE EXCEPTIONS IN ATTEMPTING TO MAKE LETTERS AS WIDE AS THEY ARE HIGH. SOMETIMES IT TAKES YEARS TO MASTER THE ART OF GOOD ARCHITECTURAL LETTERING; BE PATIENT WITH YOUR PROGRESS.

EXAMPLE: ALPHABET AND NUMERALS,

A B C D E F G H I

J K L M N O P Q R

S T U V W X Y Z

1 2 3 4 5 6 7 8 9 0

Hand lettering (pp. 25, 30, 31, 33): Student project by Kam Wong
Medium: Pencil on vellum
Courtesy of the Department of Architecture
City College of San Francisco

A graph paper underlay is an alternative to guidelines (on translucent paper).

PENCIL LINES (for architectural drafting)	GRADE OF PENCIL TO USE
PROFILE LINE	H, F, or HB
VISIBLE/ELEVATION LINES	H, F or HB
CONSTRUCTION/LAYOUT/GRID LINES	2H or 4H
SECTION LINE	H,F, or HB
SECTION LINING	H, F, or HB
HIDDEN/DASH LINES	H or 2H
CENTER LINE	2H or 4H
DIMENSION LINE / EXTENSION LINE	2H or 4H

Heavy slash marks and dots are alternatives to arrowheads for terminating dimension lines. Arrowheads are also commonly indicated by using a wide V shape, with each leg approximately 60° to the dimension line.

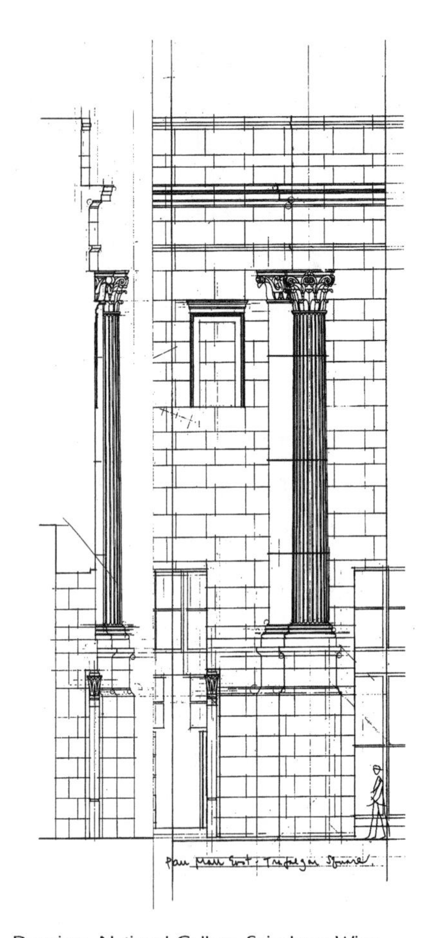

Drawing: National Gallery, Sainsbury Wing London, England
2" × 26.5" (5.1 × 67.3 cm) Scale: 1:25
Medium: Ink on vellum
Courtesy of Venturi, Scott Brown and Associates, Inc., Architects

Architectural drawing in the broad sense includes both architectural drafting and architectural sketching. Pencils are the simplest drawing medium in both areas. Pencil leads are made of compressed graphite and clay. The most common grades for architectural drafting work are 4H, 2H, F, H, and HB. To save time, it is common practice to use one lead and vary the pressure to give the desired line weight. An initially drawn line must be bold and uniform, not weak and tentative. Architectural sketching work (see p. 42) is commonly done with grades of 2B, 4B, and 6B, which are softer and allow for more expression.

Some drafting pointers:

Avoid corners that do not touch.

Keep an even line quality (see pp. 89 and 94).

A very small overlap is permissible.

Just touching is the generally accepted correct procedure.

Pointing or slightly emphasizing the ends helps to strengthen their presence.

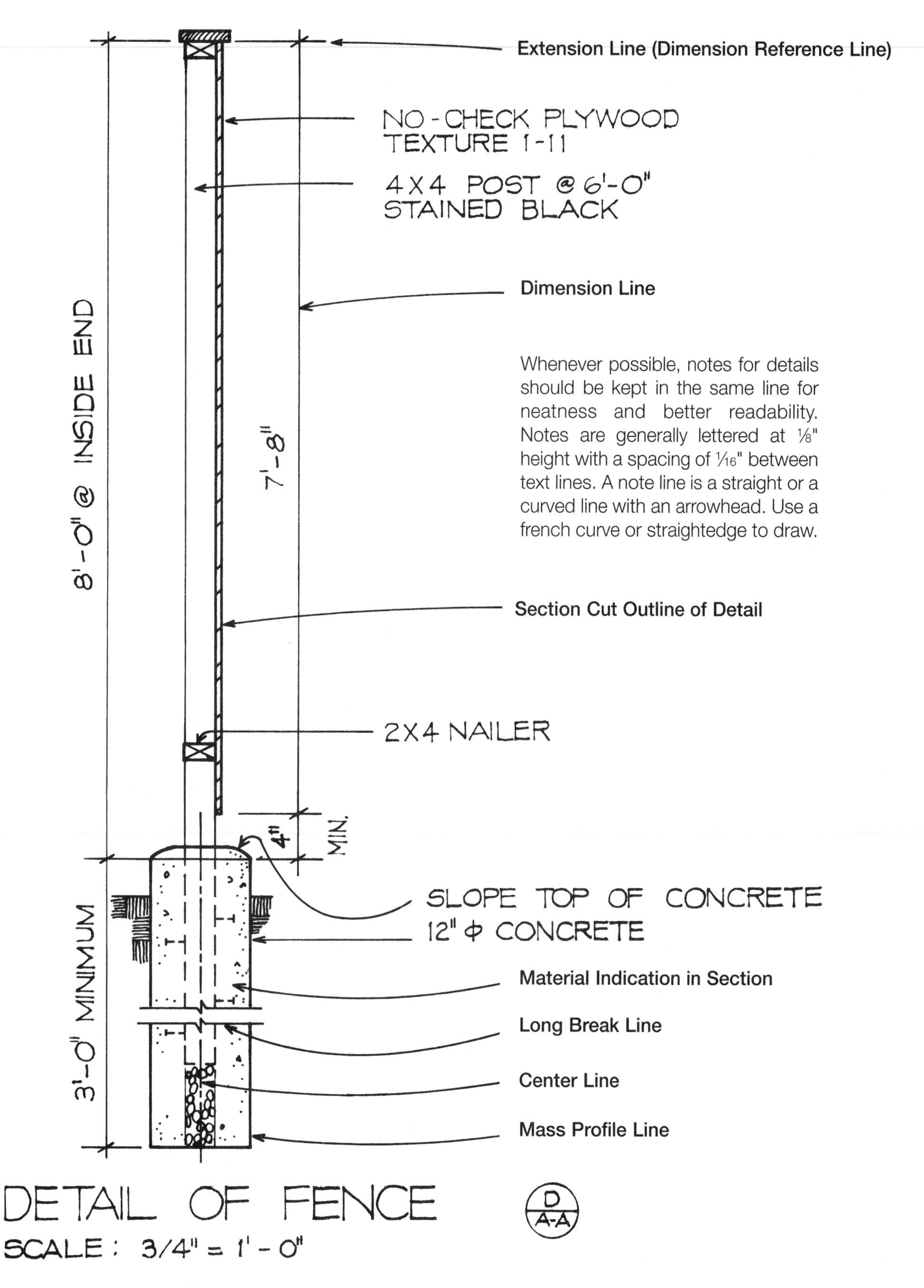

Whenever possible, notes for details should be kept in the same line for neatness and better readability. Notes are generally lettered at ⅛" height with a spacing of 1⁄16" between text lines. A note line is a straight or a curved line with an arrowhead. Use a french curve or straightedge to draw.

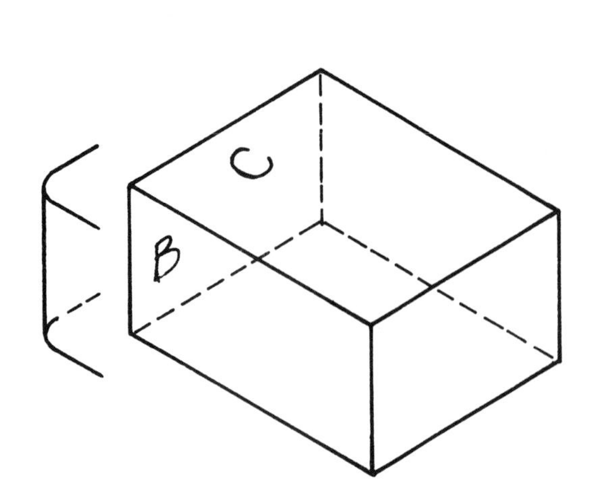

Visible line — the intersection of vertical plane B and horizontal plane C can be seen. Intersections that are not visually obstructed by solid elements of the object are defined as visible. A visible line can also be an edge of a curved surface.

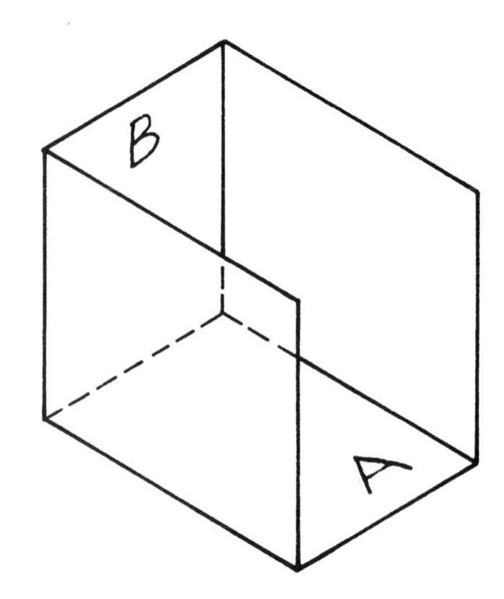

Hidden line — vertical plane B and horizontal plane A intersect, resulting in an intersection line that cannot be seen from the observer's position. This is represented by a dashed line.

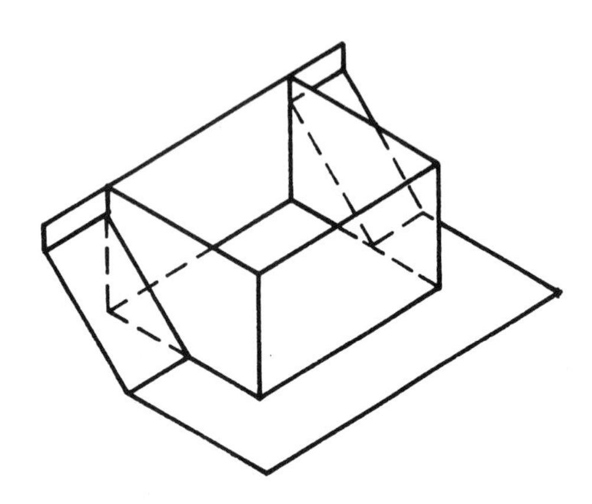

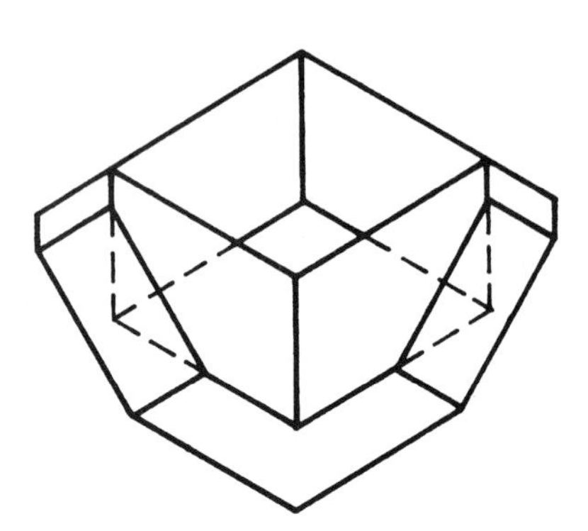

These pictorials (defined as pitch pockets) are part of construction documents for a contractor to use in the erection of a building. Note the use of hidden dashed lines to enhance the visualization of the details. When visible lines, hidden lines, and center lines coincide on a drawing, it is important to know which line takes precedence. A visible line takes precedence over a center line or a hidden line. A hidden line takes precedence over a center line.

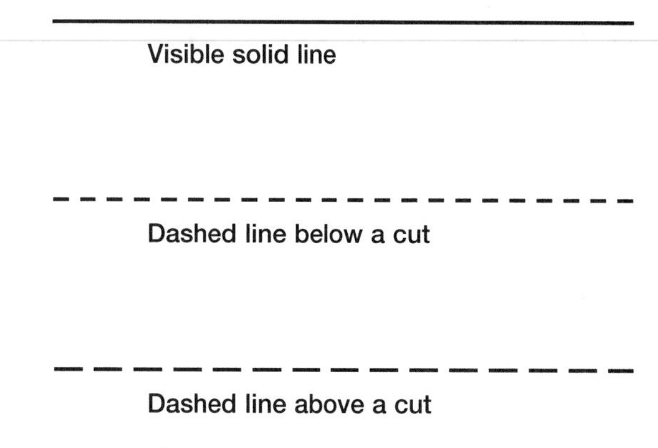

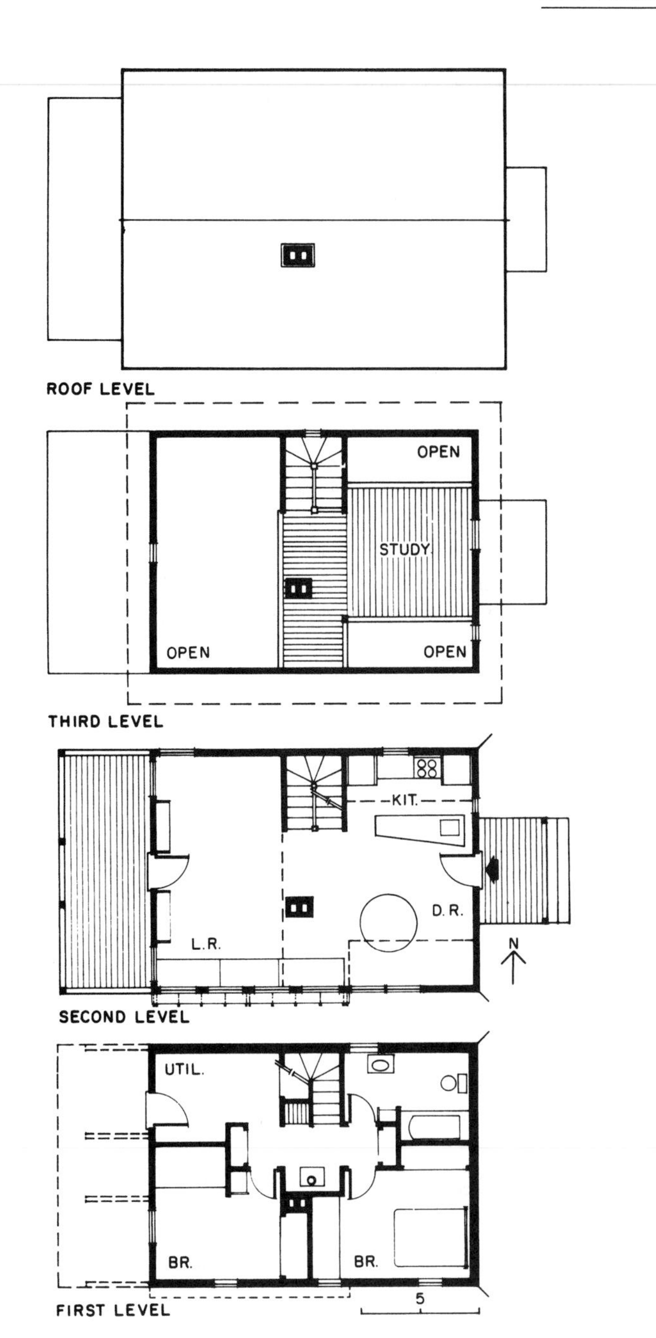

Visible solid lines and dashed hidden lines are two of the most important lines in finished architectural drawings. These lines are drawn with H, F, or HB lead weights. HB drawn lines erase easily, but they also tend to smear the most. Note that the dashed line below a cut is proportionally smaller than the one used above a cut. Strive to produce a consistent spacing and length for each dash.

Drawing: Hog Hill House
12" × 30" (30.5 × 76.2 cm) Scale ⅛"=1'0"
Medium: Ink on Mylar
Courtesy of B FIVE STUDIO

Visible lines in architectural drawings can be used for the outline of plan or section cuts (see example above) and any other intersection of planes (wall intersections in plan or elevation, etc.).

Dashed lines in architectural drawings express lines above a plan cut that the observer cannot see, such as roof overhangs (see example above), roof perforations, and skylights, as well as lines below a plan cut that are obscured by the floor, such as partitions.

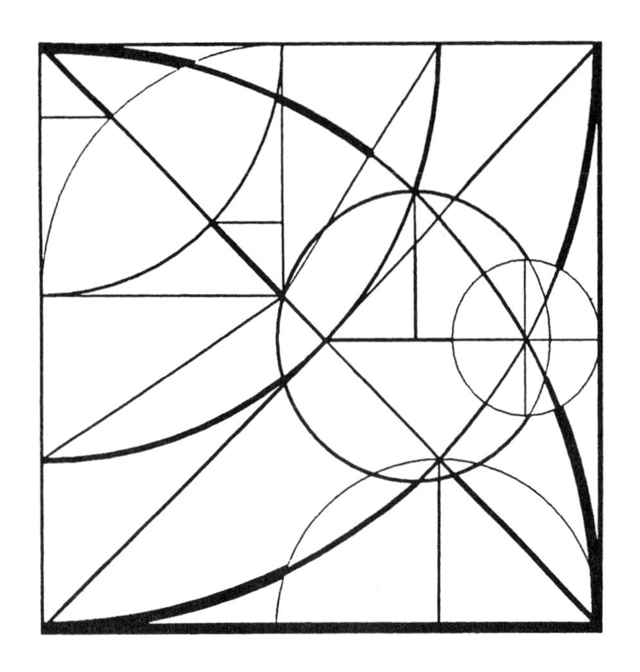

Drawing: Student project by Stephanie Slack
Medium: CAD
Courtesy of California Polytechnic State University, San Luis Obispo
College of Architecture & Environmental Design

Example Line Weights

Line quality refers to the crispness and the darkness (weight intensity) of a line. The darkness of a line is governed by the pencil used and the pressure applied. Inked lines generally have uniform value but can vary in width. It is extremely important to be consistent in drawing the same type of lines.

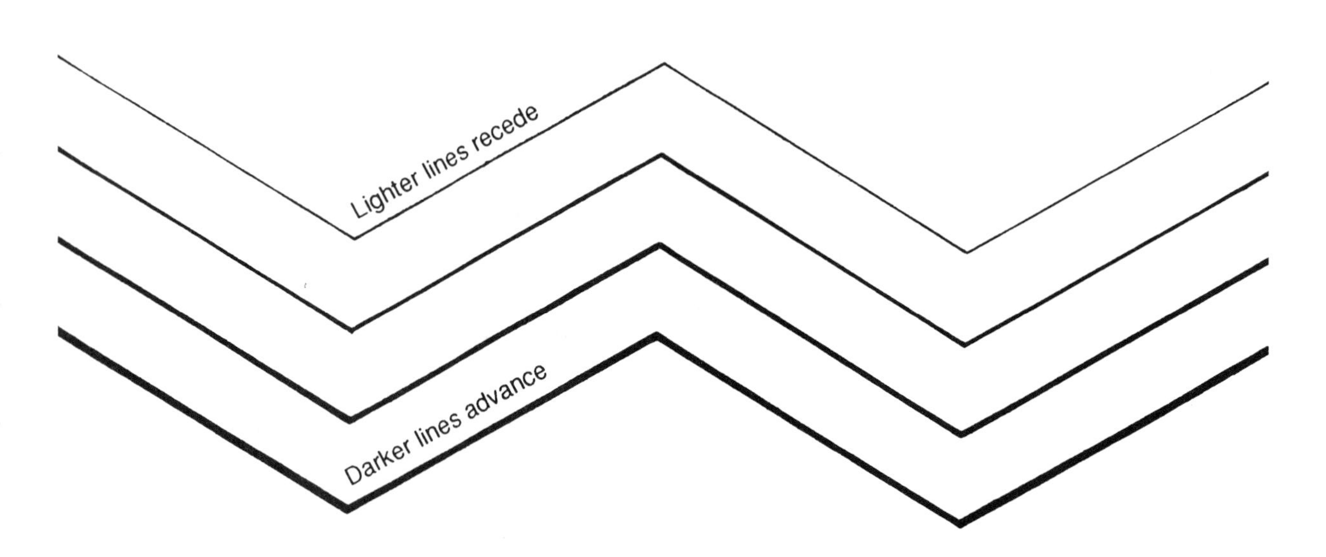

As you develop your design-drawing skills, you will realize the importance of line weight and line quality in any composition. As line weights vary, so do their impact on any composition. Design parameters such as variety, spatial depth, and visual hierarchy can be affected.

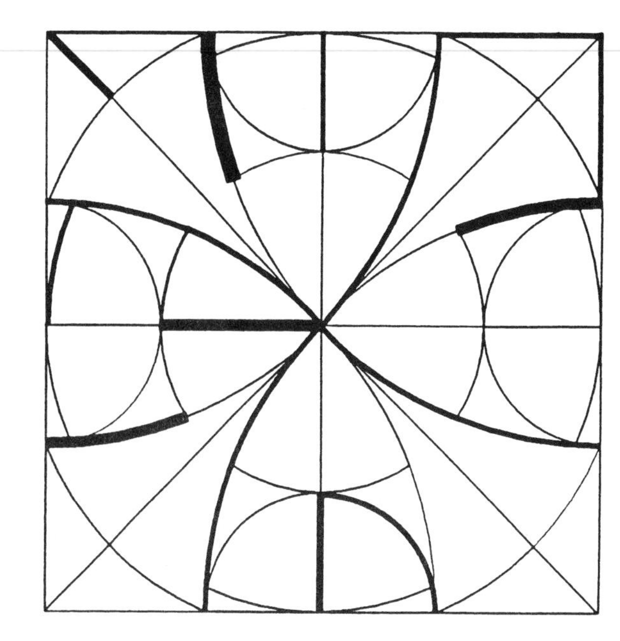

Drawings: Student project by Ben Ragle
Medium: CAD
Courtesy of California Polytechnic State University, San Luis Obispo
College of Architecture & Environmental Design

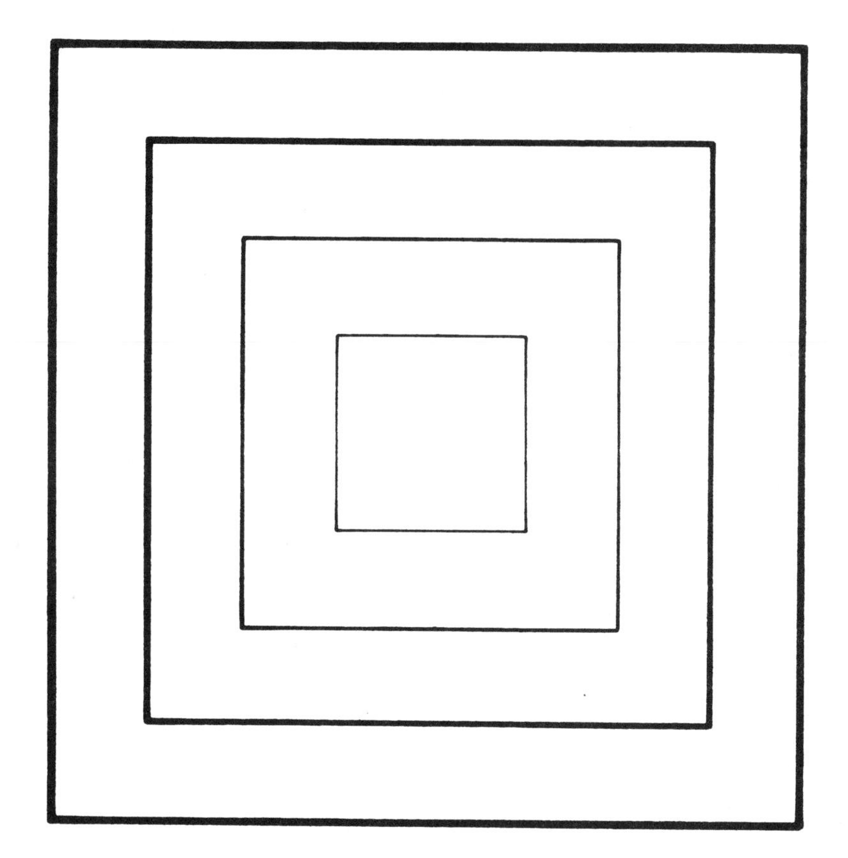

Emphasis is using line weight to create the illusion of space. The more variation of hierarchical line weight from thick to thin, the greater the implication of depth in the drawing.

3

Representational Sketching

BASICS 41
BASICS APPLIED 56

Sketches of the built environment are analytical drawings that generally convey an overall image. We do these sketches to gain a greater understanding of the nature of the urban landscape. Such sketches must be executed quickly, accurately, and with confidence.

Geometric shapes are the foundation for all derived form. Environmental form and composition is an aggregate of simple and complex forms. These forms must be graphically expressed in a visually appealing manner, whether you sketch from life or from your imagination.

The intent of this chapter is to cover the basic aspects of freehand descriptive sketching, including the types of sketching tools, line, shape, proportion, and values, as well as to examine how to observe and depict encountered environmental elements. Another goal is to hone your ability to sketch by using line, volume, texture, and tone—as well as proportional and perspective relationships—to describe various objects.

The following are some of the important skills, terms, and concepts you will learn:

Types of sketching pencils and the strokes they make
Types of sketching pens and the strokes they make
Sketching architectural elements like trees, cars, and buildings

Sighting	Blocking out	Construction lines	Contour drawing
Vantage point	Vignette	Focal point	Gesture drawing
Foreground	Middle ground	Background	Balance

Representational Sketching

TOPIC: CONTOUR DRAWING
Ching 2003.
Ching 1990, 42–45.
Dodson 1990.

TOPIC: STROKE CHARACTER
Ching 1990, 22–25.
Wang 2002.

TOPIC: VEGETATION
Wang 2002.

TOPIC: DRAWING METHODS
Crowe and Laseau 1986.
Hanks and Belliston 1977, 33–136.
Mendelwitz and Wakeham 1993.

TOPICS: HUMAN FIGURES, SIGHTING
Bridgman 2001.
Wang 2002.

TOPIC: SKETCHING WITH MARKERS
Wang 1993.

TOPIC: BUILDINGS/TRAVEL SKETCHES
Bleck 1994.
Ferriss 1986.
Ferriss 1998.
Johnson and Lewis 1999
Kliment 1984, 39–87, 105–13.
Leich 1980.
Pelli 1991.
Porter and Goodman 1985, 60–68.
Predock 1995.
Wu 1990.

Chapter Overview

In studying this chapter, you will begin to develop skills in hand representational sketching. For continued study, refer to Ching's *Drawing: A Creative Process* and Wang's *Pencil Sketching.*

Drawing from life is essential to the development of the hand-eye-brain loop. The more you draw, the more you look at the world around you. As architects, artists, and designers become more aware of their surroundings, their work becomes more formidable. Often, when students begin drawing, their work does not have "the right shape"; in other words, it is not in the correct proportions. One of the most fundamental tools for controlling proportion is called **sighting** (explained on pp. 46 and 47). This method of using a drawing instrument held at arm's length as a measuring device (essentially simulating a picture plane) is highly effective in helping the beginner to make objects in the drawing the right shape, as well as controlling distances and relative sizes in general. Looking and recording reality with the aid of sighting strengthens the visual sense and brings confidence to the drawing process.

Drawing is a process that progresses from seeing to visualizing and, finally, to expressing. The ability to see gives us the raw material for our perceptions and, ultimately, for what we draw. Visual information seen by the eye is processed, manipulated, and filtered by the mind in its active search for structure and meaning. The mind's eye creates the images we see and eventually tries to express them in the form of a drawn image. Our ability to express and communicate relies on our ability to draw.

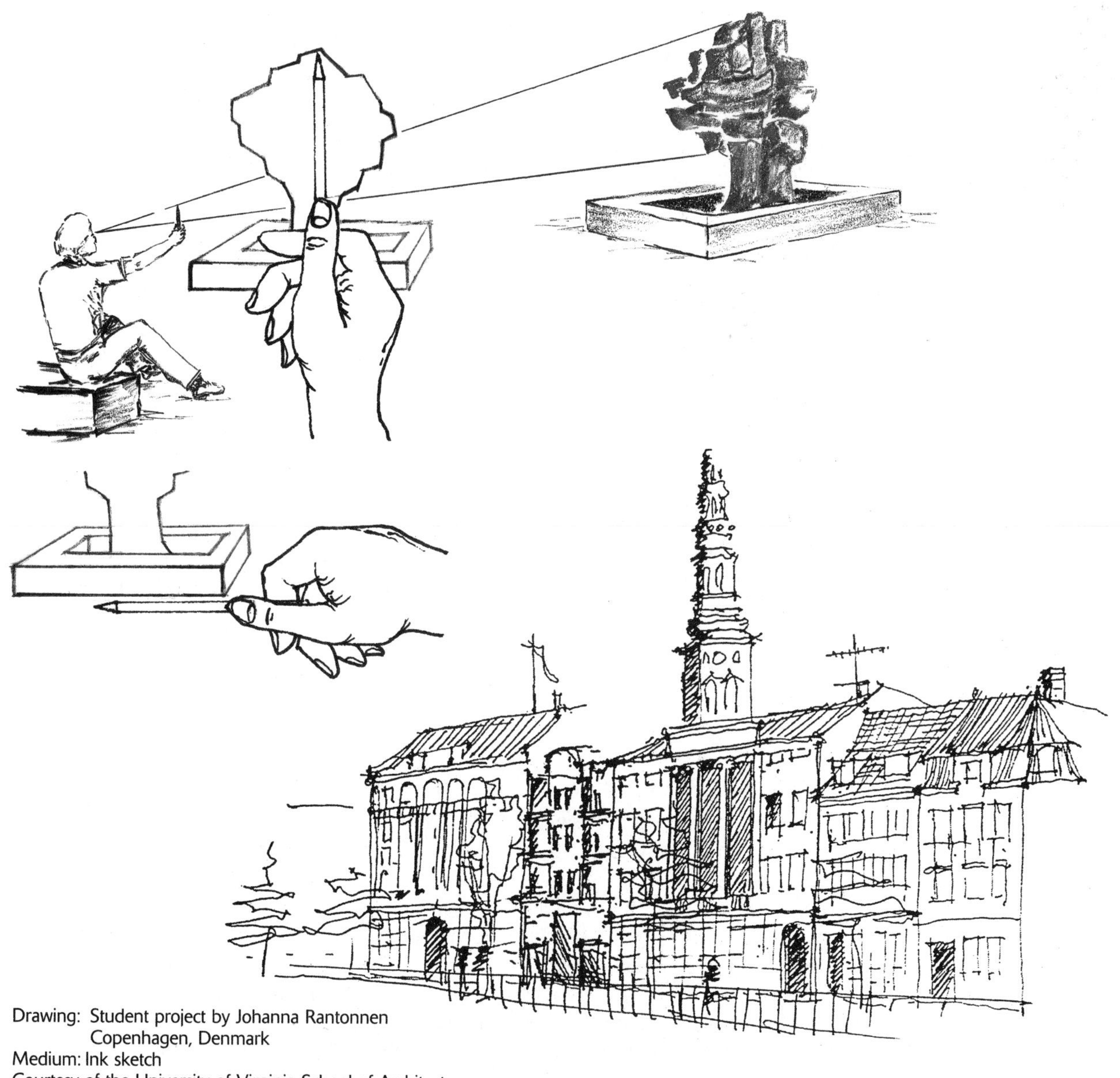

Drawing: Student project by Johanna Rantonnen
Copenhagen, Denmark
Medium: Ink sketch
Courtesy of the University of Virginia School of Architecture

FREEHAND SKETCHING PENCILS

As an introduction to this topic, this chapter will only cover noncolor representational sketching. Utilize the bibliography and Web site (Chapter 11) to explore color sketching. Some of the many quality **sketching pencils** are shown on this page. Other alternatives include charcoal sticks and Conté pencils. Experiment with different kinds of opaque **sketching paper** as well. Beginners normally use inexpensive newsprint paper as their first drawing paper. Smooth (fine-grain) sketching paper and coarse (textured) sketching paper are also commonly used. Sketched lines are more uniform and continuous on smooth paper, less uniform and more expressive on rough paper.

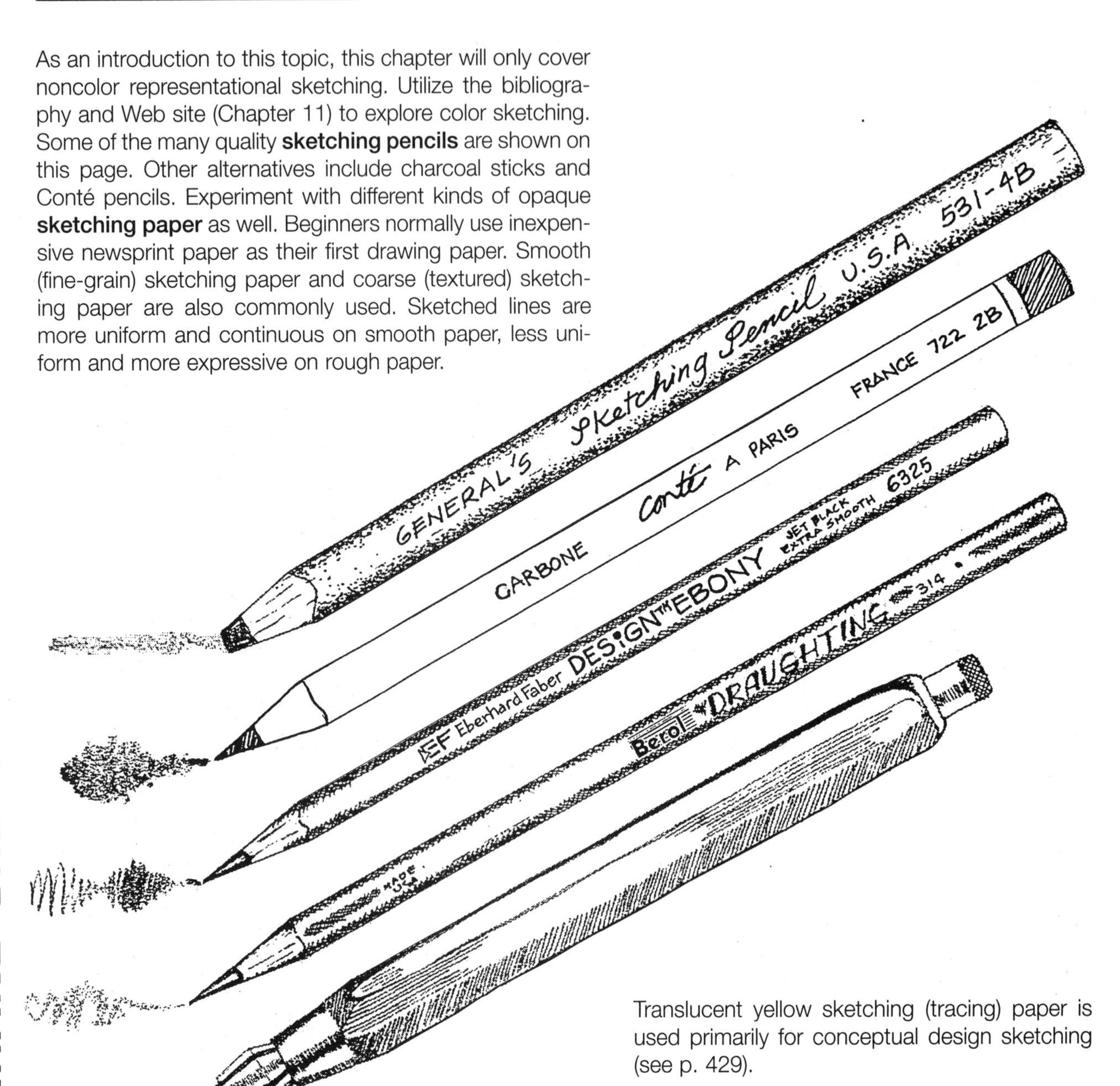

Translucent yellow sketching (tracing) paper is used primarily for conceptual design sketching (see p. 429).

Soft lead sketching pencils can have round or flat leads. A flat sketching pencil can be thick (carpenter's pencil) or medium thick (chisel pencil). Both must be sharpened by hand. Flat sketching pencils are mainly used in three degrees: 2B, 4B, and 6B. They are commonly used for covering large areas quickly, as when creating tonal indications for brick, stone, and wood. Conté pencils or sticks come in three grades of black, in four different colors, and in soft, medium, and hard. Both Conté and Ebony pencils give smooth lines. The Ebony pencil's soft core is slightly wider than that of a typical pencil. A good general-purpose sketching pencil with a soft lead is Berol Draughting 314. When round leaded pencils become too short from use, add length by using a pencil extender. An all-purpose mechanical leadholder clutch pencil can adapt its lead to almost any shape and is ideal for rapidly sketching over large areas. Other excellent brands include Derwent and Mars.

Sketch: Student project by Wan Othman
Glass study
Medium: Graphite pencil
Courtesy of Washington University
School of Architecture, St. Louis, Missouri

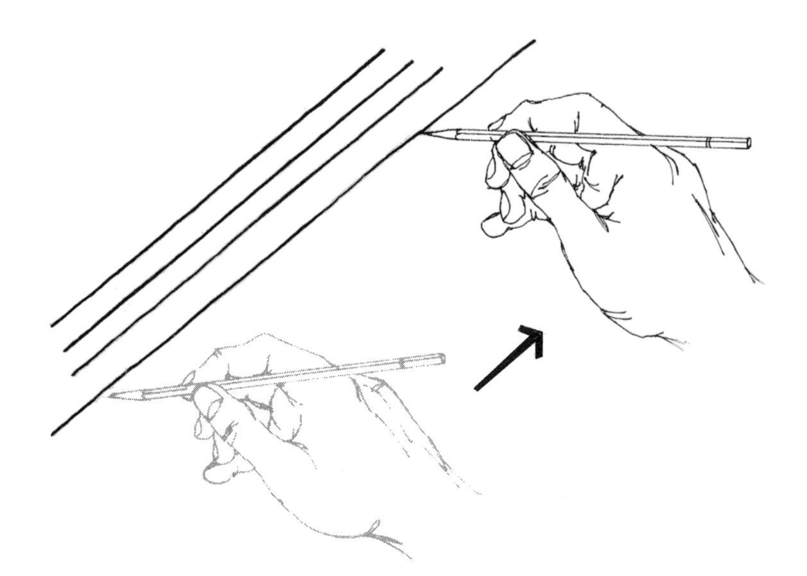

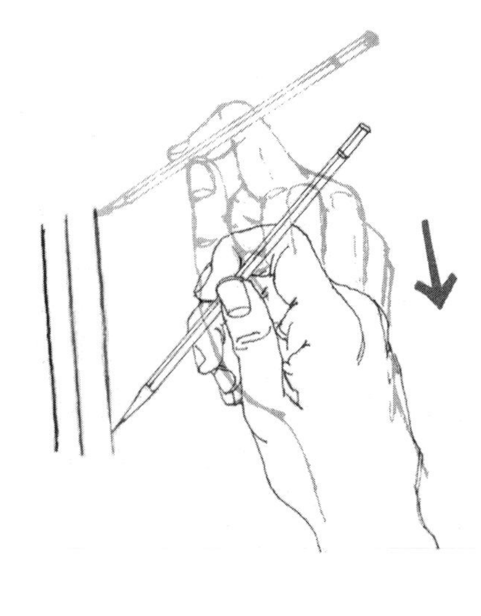

The quality of a freehand pencil stroke is determined by the hardness of the pencil lead, the character of the sharpened point, the amount of pressure applied, and the type of paper used. Compare parallel lines drawn on both smooth and rough sketching paper. Softer pencils work better with smoother paper, harder pencils with coarser paper. Architectural pencil sketching is most often done with grades such as HB, B, and 2B, though softer leads are also used. Graphite and charcoal pencils can yield variable line widths and tone. Variable tone and value cannot be achieved when sketching with pens and markers. Lighting conditions resulting in shades and shadows can be most accurately represented by using soft lead pencils, charcoal pencils, square or rectangular graphite sticks, or Conté crayons. To prevent pencil work from smudging, cover completed sections of your drawing with tracing paper or use fixative sprays.

In producing firm, steady strokes, do not rest your hand on the drawing surface as in writing. In the above illustration, only the side of the little finger is resting on the drawing surface. This allows the drawing hand to glide across the paper. The pencil should be held in a relaxed position; too tight a grip will cause hand fatigue. A wrist-and-arm movement will produce longer, continuous strokes. Use the wrist, elbow, and shoulders as pivot points. Attempt to master the control of sketching straight lines, curved lines, circular spirals, and circles. When sketching, use the whole page—draw big.

Sketch: The Garden Court of the Palace Hotel
San Francisco, California
Medium: Ink pen
Sketch by Charles Moore, Architect
Courtesy of Saul Weingarten, Executor, Estate of Charles Moore, and the Department of Architecture, UCLA School of Art and Architecture

Using **pens** or **markers** as graphic communication tools allows the architect/designer to express a wide range of images, whether they be representational, like the hotel courtyard and the Austrian street scene, or conceptual, as with the Lloyd's of London sketch. The London thumbnail sketch illustrates the loose, expressive quality that can be achieved with flexible felt-tipped markers. Contrast it with the very uniform, contoured lines delineated in the street scene with a fine-point, felt-tipped pen.

In addition to pencils, line and tone can be produced by a variety of pens and colored markers. Markers are available in a variety of halftones, but because they dry quickly, mixing tones is difficult (see Web site [Chapter 11]). Marker tips vary in size from fine to broad and in shape from pointed to chisel. Finer tips generate fine lines with more detail, whereas broader tips generate wider lines and solid tones. Technical pens are commonly used for precise mechanical lines. Razor-point pens, cartridge pens, sketch pens, and fountain pens can create loose sketching lines that are permanent. Fountain pens traditionally used for writing become quite versatile in their application of line weight simply by adjusting finger pressure. Excellent for quick sketch studies, fountain pens can also produce much thinner lines when used upside down (i.e., rotated 180°).

Sketch: Lloyd's of London, London, England
11.75" × 16.5" (29.8 × 41.9 cm)
Medium: Brown felt-tipped marker
Sketch by Laurie Abbott
Courtesy of Richard Rogers Partnership, Architects

Drawing: Street scene, Salzburg, Austria
7" × 10" (17.8 × 25.4 cm)
Medium: Felt-tipped pen on paper
Courtesy of Steven House, Architect, San Francisco

Ballpoint, felt-tipped, fiber-tipped, and roller-tipped pens can also generate a variety of line widths. In general, all types of pens create steady, fluid, smooth-flowing lines—without the need to apply pressure (unlike pencils). Remember that for architectural sketching, the width and type of the tipped nib are of most concern. Nibs can be made of felt, nylon, plastic, foam, etc. New nibs tend to be hard and become flexible after use (keep old ones for soft tones). Try to keep up with the ever-changing technology of newly developed nibs.

Felt-tipped markers are a quick, loose medium (similar to watercolors) for creating transparent presentations; they are quite effective when time is a critical factor. One of markers' advantages is that they very seldom smudge. They come in a large variety of premixed colors in addition to black and shades of gray. Markers are more suitable for smoother, harder, and heavier grades of paper, whereas pencils and colored pencils work best on medium-weight textured paper.

Pens and markers are perhaps best suited for sketching conceptual ideas (see Chapter 9). These tools give you the ability to loosen up and avoid inhibitions in the design-drawing process.

Drawing: Sacramento State Office Building, Sacramento, California
Fisher–Friedman Associates, San Francisco, California

To properly establish accurate proportions in transferring what you see to your drawing pad, you must accurately compare relative lengths, widths, and angles.

1. Observe the subject/scene that you would like to draw.
2. Close one eye, hold your head still, and extend your arm to arm's length.
3. Holding a pencil or pen, make a basic unit length measurement on any part of the viewed scene, using the distance from your drawing instrument tip to the top of your thumb as a guide to proportion.

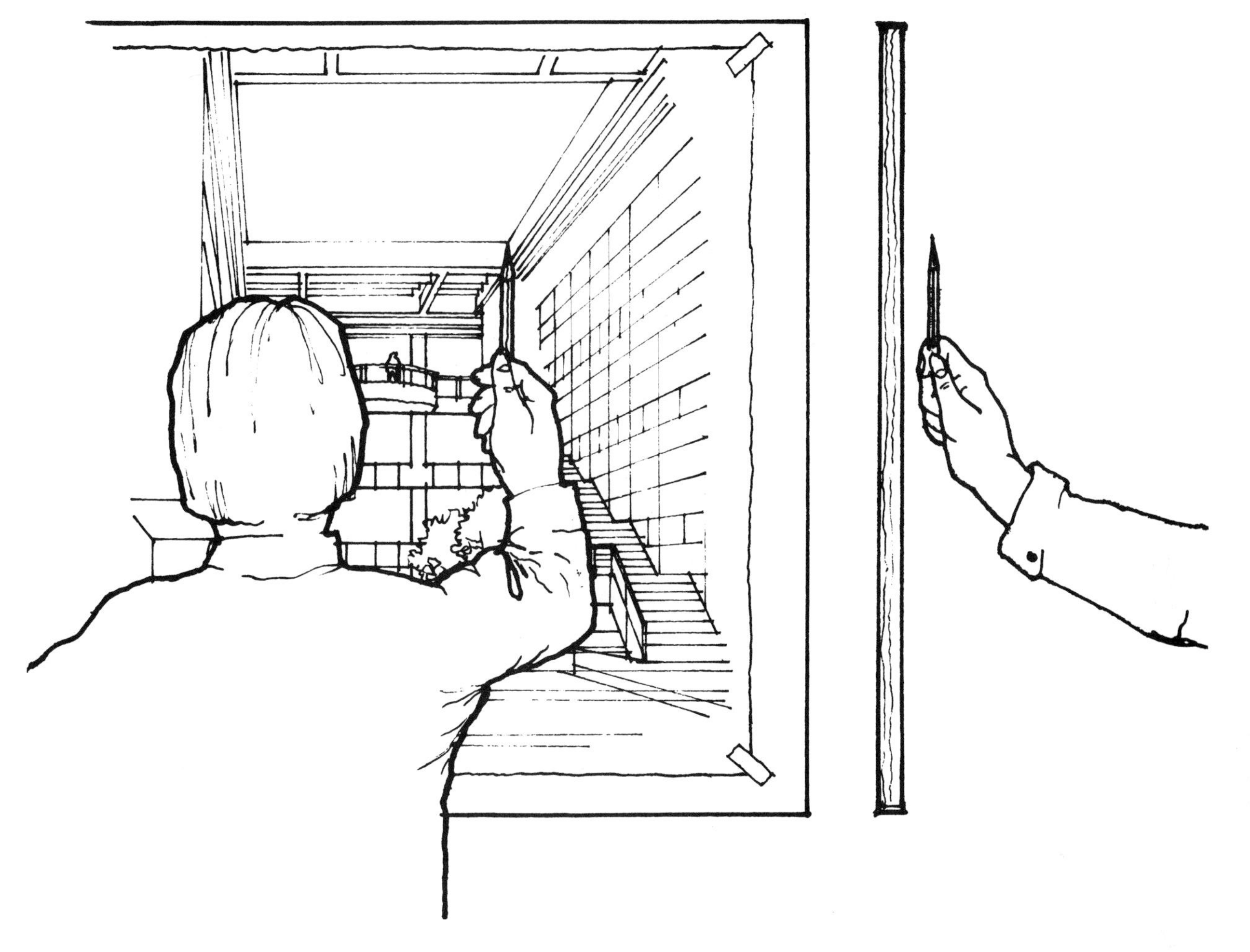

Drawing: Sacramento State Office Building, Sacramento, California
Fisher–Friedman Associates, San Francisco, California

4. Other lengths and widths can now be measured based on the smaller unit length. All of these distances must reference the basic unit in terms of relative size.
5. The drawing instrument must coincide and align with any angled line to properly transfer the same angle to the drawing pad. Measure the angle with respect to a horizontal and vertical reference that corresponds to the edges of your pad.

Remember:

- The plane of your eyes must always be parallel to the plane of your drawing instrument.
- Keep your drawing pad perpendicular to your line of sight so that your drawing instrument can lie in the same plane regardless of its orientation.
- Keep your drawing paper secured to a wood board or hard cardboard pad by using drafting tape, clips, or tacks.

Note: It is best to try to exercise your visualization skills in framing compositions. Various framing devices have been employed over the years, but the most effective, which has been used for centuries, is the use of two small cardboard L's to frame and crop views. High-tech options are also continually coming out. The ViewCatcher uses a thumb pull to give you an adjustable opening for choice of formats.

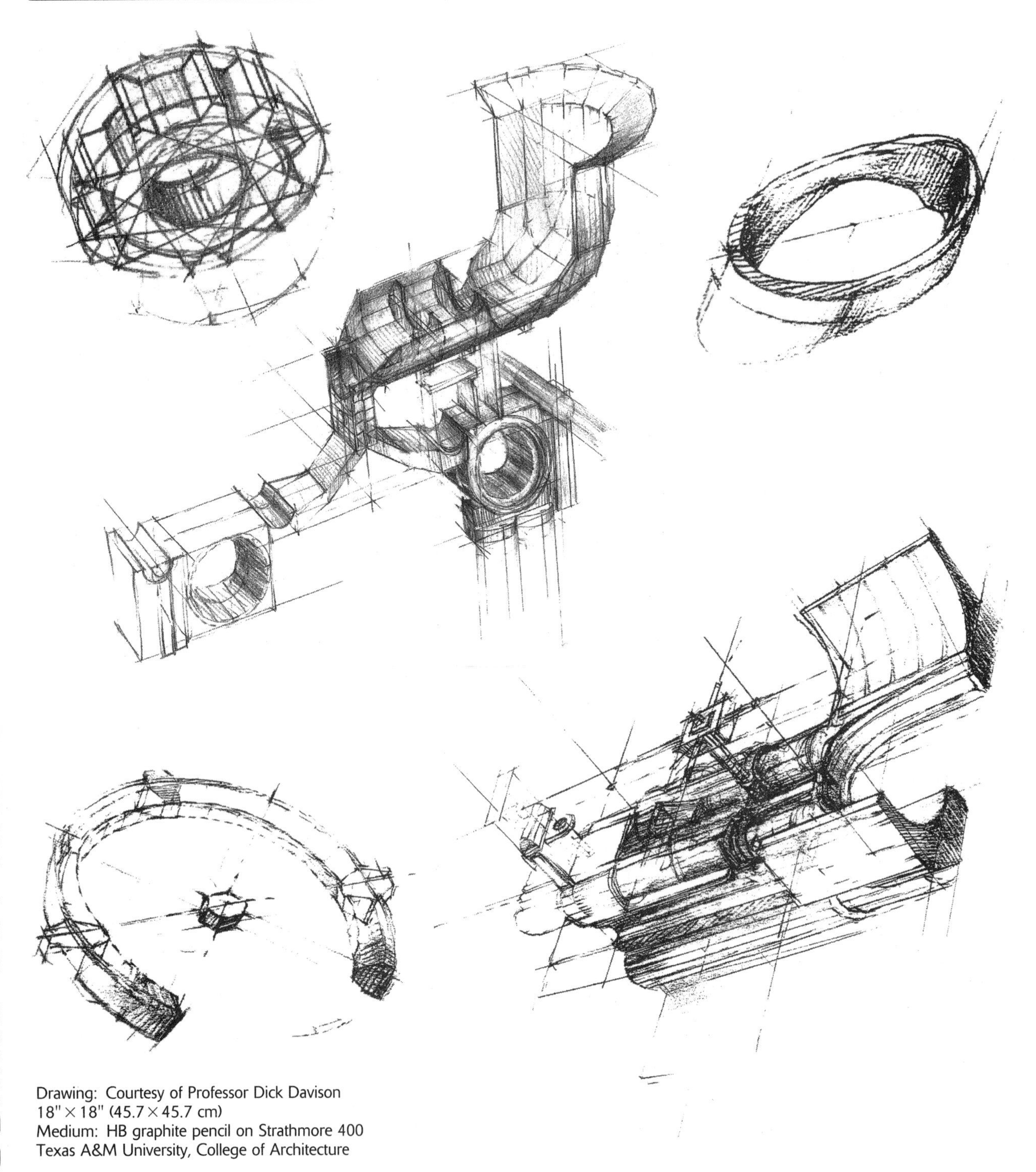

Drawing: Courtesy of Professor Dick Davison
18" × 18" (45.7 × 45.7 cm)
Medium: HB graphite pencil on Strathmore 400
Texas A&M University, College of Architecture

Objects in a composition should always be blocked out within a geometrically configured envelope. Block out a form by using lightly drawn **construction lines** that define the shape and size of the subject. Correct proportional relationships can then be regulated. Two-dimensionally, the shape can be a triangle, a circle, a square, or a 2-D polygon. Three-dimensionally, the basic element can be a cube, a sphere, or a 3-D polygon. **Blocking out** helps you compose a drawing and gives you an idea of what the end product will look like. Once an accurately proportioned composition is drawn, line weights can be adjusted or values applied to complete and finalize the drawing. An HB pencil has a lead that is in the transition zone between hard and soft and can create nice, soft tone values halfway between white and black on a value chart (scale), as shown above.

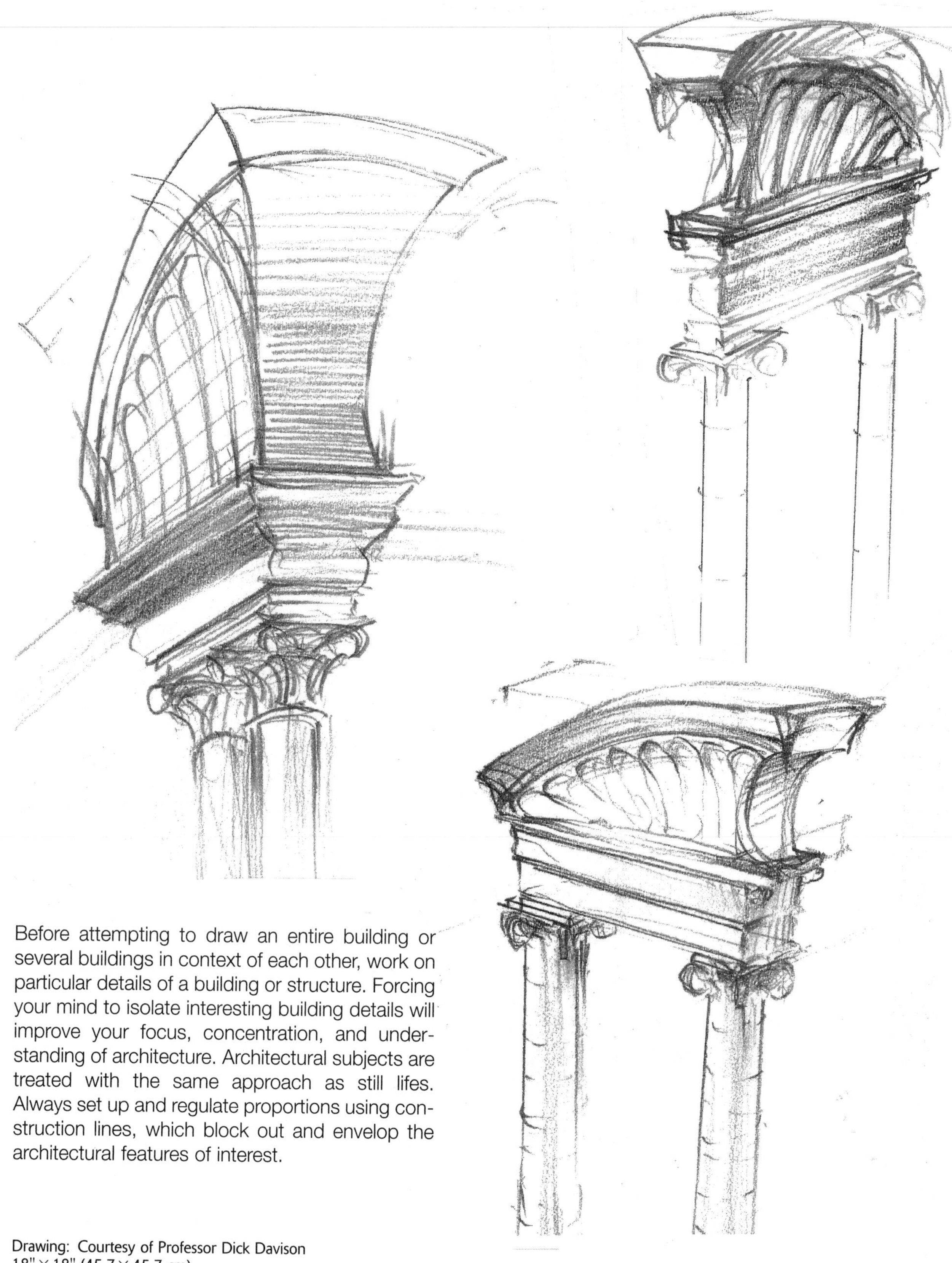

BLOCKING OUT AND CONSTRUCTION LINES

Before attempting to draw an entire building or several buildings in context of each other, work on particular details of a building or structure. Forcing your mind to isolate interesting building details will improve your focus, concentration, and understanding of architecture. Architectural subjects are treated with the same approach as still lifes. Always set up and regulate proportions using construction lines, which block out and envelop the architectural features of interest.

Drawing: Courtesy of Professor Dick Davison
18" × 18" (45.7 × 45.7 cm)
Medium: HB graphite pencil on Strathmore 400
Texas A&M University, College of Architecture

PENCIL STROKES

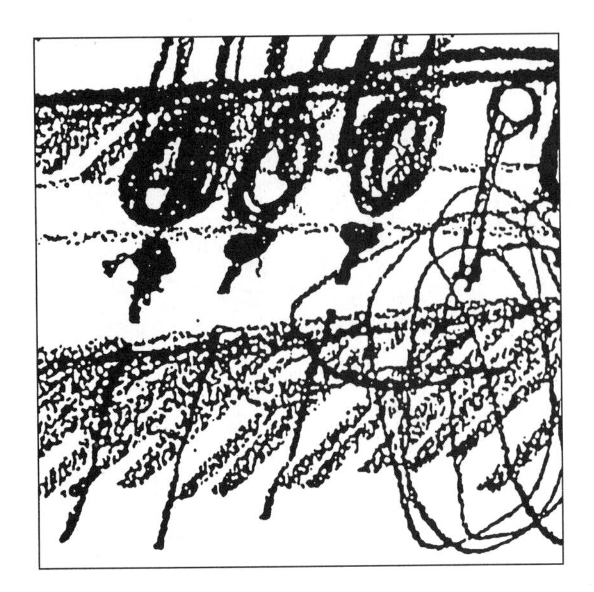

You can produce a wide variety of stroke widths with graphite pencils: from thin, light lines (H series to HB) to denser lines (B series). **Pencil strokes** can vary in direction (vertical, horizontal, angular) and in pressure intensity. The juxtaposition of closely spaced, toned lines (see close-up) creates the effect of a shaded surface. Ebony, carbon, and carpenter pencils are designed for thicker, softer leads. Soft pencil leads are used to sketch wider lines that, when blended together, produce a tonal effect. The darkness of an Ebony pencil means that less applied pressure is needed when rendering denser lines. You can smoothly render any line width with Ebony's soft graphite; you will find it receptive to most slightly toothed paper surfaces. For all pencils, experiment with stroke results based on applied pressure.

Sketch: Texas Seaport Museum, Galveston, Texas, 1991
9" × 12" (22.9 × 30.5 cm)
Medium: Ebony pencil on paper
Courtesy of David G. Woodcock, FAIA, RIBA, Professor of Architecture
Texas A&M University, College of Architecture

You can produce a clear, dark, fluid line with most pens. Unlike pencils, a pen stroke is permanent and opaque. Like pencils, pens are a convenient tool when you are sketching quickly in an unfamiliar place. They do not require extra setup time, as, for example, with watercolors. Every detailed mark and stroke is critical in the development of any drawing done with a pen. Pen strokes emphasize uniform line work and the interrelationship of the compositional shapes. Street scenes in the cityscape are always popular travel sketches. Enliven building sketches by adding visible accessories such as vegetation, people, and vehicular traffic in proper scale. Experiment with the wide range of available pens.

Sketch: Street scene, Kyoto, Japan
13" × 15" (33 × 38.1 cm)
Medium: Felt-tipped pen on good-quality white pad paper
Courtesy of Robert L. Hamilton, AIA, Professor
Department of Architecture, City College of San Francisco

STROKE CHARACTER

Sketch: Pomodoro showroom, New York City
35" × 24" (94.1 × 61 cm)
Medium: Black ink marker and sepia grease pencil
Courtesy of FTL Architects, PC

Lines in architectural sketches can be very disciplined, as in the sketch at right, or they can be very loose, as in the sketches below. Each approach conveys a different character. All of the sketches on this page use pen and ink. With this medium, the controlled cumulative effects of the strokes are the most critical.

Pen strokes often simultaneously describe different drawing elements. For example, form and volume in the Barcelona sketches combine with value and texture. Line weight (the thickness or thinness of a line) can express the "quality" of line. This quality may have the express purpose of conveying form and/or shadow. In representational sketches, lines guide the eye by delineating shapes and enclosing spaces. In drafting, lines are drawn accurately to give a literal representation of buildings. In conceptual sketches, lines are drawn freely and with rhythmic strokes.

Sketch: Student project by Susan Pruchnicki
Church of Sagrada Familia, Barcelona, Spain
10" × 12" (25.4 × 30.5 cm)
Medium: Pen and ink
Antonio Gaudí, Architect
Courtesy of Washington University
School of Architecture, St. Louis, Missouri

Sketch: Student project by Rosalino Figureras
St. Louis, Missouri
3" × 7" (7.6 × 17.8 cm)
Medium: Felt-tipped pen on bond paper
Courtesy of Washington University
School of Architecture, St. Louis, Missouri

Sketch: Student project by Kathryn Korn
Barcelona, Spain
3" × 7" (7.6 × 17.8 cm)
Medium: Felt-tipped pen on bond paper
Courtesy of Washington University
School of Architecture, St. Louis, Missouri

Sketch: Student project by Corvin Matei
Experimental train station for the D.A.R.T. (Dallas Rapid Transit Systems)
18" × 18" (45.7 × 45.7 cm)
Medium: 2B pencil on Strathmore paper
Courtesy of the University of Texas at Arlington School of Architecture

The drawing above shows precise, controlled strokes of tone value within a mechanically constructed three-point perspective (see pp. 276–79). Subtle tone values are achieved much more readily with pencil than with ink pens (facing page). Here, the drawing fades from its detailed central image. Where there is less detail, there is a hint as to how the image might continue. This type of sketch is termed a **vignette** (see pp. 67, 71, 73, 76, and 83).

A soft 2B pencil was used to emphasize the parts of the drawing that are important in order to understand the spatial architecture. It has an unfinished look.
[ARCHITECTURE STUDENT'S STATEMENT]

These two facing pages show a difference in stroke character based on the drawing instrument used. Felt-tipped or fiber-tipped markers and fountain pens usually encourage looseness in the hand and arm strokes, resulting in a less detailed representational sketch (San Francisco sketches, this page) rather than a detailed sketch of what the artist sees. A fine-point technical pen or a fine-tipped marker encourages more detail and a "copy" quality (Rome sketches, facing page).

Sketch: The Vedanta Society Building, San Francisco, California
Medium: Ink pen
Sketch by Charles Moore, Architect
Courtesy of Saul Weingarten, Executor, Estate of Charles Moore, and the Department of Architecture, UCLA School of Art and Architecture

Sketch: Palace of Fine Arts, San Francisco, California
Bernard Maybeck, Architect
Medium: Ink pen
Sketch by Charles Moore, Architect
Courtesy of Saul Weingarten, Executor, Estate of Charles Moore, and the Department of Architecture, UCLA School of Art and Architecture

Sketches: Student project by Corvin Matei, Rome, Italy
6" × 9" (15.2 × 22.9 cm)
Medium: Ink on Strathmore paper
Courtesy of the University of Texas at Arlington
School of Architecture

In architectural observation sketching, which activates the hand-eye-brain connection, the first goal is to record exactly what you see. You are sketching for yourself, to understand and analyze what you observed, as well as for your classmates or colleagues, to communicate your observations to them. Be selective in your viewing vantage point, and focus on the architectural features or details that interest you. Describe those elements using what you feel to be an appropriate medium. The sketches on this page consider particular aspects of specific buildings, whereas the sketch on the facing page examines the view from the interior to the exterior.

This sketch, done with a Micron technical pen on 9" X 12" (22.9 X 30.5 cm) white drawing paper, examines the roofline and roof details of a structure in a classical Chinese garden.

Representational sketching utilizes many basic elements, including line, value, texture, the massing of shapes and volumes, scale, and—sometimes—color. A noncolored pencil or an ink pen will result in a monochromatic sketch. In any medium, you consciously manipulate one or more of these elements. Sketches should exhibit a creative richness regardless of the technique and medium used. Your final composition in representational sketching should go far beyond accurately imitating what you see.

***Drawing** is the essence of description.*
***Drawing** connects the eye and the hand to define the world, both seen and unseen.*
[ARCHITECT'S STATEMENT]

Sketches: Manhattan, function and form
9" × 10" (22.9 × 25.4 cm)
Medium: Pen and ink
Courtesy of Hugh Hardy, FAIA, Hardy Holzman Pfeiffer Associates

Competition sketch: Rotterdam Central Station
Cambridge, Massachusetts
Medium: Ink on paper and Photoshop
Courtesy of Rafael Vinoly Architects, P.C.

An artist's choice of medium affects a sketch's character the way an author's choice of words affects the way characters are portrayed in his or her book. Before selecting a medium, try to establish the character or feeling of the sketch by deciding which words would best describe your subject or your design. Will the word or feeling be formal or informal, soft or slick? Graphite, ink, and watercolor are just a few of the possible media for architectural sketches. For color, there are many choices in addition to watercolor, such as colored pencils, colored markers, and oil pastels (see Web site [Chapter 11]). Work with the medium (dry or wet) with which you feel most at ease. Be alert to others that evolve, such as digital media that interface with manual methods (mixed media). Mixing media can be an inventive challenge.

Sketch: Boyer Center for Molecular Medicine, New Haven, Connecticut
6.25" × 9" (15.9 × 22.9 cm)
Medium: Pen and ink
Courtesy of Cesar Pelli, Architect, Cesar Pelli & Associates

Sketches and drawings can be the result of what you envision as well as representations of what you see. When you conceptualize exploratory design alternatives, you use sketched drawings to better understand your ideas. But our sketches of what we see are quite different in character from those of what we envision, and that character is also molded by the ultimate purpose of the sketches themselves. These examples are exploratory contour drawings executed with a great economy of line. As minimal as they are, they define positive and negative space clearly. Visualization sketches can convey an immense range of possibilities with respect to the viewer's sense of light, space, and form.

Drawing allows me to express the essence of a particular and dear quality of my design. This may be a play of light or color, a form or forms, a unique perspective, or most often, the relationship of my building with the sky.
[Architect's statement]

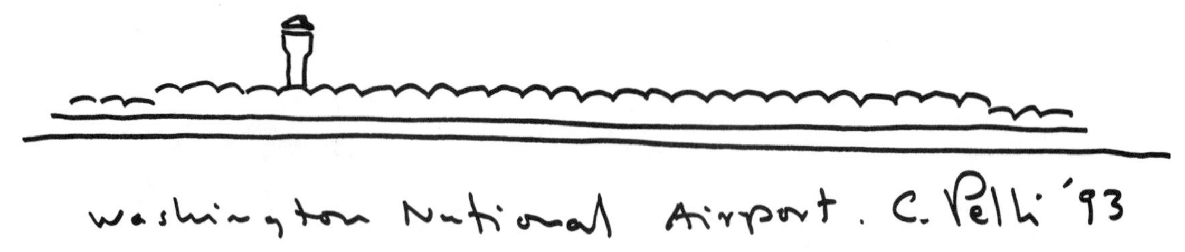

Sketch: New North Terminal, Washington National Airport, Washington, D.C.
Medium: Pen and ink
Courtesy of Cesar Pelli, Architect, Cesar Pelli & Associates

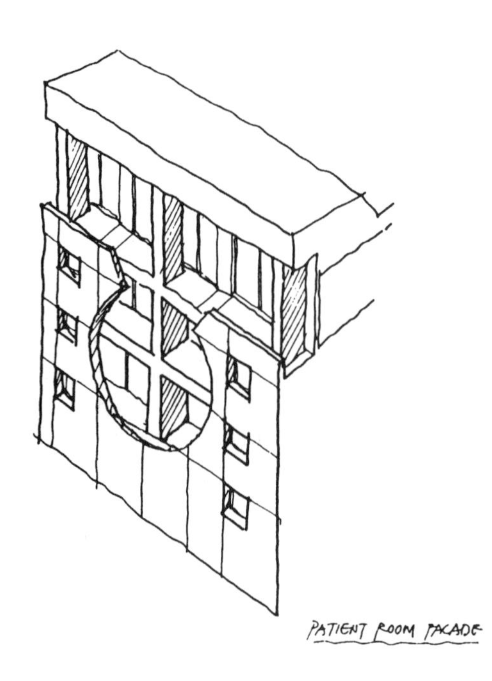

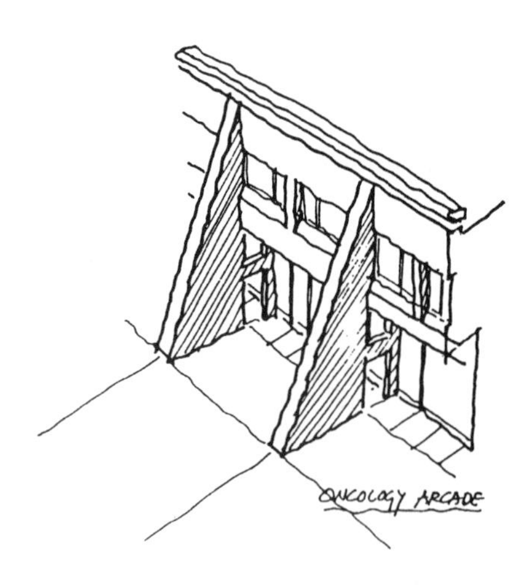

Sketches: Gleneagles Hospital and Medical Office Building
Kuala Lumpur, Malaysia
8½" X 11" (21.6 X 27.9 cm)
Medium: Ink on vellum
Courtesy of KMD/PD Architects in joint venture with the Architectural Network

Drawing: Petronas Towers, Kuala Lumpur, Malaysia
9.5" × 12" (24.1 × 30.5 cm)
Medium: Oil pastels on acid-free vellum
Courtesy of Cesar Pelli, Architect, Cesar Pelli & Associates

These rapidly sketched strokes give the soft, delicate character commonly found when pastels are used. Pastels lend themselves to compositions that are not very detailed, such as this value study. **Value** refers to the lightness or darkness of a surface. In this representational sketch, there is a high value contrast: an extremely light color (building form or figure) is placed adjacent to an extremely dark color (sky or background). A low value contrast occurs when either two (or more) light values or two (or more) dark values are placed next to each other. In the above example, this phenomenon begins to occur as the sky gradually becomes lighter toward the horizon, almost merging in value with that of the base of the towers. Classic examples of this kind of value transition can be seen in the 1920s and 1930s work of Hugh Ferriss (see Bibliography). Architect Cesar Pelli is well-known for using layered diagonal line strokes to control value and density. This expressive technique allows for complex qualities to appear, including light and shadow, volume, surface, reflections, and transparency.

STILL LIFES

1

2

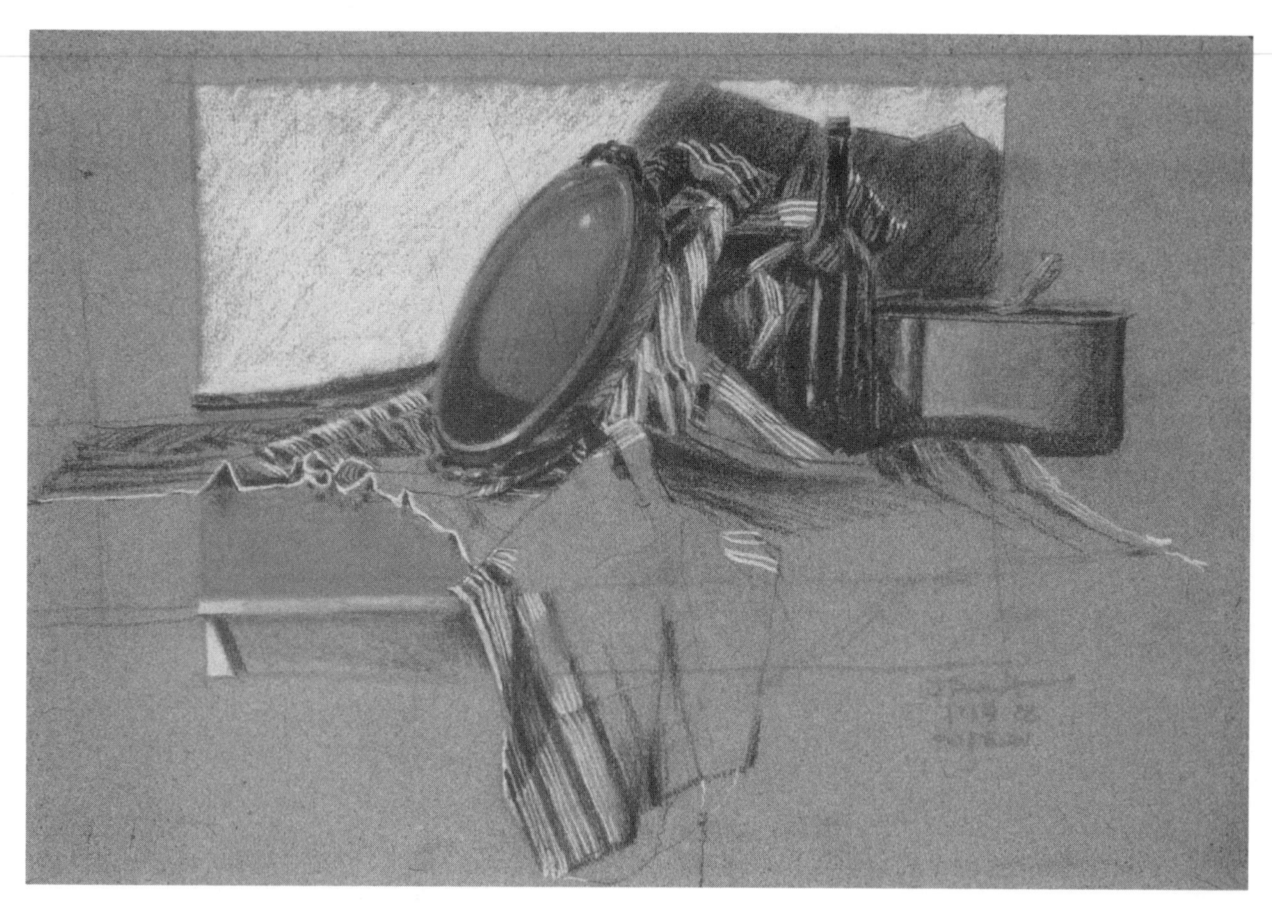

Still life: Courtesy of Jonathan Brandt, Visiting Assistant Professor
Texas A&M University College of Architecture

(Opposite page)

(1) Still life: Student project by Alysha Haggerton
Courtesy of Jonathan Brandt, Visiting Assistant Professor
Texas A&M University, College of Architecture

(2) Still life: Student project by Ryan Collins
Courtesy of Jonathan Brandt, Visiting Assistant Professor
Texas A&M University, College of Architecture

Before drawing elements in the urban landscape, you should develop basic hand-drawing skills by practicing still lifes. **Still lifes** are composed of inanimate, multishaped objects—utensils, fruits, bottles, tools, drapery, and the like—set up in a studio setting. Tables, stools, and chairs are excellent subjects for working with important negative shapes—the spaces around and between the subject. Create a visually appealing arrangement with three or more objects by balancing the elements, either symmetrically or asymmetrically. Challenge yourself by rearranging your still life compositions and drawing from a variety of vantage points.

When you delineate **contour lines,** they may show as straight or curved edges. These edges may contrast in tone and color to further define a surface outline, which is called **shape** or configuration. Experiment with a strong light source to explore the contrast of light and shade. A background value will naturally interrelate with the tonal values in the composition. Challenge yourself by using different media and seeing the results—the feeling of charcoal as opposed to white chalk, for example.

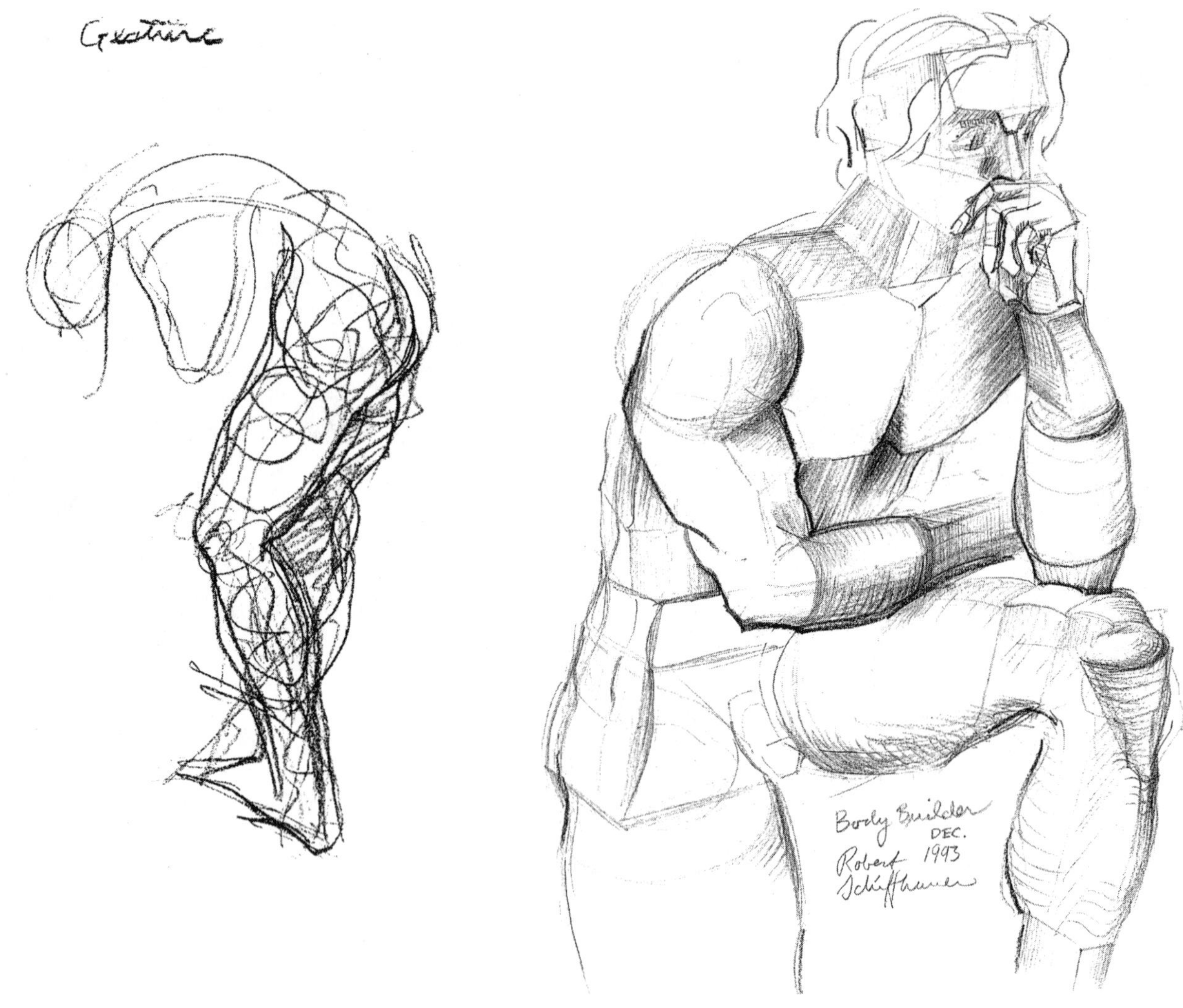

Sketches: Gesture and contour drawings
11" × 14" (27.9 × 35.6 cm)
Medium: Carbon pencil on cold-press drawing paper
Courtesy of Robert Schiffhauer, Associate Professor
Texas A&M University, College of Architecture

Gesture drawings are very quick studies that try to capture the subject's movement or energy. You draw them by responding instantaneously to what you see—without analyzing it. They help to develop rapid hand-eye coordination. **Contour** drawings are much more time consuming and precise. Your goal is to analyze and try to accurately duplicate what you see with defining exterior and interior lines. The human figure is an excellent subject for both gesture and contour drawings. The human body is basically a composite of modified geometric solids. Note the cubic, conical, cylindrical, spherical, rectilinear, and wedge-shaped volumes in the drawing on the right.

All parts of the human body are composed of many wonderful contours. As the student explores the forms of exterior human anatomy, he or she is introduced to structural considerations in a most intimate manner.

The artistic discipline of life drawing has been an adjunct to many architecture programs. Freehand representational sketching of the human body combines the intuitive fluidity of art with the geometric structural precision of architecture (see pp. 392–93, 410–11).

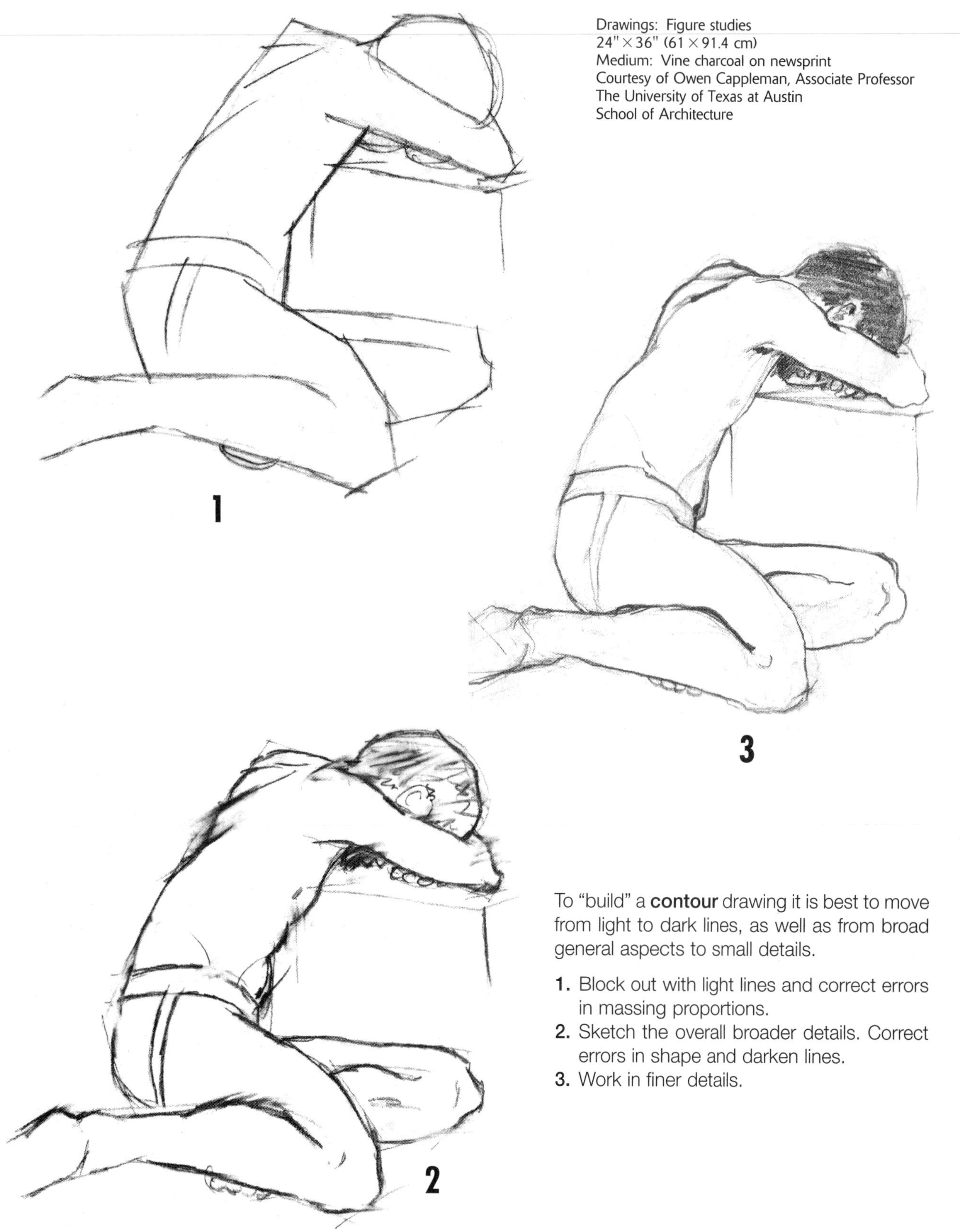

Drawings: Figure studies
24" × 36" (61 × 91.4 cm)
Medium: Vine charcoal on newsprint
Courtesy of Owen Cappleman, Associate Professor
The University of Texas at Austin
School of Architecture

To "build" a **contour** drawing it is best to move from light to dark lines, as well as from broad general aspects to small details.

1. Block out with light lines and correct errors in massing proportions.
2. Sketch the overall broader details. Correct errors in shape and darken lines.
3. Work in finer details.

By studying the proportions of the human body, we broaden our knowledge and understanding of how people fit physically with respect to the environment. This study is called **anthropometrics.**

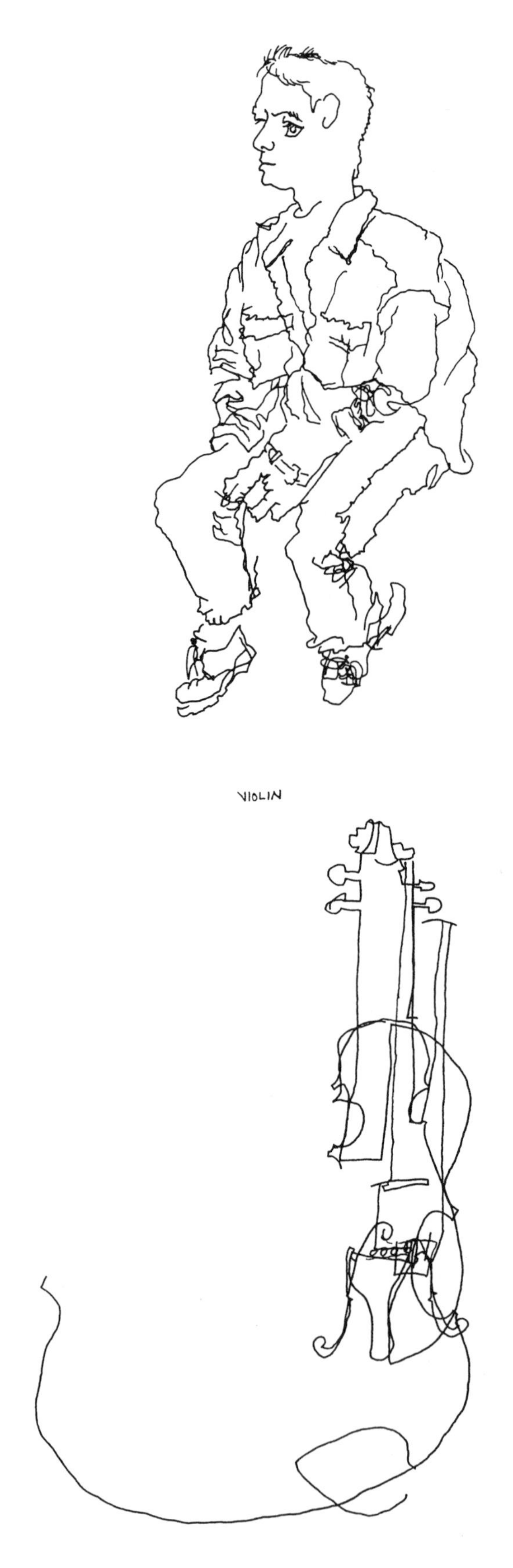

Blind contours (clockwise from top left):
Student projects courtesy of Brian Blanchard (Texas A&M University)
Dennis Martin, Amaza Lai Cheng Lam (City College of San Francisco)

Contour drawings, of which there are several varieties, attempt to use line in such a way as to express the essential form of the subject. In a good contour drawing, the line appears to wrap or traverse invisible volumes so that, as the eye follows the lines, the three-dimensionality of the subject becomes apparent. One approach is to draw the subject **"blind";** that is, while looking only at the subject and not lifting your pencil off the paper. The drawer attempts to supplant pencil with eye and track the surface of the subject. Concentrating and focusing on the subject allows you to be loose and relaxed while exploring the potential of the free-flowing contour line and enhancing your ability to observe and see.

Blind contours (clockwise from top left):
Medium: Pencil
Student projects courtesy of
Ebby Chu (City College of San Francisco)
Jennifer Sobieraj (Texas A&M University)
Dennis Martin (City College of San Francisco)

Blind drawings should be done with a minimum of conscious thought. If an edge or contour appears darker, apply more pressure; if it appears lighter, apply less pressure. This results in contour lines that are more sensitive although not proportionally accurate. Note the concentrated small areas of dark tone in which many changes of line direction took place. This is the result of exaggerated and distorted lines, common characteristics of blind contour drawings. Be patient and don't be discouraged if your drawing looks disproportionate or weird. Blind drawings usually correspond closely to your visual perception.

Drawing: Triton Museum of Art, Santa Clara, California
Courtesy of Barcelon & Jang, Architecture

A large massing of trees can be loosely rendered and the foliage made highly suggestive. Groups of trees often create a wall-like effect. Study the foliage's transparency and density. Landscaping vegetation, such as trees, plants, and shrubs, should always be complementary and secondary to the architecture to which they are adjacent.

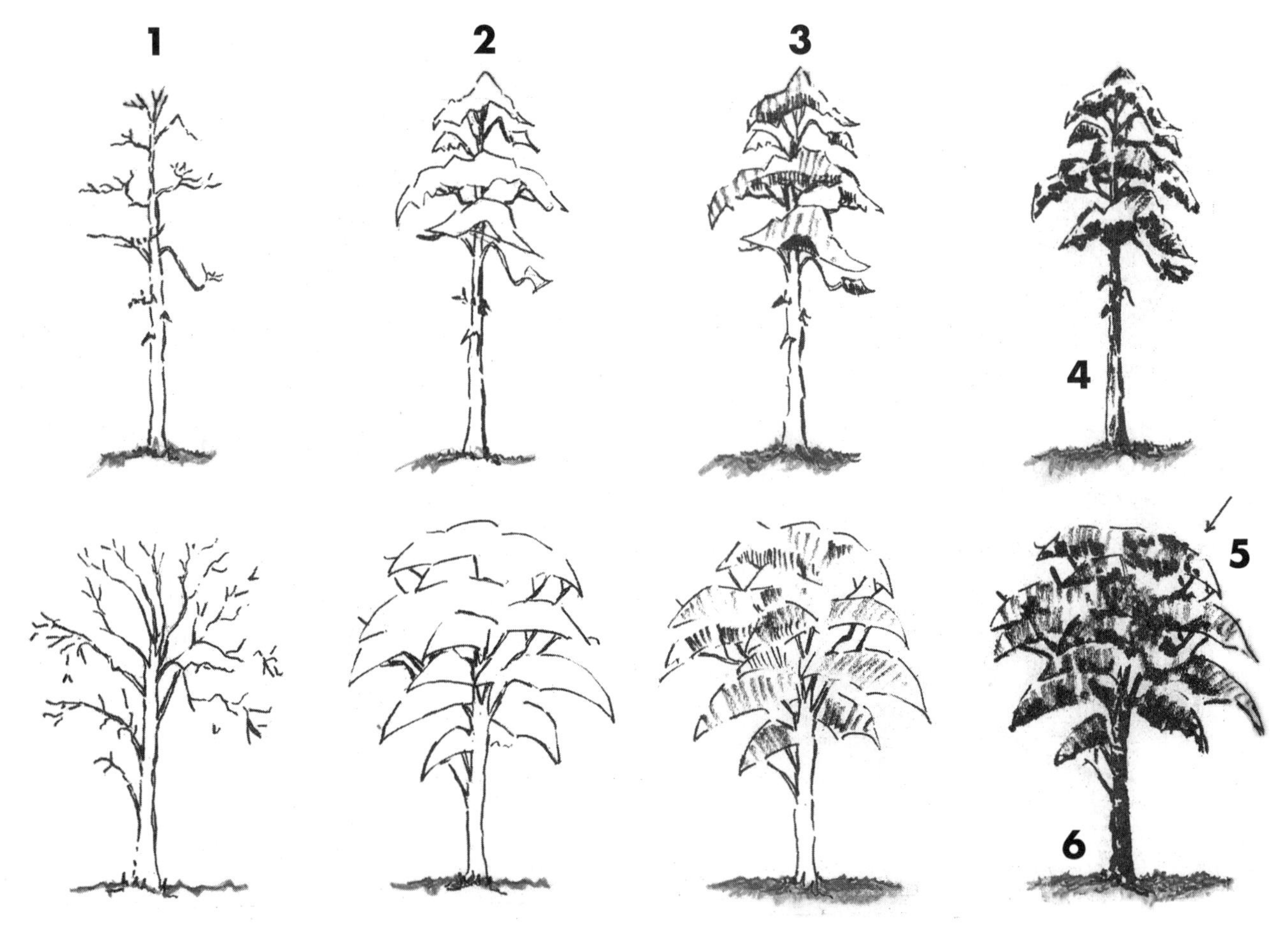

Each tree, with its initial skeletal form, has a character of its own. When sketching or composing trees, one should be aware of (**1**) the direction and pattern of growth on the branches, which is a clue to the tree's form; (**2**) the overall silhouette or shape (tall or short, bulky or thin), which is affected by gravity and wind; (**3**) the massing and pattern of the foliage; (**4**) the texture of the bark; (**5**) how the light hits and penetrates various canopy shapes, producing shades and shadows; (**6**) and the manner in which the trunk flares or tapers off. For pencil work, use 2B and HB for dark values and 2H and 4H for contour lines and light values.

Sketch: Hillside residences, San Francisco, California
Sketch by Charles Moore, Architect
Courtesy of Saul Weingarten, Executor, Estate of Charles Moore, and the Department of Architecture, UCLA School of Art and Architecture

When you are doing rapid sketch studies at a site, you may not have enough time to draw all the tree details (branches, leaves, etc.). In such situations, your objective should be to create a representational feeling of the essence of a tree or other landscape vegetation. Freehand trees can be simple and abstract. These quick sketches suggestive of trees are very effective. Sometimes it is what we leave out rather than what we put in a sketch that makes it highly expressive (see p. 583).

Sketch: Saitama Sports Arena Competition
Design offices: Takenaka Corporation, Tokyo, Japan
Cesar Pelli, Tokyo, Japan
17" × 11" (43.2 × 27.9 cm)
Medium: Prismacolor pencil
Courtesy of Lawrence Ko Leong, Architectural Illustrator

Drawing method: This was one of about forty vignette sketches done using Prismacolor pencils and eyeballing a scale model. I used a light beige-rose pencil to outline the building, plaza, and entourage, and a soft blend of greens to maintain transparency and the canopy effect of foliage. A few bright spots of color were used to highlight the people and give liveliness to the composition.
[ARCHITECTURAL ILLUSTRATOR'S STATEMENT]

SKETCHING CARS

Rapid visualization sketch
by Wenjie Chen
Medium: Watercolor
Architects: Ware Malcomb
Courtesy of Wenjie Studio

Cars range in length from approximately 14' (4.27 m) to 20' (6.1 m) and in width from 5.8' (1.77 m) to 6.3' (1.92 m). Tires range from 22" (55.9 cm) to 28" (71.12 cm) in diameter.

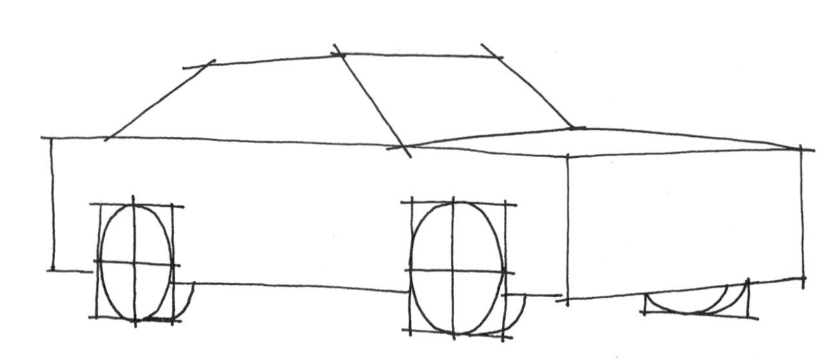

A car or any type of moving vehicle should be enclosed in an envelope of simple geometric shapes, such as truncated pyramids, rectangular solids, and cylindrical elements. Boats are similar to cars; they can be set up skeletally as a rectilinear box with shaped ends and a specific center line. Graphite is the ideal medium for layout work.

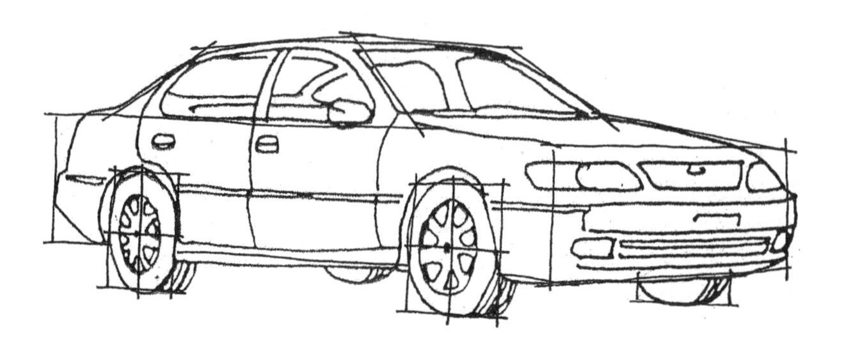

After the basic volume and form are developed with light construction lines, structural details should be sketched with a contour outline technique. To keep it simple, only major details should be added, like headlights and bumpers. The drawing can be finalized with pencil or any other rendering medium (see pp. 396–397).

Drawing: Sybase Hollis Street Campus, San Francisco, California
18" × 12" (30.5 × 45.7 cm)
Medium: Sketch watercolor on mounted presentation blackline print of pencil drawing
Robinson Mills & Williams, Architects
Courtesy of Al Forster, Architectural Illustrator

Cars in perspective should always be in scale with the rest of the drawing and secondary to major building elements. Contour outline cars are usually adequate for most architectural drawings. Add details and shaded tones in accordance with the complexity of the rendering. The roofs of cars are slightly below the eye-level line. Add visual interest by showing cars turning as well as moving in both directions.

Drawing: Ponte Vista
Architects: McLarand Vasquez Emsiek & Partners
Medium: Watercolor
Sketch by Wenjie Chen
Courtesy of Wenjie Studio

Sketch: Student project by Leigh Stringer
Movie theater
Medium: Pen and ink
Courtesy of Washington University
School of Architecture, St. Louis, Missouri

All objects can be broken down into simple **geometric solids.** For example, trees are basically spheres or cones on cylinders. Buildings are usually a combination of rectangular solids, cylindrical solids, spherical solids, and planar elements. On close observation of building forms, we see that line is in reality the joining of two surfaces or a darker surface against a lighter surface. The sketch on the left shows the buildup of line within an enclosed space to simulate texture or tonal value.

Competition sketch: Rotterdam Central Station
Cambridge, Massachusetts
Medium: Ink on paper and Photoshop
Courtesy of Rafael Viñoly Architects, P.C.

Sketch with rough thumbnail vignette: Iglesia de San Francisco, Javier, Cuautitlán, Mexico
5" × 8" (12.7 × 20.3 cm)
Medium: Black Pentel felt-tip, semidry
Courtesy of Lawrence Ko Leong, Architectural Illustrator

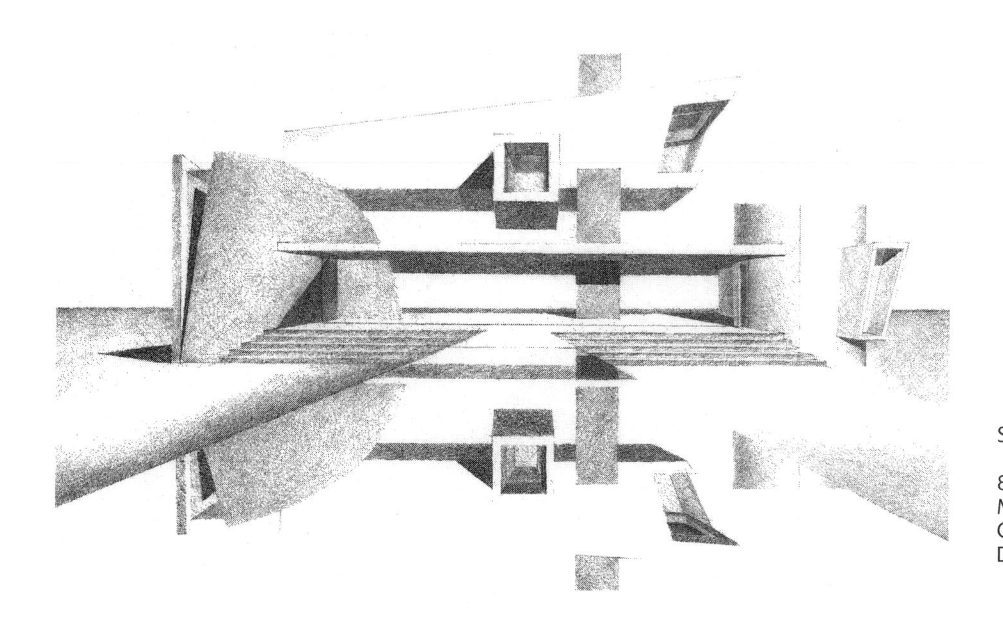

Sketch: House in Palm Springs II, Palm Springs, California
8" × 5" (20.3 × 12.7 cm)
Medium: Prismacolor
Courtesy of Kanner Architects
Drawn by Stephen Kanner

To create my drawings I lay the paper on glass, because it has a true, hard surface, and I draw and shade with the side of the sharpened point of a soft No. 2 Ticonderoga pencil. The way to get an even texture is to squint or look obliquely, never directly, at one's work. To achieve hard edges, I draw against a straightedge (see p. 81).
[ARCHITECT'S STATEMENT]

Through the medium of lead or graphite, time is transcended, as a contemporary Florence is transformed into a nostalgic moment from history.
[Professor's statement]

Pencil stroke value on buildings and streets can be made broader by producing a flat surface on the lead. Using a flat surface, a uniform width and consistent value of stroke can be achieved. Best results can be attained by moving the arm at a constant speed.

In choosing subject matter for travel sketches like these street scenes, try to focus on a center of interest and then experiment with balance and composition. Elements on the street, such as human figures, should be detailed to add a **focal point,** but not so detailed that they distract from other significant elements (e.g., buildings).

Travel sketches:
Left: Via Dei Rustic, Firenze, Italy
Above: Via Tornabuoni, Firenze, Italy
Medium: Pencil
Courtesy of Professor George S. Loli
University of Louisiana–Lafayette

A study of a drawing technique called "perspective" (see Chapter 6), in conjunction with this chapter, will help you understand why the contours you draw instinctively in your representational sketches appear the way they do. We have seen that sighting skills give you an understanding of proportions in the viewed space. The theories of perspective will accurately verify these proportions. The sketch to the right is another good example of a vignette. The continuation of the buildings is left to your imagination.

Sketch: Le Jardin Nelson, Montreal, Canada, 1993
9" × 12" (22.9 × 30.5 cm)
Medium: Ebony pencil on paper

Sketch: Galveston homes, Galveston, Texas, 1993
9" × 12" (22.9 × 30.5 cm)
Medium: Ebony pencil on paper
Courtesy of David G. Woodcock, FAIA, RIBA, Professor of Architecture, Texas A&M University, Department of Architecture

Drawing on-site is always a challenge for me, and I rarely spend more than twenty minutes on each sketch. As an architect my objective is to learn more about the subject, so I focus a lot of attention on form and materials. Ebony pencil allows me to explore shade and shadow quickly, and by keeping at least two pencils with sharp points I can still pick out critical details.
[ARCHITECT'S STATEMENT]

Sketch: Student project by Margaret Stanton
Pencil sketch of Vicenza, Italy
Courtesy of the University of Virginia School of Architecture

On-the-spot representational sketching done when traveling gives you a chance to fill your sketchbook with interesting subjects. The landscape is filled with exciting visual surprises—street scenes within a cityscape, mountain roads in a rural village, or panoramic beach views along a waterfront. Your goal may be to capture a sense of place and time at special events. Unusual and interesting views should be sought. Perspective angles can vary from traditional ground eye-level views to bird's-eye and worm's-eye views. Sketchbooks can range in size from 5" X 7" (12.7 X 17.8 cm) to 11" X 14" (27.9 X 35.5 cm). Those with a double-wire binding allow the book to lie flat.

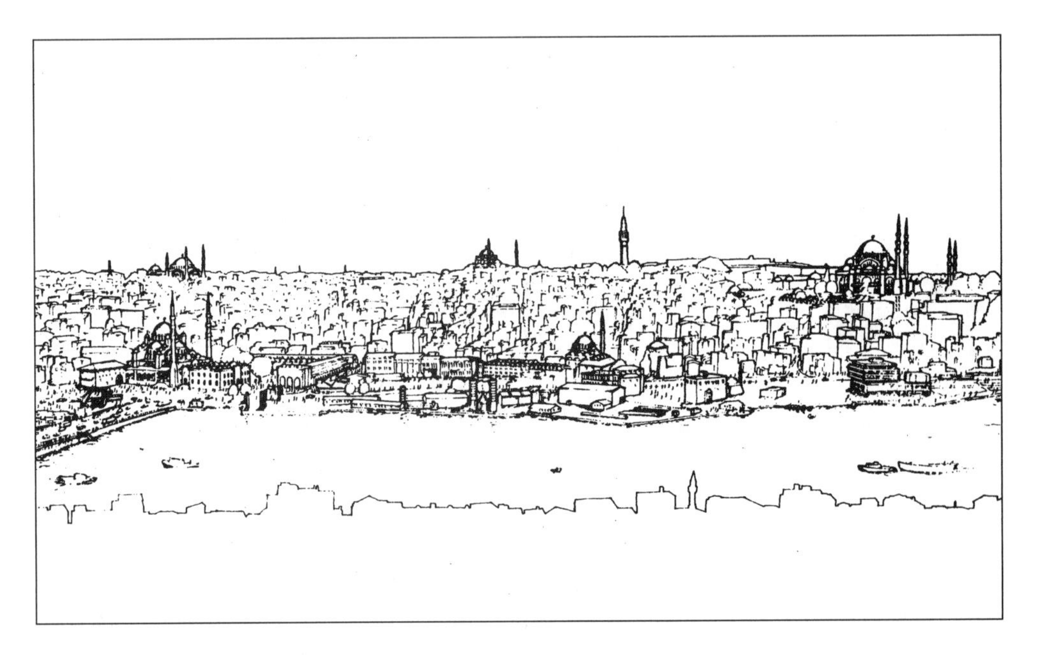

Sketch: Student project by Behan Cagri, Istanbul, Turkey
30" × 18" (76.2 × 45.7 cm)
Medium: Ink sketch on vellum
Courtesy of the University of Maryland School of Architecture

Travel sketches can trigger memories of a particular location later on. Form the habit of jotting down notes in your sketchbook or journal about the environment and your experience of the locale. Maybe it's a sound, or a smell, or the weather conditions, or chatter from curious onlookers watching you sketch.

Charcoal is a good medium for deemphasizing details. You have to work with broad strokes, so you can't be too fussy about details. Charcoal comes in both stick and pencil forms, and in a variety of grades. The long ledge of the stick form is excellent for shading large areas. After the shape and proportions of an architectural subject are sketched, focus on the surface material textures of the structure or building.

Sketched images of China, Mexico, and New Mexico (clockwise from left):

Student project by James Ke, City College of San Francisco
3" X 4" (7.62 X 10.2 cm)
Medium: Charcoal

Sketch in Mexico
5" X 5" (12.7 X 12.7 cm)
Medium: Pentel felt-tipped pen
Courtesy of Lawrence Ko Leong, Architectural Illustrator

Sketch: Santo Domingo pueblo, Santa Fe, New Mexico
Medium: Ink on paper 81/2" X 11" (21.6 X 27.9 cm)
Courtesy of Lawrence Halprin, Landscape Architect

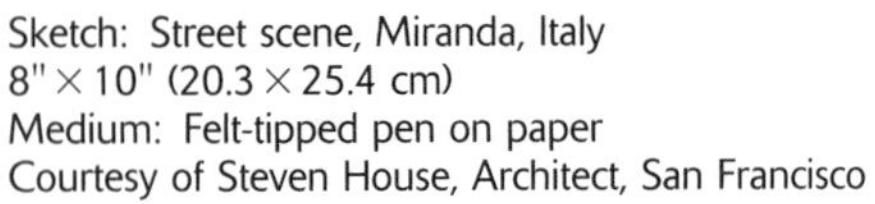
Sketch: Street scene, Miranda, Italy
8" × 10" (20.3 × 25.4 cm)
Medium: Felt-tipped pen on paper
Courtesy of Steven House, Architect, San Francisco

Sketch: Roofscape, Macau
5" × 7" (12.7 × 17.8 cm)
Medium: Pentel felt-tipped pen
Courtesy of Lawrence Ko Leong, Architectural Illustrator

Sometimes the time factor will influence the character of the sketch. Detailed sketches like the Miranda, Italy, scene may need a couple of hours of your time, whereas the European travel sketch was done in a short amount of time. Rapid sketches, also called thumbnails or vignettes (see p. 487), are needed when many studies of the same locale are required. A quick sketch lacking detail can still be highly expressive.

Sketch: European travel sketch
Medium: Ink on paper
Courtesy of Lawrence Halprin, Landscape Architect

Sketching and drawing are ways for me to have a dialogue with what I see and experience. In this interaction, I reveal my feelings about the world and my involvement with things and places and people. Sketches can influence my reactions of the moment and then lie dormant for future influences.
[LANDSCAPE ARCHITECT'S STATEMENT]

Travel sketching enables me to record the essence of time and place.... With just a few lines, a special moment can be captured forever.
[Architect's Statement]

Sketches: Taxco, Mexico
8" × 10" (20.3 × 25.4 cm)
Medium: Gray felt-tipped pen and watercolor on paper
Courtesy of Steven House, Architect, San Francisco

The examples above are serial sketches based on a visual progression or sequence through a site. Sketches done in this manner can function as a coherent group and allow for a more thorough spatial analysis of the built environment. This is analogous to the infinite number of serial views that can be called up in a computer-generated model.

Sketch: Resort Hotel, Mexico
17" × 11" (43.2 × 27.9 cm)
Medium: Black Prismacolor and thin Pilot razor-point Pentel
Shading was built up with a single line thickness
Design Office: Sandy & Babcock, San Francisco
Courtesy of Lawrence Ko Leong, Architectural Illustrator

Sketch: Central Park Boat Basin, New York City, 1991
7" × 4" (17.8 × 10.2 cm)
Medium: Pencil
Courtesy of Stephen W. Parker, Architect

Sketch: Abbey of San Galgano, Montesiepi, Italy, 1987
12" × 9" (30.5 × 22.9 cm)
Medium: Ebony pencil on paper
Courtesy of David G. Woodcock, FAIA, RIBA, Professor of Architecture
Texas A&M University, College of Architecture

The vantage point selected can affect the character and feeling of a building subject. Choice of viewpoint must be carefully considered, along with texture, lighting conditions, framing elements (like the foliage above), and the massing of forms. Studying the exact nature of light, shade, and shadow (Chapter 7) will help you understand lighting conditions as you sketch forms. Without this knowledge, your common sense and logic must help you interpret, for example, why the lighting effects on the cylindrical and prismatic forms above are quite different.

Also important in sketching the scenic environment is identifying the three "grounds" that are normally seen. These are the **foreground** (seen above as the curvilinear broadside sketched lines), the **middle ground** (seen as the heavy vegetation), and the **background** (seen as the building). In this case, as with the views on the facing page, the middle ground is emphasized to enhance the spatial quality.

Sketch: Entry at 1816 Hickory
Private residence, St. Louis, Missouri, 1992
3" × 9" (7.62 × 22.9 cm), 1992
Medium: Pencil
Courtesy of Stephen W. Parker, Architect

Sketch: Sacré Cœur Cathedral, Paris, France, 1995
4" × 9" (10.2 × 22.9 cm)
Medium: Pencil
Courtesy of Stephen W. Parker, Architect

Travel sketching has always been one of the joys of my journeys—and afterward a truer memory than what a photo can evoke in me. I strive to capture the spirit of the moment and all that defines the experience of being at a certain place, at a certain time, in a certain light, in a certain season. And all the lessons I learn, the discoveries I make with my pencil, are brought back to influence my professional artwork—opening my mind's eye to new possibilities.
[Architect's statement]

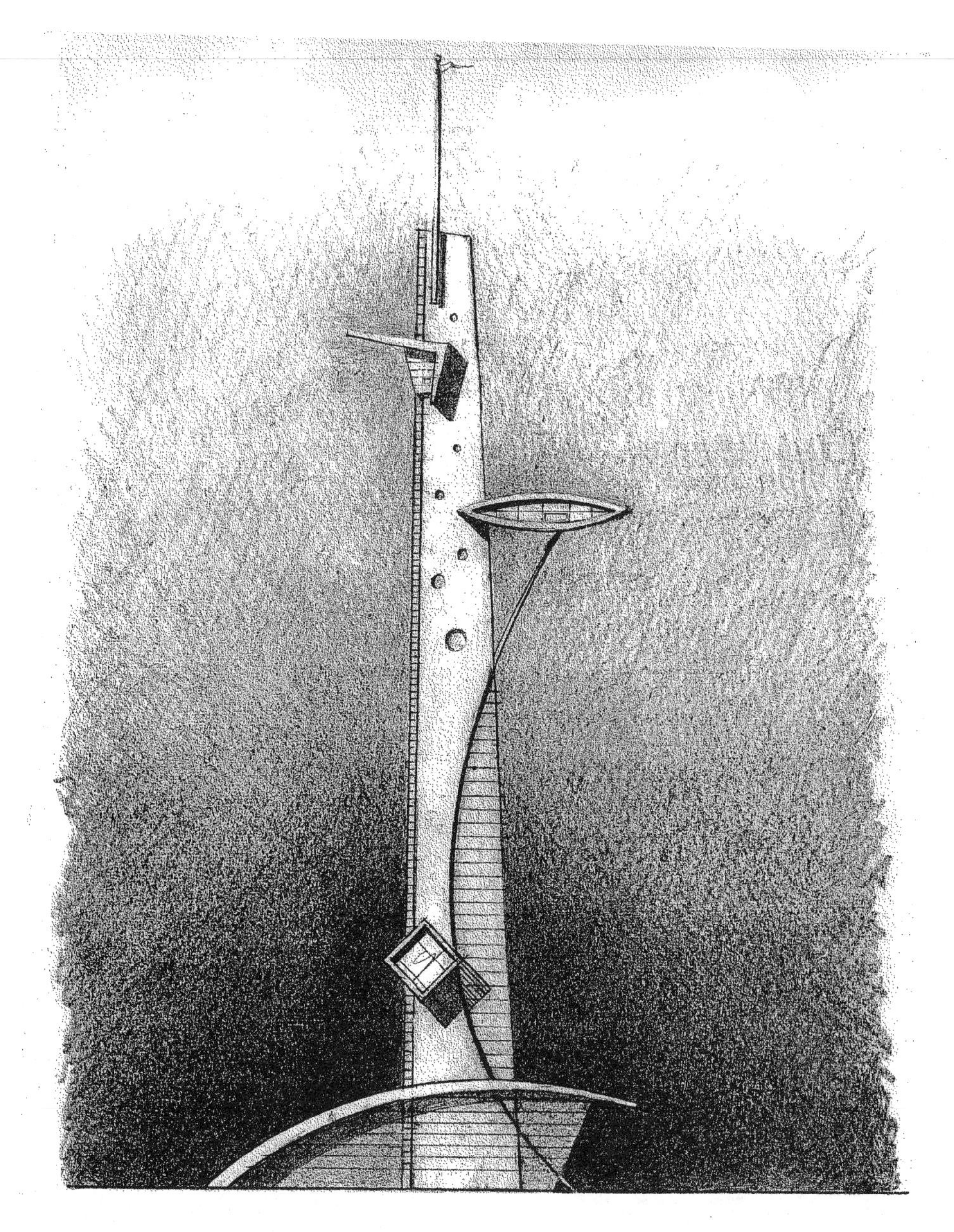

Drawing: Nan Jing Tower, Nan Jing, China
5" × 8" (12.7 × 20.3 cm)
Medium: Pencil
Courtesy of Kanner Architects
Drawn by Stephen Kanner

Conceptual sketches (see Chapter 9) are typically loose and free in execution. However, as the above drawing of a high-rise tower shows, a conceptual sketch can convey much more than might be expected—and even have the appearance of a hard-edge representational drawing. In truly efficient drawings, every line conveys information about form, light qualities, volume, and space, even if the detailing is only suggested and the surface qualities alluded to. A good conceptual sketch will often suggest possibilities that were previously unconsidered. In other words, the sketch can dictate the direction of the subsequent design. Architect Frank Lloyd Wright frequently did this kind of conceptual sketch (see Pfeiffer, pp. 7, 8, 101, and 141) by strategically using a straightedge. The result was a polished and authoritative look. He then developed the sketches into numerous preliminary studies and finally, into presentation drawings (see p. 183).

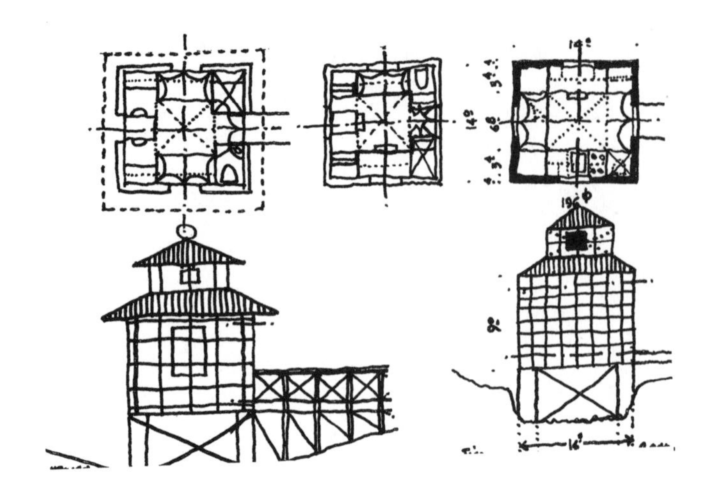

Sometimes travel sketches may not be representational. Some architects, such as Stanley Tigerman, often translate what they observe into many architectural graphic conventions. They may see a perspective view of a building, but in recording visual notes, they recode what they see into plan, elevation, section, or paraline diagrams.

My first thoughts are always recorded in my "Daler" sketchbook. I may draw anywhere from two or three to up to twenty little sketches before they move to the next level.
[ARCHITECT'S STATEMENT]

STUDY SKETCHES

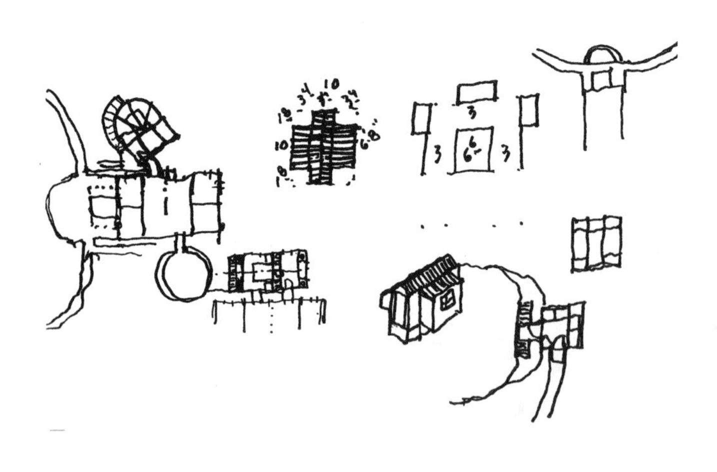

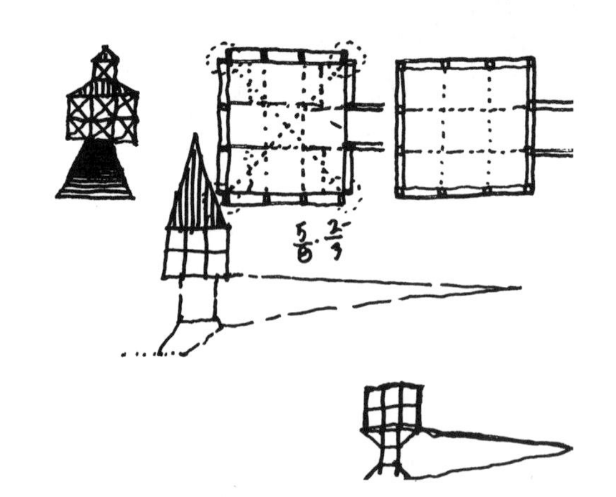

Travel sketches: Study for one-room house
Boardwalk, Michigan
3⅝" × 5¹³⁄₁₆" (9.22 × 14.76 cm)
Medium: Ink on paper

Sketches by Stanley Tigerman

Multiple interior or exterior vantage points are common in study sketches. These superimposed sketches show a variety of perspective views taken inside a house with the direction of views indicated on the sketched plan. Travel sketches can sometimes be analytical studies.

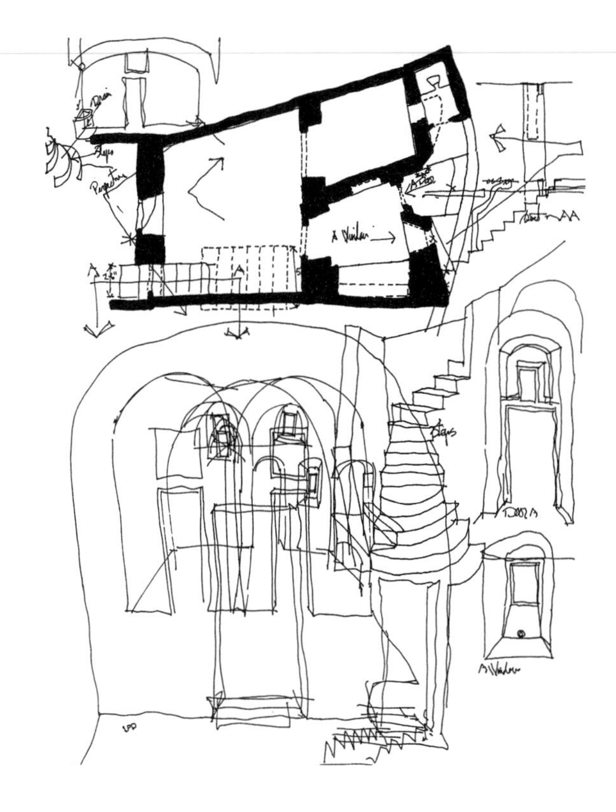

Travel sketching can offer spontaneous opportunities to document the environment. By drawing a plan view along with a series of corresponding vignettes, one can begin to capture the true essence of architectural space. These analytical studies can provide thoughtful insights into form and movement.
[ARCHITECT'S STATEMENT]

Drawing: House, Santorini, Greece
8" × 10" (20.3 × 25.4 cm)
Medium: Pen and ink on paper
Courtesy of Steven House, Architect, San Francisco

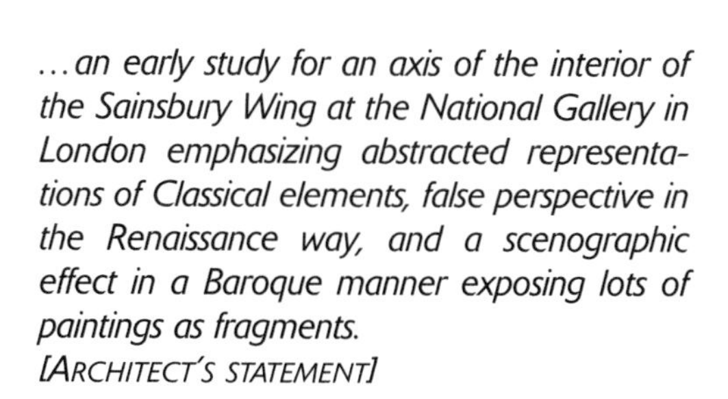

...an early study for an axis of the interior of the Sainsbury Wing at the National Gallery in London emphasizing abstracted representations of Classical elements, false perspective in the Renaissance way, and a scenographic effect in a Baroque manner exposing lots of paintings as fragments.
[ARCHITECT'S STATEMENT]

Study sketch: National Gallery, Sainsbury Wing, London, England
Medium: Felt-tipped pen
Courtesy of Venturi, Scott Brown and Associates, Inc., Architects
Sketch by Robert Venturi

4

Conventional Orthogonal Terminology

BASICS 87
BASICS APPLIED 90

Scaled plans, elevations, and sections are architectural drawing conventions that permit the representation of three dimensions at a smaller scale. These multiview drawings are the result of projecting orthographically and help to depict a three-dimensional form—like a building—in various, related two-dimensional views. With these projections, design aspects related to space, scale, and configuration can be studied. Other conventions, termed "paraline" and "perspective," are more complex and sophisticated; they are described separately in subsequent chapters.

The intent of this chapter is to introduce the potential and capabilities of multiview drawings and graphic symbols, and the kinds of information they can communicate.

The following are some of the important terms and concepts you will learn:

Orthogonal	Orthographic projection	Plan
Section	Reflected ceiling plan	Elevation
Roof plan	North arrows	Graphic scales

Conventional Orthogonal Terminology

TOPIC: CONVENTIONAL ORTHOGONAL TERMINOLOGY

Forseth 1980, 66–75.

Chapter Overview

After studying this chapter, you will have a detailed understanding of drawing conventions such as plan, elevation, and section, as well as north arrows and graphic scales. For continued study, refer to Forseth's *Graphics for Architecture.*

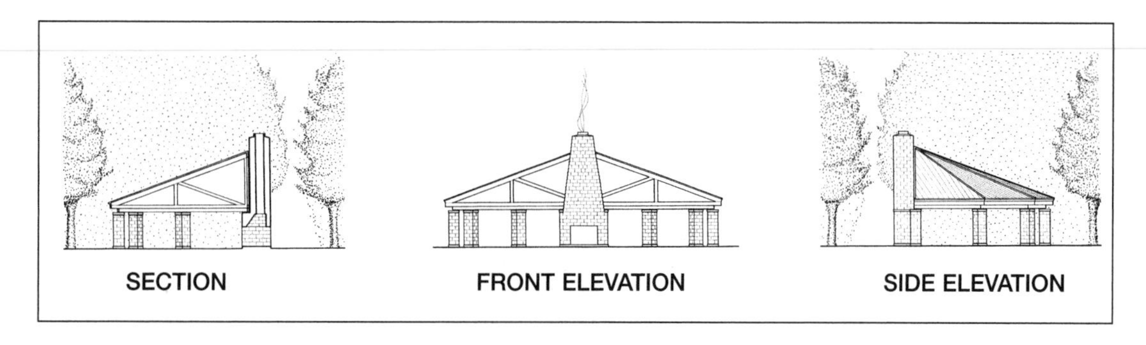

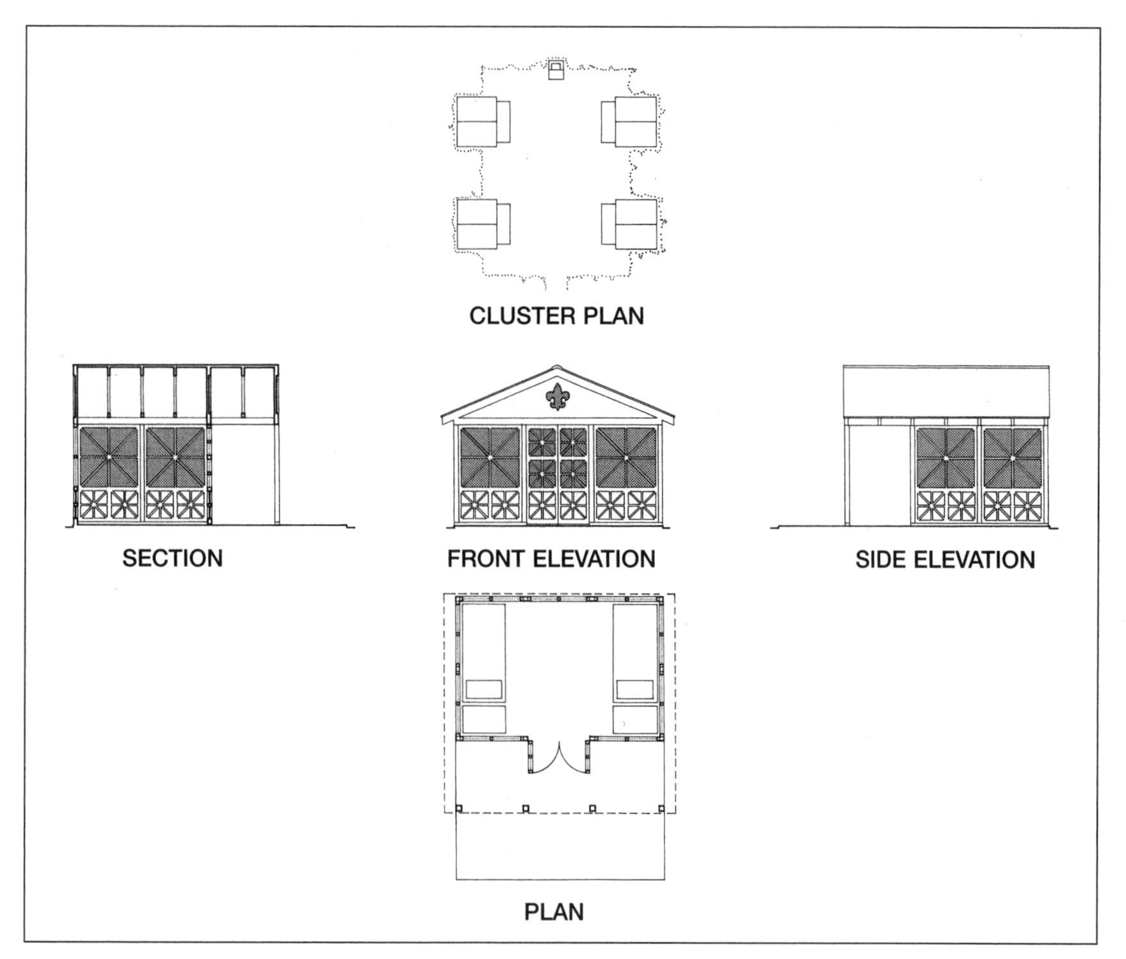

Drawings: Hoover Camping Cluster in the Hoover Outdoor Education Center
Yorkville, Illinois
Medium: Ink on Mylar
Courtesy of Tigerman McCurry Architects

Historically, buildings have been described using an **orthogonal** (right-angled) two-dimensional drawing system. The nomenclature used for the various orthogonal views is shown here. Popular architectural terminology such as "floor plan" is common knowledge for the layperson.

Small building types like residences are usually drawn orthogonally at a scale of ⅛"=1'0" or ¼"=1'0". A smaller scale (1⁄16"=1'0") can be used for larger building types such as hospitals and schools. A knowledge of orthogonal conventions and graphic symbols is necessary for architectural drawings and presentations. This chapter isolates and explores these topics in detail.

PRINCIPAL PLANES OF PROJECTION

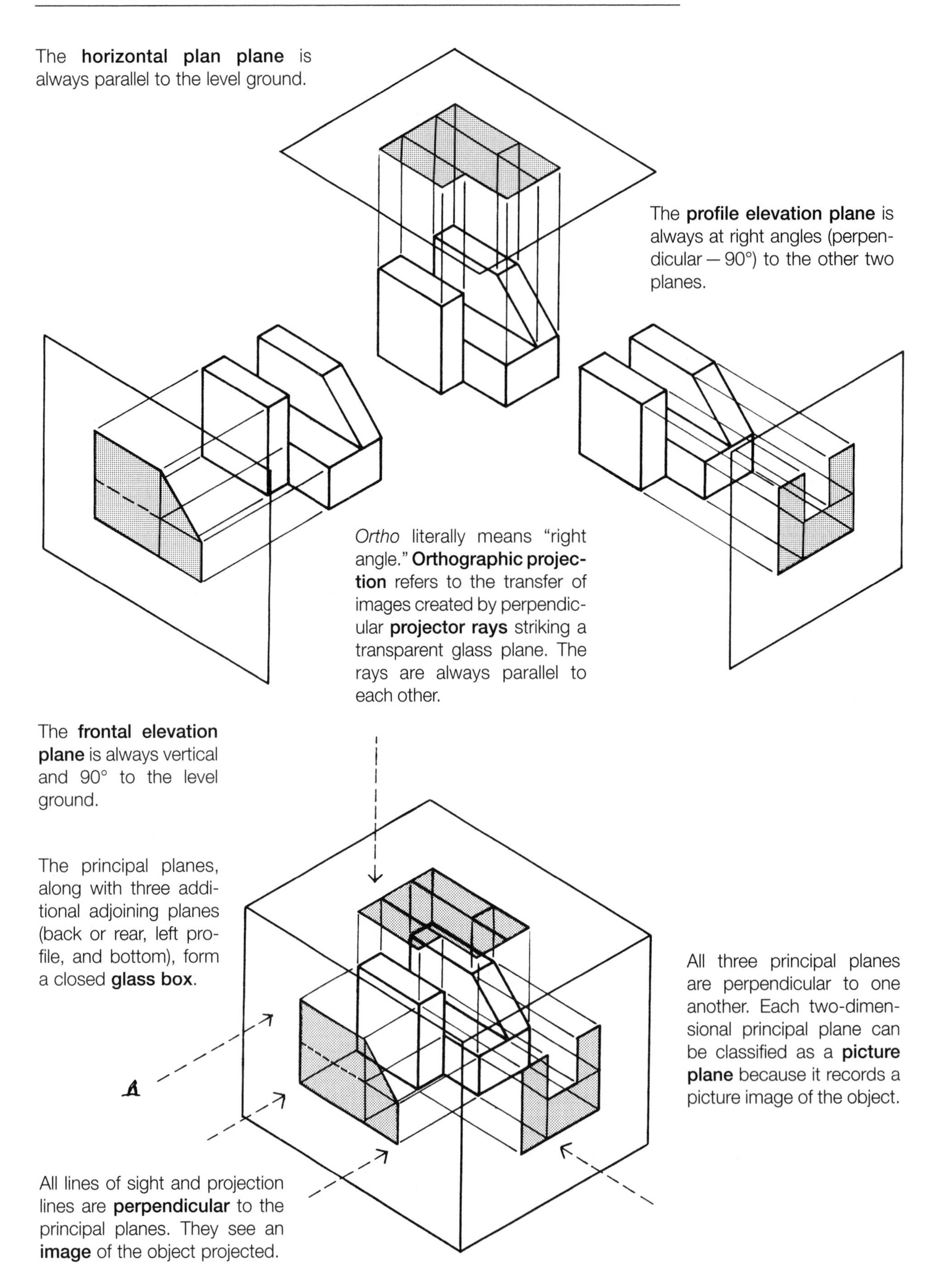

The **horizontal plan plane** is always parallel to the level ground.

The **profile elevation plane** is always at right angles (perpendicular — 90°) to the other two planes.

Ortho literally means "right angle." **Orthographic projection** refers to the transfer of images created by perpendicular **projector rays** striking a transparent glass plane. The rays are always parallel to each other.

The **frontal elevation plane** is always vertical and 90° to the level ground.

The principal planes, along with three additional adjoining planes (back or rear, left profile, and bottom), form a closed **glass box**.

All three principal planes are perpendicular to one another. Each two-dimensional principal plane can be classified as a **picture plane** because it records a picture image of the object.

All lines of sight and projection lines are **perpendicular** to the principal planes. They see an **image** of the object projected.

The **folding plane line** is the intersection of any two principal planes. If a transparent glass box is opened on its folding plane or "hinge" lines, it will become a two-dimensional surface. The plan and profile elevation planes are rotated to become a part of the frontal elevation plane's extension.

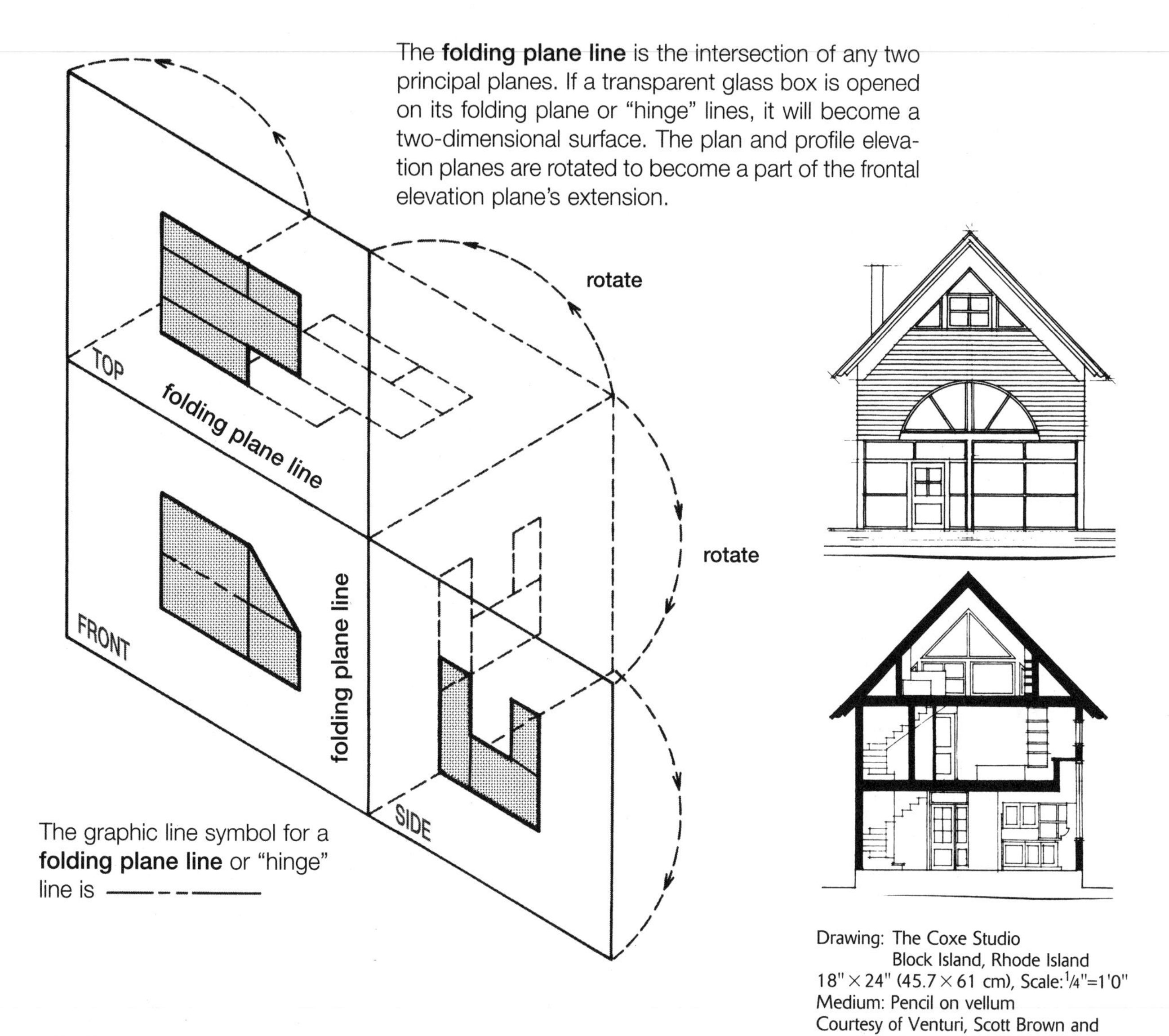

The graphic line symbol for a **folding plane line** or "hinge" line is ——— – – ———

Drawing: The Coxe Studio
Block Island, Rhode Island
18" × 24" (45.7 × 61 cm), Scale: 1/4"=1'0"
Medium: Pencil on vellum
Courtesy of Venturi, Scott Brown and Associates, Inc., Architects

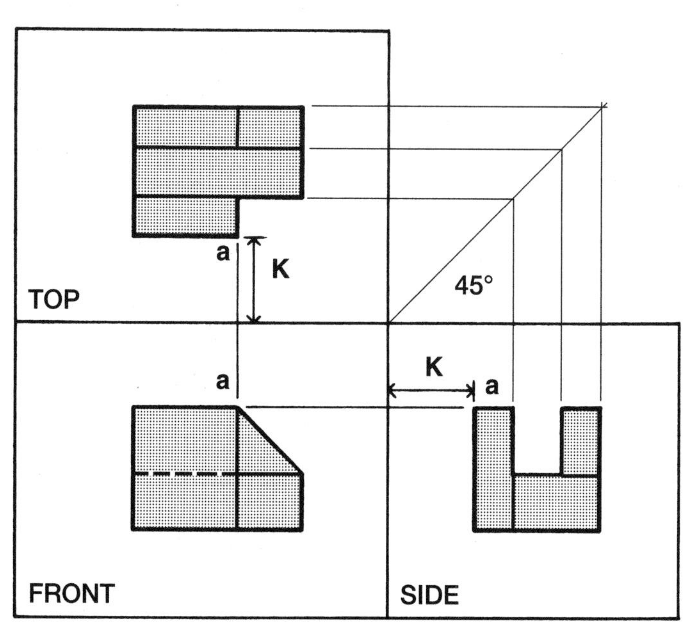

The above example shows two true-size profile views (elevation and section). **Orthographic drawings** are true-size and true-shape views that are related on a two-dimensional surface. When two planes are perpendicular to a third plane, any point in space (such as **a**) will be seen twice an equal distance **K** behind the third plane where **K** can be any distance. In constructing related orthographic views, use a **45° diagonal line** from the intersection of the folding plane lines. Proper distances can then be transferred with projector lines from the top or horizontal view to the side or profile view. See an example of this process on page 627.

In an **elevation,** the image is projected onto a vertical picture plane. A building elevation shows vertical dimension relationships, the organizational massing, and the scale of the fenestration. It also shows the location of doors and windows, as well as the pattern and textures of the construction materials (see pp. 390–91). Only the ground plane outside of the building will be shown as a solid cut line (see pp. 350 and 390) or a solid mass (see p. 104).

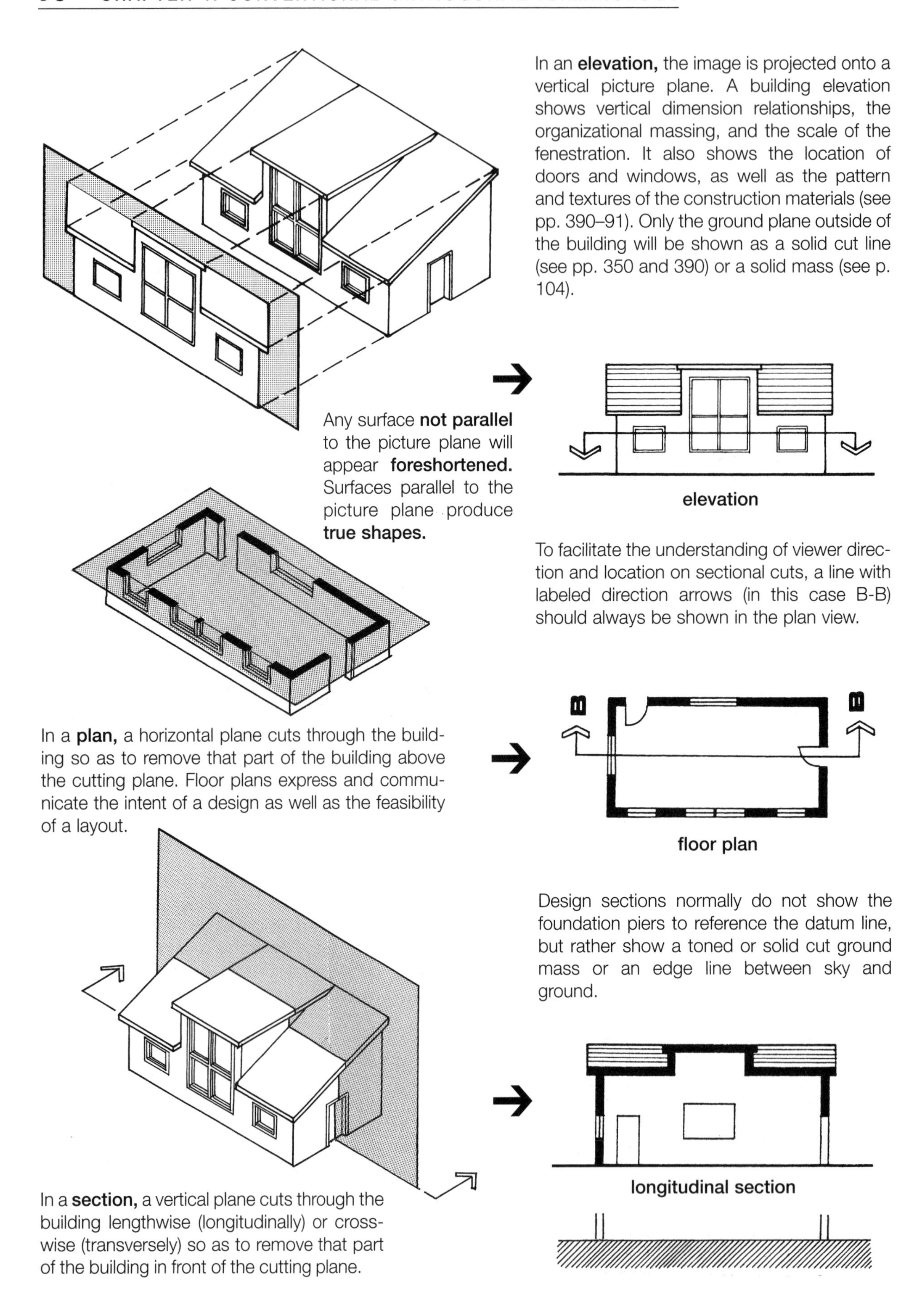

Any surface **not parallel** to the picture plane will appear **foreshortened.** Surfaces parallel to the picture plane produce **true shapes.**

To facilitate the understanding of viewer direction and location on sectional cuts, a line with labeled direction arrows (in this case B-B) should always be shown in the plan view.

In a **plan,** a horizontal plane cuts through the building so as to remove that part of the building above the cutting plane. Floor plans express and communicate the intent of a design as well as the feasibility of a layout.

Design sections normally do not show the foundation piers to reference the datum line, but rather show a toned or solid cut ground mass or an edge line between sky and ground.

In a **section,** a vertical plane cuts through the building lengthwise (longitudinally) or crosswise (transversely) so as to remove that part of the building in front of the cutting plane.

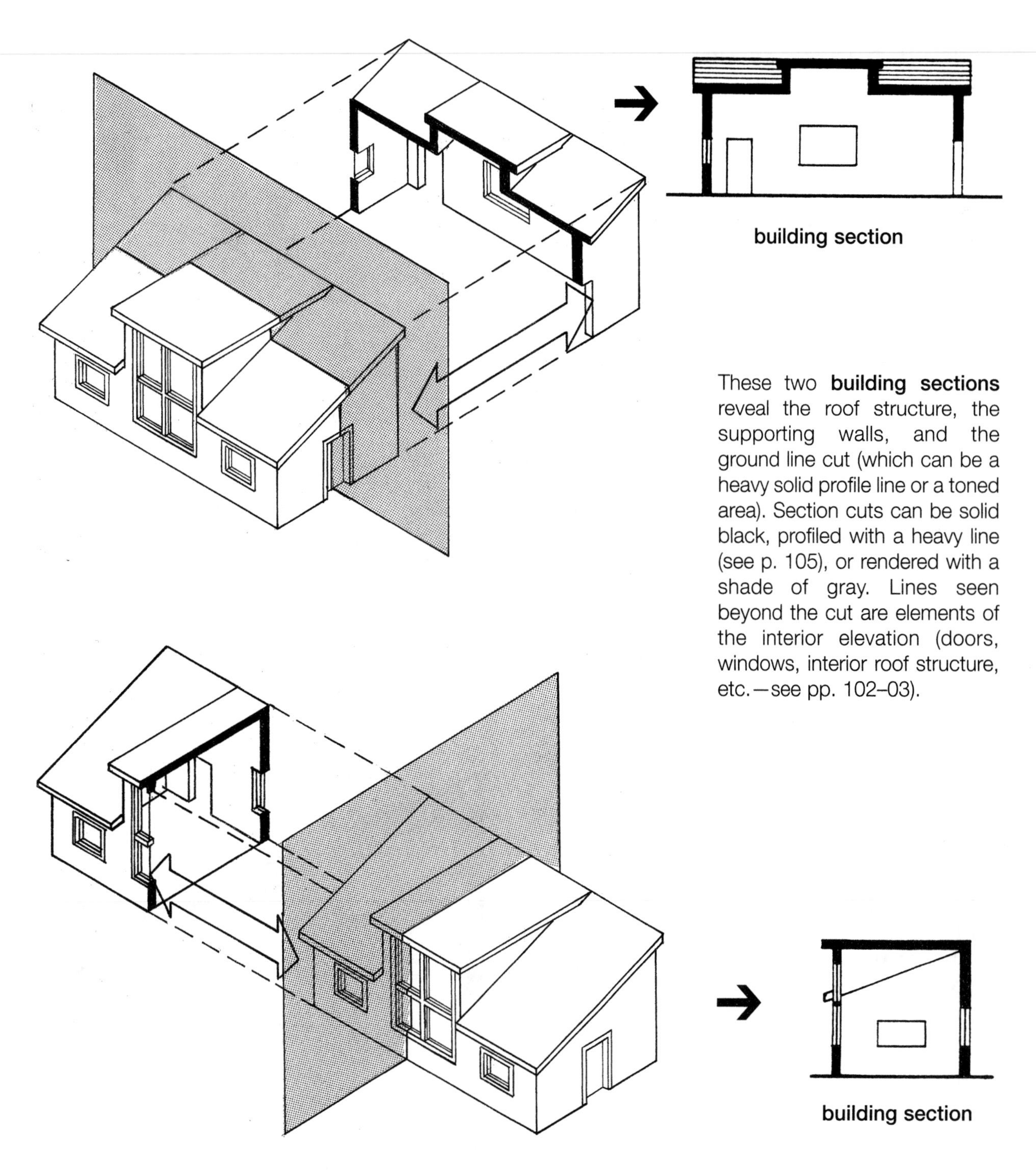

These two **building sections** reveal the roof structure, the supporting walls, and the ground line cut (which can be a heavy solid profile line or a toned area). Section cuts can be solid black, profiled with a heavy line (see p. 105), or rendered with a shade of gray. Lines seen beyond the cut are elements of the interior elevation (doors, windows, interior roof structure, etc.—see pp. 102–03).

A **building section** is analogous to the plan (horizontally cut section) except that the continuous cutting plane is **vertical.** Removing that part of the building in front of the plane reveals a cut section of the interior space. Logically, sectional cuts in architectural drawings are most often done parallel to walls in either the front or the side elevation. These sections are then properly annotated, as explained on the previous page. Other types of sectional cuts (such as offset cuts) tend to be more complex. The location of the sectional cut and the direction of view is left to the discretion of the architect/designer. Try to be very descriptive in showing the configuration and scale of the contained spatial relationships.

The contour that defines where the sky (or space above) meets the building mass and the ground line determines the configuration of any **site section.** The primary function of a site section is to relate any building design to its **contextual environment.** It is quite common to see large site sections that show multiple cut sections of the building complex in combination with elevations of the same complex (see pp. 526–27 and 541).

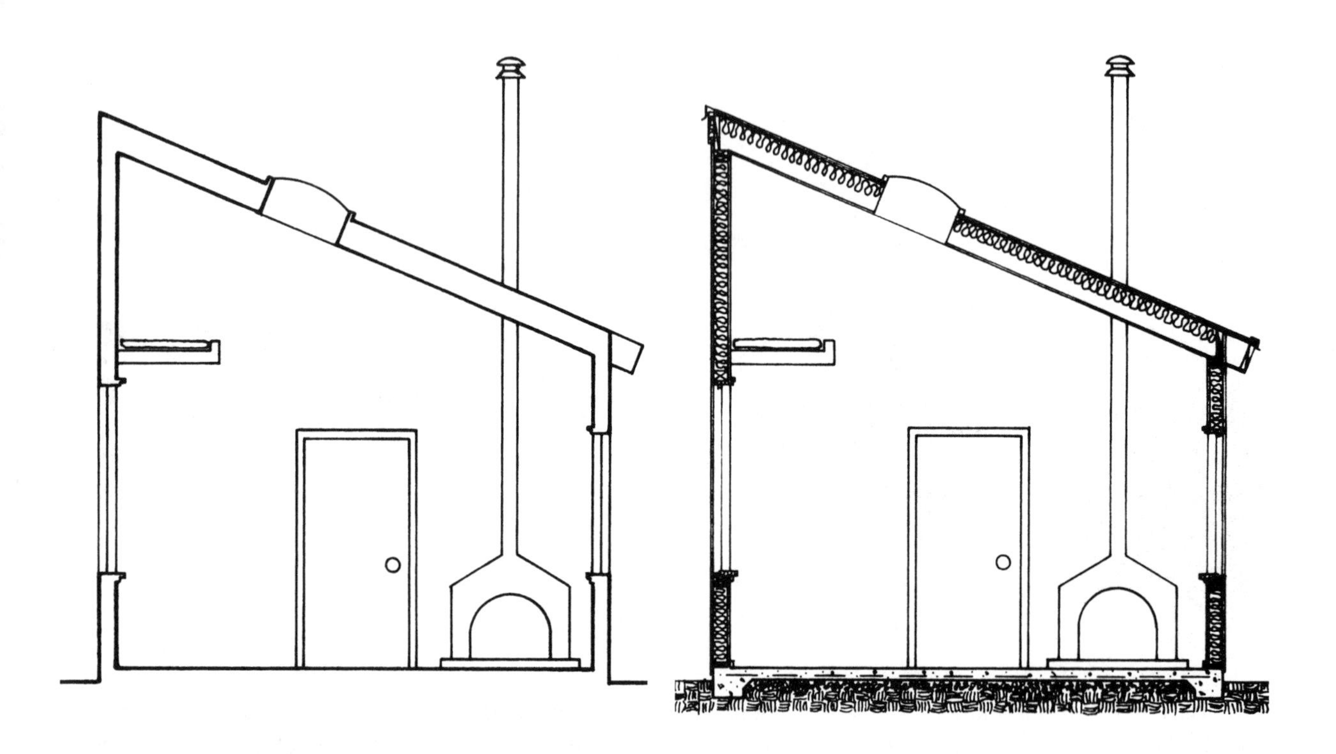

A **design section** shows no structural or construction details in the section area that is cut. The section is profiled with a heavy line to help define the interior spaces and overall form of the building. A **construction section** shows the details required to fabricate the building.

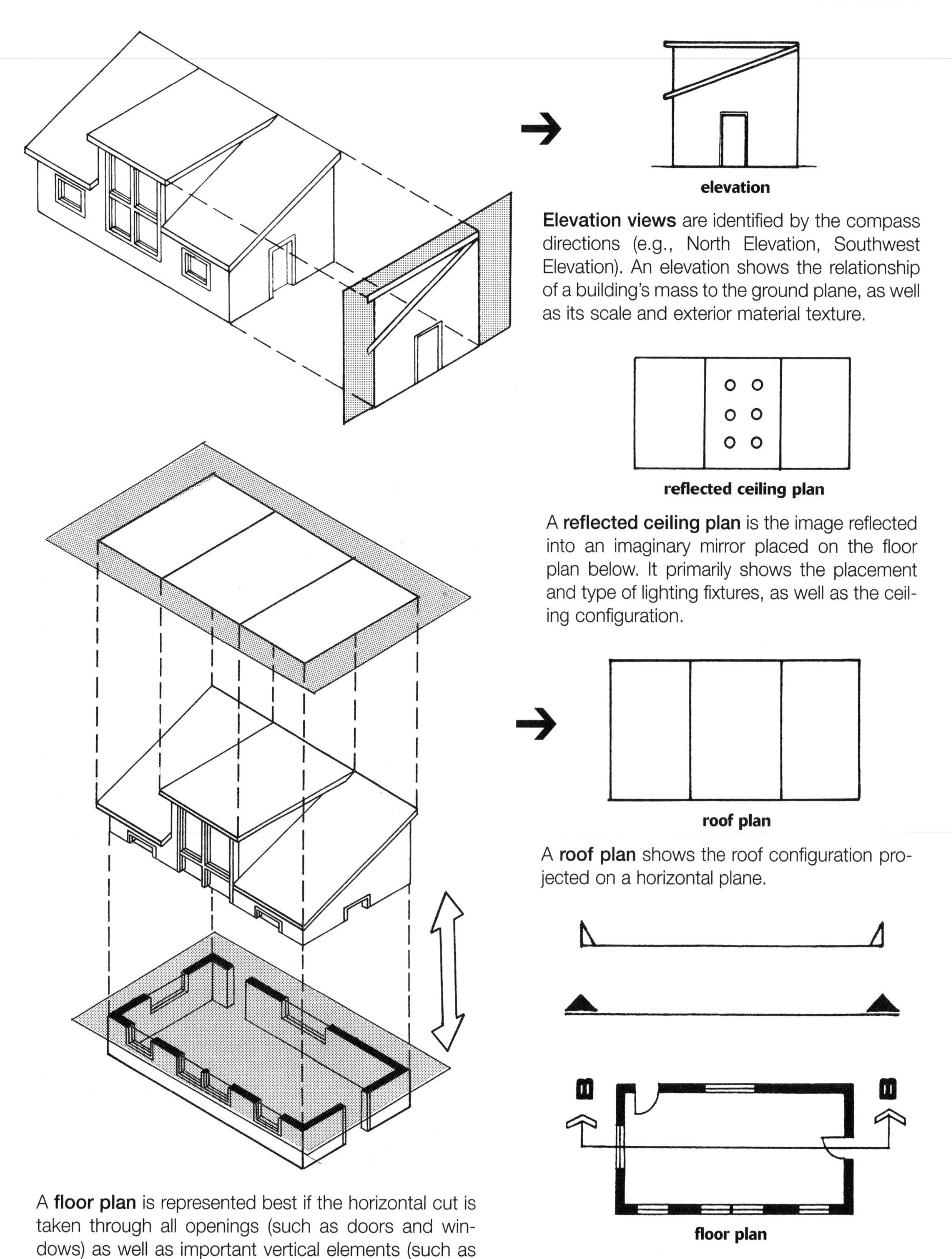

elevation

Elevation views are identified by the compass directions (e.g., North Elevation, Southwest Elevation). An elevation shows the relationship of a building's mass to the ground plane, as well as its scale and exterior material texture.

reflected ceiling plan

A **reflected ceiling plan** is the image reflected into an imaginary mirror placed on the floor plan below. It primarily shows the placement and type of lighting fixtures, as well as the ceiling configuration.

roof plan

A **roof plan** shows the roof configuration projected on a horizontal plane.

floor plan

Section arrows indicate the observer's direction of sight when viewing a building section.

A **floor plan** is represented best if the horizontal cut is taken through all openings (such as doors and windows) as well as important vertical elements (such as columns). The location of the cutting plane can vary, but normally ranges from 4' to 6' above the floor plane.

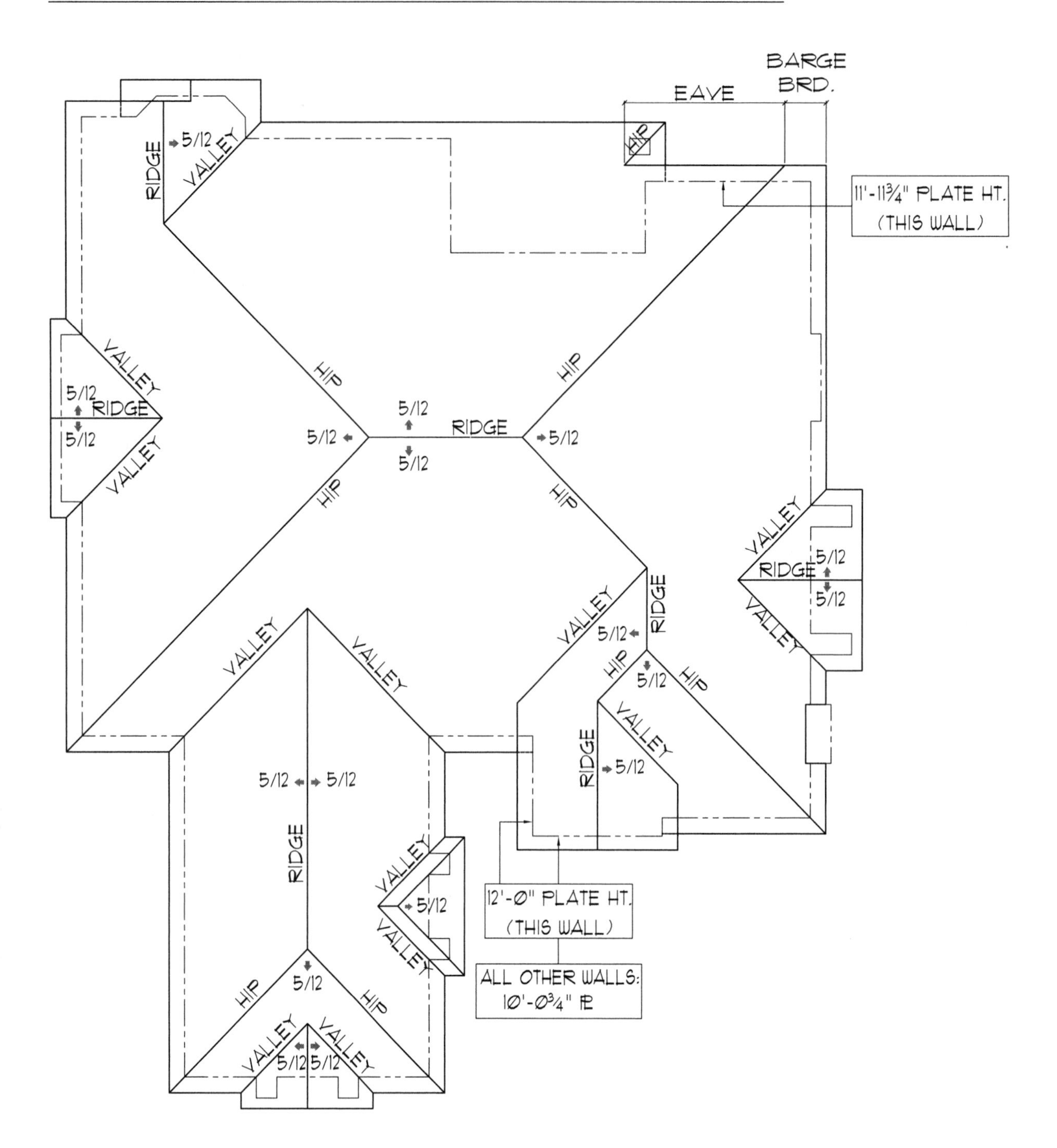

Drawing: Johnson Residence
Folsom, California
Medium: AutoCAD 2004
Courtesy of Tamano & Chaw Residential Design

A **roof plan** shows the overall shape and detailed configuration of the roof structure. In residential construction roof plans, lines are typically defined as hip, valley, or ridge. The roof's slope and the wall outline beneath the roof are also indicated. In design drawings, the material texture is indicated by symbol.

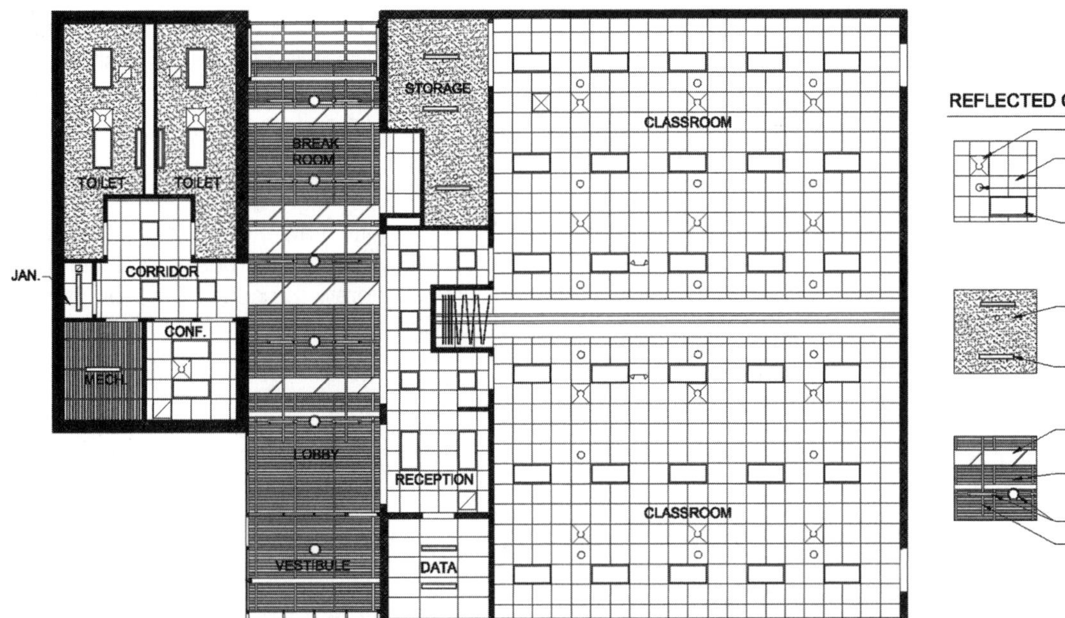

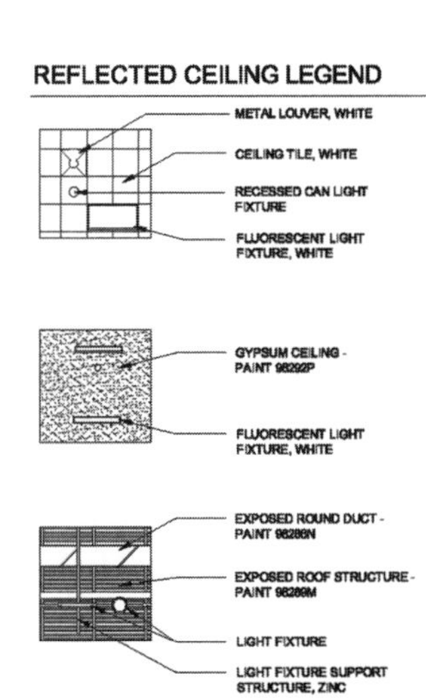

REFLECTED CEILING PLAN

Drawing: Technology and Management Center
Edwardsville, Illinois
Medium: AutoCAD
Wight & Company/Fitch-Fitzgerald, Inc.
Architects/Engineers
Courtesy of Richard Klein, SIUE

Imagine placing a huge mirror on the floor configuration shown above that matches the roof configuration. You would see the white fluorescent light fixtures, the white metal louvers, the recessed can light fixtures, and the white ceiling tiles all reflected in this mirror in their exact ceiling positions in the classrooms. The gypsum ceilings in both bathrooms and the storage area would be similarly reflected. A **reflected ceiling plan** commonly shows ceiling elements like light panels and ceiling-mounted heat registers in the same orientation as the floor plan.

Pages 96 and 97 give a step-by-step process for drawing a plan. In general, the best procedure is to draw the building shell first, then all of the elements contained within the shell. Be sure to locate the center lines of all windows and doors.

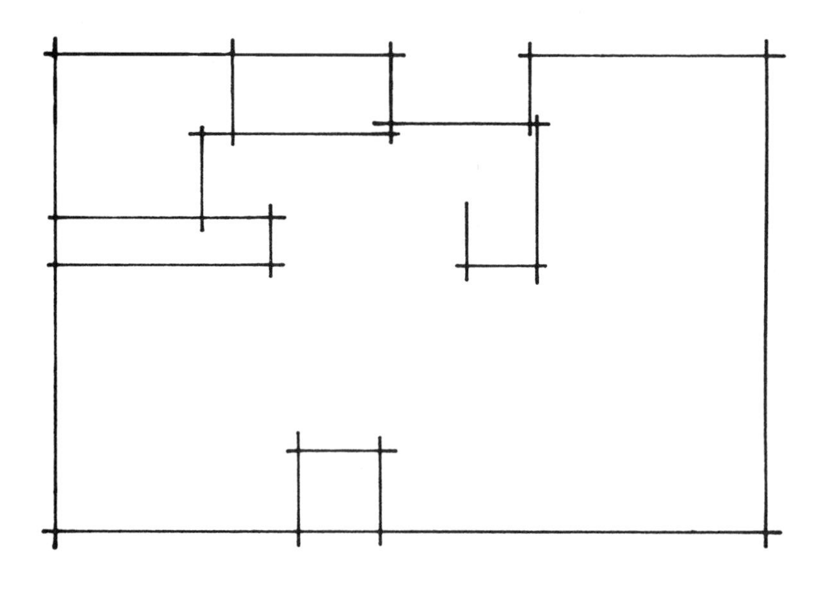

1. Lightly draw the building outline with a single line. Again using a single line, lightly draw the center lines for interior walls.

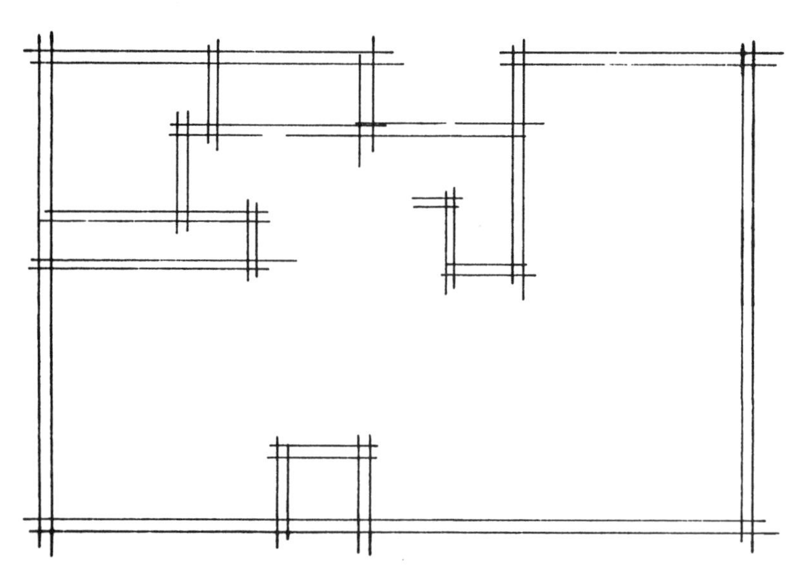

2. Add wall thickness for both exterior and interior walls.

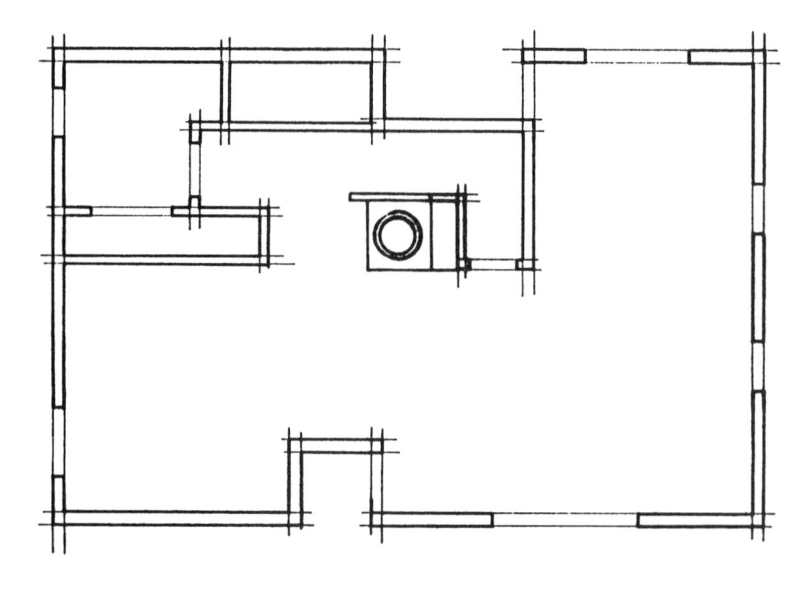

3. Locate and draw wall openings such as windows, doors, fireplaces, and stairs.

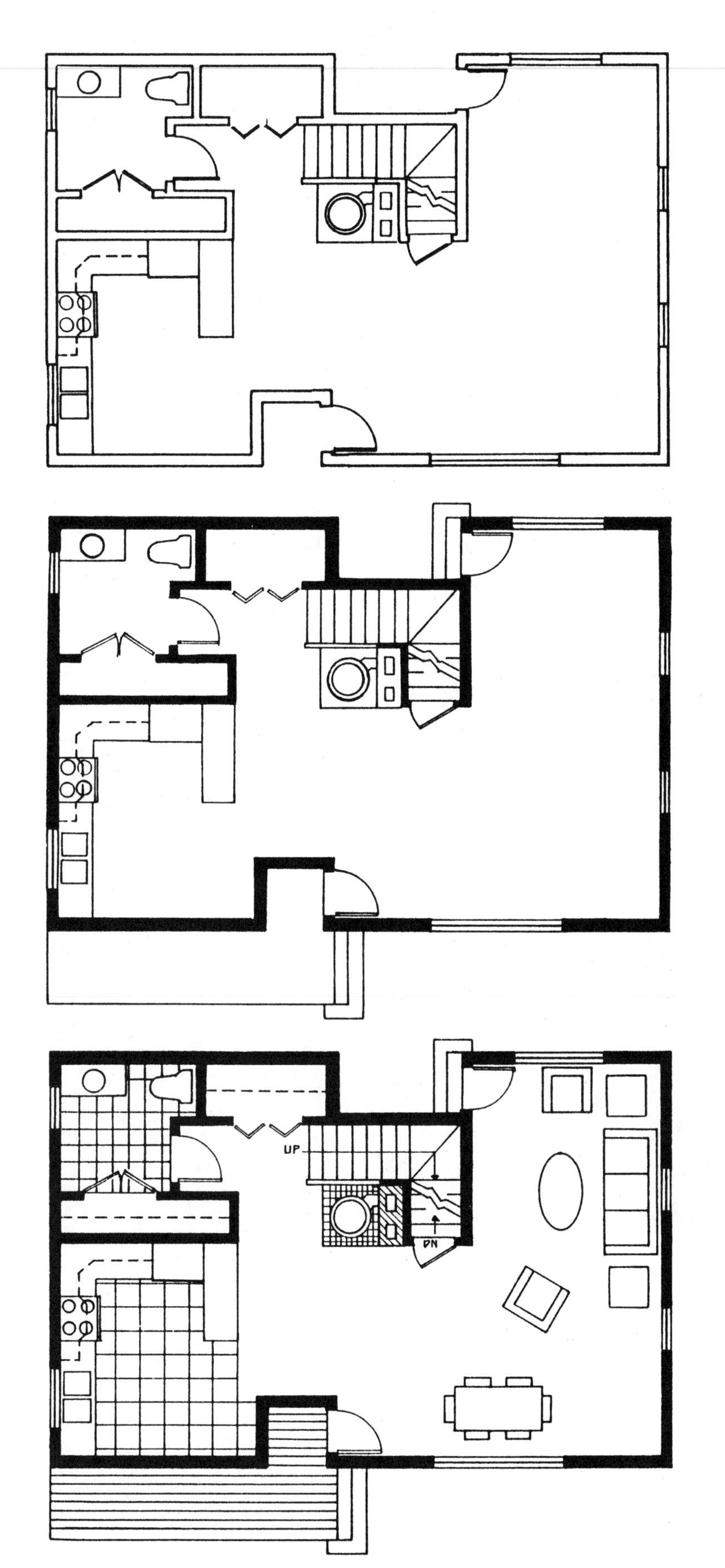

4. Locate and draw bathroom and kitchen fixtures, as well as plan details for doors and windows.

5. Draw any plan view wall indications with proper tone value (see p. 98). In this case the wall is toned solid black. If it were left white, the wall outline could be made heavier to make it read better.

Floor plans illustrate the location of walls, doors, windows, and stairs, as well as other elements below the cutting plane (countertops, toilets, etc.). Plan drawings are abstract views; at ground level, we cannot see the things they represent.

6. Draw the proper material symbol (tone and texture) for the floors in each room.

This step-by-step procedure applies to plans drawn both freehand and mechanically.

The main purpose of including furniture and built-in elements (stoves, sinks, etc.) in the plan view is to show function and scale. For an accurate interpretation, the plan view, as with all orthogonal views, must have a constant scale.

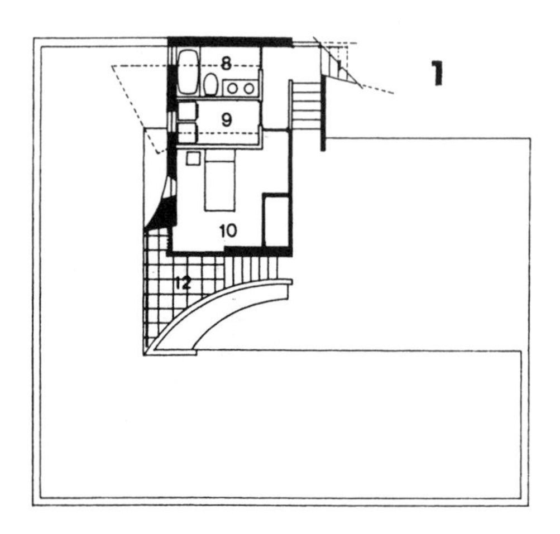

Drawing: The Hague Villa Project
The Hague, The Netherlands
8" × 10 (20.3 × 25.4 cm), Scale ¼"=1'0"
Medium: Pen and ink
Courtesy of Hariri & Hariri, Architects

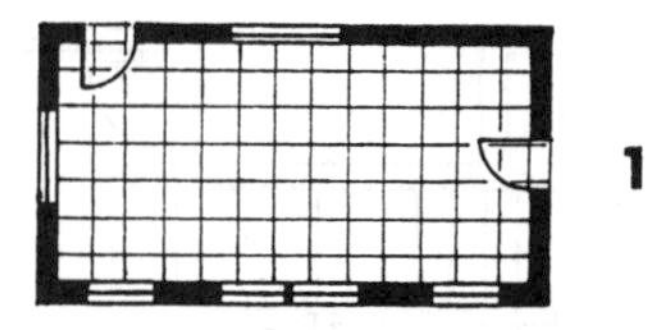

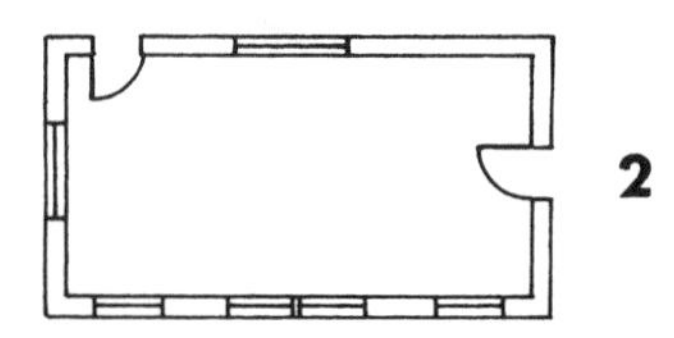

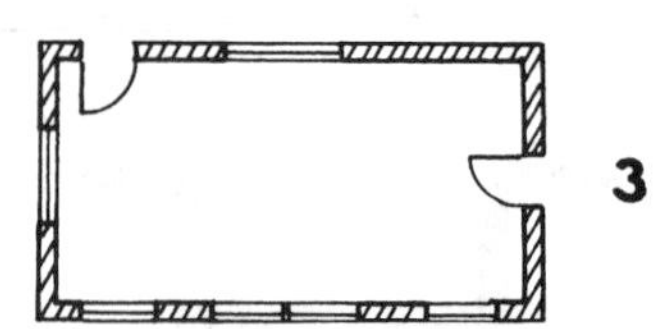

4

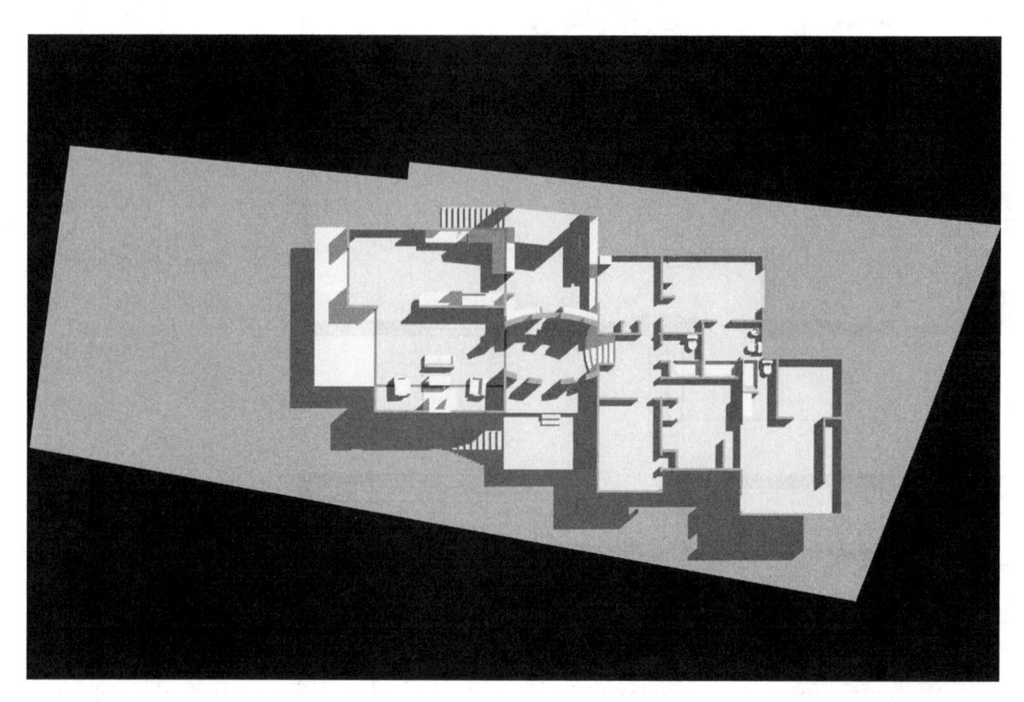

Plan study image: Nomikos residence, Berkeley, California
Courtesy of Inglese Architecture
Mark David English, Architectural Illustrator

Floor plan wall indications can be given different tonal values. In **1**, more contrast with the floorscape is desired; thus, the walls are toned solid black. In **2**, minimal contrast is needed; thus, the walls are left with no tone and a profile line. In **3**, a hatched tone is used for intermediate contrast (this can also indicate the building material). In **4**, shadows are cast within the plan view to accentuate the walls and give added contrast. The shadows also give hints as to the heights of walls and other vertical elements.

2

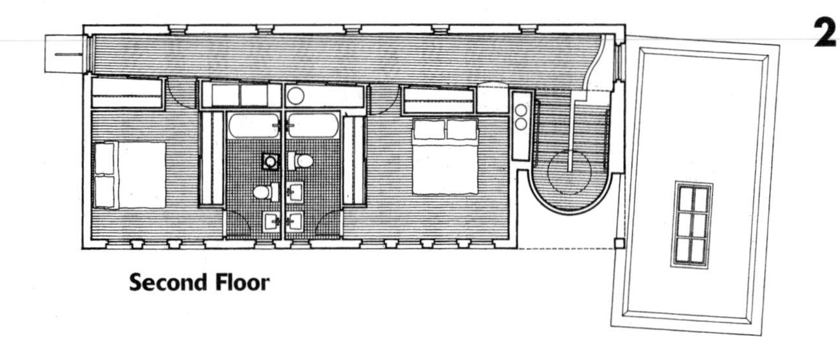

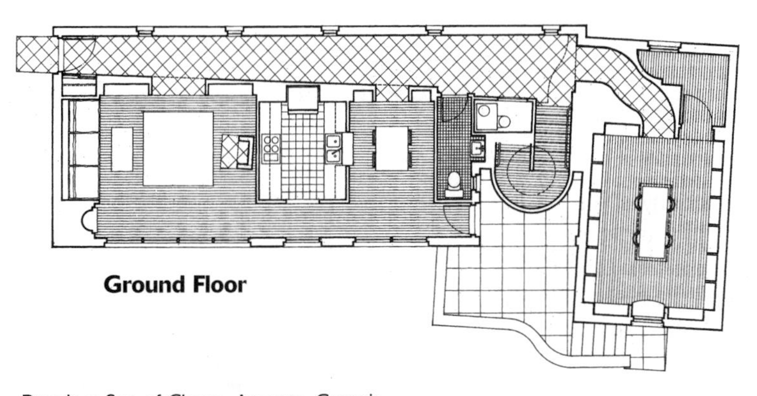

Drawing: Son of Chang, Augusta, Georgia
24" × 24" (61x61 cm), Scale ¼"=1'0"
Medium: Ink
Courtesy of Anthony Ames, Architect

The **indication** patterns, values, and colors of floor finishes (see p. 383) are equally as important as plan wall indications. In Condition **2,** the outline of the plan cut is darkened to differentiate it from the floorscape texture. In Condition **3,** the plan wall indication for concrete block is strongly defined. In Condition **4,** a solid black wall easily contrasts with many floorscapes.

In multistory buildings, floor plans are commonly drawn in a vertical **alignment** (see pp. 155 and 492) with the lowest floor at the bottom. Plans can also be drawn in a horizontally related alignment with the lowest floor plan furthest to the left.

3

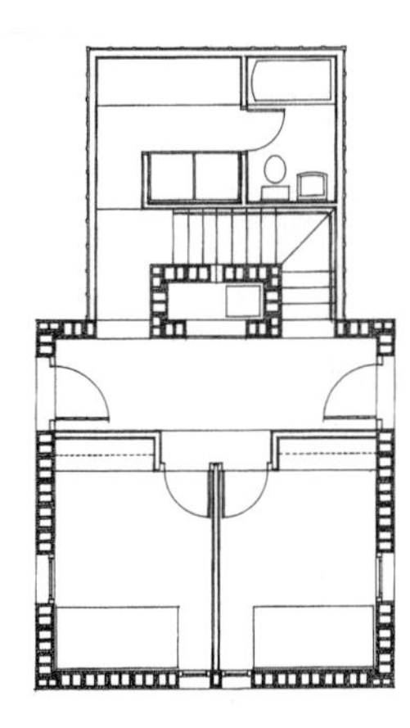

Drawing: Reid House
Johns Island, South Carolina
20" × 30" (50.8 × 76.2 cm), Scale: ¼"=1'0"
Medium: Ink on Mylar
Courtesy of Clark & Menefee, Architects

4

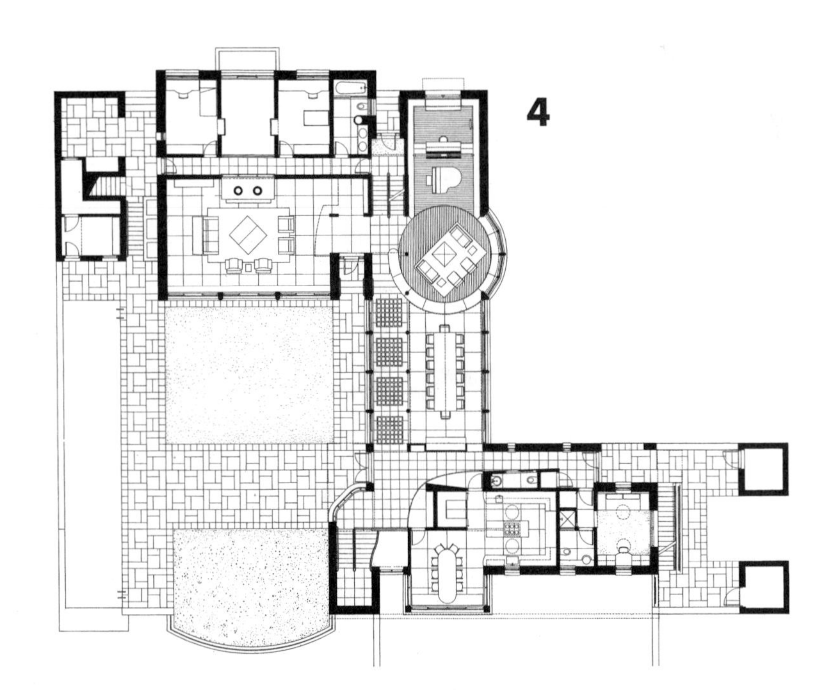

Drawing: Private residence, Zumikon, Switzerland
48" × 36" (121.9 × 91.4 cm), Scale: 1:50
Medium: Ink on Mylar
Courtesy of Gwathmey Siegel & Associates, Architects

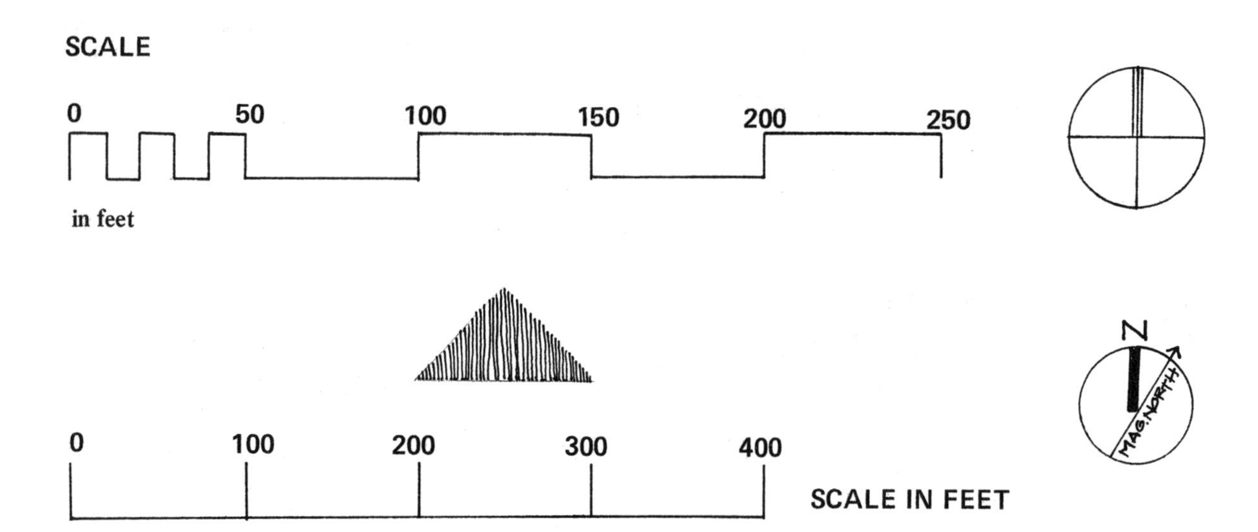

North arrows and **graphic scales** are graphic symbols that facilitate the understanding of the **orientation** and the **scale** of a building and the site it sits on. They should be placed adjacent to each other and next to the drawing they refer to in a presentation. They should be clean, simple, and legible, and must never have fancy detail or distract from the drawing itself. Section arrows are also graphic symbols (see p. 90).

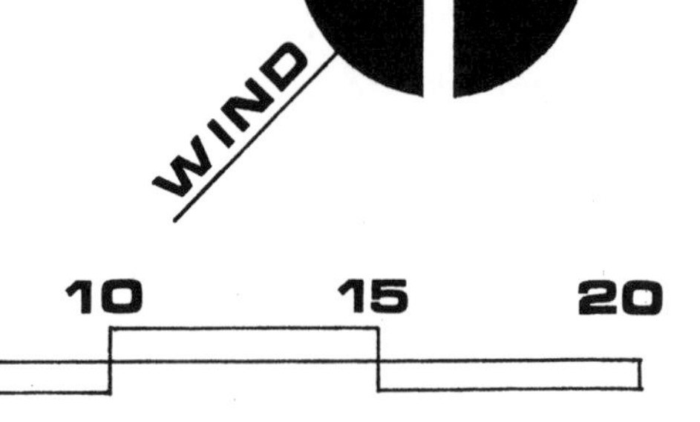

0 5 10 15 20

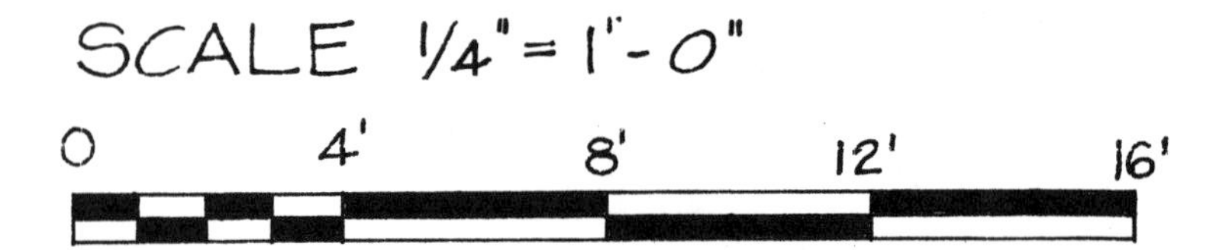

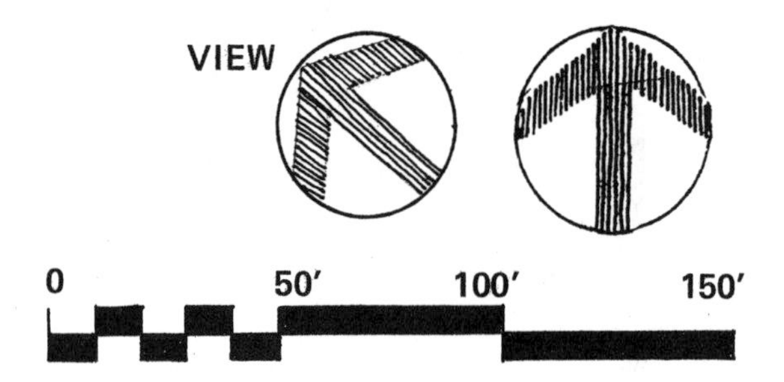

Graphic scales are lines or rectangular bars with graduations. The choice of a graphic scale size is dependent on the size and complexity of the drawing, as well as its distance from the viewer. The decision as to how many feet one inch represents is yours (i.e., 1" can be equal to 4', 5', 50', etc.).

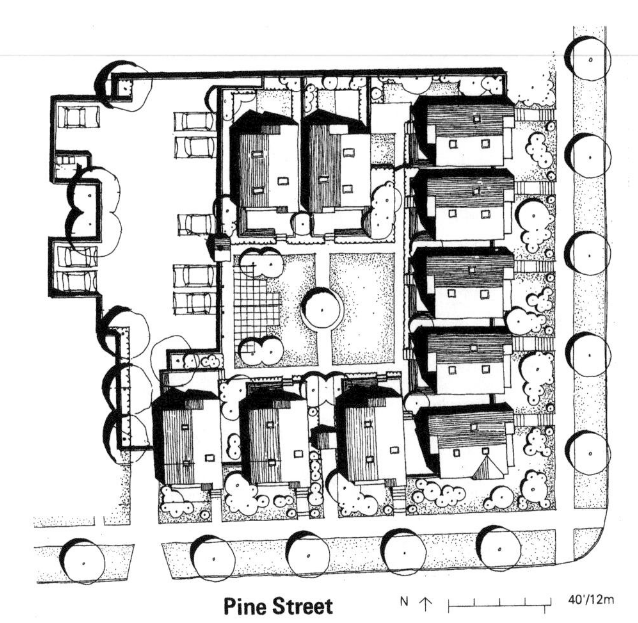

Drawing: Pine Street Cottages, Seattle, Washington
Kucher/Rutherford, Inc., Developer and Contractor
Courtesy of Marcia Gamble Hadley, Designer

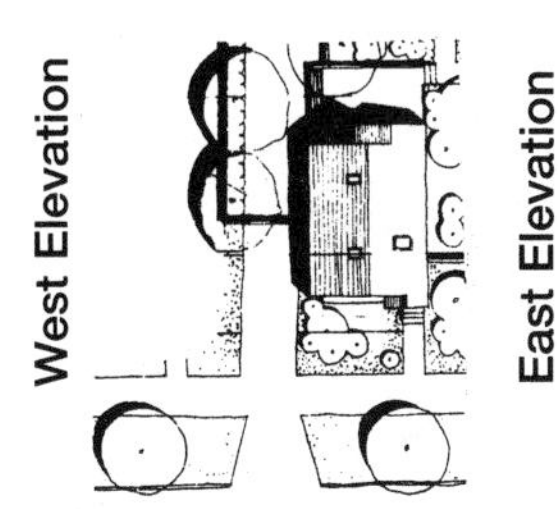

If the front of a building faces north, then the proper notation is North Elevation, and likewise for any direction the various sides of the building may face (e.g., Southwest Elevation). An important site feature, such as a major street or a body of water, can be used in place of the direction.

Site plans show the orientation and the location of a building (below) or many buildings (above). They can be precise pictorial drawings as shown on this page or schematic drawings (see pp. 431, 433, and 439). They are commonly drawn at 1⁄16"=1'0" or at engineering scales such as 1"=20', 1"=40', or 1"=50'. The boundaries of the site, which should enclose all site elements as well as the building complex, must be clearly defined as shown below. Shadows help to reveal the building's height and its overall configuration (see pp. 369 and 382).

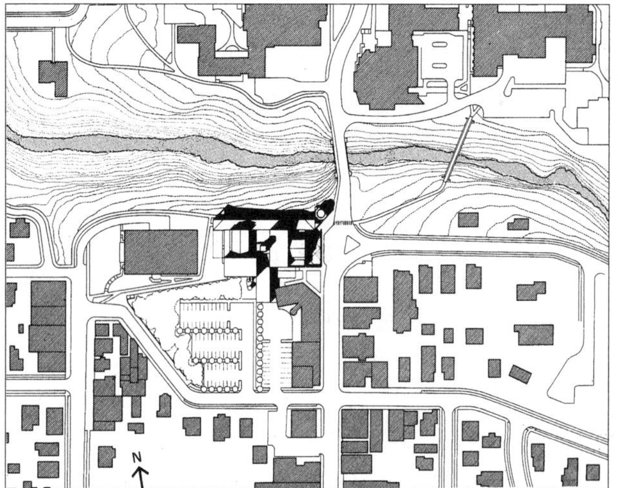

Drawing: Cornell University Center for the Performing Arts, Ithaca, New York
Scale: 1"=50'0"
Courtesy of James Stirling Michael Wilford and Associates, Architects

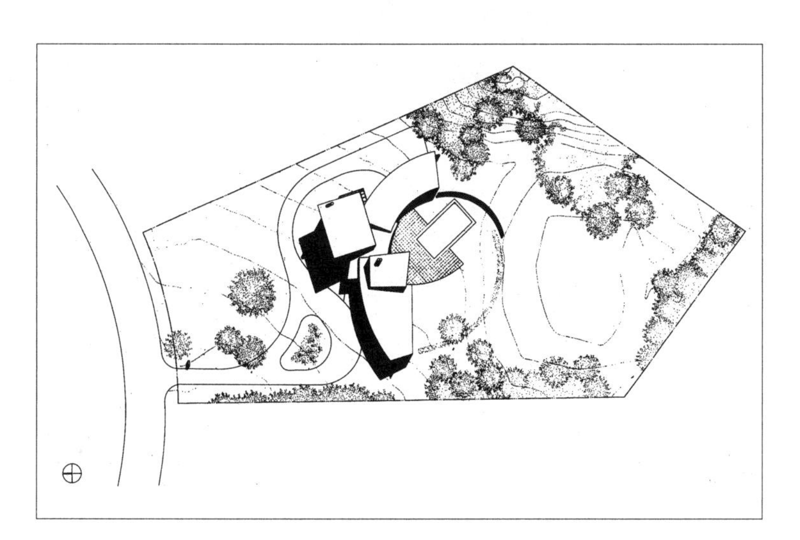

Drawing: Kreindel residence, Cresskill, New Jersey
Courtesy of Frank Lupo and Daniel Rowen, Architects

A **location plan** is a variation of the site plan that extends to include a broader, regional context. Important site features, such as transportation arteries, surrounding buildings, and the physical topography are commonly drawn. These environmental elements usually play a significant role in influencing the design of the proposed building.

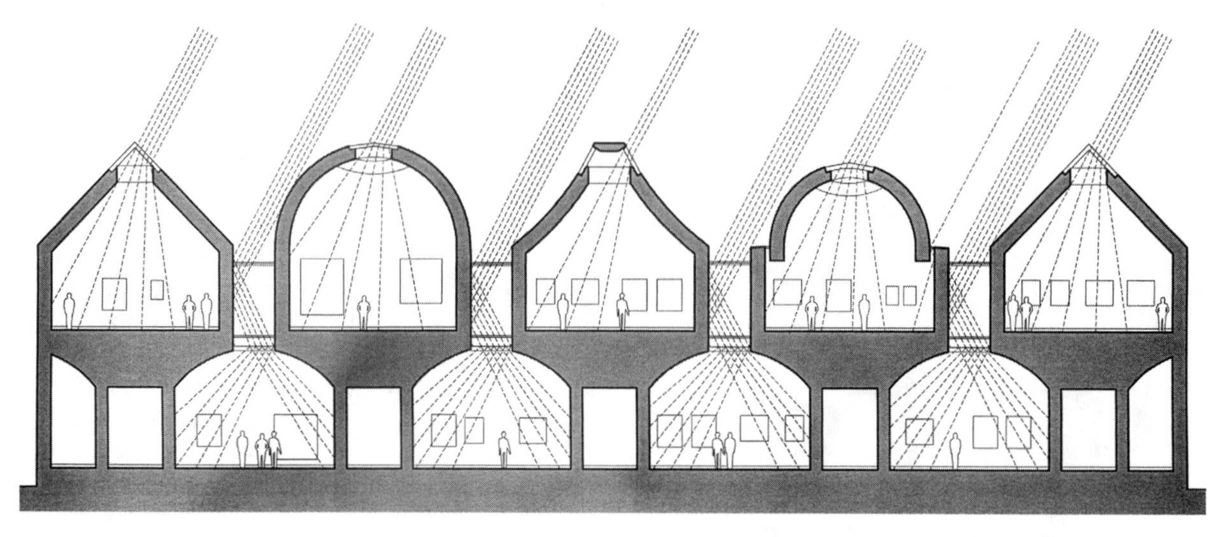

Section through upper and lower house galleries

Drawing: Peabody Essex Museum, Salem, Massachusetts
Medium: AutoCAD
Courtesy of Moshe Safdie and Associates, Inc., Architects

See companion Web site (Chapter 11) for additional drawings for this building.

A **building design section** must reveal design objectives as much as possible. To this end, slices are taken through important solids and voids. Light studies are frequently done to determine how directional sunlight comes through window or skylight openings. Architects play with how light enters an interior space and how we feel about an architectural structure's spatial quality and textural appearance. Human figures are also added to give the drawing human scale.

Sections are normally cut through (**1**) door and window openings, (**2**) circulation change of level elements (e.g., stairs and ramps), and (**3**) ceiling or roof openings such as skylights. Foundation elements may or may not be shown, depending on their significance in the overall design. Section cuts should never be made through columns.

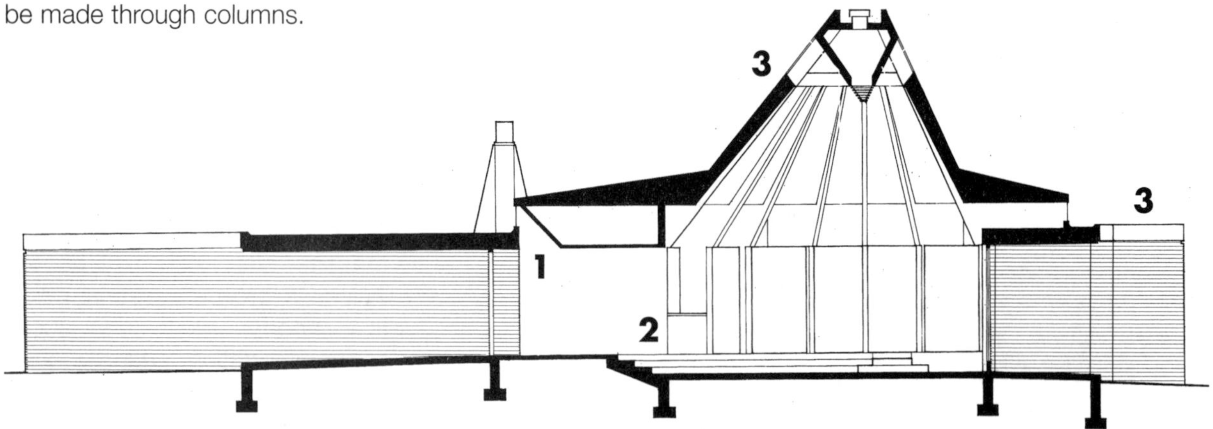

Drawing: Freeman residence, Grand Rapids, Michigan
30" × 20" (76.2 × 50.8 cm), Scale: 1/8"=1'0"
Medium: Ink on vellum
Courtesy of Gunnar Birkerts and Associates, Inc., Architects

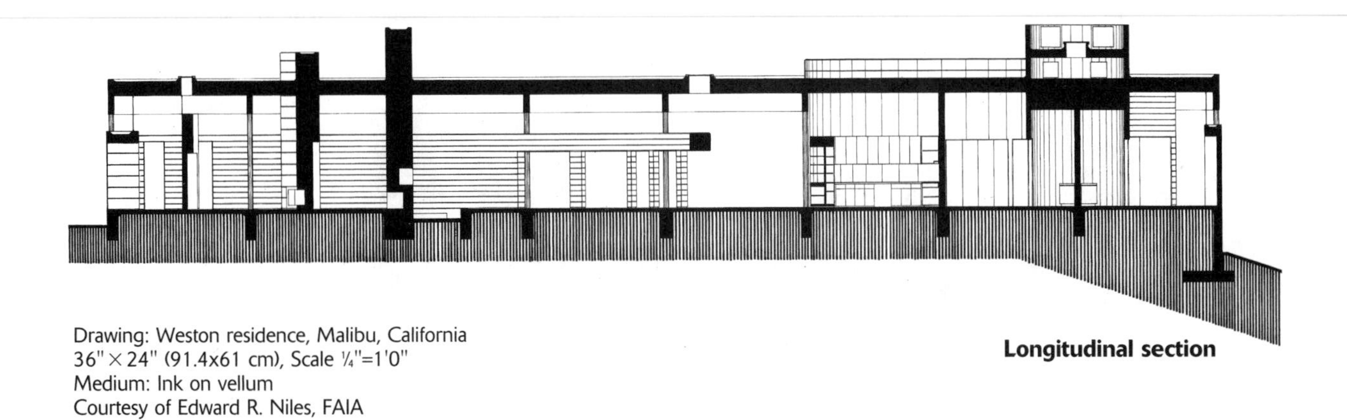

Drawing: Weston residence, Malibu, California
36" × 24" (91.4x61 cm), Scale 1/4"=1'0"
Medium: Ink on vellum
Courtesy of Edward R. Niles, FAIA

A **sectional elevation** shows elevation lines beyond the cut section. The sectional cut should be made prominent by the use of tone and hatching. Lines within the longitudinal section showing the interior elevation, above, have slightly different line-weight intensities in order to provide a greater sense of depth. The unequal spacing of fine lines in the interior elevation implies a foreshortened curved surface (see p. 315). The very close spacing of vertical lines indicates a cut ground section.

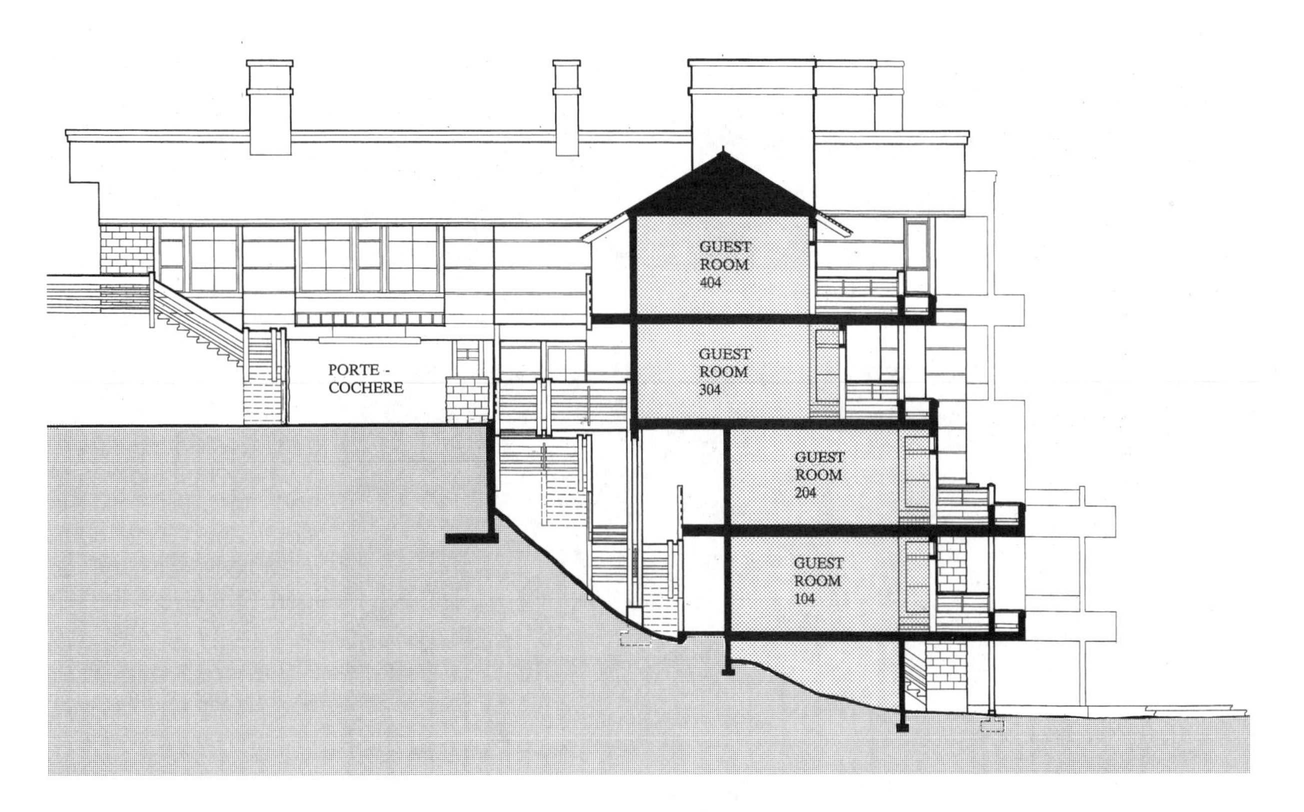

Drawing: The Inn at Langley, Whidbey Island, Washington
Courtesy of GGLO Architecture and Interior Design

It is common to see a hierarchy of elevation lines in a design section. The elevation line weights diminish in intensity as the distance from the observer increases. This contrast in line weights is an excellent depth cue.

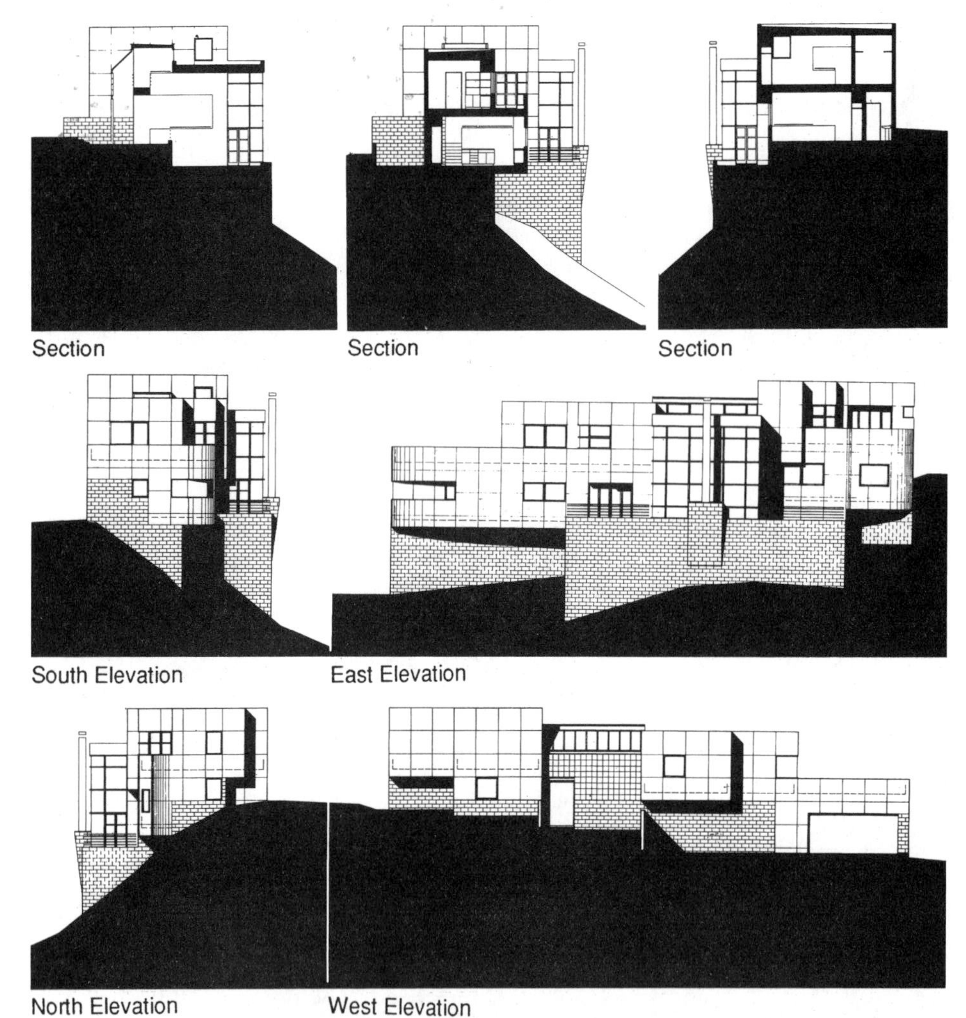

Drawings: Naiditch residence
Altadena, California
Scale: 3/8"=1'0"
Medium: Pen and ink on Mylar
Courtesy of Dean Nota Architect

In this compact presentation of sections and elevations, the sectional cut is toned solid black, which allows the viewer to see a clear relationship between the building design and the ground plane. Section cut spatial volumes can be shown from above the ground plane or from below it (i.e., from underground). See the facing page for examples. Drawings may be conveniently labeled and identified within or adjacent to the toned area of the ground mass.

Elevations are labeled based on the direction they are facing; in the south elevation, the facade of the building is facing south (see p. 101). Note that parts of the facades of the south, east, and north elevations, as well as part of the roof area in the Botta house, are foreshortened because of their curvature.

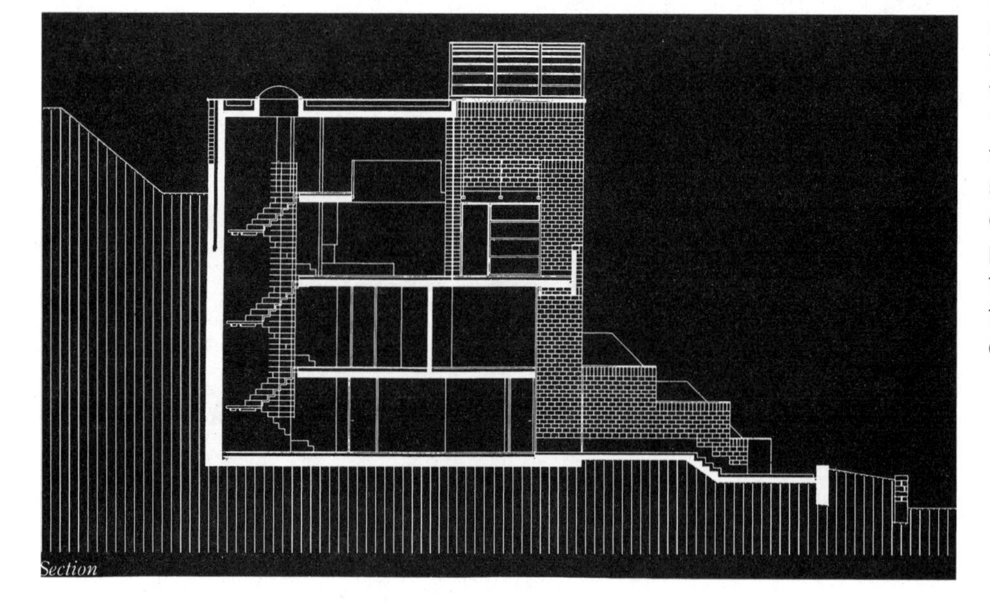

Drawing: Single-family house, Daro, Bellinzona, Switzerland
Courtesy of Mario Botta, Architect, Lugano, Switzerland

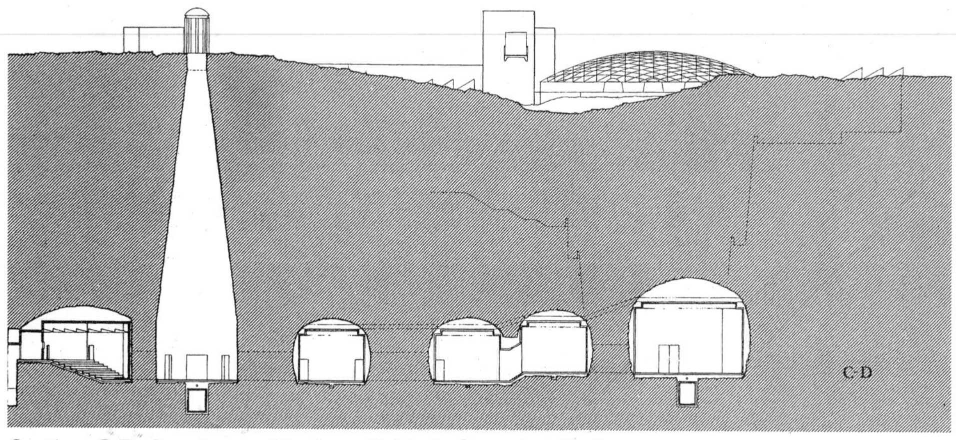

Section C-D showing auditorium, light shaft, and galleries

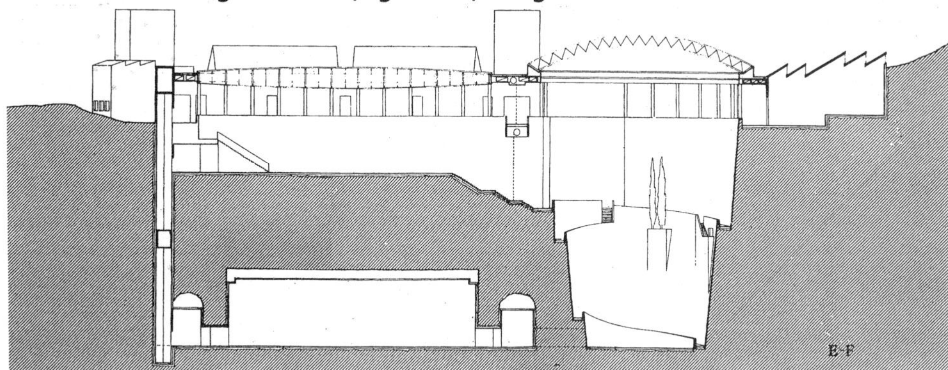

Section E-F showing "Sunk" and galleries

Drawings: The Guggenheim Museum, Salzburg, Austria
35.4" × 47.2" (90 × 120 cm), Scale: 1:50
Medium: Xerox print on paper
Courtesy of Hans Hollein, Architect

The identifications for these sections are placed within the area of the section cut through the ground mass. This creates a stabilizing effect, especially for site sections.

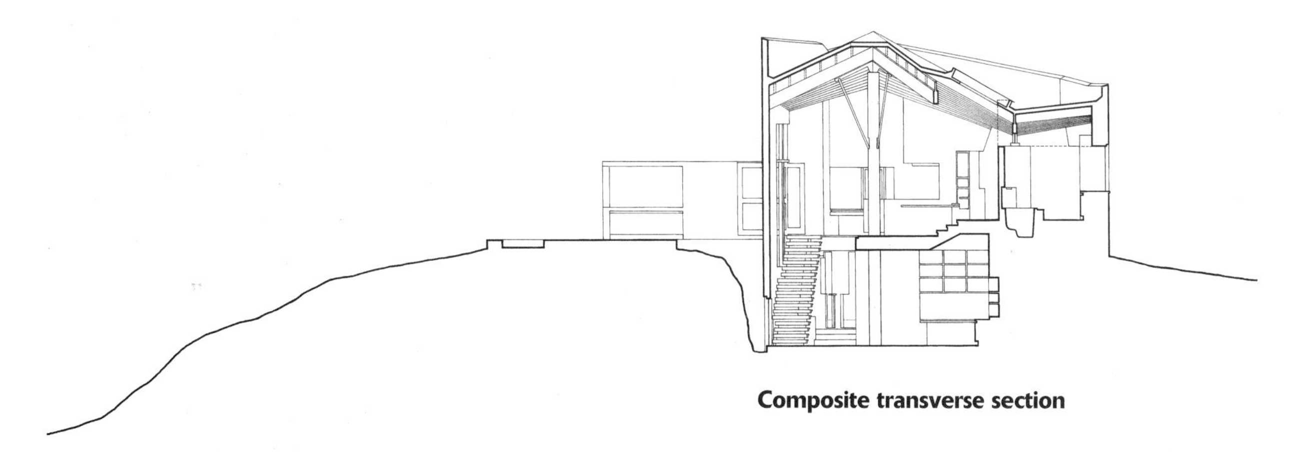

Composite transverse section

Drawing: Barnes House, Nanaimo, British Columbia, Canada
18" × 36" (45.7 × 91.4 cm), Scale: 1/4"=1'0"
Medium: Ink on vellum
Courtesy of Patkau Architects

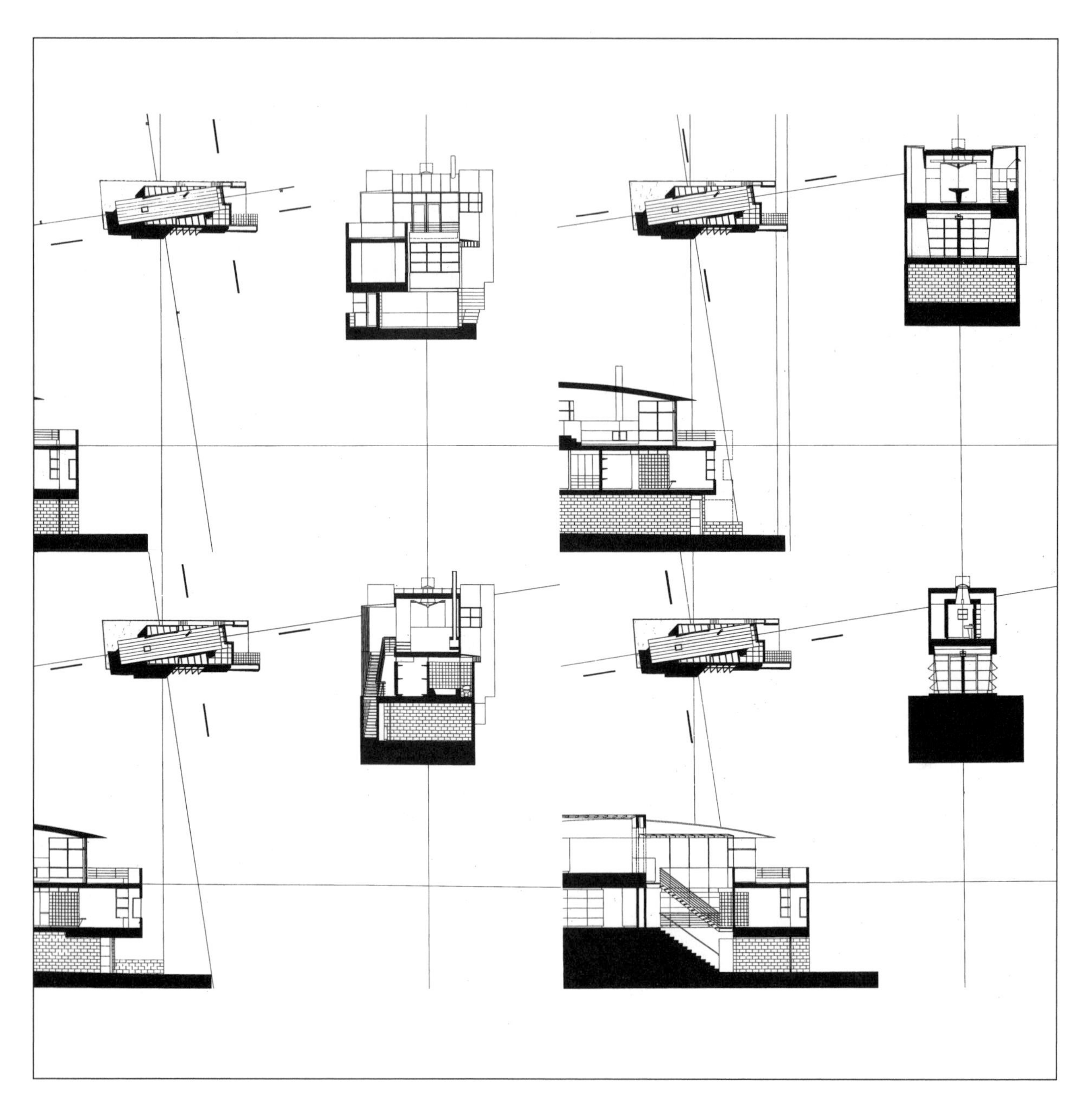

Drawings (facing pages): Elliot residence, Hermosa Beach, California
Scale: ⅜"=1'0"
Medium: Pen and ink on Mylar
Courtesy of Dean Nota Architect

Webster's Dictionary defines "composite" as something comprising a number of distinct parts or elements (see the composite drawings section in Chapter 10).

As shown above, the use of **composite sections** allows the viewer to examine a multitude of sections for a building. The cut sections are taken at selected intervals indicated in roof plan views. With the advent of computer-generated drawings, sectional cuts can be immediately examined at an infinite number of locations. This process is analogous to a CAT scan in medical technology.

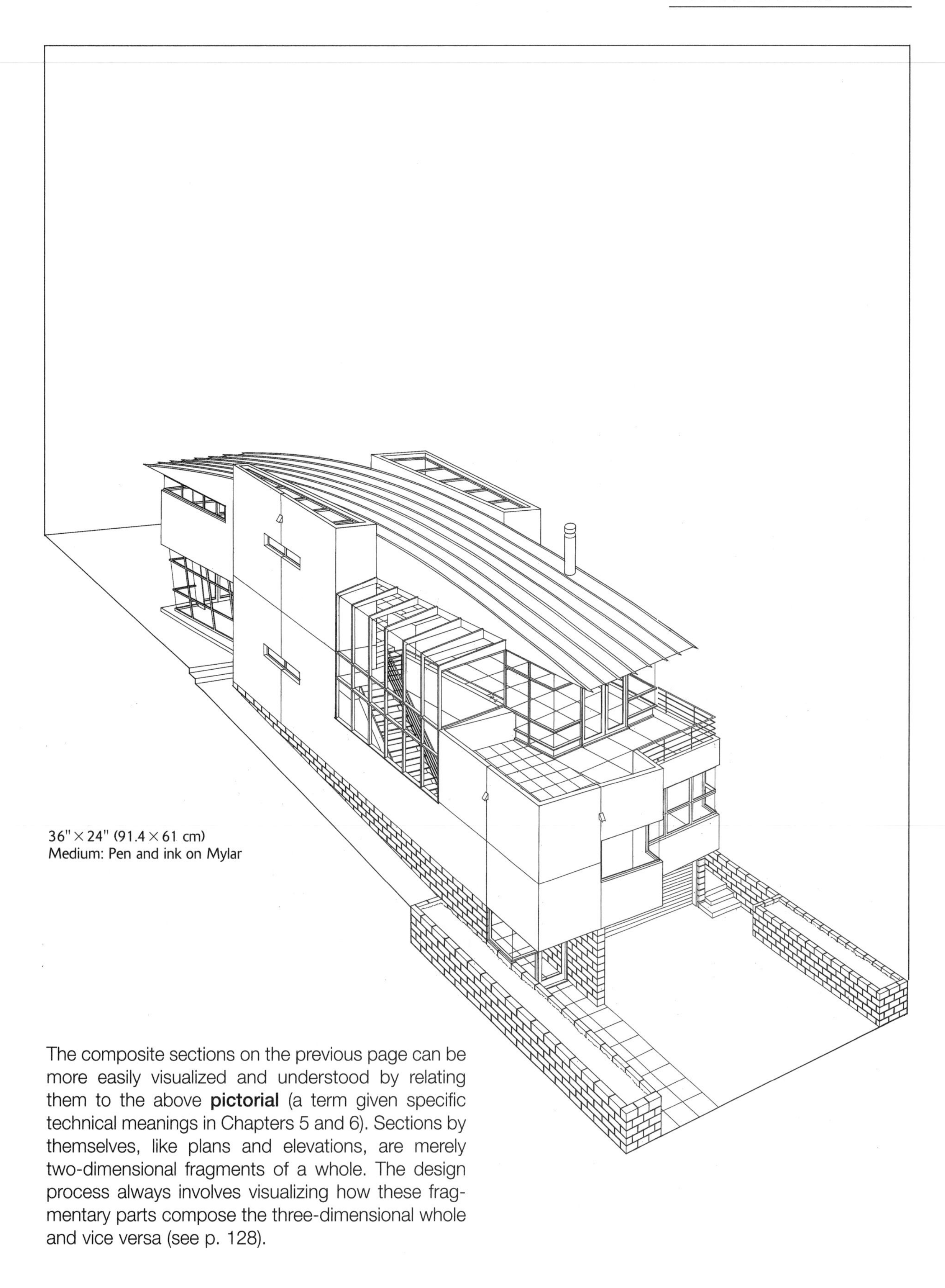

36" × 24" (91.4 × 61 cm)
Medium: Pen and ink on Mylar

The composite sections on the previous page can be more easily visualized and understood by relating them to the above **pictorial** (a term given specific technical meanings in Chapters 5 and 6). Sections by themselves, like plans and elevations, are merely two-dimensional fragments of a whole. The design process always involves visualizing how these fragmentary parts compose the three-dimensional whole and vice versa (see p. 128).

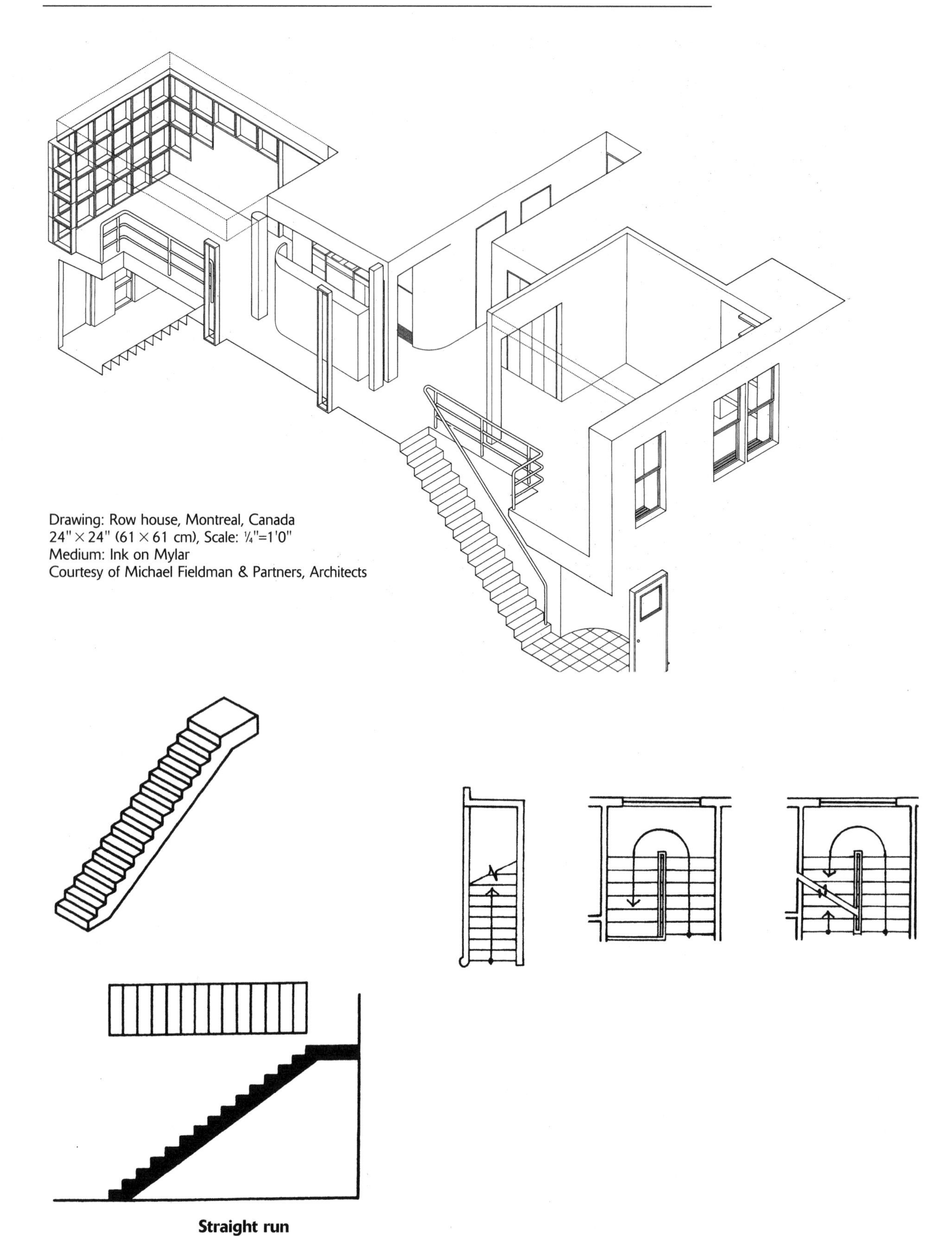

Drawing: Row house, Montreal, Canada
24" × 24" (61 × 61 cm), Scale: ¼"=1'0"
Medium: Ink on Mylar
Courtesy of Michael Fieldman & Partners, Architects

Straight run

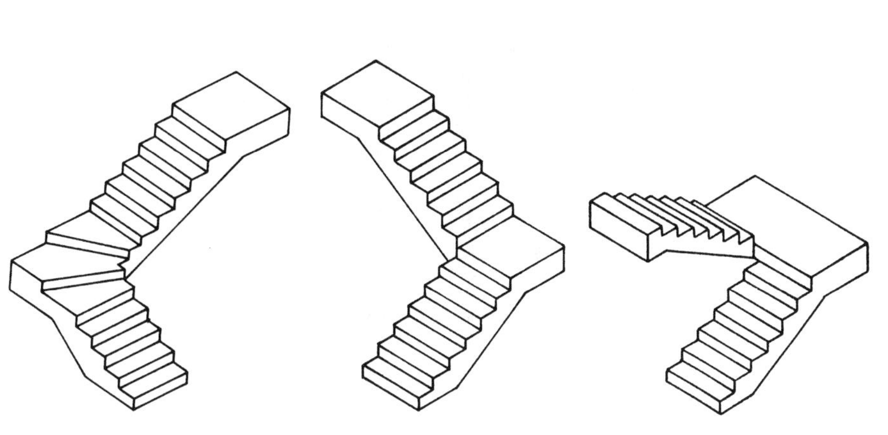

Stairs shown in pictorial
For simplicity, the handrails have been removed.

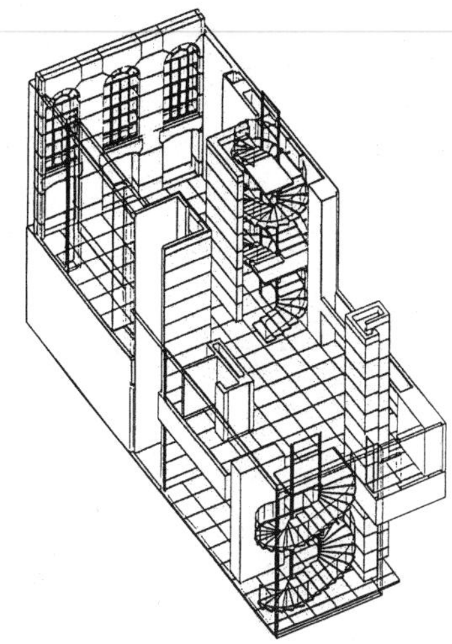

Drawings: Jil Sander Paris
Paris, France
Courtesy of Gabellini Associates

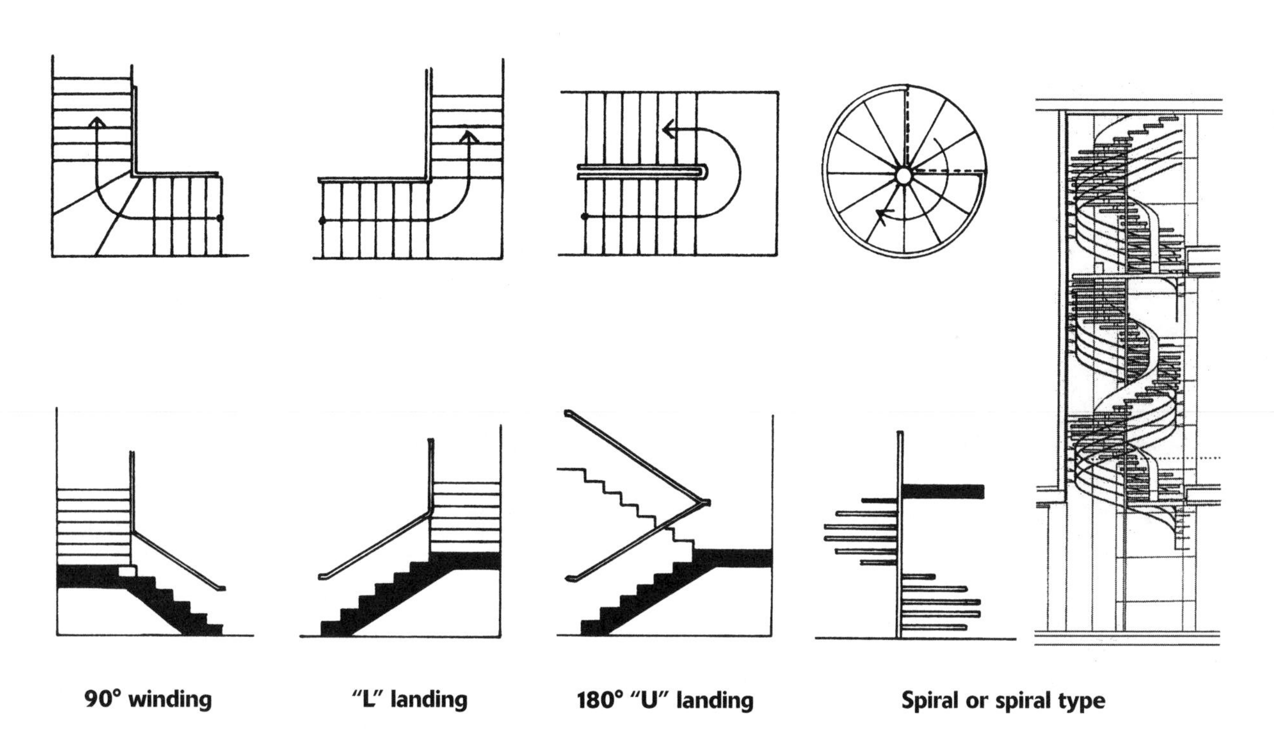

90° winding | **"L" landing** | **180° "U" landing** | **Spiral or spiral type**

Stairways are the sequences of steps that connect two or more floors in a building. The four examples above are typical stairway situations seen in plan and in section. Straight stairs are also common. In a floor plan, the up or down direction arrow is from the level of the floor plan.

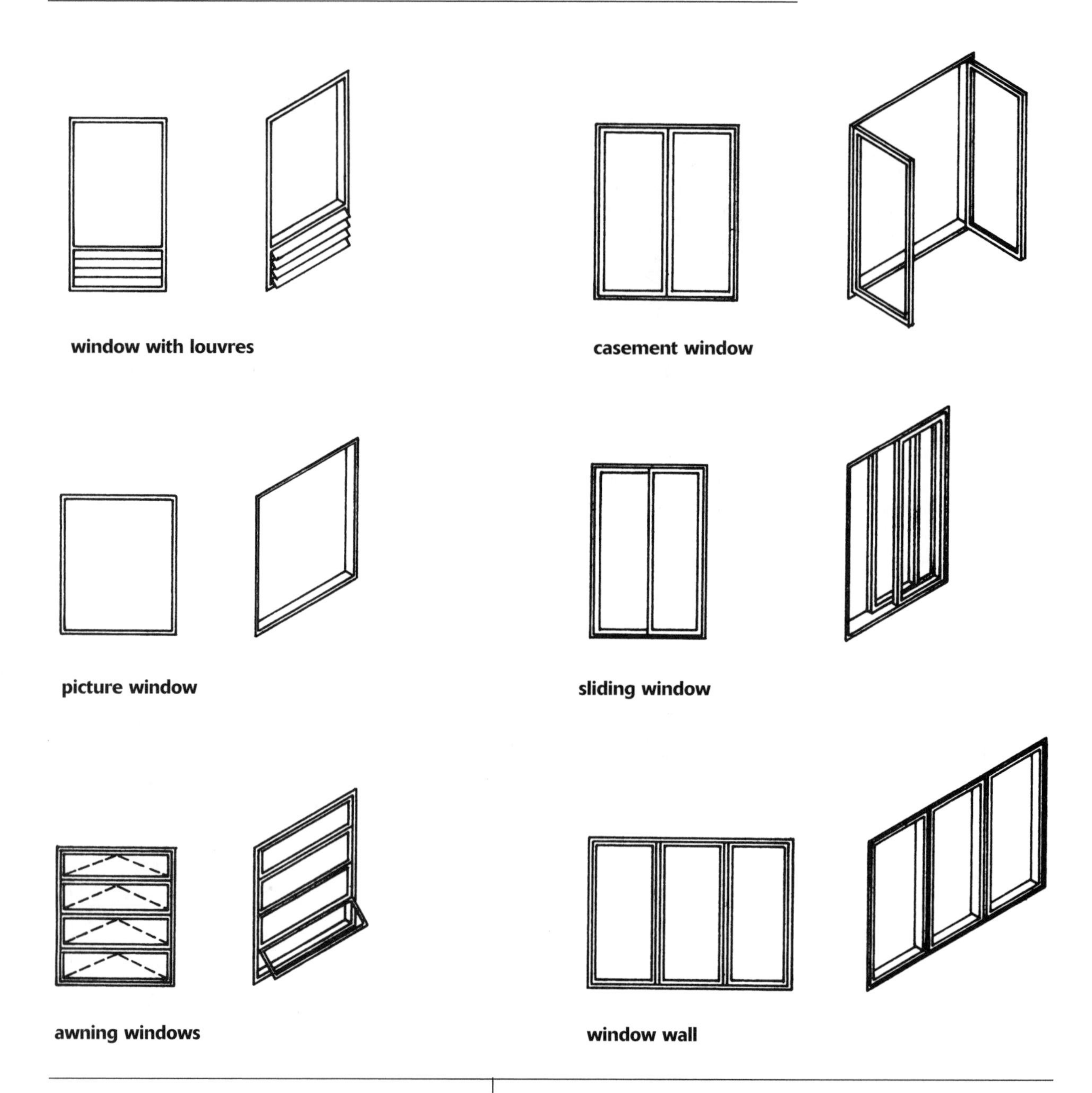

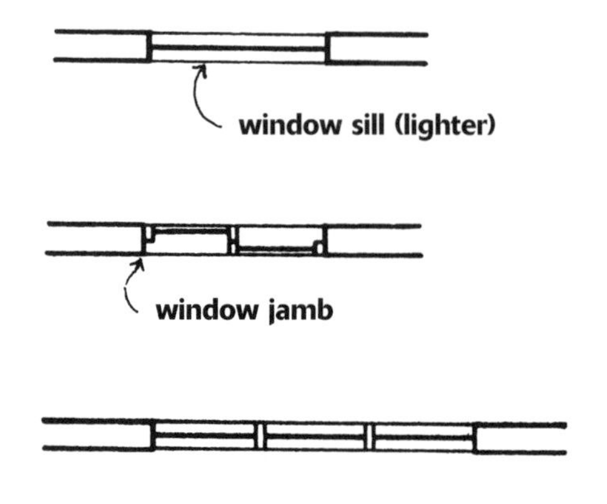

Six standard window types and five standard door types are shown in elevation and in pictorial on pp. 110 and 111. A plan window is the result of a horizontal cut through the window glass, its frame (jamb), and the wall on both sides.

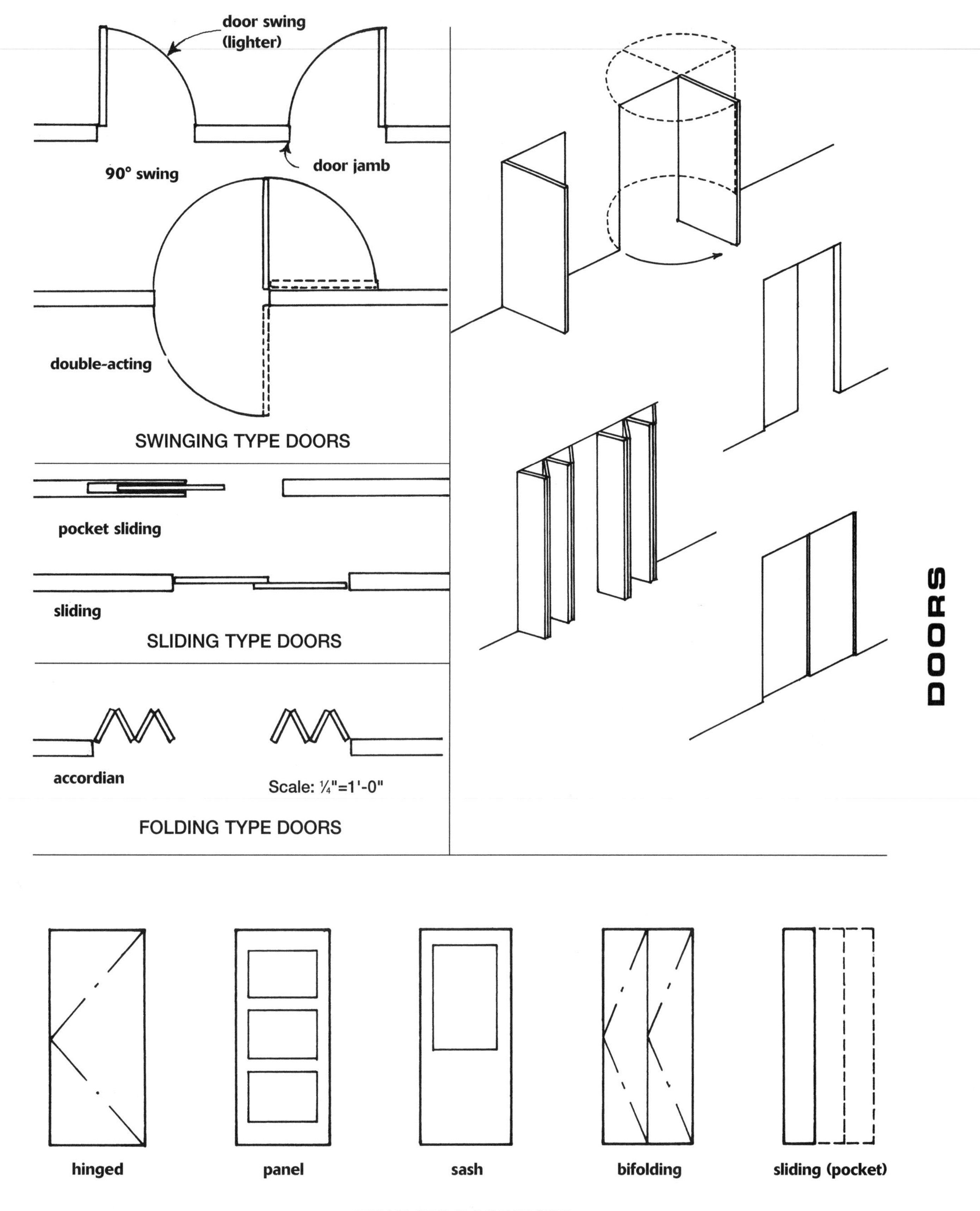
door swing
(lighter)
door jamb
90° swing
double-acting
SWINGING TYPE DOORS
pocket sliding
sliding
SLIDING TYPE DOORS
accordian
Scale: ¼"=1'-0"
FOLDING TYPE DOORS
hinged
panel
sash
bifolding
sliding (pocket)

STANDARD DOOR TYPES

5

Orthographic and Paraline Drawing

BASICS 115
BASICS APPLIED 136

It is important that students of environmental design develop the ability to visualize and graphically express forms and spaces in three dimensions. The design-drawing process begins with two-dimensional expressions in the form of orthographic sketches and drawings. These multiview drawings are the plan, elevation, and section vocabulary that an architect/designer uses. Multiviews help us accurately examine geometric configurations, spatial relationships, and the scale and proportion of a design. Multiviews by themselves cannot, however, reveal the three-dimensional pictorial configuration of an object or building, according to orthographic projection theory. For pictorial depth expression, the closely related three-dimensional, single-view drawings termed "paralines" and "perspectives" are needed. Paralines, as the name implies, are characterized by parallel lines, whereas perspectives are characterized by converging lines. Paraline drawings depict volumetric forms by combining the parameters of length, width, and depth, while simultaneously uniting plan, elevation, and section into one illustration.

The intent of this chapter is to develop your ability to visualize and communicate form and space by relating two-dimensional orthographic drawings to three-dimensional paraline drawings such as axonometrics and obliques.

The following are some of the important terms and concepts you will learn:

Orthographic drawings	Axonometric drawings	Plan oblique drawings
Paraline drawings	Isometric drawings	Elevation oblique drawings
Auxiliary views	Up views	Down views
Exploded views	Expanded views	Multioblique combinations

Orthographic and Paraline Drawing

TOPIC: ORTHOGRAPHICS

Ching 2003, 24–28.

Forseth 1980, 21–75.

Wallschlaeger and Busic-Snyder 1992, 60–61.

TOPIC: PARALINES (AXONOMETRICS AND OBLIQUES)

Ching 2003, 28–30.

Forseth 1980, 77–97.

Pérez-Gomez and Pelletier 2000, 266–80.

PARALINES (THE AXONOMETRIC CALLED ISOMETRIC)

Numerous computer games offer an opportunity to play with isometric views with and without cast shadows. The following are good examples:

Without shadows: *The Sims House Party,* Electronic Arts Inc., EA Games.

With shadows: *Age of Empires,* Microsoft Ensemble Studios.

Chapter Overview

After studying this chapter and doing the related exercises in the book's final section, you will understand how to construct orthographic views, axonometric drawings, and oblique drawings. For continued study of the principles discussed in this chapter, refer to Uddin's *Axonometric and Oblique Drawing.*

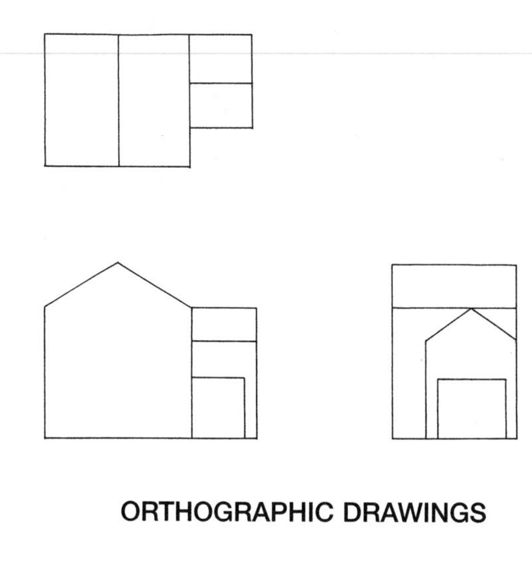

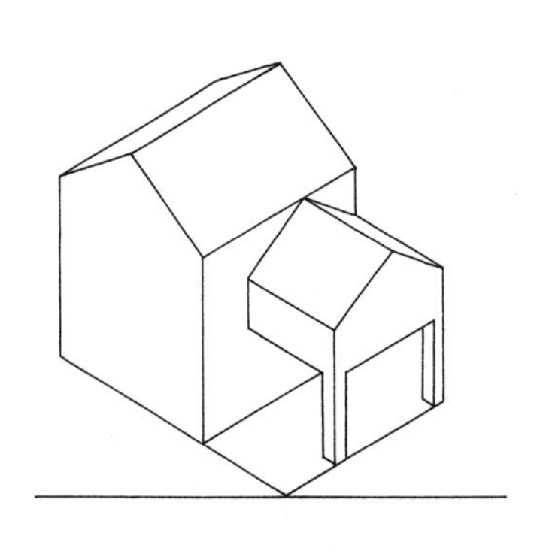

ORTHOGRAPHIC DRAWINGS

ISOMETRIC

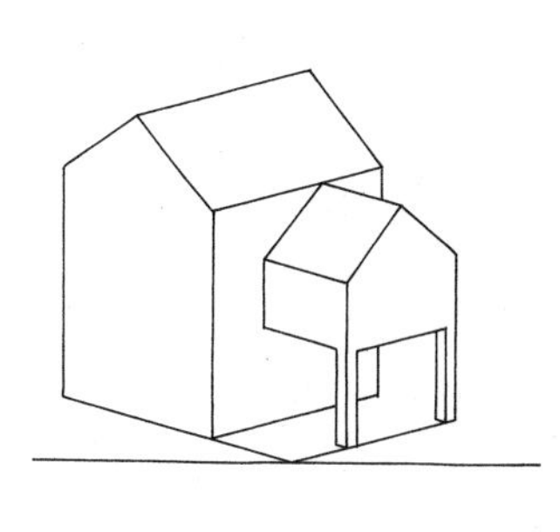

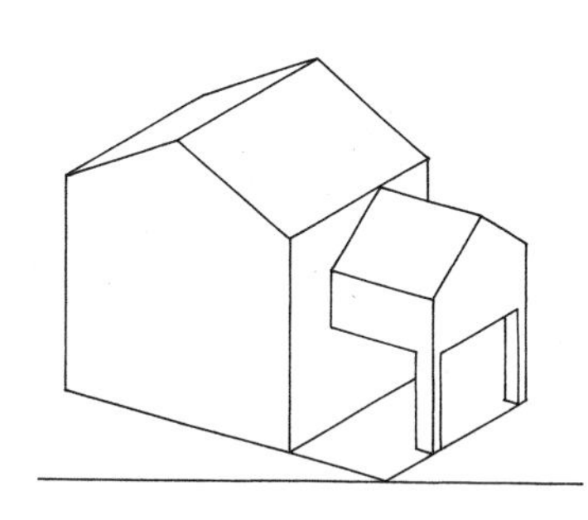

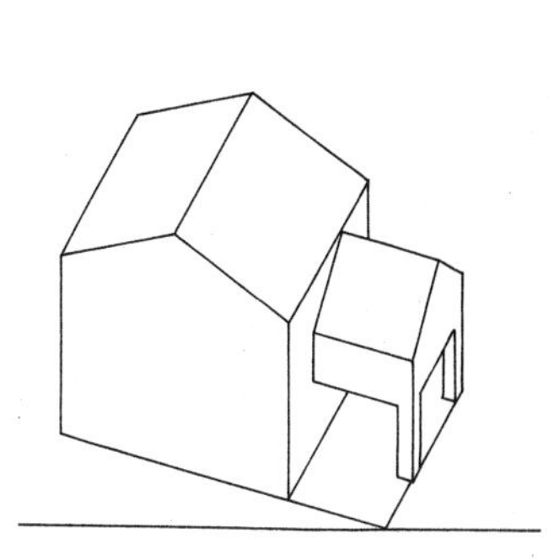

PARALINE AXONOMETRICS

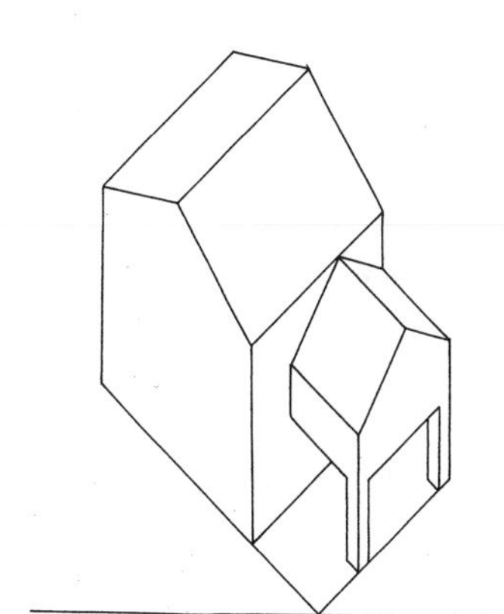

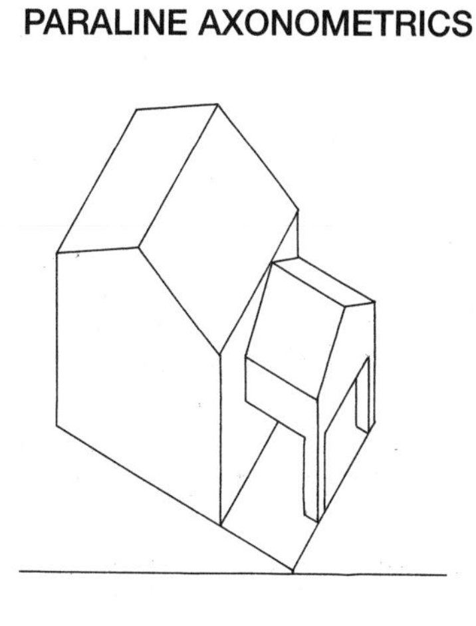

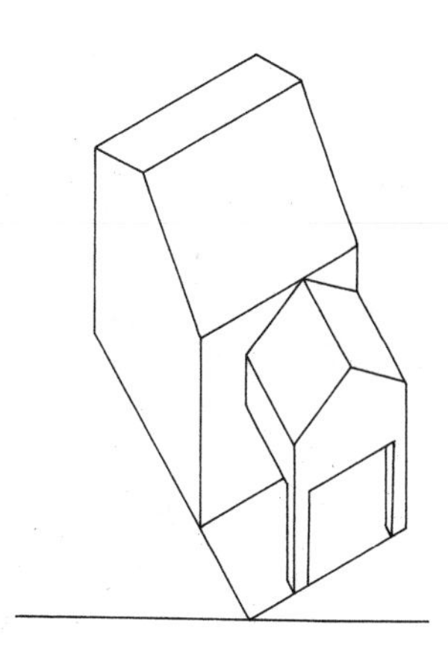

PARALINE OBLIQUES

Plans, elevations, and sections are **orthographic (multiview)** drawings (two-dimensional). In **paraline (single-view)** drawings, sets of lines are infinitely parallel to each other, giving a three-dimensional character to the pictorial. The proper preparation for the study of **orthographic–paraline drawings** consists of a proven proficiency in lettering, line quality, and handling drafting tools. This, coupled with a brief introduction to drawing conventions, provides the essential background for a survey of these types of pictorial drawings. The family of **axonometric** and **oblique** drawings, which includes **isometric** drawings, can all be classified as **paraline** drawings. Paraline axonometrics are also termed **dimetrics** and **trimetrics.**

TRUE-LENGTH AND FORESHORTENED LINES

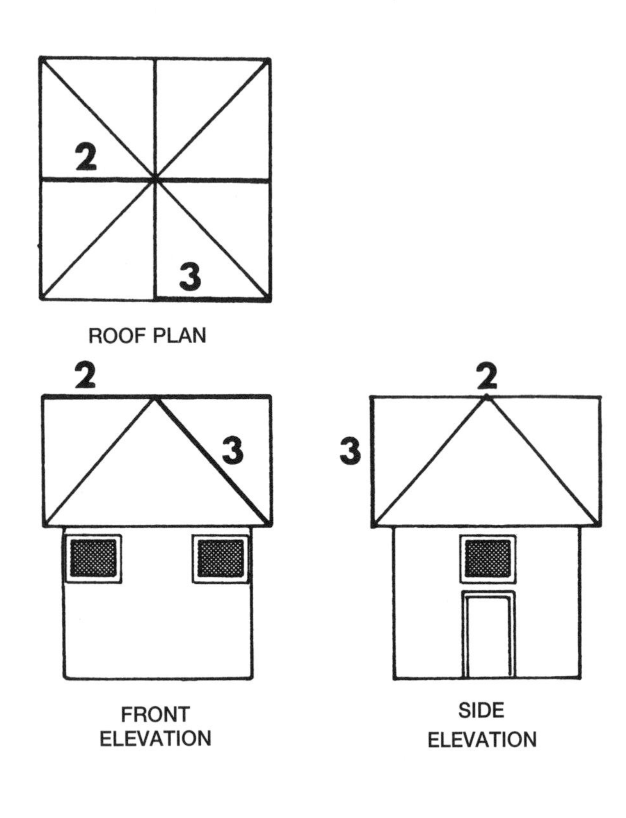

Any building form is composed of the basic elements of points, lines, and planes. We sometimes grasp intuitively why a shape appears the way it does. However, it is only through an understanding of how these geometric elements interact in orthographic projection that we can fully understand what we see. The study of this interaction is called **descriptive geometry.**

In elevation, the building form displays true-length vertical lines (**1**), which can appear as either a point or a true-length line in the adjacent views. Likewise, true-length horizontal lines (**2**) also appear as either a true-length line or a point in adjacent views. True-length inclined lines (**3**) appear foreshortened in the adjacent views.

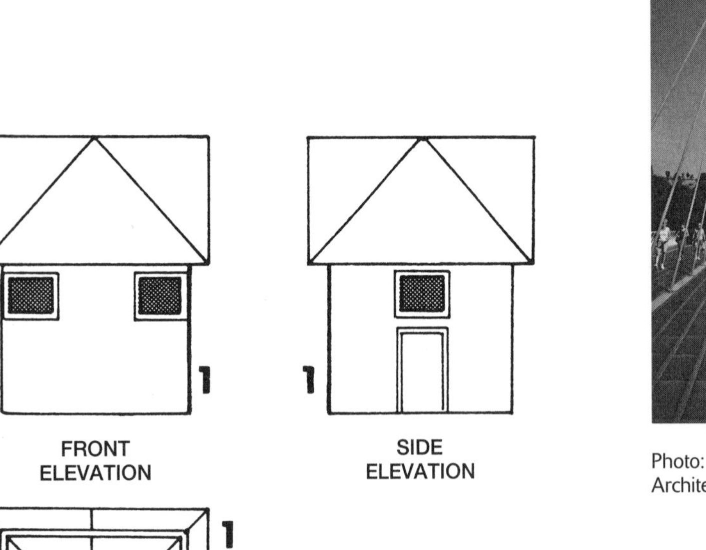

© Rendow Yee

Photo: Sundial Bridge, Redding, California
Architect: Santiago Calatrava

The 217' (66m) structural support pylon for this pedestrian bridge appears vertical from this vantage point, when in actuality it is about 60° to the horizontal plane of the walkway (when seen from a viewpoint rotated 90°). Its true length is actually seen foreshortened from the photo view. See side elevation condition (**3**).

In the drawing at bottom right, note that the edge view contains a true-length line (outer soffit line) that appears as a point. A soffit is the exposed underside feature of any overhead component of a building. Edge views of this plane show the plane as true shape in the adjacent view. The concepts of **point view** from a true-length line, **edge view** (true-length as a point), and **true shape** (true size) become readily apparent as you visualize the roof structure of this house. Correlate the orthographic views with the pictorial (true shape is the toned area).

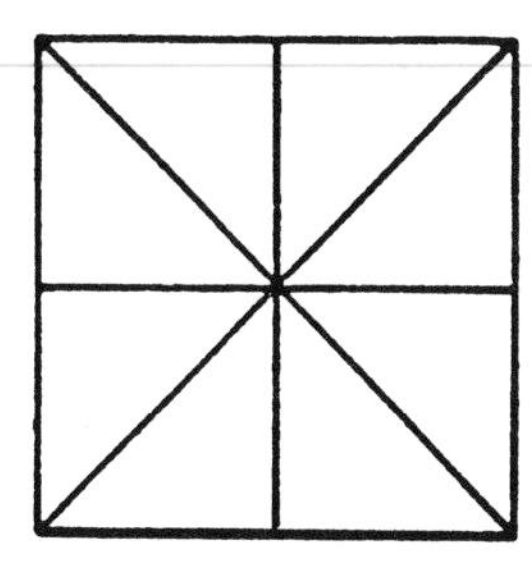

ROOF PLAN EDGE VIEW

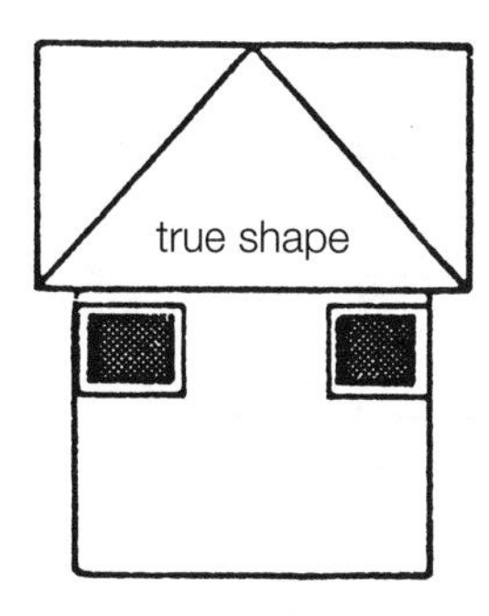

FRONT ELEVATION

SIDE ELEVATION

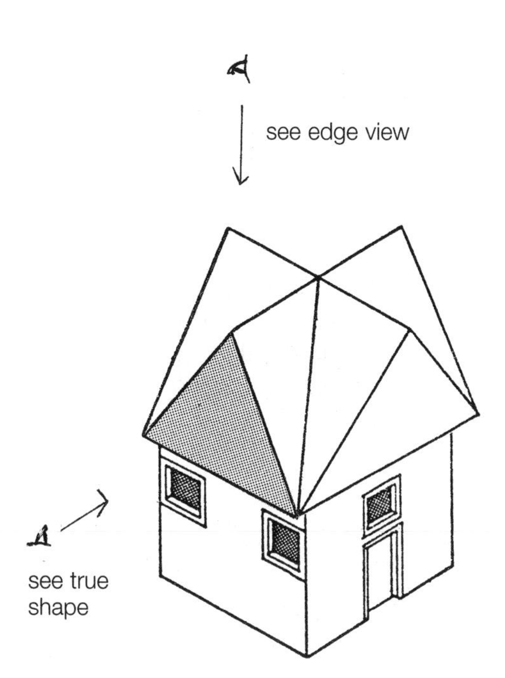

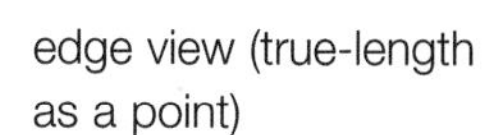

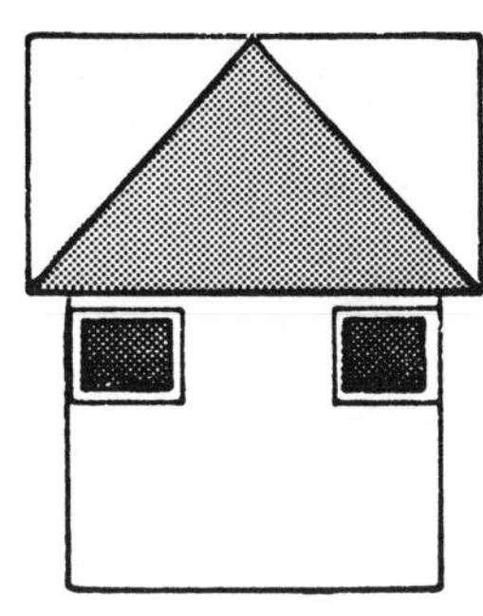

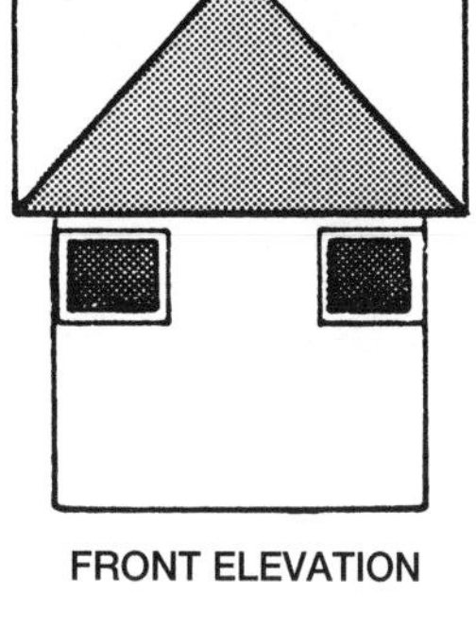

FRONT ELEVATION

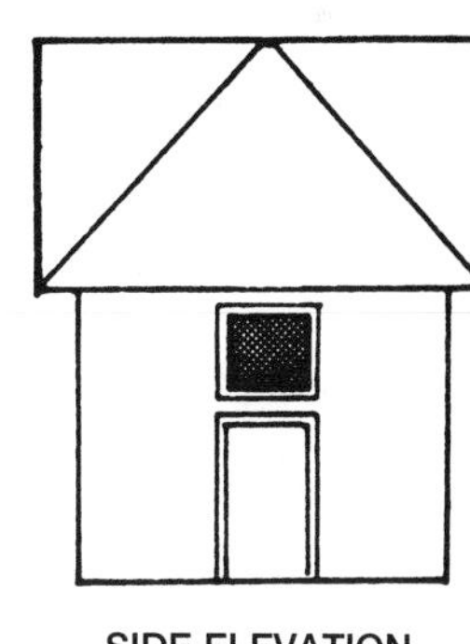

SIDE ELEVATION

Refer to the sections on basic geometric forms and the basic principles of descriptive geometry in the companion Web site's appendix.

WORM'S-EYE PLAN

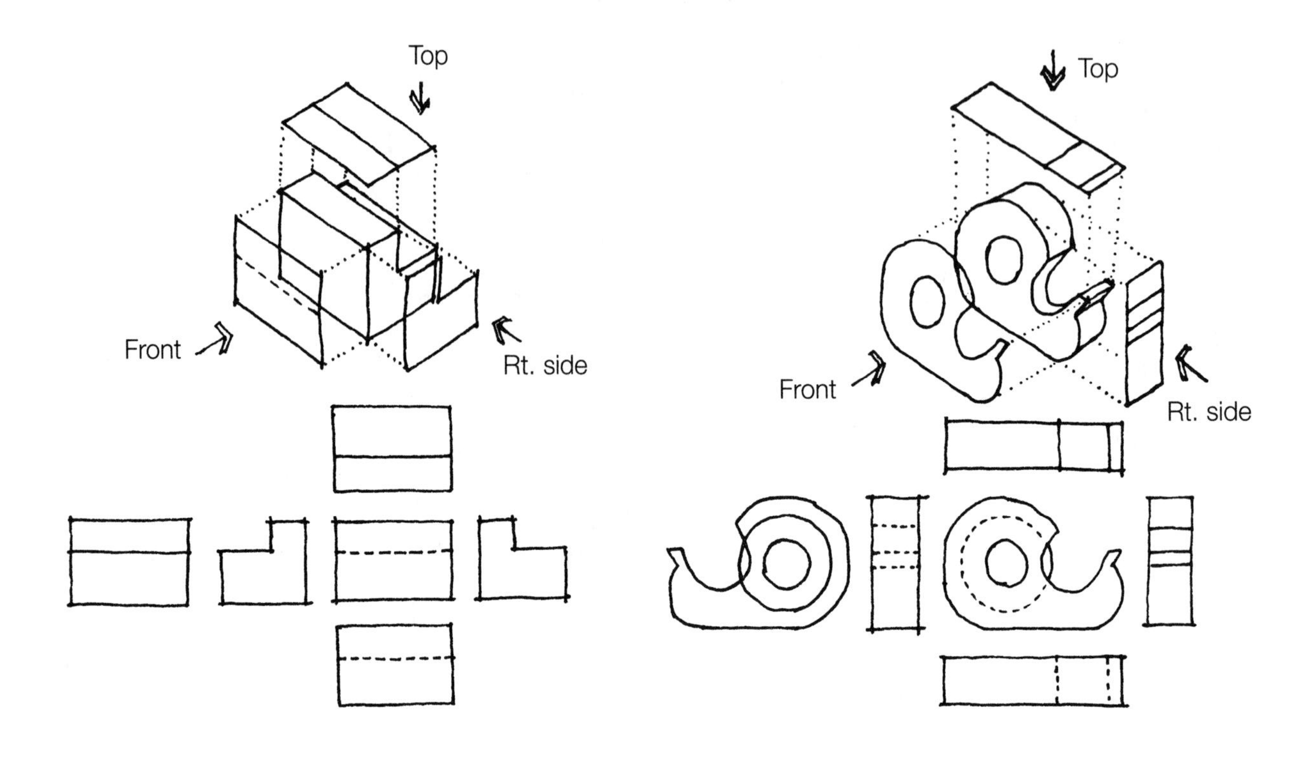

As we have seen in Chapter 4, architects and designers represent a three-dimensional building by utilizing right-angled or orthogonal views. Multiview orthogonal (orthographic) images allow us to comprehend the totality of a design. These images are produced by **visualizing** the design and then sketching the visualized shapes. The freehand graphic process begins with sketching a three-dimensional pictorial image, pulling the two-dimensional orthographic images away from the various surfaces of the object (or building form) being studied, and transferring these images to a two-dimensional orthographic drawing.

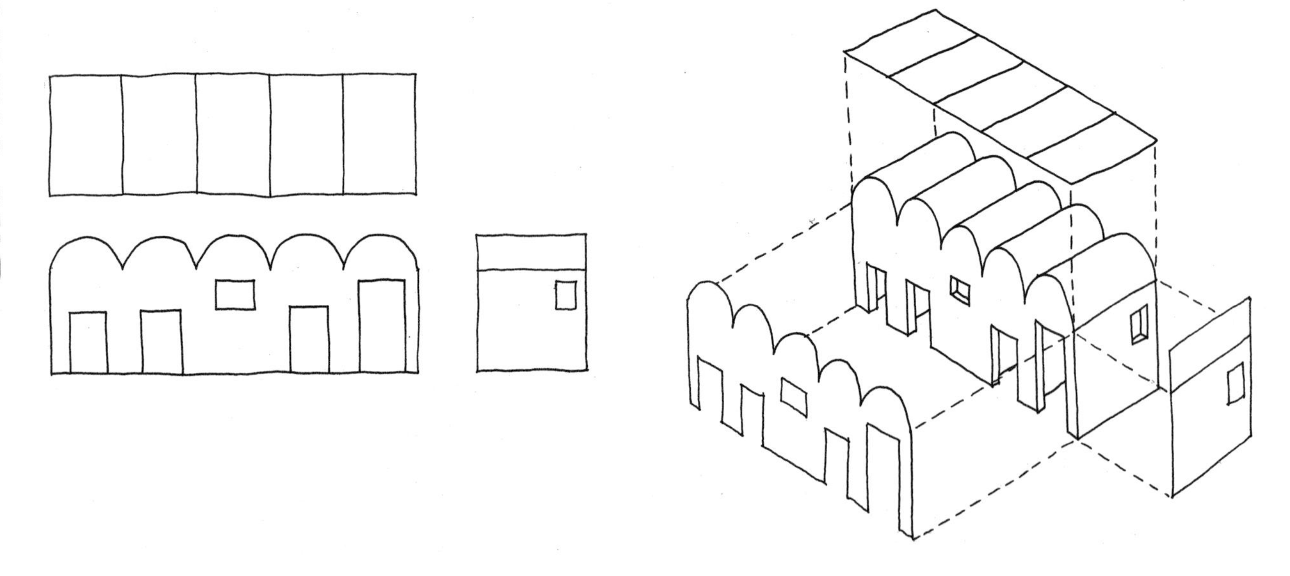

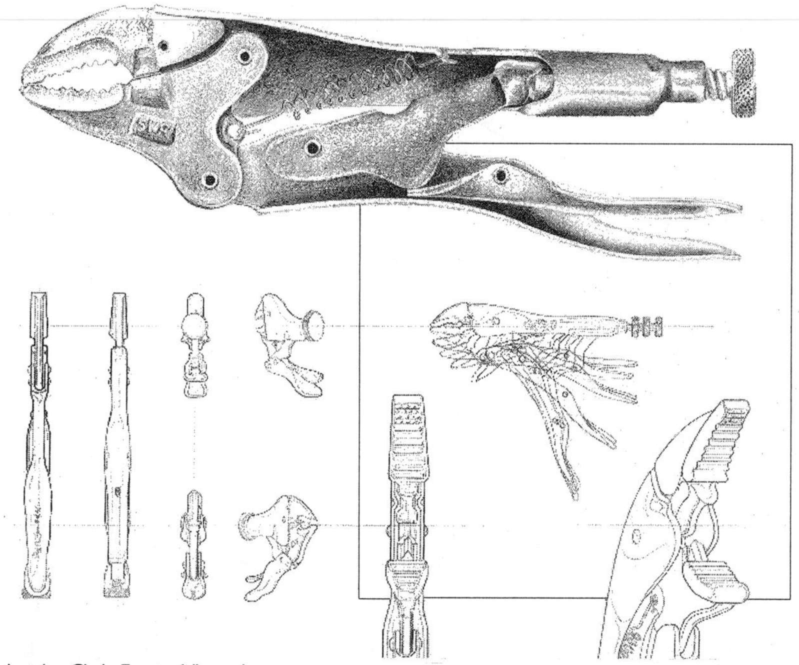

Drawing: Student project by Chris Ernst—Vise grip
Medium: Pencil
Courtesy of the University of Texas at Austin
School of Architecture

Being confident and competent in this **visualization** sketching process requires a lot of practice. The mental visualization process can begin with objects that you can hold in your hand and rotate. An orthographic image by itself cannot be descriptive enough to give us clues as to the spatial composition of the three-dimensional form, but when many orthographic views are related to each other, they become a powerful tool in describing and deciphering the object in question.

Before you can develop the skill of visualizing objects that exist only in the imagination, you must hone your skills in visualizing real objects from several different directions.

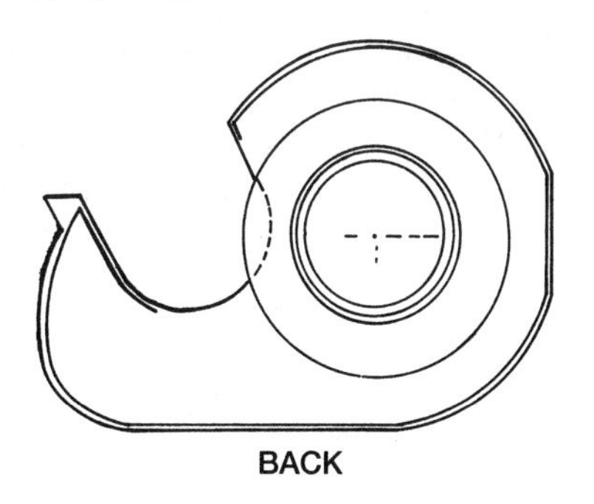

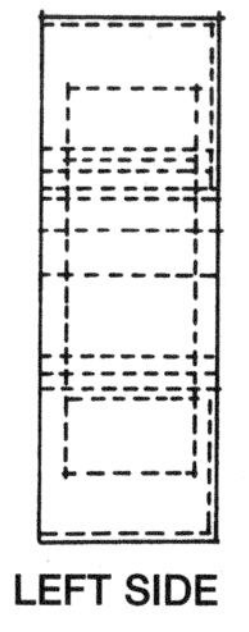

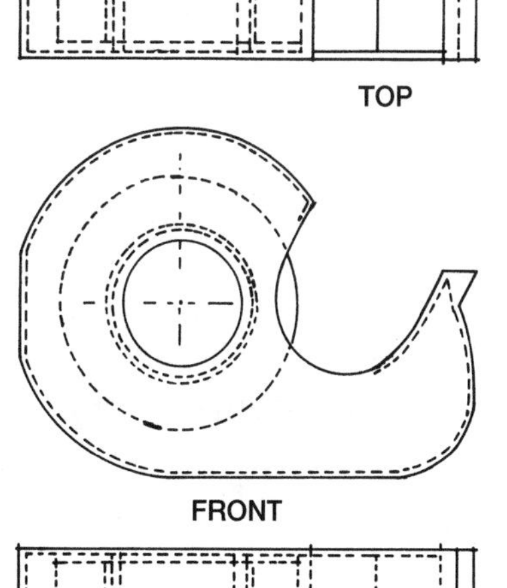

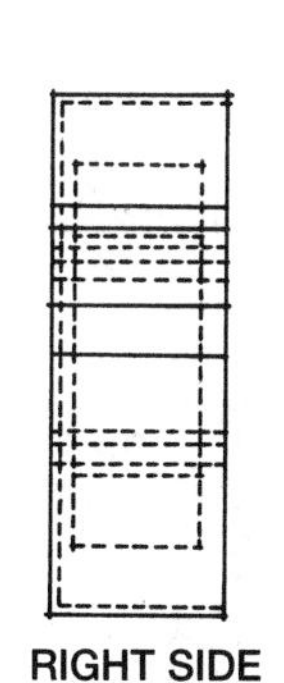

Drawing: Student project by Jacquelyn Mujica—Tape dispenser
11" × 8.5" (27.9 × 21.6 cm), Scale ¾"=1"
Medium: Pencil
Courtesy of the City College of San Francisco
Department of Architecture

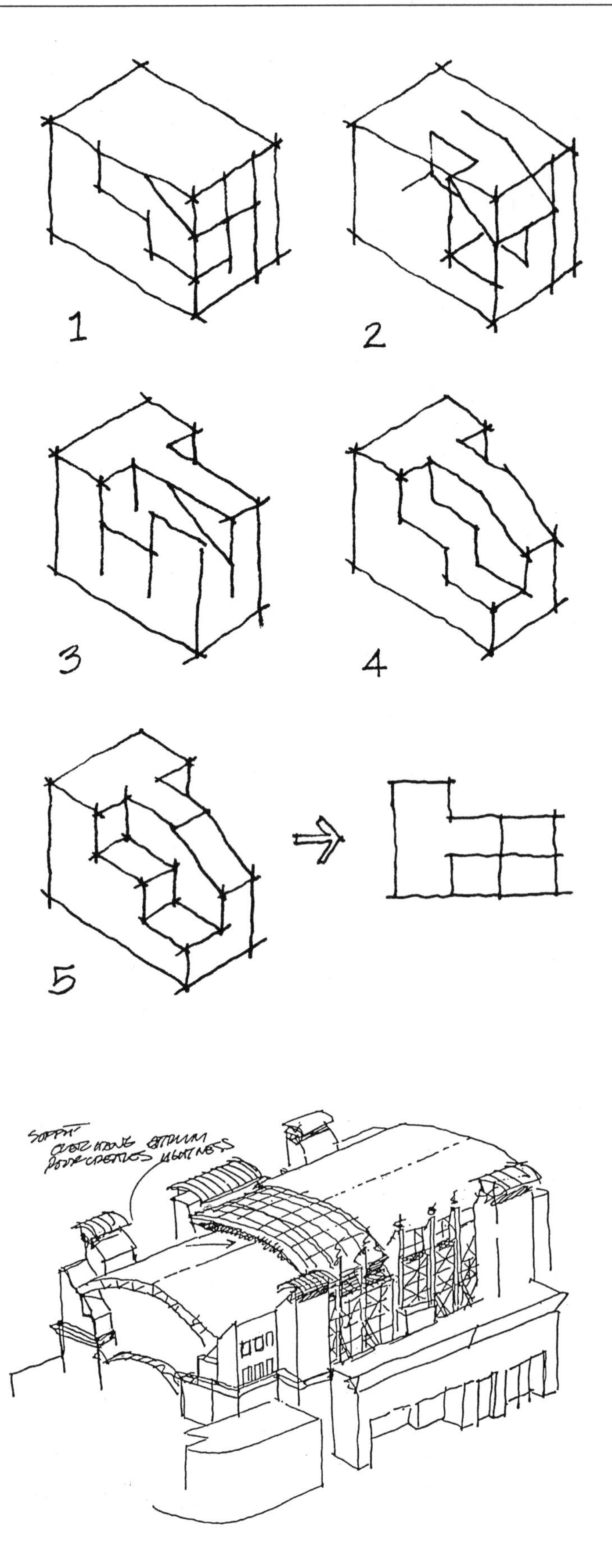

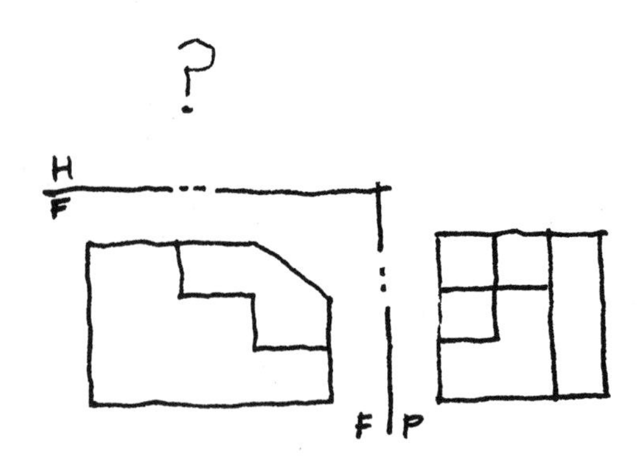

Design professionals often use paraline sketches, as well as other types of sketches, to help them visualize their designs. Refer to Chapter 3 to understand how conceptual sketching is used as a communications tool. The best way to develop your **visualization** skills is to practice seeing the relationship between orthographic and paraline drawings.

This example shows a missing horizontal (top) view. To resolve the missing view, sketch the front and profile planes as shown in sketch **1**. Project related points toward the interior of the rectilinear box. Start with the basic or rough forms as shown in sketch **2**. Proceed with more detailed parts of the object as shown in sketches **3**, **4**, and **5**.

The ability to develop **rough freehand sketches** in the orthographic-paraline conversion process will enhance visualization. When an impasse is reached in the resolution of the problem, it is much better to be loose than stiff; this helps to avoid communicative inhibitions in the design-drawing process that may develop later on.

Sketch: The redevelopment of Charing Cross Station London, England
Medium: Black ink line with colored pencil
Courtesy of Terry Farrell & Partners

Honing your skills in the visualization of simple block forms will enhance your ability to understand the building forms shown in the latter part of this chapter.

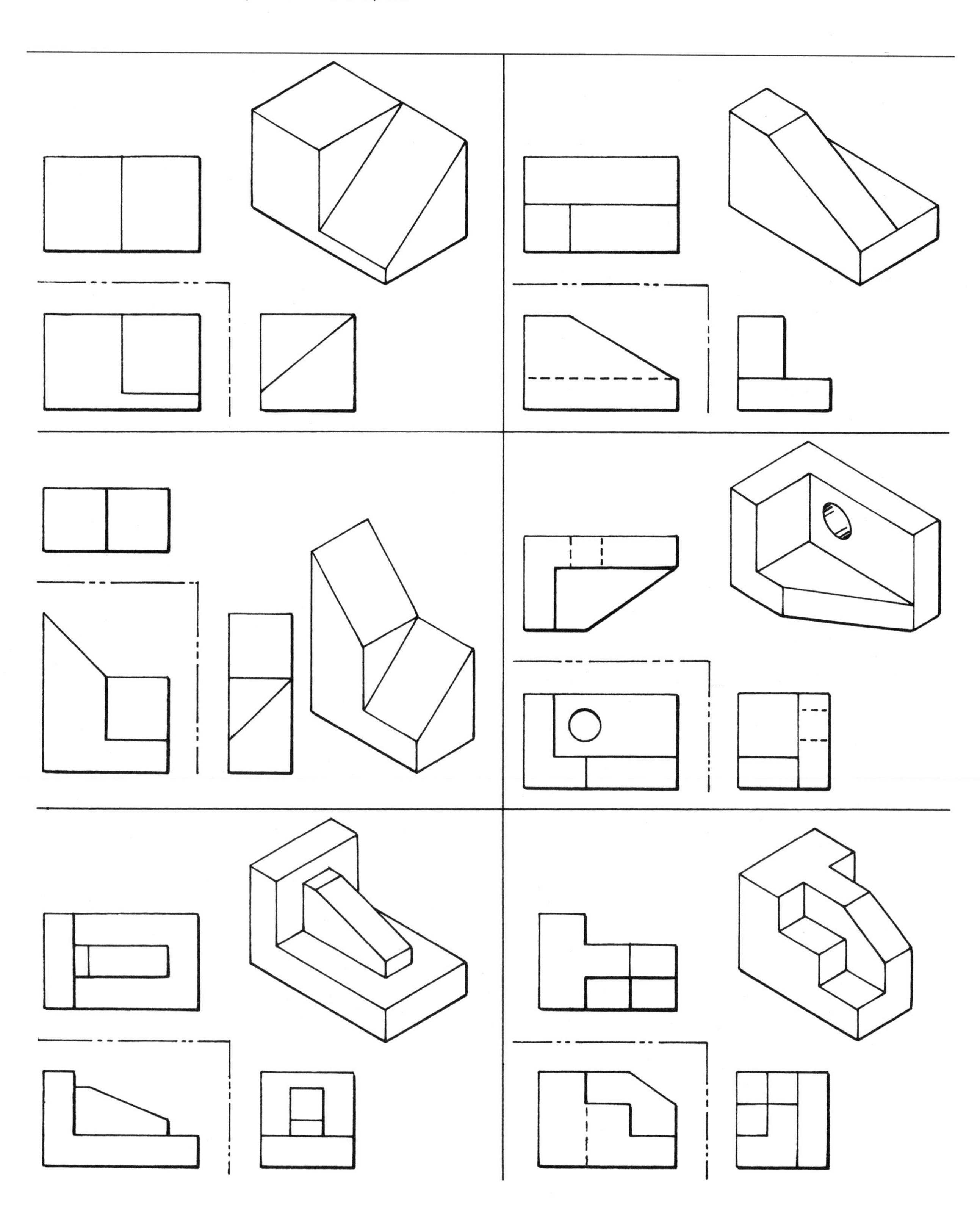

BLOCK VISUALIZATION

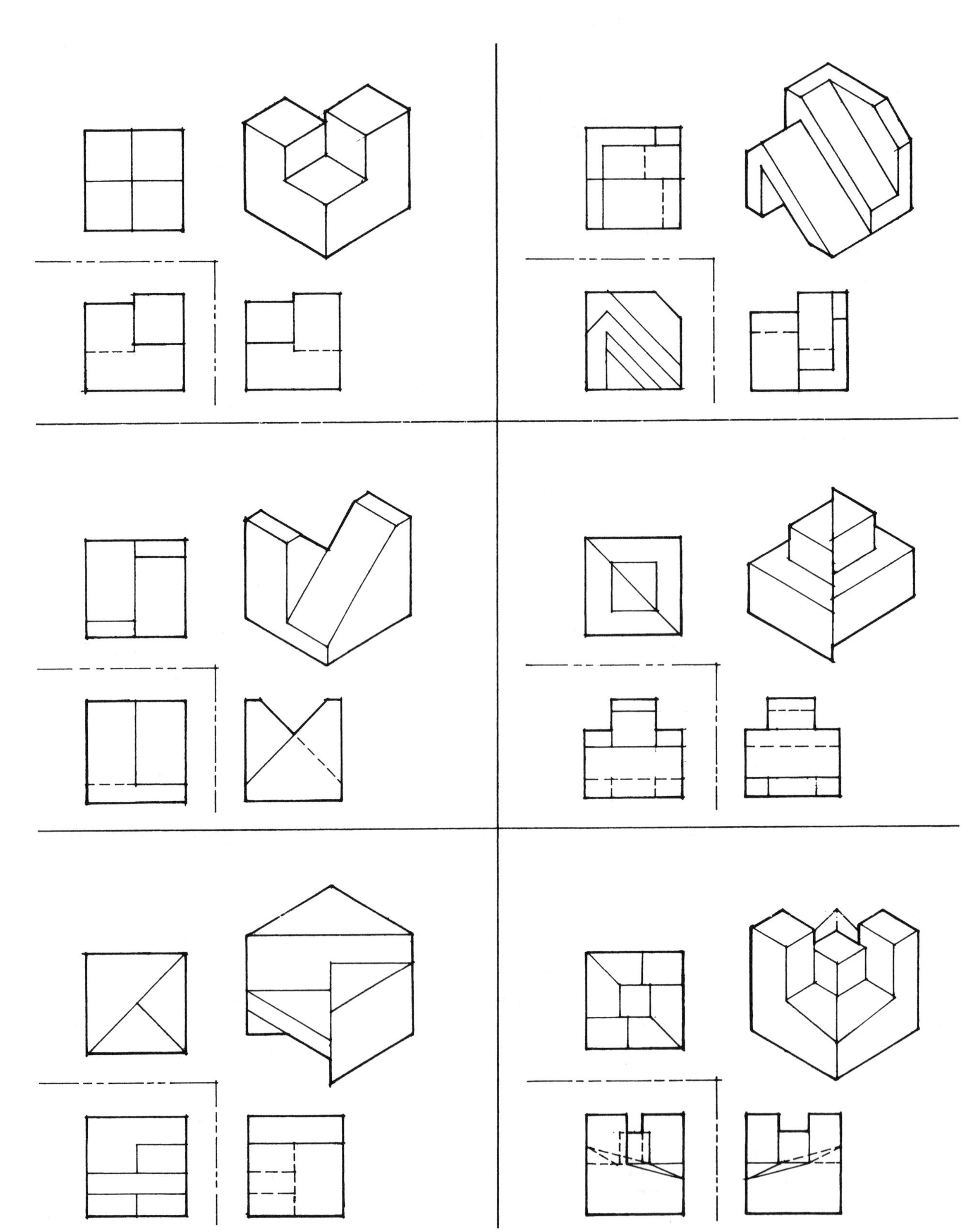

BLOCK VISUALIZATION

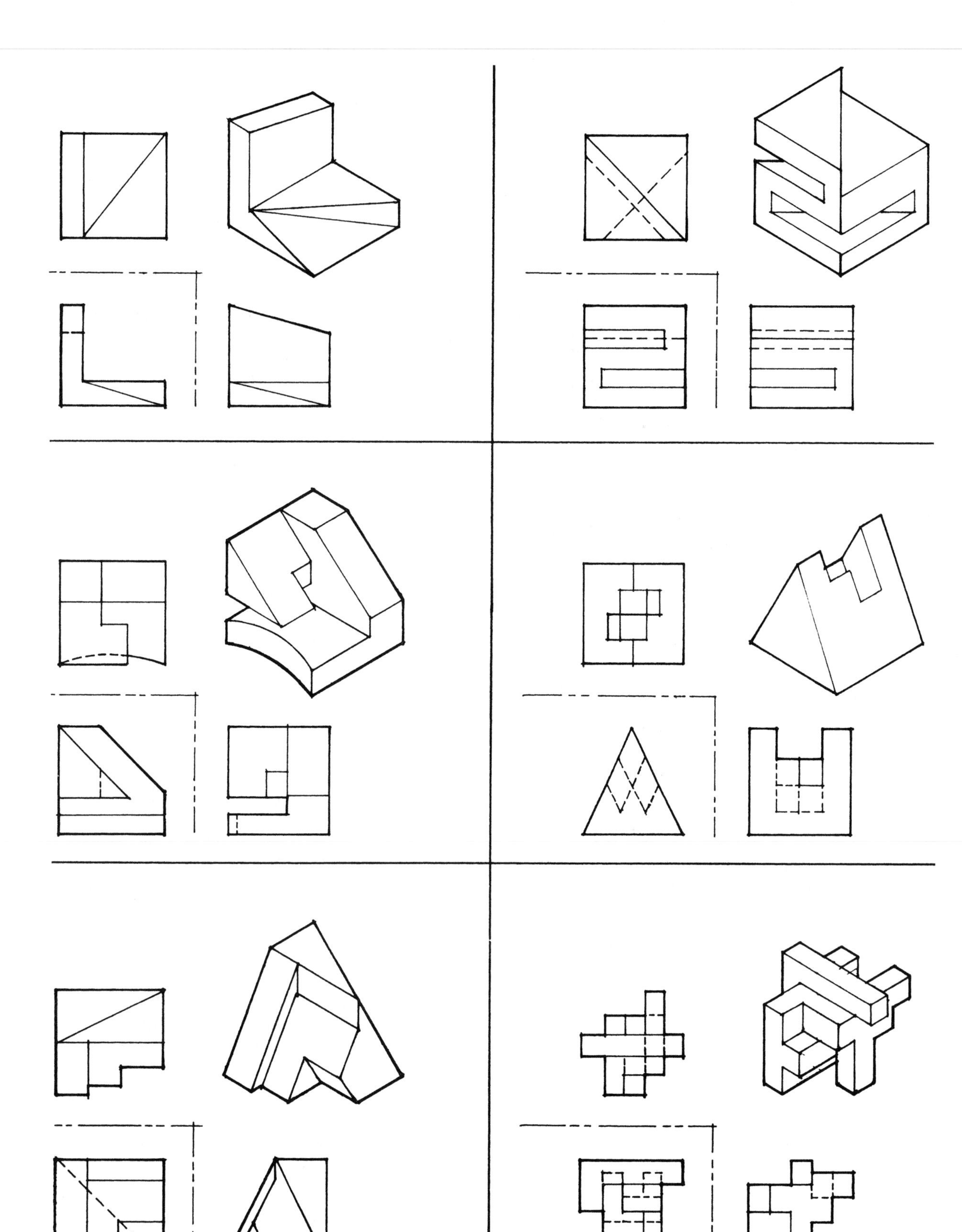

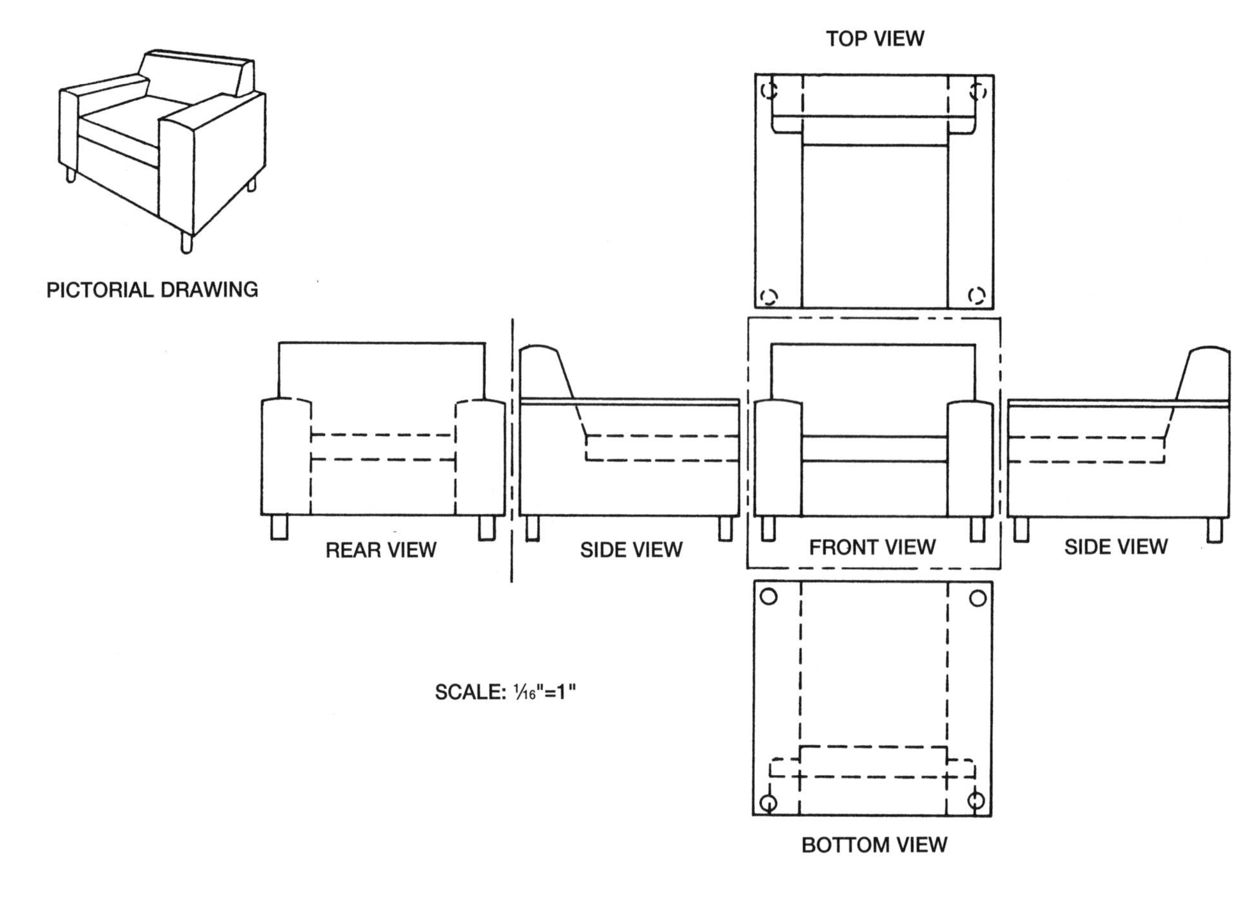

ORTHOGRAPHIC DRAWINGS

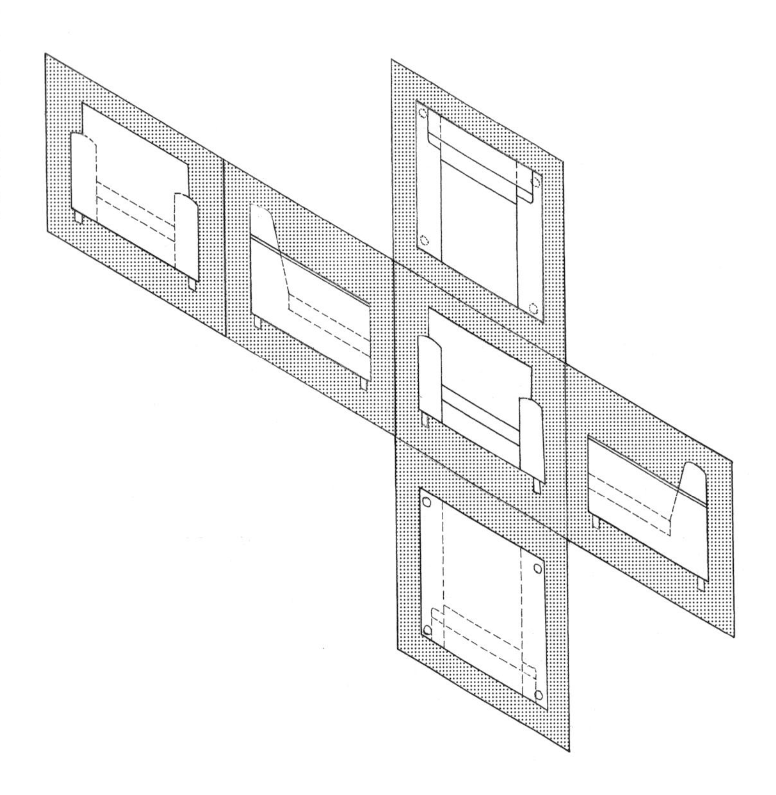

Pictorial and orthographic drawings:
Student project by Ellen Lew
Medium: Pencil on vellum
Courtesy of the City College of San Francisco
Department of Architecture

After drawing handheld-size objects, examine larger objects like furniture and small buildings and draw them with six or fewer views, as needed. The drawing at left shows six views of a chair projected on the surfaces (picture planes) of an opened glass box. In orthographic projection a folding plane line is used to help understand how the six views are positioned in relation to each other. Henceforth, this line will not be shown between views because in actual architectural practice the line is not drawn.

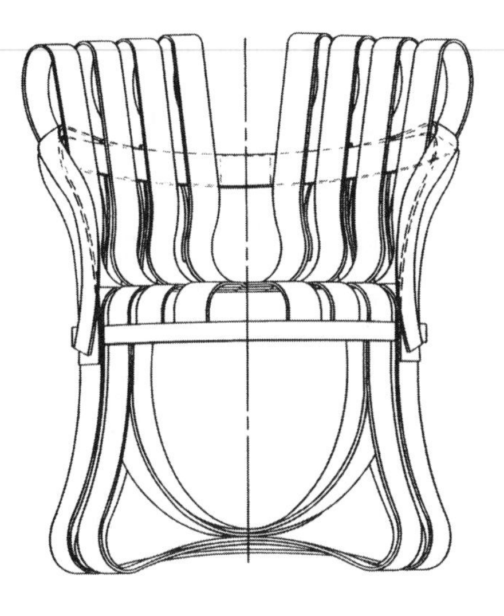

FRONT VIEW

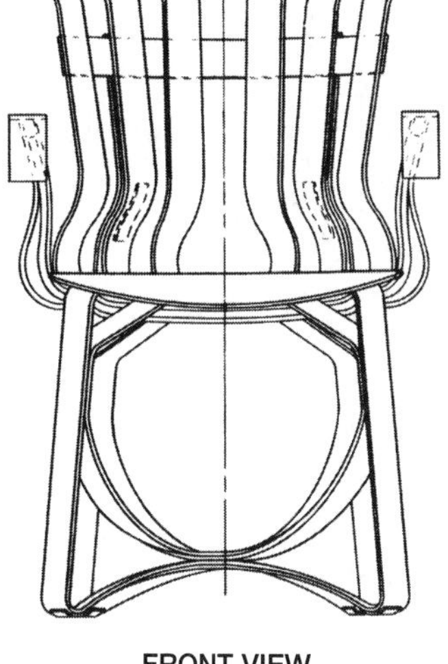

FRONT VIEW

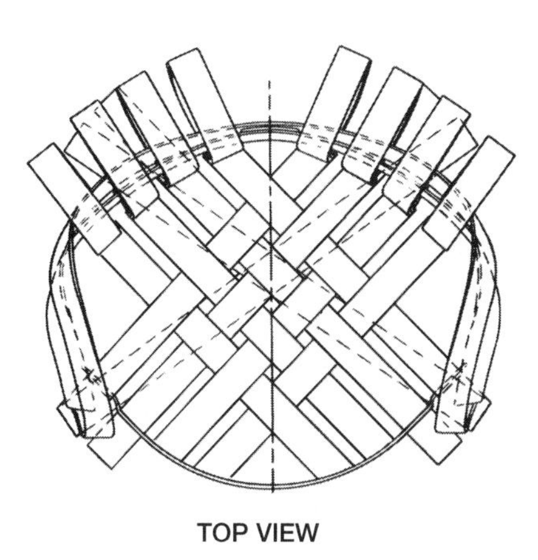

TOP VIEW

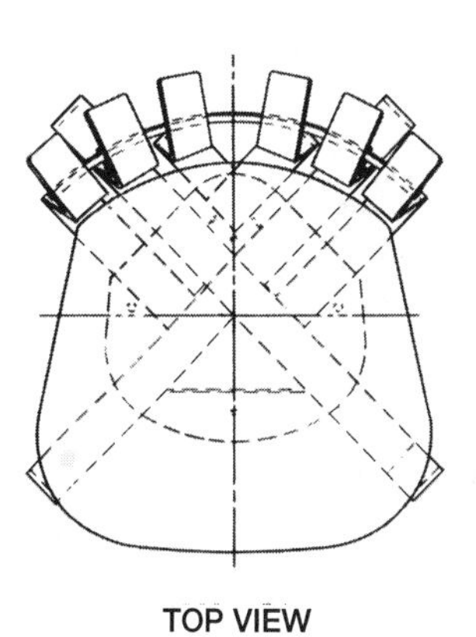

TOP VIEW

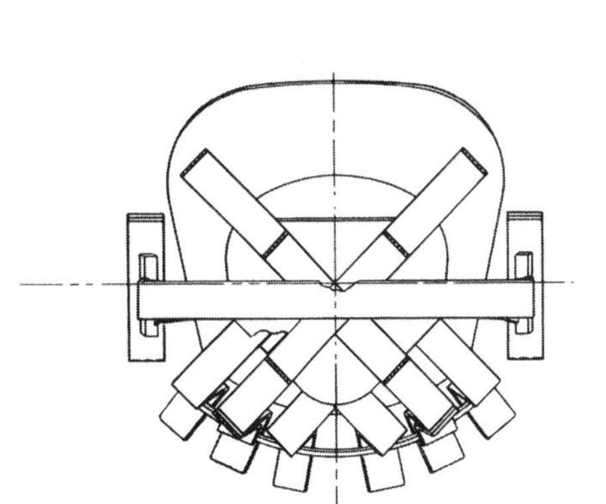

BOTTOM VIEW

Drawings: The Frank Gehry Bentwood Collection
Crosscheck armchair (above)
28" × 33.5" (72.4 × 85.1 cm), Scale: 1"=1'0"
Hat trick armchair (right)
23.4" × 33.5" (59.4 × 85.1 cm), Scale: 1"=1'0"
Medium: Ink on paper
Courtesy of Knoll

With just a front view and a top view, you can visualize the shape of most chairs and other pieces of furniture. With small objects like chairs, two or three views (top, front, and side) are adequate. With buildings, it is customary to use four or more views (see p. 129).

PROJECTION SYSTEMS COMPARED

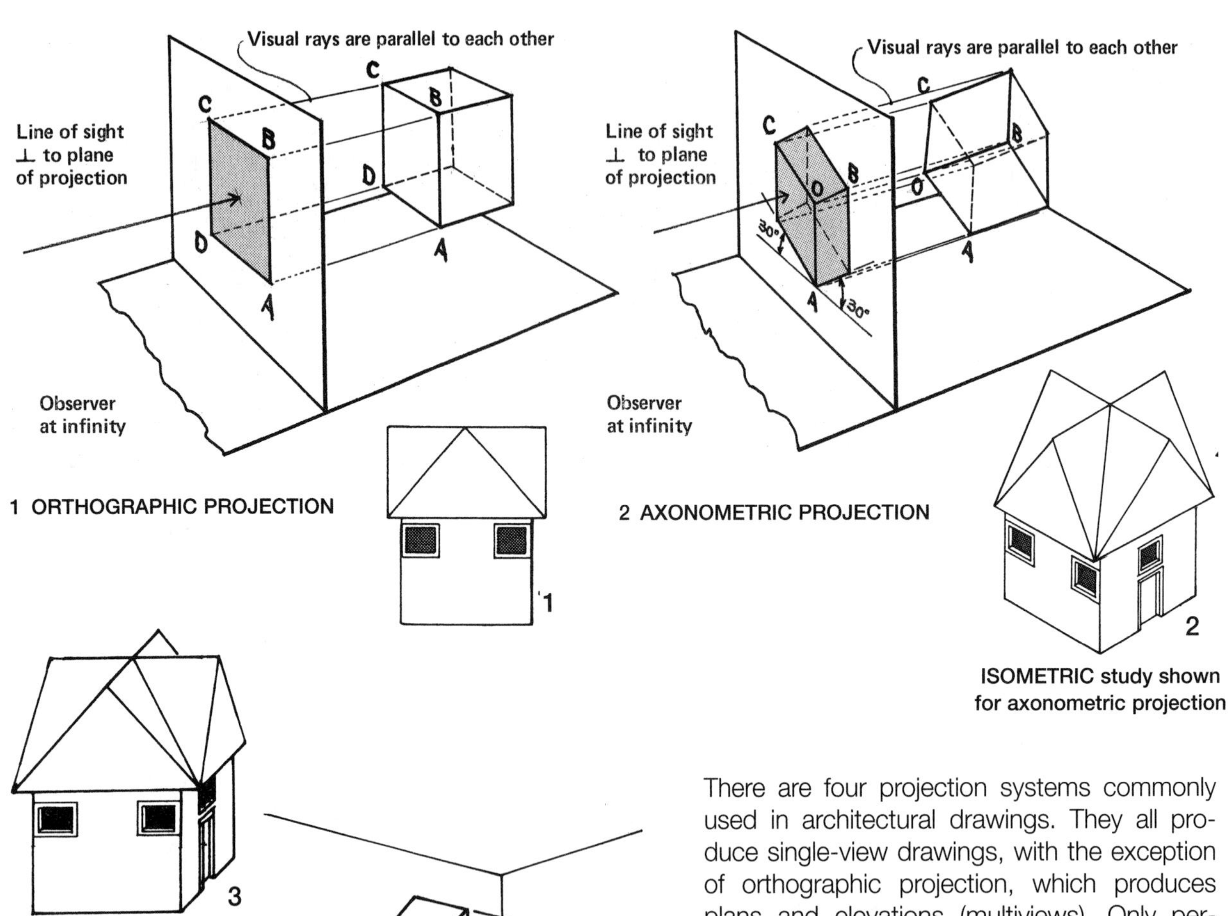

1 ORTHOGRAPHIC PROJECTION

2 AXONOMETRIC PROJECTION

ISOMETRIC study shown for axonometric projection

3

3 OBLIQUE PROJECTION

There are four projection systems commonly used in architectural drawings. They all produce single-view drawings, with the exception of orthographic projection, which produces plans and elevations (multiviews). Only perspective projection is characterized by nonparallel lines. All **projection systems** have four elements: an object, a picture plane, a viewer, and projected visual rays. **Visual rays** are the projection lines from the observer's eyes to various points on the viewed object or scene. For convenience and to save time, slightly foreshortened axonometric projection lengths are drawn true length in an axonometric drawing. Note that the symbol for perpendicular is ⊥.

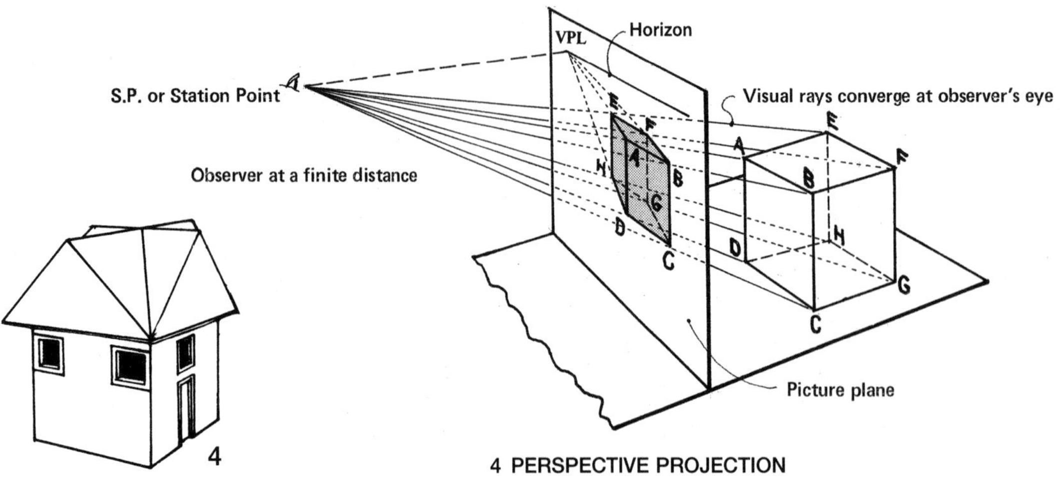

4 PERSPECTIVE PROJECTION

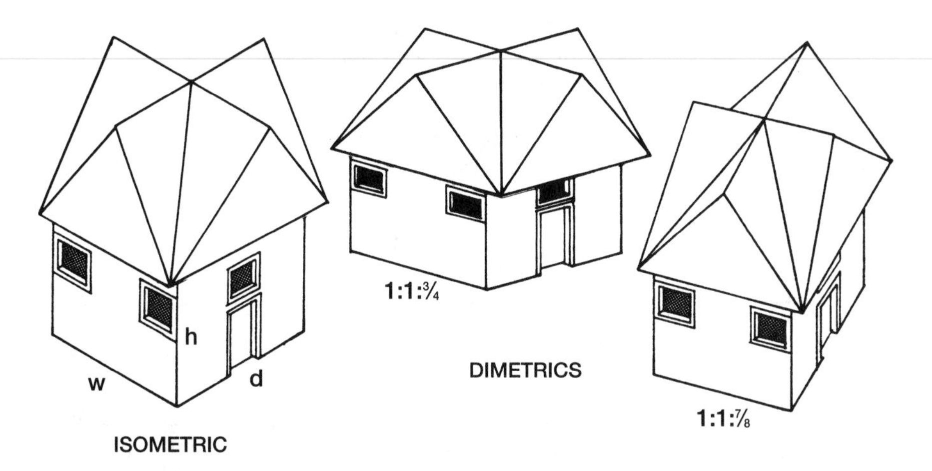

Isometric: All three primary axes are set at the same scale: 1:1:1.*

Dimetric: Any two of the three primary axes are set at the same scale. Isometric is a special case of dimetric drawing.

Trimetric: All three primary axes are set at different scales. Two viewed sides are at unequal angles to the horizontal.

Paraline axonometrics (from Greek) or **axiometrics** (from English) exhibit projectors that are **perpendicular** to the picture plane and **parallel** to each other. They exhibit a vertical front edge and nonconverging side planes.

*Scale ratios for the width (w), depth (d), and height (h) of the building.

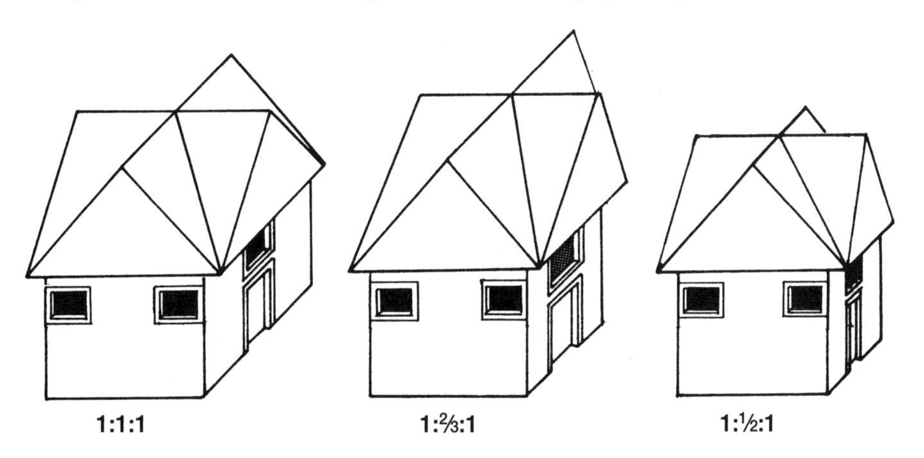

These are **elevation obliques**: one elevation is parallel to the picture plane and seen in true size and true shape. Often the receding planes seem too elongated in their true length. In practice they are usually shortened by as much as one-third to one-half to give visual comfort.

Paraline obliques (here in the form of elevation obliques) exhibit projectors that are **oblique** to the picture plane and **parallel.** They exhibit a flat, true-size frontal shape and nonconverging side planes. Historically, they derive from drawings of ancient European fortifications.

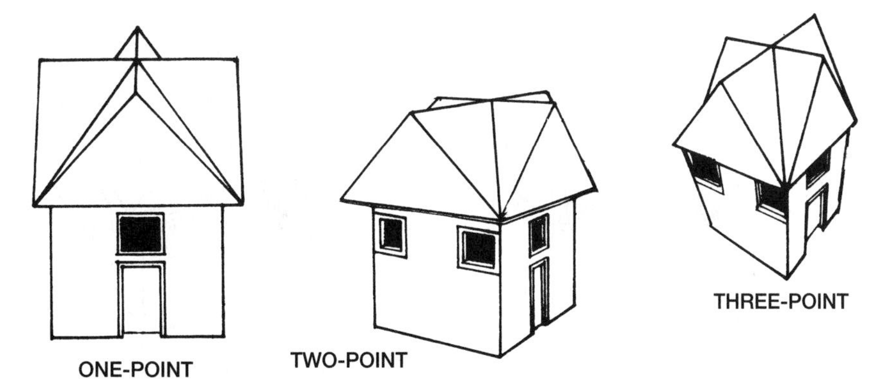

Perspectives, which will be covered in detail in Chapter 6, are single-view drawings that approach a person's optical perception. For two-point and three-point perspectives, the various surfaces are at a variety of angles to the picture plane, whereas one surface is parallel to the picture plane for a one-point perspective.

Perspectives exhibit projections that are at a variety of angles to the picture plane and display the characteristics of **point convergence.** They show converging side planes. Historically, they derive from drawings of the Renaissance.

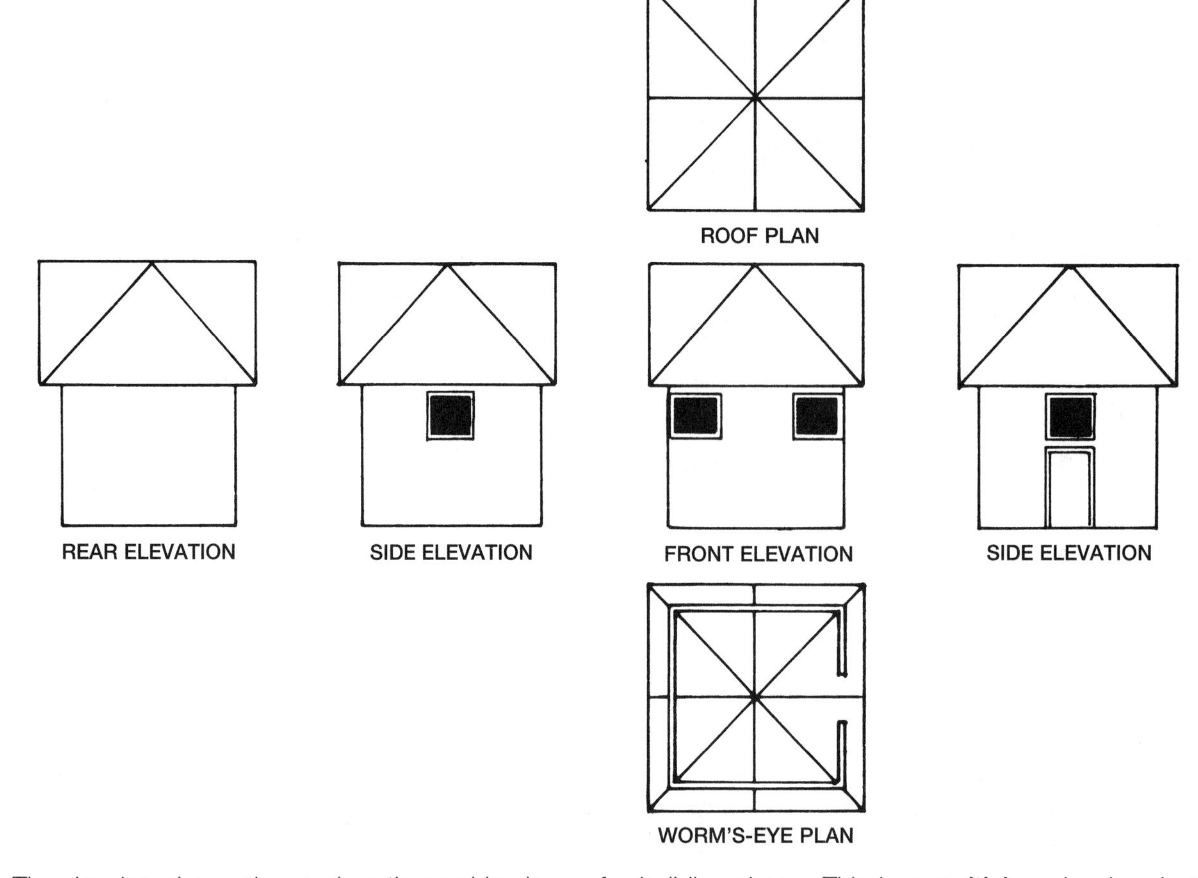

The drawing above shows six orthographic views of a building shape. This is a **multiview** drawing. In the design process, two-dimensional multiviews help us envision and communicate what the composite three-dimensional form will look like. Similarly, knowing the three-dimensional pictorial (see below) makes it easier to visualize how the multiviews lay out and relate to each other.

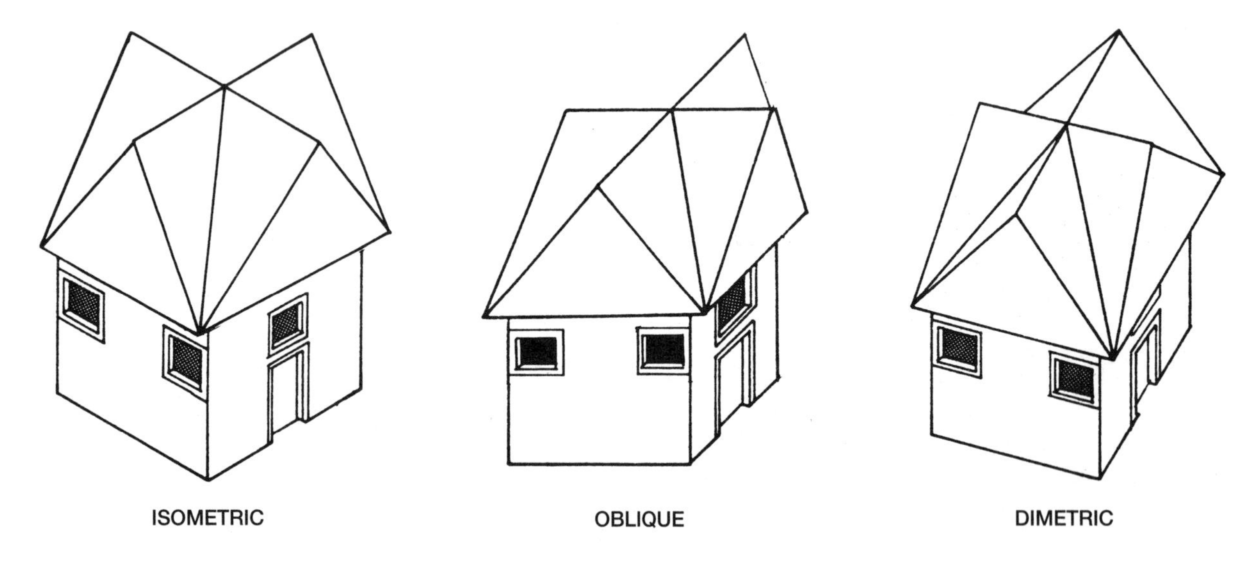

Isometric, oblique, and dimetric are three types of **single-view paraline** drawings. Unlike an isometric drawing, a **dimetric** drawing has the flexibility of being able to emphasize one or two of its primary planes. A **transparaline** is an unusual type of paraline drawing (see pp. 510, 514, and 515). Seen at the bottom on the facing page is a fourth type of single-view drawing: a perspective.

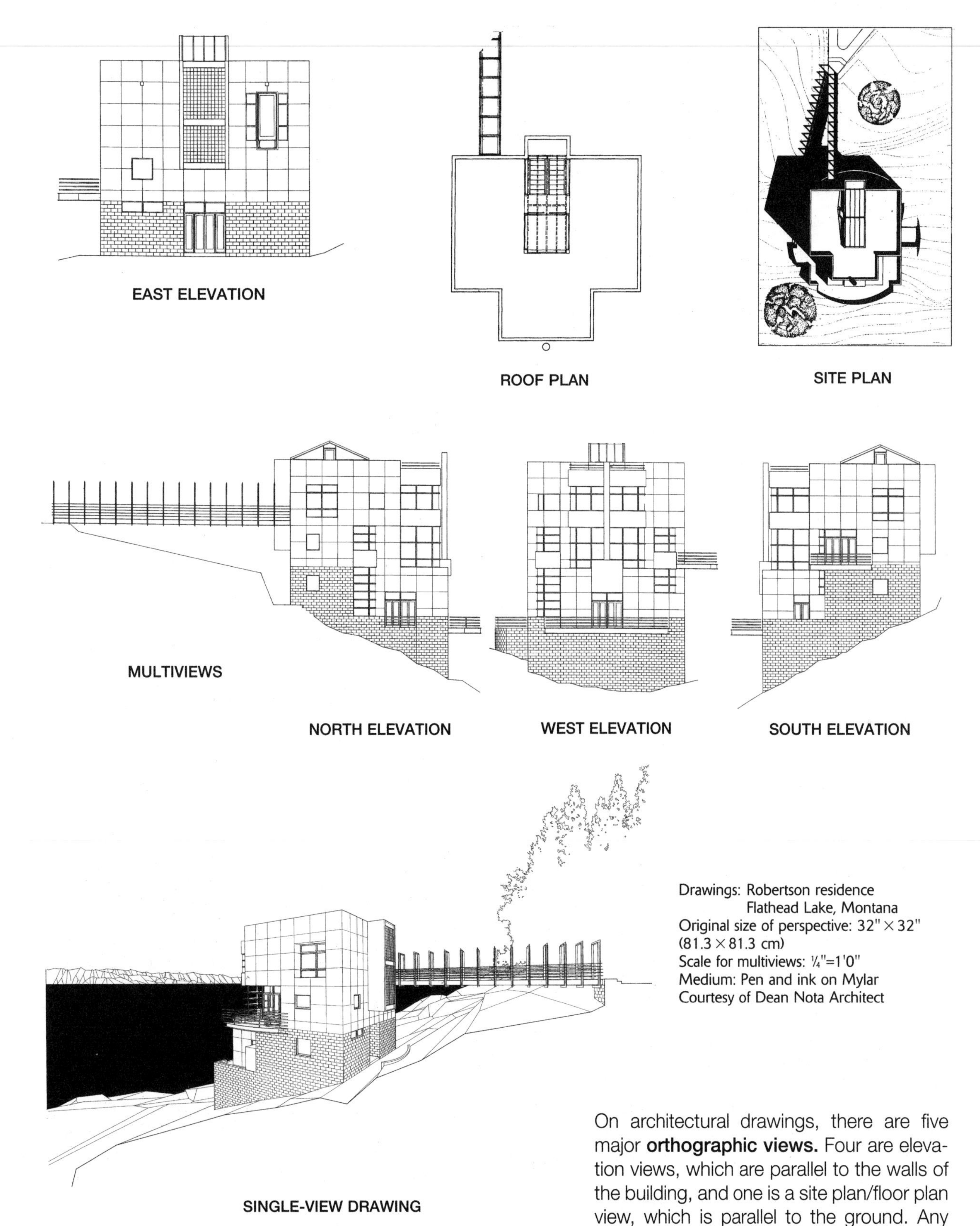

Drawings: Robertson residence
Flathead Lake, Montana
Original size of perspective: 32" × 32" (81.3 × 81.3 cm)
Scale for multiviews: ¼"=1'0"
Medium: Pen and ink on Mylar
Courtesy of Dean Nota Architect

On architectural drawings, there are five major **orthographic views.** Four are elevation views, which are parallel to the walls of the building, and one is a site plan/floor plan view, which is parallel to the ground. Any views that are not parallel to the primary walls of the building are classified as **auxiliary views.**

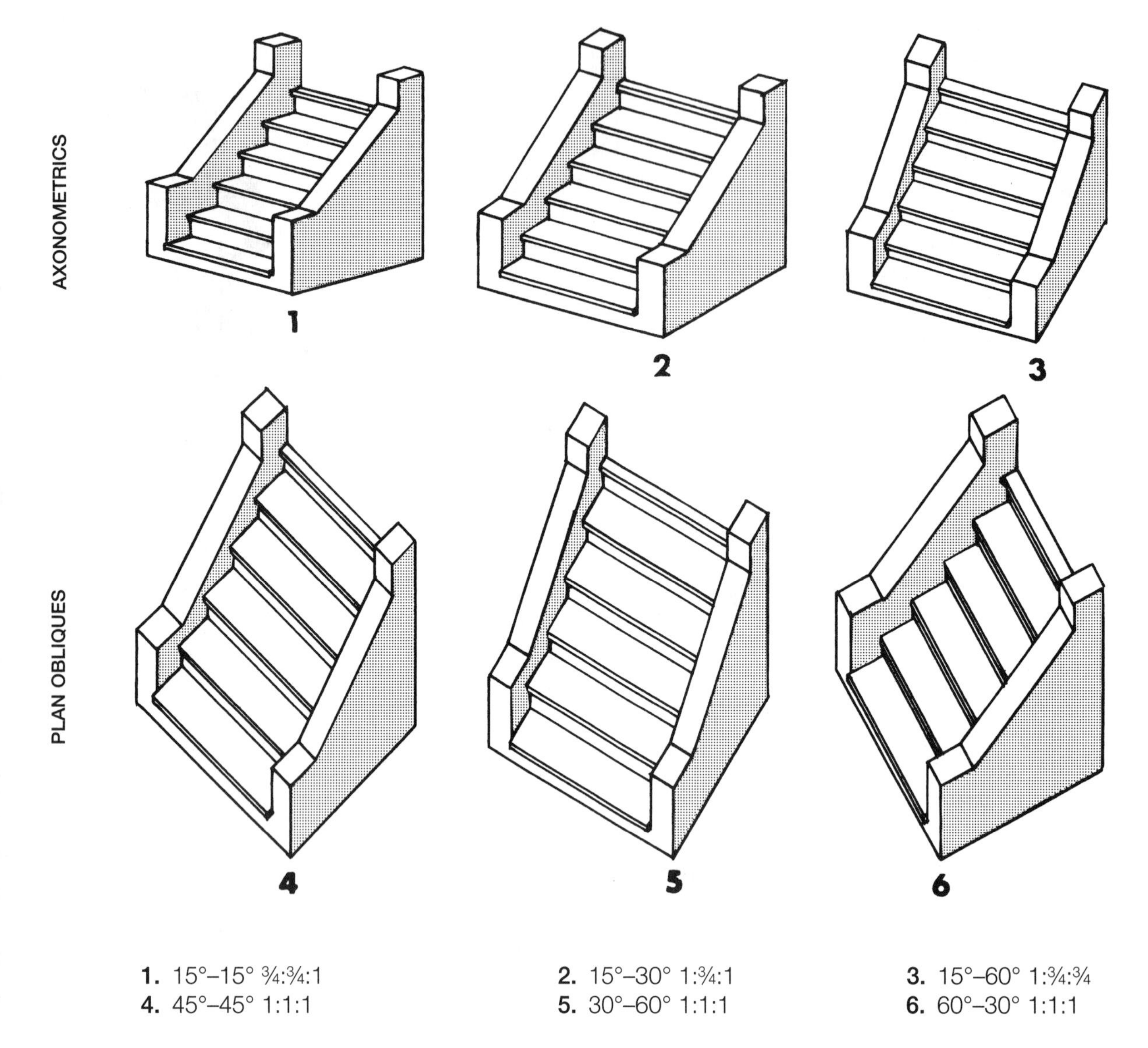

1. 15°–15° ¾:¾:1
2. 15°–30° 1:¾:1
3. 15°–60° 1:¾:¾
4. 45°–45° 1:1:1
5. 30°–60° 1:1:1
6. 60°–30° 1:1:1

Paraline **axonometrics** (axis measure) and paraline **plan obliques** allow for a great variety of choices in deciding which viewpoints are best relative to the type of object being depicted. The six alternatives shown are some of the more common angle and axes scale combinations that are used. In the oblique views of the staircase, all horizontal surfaces, such as the tread (horizontal part of the step) areas, are shown in their **true shape** and **true size** (actual plan dimensions). A small percentage of the actual riser (vertical part of the step) area is visible in the oblique situations. In contrast, note that in all of the axonometric views, the percentage of actual tread area decreases as more riser area becomes visible. You must first decide what is most important to show or emphasize before selecting the desired angle and axes scale combinations. This decision process will seem more straightforward as you study the various examples shown toward the end of this chapter. Through many years of professional usage it has become popular to classify "plan obliques" as "axonometrics." Loosely defined, the terms are interchangeable, even though they are technically two separate terms with distinct definitions.

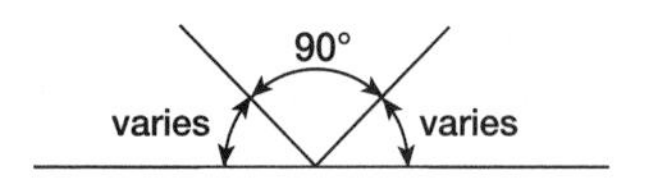

Plan obliques are quite flexible—the axes' angles can have any angular combination that you desire. An axonometric like an isometric (30°–30°) has fixed angles (see page 136).

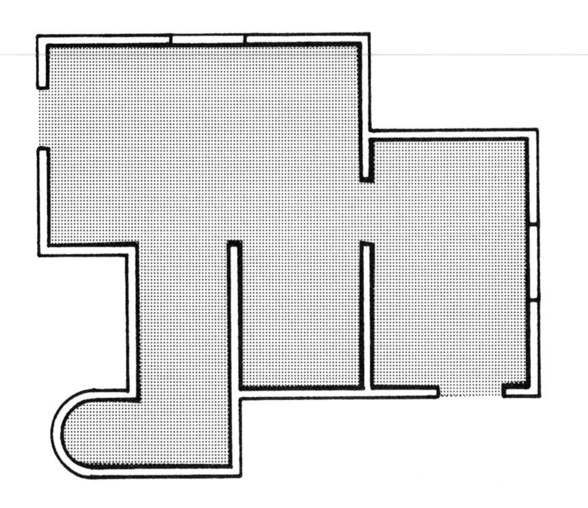

The **plan** view is essential for creating both **isometric** and **plan oblique** drawings for interior spaces. In professional practice, the plan is always available at common scales such as ¼"=1'0". This same scale would be used for plan obliques. The plan becomes a three-dimensional drawing when the vertical dimension is added. Because a plan view can be drawn quickly and easily by hand, it is especially useful for paraline oblique interiors.

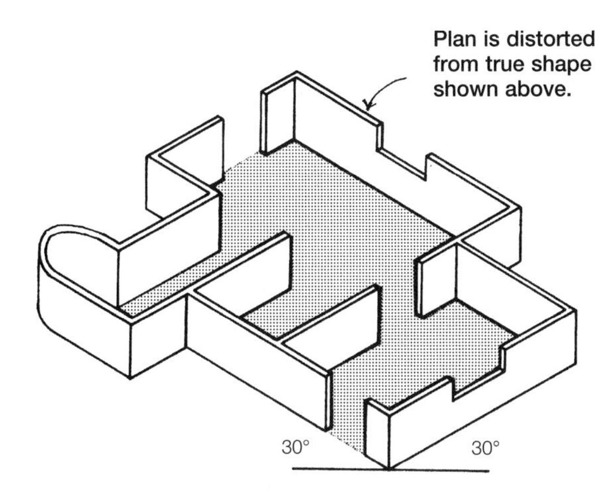
Plan is distorted from true shape shown above.
30°
30°

In a 30°–30° isometric, the interior partitions conceal large parts of the rooms, making it difficult to see the interior furniture, plants, people, etc. **Isometrics** are more commonly used for building **exteriors,** whereas **interiors** are best displayed with **plan obliques,** as shown below. An exception is the use of interior isometric drawings for transparent partitions (see p. 137). Note also that the walls are more visible in the isometric than in the 45°–45° drawing below. In plan obliques, the cut is usually taken in the range of ½ to ⅞ of the full floor-to-ceiling height.

Axes angles such as 45°–45° (see example at right), 60°–30°, and 75°–15° allow the observer to obtain a higher vantage point than the 30°–30° isometric. The partitions conceal less of the rooms in the 45° axes, and the plan becomes a **true shape.** These drawings can be termed **true-shape plan obliques**; they are simply a variation of the general oblique. As a drawing type, plan obliques give the best simultaneous representation of plan and elevation. They also give an excellent analytical view of the spatial organization of the plan. All paralines are excellent tools for verifying three-dimensional relationships.

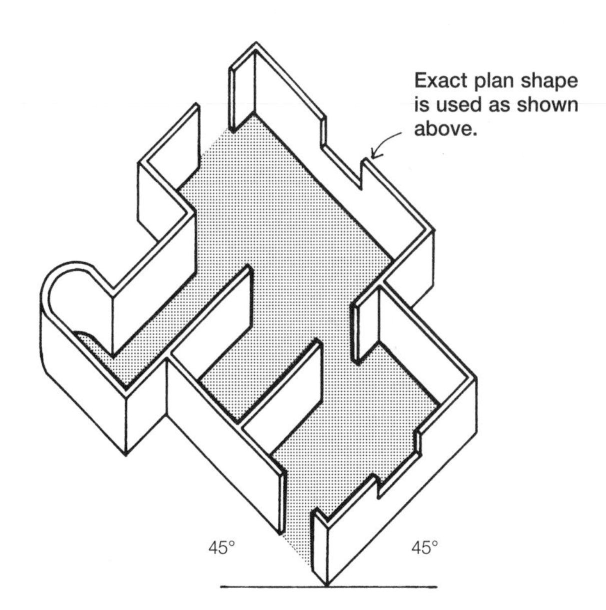
Exact plan shape is used as shown above.
45°
45°

ELEVATION OBLIQUES: A COMPARISON

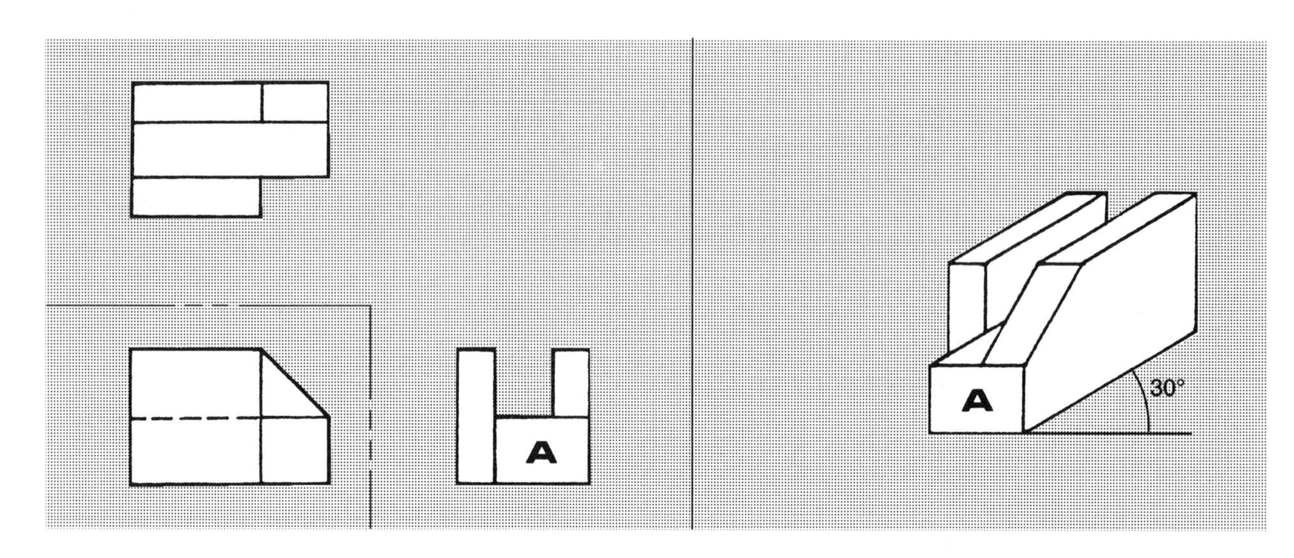

In an **elevation oblique** a chosen elevation view is seen as **true size** and **true shape.** Elevation surface **A** is used in this example. It is easy to draw elements like true-shape circles or curves on true-shape surfaces (**4** is **2** with a surface modification). The receding lines are usually drawn at 30°, 45°, or 60° angles from the horizontal. Measure the "notated" oblique angle from due north. For example **1**, this would be 90° minus 30° = 60°. The next two notations are the elevation scale and the receding line scale. For example **1**, this would be 1:1.

1. 60° — 1:1 **2.** 45° — 1:1 **3.** 30° — 1:1 **4.** 45° — 1:1 **5.** 45° — 1:⅔ **6.** 45° — 1:½

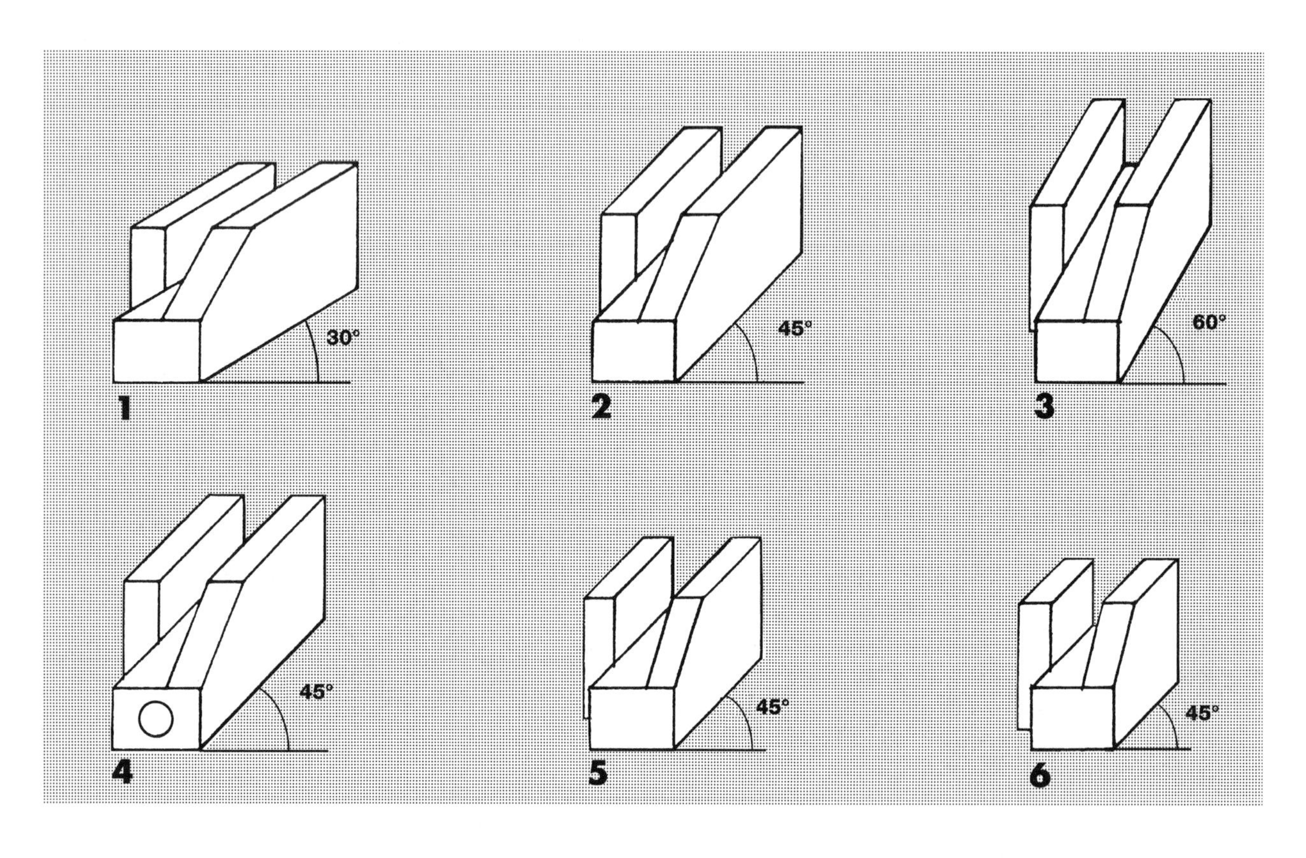

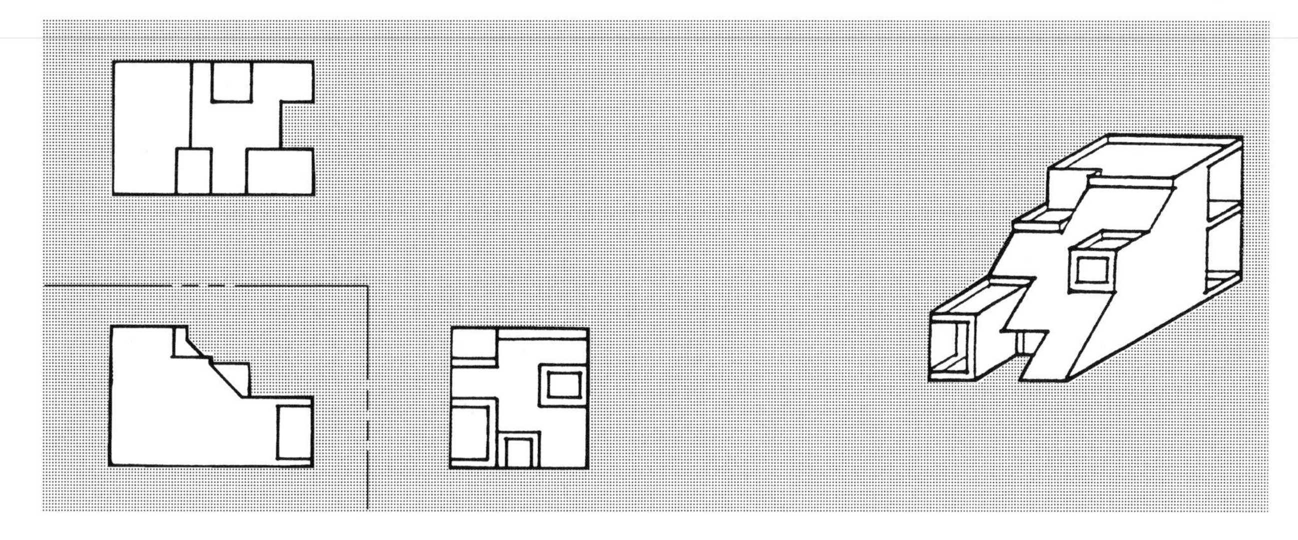

The building form shown in this example has a geometric configuration similar to that of the example shown on the opposite page. Note that all surfaces parallel to the vertical front elevation plane retain their true size and true shape and are perpendicular to the line of sight. It is common practice to show the elevation with the most irregular form as the frontal elevation. The direction of the receding lines and the scale ratio of each drawing correspond to the six drawings on the previous page. Receding lines can be set at any oblique angle.

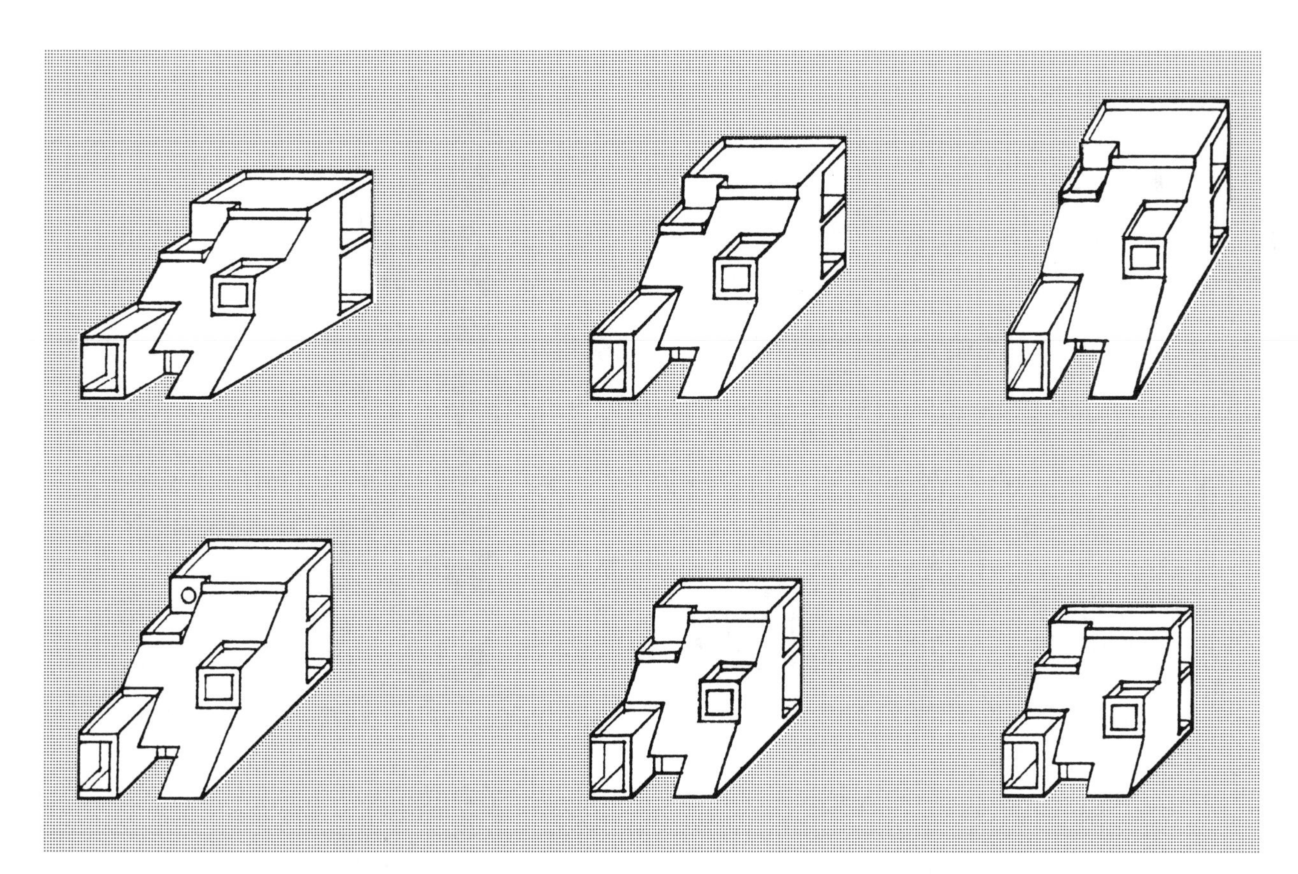

FRONTAL ELEVATION OBLIQUE 0°-1:1

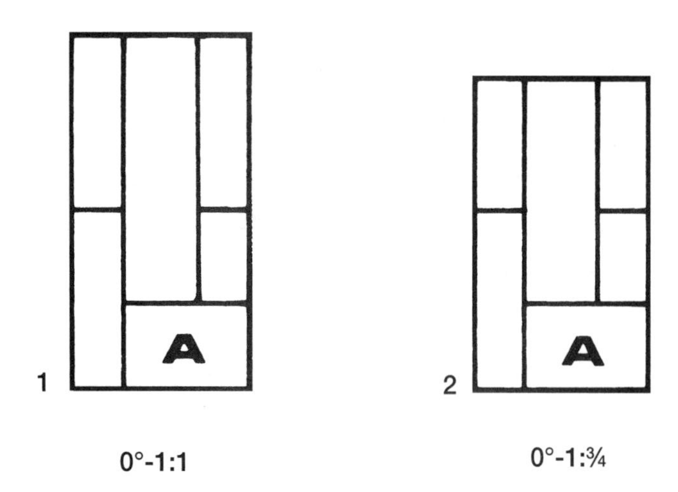

In examples **1** and **2**, the front elevation remains true size. Example **2** shows that the plan dimension is sometimes reduced from true length to generate a more realistic (foreshortened) view. This reduction can range from very little to as much as 25%. Most architects and designers, however, tend to maintain a true-size plan. Both examples below, as well as the drawings at left, show their elevations and roof plans true size and true shape. This unusual variation of an elevation oblique results when either the roof plan or floor plan (see facing page) has one of its sides parallel to the picture plane.

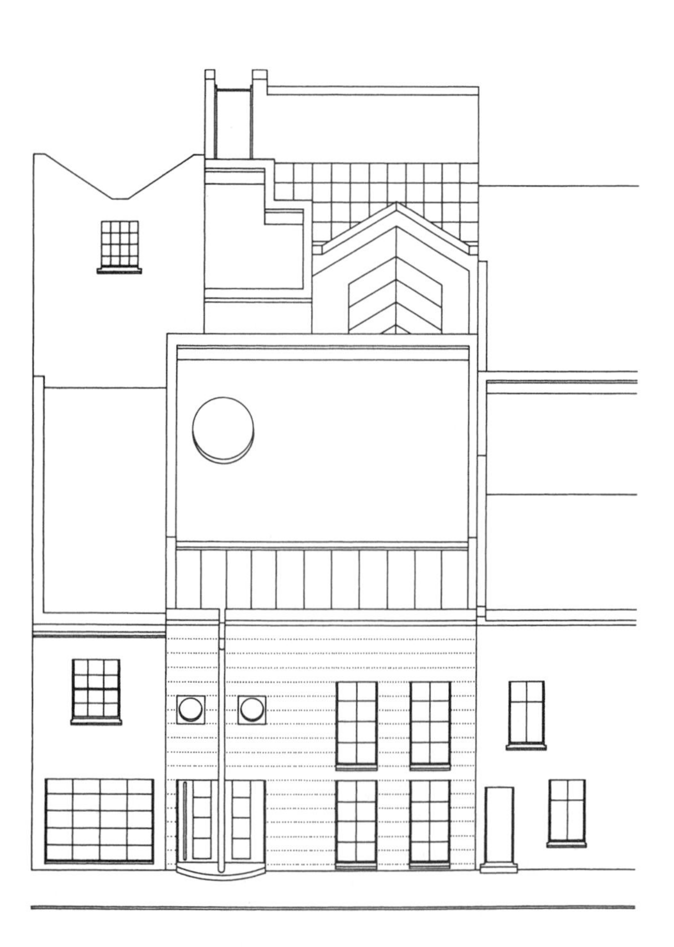

Drawing: Pond Place, London, England
Medium: Ink
Courtesy of Troughton McAslan Architects

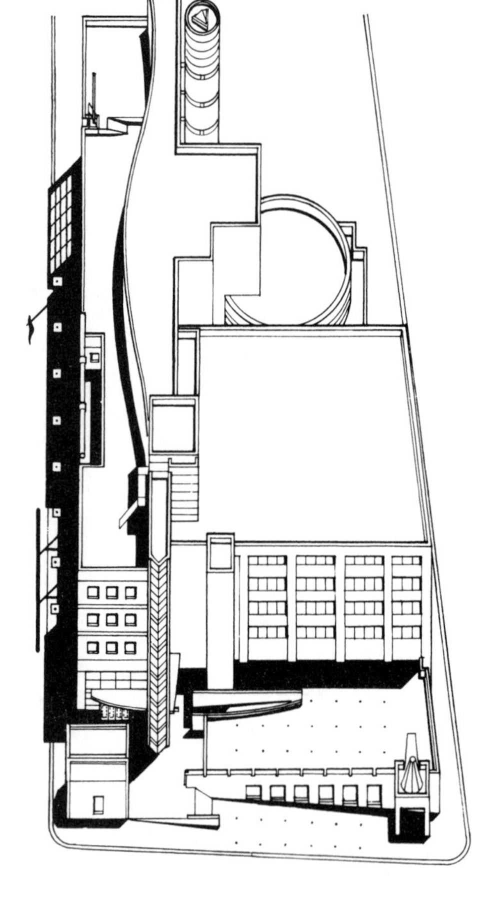

Drawing: Eugenio Maria de Hostos Community College, New York City
20" × 30" (50.8 × 76.2 cm), Scale: ⅛"=1'0"
Medium: Ink on Mylar
Courtesy of Bartholomew Voorsanger, FAIA

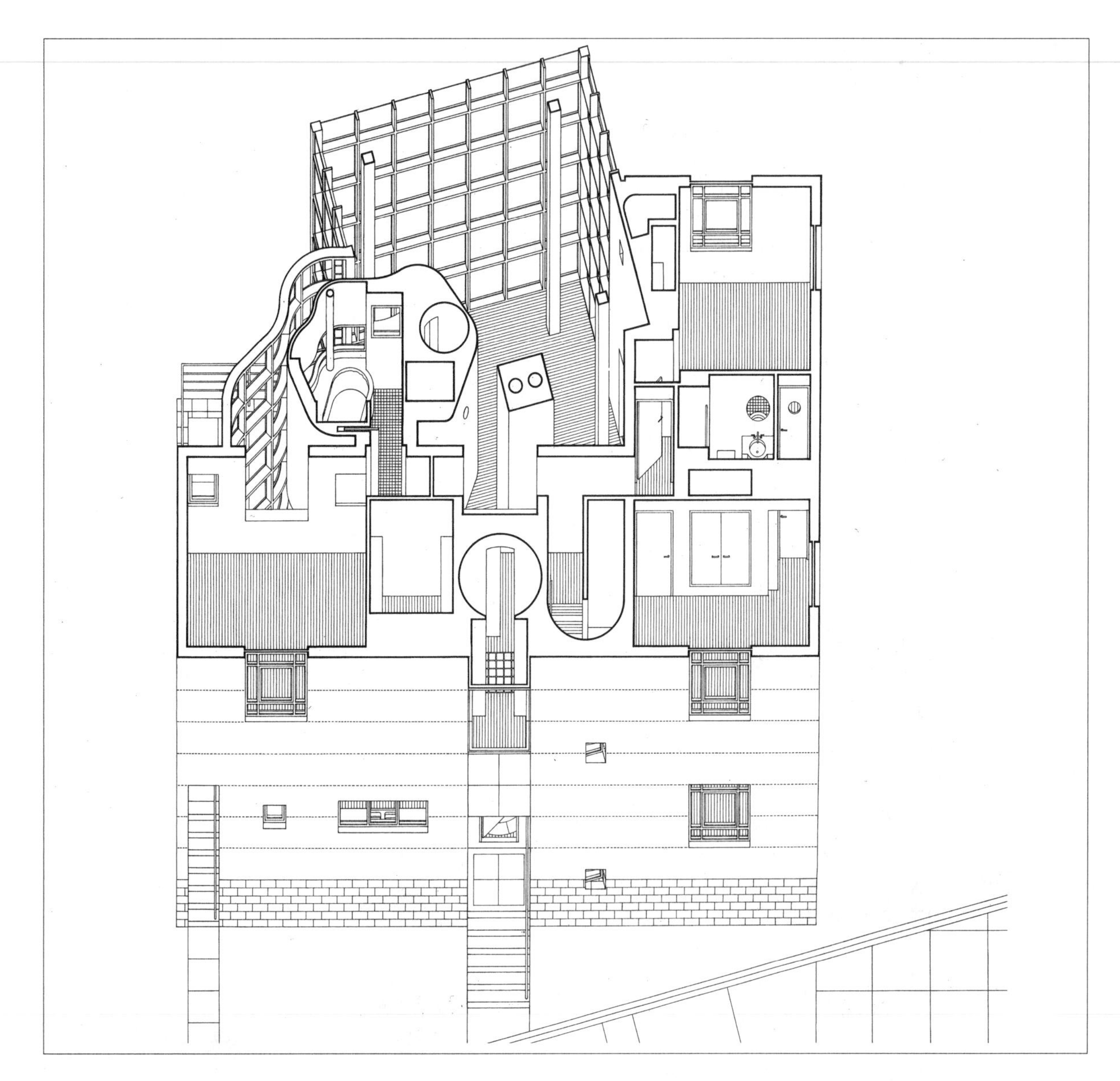

Drawing: Martinelli residence, Roxbury, Connecticut, 1989
22.5" × 22.5" (57.2 × 57.2 cm), Scale: ¼"=1'0"
Medium: Ink
Courtesy of Anthony Ames, Architect

The roof is removed from the building in this frontal axonometric drawing to illustrate the room locations on the second floor and their relationship to the double-height living and dining space, with the cloudlike element that encloses the master bathroom.
[ARCHITECT'S STATEMENT]

As with the drawings on the previous page, this frontal elevation oblique (also termed a 0° planometric) does not create the illusion of the third dimension. This type of drawing allows us to see vertical dimensions, fenestration patterns, and the roof structure configuration or plan layout simultaneously.

Isometric, when literally translated, means "equality of measurement." True-lengths parallel to any of the orthographic axes will be the same as in the isometric drawing. An isometric drawing is not composed of true angles, whereas plan oblique drawings (see p. 131) do have true angles. Isometric bird's-eye views create the illusion of parallel lines, when in reality the lines are converging. Your eyes tend to lead you to the corner of the building mass.

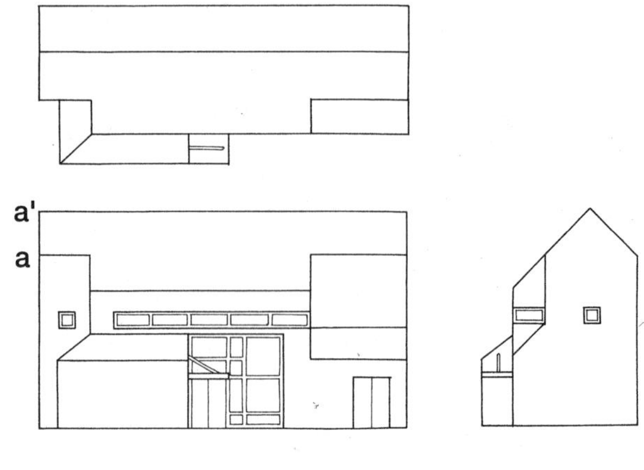

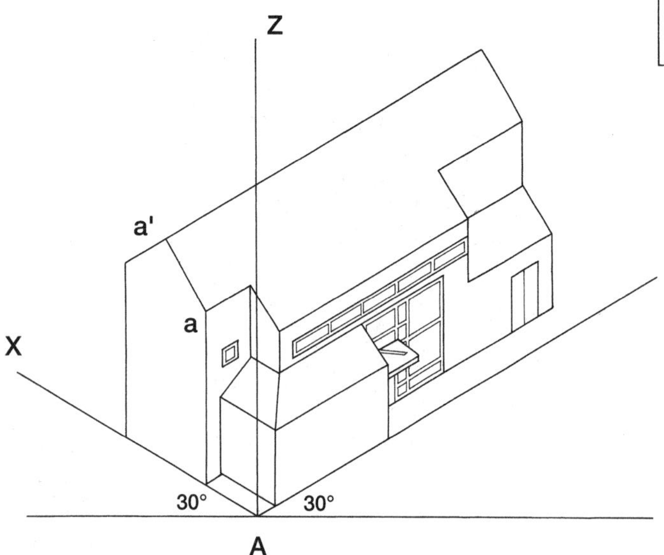

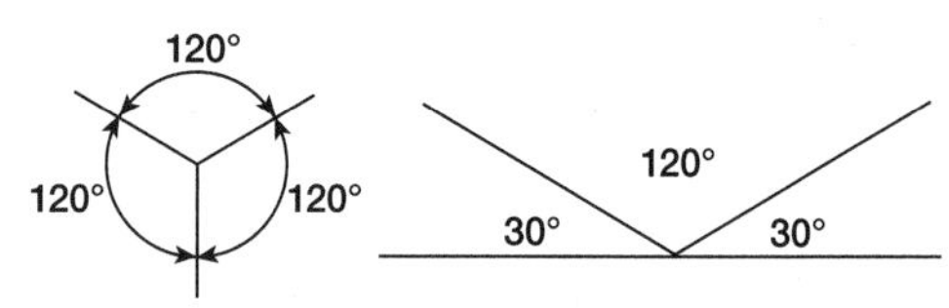

When projected on the picture plane, the three axes are always 120° apart. Conventionally and for simplicity, the two nonvertical axes are constructed 30° to a horizontally drawn line.

The **isometric drawing** is one of the most important types of **axonometric drawings.** Principles for its construction are as follows:

- The axes (*AX* and *AY*) on the ground plane are always drawn 30° from the horizontal.
- Measure all orthographic distances along the three axes *AX*, *AY*, and *AZ*, and only along these axes.
- Any lines that are not along the isometric axes (inclined or nonaxial lines) should be located and measured by locating the end points of the line (see ***a'-a*** above). These lengths will not be the same in the isometric view and the orthographic views.
- Parallel lines in an orthographic drawing remain parallel in the corresponding isometric drawing.
- Vertical lines in an orthographic drawing remain vertical in an isometric drawing.
- Hidden lines are normally not drawn in an isometric, but they can be used to help visualization.
- Corner points may be labeled in each orthographic view and in the isometric view to help visualize the isometric drawing.
- One disadvantage of the isometric is that it cannot use the orthographic view in the actual orthographic (plan/elevation) layout.

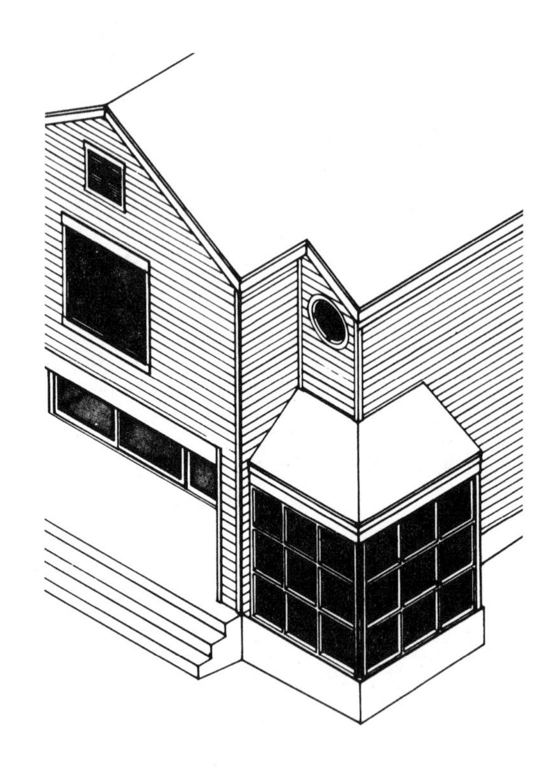

Drawing: Partial isometric
Sprague Lakehouse
Lake Cypress Springs, Texas
24" × 36" (61 × 91.4 cm), Scale: ¼"=1'0"
Medium: Ink on vellum
Courtesy of Todd Hamilton, Architect

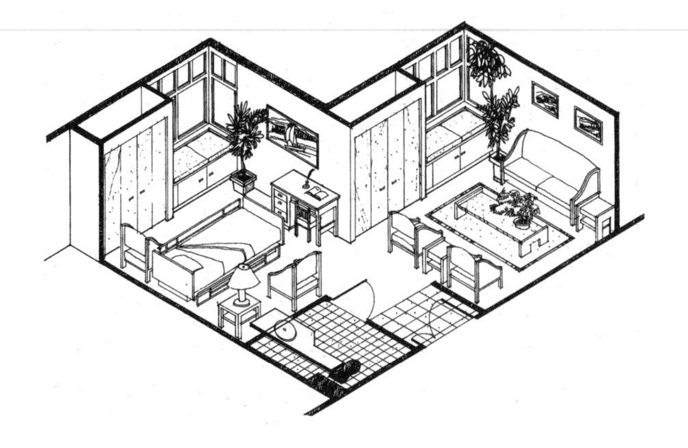

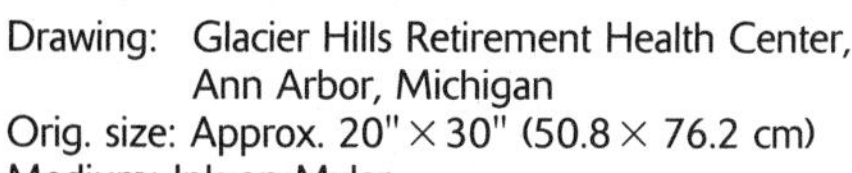

Drawing: Glacier Hills Retirement Health Center,
Ann Arbor, Michigan
Orig. size: Approx. 20" × 30" (50.8 × 76.2 cm)
Medium: Ink on Mylar
Courtesy of Ellerbe–Becket, Inc.,
Designed by Dale Tremain, AIA

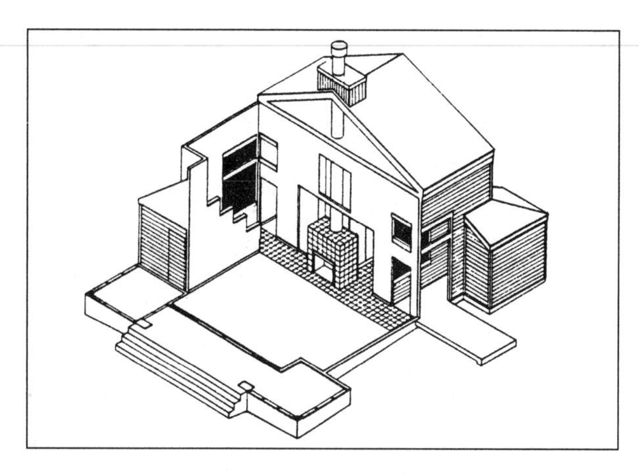

Drawing: Sprague Lakehouse
Lake Cypress Springs, Texas
24" × 36" (61 × 91.4 cm), Scale ¼"=1'0"
Medium: Ink on vellum
Courtesy of Todd Hamilton, Architect

An **isometric drawing** shows a more mechanistic type of perception. Perspective drawing, which will be studied in a later chapter, is much closer to natural human perception. Nevertheless, isometrics are used because seeing three nonconverging faces of an object is still quite beneficial in understanding its form. The observer is limited to viewing only bird's-eye views in an isometric. Due to its low angle of view (lower than plan obliques), an isometric drawing does not permit the viewer to see interior spaces unless the roof and side walls are removed. All three of these elements are absent in the examples above; they also show a partial isometric plan. The examples below show two other ways to reveal the interior configuration. The lower left drawing requires a transparent isometric (see p. xvi). The lower right drawing uses a cutaway partition as well as an isometric section.

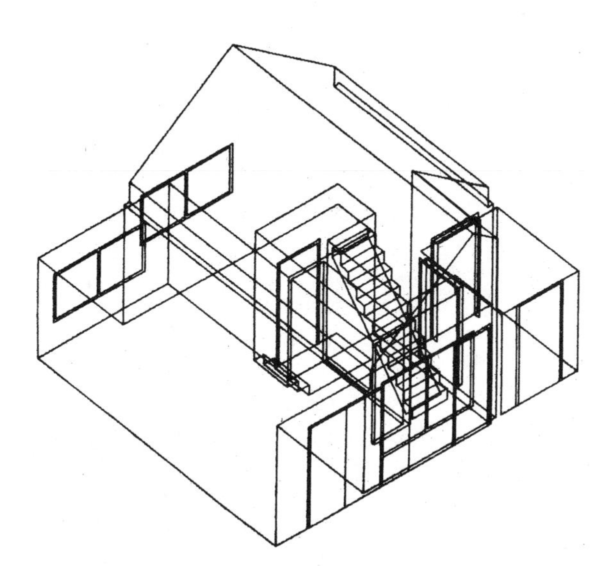

Drawing: Student project by Haden Smith
Graduate Student Housing
10" × 8" (25.4 × 20.3 cm), Scale: ¼"=1'0"
Medium: CAD
Courtesy of Washington University
School of Architecture, St. Louis, Missouri

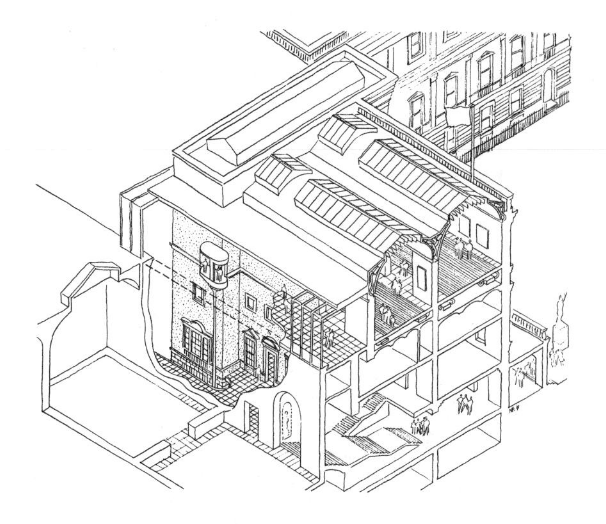

Drawing: Sackler Galleries, Royal Academy, London, England
Medium: Pencil on trace 16.5" X 11.7" (418 X 291 mm)
Courtesy of Foster and Partners
Drawn by Lord Foster of Thames Bank

PLAN OBLIQUE MEASUREMENTS

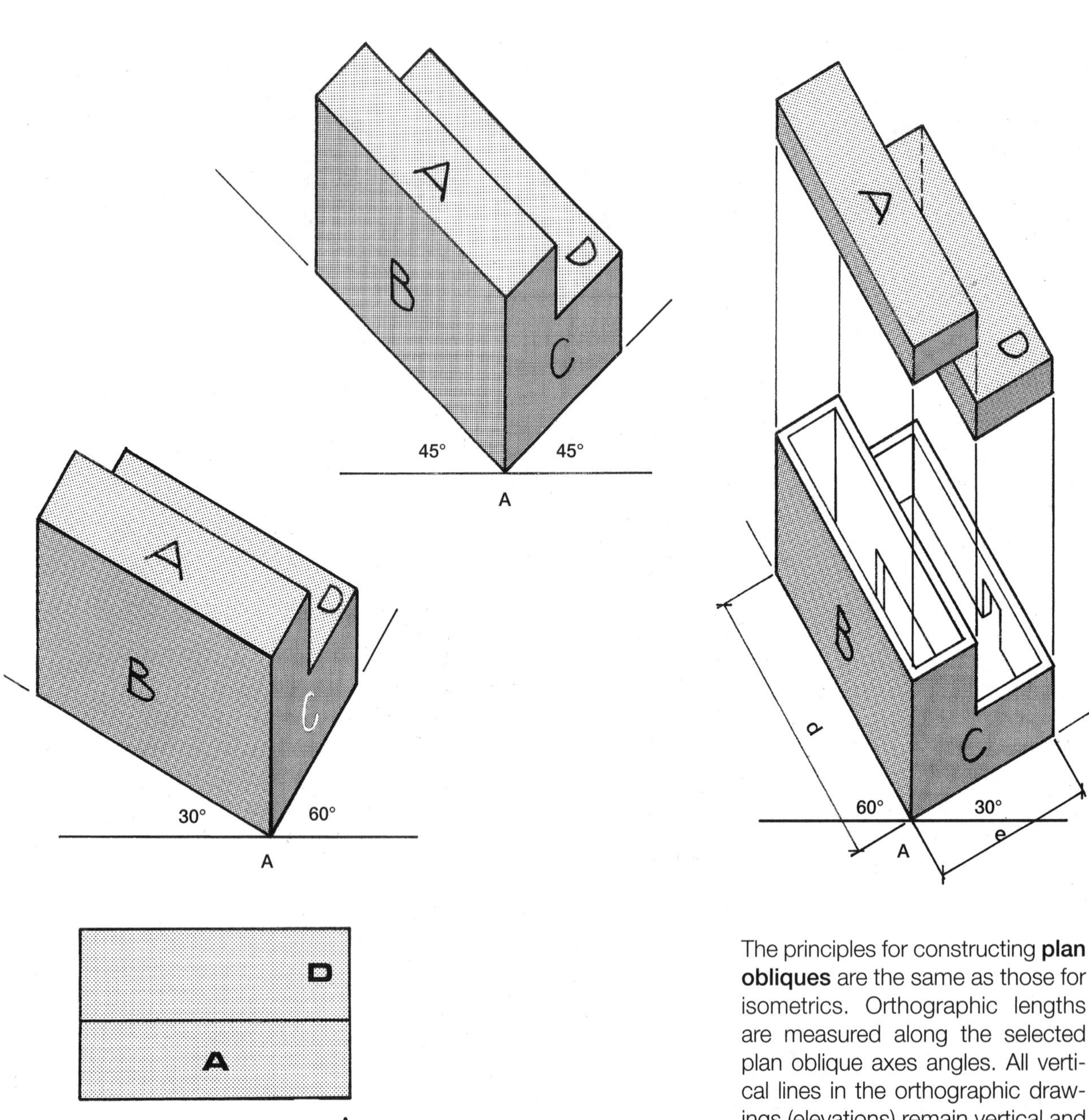

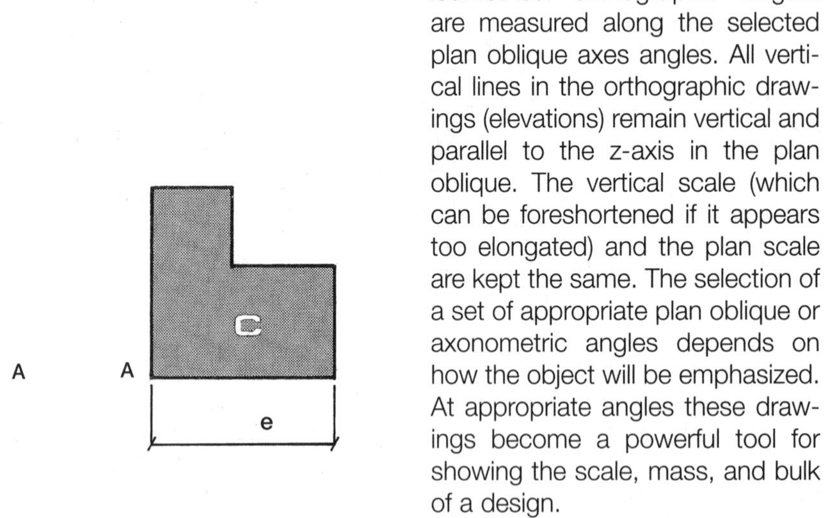

The principles for constructing **plan obliques** are the same as those for isometrics. Orthographic lengths are measured along the selected plan oblique axes angles. All vertical lines in the orthographic drawings (elevations) remain vertical and parallel to the z-axis in the plan oblique. The vertical scale (which can be foreshortened if it appears too elongated) and the plan scale are kept the same. The selection of a set of appropriate plan oblique or axonometric angles depends on how the object will be emphasized. At appropriate angles these drawings become a powerful tool for showing the scale, mass, and bulk of a design.

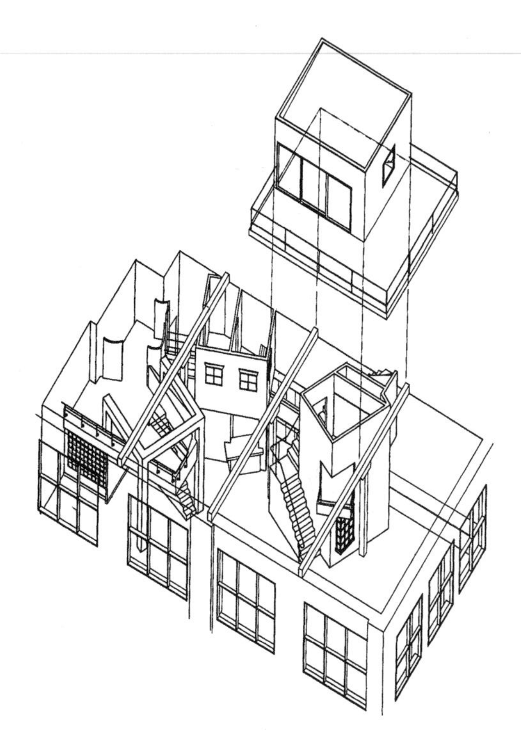

With a multitude of vertical and horizontal elements, it is most efficient to construct each element separately. No matter how complex the building, follow the basic principle of projecting the plan configuration upward to the exact elevation heights. This will result in a volumetric solid based on the plan view.

Drawing: Clybourne Lofts
Chicago, Illinois
30" × 40", (76.2 × 101.6 cm), Scale: ¼"=1'0"
Medium: Ink on Mylar
Courtesy of Pappageorge Haymes Ltd., Chicago, Architects

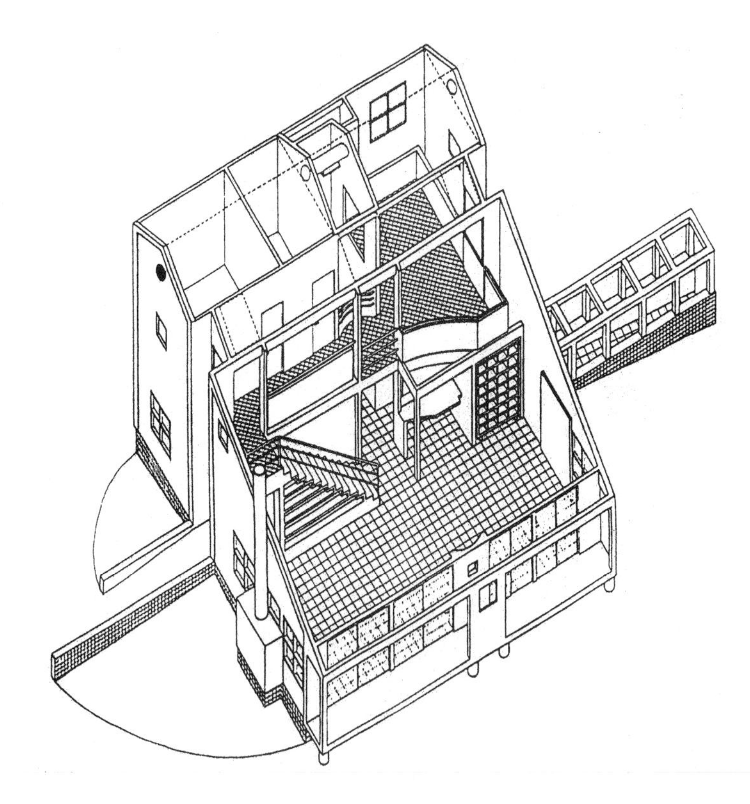

Drawing: Peele residence, North Andover, Massachusetts
±24" × 36" (61 × 91.4 cm), Scale: ⅛"=1'0"
Medium: Ink with Pantone film colors
Adam Gross, Project Associate
Courtesy of Perry, Dean, Rogers, and Partners: Architects
Reprinted from *The Compact House Book,* edited by Don Metz with permission of Storey Communications/Garden Way Publishing, Pownal, Vermont.

Removing the roof from a building form helps to reveal the interior spaces drawn at plan oblique axes angles. Plan obliques (either looking down or looking up, as on pp. 174–75) provide an unnatural but informative way of observing architecture. They make height changes and volumetric characteristics easy to understand. As a procedural rule, always construct the wall or roof outline first (as in the Clybourne Lofts, above left) before adding material wall or floor texture (as in the Peele residence, above right). Spatial definition can be enhanced by the generous use of tonal values. These values produce contrast between the horizontal and vertical planes.

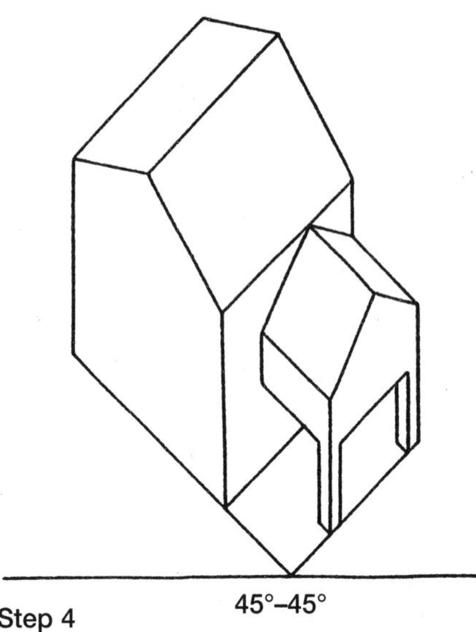
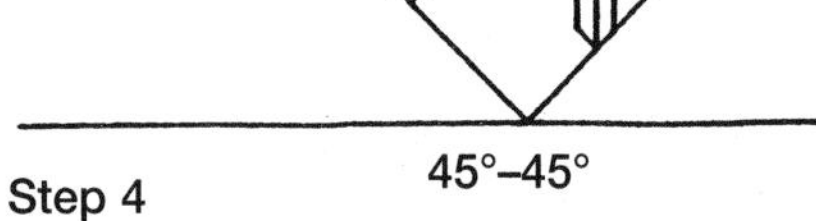

Step 4 45°–45°

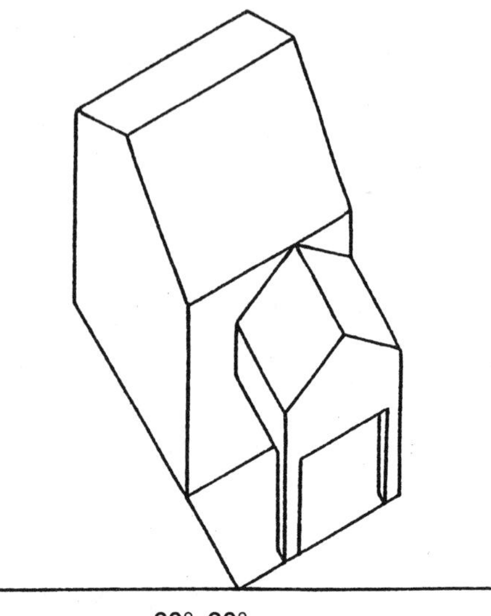

Step 4 60°–30°

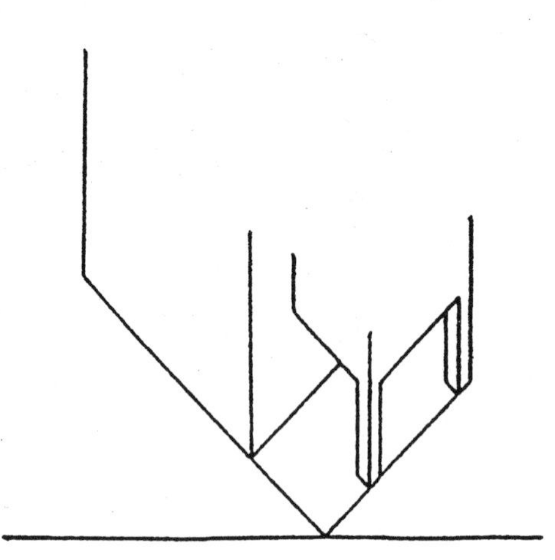

Steps 1, 2, and 3

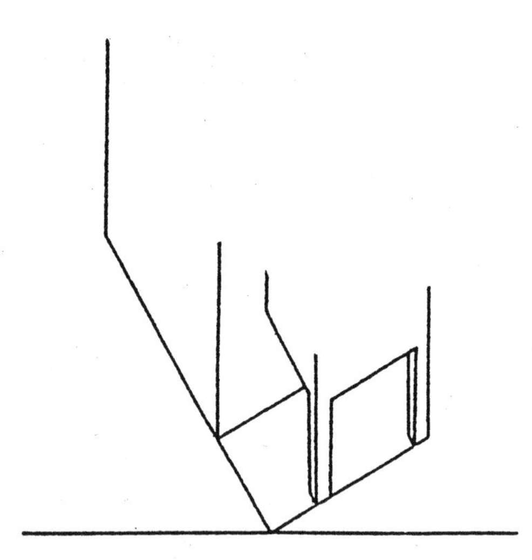

Steps 1, 2, and 3

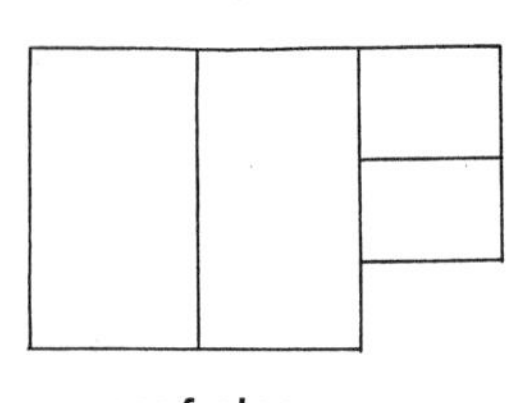

roof plan

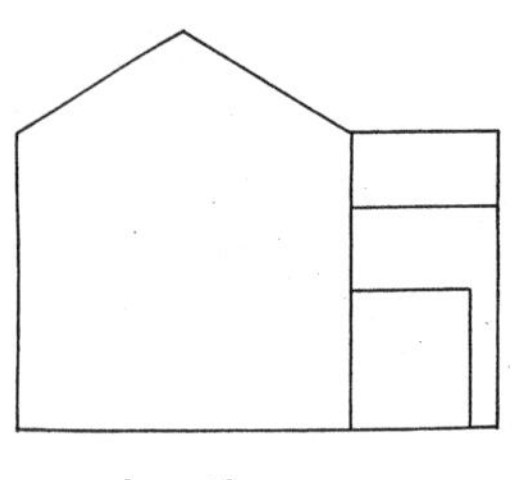
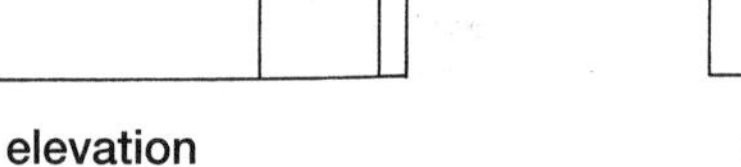

elevation

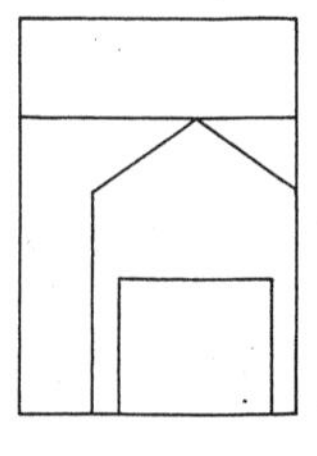

elevation

For exterior forms:

1. Access the plan configuration (roof or floor plan) and one or two elevations, all drawn to the same scale.
2. Place and rotate the plan to any axes angle combination. Construct the true-shape plan view (examples shown are 45°–45° and 60°–30°). For exteriors, some of the sides may not be visible.
3. From the elevations, scale and construct all vertical lines.
4. Complete other true-length horizontal and non-true-length lines (determined by finding their end points, as with isometric drawings).

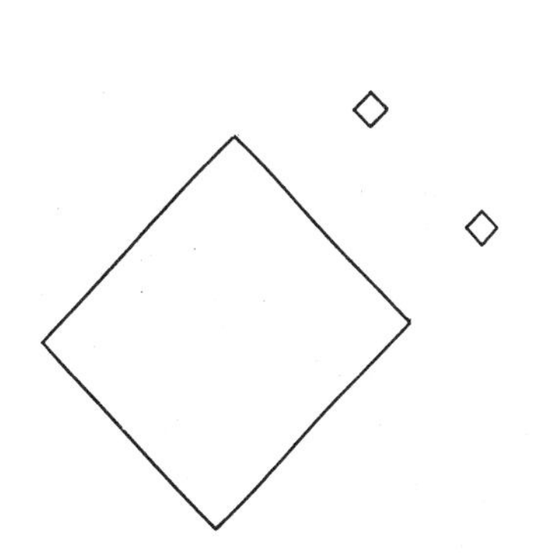

Draw the overall plan configuration (footprint) of the up view.

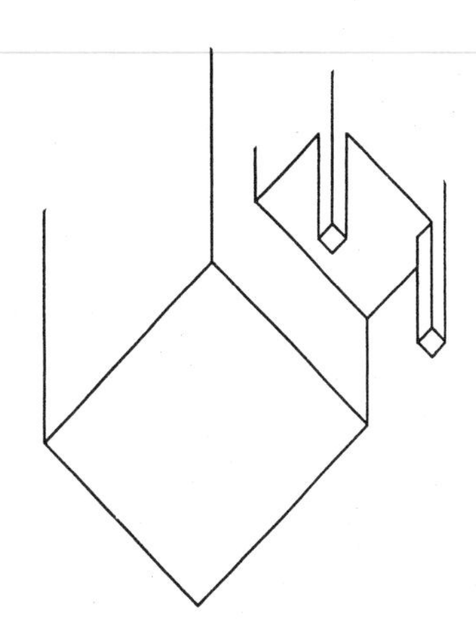

Then draw verticals and true-length horizontals.

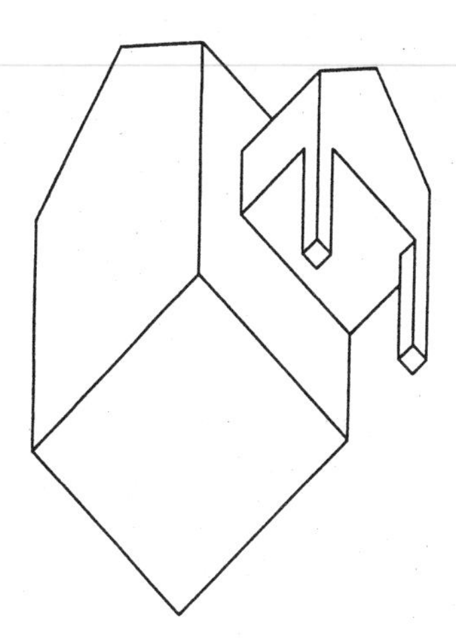

oblique up view

Then draw other non-true-length lines.

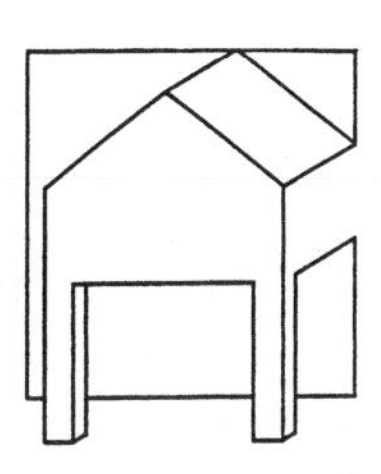

Draw the true-shape elevation view.

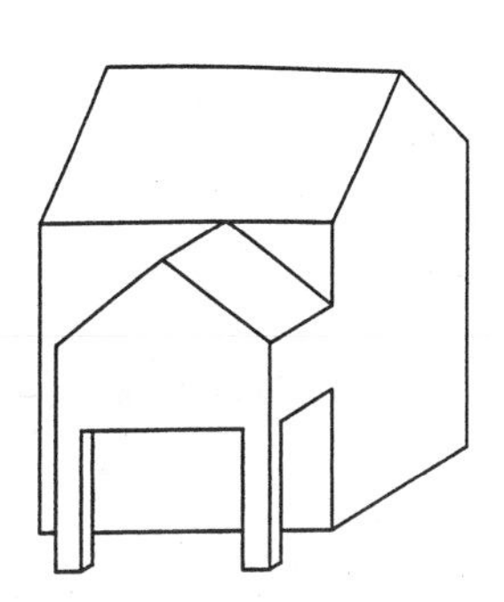

elevation oblique

Then draw all parallel receding lines and other nonparallel lines.

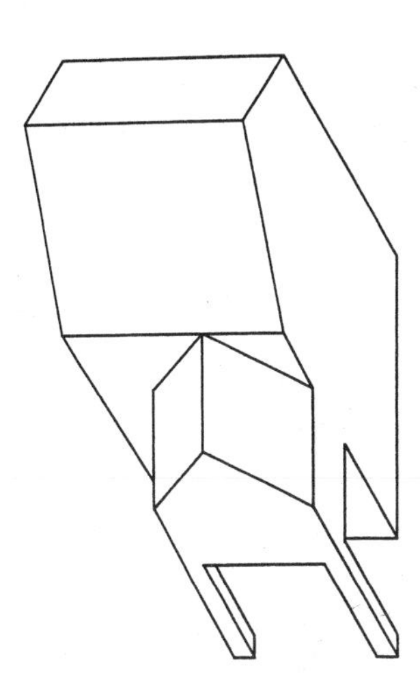

nonvertical z-axis oblique

The procedure is the same as that for other obliques, the vertical axis is swung and drawn left or right of the actual vertical.

The latter part of this chapter will introduce you to three other types of drawings that are related to the plan oblique. The construction procedure is shown above for these three types, identified as oblique up views (pp.174–77), elevation obliques (pp. 132–35 and 160–63), and non-vertical z-axis obliques (pp. 156–59).

CONSTRUCTING ISOMETRIC CIRCLES

In paraline drawings, all circles appear as ellipses except true circles—those that appear in planes parallel to the picture plane. The four-center ellipse procedure, below, is the most precise method for approximating true ellipses. See procedures to construct vertical and horizontal circles in perspective on pp. 286–87.

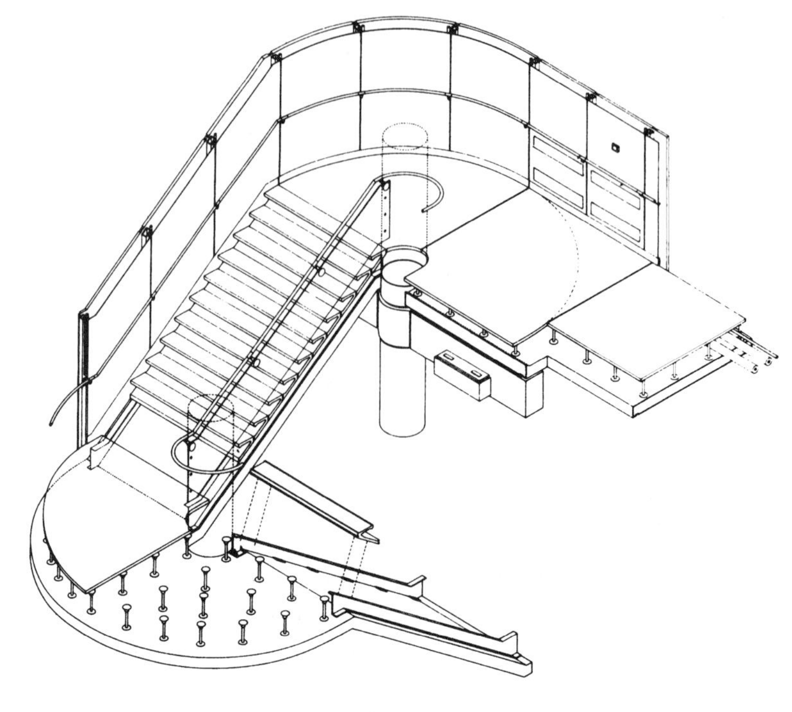

Drawing: Staircase isometric, Lloyd's of London
London, England
33" × 45.5" (83.8 × 115.6 cm)
Medium: Rottering pen on tracing
Courtesy of the Richard Rogers Partnership, Architects

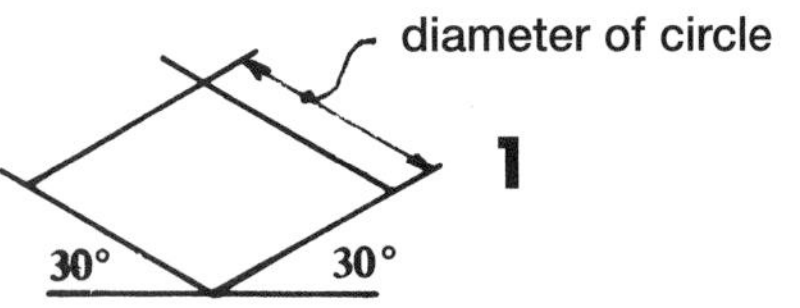

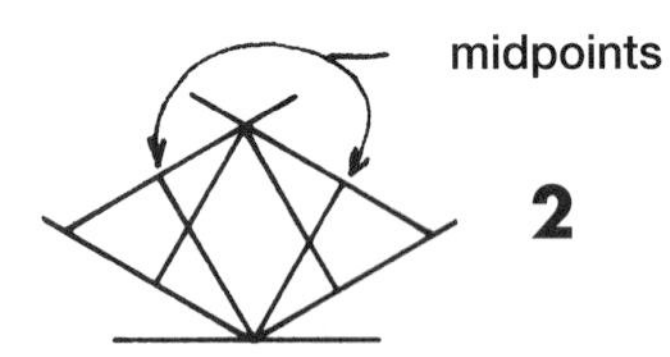

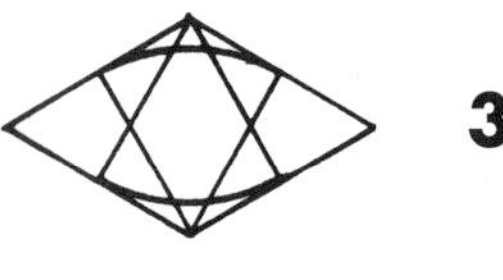

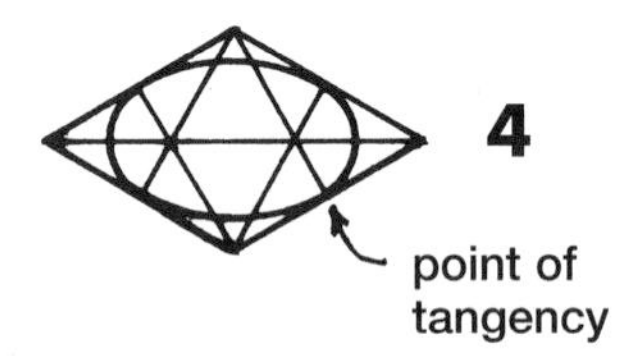

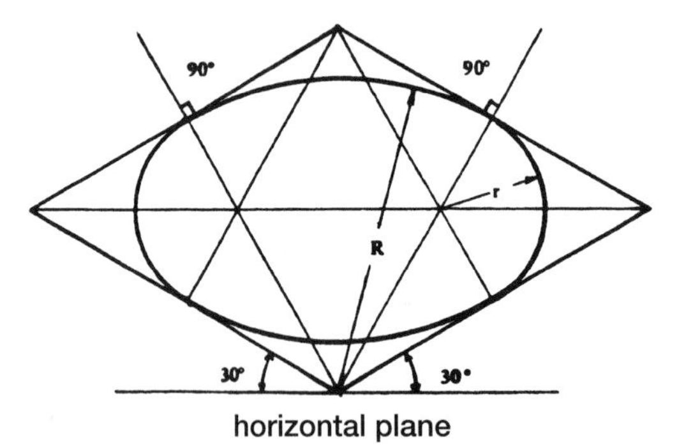

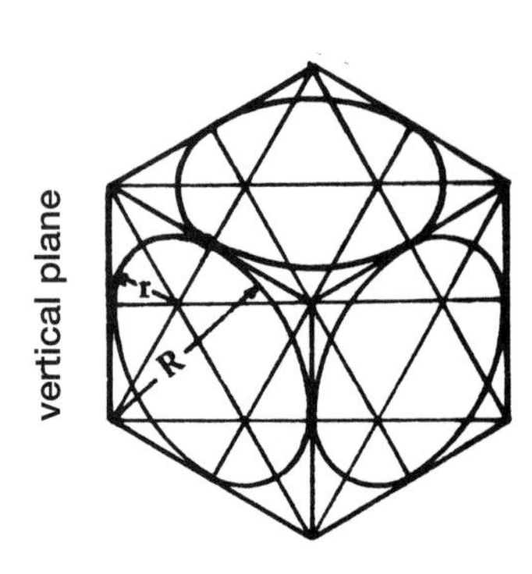

Procedure for the Four-Center Ellipse

1. Draw an isometric square using the desired circle's diameter.
2. Find adjacent side midpoints. Large radius **R** has two centers at the closest corners of the parallelogram. The intersections of the perpendiculars to both opposite sides determines the terminal points of the arc.
3. Construct the arcs.
4. Small radius **r** has two centers at the intersections of the perpendiculars within the parallelogram. These small arcs meet the large arcs to complete the ellipse.

The entire construction can be made with a T-square and 30° × 60° triangle. The same procedure applies for circles in both vertical planes and horizontal planes.

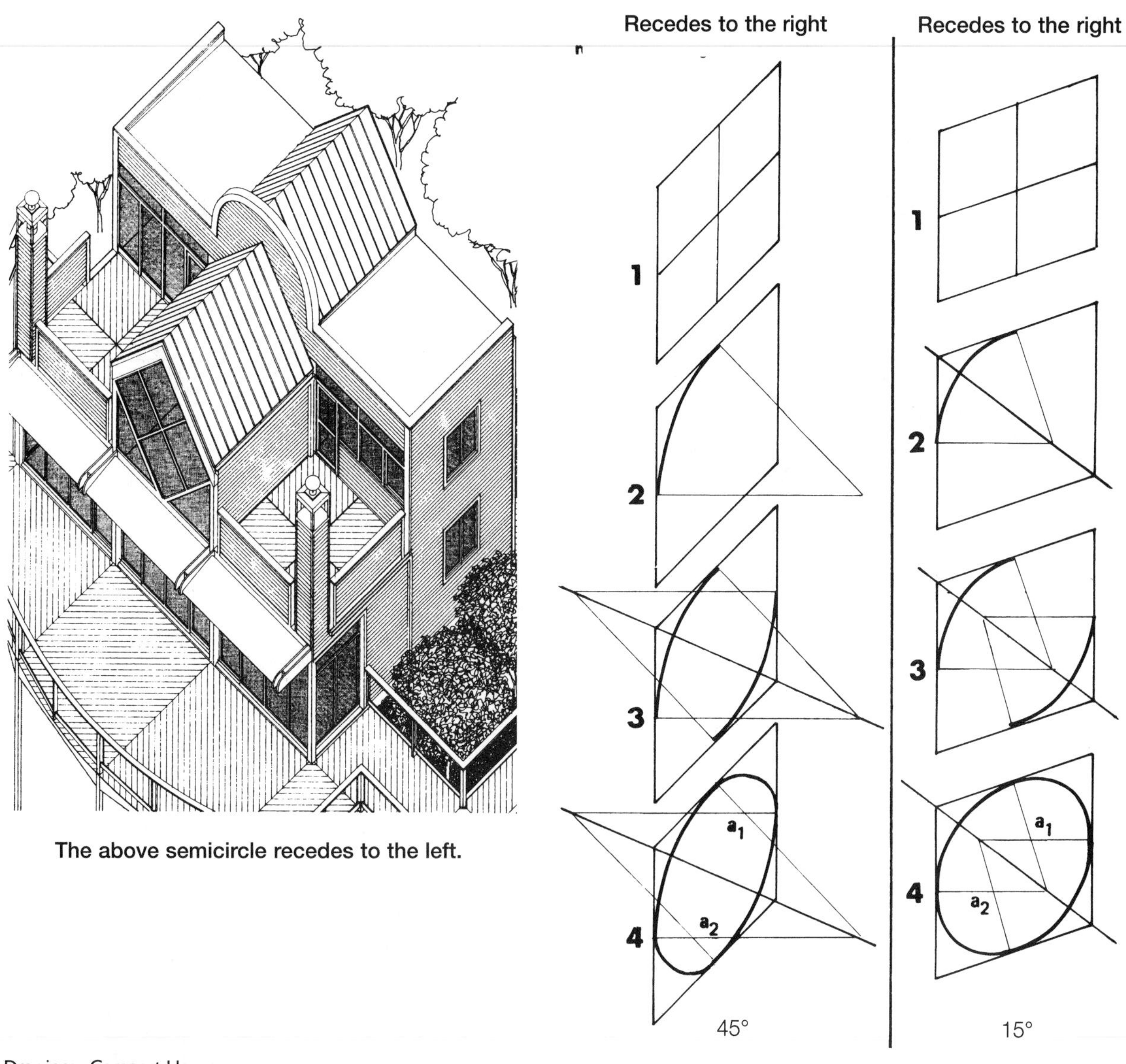

The above semicircle recedes to the left.

Drawing: Compact House,
Bayview, Lake Pend Oreille, Idaho
18" × 24" (45.7 × 61 cm), Scale: ¼=1'0"
Medium: Ink on vellum
Courtesy of David A. Harris, DHT² Architects & Planners
Reprinted from *New Compact House Designs*, edited by Don Metz, with permission of Storey Communications/Garden Way Publishing, Pownal, Vermont.

The four-center ellipse method shown on the previous page applies to non-30°–30° axonometric circles in left and right receding vertical planes only. Note that in the horizontal plane, circles are seen in true shape.

1. Draw a paraline square.
2. Find adjacent side midpoints and construct intersecting perpendiculars. The intersection becomes an arc center.
3. Repeat the process for a symmetrical mirror-image arc on the opposite side.
4. Using points $\mathbf{a_1}$ and $\mathbf{a_2}$, complete smaller arcs to accomplish the total axonometric circle.

PLAN OBLIQUE HORIZONTAL CIRCLES

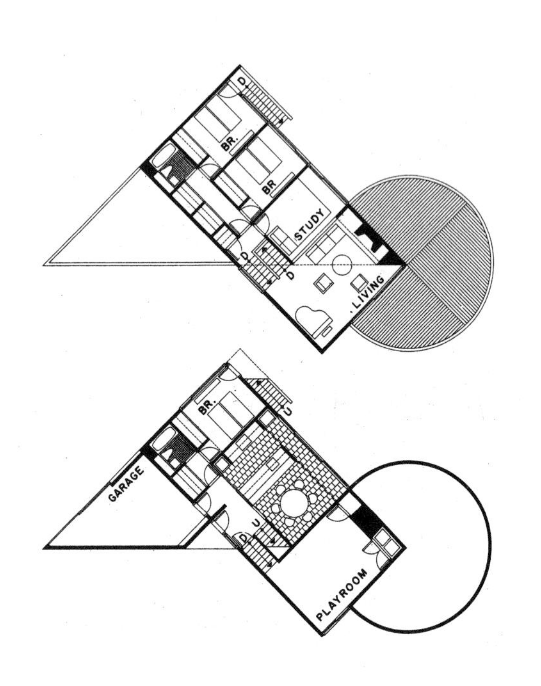

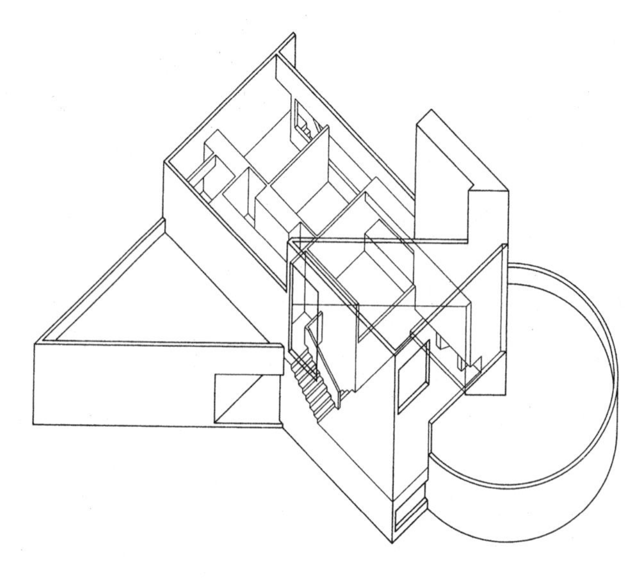

Drawings: House, Oldfield, New York
13.5" × 15.5" (34.3 × 39.4 cm), Scale: 1/4"=1'0"
Medium: Ink
Courtesy of Hobart D. Betts, Architect

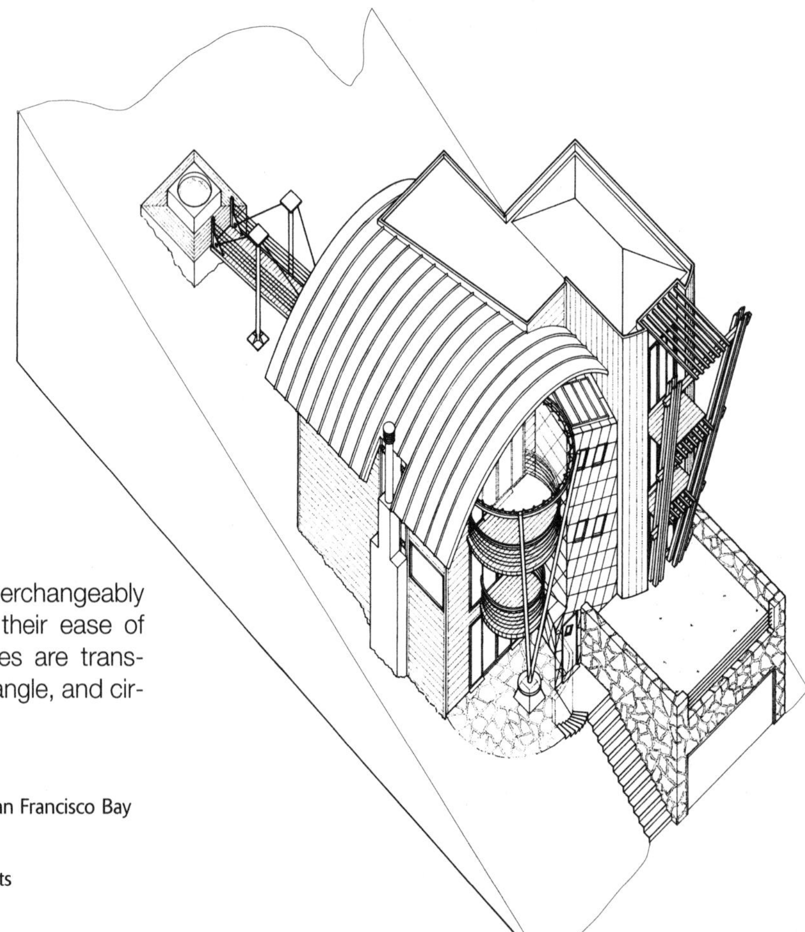

The popularity of plan obliques (interchangeably termed axonometrics) is due to their ease of construction. All geometric shapes are transferred true size (note triangle, rectangle, and circle above).

Drawing: Schuh Box (unbuilt), hills above San Francisco Bay
11" × 17" (27.9 × 43.2 cm), Scale: 1/8"=1'0"
Medium: Ink on trace
Courtesy of David Baker Associates Architects

Drawings: Meyer residence, Malibu, California
Both 24" × 36" (61 × 91.4 cm), Scale: ¼"=1'0"
Medium: Ink on Mylar
Courtesy of Gwathmey Siegel & Associates, Architects

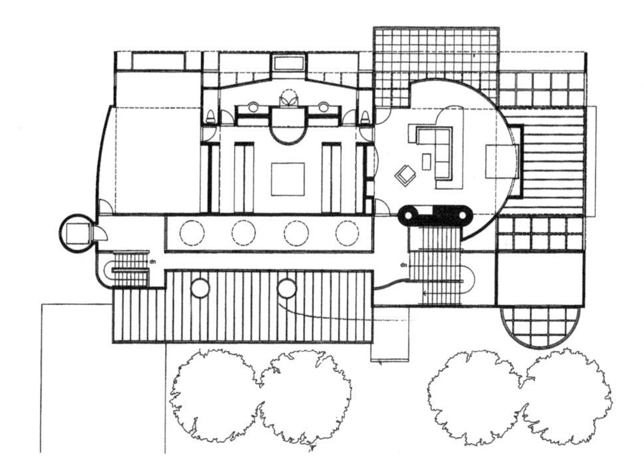

In the plan view and the plan oblique view, sometimes geometric solids are shortened (truncated) by cutting off a part. The truncated semicylinder in the above design has a circle that will appear true shape in neither the plan view (foreshortened) nor the plan oblique view. The circle must always be in the horizontal plane to be true shape in the plan view.

Regardless of the axes angles combination, **circles** and other curvilinear forms in horizontal planes retain their **true size** and **shape** in the plan oblique because the plan view is a true-shape view.

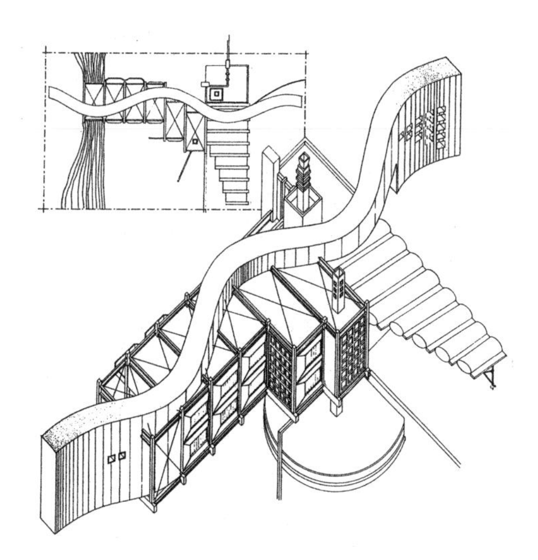

Drawing: Student project by John Crump
Dwelling with a Bridge
Medium: Ink on Mylar
M. Saleh Uddin, Professor,
Savannah College of Art and Design, Savannah, Georgia;
Southern University, Baton Rouge, Louisiana

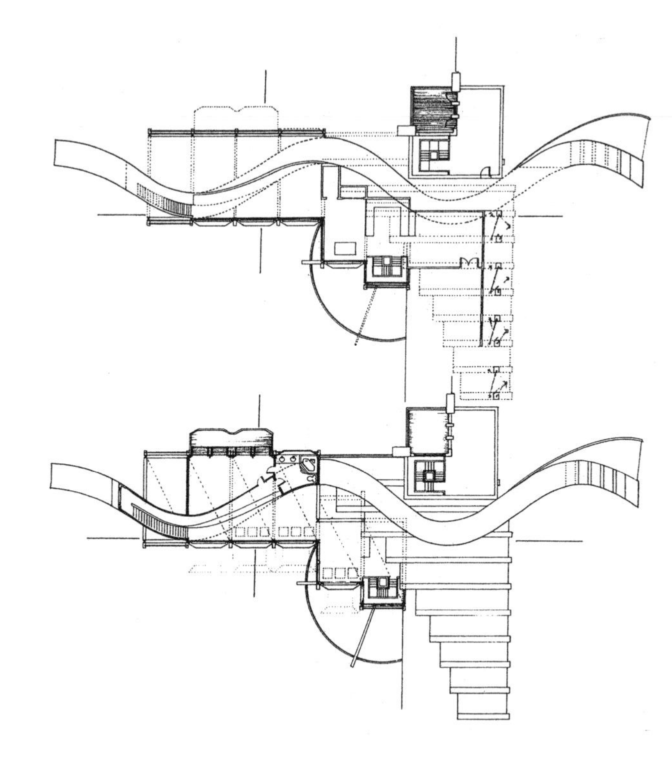

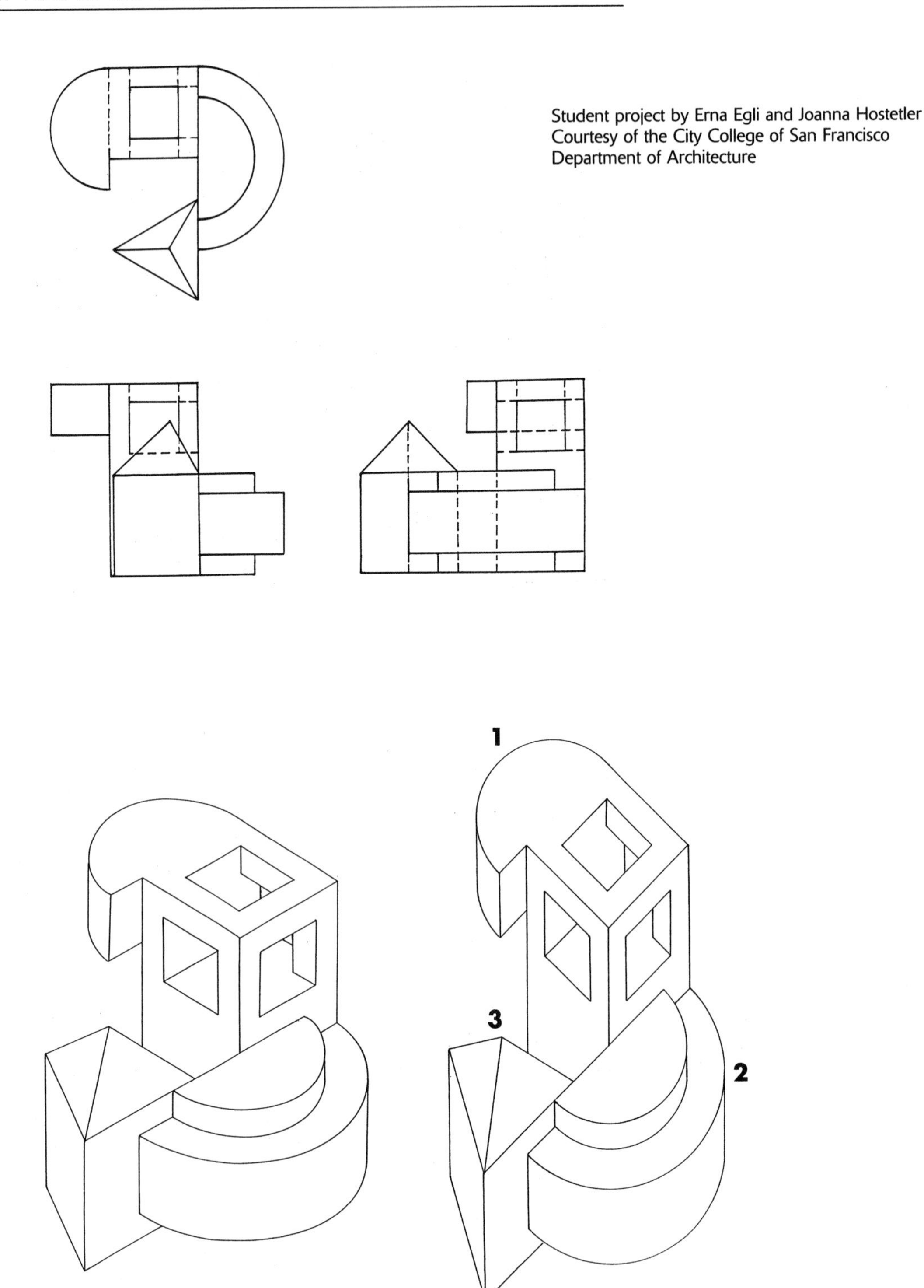

Student project by Erna Egli and Joanna Hostetler
Courtesy of the City College of San Francisco
Department of Architecture

In complex paraline drawings the order of construction can vary, but in general subordinate forms like **1** and **2** are commonly constructed as an addition to the primary form (square-shaped element). Note that the pyramid form **3** shown in this design has three non-axial lines. See if you can identify them. Linear lines in paraline drawings must either be **axial** (parallel to one of the three main axes) or **non-axial** (not parallel to any of the three main axes). When there are nonlinear elements in a design, such as circular and curvilinear shapes, these elements are frequently constructed last. Plan oblique circles, as well as plan oblique curvilinear forms, are always projected upward to their true elevation heights.

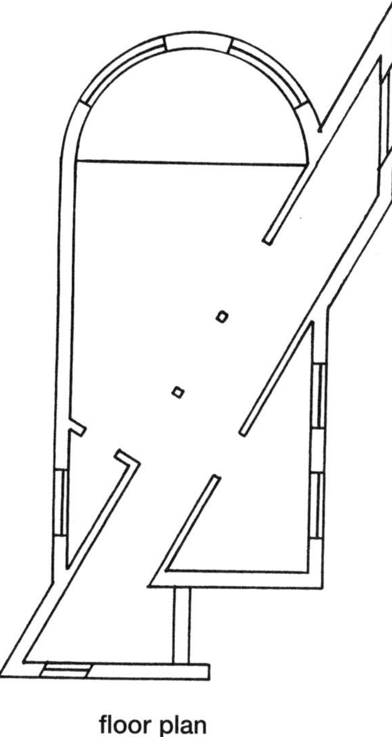

floor plan

Drawings: House, Austin, Texas
Courtesy of Kwok Gorran Tsui, an architecture graduate of the University of Texas at Austin

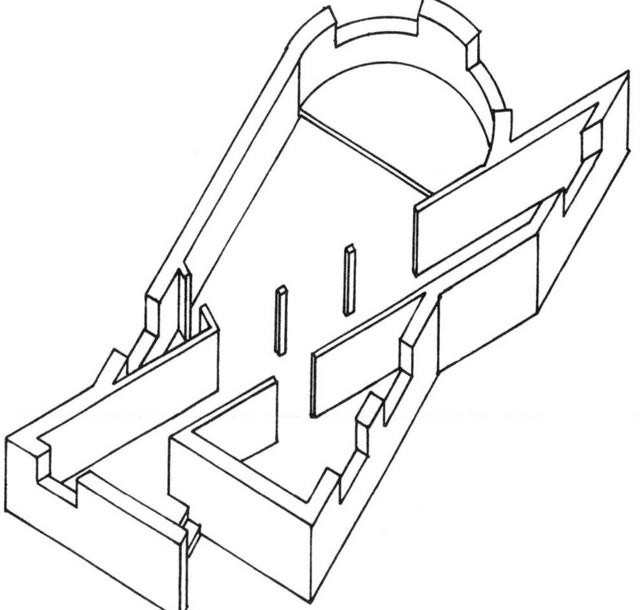

For interior spaces:

1. Access the scaled plan view.
2. Choose desired axes angles.
3. Construct scaled vertical lines to a desired height that best reveal the interior spaces.
4. Construct the true-length horizontal lines.
5. Construct any nonlinear forms.
6. Complete the same procedure for additional axes angles.

When solid elements in a building form intersect at other than 90°, it results in more than one set of plan oblique axes angles. Construct the primary volume with its one set of axes angles first, and then construct secondary volumes.

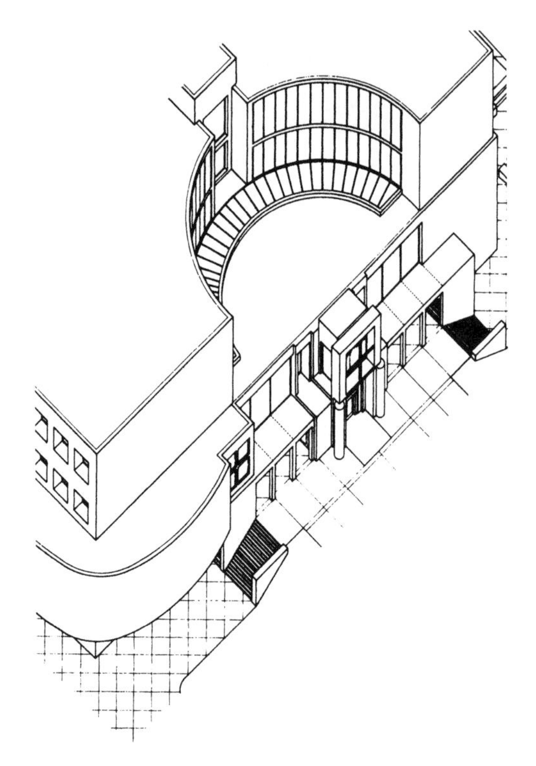

Drawing: Tallahassee City Hall, Tallahassee, Florida
24" × 36" (61 × 91.4 cm), Scale: 1/16"=1'0"
Medium: Ink on tracing paper
Courtesy of Heery International, Inc.

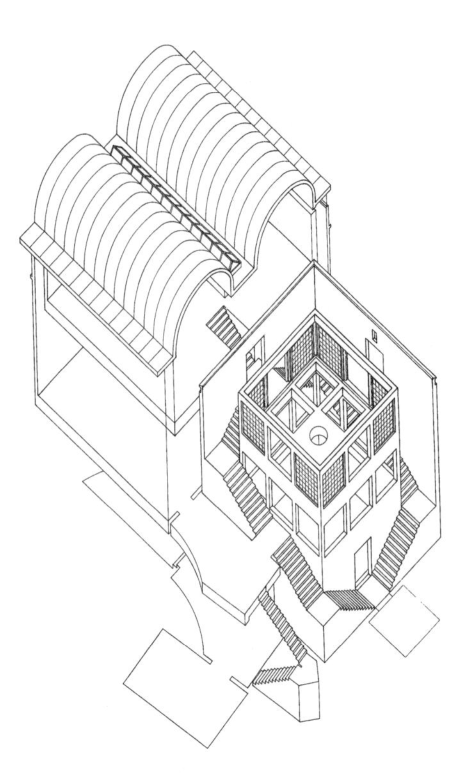

Drawing: Whanki Museum, Seoul, Korea
18" × 24" (45.7 × 61 cm), Scale 1:500
Medium: Ink on vellum
Courtesy of Kyu Sung Woo, Architect

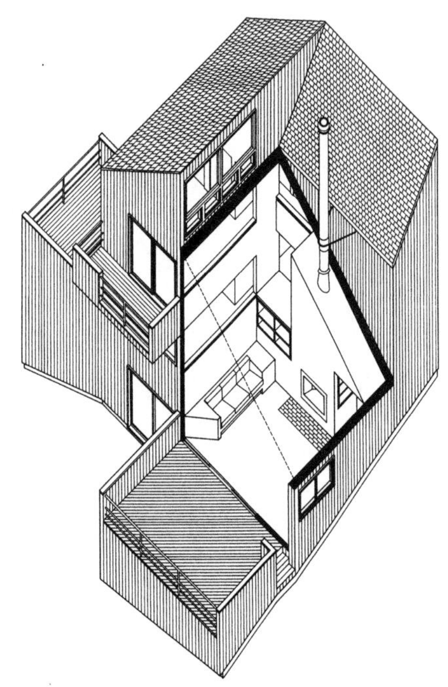

Drawing: Dattelbaum house
Kezar Lake, Center Lovell, Maine
18" × 23" (45.7 × 58.4 cm), Scale: 1/4"=1'0"
Medium: Ink on Mylar
Courtesy of Solomon & Bauer Architects Inc.

Plan obliques are commonly drawn with axes angles of 30°–60°, 60°–30°, and 45°–45°. The plan in its true shape can be quickly transferred to construct the oblique drawings. The observer's vantage point appears higher than in an isometric drawing. These plan obliques use axes angles of **45°–45°**. Facade details show equally well on either receding axis. Roof configurations and interior spaces are also clearly seen. Partial roof cutaways help to focus on the interior spaces. Detail on a nonlinear facade will show especially well (upper left). Obliques lack the size diminishment characteristic of perspectives and thus have the advantage of retaining size, detail, and information.

A dashed line indicates the volume removed in the Dattelbaum house (left). A line with short dashes or a very thin line (see p. 150, left drawing) is the accepted way of showing the **cutaway** portion that is removed.

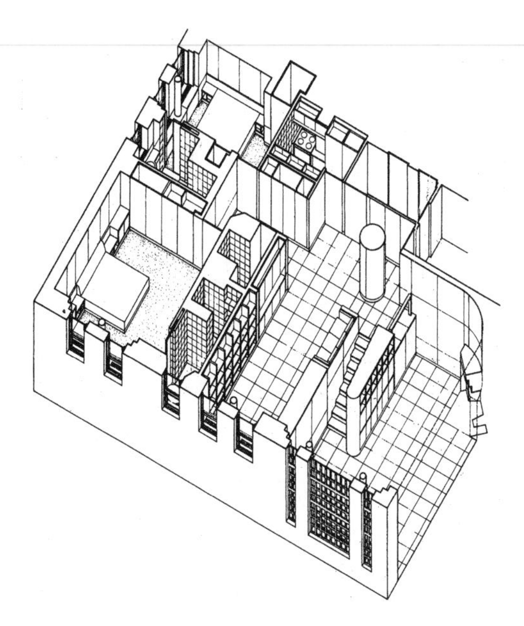

Drawing: Manhattan pied-à-terre, New York City
24" × 36" (61 × 91.4 cm), Scale: ¼"= 1'0"
Medium: Ink on Mylar
Courtesy of Gwathmey Siegel & Associates, Architects

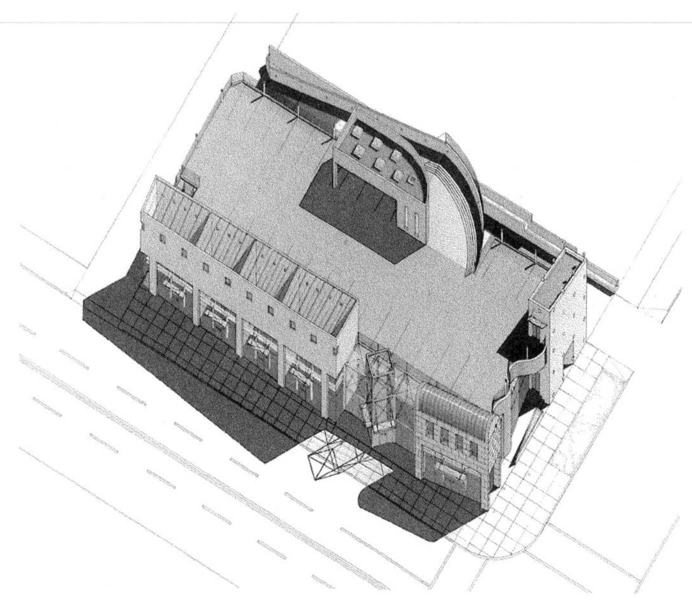

Drawing: Montana Collection, Santa Monica, California
24" × 36" (61 × 91.4 cm), Scale: ¼ = 1'0"
Medium: Ink on Mylar with Zipatone
Courtesy of Kanner Architects

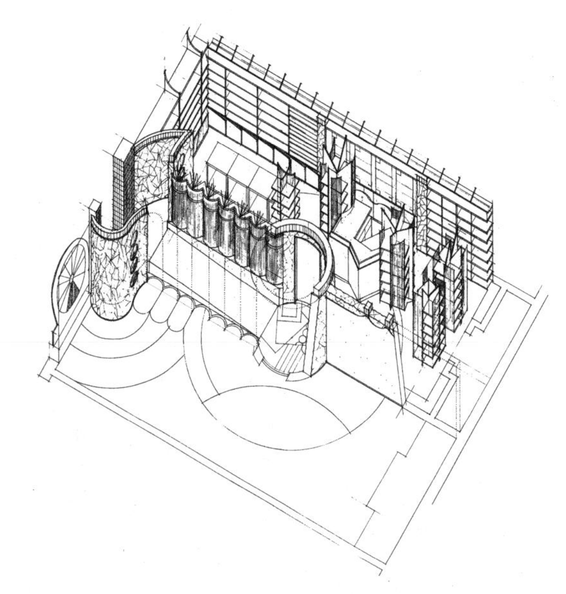

Drawing: Contemporary Arts Center Bookstore and Artware
Cincinnati, Ohio
24" × 36" (61 × 91.4 cm), Scale ½"=1'0"
Medium: Pencil on vellum
Courtesy of Terry Brown Architect

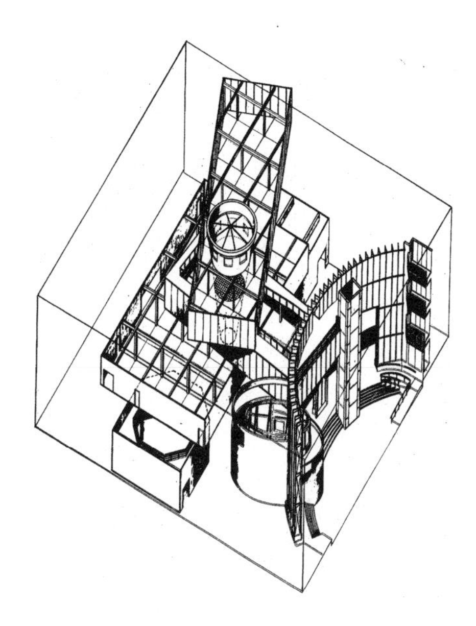

Drawing: Contemporary Arts Center
New Orleans, Louisiana
30" × 40" (76.2 × 101.6 cm), Scale: 1/16"=1'0"
Medium: Plastic lead on Mylar
Courtesy of Concordia Architects, New Orleans, Louisiana

These plan obliques use axes angles of **30°–60°**. This orientation allows the observer to clearly see interior spaces or roof configurations. Usually the 30° receding facade receives the most emphasis. However, if the facade is not linear, as with the New Orleans Arts Center, then a 60° receding axis can show the more detailed facade. The Cincinnati Arts Center, above, and the Whanki Museum on the facing page show how the interior anatomy of a building can be further revealed by dissecting it both horizontally and vertically—combining two or more section cuts. The Cincinnati building, as with previous cutaway isometric examples (see p. 137, top), shows how cutaway plan obliques can also reveal a partial footprint (plan view).

PLAN OBLIQUES — 60°-30° AXES ANGLES

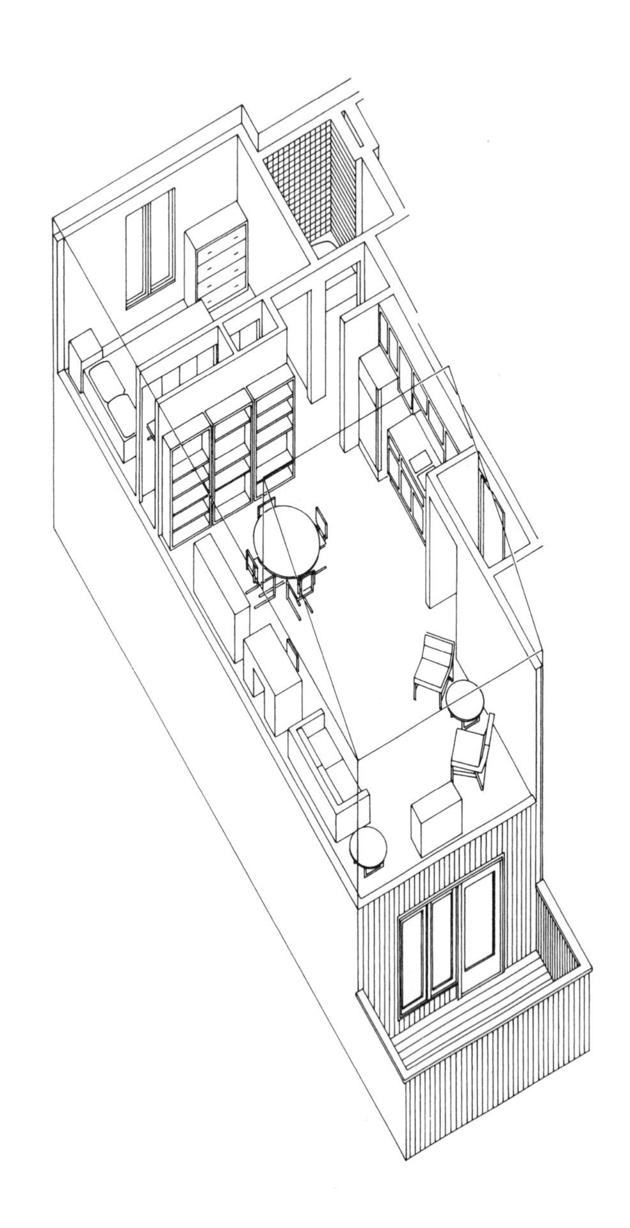

Drawing: Married student housing, University of Alaska Fairbanks, Alaska
11" × 17" (27.9 × 43.2 cm), Scale: ¼"=1'0"
Medium: Ink on Mylar
Courtesy of Hellmuth, Obata, and Kassabaum, Architects

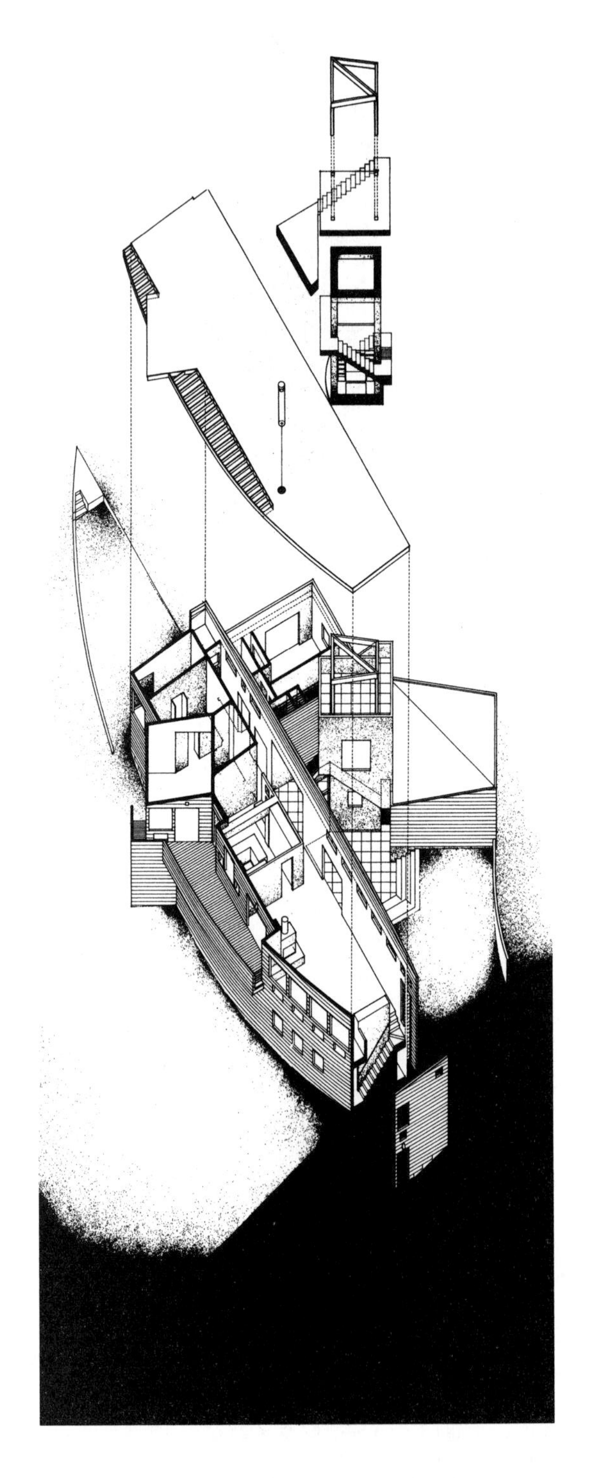

Drawing: Waldhauer residence, Woodside, California
20" × 48" (50.8 × 121.9 cm), Scale: ¼"=1'0"
Medium: India ink and airbrush on Mylar
Courtesy of House + House, Architects
Mark David English, Architectural Illustrator

These plan obliques use axes angles of **60°–30°**. Normally the 30° receding facade is emphasized. However, a lot of detail can be shown on the 60° receding facade if part of it is nonlinear. All built-in and movable furniture pieces retain their verticality and true heights (see p. 412). The 60°–30° axes angles allow the observer to see the interior spaces clearly when the roof and parts of both side elevations are removed.

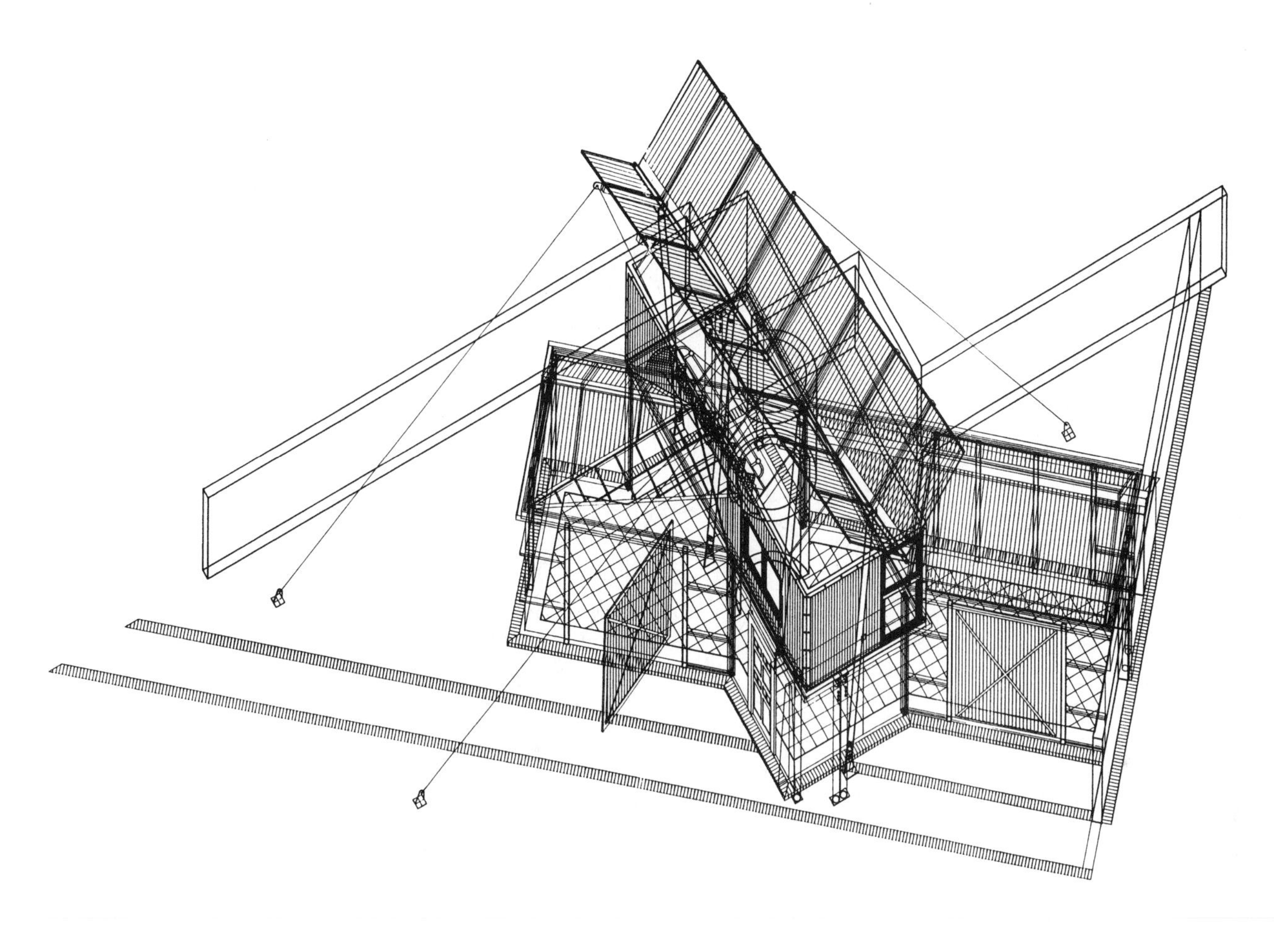

Drawing: Studio, The Ivy Villa, Pretoria, South Africa
400 × 300 mm (15.7" × 11.8"), Scale: 1:100
Medium: Ultimate CAD program
Drawn by Ian Thompson
Courtesy of Ora Joubert, Architect

This drawing has one structure with axes angles of 9°–81° and another structure with axes angles of 60°–30°. The intersection of solid elements will always require two (dual) or more sets of plan oblique axes angles. Note that the structure with the 9°–81° orientation shows details on its 9° facade extremely well, whereas its 81° facade is barely visible. Also shown above are structural cables, which are not true length in the plan oblique. All drawn elements are relatively transparent. With the design of more high-tech buildings, the drawing of dual-axes and tri-axes plan oblique angles has become commonplace.

This multidirectional section cut draw-

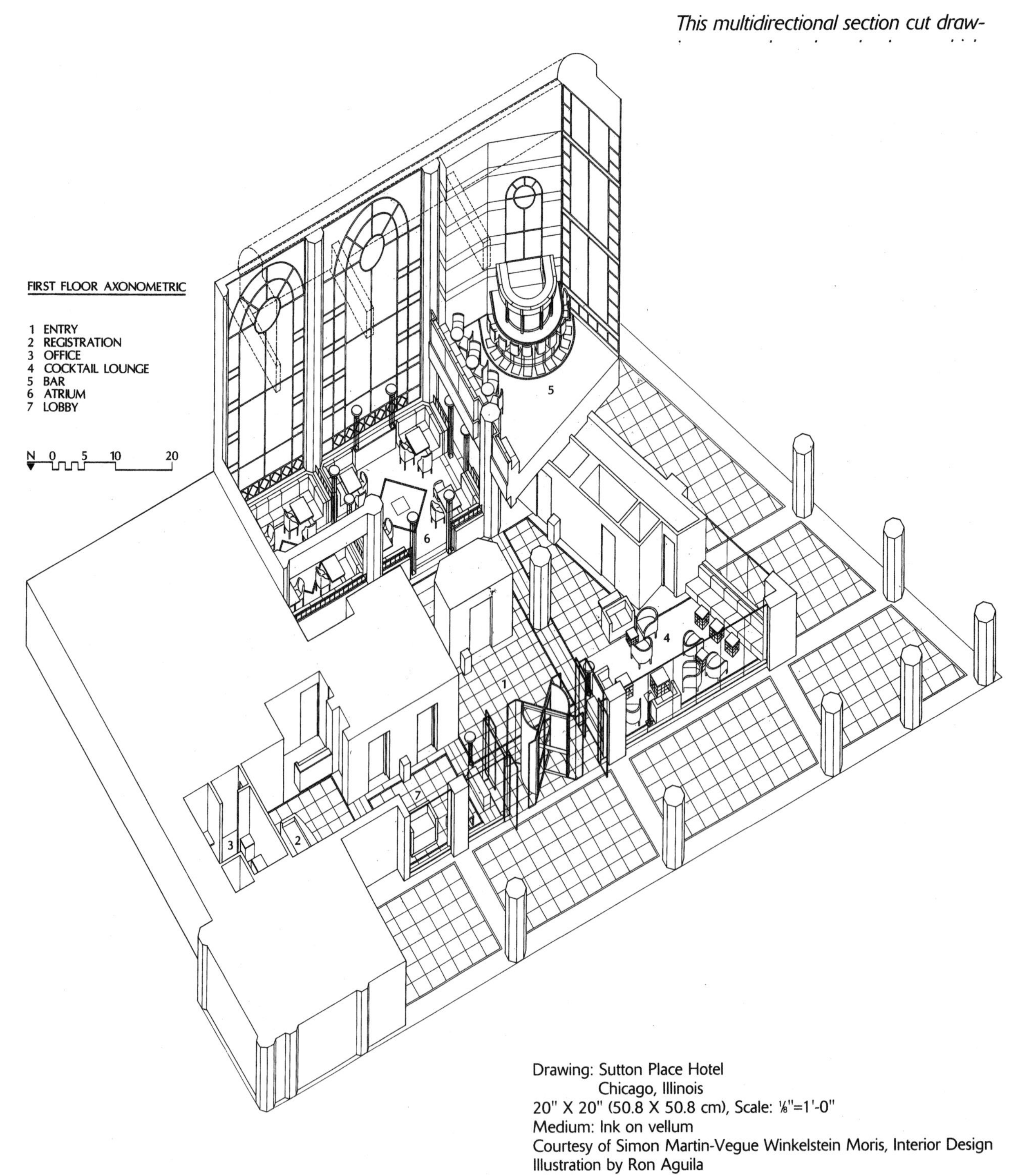

Drawing: Sutton Place Hotel
Chicago, Illinois
20" X 20" (50.8 X 50.8 cm), Scale: ⅛"=1'-0"
Medium: Ink on vellum
Courtesy of Simon Martin-Vegue Winkelstein Moris, Interior Design
Illustration by Ron Aguila

The interior anatomy of a building can be more clearly revealed by combining horizontal and vertical section cuts in plan oblique.

This composite drawing enables the professional viewer to reach an understanding of the three-dimensional relationships among the objects. Elements of the architectural vocabulary show their clear interdependence in the total composition.
[ARCHITECT/INTERIOR DESIGNER'S STATEMENT]

Chicago, Illinois
20" X 20" (50.8 X 50.8 cm), Scale: 1/8"=1'-0"
Medium: Ink on vellum (dancers: paste-up image)
Courtesy of Simon Martin-Vegue Winkelstein Moris Interior Design

PLAN OBLIQUES — INCREMENTAL GROWTH

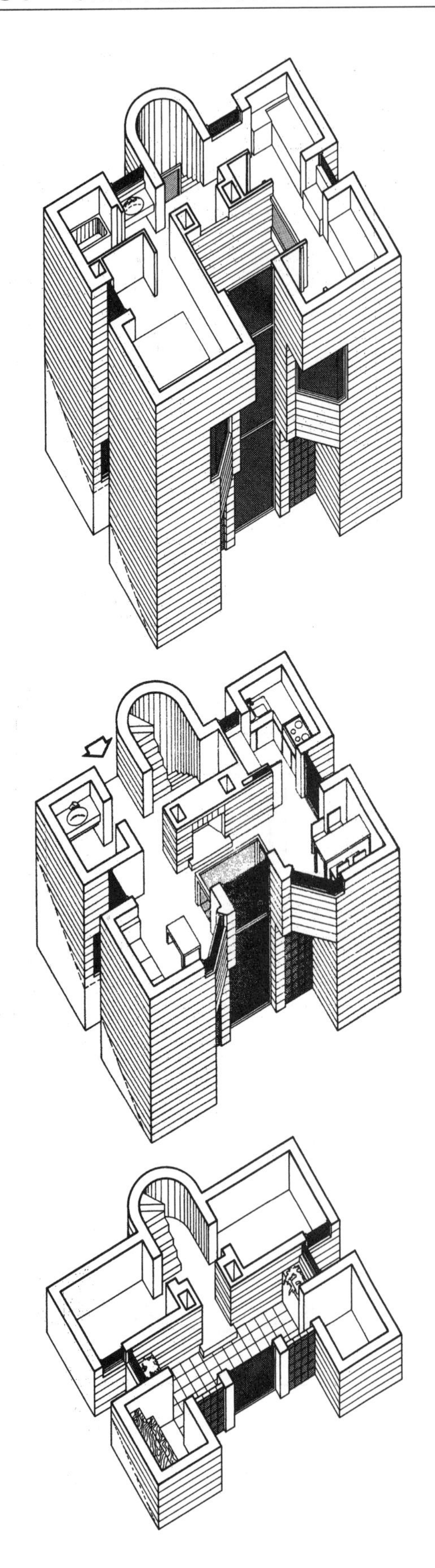

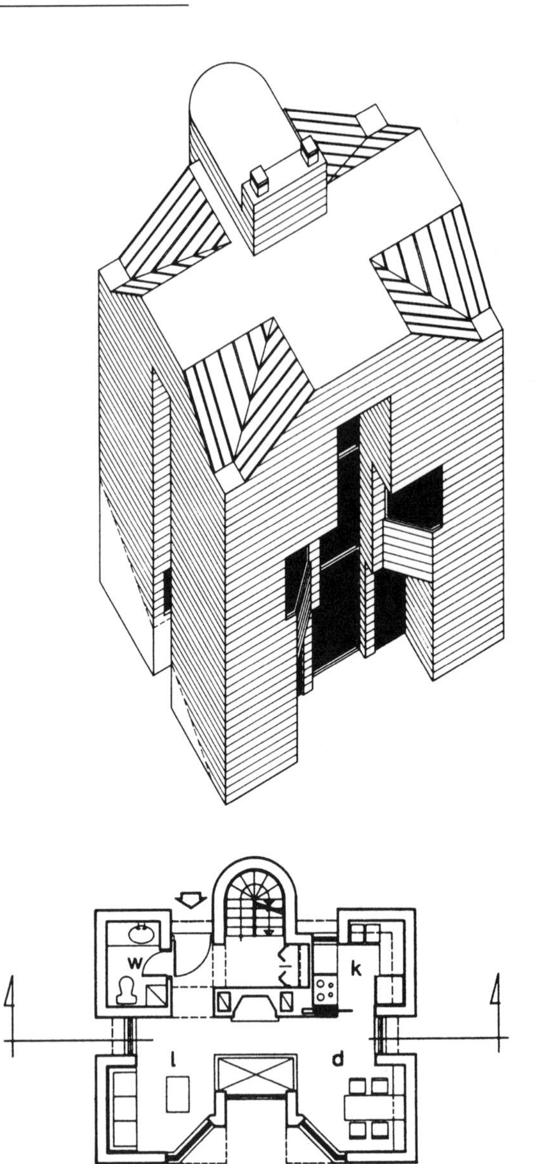

For multistory building types, the plan oblique can be effectively used for showing an **incremental growth** (layering) sequence of floor levels. Growth can begin with the first-floor plan shown at the ground plane or it can begin a few feet or meters above the ground plane, as in this example and the one on the following page. These drawings become an efficacious visual means of conveying how the entire building shell relates to the interior spaces.

Drawings: One-family prototype house, Toronto, Ontario, Canada
Courtesy of G. Nino Rico and Giancarlo Garofalo
Reprinted from *The Compact House Book*, edited by Don Metz with permission of Storey Communications/Garden Way Publishing, Pownal, Vermont.

Plan obliques illustrating incremental growth can clarify details in plan view cuts taken at different locations. Axes angles of 45°–45° were used in the example to the right, whereas 60°–30° were used in the example on the facing page.

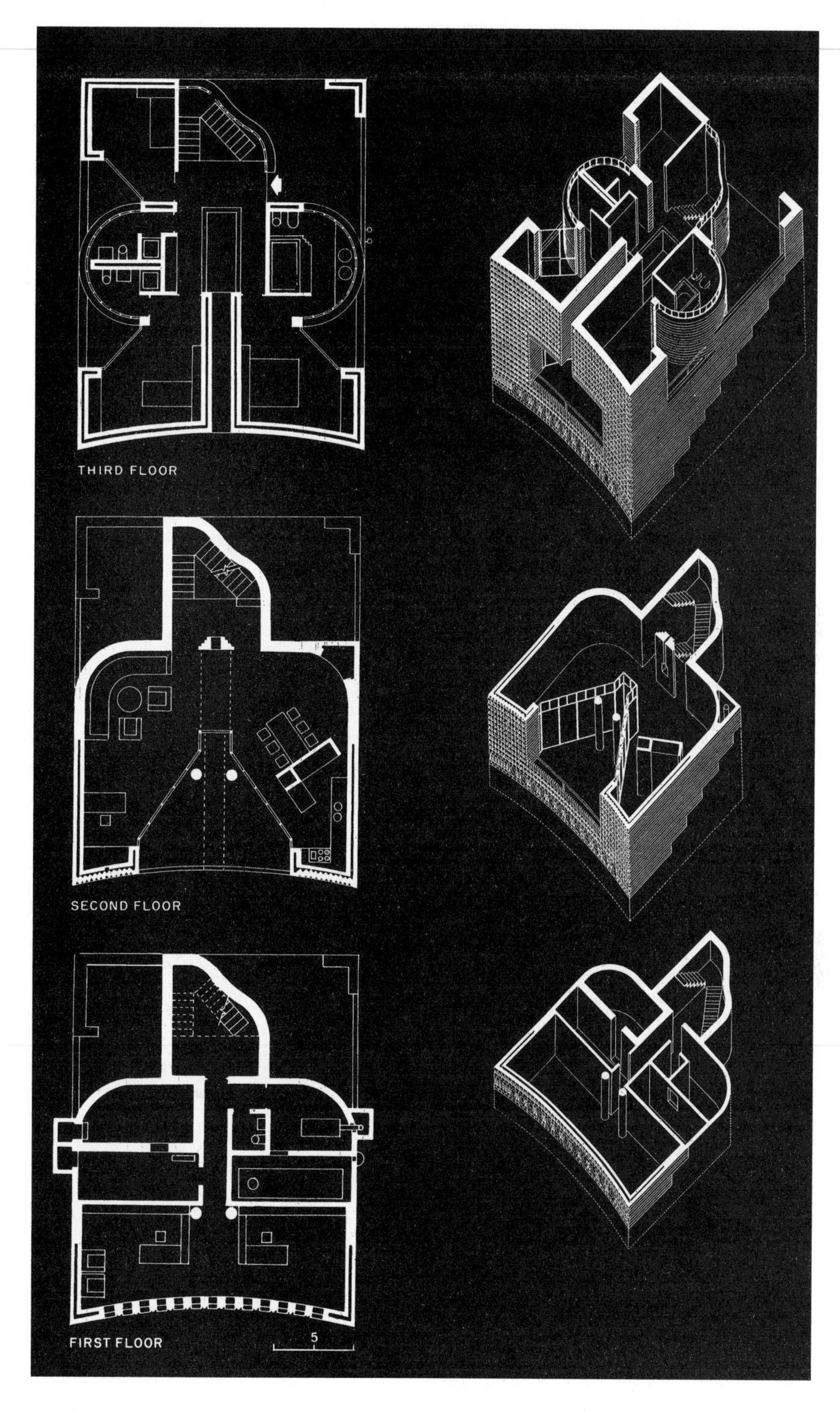

Drawings: Posteria residence, Morbio Superiore, Switzerland
Courtesy of Mario Botta, Architect, Lugano, Switzerland

PLAN OBLIQUES — NONVERTICAL Z-AXIS

A variation to the typical plan oblique is one in which the z-axis thrusts the vertical planes upward (most commonly at 45° or 60°) from the horizontal. This gives the observer a vantage point that is almost directly **overhead**. This method has the advantage of revealing more of the important horizontal planes. However, distortion appears greater than in the typical plan oblique.

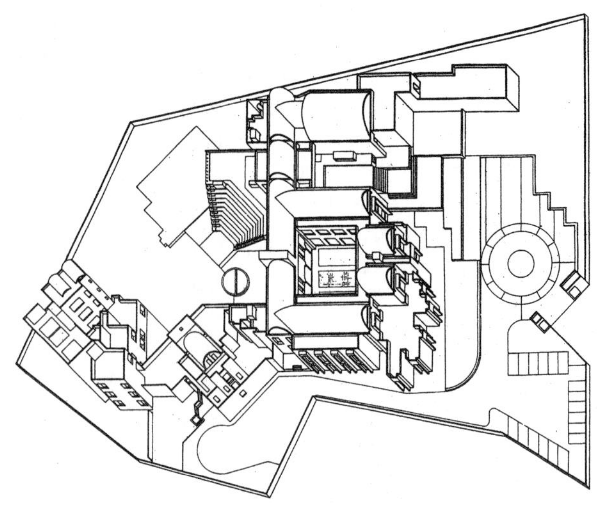

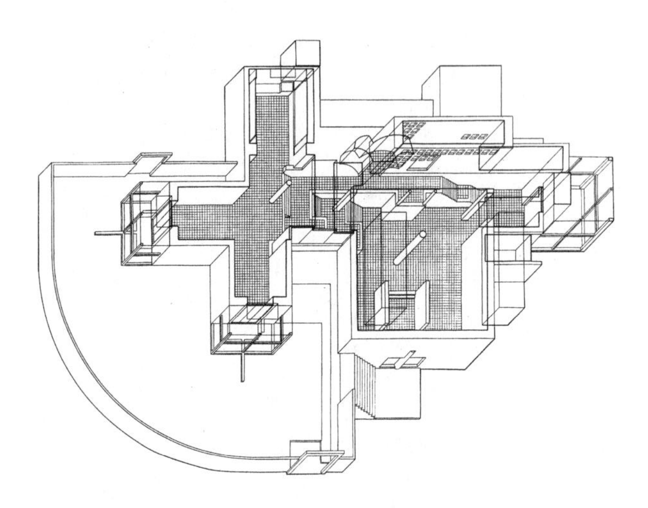

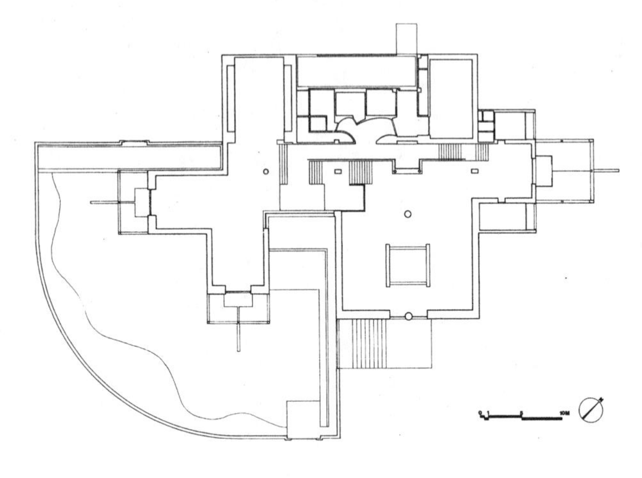

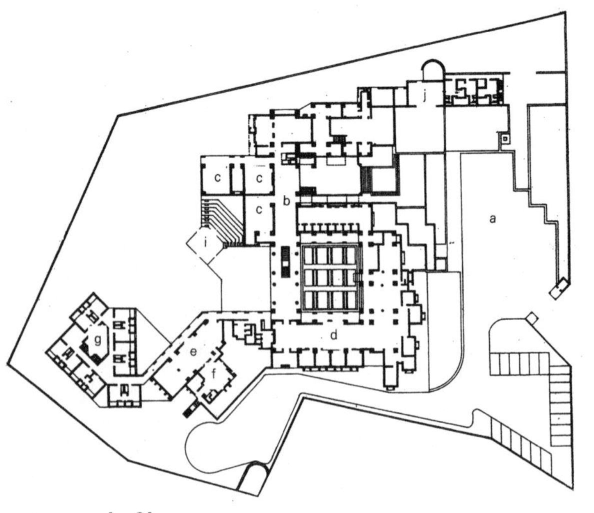

ground-floor plan

Drawing: Gandhi Labour Institute, Ahmedabad, Gujarat, India
26" × 39" (66 × 99 cm), Scale: 1:200
Medium: Ink on Gateway (tracing paper)
Courtesy of B.V. Doshi, Architect

Drawings: Iwasaki Art Museum, Kagoshima Prefecture, Kyushu, Japan
Axon: 23.2" × 16.9" (59 × 43 cm)
Plan: 28.3" × 19.7" (72 × 50 cm), Scale: 1:100
Medium: Ink on vellum
Courtesy of Fumihiko Maki and Associates, Architects

The plan oblique with a plan sectional cut (left) retains the plan geometric configuration better than does the plan oblique (above), which shows a site plan view of the roof configuration.

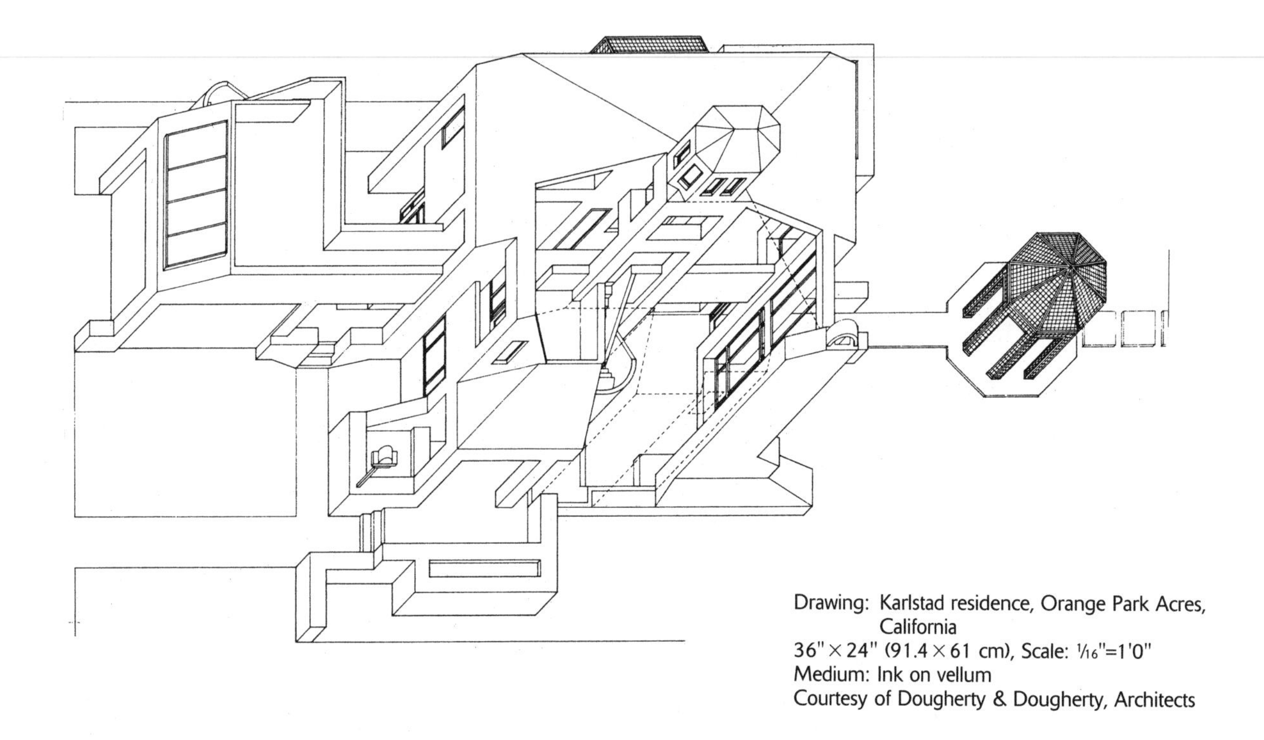

Drawing: Karlstad residence, Orange Park Acres, California
36" × 24" (91.4 × 61 cm), Scale: 1/16"=1'0"
Medium: Ink on vellum
Courtesy of Dougherty & Dougherty, Architects

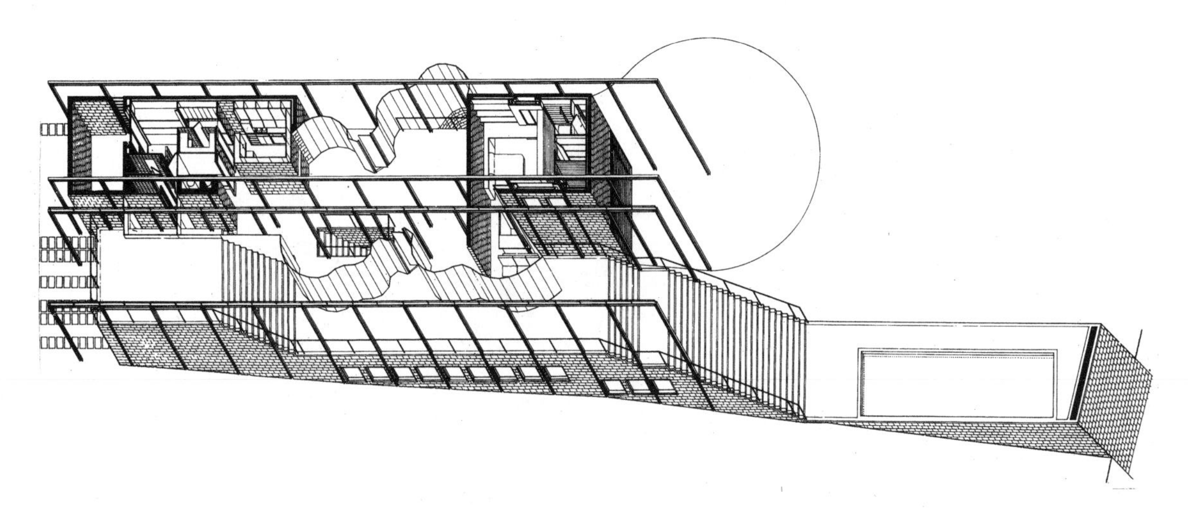

Drawing: Casa Canovelles, Granollers (Barcelona), Spain
26.4" × 54.3" (67 × 138 cm)
Medium: Ink on vellum paper
Courtesy of MBM Arquitectes
Josep Martorell, Oriol Bohigas, and David MacKay

The nonvertical z-axis can be swung either left or right of the vertical direction. These examples show that vantage points from either direction are equally effective: the choice is based on the viewing information to be conveyed.

Drawing: Curtis House (1988)
San Francisco, California
105/8" X 15" (27 X 38.1 cm), Scale: 1/4"=1'-0"
Medium: Pen, Rapidograph ink, and shading films
Courtesy of James Shay, AIA Architect

The primary spatial organization device in this house is the dark framework indicated in the drawing by line and shade. Secondary building elements, such as planes and shaded stairs, are indicated by line and film to establish context. [Architect's Statement]

Paraline drawings, more than any other type of drawing, can be utilized to explore a large number of viewpoints. Perspective drawing, although quite descriptive of pictorial depth, does not provide as many options. This page and the facing page, which shows stacked layers of floor plans, display just two of the many options and variations available for expressing a design with paraline oblique views.

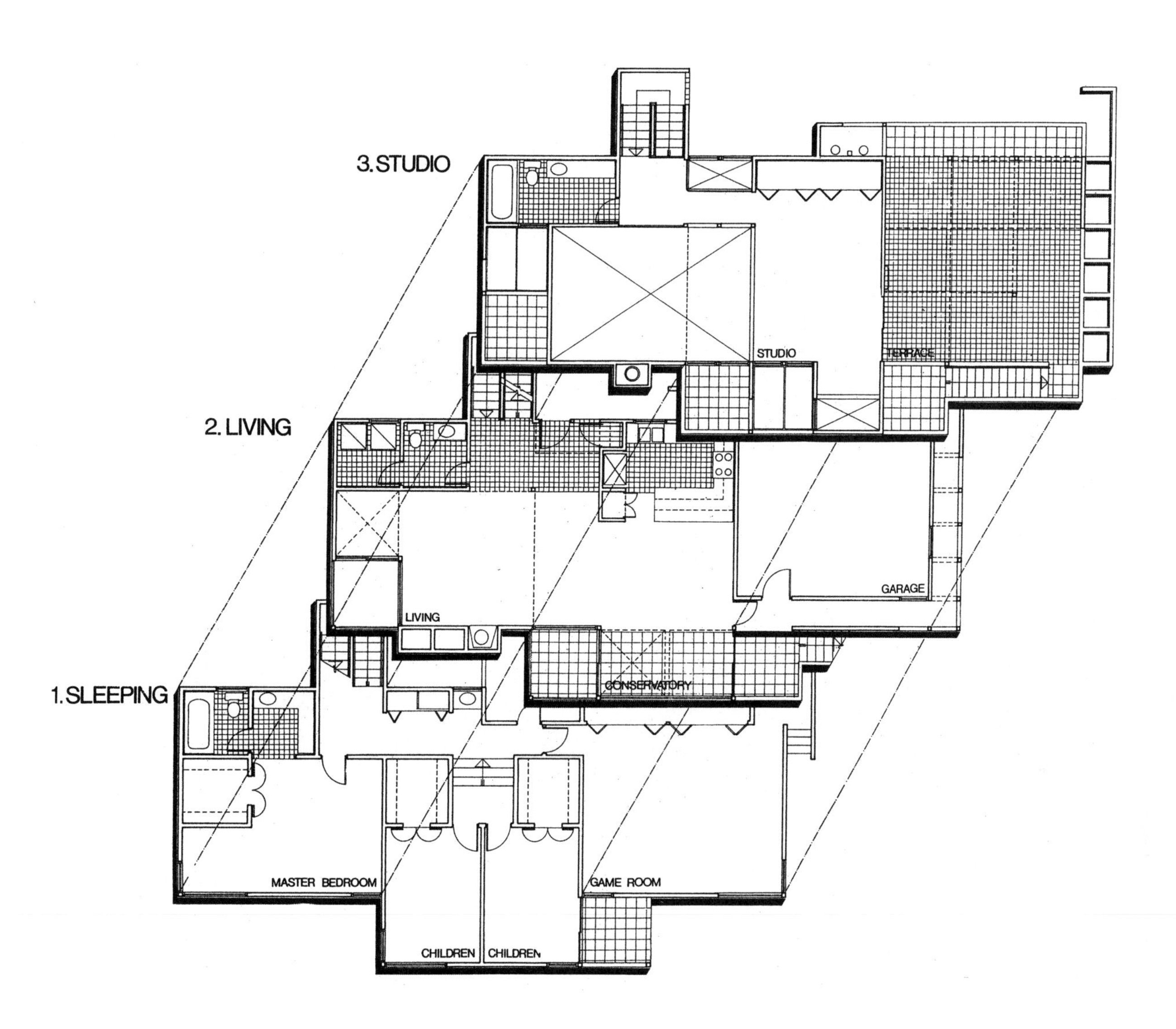

Drawing: Galor residence
Los Angeles, California
28" X 28" (71.1 X 71.1 cm), Scale: 1/4"=1'-0"
Medium: Ink
Courtesy of John V. Mutlow, FAIA, Architects

The stepped plans provide a direct interrelationship between the floors. The shaded edge of the floor identifies the service and outdoor areas and contrasts the private and public, all within the 6'-8" module and 20'-0" module.
[ARCHITECT'S STATEMENT]

Drawing: Villa dall'Ava, Paris, France
23.4" × 16.5" (59.5 × 41.8 cm)
Medium: Ink
Courtesy of Office for Metropolitan Architecture (OMA)

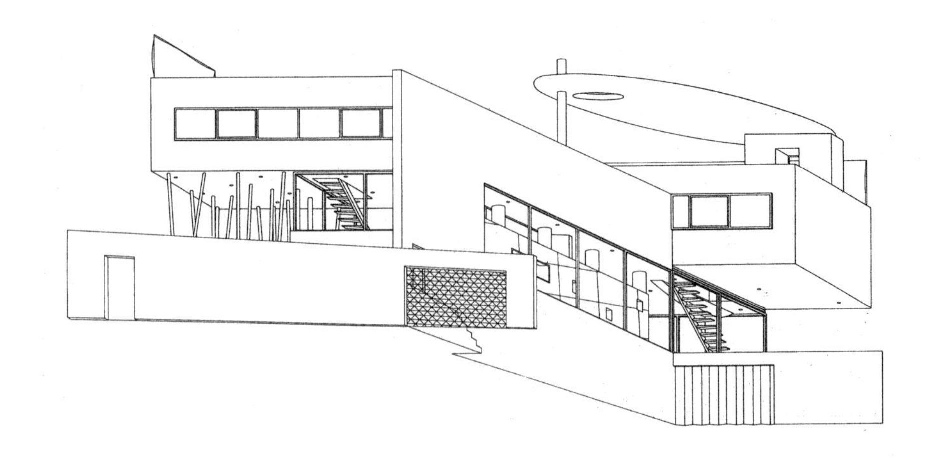

This elevation oblique of a house recedes down to the right. The result is a worm's-eye view looking up. Note that interior details can easily be seen through the receding facade.

Drawing: Boathouse, St. Andrew's School
Middletown, Delaware
18" × 6" (45.7 × 15.2 cm), Scale: ⅛"=1'0"
Medium: Technical pen
Drawing by Kim Haskell
Courtesy of Richard Conway Meyer, Architect

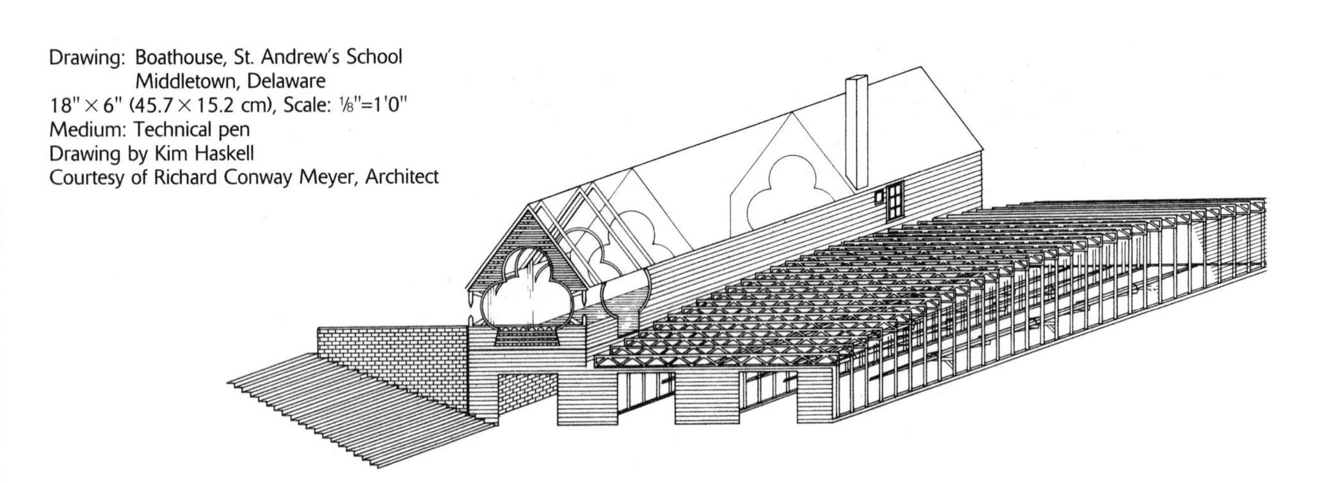

In most cases, elevation obliques recede up to the right or up to the left at a selected angle. Regular or irregular curvilinear forms are commonly seen in the true-size elevation. It is sometimes necessary to use a cutaway wall or a transparent oblique to reveal interior spaces.

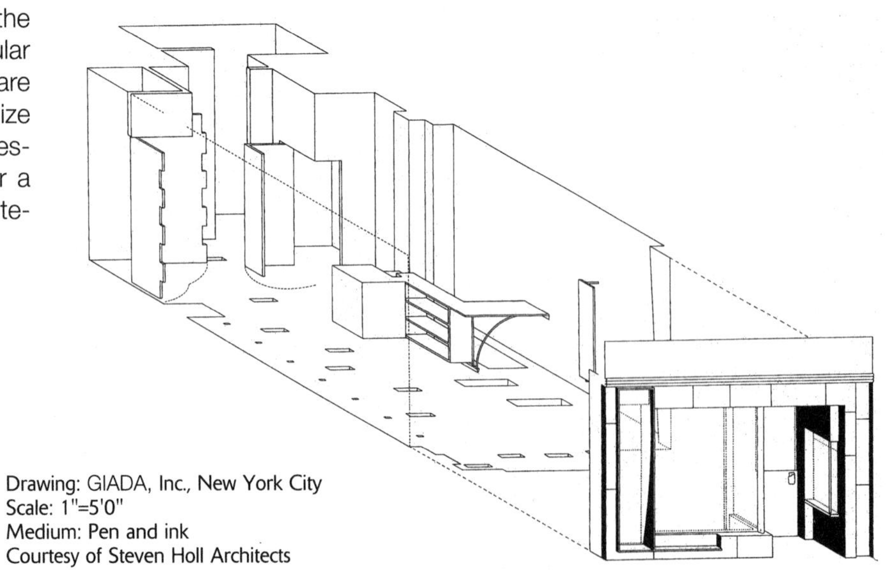

Drawing: GIADA, Inc., New York City
Scale: 1"=5'0"
Medium: Pen and ink
Courtesy of Steven Holl Architects

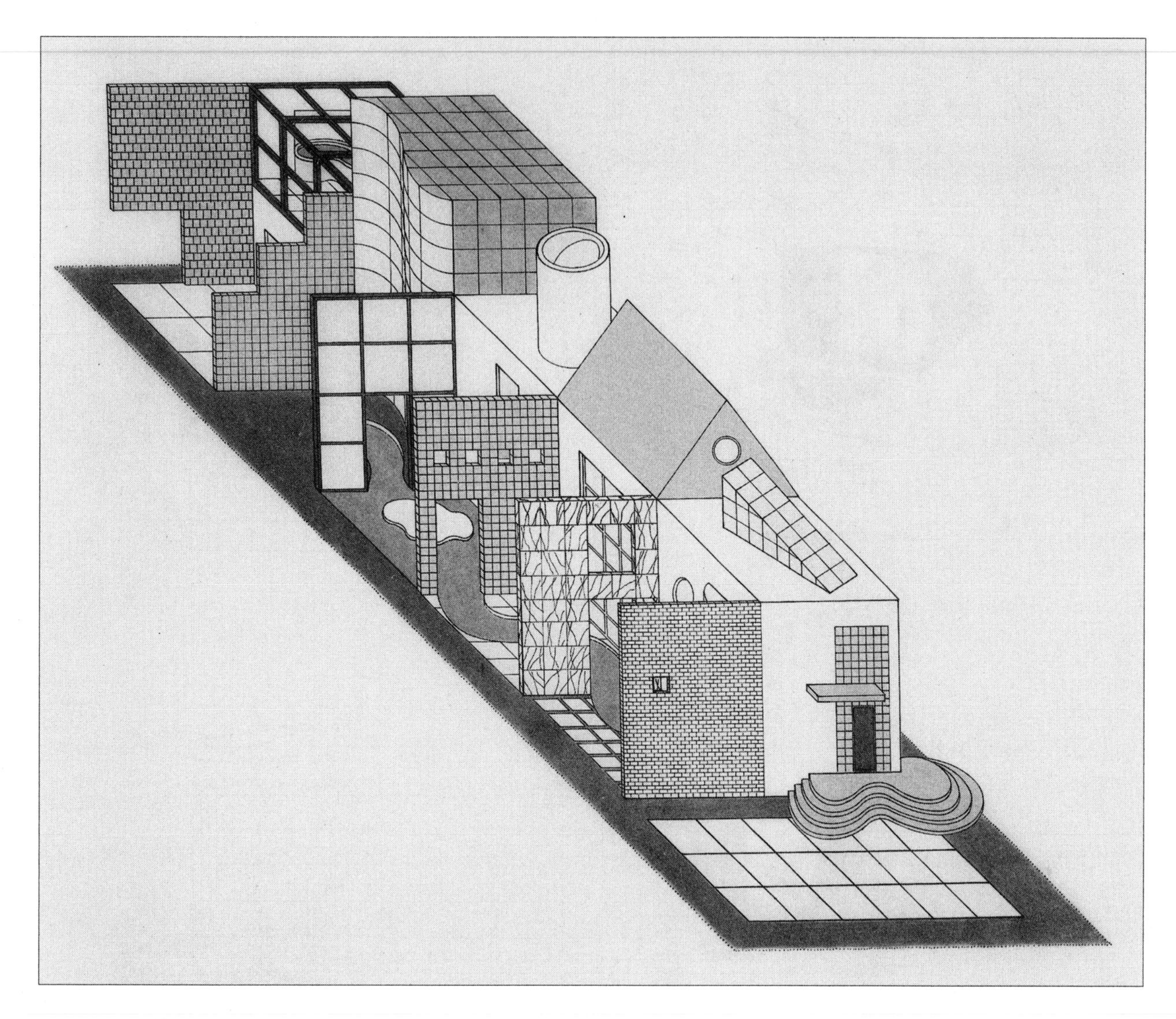

Drawing: Maba house, Houston, Texas
36" × 24" (91.4 × 61 cm)
Medium: Ink on Mylar
Courtesy of Arquitectonica International Corporation

This view was chosen because it best represented the whole house as a series of smaller cubes. The rendering was executed in 1982 on Mylar that was colored on the back. At that time this was typical of Arquitectonica's early visualization techniques. The design of the house was conceived as a series of five little houses, each with its own roof/light feature, court with walls, and different aspects of a continuous pool. The five units provide varied experiences in terms of texture, color, and light. The fenestrations vary and treat light differently within each cubic space. The courtyard of each house is varied and represents a totally unique experience within each. Water is the only element running through all of the various cubes.
[ARCHITECT'S STATEMENT]

This elevation oblique has its ground plane receding 45° to the left. It is not difficult to see why a frontal orientation was selected to best describe this house, with its numerous parallel elements of different complexities. An elevation oblique may or may not be foreshortened to avoid distortion, but a plan oblique is never foreshortened.

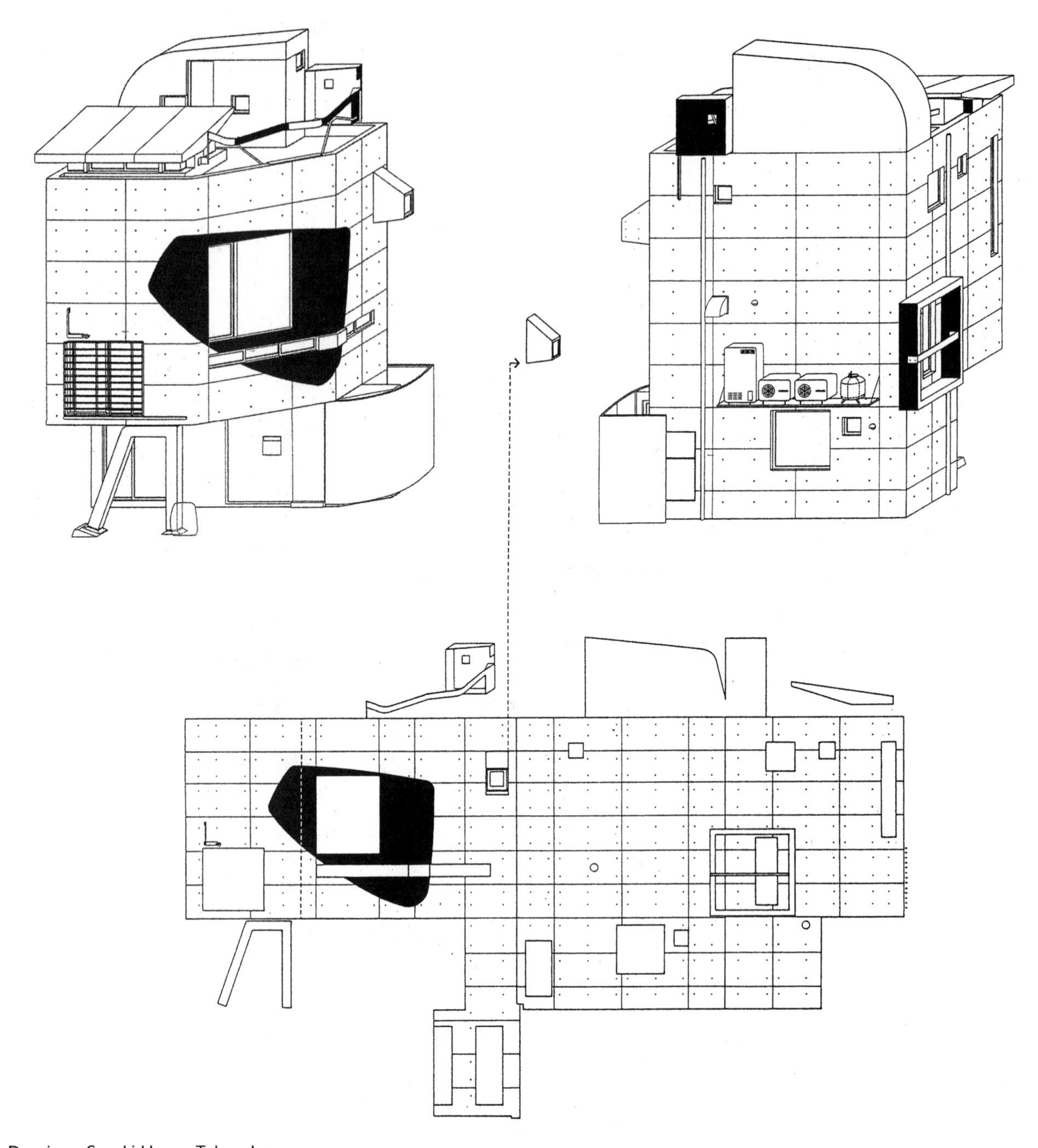

Drawings: Suzuki House, Tokyo, Japan
8.7" × 11" (22 × 28 cm), Scale: 1:30 (Japanese scale)
Medium: Ink on trace
Courtesy of Architekturbüro Bolles–Wilson + Partner

The elevation obliques above are geometrically correct in one elevation, preferable to axonometrics where the plan is true. But elevations do not show the building as experienced. In the foldout, the facade is one continuous pattern of concrete shuttering.
[ARCHITECT'S STATEMENT]

These two elevation obliques show all sides of this building, which also has its skin elevation completely unwrapped and laid out flat.

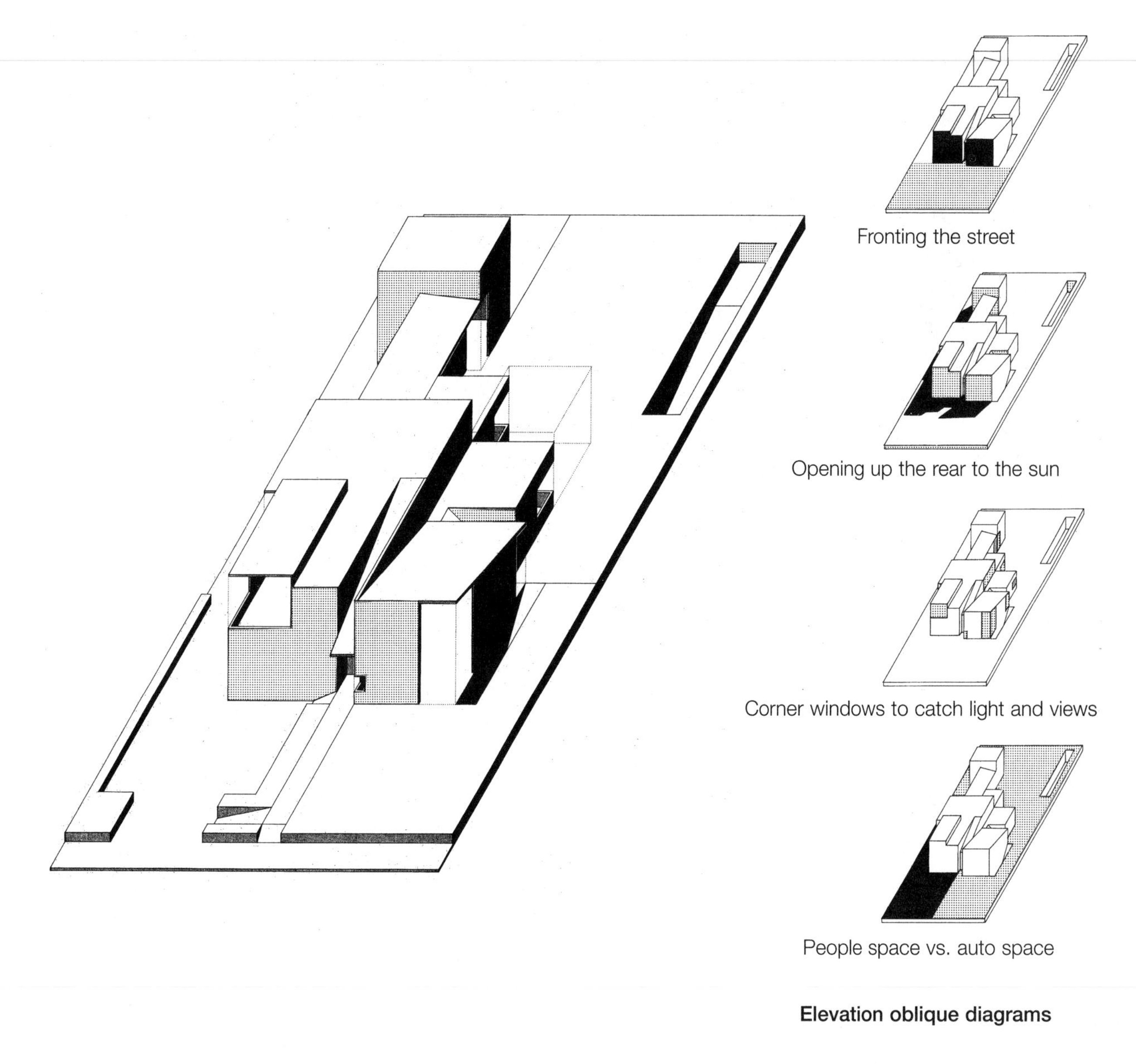

Fronting the street

Opening up the rear to the sun

Corner windows to catch light and views

People space vs. auto space

Elevation oblique diagrams

Drawing: Adelman/Llanos residence, Santa Monica, California
Medium: Ink
Courtesy of Mack Architects; Mark Mack, principal

Elevation obliques can be very effective in showing how the building design responds to various design parameters. This example shows a simple form repeated five times with an upward receding angle of 60° for the purpose of diagramming design concepts. Note the use of gray tone and black to express the parameters. The largest diagram expresses rooms as volume; in this drawing, vertical planes were toned black or gray to accentuate building components. Artificial toning can give the needed planar contrast to help enhance the understanding of a design, especially in cases where material texture is absent or not shown (see pp. 166 and 172).

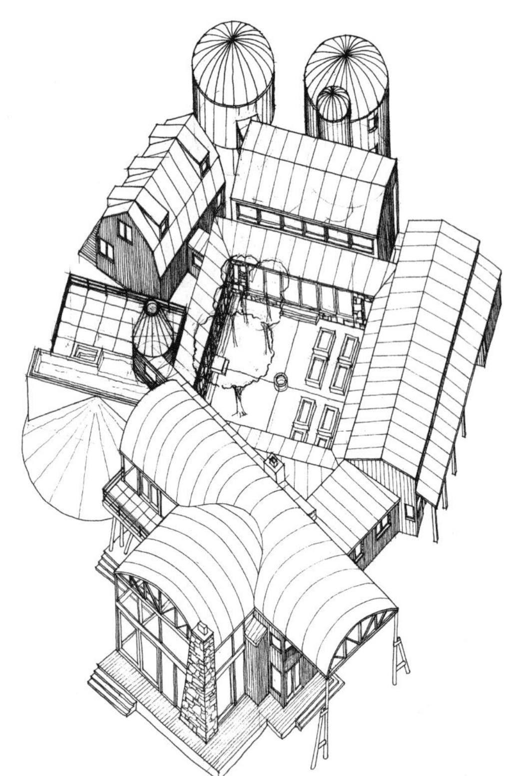

Drawing: Residence, Sun Valley, Idaho
24" × 30" (61 × 76.2 cm), Scale: 1/8"=1'0"
Medium: Pencil on vellum
Courtesy of Frederick Fisher, Architect

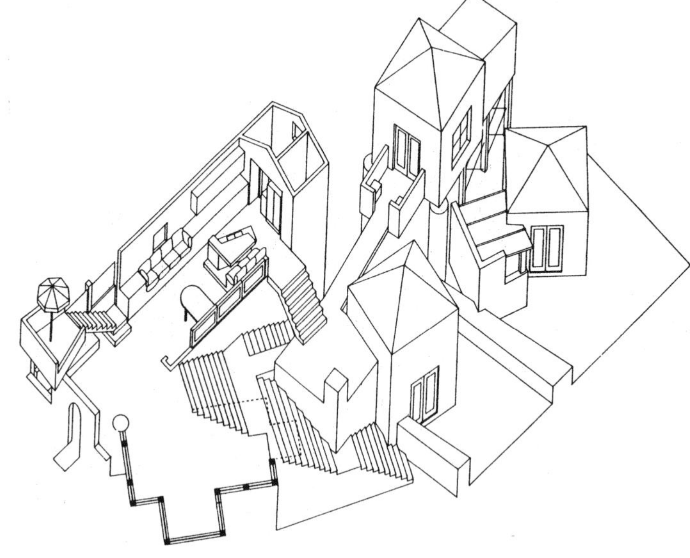

Drawing: Jaeger Beach House, La Jolla, California
24" × 36", Scale: 1"=30'
Medium: Ink on Mylar
Courtesy of Rob Wellington Quigley, Architect

It is quite common to find many building configurations that exhibit **multioblique** combinations. The addition of shades and shadows (see p. 325) gives depth to a multioblique drawing.

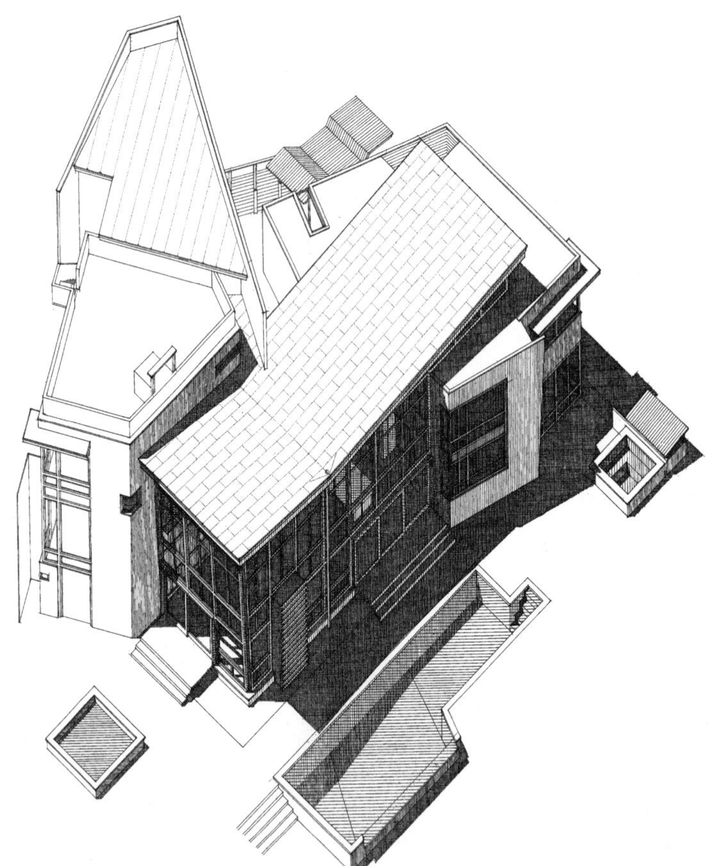

Drawing: Summer compound,
Barnegat Light, New Jersey
42" × 48" (106.7 × 121.9 cm), Scale: 1/4"=1'0"
Medium: Ink on Mylar
Courtesy of Brian Healy Architects

The rendering is done with ink on Mylar and is a representation of the many facets of the actual design. The use of ink lends a clean line to the well-defined edges and angles within the house. The composition of the drawing itself is at first a vehicle to view the many elements and geometries of the house, and is secondly a device by which the viewer is given a sense of process—the process of design and the process of experience. Airbrush is added to center the drawing at the starting point of this process.
[ARCHITECT'S STATEMENT]

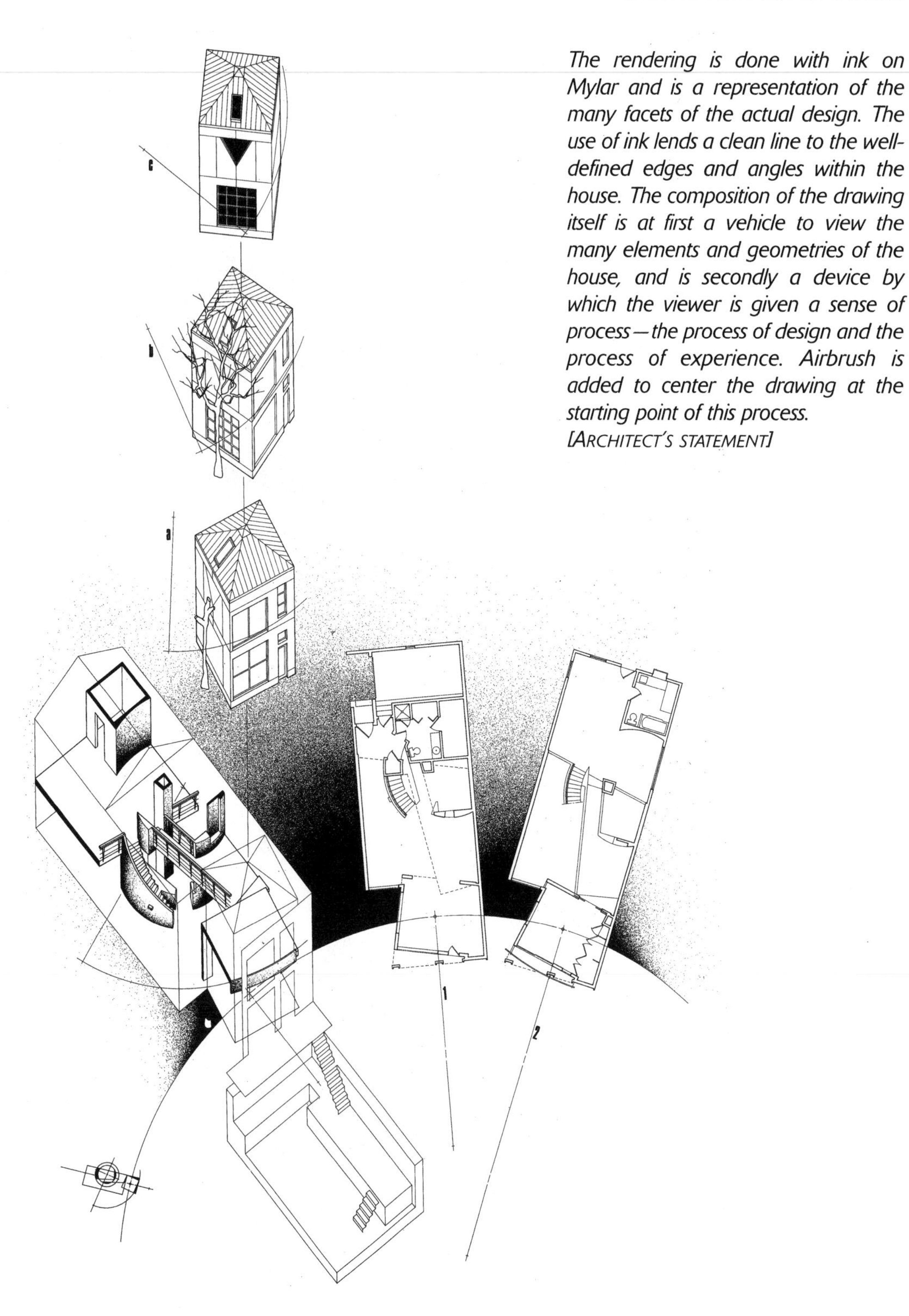

Drawing: Exploded axonometric and plan composite
Chason residence, San Francisco, California
30" × 52" (76.2 × 132.1 cm), Scale: 3/16"=1'0"
Medium: India ink on Mylar
Courtesy of House + House Architects, San Francisco
Michael Baushke, Architectural Illustrator

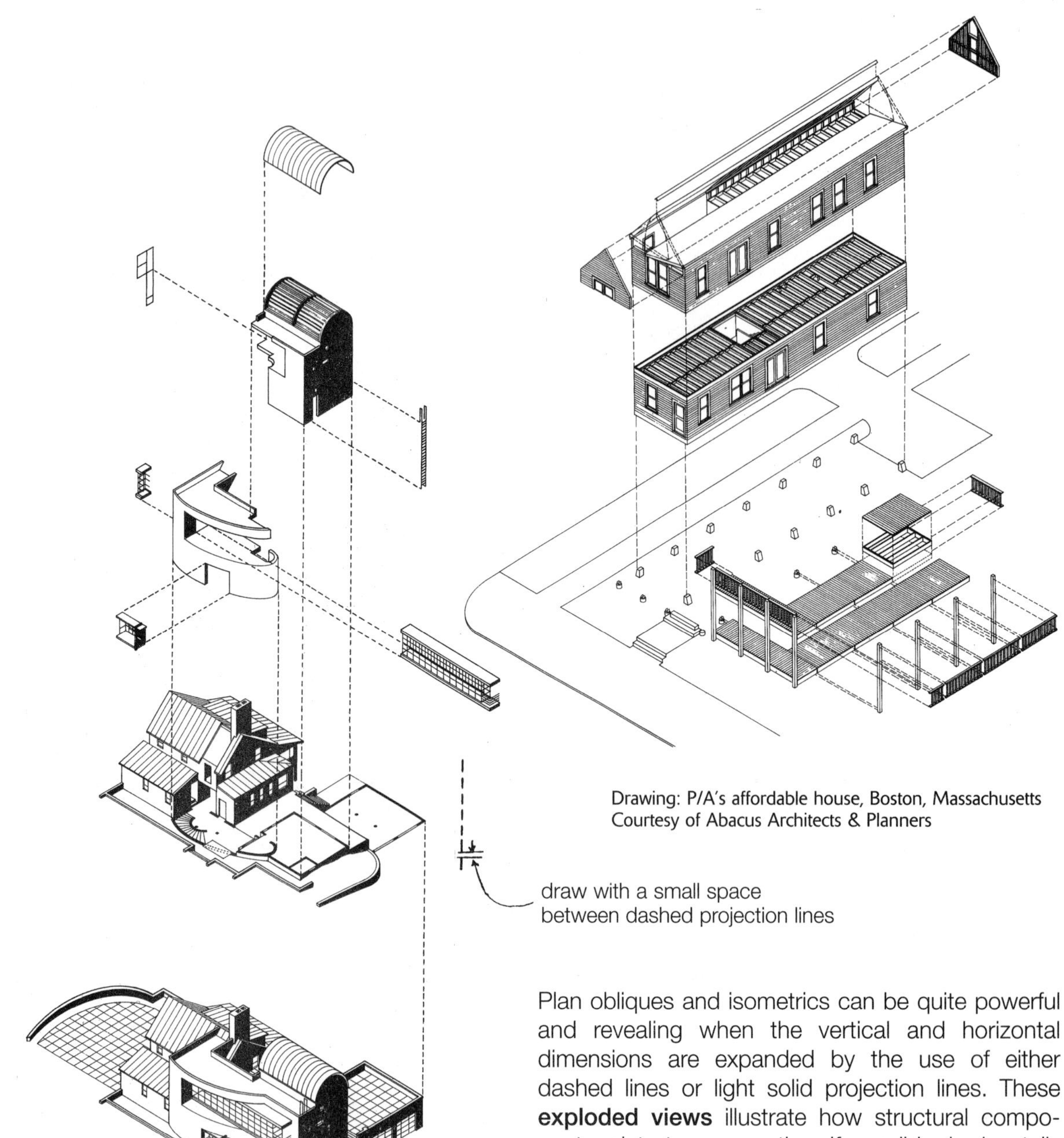
draw with a small space
between dashed projection lines

Drawing: P/A's affordable house, Boston, Massachusetts
Courtesy of Abacus Architects & Planners

Drawing: Gorman residence, New Canaan, Connecticut
24" × 36" (61 × 91.4 cm), Scale: 1/16"=1'0"
Medium: Pen and ink
Courtesy of Hariri & Hariri Design, Architects

Plan obliques and isometrics can be quite powerful and revealing when the vertical and horizontal dimensions are expanded by the use of either dashed lines or light solid projection lines. These **exploded views** illustrate how structural components relate to one another. If possible, horizontally or vertically exploded elements should not overlap. **Expanded views** (opposite page) are exploded in one direction only, as shown with the numerous roof removals on the previous pages.

The amount that the building parts are displaced (movement axes are usually parallel or perpendicular to the building axes) depends on finding the most explanatory positional relationship of the parts to each other and to the whole. Note in the Gorman residence (left) how easily the disparate elements seem to come together to make a coherent whole.

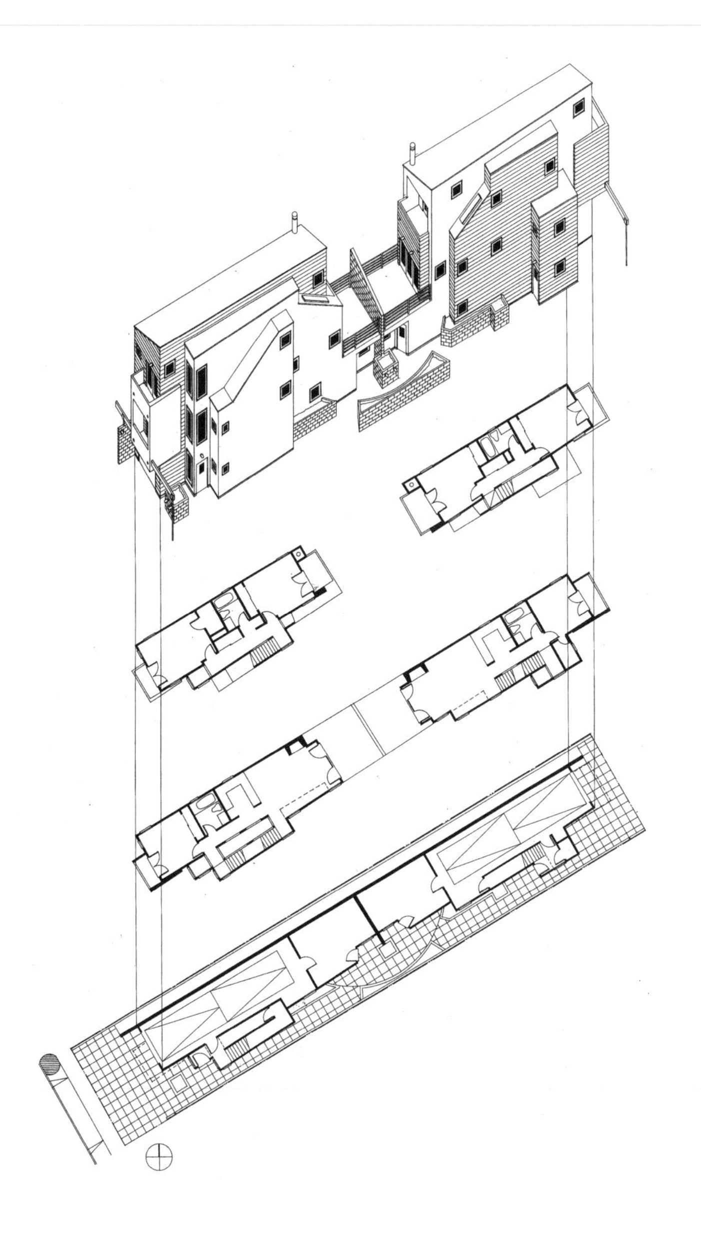

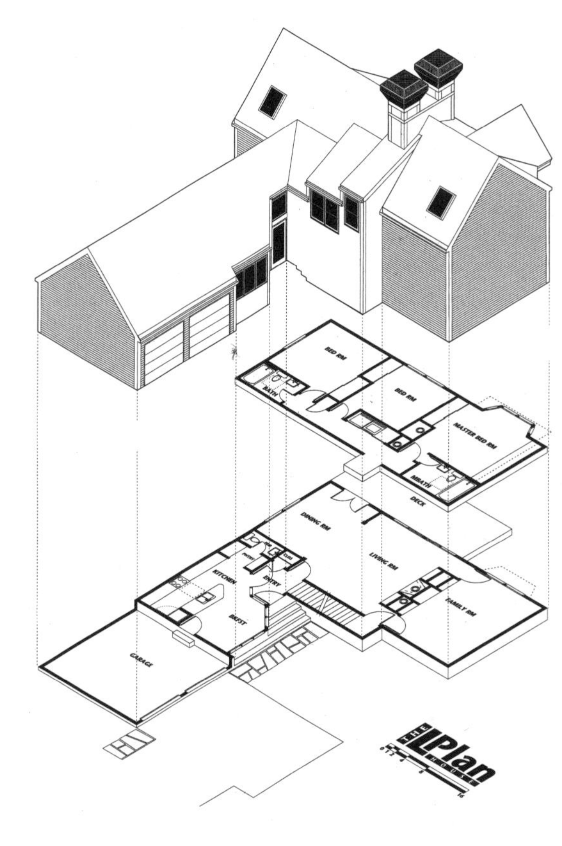

Drawing: House, Connecticut
8.5" × 11" (21.6 × 27.9 cm), Scale: 1/16"=1'0"
Originally drawn at 1/4"=1'0"
Medium: Macintosh computer in PowerDraw
Courtesy of Robert T. Coolidge, AIA, Architect

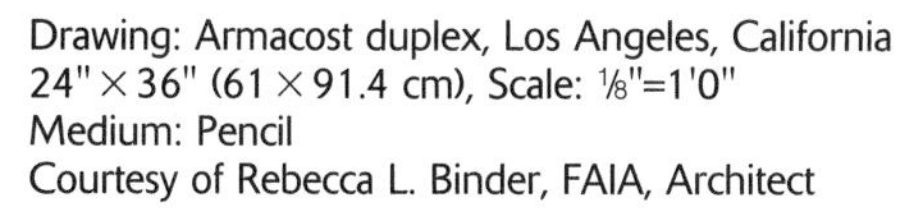

Drawing: Armacost duplex, Los Angeles, California
24" × 36" (61 × 91.4 cm), Scale: 1/8"=1'0"
Medium: Pencil
Courtesy of Rebecca L. Binder, FAIA, Architect

The concept of the expanded view in both plan obliques and isometrics is frequently applied to buildings with two or more floors. Stacked floors usually exhibit similar geometric configurations. These examples illustrate how the floor plans can be removed from the building shell to help visualize the vertical relationship of all levels in conjunction with the exterior form. Both expanded and exploded views allow us to see the internal makeup of a building. In this sense, they are quite similar to cutaway views (see pp. 148–50).

EXPLODED ISOMETRIC

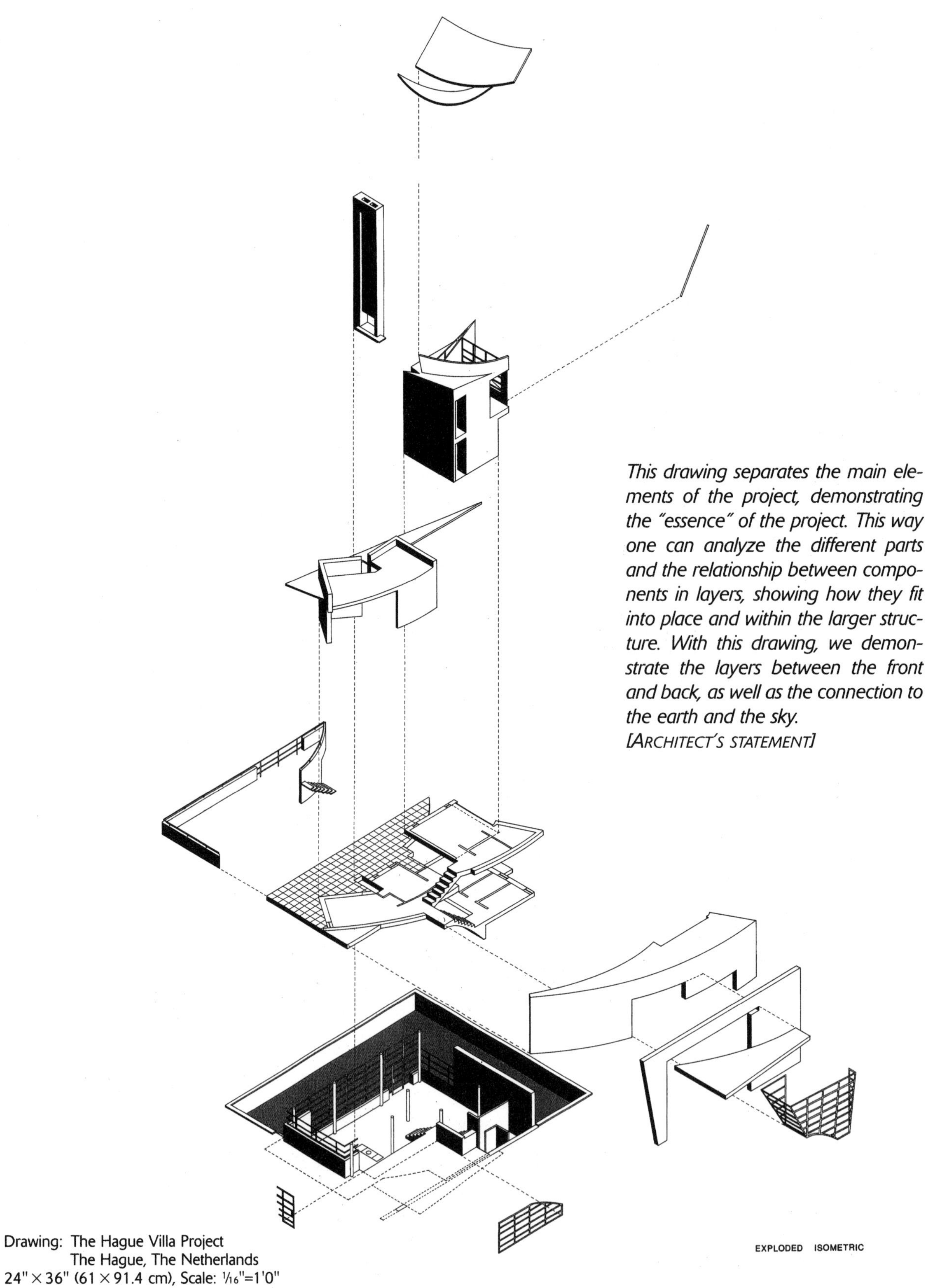

This drawing separates the main elements of the project, demonstrating the "essence" of the project. This way one can analyze the different parts and the relationship between components in layers, showing how they fit into place and within the larger structure. With this drawing, we demonstrate the layers between the front and back, as well as the connection to the earth and the sky.
[ARCHITECT'S STATEMENT]

Drawing: The Hague Villa Project
The Hague, The Netherlands
24" × 36" (61 × 91.4 cm), Scale: 1/16"=1'0"
Medium: Pen and ink
Courtesy of Hariri & Hariri, Architects

The element axonometric drawing is a composition of design elements: public street facade, private courtyard facade, axis, focal point, and circulation elements. The drawing visually analyzes the different design approaches to and the relationship between the public street and the private courtyard, and the sequence of circulation spaces that connect the major street to the inner courtyard with the linkage of the street entry porch to the rotated courtyard gazebo, the axis, and the focal point. The floor plan anchors the drawing as a basic reference.
[ARCHITECT'S STATEMENT]

Note the orderly manner in which the four expanded design elements fit together. Displaced vertically in a consistent direction, the way the elements would come back together into a cohesive whole can be visualized easily.

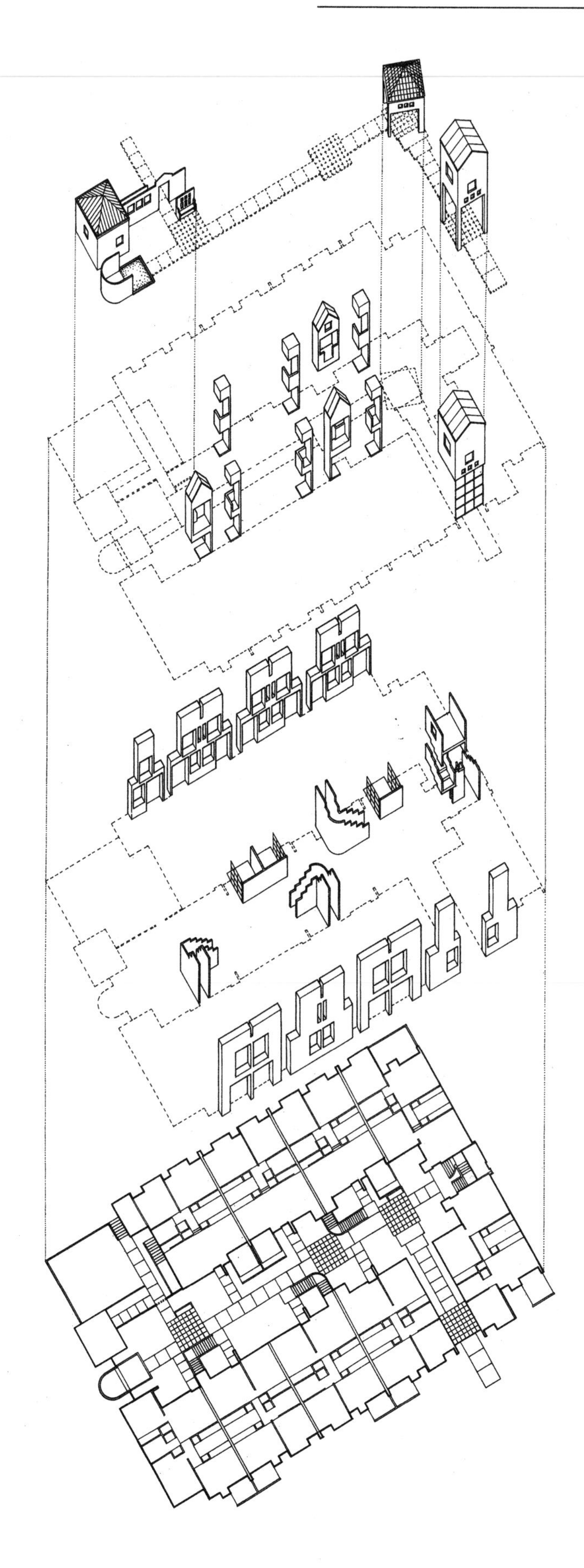

Drawing: Yorkshire Terrace, Los Angeles, California
34" × 42" (86.4 × 106.7 cm), Scale: 1/8"=1'0"
Medium: Ink
Courtesy of John V. Mutlow, FAIA, Architects

EXPANDED PLAN OBLIQUE/DIMETRIC

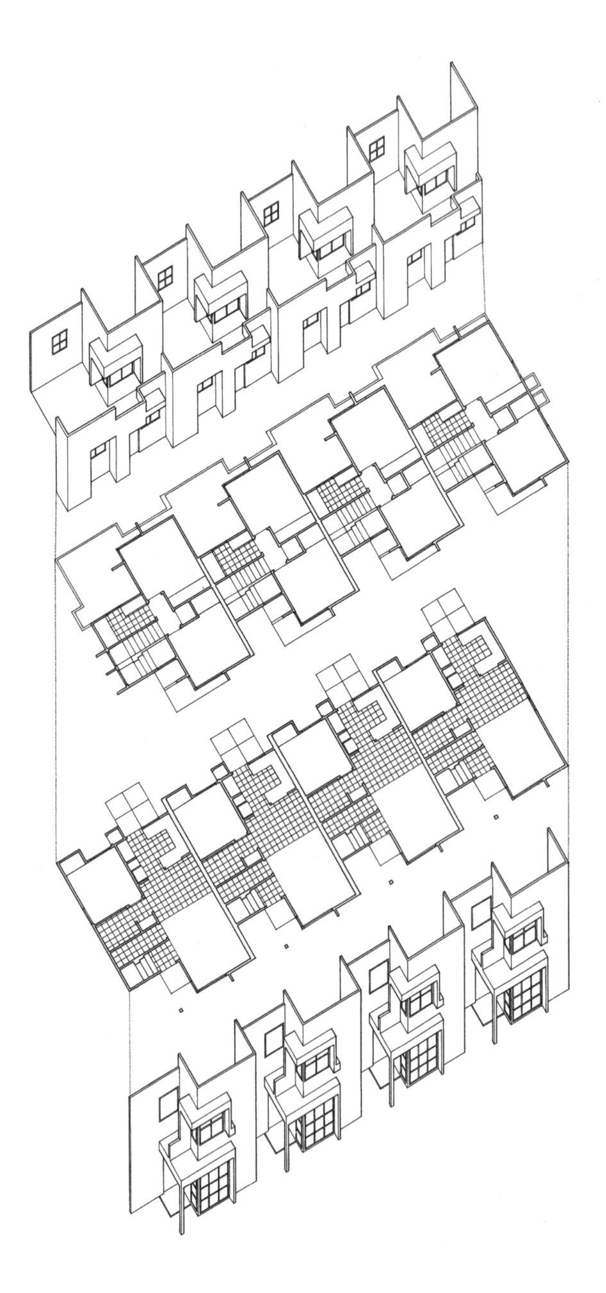

Drawing: Cabrillo Village, Saticoy, California
24" × 36" (61 × 91.4 cm), Scale: ⅛"=1'0"
Medium: Ink
Courtesy of John V. Mutlow, FAIA, Architects

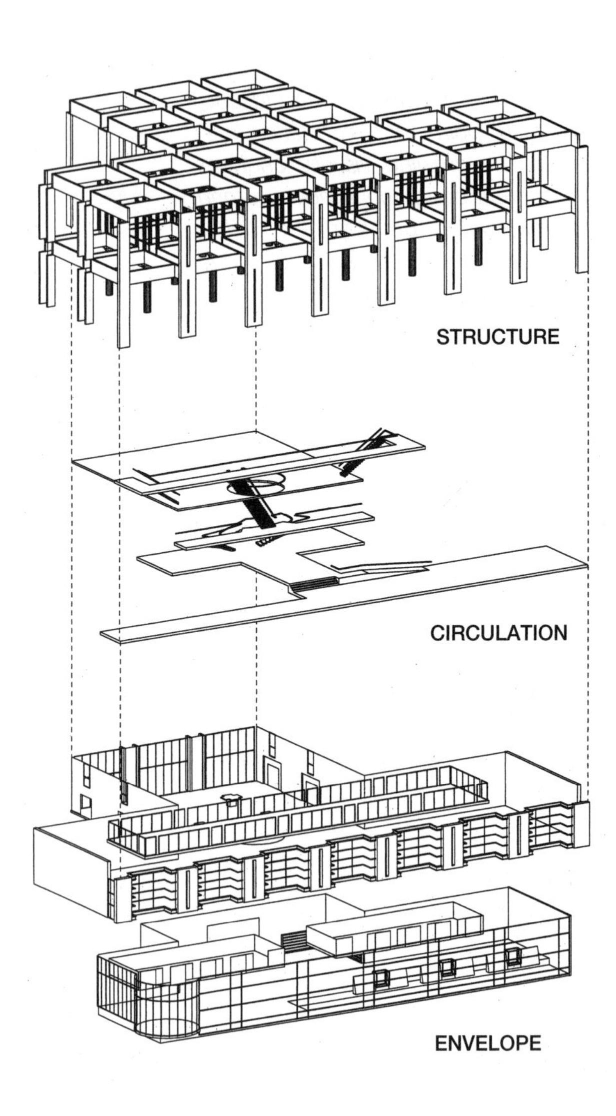

Dimetric of components

Drawing: Library, Toronto, Canada
Medium: Ink
Courtesy of A. J. Diamond, Donald Schmitt, Architects

The front and rear elevations below and above the floor plans help to project the three-dimensional richness of the facade from the two-dimensional floor plans.
[ARCHITECT'S STATEMENT]

This expanded view uses a paraline axonometric in the form of a dimetric. The lower angle of view permits one to see the linking circulation elements between floors. Dimetrics are more flexible than isometrics because a variety of viewing positions are possible.

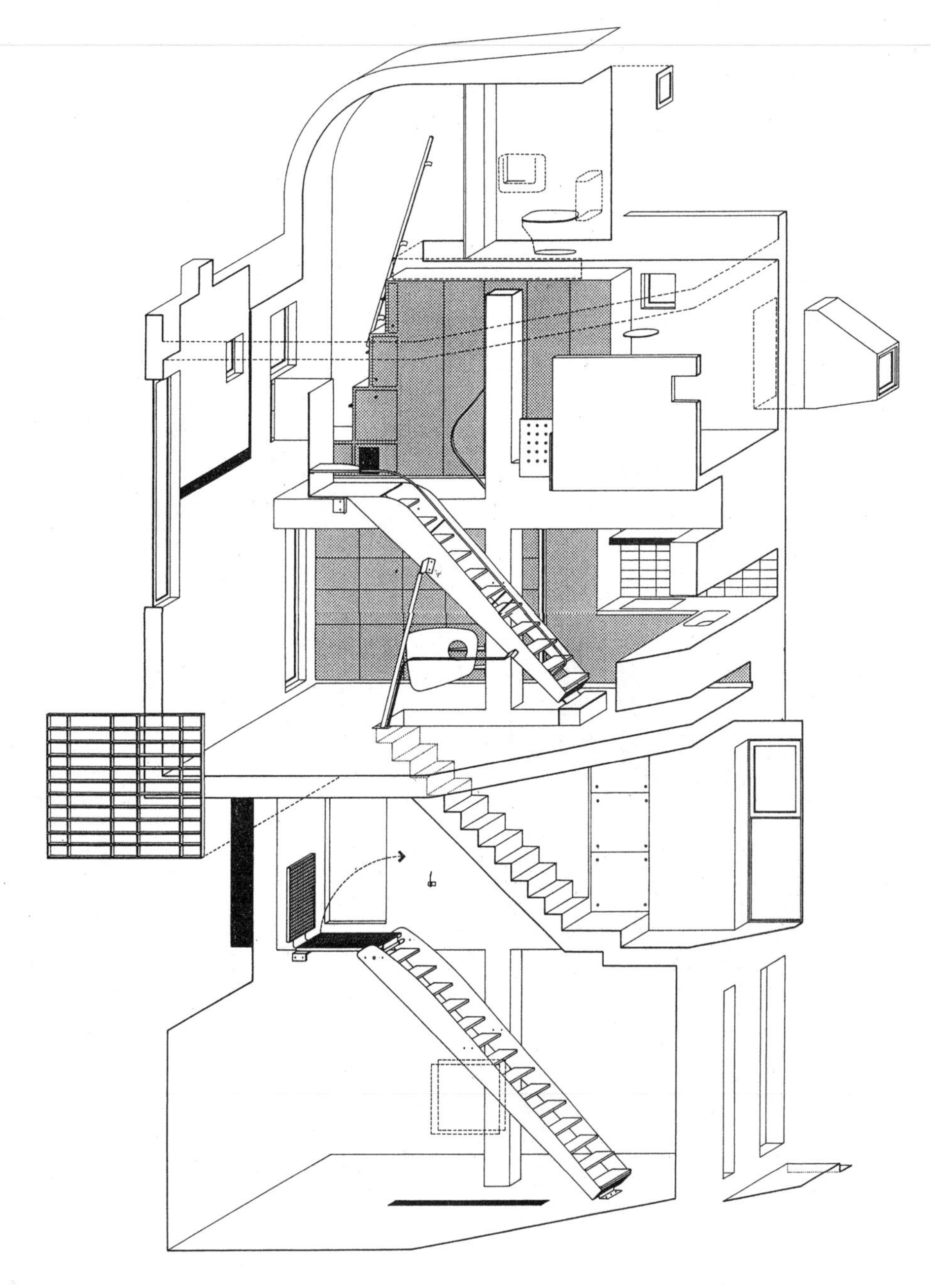

Drawings: Suzuki house, Tokyo, Japan
8.7" × 11" (22 × 28 cm), Scale: 1:30 (Japanese scale)
Medium: Ink on trace
Courtesy of Architekturbüro Bolles–Wilson + Partner

The space of the house at all levels is visible on one projection. The central stair is understood as the connecting sequence... as in Japanese painting, what is not shown is as important as what is shown.
[ARCHITECT'S STATEMENT]

Both exploded and expanded views are excellent tools for examining the way details are put together, whether they are small structural components or large building elements. This is an interior elevation oblique with exploded parts. Overlapping exploded or expanded parts is permissible, provided they do not cover important information.

EXPANDED ELEVATION OBLIQUE

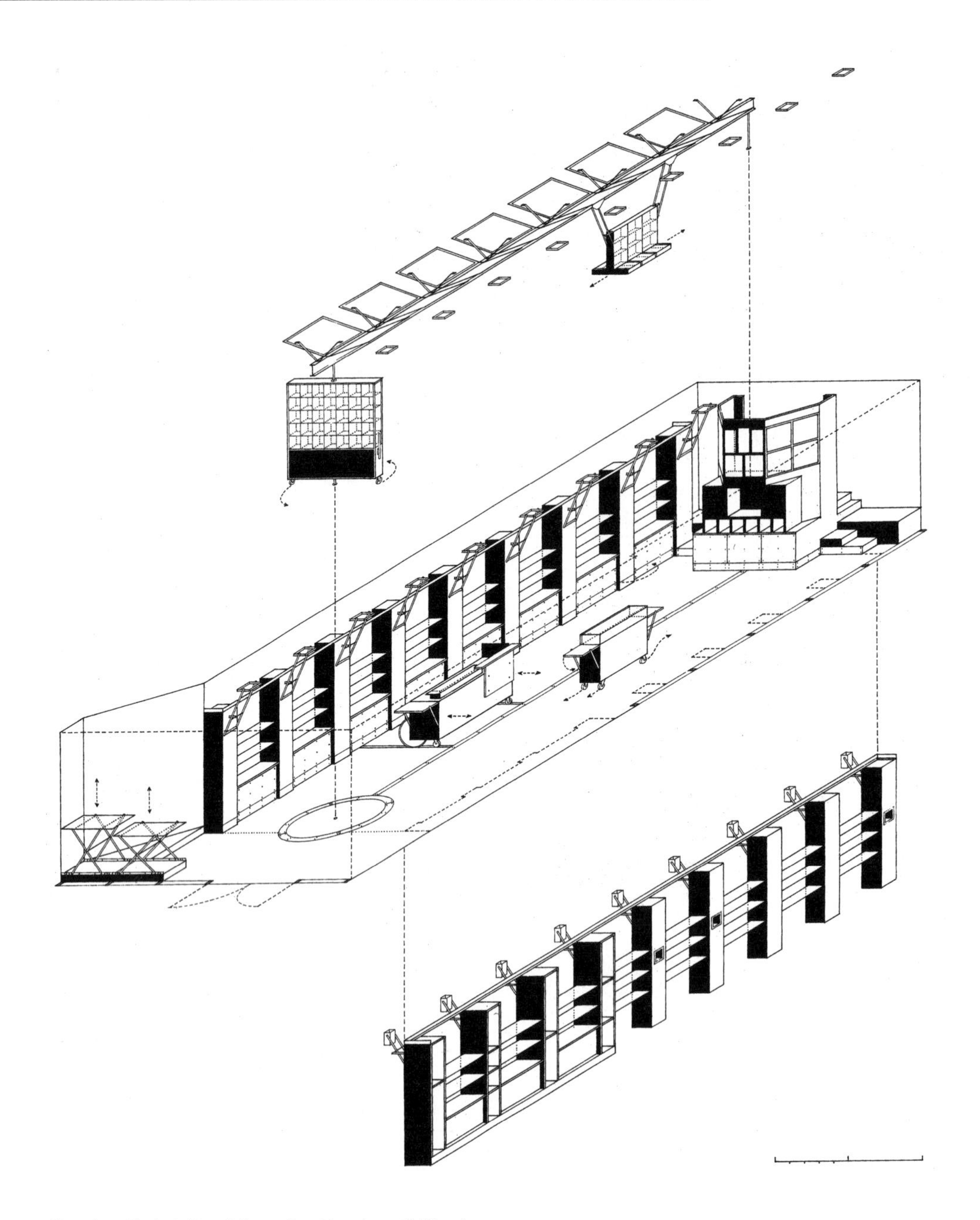

Drawing: Techsis Retail Store, San Francisco, California
17" × 22" (43.2 × 55.9 cm), Scale: ¼"=1'0"
Medium: Ink on Mylar
Courtesy of Jensen + Macy Architects

The elevation oblique was chosen because it gives more emphasis to the vertical planes (display fixtures) than the plan oblique, which emphasizes plan relationships. This drawing type has an analytical quality, allowing one to understand space–object relationships not graspable from the single, fixed vantage point of the perspective. The extensions of parts of the drawing above and below it allow a reading of the separate components of the store in the composition. [Architect's statement]

EXPANDED ELEVATION OBLIQUE UP VIEW

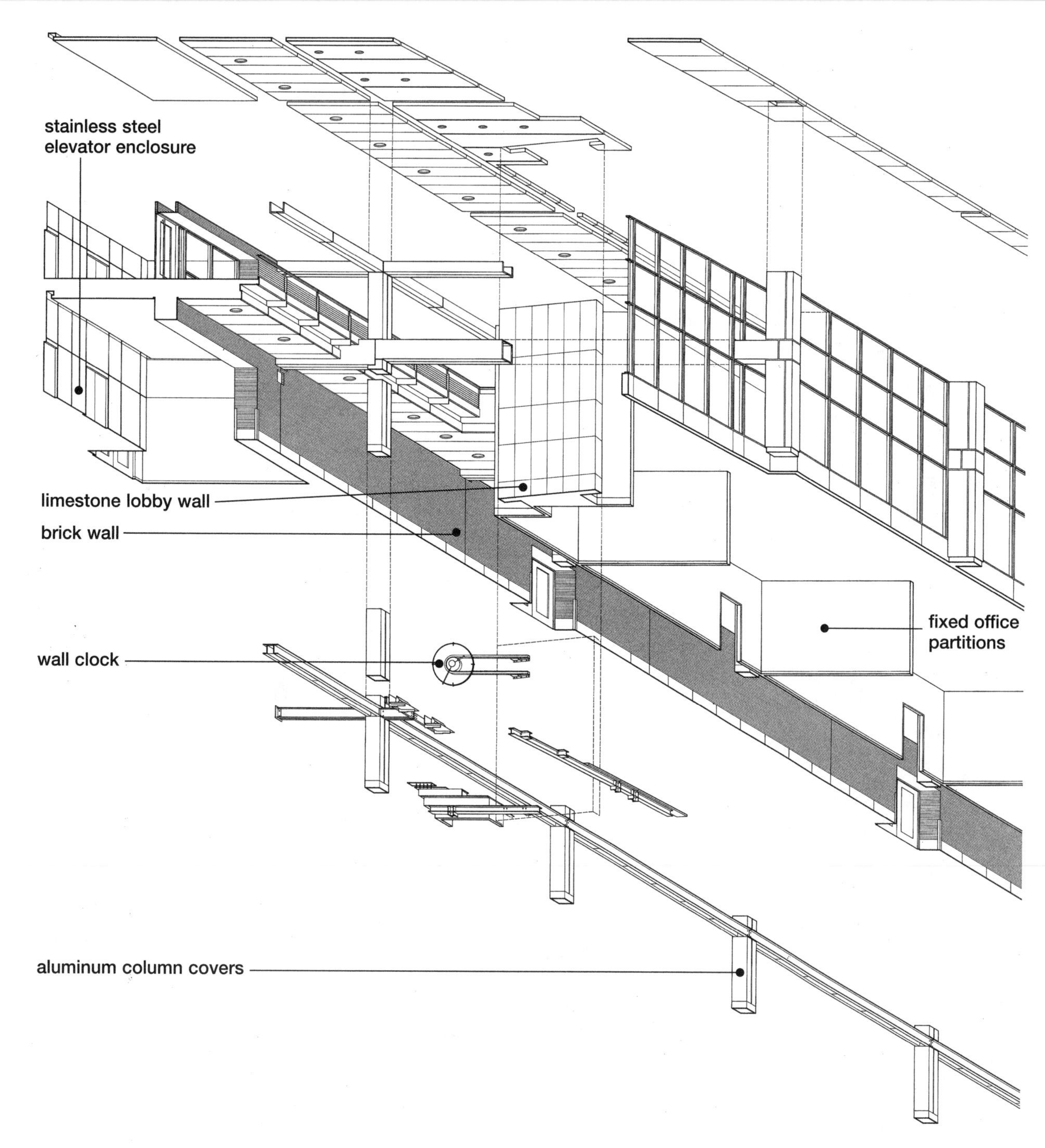

This is an expanded elevation oblique worm's-eye (up) view of the ground floor.

Drawing: New Office Building and Parking Garage for the
Pennsylvania Higher Education Assistance Agency
Harrisburg, Pennsylvania
36" × 48" (91.4 × 121.9 cm)
Medium: Ink on vellum (developed as a CADD drawing)
Courtesy of Bohlin Cywinski Jackson Architects

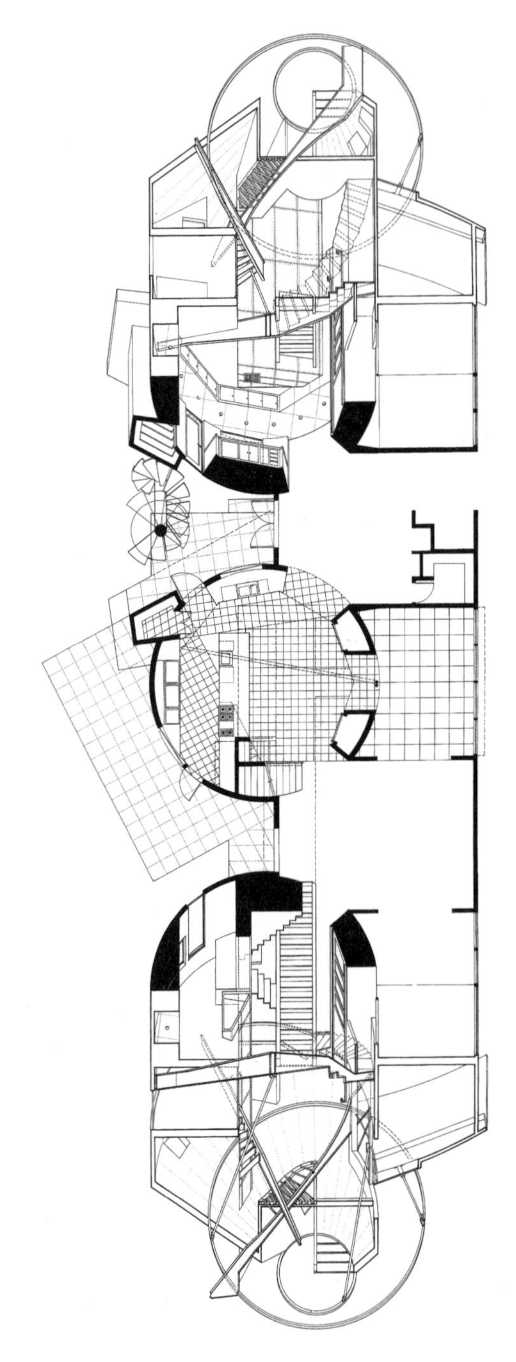

Split worm's-eye axonometric

Drawing: Lawson/Westen House, Los Angeles, California
Medium: Ink on Mylar
Courtesy of Eric Owen Moss, Architects

These dramatic worm's-eye views permit the viewer to peer upward into the buildings. This method was first developed and utilized by August Choisy in the nineteenth century. In design drawings it is sometimes necessary to show the relationship between the ceiling or the soffit and the walls. The disadvantage of this type of drawing is that it is sometimes very difficult to interpret, especially for beginning students and laypeople.

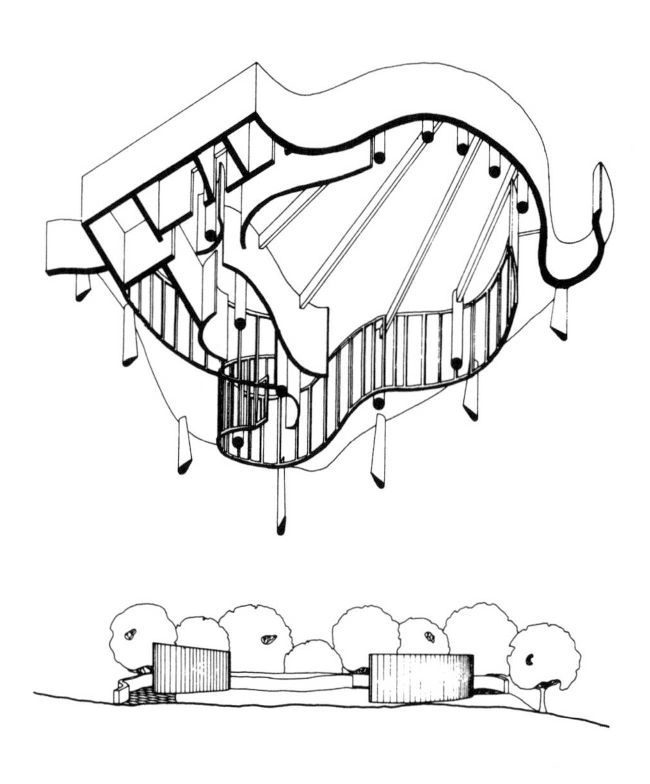

Drawing: Student project by Colin Alley
Community center
Medium: Ink on Mylar
Courtesy of Washington University
School of Architecture, St. Louis, Missouri

This drawing simultaneously allows one to understand the building's form and organization while giving clues as to how the designers conceived the building: a modest shell that bends to accommodate and encourage movement and circulation; a pure cylinder at the center of the mass as a primal gathering place; and a peaked, conical roof capping the cylinder as a distinguishing image at the center of a four-building residential village.
[ARCHITECT'S STATEMENT]

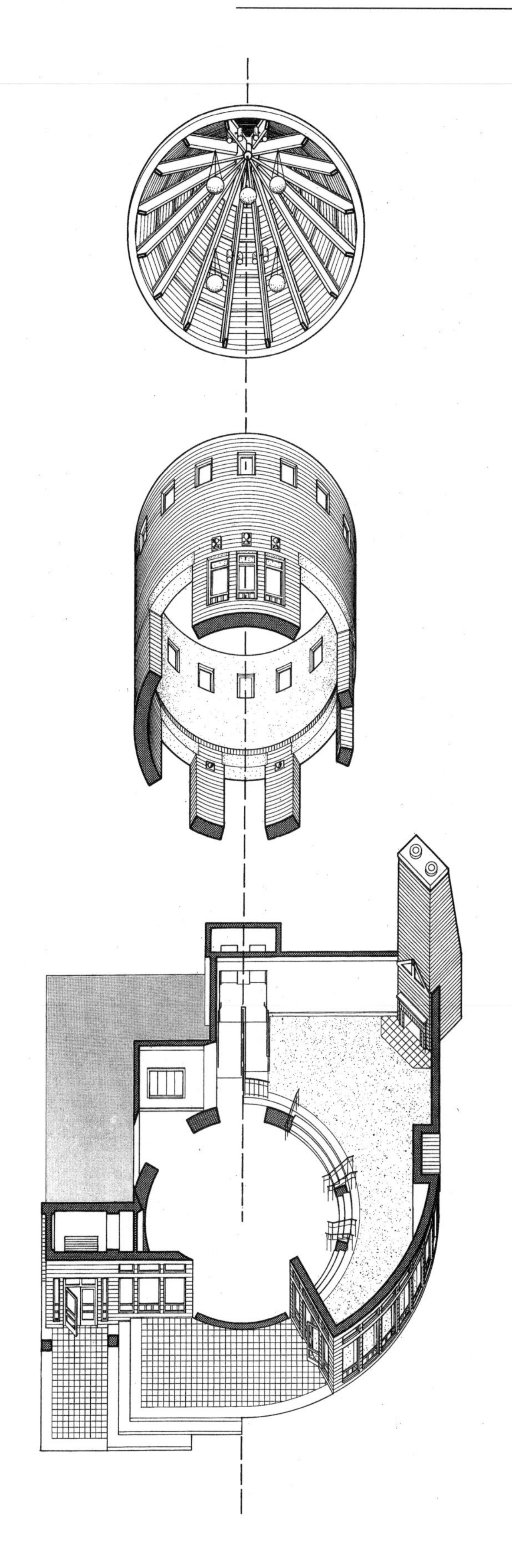

SIMULTANEOUS UP AND DOWN VIEWS

This drawing combines a plan oblique down view with plan oblique up views. Its advantage is that it allows us to simultaneously understand the total geometric configuration of a design.

Drawing: Bates College Social/Study Center
(Residential Halls project), Lewiston, Maine
12" × 30" (30.5 × 76.2 cm), Scale: ¼"=1'0"
Medium: Ink on Mylar
Courtesy of William Rawn Associates,
Architects, Inc., Boston, Massachusetts

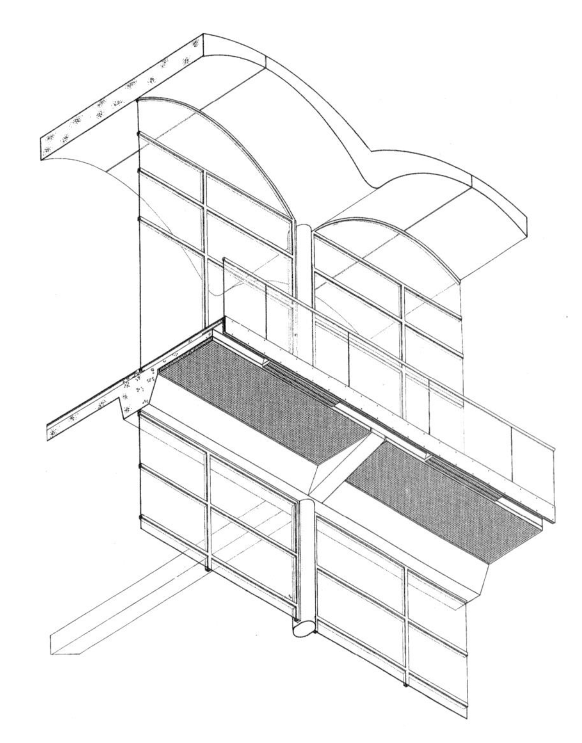

Isometric detail of balcony edge

Drawing: Lycée Polyvalent de Fréjus
Fréjus School, Fréjus, France
16.5" × 23.4" (418 × 595 mm)
Medium: Ink on film
Drawn by Keith Allen
Courtesy of Lord Foster of Thames Bank

Axonometric **up views** in the form of isometrics or dimetrics display more detail between floor levels than plan oblique up views. Note the isometric curvilinear form above and the horizontal and vertical dimetric circles shown at right. With the advantage of more vantage points, **dimetric drawings** looking up or looking down are not as inflexible and restrictive as isometric drawings.

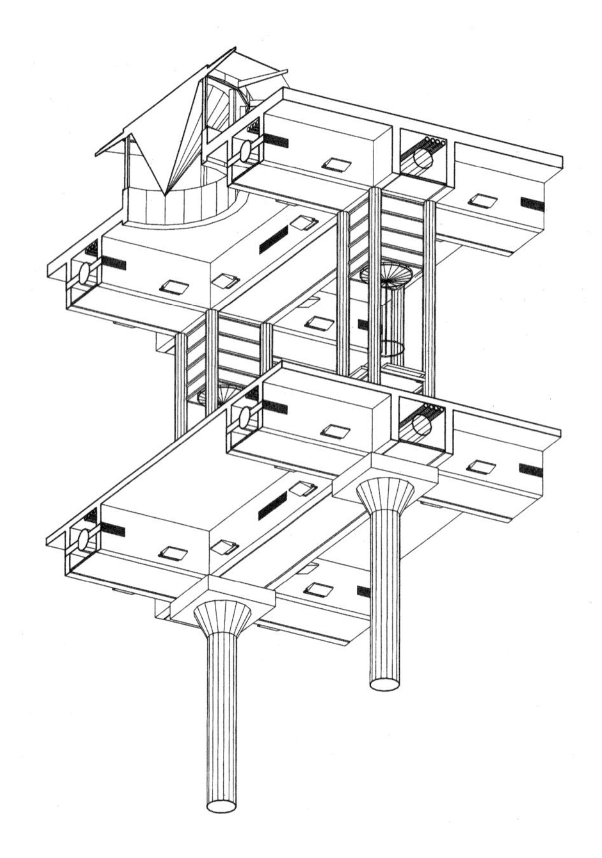

Dimetric of typical bay

Drawing: Richmond Hill Library, Toronto, Canada
Courtesy of A.J. Diamond, Donald Schmitt, Architects

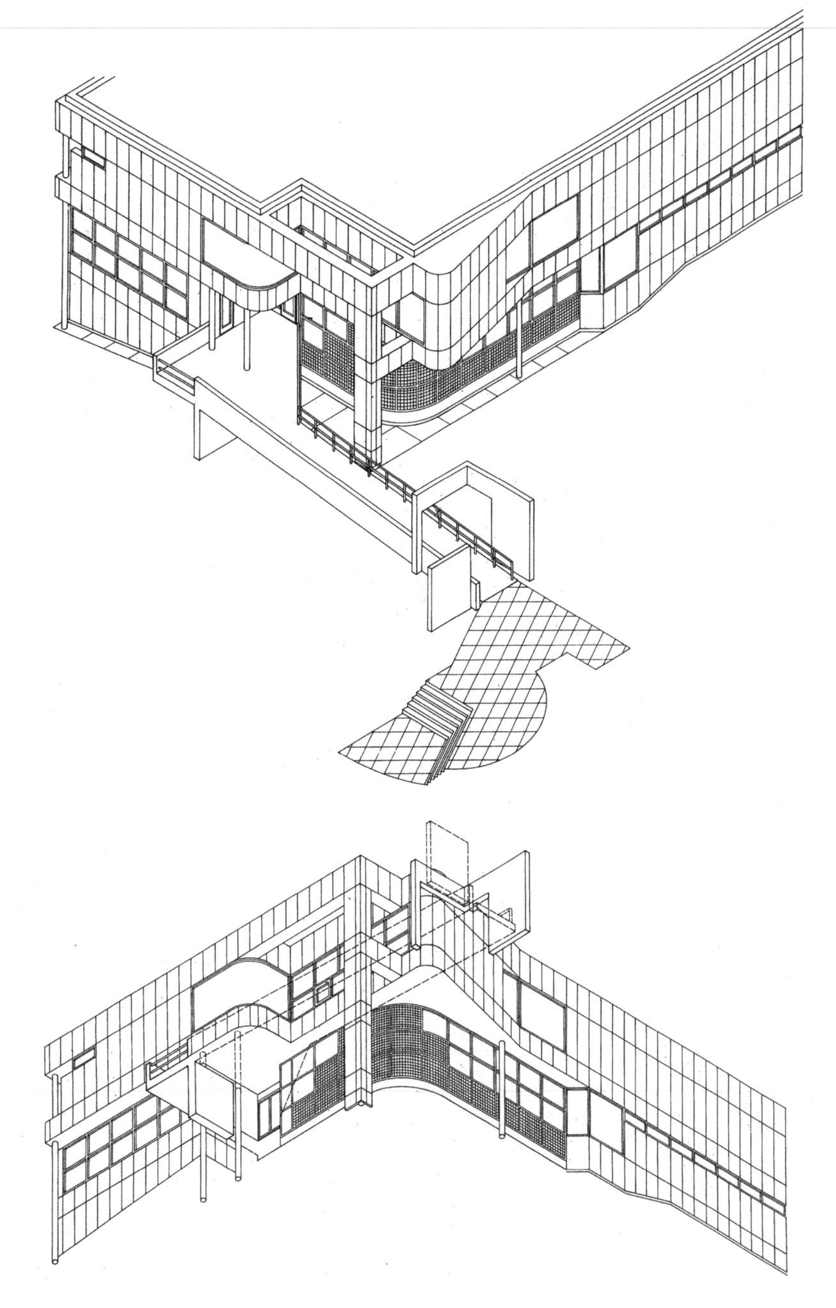

Drawings: Postindustrial factory, Dorval, Quebec, Canada
30" × 48" (76.2 × 121.9 cm), Scale: ⅛"=1'0"
Medium: Ink on Mylar
Courtesy of Michael Fieldman & Partners, Architects

A pair of axonometric views—one aerial, the other worm's-eye—were used to describe a complex 3-D corner entrance. Together they convey the spatial quality of the design.
[ARCHITECT'S STATEMENT]

SIMULTANEOUS UP AND DOWN VIEWS

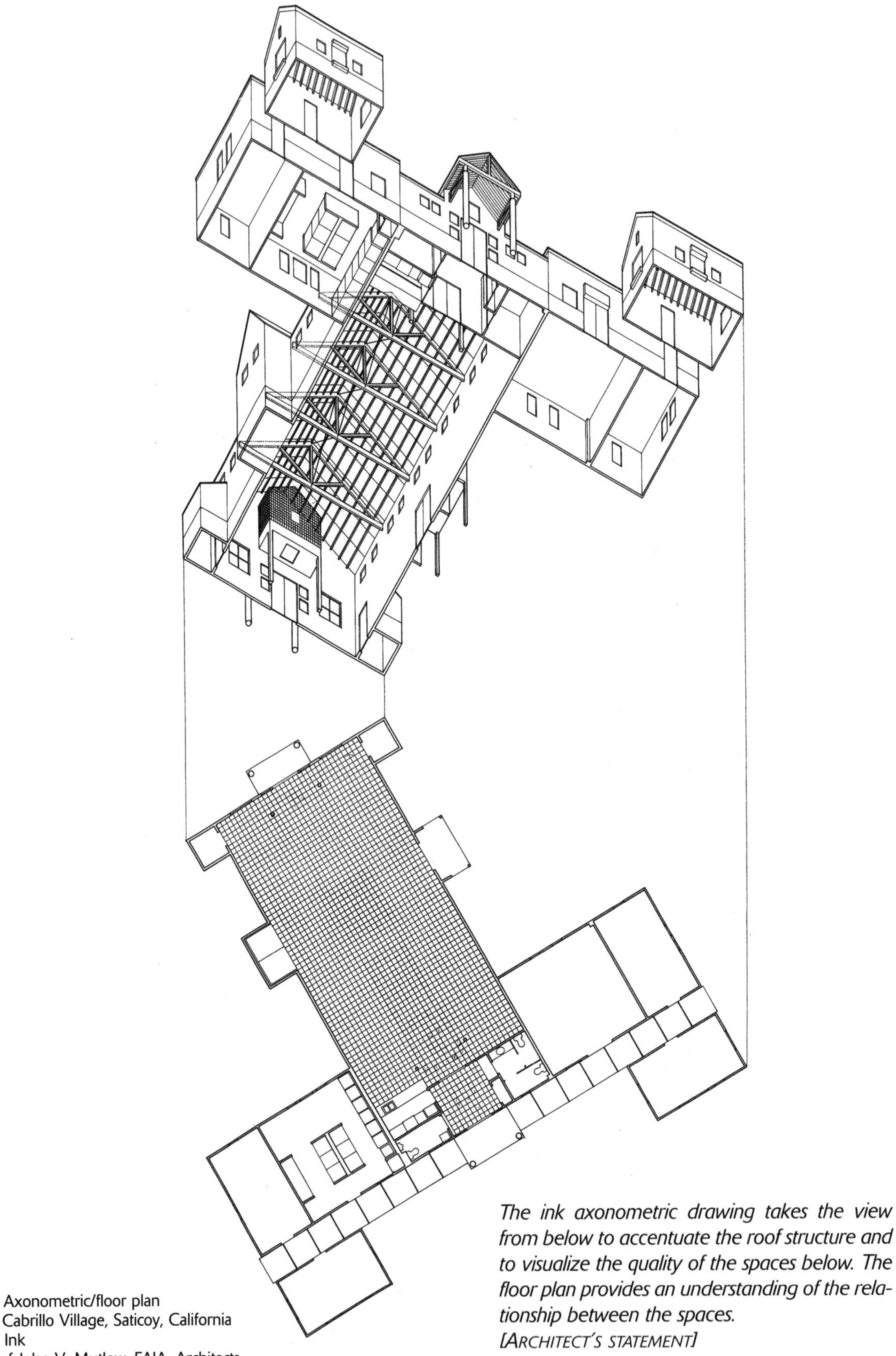

The ink axonometric drawing takes the view from below to accentuate the roof structure and to visualize the quality of the spaces below. The floor plan provides an understanding of the relationship between the spaces.
[ARCHITECT'S STATEMENT]

Drawing: Axonometric/floor plan
Cabrillo Village, Saticoy, California
Medium: Ink
Courtesy of John V. Mutlow, FAIA, Architects

Relating to and radiating out from the floor plan, these sequentially rotated views allow the observer to simultaneously experience different viewpoints. Sequentially rotated simultaneous views are also frequently seen as plan obliques radiating out from a centrally drawn floor plan. Seeing many views from different vantage points (same altitude) at one time gives a quick comprehensive overview of any structure (see p. 510).

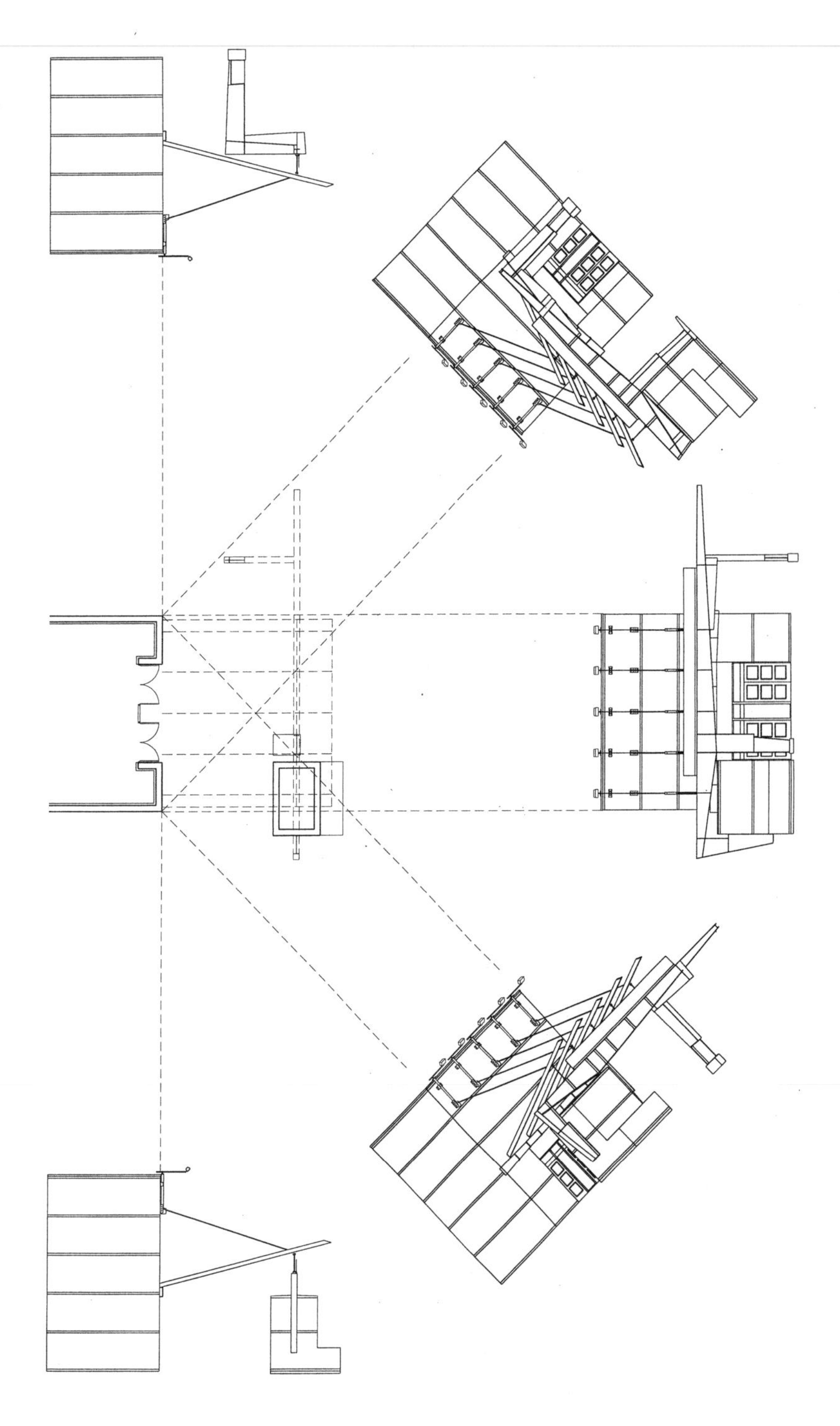

Image: Administration Building, Kennedy Senior High School
Granada Hills, California
Courtesy of Rebecca L. Binder, FAIA Architecture & Planning
Hardware: PC
Software: ACAD 14, 2000; 3D Studio

This shows the use of sequentially rotated simultaneous views to hone in on a given detail to explain its relationship to the building element.
[ARCHITECT'S STATEMENT]

6

Linear Perspective Drawing

BASICS............................183
BASICS APPLIED....................212

Perspective drawings seen from a fixed vantage point create the most realistic, lifelike views of the built environment and the urban landscape. On a two-dimensional surface, pictorial views of three-dimensional forms can be represented in a believable manner using methods characterized by diminishing sizes and defined by converging lines.

Preliminary perspective design drawings or sketches show form, scale, texture, light, shapes, shadows, and spatial order. Presentation perspective design drawings take on a more precise character from these and related components. As a final step, they may be refined into perspective renderings to complement and enhance a presentation.

The intent of this chapter is to introduce the theory of and methods for constructed architectural perspectives. It stresses the importance of visualizing in parallel (one-point) or angular (two-point) perspective from the plan and the elevation of an object. This, of course, comes with patience, perseverance, and most of all, practice.

The following are some of the important skills, terms, and concepts you will learn:

How to use one-, two-, and three-point perspectives
How to change the pictorial effect by changing the perspective variables

Station point	Picture plane	Horizon line	Ground line
Vanishing point	Line of sight	Cone of vision	Distortion
Office method	Oblique lines	Perspective circles	Measurement systems

Linear Perspective Drawing

TOPICS: CONE OF VISION

Ching 2003, 91.

TOPICS: DIAGONALS, X-, Y-, Z-AXIS, STATION POINT, PICTURE PLANE, HORIZON LINE, VANISHING POINTS, CENTER OF VISION, VERTICAL MEASURING LINE, MIDPOINT, PERSPECTIVE FIELD, PERSPECTIVE VIEWPOINT, PERSPECTIVE SETUP

Hanks and Belliston 1992, 16–19; 21–23.

Porter and Goodman 1985, 108–15.

TOPIC: ONE-POINT PERSPECTIVE USING 45° DIAGONAL LINES

Ching 2003, 99–102.

TOPICS: VERTICAL VANISHING LINES, DIAGONAL LINES, OBLIQUE LINES, OBLIQUE VANISHING POINTS, DIAGONAL VANISHING POINTS, 45° VANISHING POINTS.

Forseth 1980, 154–58.

TOPICS: ONE-POINT OFFICE METHOD, SECTION PERSPECTIVE, PLAN PERSPECTIVE, PERSPECTIVE CHARTS

Ching 1998, 234–36.

Lin 1993, 116–20, 124–34.

TOPIC: THREE-POINT PERSPECTIVE

Gill 1980, Chapter 6.

TOPICS: MULTIPLYING AND DIVIDING, CIRCLES, CIRCLES AND ELLIPSES

Ching 2003, 116, 121.

Forseth 1980, 168–69, 170.

Hanks and Belliston 1980, 122–23.

Chapter Overview

After studying this chapter and doing the related exercises in the book's final section, you will understand important perspective terms, as well as how to construct one- and two-point perspectives. For continued study of the principles discussed in this chapter, refer to Forseth's *Graphics for Architecture* and Ching's *Architectural Graphics.*

Perspective is a method of depicting the manner in which objects appear to the human eye with respect to their relative positions and distance. The optic mechanism of seeing the urban landscape is done simultaneously with both eyes, and as a result we visually experience things three-dimensionally or spatially. The term "perspective" comes from the Latin *perspectare,* which means "to view through." The origin of linear perspective theory comes from the Renaissance. The perceptual schema of Western philosophy and civilization values a drawing system that logically duplicates an individual's visual experience. Thus, linear perspective is considered "correct" in the sense that it values representation.

Architects use perspectives in both preliminary and final design stages. They utilize both drafting's traditional manual methods and computer programs to generate desired perspective views to aid in the design process. To fully appreciate perspective drawing, it is important to understand the time-consuming, hand-drawing procedures before embarking on quicker computer methods. Manually constructed methods form the basis for the computer programs used today.

In the preliminary design stages, rough freehand perspective drawings are the norm. In the final presentation stages, perspectives are accurately constructed for the purpose of rendering them (see Chapter 8). In 1949, Frank Lloyd Wright did a rendered conceptual drawing (see p. 81) for his famous Guggenheim Museum in New York City showing a tower in the background that at the time was not built. The complete dream in the perspective rendering finally came to fruition with the completion of the tower addition in 1992.

Frank Lloyd Wright
Solomon R. Guggenheim Museum (night rendering), circa 1950–1951
37" × 26" (94 × 66 cm)
Medium: Tempera and black ink on composition board
Collection Peter Lawson-Johnston
Photograph by David Heald ©The Solomon R. Guggenheim Foundation, New York

Photo: Waterfront pier
San Francisco, California

Whether we are viewing the environment or attempting to realistically depict what we see on a two-dimensional, flat drawing surface, we experience four major phenomena: (1) diminution, (2) overlapping, (3) convergence, and (4) foreshortening. **Diminution** occurs when equal-sized objects, such as the lampposts above, appear to diminish in size with distance. This can be seen on the opposite page, where a fixed observer notices that columns and arches of equal size appear to diminish with distance. Photographs require the cameraperson to view from a frozen position, much like the single vantage point of any perspective drawing. Thus, perspectives have a photolike quality.

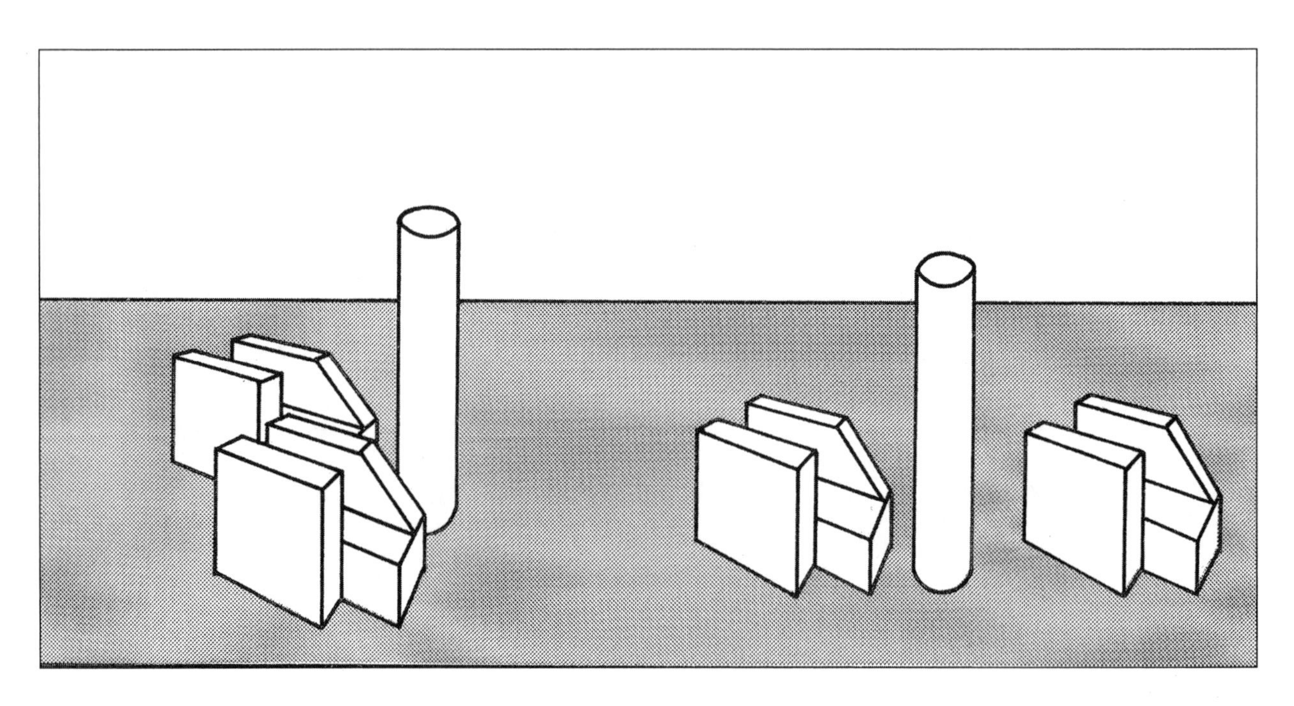

When we see objects **overlapping,** a sense of depth and space is achieved. Isolated objects provide very little sense of spatial depth—if any.

© Rendow Yee

Stanford University quadrangle, Palo Alto, California
Shepley, Rutan and Coolidge, Architects

These two photographs of a series of arches were taken from two different vantage points. The oblique angle at left is the frontal exterior side of the series of arches whereas below the angle is from behind the series of arches. In both cases a **convergence** of parallel lines occurs: the line tangent to all the arches vanishes to the same point as the line that touches the bases of all the columns.

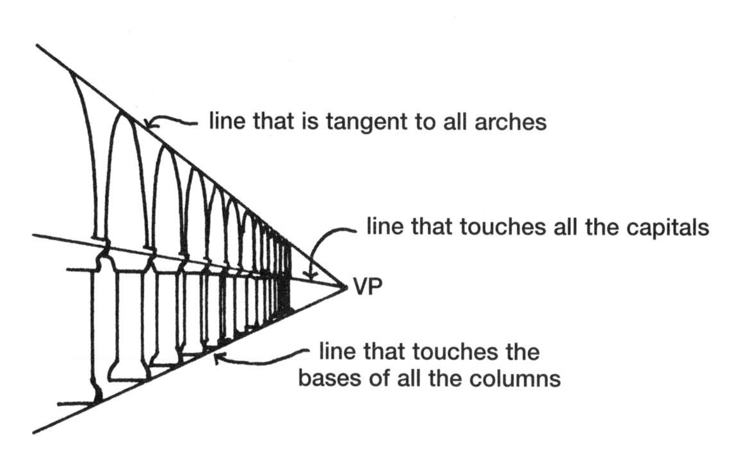

FORESHORTENED ARCHES

© Rendow Yee

The three lines that converge above would be parallel if drawn in the true-size view below.

TRUE-SIZE ARCHES

In a head-on view, there would be no illusion of perspective space because no convergence would be evident. The arches would be seen in their maximum or true size. At an oblique angle the arch size becomes **foreshortened** since it is no longer in its true size. The semicircular arch becomes elliptical in all oblique-angle positions.

Webster's Dictionary defines "cue" as a hint or intimation. We pick up visual cues all the time. The cues may not always be exactly how we see the physical environment. In general, what we see can be called "perspective" cues. The most fundamental and efficient types of drawing cues are those that employ lines to record the edges of surfaces as we experience them in reality. These are called perspective cues because they represent the relationships between the edges of surfaces at a particular point in time and space — a particular perspective on the world. Perspective cues have been codified into three drawing systems: **linear perspective, paraline perspective** (used here to include axonometric and oblique systems), and **orthographic perspective** (multiview drawings). None of these is exactly how we see the world all the time. Each represents certain perceptual and cognitive realities — some combination of what we see and what we know about things.

Linear Perspective Cues

Linear perspective is most acutely experienced in places where long rectangular surfaces begin near the observer and recede into the distance, such as long, straight roads. The essential experience is that the parallel lines seem to come together in the distance. The edges of surfaces are represented by lines that follow the rules of linear perspective and each has a line grammar. One-point perspectives have vertical lines, horizontal lines, and perspective lines (lines that go to vanishing points). Two-point perspectives have vertical lines and perspective lines. Three-point perspectives have only perspective lines.

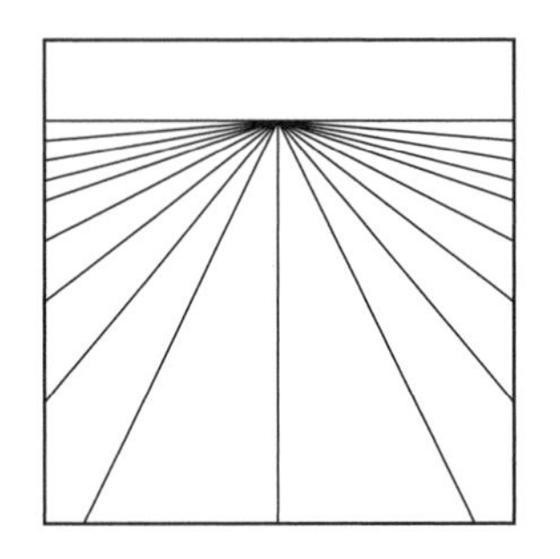

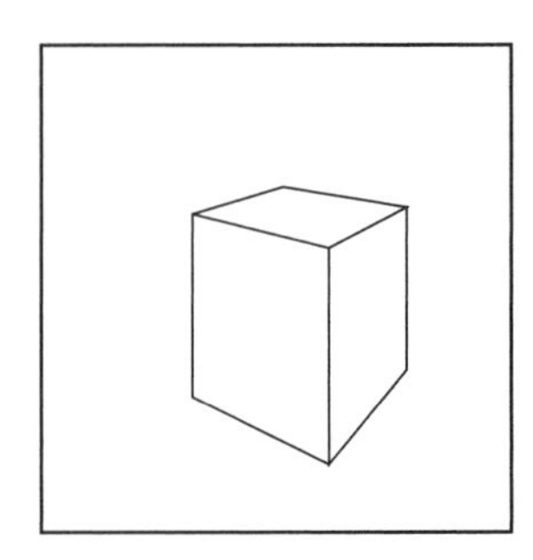

Diagrams and text: Courtesy of
William R. Benedict, Assistant Professor
California Polytechnic State University
College of Architecture & Environmental Design
San Luis Obispo, California

Paraline Perspective Cues

The Western perceptual schema is culturally biased toward linear perspective. To other cultures and in other times, a paraline drawing looked more "correct" than one using linear perspective. When things are small relative to our visual field, their edges and surfaces tend to retain their dimensions. The degree to which the edges vanish is so slight that our knowledge of their equality in length and angle can easily be more important than their adherence to the linear perspective. Paraline systems codify this view of reality. The edges of surfaces are represented by lines that follow the rules of paraline drawing conventions. The edges of parallel surfaces remain parallel and retain direct measured relationships to each other and the thing being represented. Verticals remain vertical and the other axes slope at specified angles.

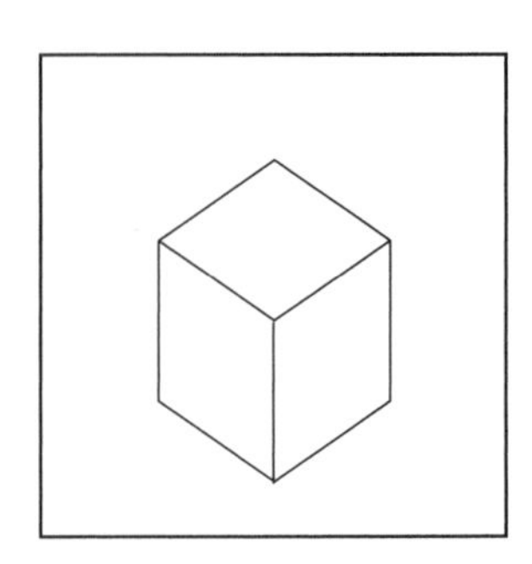

Orthographic Perspective Cues

Orthographic perspective is less acceptable to our eyes and requires experience with its conventions to be able to read it. It represents a single object with multiple drawings and requires the ability to assemble the drawings in your mind. We experience things in orthographic perspective when their surfaces are relatively flat and we are standing directly in front of and facing them. As we move away from an object, our experience more closely corresponds to an orthographic drawing. The edges of surfaces are represented by lines that follow the rules of orthoghraphic drawing. Parallel edges remain parallel and retain direct measured relationships to each other and the thing being represented. Verticals remain vertical, horizontals remain horizontal, and the depth axis is represented by a point.

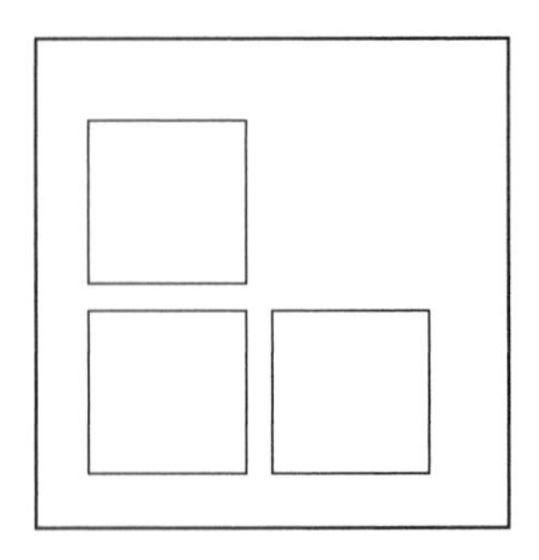

Linear perspective drawing is a tool used by the designer or delineator to make a reasonably accurate representation of a three-dimensional object on a two-dimensional surface (the drawing sheet). A linear perspective drawing is an image of an object projected upon an assumed plane (the picture plane, or PP) that is parallel to the observer's face or eyes. When used as a representational tool for the design-drawing process, it is of utmost importance not to misrepresent the physical appearance of buildings with inaccurate perspective representations. The following are the most commonly used terms in the vocabulary of perspective drawing techniques.

TERM	ABBREVIATION	DEFINITION
Station Point	SP	• A vantage point location to view an object or group of objects; the location of the observer's eye. Object projection lines (also termed visual ray or sightlines) converge to this point.
Picture Plane	PP	• A stationary, transparent, two-dimensional, vertical plane or "window." This window receives a true-size image from the projection lines that converge to the station point. It is perpendicular to the ground plane and parallel to the observer.
Line of Sight	LS	• An imaginary central axis line projected from the observer's eye (station point) that intersects the vertical picture plane perpendicularly. It is perpendicular to the observer.
Horizon Line or Eye-Level Line	HL	• The horizon line represents the observer's eye level and is recorded on the picture plane. It is the vanishing line for all horizontal lines and planes.
Ground Line	GL	• The line where the picture plane and the ground meet. The ground line lies within a ground plane from which vertical measurements are made.
Ground Plane	GP	• The reference plane where the observer is situated. It can be at any level (real or imaginary), depending on the vantage point of the perspective view.
Vanishing Point	VPL, VPR, and VP_o	• A point on the horizon line where any group of parallel horizontal lines converge in perspective. Groups of oblique (inclined) parallel lines vanish either above (sloping upward) or below (sloping downward) the horizon line. Parallel lines that are parallel to the picture plane do not converge.
Vertical Measuring Line	VML	• A vertical line within the picture plane. Vertical height dimensions are transferred from an elevation to this vertical true-length line in order to be projected into the perspective drawing.
Midpoint	M	• A point located on the horizon line that lies halfway between the vanishing points in a two-point perspective.
Horizontal Measuring Line	HML	• A horizontal line lying in the picture plane, it is therefore a true-length line.

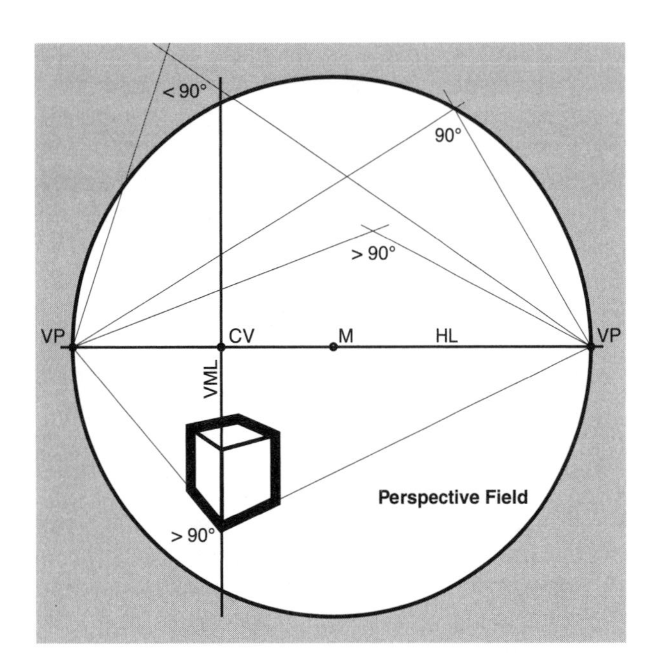

Acceptable Distortion

Linear perspective formalizes through geometry a system that attempts to represent three-dimensional reality on a two-dimensional surface—that is, it attempts to place a portion of the visual field on a page. Because it is a closed system assuming a fixed, one-eyed observer, it has limitations that must be respected if the goal is to accurately represent perceived visual reality—for the drawing to "look right." The cube that is drawn with its lead edge coinciding with the vertical measuring line (VML—the line drawn through the center of vision) and centered vertically on the horizon line is the most accurate cube in the perspective. As the cubes move away from this location, they progressively become more distorted. The question, therefore, is how far from this location does a perspective retain sufficient accuracy so as not to be visually disturbing—what are the limits within which the perspective looks right?

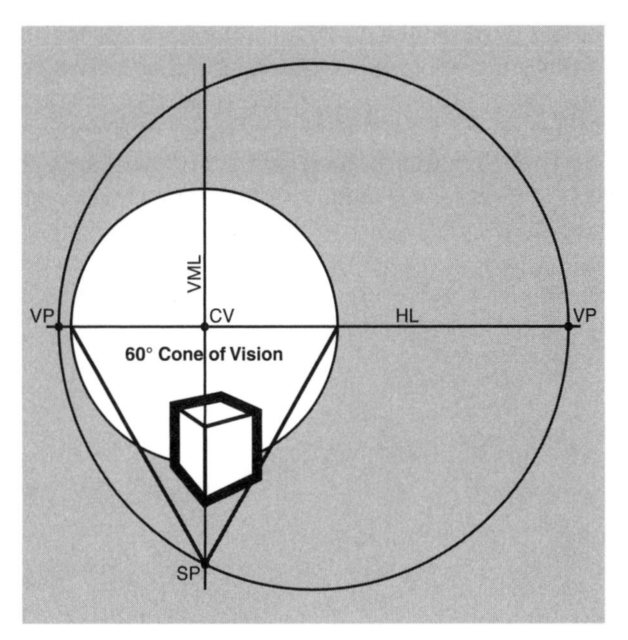

Cone of Vision

For any given perspective setup, there is a finite area surrounding the center of vision (CV), within which the perspective will look normal. The limits of this area are defined by a **cone of vision** (COV), which starts at the station point. The cone of vision links the way our eyes work and controls **distortion** within the perspective system. A 60° cone is one that extends 30° to either side of our line of sight. This illustration simultaneously shows a 60° cone of vision in both plan and perspective. For any measuring point perspective setup, the cone of vision can be constructed to establish the area within which a perspective will "look most correct."

Diagrams and text: Courtesy of
William R. Benedict, Assistant Professor
California Polytechnic State University
College of Architecture & Environmental Design
San Luis Obispo, California

Perspective Field/90° Horizontal Corner

The **perspective field** is the area defined by a circle whose center is located at the midpoint (M) and whose circumference intersects the two horizontal vanishing points in a two-point perspective. The perspective field can be used to control the near internal angle of horizontal rectangles to 90° or greater. When the angle becomes less than 90°, it does not look right. Any two lines intersecting at the circumference of the perspective field will create a 90° angle. Those intersecting beyond the circumference will create an angle of less than 90°, while those intersecting within the perspective field will create an angle of more than 90°. Therefore, the perspective field provides a guideline for establishing some limits within the linear perspective system.

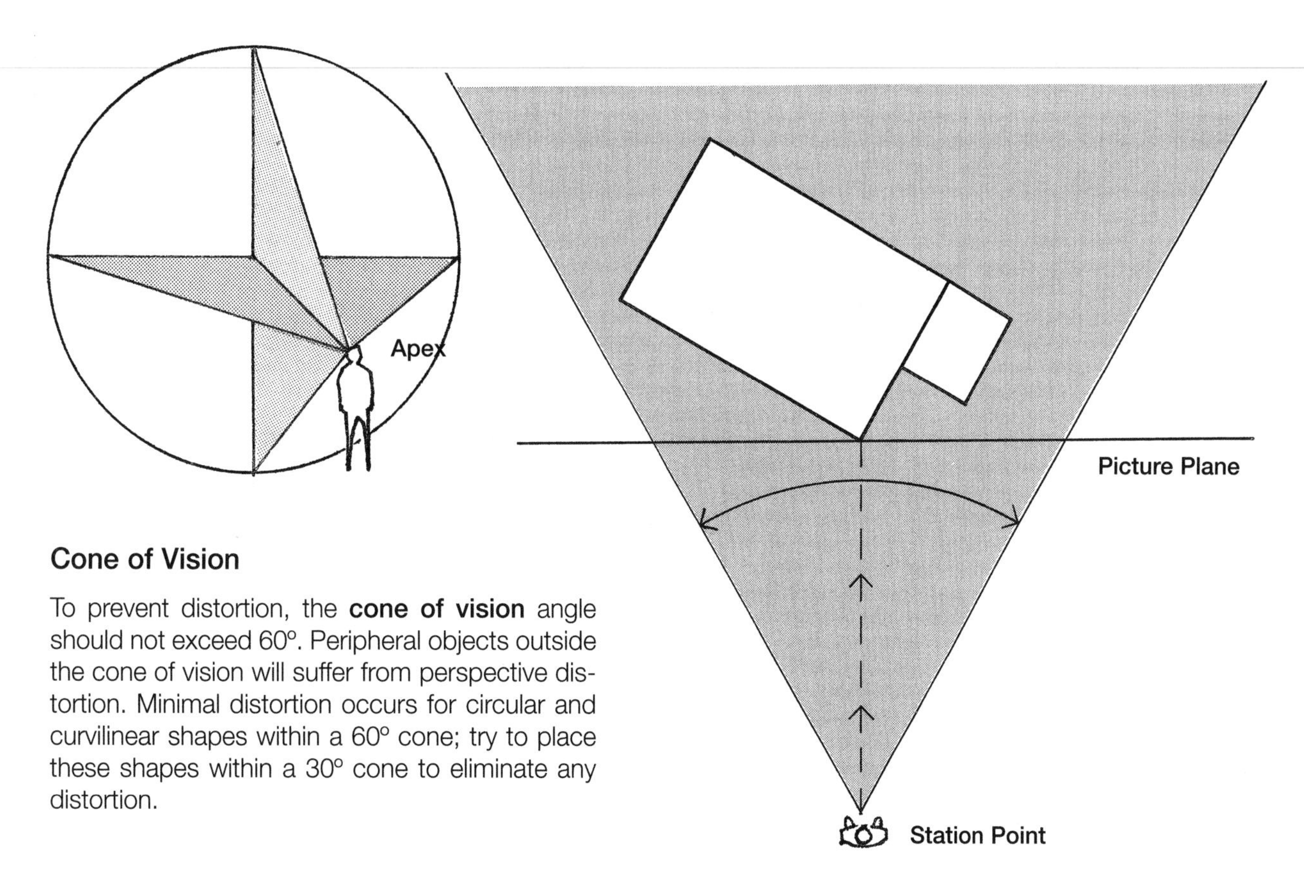

Cone of Vision

To prevent distortion, the **cone of vision** angle should not exceed 60°. Peripheral objects outside the cone of vision will suffer from perspective distortion. Minimal distortion occurs for circular and curvilinear shapes within a 60° cone; try to place these shapes within a 30° cone to eliminate any distortion.

Think of the three-dimensional **cone of vision** as what you can see without moving your eyes. The boundary of this view is the cone's surface. The area of nondistorted vision is the area of the base of the cone (a true circle) that is perpendicular to the observer's central axis line of sight. This circular area on the vertical picture plane can be seen in clear focus when the apex angle is 60° or less. The area viewed increases in size as the picture plane moves away from the observer's eyes. However, if the observer moves away from an area of constant size, the cone of vision angle becomes smaller.

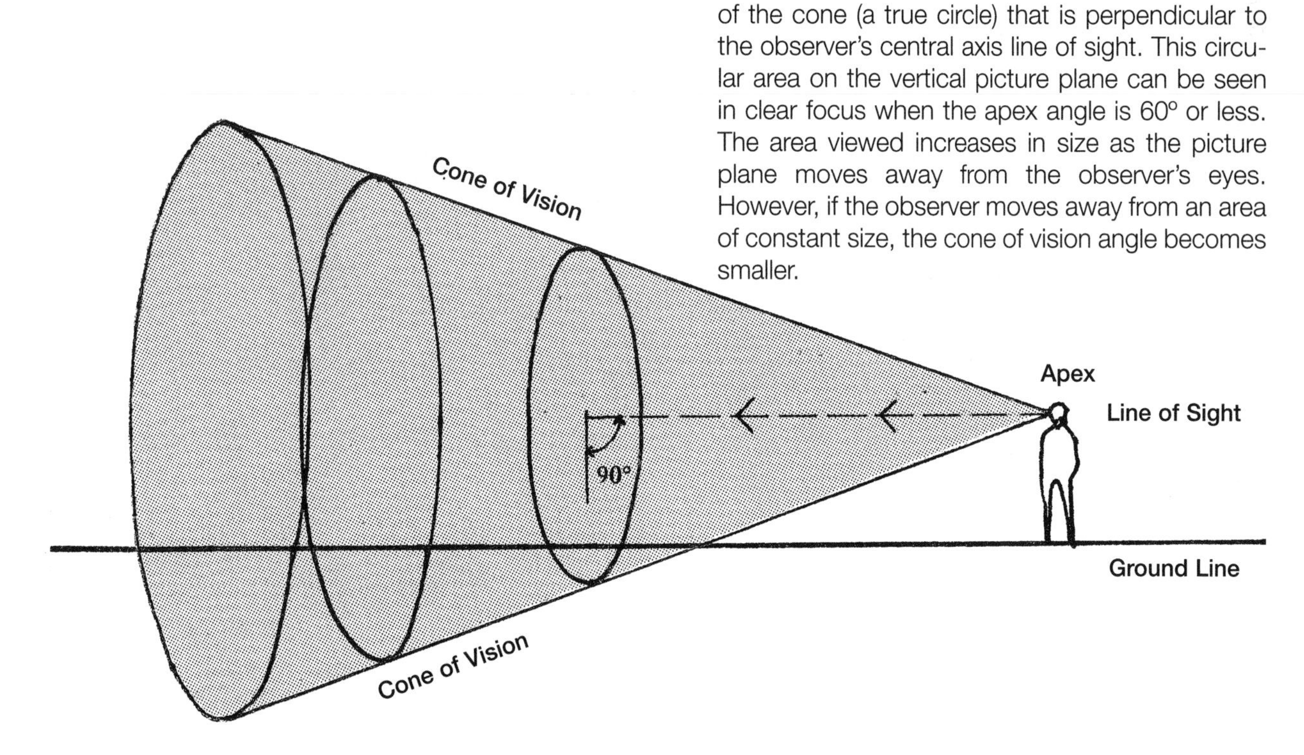

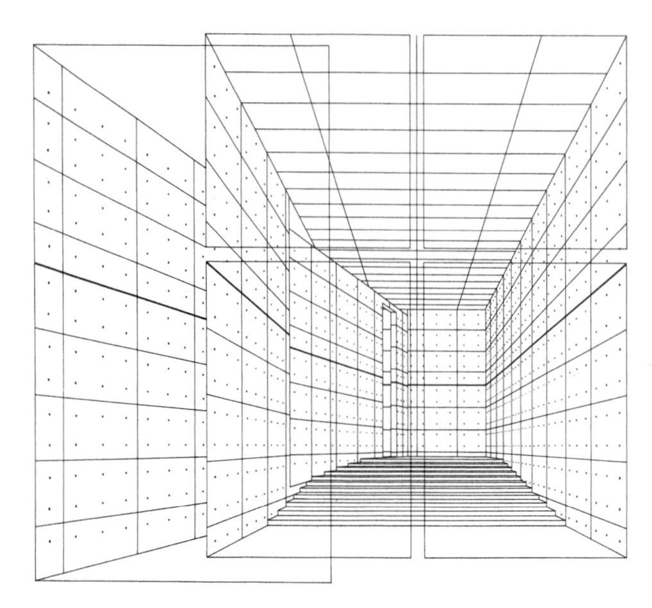

Drawing: Church of the Light, Ibaraki, Japan
23.3" × 16.5" (59.2 × 41.9 cm)
Medium: Ink
Courtesy of Tadao Ando, Architect

The Picture Plane

This transparent interior perspective shows the wall with a cross slit behind the church's altar. The wall simulates a vertical picture plane through which one can capture the perspective view. An exception to the flat, two-dimensional picture plane is the spheroidal (similar to a sphere but not completely round) picture plane used with a fish-eye lens view.

Drawing: Student project by Corvin Matei
Vasari Museum, Florence, Italy
10" × 8" (25.4 × 20.3 cm)
Medium: Ink on Mylar
Courtesy of the University of Texas at Arlington School of Architecture

A window is a fixed transparent vertical plane. When we look through a window, our eyes receive images of the three-dimensional objects we see. These images are translated onto a two-dimensional plane (the window) at an infinite number of points when our lines of sight intersect the window. Thus, the window becomes the **picture plane.** This drawing shows the viewpoint of an observer looking through a window. Note that the observer's side with the widest upper-body dimension is always parallel to the picture plane (window).

To the right is an example of parallel one-point perspective. The image of the building form is projected on the picture plane by sight lines that intersect the picture plane. Vertical and horizontal lines in the building retain verticality and horizontality in the image. Lines in the building not parallel to the picture plane will converge to a vanishing point. Because the building form is behind the picture plane, it is projected smaller than true size on the picture plane. If it were in front, it would be projected larger than true size. A one-point perspective always has a plane parallel to the picture plane. Any planes perpendicular to the picture plane vanish to one point. A two-point perspective (below) has angled planes (not parallel) to the picture plane.

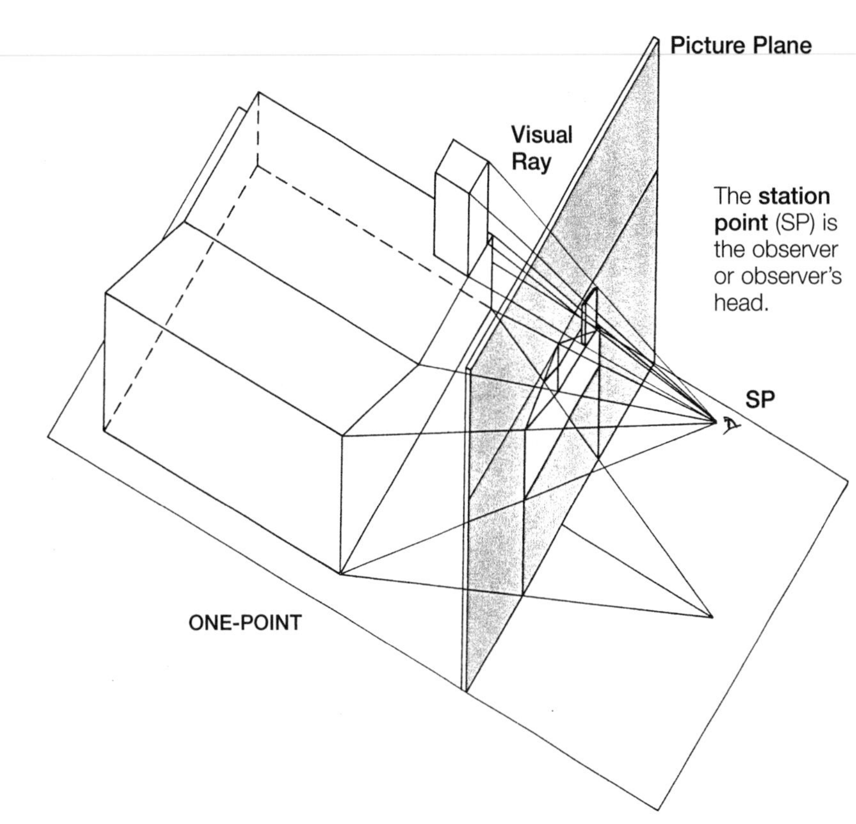

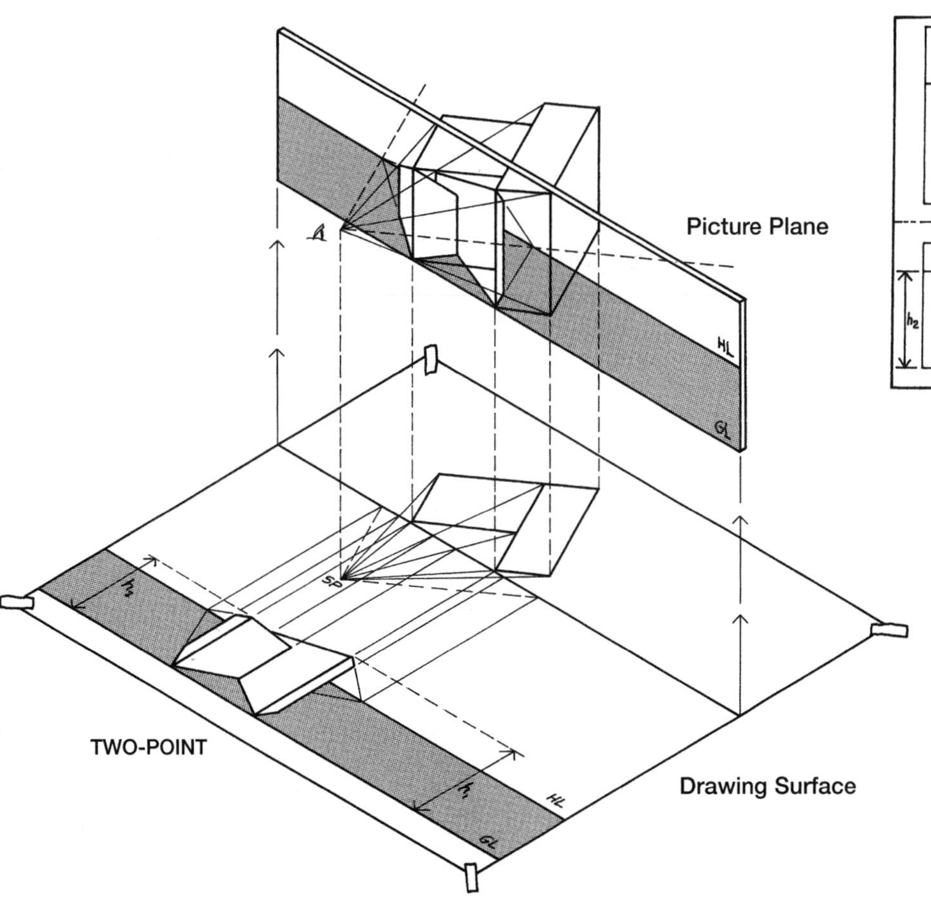

The **picture plane** is always perpendicular to the drawing surface and the central line of sight. It is represented by a **line** on the drawing. Also on the drawing, the observer reduces to a dot and the building form to a two-dimensional plan view. True heights (**h_1** and **h_2**) are always obtained from a set of orthographic drawings (plans and elevations). They are measured vertically from the ground line.

You can manipulate a perspective image by changing certain variables. These include moving the picture plane, changing the orientation, changing the station point location with respect to the object, and moving the horizon line up and down.

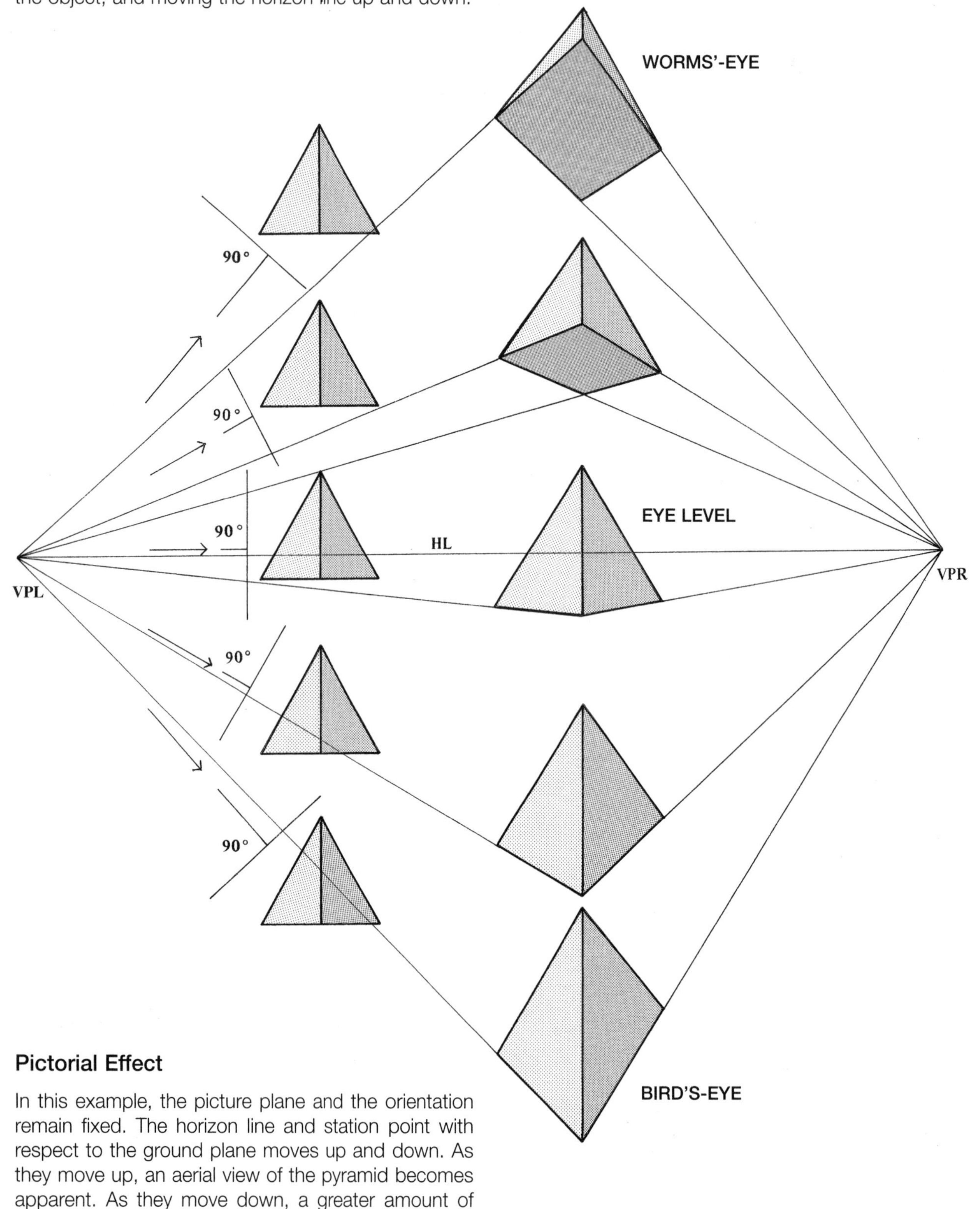

Pictorial Effect

In this example, the picture plane and the orientation remain fixed. The horizon line and station point with respect to the ground plane moves up and down. As they move up, an aerial view of the pyramid becomes apparent. As they move down, a greater amount of underside view becomes apparent.

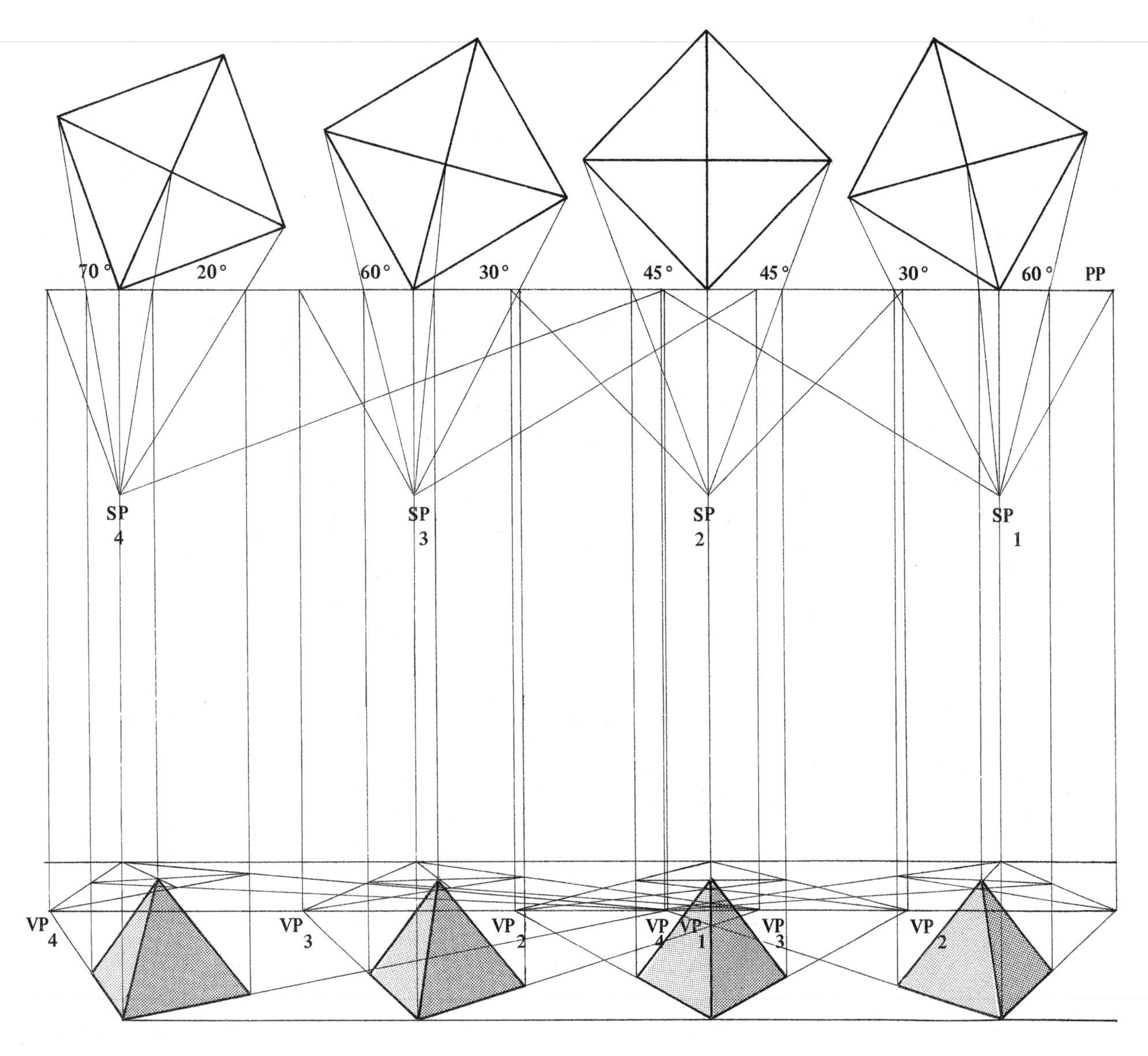

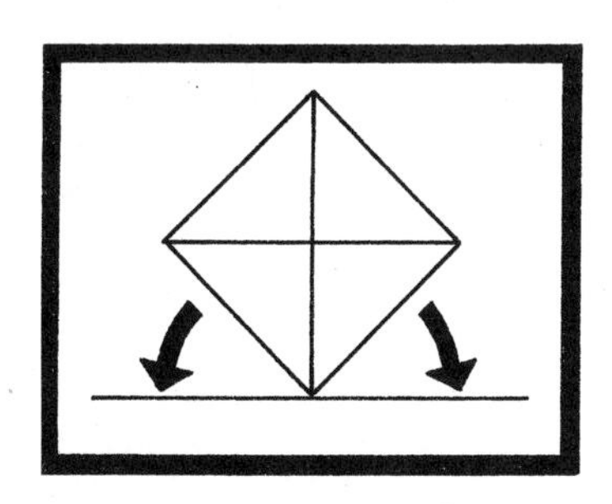

Each **orientation** change produces a new set of angles with respect to the picture plane.

In this example, the picture plane, the station point location, and the horizon line remain fixed. The orientation changes. As the plane of the pyramid sides turn away from the picture plane, you see less of its surface. In other words, it is foreshortened more.

Note that increasing the distance from the picture plane to the station point (**PP_4** to **PP_1**) causes a progressive enlargement of the perspective images that have a similar projection.

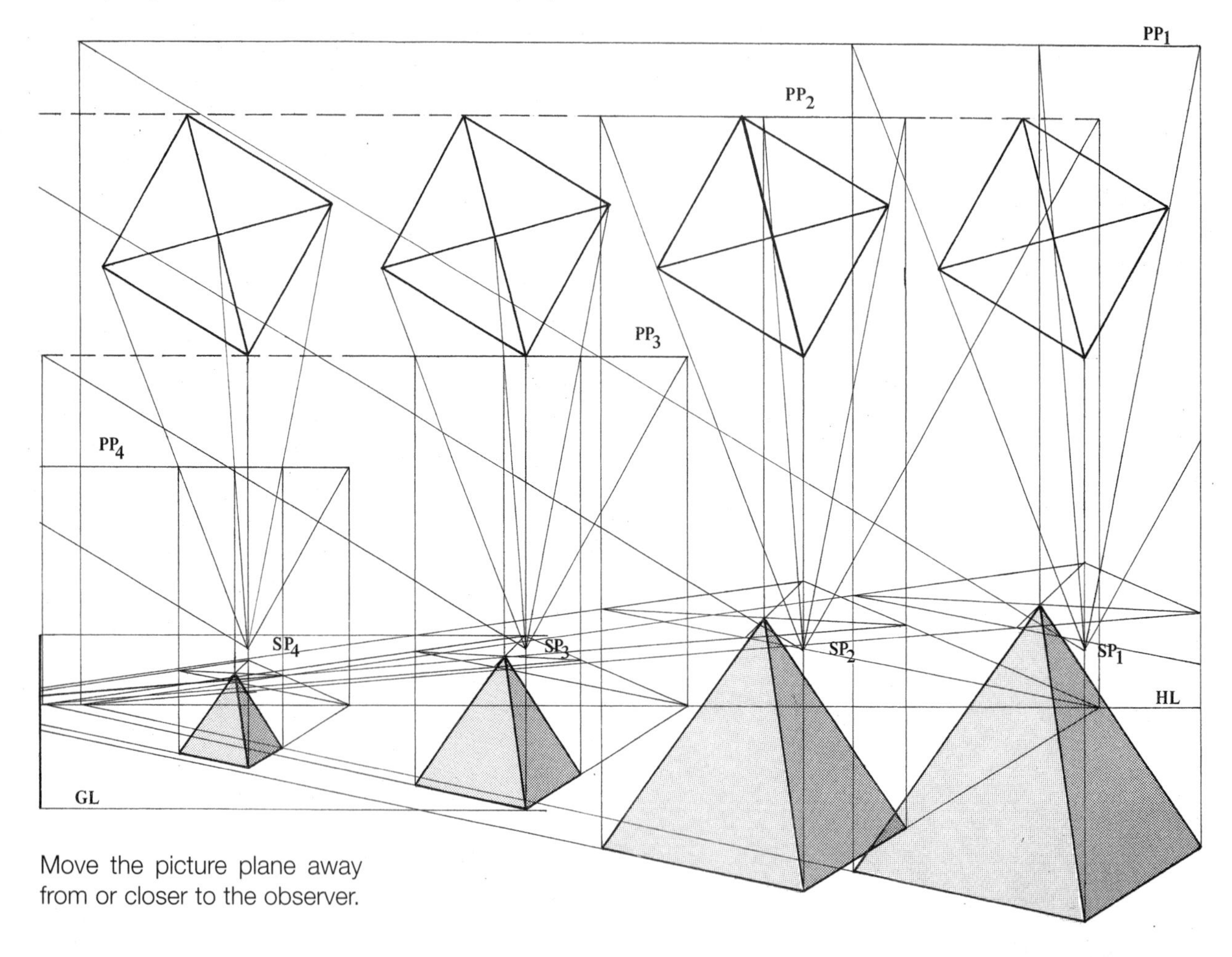

Move the picture plane away from or closer to the observer.

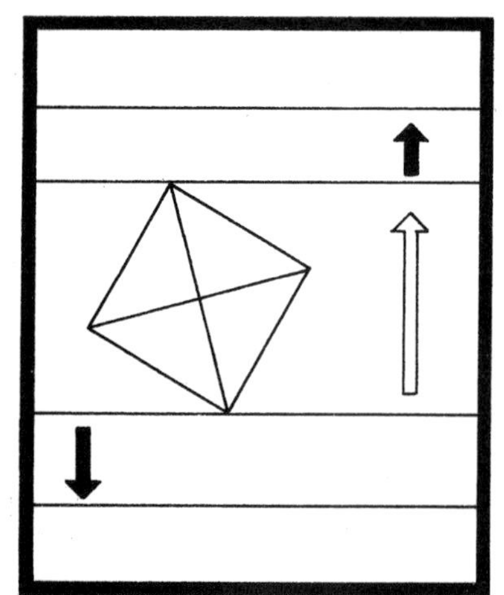

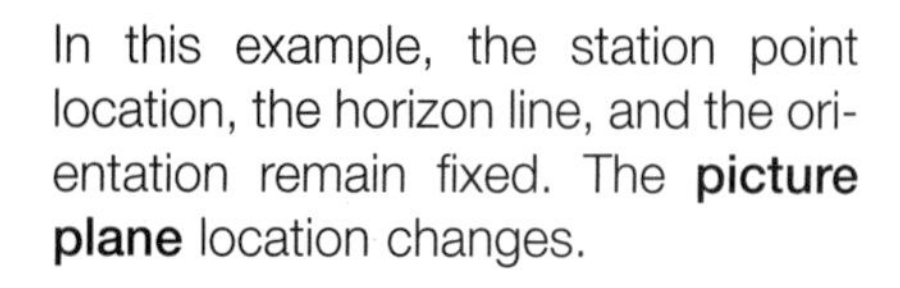
In this example, the station point location, the horizon line, and the orientation remain fixed. The **picture plane** location changes.

Drawing: The Pyramid at Le Grand Louvre, Paris, France
30" × 16" (76 × 41 cm)
Medium: Acrylic
Pei Cobb Freed & Partners / Michel Macary Architects
Courtesy of Lee Dunnette, Architectural Illustrator

Note that increasing the station point distance to the object (**SP_4** to **SP_1**) causes a decrease in foreshortening due to the two vanishing points progressively moving away from each other.

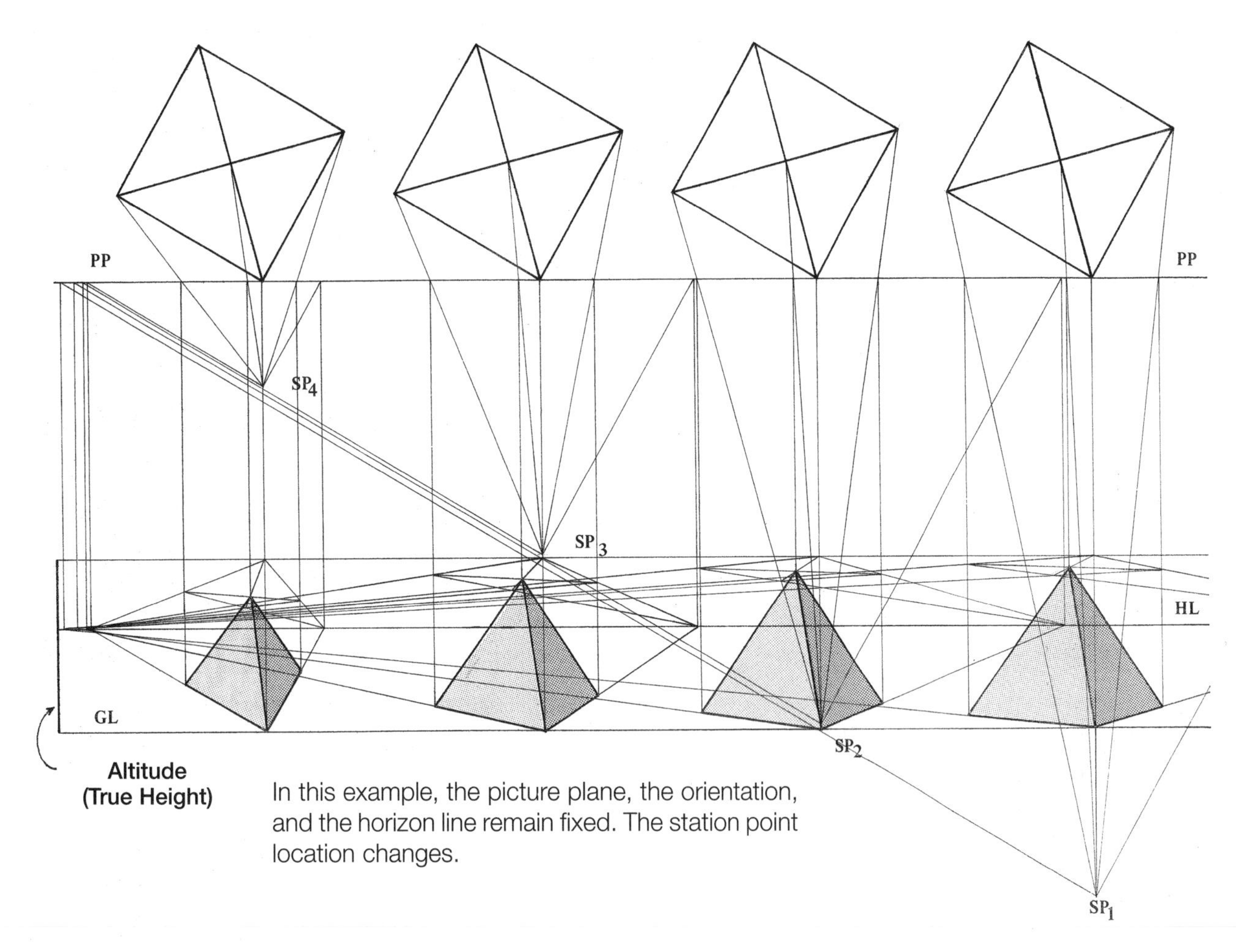

In this example, the picture plane, the orientation, and the horizon line remain fixed. The station point location changes.

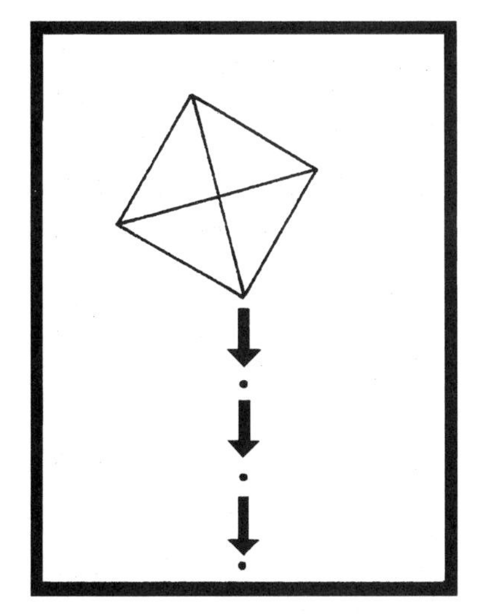

© Olallo L. Fernandez

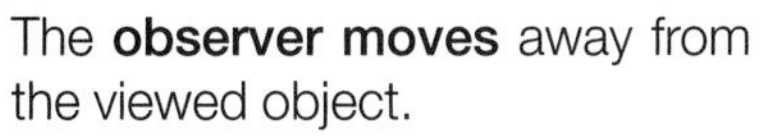

The **observer moves** away from the viewed object.

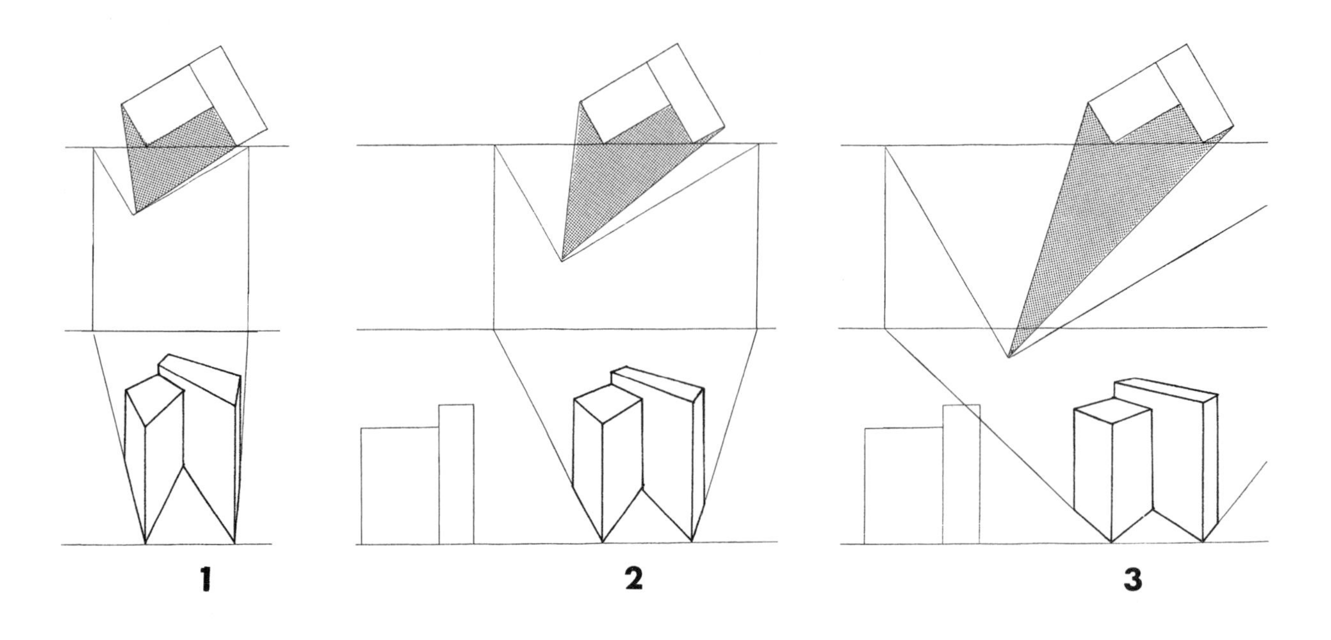

4

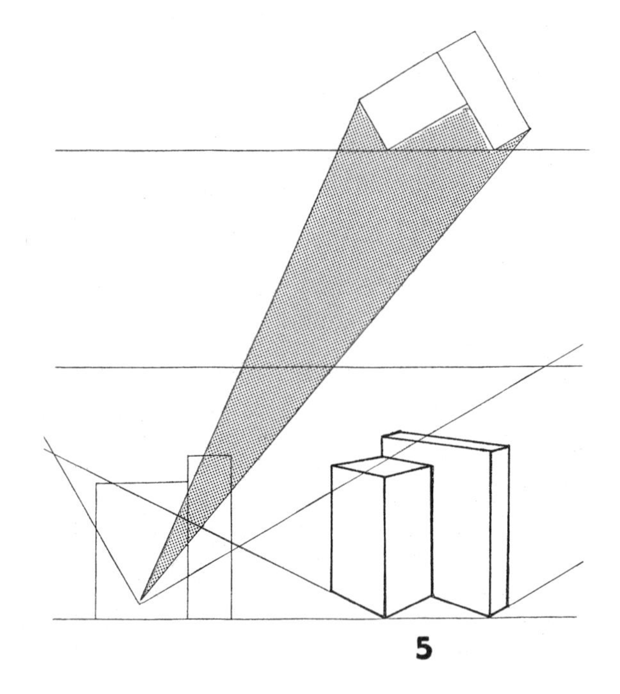

Distortion

Distortion, shown here in two-point perspective, is dependent on the spacing of vanishing points. A very close station point location with close vanishing points results in extreme convergence with a great amount of foreshortening (see **1** and **2**). A very distant station point results in minimal convergence with very little foreshortening. A more natural pictorial view is obtained by spreading the vanishing points apart (see **4** and **5**). However, try not to spread them too far apart or a distorted flatness will occur. A good distance from the SP to the PP is three times the object height, or 1.80 to 2.40 times the width of the scene or object.

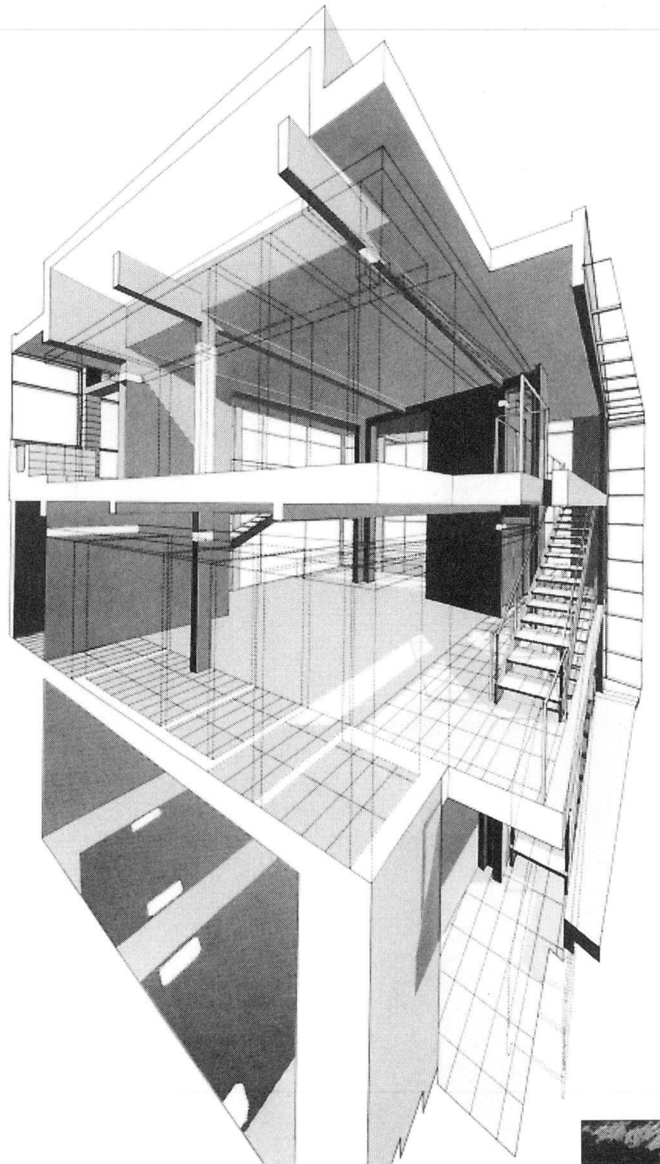

Drawing: Burnett House addition
Lake Oswego, Oregon
24" × 36" (61 × 91.4 cm)
Medium: Ink on Mylar with Zipatone
Courtesy of David Rockwood Architects & Associates

Distortion

This interior perspective shows a large amount of foreshortening with conditions similar to example **1** (opposite page). There is a point at which the vanishing points become too close with respect to the height (which relates to the cone of vision). This results in a distorted view.

Example of extreme convergence

This exterior perspective shows a small amount of foreshortening with conditions similar to example **5** on the opposite page. The vanishing points are more spread apart.

Example of a closer to natural pictorial view

Drawing: Student project by Steve Gambrel
Seafarers' Church Institute
Courtesy of the University of Virginia School of Architecture

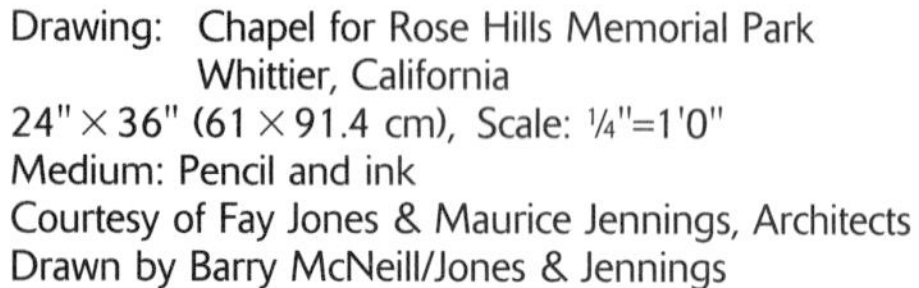

Drawing: Chapel for Rose Hills Memorial Park
Whittier, California
24" × 36" (61 × 91.4 cm), Scale: ¼"=1'0"
Medium: Pencil and ink
Courtesy of Fay Jones & Maurice Jennings, Architects
Drawn by Barry McNeill/Jones & Jennings

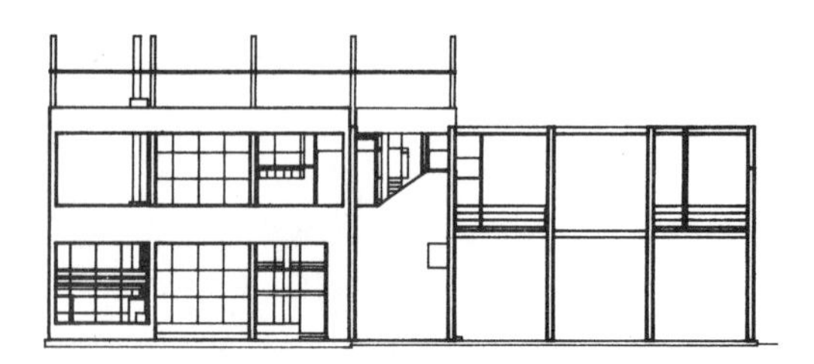

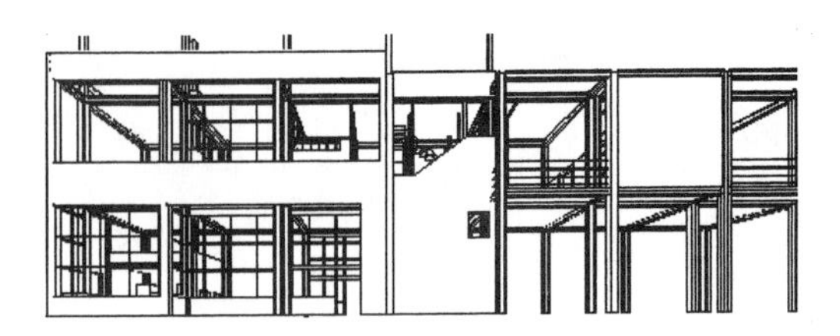

Drawings: Student project by Lois McGinnis and Michael Patrick
Shelby's Lake House—A project in CAD
Courtesy of the University of Texas at Arlington
School of Architecture

One-Point Perspective

The above one-point perspective seen at ground level is much more descriptive than its flat two-dimensional elevation.

The three main types of perspectives are classified based on the drawing's primary vanishing points. Many drawings have secondary minor vanishing points. These building examples show that all horizontal lines that recede away from the observer's eye converge to **one** vanishing point. Therefore, they can be classified as **one-point** perspectives. Note that in all three cases, one face of the building is parallel to the picture plane.

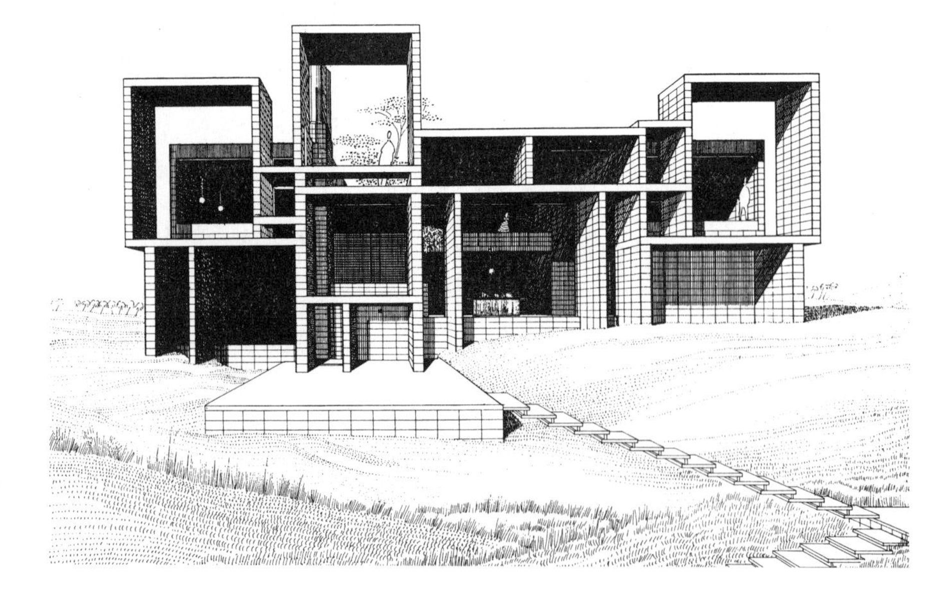

Drawing: Milam residence
St. John's County, Florida
33" × 30" (83.8 × 76.2 cm)
Medium: Ink on board,
Courtesy of Paul Rudolph, Architect

Two-Point Perspective

These building examples show their dominant facades converging on left and right sides to **two** vanishing points on their respective horizon lines. Therefore, they can be classified as **two-point** perspectives. Two-point perspectives, as in these examples, have parallel lines and edges in their dominant facades not parallel to the picture plane. With **three-point** perspectives (discussed at the end of this chapter), there is a characteristic upward or downward convergence of those same two sides to a third vanishing point (see p. 202).

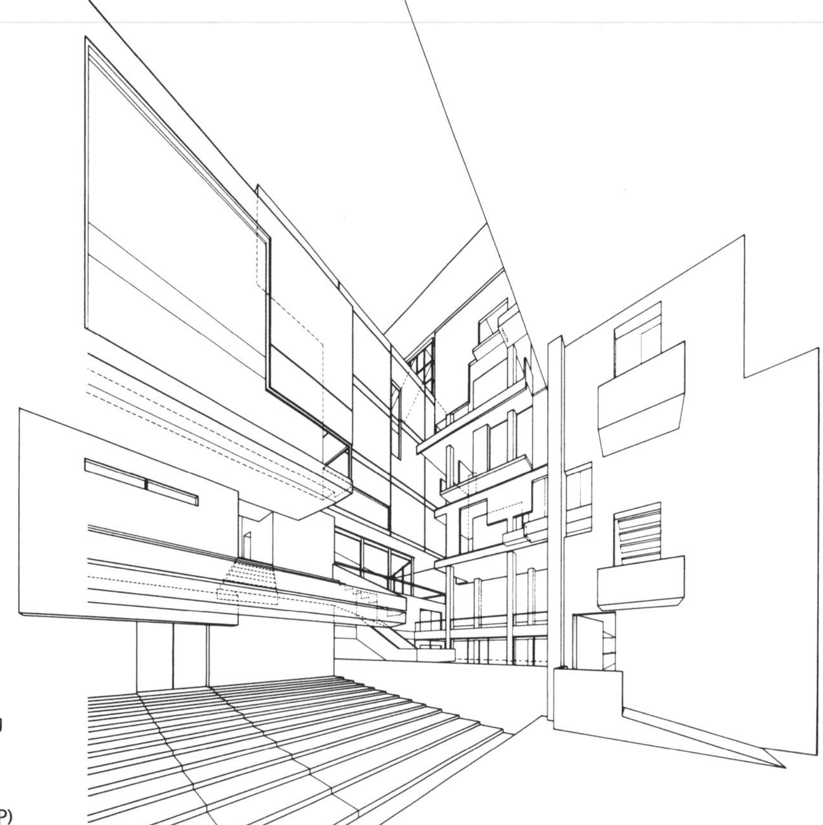

Drawing: Student project by Leopoldo Chang
Poet's Hotel, New York
Medium: Ink on Mylar
Excerpted from abstract, Columbia School of Architecture Planning and Preservation (CSAAP)

Drawing: Studio Durant (unbuilt), Berkeley, California
Medium: Computer-generated plot (size dependent on size of plot)
Courtesy of David Baker Associates Architects

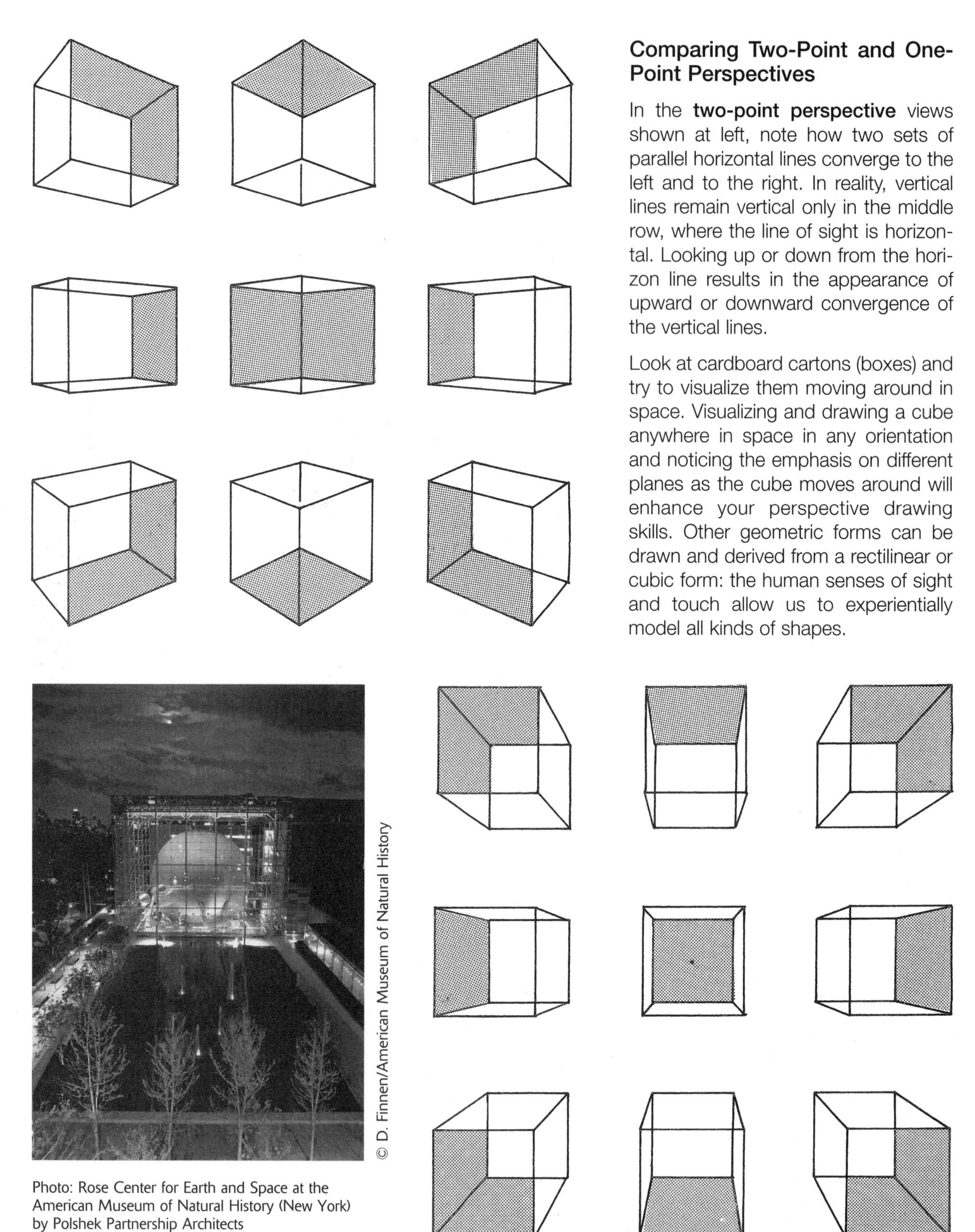

Comparing Two-Point and One-Point Perspectives

In the **two-point perspective** views shown at left, note how two sets of parallel horizontal lines converge to the left and to the right. In reality, vertical lines remain vertical only in the middle row, where the line of sight is horizontal. Looking up or down from the horizon line results in the appearance of upward or downward convergence of the vertical lines.

Look at cardboard cartons (boxes) and try to visualize them moving around in space. Visualizing and drawing a cube anywhere in space in any orientation and noticing the emphasis on different planes as the cube moves around will enhance your perspective drawing skills. Other geometric forms can be drawn and derived from a rectilinear or cubic form: the human senses of sight and touch allow us to experientially model all kinds of shapes.

© D. Finnen/American Museum of Natural History

Photo: Rose Center for Earth and Space at the American Museum of Natural History (New York) by Polshek Partnership Architects

In a **one-point perspective,** the vanishing point is on a line that is perpendicular to the picture plane and intersects the observer's eyes (station point).

Drawing: Theater lobby, Perry Community Education Village, Perry, Ohio
36" × 24" (91 × 61.4 cm)
Medium: Ink on Mylar
Courtesy of Perkins & Will, Architects

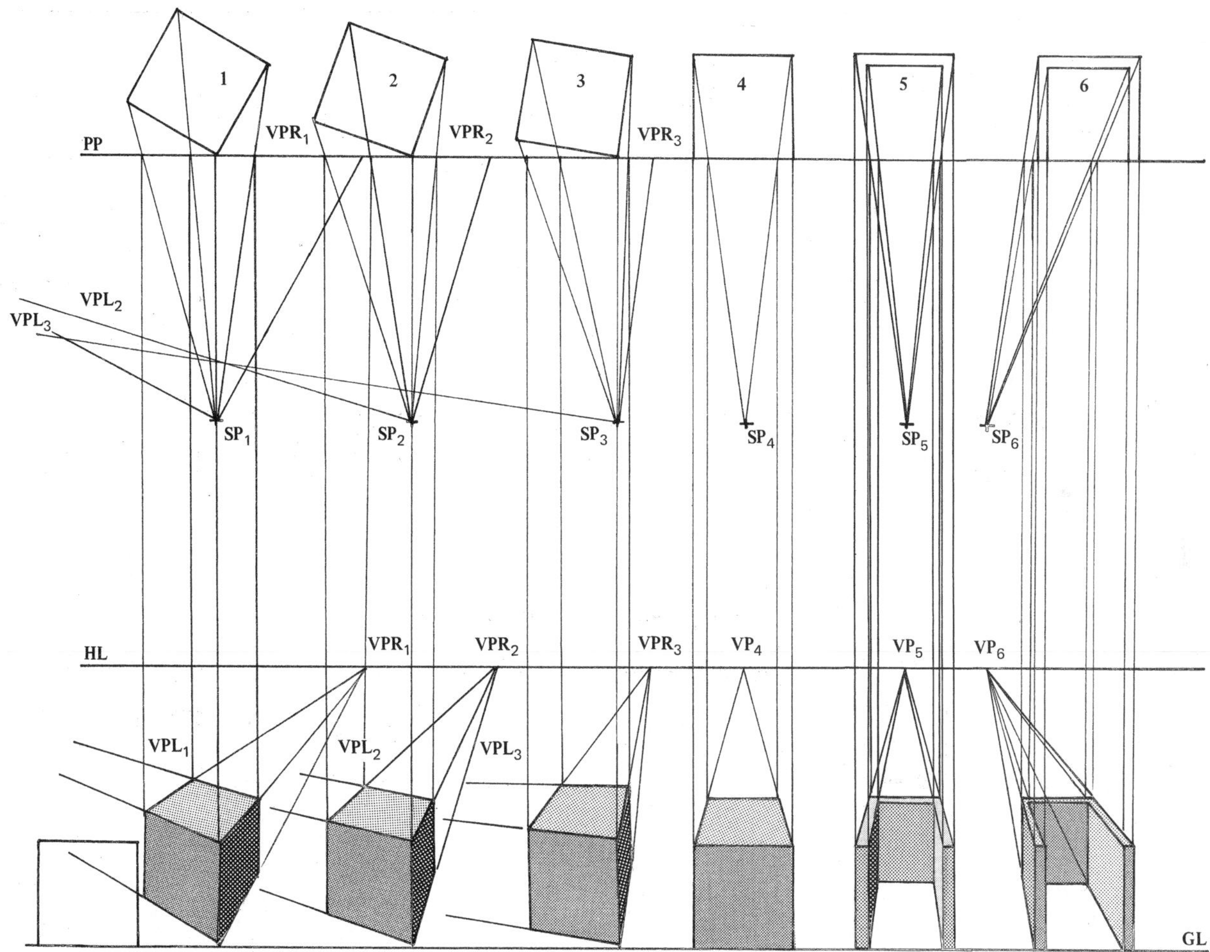

Understanding the concepts of **one-point** parallel perspective will facilitate your understanding of the construction of **two-point** angular perspectives. The construction methods of one-point perspectives are therefore presented prior to those for two-point perspectives. All horizontal and vertical lines in a one-point are parallel to the picture plane—hence the term "parallel perspective." However, all lines perpendicular to the picture plane converge to the one vanishing point (**4, 5,** and **6**). Note how the cube transforms from a two-point (**1–3**) to a one-point (**4**). The illustration at the top shows characteristics of both one- and two-point perspectives. Note the tilted ellipses (see p. 211). For both one- and two-point perspectives, construction methods using orthographic views (plans, elevations, and sections) will be shown first; this will be followed by methods used without orthographic views that use measuring points.

Bird's-Eye, Eye-Level, and Worm's-Eye Views

Because several people can't occupy the same physical space simultaneously, people will see the same object from different angles if they all look at it at the same time. Once we vacate a physical space, another person can experience the same viewpoint. The eye-level line would change as an observer sits down, stands up, or stands on top of an object to view the chair illustrated below. Notice the foreshortening of the legs of the chair below as an observer moves higher and higher. The eye-level line is always at right angles to an observer's line of sight and is theoretically located at an infinite distance from your eyes.

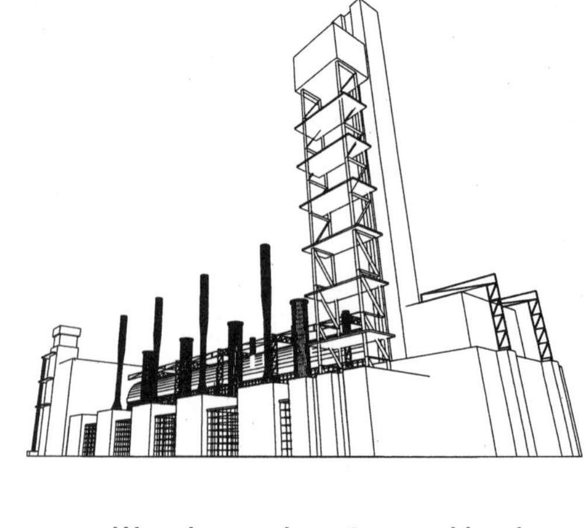

Worm's-eye view at ground level with upward convergence

CAD drawings (above and below):
Student projects by Bradford Winkeljohn and Jordan Parnass
Excerpted from abstract, Columbia School of Architecture Planning and Preservation (CSAPP)

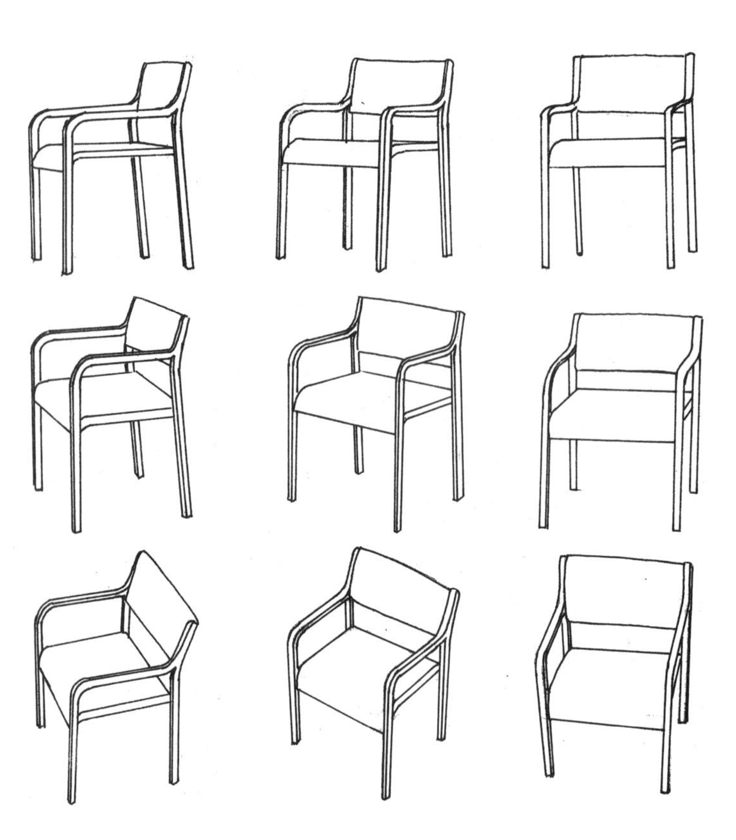

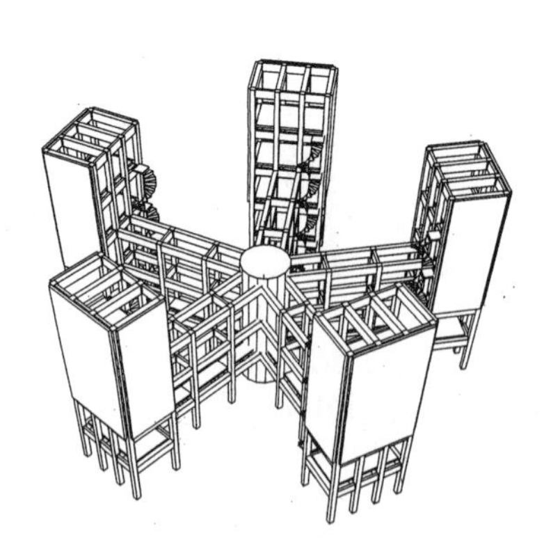

Bird's-eye view at a high angle with downward convergence

In the design-drawing process, it is important to study a design from every conceivable vantage point. For this reason, examples of other perspective views (e.g., above and below vantage points) are shown on pages 204–09.

For the most part, we view the urban environment at eye level in a standing position. The two views not at eye level are commonly termed worm's-eye and bird's-eye. Both are dramatic, although unnatural, views. A worm's-eye view can be at ground level or from below the ground plane, as shown at right.

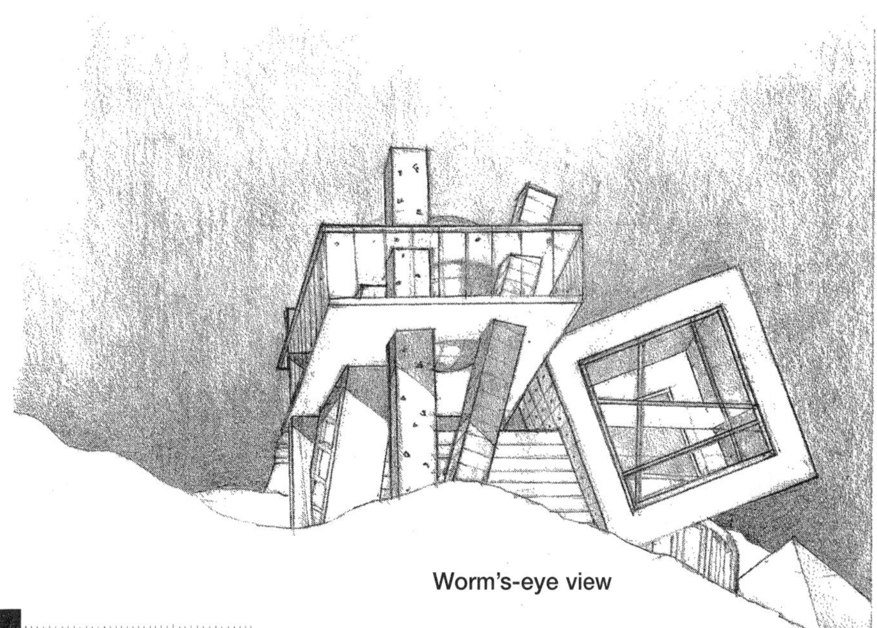

Worm's-eye view

Drawing: House in Hollywood Hills
Los Angeles, California
8" × 5" (20.3 × 12.7 cm)
Medium: Pencil
Courtesy of Kanner Architects
Drawn by Stephen Kanner

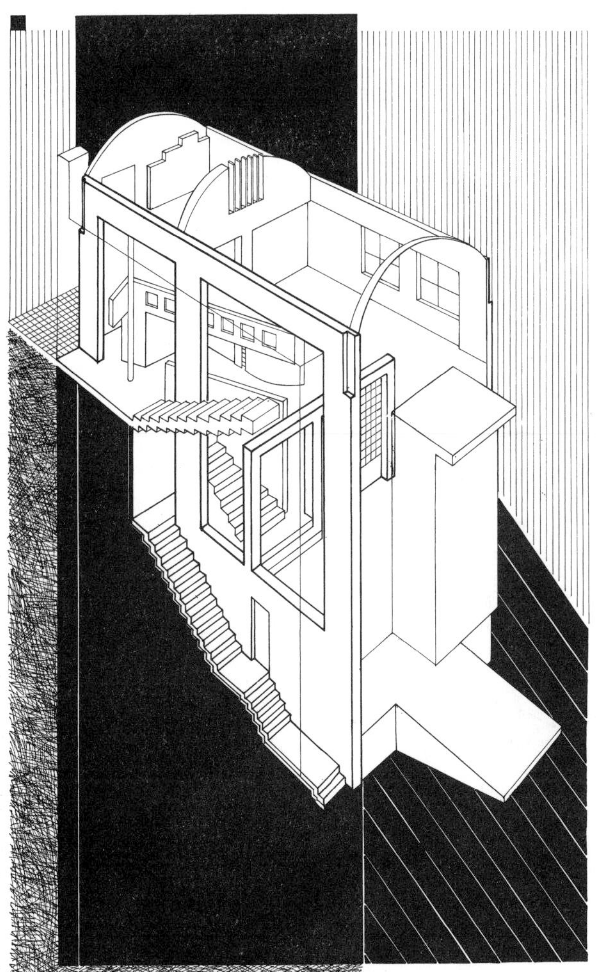

Bird's-eye view

Drawing: Shay house (1985), San Francisco, California
9.5" × 15.5" (24.1 × 39.4 cm), Scale: ⅜"=1'0"
Medium: Pen and ink
Courtesy of James Shay, AIA Architect

By stripping away exterior walls and casting the perspective as a bird's-eye, the complex interior is communicated. The rendered areas around the building are read in plan rather than perspective, creating interesting ambiguity.
[ARCHITECT'S STATEMENT]

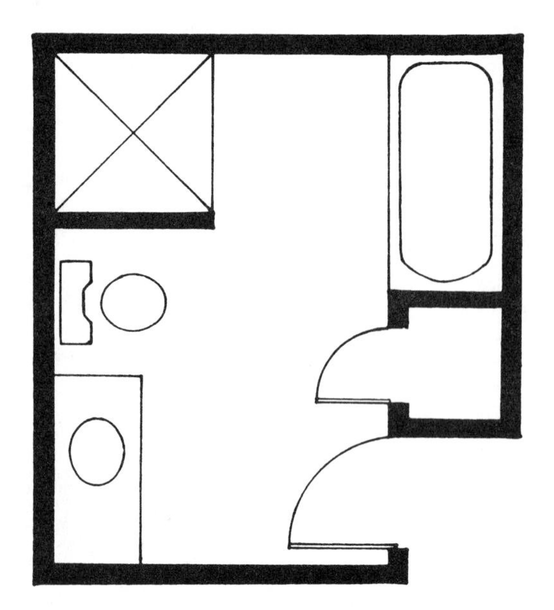

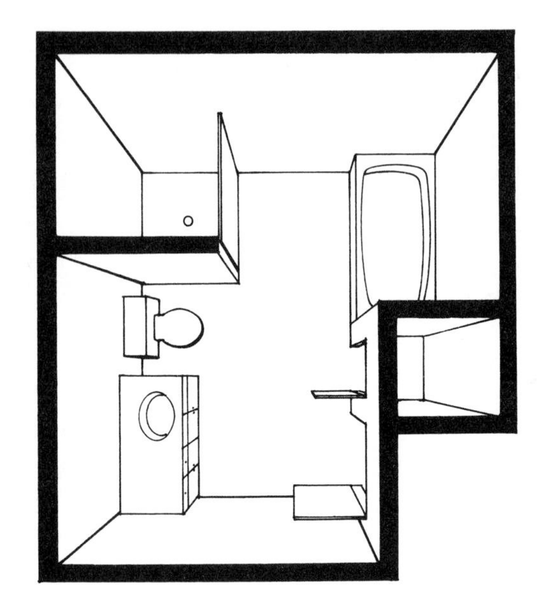

One-Point from Above

An unusual variation of the **one-point** perspective is a bird's-eye view with the line of sight perpendicular to the ground plane. This variation, which is achieved by transposing the positions of plan and elevation, is commonly used for small interior spaces and interior or exterior courtyard areas.

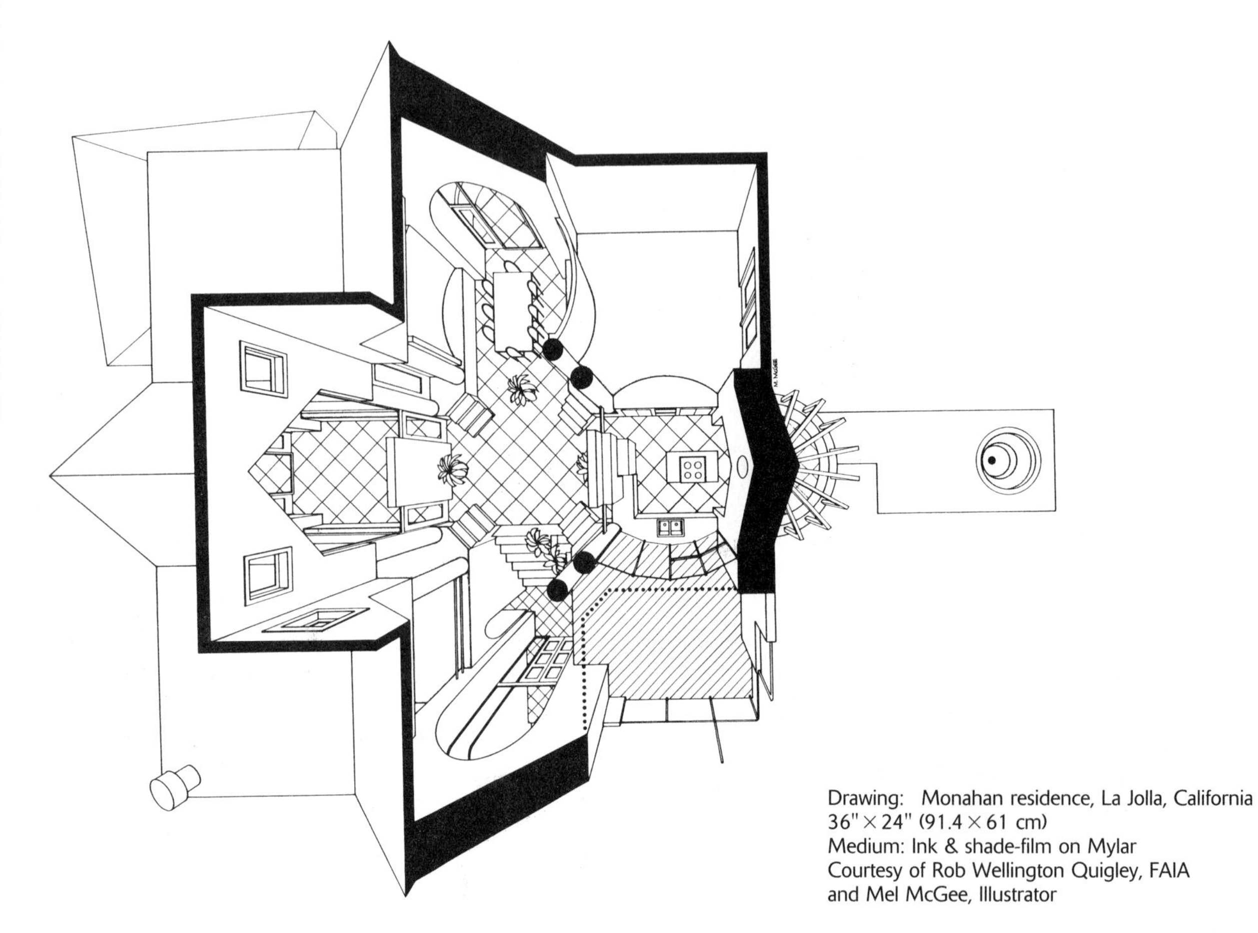

Drawing: Monahan residence, La Jolla, California
36" × 24" (91.4 × 61 cm)
Medium: Ink & shade-film on Mylar
Courtesy of Rob Wellington Quigley, FAIA
and Mel McGee, Illustrator

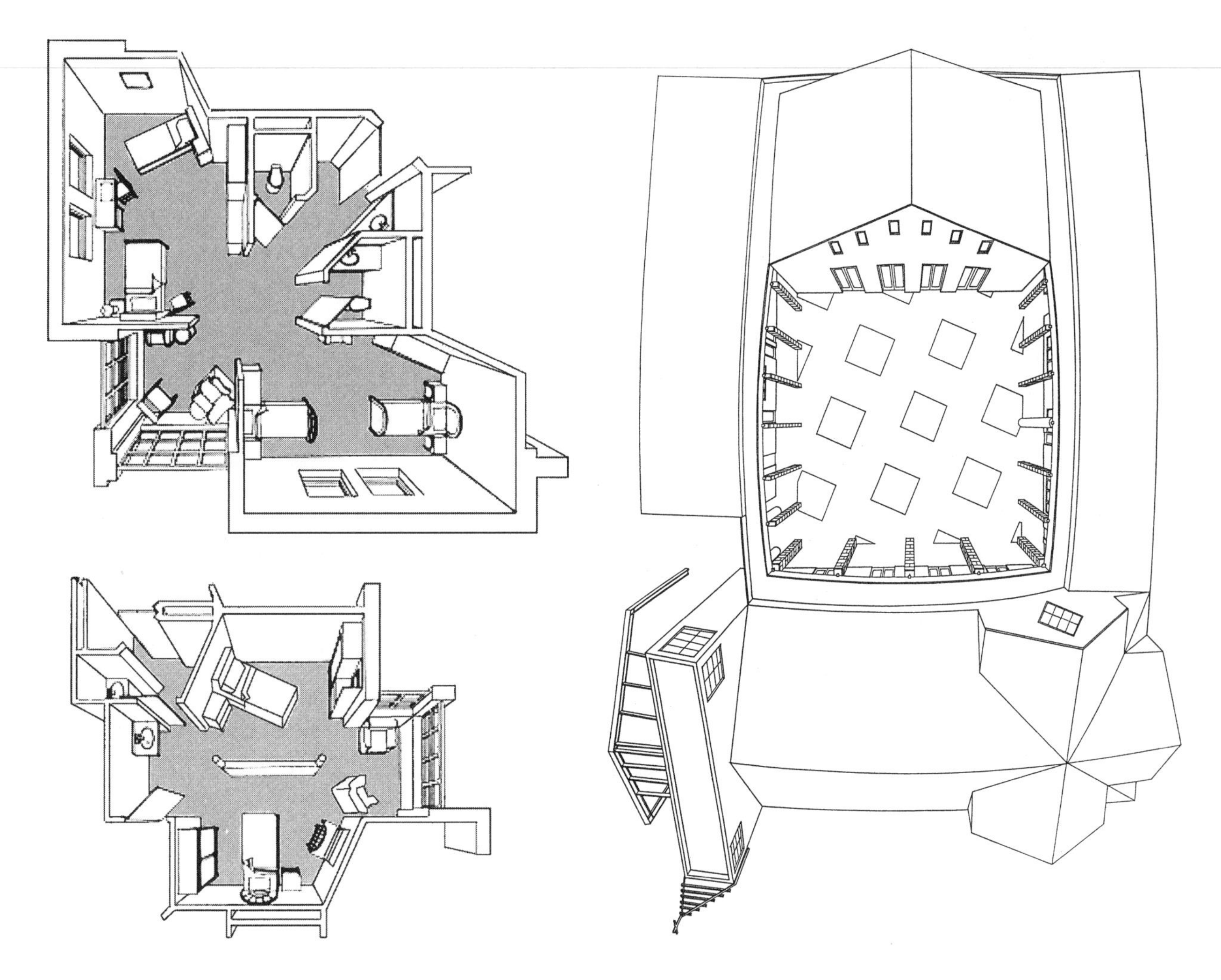

Drawings: Freeport Hospital Health Care Village, Kitchener, Ontario, Canada
Courtesy of NORR Partnership Ltd./
NORR Health Care Design Group

Drawing: New Hope Church, Duarte, California
24" × 36" (61 × 91.4 cm)
Medium: Ink on vellum
Courtesy of Rebecca L. Binder, FAIA

© Marcus Chaw

Photo: The Dueling Stairs of the Vatican Museum

One-Point from Above

Interior views from above are very descriptive and hence quite informative, especially to a person (client) who does not completely understand an architectural plan. In most cases, they simulate a one-point perspective view that one would have if the roof or ceiling of a scale model were removed. The view can be constructed quickly by placing the plan view so that it coincides with the picture plane. Vertical height lines through all corners of the plan are then drawn converging to one vanishing point in a relatively central location. Height lines are terminated where descriptively appropriate (typically where the plan section cut is taken). With the church at right above, there is no plan section cut, and the curving of the roof elements creates a fish-eye lens effect.

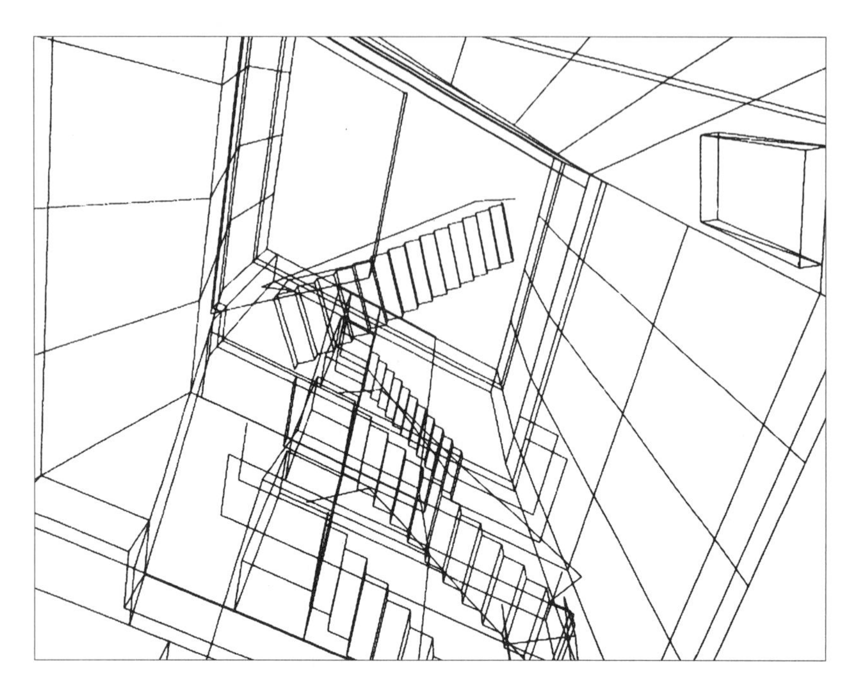

View up through tower

Drawing: 3[ER] House, Venice, California
Medium: CAD
Courtesy of COOP HIMMELB(L)AU Architects
Wolf D. Prix, Helmut Swiczinsky & Partner

One-Point from Below

This computer-generated wire-frame drawing is essentially a one-point perspective whose sides are tilted with respect to the edges of the picture plane and converging to other far-distant vanishing points. The stairs also converge to other distant vanishing points.

© Marcus Chaw

Oculus in Michelangelo's Petersdom in the Vatican

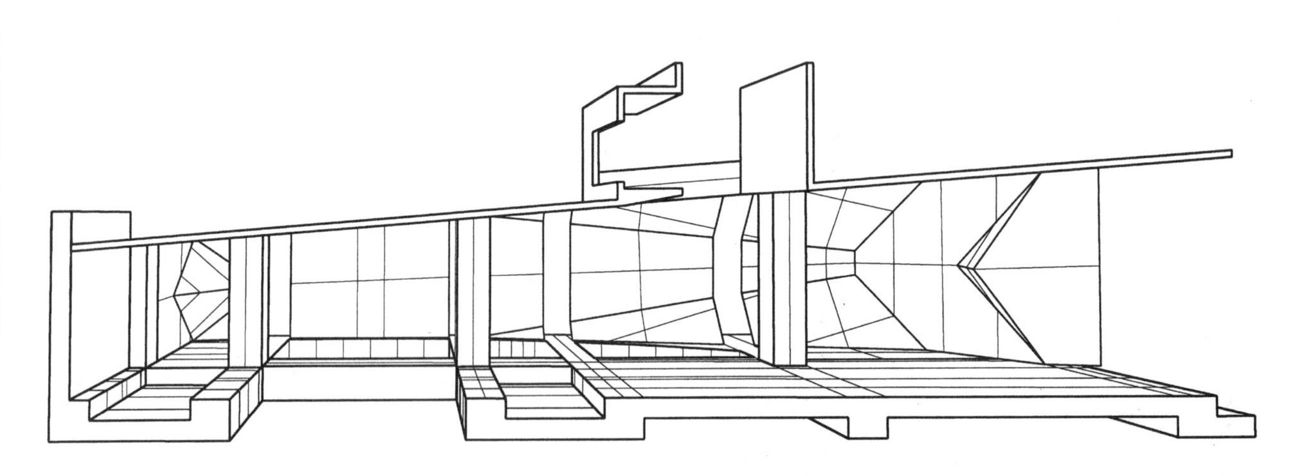

Drawing: Ackerman Student Union, University of California/Los Angeles
Medium: AutoCAD release 12
Courtesy of Rebecca L. Binder, FAIA Architecture & Planning

The entry elements and circulation in this remodel/addition project are key to the establishment of a "new" whole. The ceilings are integral to the design, articulated in finished plywood. This floor view perspective offers a clear description of this northeast entry element.
[ARCHITECT'S STATMENT]

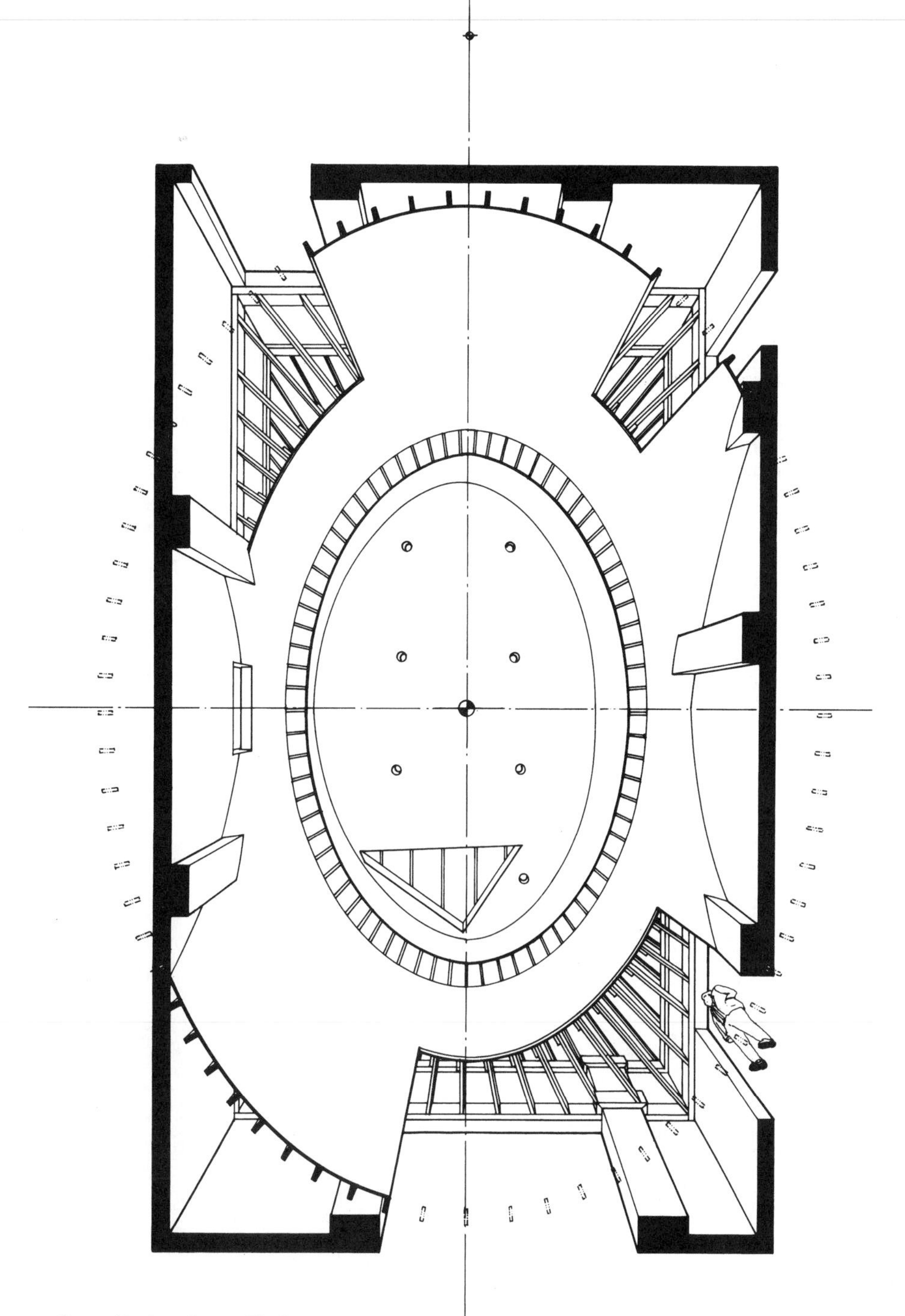

ONE-POINT FROM BELOW

One-Point from Below

This is a worm's-eye, one-point, dead-center view looking up.

This drawing illustrates the fact that symmetry is a moment in time and not a place. This is symmetrical asymmetry from the ground up. [ARCHITECT'S STATEMENT]

Drawing: Conference Room, 8522 National Boulevard
Culver City, California
Medium: Ink on Mylar
Courtesy of Eric Owen Moss, Architecct

Looking Downhill and Uphill

When the lines of sight of our bird's-eye and worm's-eye views are parallel to an inclined plane, we are looking downhill and uphill. We see downhill and uphill perspective views in the natural landscape as well as in street scenes in the cityscape. Downhill and uphill views inside or outside a building's environment are characterized by stairs, escalators, or ramps.

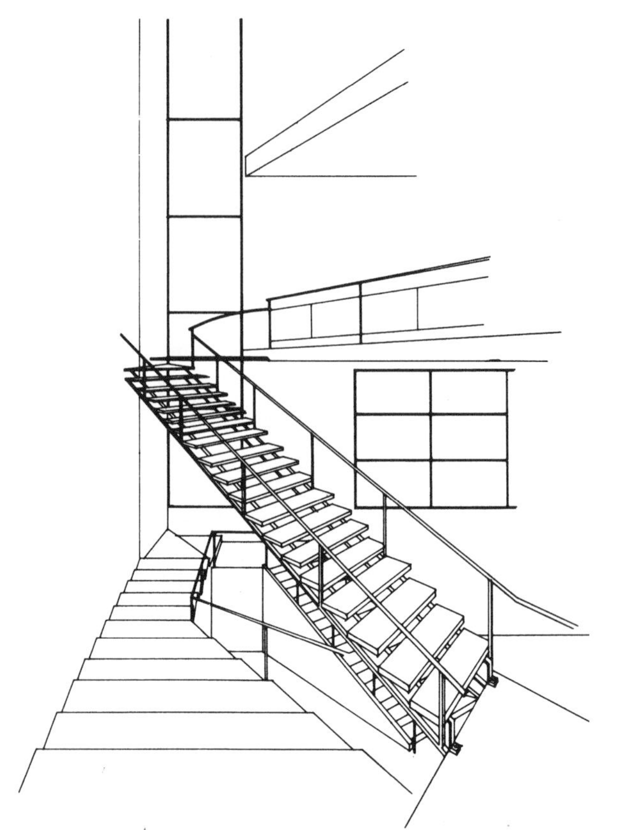

Drawing: Student project by Stacey Wenger
Barcelona studio, Barcelona, Spain
Medium: Ink on Mylar
Courtesy of Washington University
School of Architecture, St. Louis, Missouri

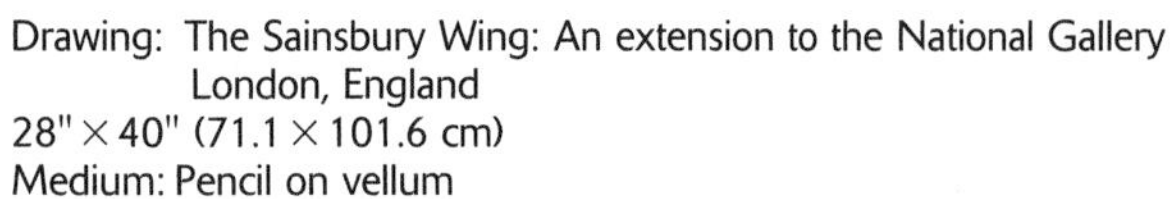

Drawing: The Sainsbury Wing: An extension to the National Gallery
London, England
28" × 40" (71.1 × 101.6 cm)
Medium: Pencil on vellum
Courtesy of Venturi, Scott Brown and Associates, Inc., Architects

Photo: The Spanish Steps leading to the Church of Trinità dei Monti
Rome, Italy

Drawings: Student project by Thanh Do
San Francisco downhill and uphill views
4" × 6" (10.2 × 15.2 cm)
Medium: Ink on vellum
Courtesy of the City College of San Francisco
Department of Architecture

© Winnie T. Leong

Photo: Great Wall of China near Beijing, China

Looking Downhill and Uphill

Downhill and uphill views produce false horizon lines. The observer's view is parallel to the sloping hills. The true horizon lines (straight-ahead, eye-level lines) are where the vanishing point of all the horizontal lines on the building facade rests. Horizontal lines on the streetcar in the downhill view (top) vanish at a point on a false horizon line below the true horizon line. Likewise, in the uphill view (left), there is a false horizon line above the true horizon line. In both the downhill and the uphill situations, the different vanishing points align themselves vertically above and below each other.

Drawing: Residence, Palm Springs, California
8" × 5" (20.3 × 12.7 cm)
Medium: Prismacolor
Courtesy of Kanner Architects
Drawing by Stephen Kanner

Perspective Circles

Circles in perspective take the form of **ellipses.** We see this form not only in architectural subjects but also in everyday things, such as bottles, dishware, pots, waste containers, coins, and wheels for transportation. Architecturally, **vertical circles** are commonly part of arches, semicircular windows, and circular vertical cylindrical forms.

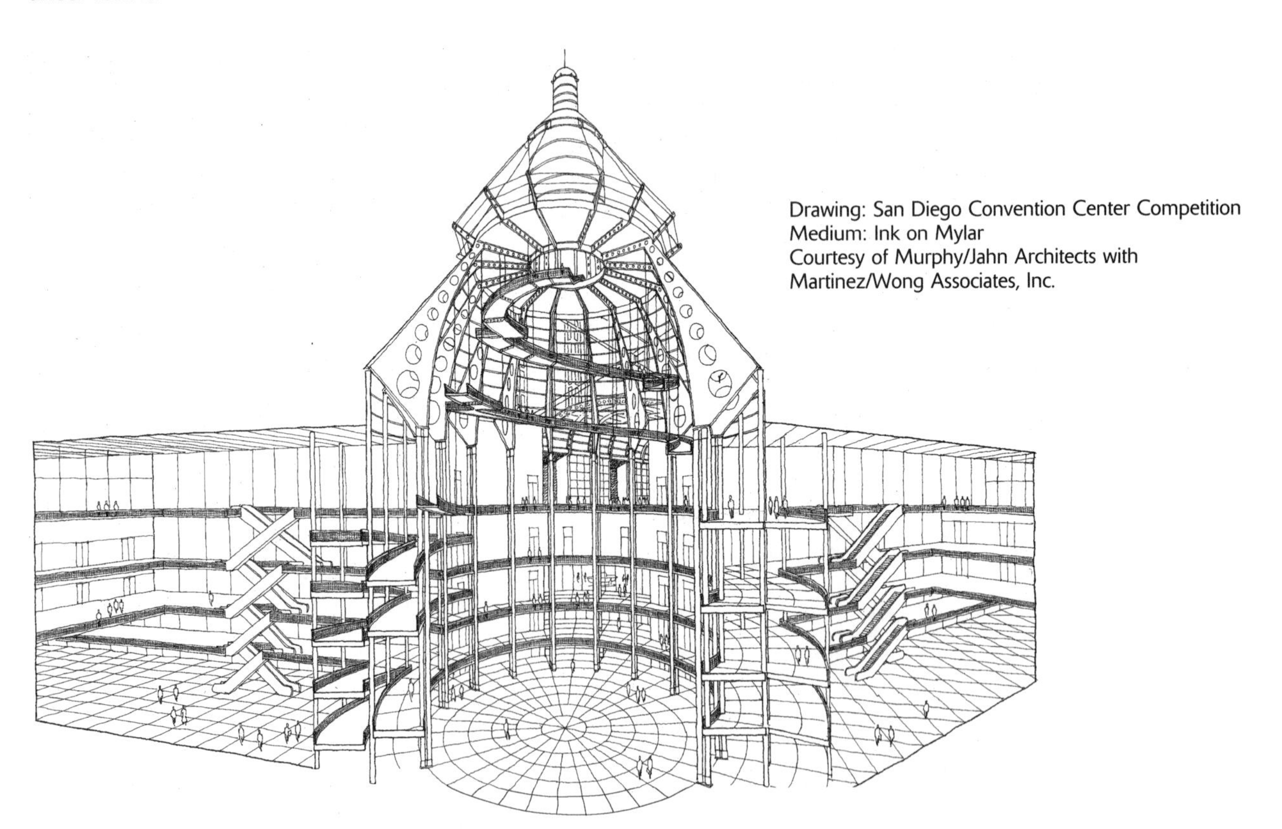

Drawing: San Diego Convention Center Competition
Medium: Ink on Mylar
Courtesy of Murphy/Jahn Architects with Martinez/Wong Associates, Inc.

Horizontal circles are commonly part of semicircular or circular skylights and semicircular or circular horizontal cylindrical forms (e.g., rotundas). See how to construct these circles on pp. 284–87.

Visualize a circle, such as a bicycle wheel. The wheel below can take the form of a **horizontal** circle as it rotates about its horizontal diameter. This diameter can be described as major (longest true length). The minor diameter (axis) is perpendicular and foreshortened and becomes progressively smaller. Or, the wheel can take the form of a **vertical** circle as it rotates about its vertical diameter. The minor diameter (axis) is perpendicular and becomes progressively smaller, as in the first case.

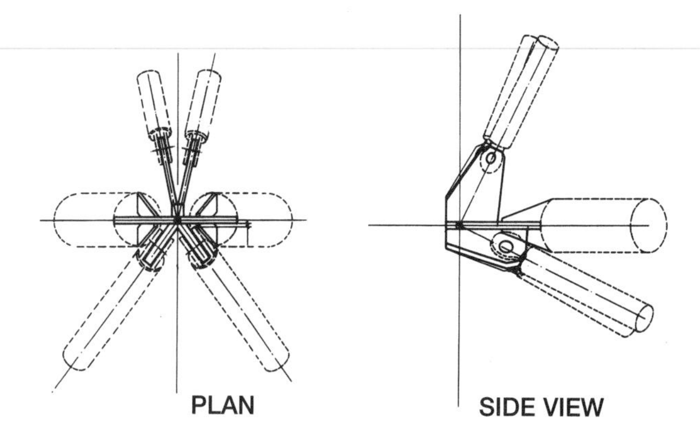

Drawing: Structural connection details
Sydney Football Stadium, Sydney, Australia
Medium: CADD, Scale: 1:10
Courtesy of Cox Richardson
Architects and Planners
Ove Arup, Structural Engineer

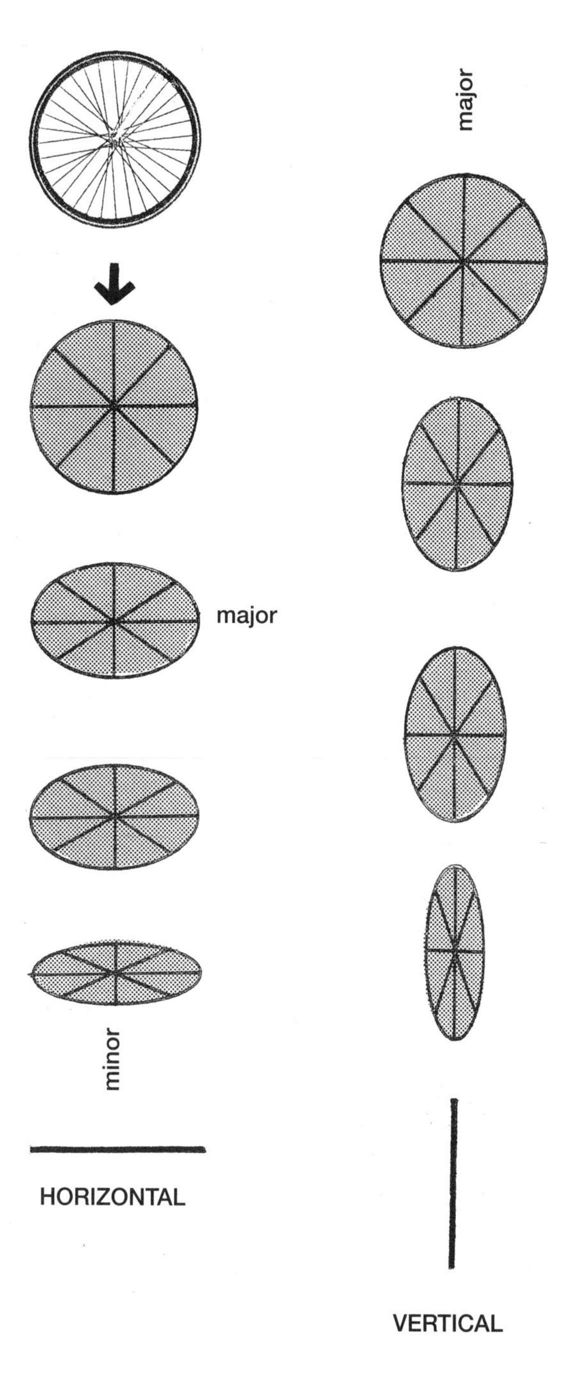

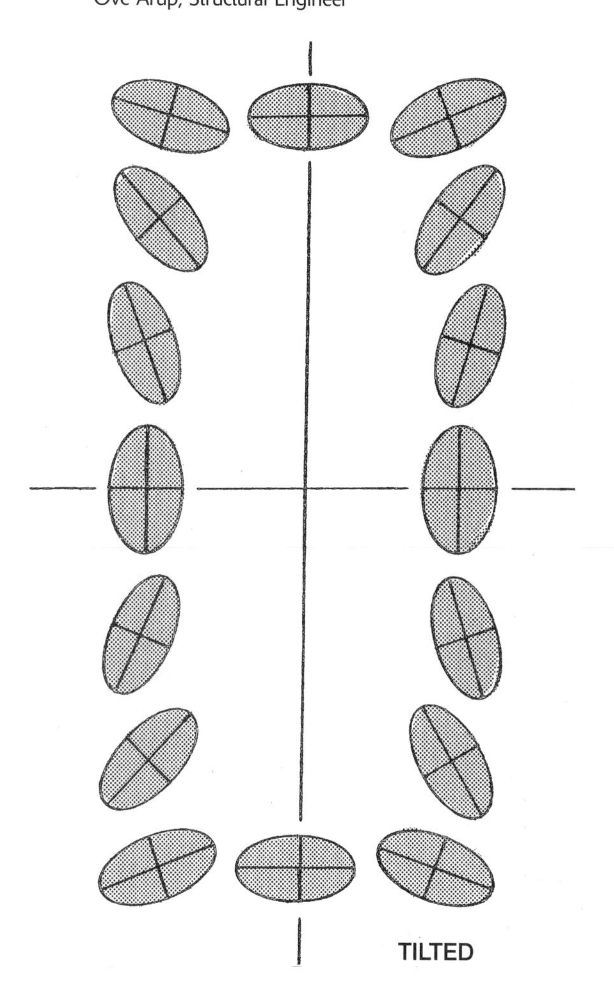

The above diagram illustrates how a circle seen in perspective as an ellipse will change in orientation from a horizontal to a vertical condition for the major axis. The intermediate conditions result in **tilted ellipses,** the degree of which depends on the inclination of the axes relative to the observer's position.

In a one-point perspective, a group of lines will vanish to one point, and this group will not be parallel to the picture plane. All vertical lines remain vertical, and all horizontal lines remain horizontal in the constructed perspective. The plan and the elevation of the room should always be traced to obtain exact dimensions.

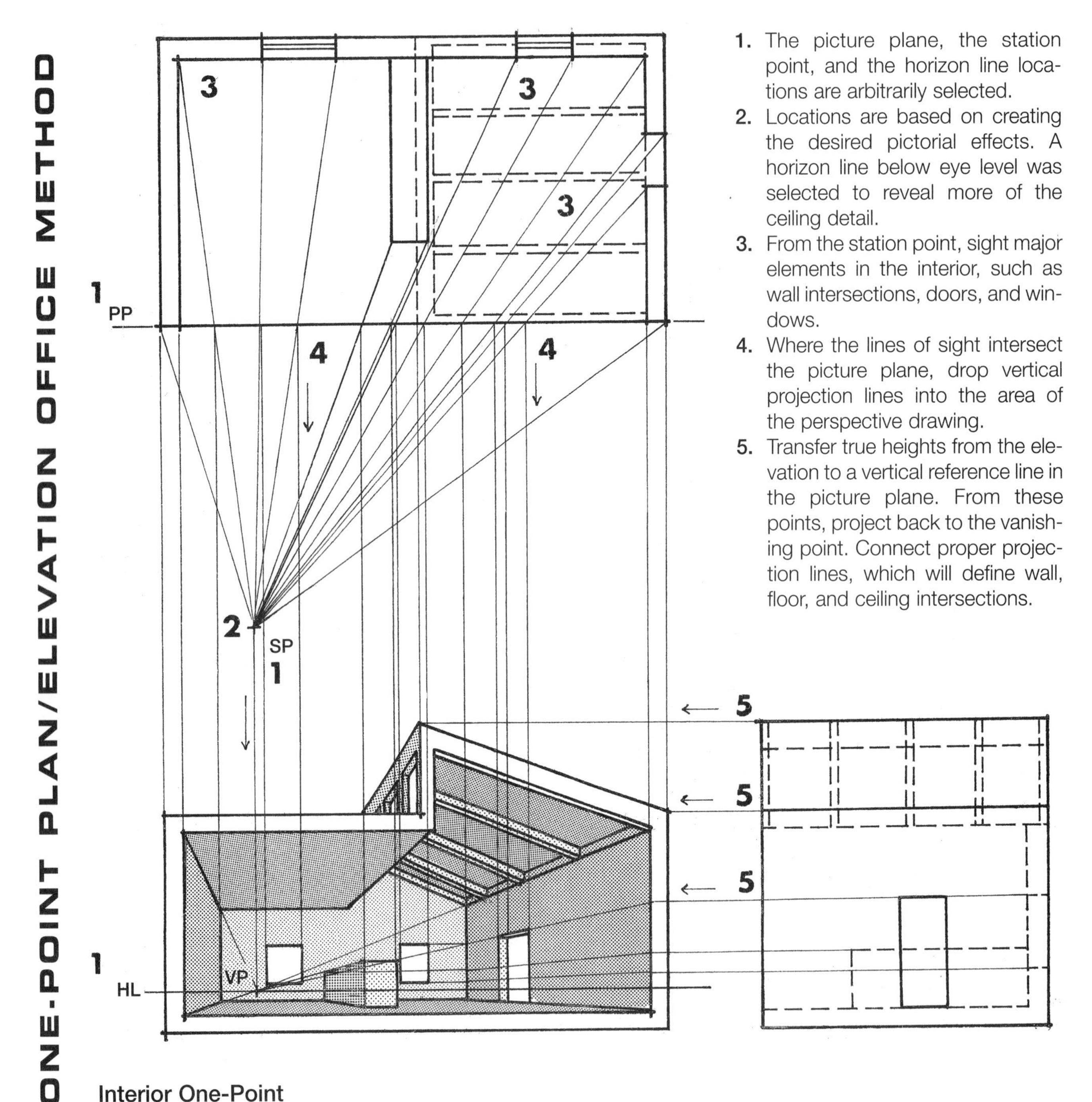

1. The picture plane, the station point, and the horizon line locations are arbitrarily selected.
2. Locations are based on creating the desired pictorial effects. A horizon line below eye level was selected to reveal more of the ceiling detail.
3. From the station point, sight major elements in the interior, such as wall intersections, doors, and windows.
4. Where the lines of sight intersect the picture plane, drop vertical projection lines into the area of the perspective drawing.
5. Transfer true heights from the elevation to a vertical reference line in the picture plane. From these points, project back to the vanishing point. Connect proper projection lines, which will define wall, floor, and ceiling intersections.

Interior One-Point

As with two-point perspectives (discussed later), the **office** or **common method** is frequently used for one-point perspectives. At least one plane of the object in a one-point is always parallel to the picture plane. This plane is always perpendicular to the observer's line of sight. For interiors, the picture plane makes a sectional cut through the building or object where the interior space to be viewed begins. See the discussion on pages 216–219.

Drawing: Student project by Richard Bacino
Housing for the elderly/day care
Medium: Ink on Mylar
Courtesy of Washington University
School of Architecture, St. Louis, Missouri

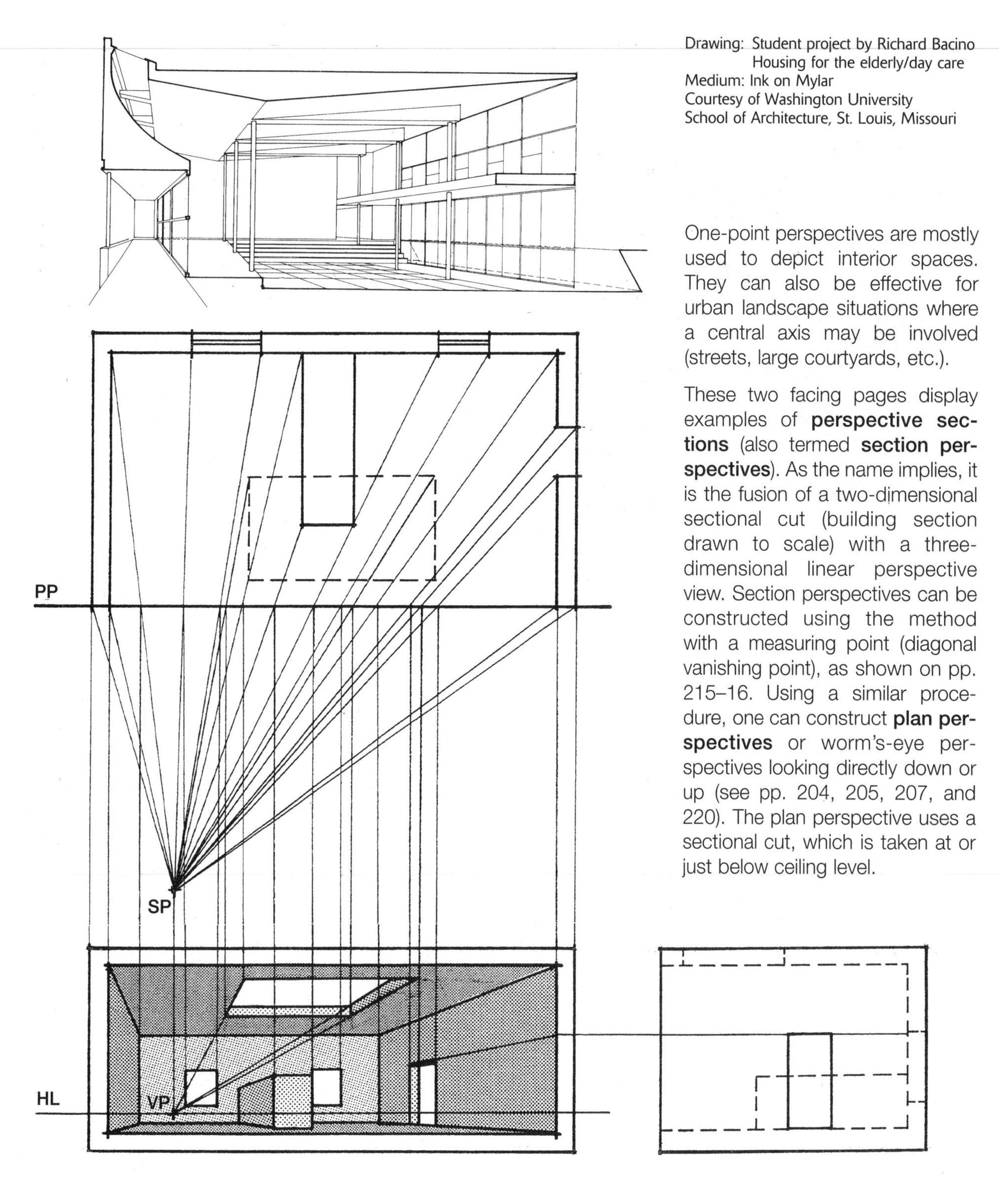

One-point perspectives are mostly used to depict interior spaces. They can also be effective for urban landscape situations where a central axis may be involved (streets, large courtyards, etc.).

These two facing pages display examples of **perspective sections** (also termed **section perspectives**). As the name implies, it is the fusion of a two-dimensional sectional cut (building section drawn to scale) with a three-dimensional linear perspective view. Section perspectives can be constructed using the method with a measuring point (diagonal vanishing point), as shown on pp. 215–16. Using a similar procedure, one can construct **plan perspectives** or worm's-eye perspectives looking directly down or up (see pp. 204, 205, 207, and 220). The plan perspective uses a sectional cut, which is taken at or just below ceiling level.

The placement of the vanishing point will govern what one sees in the interior space. If the vanishing point is high, very little ceiling will show, but much of the floor will show. If the vanishing point is near the center, an equal amount of ceiling and floor will show. If the vanishing point is low, much of the ceiling and very little of the floor will show. Moving the vanishing point to the right or to the left on the back wall has a similar effect on the side walls — that is, if near the left, more of the right wall will show, and if near the right, more of the left wall will show.

Drawing: Kiahuna Resort, Kauai, Hawaii
14" × 11" (35.6 × 27.9 cm)
Medium: Ink on Mylar
Bull Stockwell & Allen Architects
Courtesy of Chun/Ishimaru & Assoc., Architectural Illustrators

One-Point Grid

Design professionals study interior space usage. The **diagonal vanishing point** (or **measuring point**) **method** accurately locates interior elements within a plan grid layout. Unlike the office method, it doesn't require a plan and elevation; it also allows you to start with whatever perspective size you desire. The primary goal of this method is to divide a line in perspective into either equal or unequal parts. True heights are measured in the picture plane and projected back along the walls. True widths are similarly projected on the floor. Furniture and lighting elements can be positioned quickly (see opposite page) and rendered as desired.

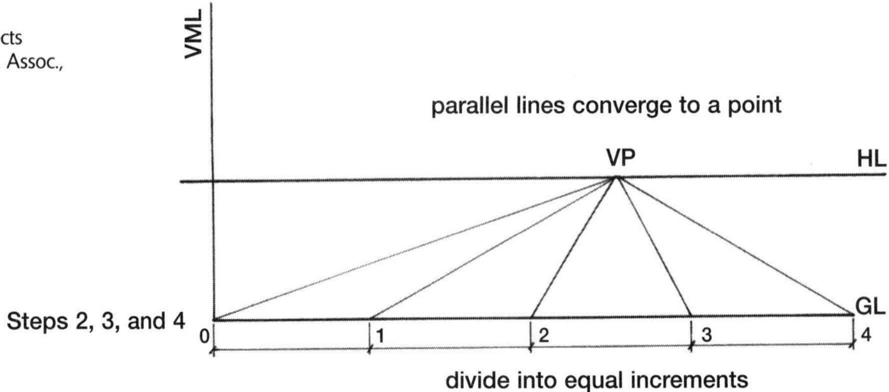

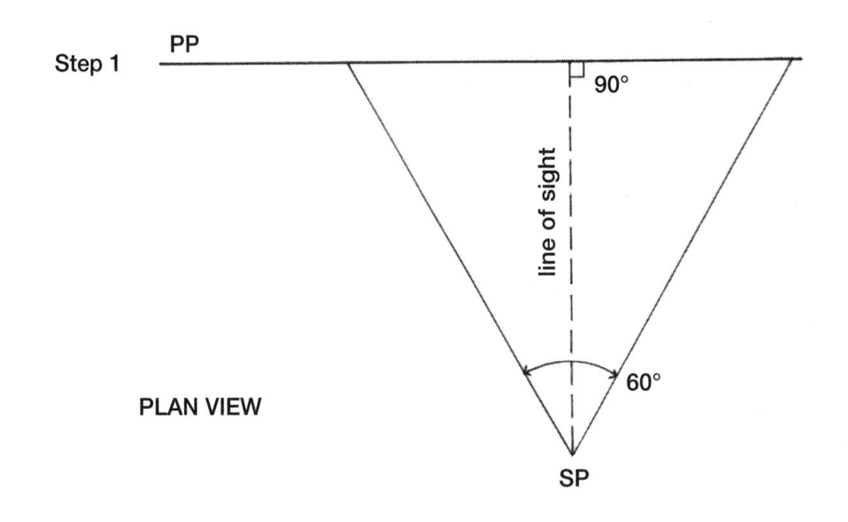

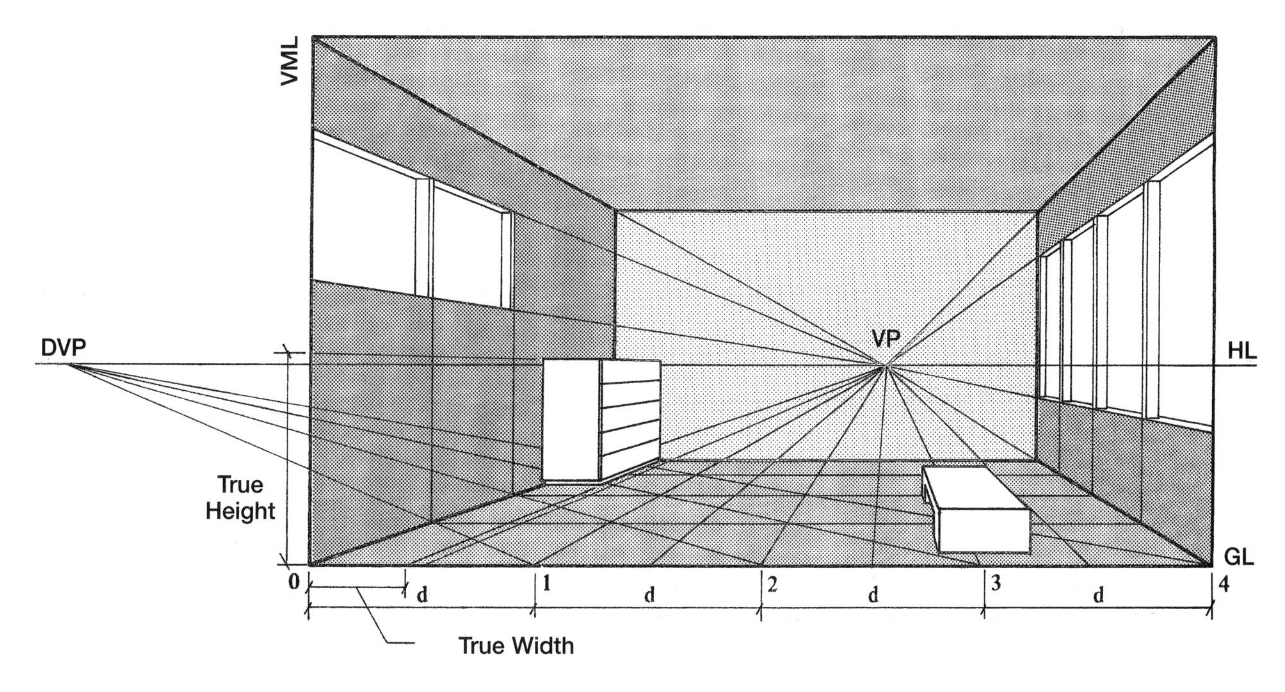

Diagonal Vanishing Point Method

These steps explain how to generate a grid in parallel perspective using a logically placed **diagonal vanishing point.** Acute perspective foreshortening will occur if you move the diagonal vanishing point too close to the vanishing point along the horizon line. A general rule is to keep the width of the drawing smaller than the distance between the diagonal vanishing point and the vanishing point. The drawing above violates this rule slightly but is still within the limits of a correctly foreshortened perspective.

1. Decide where your vantage point will be in order to establish a station point in plan view and, subsequently, a vanishing point (**VP**) in perspective. The ground line (**GL**) and horizon line (**HL**) are consequently established.
2. Draw the horizontal ground line through point **0.** The horizon line (observer's eye level) is located a true height distance along a vertical measuring line (**VML**) in the picture plane, intersecting point **0.**
3. Divide the measuring line at the **GL** where the section cut is taken into *n* equal increments (**d**), *n* being how many mullions or other interior elements must be spaced in perspective (in this case, four).
4. Generate vanishing lines (parallel in the plan view) from points **1, 2, 3,** and **4** to the vanishing point.
5. Decide on the relative depth locations of elements like mullions in the perspective. Select a diagonal vanishing point (**DVP**) location on the horizon line and draw a line to point **4.**
6. Horizontal grid lines can be located at the intersection of the diagonal vanishing lines and the line from **0** to the **VP.**
7. The diagonal line from **0** to the **VP** can also be divided unequally using the same procedures in order to locate furniture or other interior elements.

Note: For establishing depths in front of the picture plane, draw a diagonal line from the **DVP** through point **0** and proceed in the same manner.

The addition of wall, floor, and ceiling thicknesses to the plan grid measuring point drawing on page 215 would create a section cut. The cut coincides with the picture plane, and this plane frames a three-dimensional view of pictorial space that communicates an interior design. Construction of the **section perspective** saves time and space because, as with measuring point methods, no projection from a plan view is needed, and thus excess drawing space is not needed.

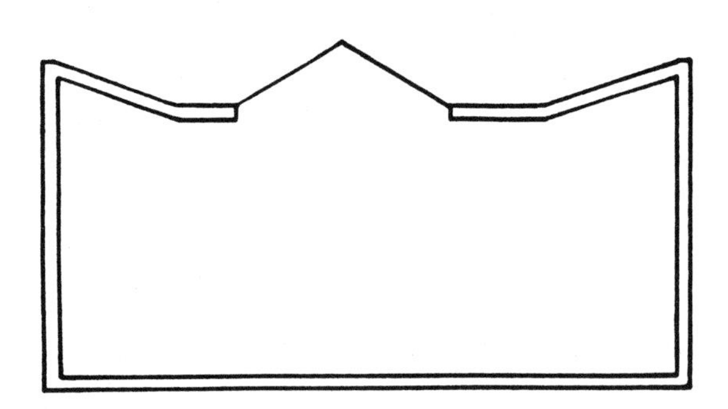

1. Determine where the section will be taken.

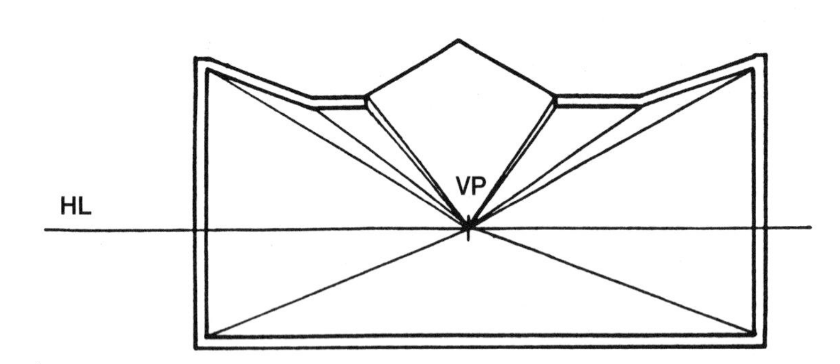

2. Establish the locations of the horizon line and the vanishing point. Project vanishing corner lines from the sectional corners.

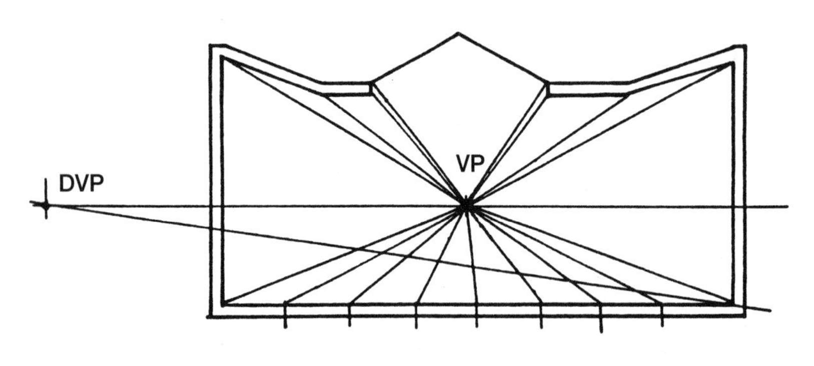

3. Mark equal increments along the sectional floor line. Select an arbitrary diagonal vanishing point (**DVP**). The farther away the diagonal vanishing point is placed from the vanishing point on the horizon line, the less the distortion. Draw a diagonal line from the diagonal vanishing point to the farthest lower corner.

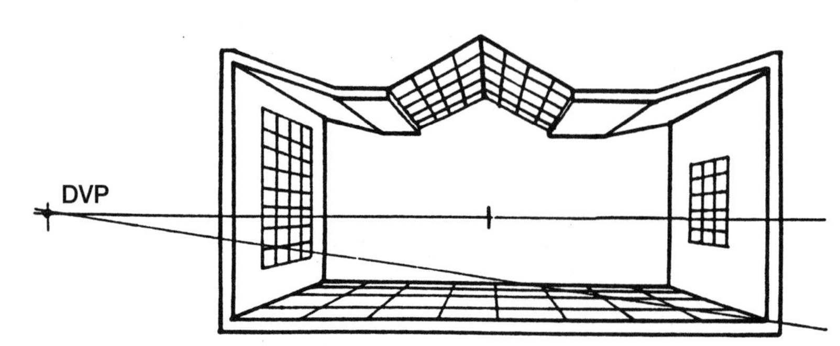

4. At the intersections of the diagonal line and the receding floor plane lines, construct horizontal lines that divide the floor, wall, and ceiling in perspective.

Generating a perspective from a building section sometimes has the drawback of exaggerating the apparent length of spaces (see p. 218).

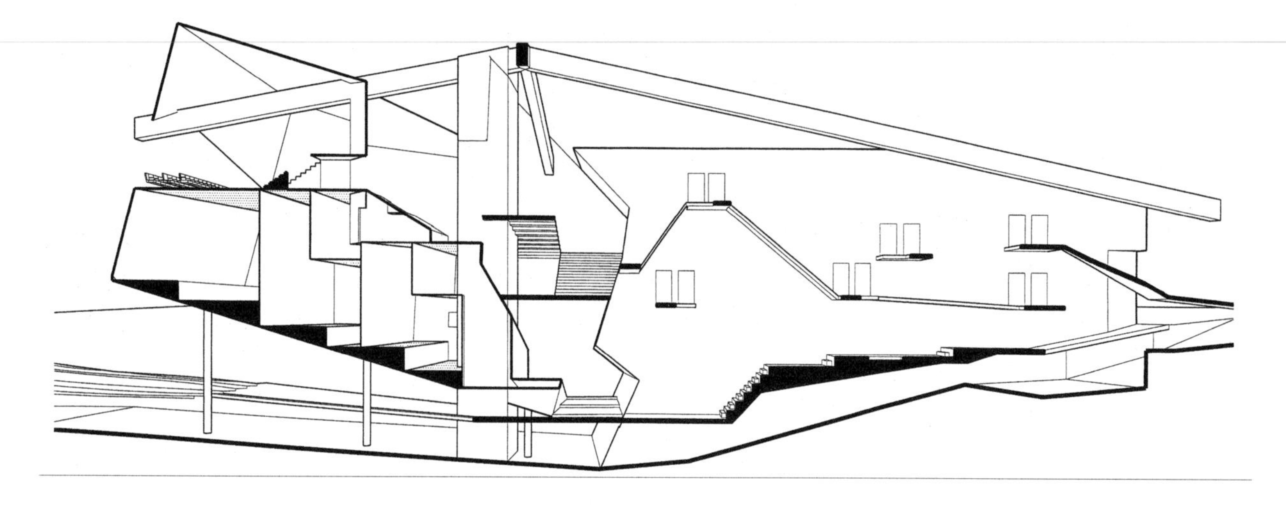

Drawing: Wagramer Strasse, Vienna, Austria
Medium: Computer generated
Courtesy of Eric Owen Moss Architects

Section Perspective Views

The perspective view above has a shallow depth of field. The perspective view (right) creates its own frame with a profile line that defines the section plane. Perspective sections are useful in making the often difficult-to-read section more communicative. Note that the vanishing point is placed within the major space. Avoid placing the vanishing point in smaller secondary spaces like the basement level shown at right.

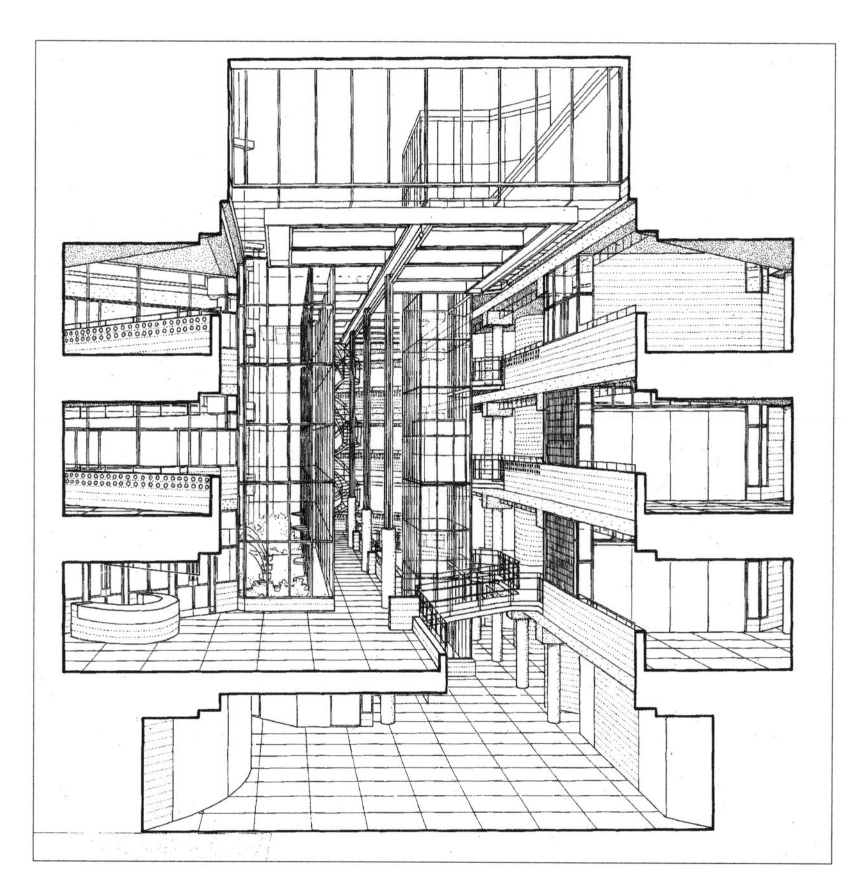

Drawing: Ministry of Social Welfare and Employment
The Hague, The Netherlands
31.5" × 31.9" (80 × 81 cm)
Medium: Ink on calque
Drawn by R. Rietveld
Courtesy of Herman Hertzberger, Architect

Competition drawing: U.S. Embassy, Berlin, Germany, Garden area
21" × 8⅜" (53.3 × 21.3 cm)
Mixed media: Colored pencil, pastel, other
Courtesy of Bohlin Cywinski Jackson
Joint venture with Sverdrup Facilities

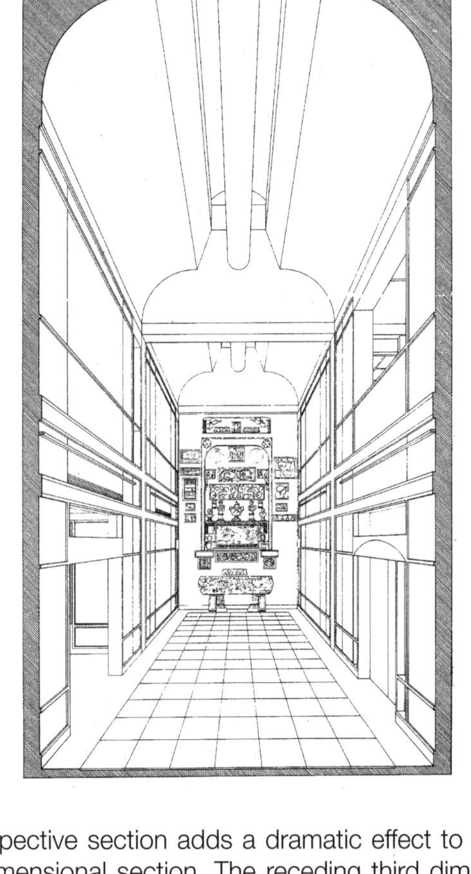

Drawing: J. B. Speed Art Museum addition
Louisville, Kentucky
Courtesy of GBQC Architects

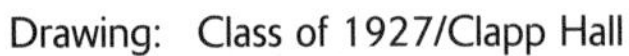

Drawing: Class of 1927/Clapp Hall
Princeton University, Princeton, New Jersey
24" × 24" (61 × 61 cm)
Medium: Ink on Mylar
Courtesy of Koetter, Kim & Associates, Inc.
Architects and Urban Designers

A perspective section adds a dramatic effect to the two-dimensional section. The receding third dimension reveals the pictorial quality of the interior spaces. The sectional perspective is more commonly seen as a one-point perspective. A two-point sectional perspective, as shown at left, is also possible but not frequently used. Emphasis should always be placed on the interior details of the cut spaces, as opposed to the structural details within the sectional cuts.

The pictorial or "real" view quality is a perspective section's strength; its weakness is that it does not convey the overall organization of spaces as well as a plan oblique (axonometric).

Drawing: Residential/commercial building, Seaside, Florida
30" × 24" (76.2 × 61 cm)
Medium: Prismacolor on blueprint paper
Courtesy of Machado and Silvetti Associates
Rodolfo Machado and Jorge Silvetti

As with shadows cast within the section view (p. 355), shadows cast in perspective sections, as shown above and in the Berlin U.S. Embassy drawing (facing page), add depth and a three-dimensional quality. Perspective sections delineate the structural profile of a building. If the purpose of the section is to show spatial relationships, then keep accessories (people, furniture, etc.) to a minimum.

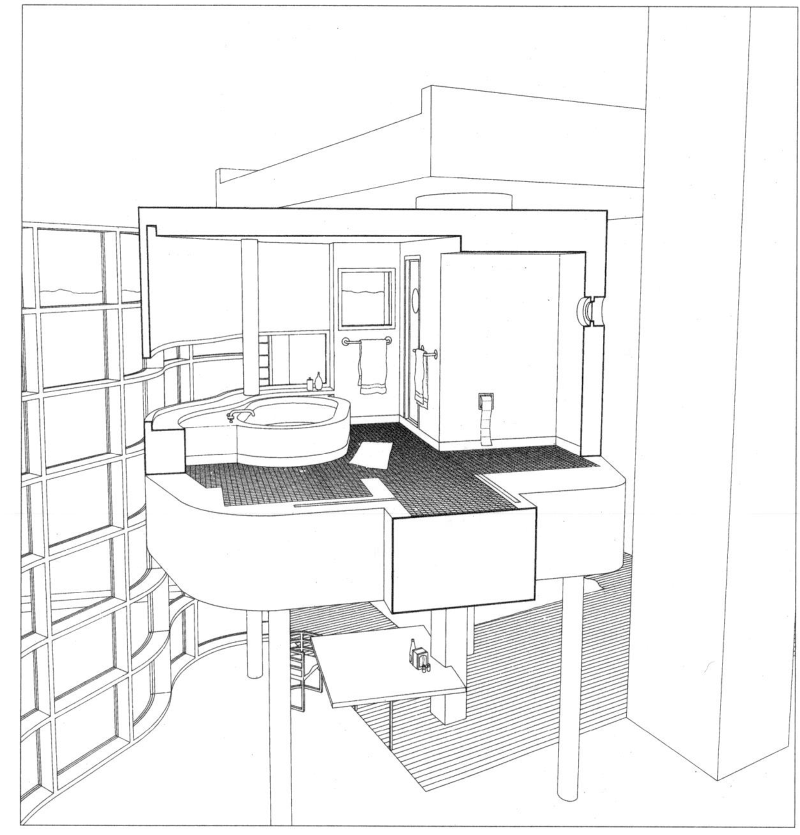

Drawing: Martinelli residence
Roxbury, Connecticut, 1989
24" × 24" (61 × 61 cm)
Medium: Ink
Courtesy of Anthony Ames, Architect

Horizontal and vertical cuts are made in the master bathroom in this perspective drawing, showing its location in a cloudlike form on columns, hovering above the dining area.

[ARCHITECT'S STATEMENT]

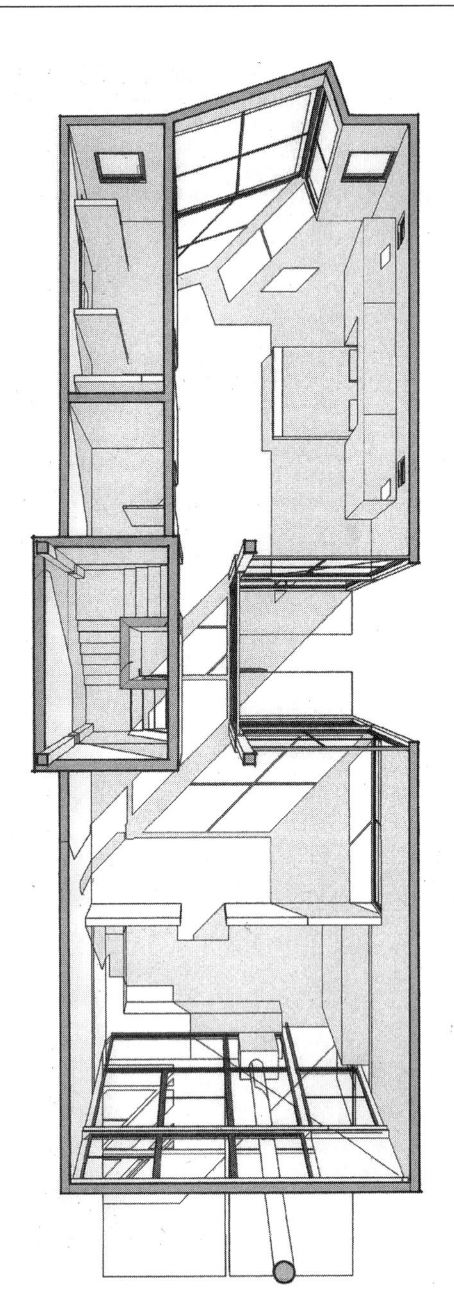

Second-Story Plan

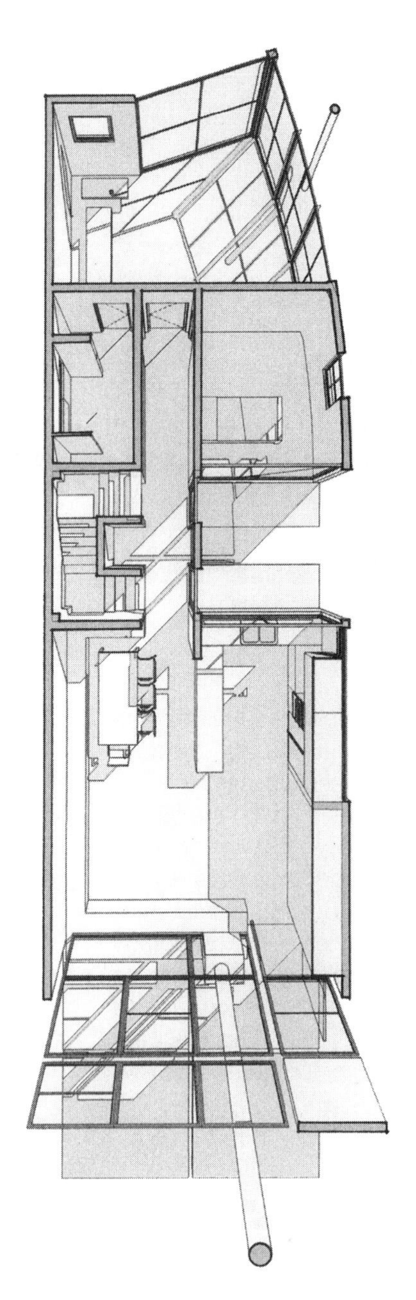

Ground-Level Plan

Images: Bernal Heights residence
San Francisco, California
Medium: Computer generated
Principal in charge: Mark English
Architectural illustrations: Star Jennings
Courtesy of Inglese Architecture

Plan Perspective Views

One-point perspective plan views are used to show the floor layout with additional volumetric information. In this case, the observer is close enough to see some window and facade details.

[ARCHITECT'S STATEMENT]

Image: The Devitt residence, Austin, Texas
Medium: Computer generated
Principal in charge: Mark English
Architectural illustrations: Star Jennings
Courtesy of Inglese Architecture

Plan Perspective Views

In keeping with the vernacular architectural traditions, the two wings of this residence are simple rectangles with gable roofs. The arrangement of building elements is anchored by a paved north-facing patio. This image is a one-point perspective showing the building and some adjacent landscape features. Our intent is to describe the floor layout as well as capture volumetric characteristics. Indications of floor pattern and material are given where clarity is required.

[Architect's statement]

One-point Grid

As we have seen with interiors (pp. 212–13), a grid in parallel or one-point perpsective is constructed using a **plan** with an **elevation** or elevation heights. In this exterior view example, you are given standing rectilinear slabs and a circular pond drawn to a specific scale (scale and heights not shown).

1. Draw both the plan grid and the perspective grid. Construct lines to the vanishing point to see how grid lines in plan converge in perspective.
2. Find where the objects in plan intersect the picture plane.
3. Establish a section image and project through the critical points to the vanishing points. Find corner points of objects by sighting corresponding plan points **(a)**.
4. Draw the completed perspective image of the first plan object selected (in this case a rectilinear slab).

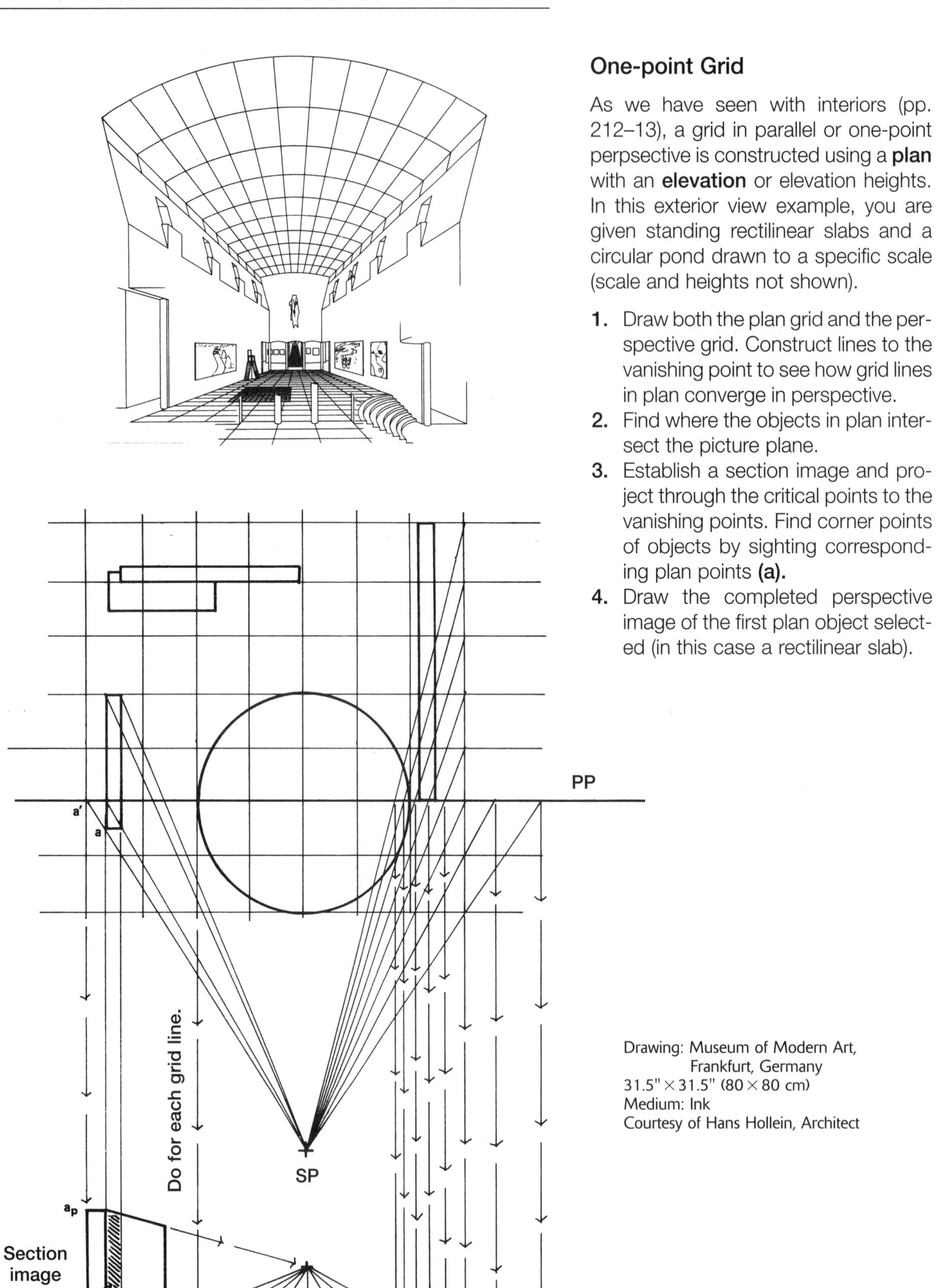

Drawing: Museum of Modern Art, Frankfurt, Germany
31.5" × 31.5" (80 × 80 cm)
Medium: Ink
Courtesy of Hans Hollein, Architect

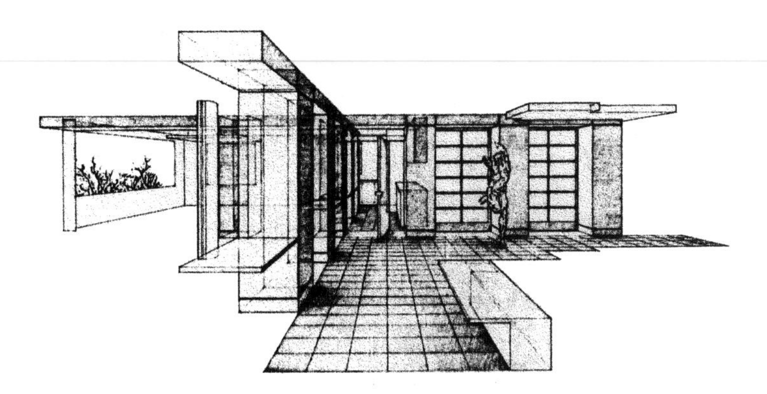

Drawing: The Rittenhouse Square apartment
Philadelphia, Pennsylvania
Medium: Ink
Courtesy of Wesley Wei, AIA, Wesley Wei Architects

5. Follow the same procedure to complete the other rectilinear objects in the perspective.
6. For the pond, enclose the circle within a square. Divide the circle into quarter-circles. Sight critical points **k, l, m,** and **n,** and project picture plane intersections into the perspective image of these same points. Use a french curve and construct the pond (it takes the form of an ellipse).

Hand-drafted grids are useful for constructing both one- and two-point perspectives. The hand-drawn grid can be blown up or reduced to a suitable scale, and design sketches can be done on trace overlays. With the development of perspective charts and especially computer-aided drafting, grids can be ready or made ready for immediate use.

Drawing: Student project by Howard Fineman
Augusta City Hall
Medium: Ink on Mylar
Courtesy of Washington University School of Architecture, St. Louis, Missouri

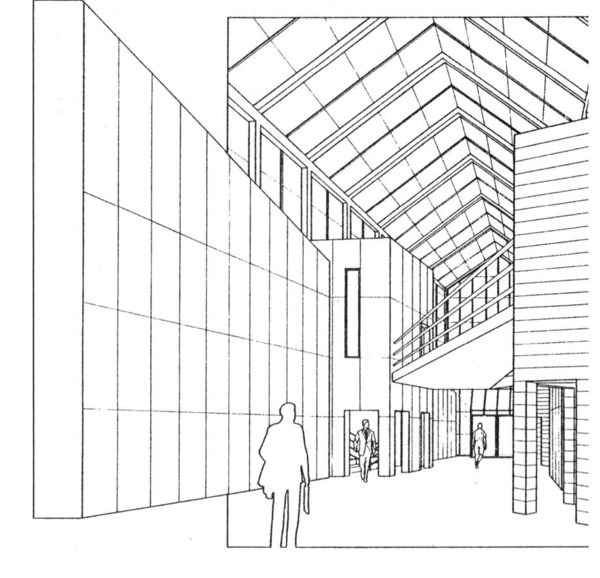

1PL
2PL PP
45° diagonal line
SP
VP
1P
2P
HL
GL

Station Point Placement

The above interior one-point places a strong visual emphasis on the left wall and the ceiling. This is because the observer is closer to the right wall. The location of the horizon line can be manipulated to emphasize either the ceiling or the floor. The manipulation zone ranges approximately from 4' to 6' above the ground. Depth enhancement is achieved by adding scaled figures.

Notation for diagram (left):

1_{PL}: plan view point 1
2_{PL}: plan view point 2
1_{P}: perspective view point 1
2_{P}: perspective view point 2

These points (**1_P** and **2_P**) are the **measuring points,** or **diagonal vanishing points (DVP).**

45° Diagonal Plan Lines

This quick procedure simply utilizes 45° diagonal plan lines from the station point. This results in an equilateral (45°) triangle. The length of the bisector from the station point will always be equal to the distance from points **1** or **2** to the picture plane intersection point. The diagonal line in perspective passes through the lower left or right corners of the picture plane. Its intersection with converging vanishing lines on the ground plane produces all the needed horizontal grid lines in perspective.

Competition sketch: Rotterdam Central Station
Cambridge, Massachusetts
Medium: Ink on paper and Photoshop
Courtesy of Rafael Viñoly Architects, P.C.

This one-point has an excellent field of view. Don't be afraid to step back when attempting to depict an interior space; most problems in distortion come from being too close to the picture plane. With interior one-points it is essential to create the feeling that you are part of the viewed space. This requires good judgment in cropping interior features on the ground plane (see pp. 395 and 406). Cropping is permitting part of the subject to be removed from within the frame of the picture.

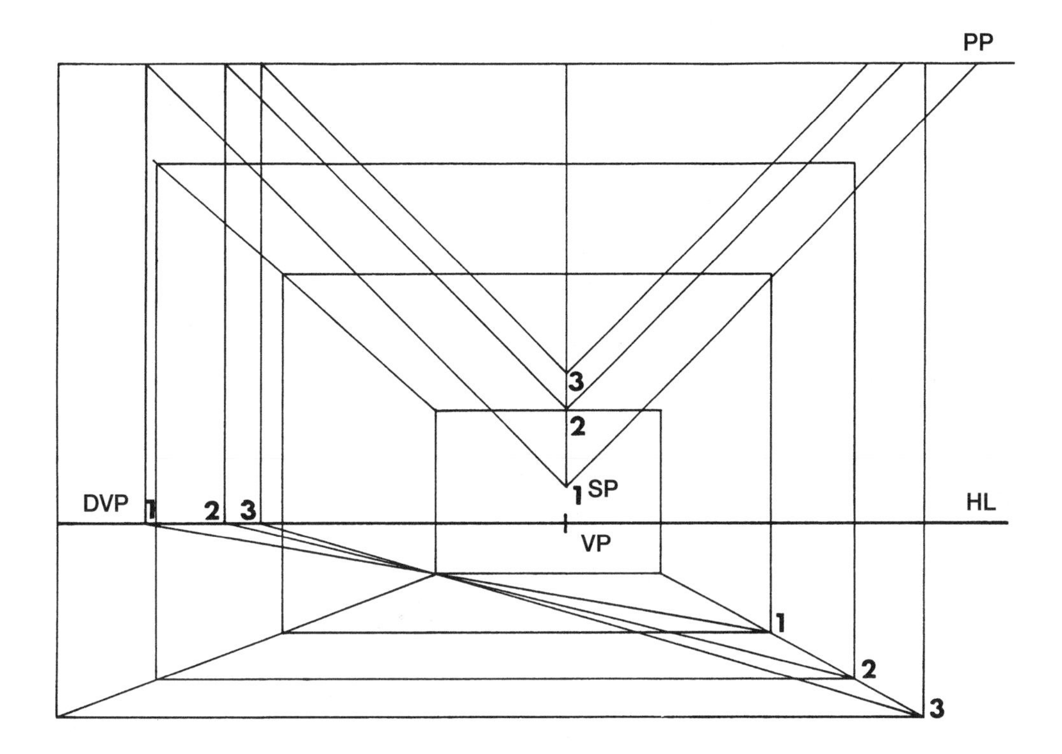

Station Point Movement

Using 45° diagonal plan lines, what will happen when the station point **(SP)** is moved along the line of sight? The station point location will affect the corresponding point location on the horizon line (and thus the picture plane). The placement of the points **1, 2,** and **3** along the horizon line controls perspective distortion of the grid. The farther the point is moved away from the vanishing point (and thus, the picture plane), the less distortion there will be. The field of view also changes as the observer moves farther away. The view is of a much larger area, and thus the cone of vision is much greater. Even though the 45° VP is a direct function of the station point distance from the picture plane, it is nevertheless variable in a one-point perspective.

This is a **simplified** method that allows the construction of an accurate but quick **one-point perspective**. It is based on the principles of the projected perspective method but takes advantage of the fact that depth can be defined from a width by using a diagonal or 45° angle. In this method, elements or objects can be constructed or placed directly in the perspective view without projecting from a floor plan.

You will construct an object with a 4' X 5' base and 4' and 10' heights on its opposite sides. You will place the object 6' to the right from the observer and 8' from the back or projection plane. Call the points on the base of this object as (a), (b), (c), and (d).

In projected perspective, images are projected onto a picture (measuring or projection) plane. Any line that lies on this plane is true length since it is on the plane itself. In this method, therefore, all measurements will be done on this picture plane, which can be placed anywhere it best suits its intended purpose. For example, it can be a wall in a space, a line defining a plane for several objects, or a street facade in an urban setting.

CONCEPT

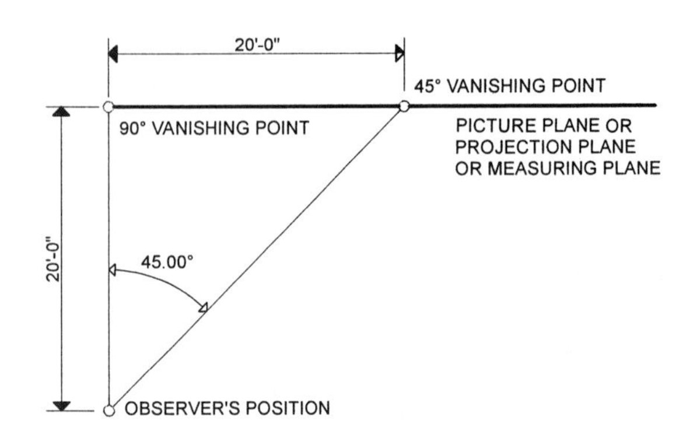

1. PERSPECTIVE SETUP AND MEASURING DISTANCE

The HORIZON LINE is a line at eye level. The BASE LINE (ground line) is the line where the picture plane intersects with the base (ground) plane.

Define the location of a line that is 6' to the right of where the observer stands. Points (a) and (b) will be on this line.

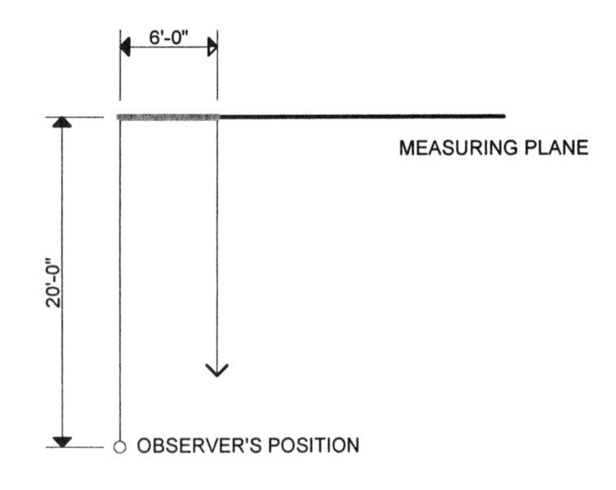

2. MEASURING DEPTH

Locate (a) at 8' from the back plane and (b) at 12'.

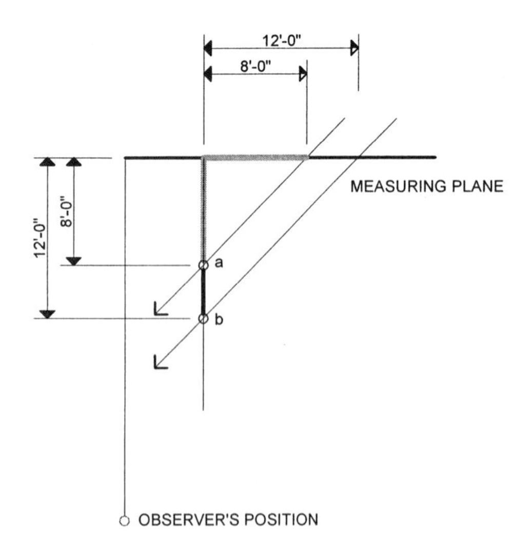

Diagrams and text (both pages):
Courtesy of Professor Arpad Daniel Ronaszegi
Savannah College of Art and Design

CONCEPT SKETCH

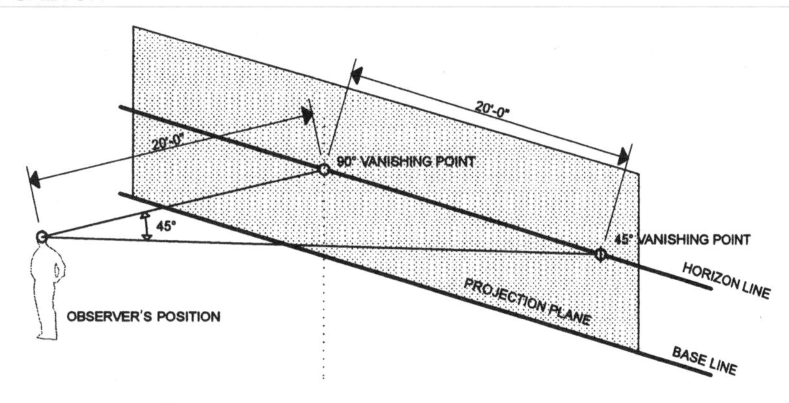

PERSPECTIVE DRAWINGS

Define the location of the HORIZON LINE and BASE LINE. The 6' distance will be measured on the back of the projection plane, where measurements are true dimensions. This distance will be projected out to the perspective space through the 90° vanishing point (VP). The resulting line is 6' to the right of the observer.

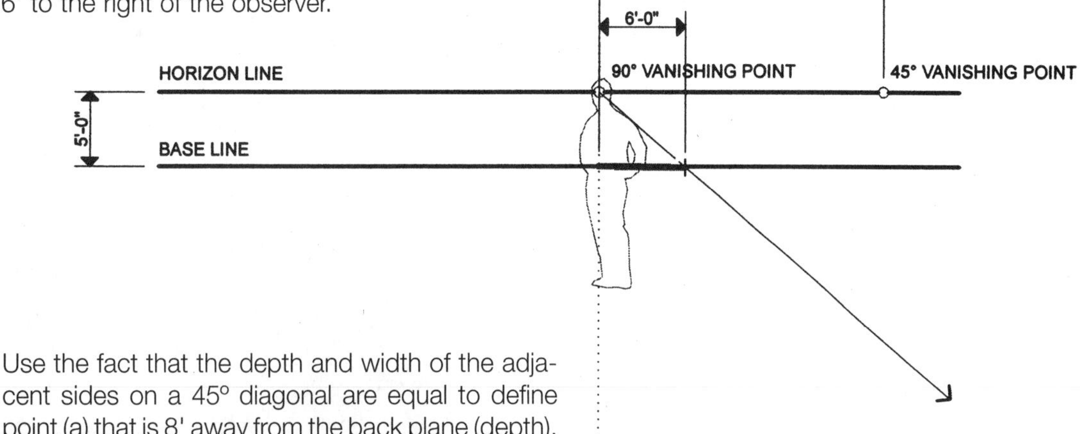

Use the fact that the depth and width of the adjacent sides on a 45° diagonal are equal to define point (a) that is 8' away from the back plane (depth). Measure an 8' width on the back plane. Project this point through the 45° VP. The intersection of this point with the line that is 6' to the right is point (a), which is 8' from the back plane. Repeat same process with 12' depth to generate point (b).

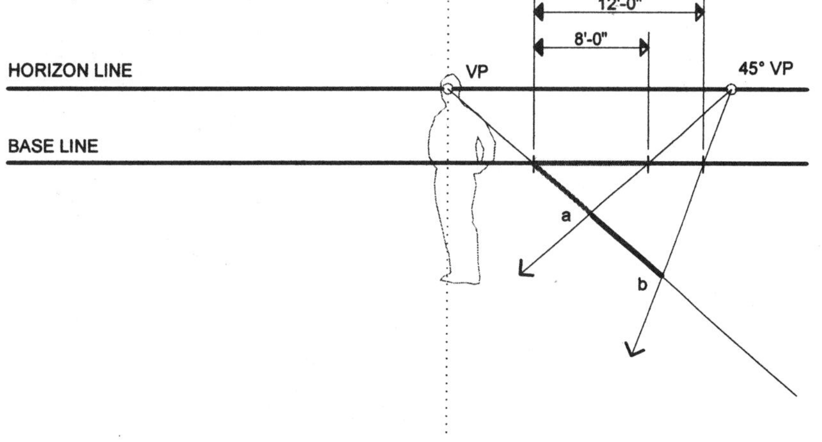

3. MEASURING WIDTH

Locate points (c) and (d) 5' to the right of line (ab).

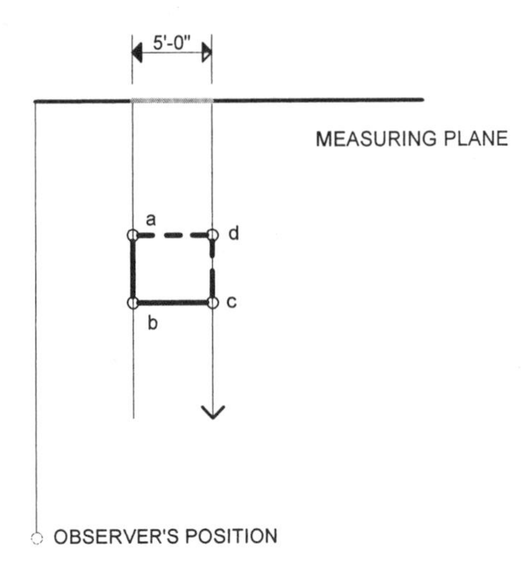

4. MEASURING HEIGHT

Define a 4' height on the line (ab) and a 10' height on line (cd).

The heights will be measured vertically on the back plane and then projected to the proper points.

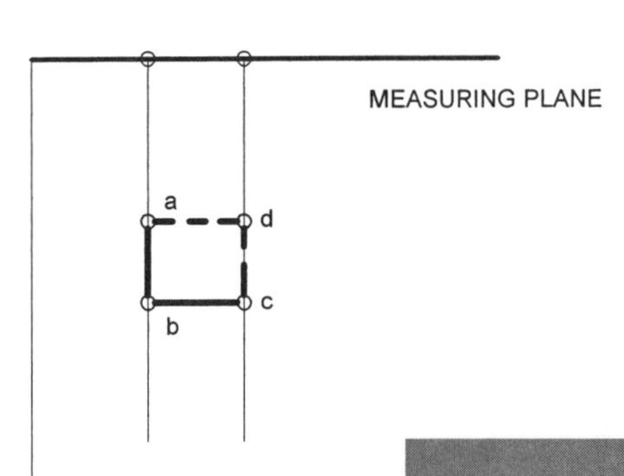

Similar to the perspective on the facing page, this building has lines that recede to one vanishing point.

Diagrams and text (both pages):
Courtesy of Professor Arpad Daniel Ronaszegi
Savannah College of Art and Design

5. FINISH OBJECT

To define points (c) and (d), which are 5' from line (ab), measure a 5' width on the back plane. Project a line through the VP. The intersection of this line with lines projected horizontally from points (a) and (b) will define points (c) and (d).

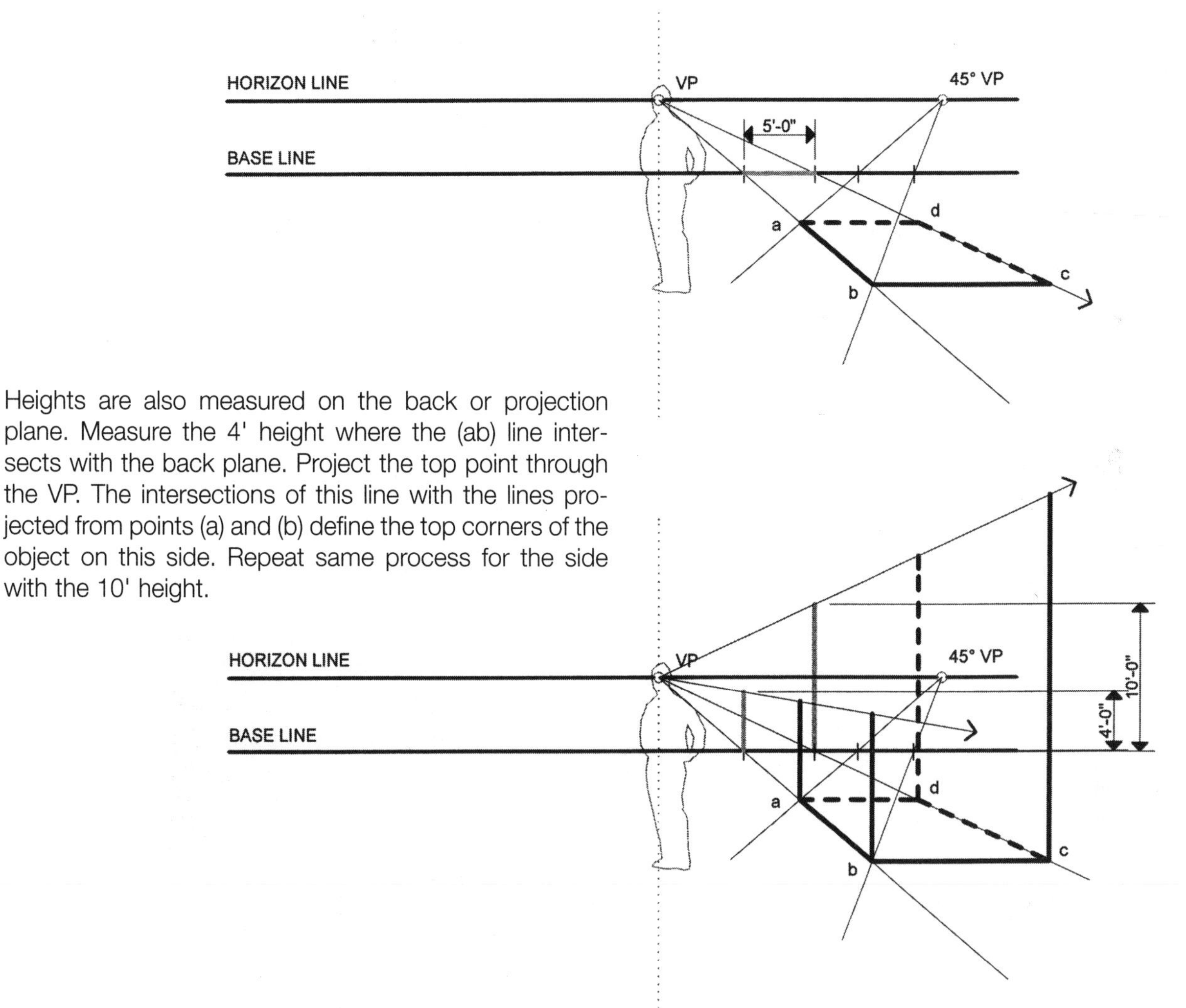

Heights are also measured on the back or projection plane. Measure the 4' height where the (ab) line intersects with the back plane. Project the top point through the VP. The intersections of this line with the lines projected from points (a) and (b) define the top corners of the object on this side. Repeat same process for the side with the 10' height.

Complete object by connecting the remaining points.

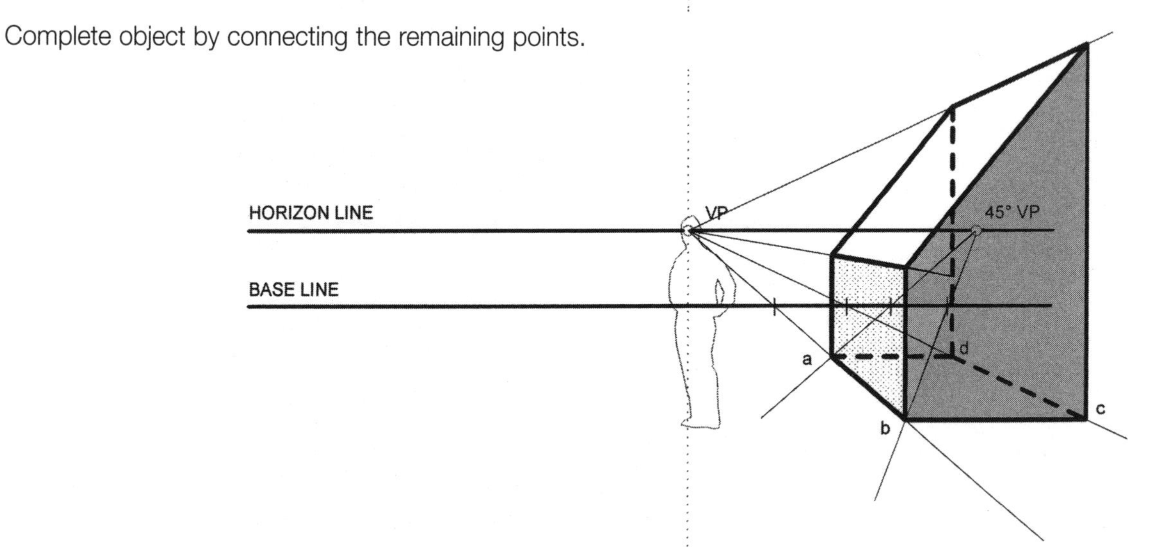

The Office Method

The **office** or **common** or **plan projection** method for constructing an accurate **two-point** perspective is a traditional one. Both sets of horizontal lines are turned at an angle to the picture plane (thus the term "angular" for the two-point system). It is dependent on both the scale of the **plan** and the scale of the **elevation.**

1. In the top or plan view, place the outline of the object or objects (buildings) with an arbitrary orientation angle θ (based on the view desired).
2. Arbitrarily locate the picture plane and the station point in the plan view to create a distortion-free view. It is advantageous to have the corner of the object touch the picture plane; this establishes a convenient vertical measuring line.
3. Adjust the station point location if necessary. Its placement controls the cone of vision and distortion. Being too close or too far away can result in extreme distortion. To minimize distortion, try to set up a cone of vision that is greater than 30° but less than 60°. The viewer's line of sight should focus on the image's center of interest.

Note: In a preliminary design drawing, an overlay of the floor plan or roof plan and elevation would be made on tracing paper. Position the plan and elevation to allow adequate space for the perspective view. When space is at a premium, place the plan and elevation closer together, keeping horizontal and vertical lines in alignment.

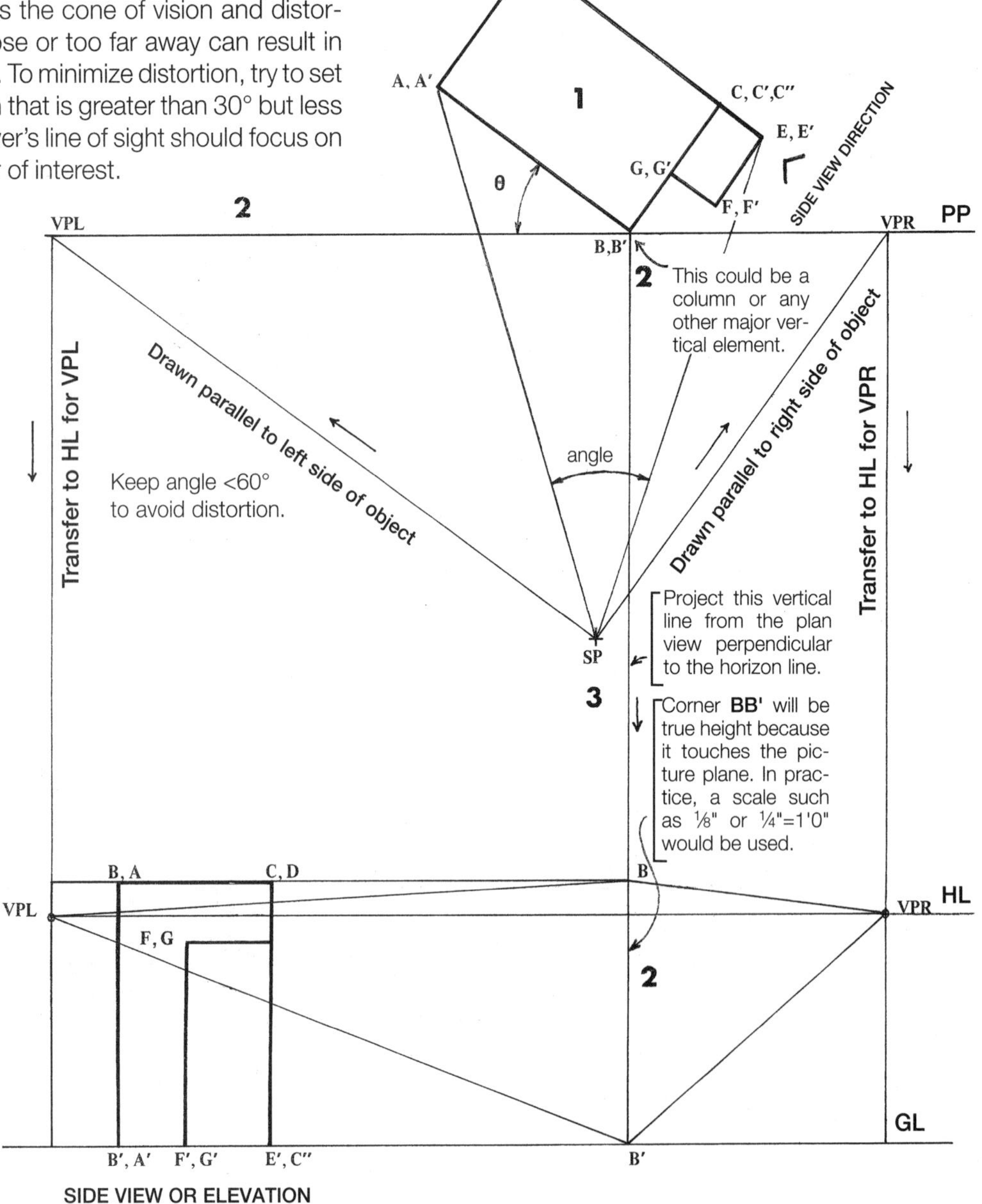

4. Draw lines parallel to the sides of the object from the station point until they intersect the picture plane. At these points, drop vertical tracer lines until they inersect the horizon line established for the perspective. The intersection points become the vanishing points for the perspective.
5. From the station point, sight all corner points, such as **A, A′,** and note where the line of sight intersects the picture plane. At this point, project a vertical line into the perspective to locate foreshortened length **A, A′.**

Note: Look for sets of parallel lines in your building or object and note where these sets will converge. **Convergence** refers to the optical phenomenon of sets of parallel lines receding to a single point at an infinite distance.

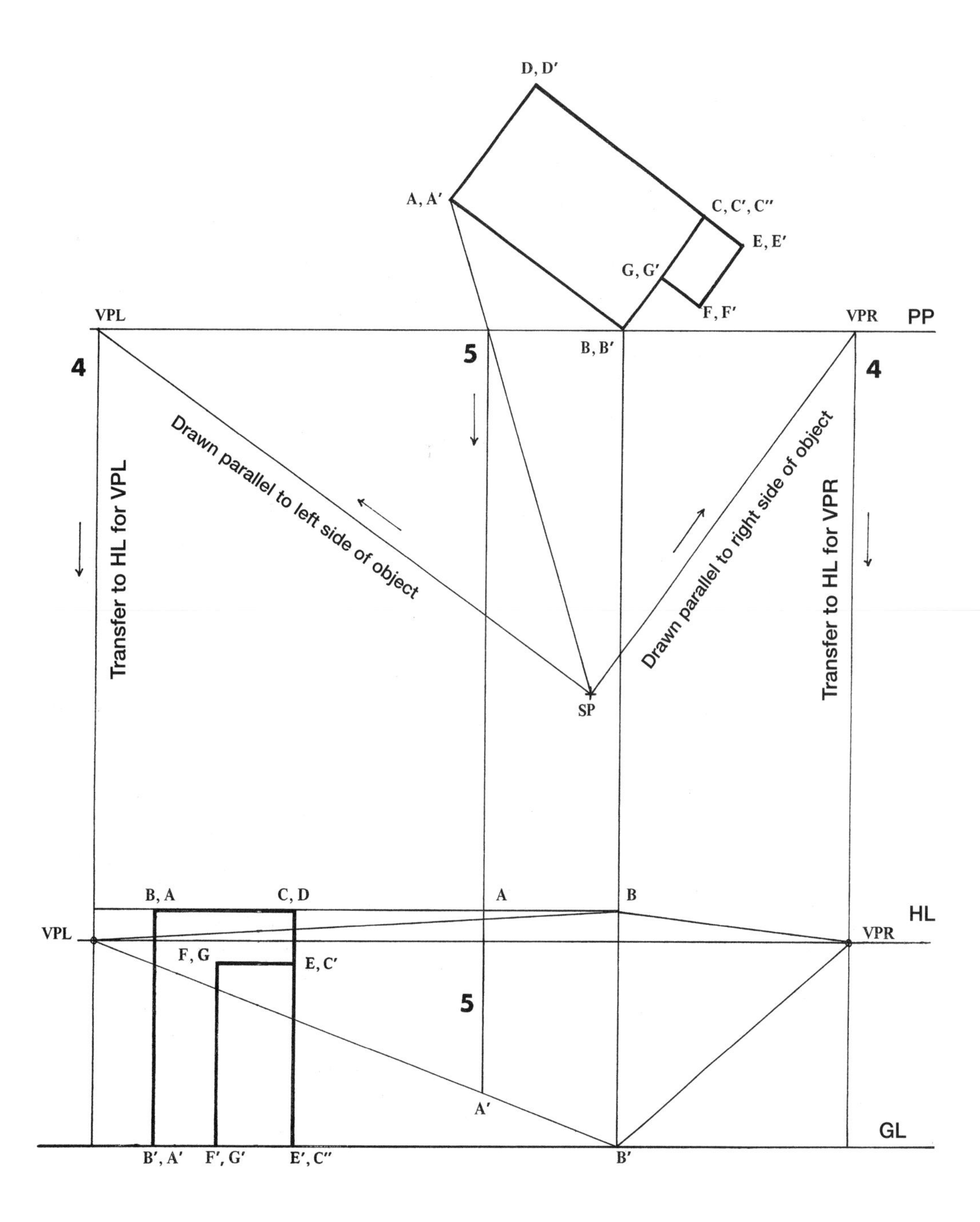

6. Project all sighting intersection points on the picture plane into the perspective in order to complete the perspective of the object. Hidden lines are optional.

Pages 230–32 show the step-by-step sequence for constructing a two-point perspective when both the building plan and the elevation are drawn at the same scale. Angular (two-point) perspective is characterized by angular planes (inclined to the picture plane) having their own separate vanishing points. All vertical lines remain vertical.

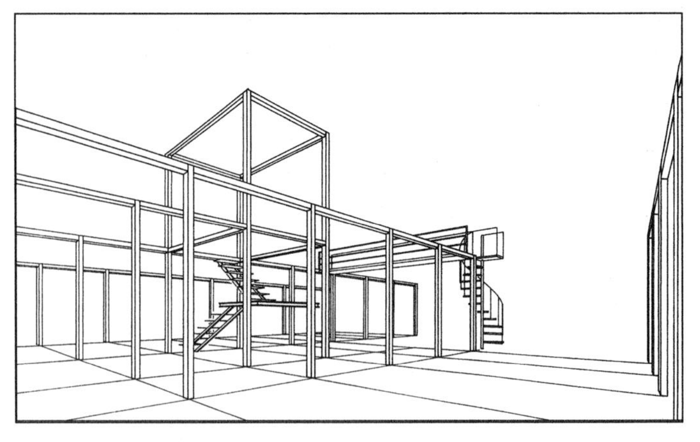

Drawing: T residence, Hayama, Kanagawa, Japan
Courtesy of Iida Archiship Studio

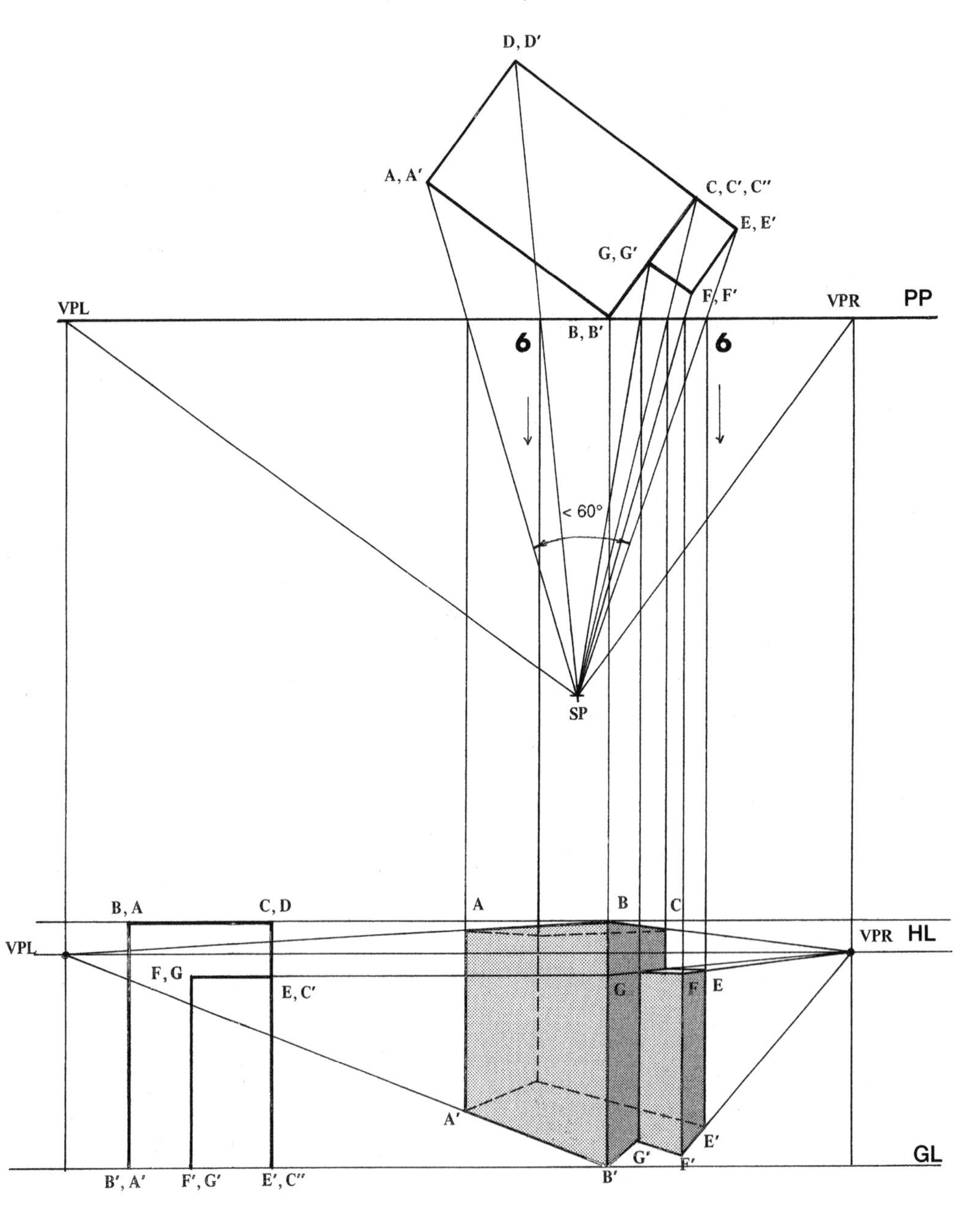

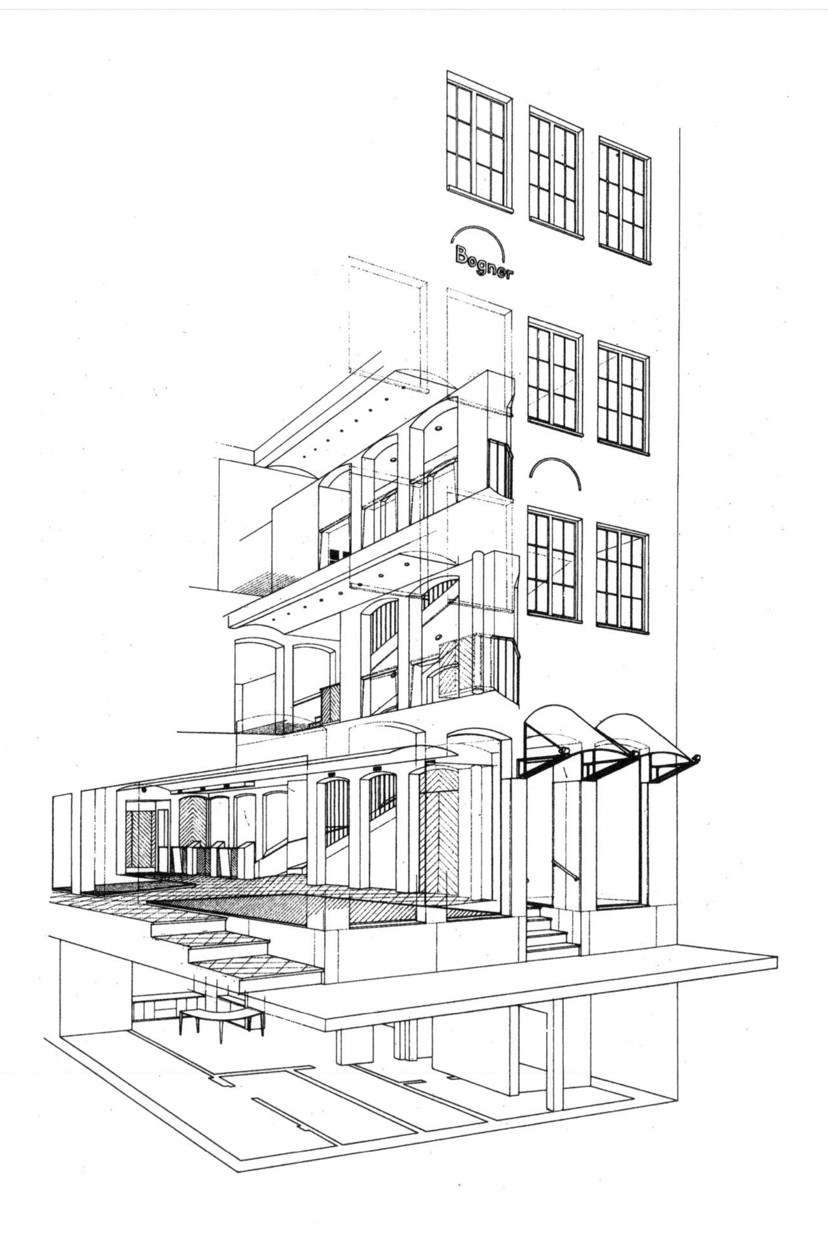

Drawing: Bogner Fashion House, Munich, Germany
Medium: Ink
Courtesy of MACK—Mark Mack, Architect
Heino Stamm Planungsbüro; Bruckner & Partner, Associated Architects

Two-Point Perspective Application

This unique, two-point cutaway sectional perspective (see pp. 218–19) has lines going to two vanishing points on a horizon line. Note that the basement level shows a partial perspective plan view. The two vanishing points on the previous page are more evenly spread apart from the observer's line of sight and the cone of vision than are the vanishing points shown above. This is because the observer's line of sight is almost exactly at the corner of the object. In the above drawing, the vanishing points are quite unevenly spread apart because the front facade is almost parallel to the observer's face, and the sectional cut surface is almost perpendicular to the observer's face (foreshortening).

Multiple Vanishing Points

1. Label each block element and find the vanishing points for each. This particular example has six vanishing points.
2. Drop true-height tracer lines (circled points) from where the object touches the picture plane. Transfer corresponding true heights from the elevation.
3. Draw lines from the top and the bottom of the true-height lines to the appropriate vanishing points.
4. From the station point, sight all object corners and follow appropriate procedures to complete the perspective view.

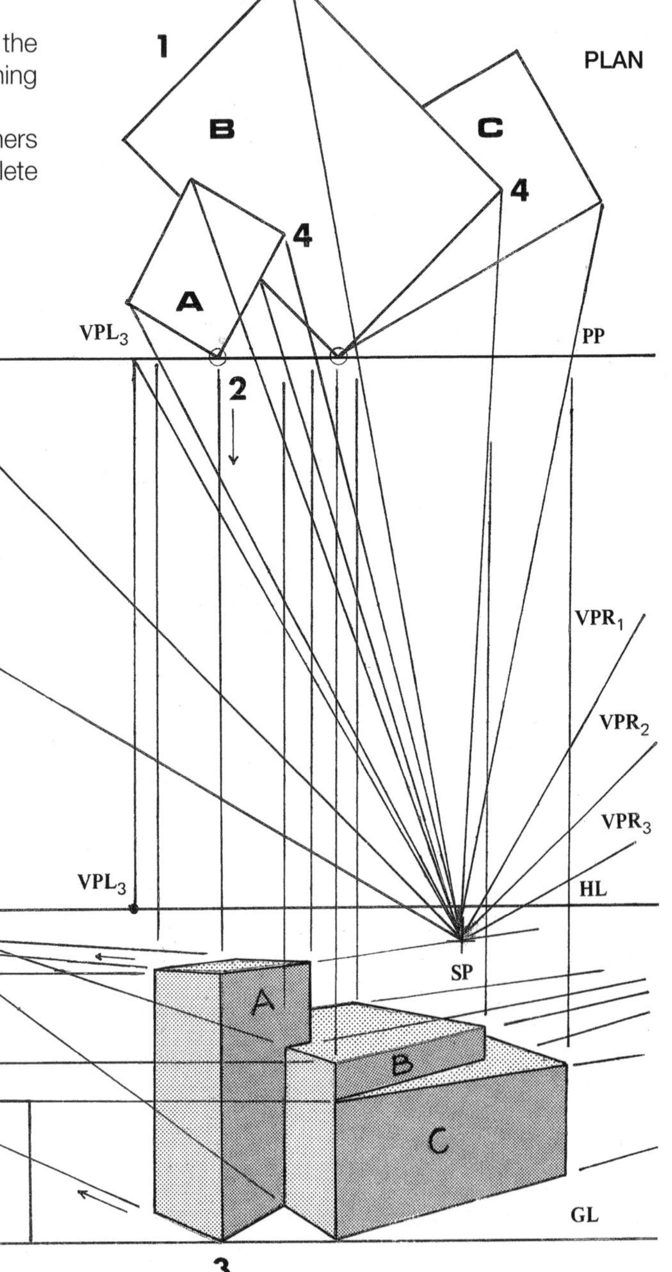

The total number of vanishing points depends on how many sets of parallel lines there are.

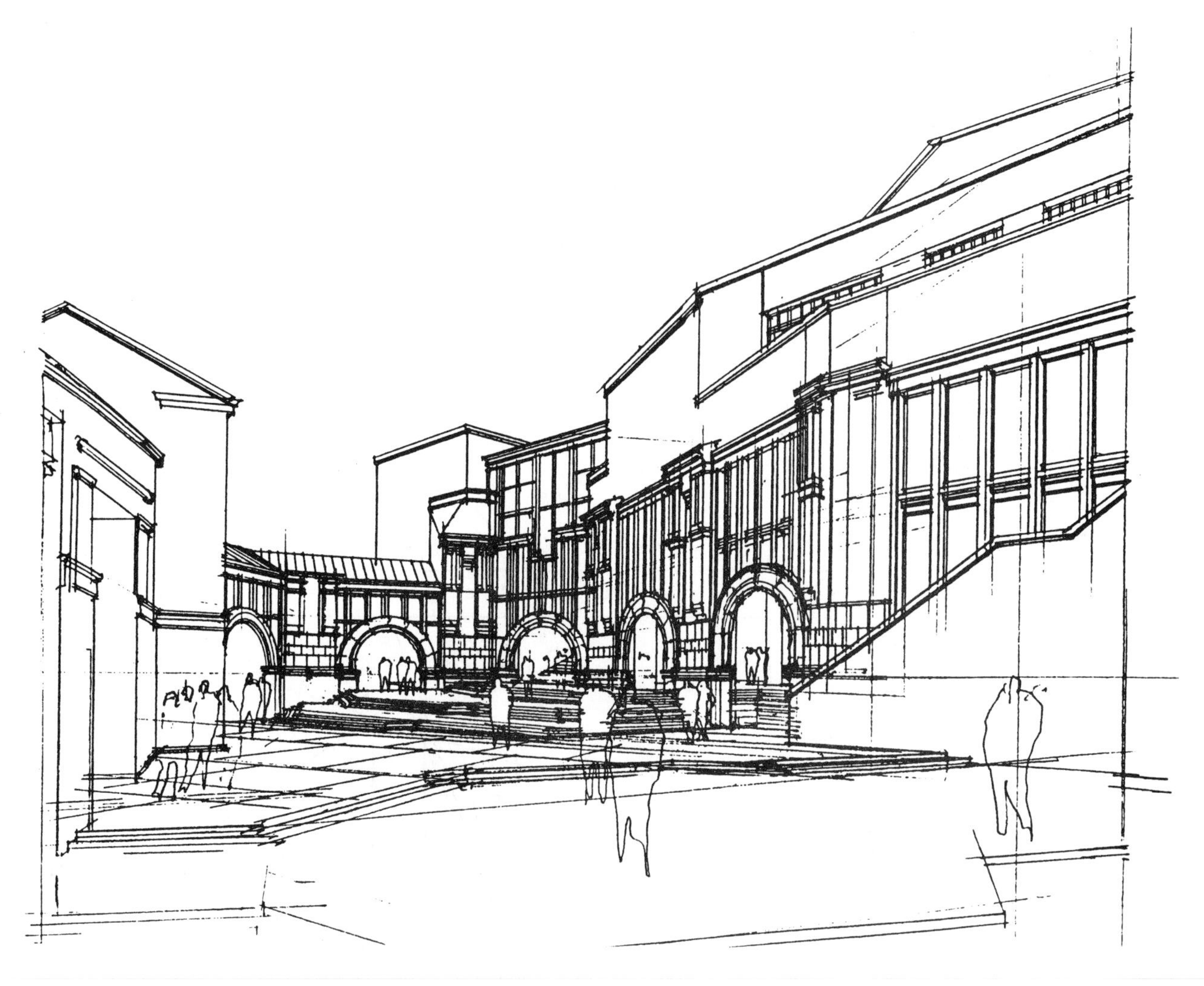

Drawing: California Center for the Arts, Escondido, California
Moore Ruble Yudell Architects
17" × 14" (43 × 36 cm)
Rough layout before a final line sketch and the use of watercolor as the medium
Courtesy of Al Forster, Architectural Illustrator

Multiple Vanishing Points

The blockout began as if there were just one ground plane. Plaza levels were added or (as in foreground) subtracted from the ground plane, and the figures in the final drawing were placed below or above the horizon line on their proper plaza levels. In a complicated drawing like this one, with multiple levels, vanishing points, and detail, it is easier to disguise certain inevitable errors than it is in a very simple drawing.
[ARCHITECTURAL ILLUSTRATOR'S STATEMENT]

This entry plaza is partially enclosed by wall planes that have multiple vanishing points on the horizon line.

1. Project extension lines from the left and right sides of the object to the picture plane and drop them vertically to the ground line.

Drawing: Lotus Mansion, Shanghai, China
16.75" × 22" (42.5 × 55.9 cm)
Medium: Watercolor by brush and airbrush on watercolor paper; linework is in pen and ink
Courtesy of Vitols Associates, Architects/Planners
Rendered by Thomas Wells Schaller of Schaller Architectural Illustrations

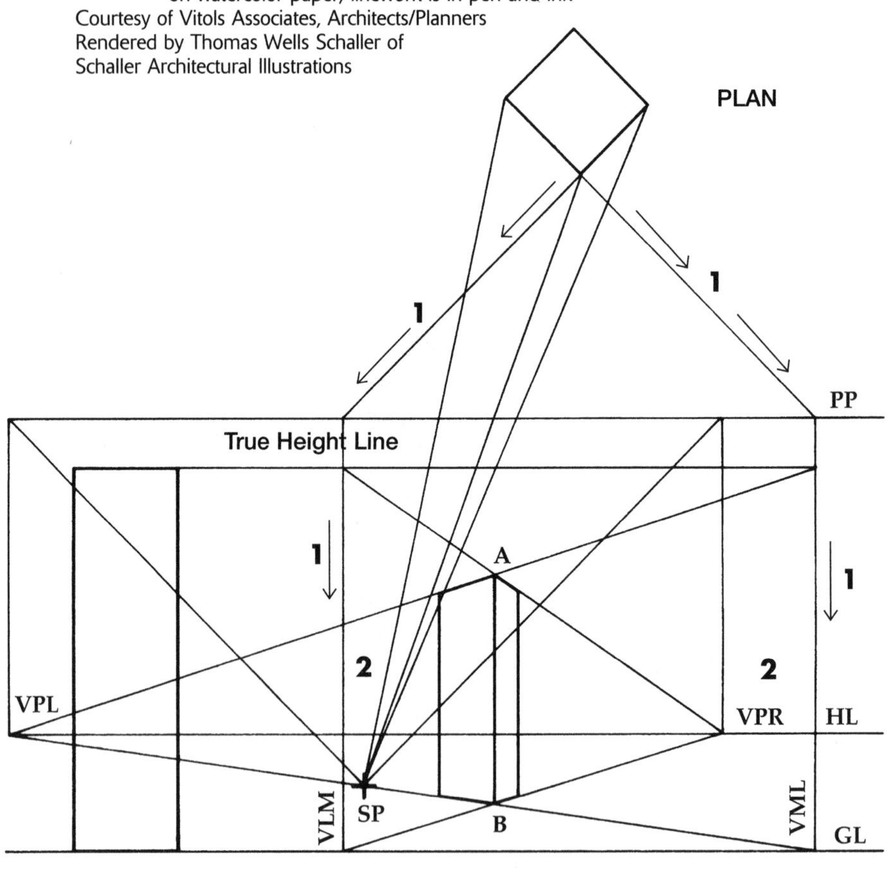

Building corner height AB is defined by the intersecting perspective planes.

2. Project the perspective planes back to VPR and VPL for both sides.

Object-PP Relationship

Objects that are behind the picture plane usually fall well within the cone of vision and show no distortion (see p. 194). The high-rise illustration was drawn with a greater degree of convergence to the left vanishing point than the example diagram to the right. Nevertheless, the view is well within the cone of vision. To find all the vanishing points when an object does not touch the picture plane, always construct (or trace) the plan view and note all the planar elements and their angles relative to the picture plane. Draw light construction lines parallel to all these planar elements, regardless of whether they are on the left or right side of the building. Drop these projection lines vertically from the picture plane to the horizon line. Relative to the station point, all left-side planar elements go to left vanishing points, and all right-side planar elements go to right vanishing points.

Drawing: Student project by A. Zainie Zainul
Medium: Ink on Mylar
Courtesy of Washington University
School of Architecture, St. Louis, Missouri

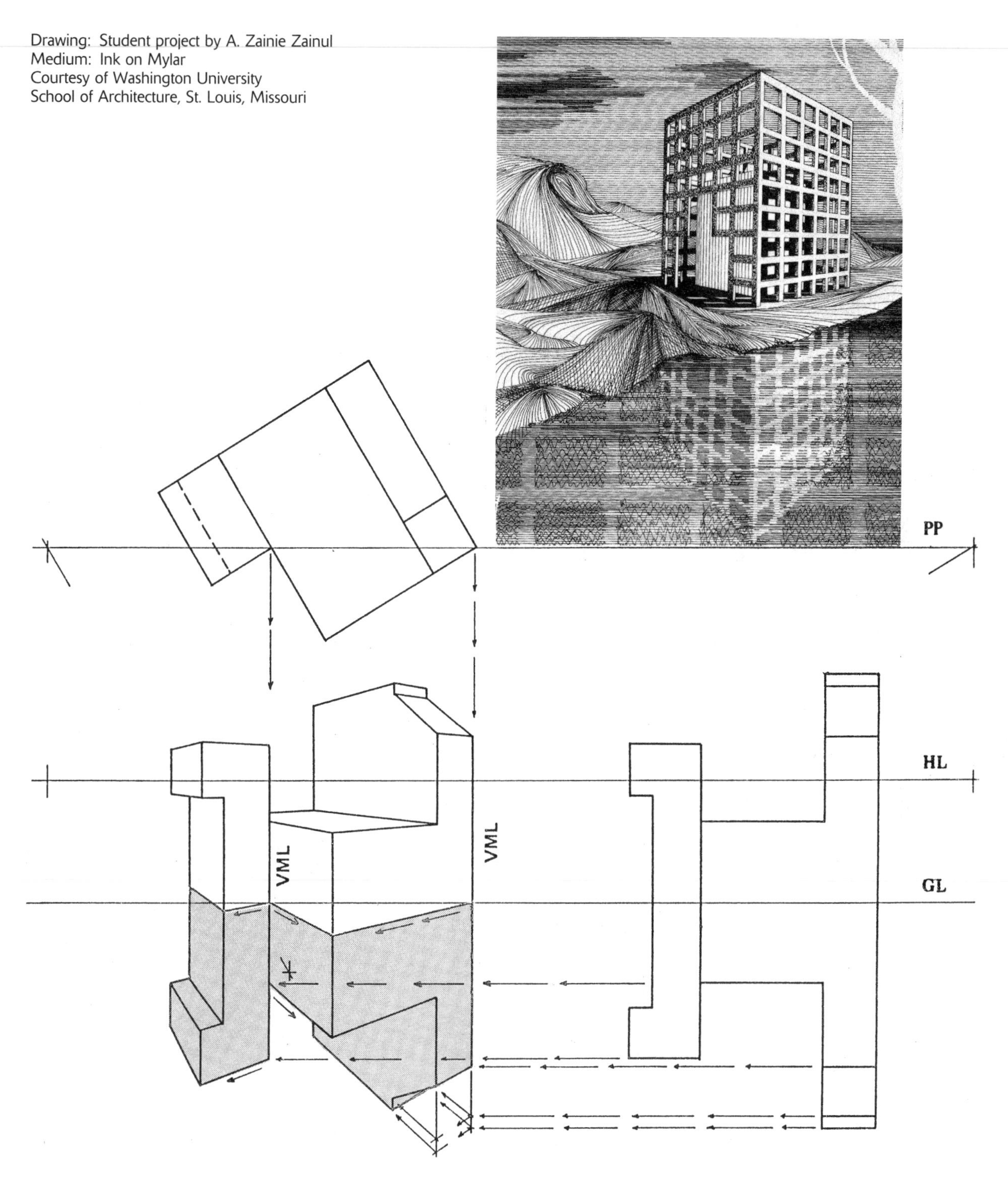

Object–Picture Plane Relationship

Objects completely in front of the picture plane will have a distorted perspective image because they begin to fall outside the cone of vision. However, partial penetration of the picture plane by an object is usually visually acceptable, as shown above. Use all **vertical measuring lines (VML)** that touch the picture plane to project construction lines into the volume in front of the picture plane. The schematic example shown has a reflection that also falls partially in front of the picture plane.

Drawing: Student project by Jennifer Kinkead
Bicycle factory, Mexico
Medium: Ink on Mylar
Excerpted from abstract, Columbia School of Architecture
Planning and Preservation (CSAPP)

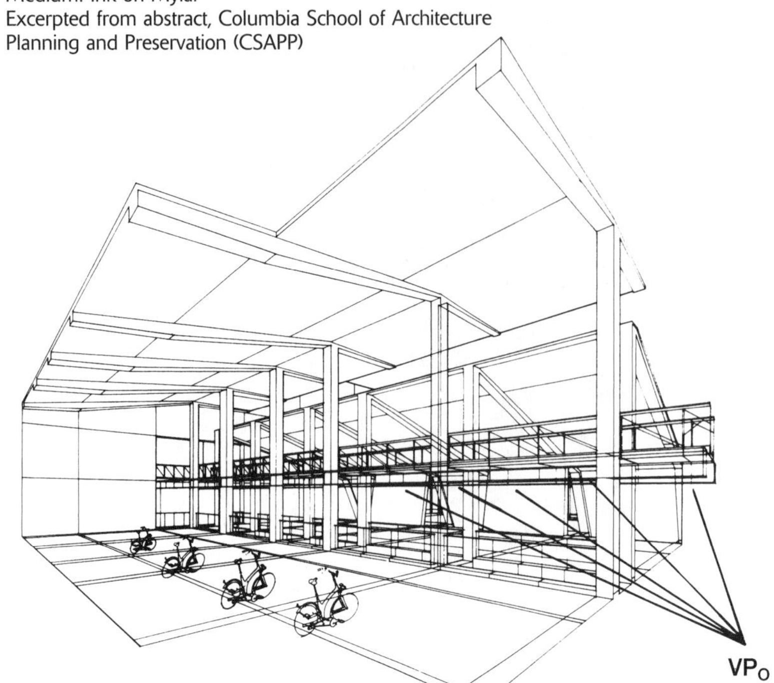

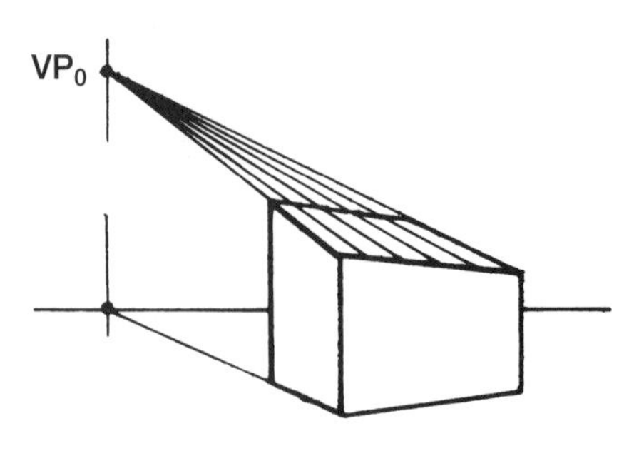

Oblique Vanishing Point

It is quite common to find a series of **oblique** (also termed "sloping" and "inclined") edges that are parallel in building forms. In such cases an oblique vanishing point **(VP_O)** expedites perspective construction.

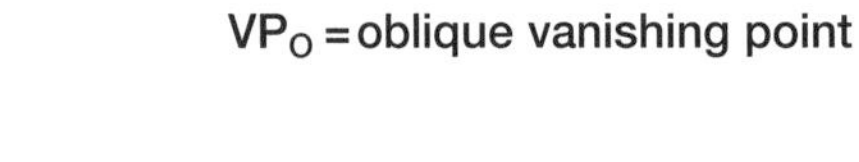

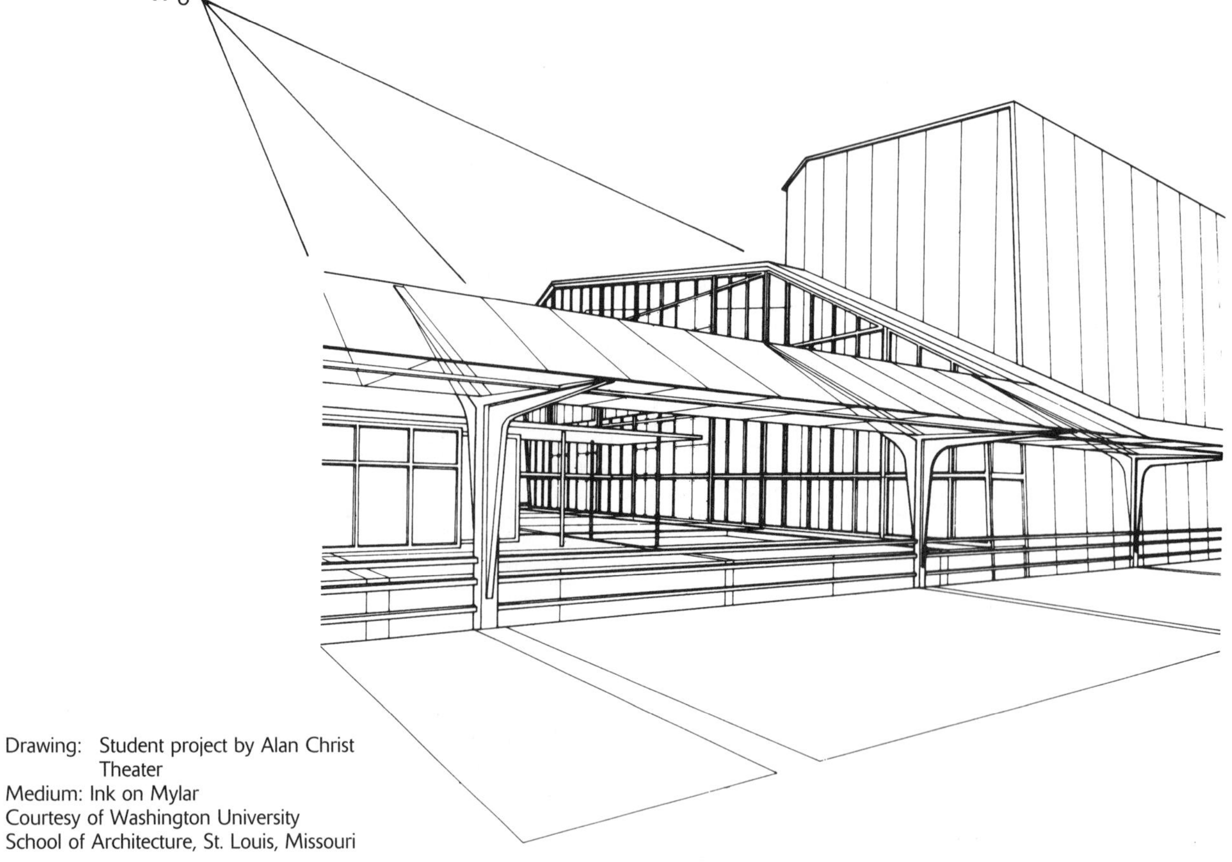

Drawing: Student project by Alan Christ
Theater
Medium: Ink on Mylar
Courtesy of Washington University
School of Architecture, St. Louis, Missouri

Drawing: Glass–Kline residence
New Paltz, New York
14" × 17" (35.6 × 43.2 cm)
Medium: Ink on vellum
Courtesy of Taeg Nishimoto & Allied Architects

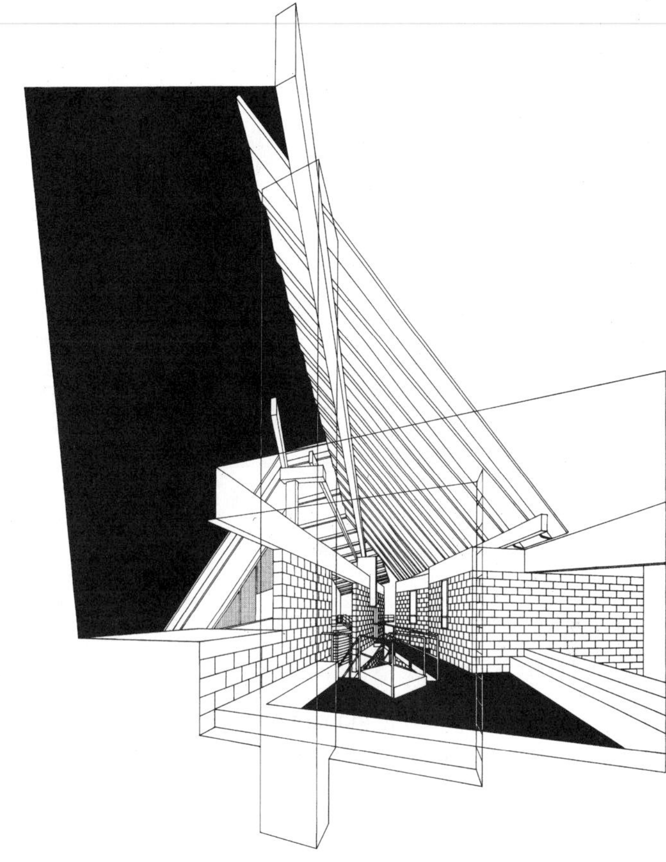

Oblique Vanishing Points

This interior perspective has structural ceiling elements that have oblique vanishing points both down to the right and down to the left.

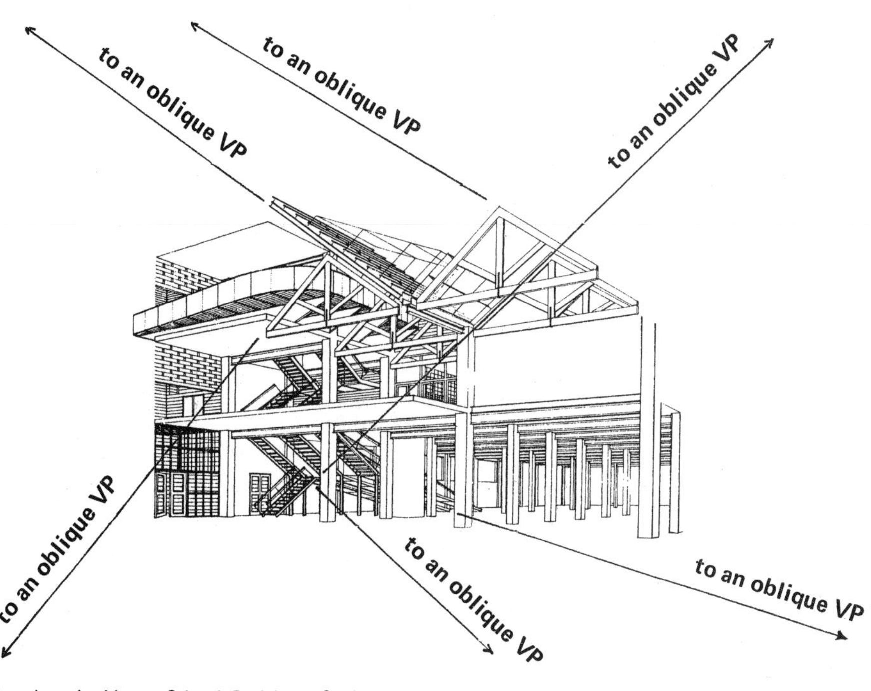

Drawing: La Llauna School, Badalona, Spain
Medium: Ink on Mylar
Courtesy of Enric Miralles & Carme Pinós, Architects

Edges that are **parallel** in an inclined plane converge to a **common** vanishing point. This vanishing point is not on the eye-level line. The vanishing points for a building's **oblique** lines fall either above or below its eye-level vanishing points. The process of determining the proper direction is discussed on the next two pages. The perspective of this building has numerous inclined lines and planes and, consequently, many oblique vanishing points. Sloping lines in perspective are a common occurrence with staircases and ramps.

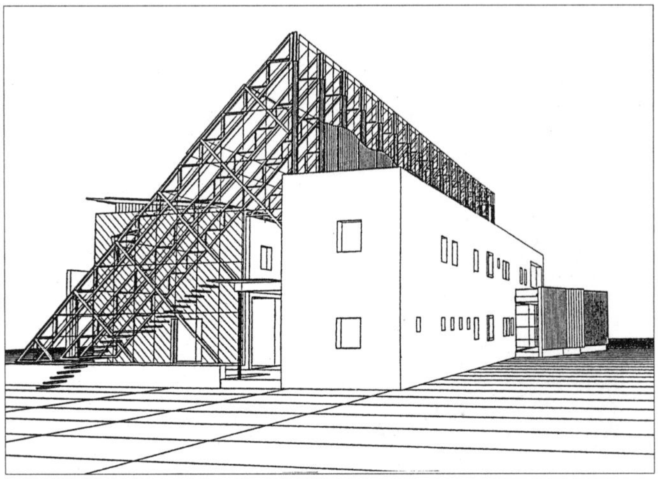

Oblique Vanishing Points

If a building has parallel inclined (slanted) edges that are neither horizontal nor vertical, as seen in the plan view below, their vanishing traces will converge to an oblique vanishing point above or below the vanishing point for horizontal lines. These trace lines are all located in the same or parallel planes.

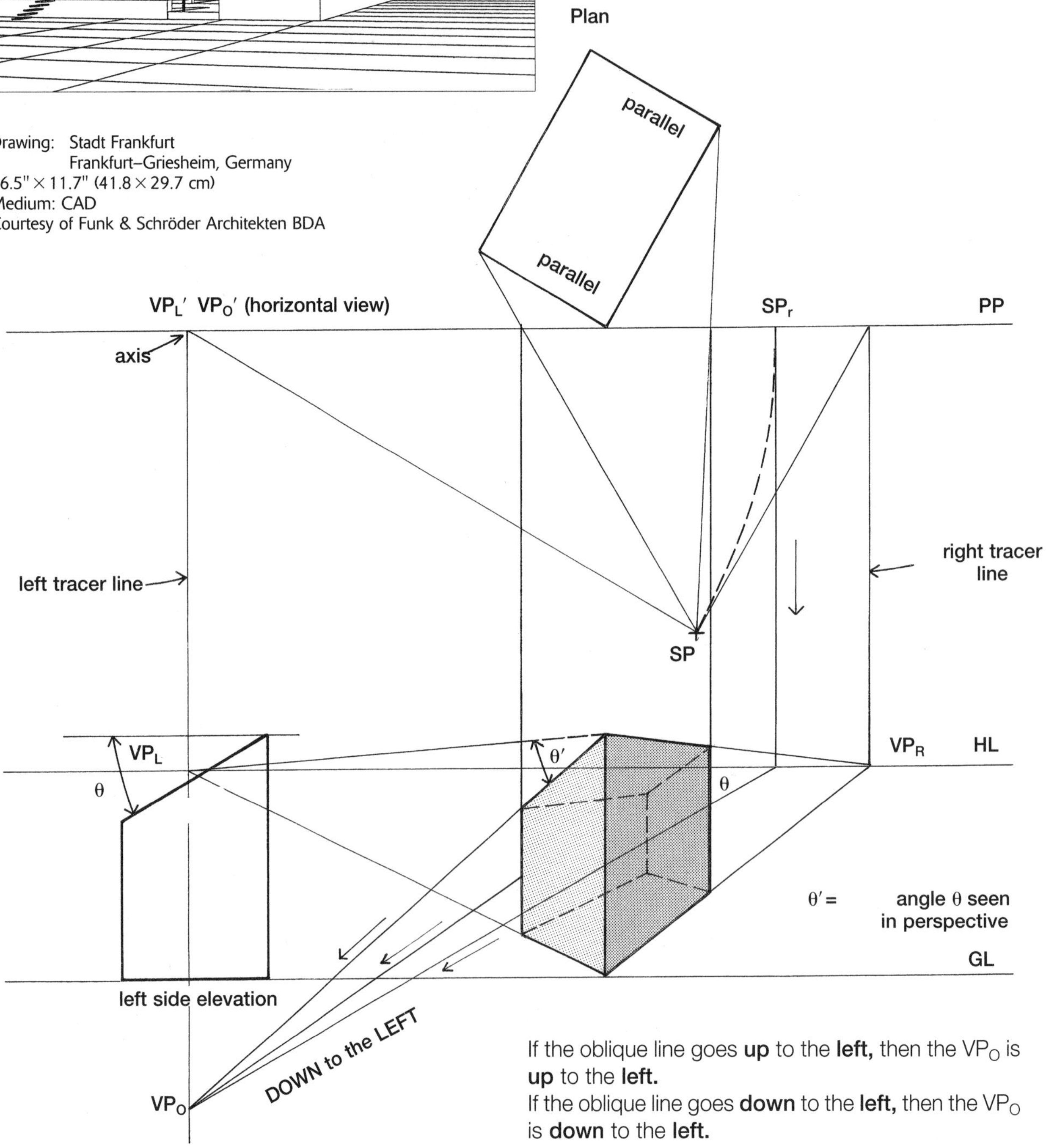

Drawing: Stadt Frankfurt
Frankfurt–Griesheim, Germany
16.5" × 11.7" (41.8 × 29.7 cm)
Medium: CAD
Courtesy of Funk & Schröder Architekten BDA

If the oblique line goes **up** to the **left,** then the VP_O is **up** to the **left.**
If the oblique line goes **down** to the **left,** then the VP_O is **down** to the **left.**

ΔABC is proportional to $\Delta SP_r\ VP_{R'}\ VP_{O'}$ where **r** means rotated.

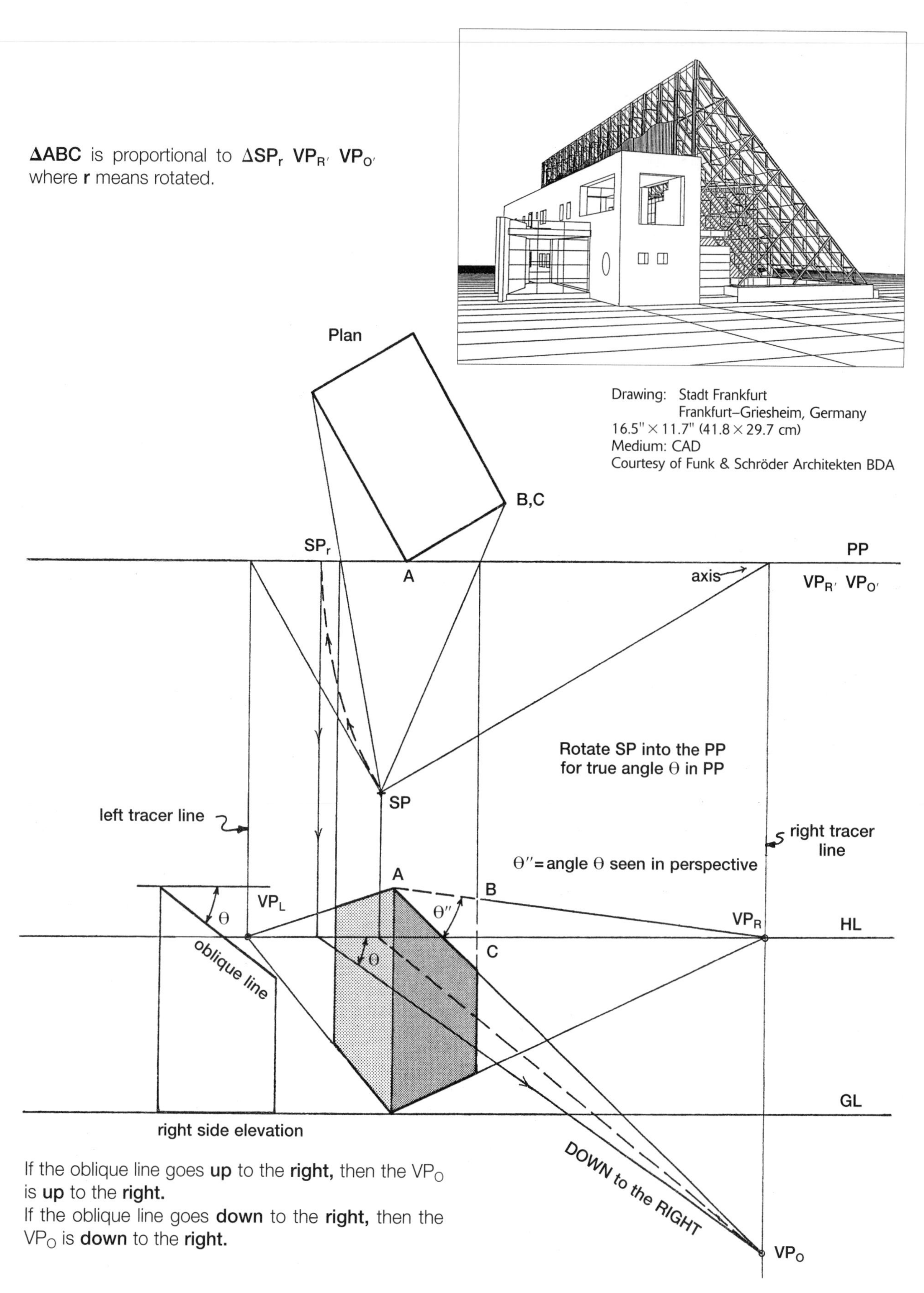

Drawing: Stadt Frankfurt
Frankfurt–Griesheim, Germany
16.5" × 11.7" (41.8 × 29.7 cm)
Medium: CAD
Courtesy of Funk & Schröder Architekten BDA

If the oblique line goes **up** to the **right,** then the VP_O is **up** to the **right.**
If the oblique line goes **down** to the **right,** then the VP_O is **down** to the **right.**

Drawing: Perry Community Education Village, Perry, Ohio
36" × 24" (91.4 × 61 cm)
Medium: Ink on Mylar
Courtesy of Perkins & Will Architects

Multiplying, Dividing, and Transferring

The plan/elevation method (for both two- and one-point) is just one of many ways to generate mechanical perspective drawings. In the future, new methods may emerge, and it is important not to be afraid to experiment with them. The balance of this chapter will, for the most part, discuss other methods.

Once an initial cube has been constructed, concepts and techniques for **multiplying, dividing,** and **transferring** dimensions in perspective space can be employed. These techniques support the development of a perspective without adding to its constructional framework. They build and reinforce an understanding of the perspective structure and the relationships among things within it regardless of the generated perspective method used. They do not require drawing space beyond the perspective itself, and they can be applied to any part of any existing perspective. Armed with this set of concepts and strategies for their employment, anything can be accurately drawn in perspective.

The application of the multiplying, dividing, and transferring techniques is of particular importance because it provides the means for linking sketching with the computer. The ability to quickly and accurately sketch within and extend a computer-generated perspective supports the exploration of alternatives and the development of presentation drawings. It allows three-dimensional modeling programs to be used to create simpler and more efficient mass models for generated perspective frameworks that can also be elaborated on by hand.

Diagram (p. 243) and text (pp. 242–43):
Courtesy of William R. Benedict, Assistant Professor
California Polytechnic State University
School of Architecture, San Luis Obispo, California

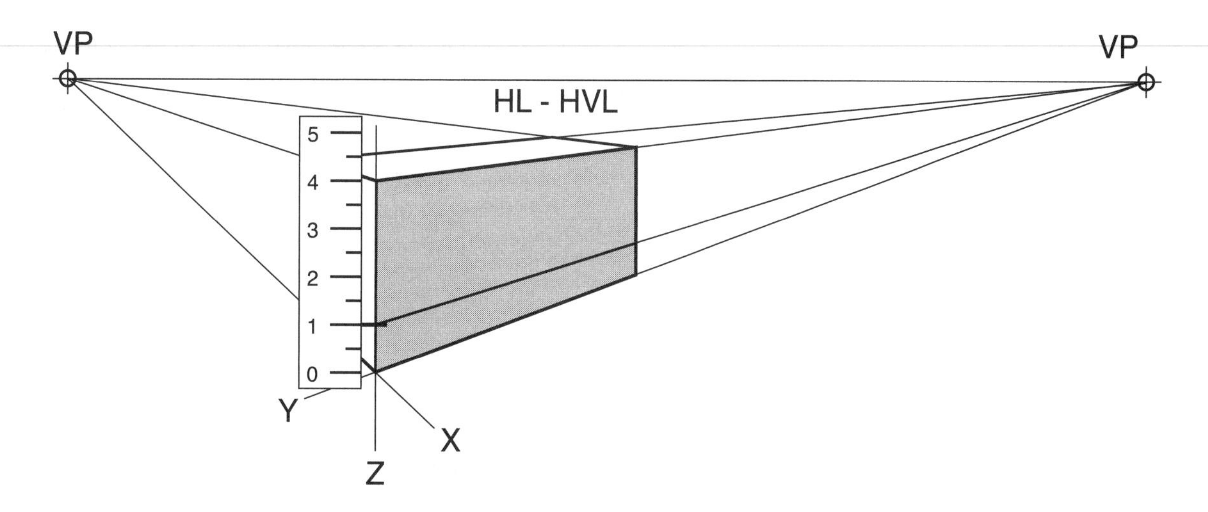

X-, Y-, and Z-Axes

The x, y, and z axes are the axes of the Cartesian coordinate system that are parallel to the three sets of parallel edges of a cube or any rectangular object or rectangular space. Moving through perspective space can be visualized as moving successively along the axes to arrive at the desired location. The z-axis is parallel to the picture plane; therefore, all lines parallel to it will retain their true orientation—that is, they will be drawn as vertical lines.

Dividing by Measuring

A common need in drawing is to give a line some scale and establish dimensions along it. You may have a line of some length that you wish to call a specific dimension (give a specific scale), say 4', and then establish a point on the line that is one foot from one end.

Three techniques can be used: direct measurement, vanished transfer, and parallel transfer. All three techniques are intended to give a line scale and locate specific dimensions. Once this has been done, other techniques must be used to move the dimensions within the drawing. Direct measurement, parallel transfer, and a variation of parallel transfer with vertical and horizontal lines will be discussed.

Direct Measurement

This technique involves directly measuring the line. It is used when establishing dimensions through visual judgment or direct measurement with a scale. Direct measurement with the eye involves making visual judgments that proportionally divide the line. For example, if the line is assumed to be 4' long and a 1' increment is needed, you can visually divide the line in half and then in half again to demarcate 1'. This works very well because we can accurately judge the middle of things. With practice you can also divide a line into thirds or fifths. By combining judgments of halves, thirds, and fifths, you can easily and accurately use your eye to establish dimensions in a drawing.

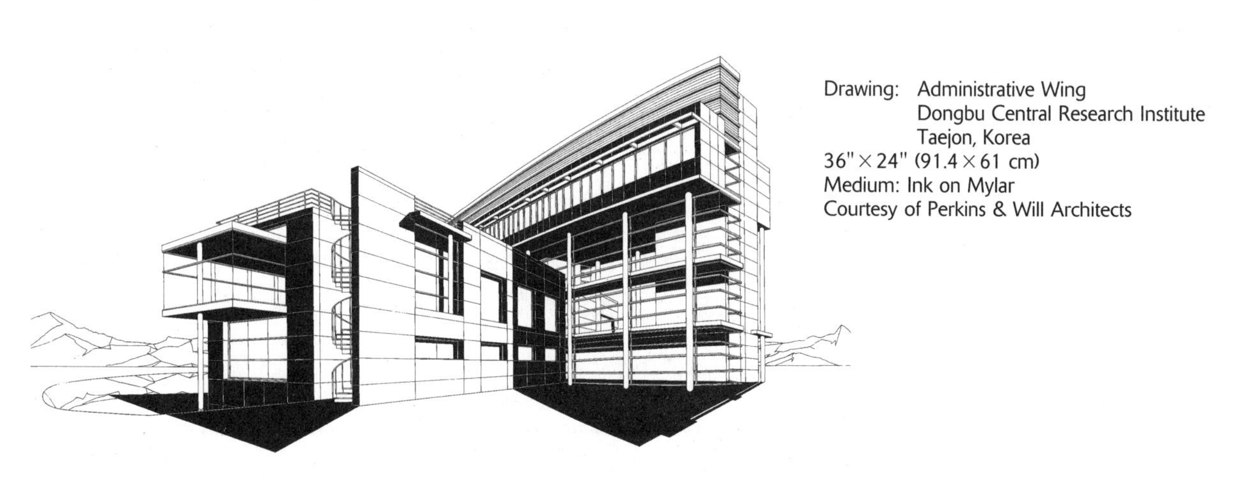

Drawing: Administrative Wing
Dongbu Central Research Institute
Taejon, Korea
36" × 24" (91.4 × 61 cm)
Medium: Ink on Mylar
Courtesy of Perkins & Will Architects

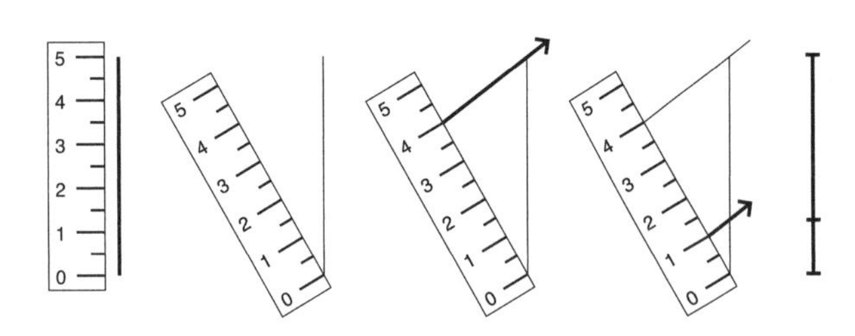

Parallel Transfer

Suppose the existing line is of a dimension not readily divisible by four. Identify the line parallel to the picture plane that you want to make equal to that dimension.

Choose a scale reasonably close to the actual length of the line. Align the zero mark on the scale to one end of the line to be dimensioned. Angle the scale away from the line. Mark the desired dimensions along the edge of the scale, including the one that designates the full length of the line.

Draw a line from the full-length dimension along the scale to the end of the line you want to dimension. The angle of this line will be used to transfer all other dimensions from the scale to the line. Draw lines that are parallel to the line created in the preceding step between all dimensions along the scale and the line you are dimensioning (i.e., 1'). You have now proportionally dimensioned the base line and can proceed with the drawing construction using other techniques.

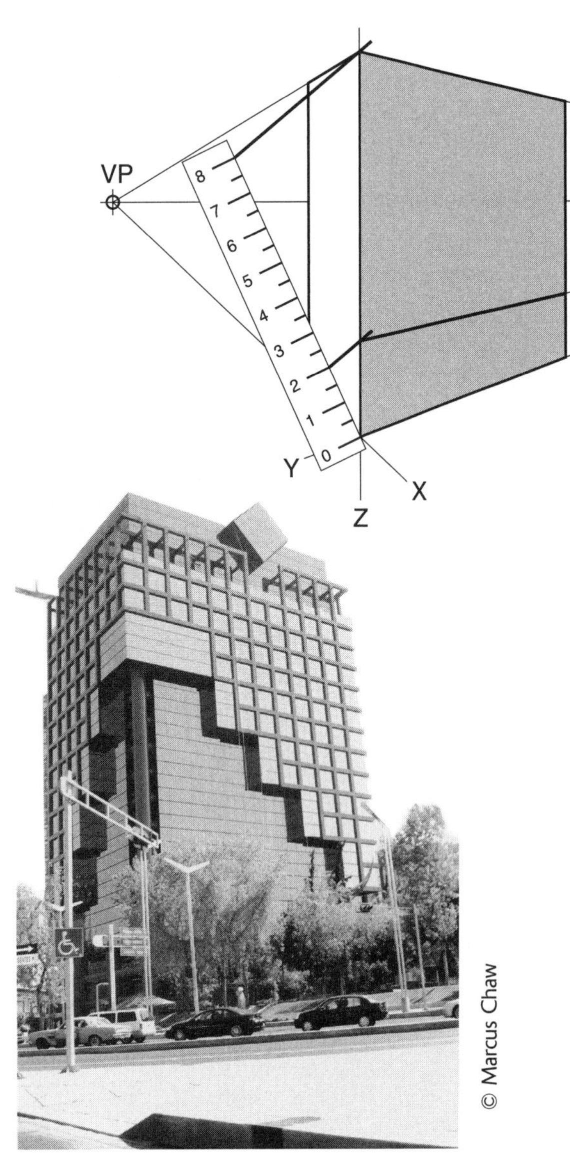

Photo: Reforma 164 Building, Mexico City, Mexico

Vertical and Horizontal Lines

The parallel transfer technique translates directly to any line that is parallel to the picture plane, such as those that are vertical and horizontal. The perspective example above shows the technique being used for a vertical edge — a condition that occurs in both one- and two-point perspectives.

Note: The photo of this eighteen-story high-rise building shows that the parallel vertical lines appear to converge upward when seen by an observer at ground level.

Diagrams and text (pp. 243–45):
Courtesy of William R. Benedict, Assistant Professor
California Polytechnic State University
School of Architecture, San Luis Obispo, California

Multiplying by Measuring

The assumption is that you have a visually and proportionally correct square and wish to generate additional squares above or below.

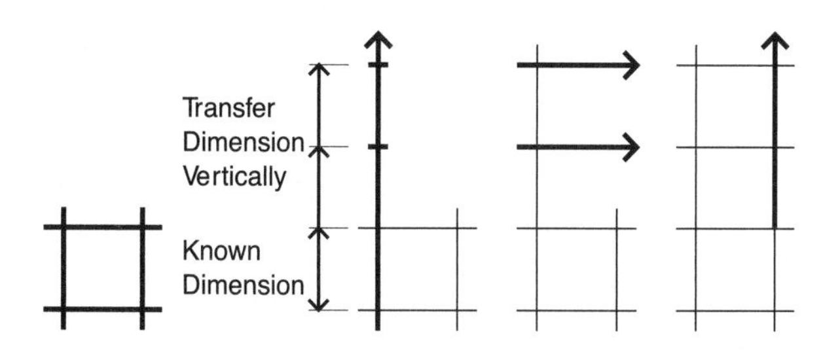

Draw or identify the base square whose vertical edges are parallel to the picture plane. All edges are parallel in orthographic drawings.

Extend a vertical edge of the base square to function as a measuring line. Transfer the height of the base square (the known dimension) along this edge. You can transfer dimensions above and/or below the base square as many times as needed.

Principle: Vertical lines in both one- and two-point perspectives represent edges that are parallel to the picture plane — they do not vanish. This means that a dimension or portion of the dimension (½, ¼, etc.) established on any vertical line within a perspective can be transferred vertically along that line.

Draw horizontal lines through these points (orthographic) or lines that go to the vanishing point for the plane (perspective).

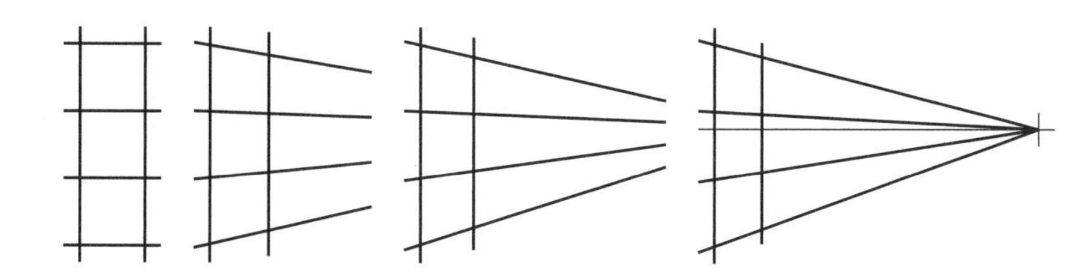

Principle: In both one- and two-point perspectives, sets of parallel horizontal lines not parallel to the picture plane vanish to a common vanishing point on the horizon line. This means that dimensions can be transferred horizontally between vertical lines on the same plane by using the vanishing point for horizontal lines for that plane.

Extend the remaining vertical edge to complete the additional squares.

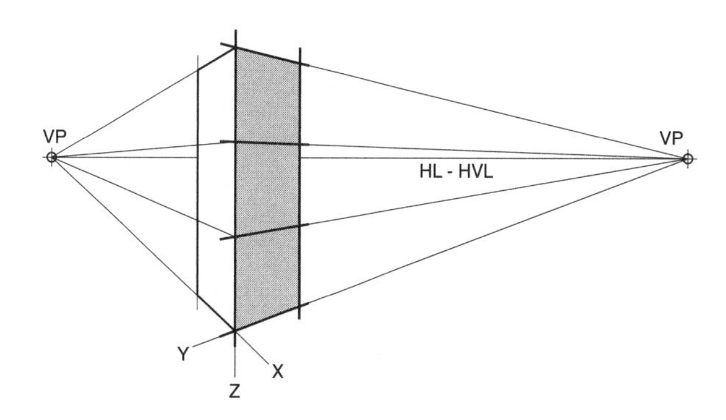

Drawing: Torre de Telecomunicacions de Montjuïc
Barcelona, Spain, 1992
Santiago Calatrava, Architect
4.5" × 7" (11.4 × 17.8 cm)
Medium: Ink on vellum
Drawn by Kwok Gorran Tsui, architecture graduate, University of Texas at Austin

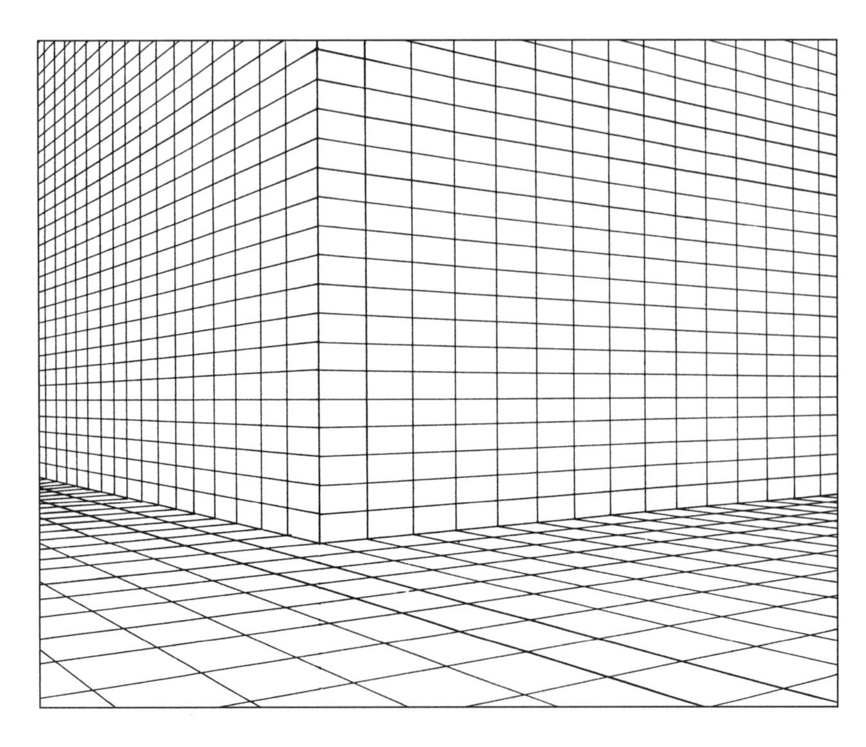

This is part of a typical two-point perspective grid chart. Grids for exteriors and interiors are rotated at specific angles (30°, 45°, etc.) from the picture plane to allow various views. Using manual methods, a perspective plan can be constructed to simulate a grid chart (see below). Constructed grids should be saved for future use. Grids are ideal for plotting points on axial lines or within axial planes to facilitate drawing exterior or interior views. The selected scale can be any unit of length.

Perspective Grid Charts (Pros and Cons and View Development)

Perspective charts (such as Lawson charts, which include metric applications) are commercially available. They save time when you need to generate many similar images; they are also space savers, especially when a large layout is required (residential layouts, for example, may need 5' or more). The scale of the grid lines on perspective charts is flexible, and the observer's relationship to the horizon line (bird's-eye, worm's-eye, eye-level, etc.) can always be adjusted. Perspective charts restrict the placement of the SP and PP, however, and have limited viewing angles. Charts that are made for both one- and two-point perspectives are divided into two categories: those with a relatively high HL and those with a relatively low HL. (See the discussion of three-point perspective charts on p. 275.) Although they are handy for quick studies, perspective charts are becoming dated by digital technology.

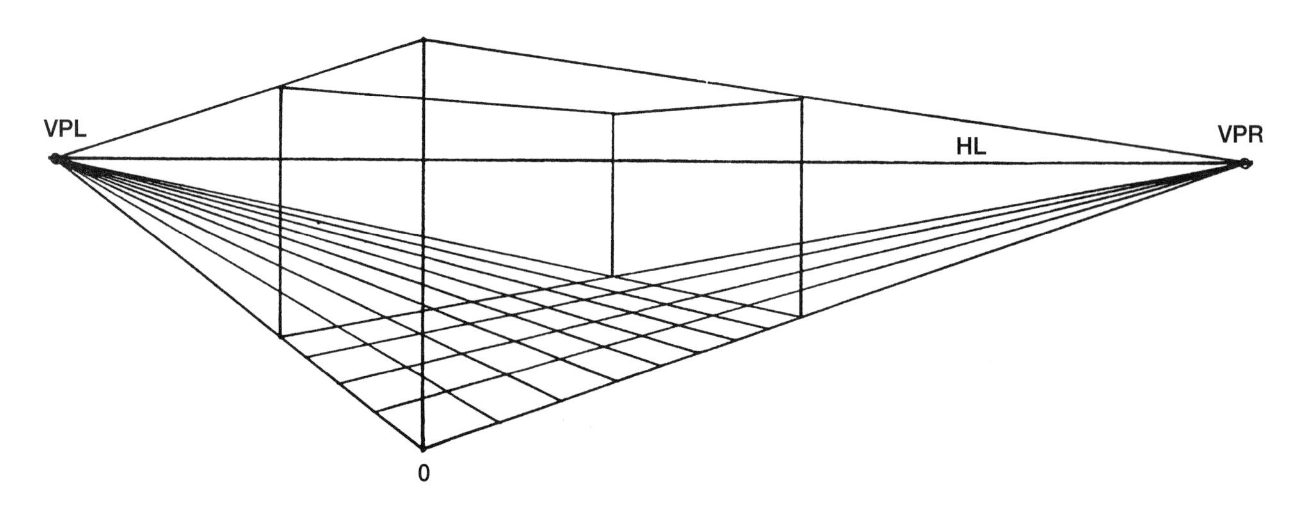

Briefly, the sequential process for developing a view begins with (**1**) determining the SP location; (**2**) choosing an angle of view; (**3**) selecting an appropriate chart; (**4**) locating architectural elements such as ceilings, doors, and windows from major vertical dimensions (heights) using elevations, etc.; and (**5**) adding accessories such as human figures and furniture (if drawing an interior scene) in their accurate relative positions (see p. 406).

Sample Perspective Charts

Perspective charts are excellent for developing quick sketches. Eight easy-to-use charts comprise the set of Lawson perspective charts. Charts 1 through 4 are more suitable for drawing interiors and elements within the interior space, such as furniture. Charts 5 through 8 are usually used for exterior views or large-size subjects. The 45° two-point chart shown here lends itself to views showing two interior walls with equal emphasis. The one-point perspective chart shown below emphasizes one important (parallel) side, with two other sides of secondary interest.

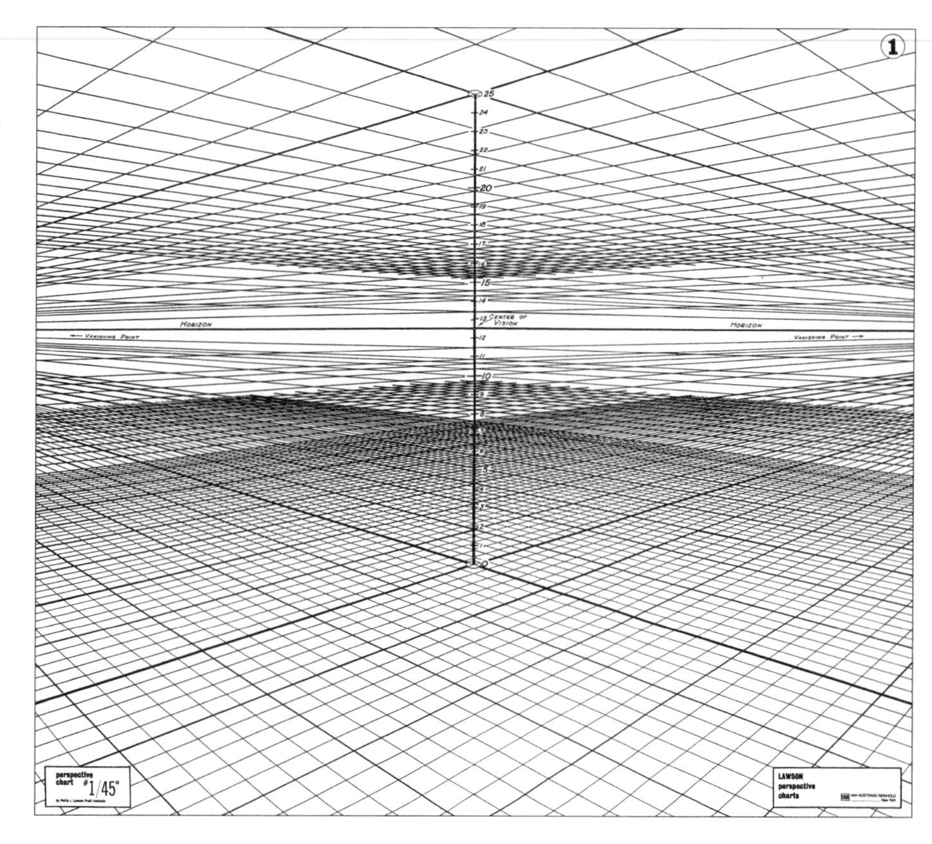

Use the bold vertical measuring lines given on all charts to measure and project true heights. The true heights are then projected on axial lines along true-height vertical grid planes and eventually, into the perspective view. Circles (p. 223 and p. 287) and non-circular curves (p. 289) can be constructed using plotted points on the grid. The recommended value for general work in the metric system is 15 cm (6") per unit; for drawing interiors, it is 12.5 cm (5") per unit. Use smaller units (5 cm or 3" per unit, etc.) for small furniture objects.

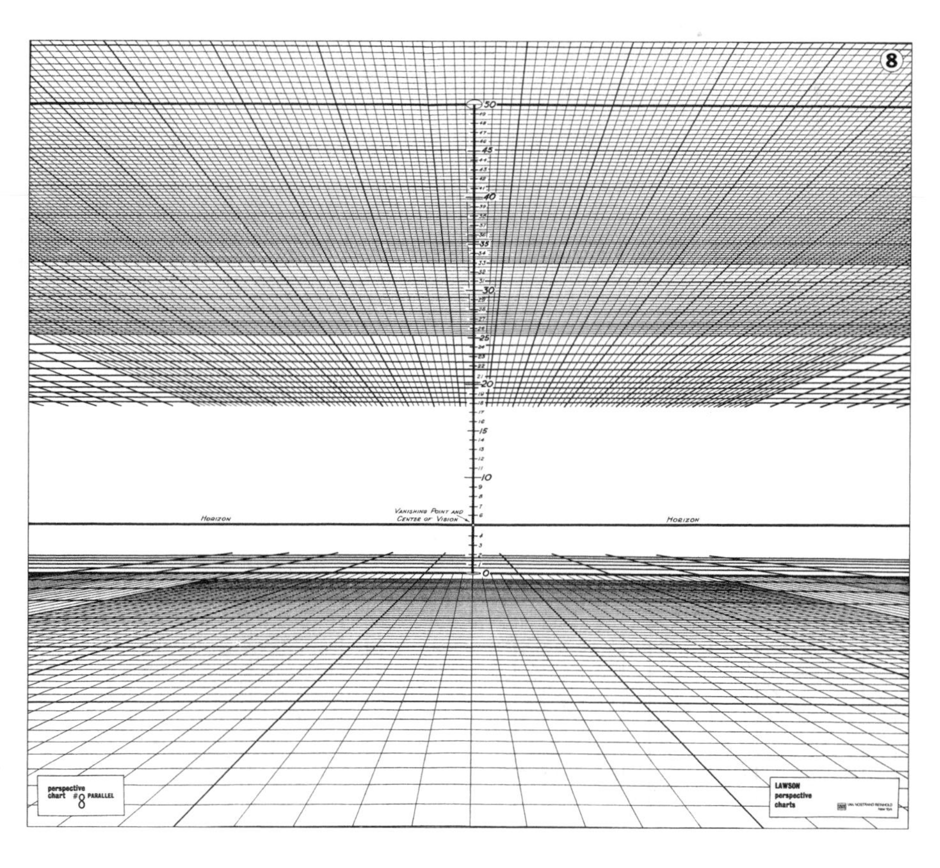

Lawson Perspective Charts: Courtesy of Margaret Cummins, Senior Editor John Wiley & Sons, Inc.

Transferring with the Diagonal

Suppose that you have a visually and proportionally correct square with dimensions located on one side that you want to transfer to an adjacent side.

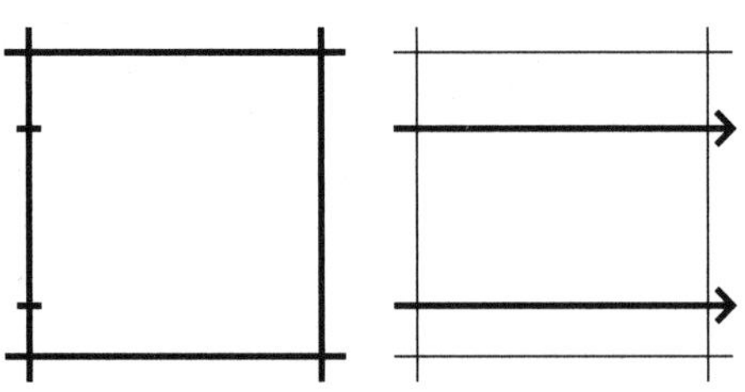

Draw or identify the base square and the dimensions. The vertical edges are parallel to the picture plane. All edges are parallel in orthographic drawings. Extend the dimensions across the square. Draw one of the diagonals of the square. Draw lines that intersect with the sides of the square through the intersections of the diagonal and dimension lines.

Principle: A 45° line drawn through the intersection of two perpendicular lines will transfer dimensions from one line to the other. The diagonal you choose to draw will control the side to which a dimension is transferred. This technique has slightly different results when used in a square, as illustrated, than when used in other rectangles. The diagonal of a square will transfer the exact dimensions (2' to 2'), while the diagonal of a rectangle will transfer only proportions (¼ to ¼) .

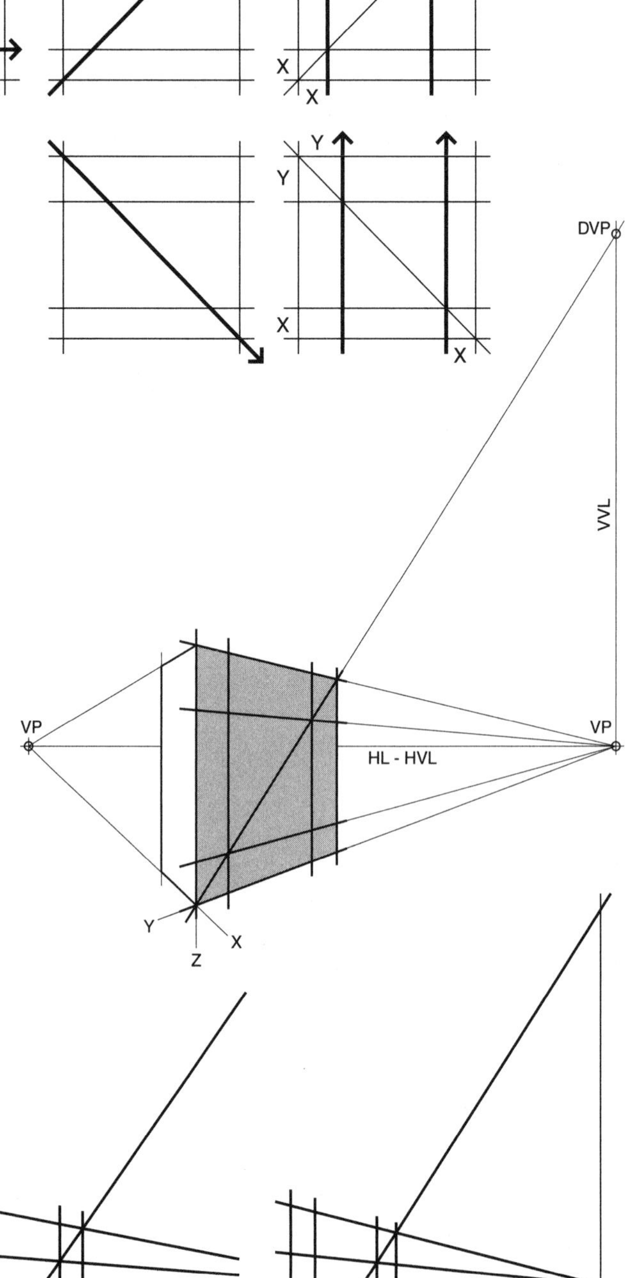

Diagrams and text (both pages): Courtesy of William R. Benedict, Assistant Professor California Polytechnic State University College of Architecture & Environmental Design San Luis Obispo, California

Multiplying by Measuring Plus the Diagonal

Suppose that you have a visually and proportionally correct square and wish to generate additional squares to one or more sides. The strategy combines the vertical transfer of dimensions introduced in Multiplying by Measuring, p. 245, with transferring the diagonal of a square.

As the illustrations show, the diagonal can be further extended to intersect a vertical line **(VVL)** drawn through the vanishing point **(VP)** for the horizontal lines. This creates a diagonal vanishing point **(DVP)** to which all parallel diagonals will converge. You do not need to create the diagonal vanishing point to use this technique. The diagonal vanishing points may be above or below or to either side of a VP.

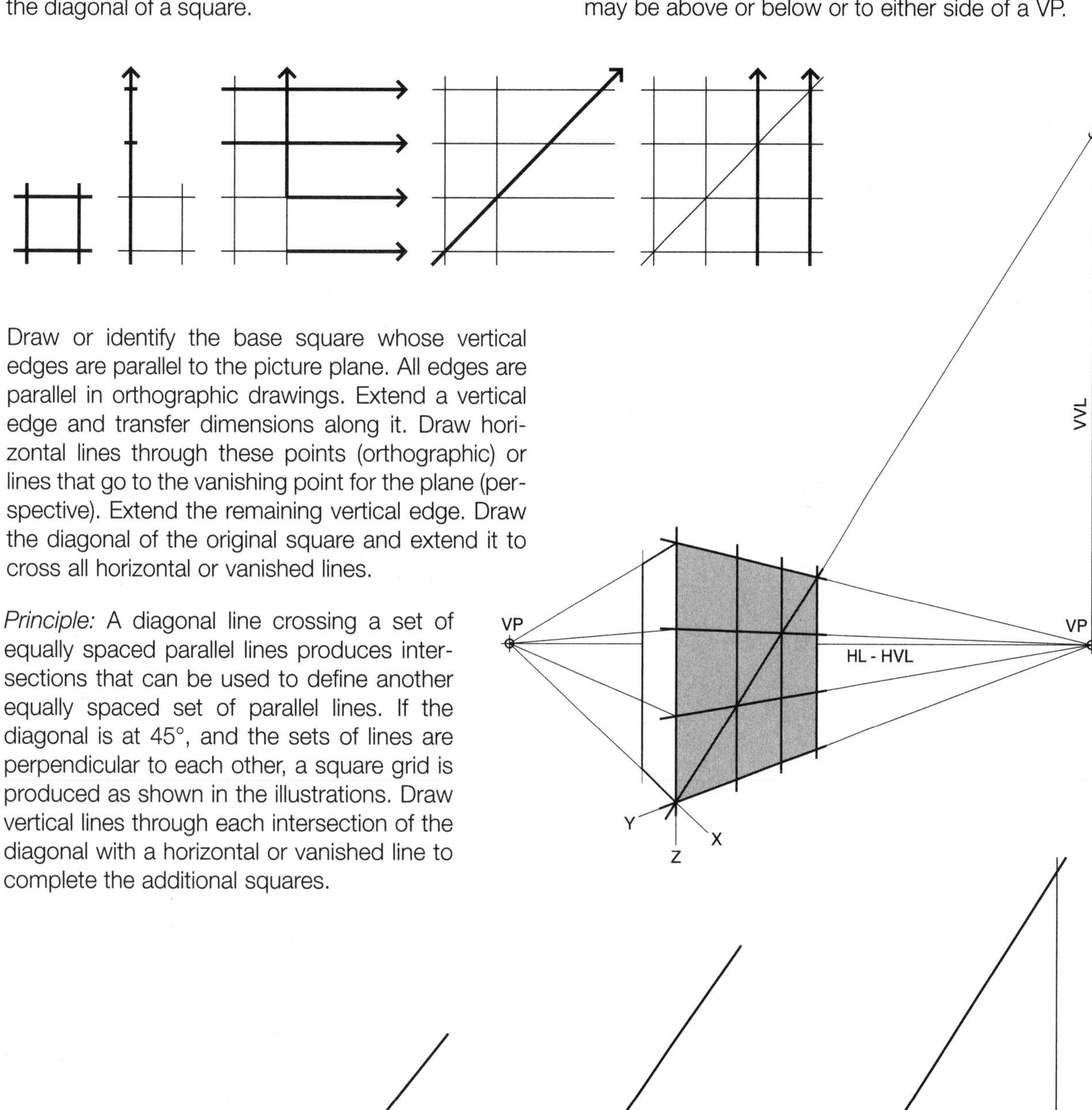

Draw or identify the base square whose vertical edges are parallel to the picture plane. All edges are parallel in orthographic drawings. Extend a vertical edge and transfer dimensions along it. Draw horizontal lines through these points (orthographic) or lines that go to the vanishing point for the plane (perspective). Extend the remaining vertical edge. Draw the diagonal of the original square and extend it to cross all horizontal or vanished lines.

Principle: A diagonal line crossing a set of equally spaced parallel lines produces intersections that can be used to define another equally spaced set of parallel lines. If the diagonal is at 45°, and the sets of lines are perpendicular to each other, a square grid is produced as shown in the illustrations. Draw vertical lines through each intersection of the diagonal with a horizontal or vanished line to complete the additional squares.

Multiplying with the Diagonal

Suppose that you have a visually and proportionally correct square and wish to generate additional squares to either adjacent side, or above, or below.

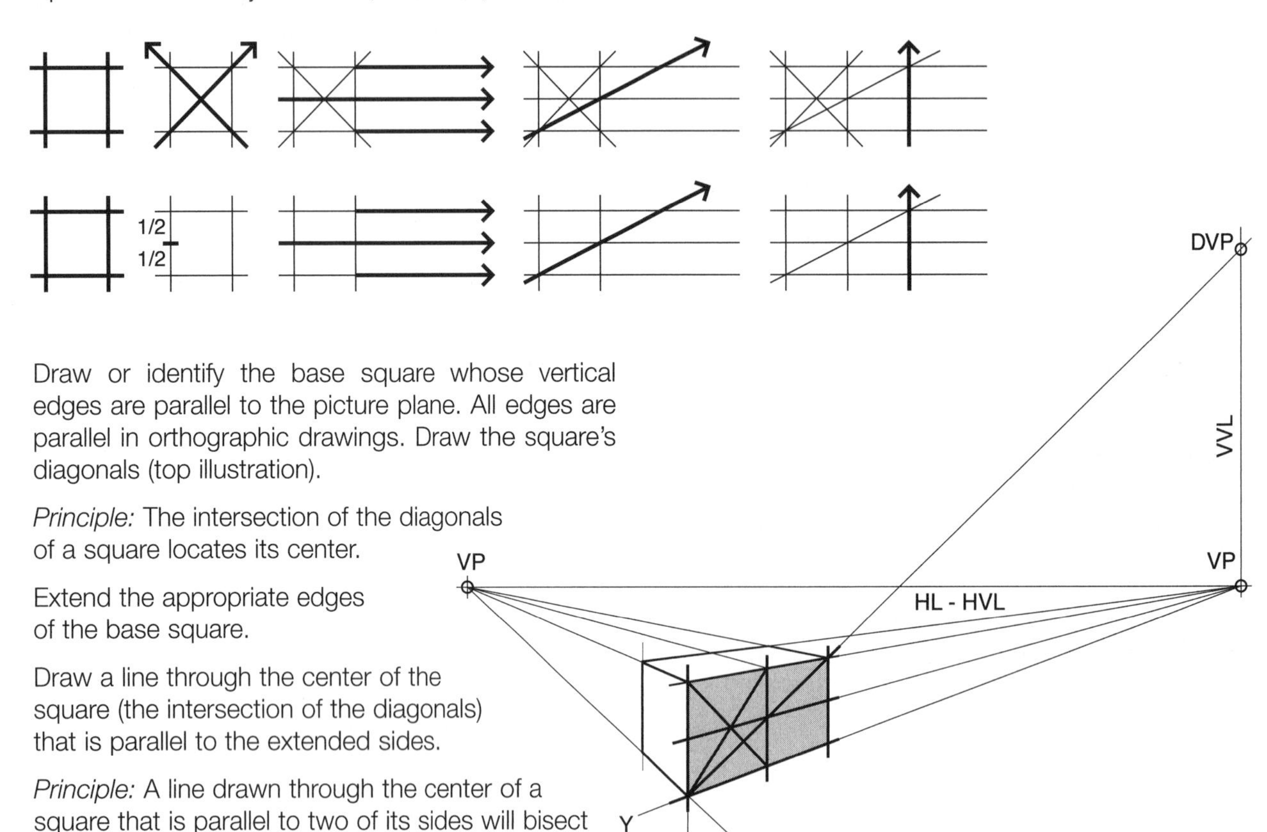

Draw or identify the base square whose vertical edges are parallel to the picture plane. All edges are parallel in orthographic drawings. Draw the square's diagonals (top illustration).

Principle: The intersection of the diagonals of a square locates its center.

Extend the appropriate edges of the base square.

Draw a line through the center of the square (the intersection of the diagonals) that is parallel to the extended sides.

Principle: A line drawn through the center of a square that is parallel to two of its sides will bisect the other two sides.

Alternative (bottom illustration): Sometimes it is faster to divide a vertical edge with a scale or by visual judgment. In this case, draw a line through the center of the side that is parallel to the extended sides.

Draw a line from one corner of the square through the center of an opposite side. Extend this line until it intersects one of the extended sides. This line is now the diagonal of a rectangle that is twice as wide as the original square.

Draw a line through the intersection of the line just completed and the side of the square to define the new square.

As the illustrations show, the diagonal of the double-wide rectangle can be further extended to intersect a vertical line **(VVL)** drawn through the vanishing point for the horizontal lines. This creates a diagonal vanishing point **(DVP)** to which all similar diagonals will converge. You do not need to create the diagonal vanishing point to use this technique.

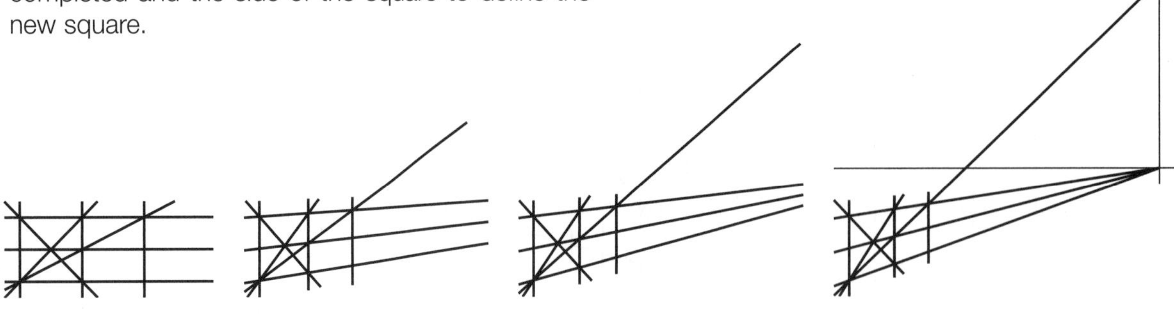

Dividing with the Diagonal

It is a good strategy to draw the largest inclusive form possible as a first step in constructing a perspective and then to subdivide that form to locate smaller elements. This technique assumes that you have a visually and proportionally correct square and wish to divide it into halves, quarters, eighths, etc.

As the illustrations show, the diagonals can be further extended to intersect a vertical line **(VVL)** drawn through the vanishing point **(VP)** for the horizontal lines. This creates a diagonal vanishing point **(DVP)**. You do not need to create the diagonal vanishing point to use this technique. The diagonal vanishing points may be above or below or to either side of a VP.

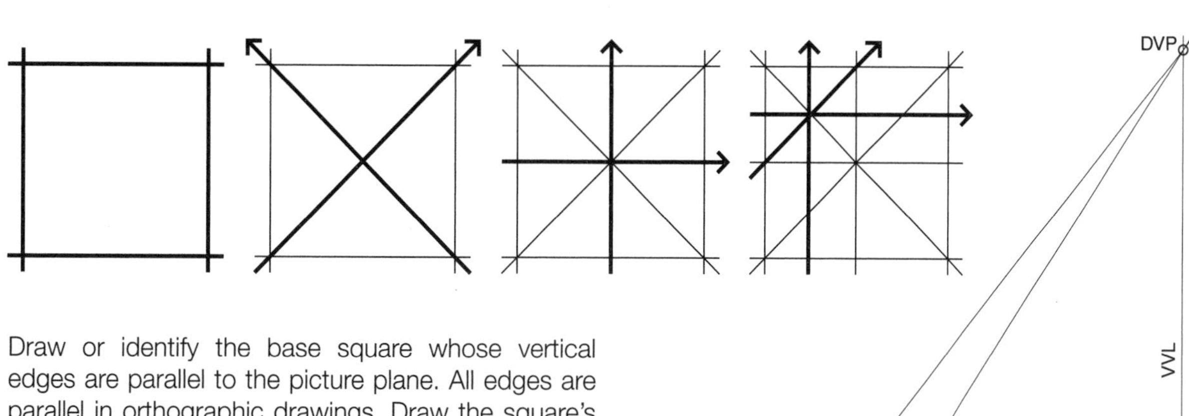

Draw or identify the base square whose vertical edges are parallel to the picture plane. All edges are parallel in orthographic drawings. Draw the square's diagonals.

Principle: The intersection of the diagonals of a square locate its center.

Draw a vertical and a horizontal line through the intersection of the diagonals. In perspective, the horizontal line vanishes to the vanishing point for horizontal lines on that surface.

Principle: A line drawn through the center of a square that is parallel to two of its sides will bisect the other two sides.

The vertical and horizontal lines have defined four smaller squares that have the same proportions as the original but are one-quarter the size. This process can be repeated within each progressively smaller square until the desired subdivision is produced. Each subdivdsion halves the square (e.g., a 12' square becomes four 6' squares.

Diagrams and text (both pages): Courtesy of William R. Benedict, Assistant Professor California Polytechnic State University College of Architecture & Environmental Design San Luis Obispo, California

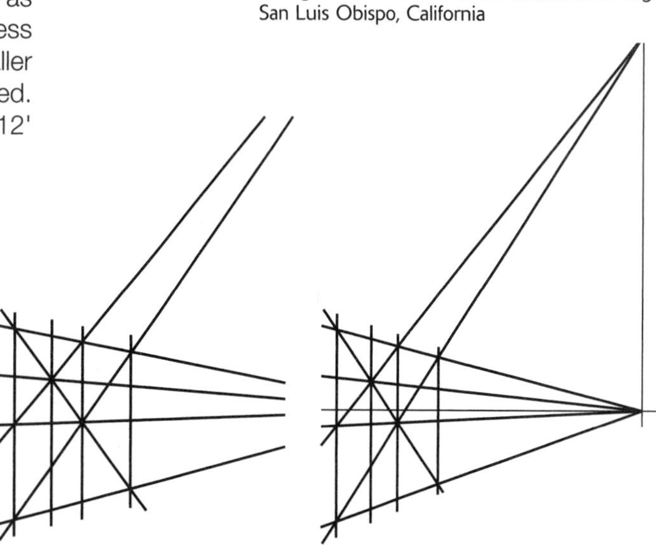

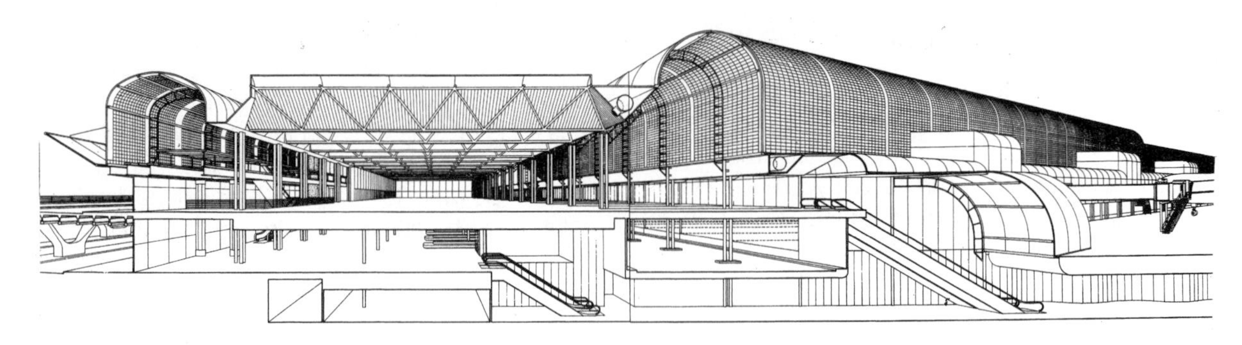

Drawing (above): United Airlines Terminal, Chicago, Illinois
34" x 22" (86.4 x 55.9 cm)
Medium: Sepia ink on 1000H paper
Courtesy of Murphy/Jahn, Architects
with A. Epstein & Sons, Architects

Drawing (left): Storrow Drive, Boston, Massachusetts
30" × 24" (76.2 × 61 cm)
Medium: Ink on Mylar
Courtesy of Koetter Kim & Associates, Inc.
Architects and Urban Designers

Projected Depths

The principles for multiplying and dividing with diagonals are frequently used on the fenestration of buildings to distribute elements along a plane.

In building structures of great lengths (institutional, commercial, etc.), it is common to have **equally** spaced repetitious elements. Perspective construction can be expedited by the use of **diagonals;** this is possible because all diagonals of squares and rectangles intersect in the exact center of the figure (see pp. 250–51).

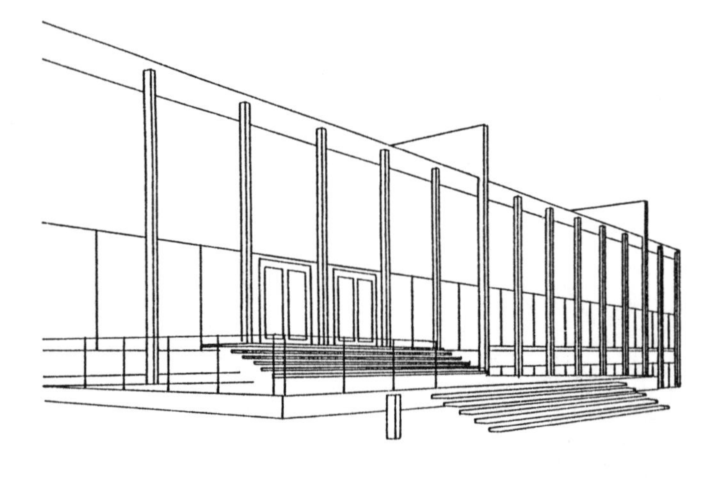

Drawing: Crown Hall, Illinois Institute of Technology, Chicago, Illinois
Ludwig Mies van der Rohe, Architect

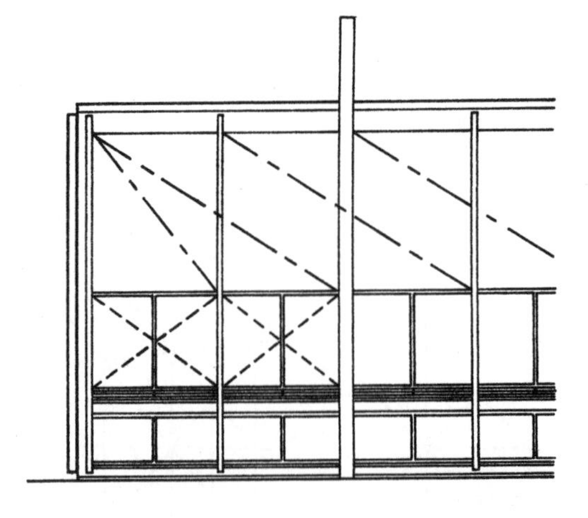

TYPICAL PARTIAL ELEVATION

1. Decide on the spacing between two primary window mullions, **a** and **b**.
2. Draw diagonals between **a** and **b** to determine the mullion midline bisector.
3. Locate mullion **c'c** by drawing a line from **a'** through the midpoint of **b'b**.

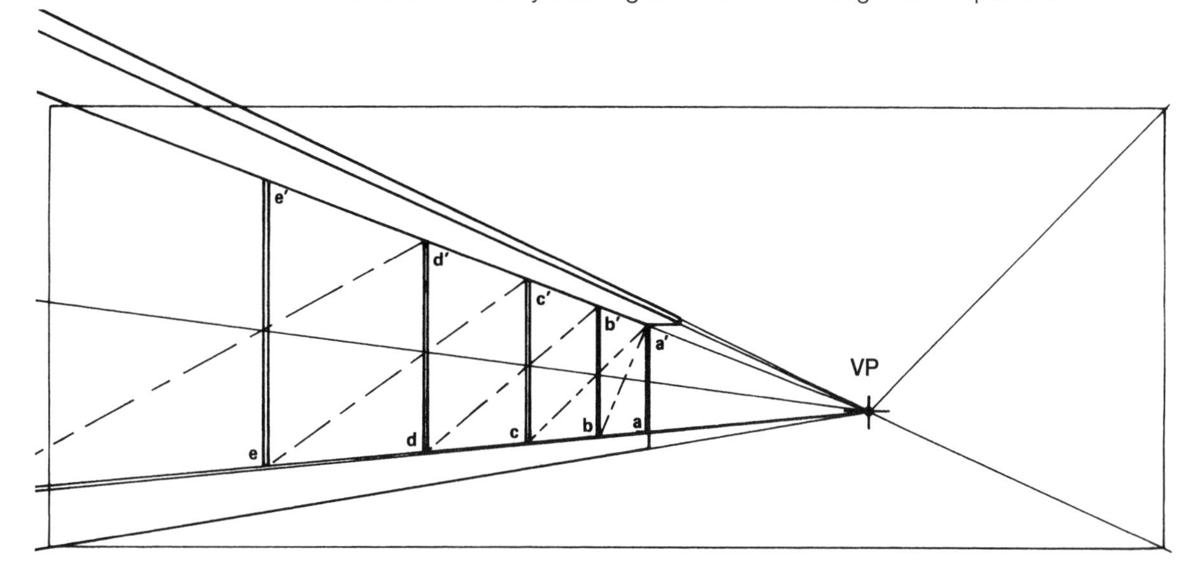

4. Repeat the procedure in Step 3 to locate **d'd** starting from **b'**, **e'e** starting from **c'**, etc.
5. Locate secondary window mullions **1'1**, **2'2**, **3'3**, etc., by drawing diagonals between the primary window mullions.

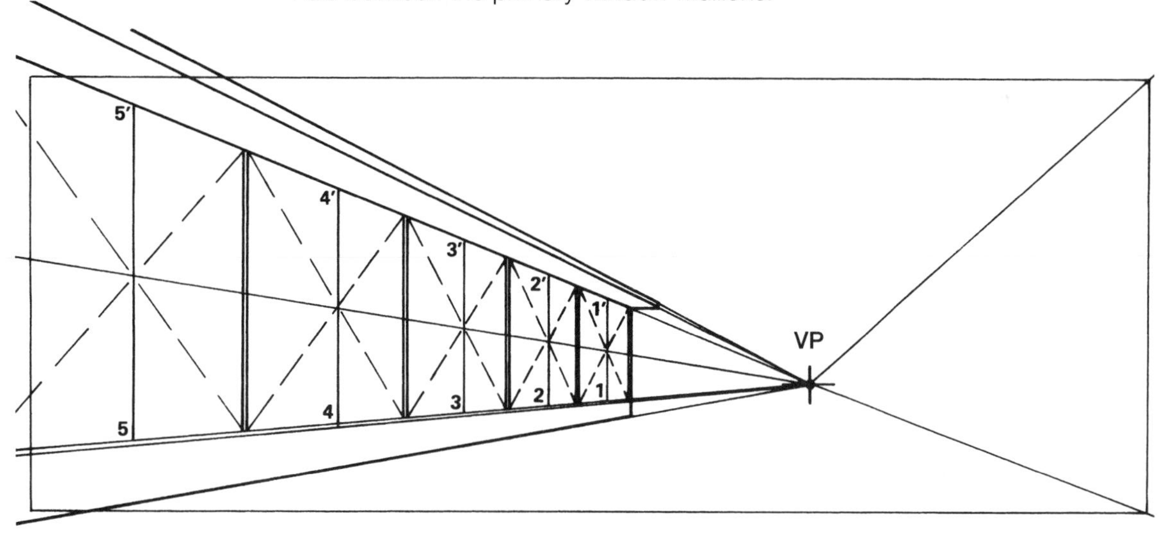

NOTATION — - — - — - — **Diagonal lines locating primary window mullions**

— — — — — — — **Diagonal lines locating secondary window mullions**

Follow Steps 1 through 5 to accurately locate equally spaced lines in perspective. In both one-point (above example) and two-point perspectives, it is frequently necessary to repeat lines that are equally spaced. For example, window mullions seen in both exterior or interior perspective views are often equally spaced, as are lampposts, parking meters, telephone poles, building types with repetitious units, columns in a colonnade, and sidewalk units. **Diagonals** provide the best method of determining projected depths in perspective.

Diagrams and text (both pages): Courtesy
of William R. Benedict, Assistant Professor
California Polytechnic State University
College of Architecture & Environmental Design
San Luis Obispo, California

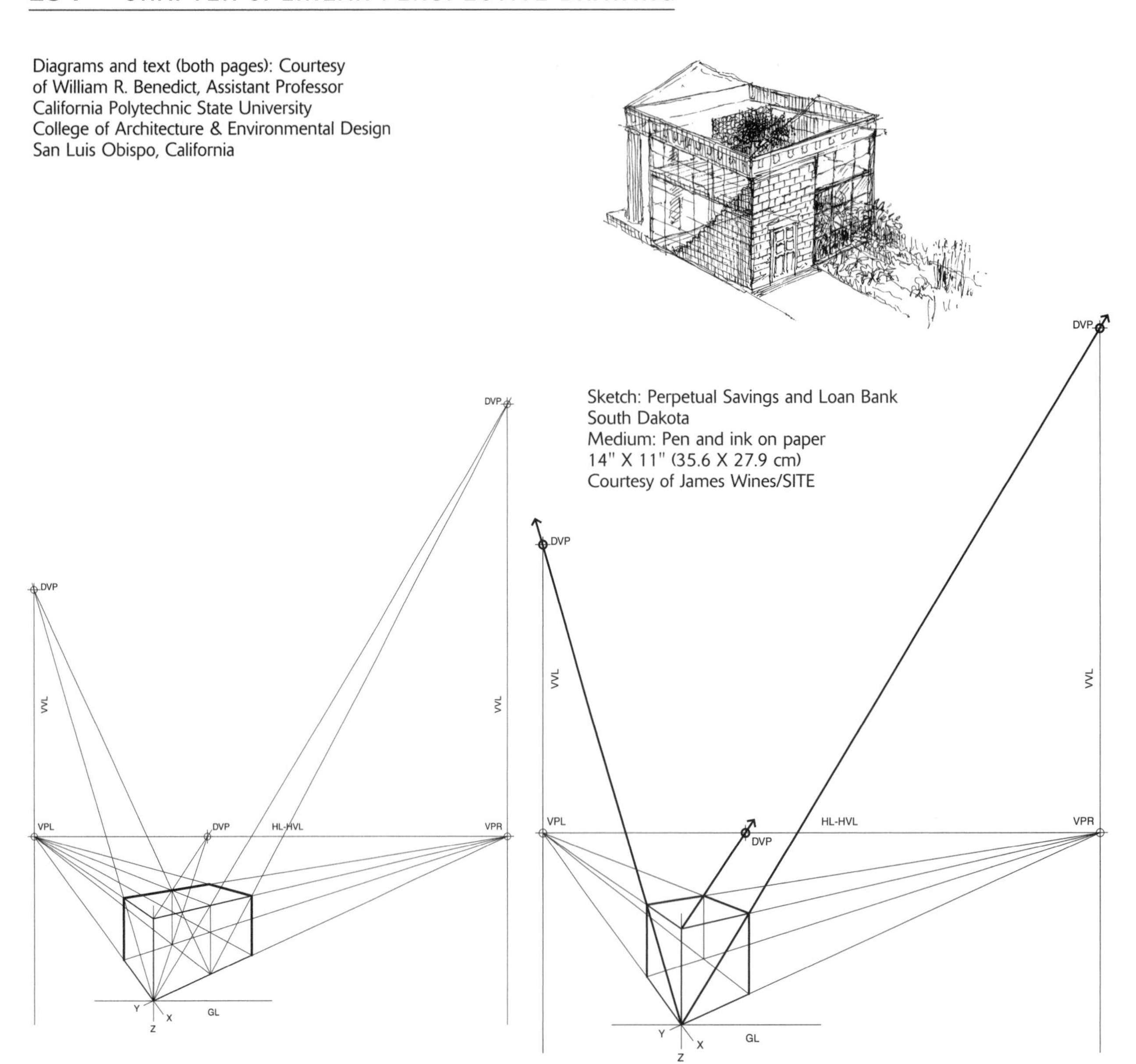

Sketch: Perpetual Savings and Loan Bank
South Dakota
Medium: Pen and ink on paper
14" X 11" (35.6 X 27.9 cm)
Courtesy of James Wines/SITE

The techniques of multiplying, dividing, and transferring discussed on pp. 248–51 are especially applicable to constructing two-point perspectives. These techniques have the advantage of requiring fewer construction lines than the plan-elevation cone of vision method.

Diagonal Vanishing Points

Draw and extend the diagonals of the visible faces of the cube until they intersect with their respective vanishing lines. Label the diagonal vanishing points **(DVP)**. There are two possible diagonal vanishing points for each square face. One will be above and one below the horizon line on the vertical vanishing lines. The illustrations show only one set to save space, and we usually draw only one for the same reason. The decision to draw one or the other or both depends on what is useful in constructing a specific perspective.

The illustration above left shows that the diagonals of the opposite faces of the cube go to the same vanishing point because they are parallel; therefore, their diagonals are parallel. All parallel lines go to the same vanishing point. The use of the diagonal to generate (multiply) a new cube is also illustrated.

If you become confused as to which diagonal vanishing point to use, first find the vanishing point for horizontal lines on the same plane. The vanishing line for the diagonals will pass through the vanishing point for the horizontal lines on the plane.

Drawing (partial): D.O.M. Headquarters
Cologne, Germany
Medium: Ink on Mylar
Courtesy of Machado & Silvetti Associates
Rodolfo Machado and Jorge Silvetti

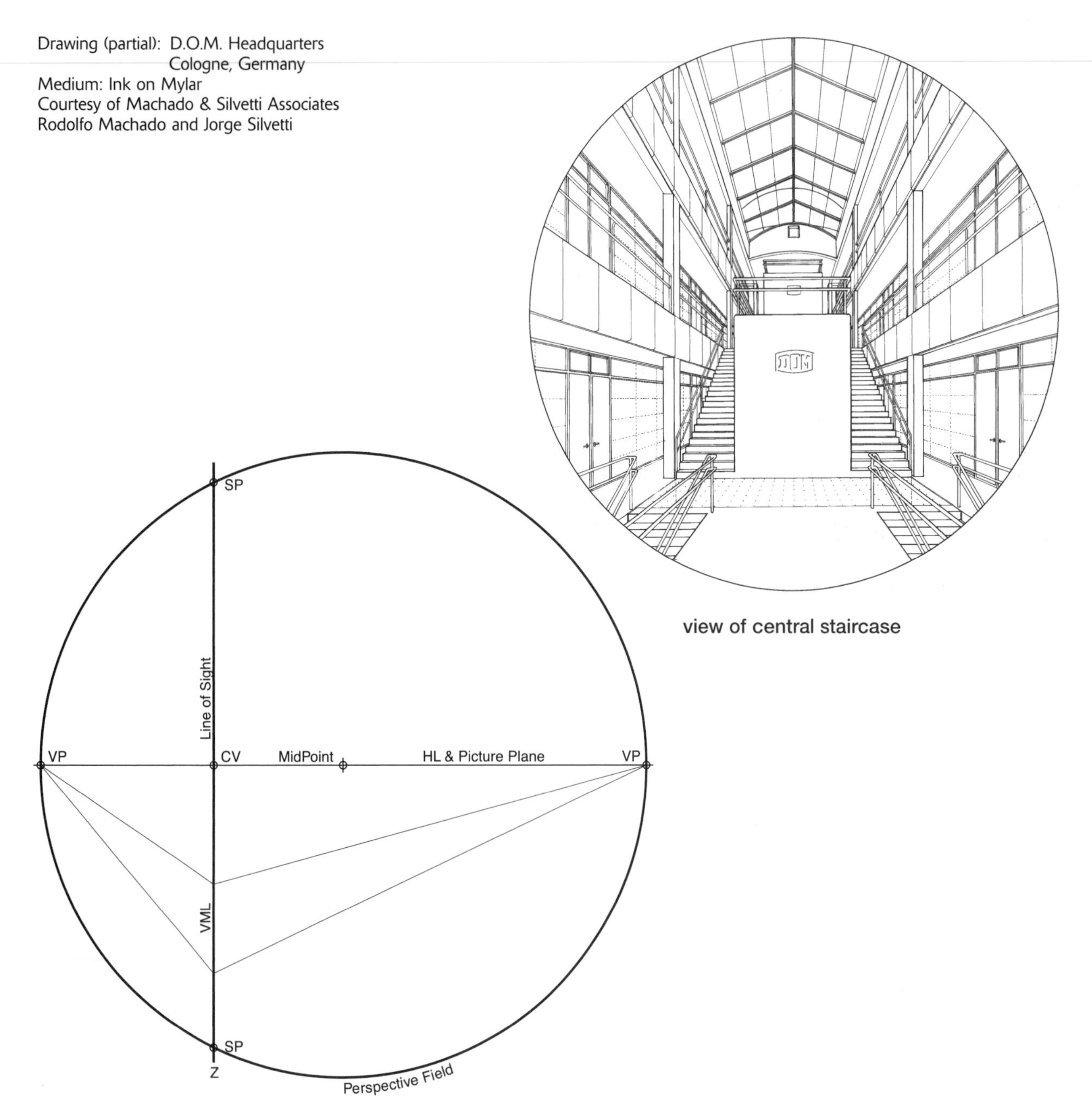

view of central staircase

Midpoint and Perspective Field of View

Locate the midpoint between the two vanishing points, and use it to draw a circle that passes through the two vanishing points to construct the perspective field of view. The intersection of the perspective field and the vertical line through the center of vision (the line of sight) locates the station point **(SP)**.

The perspective field of view is the interface between our visual experience of the world and the geometry of the linear perspective. The vanishing points for the horizontal edges of an object within our visual field can fall anywhere along the perceived horizon line from directly in front of us to the limits of our peripheral vision. The perspective field of view encompasses the two vanishing points for a specific rectilinear object within our visual field, or the one vanishing point in a one-point perspective, as shown above.

Center of Vision (CV): This is the point created by the orthogonal (90°) intersection of the line of sight and the horizon line on the picture plane. The **CV** in the example above is near the circle's center.

The vertical lines in the diagram below are parallel. In reality, these lines would begin to converge to a third vanishing point far below the horizon line, as seen in the illustration at right (see also pp. 276–79).

Drawing: National Audubon Society's National Headquarters, New York City
9" × 13" (22.9 × 33 cm)
Medium: Wax-based pencil
Courtesy of Paul Stevenson Oles, Architectural Illustrator
Croxton Collaborative Architects

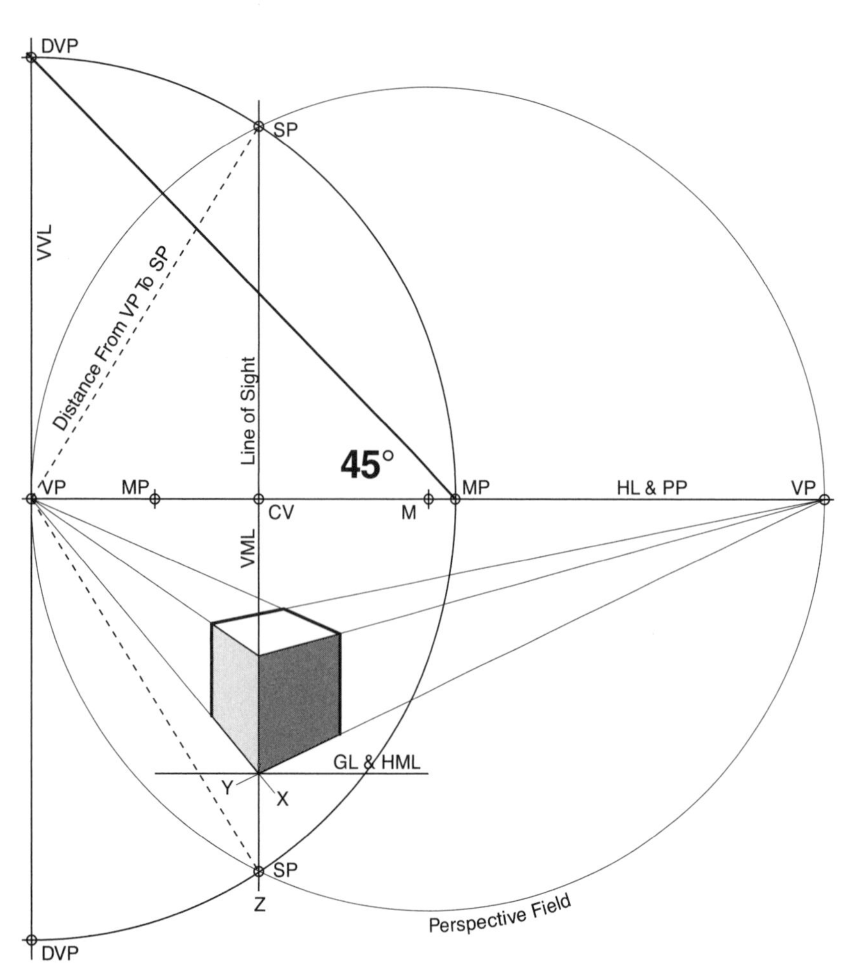

Note: For background material, refer to the discussion of vertical vanishing lines (**VVLs**), measuring points (**MPs**), and the measuring point system in the companion Web site's appendix.

Measuring Points and Oblique Lines

Combine and examine the construction processes for determining the locations of the diagonal vanishing points for the faces of the cube and its measuring points. A 45° line connects the corresponding **MPs** and **DVPs**. Once the location of the measuring points is known, you can construct the 45° diagonal vanishing point by drawing the vertical lines and then extending 45° lines through the measuring points until they intersect their respective vertical vanishing lines (the ones farther away).

It is necessary to construct the measuring points before this technique can be employed. The concept works for sloped planes whose edges are parallel to the x- or y-axis. The vanishing point for the inclined edges or lines can be found by drawing a line at the corresponding slope through the appropriate measuring point until it intersects with the corresponding vertical vanishing line.

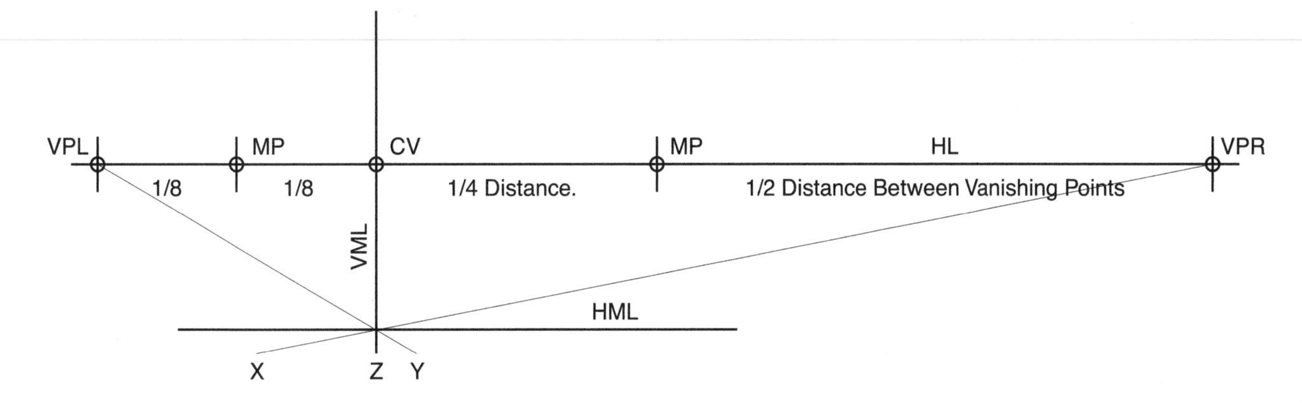

Measuring Points — 30°/60° Shortcut

One of the liabilities of the measuring point system is the space and scale of instruments required to construct the framework — especially the diagonal vanishing points. This can be overcome by making a small drawing of the setup to establish the relative dimensions within the framework and then enlarging it proportionally to support the actual construction of the perspective.

The 30°/60° setup provides another way around the problem. Perspectives in which the plan is oriented in a 30°/60° relationship to the picture plane are common and produce a simple set of geometric relationships between the vanishing points, measuring points, and center of the drawing above. By drawing the horizon line, establishing the vanishing points, and subdividing the distance between them accordingly, you can quickly generate the full component of information necessary to construct an accurate perspective framework at any scale. The process simply divides the distance between the vanishing points into successively smaller halves.

Remember that the distance from a vanishing point to the farther measuring point is equal to the distance from that vanishing point to the diagonal vanishing points above and below it on the vertical vanishing line.

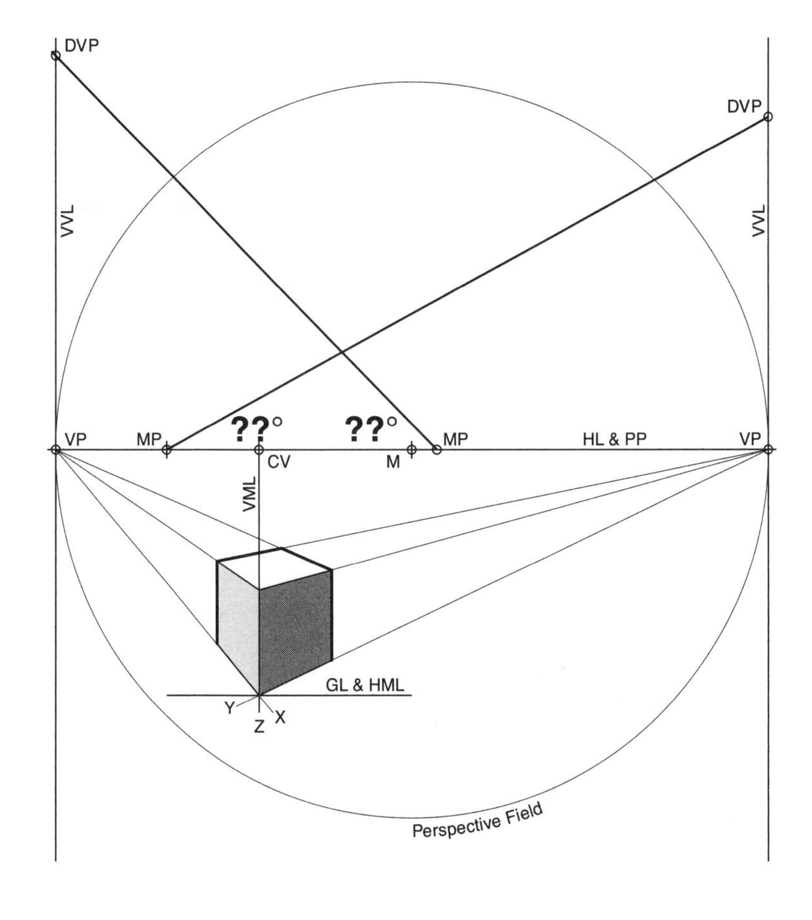

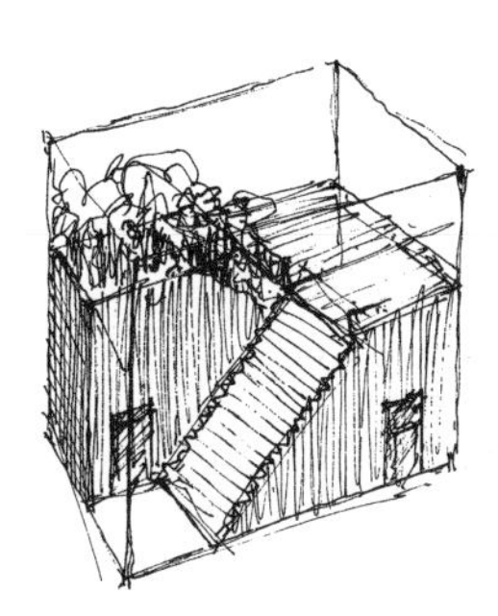

Sketch: Perpetual Savings and Loan Bank
South Dakota
Medium: Pen and ink on paper
14" X 11" (35.6 X 27.9 cm)
Courtesy of James Wines/SITE

Diagrams and text: Courtesy of
William R. Benedict, Assistant Professor
California Polytechnic State University
College of Architecture & Environmental Design
San Luis Obispo, California

Diagrams and text (both pages): Courtesy of William R. Benedict, Assistant Professor California Polytechnic State University College of Architecture & Environmental Design San Luis Obispo, California

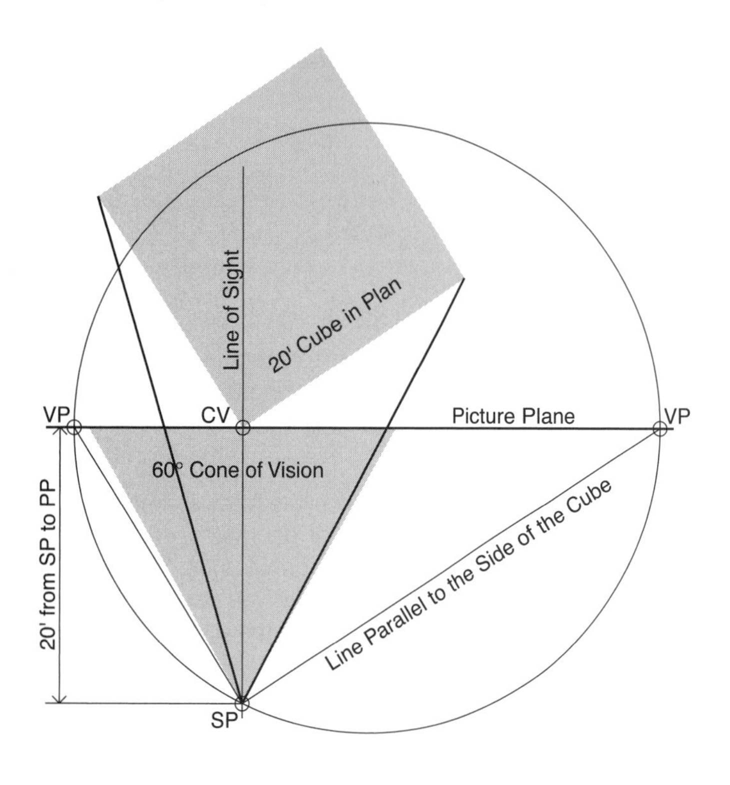

Establishing Scale in Two-Point Perspectives

When the measuring point method is used to construct a perspective using a plan drawing, the scale of the perspective is established by the scale used to construct the drawing (plan, picture plane **[PP]**, center of vision **[CV]**, station point **[SP]**, etc.). The goal is to make the perspective as large as possible while keeping the image projected on the picture plane within a 60° cone of vision. The problem comes when we want to draw a perspective without a plan or before a plan exists. The question is: What rule of thumb can be used to develop a two-point perspective framework for sketching, given only the general dimensions of the form or space?

The rule of thumb can be found in the illustration at left. Notice that when the distance from the station point to the picture plane is equal to the horizontal dimension of the subject, the projected image just fits within the 60° cone of vision. This 1:1 relationship means that to draw a perspective of a 20' wide object, the station point is located 20' back from the picture plane, assuming that the object also touches the picture plane as shown. More generally, the greatest horizontal dimension of the subject establishes the distance from the station point to the picture plane and produces a perspective that will fall within a zone of acceptable distortion.

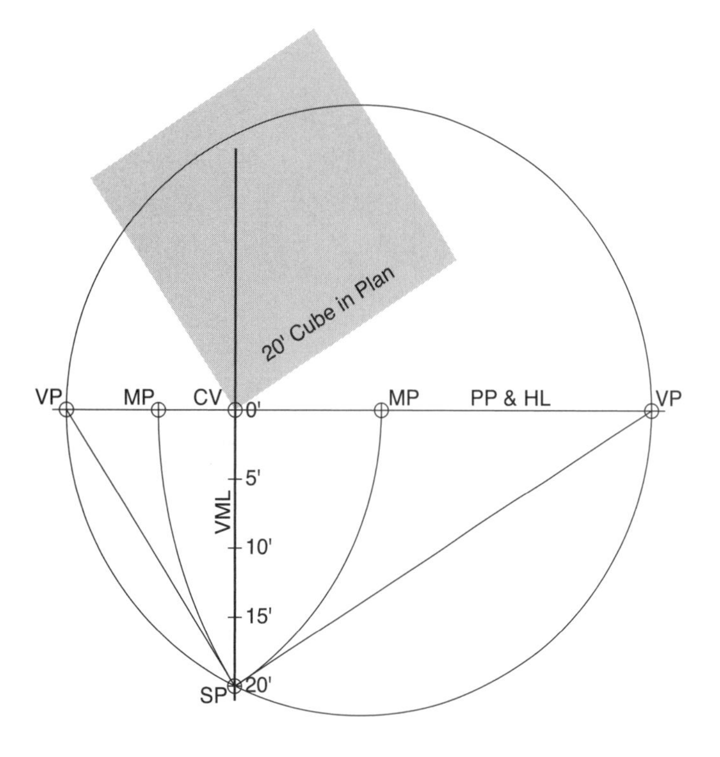

Basic Setup

Draw a horizon line **(HL)** and vanishing points **(VPs)** and locate the center of vision **(CV)**, station point **(SP)**, and measuring points **(MP)**. The vanishing points are located arbitrarily to fit on the sheet of paper being used — the layout has no inherent scale. Given the 1:1 ratio as a guide, scale can be introduced by making the distance from the station point to the picture plane equal to the greatest horizontal dimension of the object being drawn (20' in the example). The distance between the **SP** and the **PP** is proportionally divided along the **VML** to create a scale for the drawing.

Ground Line and Dimensions

The proportional scale created along the **VML** is used to locate the ground line (**GL**), which is also a horizontal measuring line (**HML**). In the example, the ground line is located 5' below the horizon line to create an eye-level perspective. The scale created on the **VML** is then transferred along the **VML** and **HML** to locate the needed dimensions.

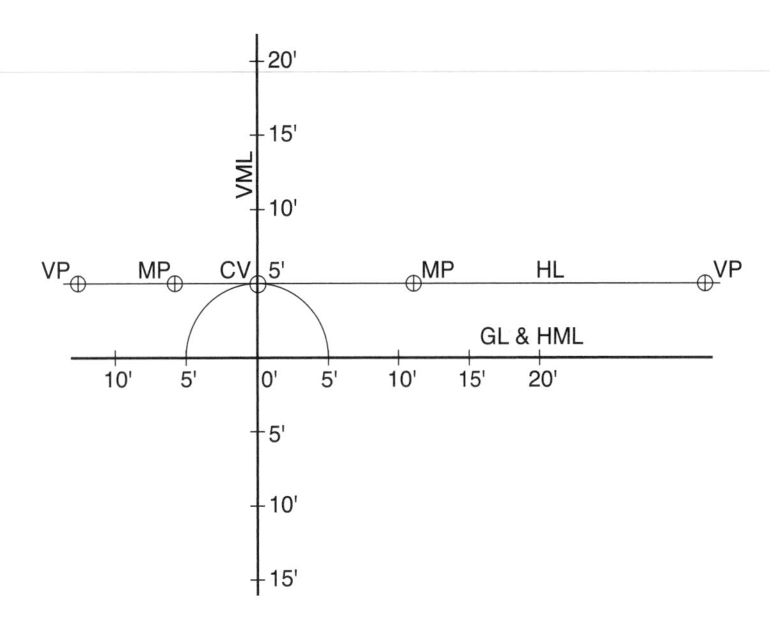

Perspective Construction

Once the dimensions have been established, the perspective can be developed using the measuring point and other construction techniques previously discussed. The resultant drawing will fall within an acceptable zone of distortion. Note that the cube extends vertically beyond the 60° cone of vision for an eye-level perspective, and therefore, if the subject is significantly taller than it is wide, its height should be used to establish the scale. The 1:1 rule of thumb must be adjusted in response to the subject and the desired communication.

Note: That the cube's vertical edges pass through the measuring points is coincidental.

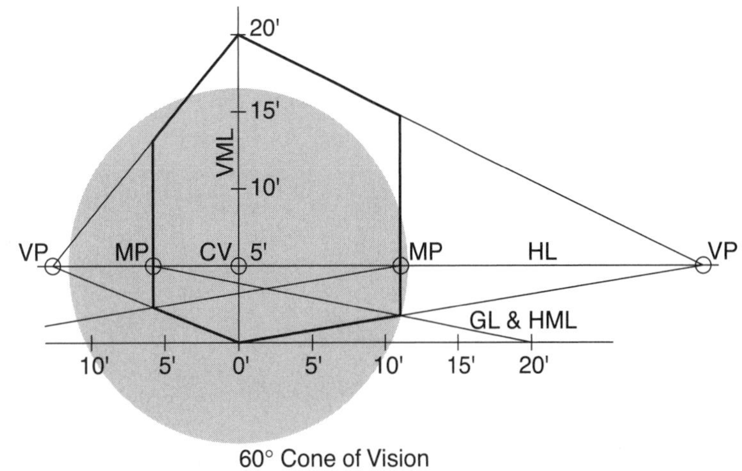

60° Cone of Vision

The Hypotenuse

The points identified as **SP, CV,** and **VP** define two right triangles whose hypotenuse is **VP-SP** (see gray triangle). The hypotenuse establishes a proportional relationship between the two other sides of a triangle. Therefore, if a line parallel to the hypotenuse is drawn through the center point of one side, it will pass through the center of the other side, as illustrated. This permits the establishment of scale in some two-point perspectives without locating the station point.

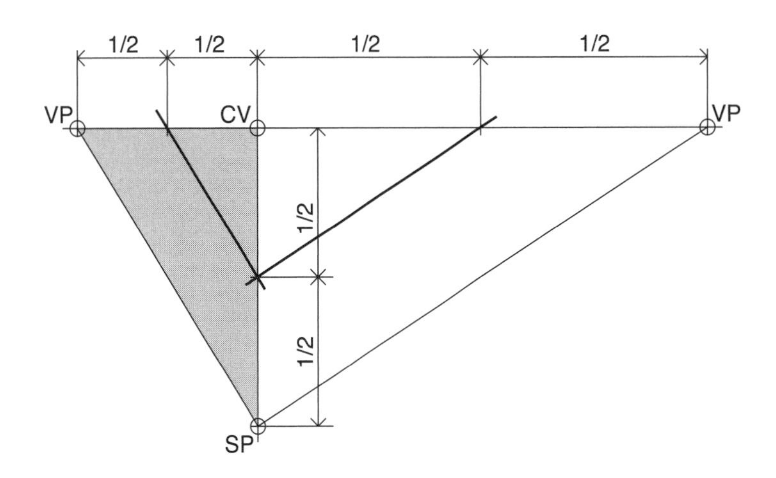

Drawing: Boston Ballet School and Studios
Boston, Massachusetts
30" × 28" (76.2 × 71.1 cm)
Medium: Watercolor on rendering paper
Architect: Graham Gund Architects, Inc.

30°/60° Shortcut Perspective

Draw a horizon line and locate the vanishing points to fit on the sheet of paper being used. Locate the measuring points and center of vision for a 30/60° perspective using the proportions as illustrated and described in the section on the 30/60° shortcut method (see p. 257).

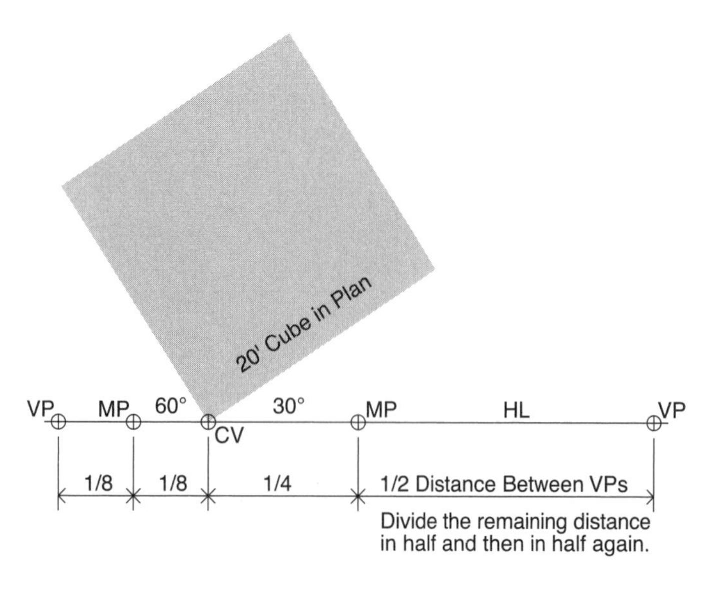

Establishing and Transferring the Scale

Given this approach, there is no station point or line that connects it to the picture plane. In its place, the distance from a vanishing point to the center of vision will be used. Given the 1:1 ratio, scale can be introduced by making the distance from a vanishing point to the center of vision equal to the greatest horizontal dimension of the object being drawn (20' in the example). The distance is then proportionally divided to produce useful dimensions (e.g., the distance from the horizon line to the ground line). Next, the dimension must be transferred to the vertical measuring line that passes through the center of vision. This is accomplished by drawing a line parallel to the hypotenuse of the corresponding **SP, CV, VP** triangle through the known dimension so that it intersects the vertical measuring line. For a 30/60° perspective, the hypotenuse will be at either 30° or 60° (the 60° triangle is being used in the example). In the illustration, a 5' distance is being transferred to locate the ground line and establish an eye-level perspective.

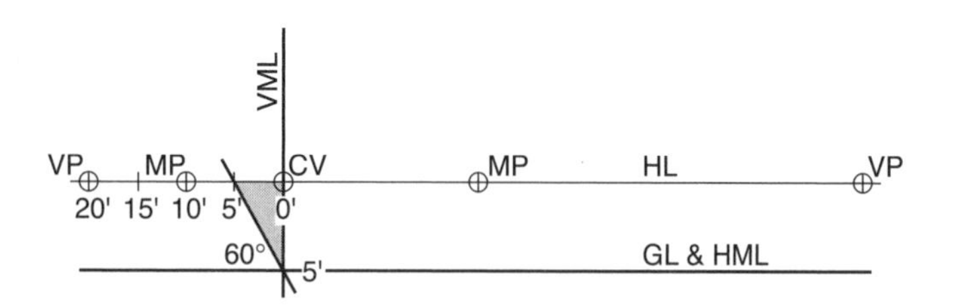

Diagrams and text (both pages): Courtesy of William R. Benedict, Assistant Professor California Polytechnic State University College of Architecture & Environmental Design San Luis Obispo, California

Drawing: Scripps Memorial Hospital
View of entrance
Chula Vista, California
23" × 24" (58.2 × 61 cm)
Medium: Ink on Mylar
Courtesy of Perkins & Will Architects
Associate Architect James A. Leary
Architecture & Planning

Dimensions

The dimensions transferred to the vertical measuring line establish a scale for the drawing. These dimensions can then be transferred along the vertical and horizontal measuring lines to locate the needed dimensions.

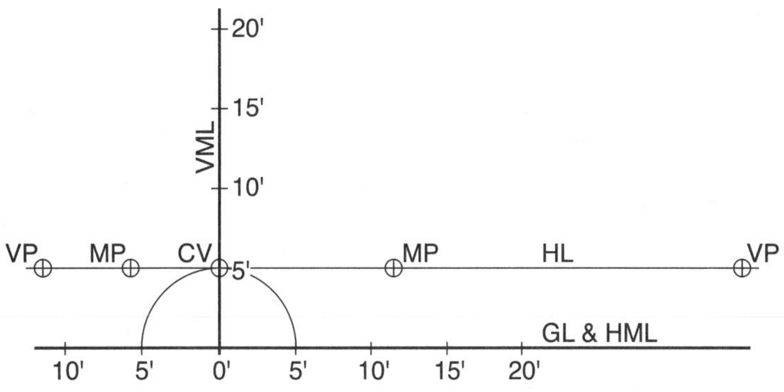

Perspective Construction

Once the dimensions have been established, the perspective can be developed using the measuring point and other construction techniques previously discussed. If it is desirable to have the perspective fall more completely within the cone of vision, then the controlling dimension is set to something greater than the width of the subject (e.g., 30').

A standard 6' figure is excellent for sizing objects in a perspective. In developing a perspective view (see pp. 298–303), remember that all views start with a horizon line and a scaled figure that seems appropriate. There is no scale other than the putative 6' figure.

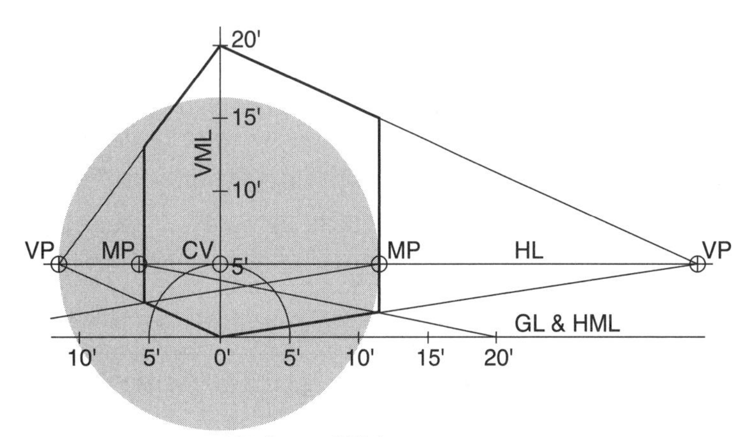

60° Cone of Vision

Drawing: Student project by Greg Stackel
Housing in Greenwich Village
Manhattan, New York
Medium: Ink on Mylar
Excerpted from Abstract, Columbia School of Architecture Planning and Preservation (CSAPP)

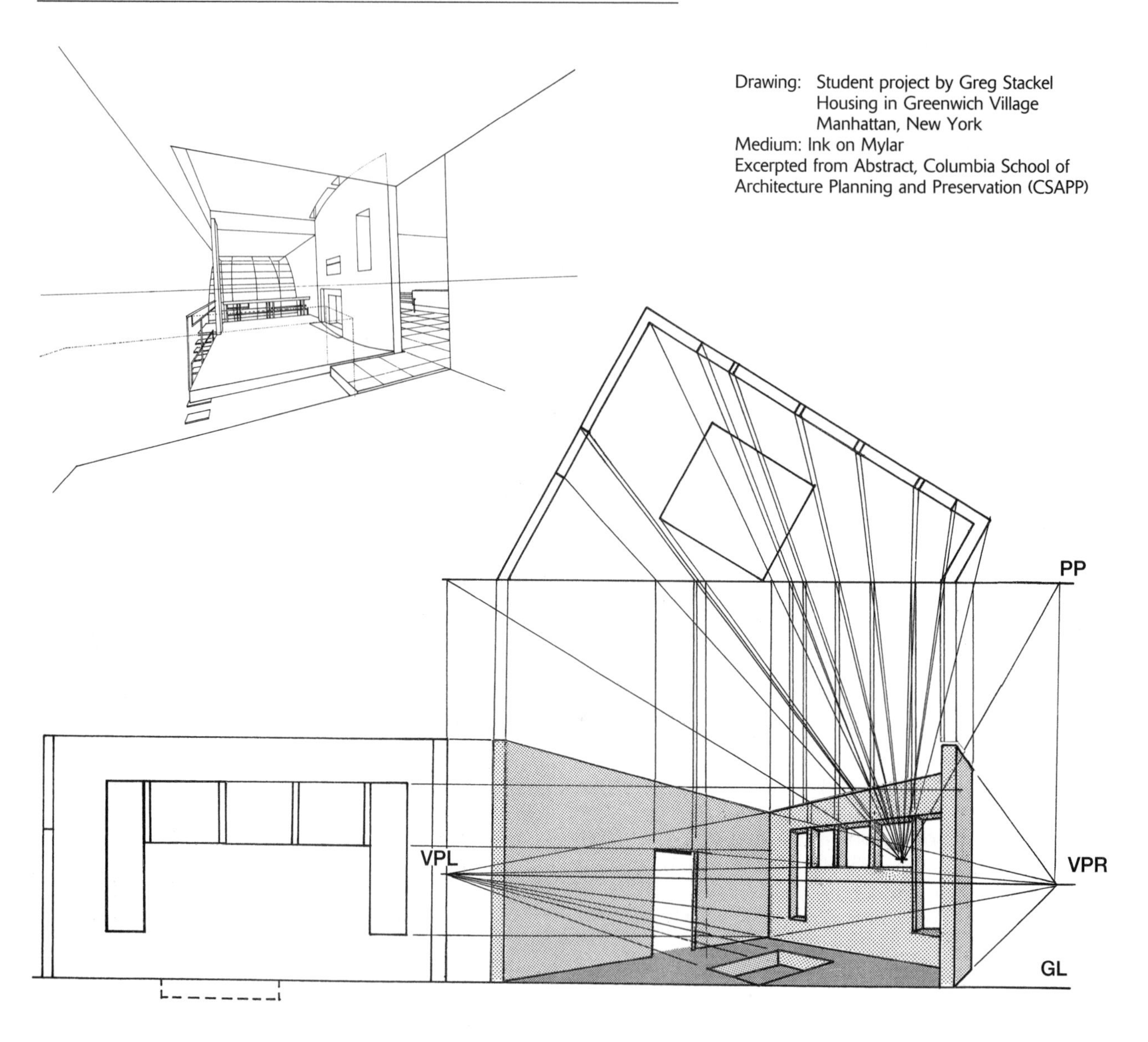

Interior Two-Point

Let's examine the two-point **plan-elevation** office method (pp. 230–32) again. These perspectives are commonly constructed for both exterior and interior two-point perspectives. The method is basically the same in both cases. This method can also be applied to exterior and interior one-point perspectives. Choose a station point that best describes the important interior elements and the feeling you would like to convey. Frank Lloyd Wright favored the two-point interior view, which is essentially a one-point made slightly oblique to the picture plane, resulting in a very long second vanishing point (see p. 407). Avoid placing the eye-level horizon line in a position where it coincides with any horizontal structural element (e.g., the windowsill shown above).

1. Select locations of the **SP**, **HL**, and **PP** based on the perspective desired.
2. Select a **PP** that will cut both walls of an interior space and will intersect the corners of important or major interior elements.
3. Construct the appropriate parallel lines to find the vanishing points.
4. Transfer the true heights from the elevation view to the vertical tracers from the interior wall intersections.
5. Converge the wall planes to their appropriate vanishing points and then construct the details of the interior space.

Compare this method to the one-point office procedure (pp. 212–13 and 222–23).

Image: A new Coach store, 342 Madison Avenue
New York City
Medium: Ink on Mylar
Courtesy of Kennethpark Architecture • Planning • Interiors

This interior two-point was created during the design development phase using AutoCAD Release 14 and Photoshop for rendering color. It was extremely useful in communicating and showing the design ideas discussed in meetings. It helped to catch desirable and undesirable aspects of the design; the client was able to see what they liked or didn't like. Ultimately, this helped to speed the design process along and gave the client a workable model to refine and shape.
[ARCHITECT'S STATEMENT]

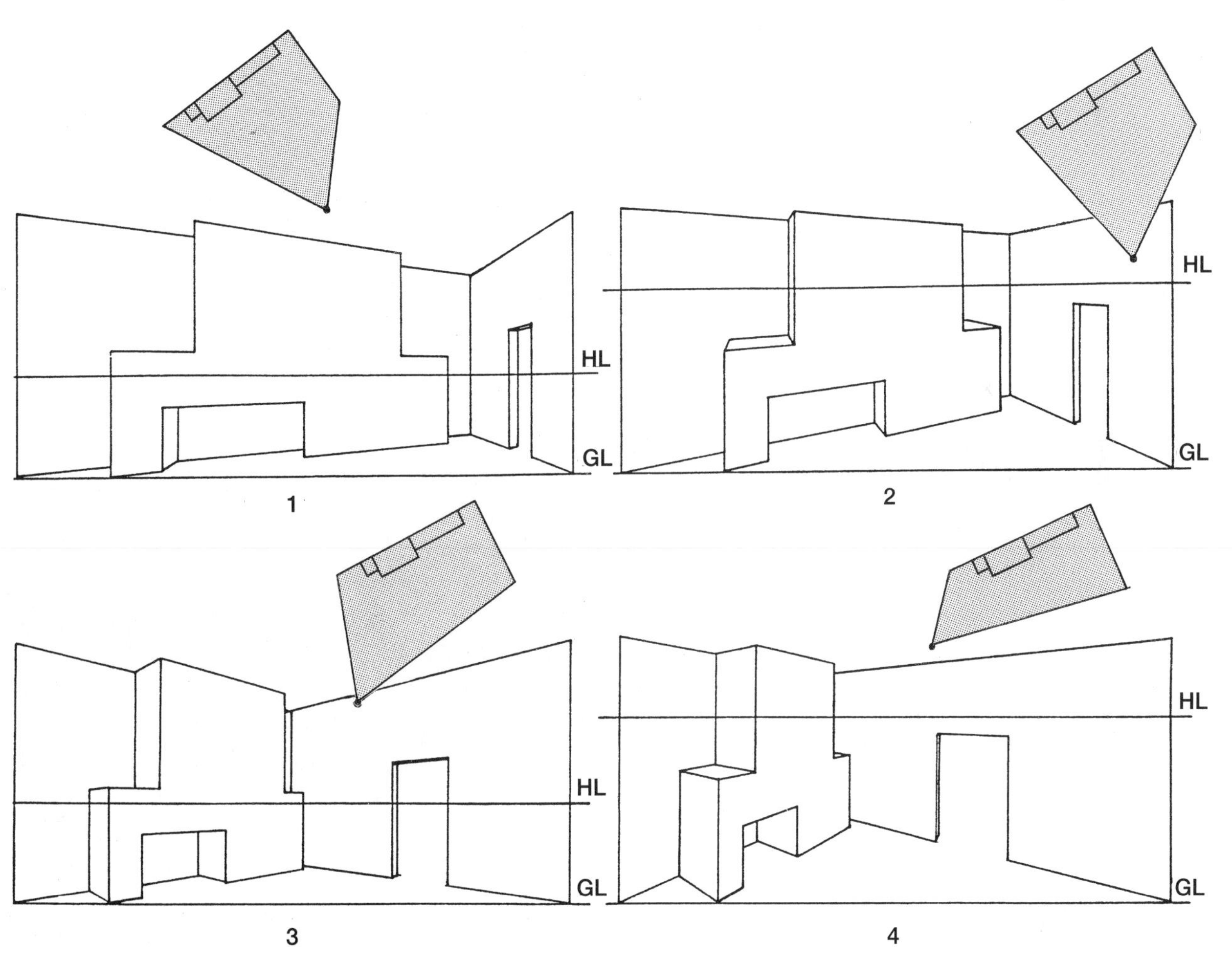

In any interior perspective, visual emphasis on the left or right wall is governed by the **variable station point.** The station point also dictates whether the wall vanishing points fall within or out of the drawing. Note how the images of the fireplace and the door change as one moves from being close to the wall with the door (**1**) to being close to the fireplace wall (**4**). Also note that the higher horizon line in **2** and **4** allows the viewer to see more floor and less ceiling (above normal eye level).

Drawings: Canadian Museum of Human Rights, Winnipeg, Manitoba, Canada
Medium: Vectorworks, form-Z, InDesign, and Photoshop
Area: 23,200 sq. m
Courtesy of Antoine Predock, Architect

These beautiful interior perspectives, which are part of a set of winning competition drawing panels (see Web site, Chapter 12), have a greater sense of enclosure than the interiors on the previous page simply because a third wall or third side is included. This third element has its own vanishing point.

Drawing: Carnegie Mellon Research Institute
Pittsburgh, Pennsylvania
11" × 8.5" (27.5 × 21.5 cm)
Medium: Pantone on Photostat
Courtesy of Peter D. Eisenman, FAIA, of Eisenman Architects

The interior at left is primarily a one-point perspective. It is modified by an additional wall element that has its own vanishing point. The lobby below has essentially only one vanishing point, but the interior corridor in the background is curvilinear and has multiple vanishing points. These drawings can be called **modified one-points** in the sense that they have one vanishing point in the picture area, even though the total drawing is a multipoint perspective.

Drawing: GSA-IRS Competition project
Original size: approx. 18" × 17" (45.7 × 43.2 cm)
Scale used: 1/8" and 1/4"=1'0"
Medium: Pen and ink with colored pencil on vellum paper
Perkins & Will Architects
Courtesy of Manuel Avila, Architectural Illustrator

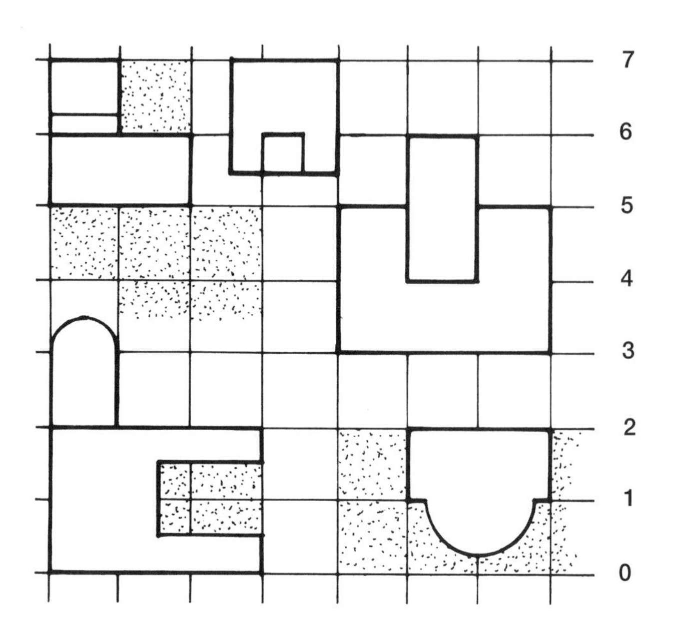

Bird's-Eye View

Technically, the terms **bird's-eye** and **aerial** are synonymous.

A grid procedure for bird's-eye perspectives is advantageous when the building complex or urban landscape is in a predominantly regular arrangement. After transposing the elements from plan grid to perspective grid, structural forms can be eyeballed and sketched using appropriate heights. The plan grid and perspective grid can be at different scales, but the total number of grid lines must correspond. Relate the plan shown at the left to the selected aerial perspective view shown below. Note that the eight (**0** to **7**) grid lines correspond.

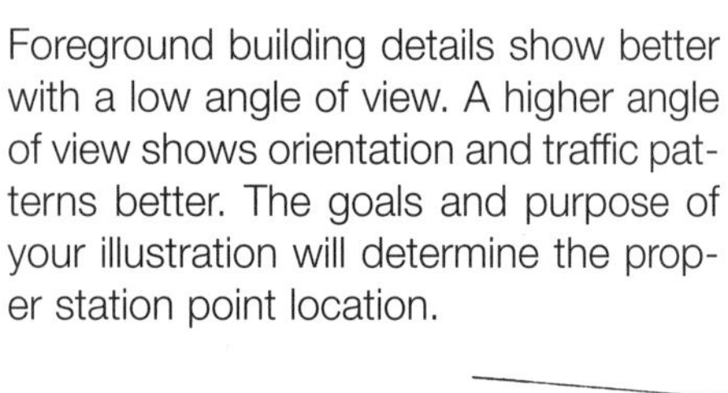

Foreground building details show better with a low angle of view. A higher angle of view shows orientation and traffic patterns better. The goals and purpose of your illustration will determine the proper station point location.

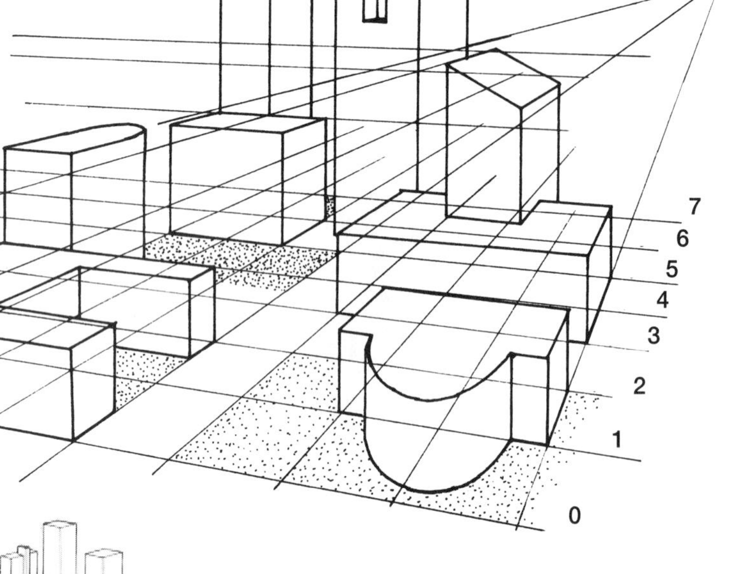

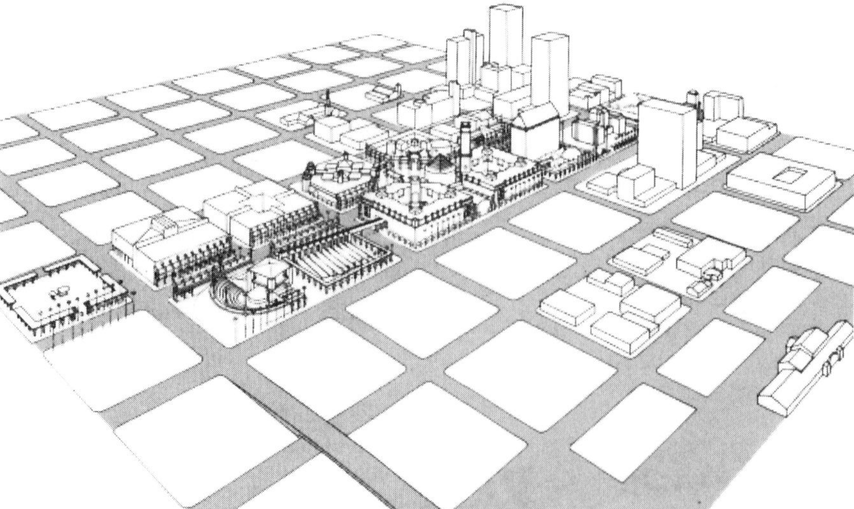

Drawing: Master-plan concept
Phoenix Municipal
Government Center
Phoenix, Arizona
Courtesy of John Schreier,
Barton Myers Associates, Architects

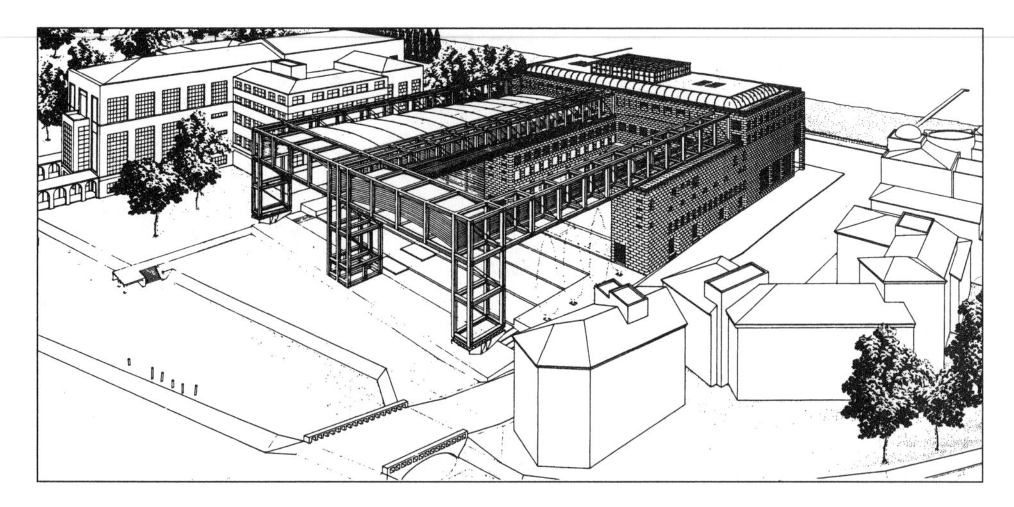

Drawing: A Film Palace
Venice, Italy
Courtesy of Oswald Mathias Ungers, Architect

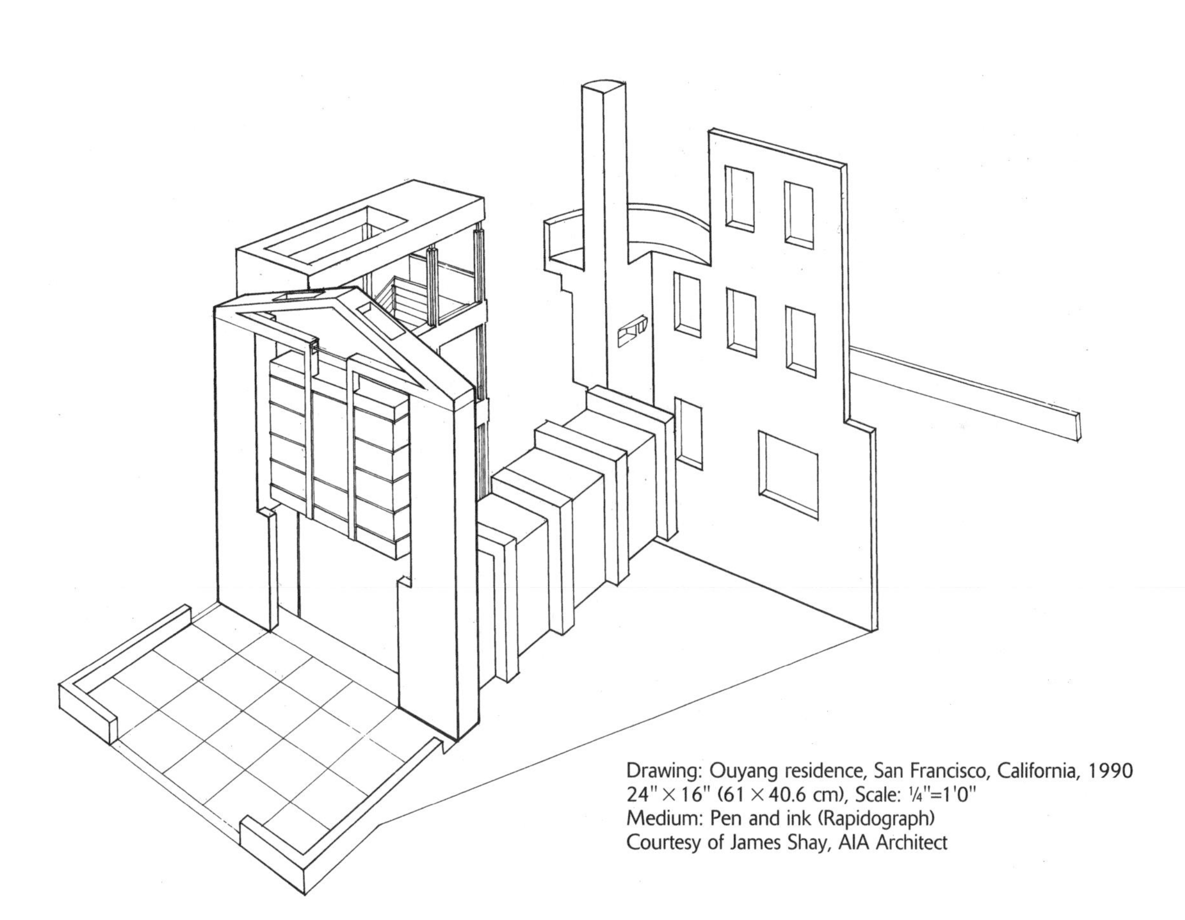

Drawing: Ouyang residence, San Francisco, California, 1990
24" × 16" (61 × 40.6 cm), Scale: ¼"=1'0"
Medium: Pen and ink (Rapidograph)
Courtesy of James Shay, AIA Architect

This is drawn to show important parts of the house without showing the entire building. This enables the architect to clearly communicate what he or she regards as most important.
[ARCHITECT'S STATEMENT]

Most bird's-eye view perspectives that are slightly above roof level are characterized by a horizon line that is in the range of 40' to 80' above the ground plane. Unlike an eye-level perspective, it reveals the surrounding landscape (trees, group of buildings, townscape, etc.) as well as unexpected roof line details.

Drawing: First Street Plaza, Los Angeles, California
Courtesy of First Street Plaza Partners
and TAC, The Architects Collaborative
Renderer: Jim Arp

Bird's-Eye Perspective

Large-scale bird's-eye views are used frequently, not only by architects but also by city planners, urban designers, environmental analysts, landscape architects, and site engineers. These design professionals need both precise renderings as well as conceptual visualization studies of aerial cityscape views. Cityscape views are most informative when the angled vantage point is approximately 60° to 75° from the horizontal ground plane. Compare the above bird's-eye perspective to the bird's-eye plan oblique (axonometric) on the facing page. The perspective reveals more building facade (see p. 543), whereas the plan oblique shows more of the pedestrian streetscape and the open spaces between buildings.

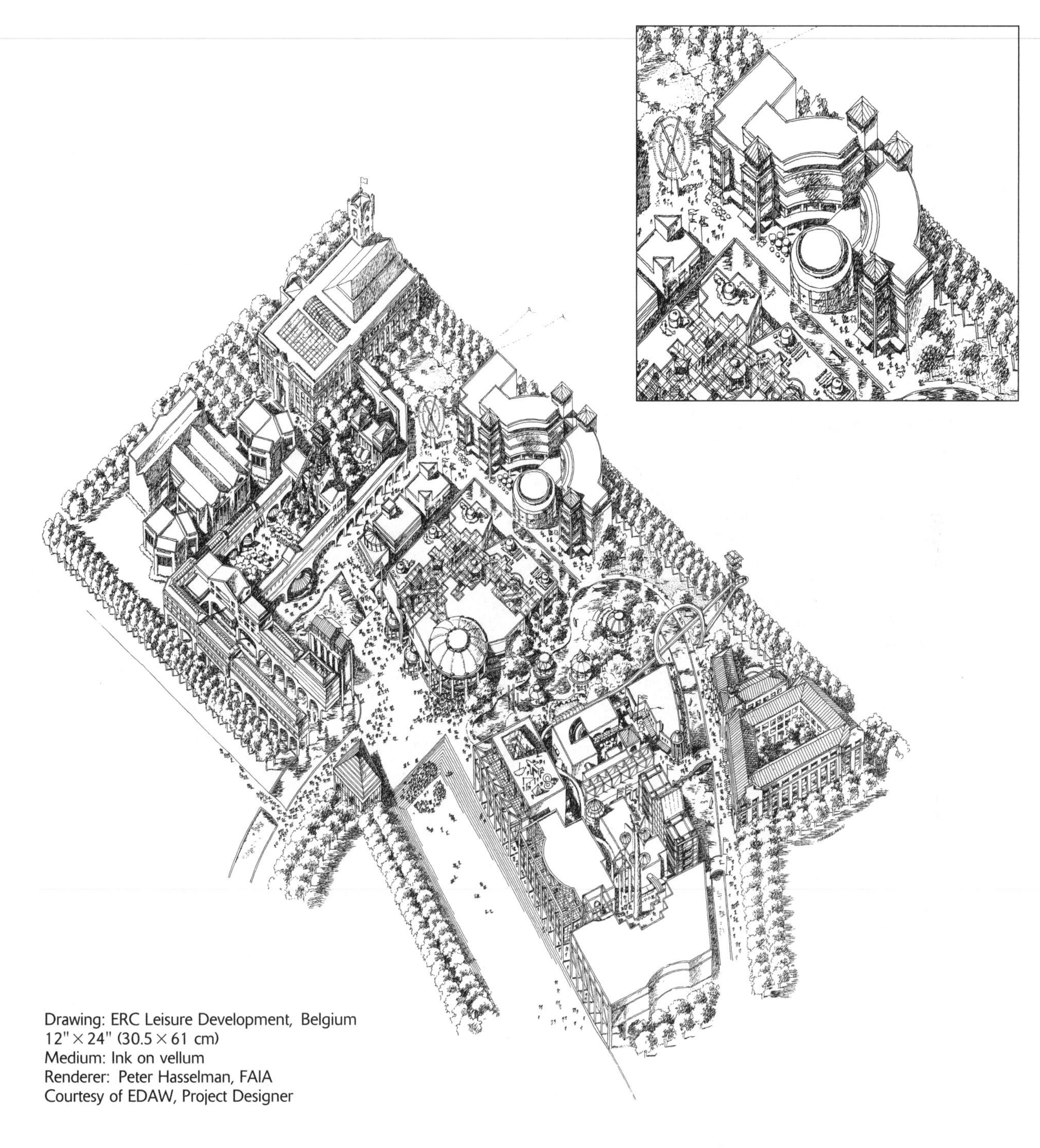

Drawing: ERC Leisure Development, Belgium
12" × 24" (30.5 × 61 cm)
Medium: Ink on vellum
Renderer: Peter Hasselman, FAIA
Courtesy of EDAW, Project Designer

Bird's-Eye Plan Oblique

Bird's-eye plan obliques are similar to steep angled perspectives. Landscaping patterns, as well as vehicular and pedestrian circulation patterns, are usually more easily visible with an oblique view. As with faraway aerial perspective entourage (trees, vehicles, people, etc.), plan oblique entourage must add character without much detail. The drawback of time-saving digital drawings is that the entourage usually lacks character.

PERSPECTIVE UNDERSIDE VIEW

Phaeno Science Center, Wolfsburg, Germany
Medium: Computer generated
Courtesy of Zaha M. Hadid Architects

In the perspective **underside view,** the observer looks up; his or her station point is subterranean. This creates an effect similar to that of the paraline up view's.

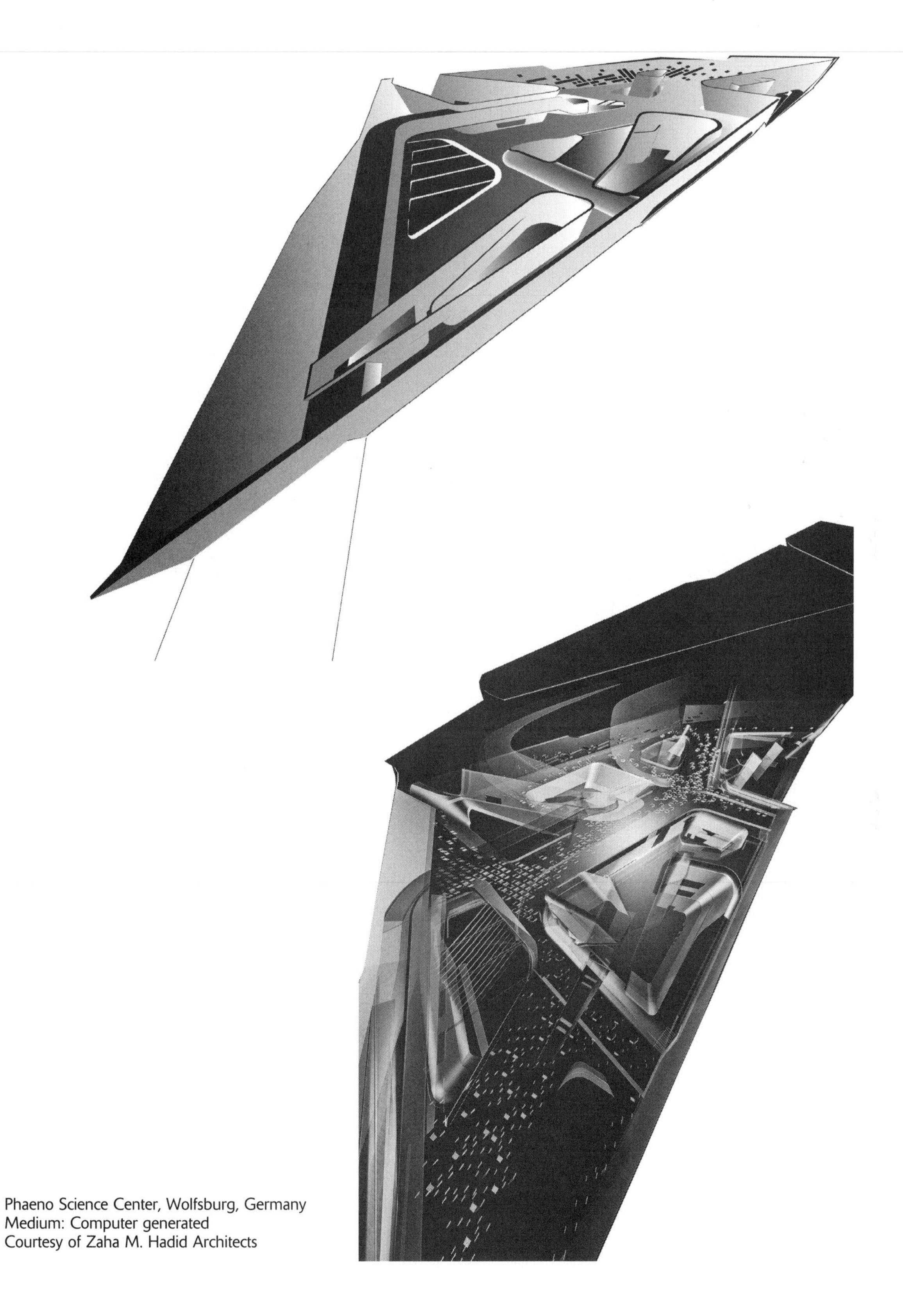

Phaeno Science Center, Wolfsburg, Germany
Medium: Computer generated
Courtesy of Zaha M. Hadid Architects

As with the underside view, this section perspective underside view renders this building interior quite dramatically. The low-angle bird's-eye view of the building interior creates a similar feeling.

LOOKING UP AND LOOKING DOWN

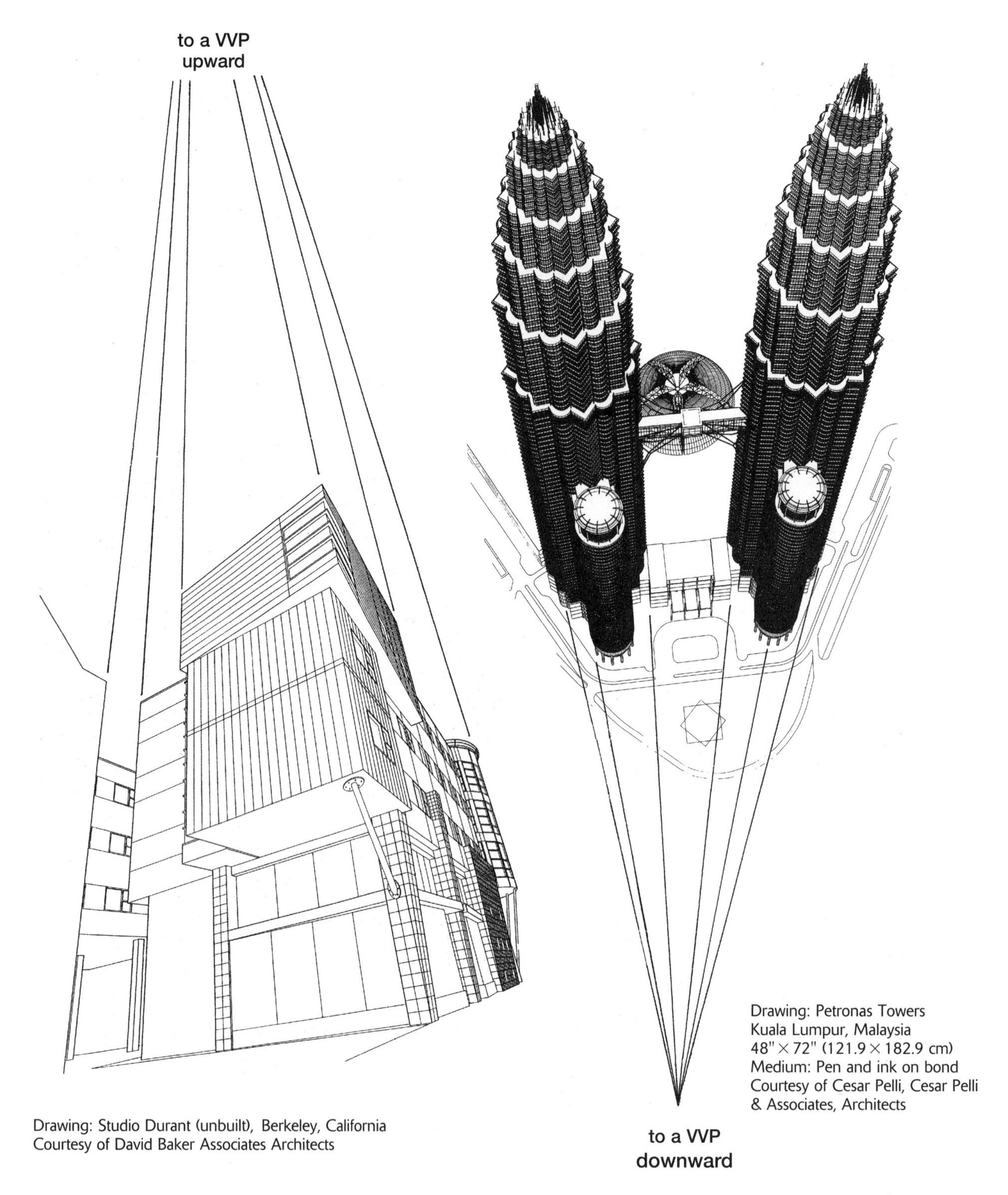

Drawing: Studio Durant (unbuilt), Berkeley, California
Courtesy of David Baker Associates Architects

Drawing: Petronas Towers
Kuala Lumpur, Malaysia
48" × 72" (121.9 × 182.9 cm)
Medium: Pen and ink on bond
Courtesy of Cesar Pelli, Cesar Pelli & Associates, Architects

Looking up results in an upward convergence of vertical lines; **looking down** results in a downward convergence of vertical lines. A view with upward or downward convergence has the characteristic of a tipped or tilted picture plane. The picture plane is inclined at an oblique angle to the ground plane—not perpendicular to it, as with one- and two-point perspectives. Therefore, the three typical planes (horizontal, frontal, and profile) are not parallel to this picture plane. The vertical vanishing points above and below are usually placed closer to the ground plane than they normally would be in order to exaggerate the soaring (see pp. 80 and 522) or plunging (see p. 53) effect. See the discussion on three-point (sometimes called oblique) perspectives on the following pages.

Looking Up and Looking Down

In comparison with the images on the opposite page, these show a less exaggerated, more natural view of downward and upward convergence.

Images: Merrill Lynch headquarters, Jersey City, New Jersey
Client: Merrill Lynch
Courtesy of Fox & Fowle Architects

A strong commitment to the integration of computer-aided design (CAD) technology into the firm's design and production processes has allowed this system to grow into more than 65 advanced CAD workstations, all part of the firm's local area network of more than 80 computers. CAD technology is applied through every phase of architectural design and construction document production. Digital zoning studies and area analyses become 3-D massing models and spatial studies, which in turn are developed into computer-rendered presentations. These renderings can be either highly stylistic or photorealistic.
[Architect's statement]

Upward Convergence

Any object seen in a three-point perspective is characterized by projection lines, which are extensions of vertical lines in the object converging upward or downward to a vertical vanishing point (**VVP**). Note that the ski resort is actually a more than three-point (multi-vanishing point) perspective, due to other sets of parallel horizontal lines vanishing left or right (see below).

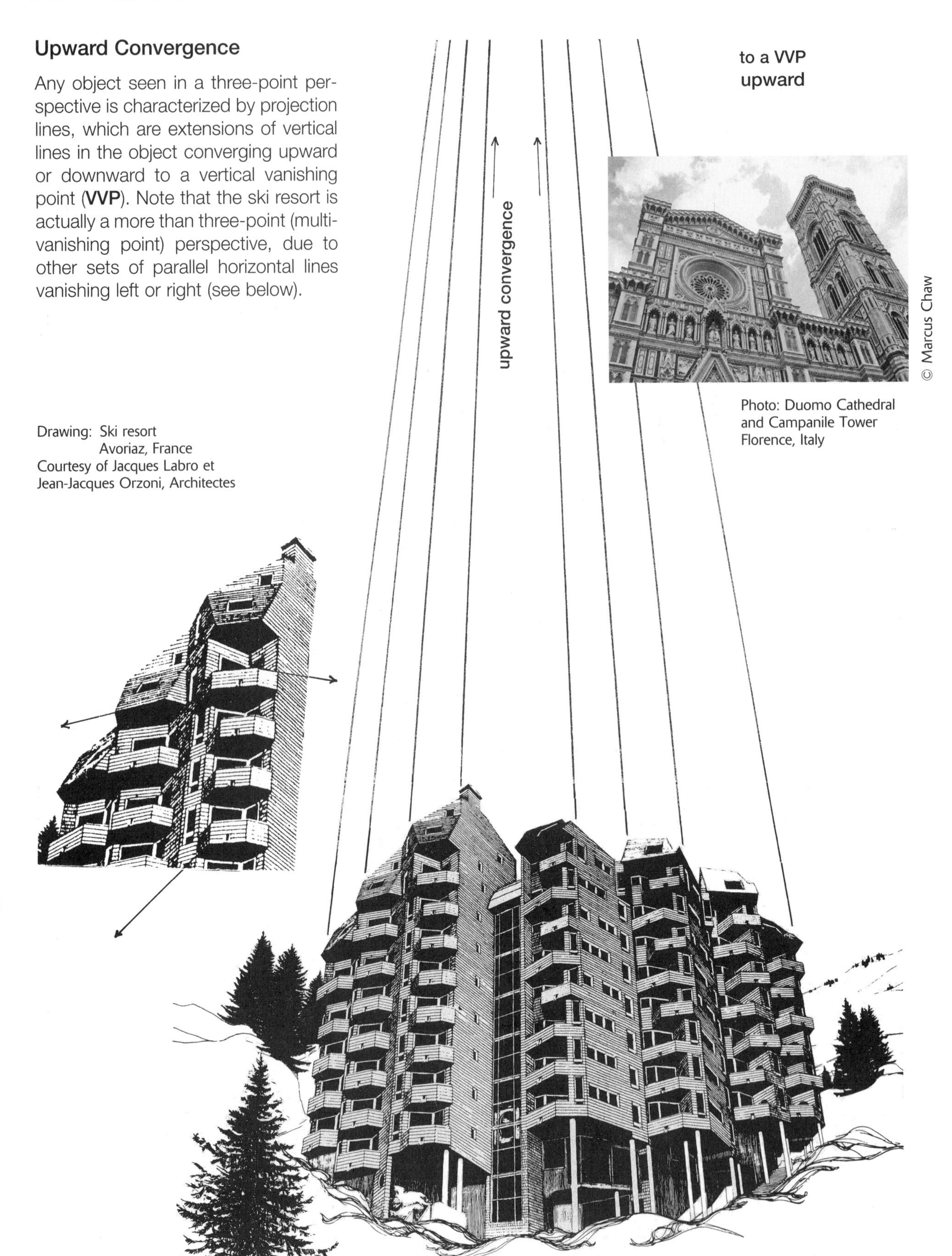

Photo: Duomo Cathedral and Campanile Tower Florence, Italy

Drawing: Ski resort Avoriaz, France
Courtesy of Jacques Labro et Jean-Jacques Orzoni, Architectes

Drawing: Victoria peak vantage point
Hong Kong aerial,
Hong Kong, China
A3-size tracing paper 16.5" x 11.5"
(41.9 x 29.2 cm)
Medium: Color pencil with black marker and overlaid paint highlights (spirit-based)
Courtesy of Peter Edgeley, Architectural Illustrator

The drawing and the photo are from slightly different vantage points from the same Victoria peak. They show that the illustrator took the liberty to exaggerate the lines of downward convergence from what is actually seen.

© Monika Waronska

This drawing was used as a planning document to explain preliminary design studies of the Hilton Hotel and to explain softening landscape elements to the surrounding streetscape (the Hilton Hotel is the bronze-clad building).

1. An impressionistic technique was chosen to match the preliminary nature of the submission as part of a discussion paper. A hard-edge photographic effect was avoided.

2. The hills in the background were treated by broad soft strokes of crayon, whilst closer buildings and rows of street trees were given finer details and more contrast. This helped focus the attention where the main decisions of master planning and landscape architecture were being made.

[ARCHITECTURAL ILLUSTRATOR'S STATEMENT]

Downward Convergence

This is an example of a very high vantage point view looking down, with a lot of downward convergence. Architects and architectural illustrators use such vantage points to increase the dramatic effect of a rendering. They can use three-point perspective grid charts where the third vanishing point has already been set to quickly add detail and create downward or upward views. Similar to rough digital wire-frame methods, charts are much faster than the rigorous plan-elevation projection method for constructing a three-point perspective (see pp. 278–79).

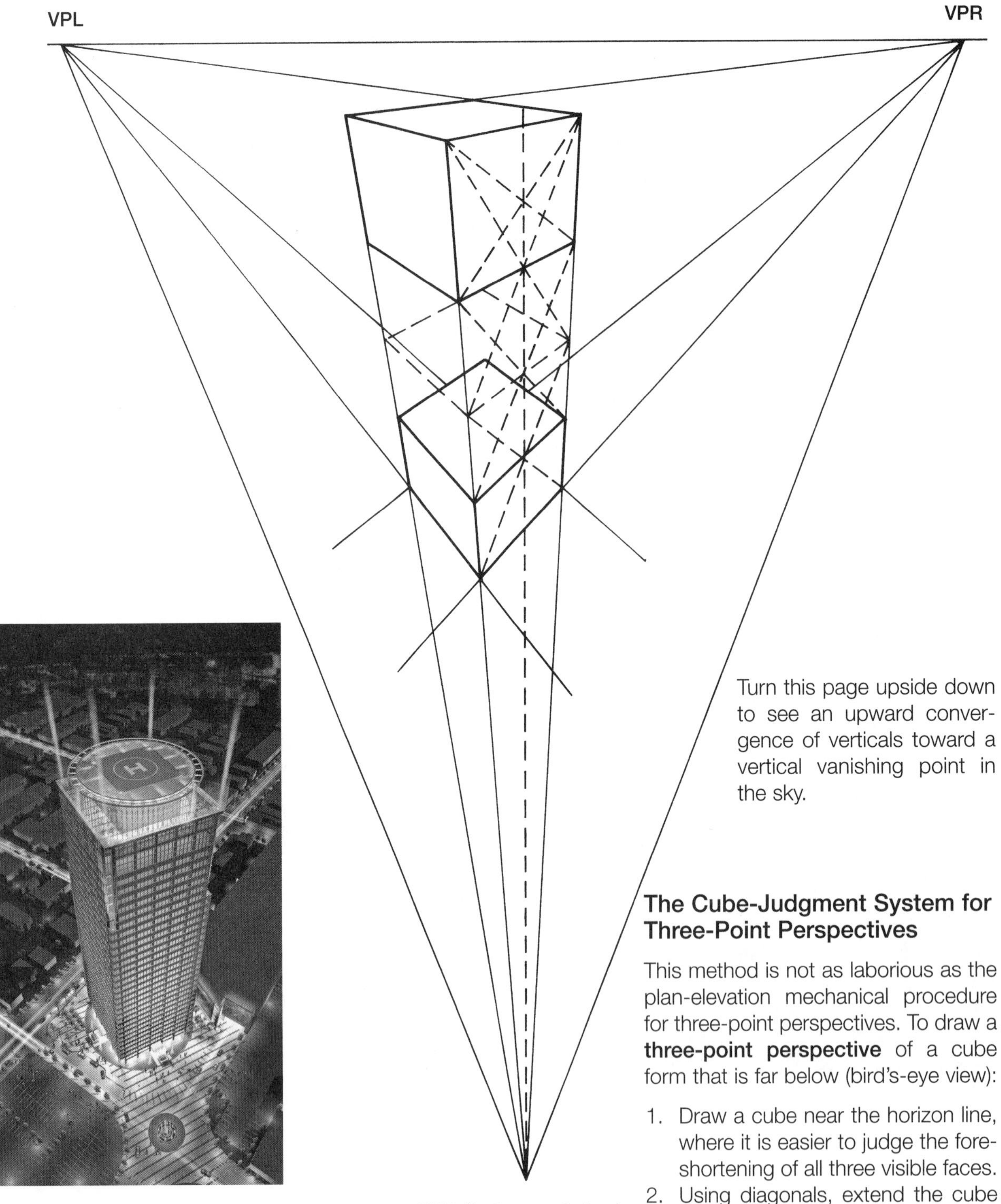

Turn this page upside down to see an upward convergence of verticals toward a vertical vanishing point in the sky.

Digital drawing: One Broadway Plaza
Santa Ana, California
Architects: carrierjohnson
Medium: 3DStudio Max and Photoshop
Courtesy of Wenjie Studio

Diagram and text: Courtesy of Dik Vrooman, Professor
Texas A&M University
Department of Architecture

The Cube-Judgment System for Three-Point Perspectives

This method is not as laborious as the plan-elevation mechanical procedure for three-point perspectives. To draw a **three-point perspective** of a cube form that is far below (bird's-eye view):

1. Draw a cube near the horizon line, where it is easier to judge the foreshortening of all three visible faces.
2. Using diagonals, extend the cube module system downward to draw the correct perspective of the cube on the ground.
3. Also using diagonals, extend this system laterally.
4. Building design shapes other than cubes are then measured from these cubes.

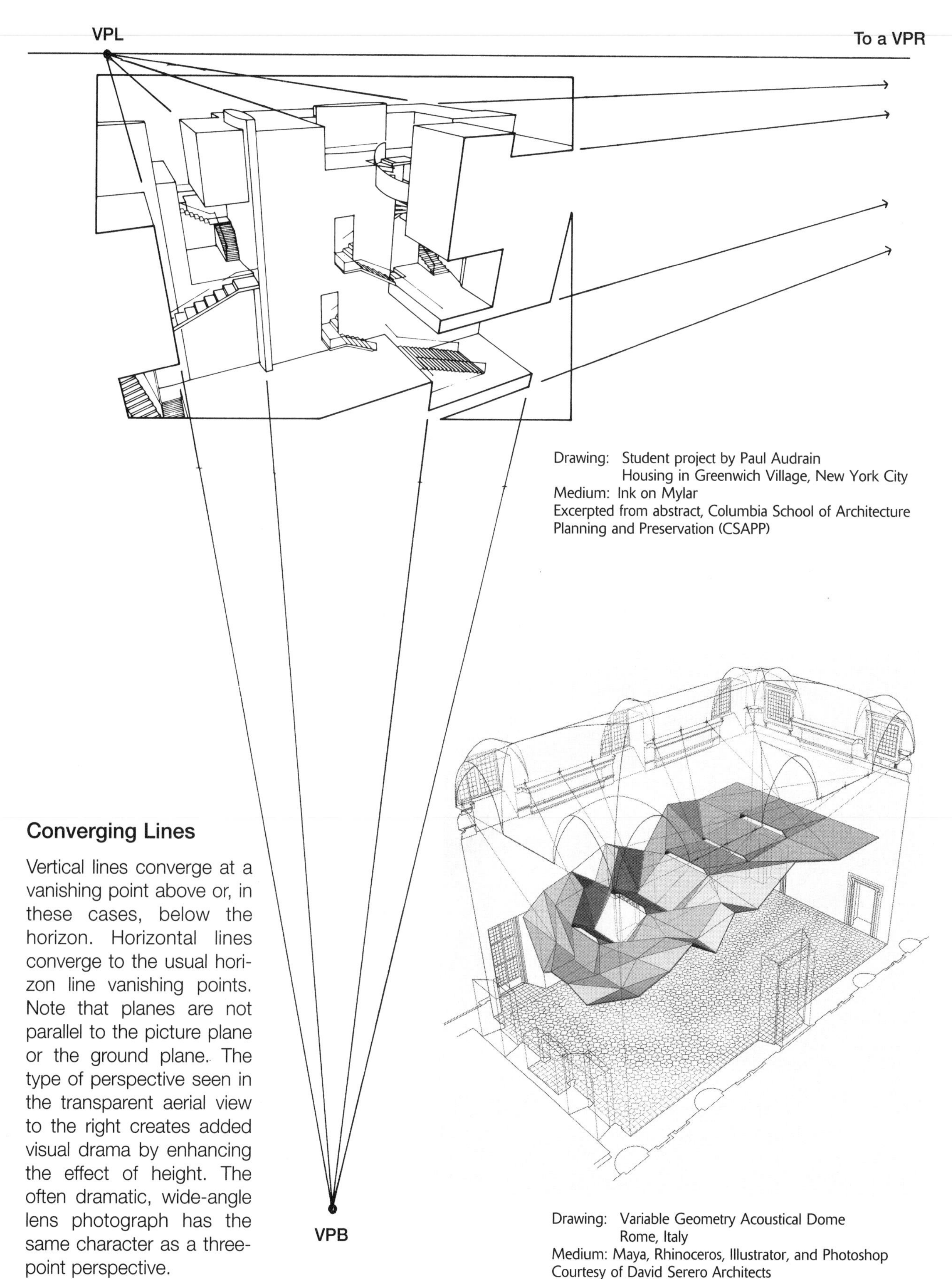

Drawing: Student project by Paul Audrain
Housing in Greenwich Village, New York City
Medium: Ink on Mylar
Excerpted from abstract, Columbia School of Architecture Planning and Preservation (CSAPP)

Converging Lines

Vertical lines converge at a vanishing point above or, in these cases, below the horizon. Horizontal lines converge to the usual horizon line vanishing points. Note that planes are not parallel to the picture plane or the ground plane. The type of perspective seen in the transparent aerial view to the right creates added visual drama by enhancing the effect of height. The often dramatic, wide-angle lens photograph has the same character as a three-point perspective.

Drawing: Variable Geometry Acoustical Dome
Rome, Italy
Medium: Maya, Rhinoceros, Illustrator, and Photoshop
Courtesy of David Serero Architects

This method of construction produces an accurately measured **three-point perspective** drawing. The principle is based on the measured two-point perspective method: The image is generated on a picture plane by projecting lines from the object to a single eye point. In three-point perspective, the picture plane will be tilted at an angle, as one would tilt a camera to photograph a tall object. When the picture plane (and the camera) are tilted, the lines in the vertical direction will converge as well. The principle is illustrated in the diagram at right. Using a scale for the perspective layout allows control of the image. In the example, 1"=50' scale was used.

1. Determine the distance of the observer (the eye point **E**) from the picture plane. A larger distance will produce a smaller but less distorted image. This distance is the radius of the circle drawn.
2. To generate the vanishing point for the vertical lines **(VVP)**, the eye point (E) must be rotated around the centerline **(CL)** from the center of the circle **(c)** into the surface of the picture plane. The point received **(EV)** will be used for generating measurements in the vertical direction.
3. Determine the tilt of the picture plane. A larger angle produces a closer vanishing point. In the example, the angle is 20°. Draw a line **(h)** with the angle from EV. The intersection with the centerline (CL) gives the location of the horizon line. Perpendicular to the line (h), draw a line **(v).** The intersection with the center line (CL) will give the vanishing point (VVP) for the vertical lines. Note that the tilted picture plane is the surface of the paper; thus, the horizontal and vertical lines (h and v) must be drawn tilted instead.
4. Rotate the EV eyepoint around point H into the centerline (CL) to generate the eye point **(EH)**. This point will be used to construct the perspective in the horizontal direction.
5. Determine the distance of the base plane from the horizontal plane. In the example it is 60'. In this perspective, the base plane was selected at the top of the object to reduce the drawing size. The **baseline** (BL)—the intersection of the base plane and the picture plane—is drawn in scale 60' below the **horizon line** (HL).

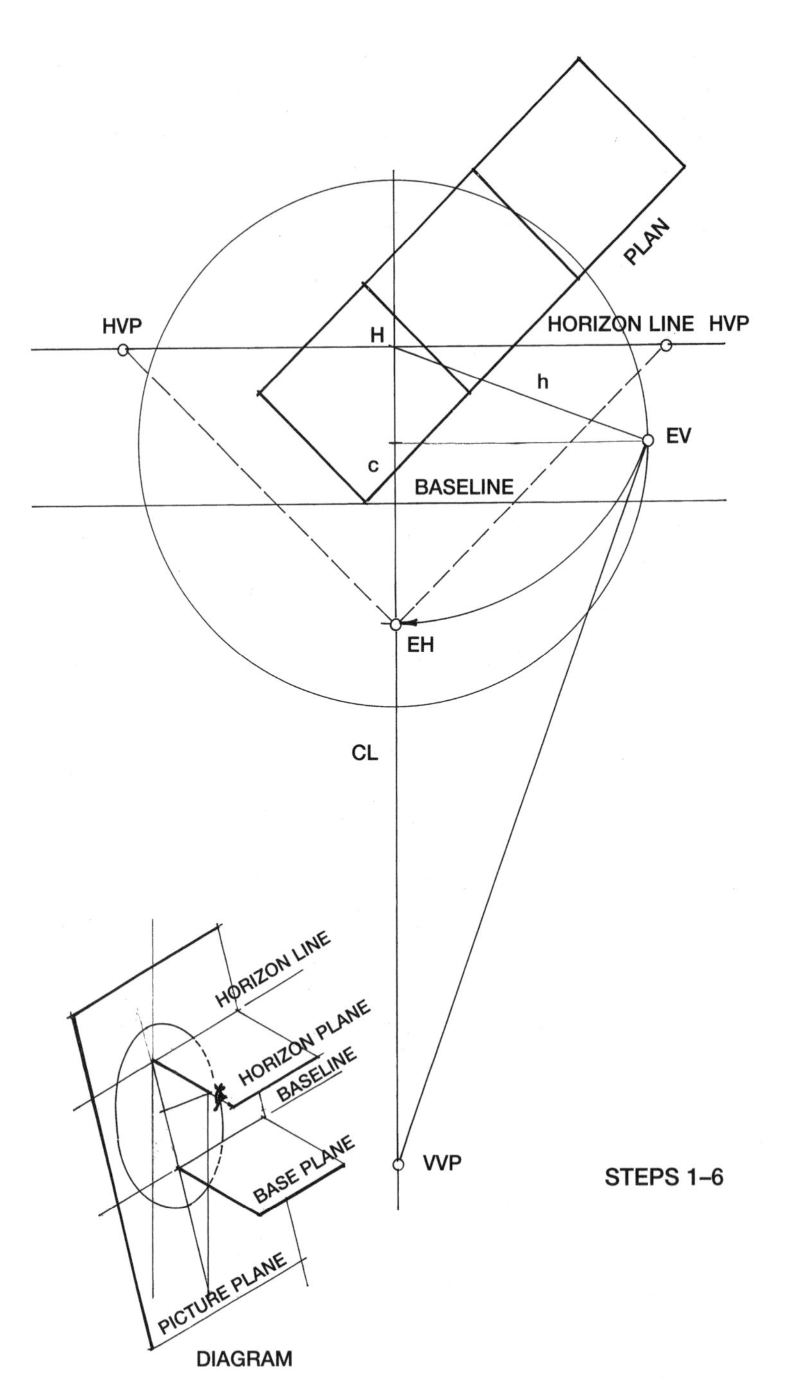

Text and diagram: Courtesy of Arpad Daniel Ronaszegi, Assistant Professor Andrews University Division of Architecture

6. Position the plan on the base plane. Here, the object was placed behind the picture plane with one corner touching it. From EH you can construct the vanishing point **(HVP)** by drawing parallel lines with corresponding sides and intersecting with the horizon line (HL).

7. Construct the perpsective image of the plan by connecting lines to the appropriate horizontal vanishing points (HVP). The lengths of the lines will be measured by connecting points to the eye point (EH) and intersecting them with the corresponding lines.
8. The image of vertical lines can be constructed by connecting points from the plan image to the vertical vanishing point (VVP).
9. The heights in the vertical direction will be generated from the vertical measuring line **(VML).** Draw a line parallel to line **v,** starting from the point where the plan touches the picture plane (**BL** on the drawing). On the line generated **(vml),** the actual heights can be measured out. In this example, the elevation is drawn orthogonal to the VML and then projected onto it.

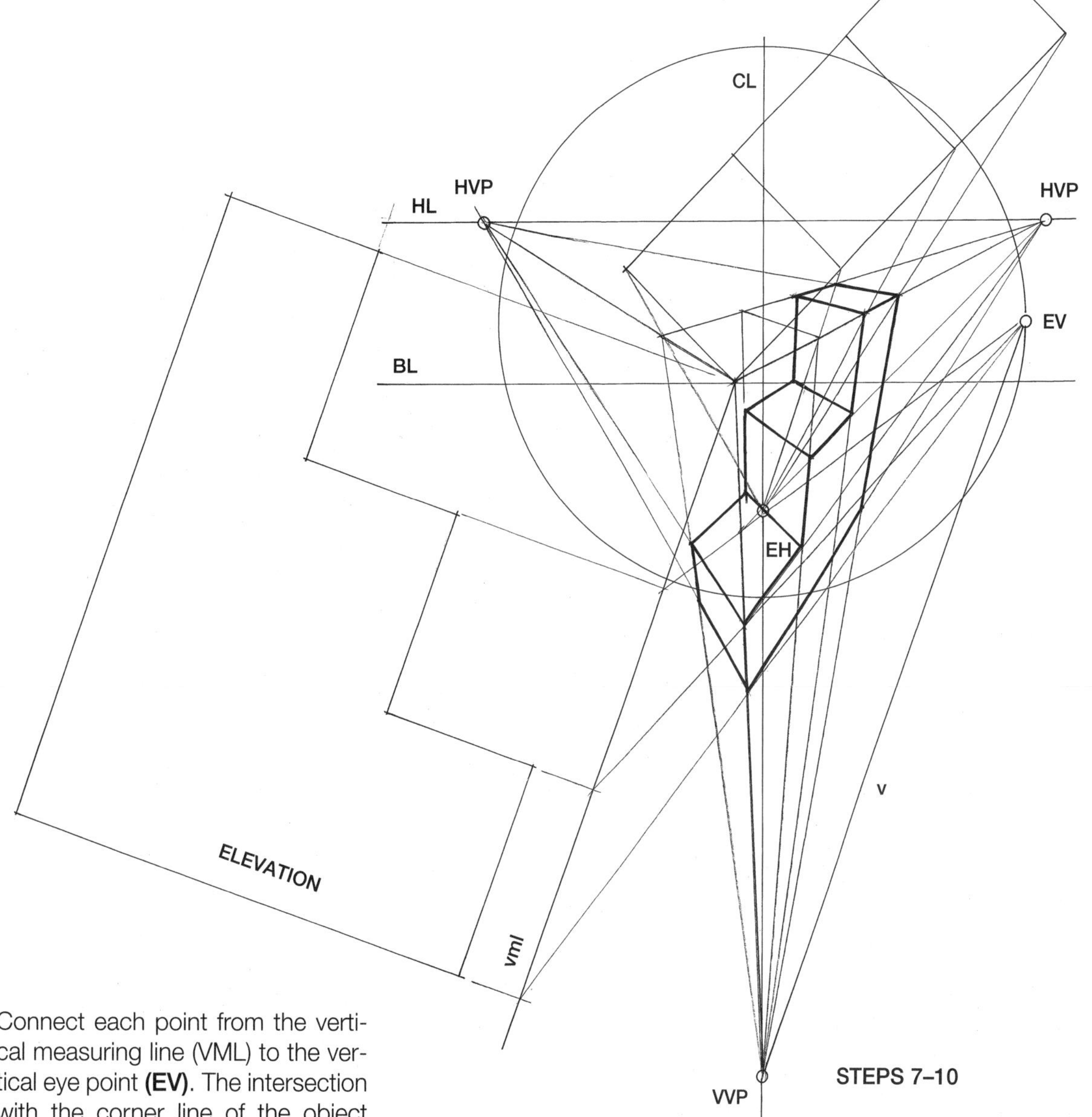

STEPS 7–10

10. Connect each point from the vertical measuring line (VML) to the vertical eye point **(EV)**. The intersection with the corner line of the object gives the points for the heights in perspective. These points can be connected to the appropriate HVP points to finish the construction of the image.

Text and diagram: Courtesy of Arpad Daniel Ronaszegi, Assistant Professor Andrews University Division of Architecture

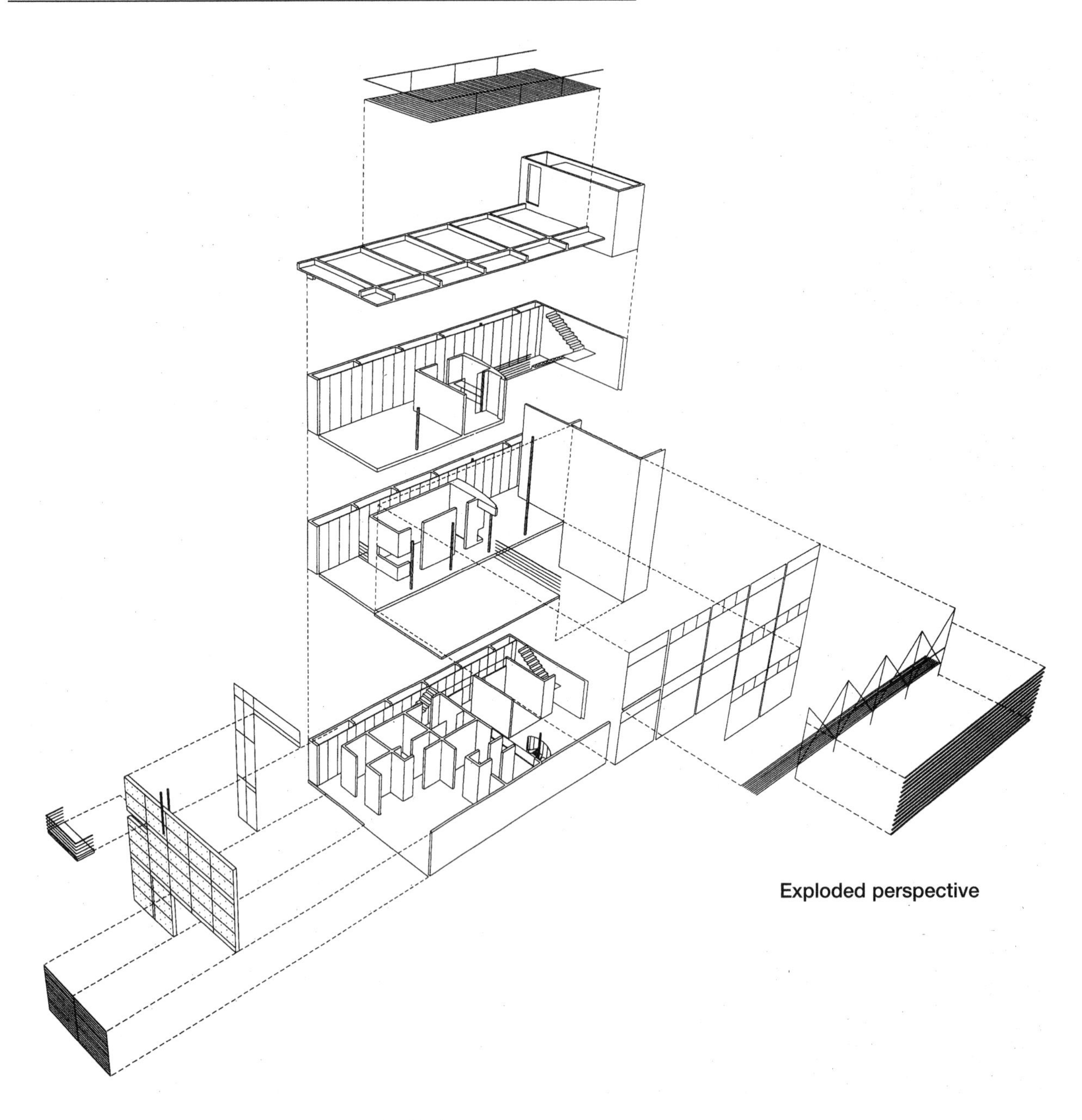

Exploded perspective

Drawing: HOUSE LE, Colonia Condesa, Mexico City, Mexico
Courtesy of TEN Arquitectos-Enrique Norten
Bernardo Gomez-Pimienta, Carlos Ordoñez, project coordinators

Exploded Perspective

Each layer in this exploded perspective gives an unimpeded view of the interior and exterior details of the house. The individual layers must be far enough apart to distinguish each layer (horizontal and vertical), yet be close enough so that they read as a coherent whole.

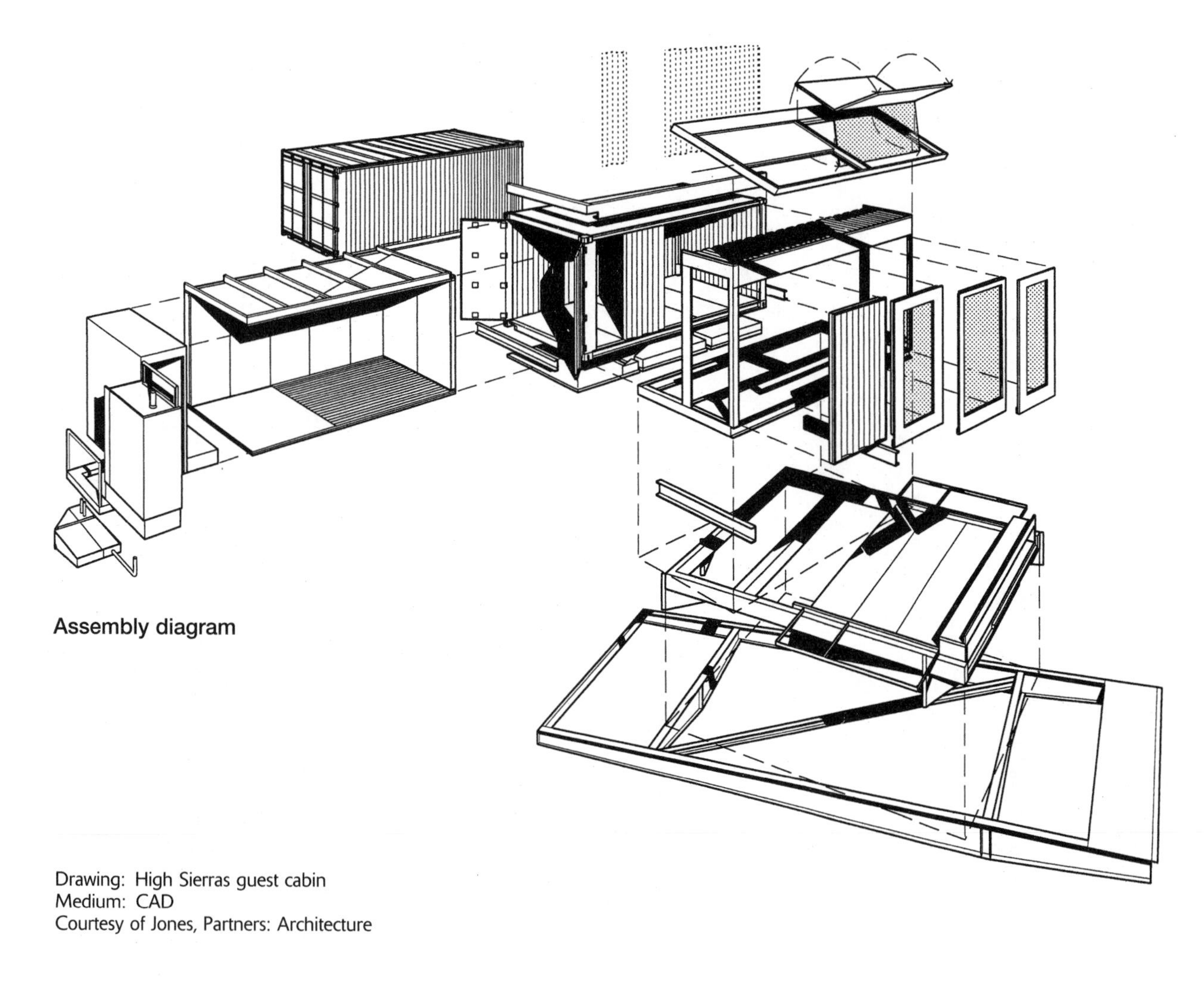

Assembly diagram

Drawing: High Sierras guest cabin
Medium: CAD
Courtesy of Jones, Partners: Architecture

Exploded Assembly Drawing

The use of the exploded view highlights the nature of this structure as an assemblage of standardized parts and shows the genesis of the primary building module in the standard 20′ shipping container. The primary modular assembly occupies the horizontal plane established by the existing container in the background, while accessory elements are, where possible, exploded along the vertical axis. Corrugated steel removed from the existing container is shown dotted in. [ARCHITECT'S STATEMENT]

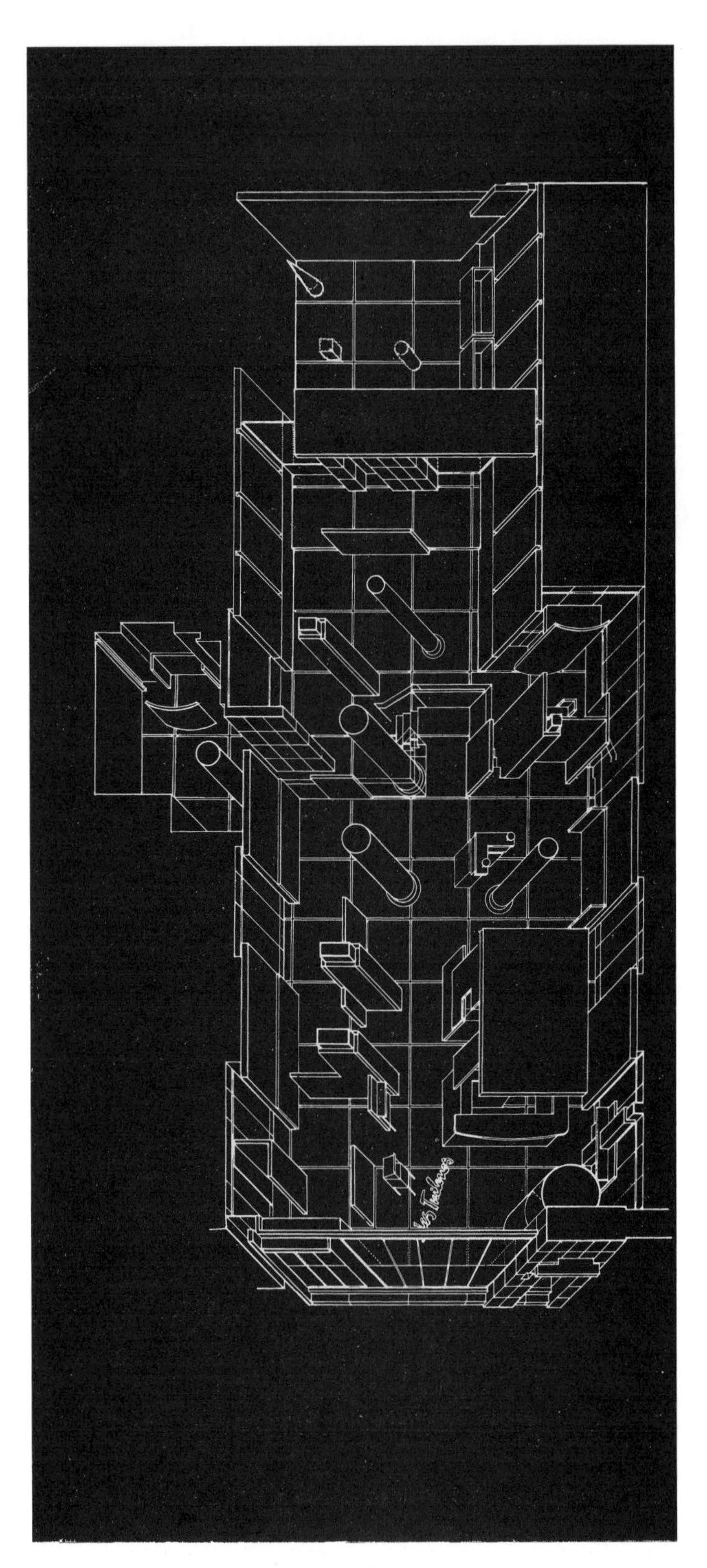

Drawing: Les Tuileries Restaurant, New York City
20" × 30" (50.8 × 76.2 cm), Scale: 1/4"=1'0"
Medium: Ink and Mylar
Courtesy of Diane Lewis, Peter Mickle, and Christopher Compton, R.A., Designers

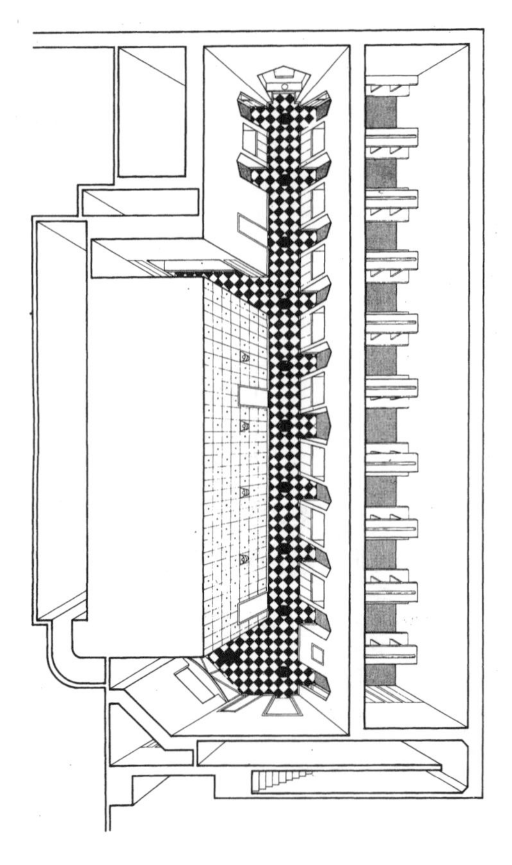

Drawing: The WEB (Workstations in Evans Basement)
University of California, Berkeley
12" × 18" (30.5 × 45.7 cm), Scale: 1/8"=1'0"
Medium: Ink on Mylar
Courtesy of Sam Davis, FAIA, of Davis & Joyce Architects

An aerial one-point perspective shows the organization of the various rooms as would a simple plan, while also showing the volumetric relationships of the spaces. Certain liberties are necessary in the construction of such a drawing, but revealing so much conceptual information at a single glance is often valuable.
[ARCHITECT'S STATEMENT]

Hybrid Drawings

When drawing types are superimposed, the result is a **hybrid** drawing. These two hybrid drawings with unusual overhead views combine the principles of paraline and perspective drawing. At first glance, they appear to be overhead one-point perspectives. On closer examination, however, one notices many internal structural elements having infinitely parallel lines.

ENLARGED AND EXPANDED VIEW

Hybrid Drawing

This hybrid drawing combines a one-point persective with a vertically expanded plan oblique. Note that the perspective convergence results in the plan being enlarged, allowing for a clearer view of many details.

This drawing was made to illustrate a relation between a plan (in this case a floor plan) and certain three-dimensional elements contained within that plan. The plan is made as a figure/ground drawing in which the central void space of the office is highlighted. It is out of that void space that the three-dimensional parts are drawn as an axonometric projection. [ARCHITECT'S STATEMENT]

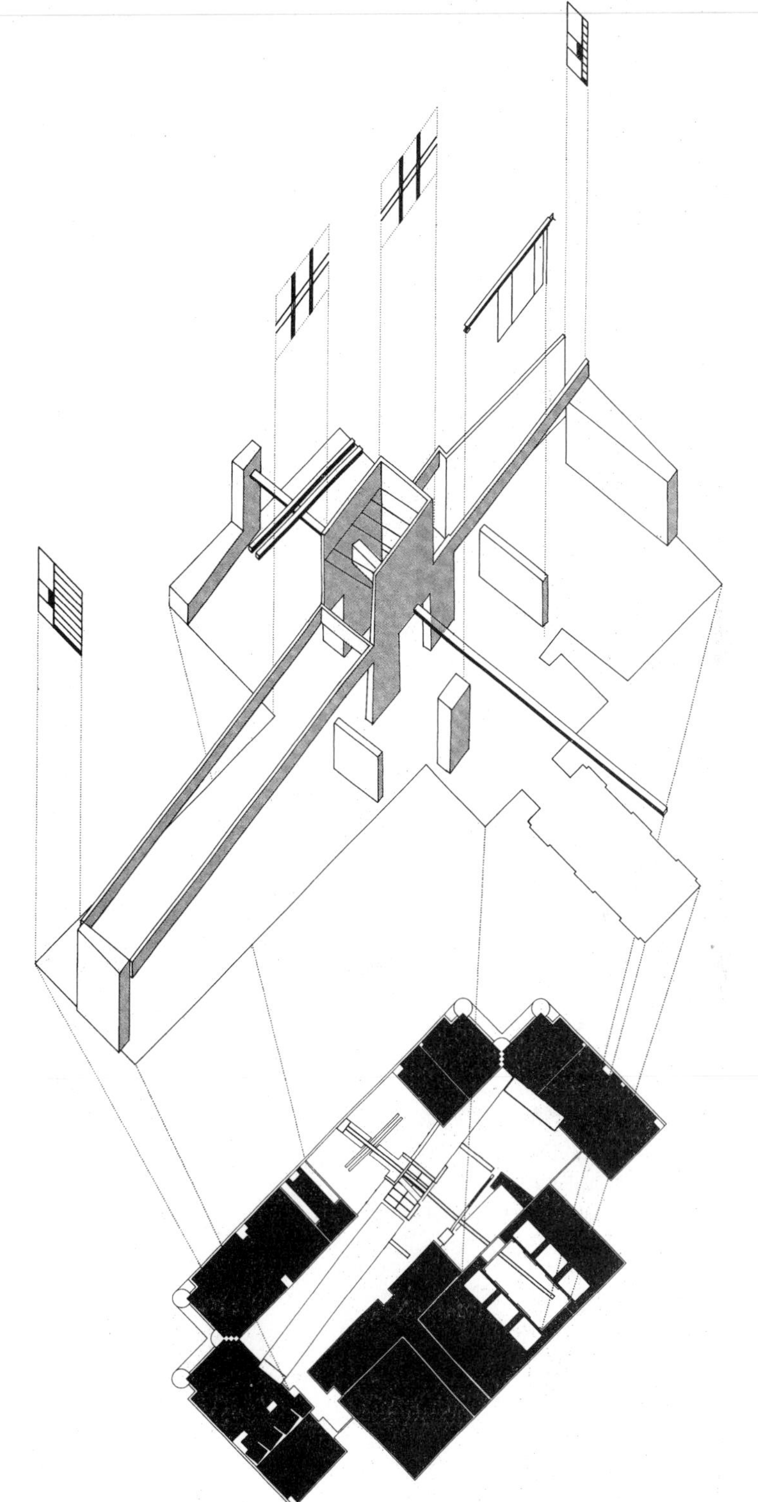

Drawing: World Savings Center Executive Suite, Oakland, California
14" × 26" (35.6 × 66 cm), Scale: 1/8"=1'0"
Medium: Ink on vellum
Courtesy of Jim Jennings, Architect, of Jennings + Stout, Architects
Drawn by Jim Jennings

Drawing Perspective Circles

To draw a circle or a portion of a circle accurately in perspective requires that you first draw its circumscribing square. With experience and practice, you will be able to derive from the square all the reference that is needed for quick sketches. However, as accuracy requirements and circle size increase, so does the need to construct additional points of reference to assist in constructing the circle. The following sections describe the four-, eight-, and twelve-point techniques for constructing circles.

Photo: St Mark's Cathedral
Venice, Italy

The Four-Point Perspective Circle

The four-point technique locates the points of tangency between the circle and square.

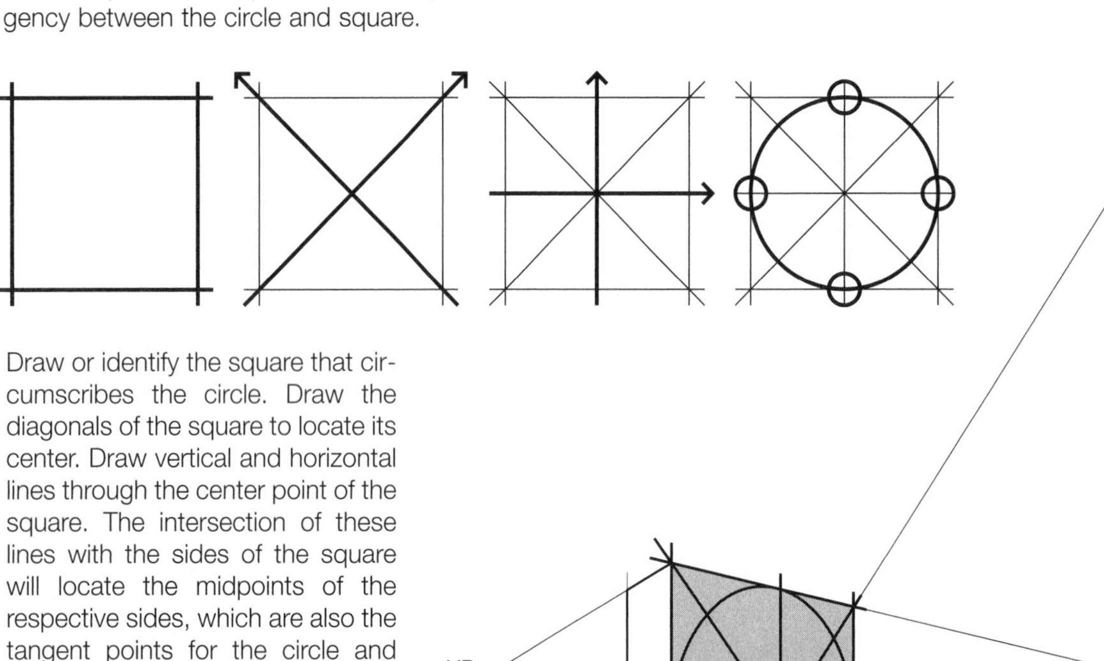

Draw or identify the square that circumscribes the circle. Draw the diagonals of the square to locate its center. Draw vertical and horizontal lines through the center point of the square. The intersection of these lines with the sides of the square will locate the midpoints of the respective sides, which are also the tangent points for the circle and square. Draw a smooth curve that connects the four points to create a circle in perspective. Visually adjust the circle until it looks correct.

Note that the highest and lowest points of the circle are to the near side of their respective tangent points.

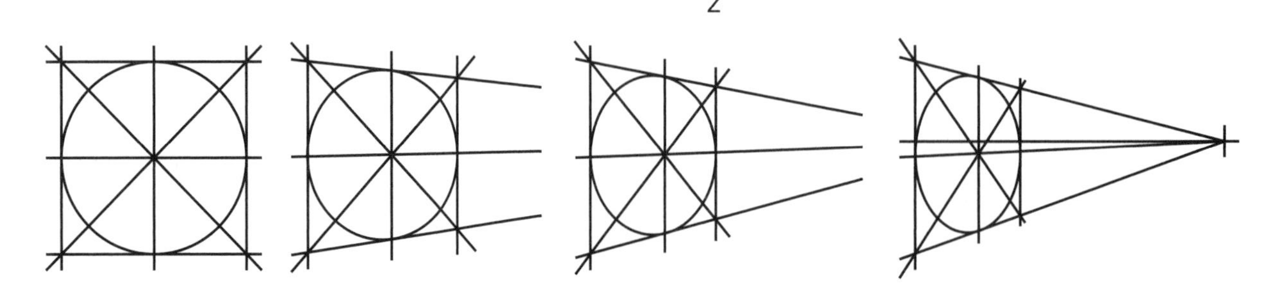

The Eight-Point Perspective Circle

The eight-point technique builds directly on the four-point system with a visual approximation that provides four more points.

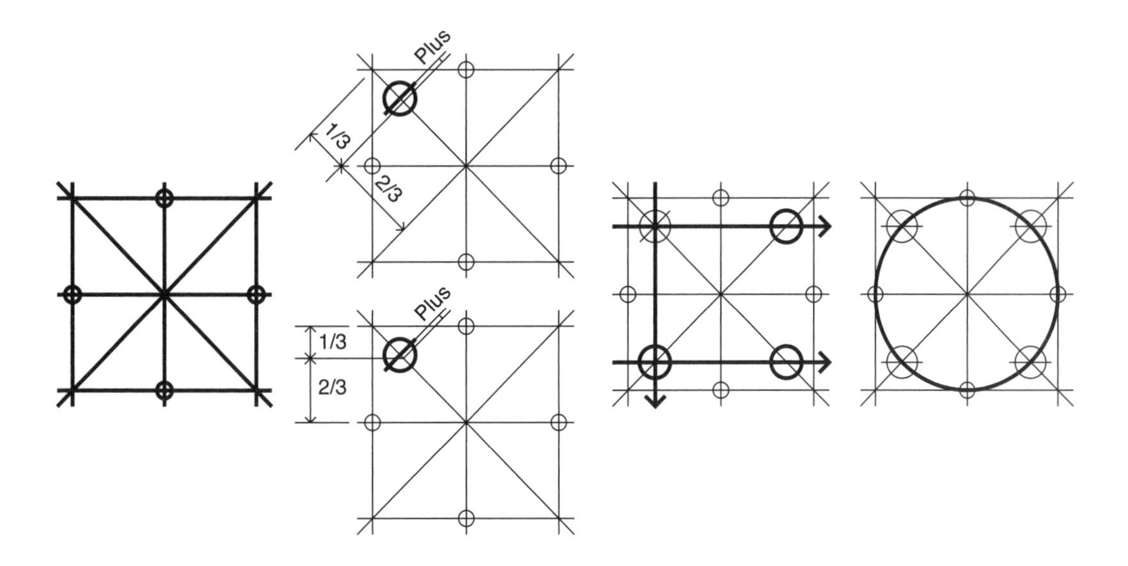

Follow the four-point procedure to locate the first four points. The diagonals used in this process are now divided to locate the additional points.

Divide the near half of one of the diagonals into thirds to locate the two-thirds point as shown. This can be done either directly along the diagonal or along the corresponding half of the square's side. If you use the square's side, you must transfer the two-thirds mark to the diagonal.

Mark a point just beyond the two-thirds point of the diagonal. This locates the point at which the circle will intersect the diagonal.

Transfer this point to the other diagonals with lines that are parallel to the respective sides. This locates the other three points, giving you eight points to guide your circle construction.

Draw a smooth curve that connects the eight points to create a circle. Visually adjust the circle until it looks correct.

Drawing (partial): The Peninsula Regent, San Mateo, California
16" × 24" (40.6 × 61 cm)
Medium: Ink on Mylar
Courtesy of Backen Arrigoni & Ross, Inc.
Architecture, Planning & Interior Design
Peter Szasz, Architectural Illustrator

Drawing: Student project by Duke Wilford
Wine Growers Association
30" × 30" (76.2 × 76.2 cm)
Medium: Technical pen (latex ink) on Mylar
Courtesy of Washington University
School of Architecture, St. Louis, Missouri

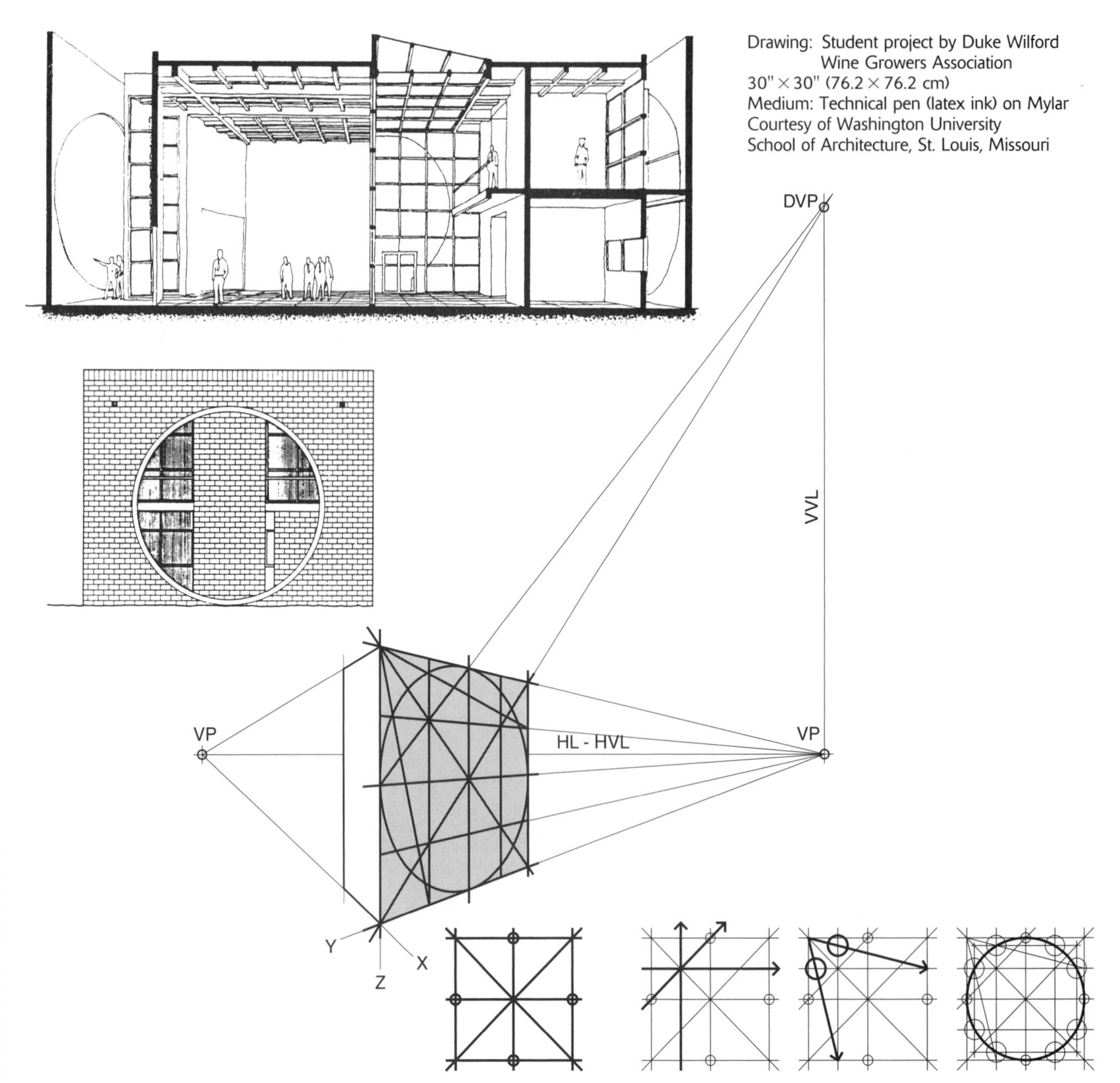

The Twelve-Point Perspective Circle

Follow the four-point procedure to locate the first four points.
Draw a diagonal through a near quarter of the original square to find its center. Draw vertical and horizontal lines through this point.

Draw lines from the corner of the original square to the one-quarter points on the opposite sides as shown. The intersection of these lines with the nearest horizontal or vertical one-quarter line defines two new points on the circle.

Use transfer techniques to create the other vertical and horizontal lines, and then transfer the location of the two new points on the circle to the appropriate lines. This locates the other six new points and provides twelve points to guide circle construction. Draw a smooth curve that connects the twelve points to create a circle. Visually adjust the circle until it looks correct.

Diagrams and text: Courtesy of William R. Benedict, Assistant Professor
California Polytechnic State University School of Architecture
San Luis Obispo, California

The **twelve-point** procedure is equally effective in constructing a horizontal perspective circle. It can also be used to construct an isometric circle. (See construction of isometric circles on p. 142).

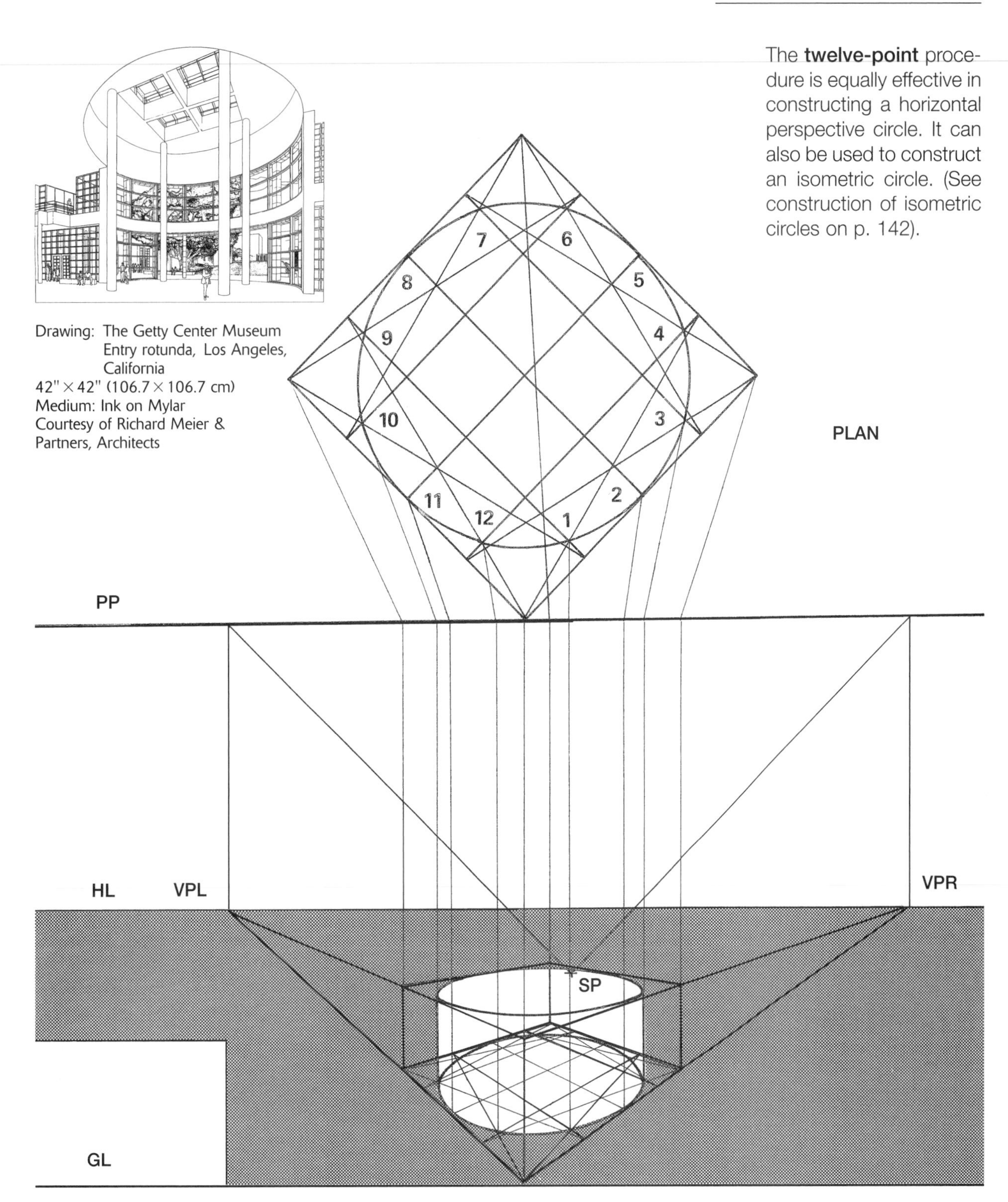

Drawing: The Getty Center Museum Entry rotunda, Los Angeles, California
42" × 42" (106.7 × 106.7 cm)
Medium: Ink on Mylar
Courtesy of Richard Meier & Partners, Architects

The Twelve-Point Perspective Circle

1. Divide the encompassing square into sixteen squares of equal size.
2. Project lines from the four major corners to the farthest corner of each smaller corner square.
3. Intersection points (8) for the circle occur at the intersection of the major corner line and the opposite side of the first smaller square.
4. The other four points are the tangent points. Carefully draw the elliptical curve connecting the twelve points.

Noncircular curvilinear forms in architecture can be elliptical or even undulating (a wavelike continuum), as seen in the work of Alvar Aalto.

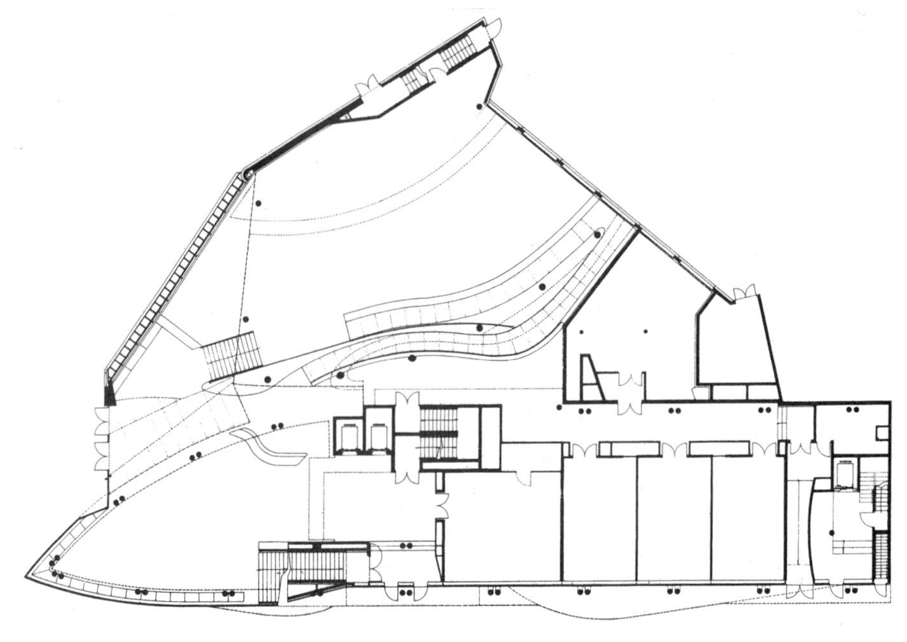

Ground-floor plan

Interior perspective: entrance hall

Noncircular curvilinear horizontal or vertical forms can be plotted by using a similar point-by-point technique, as shown with perspective circles. Contemporary graphic strategies dictate that its expeditious accurate plotting be computer-generated or approximated by eye using freehand techniques. These curves in the horizontal plane are much easier to draw in plan obliques because they are seen in true shape and true size.

Drawings: Maison du Sport Français
Paris, France
Courtesy of Atelier Henri Gaudin, Architect

NONCIRCULAR CURVES IN PERSPECTIVE

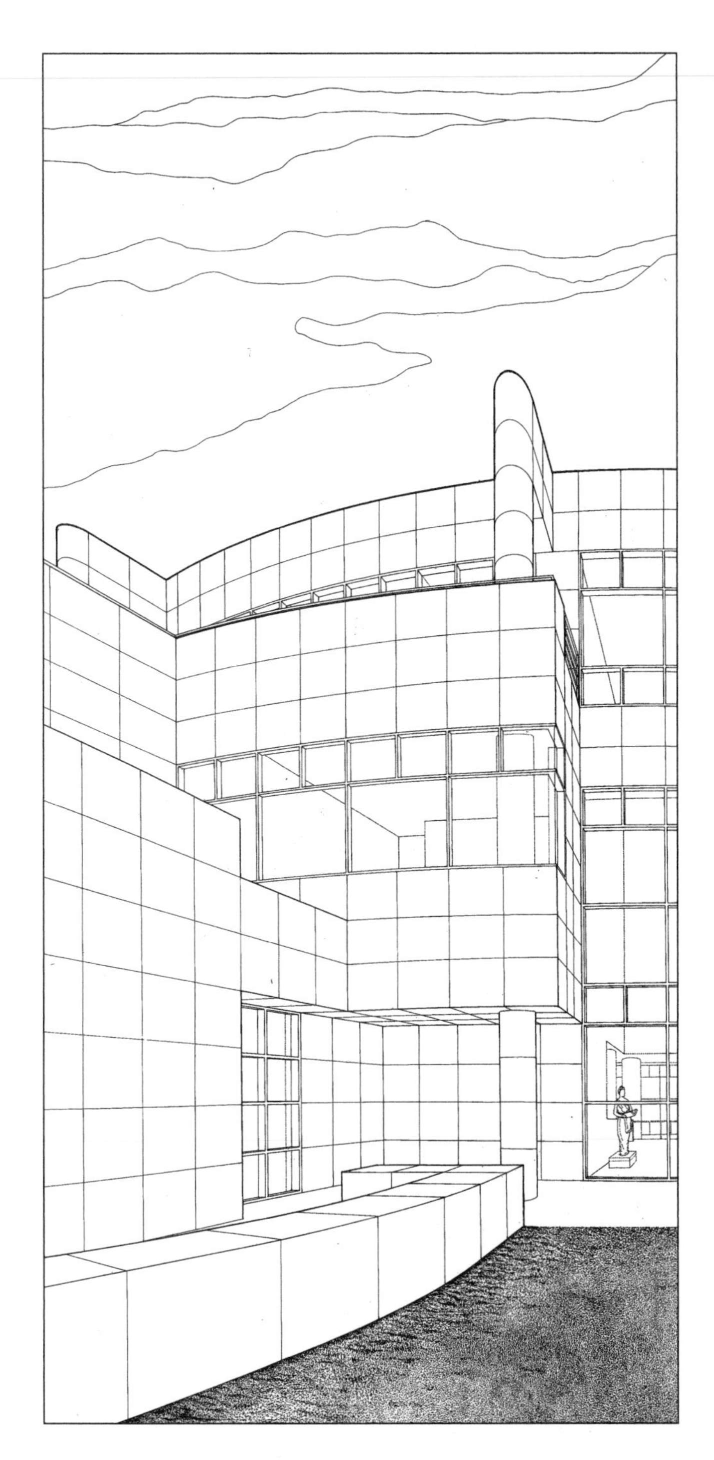

Drawing (partial): The Getty Center for the History of Art and the Humanities, Los Angeles, California
Medium: Ink on Mylar
Courtesy of Richard Meier & Partners, Architects
Reprinted from The Getty Center Design Process with permission of The J. Paul Getty Trust

Drawing: Student project by Cort Morgan
Film Institute in Vicenza, Italy
Medium: Ink on Mylar
Courtesy of the University of Texas at Arlington School of Architecture

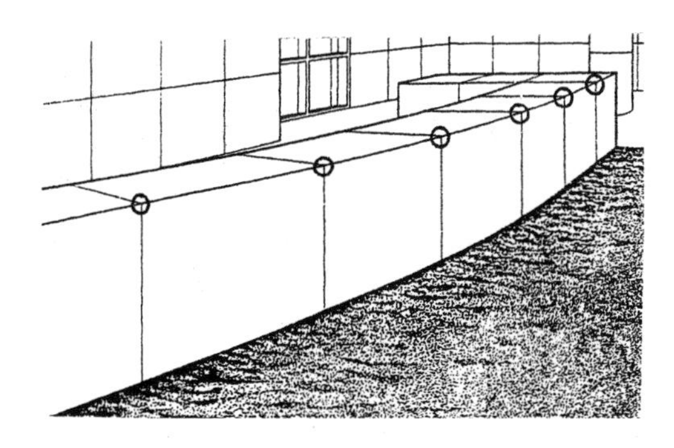

Where the ground plane (in this case the dark area) meets the curvature of the building or object, plot a series of points on the plan grid. The connection of these points determines the proper curvature. Find the proper location of any elevated points in perspective (the circled points in this example) by projecting from a vertical grid or transferring from a true-height line intersecting the horizon line.

© Rendow Yee

Oakland Museum pool structure, Oakland, California
Oakland Museum
Kevin Roche, John Dinkeloo, and Associates, Architects

Reflections

In most cases, a reflecting surface causes a visually interesting and appealing phenomenon. Reflections in architecture are associated with water, glass window panes, glass mirrors, wet pavement, and materials with a shiny surface, such as polished granite. Light causes the phenomenon of reflections. A **reflecting surface** results in an **extension** of any viewed perspective. The rendering of reflections (pp. 296–97, 398–401) furthers the understanding of a building within its contextual setting. The analytical drawing of the sculpture and its reflection is the optimal case of a reflected inverted object identical in size to the object itself. In reality, a horizontally reflected object does not create an exact mirror image in its reflected perspective, because the observer's eye level is always above the ground (reflecting surface) line. This results in different distances between the eye and any point, and its corresponding reflected point on the inverted image.

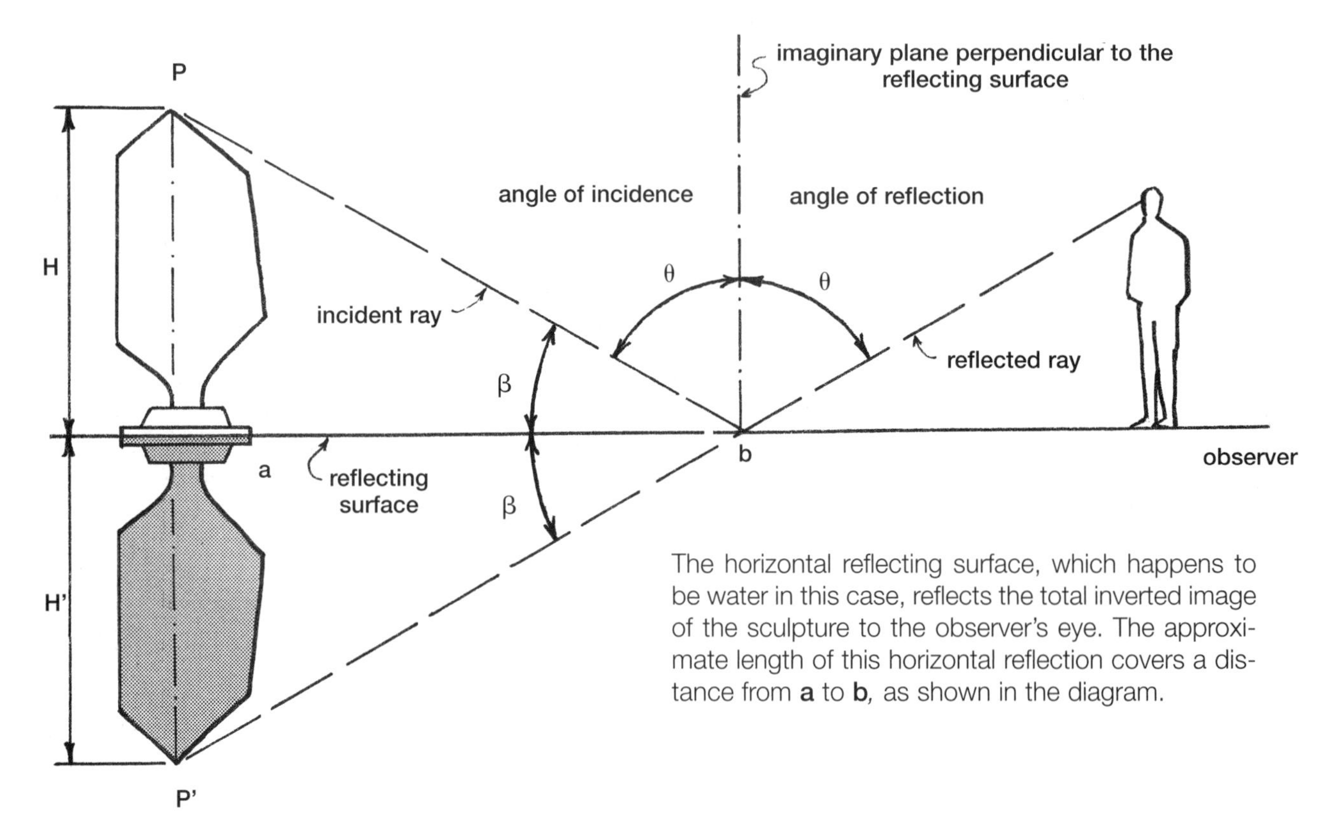

The horizontal reflecting surface, which happens to be water in this case, reflects the total inverted image of the sculpture to the observer's eye. The approximate length of this horizontal reflection covers a distance from **a** to **b**, as shown in the diagram.

Building Touching the Reflective Surface

1. Construct the perspective of the building.
2. Extend all vertical lines into the reflection. The reflected lengths will be equal to the existing building verticals (aa'= aa").
3. Horizontal lines in the reflection vanish to the same vanishing points as their corresponding horizontal lines in the existing building.

Photo: Team Disney Building
Lake Buena Vista, Florida
Courtesy of Arata Isozaki & Associates, Architects

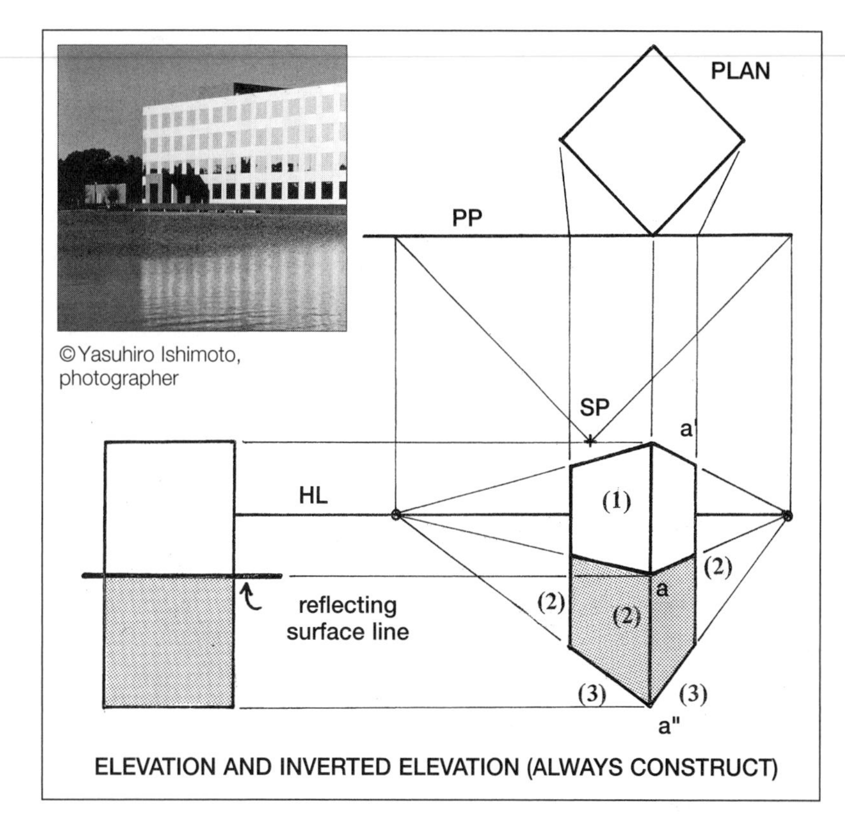

©Yasuhiro Ishimoto, photographer

Building Not Touching the Reflective Surface

1. Construct the perspective of the building.
2. The reflecting surface does not extend under the building; therefore, parts of the reflection will be concealed. Construct the projection of the building onto the plane of the reflecting surface. The verticals are measured to the plane of the reflecting surface.
3. These vertical distances are duplicated to construct the reflection.

Photo: Dolphin and Swan Convention Hotels
Orlando, Florida
Photo by Bill Whitehurst
Courtesy of Michael Graves, Architect, and Courtesy of Tishman Realty & Construction Company

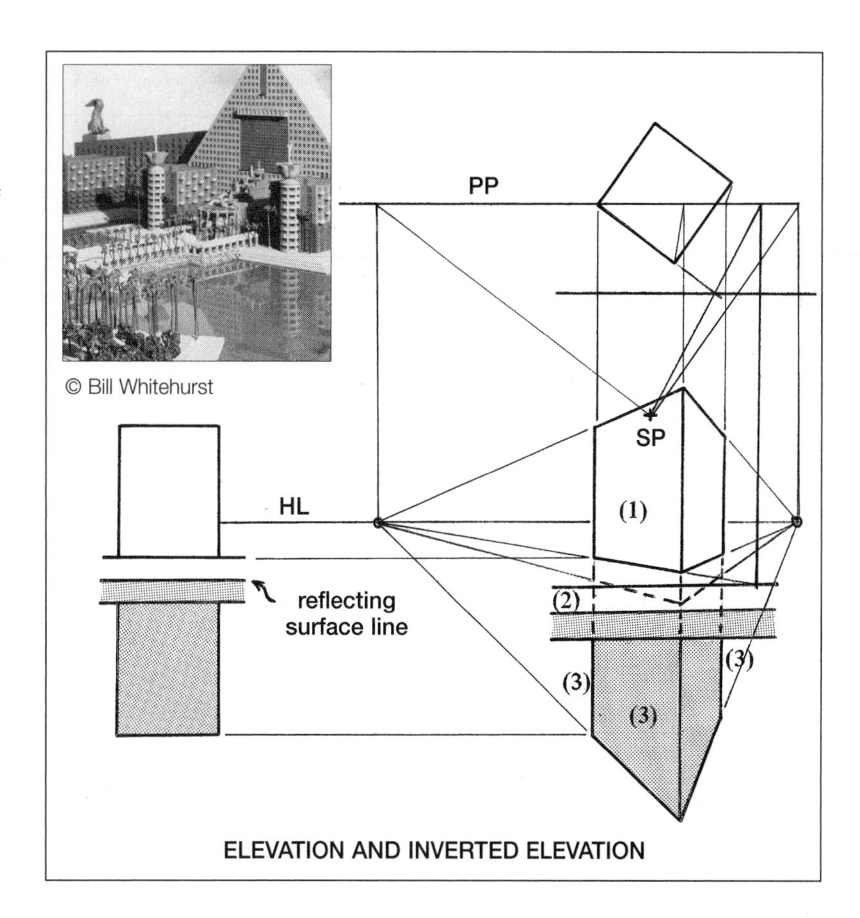

© Bill Whitehurst

If a building has parallel inclined edges, as seen in the plan view at right, the vanishing trace lines will converge to an oblique vanishing point above or below the vanishing point for horizontal lines. These trace lines are all located in the same or parallel planes.

Line **AB** is part of an inclined surface that has its own vanishing point oblique. Its reflected image (**A'B'**) vanishes at an oblique vanishing point that is an equal distance above the **HL** as its nonreflected counterpart **VP$_O$** is below.

Horizontal reflections in perspective are always seen with the horizon line higher than the reflecting surface line, resulting in the reflected lines always sloping at a sharper angle than those of the building itself.

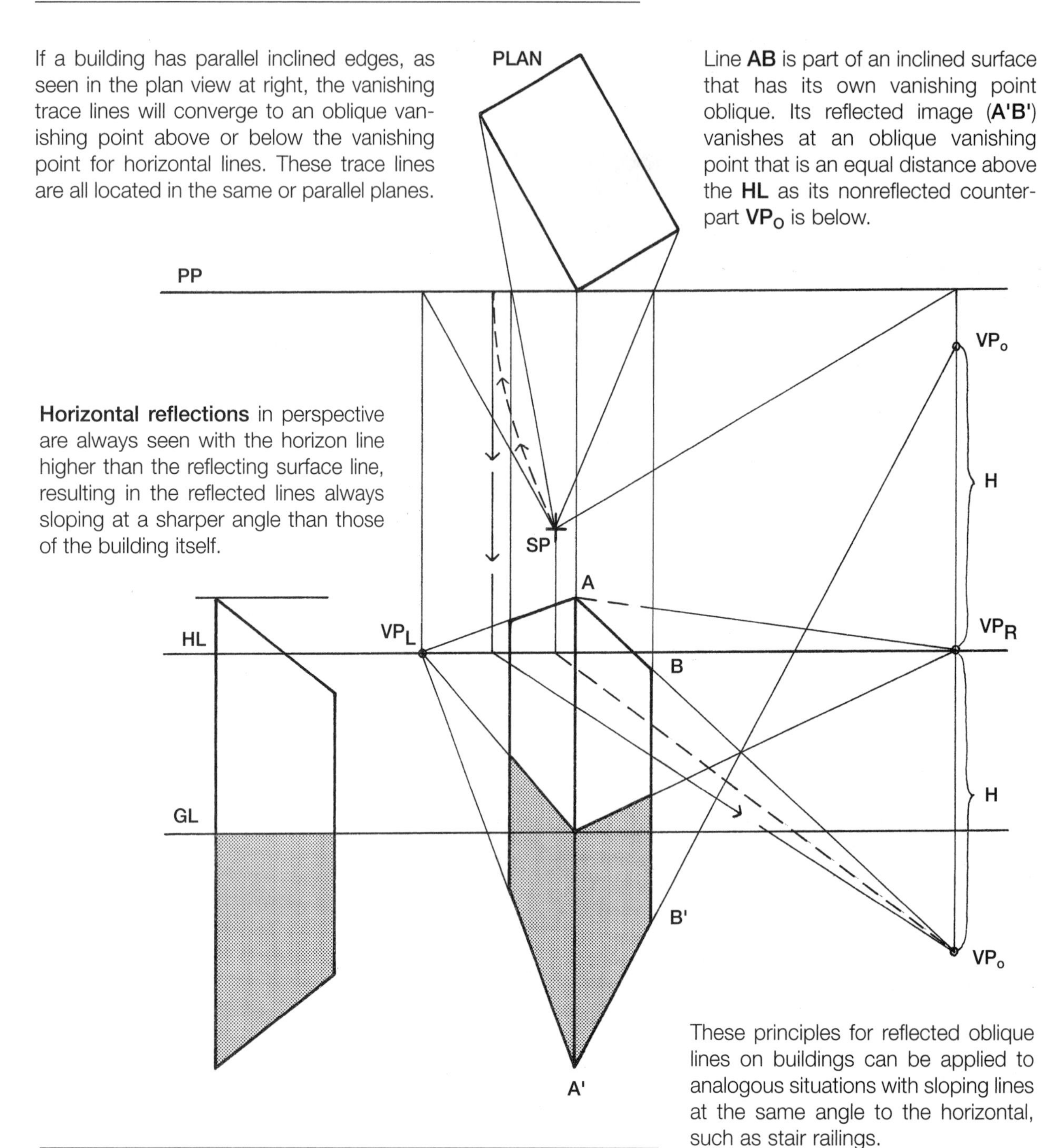

These principles for reflected oblique lines on buildings can be applied to analogous situations with sloping lines at the same angle to the horizontal, such as stair railings.

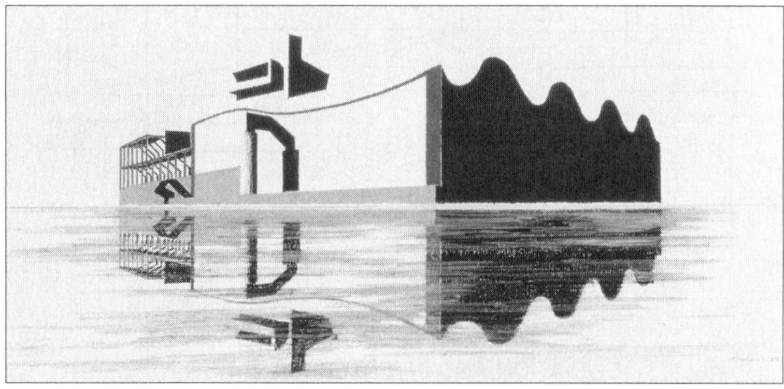

Drawing: Kitakyushu International Conference Center
Kitakyushu, Fukuoka, Japan
23.4" × 18.9" (59.4 × 48.1 cm)
Medium: Crayon paint
Courtesy of Arata Isozaki & Associates, Architects
Drawn by Arata Isozaki

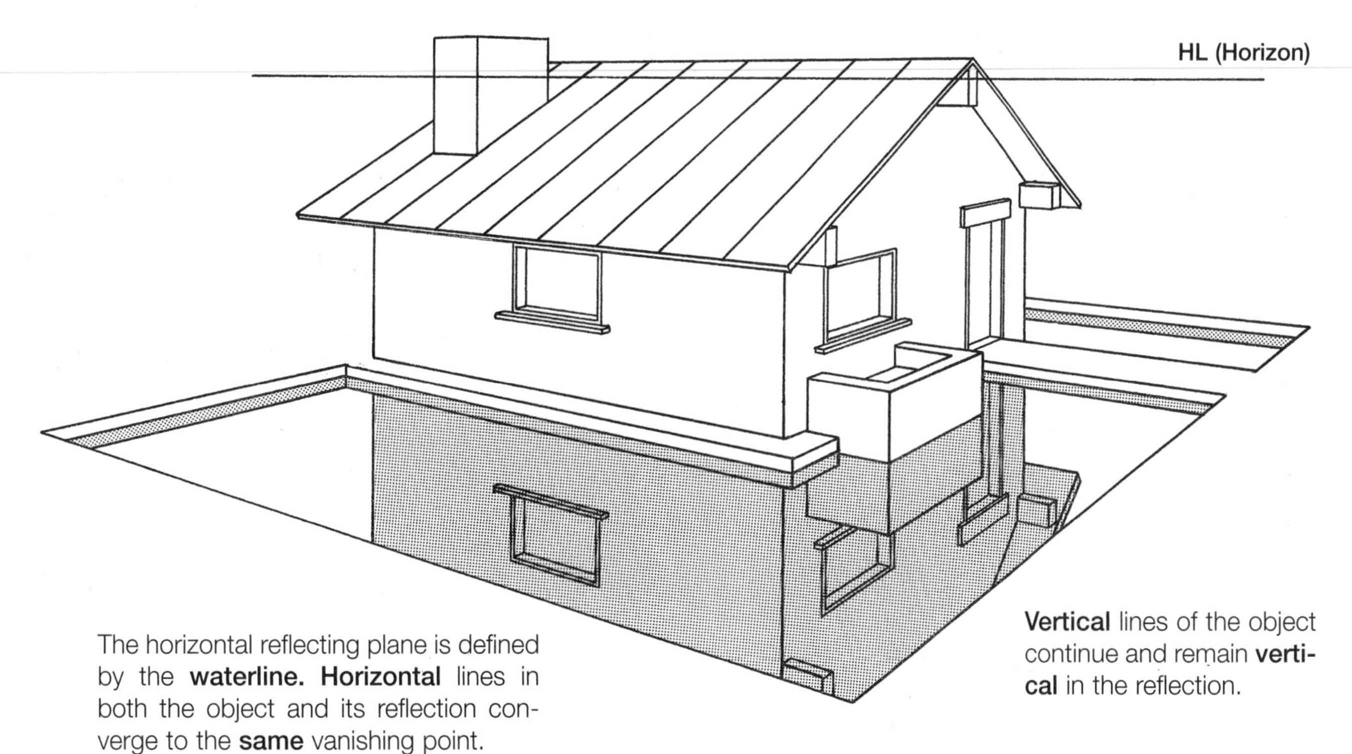

The horizontal reflecting plane is defined by the **waterline. Horizontal** lines in both the object and its reflection converge to the **same** vanishing point.

Vertical lines of the object continue and remain **vertical** in the reflection.

Artificial reflecting pools commonly display **partial** reflections because of the pool's enclosing elements. Natural bodies of water display almost total reflections. The bottom of the reflected image above is concealed by the area around the pool's edge, whereas the top of the reflected image is hidden by the pool's deck in the photo below.

© Norman McGrath, Photographer

Photo: Sklar House
Westchester County, New York
Courtesy of Christopher H.L. Owen, Architect
and Norman McGrath, Photographer

The soft light of a late fall day established the mood of this photograph. The selection of a low viewpoint captures an almost complete reflection of the house and emphasizes the strong geometry of the design. A conscious effort was made to establish the sympathetic relationship of the house setting with freshly fallen leaves around and on the pool's surface. Some photographers might have cleaned it up, producing a stiffer, more formal result. Recognizing and taking advantage of unpredictable circumstances such as those shown here can produce images that are both aesthetic and informative. A 4″×5″ view camera with a wide-angle lens was used to produce this photograph.
[ARCHITECTURAL PHOTOGRAPHER'S STATEMENT]

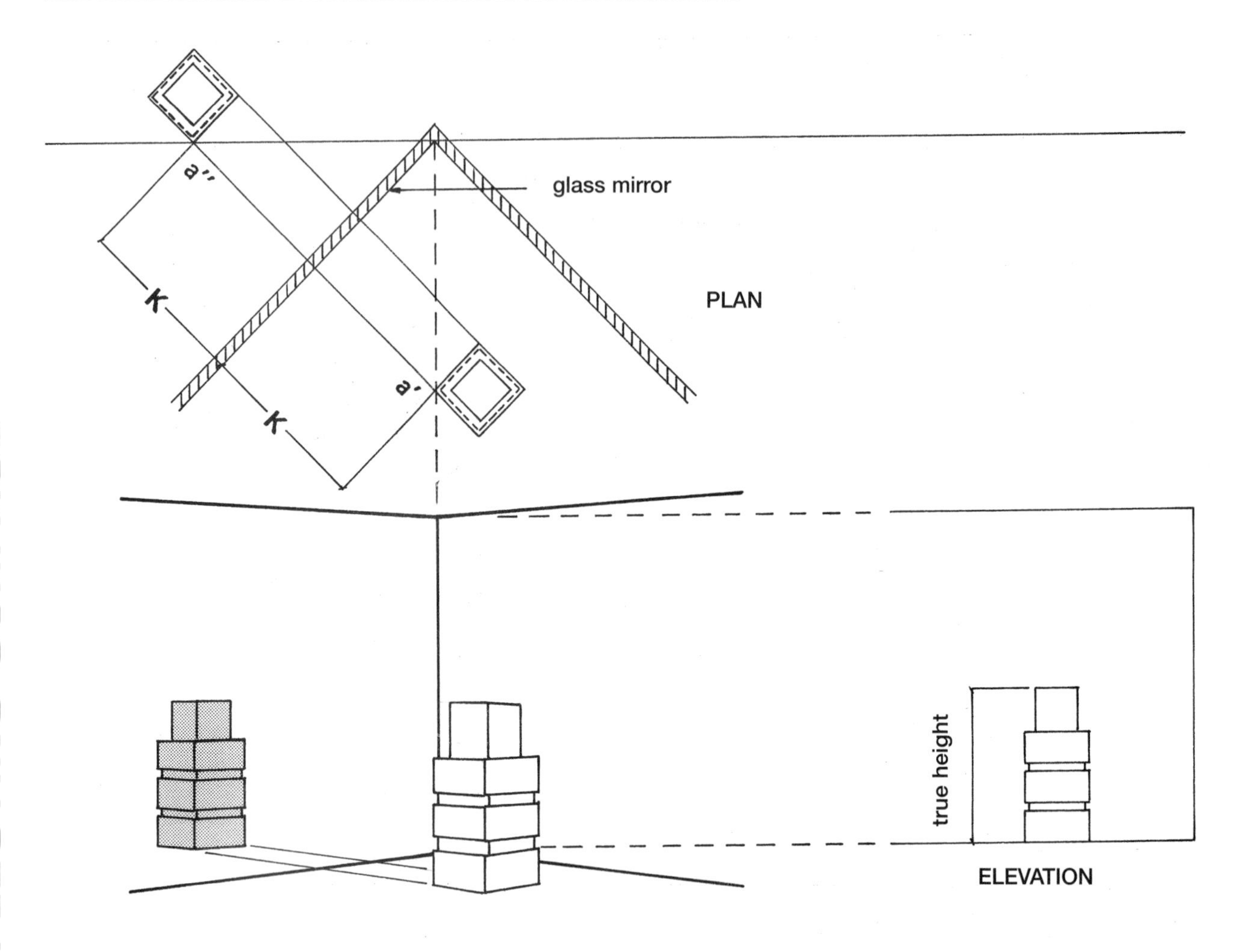

Drawing: Pico Partners, San Clemente, California
Courtesy of Architect: ARC-ID Corporation
Renderer: Robert J. Reynolds

It is common to have either interior perspective **views or urban landscape** perspective views where vertical reflecting surfaces (such as a mirror in this case and a building facade in the case study on the opposite page) give an added dimension to the perspective. The added dimension for a mirror is the optic expansion of a small interior space. This enlargement seen in the mirror usually shows parts of the room not seen from the perspective vantage point. For vertical reflections, the most important principles to remember are:

- A point such as **a'** in front of a reflecting surface is reflected back an **equal distance (K)** to its reflected image **a"**.
- A point **a'** and its corresponding reflected image **a"** always lie on a line **perpendicular** to the reflecting surface.
- The object and its reflected image follow the same rules for perspective construction.

This aerial view shows buildings being reflected into other buildings in a three-point perspective.

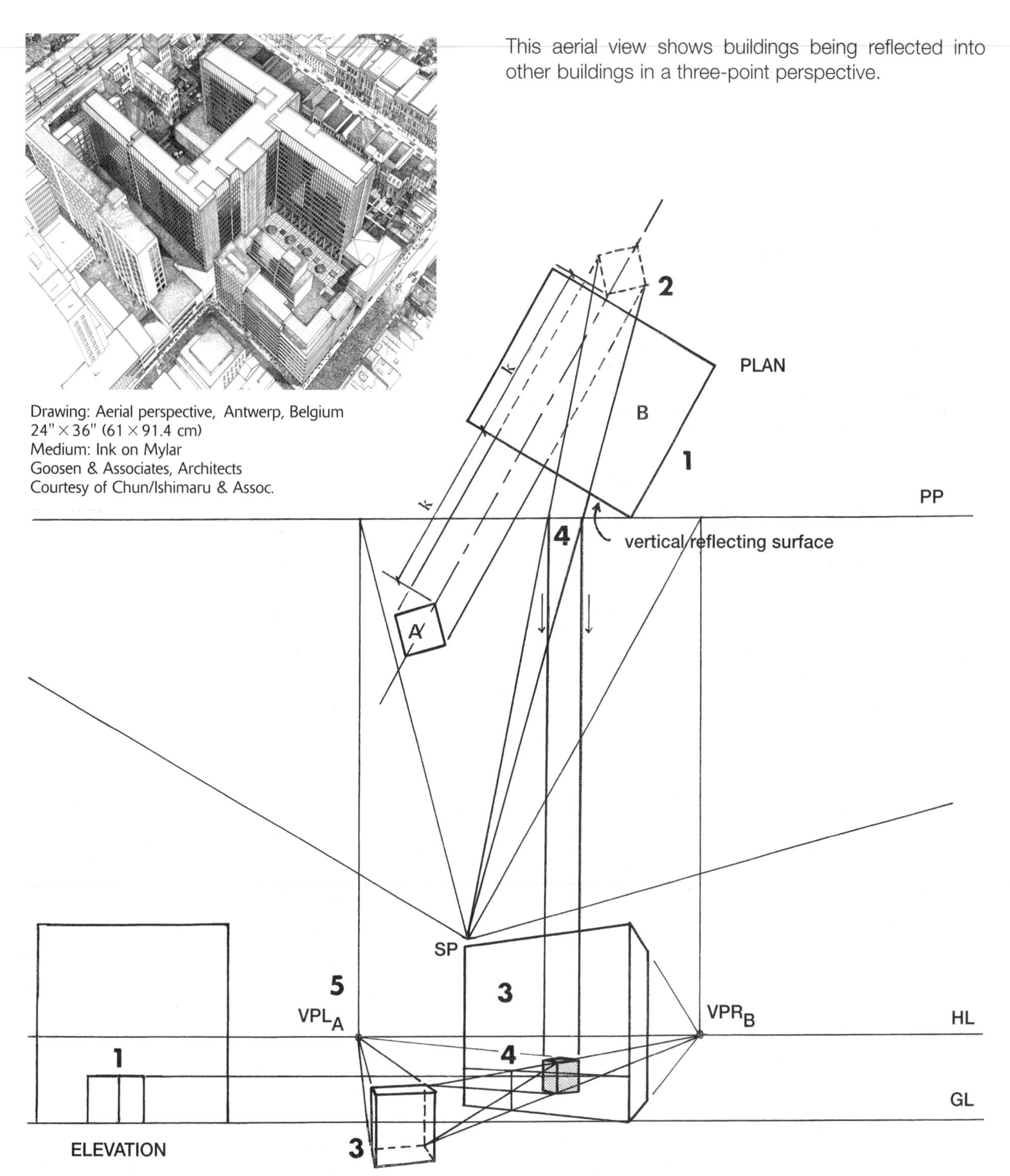

Drawing: Aerial perspective, Antwerp, Belgium
24" × 36" (61 × 91.4 cm)
Medium: Ink on Mylar
Goosen & Associates, Architects
Courtesy of Chun/Ishimaru & Assoc.

1. Construct plan and elevation views of the buildings (**A** and **B**) involved.
2. Construct the plan view of the building (**A**) reflected in a reverse image, an equal distance (k) beyond the reflecting surface.
3. Construct a two-point perspective of the reflecting surface and the building (**B**) being reflected.
4. Construct the reflected reverse image by first finding an image height on the reflecting surface and then projecting rays from the **SP** through the **PP** and down into the perspective view.
5. The reflected reverse image of the building uses the same set of vanishing points as the building itself.

The pavement in front of the building often occupies a significant portion of a perspective drawing. This seeming liability can be turned into an asset through the use of reflections. In this example, the reflections in the wet pavement are almost as detailed as the building and cars themselves and must be plotted as carefully as the rest of the drawing. When rendered, the reflection gradually fades away as it extends downward. The effect can be quite striking.
[ARCHITECTURAL ILLUSTRATOR'S STATEMENT]

Drawing: The Lytton Building, Palo Alto, California
Korth Sunseri Architects
Medium: Watercolor, 20½" X 12" (52.1 X 30.5 cm)
Courtesy of Stephan Hoffpauir, AIA

When there is very little air movement, reflections on a body of water become very sharp. In such instances a building at the water's edge will look almost as though it is being reflected in a mirror. The mood created under these conditions is one of placid tranquility.

To recreate this effect in an illustration, simply draw the building upside down. The reflection of the building should be rendered slightly darker than the building itself, and the vertical lines made somewhat wavy. This technique is particularly successful in elevations and has the advantage of being both easy and dramatic. [ARCHITECTURAL ILLUSTRATOR'S STATEMENT]

The circle in the water was to be a reflection of the moon. As the renderer completed the composition, he decided to omit it.

Drawings: Edoff Memorial Bandstand
Proposed reconstruction and seismic retrofitting
Oakland, California
12" × 21" (30.5 × 53.3 cm)
Medium: Watercolor
Courtesy of Stephan Hoffpauir, AIA

Step 1

Step 2

Once you understand linear perspective drawing, you can develop perspective views—from the rough to the finished form. In the profession of architectural illustration, this requires an understanding of the design of the project being illustrated, as well as skills in managing the balance, composition, and arrangement of a drawing's many elements. These drawings depict the process, from a rough layout to a line transfer to a detailed line drawing. The architectural illustrator must decide which way of representing a project will be most likely to lead the client to accept the design concept.

The project site was a narrow street/mall. The rough layout was done to determine the view and the relationship to the background building. The view of the final line transfer was done from a photograph supplied by the client to each competitor so that each scheme could be compared from the same fixed station point. Note the actual amount of background building that shows versus the perceived amount of the building that shows in the rough layout.
[ARCHITECTURAL ILLUSTRATOR'S STATEMENT]

Drawings: Peek & Cloppenburg Department Store competition winner
Leipzig, Germany
14" X 17" (35.6 X 43.2 cm)
Medium: Full watercolor over pencil line transfer
Moore Ruble Yudell, Architects
Courtesy of Al Forster, Architectural Illustrator

Step 3

Step 1

View Development

Step 1: For the rough block-out, human figures, cars, and tree forms are sketched in for scale, depth, and possible (or actual) placement.
Step 2: An entourage tracing paper overlay is used for clean figures, cars, etc. This can be done directly onto the rough block-out from Step 1.
Step 3: A final line sketch or pencil transfer incorporates building and entourage together. More tree detail is now added, as well as small, distant hand-drawn figures not necessarily on the entourage overlay.
[ARCHITECTURAL ILLUSTRATOR'S STATEMENT]

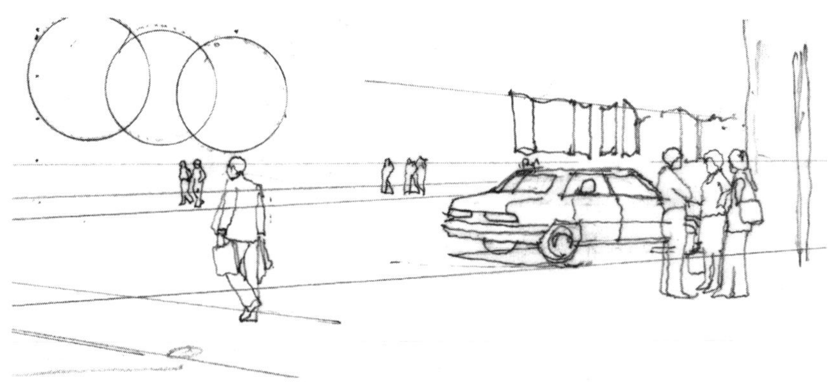

Step 2

Drawings: Sybase Hollis Street Campus
San Francisco, California
18" X 12" (45.7 X 30.5 cm)
Medium: Sketch watercolor on mounted presentation blackline print of pencil drawing
Robinson Mills & Williams, Architects
Courtesy of Al Forster, Architectural Illustrator

The advantage of a constructed perspective layout is that before the tone and values are finalized, the renderer can experiment with additions, deletions, and corrections to apparent distortions. Using overlays, tonal values and color can also be applied in varying degrees to help determine how to finalize the rendering.

Step 3

Written comments on the rough layout allow on-the-spot corrections, refinements, and adjustments and provide a record that can become a legal document for disputes that might arise later.
[ARCHITECTURAL ILLUSTRATOR'S STATEMENT]

Before

Drawings: Concept study, Riverwalk
Mixed-use project, San Diego, California
14" X 17" (35.6 X 43.2 cm)
Medium: Full watercolor over pencil line transfer
Robert A. M. Stern with Fehlman LaBarre Architects
Courtesy of Al Forster, Architectural Illustrator

View Development

An architect, designer, or renderer can experiment with a perspective layout by adding accessories such as cars, trees, and human figures (see Chapter 8, "Delineating and Rendering Entourage," for a more detailed coverage of perspective accessories). Even in the age of digital imaging, it is of utmost importance that students and design professionals develop good freehand techniques to draw accessories.

Compare the development of individual parts and pieces of the drawing in the before and after examples, as well as the illustrator's response to actual comments.
[ARCHITECTURAL ILLUSTRATOR'S STATEMENT]

After

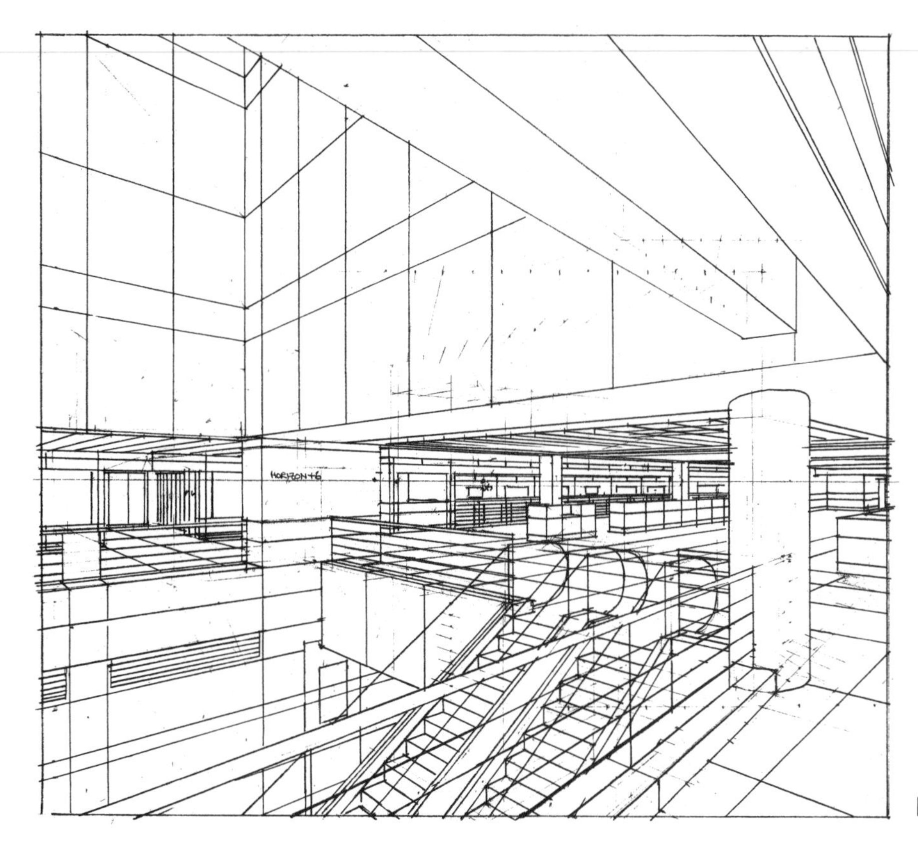

After providing a series of different preliminary layouts to find the most compelling and descriptive space view, this one was chosen for development. All the details and design elements were then drawn in collaboration with the architects so all the correct information would be included. The layout was completed by hand. By the time the illustrator was ready to draw the final black-and-white illustration, the layout was completed and ready to be rendered.
[ARCHITECTURAL ILLUSTRATOR'S STATEMENT]

Before

After the layout is completed, the rendering is done in pen and black ink. The focus of the drawing is, first of all, to show the main floor amenities; second, to show how busy the space is—people moving, buying stamps, using mailboxes; and finally, to draw attention to the multistory lobby that precedes the main floor.
[ARCHITECTURAL ILLUSTRATOR'S STATEMENT]

After

Drawings: Sears Tower Renovation Project, Chicago Main Post Office, Chicago, Illinois
Original size: (approx.) 24" X 20½" (61 X 52.1 cm), Scale used: ¼"= 1'-0"
Medium: Pen and ink
Courtesy of Knight Architects Engineers Planners, Inc., and
Manuel Avila Associates, Architectural Illustrator

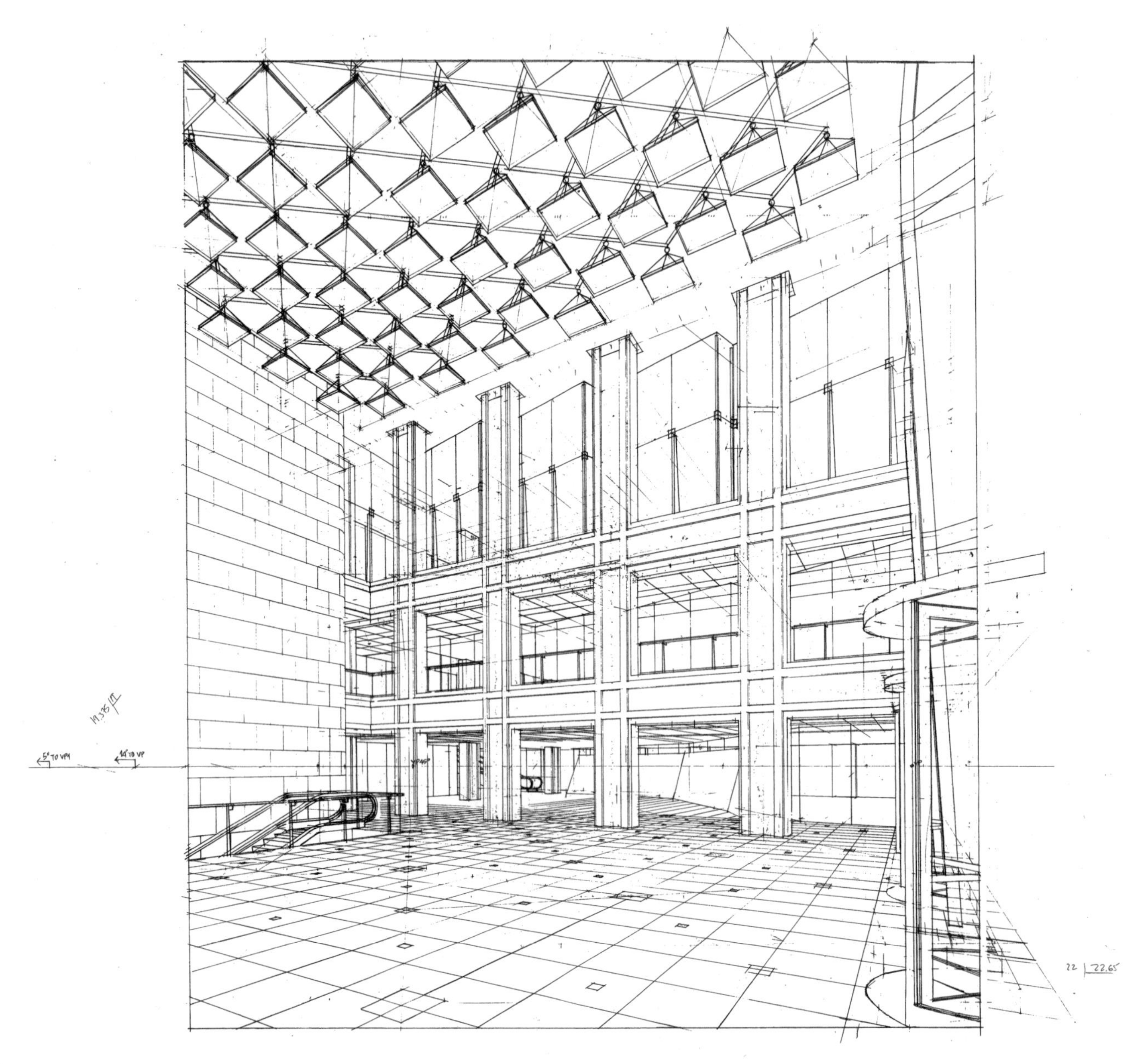

Drawing: Sears Tower Renovation Project, Chicago, Illinois
DeStefano & Partners, Architects
Courtesy of Manuel Avila Associates, Architectural Illustrator

To establish the proportions and the size of the new, enlarged interior space (the original space consisted of only two floors, not three), we set ourselves as close to the entrance wall as we could to show the full extension of the room, with all the new floor materials, new clad columns, and glass walls. We always try to show three sides of a room to communicate enclosement (see p. 264). Although the entrance wall can only be partially seen, we emphasized its presence with the sunlight coming in.
[Architectural Illustrator's statement]

Drawing: Sears Tower Renovation Project, Chicago, Illinois
DeStefano & Partners, Architects
Courtesy of Manuel Avila Associates, Architectural Illustrator

In this interior, the space was flooded with shadows to establish different levels of contrast because the materials used were basically light. The different levels of contrast in shadows and reflections were achieved first by the use of pen and ink, followed by the use of colored pencil to saturate and emphasize forms. To make the illustration more complete, people were drawn very carefully and in detail, to bring more reality to the floor activity.
[ARCHITECTURAL ILLUSTRATOR'S STATEMENT]

7

Light, Shade, and Shadow

BASICS. 307
BASICS APPLIED 334

Light allows us to have vision. With light we can structure and put order into the environment. It enhances our senses for experiencing architecture as we move through space over a period of time. The experience of the three-dimensional or sculptural quality of a building largely depends on the direction of sunlight hitting its surfaces. Buildings become alive when light strikes them at different angles. Your awareness of this aids in your design decisions. A thorough knowledge and understanding of light and the application of shades and shadows to presentations of the built environment helps to further client–architect understanding during the design process. Shadows accent orthographic (particularly elevations and site plans), paraline, and perspective drawings, adding a sense of clarity and substance to the represented forms.

The intent of this chapter is to develop your ability to draw and construct shades and shadows in plan, elevation, paraline, and perspective drawings.

The following are some of the important terms and concepts you will learn:

How to construct shades and shadows in plans, elevations, axonometrics, obliques, and perspectives

Light	Shade	Shadow	Casting edge
Altitude	Azimuth	Sun's bearing	Vanishing point of sun's rays

Light, Shade, and Shadow

TOPICS: CASTING EDGE, VERTICAL CASTING EDGE, ALTITUDE AND AZIMUTH, SUN'S BEARING, SUN BEARING VANISHING POINT, SUN'S RAY, SUN RAY VANISHING POINT, SUN RAY TRIANGLE, HORIZONTAL CASTING EDGE, SHADOWS IN PLAN

Ching 2003, 144–56.

Ching 1990, 130–33.

Pérez-Gomez and Pelletier 2000, 111–24.

Porter and Goodman 1985, 22–27.

Chapter Overview

After studying this chapter and doing the related exercises in the book's final section, you will learn how to cast shadows in plan, in elevation, in paralines, and in perspectives. For continued study, refer to Forseth's *Graphics for Architecture* and Lockard's *Design Drawing.*

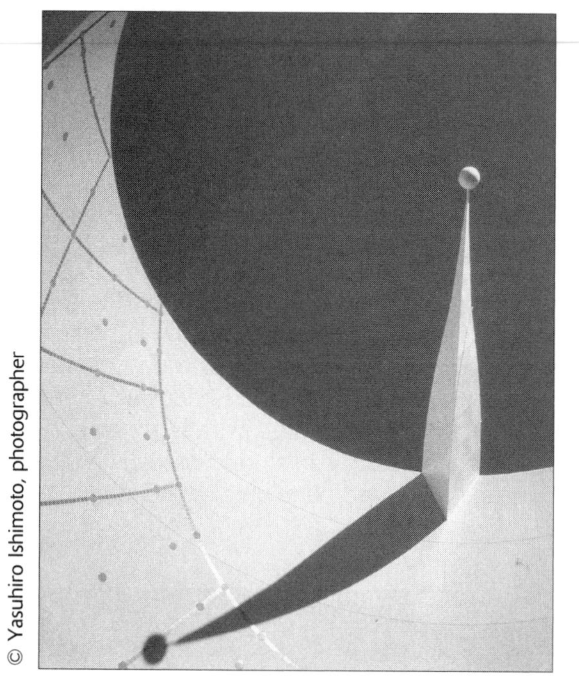

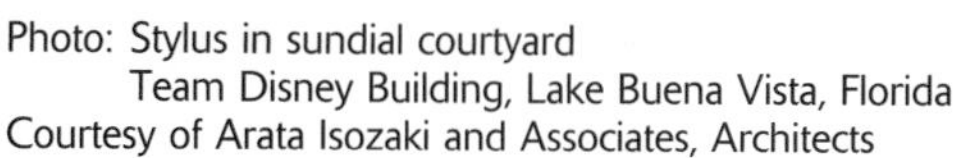
Photo: Stylus in sundial courtyard
Team Disney Building, Lake Buena Vista, Florida
Courtesy of Arata Isozaki and Associates, Architects

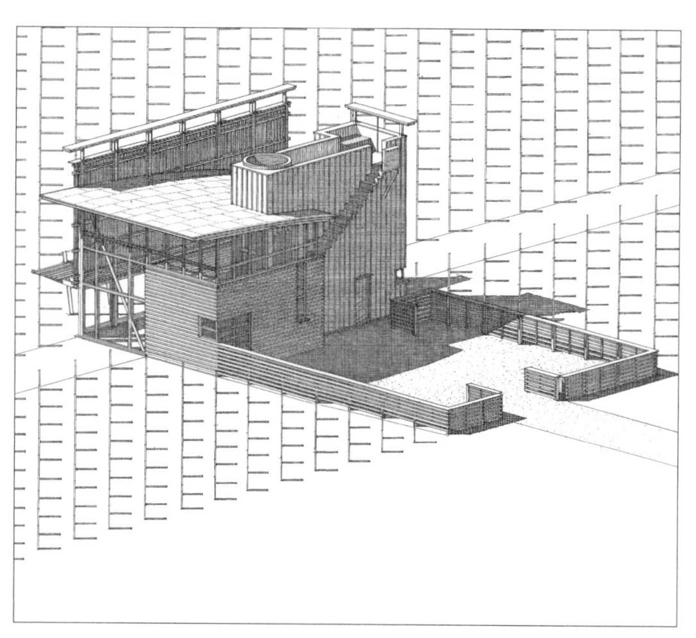
Drawing: A small lodge, Saint Helena, California
24" × 24" (61 × 61 cm), Scale: ¼"=1'0"
Medium: Ink on Mylar
Courtesy of Brian Healy Architects

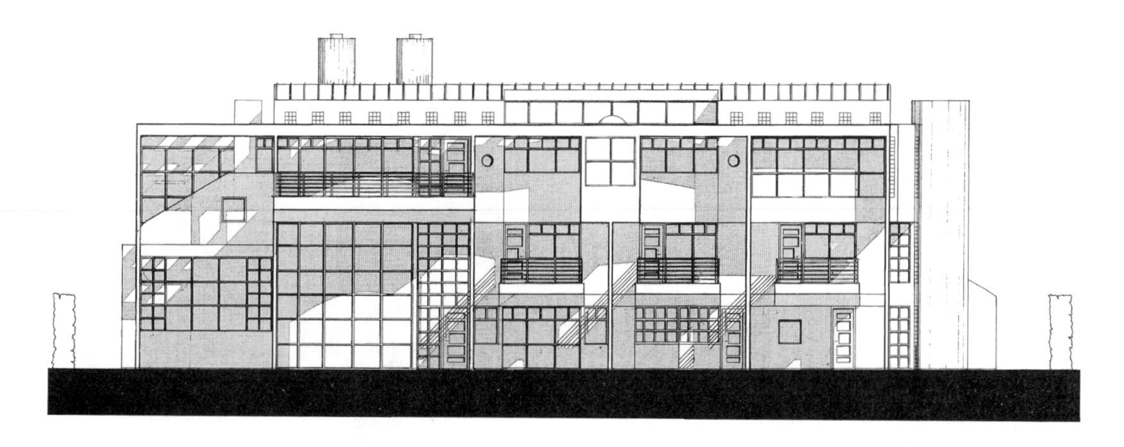
Drawing: Meyer residence, Malibu, California
Medium: Ink on Mylar
Courtesy of Gwathmey Siegel & Associates, Architects

During the day, our shadow is our constant companion, whether or not we are aware of it (see p. 209). There is also constantly shade on those parts of our bodies not in direct light. We perceive shades and shadows on both animate and inanimate objects. From experience, most of us can sense why an object's shadow takes on a certain geometric configuration. However, that shadow sense is inadequate for architectural students, architectural illustrators, and architects. To properly convey a design concept, it is imperative to learn how to construct precise shadow drawings.

Four terms can appropriately describe our timeless response to and interpretation of shadows: (1) mysterious, (2) vague, (3) dramatic, and (4) dimensional. Dimensional refers to a shadow's unique property of delineating form and scale in the urban landscape. Shades and shadows were of utmost importance in providing depth to the facades for front elevations during the early periods of architecture. The added illusion of depth was aesthetically pleasing. It clarified overlapping elements on the facade to the layperson. Knowing how to delineate and draw shades and shadows helps us to better understand spatial concepts in our designs. **Sciagraphy** is the science of shade and shadow graphics and is an indispensable tool for architects, designers, and delineators. Sciagraphy provides a tool for obtaining a finished and realistic appearance to any drawing.

The illustration below left emulates the work of the late professional renderer Hugh Ferriss. It is rendered to give form to a lighting quality that has mystery and drama. The other illustration typifies the meticulous delineation techniques that were instilled by the nineteenth-century École des Beaux Arts. Light, shade, and shadow are purposely articulated to create artificial lighting effects for compositions of classical details. Shadows play an important role in conceptual design stages of contemporary graphic strategies. Fenestration patterns on conceptual elevations are visually articulated and enhanced by the use of shadows. These studies of the interplay of solids, voids, and inclined planes give a surface modulation to make interrelated parts understandable.

Drawing: Student project by Ed Yeomans
Rudder Tower
18" × 24" (45.7 × 61 cm)
Medium: Charcoal
Courtesy of Texas A&M University
Department of Architecture

Drawing: Student project by Eberhard Lenz
Classical details
18.5" × 25.5" (47 × 64.8 cm)
Medium: Ink wash
Courtesy of Washington University
School of Architecture, St. Louis, Missouri

The application of sciagraphy is of great importance to the design professional. Light, shade, and shadow define form and space. A **shadow** indicates the shape of the object casting the shadow and can in many ways indicate the texture of the surface receiving the shadow. When **light rays** are intercepted by an object, the portion of the object on the light side will be illuminated, while the portion opposite the light side will be protected from the light rays. This shielded portion can be defined as **shade.** The boundary line that separates light from shade determines the **shadow line** on a receiving surface. The boundary of the shadow line determines the dark area cast onto the surface on which the object rests and which receives the cast **shadow.** To produce a shadow, three conditions are required:

1. A **light source**
2. An **object** to cast the shadow line, or to intercept the light ray
3. A **surface** to receive the shadow line and shadow

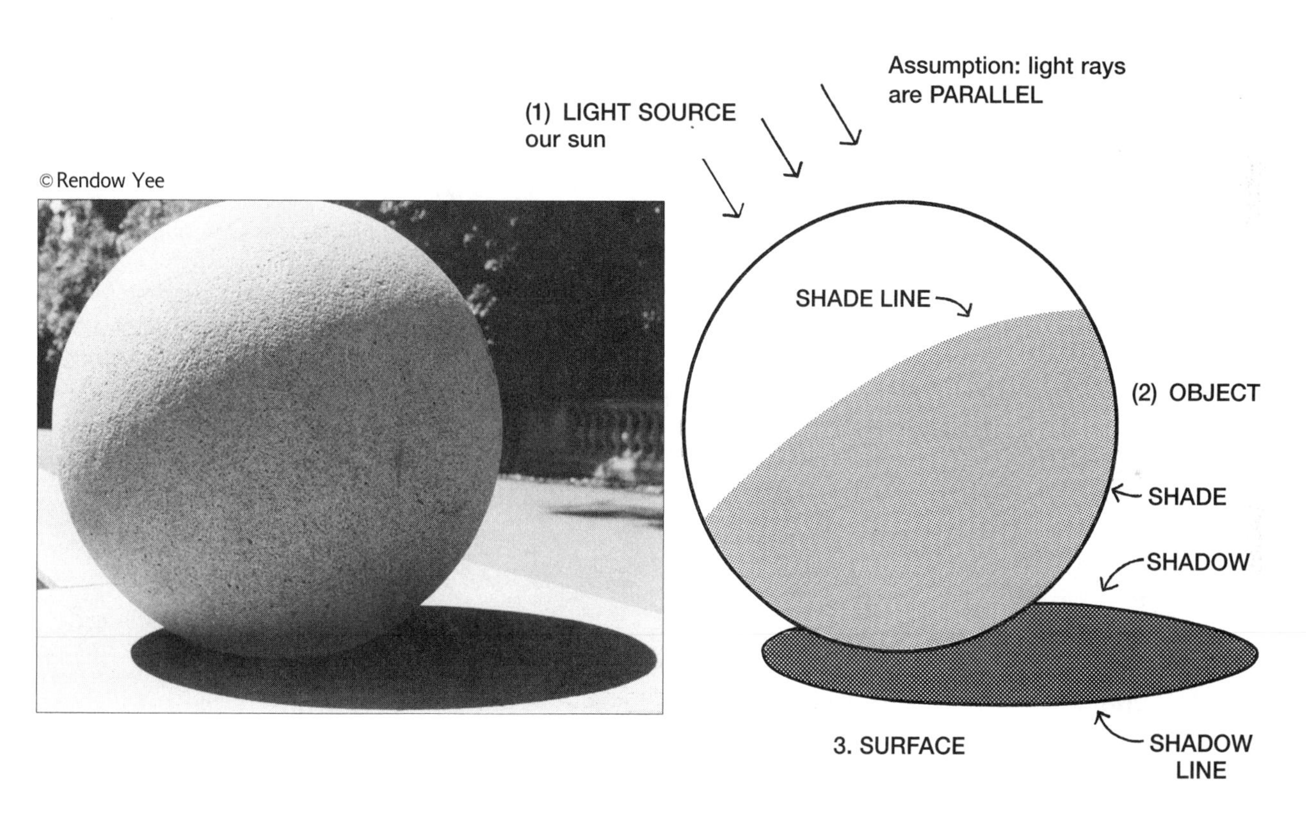

Basic Shadow Concepts

Due to the enormous distance of the earth from the sun, the light rays from the sun are considered to be parallel (in reality, the rays are divergent). This condition can be contrasted with artificial light, which produces radiating rays of light because of the proximity of the light source. The photograph of the spherical solid above shows that humans see shade and shadow at approximately the same value intensity or darkness. When sketching, the gradual transition in tone from shade to light seen in the photo is described as a "soft-edge" area. A sharply defined border such as the edge of the shade area is described as "hard edge." In architectural drawings, shadow is usually shown darker than shade, regardless of the sketching or rendering medium.

The direction of solar rays is identifed by two angles described as **bearing** and **azimuth.** Both bearing and azimuth are measured only in the plan view. The bearing acute angle of an inclined line is always measured in degrees.

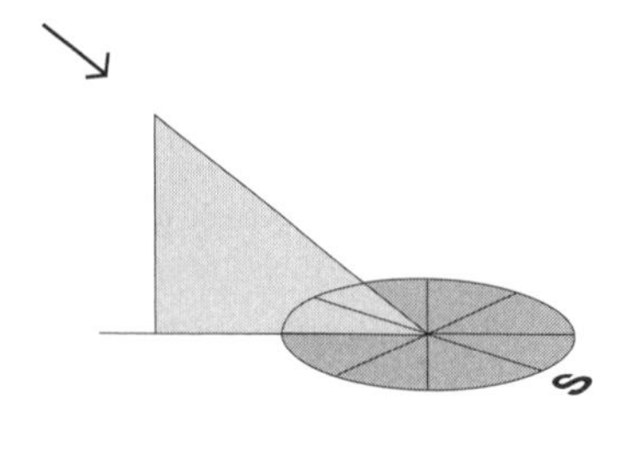

Example
N 45° W is a bearing
or
315° azimuth

Light rays are notated by their **bearing** relative to due north or south, and their **azimuth** is measured clockwise from due north.

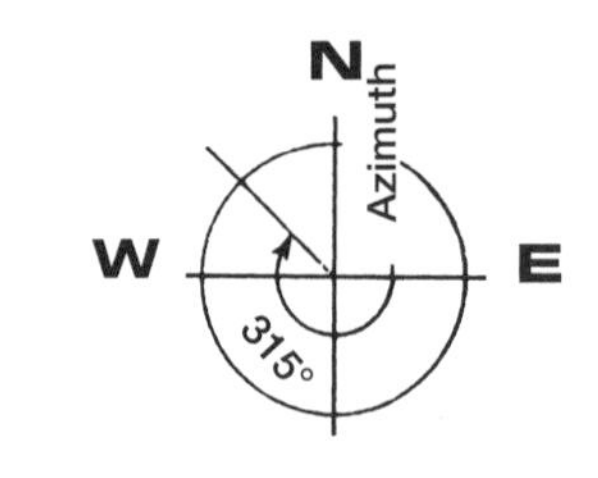

Altitude is the angle between the sun's position in the sky vault and the earth's horizontal plane for a given latitude.

Azimuth is the angle between the sun's bearing and a horizontal line that is in a plane perpendicular to the horizontal plane of the earth's surface.

Latitude is the angular distance north or south from the equator measured in degrees on the meridian of a point.

Longitude is the angular distance east or west between the meridian of a particular place and that of Greenwich, England, expressed in degrees.

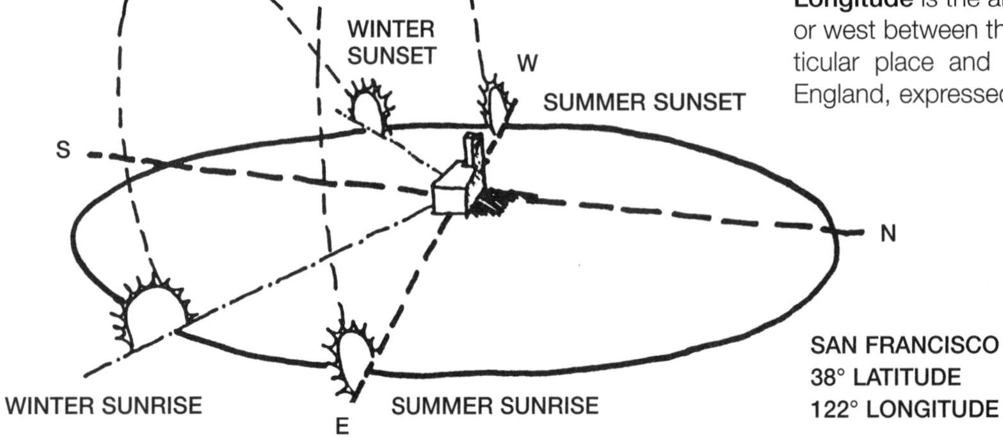

SAN FRANCISCO BAY AREA
38° LATITUDE
122° LONGITUDE

Sun path diagram: Courtesy of Thomas L. Turman, Professor
11" × 8½" (27.9 × 21.6 cm)
Medium: Ink (freehand)
Laney College Department of Architecture

Solar Angle Diagrams/Definitions

One of the most important factors in architectural design is natural sunlight. How the sun moves across the sky in different geographic locations affects how architects design for each place, because architects are concerned about radiant heat energy and the design of shading devices for buildings.

Solstice is defined as either of the two times a year when the sun is at its greatest distance from the celestial equator. The summer solstice occurs about June 21, and the winter solstice occurs about December 21. In North America, which is in the Northern Hemisphere, June 21 marks the sun's highest point in the sky and thus the longest solar day, whereas December 21 marks the sun's lowest point in the sky and thus the shortest solar day. A solar day is from 12 o'clock noon to 12 o'clock noon. The simple diagram above is for the San Francisco Bay Area in the United States.

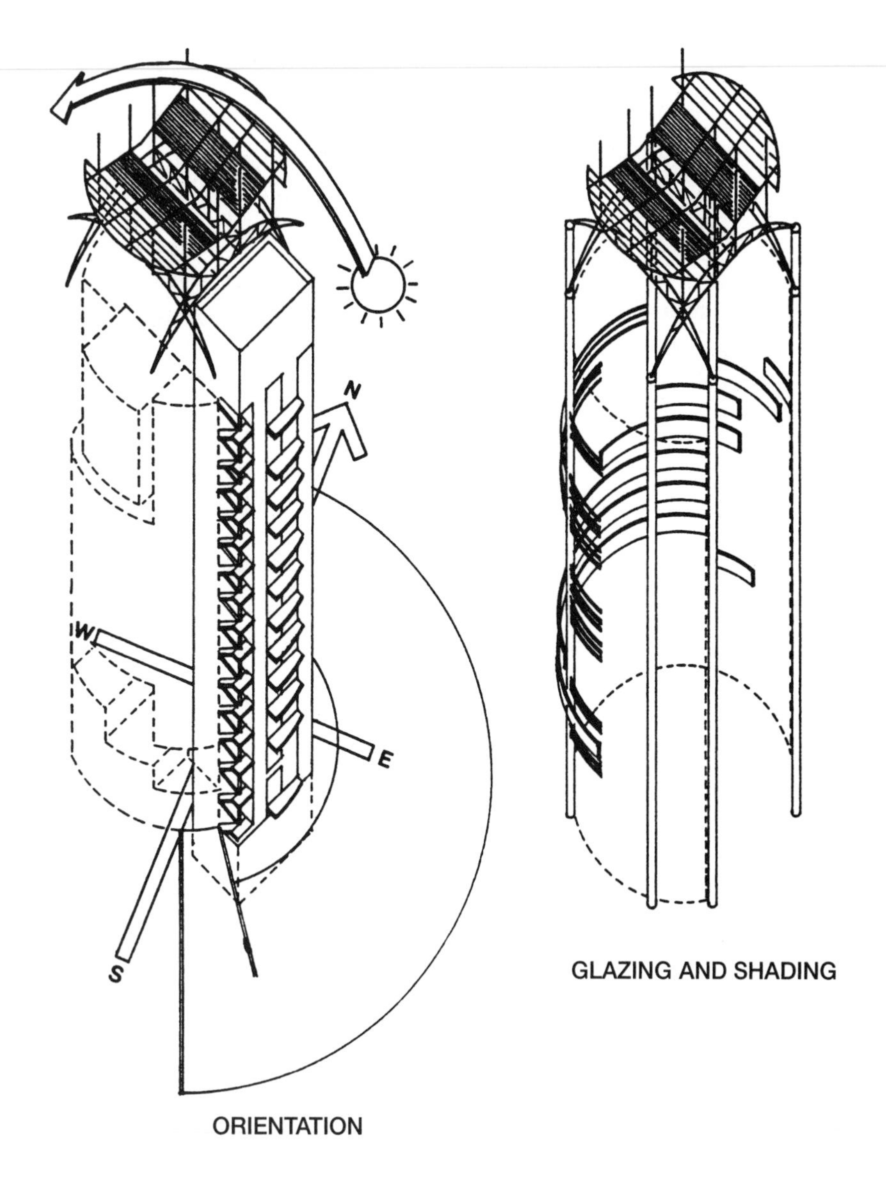

ORIENTATION

GLAZING AND SHADING

Drawing: Menara Mesiniaga (IBM Tower)
Selangor, Malaysia
T. R. Hamzah & Yeang, Architects

Solar Angle Diagrams

Tall buildings are more exposed to the full impact of the sun and heat than low-rise structures. Office towers throughout the world do not adapt to their local climates; they fight them, using the twentieth century's arsenal of mechanical systems such as air conditioning, artificial light, and heating.
[ARCHITECT'S STATEMENT]

Perspective solar angle diagrams are the most difficult and most complex of all shadow diagrams for the beginner. For this reason, this chapter progressively examines shadow constructions, starting with prismatic forms in orthographic views. It then focuses on common construction situations in elevations, such as overhangs, canopies, colonnades, arcades, stairs, niches, dormers, and inclines. This is followed by a study of paraline shadow constructions, and, finally, perspective shadow constructions. Rendering techniques for using shades and shadows to accentuate architectural form and space are explored in Chapter 8.

Drawing: West Adams Place, Los Angeles, California
36" × 24" (91.4 × 61 cm)
Medium: Ink
Courtesy of John V. Mutlow FAIA, Architects, and Iraj Yamin Esfandiary, Illustrator

These building solids cast shadows and show shade with a line hatching technique (shadow darker than shade). The foreground road has the heaviest hatching.

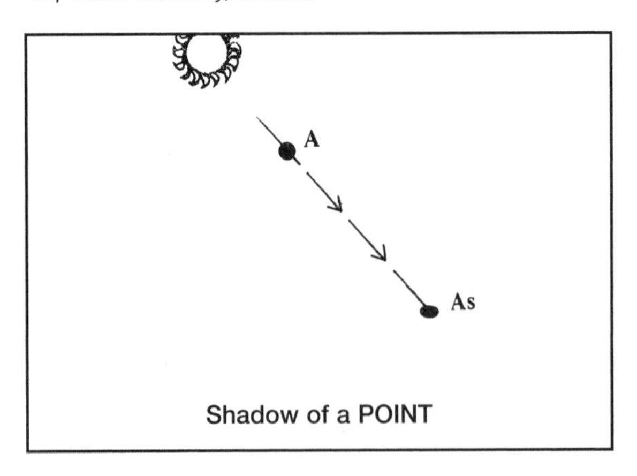

Shadow of a POINT

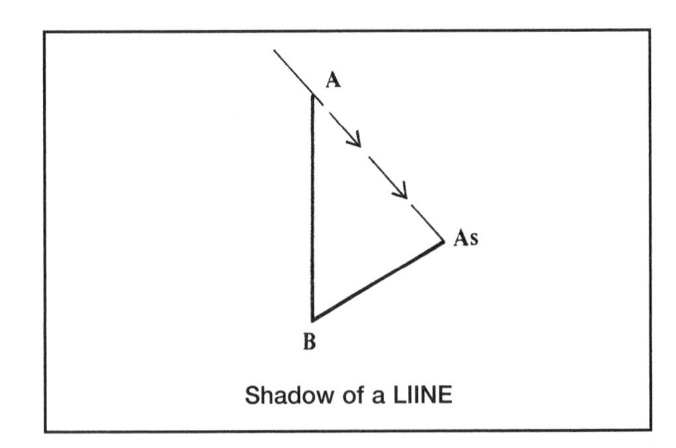

Shadow of a LIINE

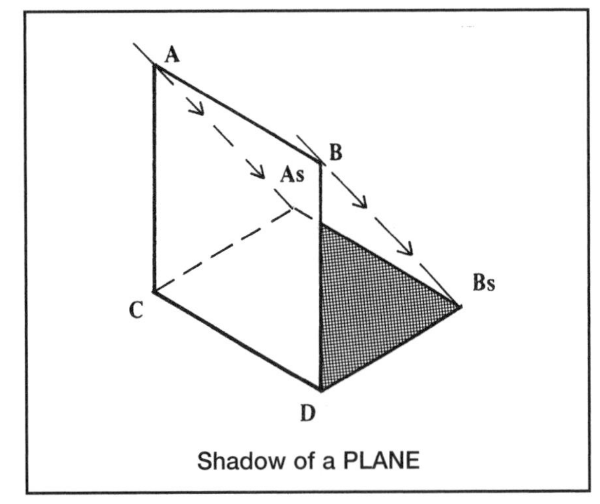

Shadow of a PLANE

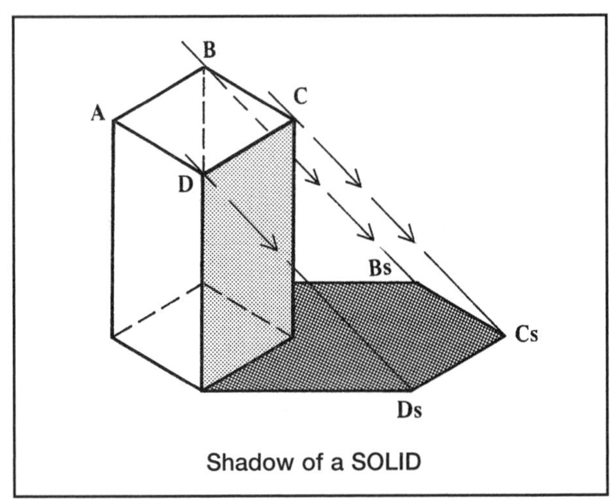

Shadow of a SOLID

Shadow development can be analyzed by studying shadow progressions from points to lines to planes and finally to solids. Begin by studying point shadows, since a finite series of points will ultimately:

1. Determine shadows of **lines** (lines being composed of points)
2. Determine shadows of **planes** (planes being composed of lines)
3. Determine shadows of **solids** (solids being composed of planes)

The shadow of a line, a plane, or a solid is most efficiently determined by locating the shadows of the **critical** points of the line, plane, or solid.

Drawing: Site plan of housing at Shakujii Park
Tokyo, Japan
Medium: Ink on Mylar
Courtesy of Shigeru Ban Architects

Shadow Principles

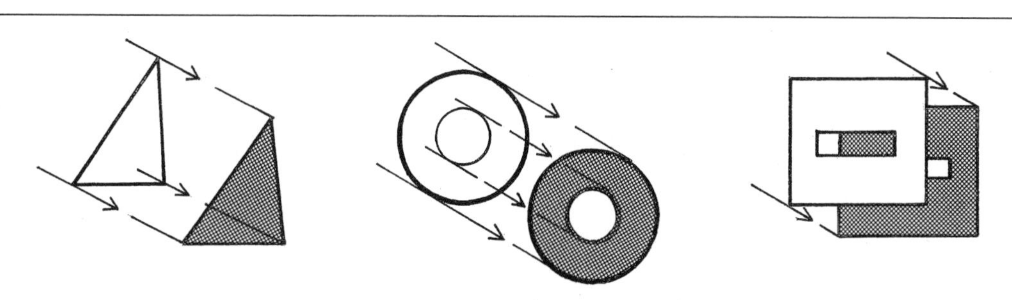

The shadow of a plane figure on a parallel plane is identical in size, shape, and orientation to the figure. The more distant the parallel plane (triangle and donut), the more shadow will show.

For architectural graphics, a 45° angle light ray direction from the left in plan and in elevation is conventionally used. In cubic form this can be represented by the diagonal of a cube with a slope of 35°15'52" (θ). Also commonly used is a 45° angle light ray direction from the right. Note that the **slope** angle of the light ray is the inclination relative to the horizontal plane.

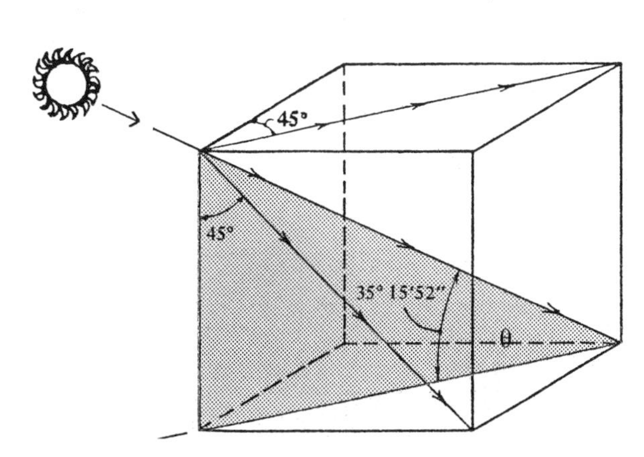

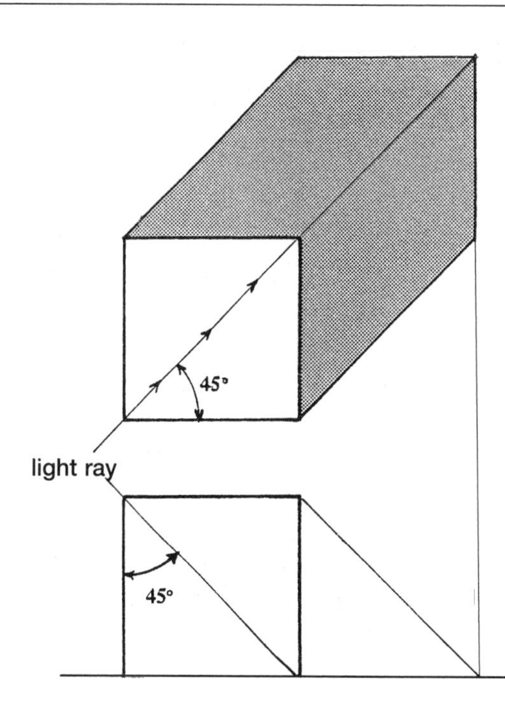

Drawing: Erectheum house, San Francisco, California
12" × 20" (30.5 × 50.8 cm), Scale: ¼"=1'0"
Media: Pencil, Prismacolor, pastel, Zipatone
Courtesy of Kotas/Pantaleoni, Architects
Jeremy Kotas

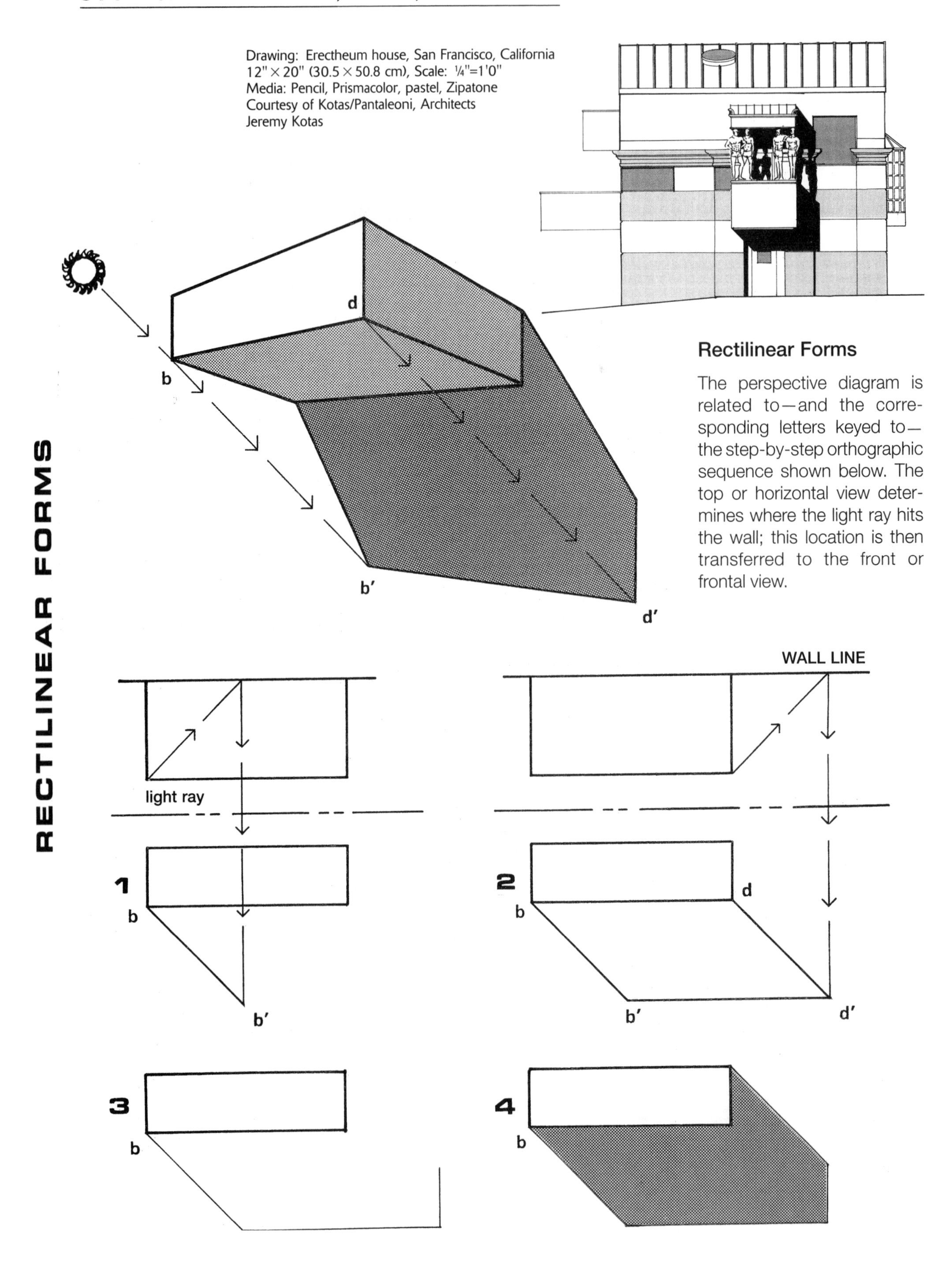

Rectilinear Forms

The perspective diagram is related to—and the corresponding letters keyed to—the step-by-step orthographic sequence shown below. The top or horizontal view determines where the light ray hits the wall; this location is then transferred to the front or frontal view.

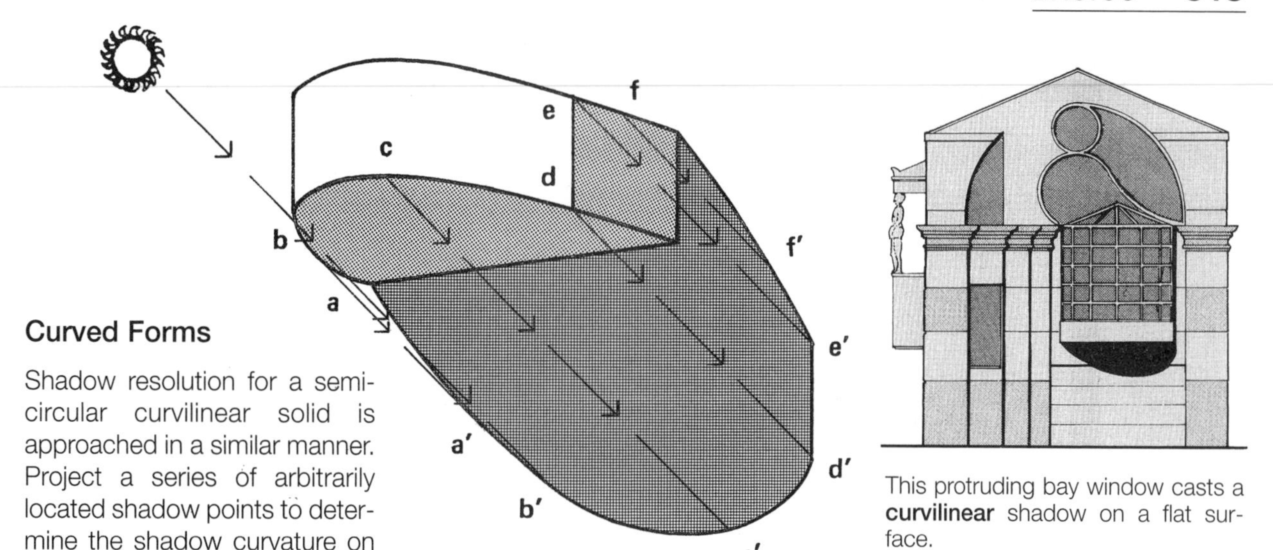

This protruding bay window casts a **curvilinear** shadow on a flat surface.

Drawing: Erectheum house, San Francisco, California
12" × 20" (30.5 × 50.8 cm), Scale: ¼"=1'0"
Media: Pencil, Prismacolor, pastel, Zipatone
Courtesy of Kotas/Pantaleoni, Architects
Jeremy Kotas

Curved Forms

Shadow resolution for a semicircular curvilinear solid is approached in a similar manner. Project a series of arbitrarily located shadow points to determine the shadow curvature on the wall. Remember that every point on the line that separates light from shade **(shade line)** will cast a shadow point on the **shadow line.**

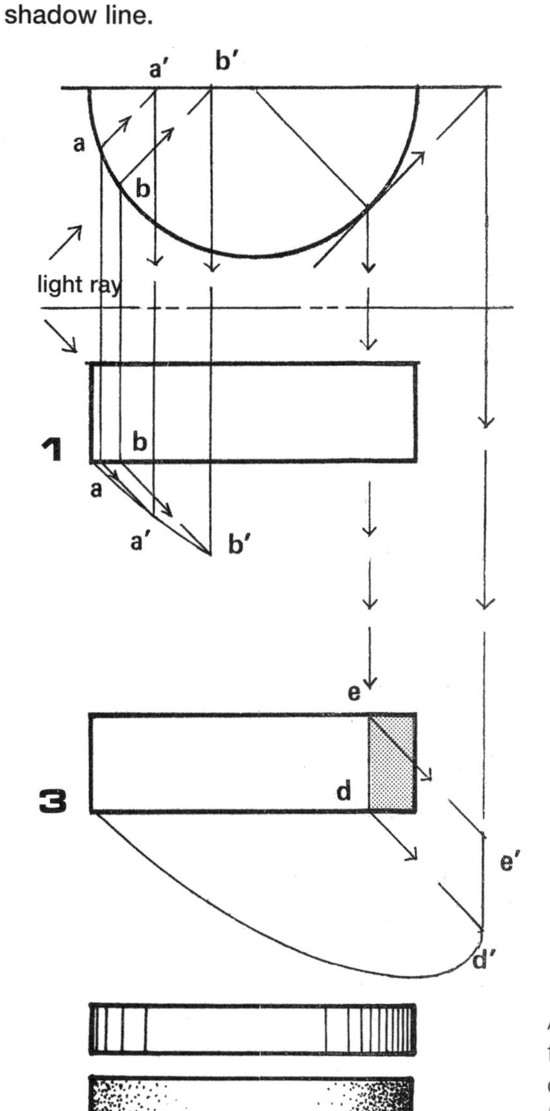

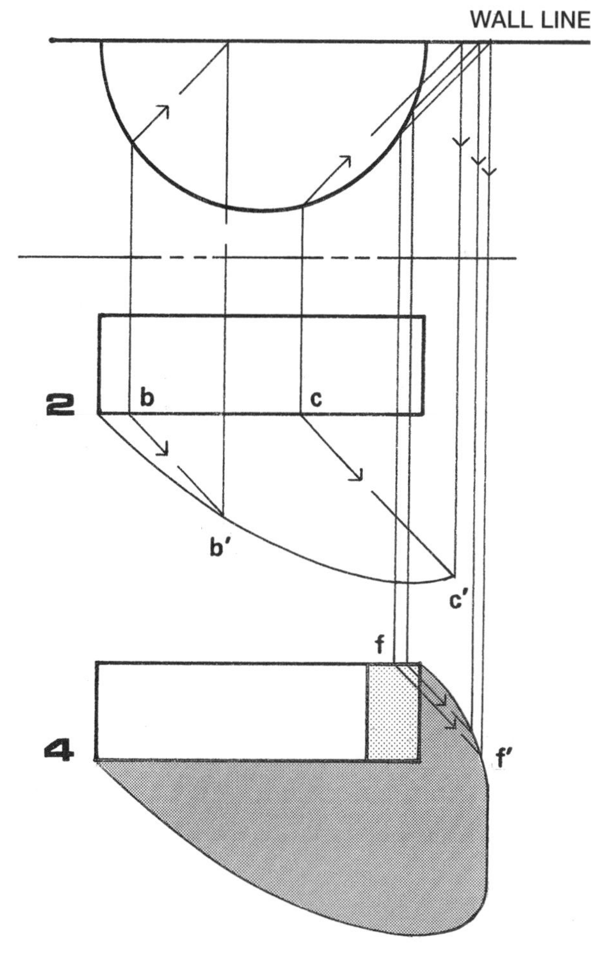

A cylindrical or curvilinear surface always appears flat in the front elevation. Use a series of unequally spaced fine lines or increasing dot density instead of a uniform shade density to create a feeling of depth (see pp. 103–04).

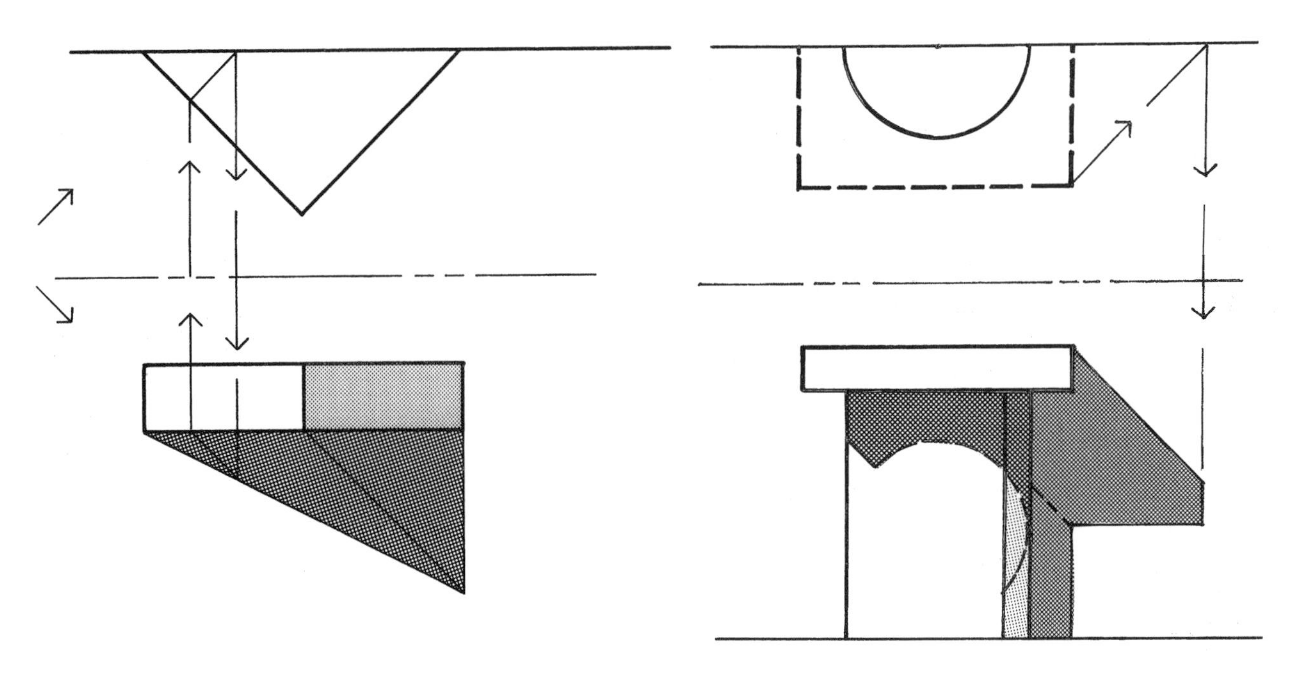

Elevation View Shadows

The study of wall condition shadows for various geometric forms, such as the previously described rectilinear and curvilinear forms and the variety shown on this page, provides the necessary framework for the analogous situations encountered in site plan and roof plan shadows. This analogy becomes apparent by turning any wall condition drawing upside down: the "wall line" then becomes the "ground line," and the "wall object" becomes the object seen in the plan view.

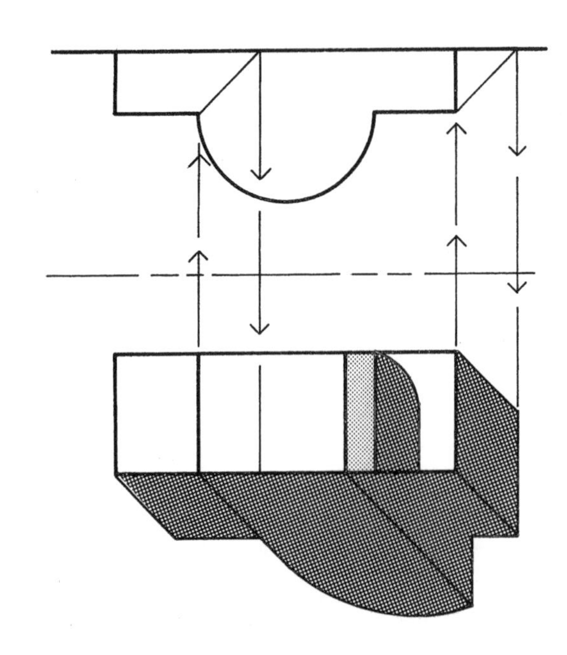

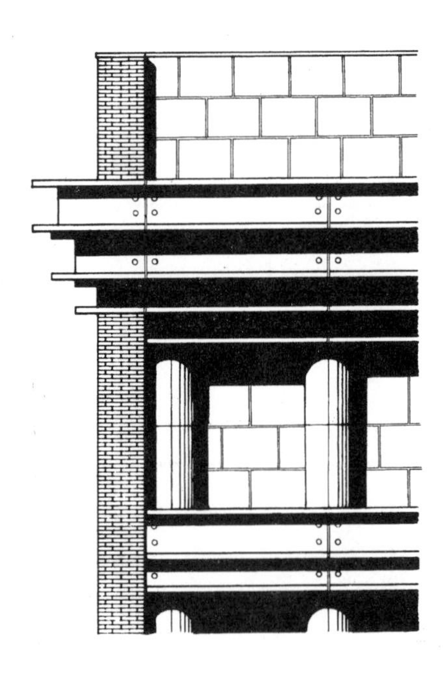

Partial elevation: Hotel Il Palazzo
Fukuoka, Japan
18" × 24" (45.7 × 61 cm), Scale: 1:50 m
Medium: Black ink on Mylar
Courtesy of Aldo Rossi, Studio di Architettura
New York, Architect

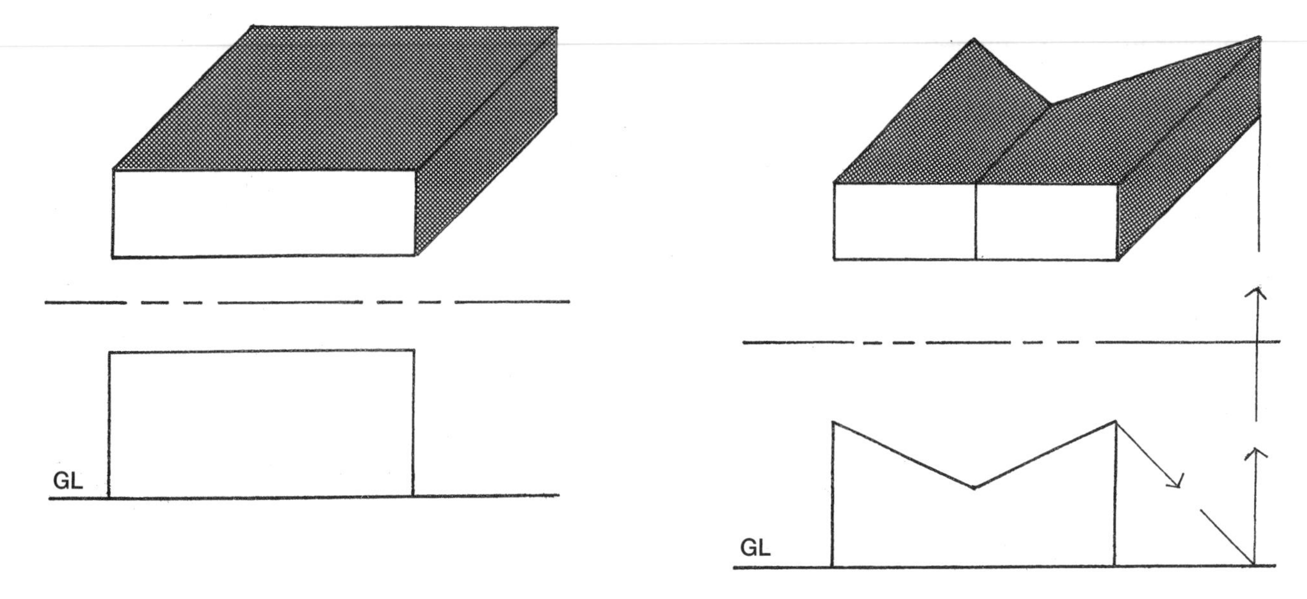

Plan View Shadows

These drawings illustrate the analogy between wall elevation shadows and site/roof plan shadows. The height of the solid forms above the "ground line" determines the length of the shadow cast in the plan view. Note that by simply turning the drawing upside down and switching the plan and elevation views, wall elevation conditions result.

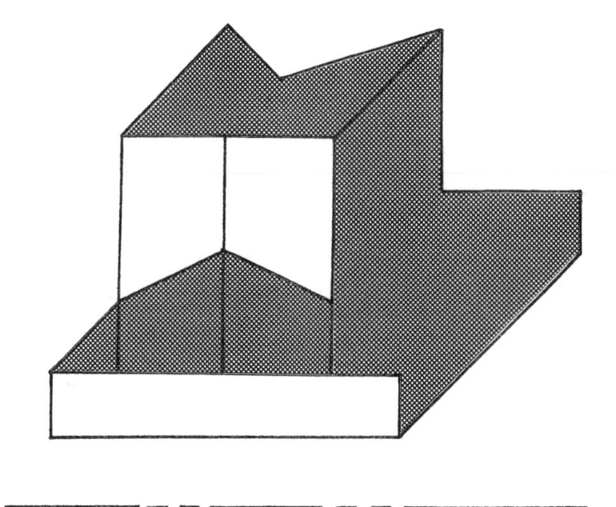

Drawing: Town Square, four houses and chapel
Port Ludlow, Washington
Scale: 1"=40'0"
Medium: Pen and ink
Courtesy of Steven Holl Architects

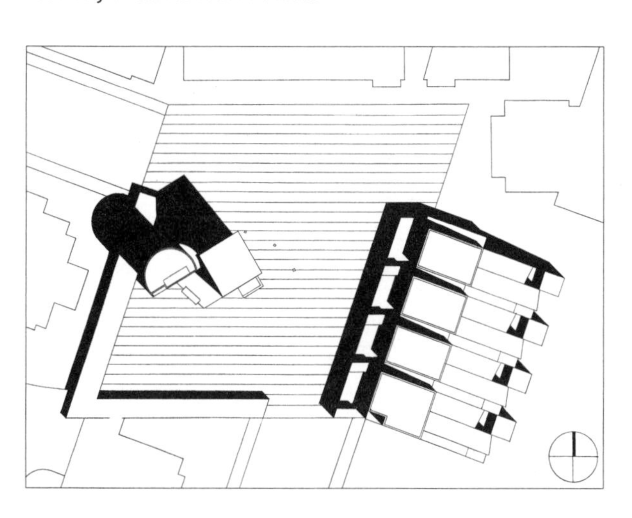

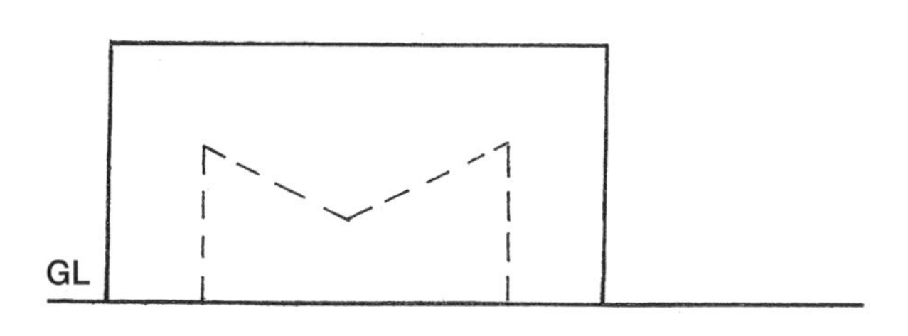

Singular Forms Combined

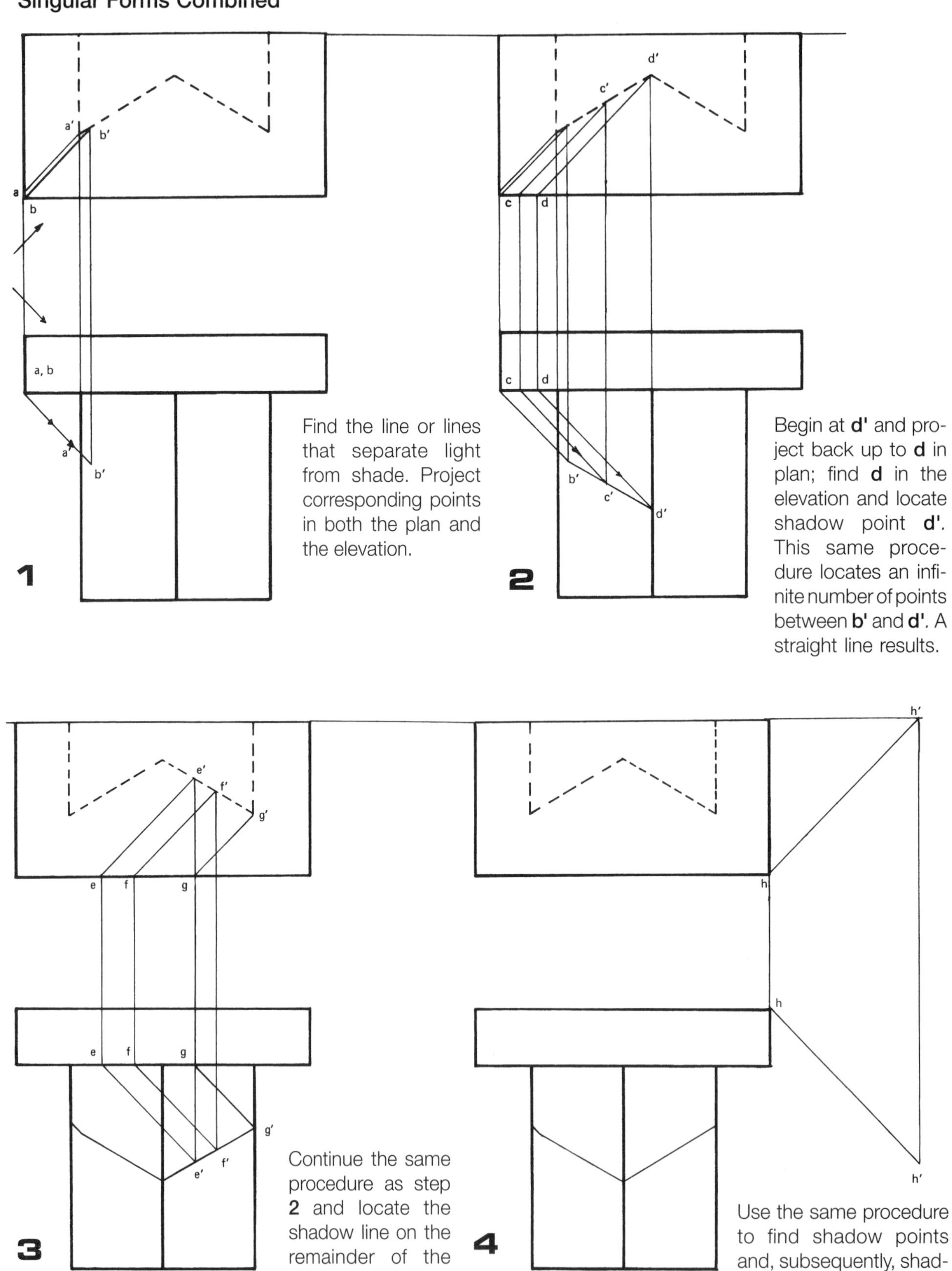

Find the line or lines that separate light from shade. Project corresponding points in both the plan and the elevation.

Begin at **d'** and project back up to **d** in plan; find **d** in the elevation and locate shadow point **d'**. This same procedure locates an infinite number of points between **b'** and **d'**. A straight line results.

Continue the same procedure as step **2** and locate the shadow line on the remainder of the object.

Use the same procedure to find shadow points and, subsequently, shadow lines on the wall.

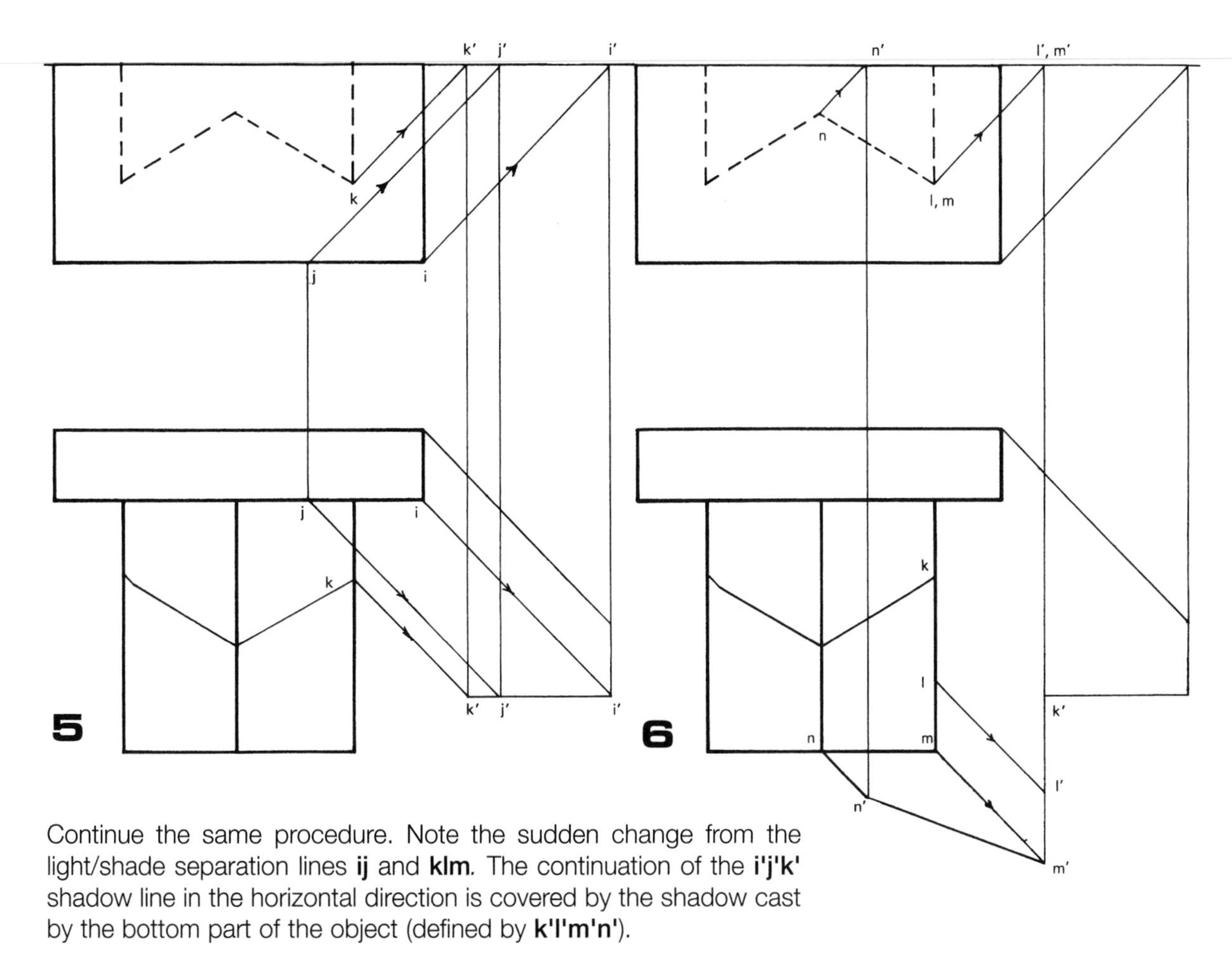

Continue the same procedure. Note the sudden change from the light/shade separation lines **ij** and **klm**. The continuation of the **i'j'k'** shadow line in the horizontal direction is covered by the shadow cast by the bottom part of the object (defined by **k'l'm'n'**).

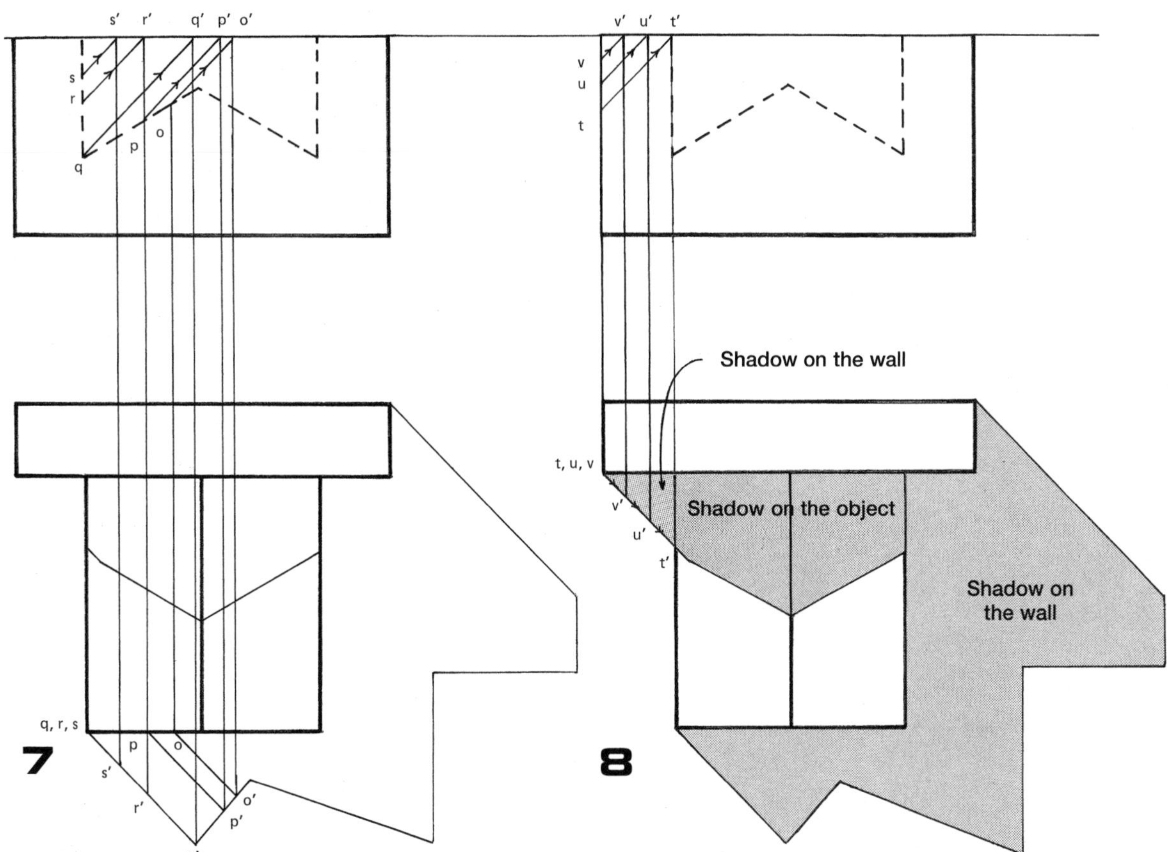

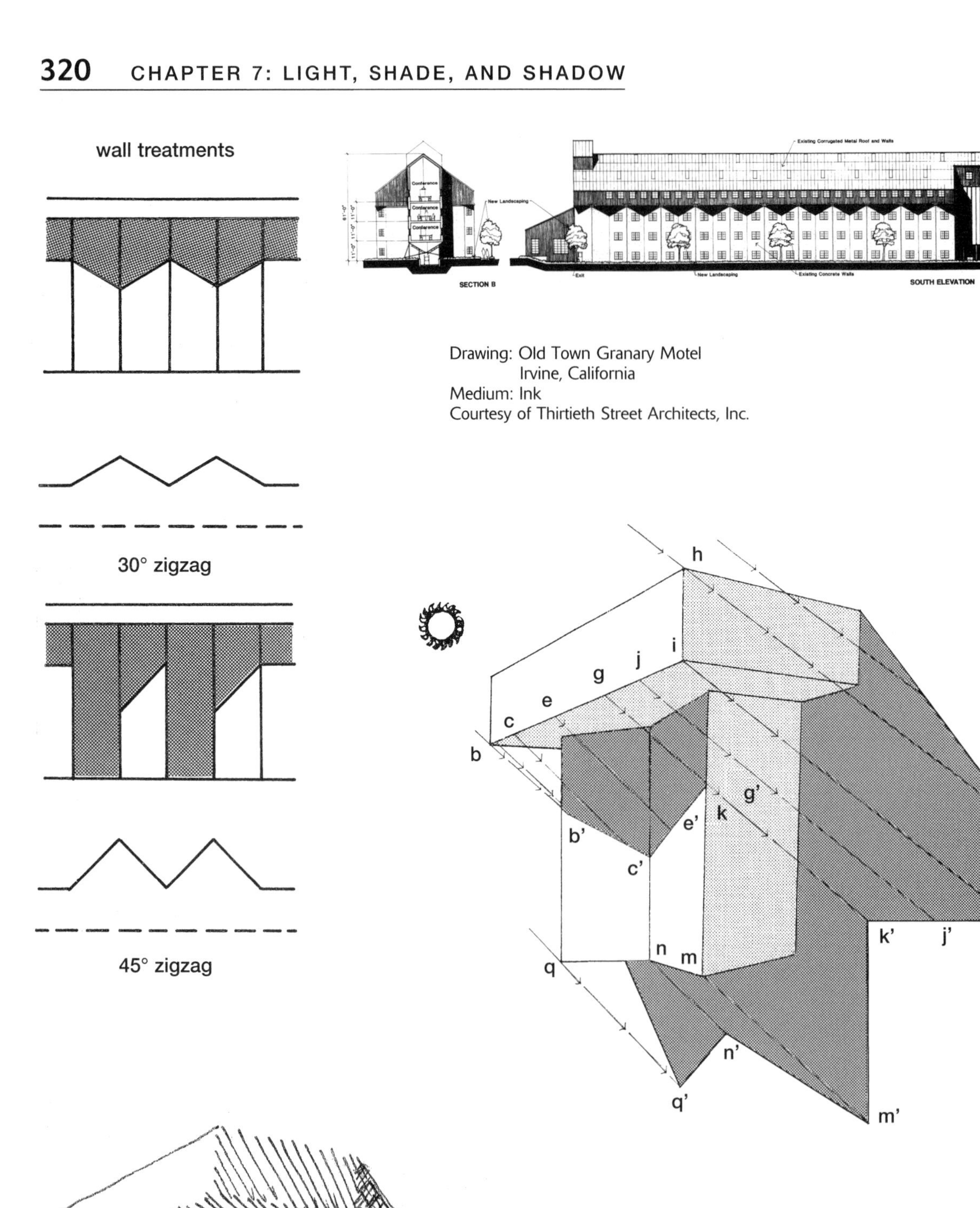

Drawing: Old Town Granary Motel
Irvine, California
Medium: Ink
Courtesy of Thirtieth Street Architects, Inc.

Visualizing Shadows/Zigzag Shadows

To visualize problems with shades and shadows, quickly sketch the object in a three-dimensional perspective setting. It may take many such preliminary sketches to resolve a problem with shadows. The sequential drawings on the previous pages can be more easily understood with the aid of a typical sketch (left) and verified by point analysis (above). Labeling corresponding points in a perspective diagram will enhance your understanding of any shadow configuration.

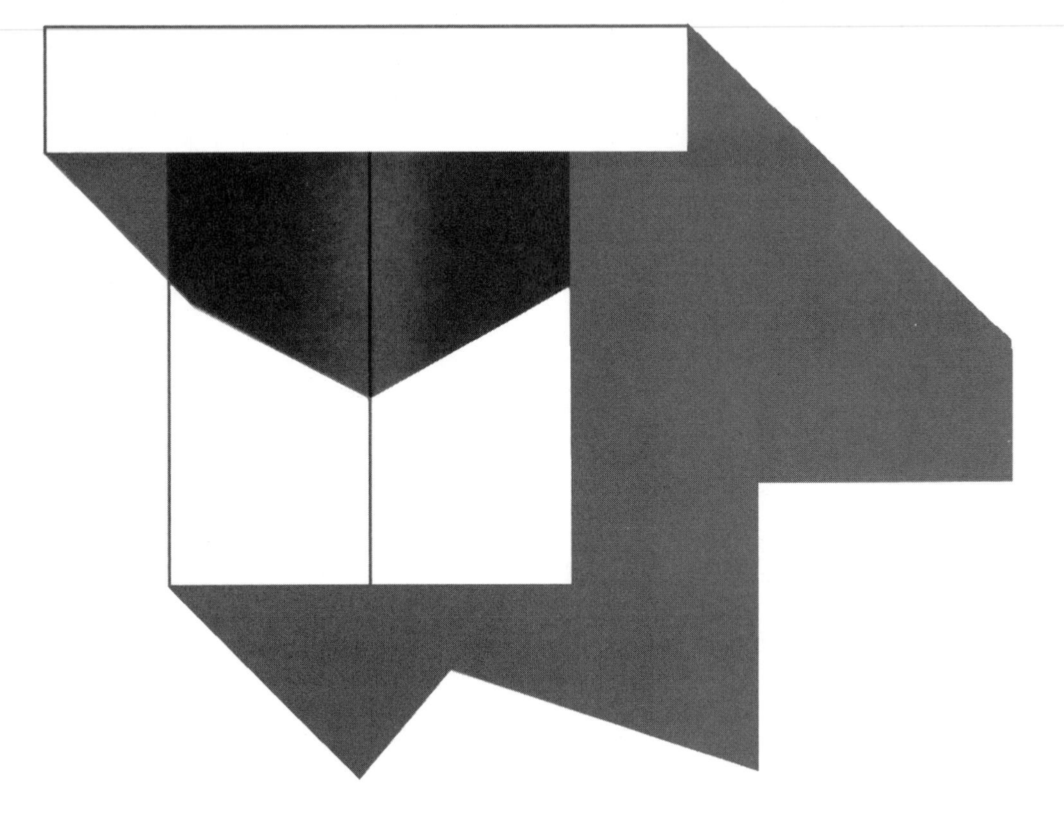

Airbrush rendering: Student project by Steven Toy
Courtesy of the Department of Architecture
City College of San Francisco

Shadow Intensity on Receding Surfaces

The rendering above is of the wall elements shown in the sequence diagrams on the previous pages. It was done with an airbrush in order to best display the tone intensity cast by a shadow on its various surfaces. An airbrush sprays paint, using compressed air to create large areas of flat color or gradations of color. Refer to the extensive coverage on airbrush techniques in the companion Web site (Chapter 11). The contrast is greater on surfaces closer to the observer's eye because a surface appears brighter when it is closer, whereas the actual difference may be insignificant. The illustration to the right clarifies this concept: receding surfaces are rendered with less contrast.

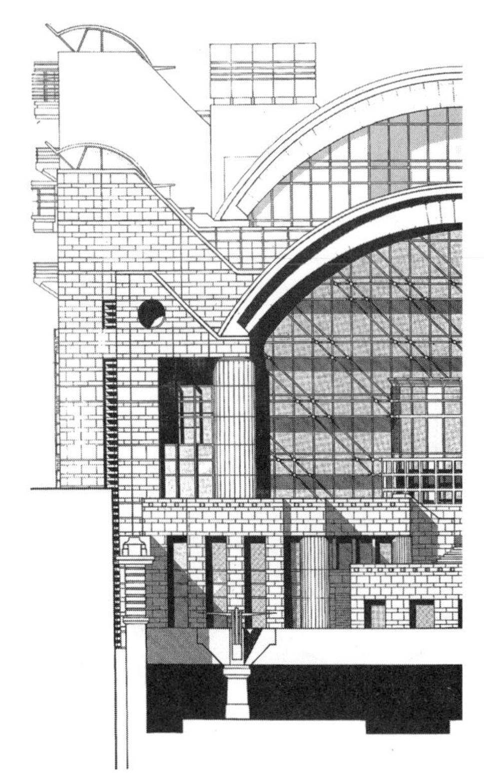

Drawing: Embankment Place
London, England
Medium: Letratone
Courtesy of Terry Farrell & Partners, Architects

Forty-five degree light ray condition:
Paraline conditions exhibit light rays parallel to the picture plane.

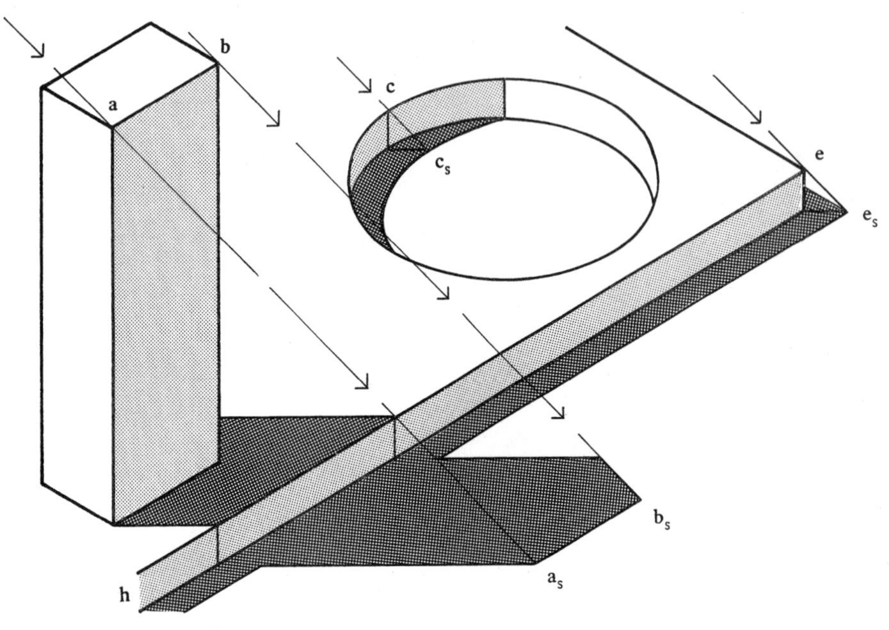

Drawing: Faculty Housing
The Rockefeller University
Pocantico Hills, New York
Partial drawing is shown
30" × 48" (76.2 × 121.9 cm)
Scale: 1/8"=1'0"
Medium: Oil paint and colored pencil on black line diazo print
Courtesy of Michael Fieldman & Partners, Architects

Isometric Paraline Shadows

Critical paraline shadow points are determined by constructing triangular planes parallel to the picture plane. A vertical drop or rise **(h)** in the horizontal surface connects paraline shadows on different horizontal surfaces. A drop in a horizontal receiving surface always results in a longer shadow. A rise in a horizontal receiving surface always results in a shorter shadow.

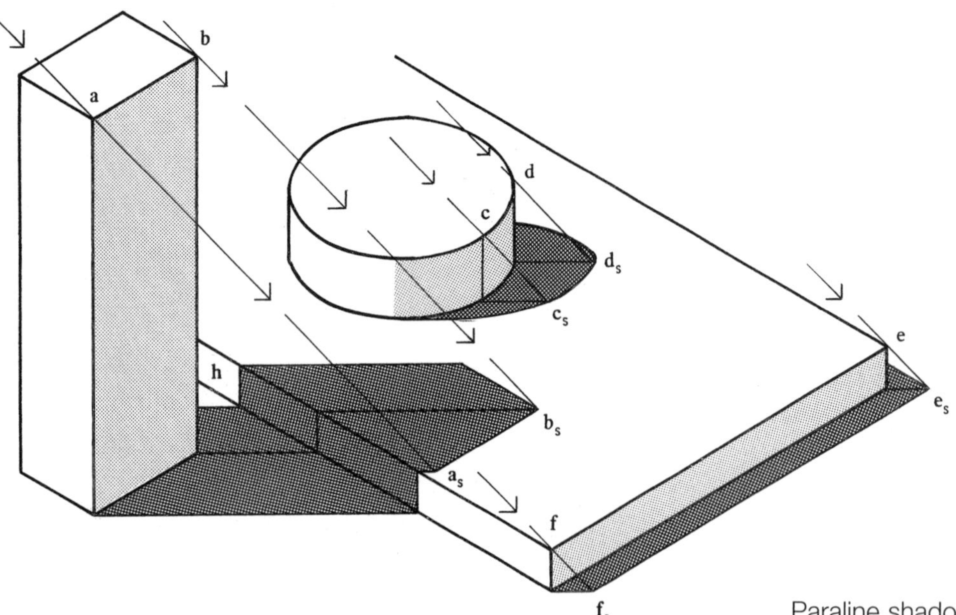

Paraline shadows of cylindrical forms can be determined by finding and plotting a series of arbitrary points (**c** and **d**) on the light/shade boundary.

Forty-five degree light ray condition: Paraline conditions exhibit light rays parallel to the picture plane.

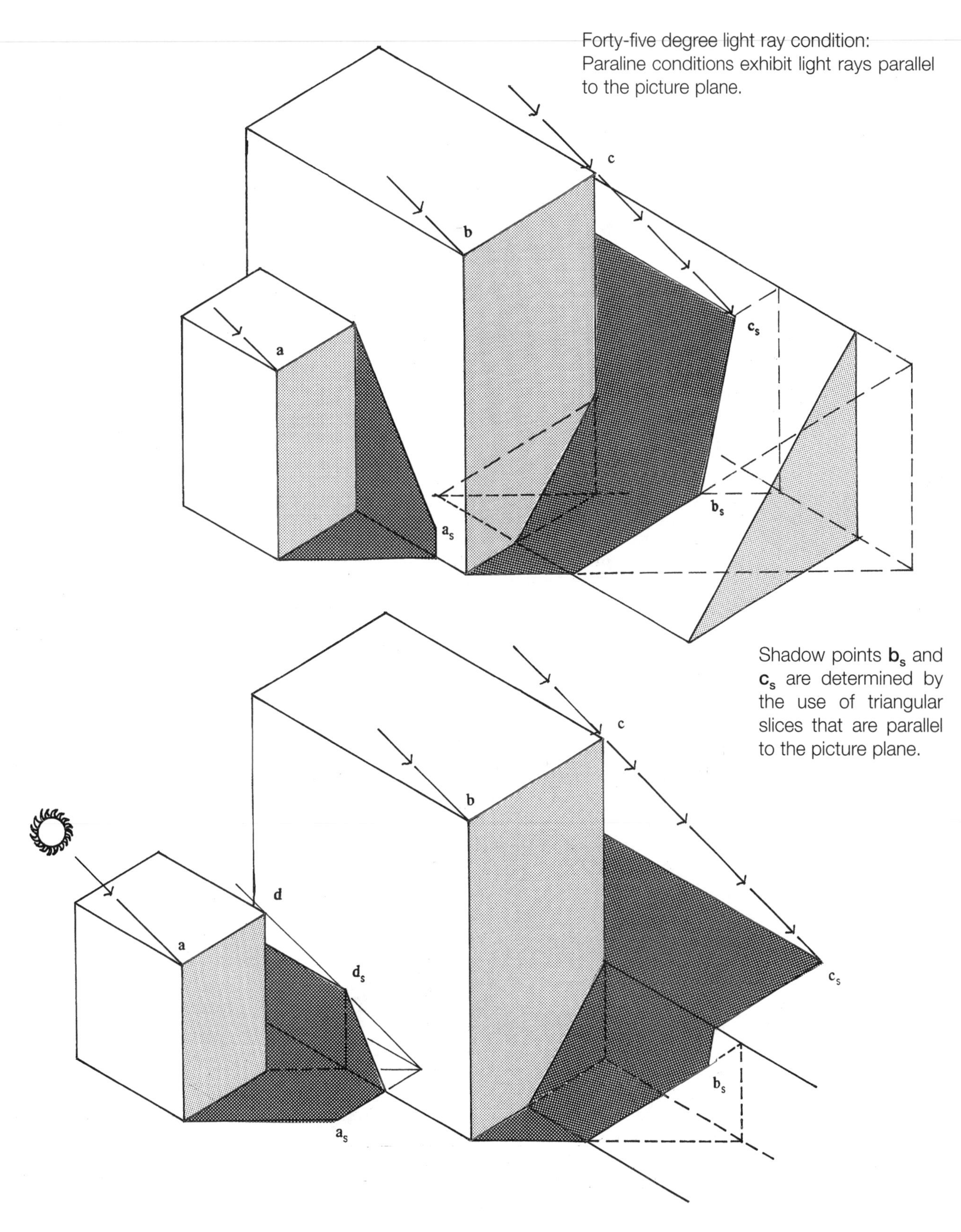

Shadow points $\mathbf{b_s}$ and $\mathbf{c_s}$ are determined by the use of triangular slices that are parallel to the picture plane.

To determine the shadow on the vertical wall above, cast a shadow on the ground as if there were no wall. Then project horizontal and vertical trace lines until they intersect the light-bearing rays.

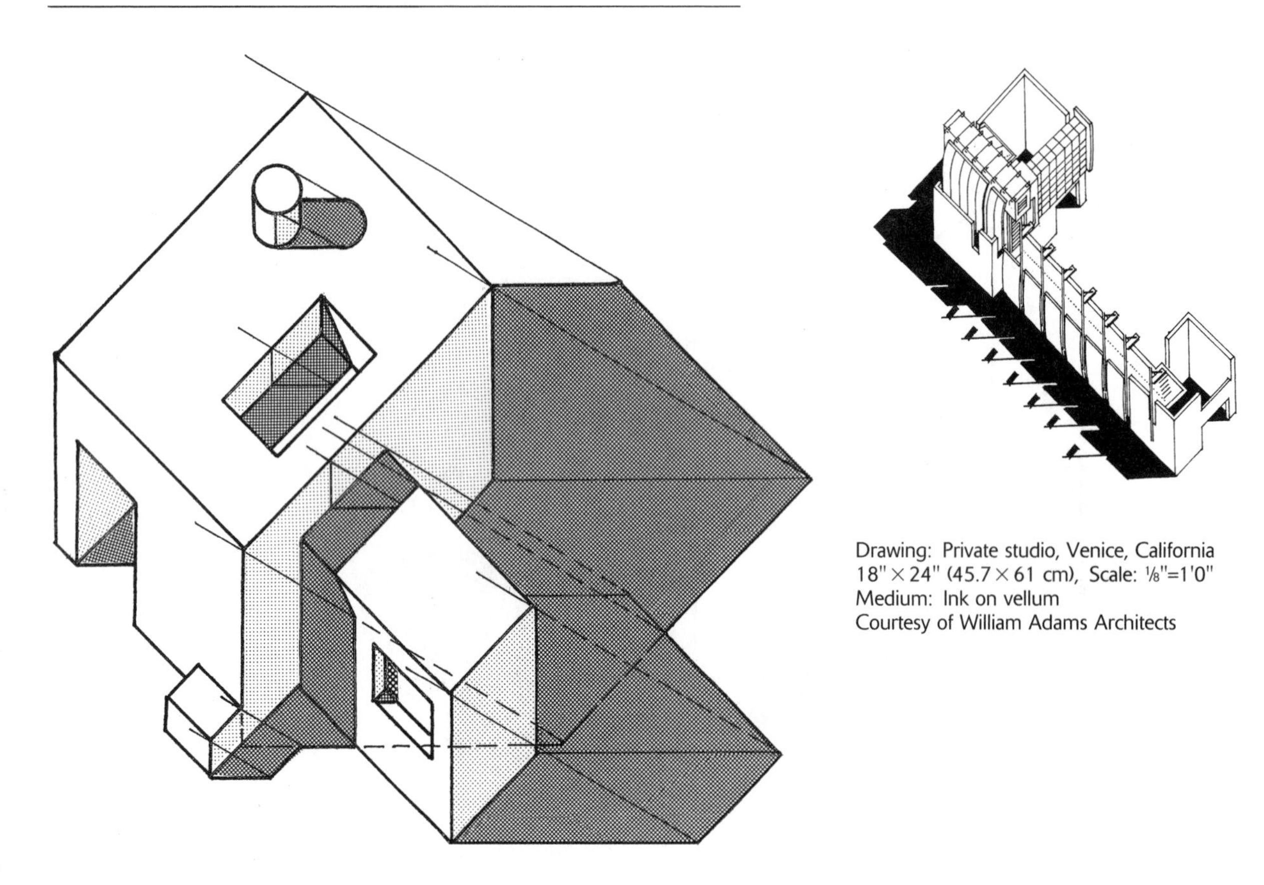

Drawing: Private studio, Venice, California
18" × 24" (45.7 × 61 cm), Scale: 1/8"=1'0"
Medium: Ink on vellum
Courtesy of William Adams Architects

Plan Oblique Paraline Shadows

These plan oblique (45°–45°) drawings exhibit shadows cast from light rays that are parallel to the picture plane. Critical shadow points on the ground are determined by the intersection of sloping light rays from a casting edge (height or altitude) and the bearing line on the ground. In the above example, the small building elements intercept the light rays cast by vertical and horizontal casting edges of the large building element. This results in a shadow line that climbs across the small element.

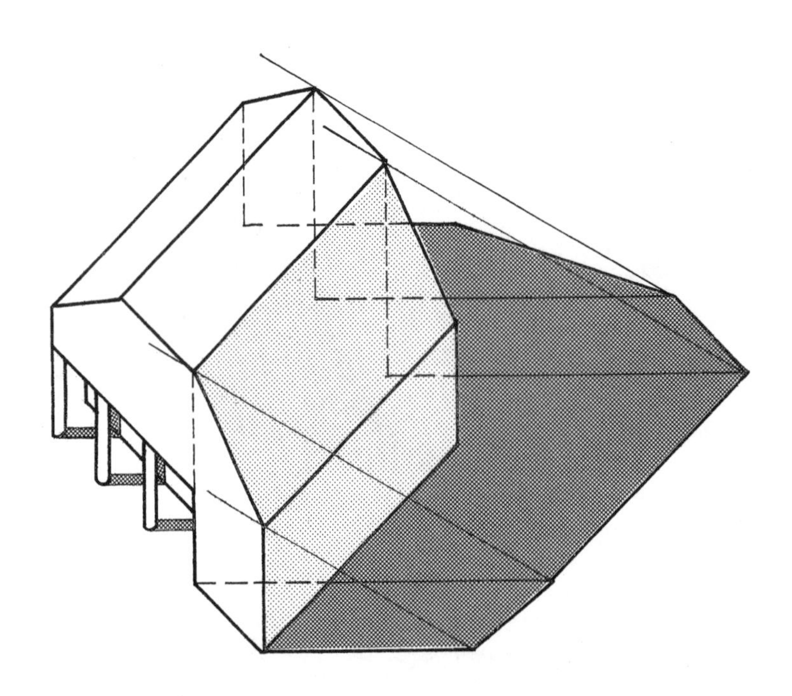

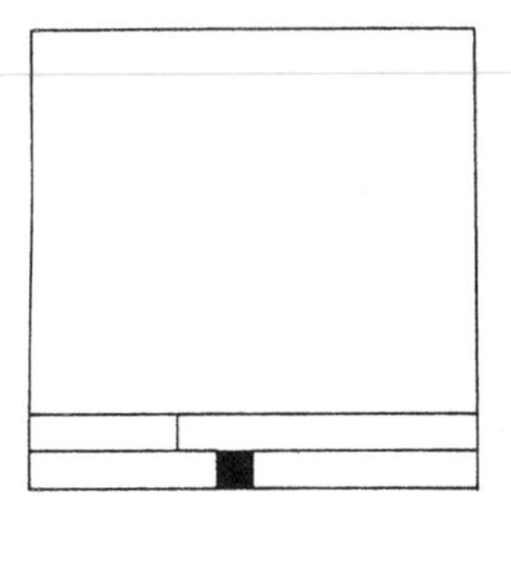

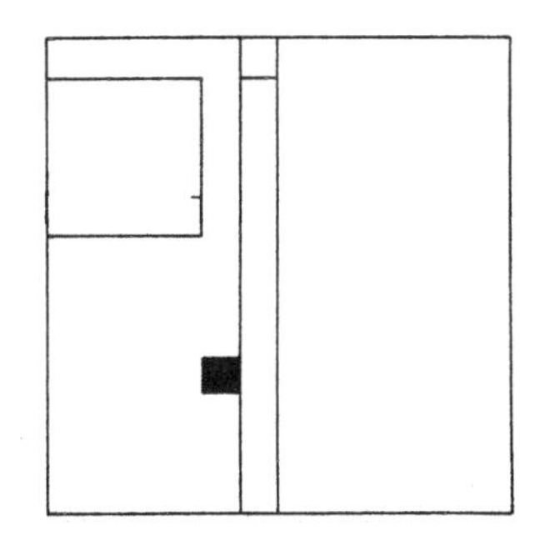

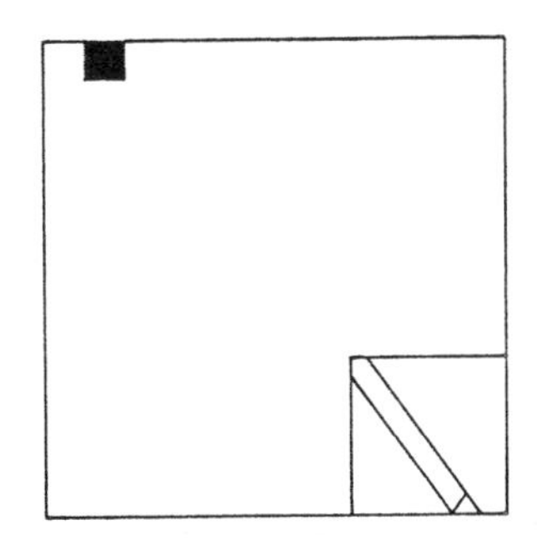

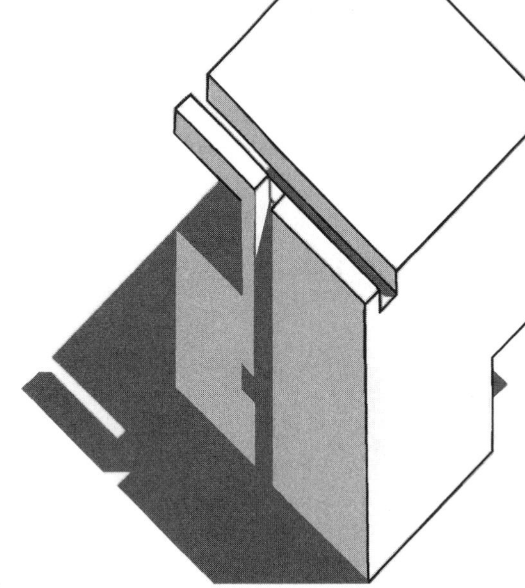

Drawing: Student project by Andrew Von Mauer, Solid–void relationship investigation
17" × 11" (43.2 × 27.9 cm), Scale: Full-size after model
Medium: Ink on Mylar
Courtesy of Andrews University, Division of Architecture, first-year Graphics Studio
Studio Professor: Arpad Daniel Ronaszegi; Assistant: Tom Lowing

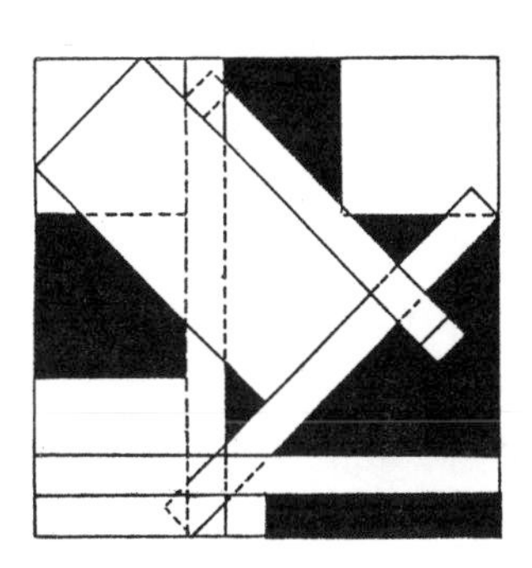

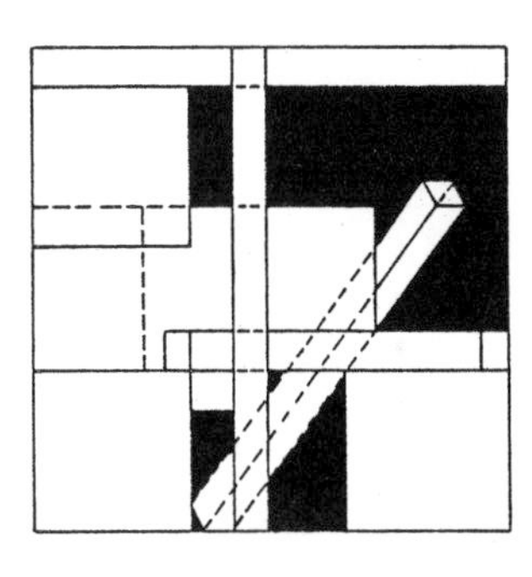

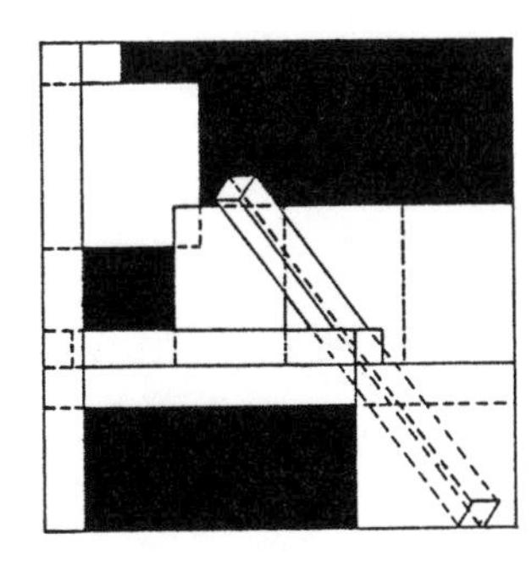

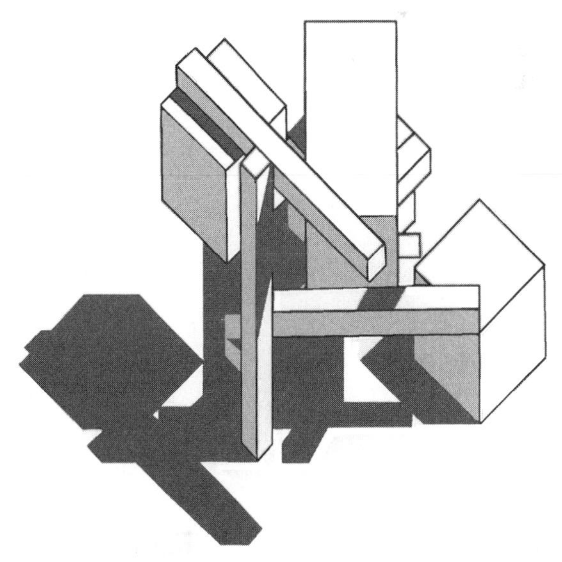

Drawing: Student project by Andrew Von Mauer, Solid–void relationship investigation
17" × 11" (43.2 × 27.9 cm), Scale: Full-size after model
Medium: Ink on Mylar
Courtesy of Andrews University, Division of Architecture, first-year Graphics Studio
Studio Professor: Arpad Daniel Ronaszegi; Assistant: Tom Lowing

Select the location of the vanishing point of the sun's rays on the vertical tracer line. The vanishing point of the shadow will also fall on this line. Note that the small triangle **(ABC)** and the large triangle are similar.

VP_S or **VPS** is the vanishing point of the shadow.

VP_{SR} or **VPSR** is the vanishing point of the sun's rays.

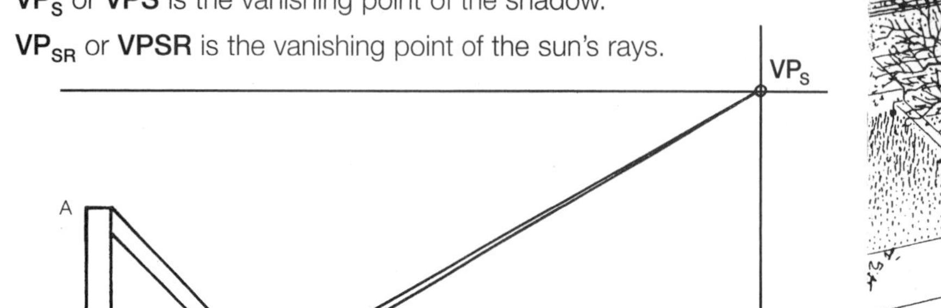

Drawing: Skid Row Development Corporation
Los Angeles, Caifornia
Medium: Ink
Courtesy of Ron Silveira, AIA, Architect;
James Bonar, FAIA; and the
Los Angeles Community Design Center

Perspective Shadows

Shadow casting in **perspective** is similar to paraline shadow casting. The difference is that the sun's rays and the shadow lines (outlines) converge to vanishing points. The light rays can either be parallel or oblique to the picture plane (see pp. 328–33).

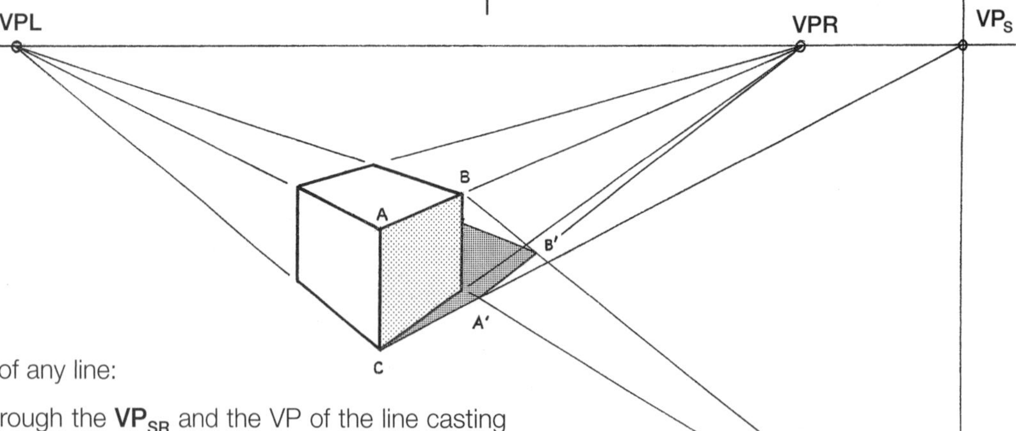

Locating the **VP_S** of any line:

1. Draw a line through the **VP_{SR}** and the VP of the line casting the shadow.
2. The line intersects the plane receiving the shadow at the horizon line.
3. This intersection is the VP of the required shadow line.

NOTE: **A'B'** is parallel to **AB** in the plan view; therefore, they vanish at **VP_R** in perspective. Vertical line **AC** casts shadow line **A'C**. **A'C** will vanish on the horizon at **VP_S**; therefore, all vertical lines will cast shadows that vanish at **VP_S**.

Photo: Notre Dame Catholic Church, Kerrville, Texas
Courtesy of Tapley/Lunow Architects,
Gerald Moorhead FAIA

Shadows Cast on a Combination of Horizontal and Vertical Surfaces

1. Vertical light/shade line **ab** casts shadow line **ab$_S$** on the ground and this line vanishes at the **VPS**.
2. Vertical light/shade line *bc* casts shadow line **b$_S$c$_S$**. This is a case of a vertical line casting a shadow line on a vertical surface.
3. Horizontal light/shade line **cd** casts shadow line **c$_S$d$_S$**, which vanishes at the intersection of the line through the **VPSR** and the **VPR** and the vertical traces through the **VPL**.
4. Vertical light/shade line **de** casts shadow line **d$_S$e$_S$** following the principle stated in Step 2.

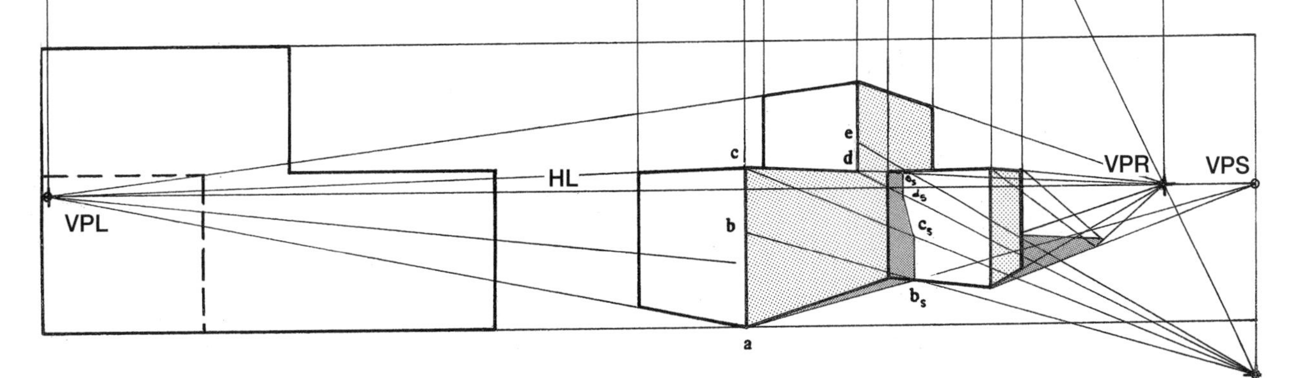

Photo (right): Newport Center/Fashion Island
Newport Beach, California
Courtesy of the SWA Group

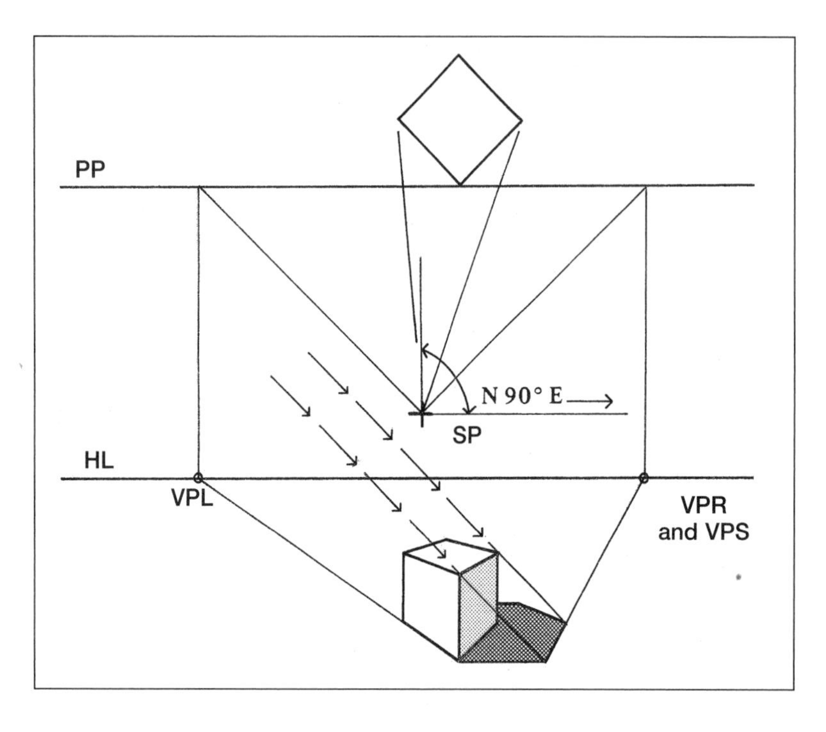

Light rays parallel to the picture plane

Light rays **parallel** to the picture plane can be cast at any convenient angle, such as 45°, depending on the effect desired. A **vertical line** casts a shadow line that is **parallel** to the **HL** and the **PP** in the direction of the bearing of the light rays. Lines **parallel** to the ground plane cast shadow lines that are **parallel** to the line casting the shadow line.

PP
VPSR
S 60° W
SP
HL
22° slope
VPL
VPR
VPS

Light rays oblique to the picture plane

Given conditions:
Bearing of light rays = S 60° W
Slope = 22°

Note that the **VPSR** is **above** the **HL**.

The vanishing point of the sun's rays **(VPSR)** is located by **rotating** the bearing line into the **PP** and dropping a vertical to locate the corresponding point on the **HL**. From this point the slope of the light ray is drawn until it intercepts the vertical tracer line drawn from the penetration point on the **PP** by the bearing of the light rays. The vanishing point of the shadow **(VPS)** lies at the intersection of this vertical tracer and the **HL**.

BEARING — the direction of the line (in this case a light ray) relative to due north or south. It is always measured in the plan view and expressed in degrees.

SLOPE — the slope angle of a line measured in the elevation view relative to the horizon line and expressed in degrees.

View from west

Perspective Shades and Shadows

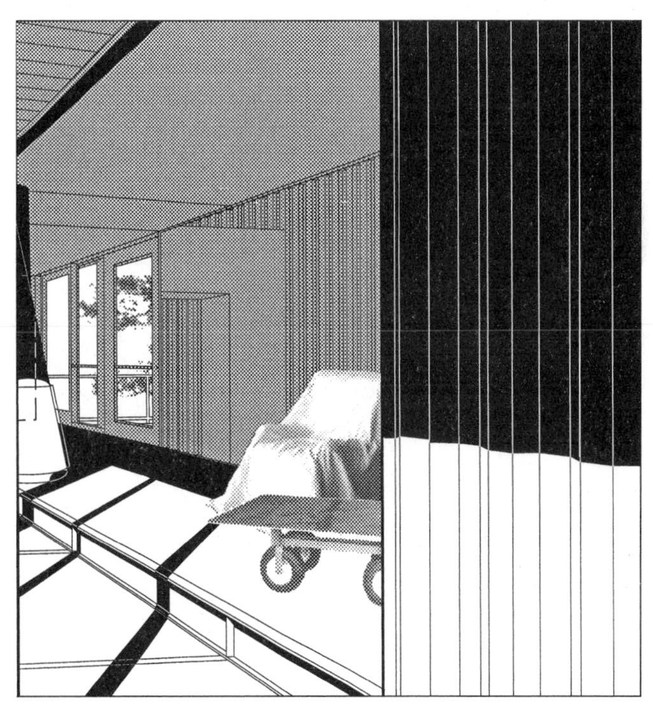

View from northwest

Drawing: High Sierras Meadow's Edge Cabin
Medium: CAD
Courtesy of Jones, Partners: Architecture

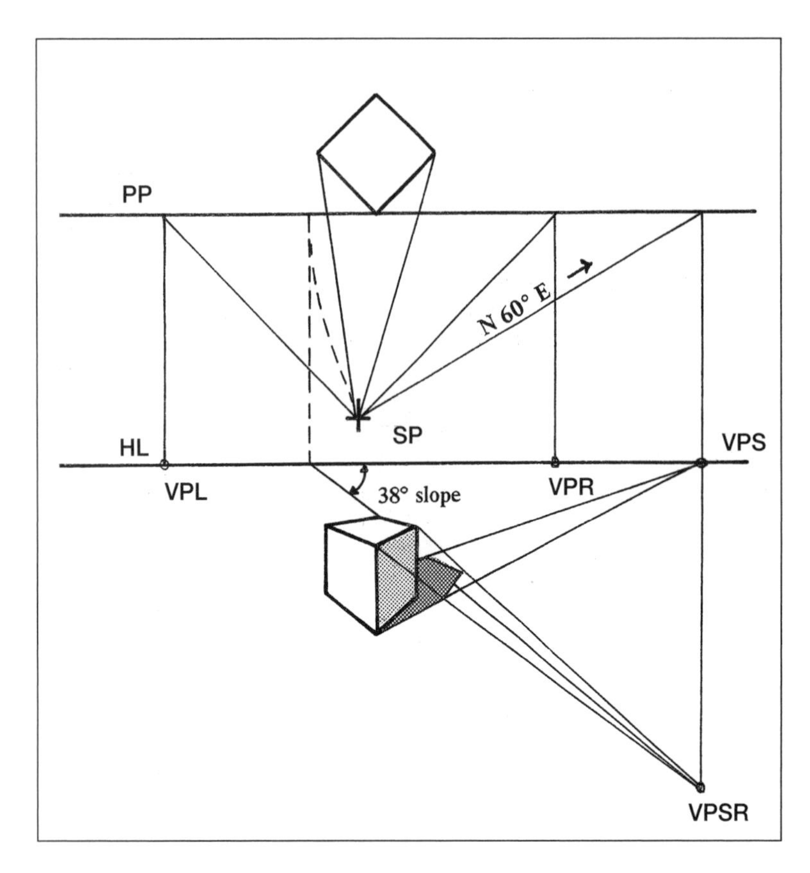

Light rays oblique to the picture plane

Given conditions:

Bearing of light rays = N 60° E
Slope = 38°

Note that the **VPSR** is **below** the **HL.**

Photo: Bollard, Alcoa Building Plaza
(Maritime Plaza)
San Francisco, California
Courtesy of the SWA Group

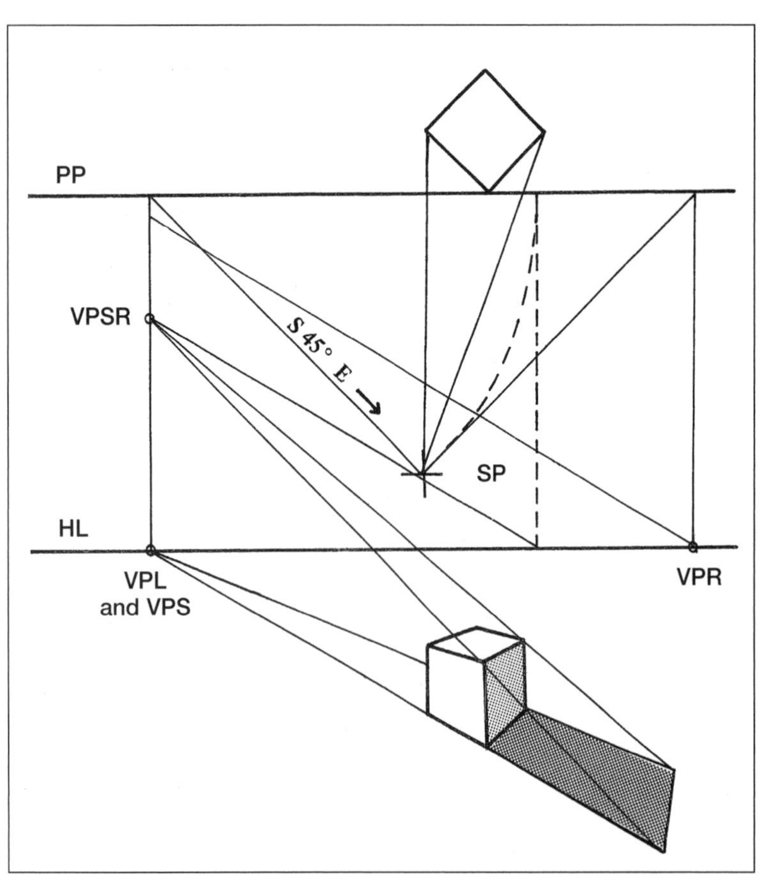

Light rays oblique to the picture plane

Given conditions:

Bearing of light rays = S 45° E
Slope = 30°

Note that the **VPSR** is **above** the **HL.**

Photo: Garden area of Pitney Bowes
World Headquarters
Stamford, Connecticut
Courtesy of I. M. Pei & Partners, Architects
© 1987 Steve Rosenthal

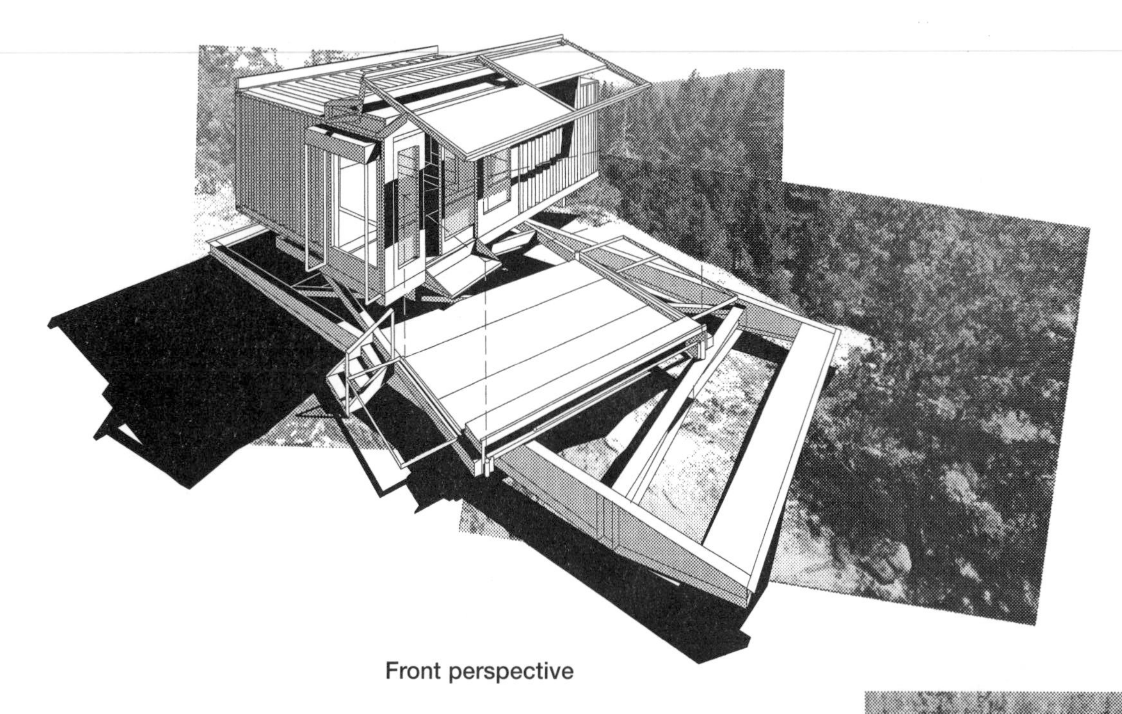

Front perspective

Perspective Shades and Shadows

Rear perspective

Drawings: High Sierras Guest Cabin
Medium: CAD
Courtesy of Jones, Partners: Architecture

Integral to this project is the contrasting nature of human-generated systems [as represented by the modular container element] and naturally generated systems [the site environs]. The juxtaposition of hardline, shadowed rendering with scanned photographic information underscores this dichotomy. The representation of shade and shadow provides a link between these two graphic modes.
[ARCHITECT'S STATEMENT]

Perspective Shades and Shadows

The separation of the two block forms (below left) causes shadows to be cast on both horizontal and vertical surfaces in a manner similar to the shadows on the two building elements of the Swan House. Light rays are parallel to the picture plane for these two perspective conditions. Triangular slice **rst** is in a plane parallel to the picture plane. Its location is determined by horizontal line **qrt**. Line **rs** determines the locus of piercing points for a variety of light ray angles.

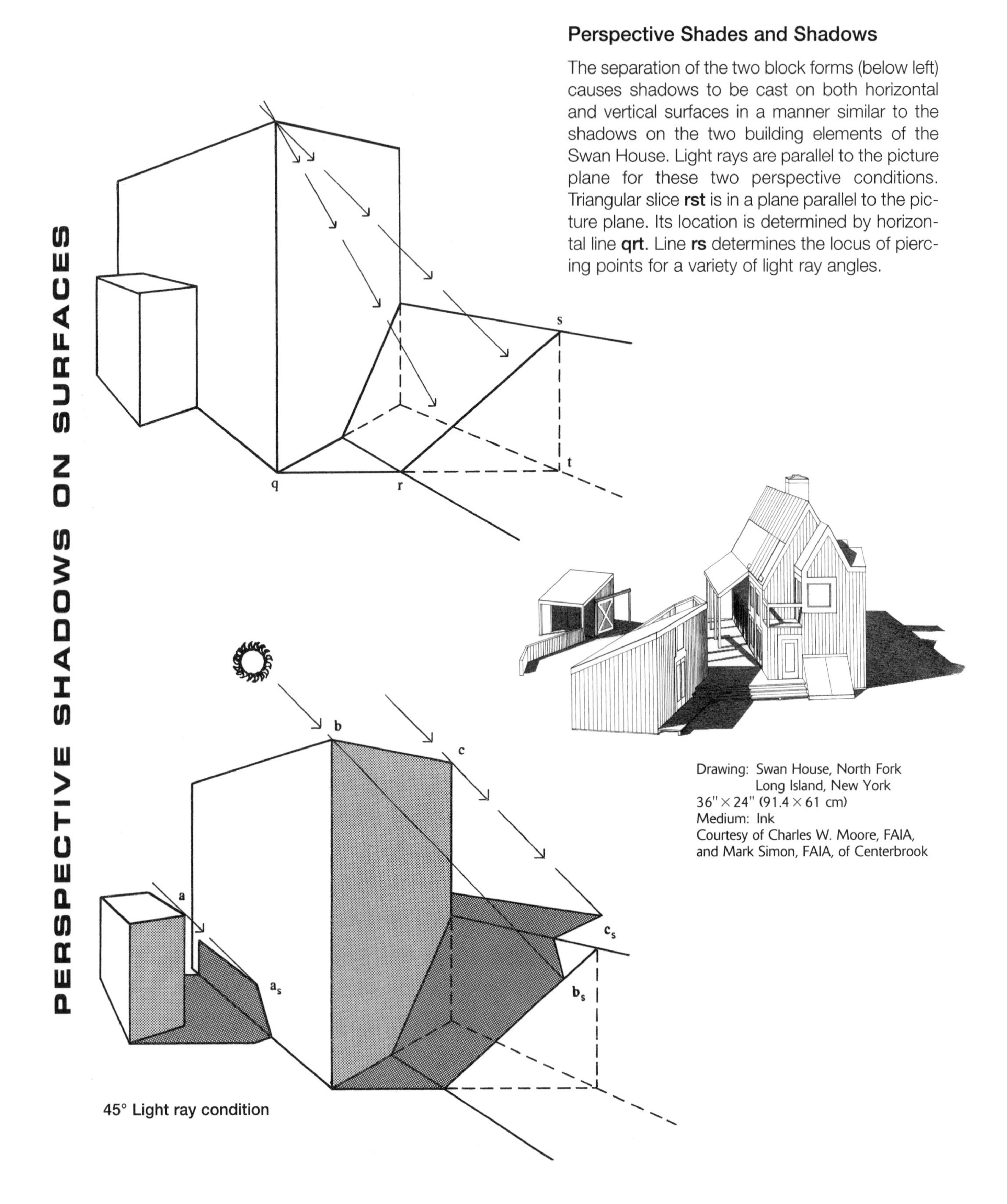

45° Light ray condition

Drawing: Swan House, North Fork Long Island, New York
36" × 24" (91.4 × 61 cm)
Medium: Ink
Courtesy of Charles W. Moore, FAIA, and Mark Simon, FAIA, of Centerbrook

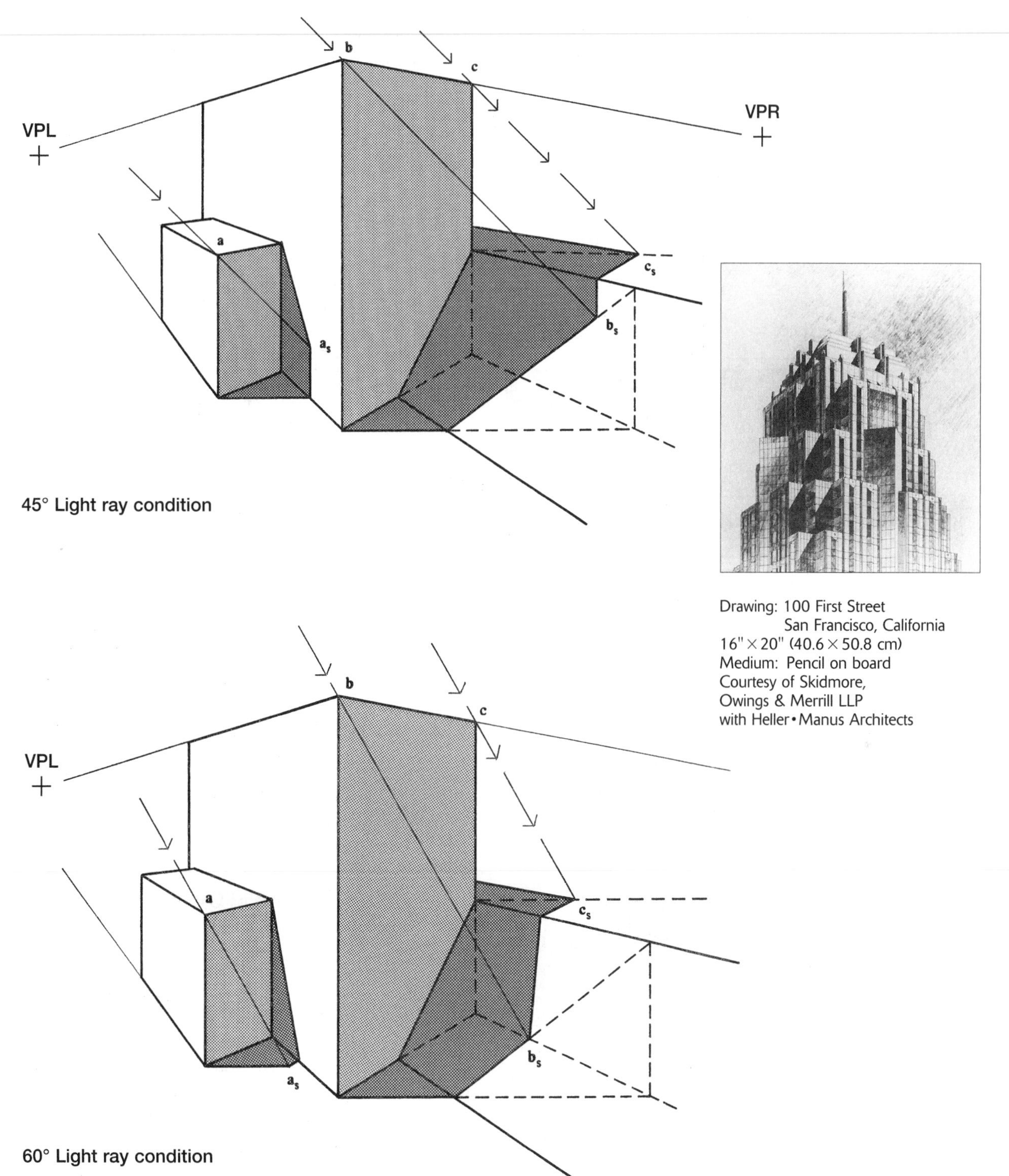

45° Light ray condition

60° Light ray condition

Drawing: 100 First Street
San Francisco, California
16" × 20" (40.6 × 50.8 cm)
Medium: Pencil on board
Courtesy of Skidmore,
Owings & Merrill LLP
with Heller • Manus Architects

Perspective Shades and Shadows

As on the previous page, light rays for these two perspective conditions are parallel to the picture plane, and they are also parallel to each other. To determine the critical shadow piercing point on the sloping surface $\mathbf{b_s}$, set up a triangular slice (dashed lines) parallel to the picture plane. Critical point $\mathbf{c_s}$ also lies in a plane that is parallel to the picture plane.

Drawing: Parkview Commons, San Francisco, California
36" × 24" (91.4 × 61 cm), Scale: 1/8"=1'0"
Medium: Ink on Canson paper
Courtesy of David Baker Architects

SOLID OVERHANG SHADOWS

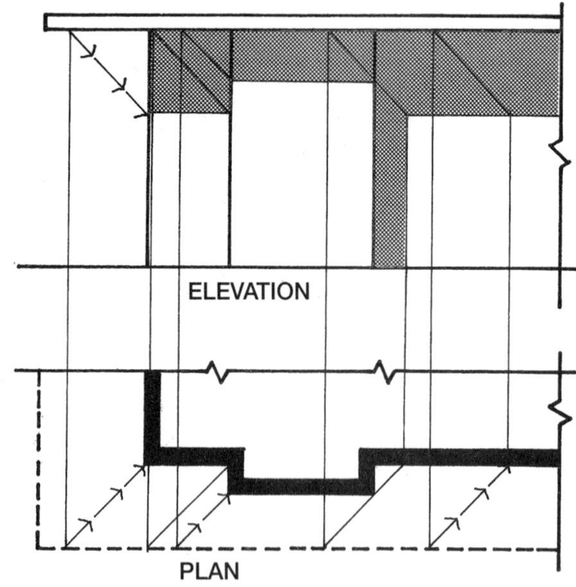

Flat overhang parallel to wall

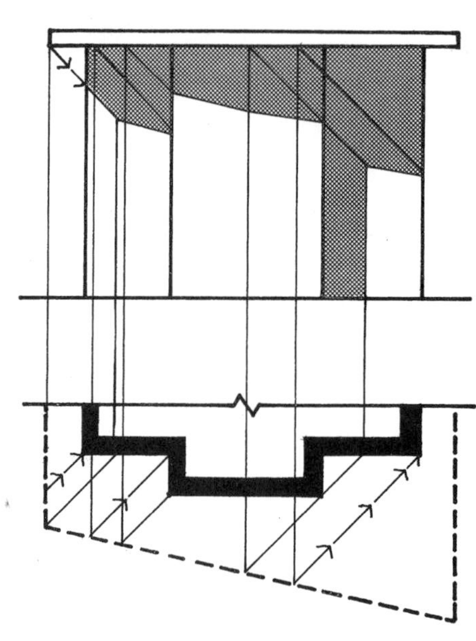

Flat overhang oblique to wall

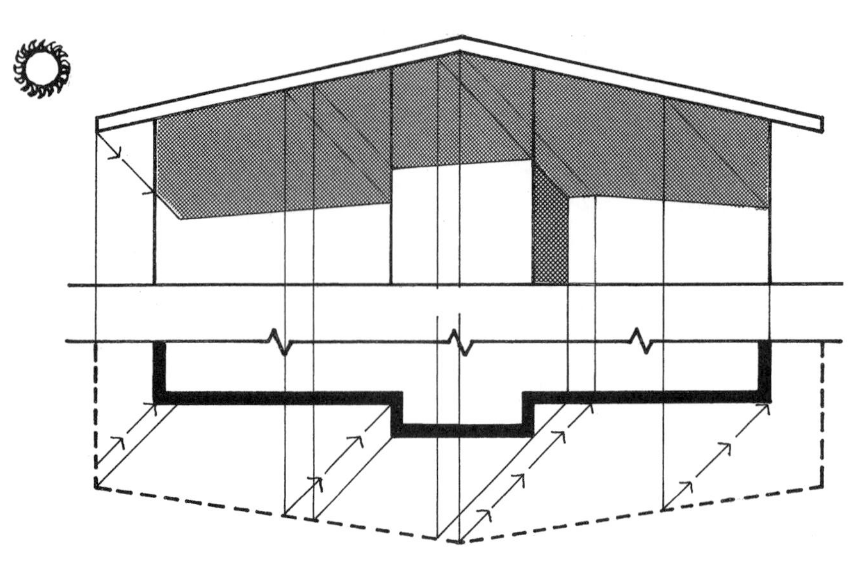

Inclined overhang oblique to wall

Solid Overhang Shadows

It is common to encounter buildings that have either flat or inclined solid overhangs. The edge casting the shadow line on the vertical wall can be either parallel or oblique to the wall. The previously explained shadow-casting principles for objects on a vertical wall also apply to overhangs. Use the plan view to transfer critical points into the elevation. As the angle of the light ray with respect to the ground line becomes steeper, the length of the resulting shadow will become longer.

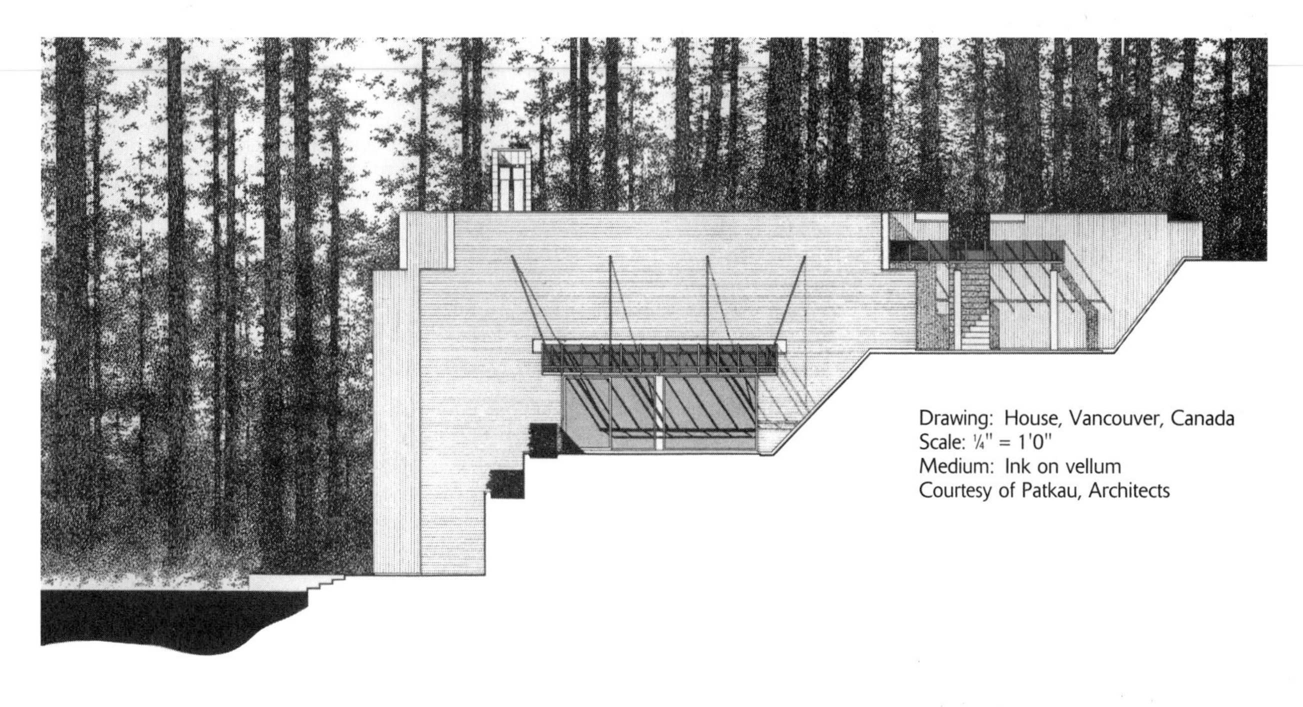

Drawing: House, Vancouver, Canada
Scale: ¼" = 1'0"
Medium: Ink on vellum
Courtesy of Patkau, Architects

Perforated Overhang Shadows

This overhang condition is characterized by openings or perforations. To cast the shadow in elevation, construct the plan, the elevation, and a sectional elevation in profile. Critical shadow points are located by transferring corresponding points between views.

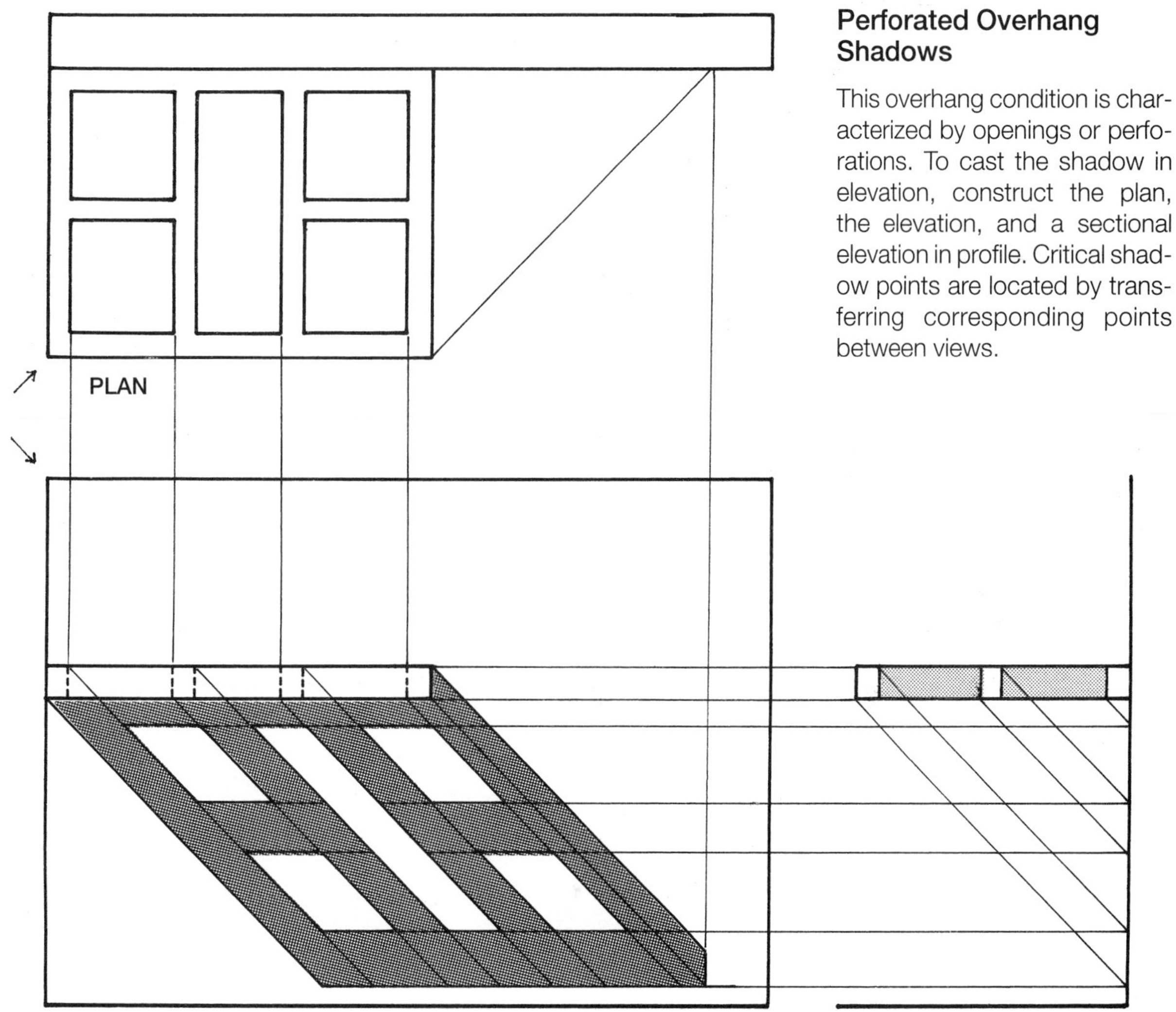

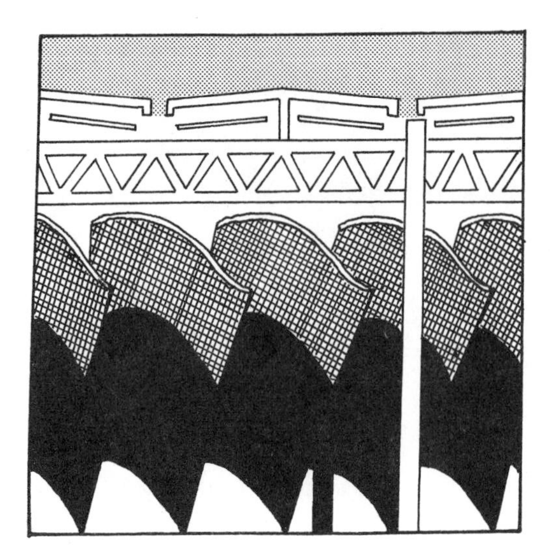

Drawing: Student project by Gorran Tsui
2.5" × 2.5" (6.4 × 6.4 cm)
Medium: Ink and Zipatone on vellum
The Menil Collection Museum, Houston, Texas
Courtesy of Renzo Piano Architect, Piano & Fitzgerald, Houston and the City College of San Francisco Department of Architecture
Structural Consultant: Ove Arup

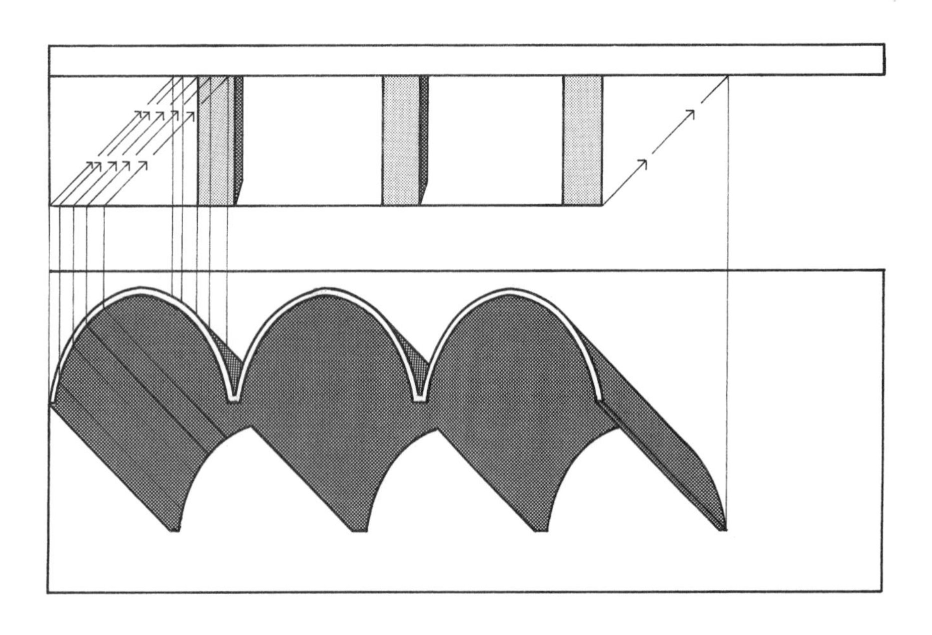

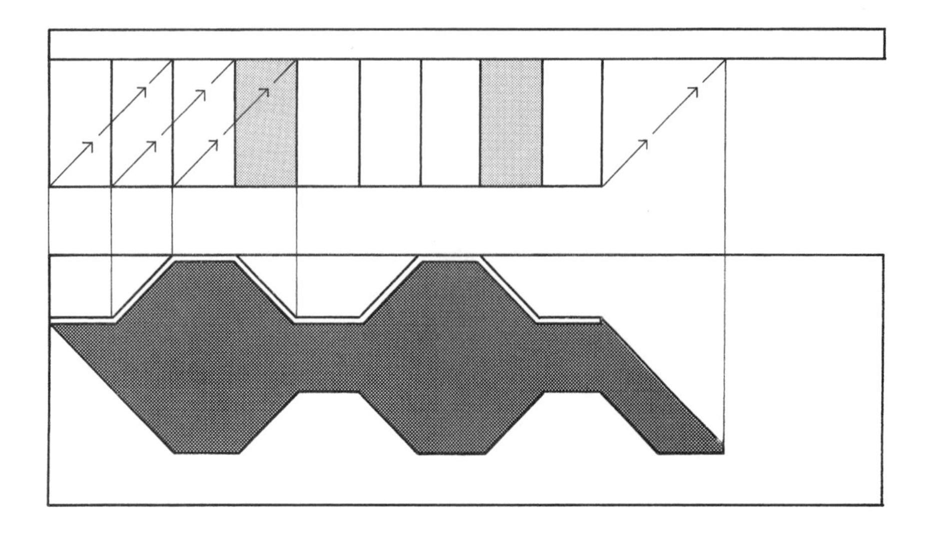

Canopy, Colonnade, and Arcade Shadows

The ways a plane figure casts a shadow on a parallel plane is demonstrated on these two facing pages. The bottom edges of the canopies cause a wall shadow line that has the same orientation and configuration as the canopy forms. Likewise, the geometric shapes of the arcade and the colonnade are cast on the recessed wall shadows. The repetition of geometric forms in all cases creates a shadow rhythm on the receiving surfaces. Note the shade on the underside of the sinuously curved roof canopy (upper left).

Drawing: San Francisco Waldorf School
36" × 24" (91.4 × 61 cm)
Scale: ¼"=1'0"
Medium: Ink on Mylar
Courtesy of Tanner Leddy Maytum Stacy, Architects

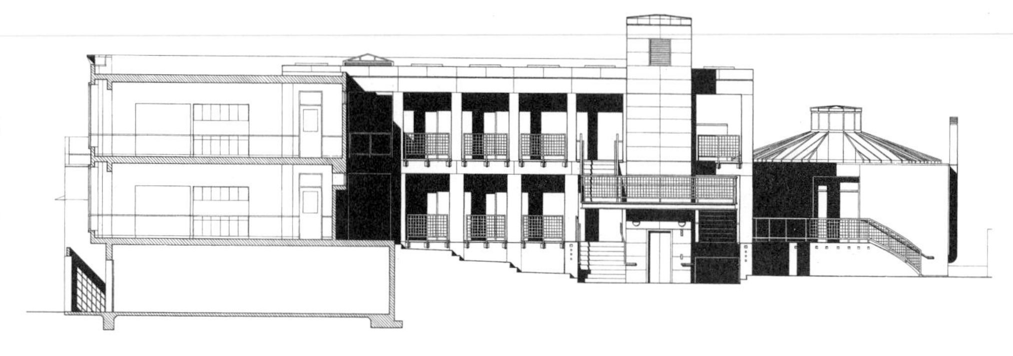

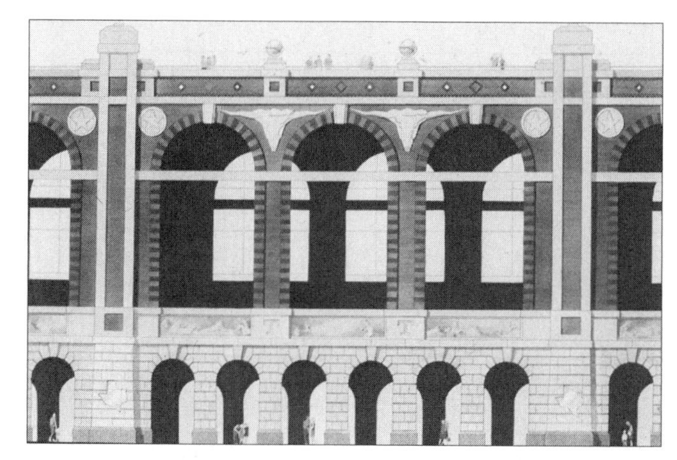

Drawing: Texas Rangers Ballpark, Arlington, Texas
24" × 18" (61 × 45.7 cm), Scale: ¼"=1'0"
Medium: Watercolor and pencil on mounted Bristol paper
Courtesy of David M. Schwarz/Architectural Services

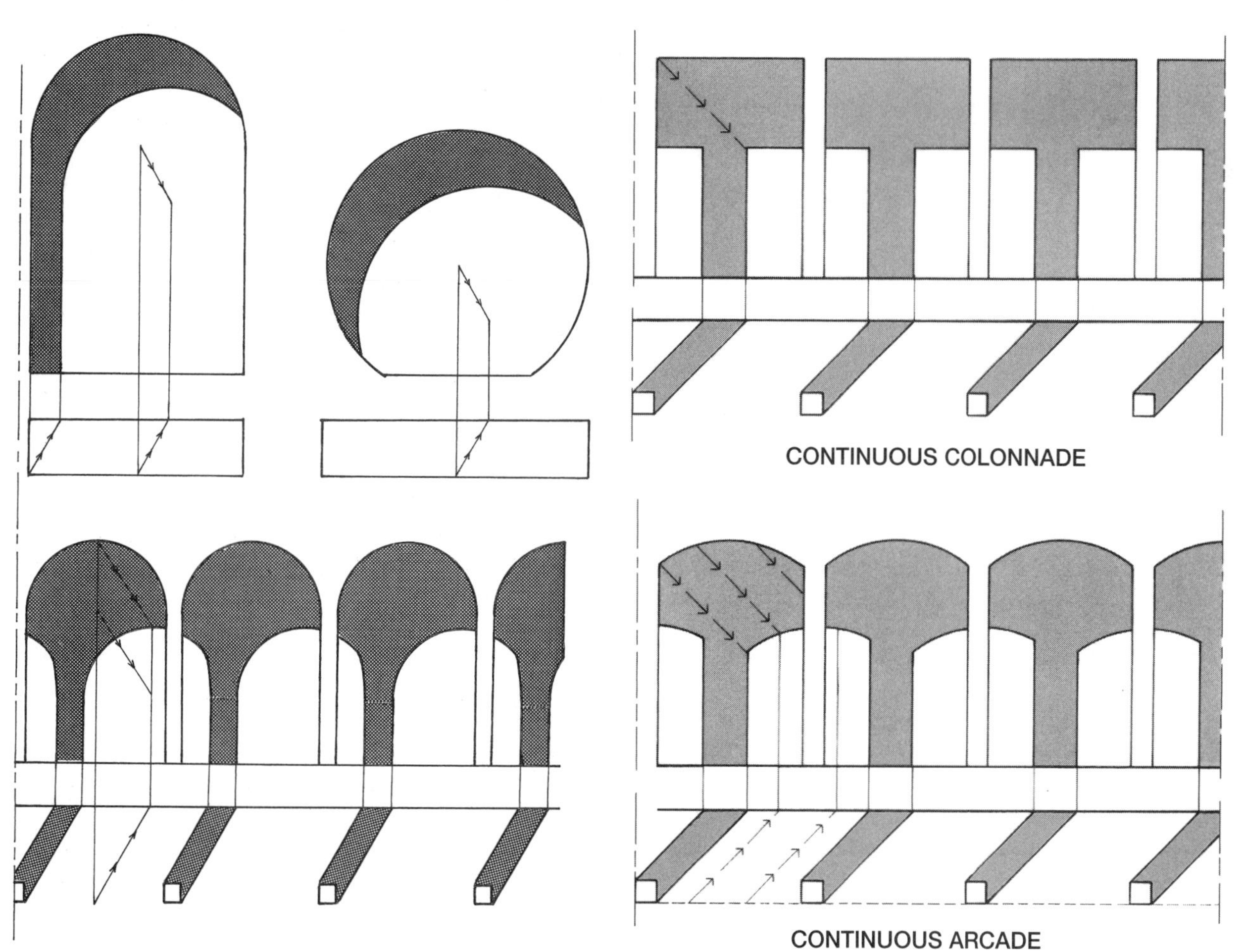

CONTINUOUS COLONNADE

CONTINUOUS ARCADE

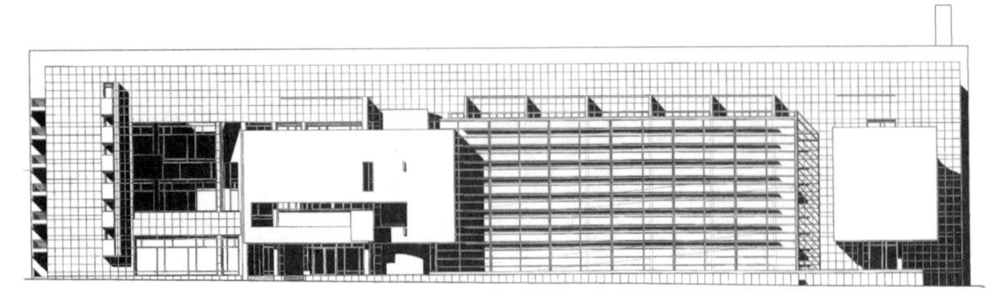

Drawing: Museum of Contemporary Art
Barcelona, Spain
36" × 48" (91.4 × 121.9 cm)
Medium: Ink on Mylar
Courtesy of Richard Meier
& Partners, Architects

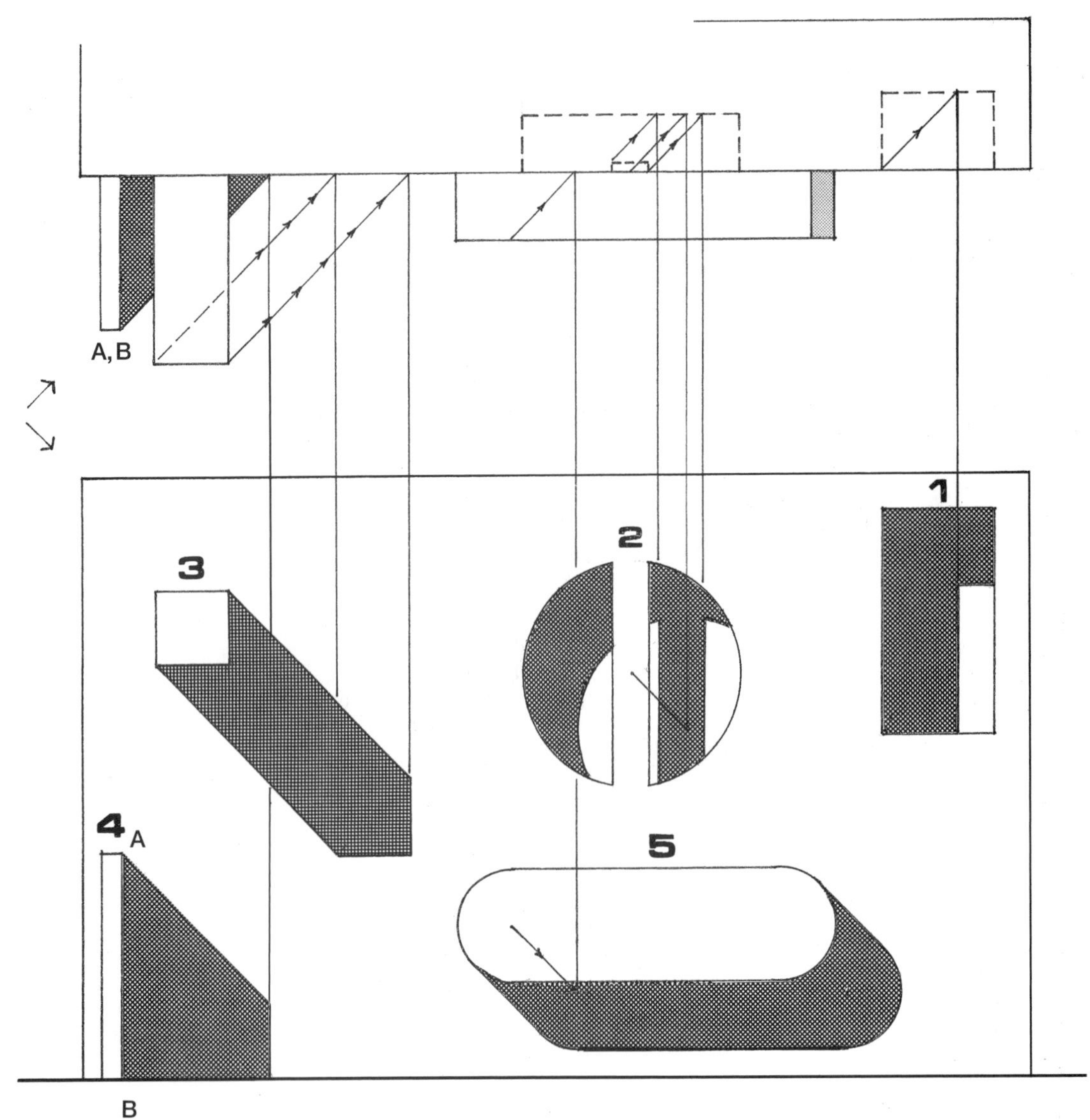

Nonoverlapping Shadows

In the wall of shadows shown above, the light source is coming from the left at 45° (see direction arrows in the elevation and the plan views). When the general rule that shadows of plane figures on parallel planes cause shadows of the same size, shape, and orientation is applied, the shadow configurations seen in conditions **1** and **2** become readily apparent and are easily understood. When edges are perpendicular to a vertical wall as in condition **3** and the top edge of condition **4**, the shadow line produced is in the sunlight-bearing direction. Likewise, edge **AB** is perpendicular to the horizontal ground surface, and the shadow line produced on the ground is in the sunlight-bearing direction (plan view) as well as parallel to edge **AB** when it is intercepted by the vertical wall (elevation view). Condition **5** follows the aforementioned rules.

© Markova Nadine, photographer

Photo: Renault Factory (partial elevation)
Gómez Palacio, Durango, Mexico
Courtesy of Legorreta Arquitectos: Ricardo Legorreta, Victor Legorreta, Noé Castro

This photograph was taken early in the morning in order to obtain hard shadows. Facade details were taken with a 200 mm telefoto lens. I used a Minolta camera with a polarizing filter.
[Architectural Photographer's Statement]

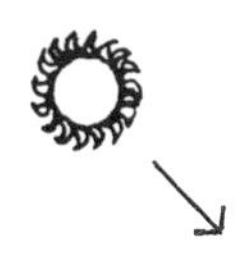

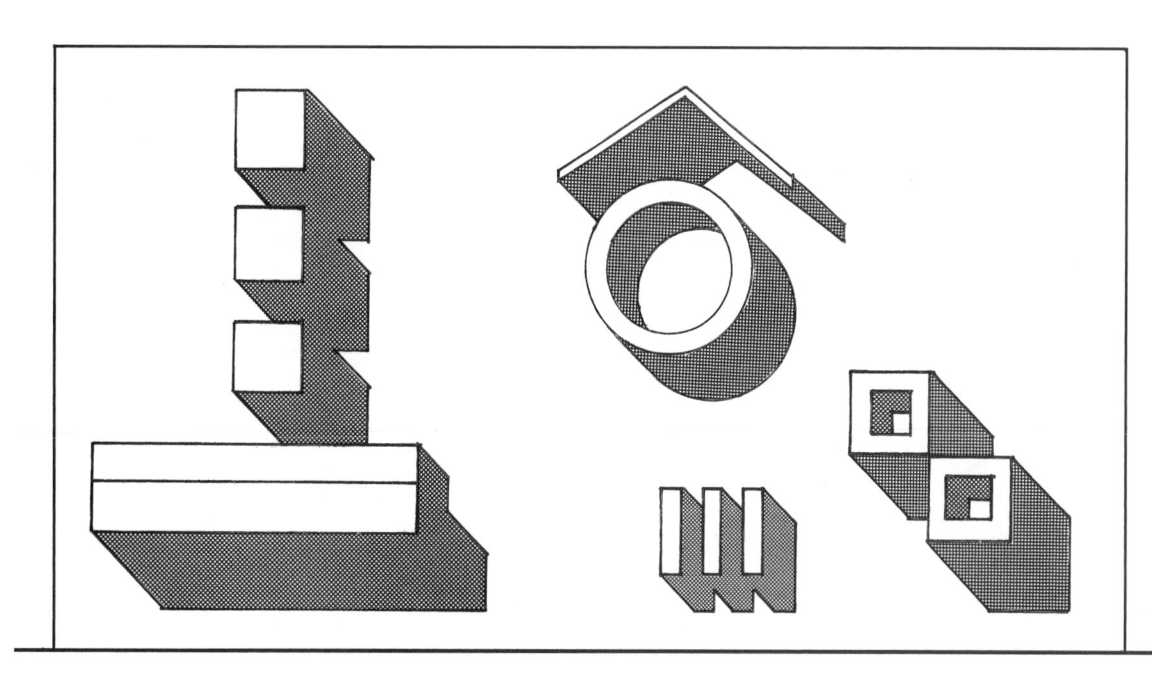

Drawing: Student project by William Xie and Daniel Orona
Design of a sculptural wall of shadows
Studio professor: Pershing C. Lin
Courtesy of the City College of San Francisco
Department of Architecture

Overlapping Shadows

When casting shadows of protruding elements that are in close proximity to each other, it is common to find shadows that are interrupted before they hit the major receiving surface. The shadow lines that we do not see sneak across the lighted surface closest to their neighbor.

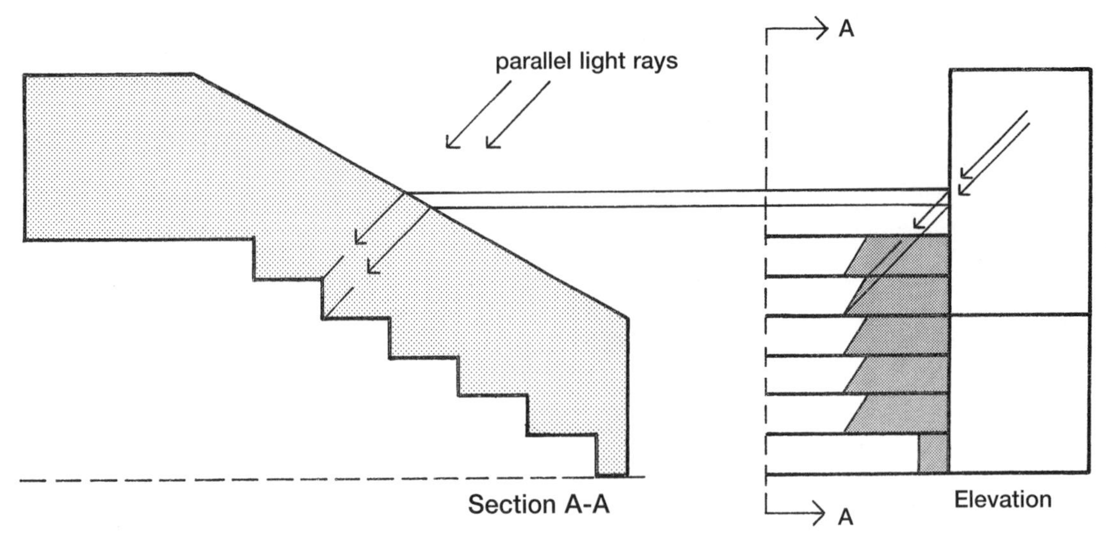

Stairway Shadows

Project corresponding points to find the shadow line of an oblique line on the steps above. Light rays maintain a parallel condition regardless of the geometric configuration of the receiving surface. See condition **A** in both elevation and plan below. A horizontal edge is seen as a point in the elevation **1**. It causes shadow line **A** seen in elevation.

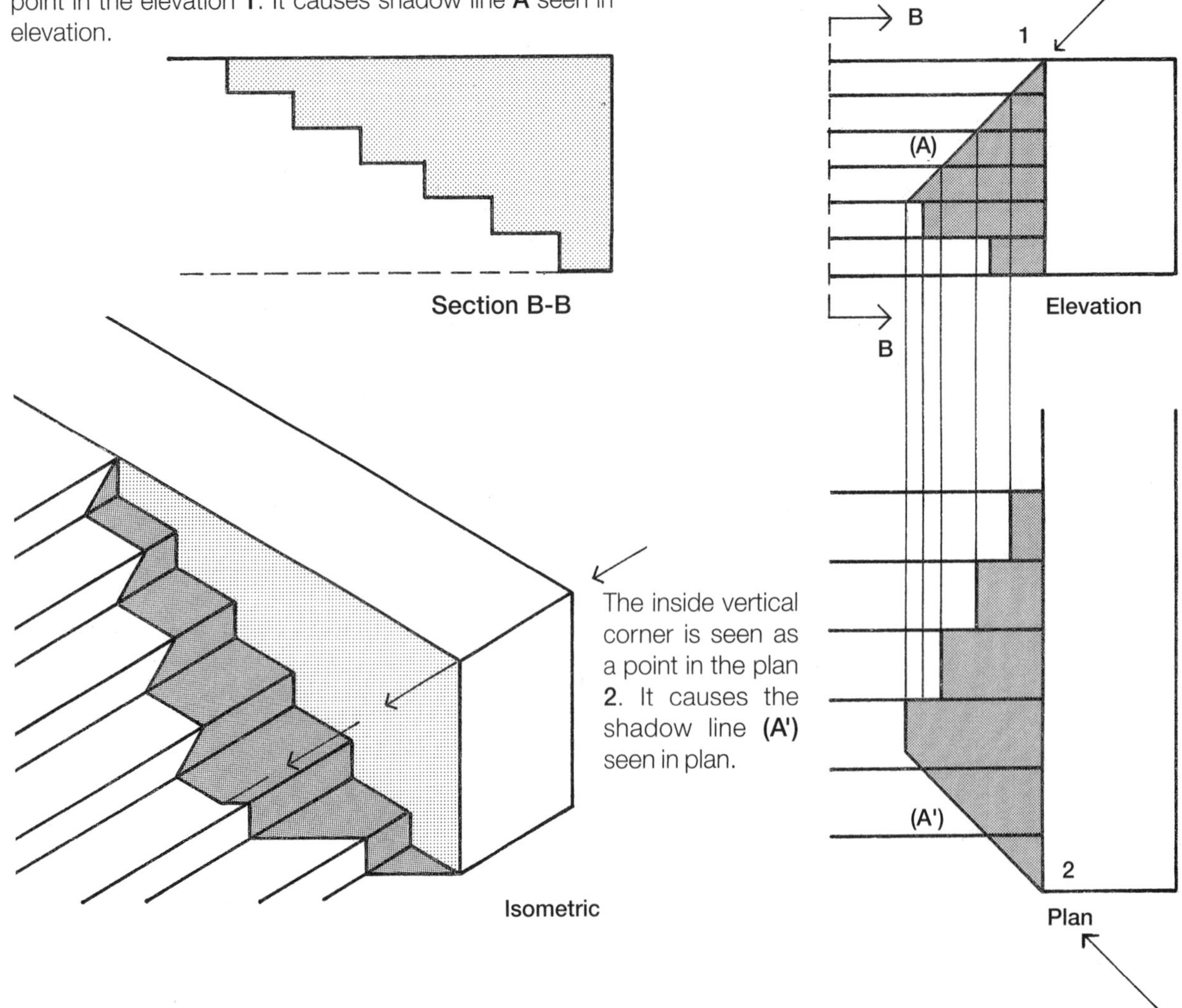

The inside vertical corner is seen as a point in the plan **2**. It causes the shadow line **(A')** seen in plan.

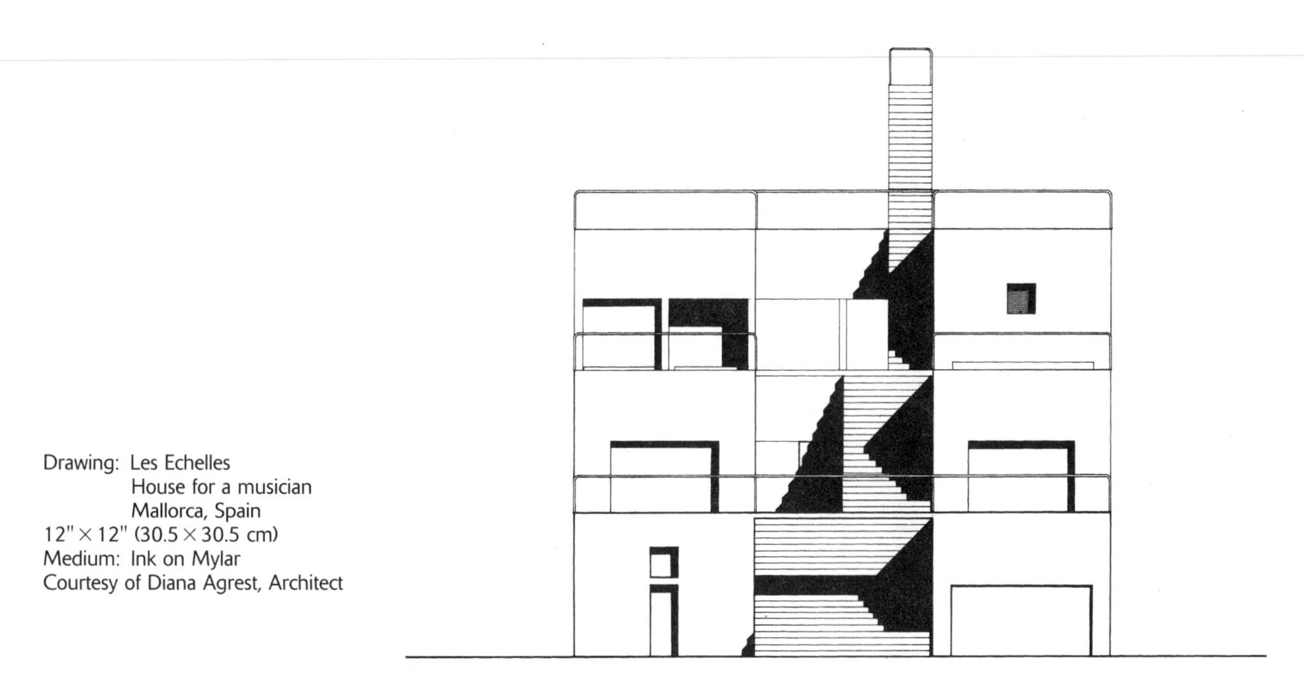

Drawing: Les Echelles
House for a musician
Mallorca, Spain
12" × 12" (30.5 × 30.5 cm)
Medium: Ink on Mylar
Courtesy of Diana Agrest, Architect

There are three parallel angled shadow lines cast on the building elements above. The three horizontal edges casting these lines all appear as points (see **1** on the facing page). This fact helps us understand that each floor level must step back and that we are not seeing a continuous vertical facade. Shadows model a building form and give us clues to its shape and disposition. Note that the elevation shadows on the stairway take the same configuration (see facing page) regardless of the direction of the sun's rays. Sometimes stairway configurations protrude from a vertical surface (see below left).

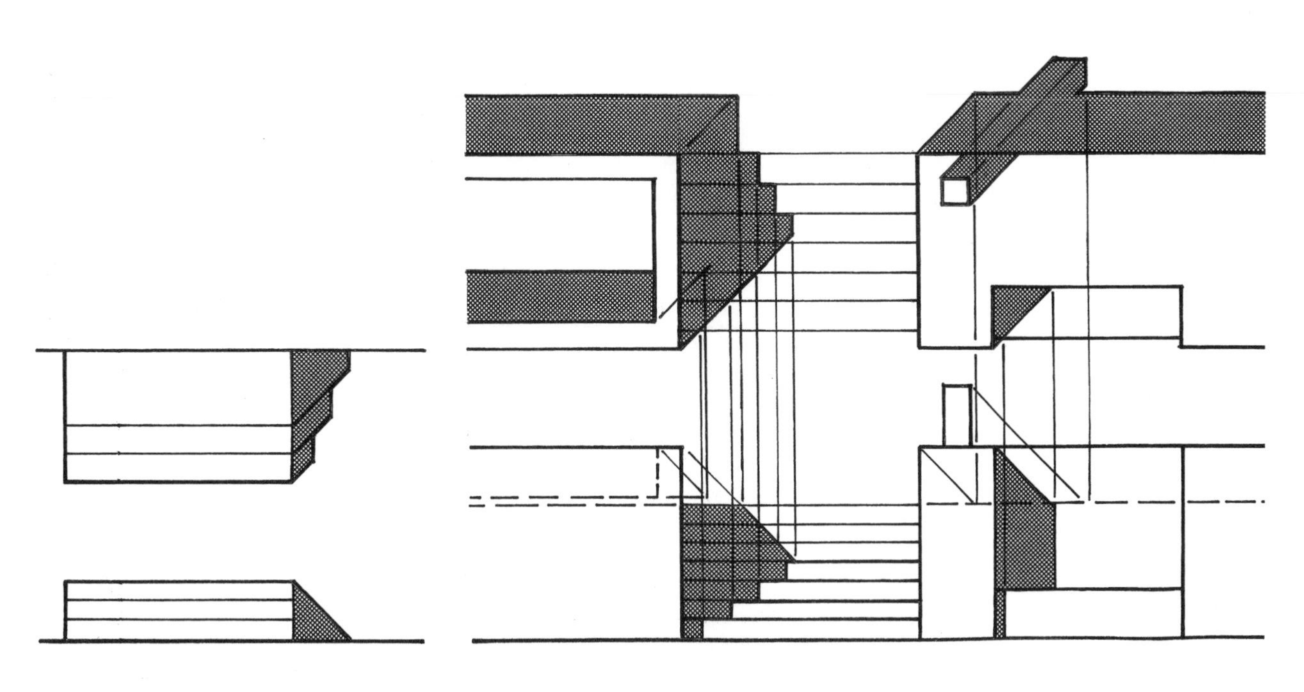

Shadows on Cylindrical Forms and Niches

Triangular and trapezoidal niches and cylindrical forms produce interesting shadows. The protruding element on this facade is slightly larger than a semicylinder, producing a shadow that begins in a hidden position, as seen in the frontal elevation.

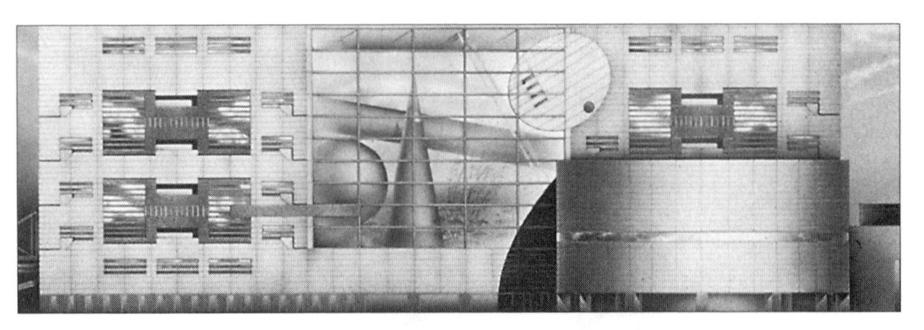

Drawing: Kunibiki Messe, Matsue, Shimane, Japan
48.6" × 33.1" (118.9 × 84.1 cm)
Medium: Airbrush
Courtesy of Shin Takamatsu Architect & Associates, Kyoto

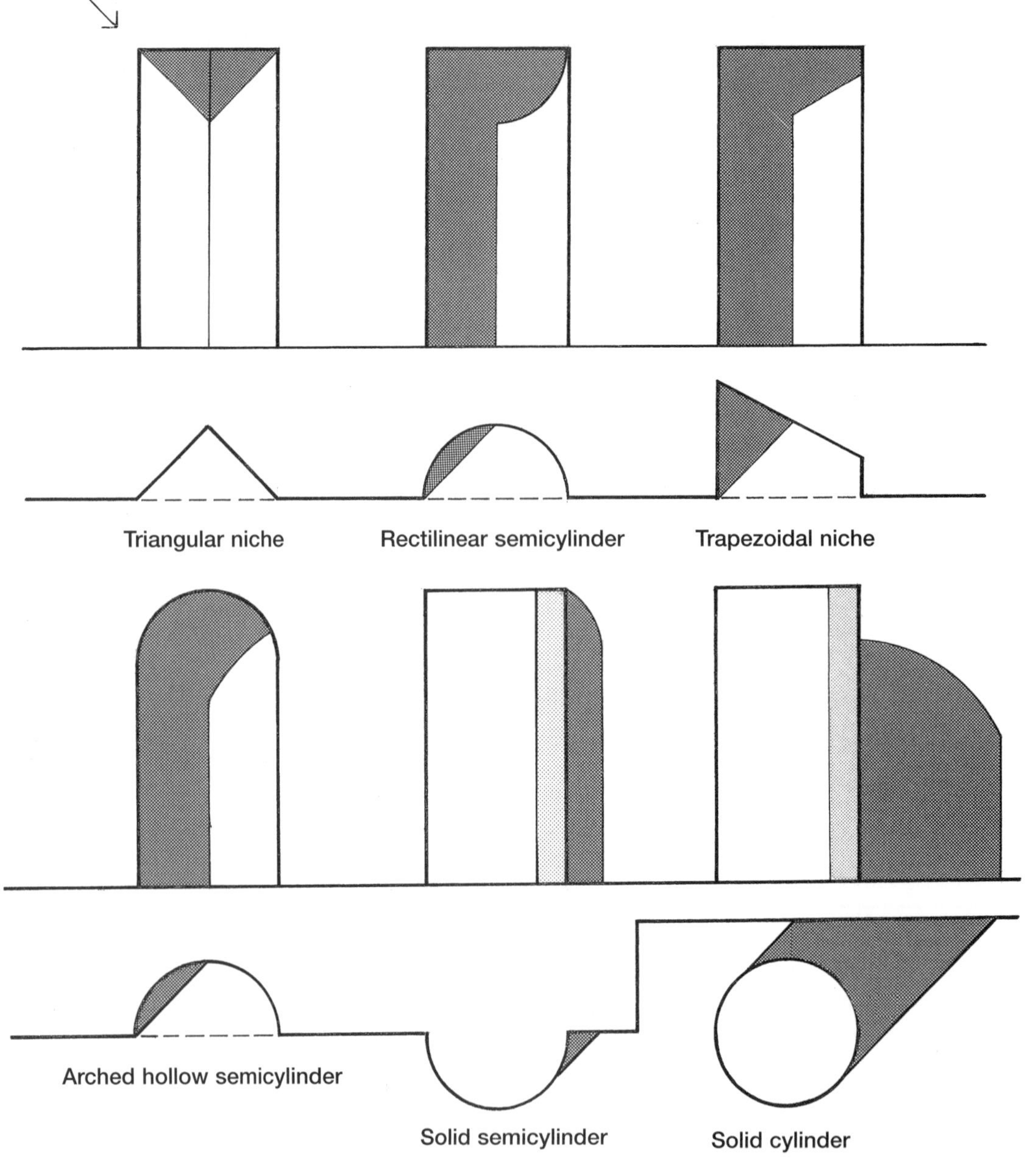

Shadow designs (two facing pages): Courtesy of Ann Cederna, Associate Professor
8½" × 11" (21.6 × 27.9 cm)
Original medium: Pencil
The Catholic University of America School of Architecture & Planning

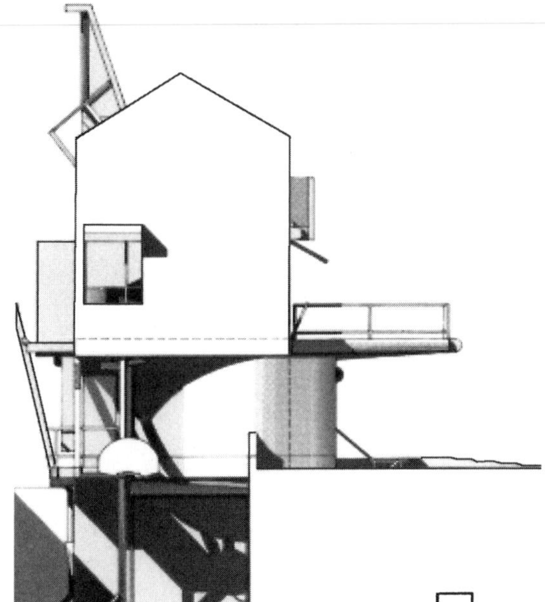

Drawing: Tract House
Manhattan Beach, California
11" × 11" (43.2 × 27.9 cm), Scale: ¼"=1'0"
Medium: Ink on Mylar with Zipatone
Courtesy of Holt Hinshaw Pfau Jones, Architecture

Shadows on Niches, Recessions, and Protrusions

We see overhangs and niches (see following two pages) primarily as elevation views. The shadows they cast give us hints as to the depth of overhangs and the amount of recessions.

Rectilinear niches and overhangs also produce interesting shadows. Overhangs in this example cast shadows on both flat and curvilinear surfaces. The curvilinear shape beneath the flat facade results in a curvilinear shadow line.

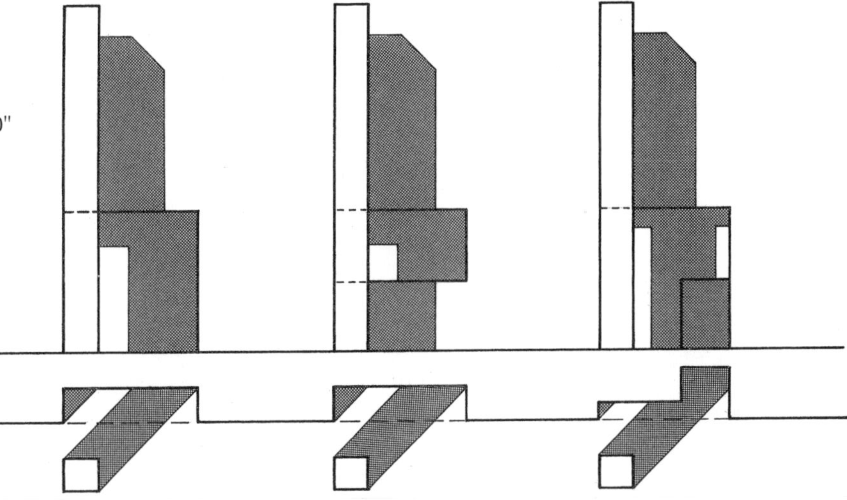

Rectilinear columns casting shadows on rectilinear niches

© Charles Yim

The shadow conditions on the buildings on these facing pages are combined in this photo and are shown as crisscrossing shadows.

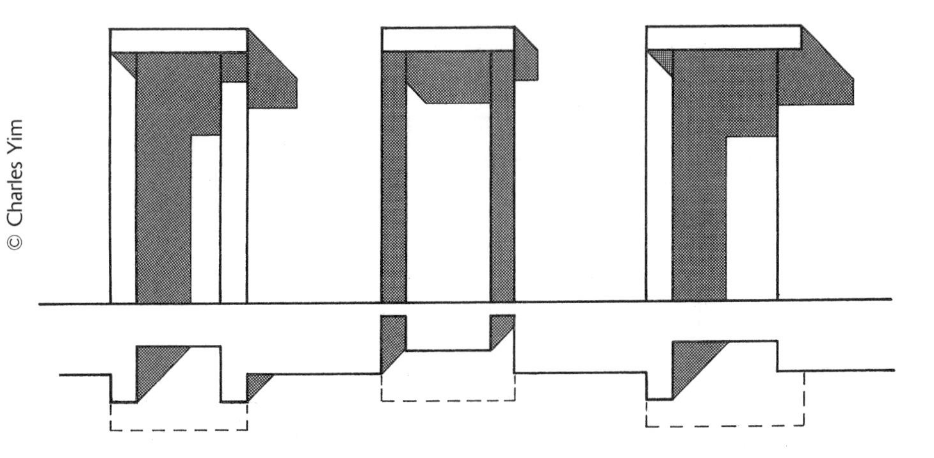

Overhangs casting shadows on rectilinear wall recessions and protrusions

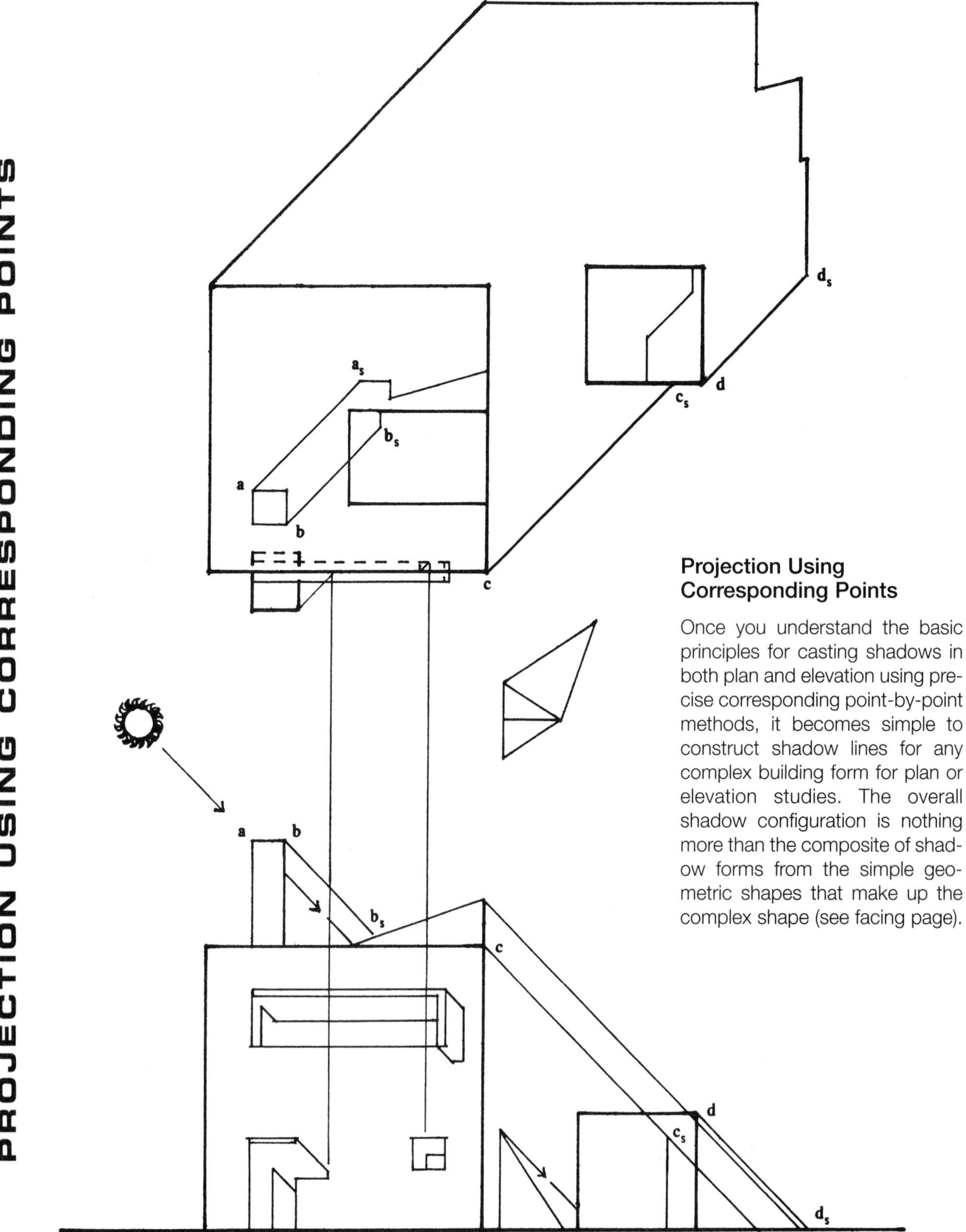

Projection Using Corresponding Points

Once you understand the basic principles for casting shadows in both plan and elevation using precise corresponding point-by-point methods, it becomes simple to construct shadow lines for any complex building form for plan or elevation studies. The overall shadow configuration is nothing more than the composite of shadow forms from the simple geometric shapes that make up the complex shape (see facing page).

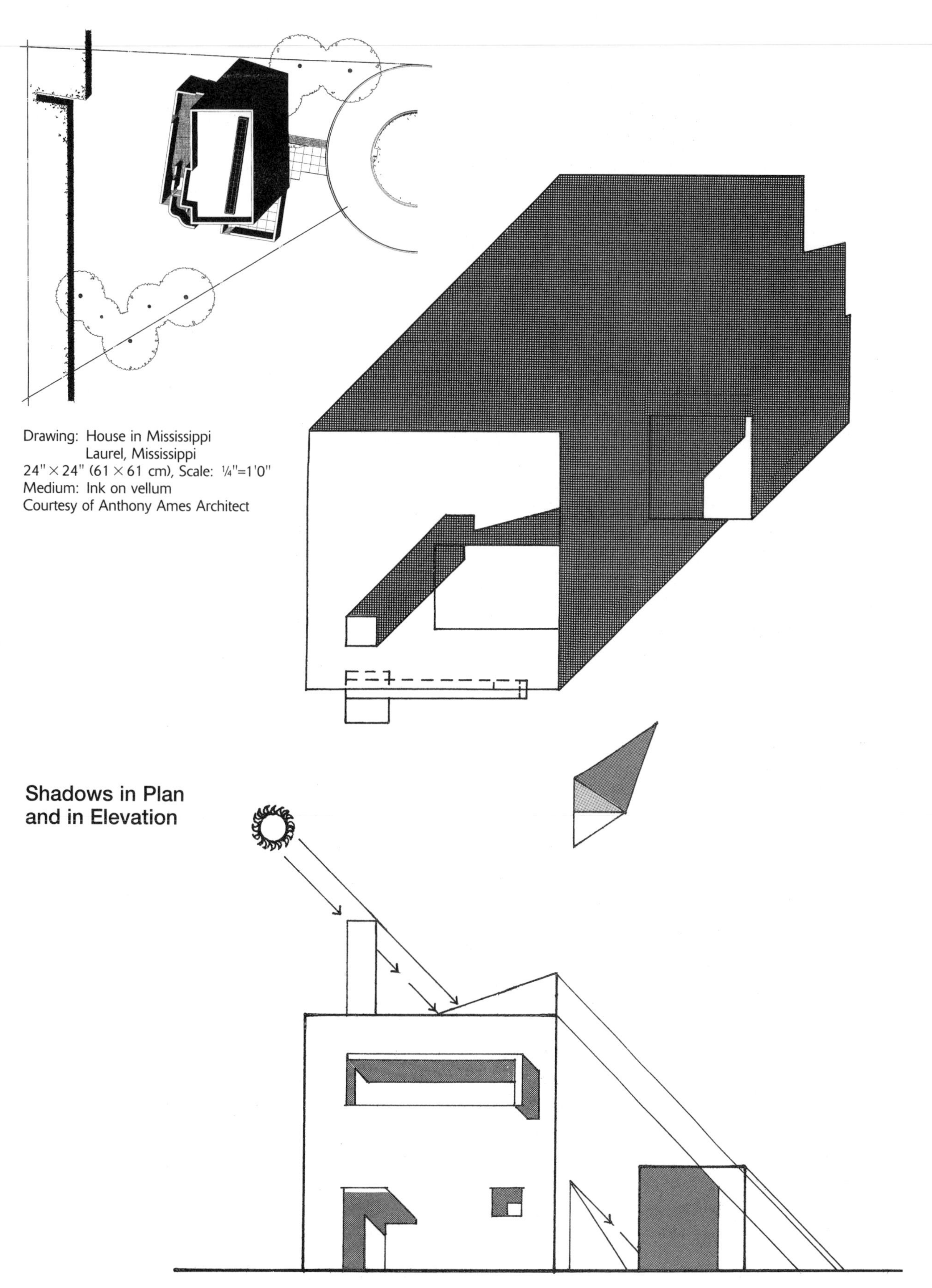

Drawing: House in Mississippi
Laurel, Mississippi
24" × 24" (61 × 61 cm), Scale: ¼"=1'0"
Medium: Ink on vellum
Courtesy of Anthony Ames Architect

Shadows in Plan and in Elevation

SHADOWS IN PLAN AND IN ELEVATION

Drawing: Villa Gables
Meersbusch near Dusseldorf, Germany
Southwest facade 15" × 9" (381. × 22.9 cm), Scale: 1:50
Medium: Colored pencil on yellow tracing paper
Courtesy of Michael Graves, Architect
Photo credit: Marek Bulaj

The representational style that architect Michael Graves uses in his soft, colored pencil drawings is characterized by predominantly frontal views such as elevations (see Bibliography).

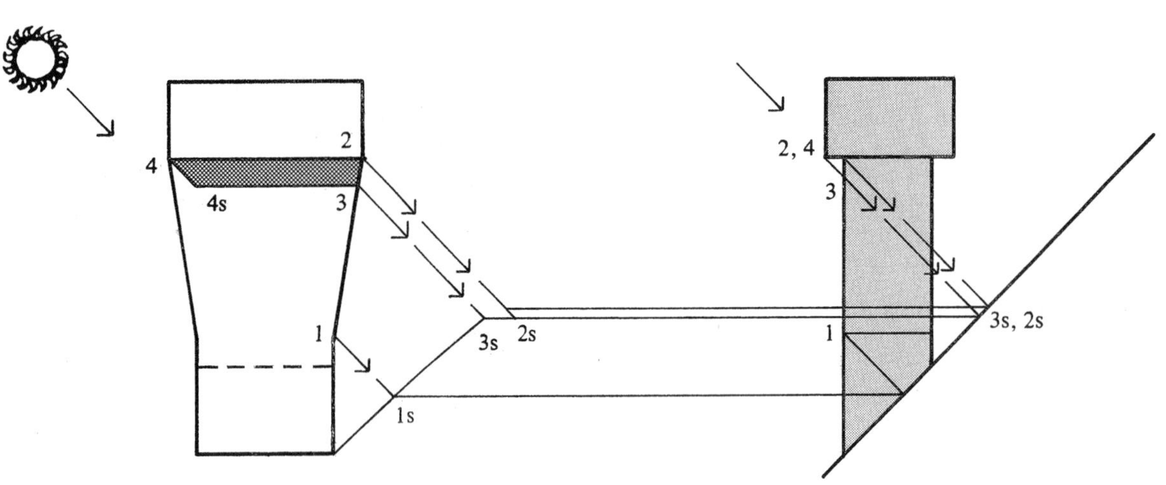

Shadows on Inclined Surfaces

Chimneys are commonly seen casting shadows on a roof plane that is inclined. Most chimney shapes are rectilinear; this example shows a slight variation. With two or more elevations, you can project shadow construction lines from one to the other to determine the proper shadow configuration. Always label the critical points in all views and be systematic in your convention.

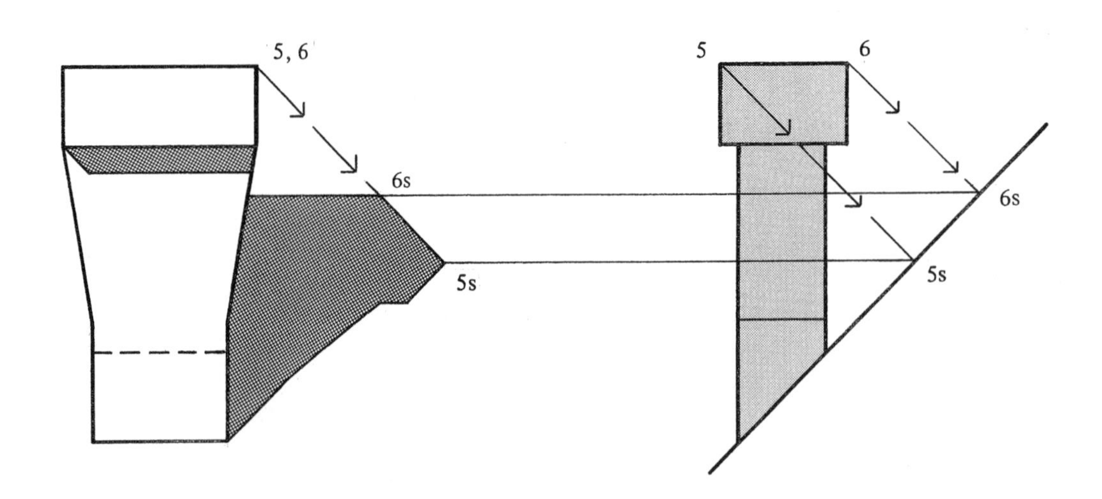

Drawing: Villa Gables
Meerbusch near Dusseldorf, Germany
Northwest facade 14" × 9" (35.6 × 22.9 cm), Scale: 1:50
Medium: Colored pencil on yellow tracing paper
Courtesy of Michael Graves, Architect
Photo credit: Marek Bulaj

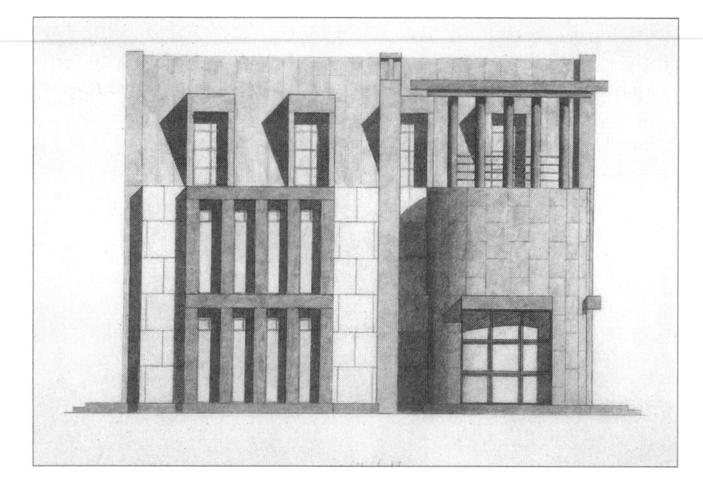

A dormer is characterized by a projection that extends above a wall and intersects a sloping roof. Windows on its front vertical face provide light, ventilation, and attic space. These two examples show typical shade and shadow conditions.

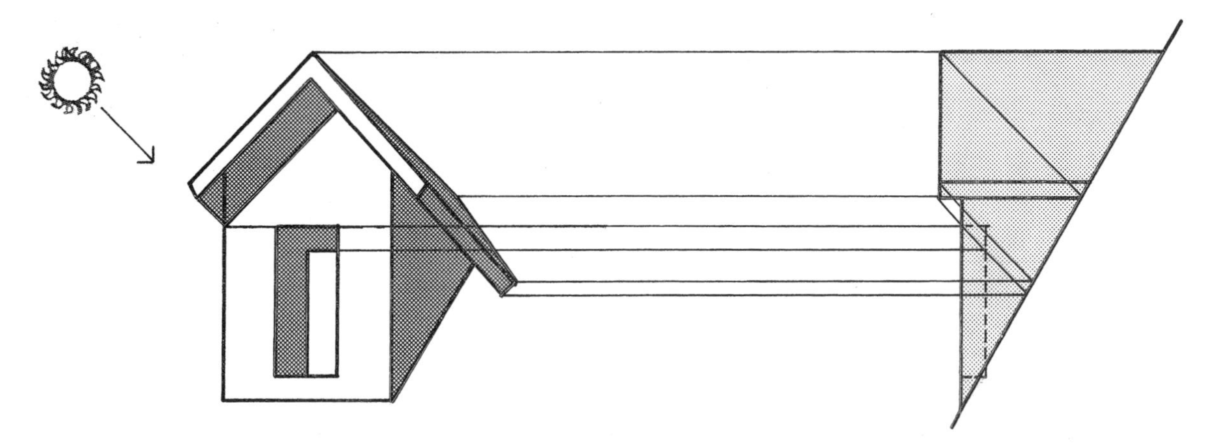

Dormers exhibit a combination of shadows on vertical and inclined surfaces seen in elevation. The profile of the side elevation of the dormer that is seen in shade will cast critical points on the sloping roof. These points are horizontally projected back into the front elevation in order to locate the same critical points seen in the front elevation view.

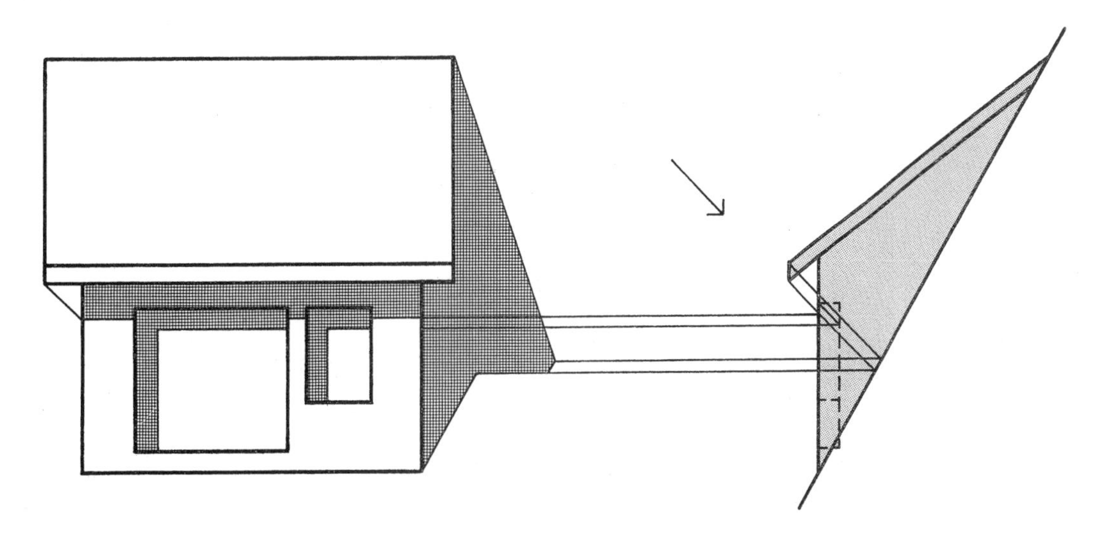

Since the sun's light rays are assumed to be **parallel,** they cause vertical (parallel) object lines to cast **parallel shadow lines** on flat or inclined surfaces. This is always true for shadow lines seen either in the plan view or in the elevation view (see the example at right).

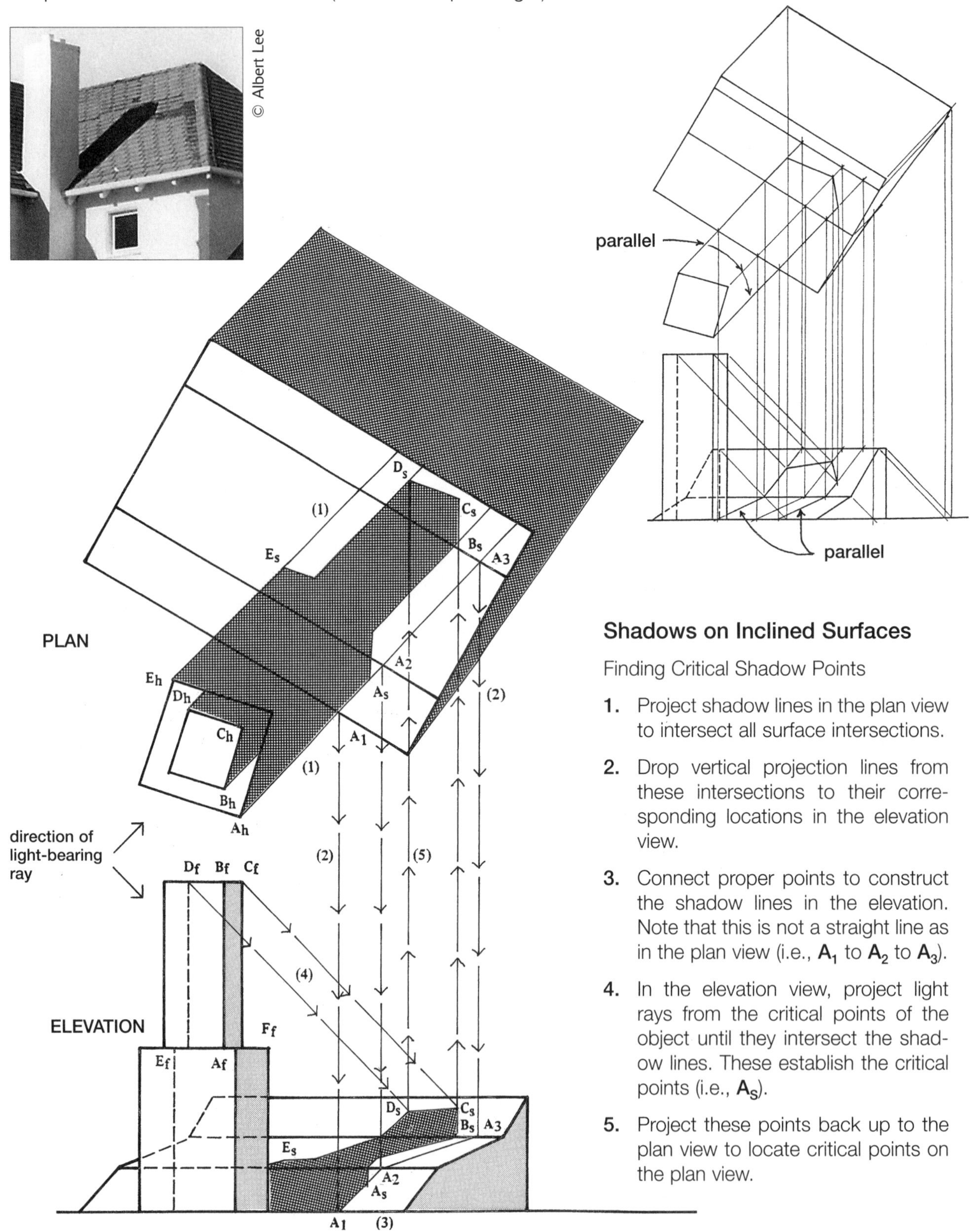

Shadows on Inclined Surfaces

Finding Critical Shadow Points

1. Project shadow lines in the plan view to intersect all surface intersections.
2. Drop vertical projection lines from these intersections to their corresponding locations in the elevation view.
3. Connect proper points to construct the shadow lines in the elevation. Note that this is not a straight line as in the plan view (i.e., $\mathbf{A_1}$ to $\mathbf{A_2}$ to $\mathbf{A_3}$).
4. In the elevation view, project light rays from the critical points of the object until they intersect the shadow lines. These establish the critical points (i.e., $\mathbf{A_S}$).
5. Project these points back up to the plan view to locate critical points on the plan view.

This curvilinear roof fenestration casts a strong shadow in the sectional elevation. This is another nice example of shadows cast within the section.

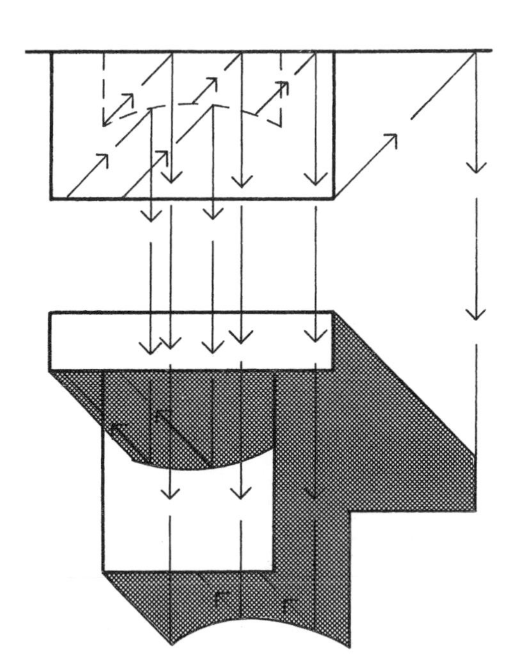

Shadows on Curvilinear Surfaces

Curvilinear surfaces differ from inclined surfaces because a series of points, rather than just end points, are needed. Shadow lines on a curvilinear surface cast by a horizontal line can be determined by plotting arbitrary points. Likewise, the same procedure applies for a curvilinear line casting a shadow line on a horizontal surface.

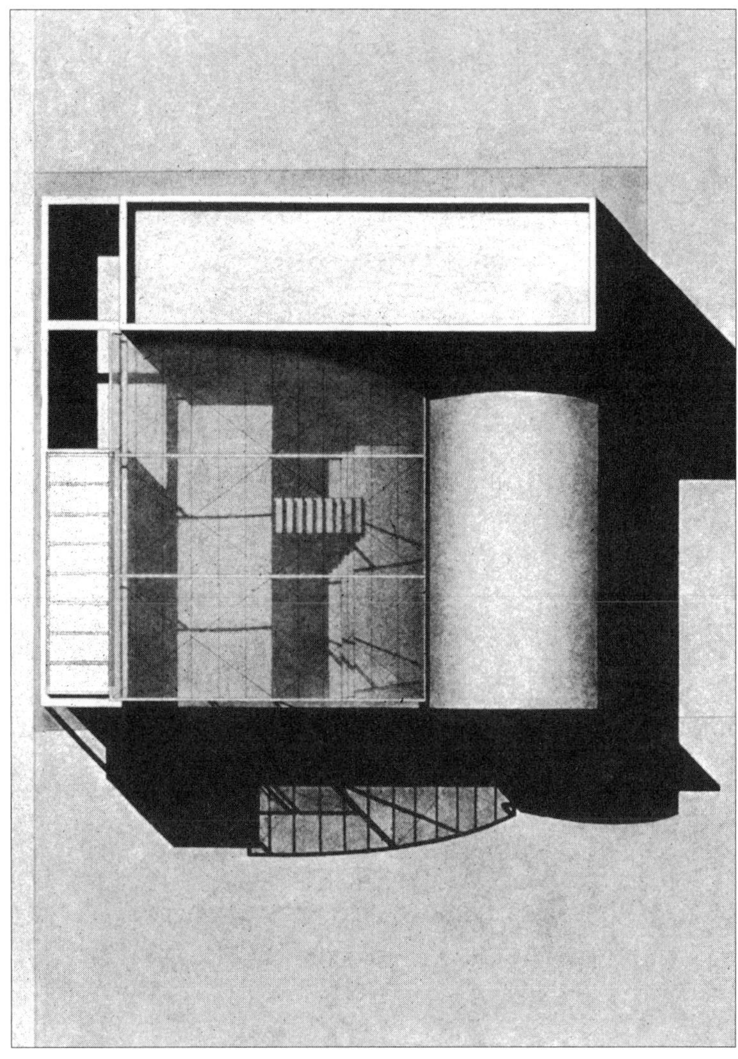

Drawings: Sugita House, Katsushika-ku, Tokyo, Japan
9.88" × 13.88" (25.1 × 35.3 cm), Scale: 1/30"=1'0"
Medium: Charcoal
Courtesy of Riken Yamamoto & Field Shop, Architects
Drawing by Monica Shanley

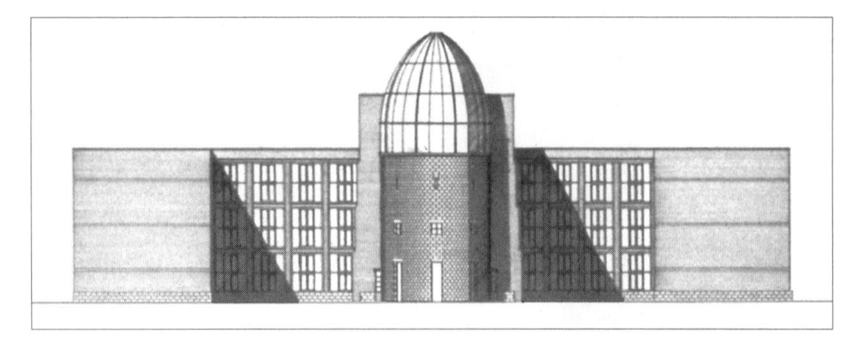

Drawing: Bonnefanten Museum
Maastrich, Holland
33.25" × 23.5" (84.1 × 59.4 cm), Scale: 1:200
Medium: Black and red ink on vellum
Courtesy of Aldo Rossi, Architect
with Etienne van Sloun & Gregor Ramaekers

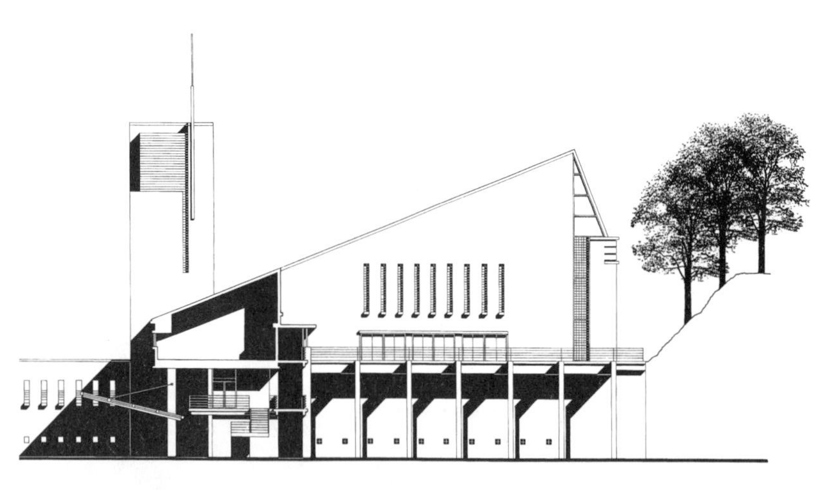

Drawing: Singapore American School, Singapore
36" × 24" (91 × 61.4 cm)
Medium: Ink on Mylar
Courtesy of Perkins & Will Architects

Shadows in Elevation

The form displacement and composition of the fenestration on building facades cannot be rendered without shadows. Intersecting 90° exterior walls (above) produce a continuous shadow line. Intersecting exterior walls at uneven heights produce a broken shadow line. If a cylindrical form has a shaded side, as shown above, no shadow can fall on the shaded area.

Shadows provide clues as to how a facade articulates. For example, the wider the shadow on a receiving surface, the more the protruding element casting that shadow will extend outward. Shadows on elevations are an effective means of showing the massing and character of protruding and recessed elements. All of these examples have deeply cast shadows; they illustrate how two-dimensional elevations can be given a three-dimensional feeling and quality.

The purpose of elevation shadows in presentation drawings is to provide contrast in order to suggest a third dimension. In practice, the designer or delineator is free to choose the sunlight's direction and is not required to hew to convention: a light ray from behind the left shoulder of the viewer at a 45° angle. Select a position for the sun that accentuates the architectural design.

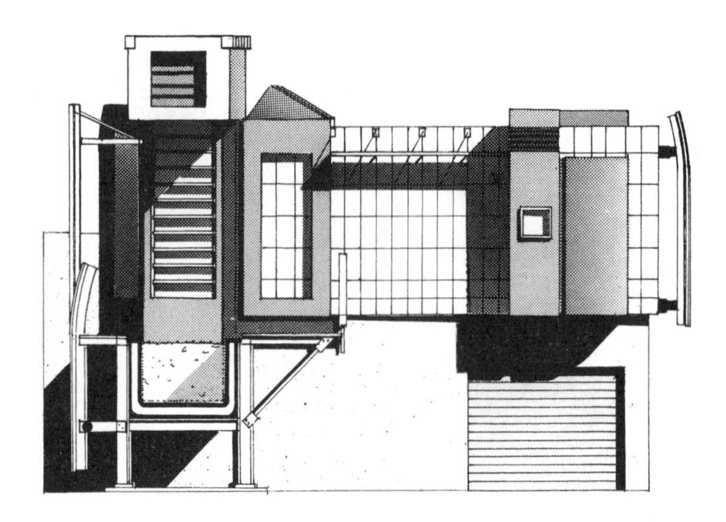

Drawing: Private studio, Venice, California
10" × 8" (25.4 × 20.3 cm), Scale: ⅛"=1'0"
Medium: Vellum, ink, and Zipatone
Courtesy of William Adams Architect

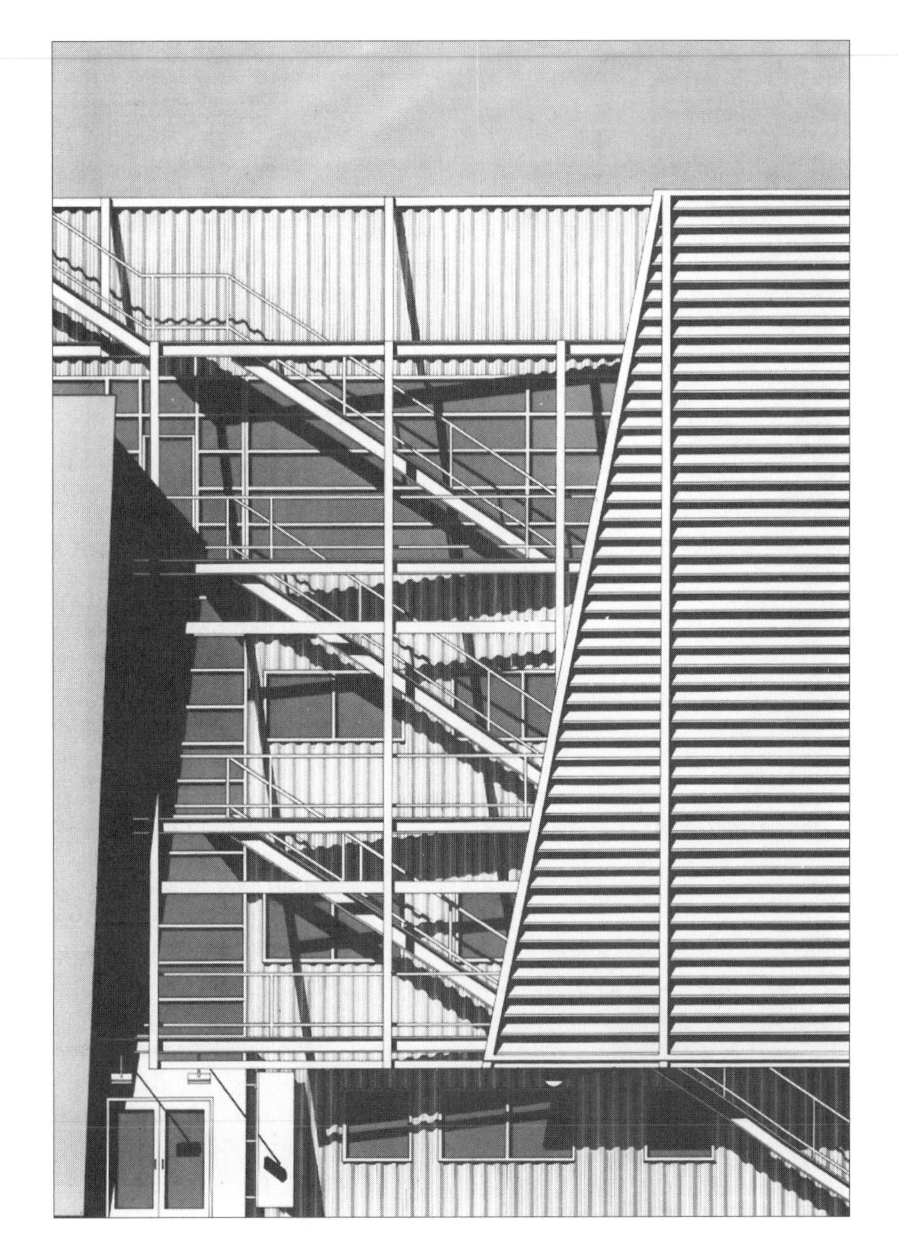

Drawing: Central Chiller Plant and Cogeneration Facility, UCLA
North elevation detail
24" × 30" (61 × 76.2 cm), Scale: ½"=1'0"
Medium: Ink on Mylar and Zipatone
Courtesy of Holt Hinshaw Pfau Jones Architecture

This north elevation has no true solar orientation. Therefore, in order to create a convincing portrayal of the complex building planes, the shade and shadow were constructed intuitively to best illuminate the juxtaposition of the orthogonal and nonorthogonal geometries.
[ARCHITECT'S STATEMENT BY PAUL C. HOLT]

The tight composition of this drawing allows it to be read both as a representation of three-dimensional space and as an abstract two-dimensional composition. Due to the fact that the corrugated receiving surface slopes away from the viewer, the cast shadows rake across it, introducing a secondary geometry to this otherwise orthogonal composition. Moreover, they afford a greater sense of depth to a drawing format that traditionally tends to compress space.
[ARCHITECT'S STATEMENT BY WES JONES]

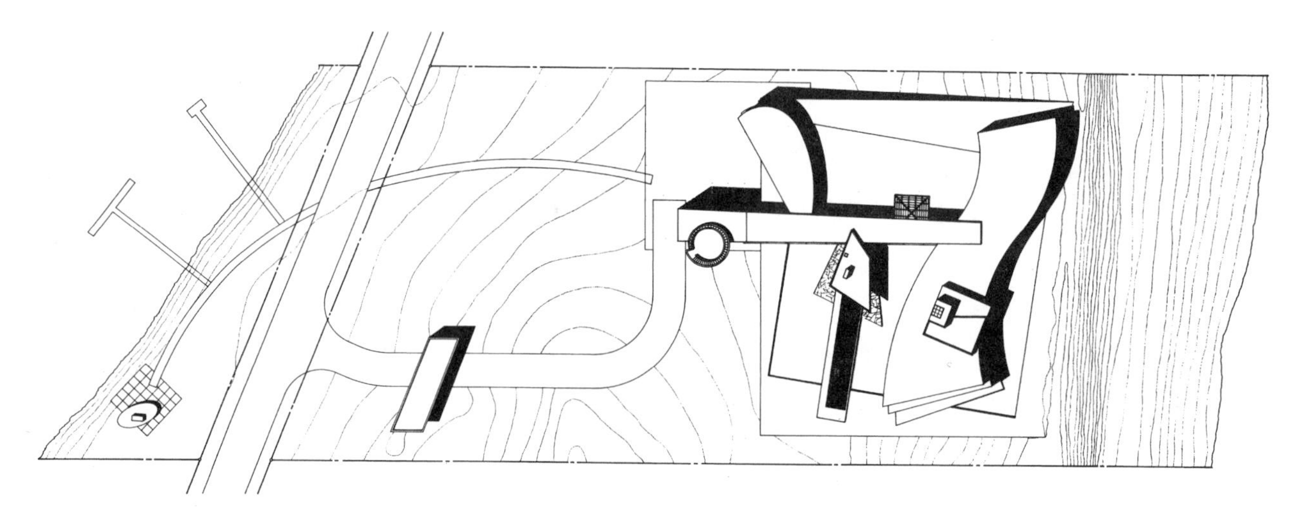

Drawing: Worrel residence, Hillsborough, Florida
36" × 24" (91.4 × 61 cm)
Medium: Ink on vellum
Courtesy of Arquitectonica International Corporation

Shadows on Roof and Site Plans

When a site plan contains many elements, as in these examples, the resolution of their proper shadow lengths will require both the plan and the elevation (height) of each element. The procedure is analogous to resolving shadow lengths for wall elements seen in elevation. Note that the shadows cast by the structures above mimic the size, shape, and orientation of the structures' roof lines. We can infer that the structures are all about the same height above the ground plane, which for the most part has a flat topography.

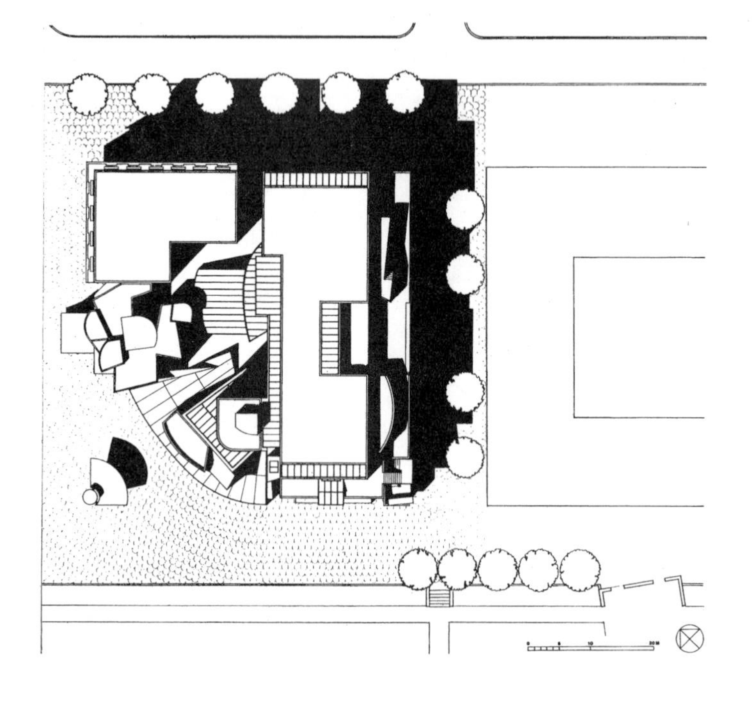

Drawing: American Center, Bercy Park, Paris, France
30" × 40" (76.2 × 101.6 cm)
Medium: Ink on Mylar
Courtesy of Frank O. Gehry & Associates, Architects

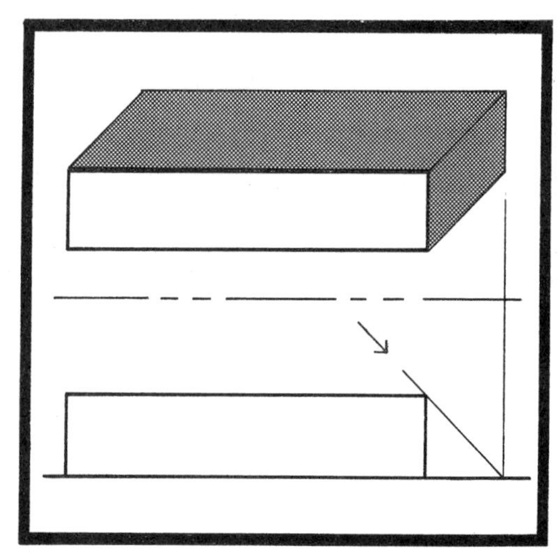

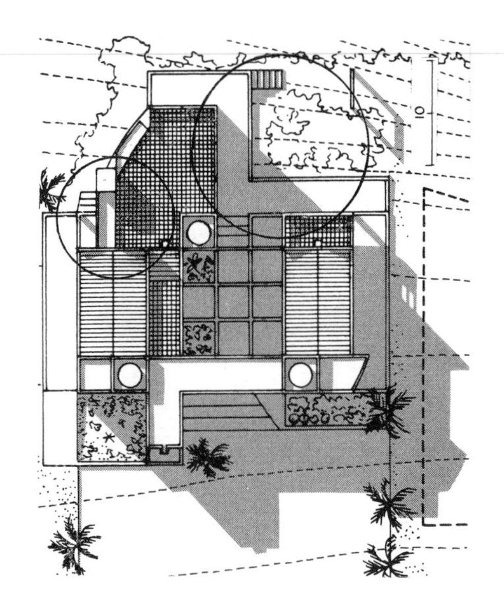

Drawing: Lohmann House
Akumal, Yucatan, Mexico
16" × 24" (40.6 × 61 cm), Scale: 1:100
Medium: Ink and Zipatone
Courtesy of George C. T. Woo, Architect, FAIA

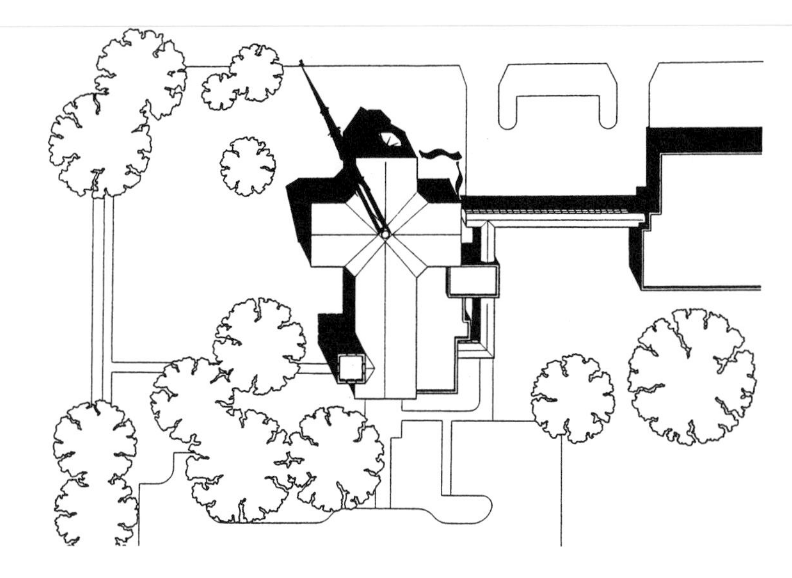

Drawing: The Church of St. Therese
Wilson, North Carolina
9.5" × 7" (24.1 × 17.8 cm), Scale: 1"=20'0"
Medium: Ink on Mylar
Courtesy of Allen, Harbinson & Associates, Architect

Circled situations in the above left site plan adhere to the following principles: In the plan view, light rays and shadow lines cast by **vertical** light/shade lines remain **parallel** regardless of the receiving surfaces' geometric configuration. The shadow line retains continuity in a straight line when it strikes the receiving geometric forms. The shadows of all the posts in the drawing at right are parallel to each other as well as to the shadows of the other structural elements, following the same principle.

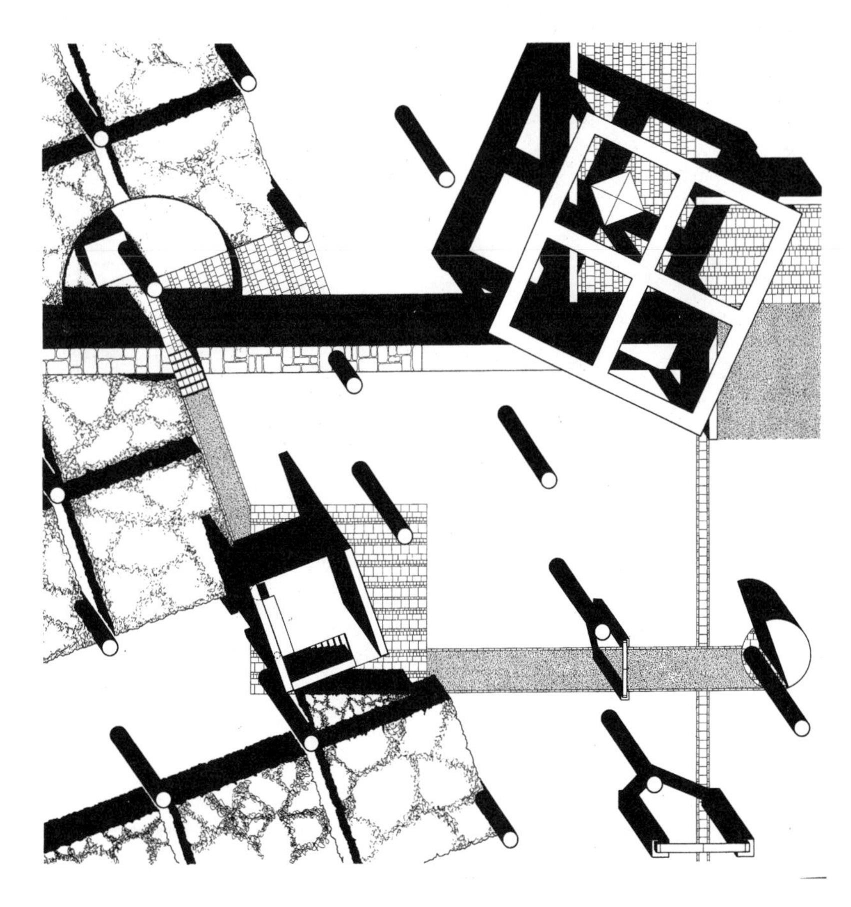

Drawing: Student project by Stephen Roberts and Doug Lincer
Garden intervention
Medium: Ink on Mylar
Courtesy of the University of Texas at Arlington School of Architecture

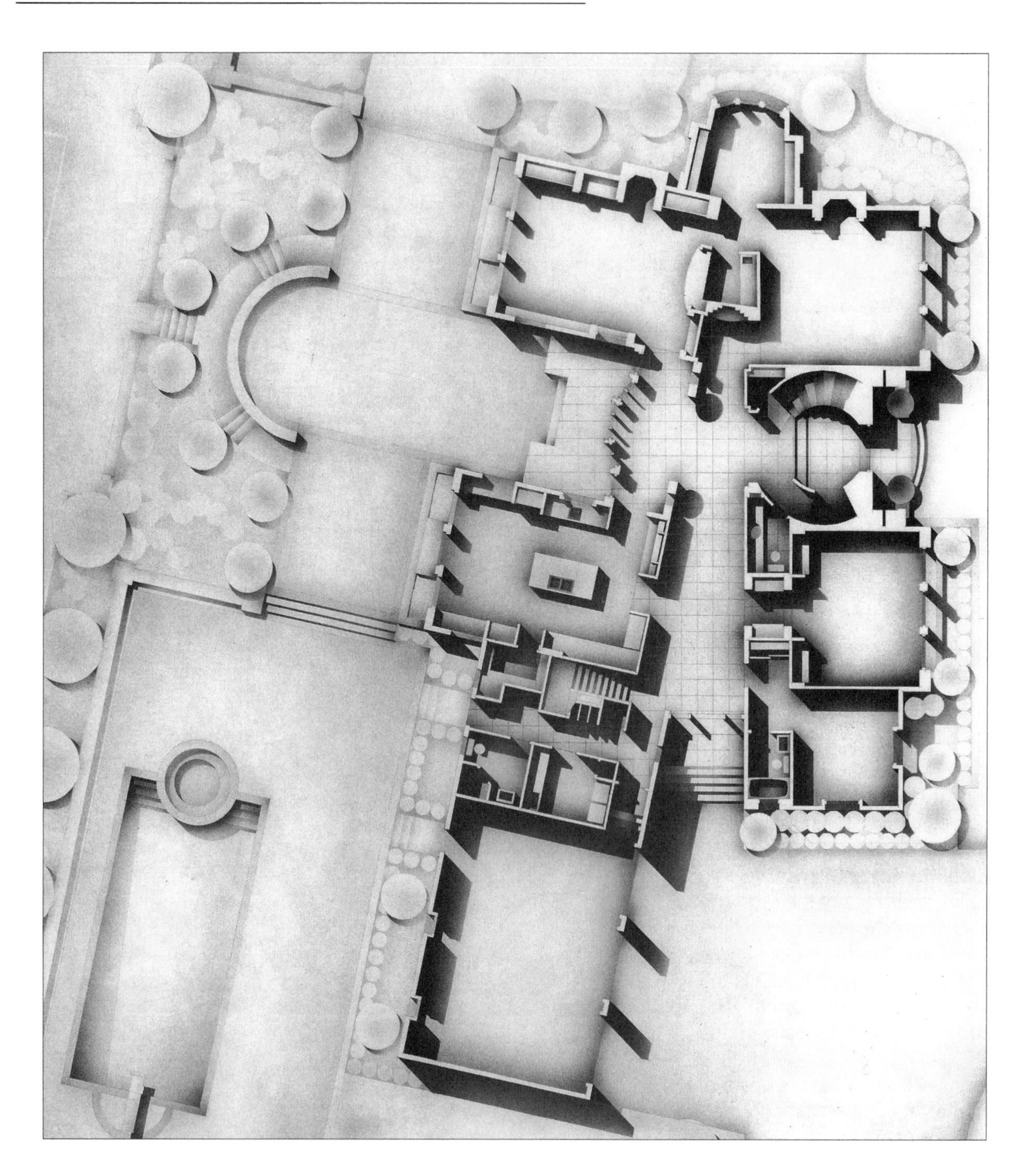

Drawing: Kahn residence, Hillsborough, California
24" × 30" (61 × 76.2 cm), Scale: ¼"=1'0"
Medium: Airbrush using acrylic inks over latex paint on Masonite board
Courtesy of House + House, Architects, San Francisco
Mark David English, Architectural Illustrator

Shadows Cast within the Plan

This drawing shows shadows cast in the plan view by vertical elements cut in plan. The purpose is to make the drawing read better by accentuating the heights of the elements (walls, columns, etc.). This creates a greater feeling of depth and eliminates the flatness of the plan view.

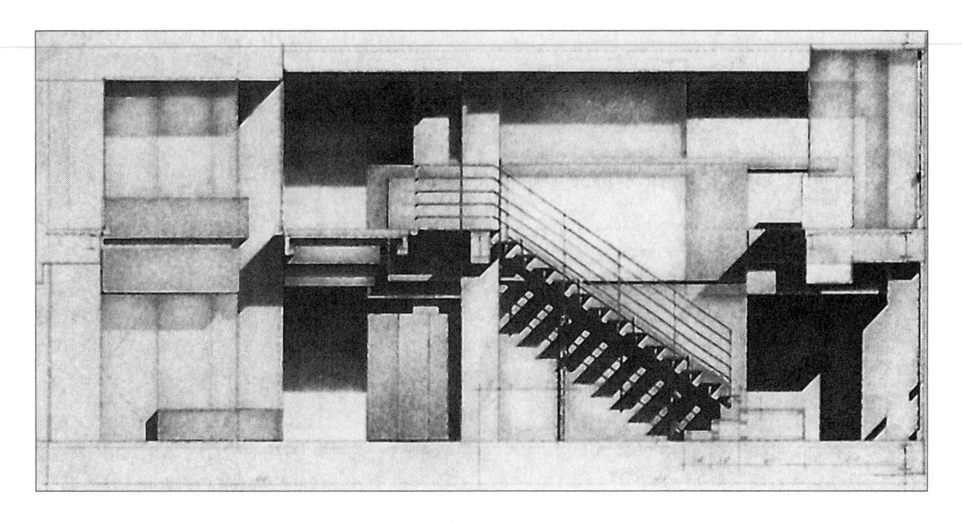

Drawing: The Stainless Steel Apartment, Chicago, Illinois
36" × 24" (91.4 × 61 cm), Scale: ½"=1'0"
Medium: Colored pencil
Courtesy of Krueck & Sexton, Architects, and
Ludwig Mies Van der Rohe, Building Architect

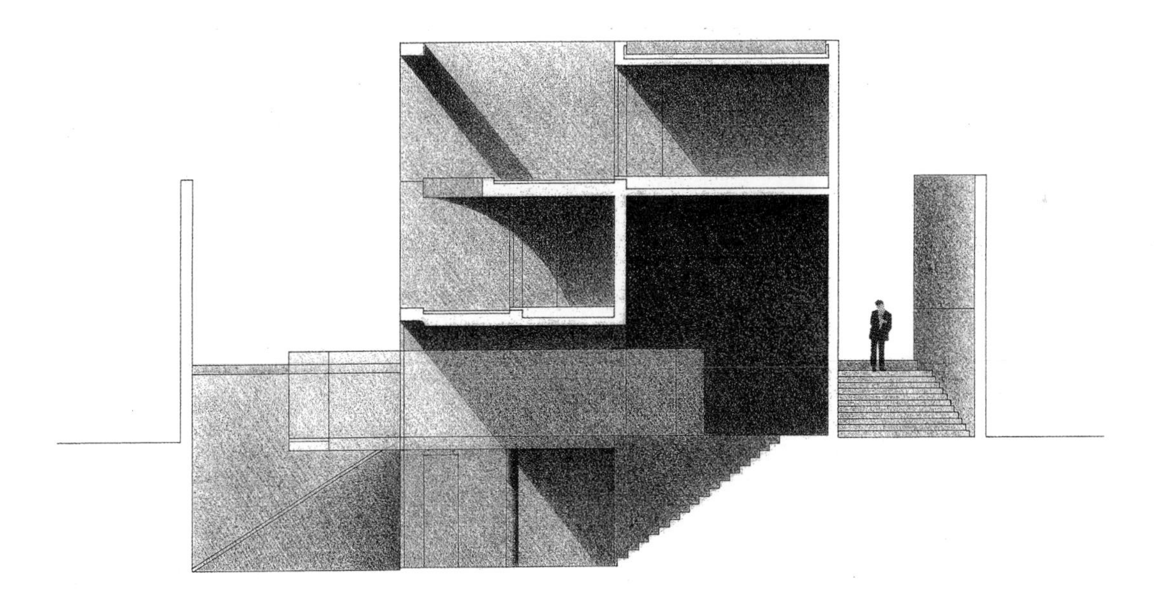

Drawing: I Gallery, Tokyo, Japan
429 × 297 mm (16.9" × 11.7"), Scale: 1:100
Medium: Colored pencil on the copy of the inked drawing
Courtesy of Tadao Ando, Architect

Shadows Cast within the Section

These drawings show shadows cast in a cut section. All elements that protrude (wall, floor, roof, stairs, built-in furniture, etc.) cast a shadow. This allows a normally flat two-dimensional section to "punch out." In the gallery drawing, note the gradual change in the tonal value of the shadows cast. This rendering technique helps to more clearly define the interior spaces. Architects and designers use shadows to help accentuate and articulate their design ideas and goals.

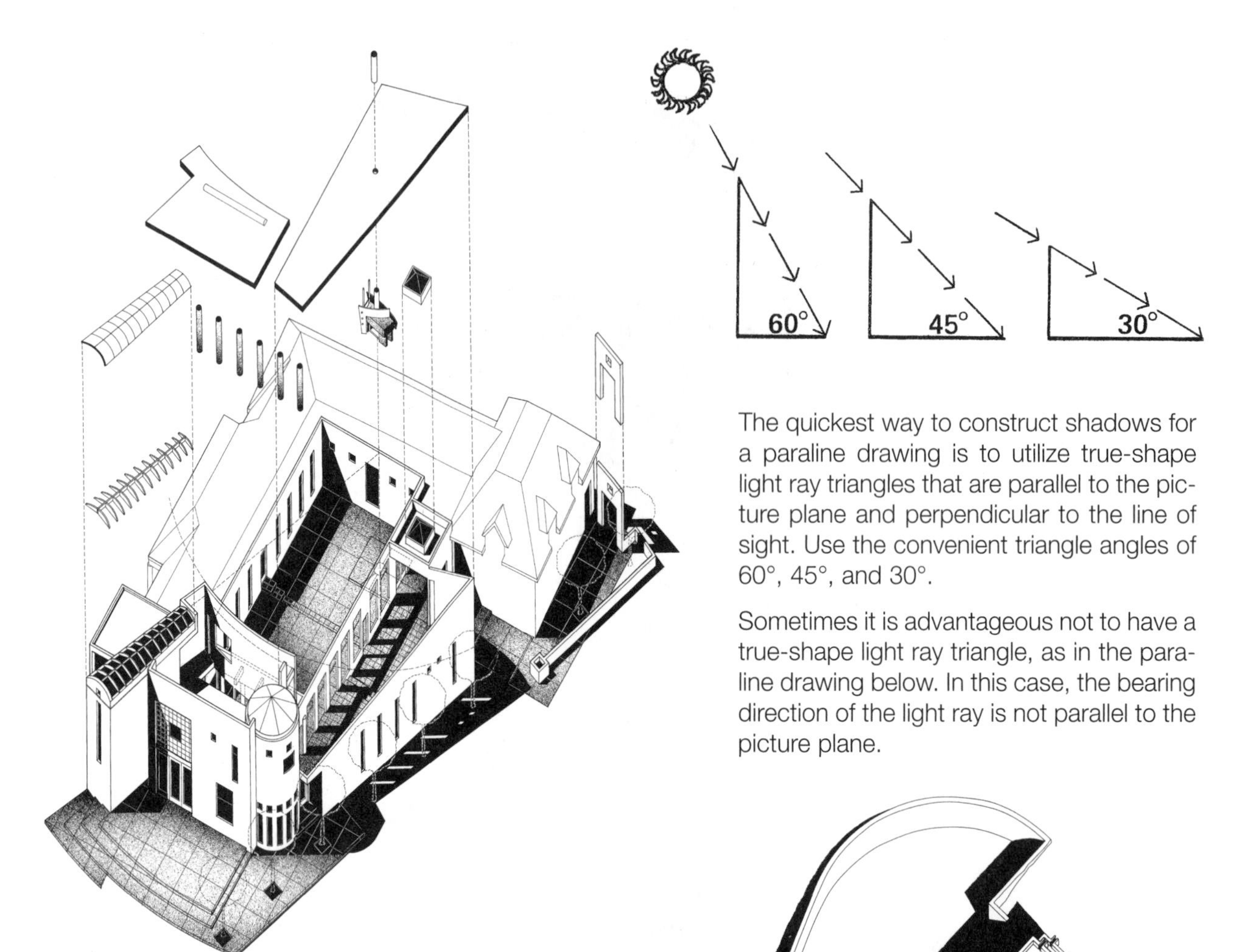

The quickest way to construct shadows for a paraline drawing is to utilize true-shape light ray triangles that are parallel to the picture plane and perpendicular to the line of sight. Use the convenient triangle angles of 60°, 45°, and 30°.

Sometimes it is advantageous not to have a true-shape light ray triangle, as in the paraline drawing below. In this case, the bearing direction of the light ray is not parallel to the picture plane.

Drawing: Shamash residence, Hillsborough, California
20" × 28" (50.8 × 71.1 cm), Scale: ⅛"=1'0"
Medium: Pen and ink and airbrush on Mylar
Courtesy of Steven House, Architect

Shadows Cast in Paraline Drawings

Shadows on buildings in paraline drawings create a strong three-dimensional feeling, as shown in these examples. A paraline drawing without shadows is relatively flat. Absent or just lightly rendered shade on planes is permissible when fenestration detail must be clear (see above). Always choose a convenient angle (45° or 60°) and direction for the slope of the light rays. Complex configurations can best be resolved by a series of shadow-point-casting triangles.

Drawing: Kress residence, Albuquerque, New Mexico
20" × 30" (50.8 × 76.2 cm), Scale: ¼"=1'0"
Medium: Ink on vellum
Courtesy of Robert W. Peters FAIA,
Alianza Arquitectos/An Architect's Alliance

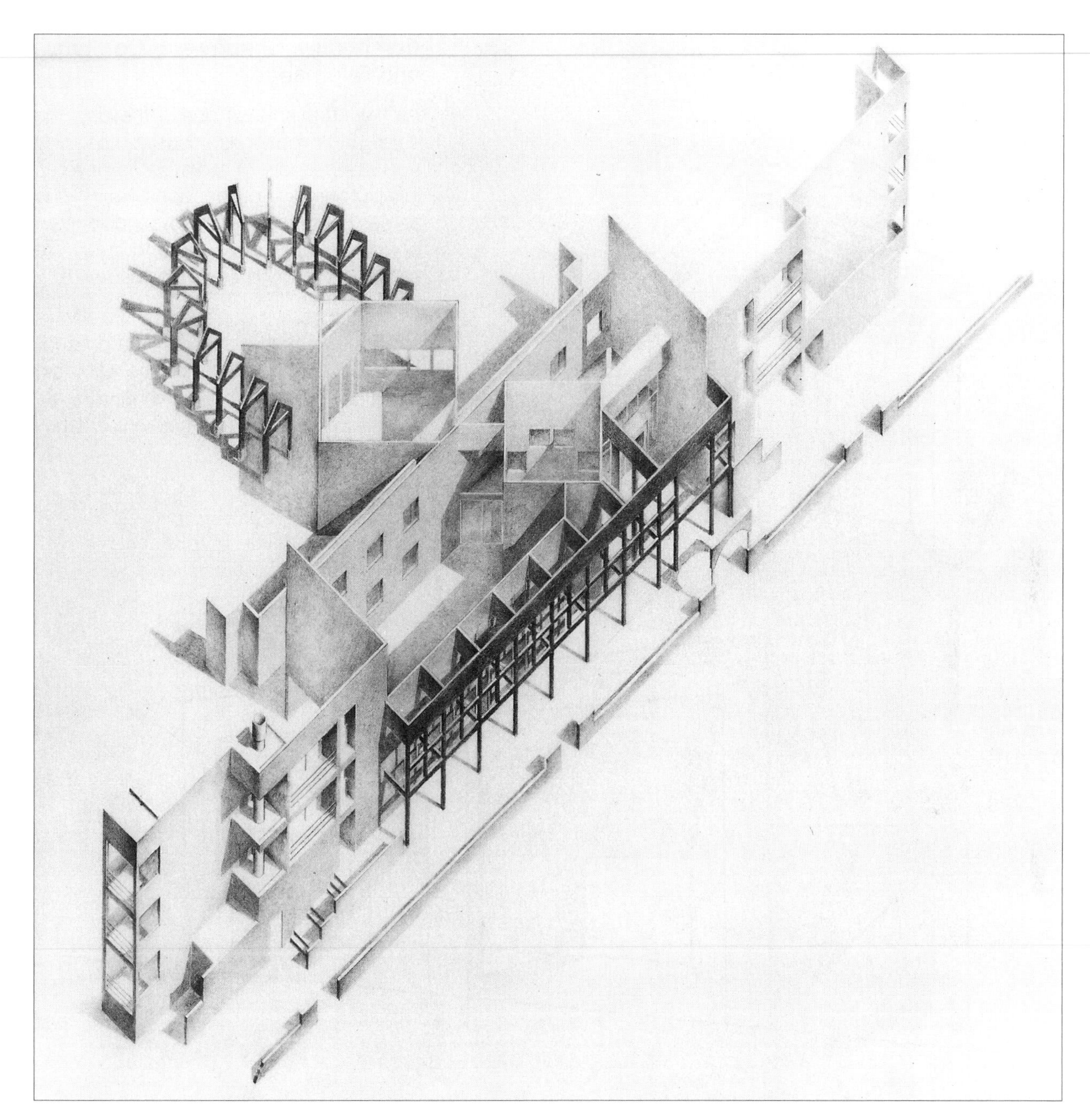

Drawing: Verdugo Hacienda Housing for the Elderly, Sunland–Tujunga, California
24" × 24" (61 × 61 cm), Scale: 1/8"=1'0"
Medium: Ink and colored pencil
Courtesy of John V. Mutlow FAIA, Architects

To articulate the basic premise of this courtyard building, only the important public spaces and enclosure planes were selected for delineation. The brise-soleil *shades the south-facing front elevation, and the rotating volumes connect the off-center enclosure to the axial courtyard and lanai. The shadows were then cast in order to best articulate the building form and movement sequence.*
[ARCHITECT'S STATEMENT]

This drawing does not use a true-shape light ray triangle. Note the use of soft shadows.

Perspective Shadows of Dormers and Overhangs

As the earth rotates during the day, the solar angle changes, causing the perspective shadow of a dormer to have an infinite number of positions as it falls across a sloping roof. Two conditions on opposite uphill sides of a dormer are shown on this and the facing page.

Dormer shadows sloping uphill are always shorter than they would be on a horizontal surface, regardless of the light ray direction. When sloping downhill, they are always longer than on a horizontal plane.

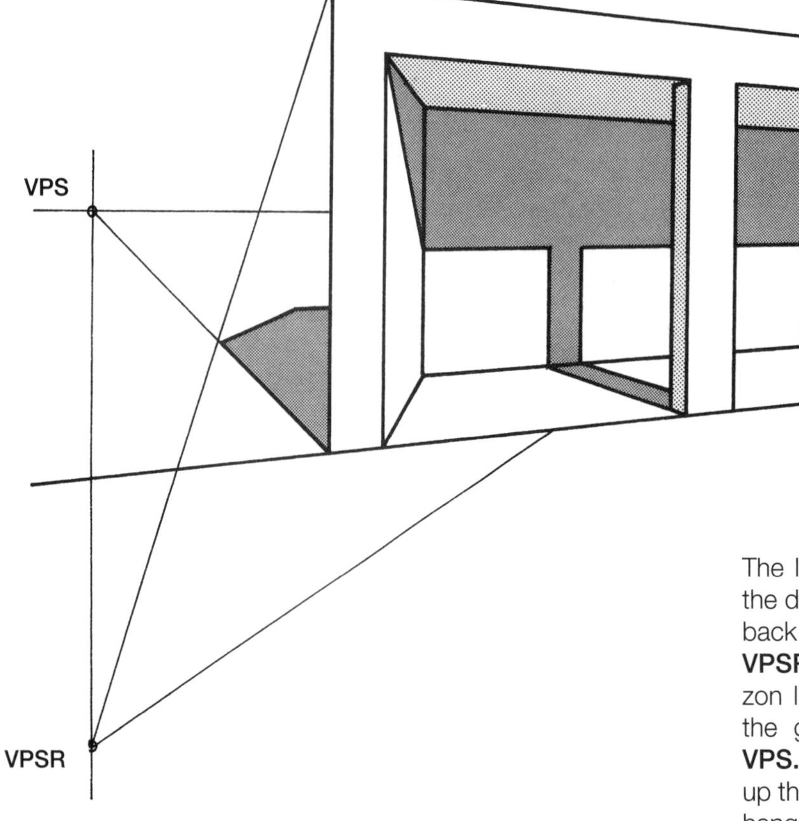

The location of the **VPSR** will determine the depth of the overhang shadow on the back wall. A vertical line through the **VPSR** will determine the **VPS** on the horizon line. The columns cast shadows on the ground; their edges vanish at the **VPS.** Then the shadows creep vertically up the back wall and connect to the overhang shadow.

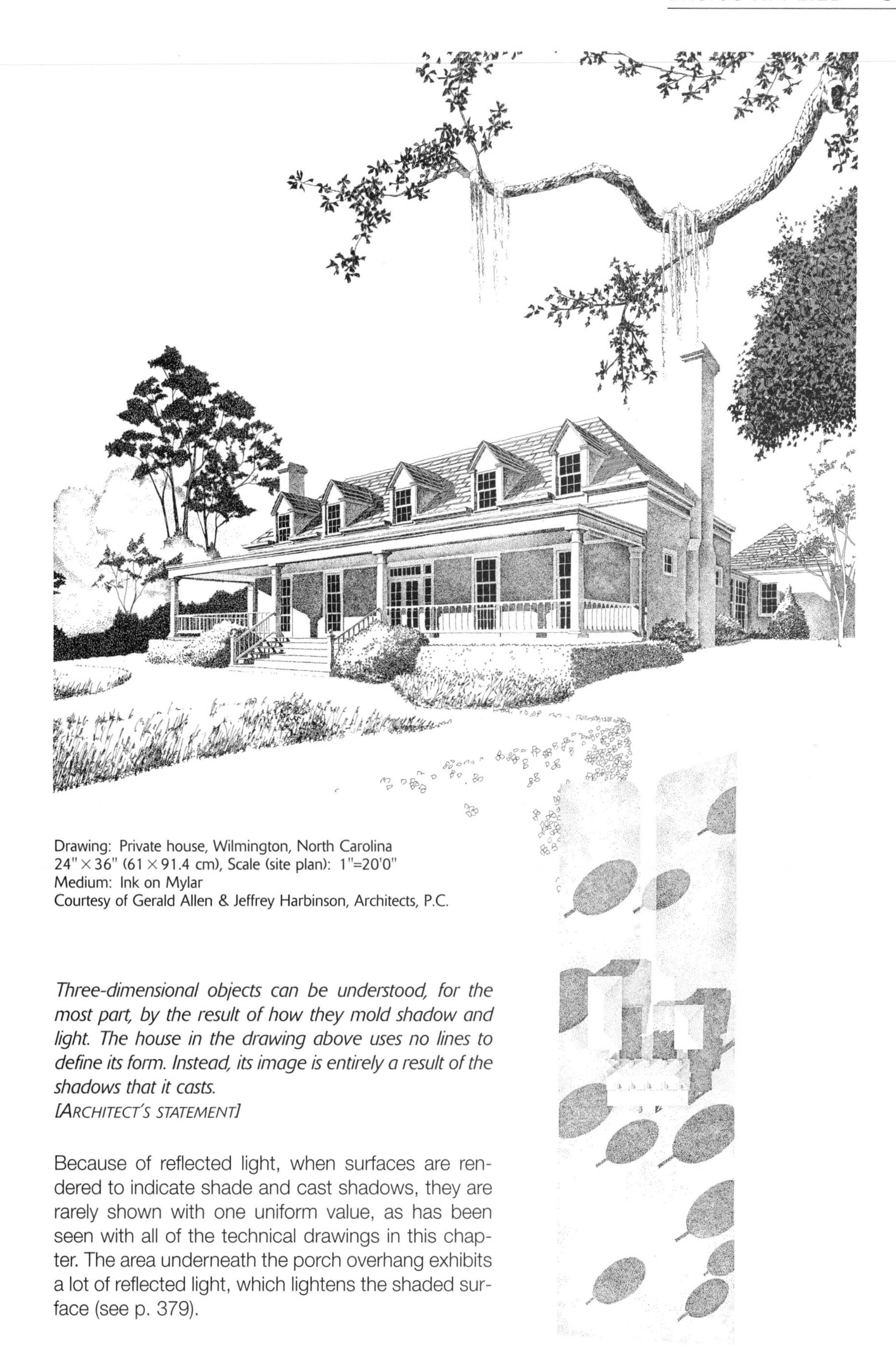

Drawing: Private house, Wilmington, North Carolina
24" × 36" (61 × 91.4 cm), Scale (site plan): 1"=20'0"
Medium: Ink on Mylar
Courtesy of Gerald Allen & Jeffrey Harbinson, Architects, P.C.

Three-dimensional objects can be understood, for the most part, by the result of how they mold shadow and light. The house in the drawing above uses no lines to define its form. Instead, its image is entirely a result of the shadows that it casts.
[Architect's statement]

Because of reflected light, when surfaces are rendered to indicate shade and cast shadows, they are rarely shown with one uniform value, as has been seen with all of the technical drawings in this chapter. The area underneath the porch overhang exhibits a lot of reflected light, which lightens the shaded surface (see p. 379).

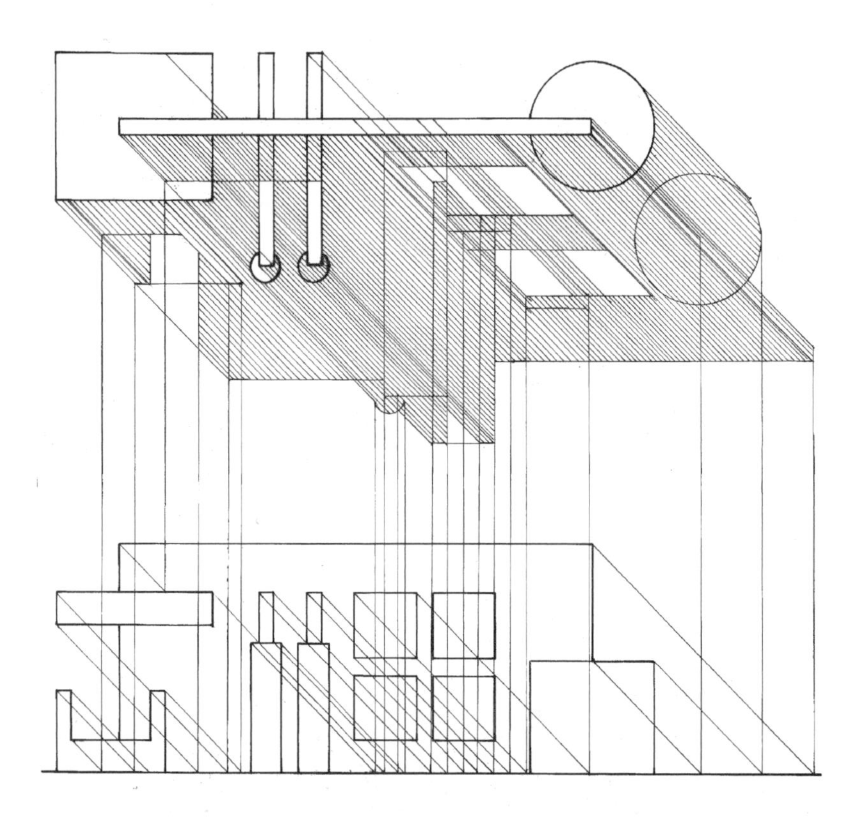

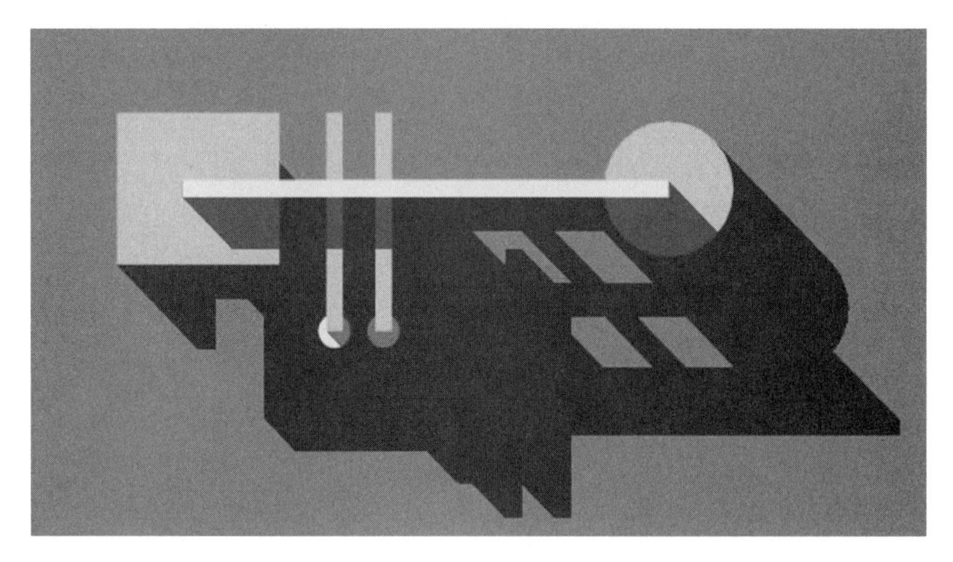

Student: Mark Stegeman
Professor: M. Saleh Uddin
Course: Design Communication I
Courtesy of University of Missouri–Columbia
Department of Environmental Design

Comparing Manually Cast and Digital Shadows

Hand-constructed shadows can be verified by casting the same shadow in a 3-D computer environment. The top drawing shows a manually constructed shadow using the principle of corresponding points. The bottom drawing shows a computer-generated shadow. A sun-altitude and bearing angle of 45° was used for both the plan and elevation. [PROFESSOR'S STATEMENT]

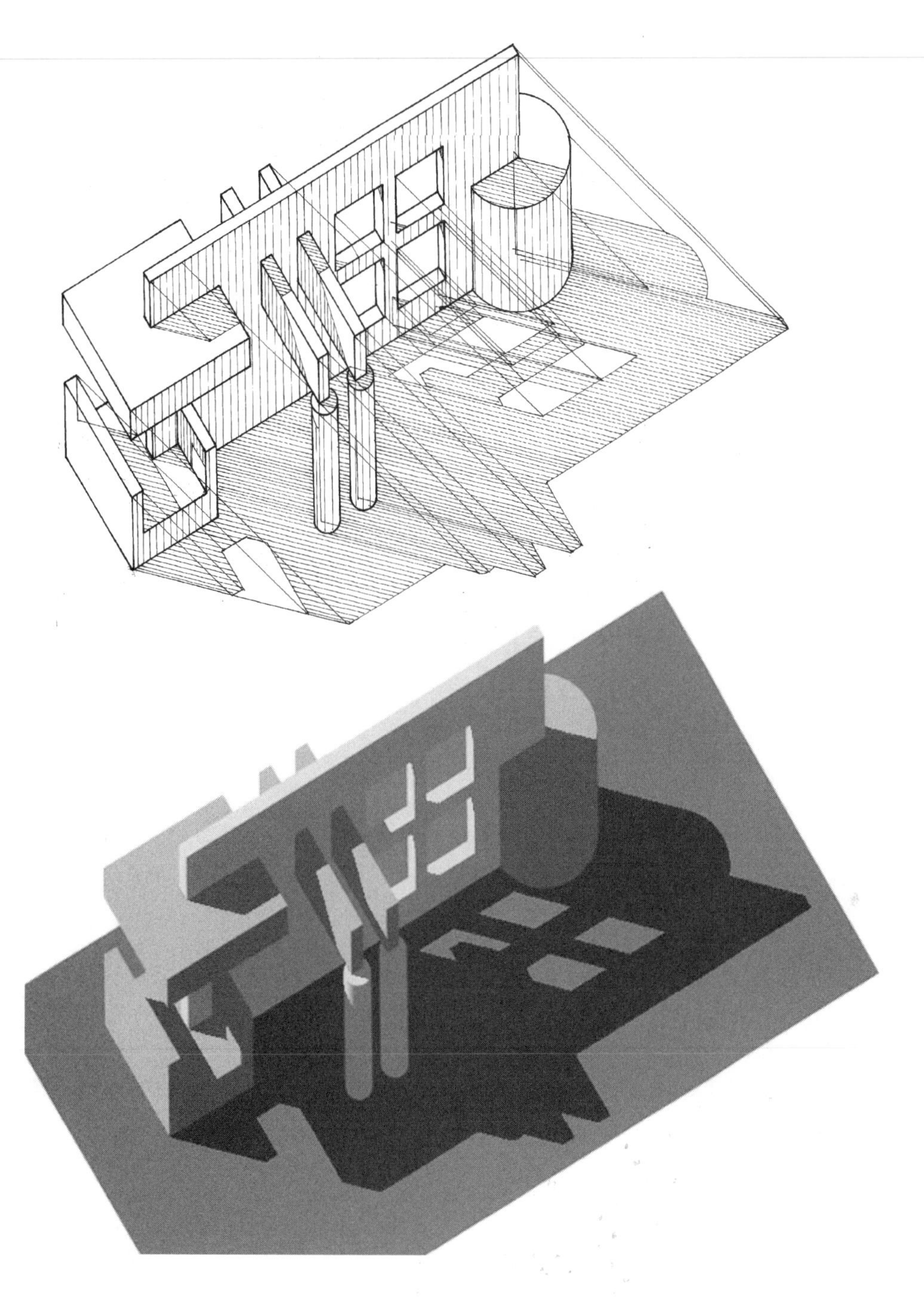

Student: Mark Stegeman
Professor: M. Saleh Uddin
Course: Design Communication I
Courtesy of University of Missouri–Columbia
Department of Environmental Design

As on the facing page, the manual projection (top) was compared with the computer projection (bottom) for this plan oblique drawing. The sun-altitude and bearing angles in these examples were also 45°. One of the casting edges is hidden when the shadows are cast by a thick vertical plane. With wall openings, it is necessary to cast shadows by all of the horizontal and vertical edges to resolve the correct shadow configuration.
[PROFESSOR'S STATEMENT]

1

2

3

Section perspective

1

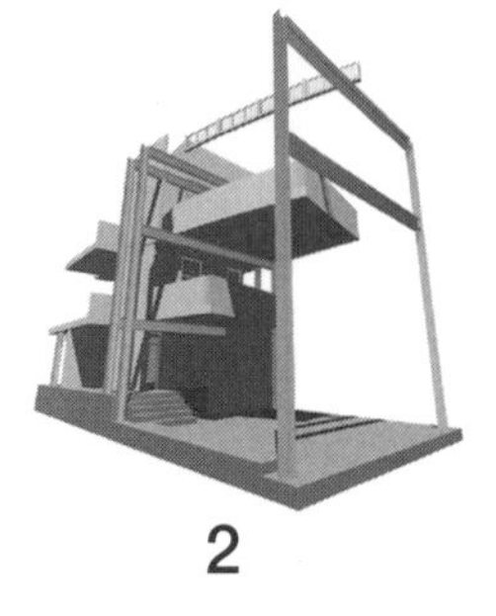
2

3

The top row on these two facing pages shows a nice use of the two-point perspective section in sequence (**1** to **6**) to reveal a dissected model of the residence and important details of the interior spaces. The bottom row on this page shows a three-point perspective used in the sequence (**1** to **3**) of analytical perspectives. Also note the beautiful use of computer-generated shadows in the one-point perspective section (with slight upward convergence).

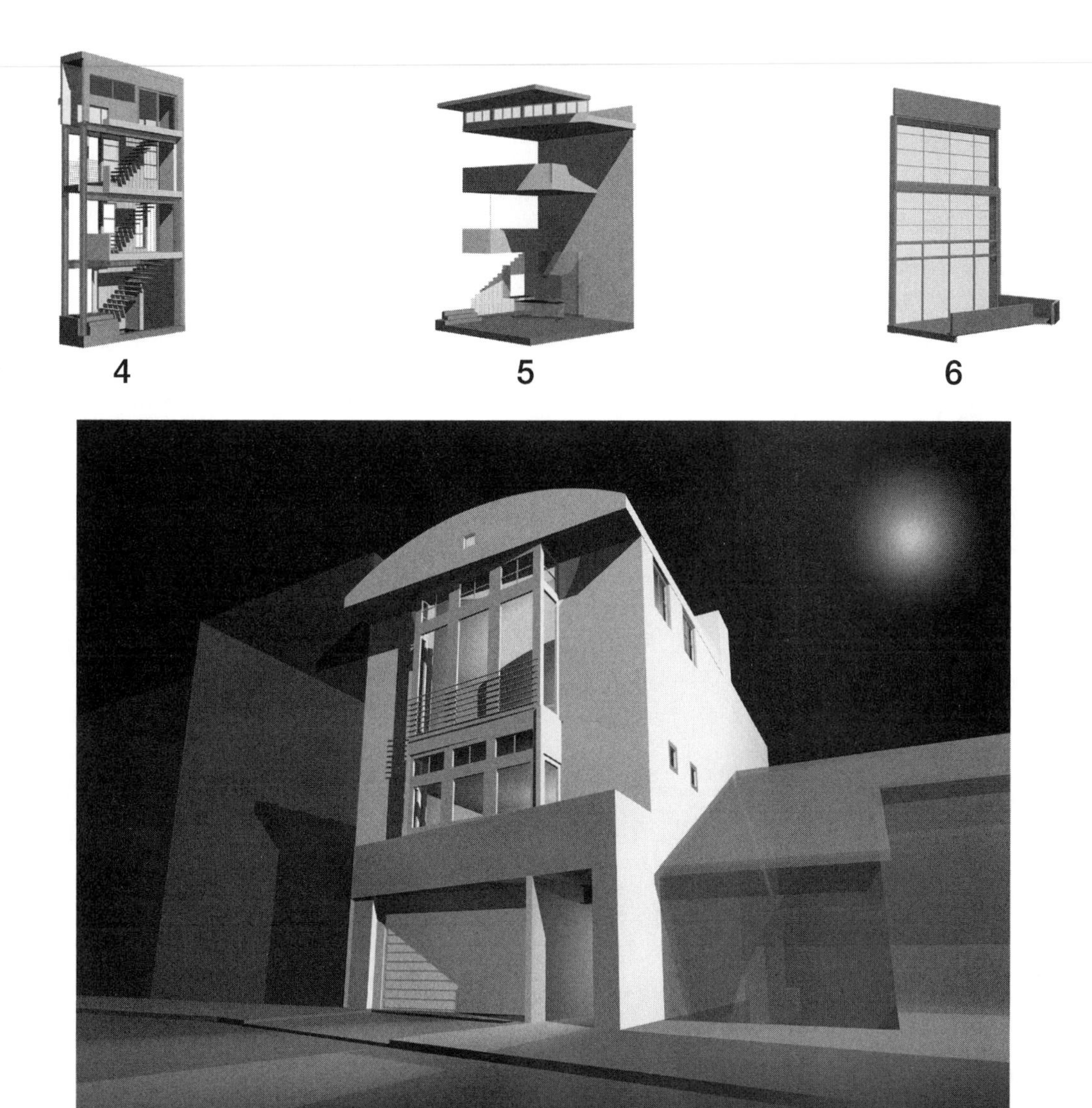

Night perspective

Images: Buena Vista residence, San Francisco, California
Principal in Charge: Mark English
Architectural Illustrations: Star Jennings
Courtesy of Inglese Architecture

All design and construction documents produced in the office are digitally created or manipulated. The CAD program used for the creation of three-dimensional drawings is ArchiCad 6.0, in conjunction with Artlantis Renderer and Photoshop. The hardware used is the Macintosh G4, Umax 1200s scanner, and Epson Stylus Photo 1200 printer.

Inglese is a young design firm located in San Francisco's Jackson Square District. The firm is dedicated to fine residential, commercial, and civic architecture and interior design. Mark English and associates Star Jennings, Alessandro Miramare, and Ani Balarezo follow a team approach to design wherein talented builders and artisans are involved as collaborators from the beginning of the design process through construction.

[ARCHITECT'S STATEMENT]

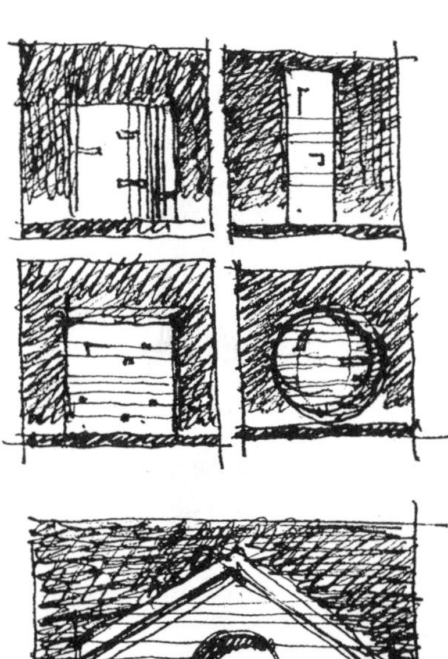

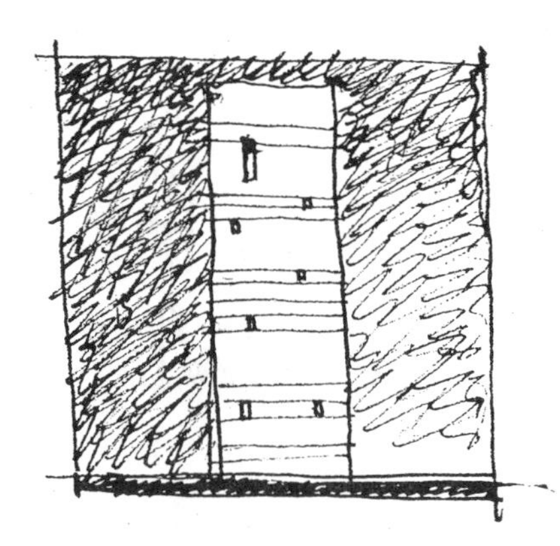

Shades and Shadows in Sketches and Renderings

One says that a colored picture is harmonious only if its black-and-white illustration is correct as well. Therefore, I use shadows in my preliminary black-and-white sketches to develop and bring out the contrasts of the picture and the profiles of the architectural objects.

My renderings are about the world of fantastic architectural visions. At the same time, they are an important part of my "real" projects' realization.

The layers of the city skyline—old or new—and of watercolor and brushstrokes—transparent or opaque—traverse and create an ever-changing intersection between the old and the new.

[Architectural Illustrator's Statement]

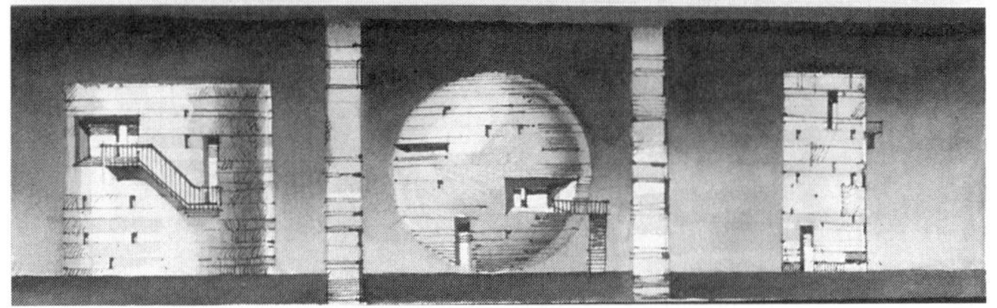

Shadow studies and rendering: The simple forms, 1999
16" × 24" (41 × 61 cm)
Medium: Watercolor, pen, and sepia ink
Courtesy of Sergei Tchoban, Architectural Illustrator

Shadow study and rendering: Bridges, 1/2000
8.5" × 40" (30 × 100 cm)
Medium: Watercolor, pen, and sepia ink
Courtesy of Sergei Tchoban, Architectural Illustrator

Render facade textures before rendering any shadows on the exterior elevations.

Shadow studies and rendering: The life on the back side, 1993
24" × 24" (60 × 60 cm)
Medium: Watercolor, pen, and sepia ink
Courtesy of Sergei Tchoban, Architectural Illustrator

Shades and shadows are often used to embellish conceptual elevations and paraline/perspective massing studies. The introduction of shadows makes these images less diagrammatic.

8

Delineating and Rendering Entourage

BASICS. 369
BASICS APPLIED 380

The major communicative drawings (plan, elevation, section, paralines, and perspectives) are part of a presentation package. It is of utmost importance to accentuate these drawings with the use of contrast so that they "read" for the prospective client. This process of delineating and rendering is critical in the presentation phase of a design project. Contrast must be properly balanced for a presentation to be clear; thus, different shades of dark values must be played against various degrees of light values. The amount of rendered contrast is based on the contextual relationship of the adjacent forms.

The intent of this chapter is to introduce techniques of delineation and rendering as applied to contextual elements — or, to use the Beaux Arts term, "entourage" — such as landscaping, human figures, furniture, cars, and building materials.

The following are some of the important terms, skills, and concepts you will learn:

Rendering	Value	Contrast	Entourage
Ground textures	Scribbling	Spatial profiling	Stippling
Hatching	Foliage textures	Delineating figures	Delineating cars

Delineating and Rendering Entourage

TOPIC: CONTOUR & FORM LANGUAGE
Ching 2003, 134–35.

TOPIC: BASIC VALUE LANGUAGES
Ching 2003, 125–43.

TOPIC: RENDERING HUMAN FIGURES
Ching 2003, 158–61.

TOPIC: RENDERING ENTOURAGE (OTHER THAN PEOPLE)
Wang 1997.
White, E. T., 1972.

Chapter Overview

After studying this chapter and practicing the techniques discussed, you will be able to delineate and render various types of drawings. For continued study, refer to Lockard's *Design Drawing Experiences,* Porter and Goodman's *Manual of Graphic Techniques 4,* and Lin's *Drawing and Designing with Confidence.*

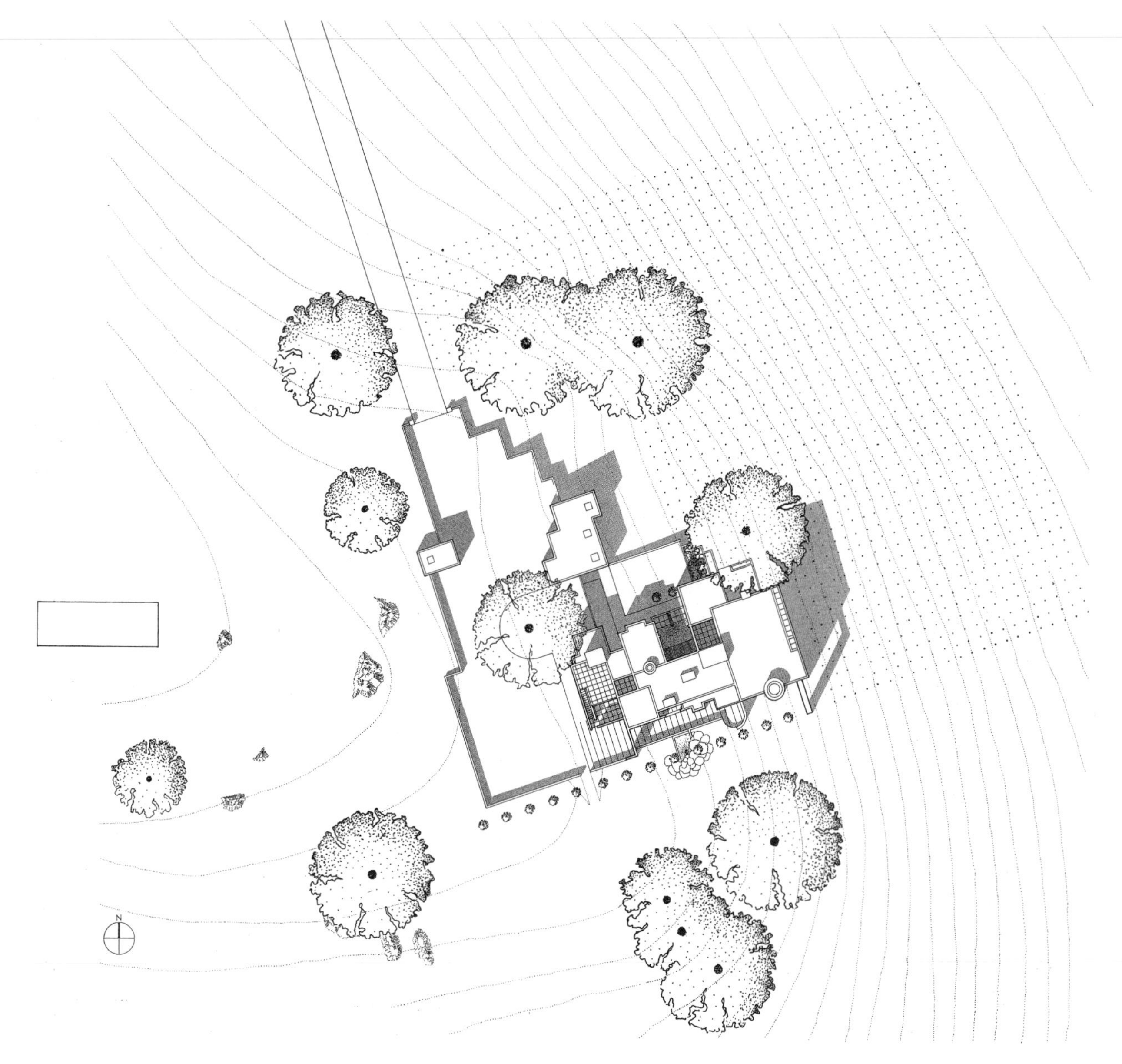

Drawing: Private residence, Healdsburg, California
24" × 36" (61 × 91.4 cm), Scale: ⅛"=1'0"
Medium: Ink on Mylar
Courtesy of Sandy & Babcock, Inc.
Architecture & Planning

SITE PLAN

When there is a dark field caused by tonal values in the surrounding contextual environment, a site plan's figure–ground, light–dark, positive–negative areas yield better depth because of **contrast.** We see this strong contrast in the drawing of architect William Kessler's house on p. 382. The rendering above lacks this contrast, but instead shows soft shadows cast by the building that cause the plan to "punch out." Contrast in architectural drawings is achieved by **rendering:** the application of artistic delineation to site plans, elevations, paralines, perspectives, and other architectural drawings. The objective of rendering drawings is either to enhance client understanding of the proposed design or for publicity and promotion. This chapter and Web site Chapter 11 provide only a brief introduction to this complex topic. Refer to the Bibliography for many excellent resources in this subject area.

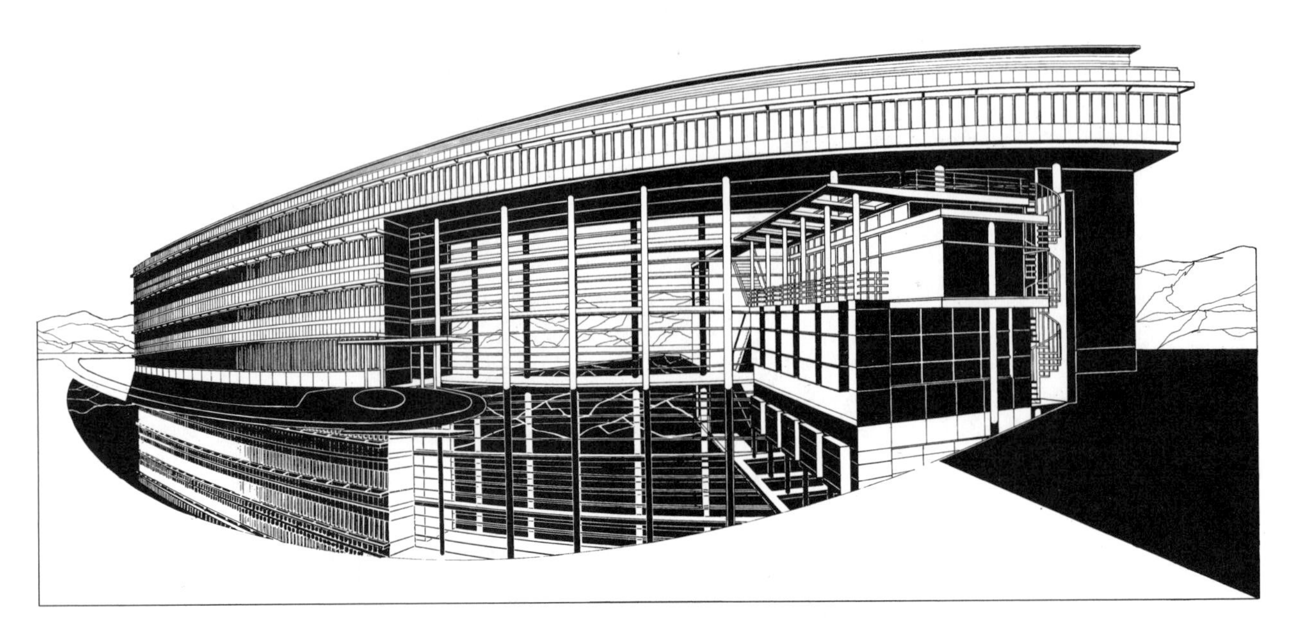

Drawing: Dongbu Central Research Institute, Taejon, Korea, view from south
36" × 24" (91.4 × 61 cm)
Medium: Ink on Mylar
Courtesy of Perkins & Will Architects

Diagrams and text: Courtesy of William R. Benedict, Assistant Professor California Polytechnic State University College of Architecture and Environmental Design, San Luis Obispo, California

Basic Value Types

A value is any technique that directly describes a surface rather than its edges. The edges are made visible by the limits of and/or a sharp change in value. A value (sometimes called a tonal value or tone in drawing) can be a continuous value or created by lines. A **continuous** value is even, small in scale, and fine in implied texture. A **value of lines** has texture that is significant in scale and composed of individual marks that retain their identity within the value. These marks include stippling, lines, cross-hatching, scrubbing, scrubbing over texture, and scribbling. The classification of a value as continuous or created by lines depends on the media and application technique employed.

The role of value in a drawing includes describing the area of a surface, the gradations produced by the surface's texture, the orientation of the surface to the light source, and the surfaces's attributes — materiality, texture, uniformity, reflectance, transparency, color, etc. In representing these qualities, the scale, coarseness, form, and hue of the value can be manipulated. Gradations are value changes on a surface or form.

VALUE SCALES USING VALUE-GRADING TECHNIQUES

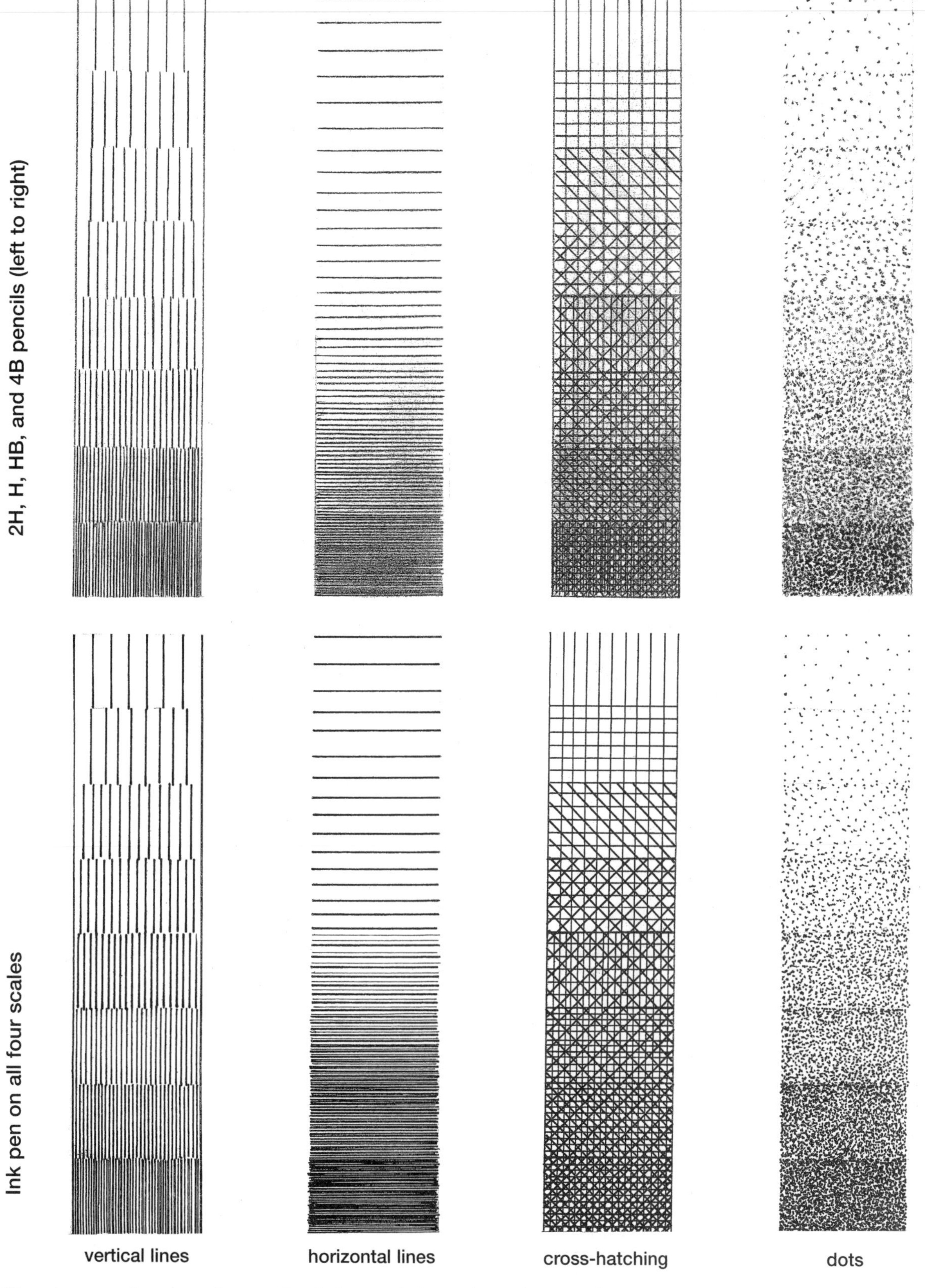

The use of dots is also termed "stippling" (see pointillism, p. 378)

The above scales show four methods for rendering value using pencil or ink pen. Other value-producing media are ink wash, watercolor wash, markers, and dry-transfer Zipatone.

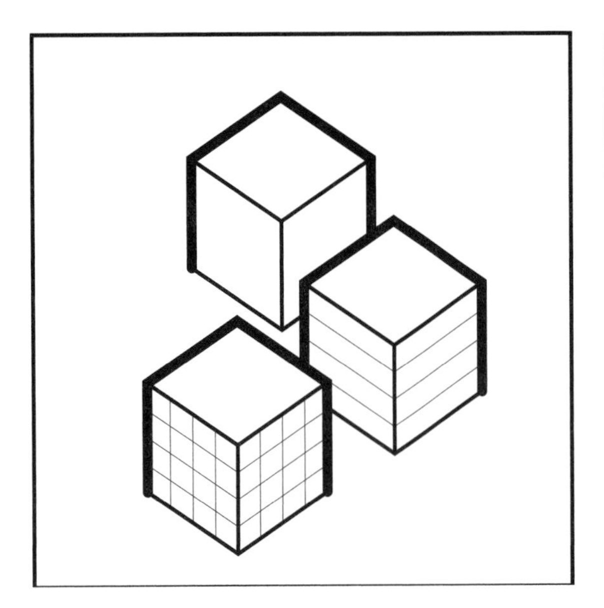

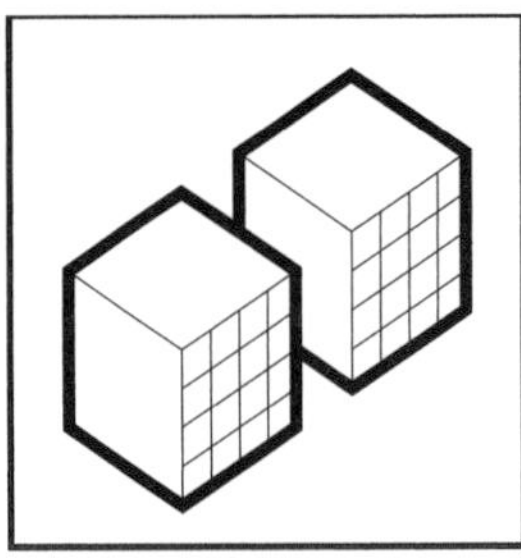

Primary Contours

Primary contours define the outermost extremities of a form—they record the outline or profile of an object. They are edges formed by the meeting of two surfaces when only one surface can be seen. They respond to and record all edge textures and irregularities. Drawing only the profile of an object tends to flatten the object.

Secondary Contours

Secondary contours describe the edges of surfaces when both surfaces are visible. They respond to and record all edge textures and irregularities.

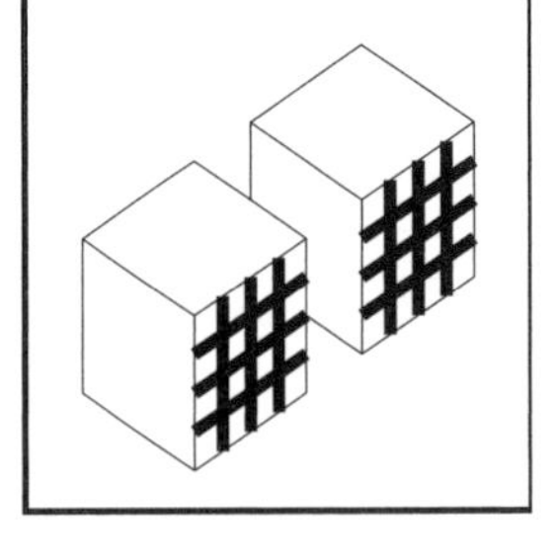

Tertiary Contours

Tertiary contours describe changes in the uniformity of a surface or plane. They respond to and record linear markings on a surface and the edges of values, shadows, textures, and colors. Tertiary contours disclose the volume of an object. They are plastic and emphasize the three-dimensionality of the object.

Contour and Form

The language of contour and form relates line-weight choices to the aspect of the form that they are representing. The language identifies primary, secondary, and tertiary edge conditions using a vocabulary of three different line weights, with the grammar defining primary contours as heavy, secondary contours as medium, and tertiary contours as light.

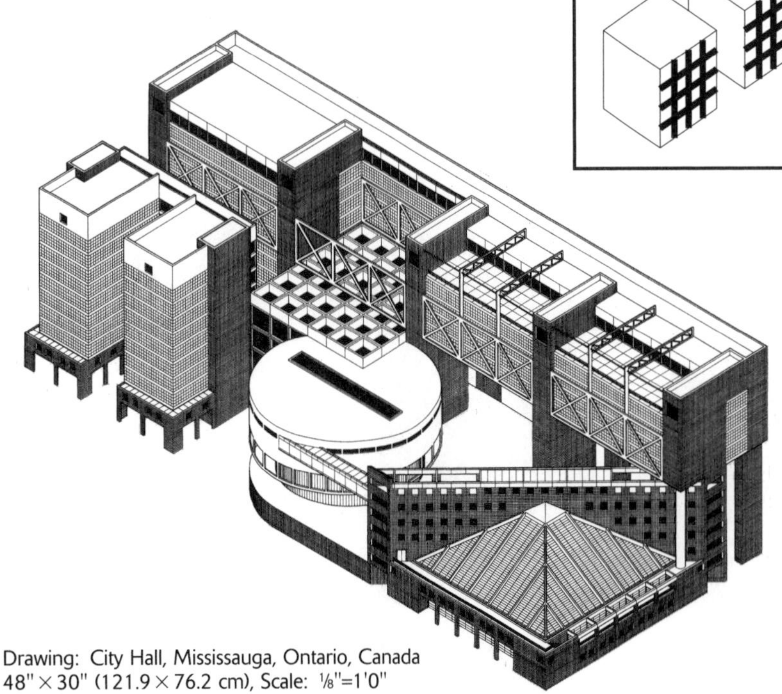

Drawing: City Hall, Mississauga, Ontario, Canada
48" × 30" (121.9 × 76.2 cm), Scale: ⅛"=1'0"
Medium: Ink on Mylar
Courtesy of Michael Fieldman & Partners, Architects

Diagrams and text (both pages): Courtesy of William R. Benedict, Assistant Professor
California Polytechnic State University
College of Architecture & Environmental Design
San Luis Obispo, California
Software: Aldus Freehand

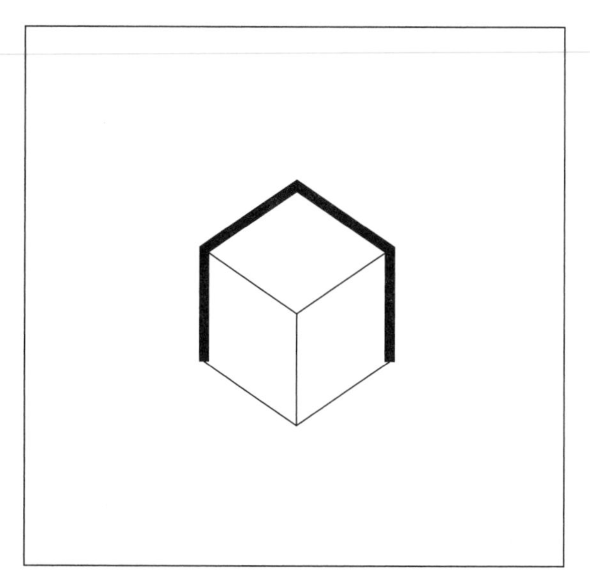

Spatial Profiling

Edges are perceived under two conditions: when both surfaces defining the edge are visible and when only one surface is visible. Lighter lines indicate an edge between two planes when both can be seen. Heavier lines — profile lines — indicate an edge between two planes where only one plane can be seen. To one side of a profile edge you are looking through space to some distant surface. The greatest spatial differential — the heaviest profile line — occurs at the edge between the object and the sky and earth (the object's environment or background). Lines become heavier as the distance between the edge they represent and the surface against which the edge is seen increases.

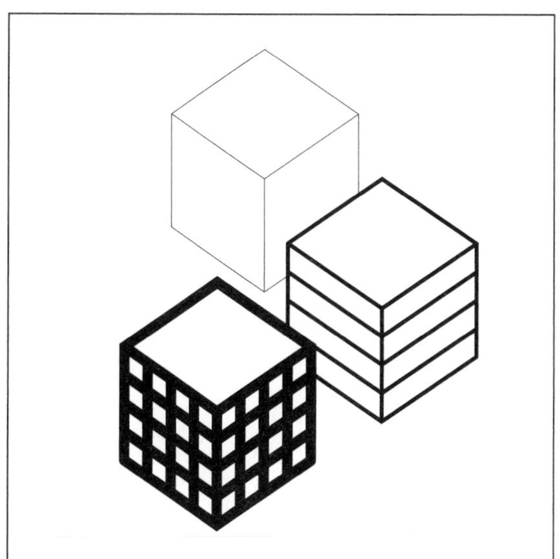

Contours and Distance

A heavy black line on a white sheet of paper reads as closer than a light line due to its size and our experience with the effect of aerial perspective on contrast. A thin black line appears lighter in value than a thick black line because it has less surface area with which to communicate its value. The closest contours, therefore, are the heaviest, and weight decreases with distance. Lines of varying distance can taper. The illustration at left categorizes all the lines of a cube as the same, but this language can become much subtler by further varying the line weights within each cube.

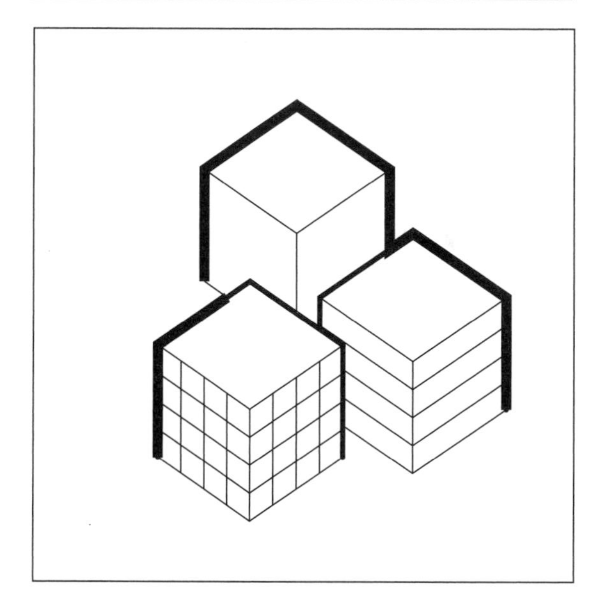

Contours and Depth

Primary contours define the edges of surfaces that can be seen. To one side of the contour is the surface that the contour defines; to the other, some distance or depth of space until another surface is encountered. The greater the depth, the heavier the contour line. This language is a development of spatial profiling cues.

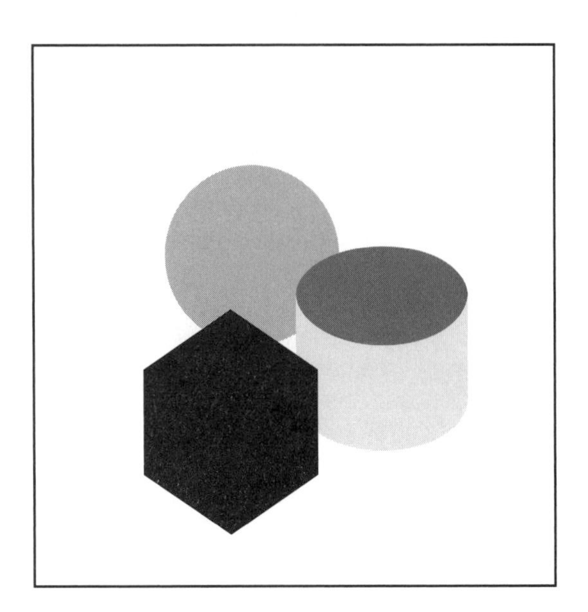

Value and Color

Value directly represents the color of a surface. Whatever color (value, hue, chroma) that a surface possesses is represented in the drawing. If the surface is dark red, it is drawn dark red. Issues of relative illumination and orientation of the surface are not considered. The liability of this language is that it tends to flatten and disguise form, as indicated in the illustration at left.

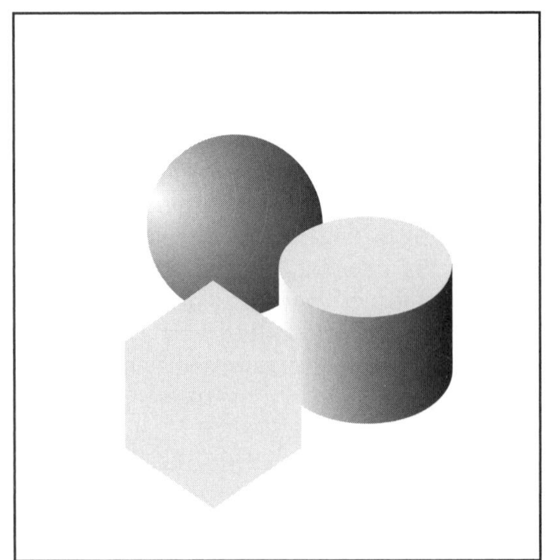

Value and Form

Value can delineate form by defining and differentiating surfaces. The simplest value and form language represents flat surfaces with uniform values and curved surfaces with tonal gradations. As in the value and color language, issues of relative illumination and orientation of the surface are not considered; here, too, the liability of the language is that it can flatten and disguise form, as indicated in the illustration at left.

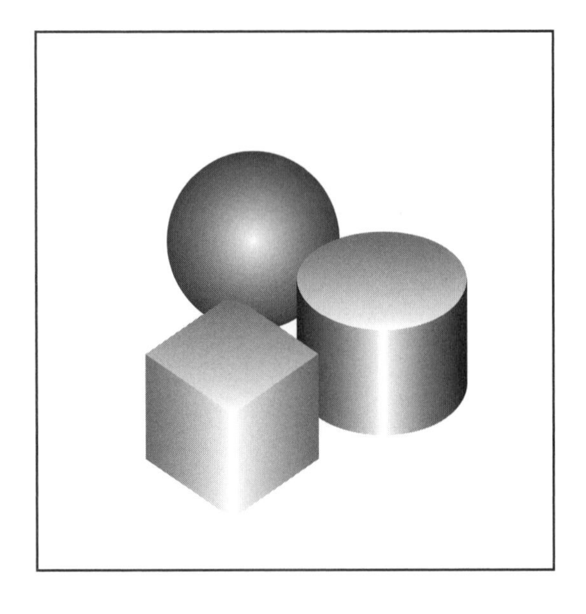

Value and Texture

If a surface has some perceivable textural qualities, then value can represent the surface's textural gradients. A surface that is directly facing the observer has a uniform textural gradient and is represented by a uniform value. A surface that is oblique to the observer has a varying textural gradient and is represented by a gradation that goes from light to dark as it moves away from the observer. A textured surface will also appear darker as it turns away from the observer — as it moves from perpendicular to parallel to the observer's line of sight.

Diagrams and text (both pages): Courtesy of William R. Benedict, Assistant Professor
California Polytechnic State University College of Architecture & Environmental Design, San Luis Obispo, California

Value and Orientation

A surface's value corresponds to its orientation to the light source. In this example, flat surfaces are represented by uniform values. The values are then adjusted to represent the surface's orientation to the assumed light source. The surfaces most directly facing the source are the lightest, and the surfaces facing most directly away from the source are darkest. Surfaces with the same orientation receive the same value no matter where they are within the drawing.

Value and Shadow

This language builds on the orientation language. The orientation of the surfaces to the light source must be established before shadows can be cast. Once the orientation is established, shadows are cast and values are adjusted for reflected light. The example at left shows all values as flat or even. In reality, bounced light modifies the values.

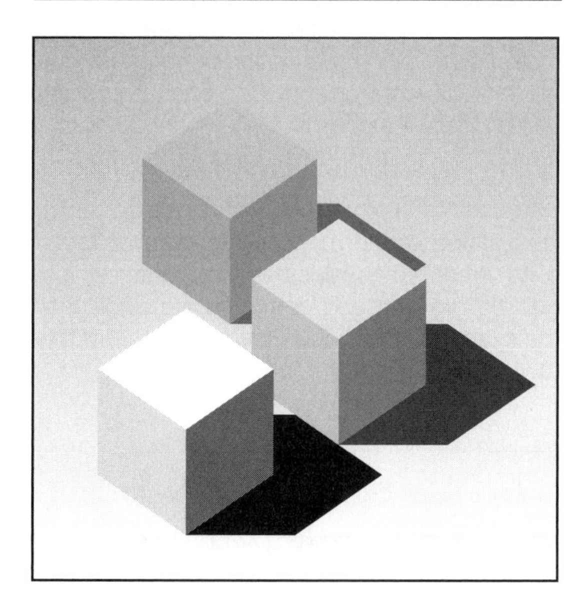

Value and Distance

Value is also affected by the aerial cues of contrast and blueness. The closest cubes will have the greatest contrast within themselves and to the environment, while those farther away will have less. Furthermore, as the cubes get farther away, they move toward a middle gray because of the intervening atmosphere.

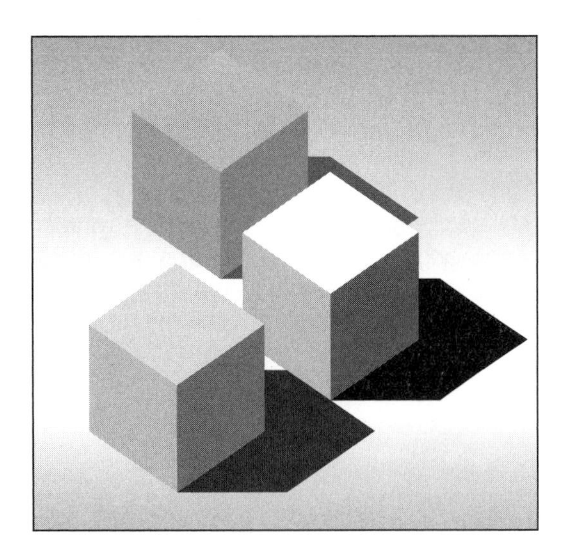

Sun, Shade, and Shadow

This language employs an abbreviated vocabulary and grammar. The vocabulary consists of only three continuous values and responds to three formal conditions. The surfaces in direct sunlight are white, those in shade are gray, and those in shadow are black. This language tends to abstract reality and create strong graphic images with sharp contrast. It is useful in compositional and massing studies.

Orientation, Shadow, and Texture

In this combination the orientation and shadow languages have been enriched to include gradations created by the surfaces' textures. The textural gradations cause the surfaces to get darker as they move away from the viewer. This is true for all surfaces not parallel to the face of the viewer. The greater the angle, the more dramatic the gradation.

Created in Fractal Design Painter

Value and Expression

The technique used, media, key (value or tonal range), and distribution of values within a drawing can support different moods — freehand is different from drafted, pen is different from pencil, high key is different from low key, and variegated is different from uniform. Each combination will create a different mood.

In a high-key drawing, all the values are at the light end of the value scale; a low-key drawing is the opposite.

The scale and shape of the marks — the style or technique used to create the values — also influence the expression of the drawing and communicate additional meaning. The example at left feels very different from the previous drawings.

Diagrams and text (both pages): Courtesy of William R. Benedict, Assistant Professor
California Polytechnic State University College of Architecture & Environmental Design, San Luis Obispo, California

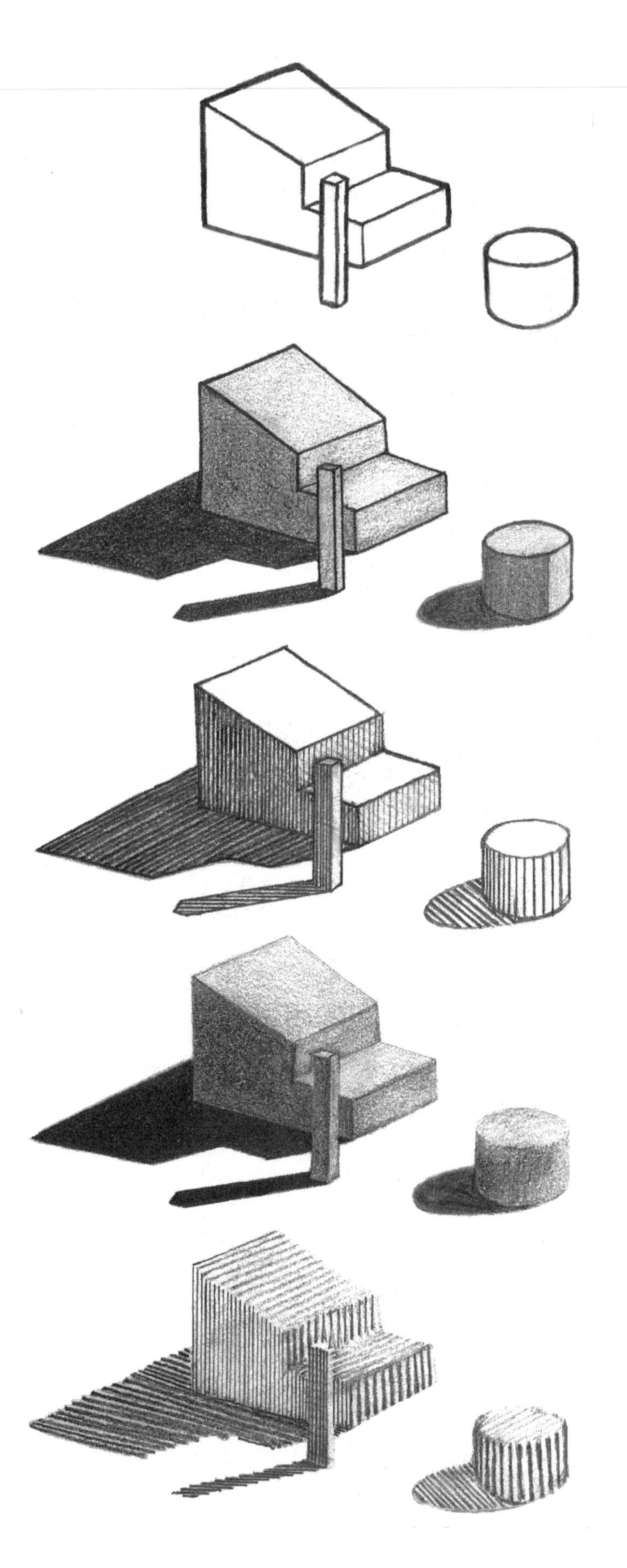

Line with space-defining edges accented (profiled)

Profiling or silhouetting gives a needed contour to help define any form against negative space.

Line with value

Shadow is rendered darker than shade. Silhouetting is normally not done against negative space.

Line with value of lines

Planar edges are defined by both line and value of lines. Silhouetting is normally not done against negative space. For directional reinforcement, use vertical lines for vertical planes and horizontal or near-horizontal lines for horizontal planes.

Value

Planes rendered with different pure values define planar edges. Shadow is rendered darker than shade.

Value of lines

Planar edges are defined when two planes, each with a value of lines, meet. A flat plane uses evenly spaced lines. A curvilinear form uses unevenly spaced lines (see p. 315).

Stippling is used to build up shade and value. Its objective—to model form—is the same as that of the linear technique of cross-hatching (see p. 371). By varying the size and spacing of dots, tone values and model form can be created. This dot technique is called "pointillism" and originated with French painters, such as Georges Seurat, who experimented with light and vision in their work. Although quite time-consuming, this method provides excellent control over gradations and produces a copylike quality. Note the stippling for the sky area in the villa rendering and on the building exterior on the facing page.

Hatching is the use of approximately parallel (short or long) lines in a tonal arrangement in order to portray surface or form. It can describe light, space, and material as an abstraction of reality (see the sky and glass on p. 415). Adding layers of hatching increases tone density. This is especially effective for nuances in shadow tones.

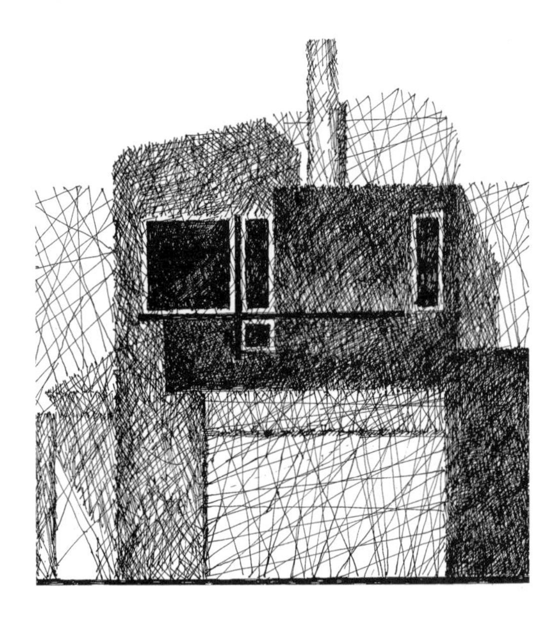

Drawing: Van Kirk House, San Francisco, California, 1991
7.5" × 7.5" (19.1 × 19.1 cm), Scale: ¼"=1'0"
Medium: Pen and ink
Courtesy of James Shay, AIA, Architect

This style of rendering communicates visual tonal values very effectively. The high contrast achieved creates a lot of visual "snap."
[ARCHITECT'S STATEMENT]

Rendering: Filothei Villa, Greece
24" × 36" (61 × 91.4 cm), Scale: ⅛"=1'0"
Courtesy of Hugh Newell Jacobsen, FAIA, Architect, and Stephen S. Evanusa, Architect

Scribbling is used to produce a tonal value by applying randomly directed lines that appear haphazard in their arrangement (see foreground, above). Pen and ink is an excellent medium for producing a variety of stroke patterns. These illustrations show the use of straight and curved lines, cross-hatched lines, and dots yielding excellent tonal values. Regardless of the technique, the density of tone produces the needed contrast. Different stroke techniques are often used in combination to depict shape clusters. The number of techniques employed depends on how much detail and precision is desired. Spontaneous loose, imprecise strokes are more suggestive and symbolic. Fine-point felt-tip pens and fountain pens are best suited for hatching and scribbling, whereas pens with a more flexible point are best suited for stippling.

Drawing: Student project by Richard Tsai
Interior study
Medium: Ink on Mylar
Courtesy of Washington University
School of Architecture, St. Louis, Missouri

The rendering at right was drawn using only dots of varying intensity and dimension. The student began this exercise by carefully studying shade and shadow conditions on the building with the objective of creating a line drawing.

Shades or cast shadows on surfaces should have a transparent quality. We should be able to see through the applied value and recognize the detailed aspects of the surfaces' form and texture.

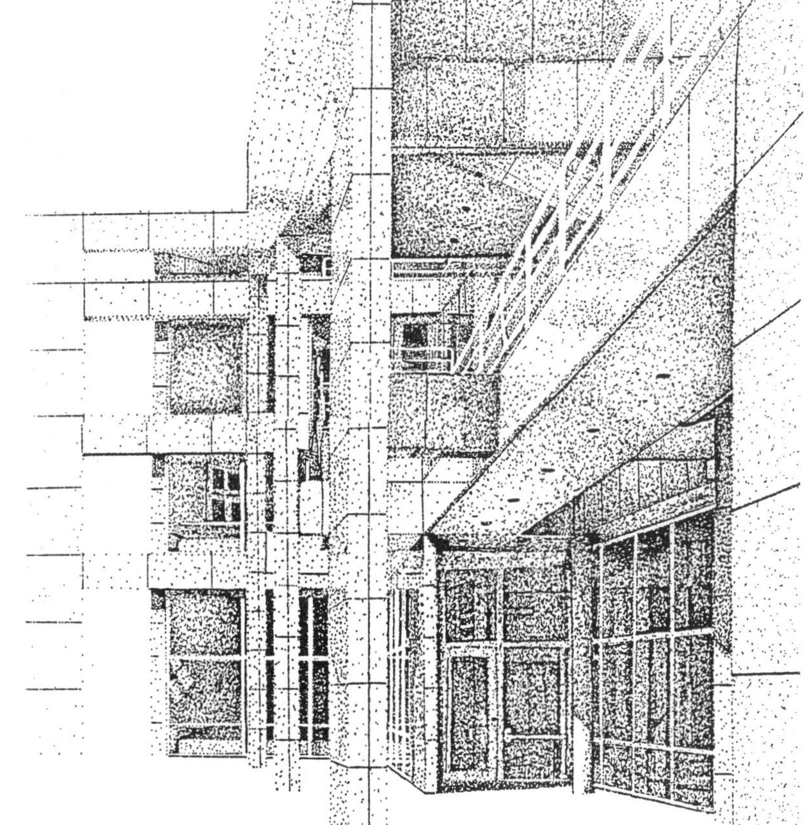

Drawing: Student project by Roosevelt Sanders
Medium: Ink on Mylar
M. Saleh Uddin, Professor, Savannah College of Art and Design, Savannah, Georgia; Southern University, Baton Rouge, Louisiana

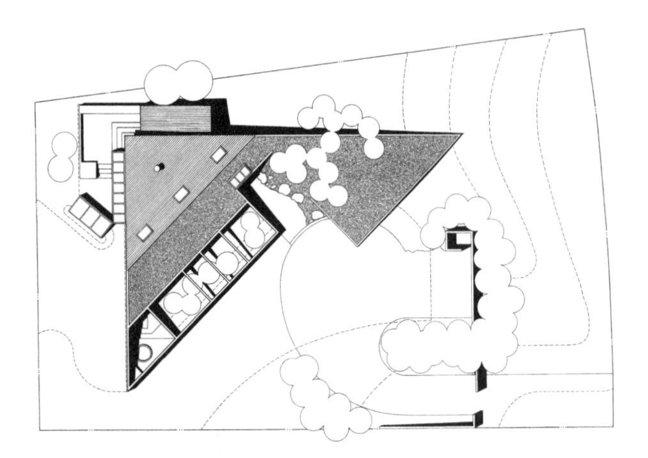

Drawing: Brugler residence, The Sea Ranch, California
20" × 15" (50.8 × 38.1 cm), Scale: ⅛"=1'0"
Medium: Rapidograph ink pen
Courtesy of Obie G. Bowman, AIA, Architect

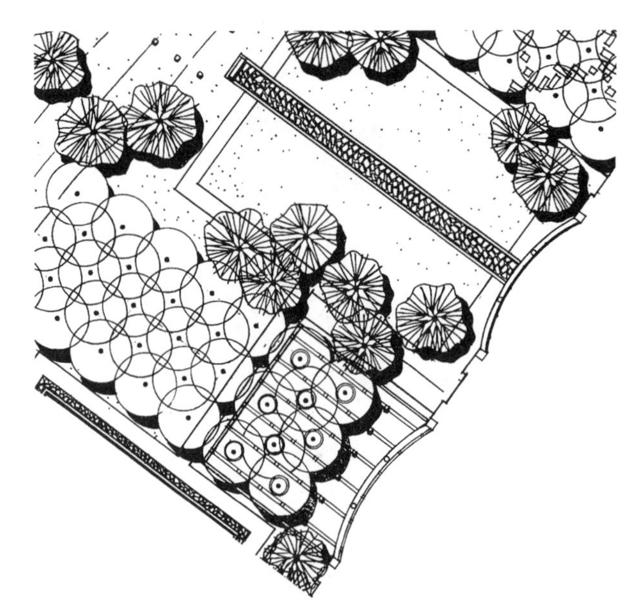

Drawing (partial): Takamiya Country Club Hiroshima, Japan
Medium: Pencil
ED2 International Architects
Courtesy of the SWA Group

There are numerous ways to depict an abstract rendered tree in plan. The nature and quantity of abstract detail is dependent on the scale and objective of the drawing. Different types of plan trees can be interchanged. Deciduous and coniferous trees are commonly rendered. Coniferous trees (below middle) are delineated with radiating lines that look like bicycle spokes. Sometimes smaller trees and shrubs are clustered as a group with one continuous outline.

Note the range of plan tree types, above—from a simple circle to more elaborate forms. Ground textures can yield a value contrast that causes the trees to have distinct edges. Trees, ground textures, and other plan entourage should always complement (and be secondary to) the architectural building elements to which they are adjacent. Site plan entourage provides vital field–background (dark–light) tonal contrast, giving added depth to a drawing. Render ground textures before rendering shadows over the texture.

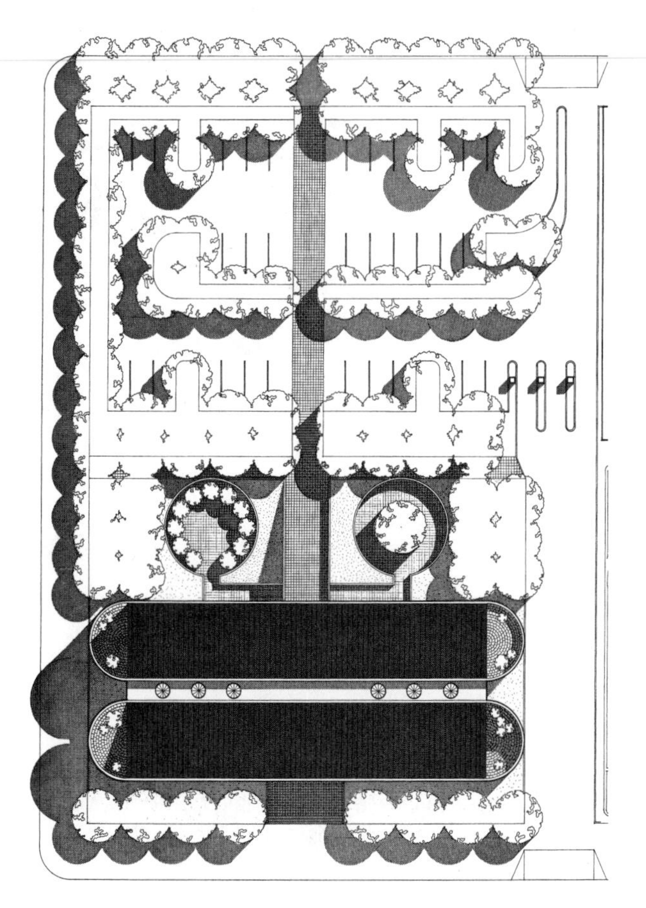

Drawing: Savings Association Headquarters
Denver, Colorado
24" × 32" (61 × 81.3 cm), Scale: 1/10"=1'0"
Medium: Ink on vellum with pressure-applied screens (Zipatone)
Courtesy of James Ream FAIA, San Francisco, California

At left, both tree plan and much smaller shrub plan symbols are used. These, along with ground-cover texture symbols, constitute the three most important landscape vegetation symbols. The trees shown in both of these rendered site plans nicely complement the building forms that they are near. Depth is added to both site plans by the use of cast shadows. Circular trees cast circular shadows. Draw them with a circle template. A sense of depth can be achieved by a slight displacement of one circle, forming two intersecting circles. When circular shadows are cast as a whole group (left), the sense of depth achieved can be very effective.

Trees in plan fall into two categories: (1) sectional trees, as shown on the facing page, where a horizontal cut reveals branching, trunk size, and foliage (or a lack thereof); and (2) nonsectional trees (view from above), where shade on the foliage gives a three-dimensional effect. When plan tree symbols overlap, as in the Takamiya Country Club drawing on the facing page, care must be taken not to obscure or completely block any plan symbol.

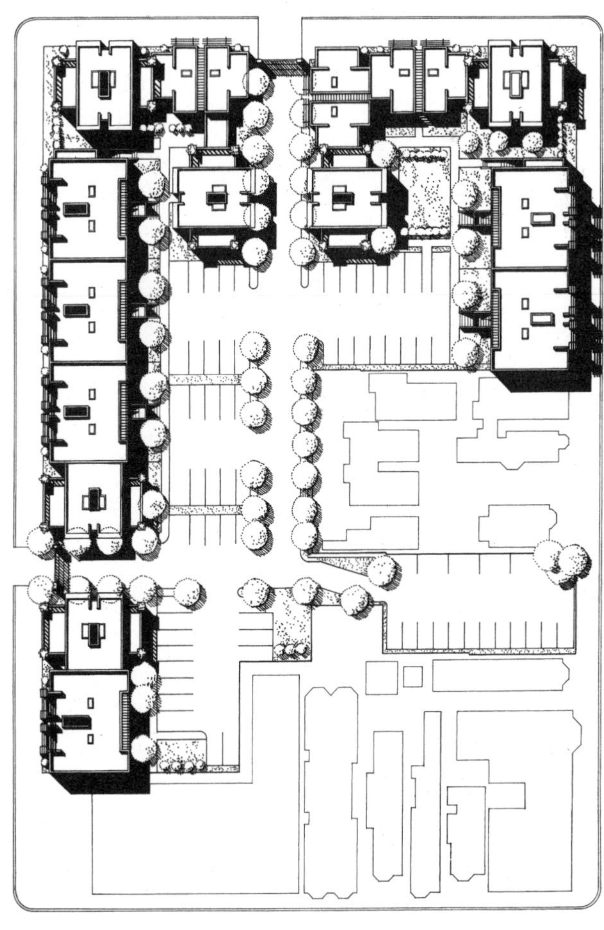

Drawing: Amancio Ergina Village
San Francisco, California
24" × 36" (61 × 91.4 cm), Scale: 1/16"=1'0"
Medium: Ink on vellum
Courtesy of Daniel Solomon, FAIA

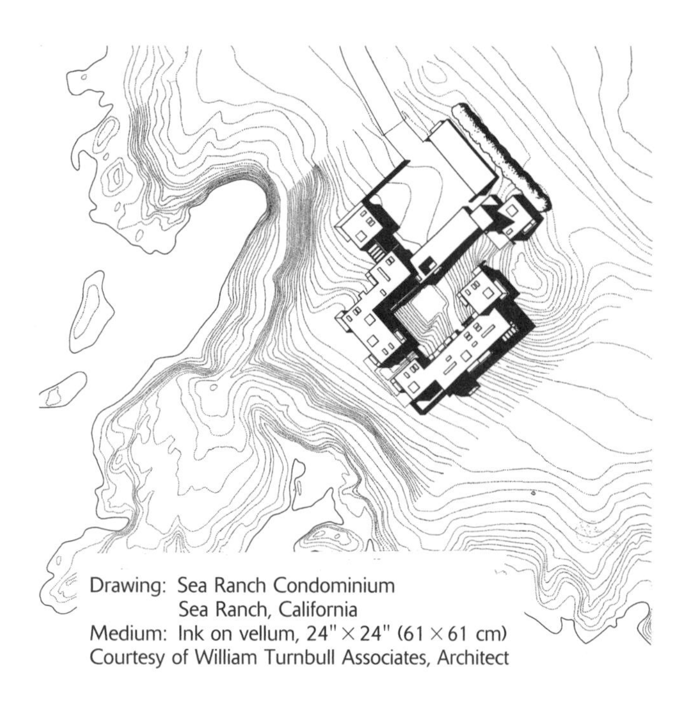

Drawing: Sea Ranch Condominium
Sea Ranch, California
Medium: Ink on vellum, 24" × 24" (61 × 61 cm)
Courtesy of William Turnbull Associates, Architect

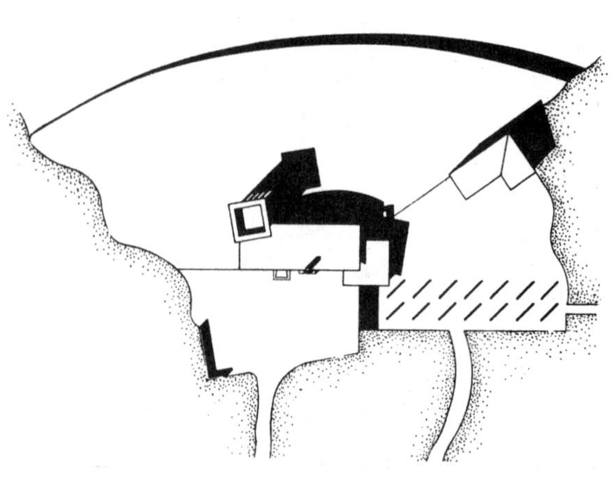

Drawing: Bargonetti, Kent, Connecticut
11" × 14" (27.9 × 35.6 cm), Scale: 1"=32'0"
Medium: Ink on Mylar
Courtesy of Steven Harris & Associates, Architect

There are many ways to indicate ground cover for soft surfaces, such as grass. Upper left: (1) contour lines; (2) upper and lower right: dot clusters; and (3) lower left: short lines ordered into layers defining contours. When rendering ground line textures, it is less confusing when the lines are even and consistent in line width.

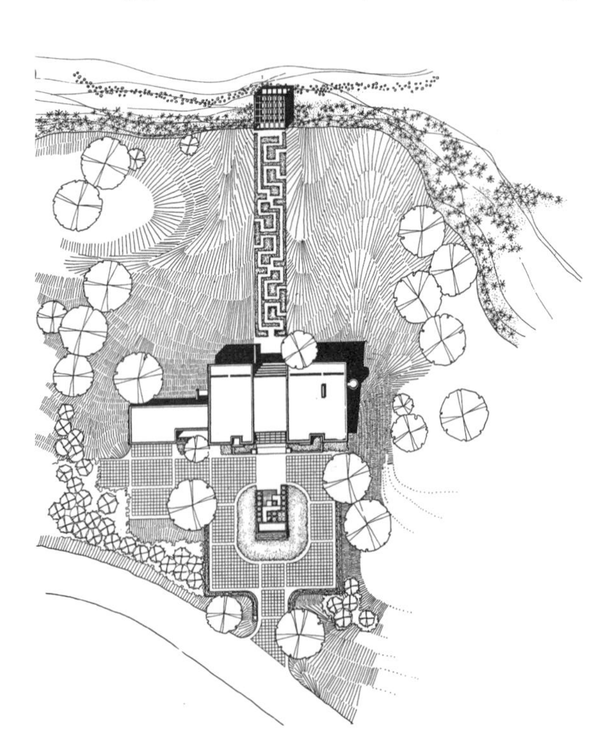

Drawing: Private house, southeastern Michigan
20" × 30" (50.8 × 76.2 cm), Scale: 1"=30'0"
Medium: Ink on vellum
Courtesy of William Kessler and Associates Architects

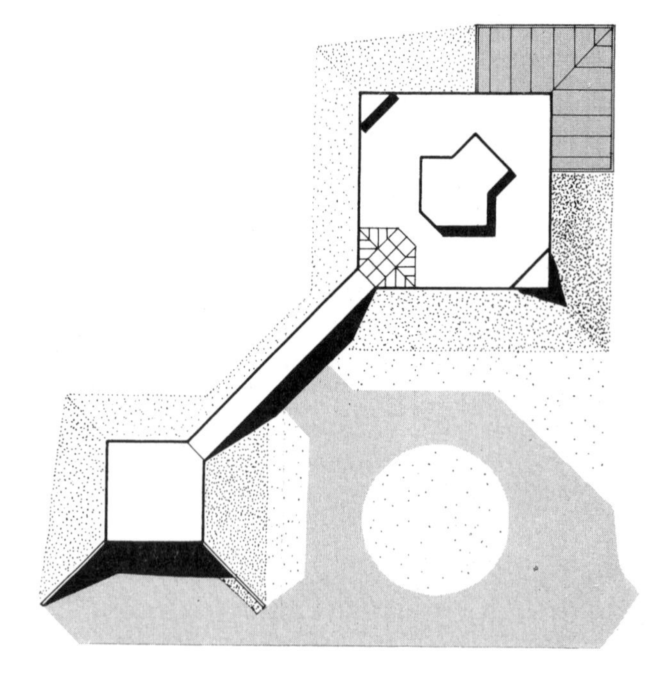

Drawing: Private residence, Gainsville, Florida
24" × 24" (61 × 61 cm), Scale: ⅛"=1'0"
Medium: Ink on Mylar film with Zipatone shading
Courtesy of William Morgan FAIA,
William Morgan Architects, P.A.

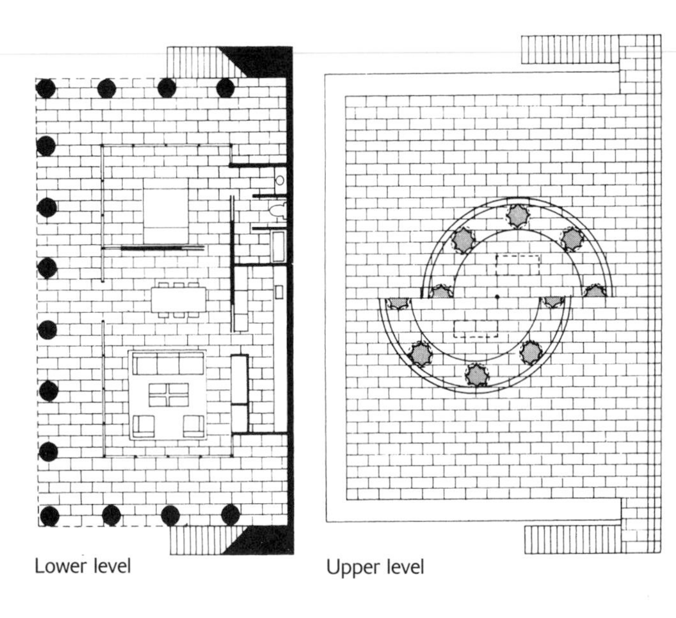

Lower level   Upper level

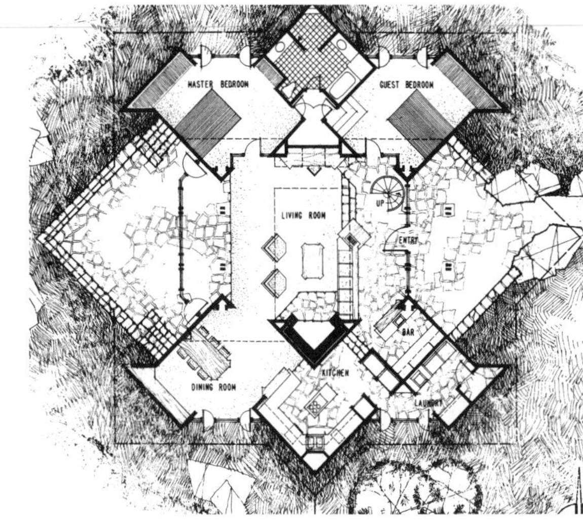

First floor

Drawing: Two crypts near Athens, Greece
24" × 36" (61 × 91.4 cm), Scale ⅛"=1'0"
Courtesy of Hugh Newell Jacobsen, FAIA

Drawing: Davenport house, Evergreen, Colorado
18" × 24" (45.7 × 61 cm), Scale: ¼"=1'0"
Medium: Ink on vellum
Courtesy of Fay Jones + Maurice Jennings, Architects

Landscaping indication symbols for hard surfaces should be consistent with the interior floor material of the building they surround. These symbols provide a clue as to how the interior relates to its adjacent transitional spaces, as well as to its external landscape and environment.

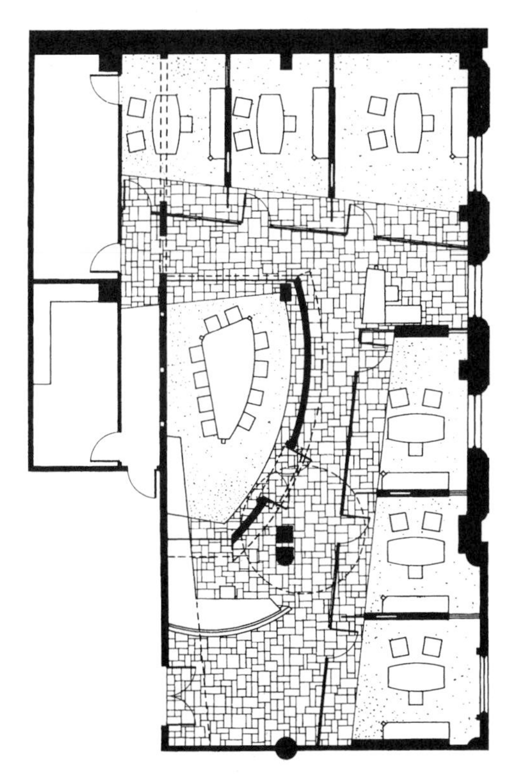

Drawing: Shinko Management, Beverly Hills, California
24" × 36" (61 × 91.4 cm), Scale: ¼"=1'0"
Medium: Ink on Mylar
Courtesy of David Kellen, Architect

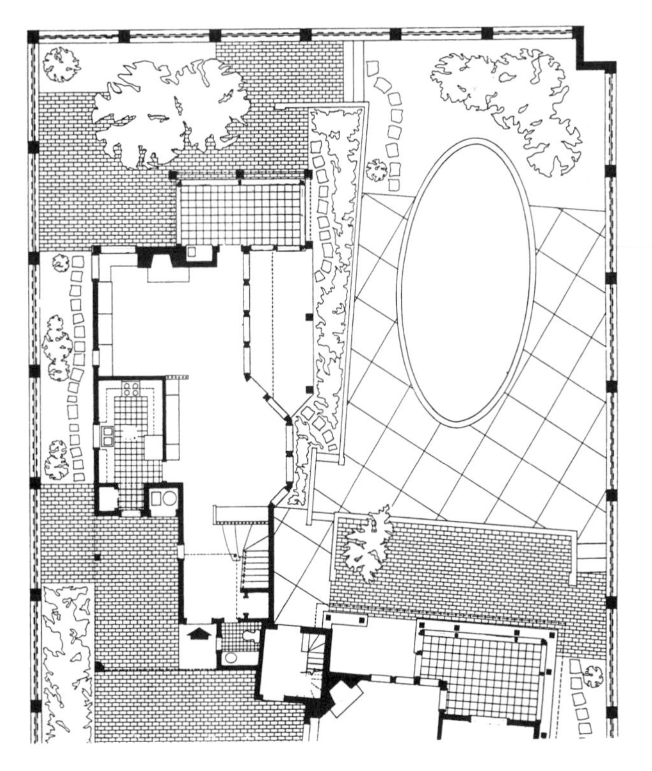

Drawing: Salasky/Sedel house, Virginia Beach, Virginia
30" × 40" (76.2 × 101.6 cm), Scale: ⅛"=1'0"
Medium: Ink on Mylar
Courtesy of B FIVE STUDIO

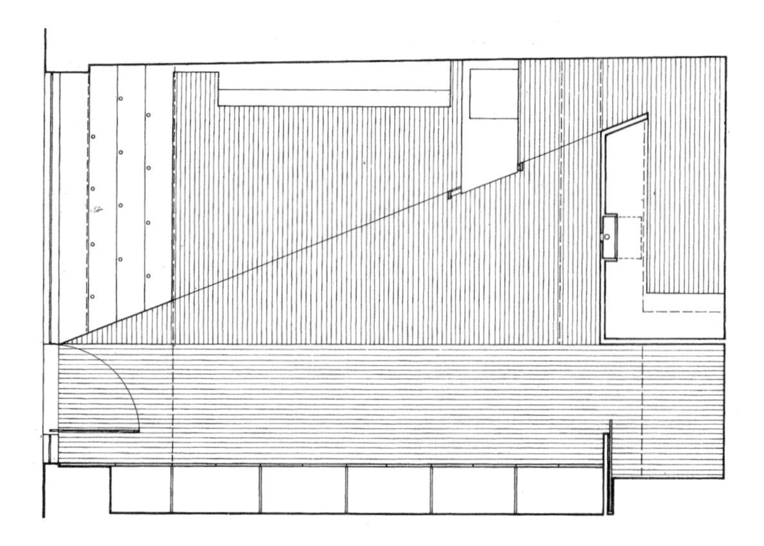

Drawing: Kinder Kind Shop I
Repulse Bay, Hong Kong, China
14" × 10" (35.6 × 25.4 cm)
Medium: Ink on Mylar, Scale: 1:20
Courtesy of Tsao & McKown Architects

As with ground textures, rendering materials within the plan view gives depth through contrast to an otherwise flat, two-dimensional plan. Major circulation areas can be quickly identified when defined with a uniform tone value (see below). Floorscape is normally the material symbol of the actual material presented in a simplified technique.

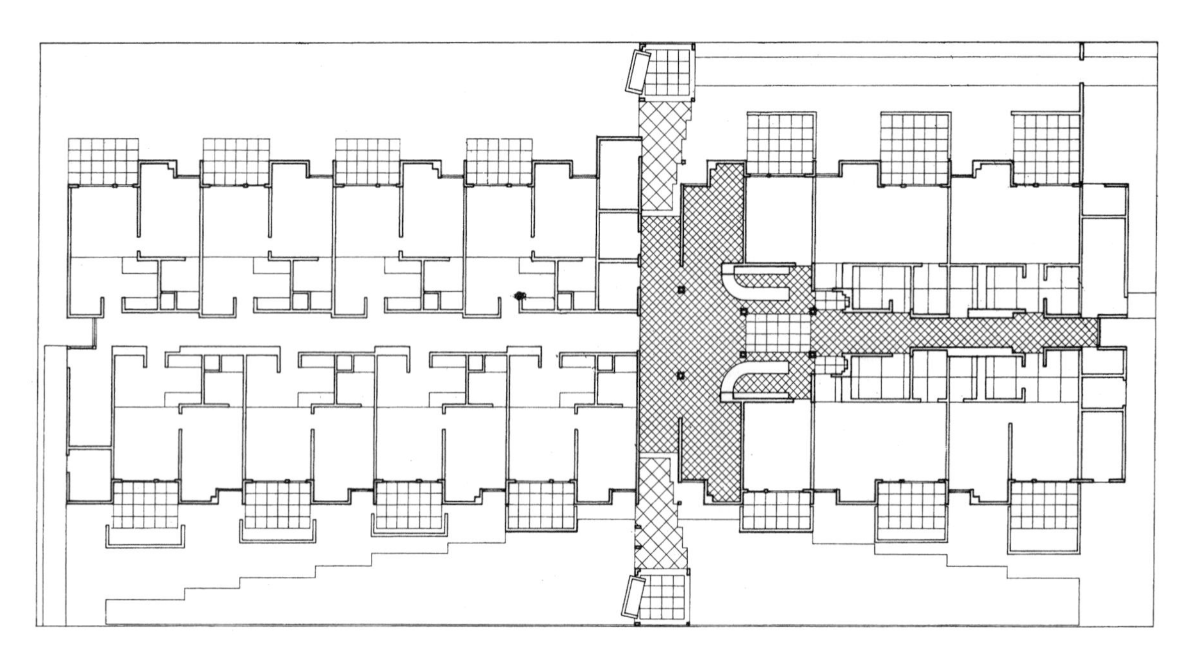

Drawing: Plymouth Place Housing, Stockton, California
31" × 36" (78.7 × 91.4 cm), Scale: ⅛"=1'0"
Medium: Ink
Courtesy of John V. Mutlow, FAIA, Architects

The rendition of floor patterns in a two-dimensional plan assists in the understanding of the design intention of the project. The floorscape identifies the areas of public circulation space and the sequence of the public spaces, and accentuates the principle elements, the major axis, and the circulation. The variation in floor pattern intensity differentiates the inside space from the outside, the diagonal to the square pattern, and the public to the private.
[Architect's statement]

Most ground-floor plans show the relationship of the interior floorscape to the immediate exterior landscape. Thus, the surrounding area not occupied by the building plan should be rendered with a ground texture (see the Salasky/Sedel house on the previous page).

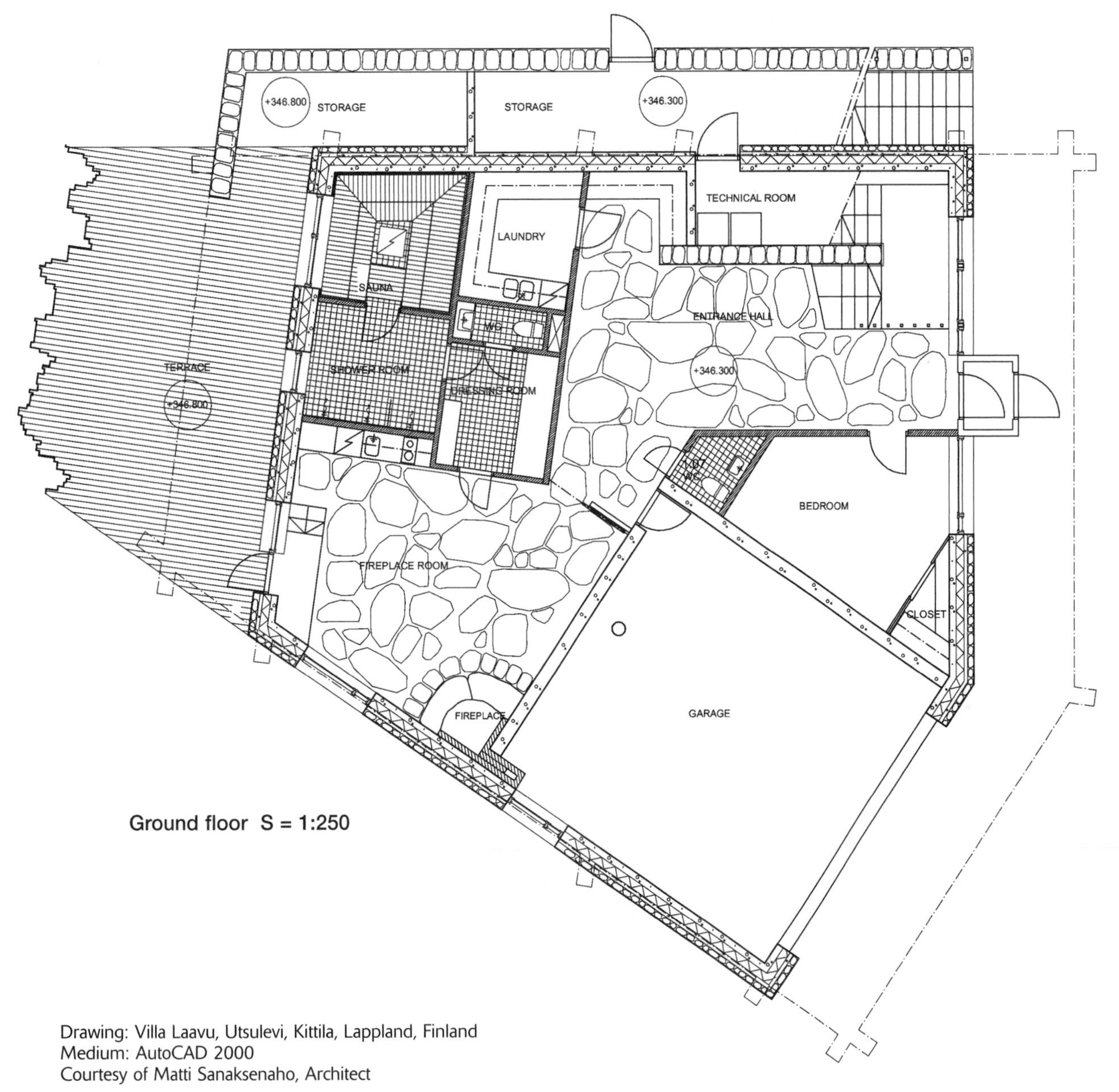

Drawing: Villa Laavu, Utsulevi, Kittila, Lappland, Finland
Medium: AutoCAD 2000
Courtesy of Matti Sanaksenaho, Architect

To better understand how to represent floorscape and the surrounding groundscape, observe how artificial light and sunlight affects them. Make a careful study of interior floor materials, as well as exterior masonry and cobblestone walks, concrete paving, rock and gravel beds, wooden decks, and patios. Develop a graphic representation of an exterior material while it is illuminated by natural light. Practice rendering abstract graphic representations for all of these materials, using both pen and pencil.

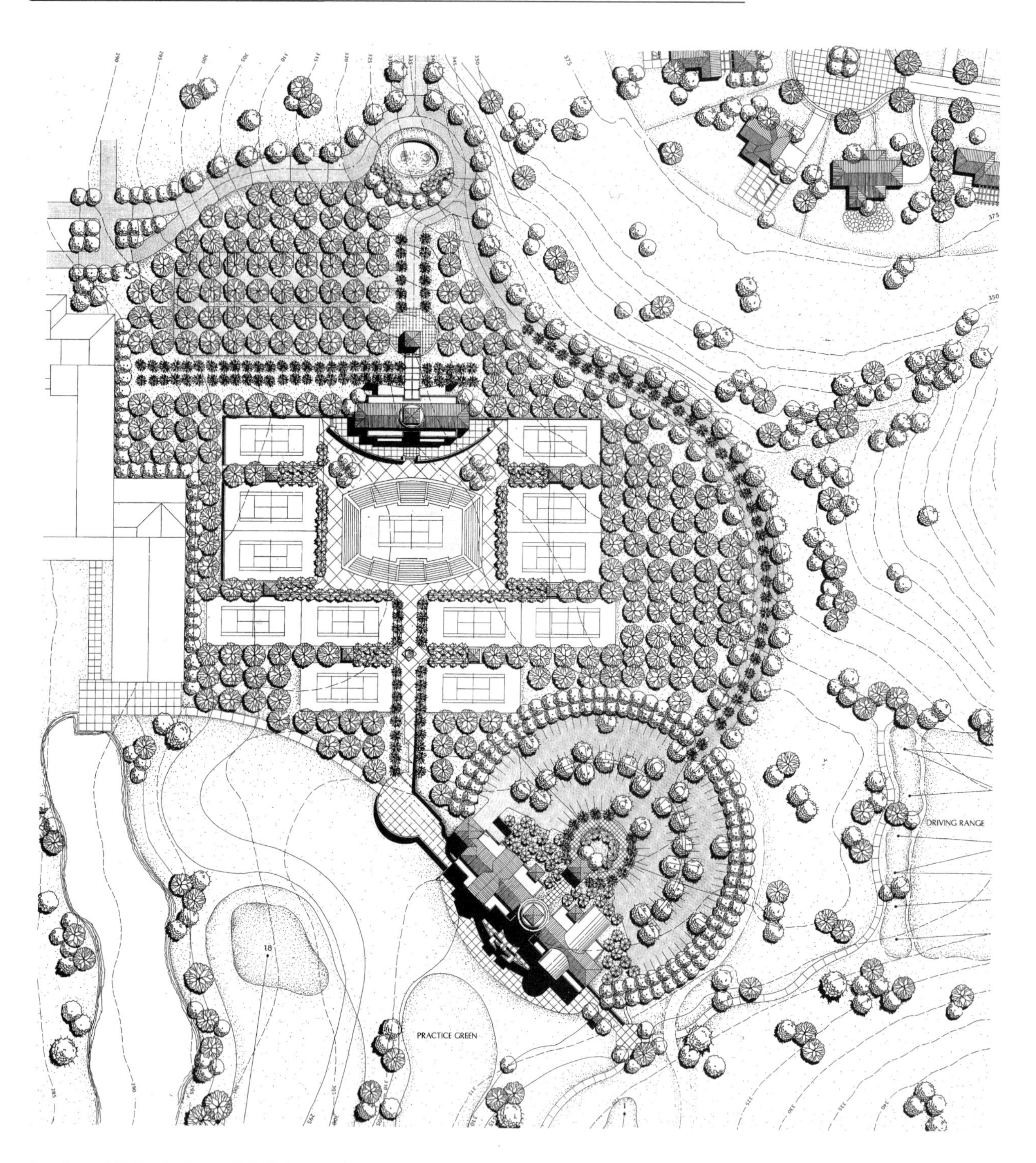

Drawing: ATP Tennis Center/TPC Clubhouse, Black Mountain Ranch
San Diego County, California
30" × 42" (76.2 × 106.7 cm), Scale: 1"=40'
Medium: Ink on Mylar
Courtesy of Sandy & Babcock Inc., Architecture & Planning

As the size of a site plan becomes larger and larger, less and less detail is needed to indicate a tree in plan. Regardless of the scale, a value differentiation between the trees and the ground cover must be maintained.

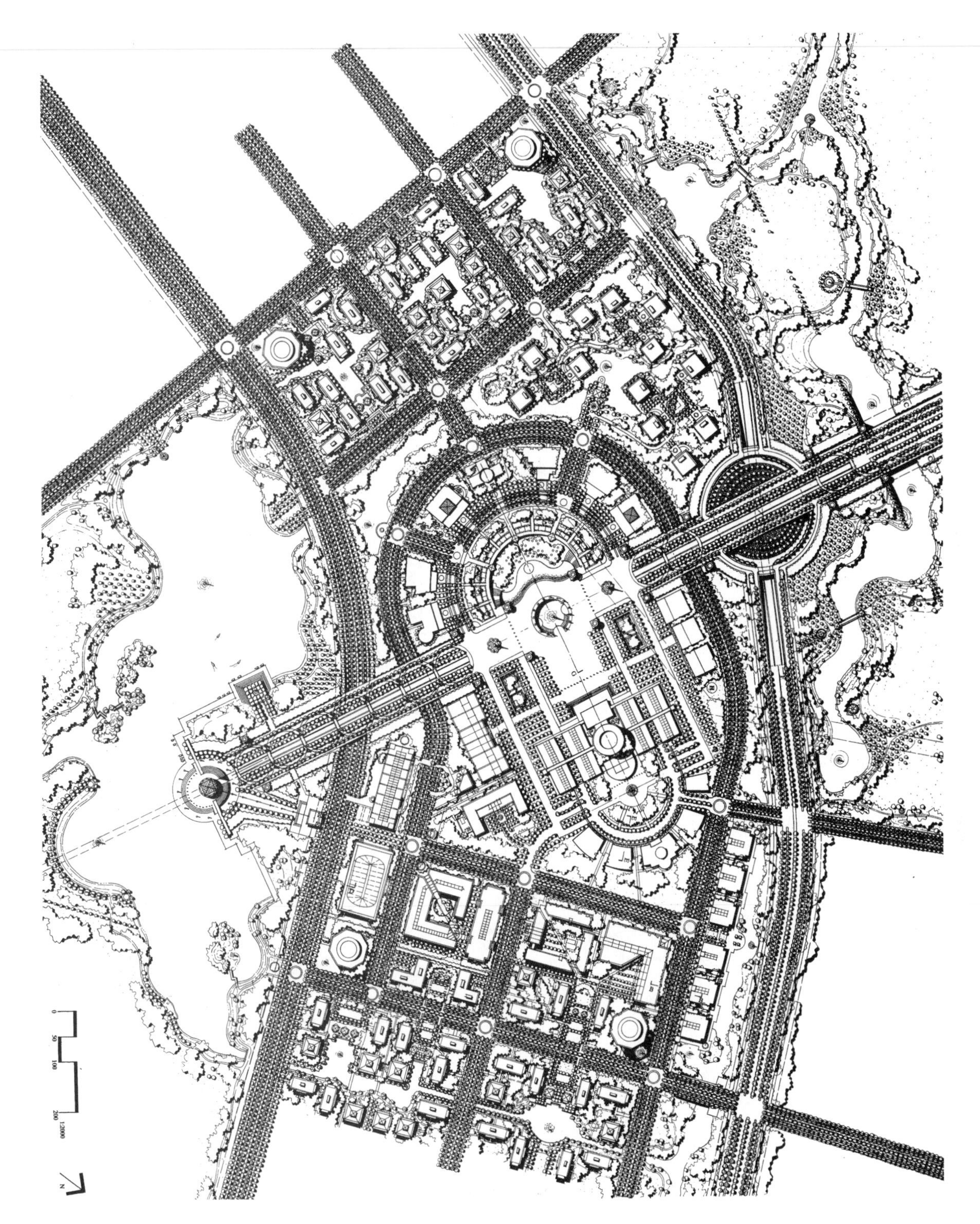

Drawing: Shanghai Civic Center District, Shanghai, China
36" × 48" (91.4 × 121.9 cm), Scale: 1:2000
Medium: Pencil
Drawn by John L. Wong, Landscape Architect
Courtesy of The SWA Group

In this site plan, the trees no longer read individually, but rather as clustered groups that produce a dense value and a circulation pattern.

Drawing: The Moir Building
San Jose, California
36" × 42" (91.4 × 106.7 cm)
Medium: Pentel on vellum
Courtesy of Jerome King, AIA
Renderer: Barney Davidge Associates

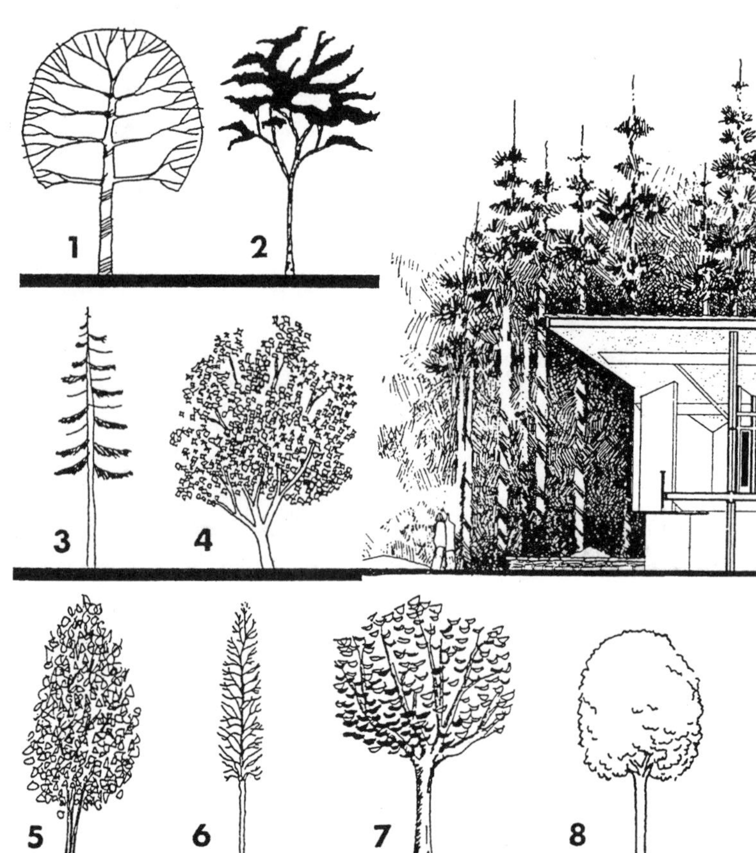

Drawing: Rendered trees, Davenport house,
Evergreen, Colorado
18" × 24" (45.7 × 61 cm), Scale: ¼"=1'0"
Medium: Ink on vellum
Courtesy of Fay Jones + Maurice Jennings, Architects

Rendered trees can show branching (**3** and **6**), branching with outline (**1**), partial texture with outline (**8**), full texture (**2**, **4**, and **5**), or full texture with shade (**7**). Texture with shade is based on directional sunlight. Trees form a parachute shape as they react to gravity.

Drawing: Foliage texture for foreground trees
Medium: Ink on vellum
Herbert Cuevas, AIA, Architect
Courtesy of Brigette Nalley

Symbolic trees can be abstract or representational. They should always complement rather than compete with or overpower the human-built environment they are surrounding. Trees can be made darker (top right) or lighter than the building they are behind to give more contrast. Tracing existing high-quality examples will build your graphic vocabulary of these symbols.

Drawing: The Peninsula Regent, San Mateo, California
24" × 24" (61 × 61 cm)
Medium: Ink
Courtesy of Backen Arrigoni & Ross, Inc. Architecture, Planning & Interior Design
Peter Szasz, Architectural Illustrator

Trees and other vegetation, human figures, furniture, moving vehicles, and ground textures are defined as **entourage** (French for "surroundings") in an architectural rendering. These supporting elements should always complement the human-built environment, not compete with it. Accurately drawn entourage also helps to give scale to the drawing.

The trees in this illustration are quite detailed and realistic in appearance. When delineating abstract or realistic trees in perspective, you can create more visual interest by changing the height of the trees; and you can add more depth to the rendering by casting ground shadows (see p. 404).

ELEVATION MATERIAL SYMBOLS

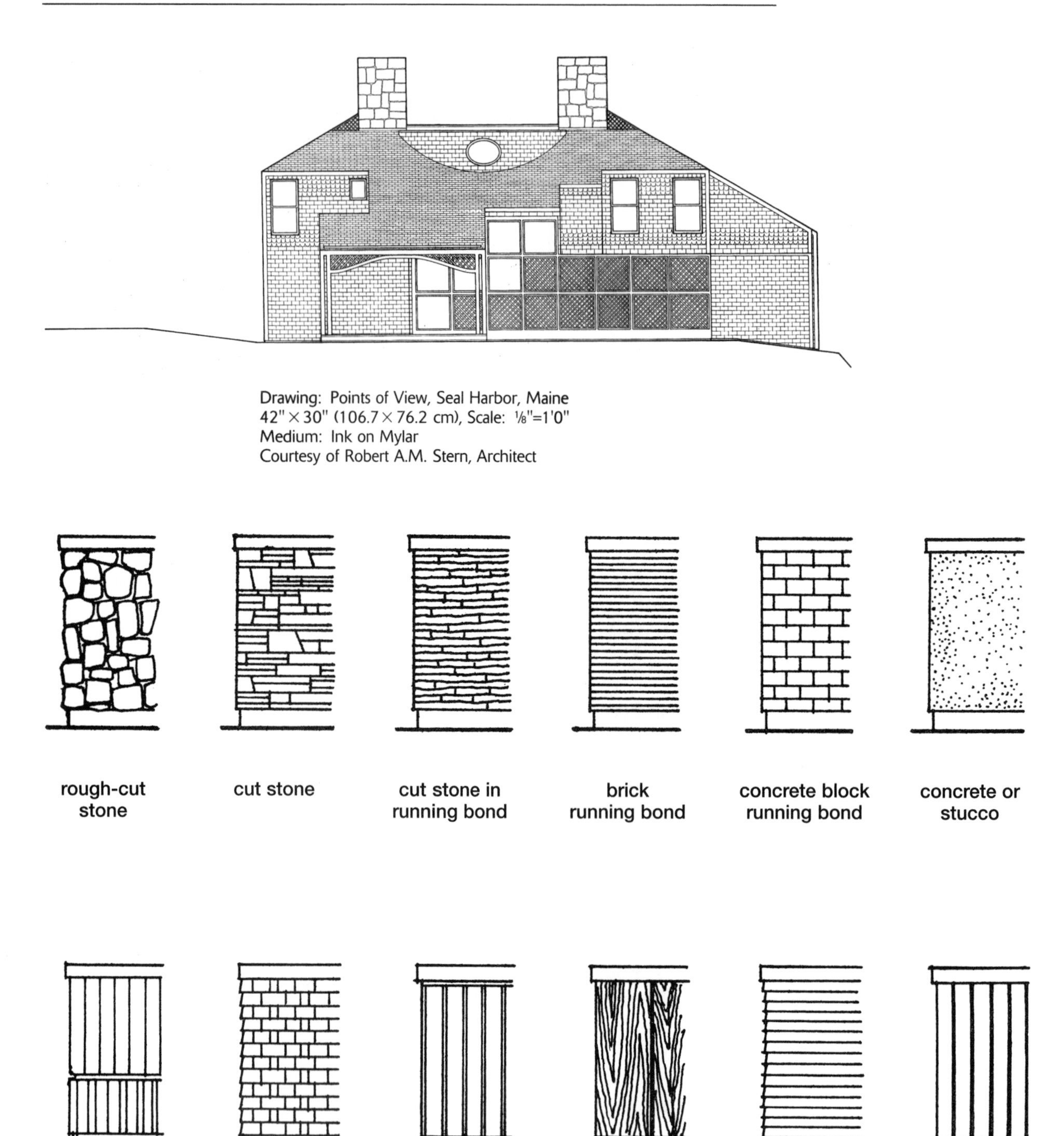

Drawing: Points of View, Seal Harbor, Maine
42" × 30" (106.7 × 76.2 cm), Scale: 1/8"=1'0"
Medium: Ink on Mylar
Courtesy of Robert A.M. Stern, Architect

As with floorscapes, building elevations are commonly rendered with material symbols in order to accentuate their typical flatness and communicate building material choices. Generally, the drawings are simplified because of the small scales used, and tonal values are not shown. The examples above are selected material structural texture indication symbols. Material textures rendered on plan obliques and perspectives are, for the most part, similar to their corresponding elevation textures (see the many examples in this chapter).

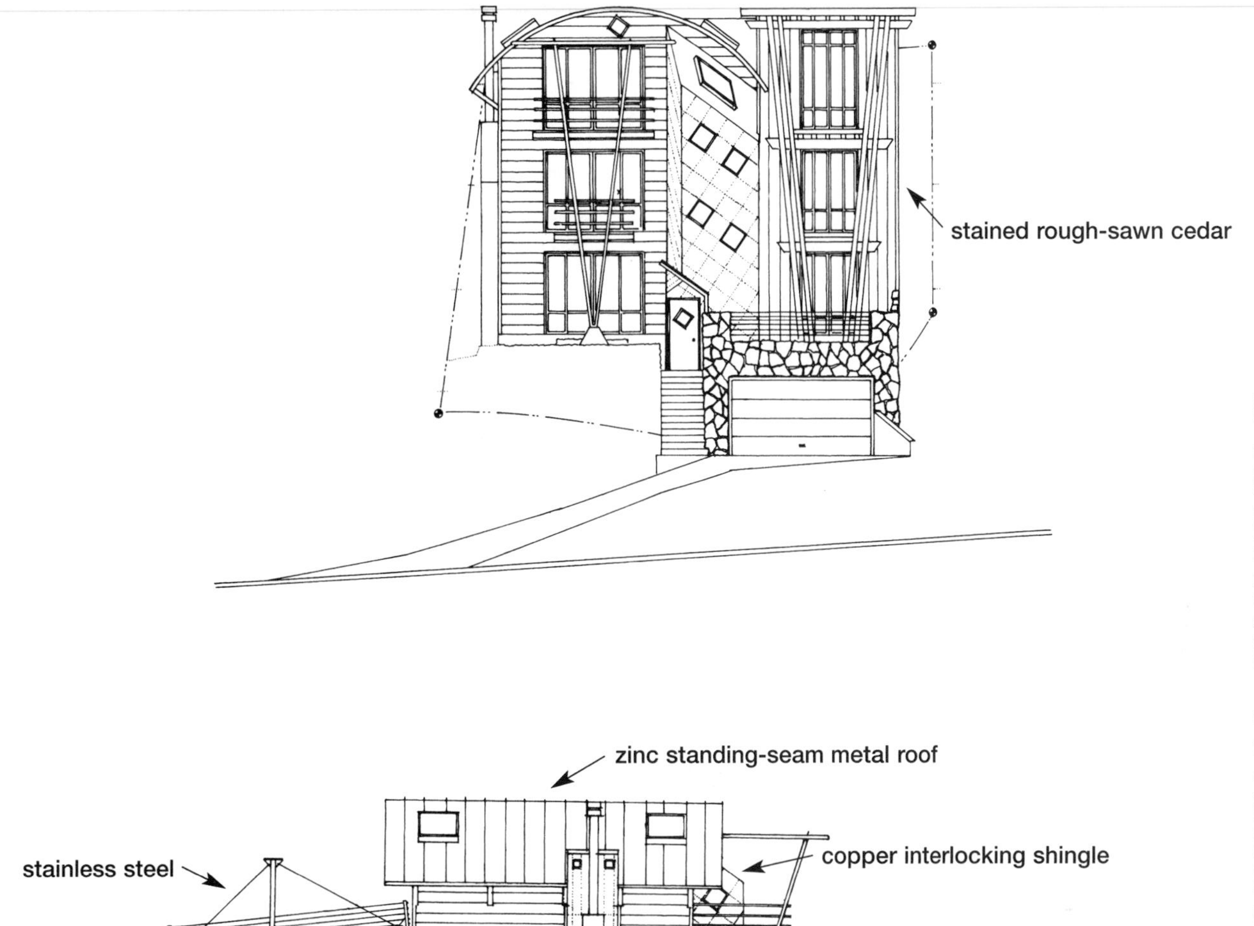

Drawing: Schuh Box (unbuilt), hills above San Francisco Bay
Medium: Ink on trace
Courtesy of David Baker Associates Architects

Distinct natural-finish materials, such as copper, zinc, stainless steel, transparent stain on rough-sawn cedar, smooth redwood, and Arizona sandstone, are used to code the distinct volumetric elements that compose this design.
[ARCHITECT'S STATEMENT]

In the twenty-first century, construction materials with new materiality and tectonics will be developed (see *Architectural Record,* "Innovation," November 2005, p. 36). This is inevitable, especially with the development of nanotechnology which, through molecular manipulation, will allow existing materials to transform into other building materials. With the advent of new materials will come the need to create new representational symbols, and these symbols will be added to the current architectural nomenclature.

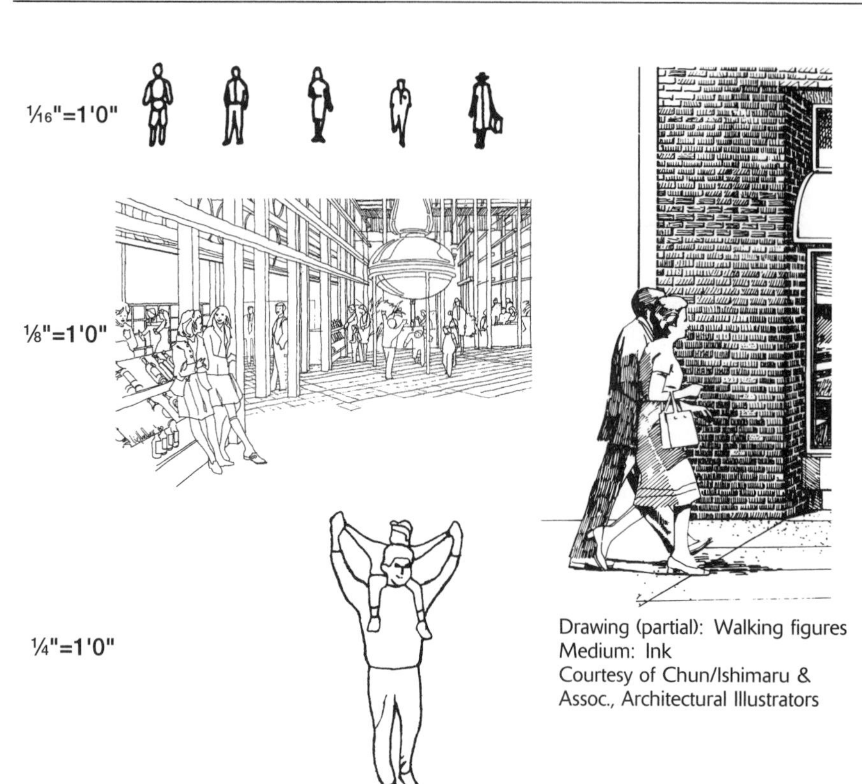

Drawing (partial): Walking figures
Medium: Ink
Courtesy of Chun/Ishimaru & Assoc., Architectural Illustrators

Keep the following in mind when using human figures:

- Figures show the scale of a drawing.
- Figures are secondary to the architecture.
- Figures should not cover space-defining intersections.
- Figures should imply activity yet not be overactive.
- Figures should have simple details for clothes.
- Grouped figures should show overlap (see pp. 410–11).
- Figures should be developed using properly proportioned, contoured bubble forms to depict activity (standing, walking, sitting, etc.).
- Figures should be drawn as an integral part of any rendering (not pasted in, resulting in a cookie-cutter look).

Keep a reference clipping file of photographs and drawings of people in different poses alone as well as in groups. Use a Polaroid camera or a digital camera (with a computer and printer) to freeze figure images for future reference. These photos can be reduced or enlarged to suit the size of your drawing.

⅜"=1'0"

Grouped figures (2nd row left)
Medium: Ink
Courtesy of Martin Liefhebber, Barton Myers Associates, Architects

Grouped figures (5th row left)
Medium: Ink
Courtesy of Chun/Ishimaru, Architectural Illustrators

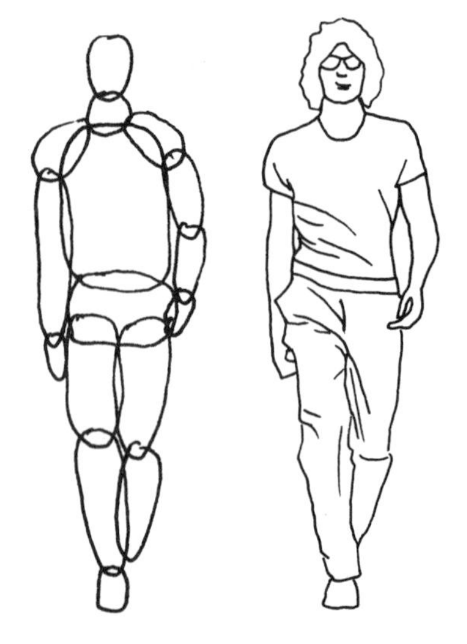

½"=1'0"

The people in the drawing at right are abstract, with little or no clothing detail. Abstract figures (either with contour outline or with gray shades) are usually adequate for most drawings. Clothing detail for figures is dependent on the scale, style, and intent of the drawing.

Drawing (partial): East Wing of the National Gallery of Art
Washington, D.C.
Entire original: 21" × 14" (53.3 × 35.6 cm)
Medium: Black Prismacolor on vellum
Pei, Cobb, Freed, and Partners, Architects
Courtesy of Paul Stevenson Oles FAIA, Renderer

Drawing (partial): Waterfront Development Plan
Asbury Park, New Jersey
Medium: Ink
Courtesy of Koetter, Kim & Associates, Inc.
Architects and Urban Designers

As the scale of the human figure increases in size, a simple form without clothing detail is no longer adequate. Keep added clothing detail minimal to avoid distracting from the architectural subject. The drawing at right successfully adds important human scale for the background building while avoiding extremes in clothing fashion that can be eye-catching.

Allow digitally generated people to be transparent so as not to obscure important architectural features (see pp. 544, 546).

Drawing: Renovation of Santa Fe Depot, San Diego, California
Hanna/Olin Ltd. Landscape Architecture
16" × 24" (40.6 × 61 cm)
Medium: Full watercolor over pencil line transfer
Courtesy of Al Forster, Architectural Illustrator

Drawing: Villa Sheraton Senggigi Indonesia
17" × 11" (43.2 × 27.9 cm)
Medium: Felt pen, markers, and pencil crayons on white tracing paper
Courtesy of the Timothy Seow Group Architects

In interior space design, furniture and materiality depiction is the best way to animate a space because these are the elements to which users relate. Sofas and chairs are commonly seen in groups of two or more. Become familiar with good furniture design. Outstanding furniture has been designed by many noted architects, including Alvar Aalto, Marcel Breuer, Charles Eames, Frank Gehry, Richard Meier, Eero Saarinen, and Frank Lloyd Wright. As with people and cars, keep a reference photo file.

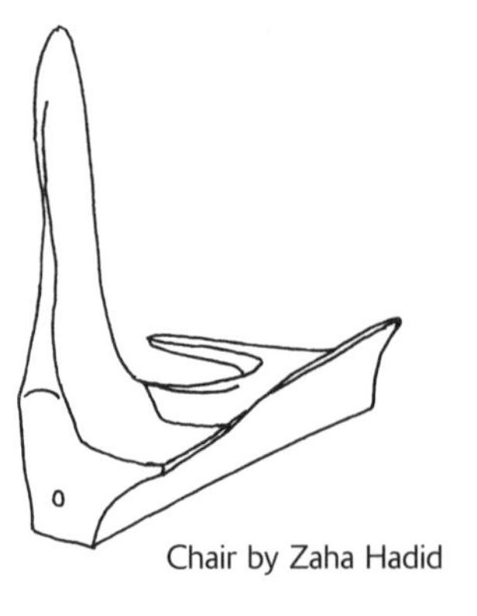

Chair by Zaha Hadid

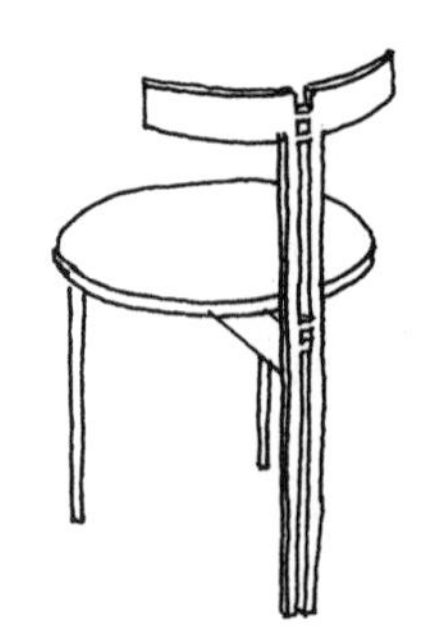

Furniture study by Richard Meier

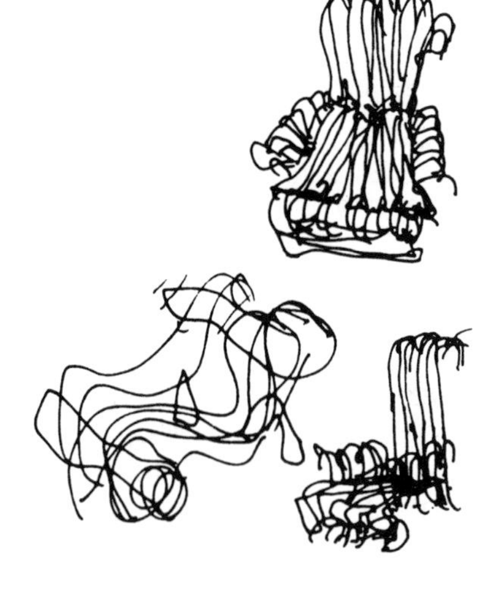

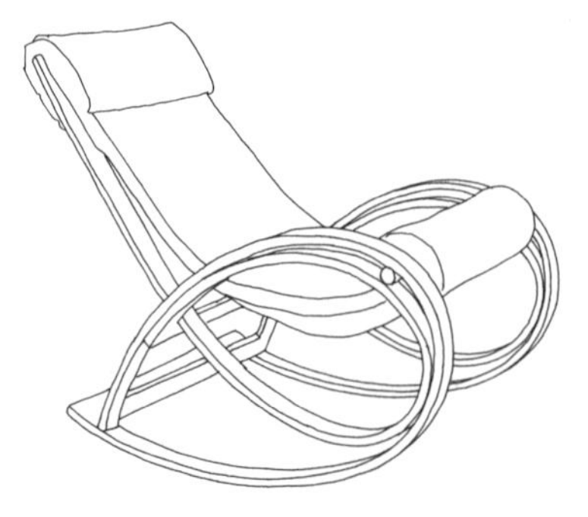

Chair by Gaetana Aulenti

Chair by Charles Eames

Concept sketches: Courtesy of the Frank Gehry Bentwood Collection
9" × 12" (22.9 × 30.5 cm)
Medium: Ink on paper
Courtesy of Knoll

Drawing: The Peninsula Regent
San Mateo, California
20" × 24" (50.8 × 61 cm)
Medium: Pencil on vellum
Courtesy of Backen Arrigoni & Ross, Inc.,
Architecture, Planning and Interior Design
Jim Gillam, Architectural Illustrator

Furniture accessories, such as lighting elements, chairs, sofas, and tables, should complement the interior architecture and show how interior space is used. The size and scale of an interior space can be indicated when human figures are added with the furniture. Drawing properly scaled people in the interior space will help in drawing properly scaled furniture. It is easier to start by drawing a scaled figure, and then drawing the piece of furniture on which the figure is sitting (see p. 407).

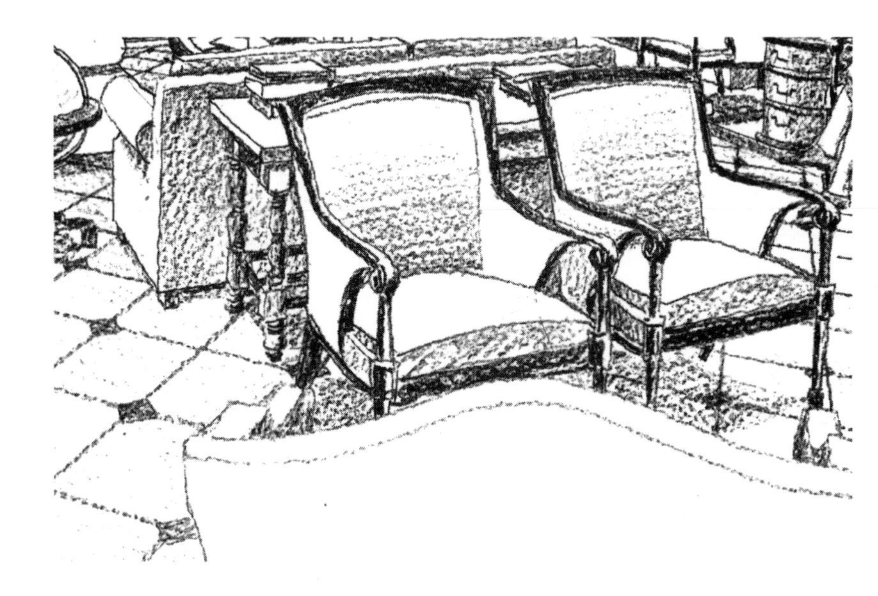

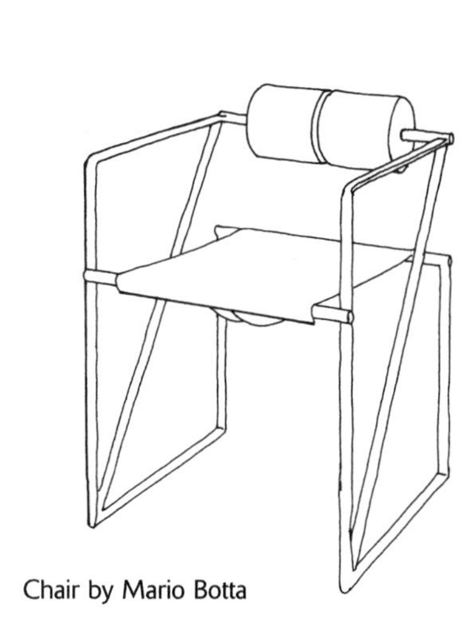

Chair by Mario Botta

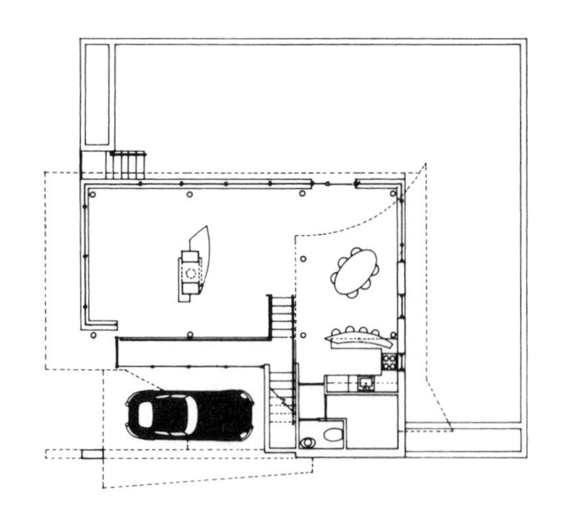

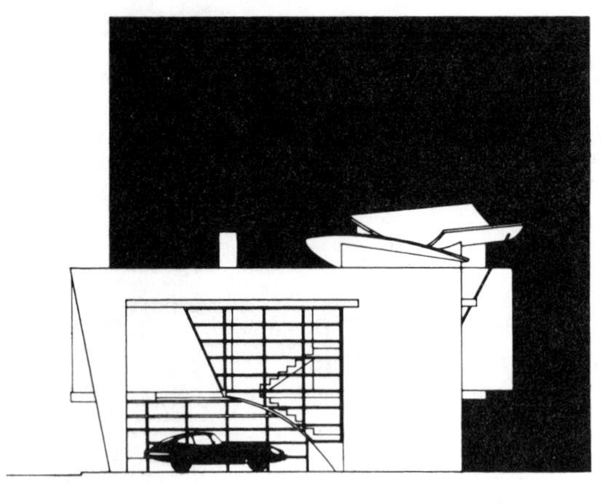

Drawings above: The Hague Villa Project
The Hague, The Netherlands
10" × 8" (25.4 × 20.3 cm), Scale: ¼"=1'0"
Medium: Pen and ink
Courtesy of Hariri & Hariri, Architects

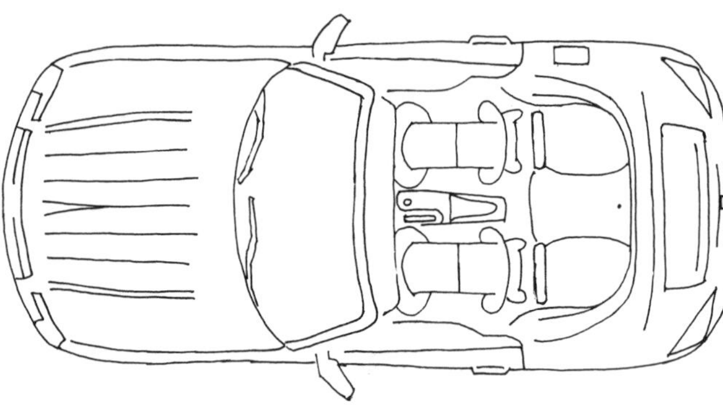

Cars seen in the plan view are good scale indicators when placed on driveways and roadways in site plans. Likewise, cars seen in elevation, as with human figures, are good scale indicators for buildings. They can be symbolic, as shown above, or delineated with more detail.

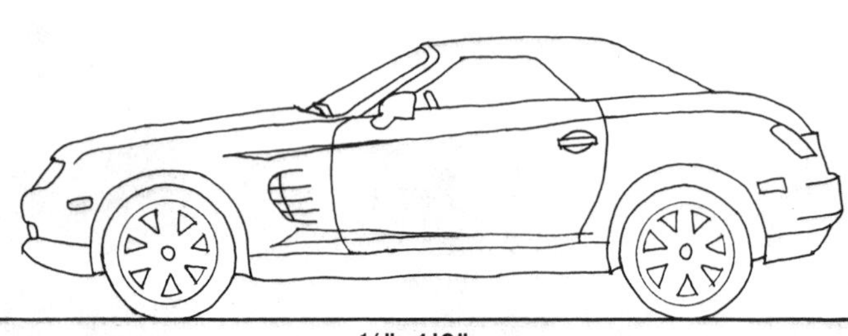

¼"=1'0"

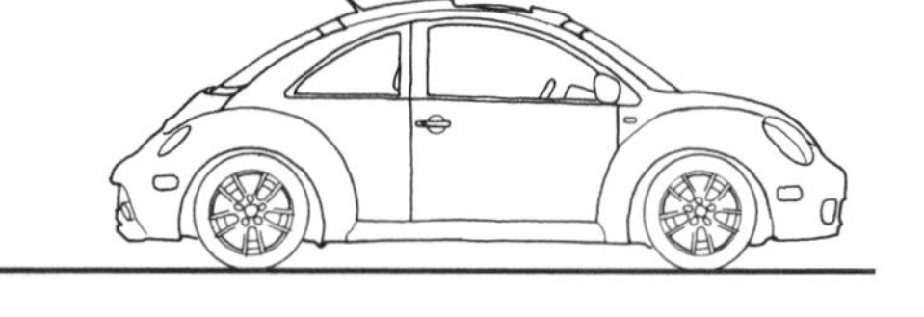

⅛"=1'0"

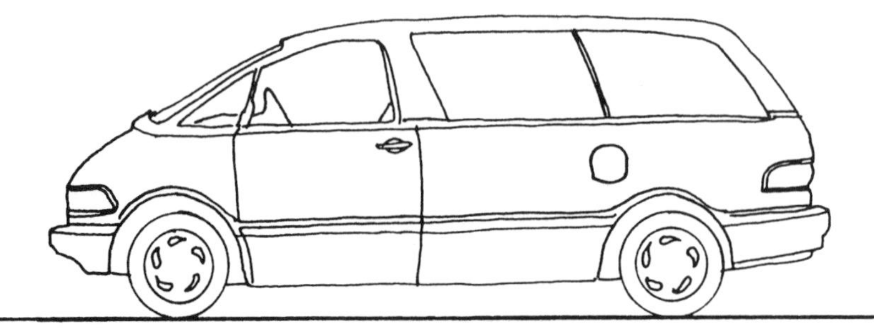

¼"=1'0"

Drawing: Off-Track Betting
Chicago, Illinois
Architects: Ware Malcomb
Medium: Watercolor 11" X 17" (27.9 X 42.2 cm)
Drawing by Wenjie Chen
Courtesy of Wenjie Studio

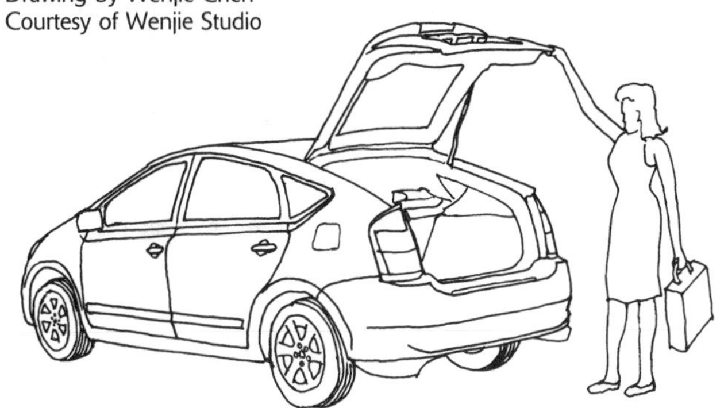

Car shapes in plan and in elevation are essentially rectangles. Cars in perspective can be simplified into rectangular boxes (see p. 68). Standing human figures are usually drawn in perspective with cars in order to indicate an appropriate scale.

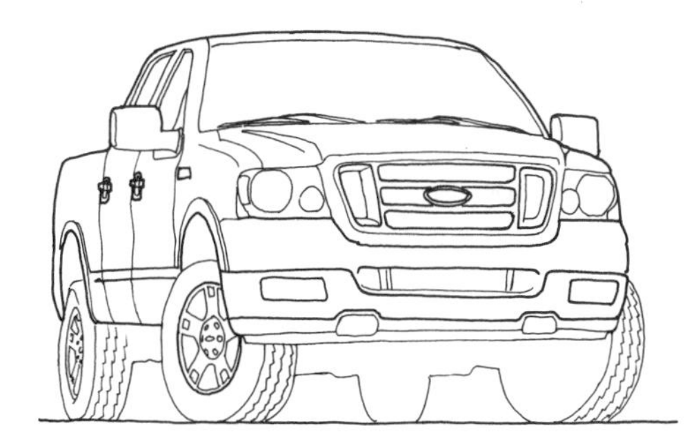

As with people and landscaping entourage, cars should complement the architecture. Keep a reference file of photos and drawings for cars. Periodically update this file with the latest car designs.

Drawing: Project, Japan
Courtesy of Projects International, Palo Alto
and Christopher Grubbs, Illustrator

Both water reflection drawings measure 8″ × 5″ and were drawn with a Uniball Micro pen on Clearprint. These images represent the first of a two-step process in which the drawings were copied and Prismacolor was applied to the copies for a color version.
[Architectural Illustrator's statement]

Buildings or small structures in the urban landscape appear light in daylight, and their reflections should be shown lighter than the value of the body of the water. The above example shows these elements reflected as pure white, with minimal horizontal strokes within the white area. The reflection of the dark part of the landscape (background trees) in the water is depicted with closely spaced, short horizontal marks. The water reflections on both of these pages show slight agitation, but with a general feeling of calmness and serenity. A horizontal reflection actually begins where the object reflected meets the reflecting surface. If the horizontal surface is above the reflecting surface that is horizontal and is part of a solid construction, you won't see the surface in the reflection (see the steps at lower left in the drawing above).

Drawing: Saigon City, Vietnam
Courtesy of Skidmore, Owings, and Merrill, San Francisco
and Christopher Grubbs, Illustrator

Shifting reflective water surfaces tend to intimidate the artist. But water is just as tangible a material as brick. The first rule is not to overdraw the surface. This is best achieved by planning ahead. In the preliminary drawing, flip upside-down those elements that will best express reflections. Anticipate the scale change of big strokes (foreground waves) versus tiny strokes (distant waves). Since water surfaces are so varied and quick to change, it's very important to establish a specific instant of time or condition for your scene and to anticipate the graphic implications: Is there a breeze rippling the surface or is it glassy? Is this a pond or an ocean?
[Architectural Illustrator's statement]

Water can be rendered either as **still** or with **ripples.** Still water is best illustrated with precise parallel horizontal lines. These can be equally or unequally spaced at increasing intervals, depending on the nature of the body of water. Wave ripples have a convex and concave form that reflects objects at different angles. The resulting visual phenomenon is that of irregular stripes. Small, **wavy** freehand lines produce the best results for depicting agitated water. In this river scene, the darker value of the boats reflects darker than the background foliage. Also note the multiple directions for the wavy lines to represent agitated water.

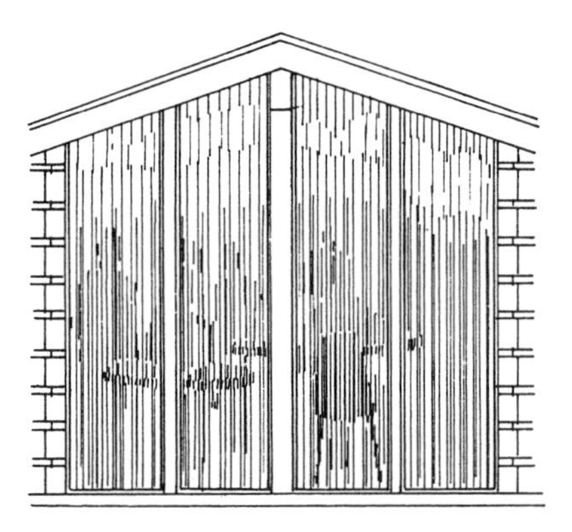

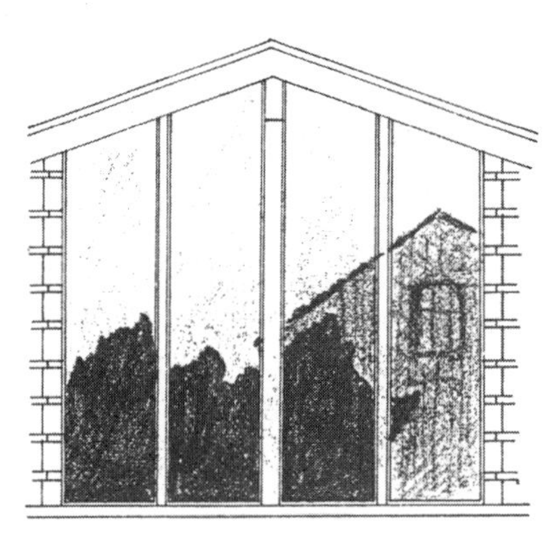

Glass usually creates reflections. When glass is **nonreflective,** it is transparent. Show human figures, vegetation, and furniture seen in the interior space to create a realistic effect. Reflections show objects behind the observer, such as trees, buildings, vehicles, and the sky condition. In a **partially reflective/partially transparent** situation, objects behind the observer as well as human figures and furniture within the space are seen.

Drawing: New England Sunbox
Methuen, Massachusetts
9" × 11" (22.9 × 27.9 cm)
Medium: Black Prismacolor on vellum with watercolor paper underlay
Courtesy of Interface Architects
Illustration: Paul Stevenson Oles, FAIA

This drawing is a straightforward example of wax-based pencil on vellum with a watercolor paper underlay. The reflections in the glazing were carefully plotted using a folded tracing device. Plan elements to be reflected were traced. Then the tracing was folded 180° about the axis (in plan) of the reflecting surface (glass in this case), and the perspective image was constructed beyond the glass in the usual way. Deciding on tonal values for superimposed images (real and virtual) is a little tricky and requires some analysis, but intuitive judgments allow a reasonably convincing depiction of transparent and reflective glazing.
[ARCHITECTURAL ILLUSTRATOR'S STATEMENT]

Drawing: Student project by Corvin Matei
D.A.R.T. (Dallas Rapid Transit Systems)
18" × 18" (45.7 × 45.7 cm)
Medium: 2B pencil on Strathmore paper
Courtesy of the University of Texas at Arlington
School of Architecture

This drawing is an investigative study rather than a straightforward representation of a space. It tries to convey the differences and similarities between "virtual" and "real." This is done by assigning different textures only to the surfaces important to the study. The glass, which is the focus of this drawing, is assigned the darkest tone, while other, unimportant areas are left blank. The sketches at the lower right are section and plan studies done simultaneously with the perspective; they become part of the study and help to better understand and develop the design of the piece.
[ARCHITECTURE STUDENT'S STATEMENT]

This reflection is typical of a night scene (dark exterior) and is caused by the artifical illumination inside the train. This is analogous to observed reflections on windows separating a dark interior from a sunlit exterior. In the daytime, a train traveller would experience completely transparent glass.

Floor and elevation material symbols are commonly shown in pictorial drawings such as obliques, axonometrics, and perspectives. In these examples, wall and floor material textures enhance the powerful spatial quality that is created. Note the extensive use of material texture (porcelain enamel panels, concrete blocks, etc.) on both horizontal and vertical planes.

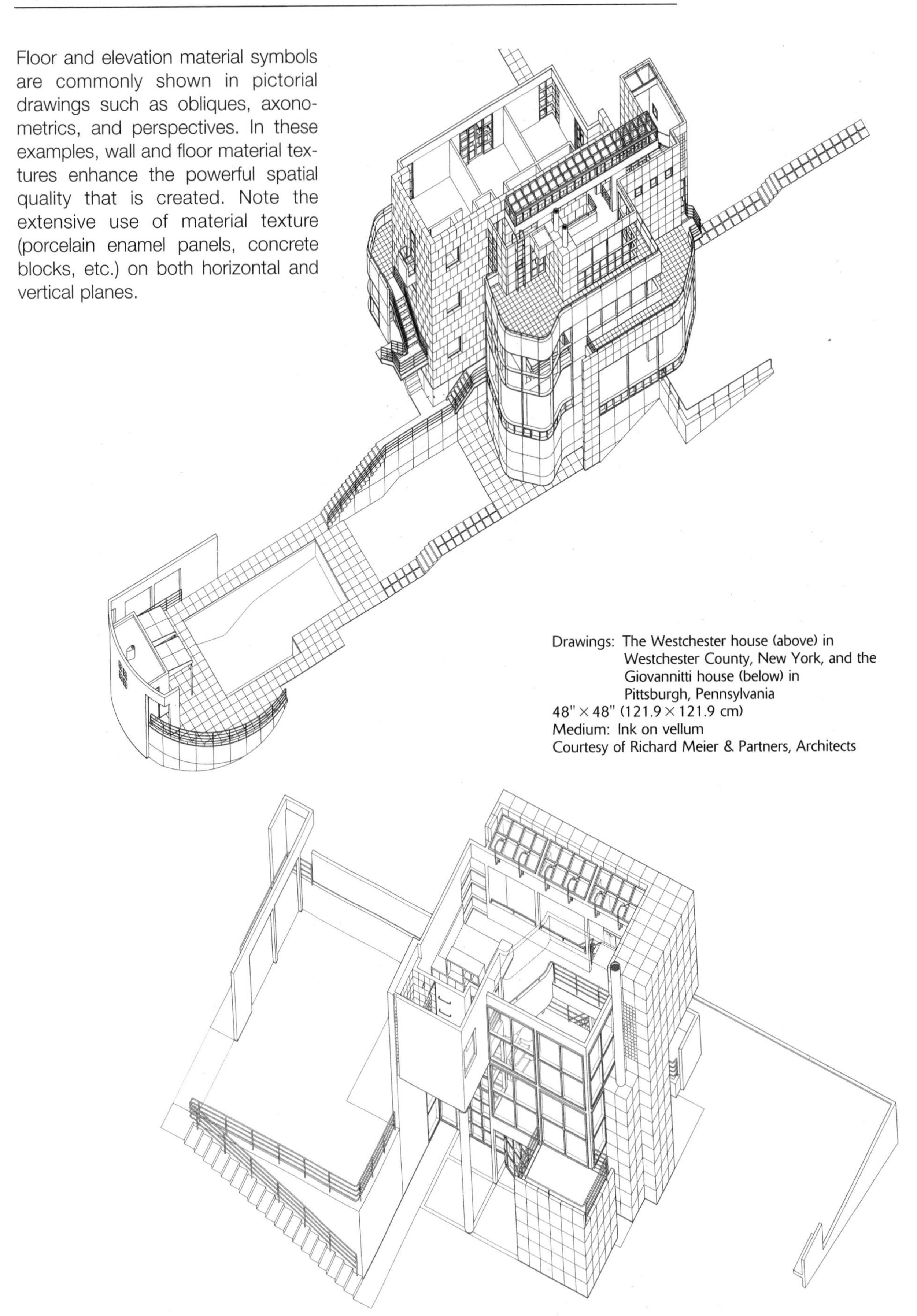

Drawings: The Westchester house (above) in Westchester County, New York, and the Giovannitti house (below) in Pittsburgh, Pennsylvania
48" × 48" (121.9 × 121.9 cm)
Medium: Ink on vellum
Courtesy of Richard Meier & Partners, Architects

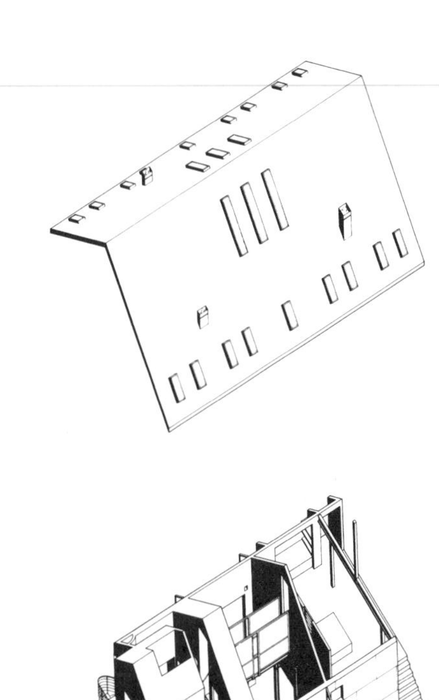

This exploded drawing of the design scheme of a "box inside a box" shows a small box faced with cherrywood inside a large rough stone shell. The material symbols on the walls are easily identifiable.

Material texture symbols retain a uniform, repetitive appearance in obliques and axonometrics; however, because of the diminution factor in perspectives, textures are gradually simplified from foreground to distant background areas (see the examples of the rendering of brick on pp. 404 and 417).

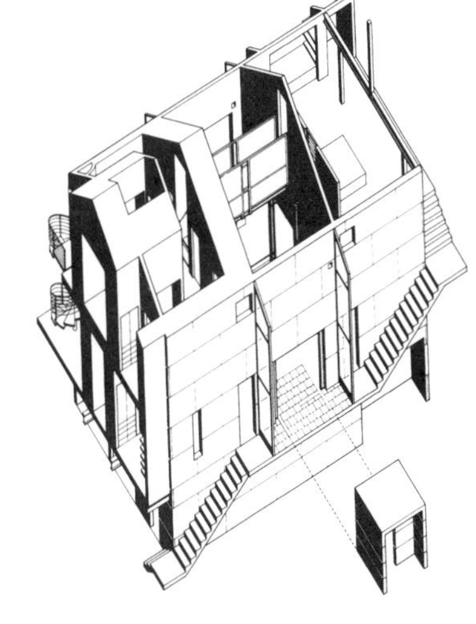

The exploded axonometric view was selected to express the conceptual basis of this design: the creation of a tectonic dialogue between past and present. A contemporary dwelling, articulated as a new wooden "box," is inserted within the old stone shell of a Pennsylvania barn. A family of other new elements, clad in metal and abstracted from nearby agrarian forms, engage the exterior of the stone shell at various places.
[ARCHITECT'S STATEMENT]

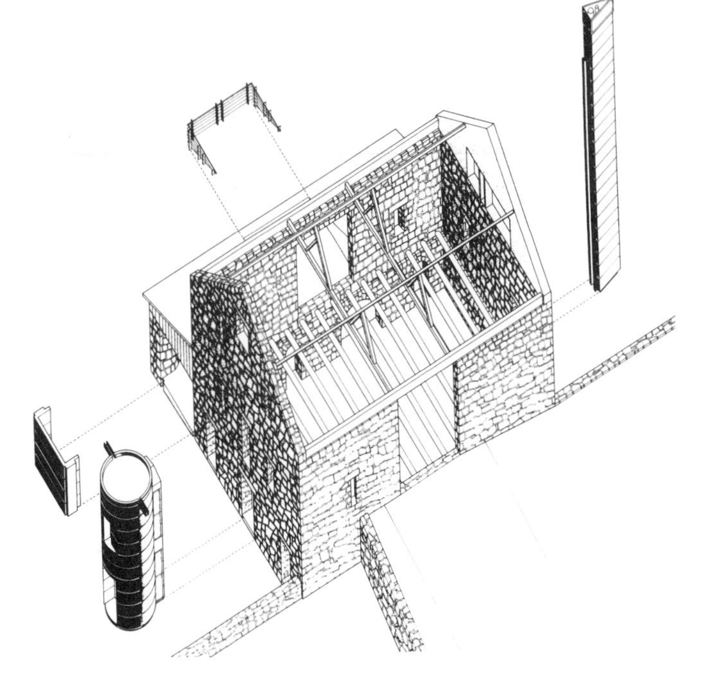

Drawing: Martin residence
Kennett Square, Pennsylvania
20" × 48" (50.8 × 121.9 cm), Scale: ¼"=1'0"
Medium: Ink on Mylar
Courtesy of Tanner Leddy Maytum Stacy Architects

Drawing: Burnett residence, 17 Mile Drive, Pebble Beach, California
36" × 24" (91.4 × 61 cm)
Medium: Pen and ink on Mylar
Simpson Gumpertz & Heger, Inc., Architects
Courtesy of Markus Lui & Associates, Architectural Illustrators

Foliage texture for foreground trees should exhibit more detail. The more highly detailed a symbolic tree, the more time-consuming it will be to draw. These foreground trees frame the buildings in the background and balance the vertical elements in both buildings. The sun is behind the observer, causing ground shadows cast away from the observer. This location for the light source permits both sides of the building to be in sunlight, giving a sense of depth to the overall drawing. The foreground tree trunk bark texture and the foreground grass are both rendered darker than the background tree trunks and background grass.

Drawing: CBS-Morningstar
Chicago, Illinois
Gensler Chicago and Perkins and Will, Architects
Courtesy of Manuel Avila Associates, Architectural Illustrator

This illustration was basically produced in the mixed-media technique of color pencil, airbrush, and black ink. However, for the trees, different ink colors were applied to create the desired depth and effect.
[Architectural Illustrator's statement]

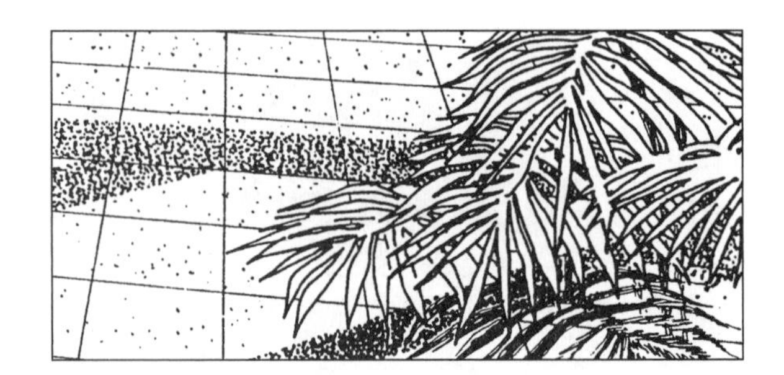

Drawing: 1333 Broadway, Oakland, California
36" × 24" (91.4 × 61 cm)
Medium: Pen and ink on Mylar
ED2 International, Richard Hom, Architects
Courtesy of Markus Lui & Associates, Architectural Illustrators

Interior vegetation should complement and not overpower interior architecture. The plant in the right foreground, above, increases the feeling of perspective depth in the interior space. The bottom perspective on the facing page is a good example of a "fudged one-point," also called a "soft two-point"—essentially a one-point view with a very long second vanishing point. The effect is basically of a one-point, but is less static. This very natural drawing type was a favorite of Frank Lloyd Wright (see Bibliography).

Drawing: Twelve-plex motion picture theater, Gateway Center, Arizona
36" × 24" (91.4 × 61 cm)
Medium: Pen and ink on Mylar
Vincent Raney, AIA, Architect
Courtesy of Markus Lui & Associates, Architectural Illustrators

Like trees, plant and shrub vegetation can be simply symbolic or realistically detailed.

Drawing: Cheeca Lodge Resort, Islamadora, Florida
24" × 13" (61 × 33 cm)
Medium: Pencil on vellum
Courtesy of Simon Martin–Vegue Winkelstein Moris
Interior design and illustration by G. Lawrence Saber

Drawings: AQIS (Australian Quarantine Inspection Service)
Brisbane, Australia
23.6" × 11.8" (60 × 30 cm)
Medium: Ink, pencil, and pastel
Architect: Donovan Hill
Client: Brisbane Airport Corporation
Courtesy of Jane Grealy, Architectural Illustrator, 2000

This is a recent project for which I used a different approach. I had been studying the illustrations of urban theorist and designer Gordon Cullen (1914–1994). His work was always beautifully composed, and I was particularly attracted to the textural qualities of the Biot series (1967). I resolved to concentrate on the composition of my drawing, completing four or five studies of four different views. Small-scale studies were done quickly by overlaying the computer-generated line drawing with detail paper and by adding tone using a black drawing pencil. I used two (right-angled) cardboard mats to frame the drawing and experimented until I found a composition that had some potential for further development. Two views were chosen, and they were enlarged so that they could be placed on the full-size sheet layout.

Attention was paid to the landscaping detail, and the black-and-white part of the perspective was hand drawn using black felt pen and pencil. This was printed onto acetate and placed over a sheet of gray Stonehenge paper, onto which the background color of pastel and pencil was applied. When choosing the color palette, I wanted a restrained, almost monochromatic effect to reflect the colors of the building materials used. I experimented with color combinations, often referring to landscape photographs where such palettes might occur naturally. The drawing was intended to be viewed with the black line and tone as dominant and the color muted and subtle. It is interesting to see the line drawing and color drawing as separate and supplementary images. It has been said that this drawing has a sixties feel, so perhaps Gordon Cullen's influence is showing through!

[Architectural Illustrator's statement]

Drawing: University of Maryland Center for the Performing Arts competition winner
Moore Ruble Yudell Architects
18" × 12" (45.7 × 30.5 cm)
Medium: Sketch watercolor on mounted presentation
blackline print of ink line drawing
Courtesy of Al Forster, Architectural Illustrator

In the perspective above, almost all of the human heads are on the observer's horizon line—it doesn't matter whether the figure is closer to or farther away from the observer. In such instances, the horizon line tends to be read as the eye level of the observer. If the human figure is taller than the observer, or located above the scene, its eyes will be above the horizon line. The same is true for a shorter human figure. On the facing page, the standing children's heads are below the horizon line. Figures on higher elevations (see the staircase above) are far above the observer's eye level.

Drawing: Proposed NTC Navy housing playground area
San Diego, California
Fehlman Labarre Architecture & Planning
18" × 12" (45.7 × 30.5 cm)
Medium: Full watercolor over pencil line transfer
People overlay courtesy of Al Forster, Architectural Illustrator

Human figures should be well distributed in a perspective drawing in order to create the proper sense of depth. This distribution should be in three zones: the **foreground,** or the area nearest to the observer; the **middle ground,** or the area that has the observer's attention (the building on the facing page and the playground structure above); and the **background,** or the area farthest from the observer (with smallest figures). When possible, carefully insert figures—whether alone or in a group—into these three distinct areas. The gestures made by figures in a drawing can lend the building a sense of use and occupancy.

75°–15°

Drawing: Arcadia Clinic
Arcadia, California
Medium: Ink
Group Four Architecture, Research, and Planning
Courtesy of Robin Chiang, Architect and Architectural Illustrator

The projected drawing shown here depicts actual (to scale) room dimensions...including heights of walls and counters. As a preliminary sketch, this was an efficient method of presentation...giving an idea of the sorts of activities while allowing users to measure proposed scales. With one drawing, it was possible to convey information on a single sheet that was copied and distributed to fourteen users.
[Architect's statement]

The plan oblique down view is the appropriate view when communicating interior accessories such as furnishings and examining how the walls meet the floor plane. Compare this with the up views on pp. 174 and 178, where the walls meet the ceiling plane and ceiling structure.

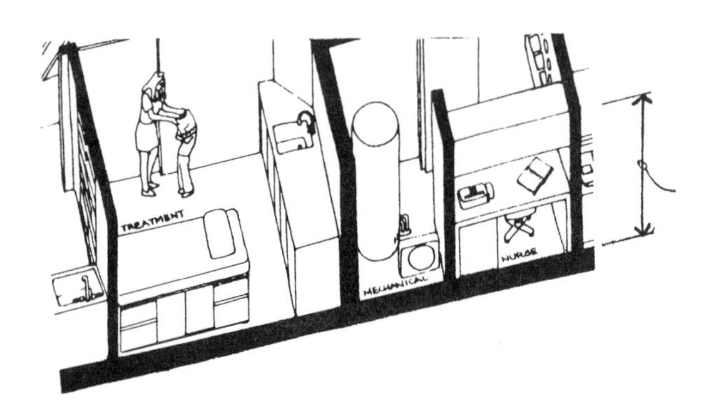

The height of the horizontal section (plan view) cut is usually taken slightly below the ceiling height (7' to 8'). This allows a clear view of important interior elements. People, plants, furniture, and columns retain verticality.

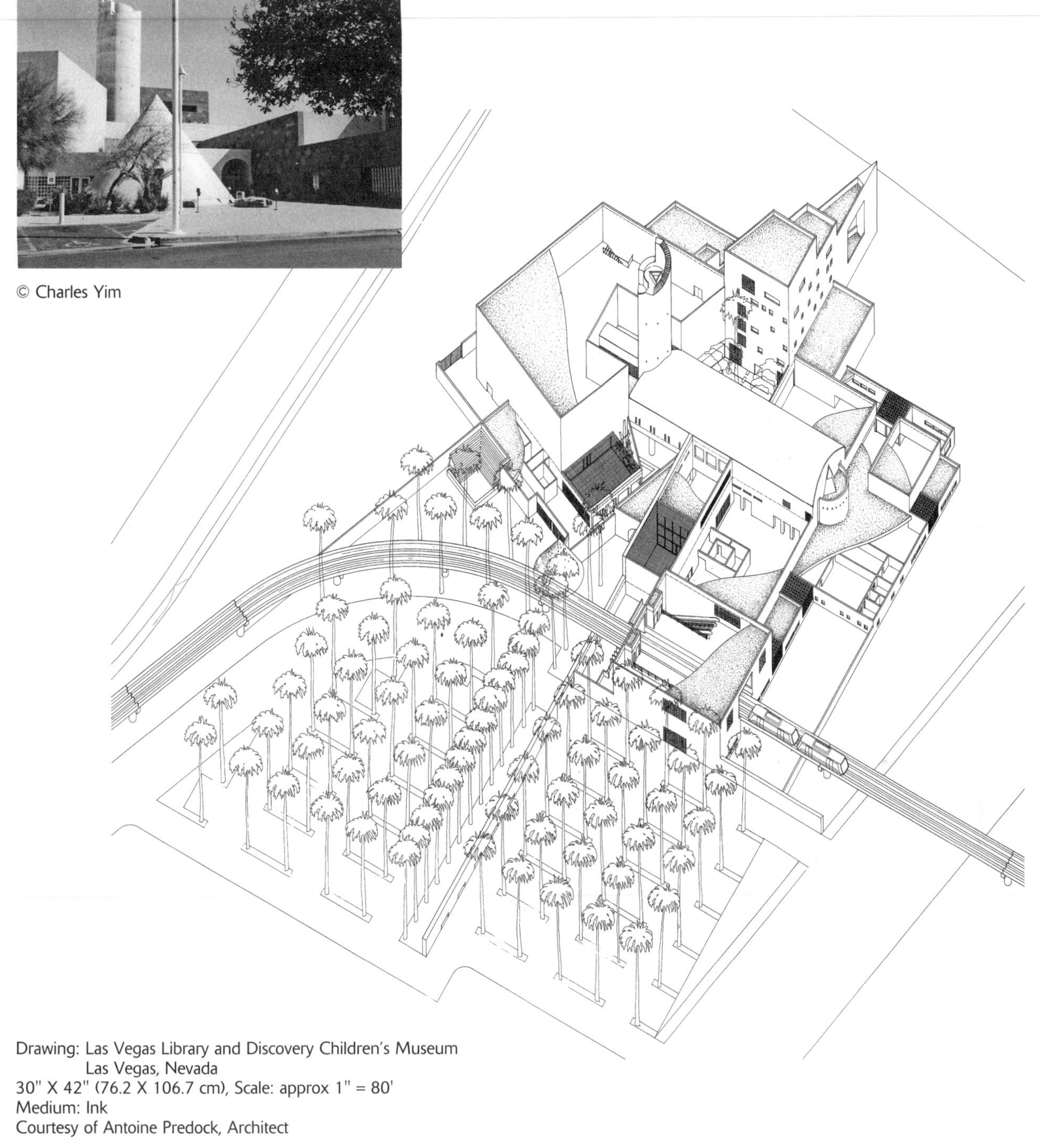

© Charles Yim

Drawing: Las Vegas Library and Discovery Children's Museum
Las Vegas, Nevada
30" X 42" (76.2 X 106.7 cm), Scale: approx 1" = 80'
Medium: Ink
Courtesy of Antoine Predock, Architect

The fragility of both the desert and the communities that colonize it is apparent when one views Las Vegas, Nevada, from the air. This confluence of nature, fantasy, urbanization, and science underscores the complexities of the desert environment and the task of making architecture responsive to its many faces.
[Architect's Statement]

Trees retain their verticality in plan obliques. In this drawing, a group of trees complements the building complex. Moving vehicles (trains, cars, etc.) also retain their verticality. Removing part of the roof allows the building to retain the feeling of a complete enclosure while at the same time permitting glimpses of the interior spaces.

Drawing: San Francisco Ballet building
40"×30" (101.6×76.2 cm)
Medium: Pencil
Rendered by J. Poey
Courtesy of Beverly Willis, FAIA

This nicely rendered two-point perspective shows a combination of reflective glass on the windows at the top and transparent glass on the windows below. The interior ceiling lighting fixtures dominate the balcony shadows. The opera house building (left) is visible and "ghosted" over the part of the building that the ballet building would obscure. This shows reflective glass seen from an interior space. Ghosting is a technique that portrays the complete exterior shape of a building as well as building forms hidden behind or within the major building. Successful ghosting depends on subtle color shading changes that do not favor the building exterior, the building interior, or the hidden building beyond.

Drawings: Bank of Tokyo of California
Headquarters building
San Francisco, California
Medium: Pen and ink
Rendered by Carlos Diniz Associates
Visual Communication

For high-rise buildings with a predominantly glass facade, the sky and clouds will generally reflect in the windows up high, and the surrounding urban landscape will reflect in the windows below.

Hatching techniques can effectively indicate reflections in glass. A series of approximately parallel thin marks or lines are hand-drawn to simulate tone. Lines spaced closely create a dark tone or value; lines spaced farther apart create a light tone or value. **Hatching** or **cross-hatching** (crisscrossing hatched lines) makes a rendered surface seem more animated than if it were toned a solid shade. Here, the renderer has given the feeling of an overcast sky by using a cross-hatching technique to create tone density.

Drawing: New England Sunbox
Methuen, Massachusetts
Medium: Black Prismacolor on vellum
Courtesy of Interface Architects
Illustration: Paul Stevenson Oles, FAIA

The three horizontal shiny surfaces (floor, table, counter) are indicated as partially reflective by repeating the high-contrast patterns of the bright openings with their vertical edges and mullions. The nearer reflections become less precise and contrasty because the angle of incident view is greater. The smooth, vertical surface (picture glazing on the left) is very bright and precisely reflective because of the extremely raking angle of incident view.
[ARCHITECTURAL ILLUSTRATOR'S STATEMENT]

Drawing: Dolby Building
San Francisco, California
18" × 24" (45.7 × 61 cm)
Medium: Ink on Mylar
Courtesy of Chun/Ishimaru &
Assoc., Architectural Illustrators

Note the simplification of the material texture rendering of brick, from heavily toned in the bottom right foreground to a series of continuous lines in the background.

The most important purpose of any rendering to us is the readability of the space. We will purposely manipulate shadows and reflections to further this end. In the final analysis, it is a matter of simple composition and the use of darks against lights and lights against darks.... This is true for any medium. Interiors are more difficult to illustrate because there are so many options and choices of light sources. Exteriors are rather simple because once the light source direction is determined, it is just a matter of putting in lighted surfaces, shaded surfaces, and shadows.
[Architectural Illustrator's statement]

Drawing: Ahmanson Theater renovation
Los Angeles, California
24" × 24" (61 × 61 cm)
Medium: Pen and ink with oil and acrylics
Ellerbe Becket, Architects
Courtesy of Art Zendarski, Architectural Illustrator

The new music center was designed by Frank Gehry. The rendering had to meet two requirements. The drawing needed to communicate the design renovation to the music center administrators. And it would be incorporated into a marketing package used for fund-raisers seeking private and public donations to cover the cost of construction.

Expressing the architect's complex, unconventional design to first-time viewers posed quite a challenge. Numbers of study views were analyzed to capture just the right vantage point. The study views and initial perspective blockout were created by computer. To clearly and accurately depict the complexity of the ceiling acoustic forms, lighting design elements, and also the additional balcony and box seating, I used pen and ink on vellum. The ink-line drawing was then transferred photographically onto photomural paper. Oils and acrylics were used to complete the rendering. Working in pen and ink also helped in meeting marketing specifications that called for the rendering to provide both black-and-white and color reproduction capabilities.

The rendering was meticulously detailed to provide a true and accurate portrayal. Also, the drawing needed to depict a level of excitement that would get potential investors enthusiastic about the project. The artificial lighting is a strong visual element used to build this excitement. The diagonal thrust of light from the ceiling onto the stage is a composition device that creates a sense of drama and a focal point for the drawing while prominently featuring the new lighting design elements. The careful composition of the viewpoint that draws the viewer into the interior space, the texture, the on-stage scene from the popular play Les Misérables, *and the animation of the people in the audience, were all added to give the drawing a sense of reality.*
[Architectural Illustrator's statement]

The purpose of this illustration was to portray the drama and monumental scale of the elliptical entrance rotunda. An exaggerated shaft of light emanating from the dome's oculus was chosen to achieve a dramatic quality, while the low station point emphasizes the monumental scale of the space.
[ARCHITECTURAL ILLUSTRATOR'S STATEMENT]

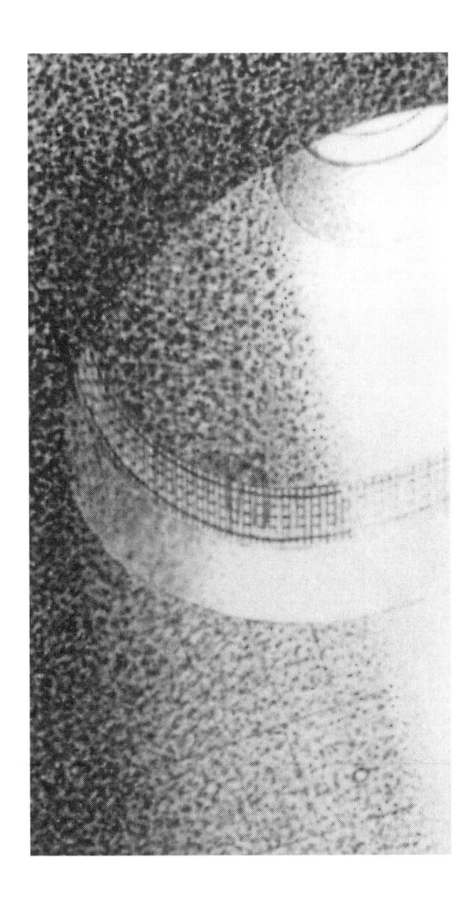

The rendering of both artificial light and natural light helps to create an ambience in interior spaces. Artificial exterior light (spotlights, etc.) can produce dramatic sky patterns and enliven a rendering. The artificial interior light on the facing page helps to highlight the architectural design of the interior space. Natural solar light shown on this page functions in a similar manner.

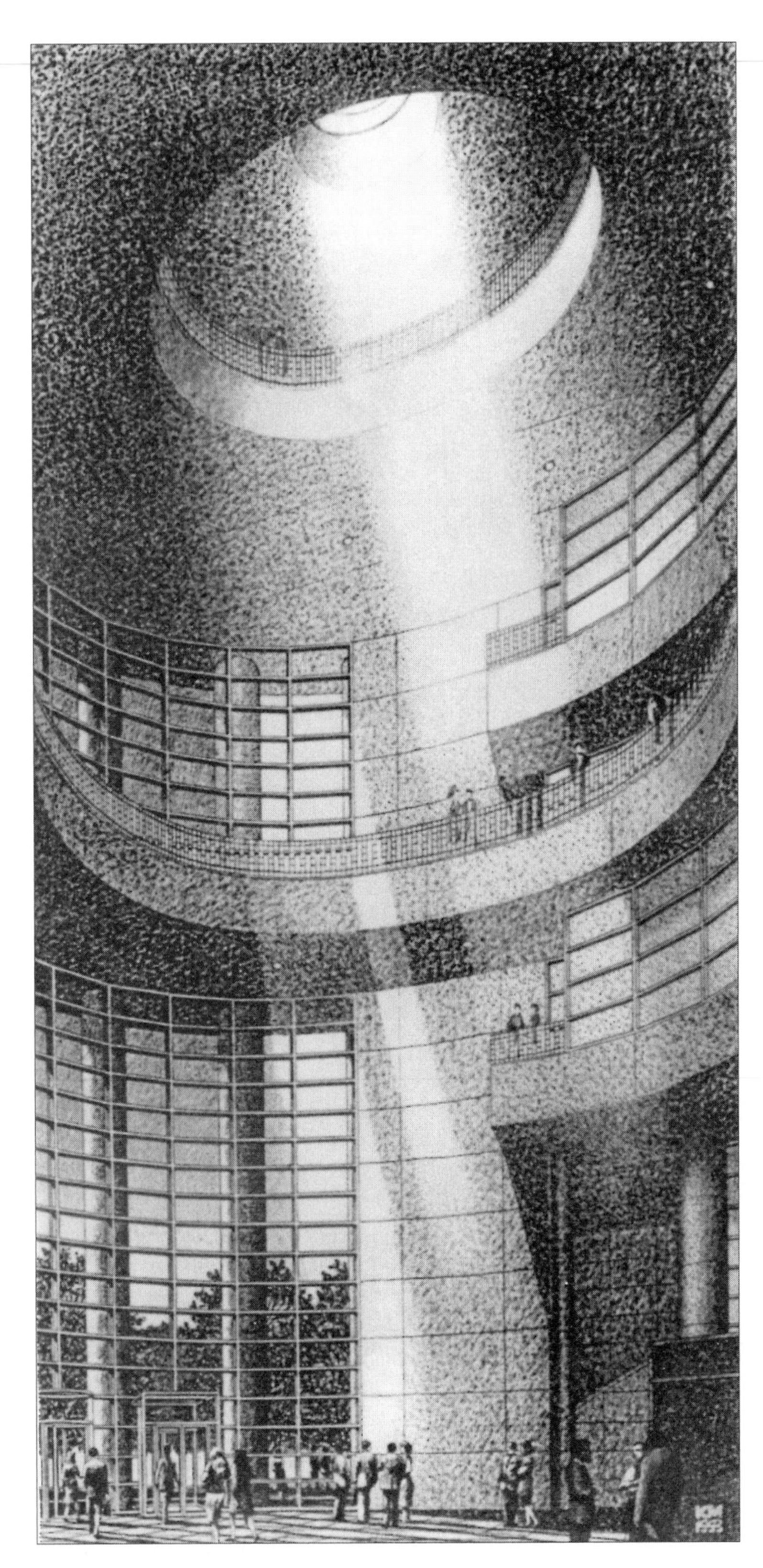

Drawing: Federal Courthouse, St. Louis, Missouri
9½" × 20" (24.1 × 50.8 cm)
Medium: Pencil on vellum
Architect: Hellmuth, Obata & Kassabaum, Inc.
Courtesy of Kenneth E. Miller, Architect, Architectural Illustrator

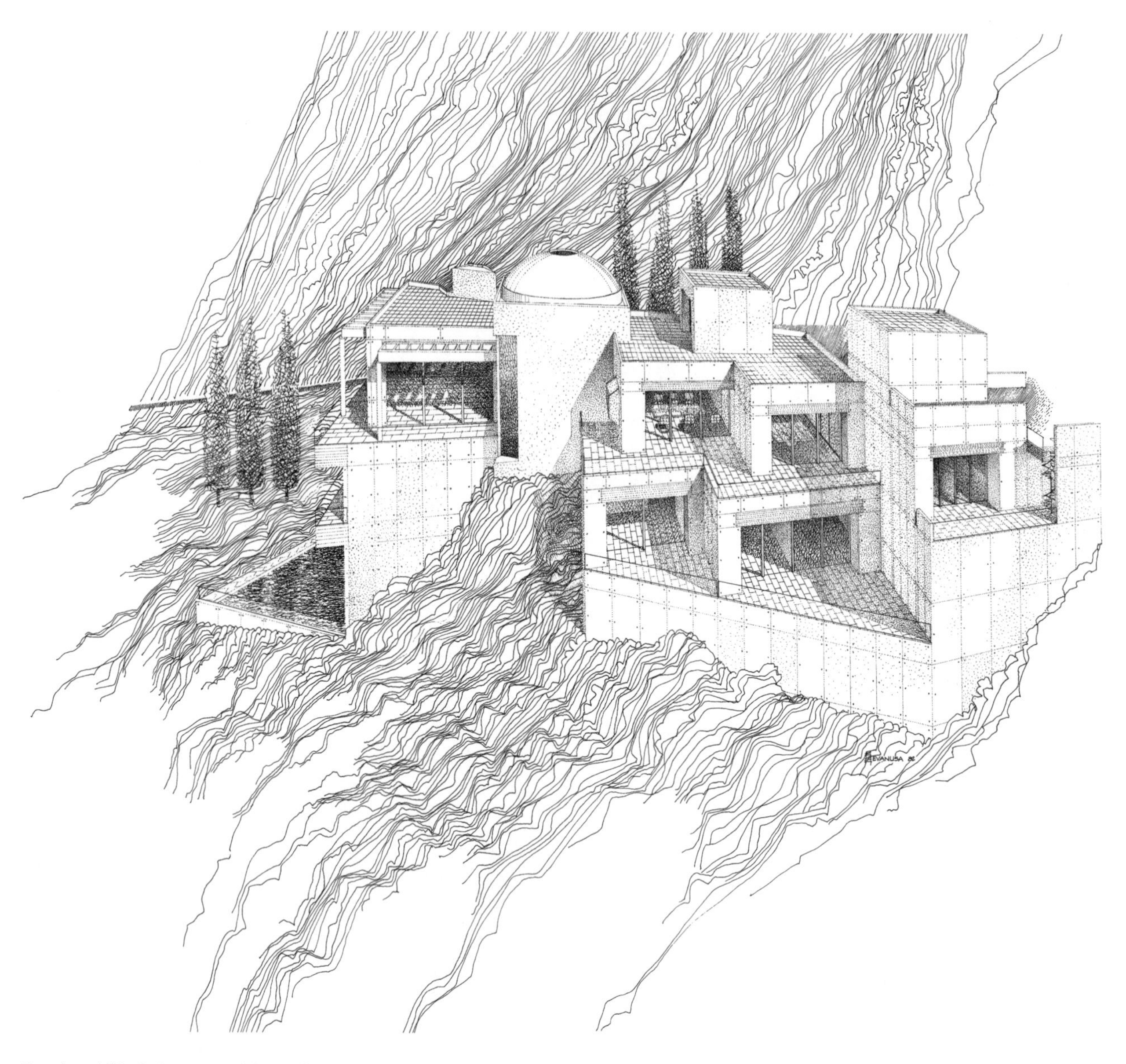

Drawing: Villa Syrigos, near Athens, Greece
36" × 24" (91.4 × 61 cm), Scale: ⅛"=1'0"
Medium: Ink on Mylar, Rapidograph pen
Courtesy of Hugh Newell Jacobsen, FAIA, Architect
Rendered by Stephen S. Evanusa, Architect

The careful study of shadows and reflections is an essential element in this rendering.
[DELINEATOR'S STATEMENT]

This rendering derives its character from the interplay of line and tone. Note the stippled texture on the house and the long, closely spaced continuous lines on the hillside. Rendering convincing textures requires creative imagination. Because design drawings are made during a developmental stage, they take less time to produce than rendered drawings made for a final presentation to a client. Finalized rendered delineations can be (and often are) manipulated to obscure design flaws and increase the design's acceptability and marketability. Architects frequently contract out renderings for their designs to specialists called delineators or architectural illustrators. Their primary goal is to generate a drawing that will sell a design to a potential client.

Drawing: Pedestrian streetscape
Medium: Pen and ink on Mylar, 24" × 36" (61 × 91.4 cm)
Courtesy of Markus Lui & Associates, Architectural Illustrator

This rendering makes extensive use of dot-tone density (stippling) and lines to give value to the building structures. The well-delineated palm trees and the cropping give the viewer a feeling that he or she is actually in the scene. Hand delineation of any kind of tree foliage always involves imitating what you see (leaves, groupings on branches, etc.). Always start with the branch structure and finish with the leaves. There is no shortcut to detailed delineation; it requires a lot of repetition, hard work, and most importantly, practice.

Images: Asian Studies building
University of California at Berkeley
Tod Williams Billie Tsien Architects
Courtesy of Lawrence Ko Leong, Architectural Illustrator

The assignment was familiar: Create an image to generate project funding without much design development information. We wanted to suggest the proposal's potential without committing to too much detail. Throughout the short two-week timeframe, the preliminary layouts were transferred to the design architects, who used them as study overlays for their conceptual design input. At the same time, reviews with the university facilities management, development offices, and the Asian Studies department took place.

I chose to use the computer overlay technique of compositing. First, an image based on a highly abstract massing CAD model that the architects had produced was hand drawn. Then it was scanned and placed onto a site photograph showing adjacent context to which people familiar with the site could relate scale and space. This showed the proposal in context while providing artistic control and an ethereal quality. Creating the image digitally meant a flexible reproduction process: In-process images and final output could either be distributed electronically (by inserting them into a layout program) or on a presentation enlargement board.

[Architectural Illustrator's statement]

Images: Asian Studies Building
University of California at Berkeley
Tod Williams Billie Tsien Architects
Courtesy of Lawrence Ko Leong, Architectural Illustrator

To take the hard edge off the context photo, an overlay was softly delineated with hand-drawn Prismacolor pencil and composited over the background photo, which was filtered in a digital photoediting program. The various layers are the filtered background photo, the sketched background overlay, the hand-drawn new proposal, and the color and final touchups using the digital editing tools.
[ARCHITECTURAL ILLUSTRATOR'S STATEMENT]

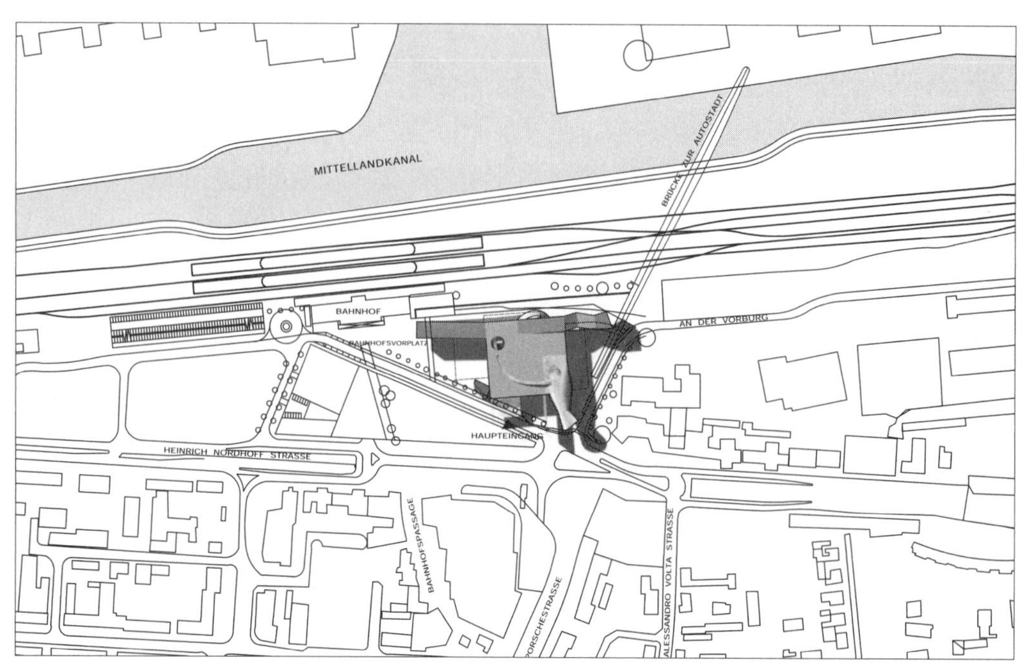

Site plan

©by Armin Hess, A-1060 Vienna, Morizgane 8/21 fon + fax: 0043 1 9610363

Bird's-eye perspective

©by Armin Hess

Computer renderings: Top—Site plan Bottom—Aerial perspective
Science Center, Wolfsburg, Germany
Medium: AutoCAD and form-Z
Courtesy of COOPHIMMELB(L)AU

This office does perspective renderings rather than elevations as part of their competition drawings, which are always computer generated. Note the transparency of these digitally generated buildings.

Eye-level perspective

©by Armin Hess

Eye-level perspective

©by Armin Hess

Close-up of large entrance staircase

©by Armin Hess

Computer-rendered perspectives: Science Center, Wolfsburg, Germany
Medium: AutoCAD and form-Z
Courtesy of COOPHIMMELB(L)AU

The mutation of the form from rigid solids into malleable, fluid forms is a metaphor for the infinite scientific process of gaining knowledge that is the center's program. Research is understood as a cyclical process between basic scientific knowledge and discovery through the introduction of hypothetical solutions. Through the dramatic combination of completely different bodies and their hybridization, the building represents in architecture what recent theories in the sciences do: It rejects the idea of boundaries as being hard and definite; rather, they are seen as soft and transient, like osmotic membranes. [ARCHITECT'S STATEMENT]

9

Diagramming and Conceptual Sketching

BASICS............................429
BASICS APPLIED....................444

Diagrams and conceptual sketches are integral parts of the design-drawing process. They are the means by which the designer generates, organizes, and formalizes options for his or her ideas.

Conceptual diagrams constitute an abstract language that must be understood and used properly within the design community. It is through graphic diagramming that one develops a design vocabulary and can convey an understanding of the design concept. Elements like arrows, nodes, lines, and other symbols help the beginner use graphic techniques to explore ideas.

Conceptual (or design) sketches are quickly drawn syntheses that represent a range of alternative design ideas for an imagined conception. Such visualizations may be crude initial images or somewhat more refined, developed drawings. Although tentative in nature, conceptual sketches are attempts to depict the reality of the design in its idealized and essential state.

This chapter introduces the vocabulary of diagramming and shows a wide range of professional examples of both diagrammatic models and conceptual sketches.

In summary, following are some of the important terms and concepts you will learn:

Graphic diagram	Circulation	Node	Visualization
Thumbnail sketch	Arrowed line	Ideational drawing	Conceptual thinking
Parti diagram	Line	Symbolic language	Site diagram
Programmatic diagram	Formal/spatial diagram	Environmental control diagram	

Diagramming and Conceptual Sketching

TOPIC: DIAGRAMMING

Brooks 1997.

Ching 2003, 200–205.

Clark and Pause, 2005.

Kasprisin and Pettinari 1990.

TOPIC: DESIGN SKETCHING EXAMPLES

Herbert 1993.

Jeanneret-Gris 1981.

Lin 2000.

Paulo dos Santos 1994.

Pfeiffer 1996, 7–8, 99, 141.

Portoghesi 2000.

Rappolt and Violette 2004.

Robbins 1997.

Soleri 1971.

Zardini 1996.

Chapter Overview

After studying this chapter, you will have a better understanding of why diagramming and conceptual sketching are important in design communications. For continued study, refer to Laseau's *Graphic Thinking for Architects and Designers.*

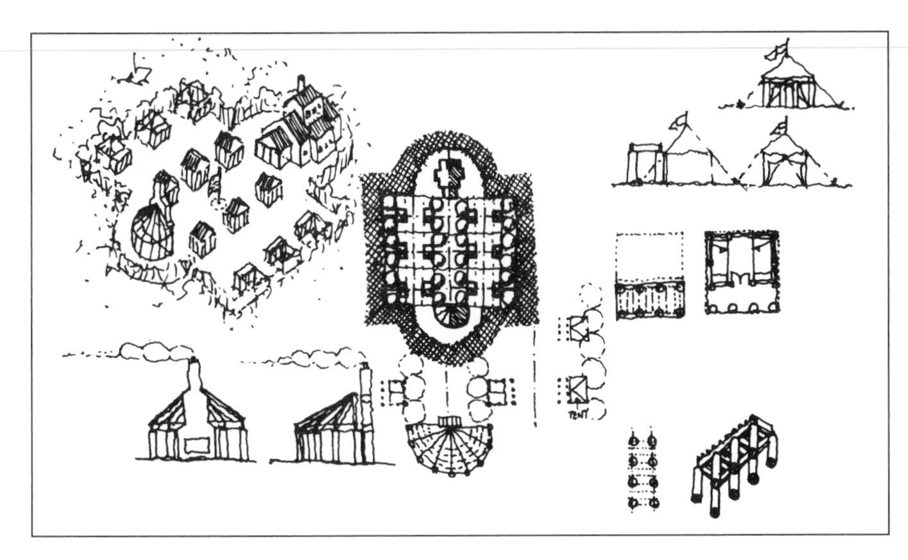

Preliminary schematic diagrams frequently contain the seeds for the final design and, ultimately, the built project. They can take a two-dimensional or three-dimensional configuration, as shown in the Hoover Center. The diagrams below use a combination of point, line, and two-dimensional zone to explain the design concept.

Diagrams: Hoover Outdoor Education Center, Yorkville, Illinois
Medium: Felt-tipped pen on trace
Courtesy of Tigerman McCurry Architects

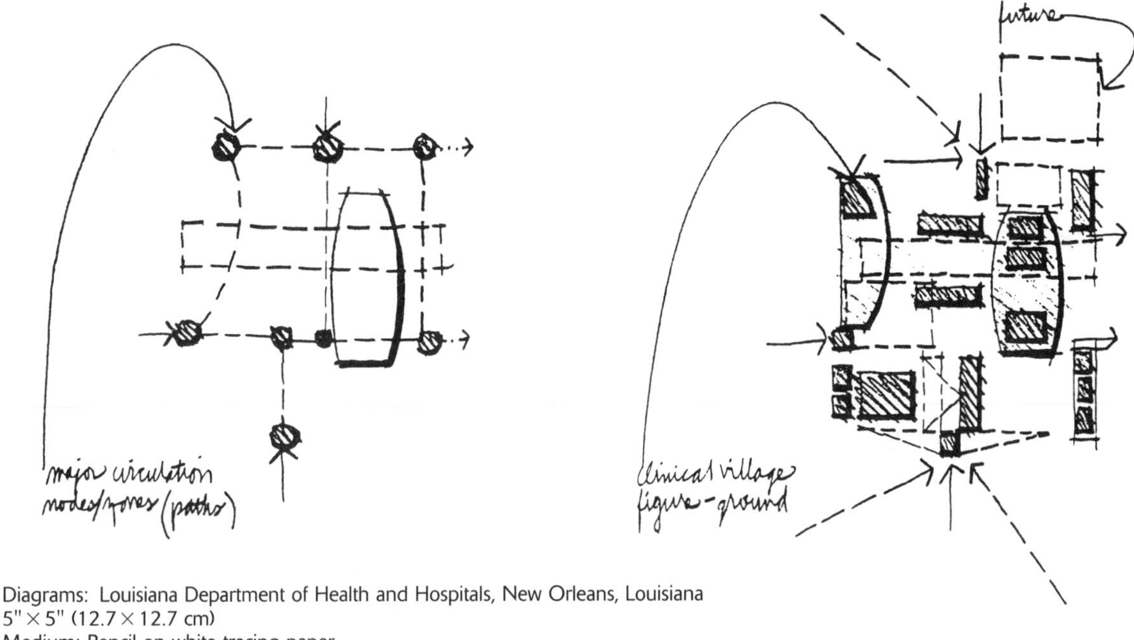

Diagrams: Louisiana Department of Health and Hospitals, New Orleans, Louisiana
5" × 5" (12.7 × 12.7 cm)
Medium: Pencil on white tracing paper
Courtesy of R-2 ARCH Designers/Researchers
Ben J. Refuerzo and Stephen F. Verderber

Once an architecture student's freehand graphics skills are honed, he or she will begin to appreciate the potential of these skills not only in drawing contextual elements (people, vegetation, cars, etc.) but also in drawing **conceptual diagrams.** Students are immediately confronted with developing sketches on tracing paper (termed yellow trace, flimsy, or bumwad [British]) as part of the design process in a design studio project. Beginning with the first course in architectural design and continuing throughout their academic careers (and professional lives), students will face the task of developing numerous alternative ideas or schemes for each design problem. The ability to do quick freehand graphics in the form of scribbles and doodles is essential. These **graphic diagrams** explore alternative solutions and encourage **visualization, visual thinking,** and **transformative understanding.**

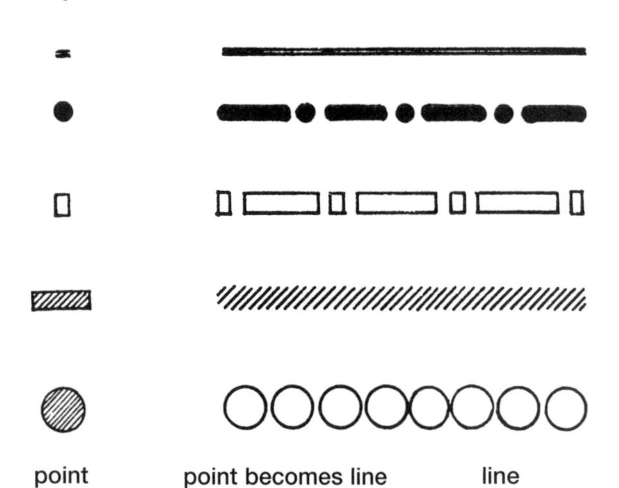

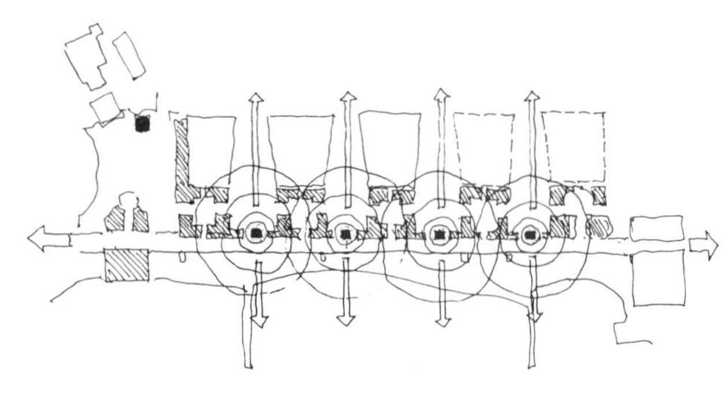

Diagram: Waterfront Development Plan
Asbury Park, New Jersey
6" × 3" (15.2 × 7.6 cm)
Medium: Ink on trace
Courtesy of Koetter, Kim & Associates, Inc.
Architects and Urban Designers

Every drawing type can be used as a conceptual analytical diagram. **Graphic diagrams** can be two-dimensional or three-dimensional in their abstract communication of a design scheme. Through point, line, symbol, and zone diagrams, a building's organization can be represented in terms of user movement (**circulation**), space usage (**zoning**), site plan and site section analysis, structural analysis, and volumetric enclosure (geometric configuration). The use of diagrams early in the design process allows for the creative exploration of an array of alternatives unfettered by rigid programmatic constraints.

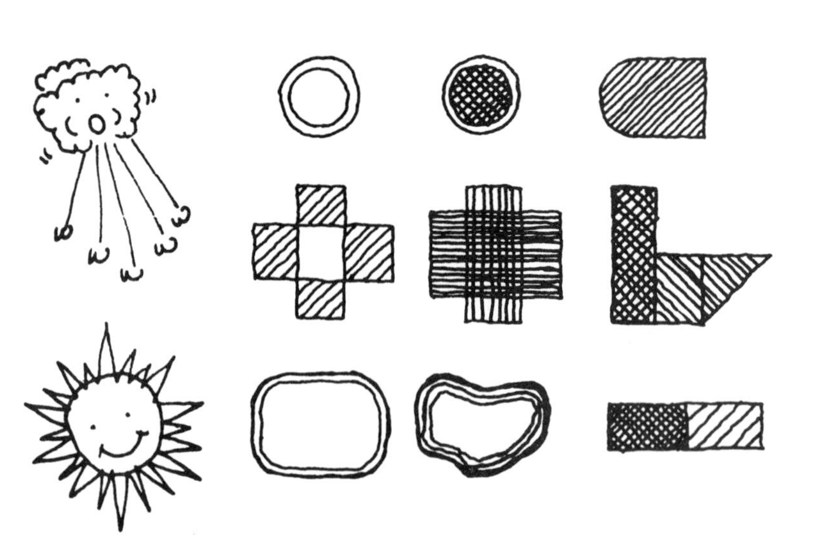

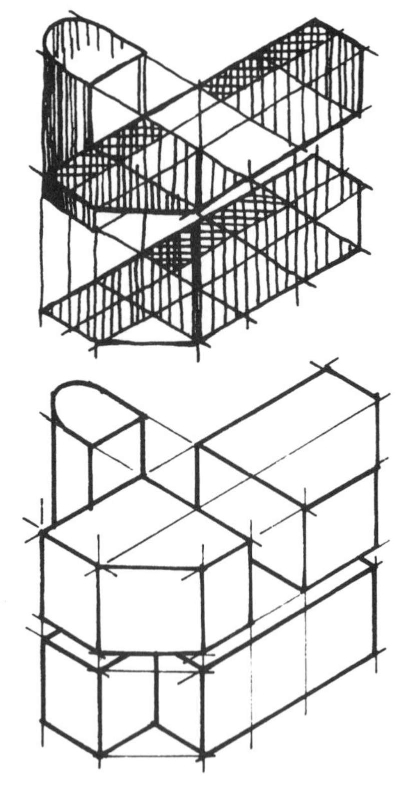

Pictorial symbols

Two-dimensional zone diagrams

Three-dimensional zone and volume diagrams

Students hear a new vocabulary in the design studio. Terms like "bubble diagram," "schematics," "flow," "circulation," "zoning," "hierarchy," and "metaphor" become commonplace. The many new terms of this studio language, coupled with incessant demands for an abundance of ideas, sometimes overwhelm beginning students. An understanding of the language comes with reading architectural literature.

Diagram: Scheme C
Gleneagles Hospital and Medical Office Building
Kuala Lumpur, Malaysia
17" × 11" (43.2 × 27.9 cm)
Medium: Ink on bond paper
Courtesy of KMD/PD Architects
Joint venture with the Architectural Network

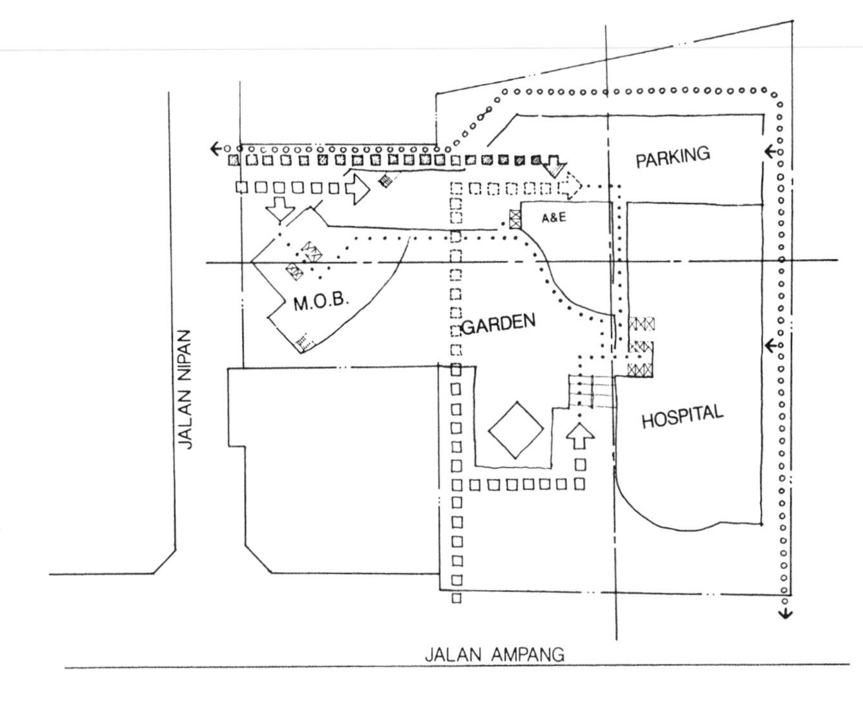

This is a good example of a circulation analysis in an early schematic stage of the design process. Note that each type of movement has a different symbol. A **symbol** is something that represents something else—in this case, the condition of movement on a site plan. A clear **symbolic language** is essential to communicating graphically important collected data.

KEY OF SYMBOLS

- PUBLIC ACCESS
- EMERGENCY ONLY
- SERVICE/FIRE/STAFF
- PEDESTRIAN

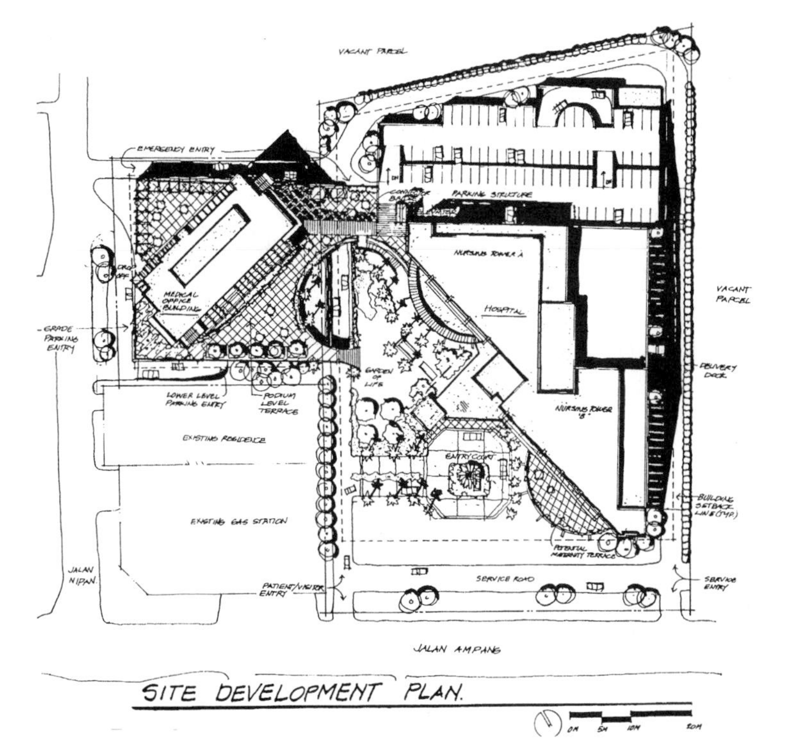

Site development plan for scheme C
24" × 36" (61 × 91.4 cm), Scale: 1:300
Medium: Ink on vellum

Circulation traces the path and flow of user movement two-dimensionally in plan and in section, and three-dimensionally in pictorial diagrams (see p.170). The movement can be horizontal or vertical. Points where movement begins are called **nodes.** A node is a point of focus for other diagrammatic symbols. On diagrams nodes (central points or points of concentration) are frequently connected by lines of movement. Nodes can also be the intersection points of lines of movement. The above diagram also shows symbolic lines for the site's property lines and axial arrangement.

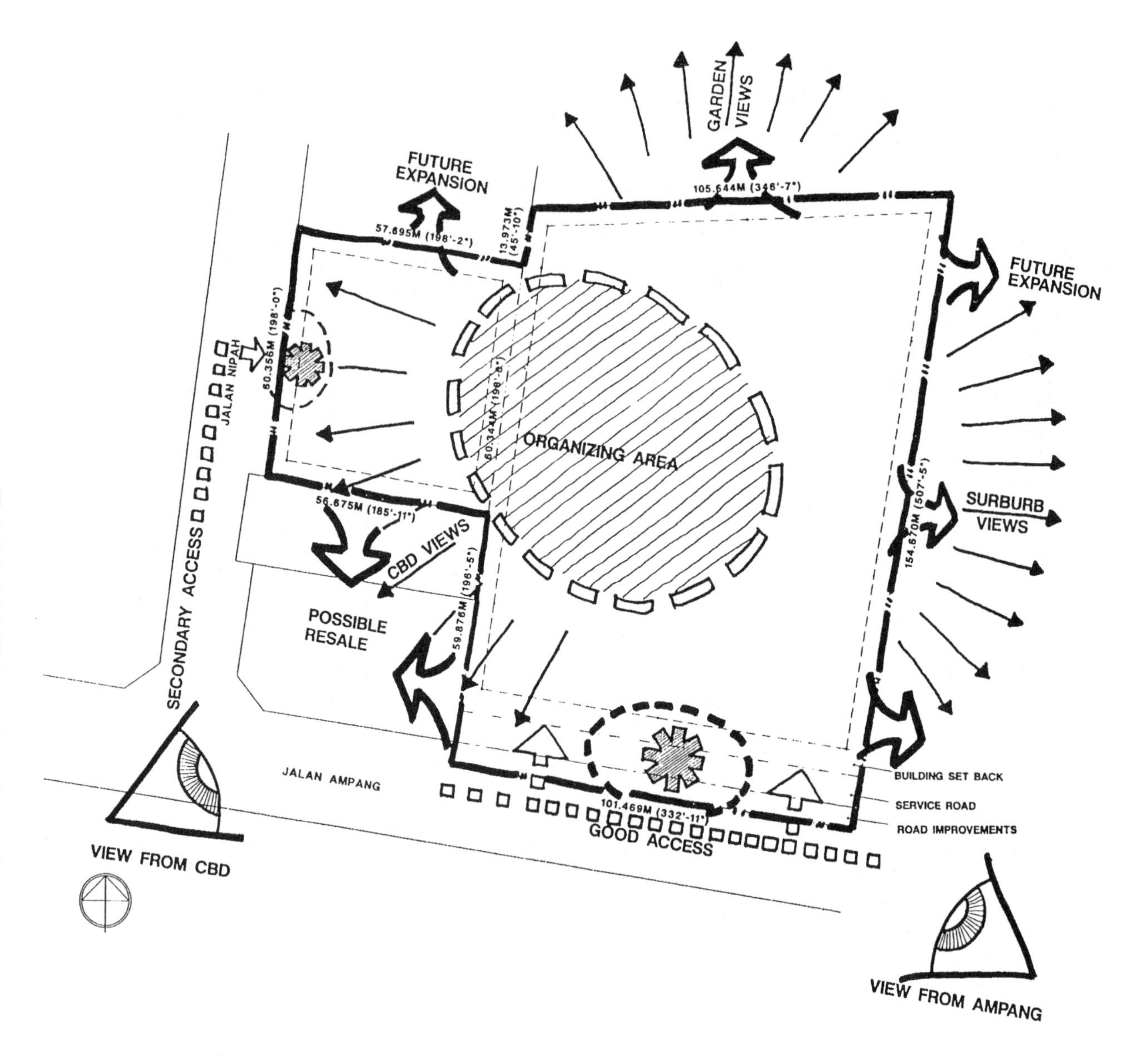

Diagram: Site analysis, Gleneagles Hospital and Medical Office Building, Kuala Lumpur, Malaysia
36" × 24" (91.4 × 61 cm)
Medium: Ink on vellum with Kroy type
Courtesy of KMD/PD Architects
Joint venture with the Architectural Network

Analytical diagrams such as site (see above and pp. 438–39), program and function (p. 440), and formal/spatial (p. 441) diagrams, are generated in the earliest stages of the design process. Diagrammatic study drawings are some of the most important types of drawings for the designer; paradoxically, they are rarely (if ever) seen by the client. **Diagrams** are abstract: they use symbols to simplify pictorial reality. This abstraction aids in the analysis stage of the design process. Diagrams are a visual means for collecting and sorting information, for testing ideas and exploring alternative solutions—for looking into the very heart of a design problem. They represent that crucial, intimate conversation with oneself, a conversation conducted in a very specific language that has its own vocabulary, grammar, and syntax. They also communicate your ideas to your classmates or professional peers so that their soundness can be tested.

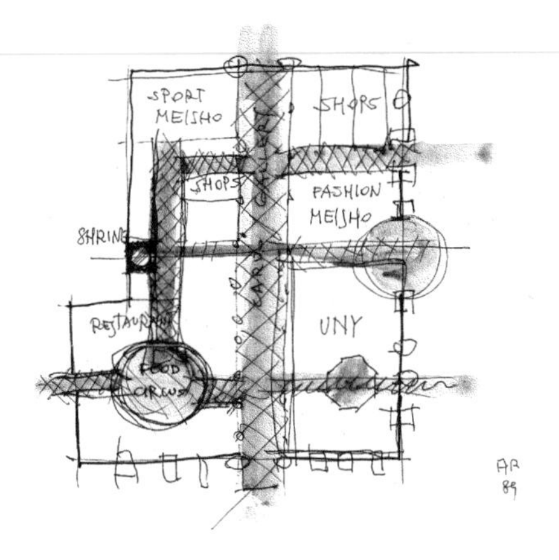

Plan sketch diagram: Shimizu Corporation
Nagoya, Aichi, Japan
Courtesy of Aldo Rossi, SDA, Architect

The drawing at left is a diagrammatic schematic plan sketch showing pedestrian pathways. Note the use of node symbols. The four different schemes sketched below were evaluated with respect to vehicular and pedestrian movement (circulation). Graphic symbols for flow and bubbles are scaleless and are thus ideal for both small- and large-scale projects.

Straight or curved **lines** on diagrams are commonly used as boundaries (see pp. 432 and 438), as axial elements (as seen below), or as organizing elements for conceptual ideas on site, relationship, and circulation diagrams (see pp. 436 and 474–75).

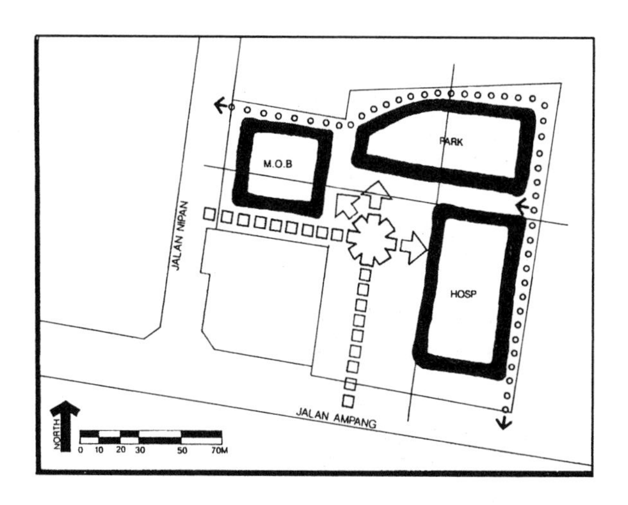

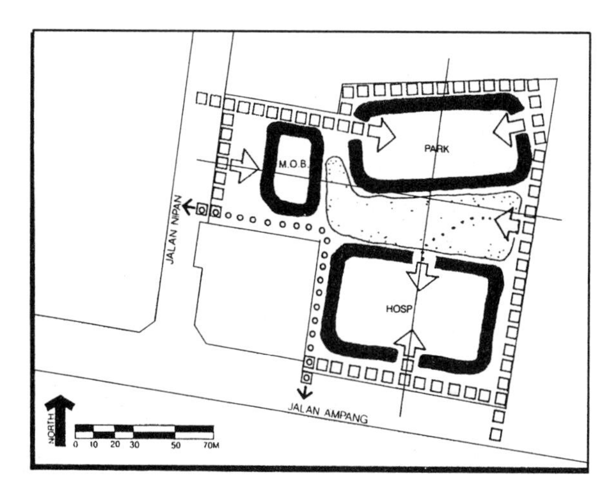

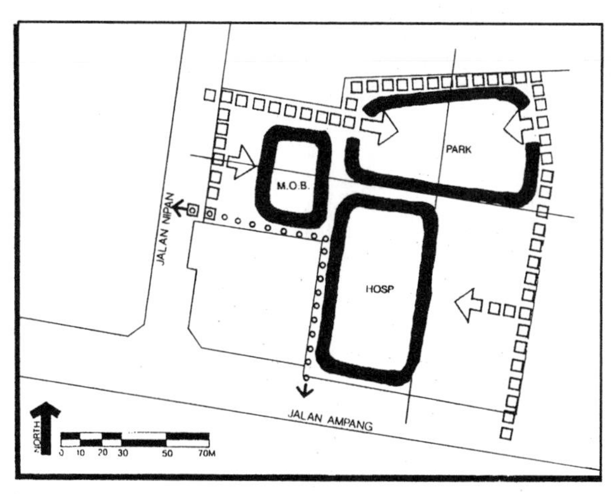

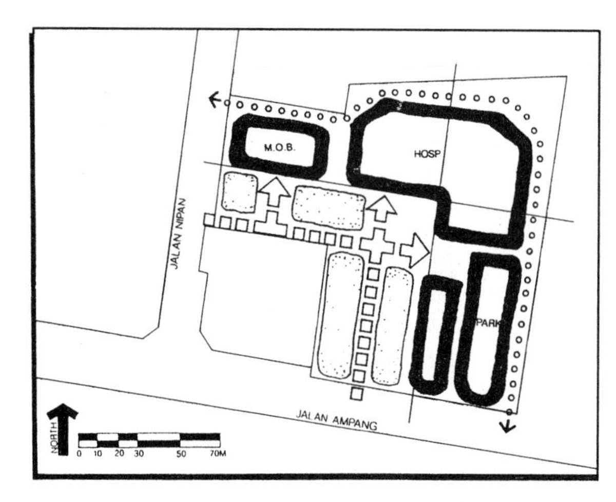

Diagrams: Four alternative schemes
Gleneagles Hospital and Medical Office Building, Kuala Lumpur, Malaysia
Each drawing 17" × 11" (43.2 × 27.9 cm), reduced and composed on 36" × 24" (91.4 × 61 cm)
Medium: Ink on bond paper
Courtesy of KMD/PD Architects
Joint Venture with the Architectural Network

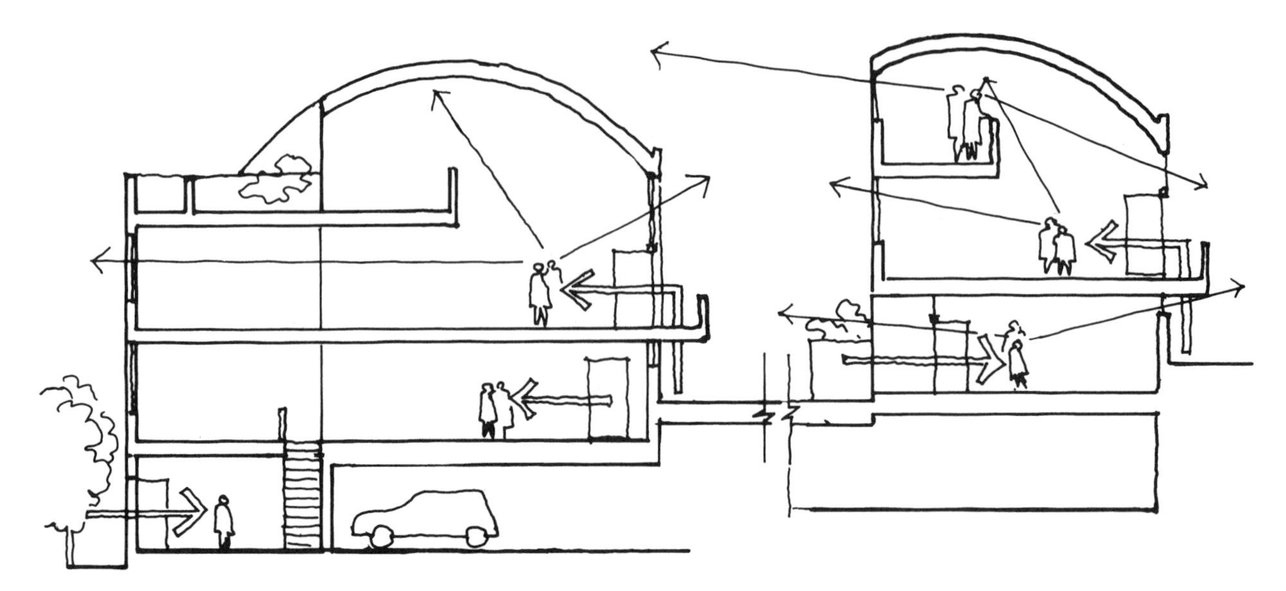

Diagram sketch: Franklin/La Brea Family Housing, Los Angeles, California
6" × 6" (15.2 × 15.2 cm), Scale: 1/16"=1'0"
Medium: Technical pen on Mylar
Courtesy of Adèle Naudé Santos and Associates, Architects

The section diagram clearly shows user view (thin arrowed line) and user movement (thick arrowed line). The **arrowed line** can symbolize the direction of an action or a movement; it can be one-way or-two way.

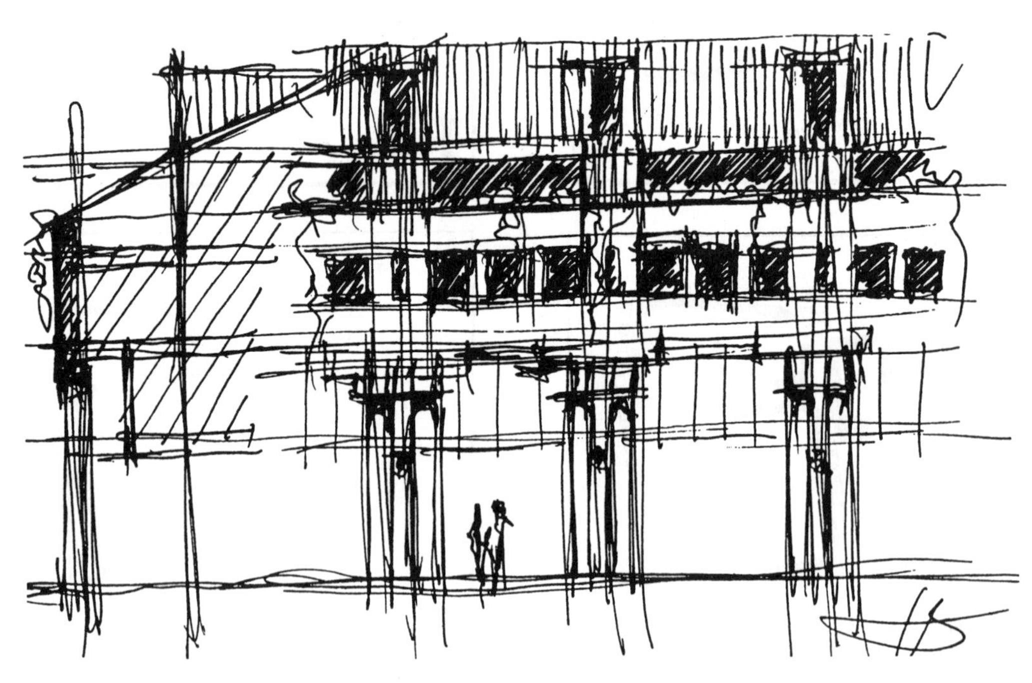

Diagram sketch: Mixed-Use Center, Turin, Italy
8" × 6.5" (20.3 × 16.5 cm)
Medium: Black marker pen on smooth paper
Courtesy of Gunnar Birkerts and Associates, Inc., Architects

Graphic diagrams should be drawn with loose, fluid line strokes. The looser the line quality, the more evocative the image is to the viewer. Sectional diagrams should include human figures to give scale to the sketches.

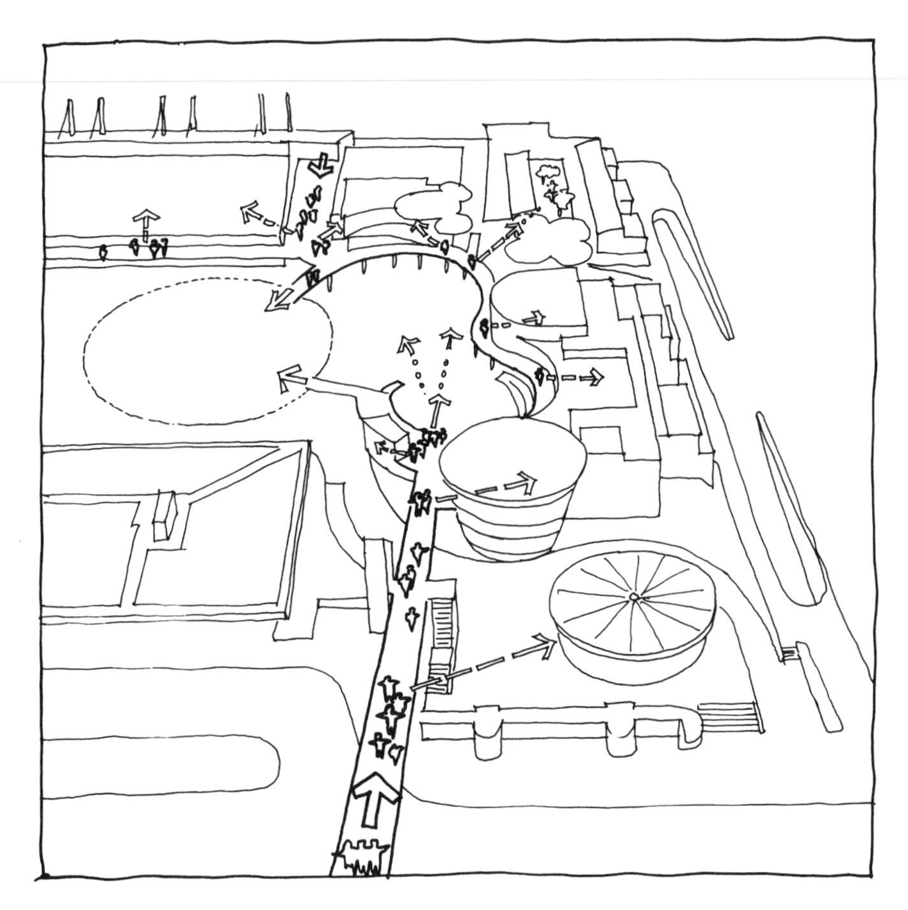

These diagrams are part of a series that was used to engage the users of the site and facilities in a public design process. Specifically, the diagrams describe routes through the site and a sequence of visual experiences. They were keyed to vignettes depicting views of the buildings and the activities observed within.
[ARCHITECT'S STATEMENT]

These diagrams make extensive use of a point and an arrow symbol to depict pedestrian movement. Arrowed lines can vary in thickness (see p. 432) and tone intensity (see p. 438) depending on what is being depicted (thin arrowed lines for view and thick arrowed lines to depict wind direction and future expansion).

Movement diagrams: Yerba Buena Gardens Children Center
San Francisco, California
6" × 6" (15.2 × 15.2 cm)
Medium: Technical pen on vellum
Courtesy of Adèle Naudé Santos and Associates, Architects

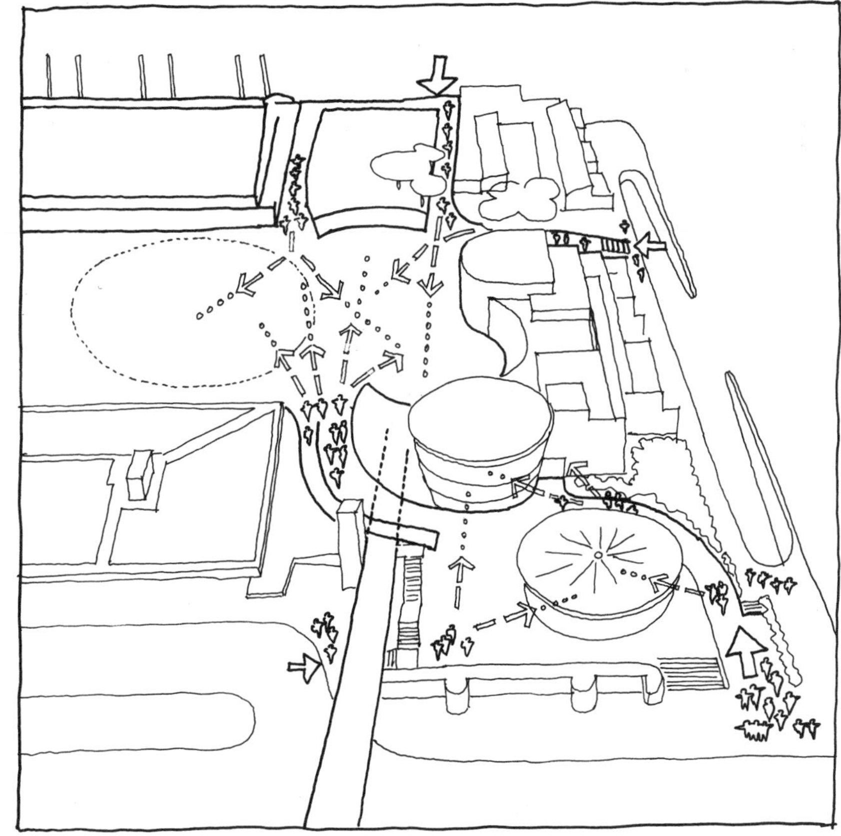

The bird's-eye view is more descriptive than a site plan in showing user circulation. Three-dimensional diagrams, such as perspectives and plan obliques, are as depictive as two-dimensional diagrams. Sometimes the same diagram can be used to explain different sets of information. These diagrams can be presented individually or as a set using transparent overlays. A composite set should present the information under consideration in a clear hierarchy to avoid information overload.

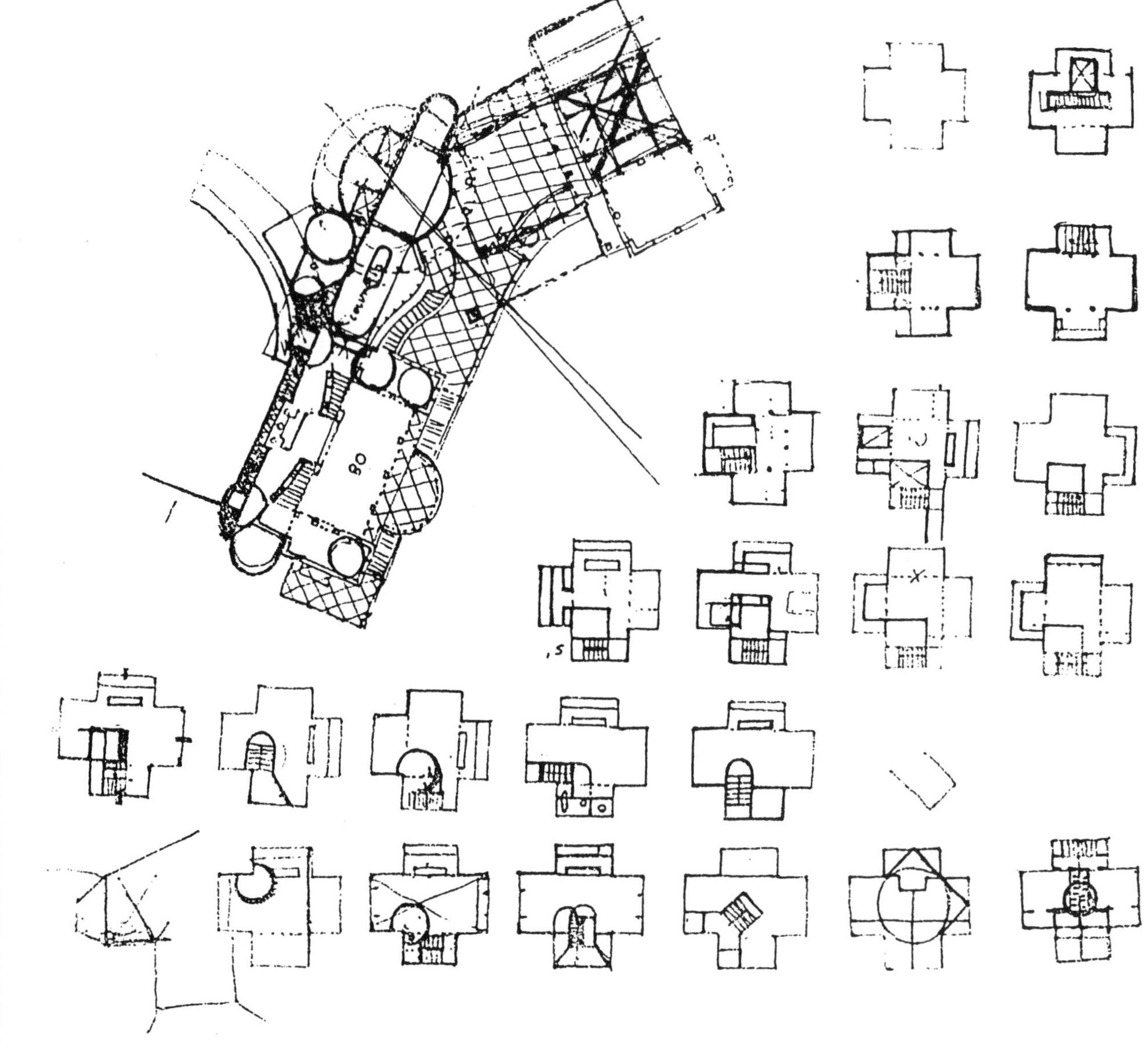

Conceptual diagrams: Villa Linda Flora (unbuilt), Bel Air, California
8½" × 11" (21.6 × 27.9 cm)
Medium: Ink on sketch paper
Courtesy of Hodgetts + Fung Design Associates

In any design project, there are numerous alternative solutions to analyze. Seen above is a juxtaposition of diagrams showing potential alternatives. During the design process, **design drawings** (diagrams, design sketches, etc.) are crucial for testing alternative schemes and themes. This project shows the wide range of possible stairway types and locations within the same geometric plan configuration. Diagrams are frequently drawn with a consistent graphic format, as shown above. This allows you to analyze a particular problem or focus on one specific issue (in this case, stairway location) by comparing one alternative with another.

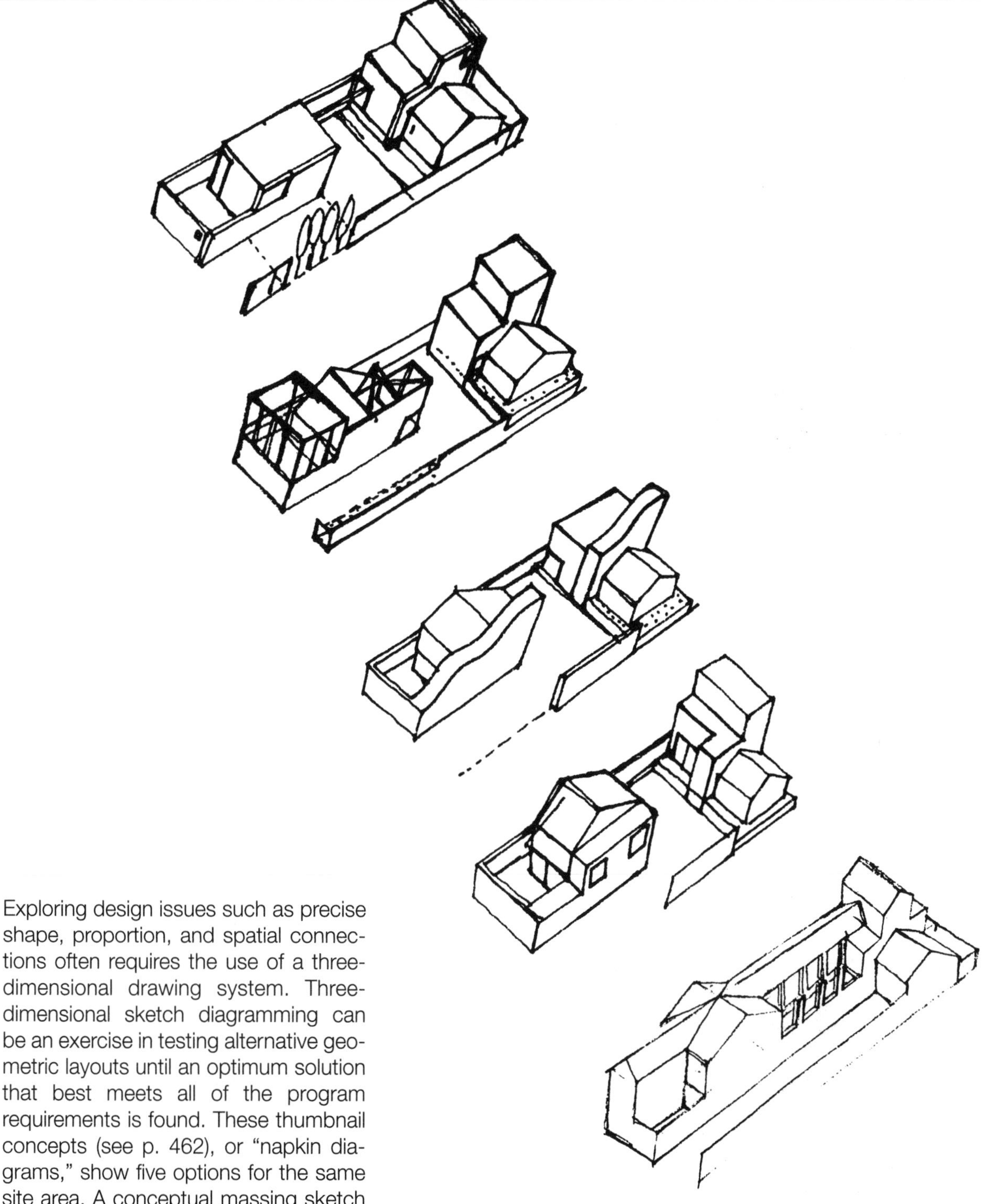

Exploring design issues such as precise shape, proportion, and spatial connections often requires the use of a three-dimensional drawing system. Three-dimensional sketch diagramming can be an exercise in testing alternative geometric layouts until an optimum solution that best meets all of the program requirements is found. These thumbnail concepts (see p. 462), or "napkin diagrams," show five options for the same site area. A conceptual massing sketch should show fairly accurate proportions, but it should not be overly detailed. As with a massing volume, details can be finalized later on. These diagrams help the designer to solidify a strong formal strategy from which to move on to more detailed planning.

Alternative diagrams: Click Agency, West Hollywood, California
Medium: Ink on sketch paper
Courtesy of Hodgetts + Fung Design Associates

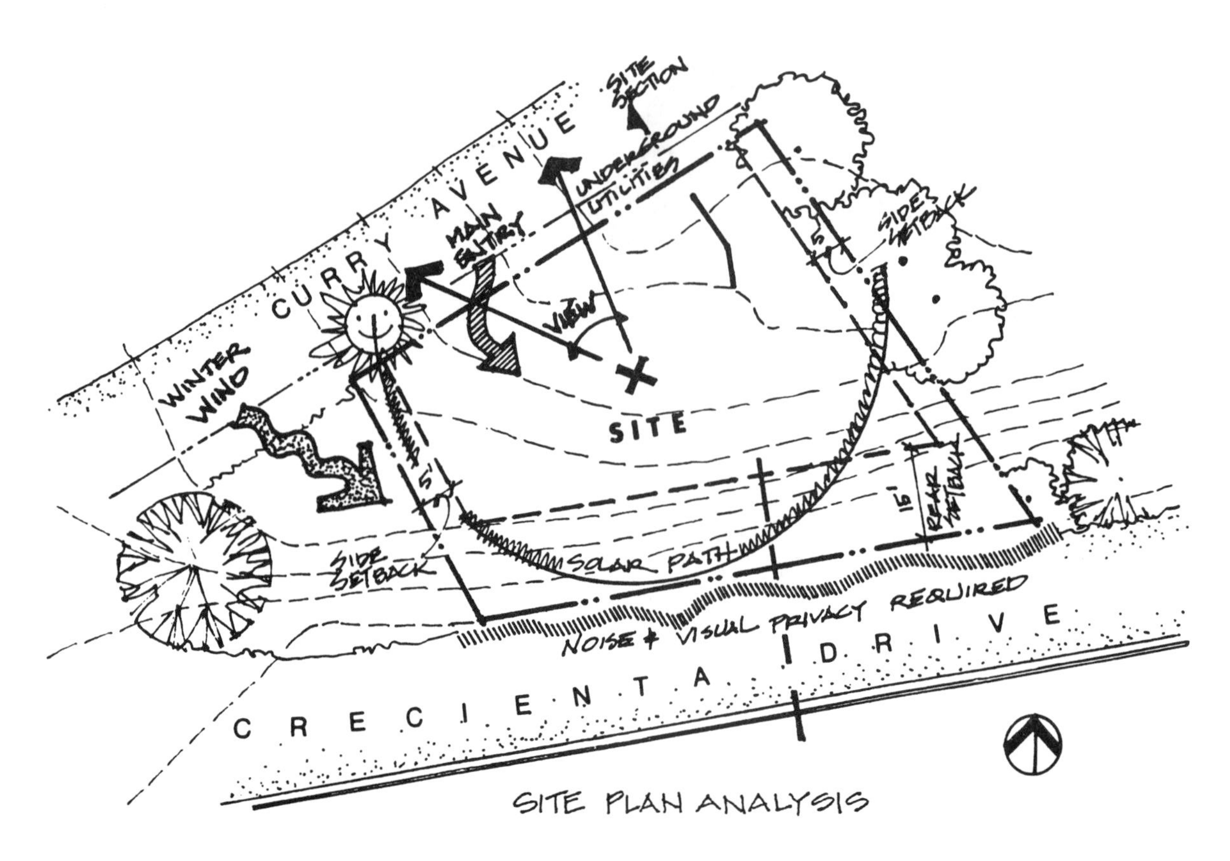

SITE PLAN ANALYSIS

Schematic analytical diagrams for site plans and site sections are frequently sketched in the design-drawing process. **Site diagrams** commonly have pictorial **symbols** like those for the sun and the plan trees, above, which represent an abstract simplification of physical reality. By using diagramming symbols, influential site factors, such as contours, traffic circulation, view, solar and wind conditions, noise, zoning regulations, property lines, land use, and adjacent landscaping, can be graphically recorded and analyzed quickly. This helps to set the external design constraints.

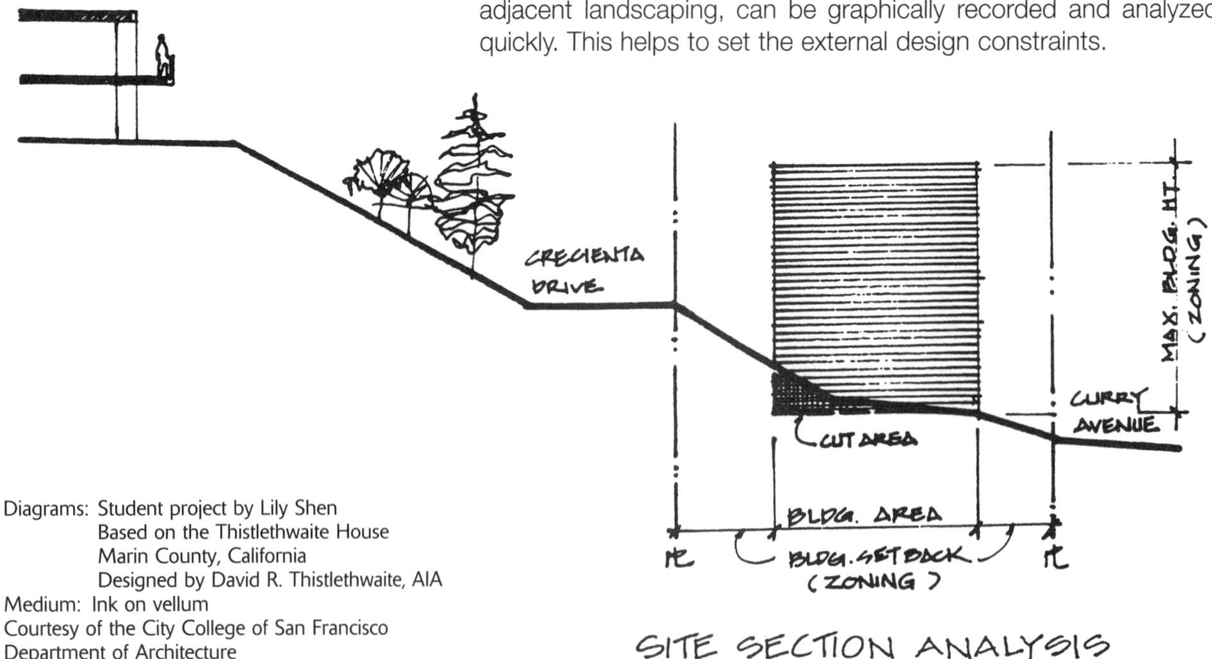

SITE SECTION ANALYSIS

Diagrams: Student project by Lily Shen
Based on the Thistlethwaite House
Marin County, California
Designed by David R. Thistlethwaite, AIA
Medium: Ink on vellum
Courtesy of the City College of San Francisco
Department of Architecture

Diagrams: House in Northern California
Medium: Pencil on trace
Courtesy of Legorreta Arquitectos, Ricardo Legorreta, Victor Legorreta, Noe Castro

Design drawings document the design process. The initial stages are frequently sketched in black-and-white with the goal of describing only the architectural form and its relation to surrounding conditions. Later stages may incorporate color.

Diagrams simplify reality so specific aspects can be examined. As reality is simplified, it is abstracted. These graphic diagrams of a location plan, a site plan, a site section, and an elevation are precursors for the more three-dimensional diagrams of paraline and perspective sketches. It is important that designers acquire the ability to relate the size and proportion of various architectural elements to buildings and their site conditions. Note the use of various scales in this study.

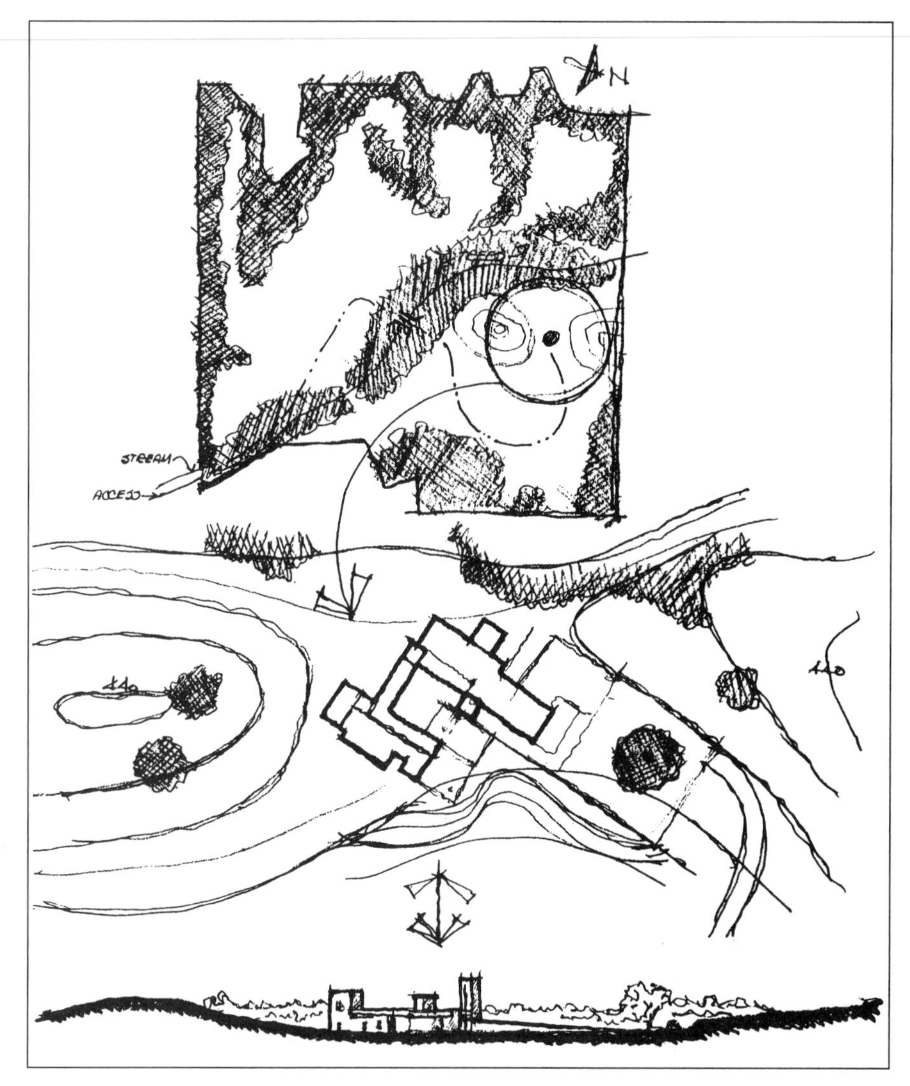

Site plan, location plan, and site section diagrams

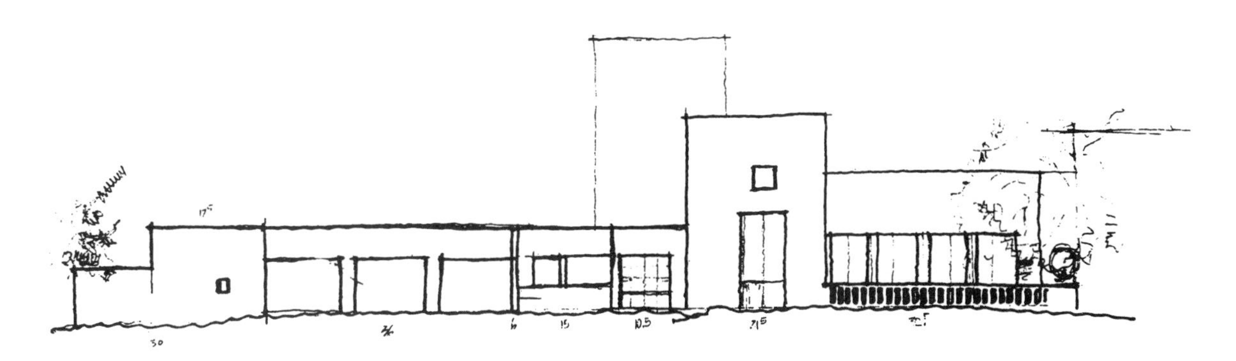

Elevation study, Scale: ⅛"=1'0"

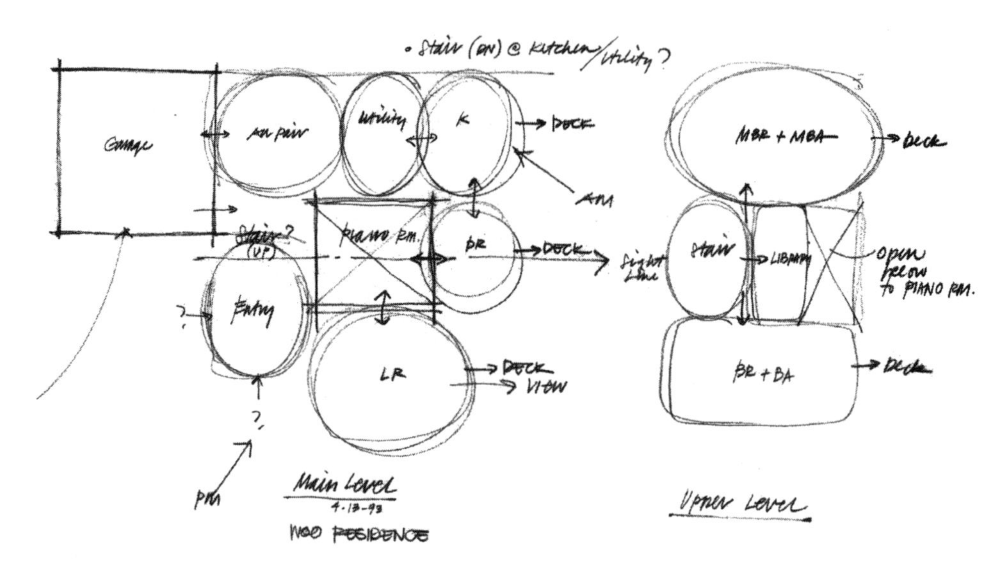

Diagram: Woo residence, Oakland, California
Medium: HB pencil
Courtesy of Kenzo Handa, Architect

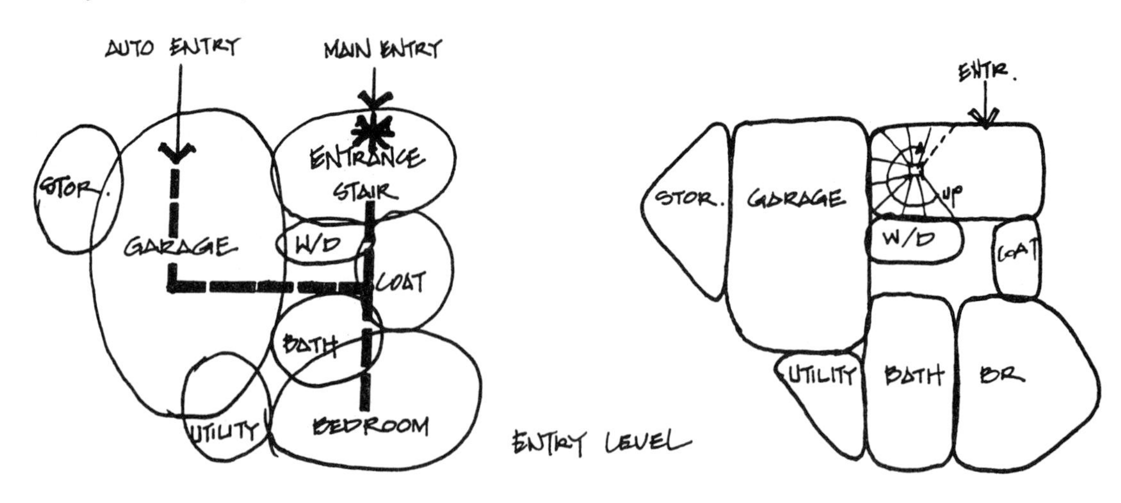

Bubble diagrams relate the program functions and relative sizes of spaces to each other and to external site determinants. Circulation linkages can be analyzed and evaluated quickly.

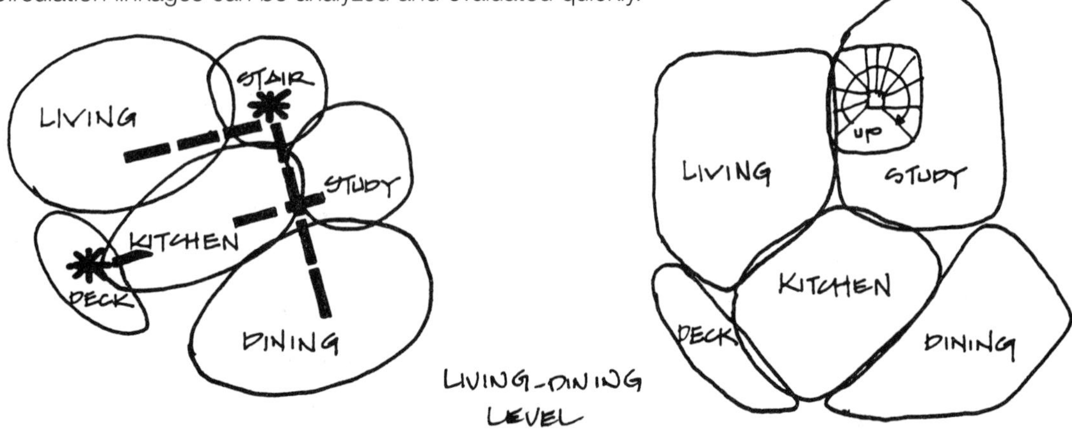

With an area program (square footage or square meters), it is important to set up functional zone adjacencies. These diagrams hint at the proximity relationships and the possible arrangements for a final solution.

Sketches: Student project by Charles Roberts
Courtesy of studio professor William W. P. Chan
Institute of Architecture and Planning
Morgan State University

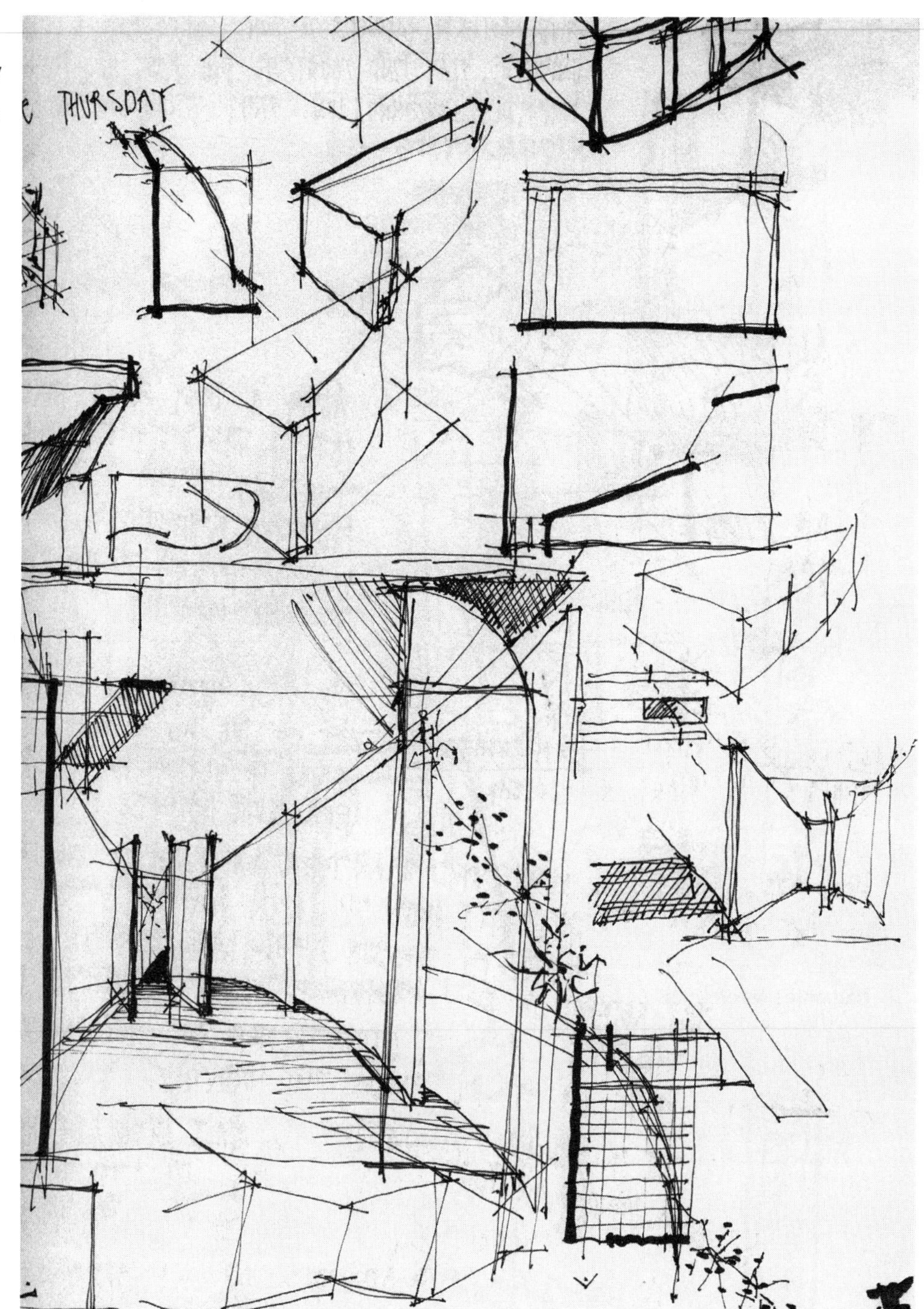

Formal/spatial diagrams delve into the analysis of a design's scheme. The elements for the analysis and diagramming examine numerous characteristics. Some of these elements include natural daylighting, structure (the support system of a building), axial arrangement (and thus symmetry and balance), spatial usage and circulation (entry and path), geometric configuration (proportion) and massing, plan and its relationship to vertical configurations (section/elevation), and hierarchy (a rank order such as a major–minor relationships).

ENVIRONMENTAL CONTROL DIAGRAMS

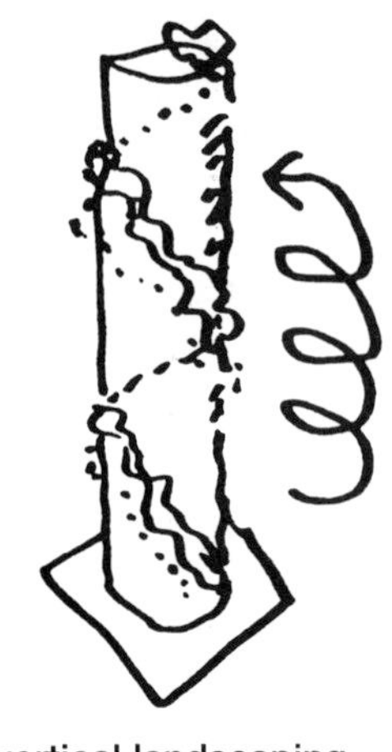

vertical landscaping

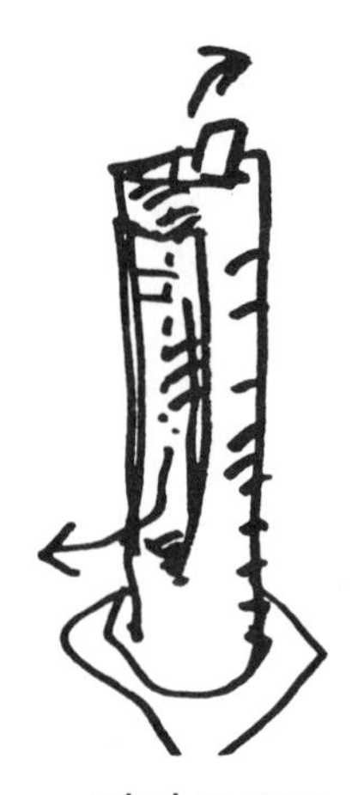

wind scoops

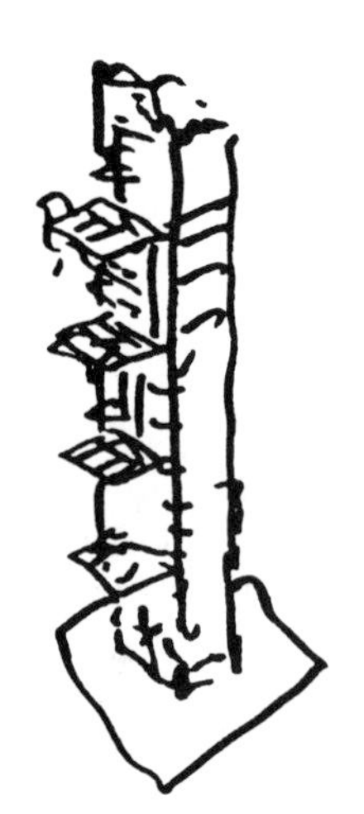

balconies & terraces

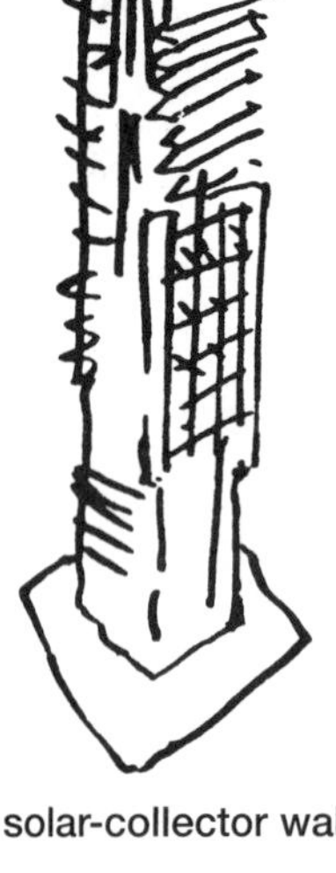

solar-collector wall

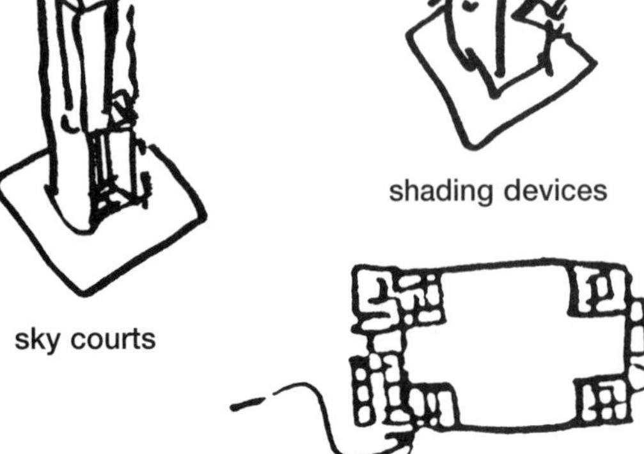

sky courts

shading devices

Photo: Menara Mesiniaga (IBM Tower)
Selangor, Malaysia
Courtesy of T. R. Hamzah & Yeang, Architect

Structure, elements of enclosure, and the control of sunlight are vital issues in an environmental control diagram. These issues are clearly seen in the diagrams for the IBM Tower design, which responds to regional bioclimatic principles through low energy consumption. These diagrams relate to an agenda for high-rise buildings that alter highly industrialized societies' relationships to artificial mechanical systems such as air-conditioning.

Diagrams: Design principles and agenda
Courtesy of T. R. Hamzah & Yeang, Architect
Tengku Robert Hamzah and Dr. Kenneth Yeang, Partners

The use of light, both natural and artificial, is central to the conception of the Getty Museum and is therefore the focus of these sketches. These drawings explore the uses of light and its ability to mediate between the building's exterior and interior.
[Architect's statement]

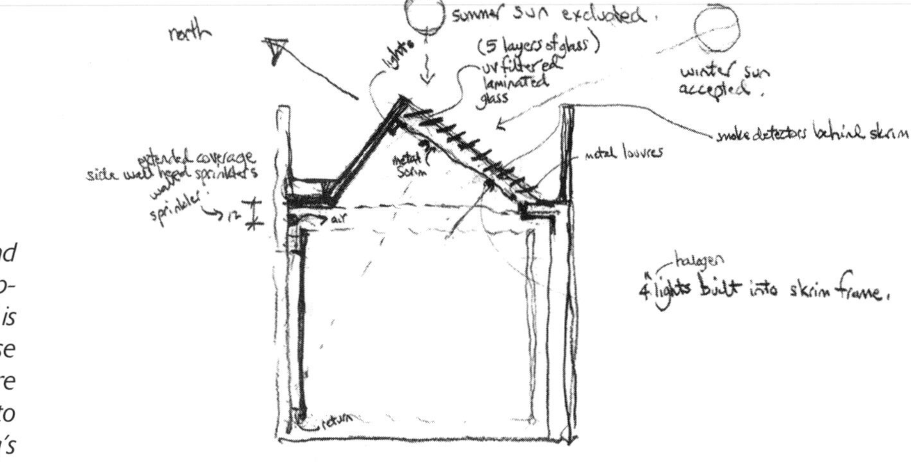

The environmental control diagram at the top uses a sun symbol with directional arrows to show the effect of winter and summer solar angles. Arrow symbols are frequently used in diagrams, especially in plan and section diagrams. Light direction is represented by a directional arrow to enhance the viewer's understanding of how light enters the museum's space. Note also the integration of an architectural design concept with structural section/environmental control diagrams.

Drawings: Diagram sketch studies of museum sections
The Getty Center Museum
Los Angeles, California
Both 18" × 18" (45.7 × 45.7 cm)
Medium: Graphite pencil on yellow trace
Courtesy of Richard Meier & Partners, Architects
Reprinted from The Getty Center Design Process
with permission of The J. Paul Getty Trust

PLAN DIAGRAM

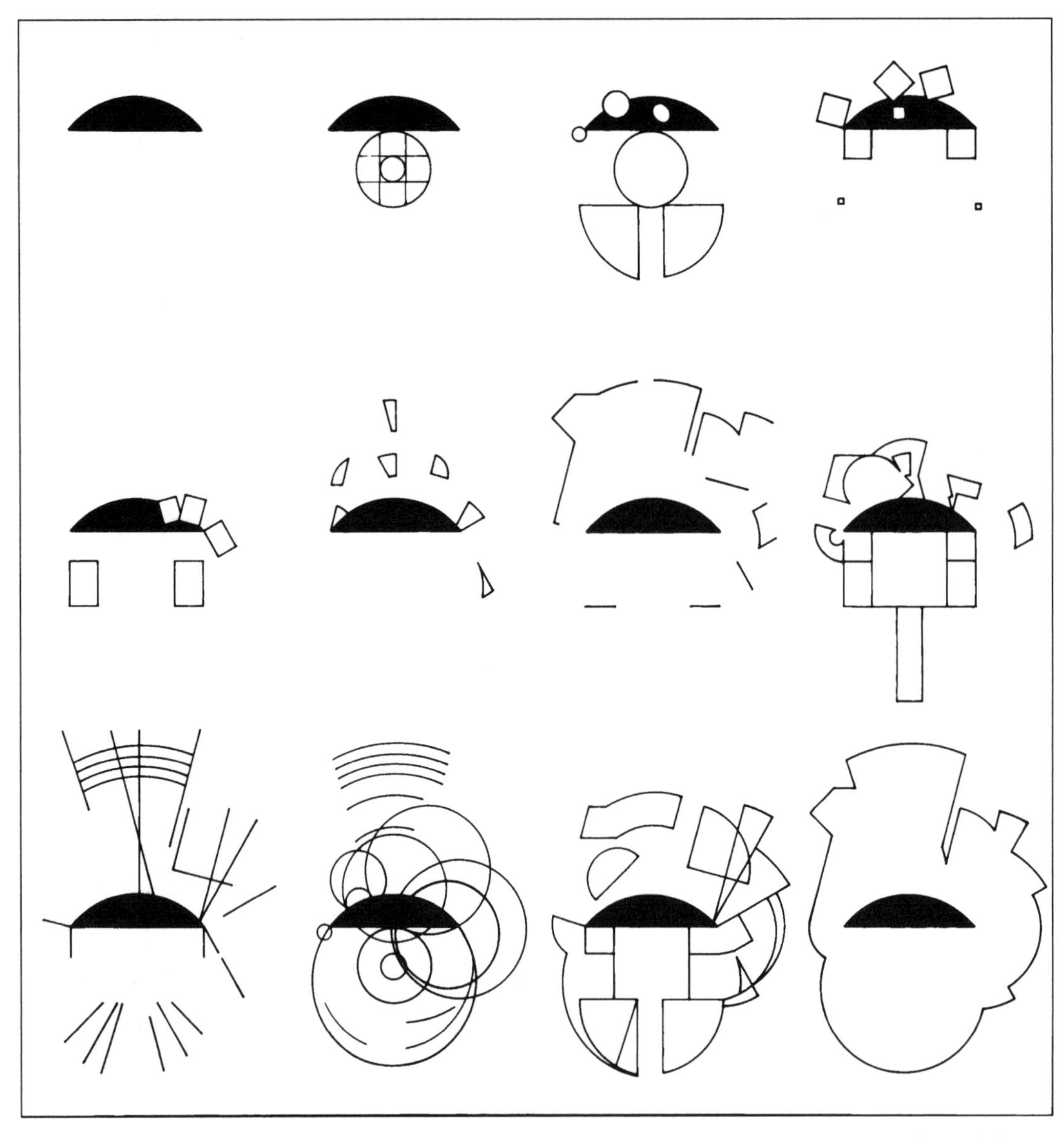

ELEMENTS DEVELOPMENT

Diagrams: Private residence, Illinois (1988–1990)
Medium: Ink
Courtesy of Stanley Tigerman, Architect

Storyboard showing the evolution of elements. The house begins with a wedge, generating other forms that tumble off of it.
[ARCHITECT'S STATEMENT]

In addition to the site analysis and site synthesis diagrams shown on the preceding pages, the plan diagrams, section diagrams, and elevation diagrams shown on the following pages are most often used during the initial phase of the design process. These diagrams attempt to effectively understand the organizing idea of the design concept by addressing a variety of issues. As the design process continues, layers of tracing paper are used to refine the development of ideas.

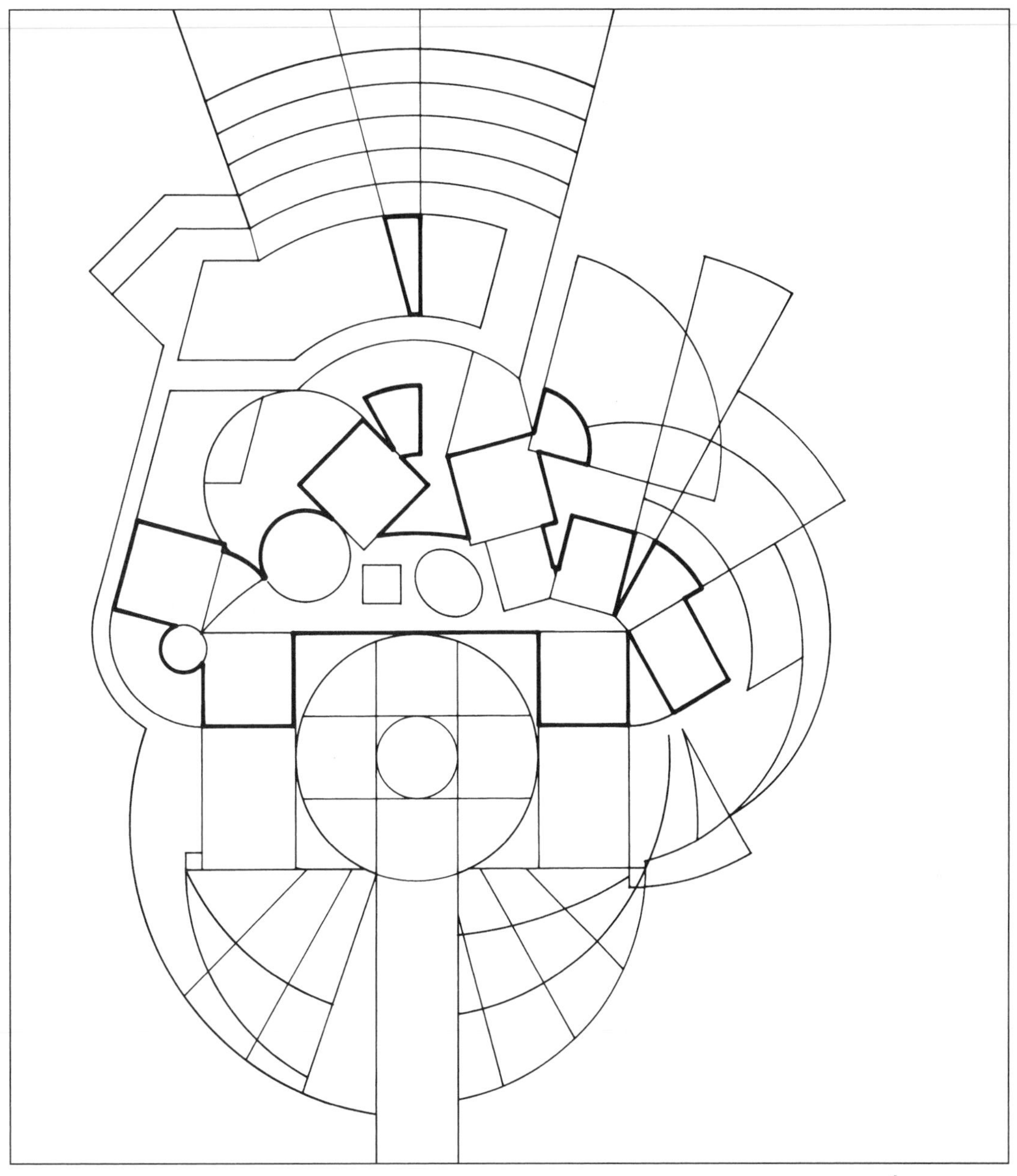

PARTÍ DIAGRAM

Diagram: Private residence, Illinois (1988–1990)
Medium: Ink
Courtesy of Stanley Tigerman, Architect

In the partí diagram, the house expands into the site, and geometric repetitions radiating from the home into the landscape are indicated.
[ARCHITECT'S STATEMENT]

A ***partí* diagram** shows the basic schematic assumption of a plan. It is the fundamental overarching or big idea (scheme) of a plan. A strong *partí* (see p. 487) can withstand design transformations. The elements in Tigerman's design are the determinants that shape the final resolved form. The ongoing refinement process allows for the evolution of a mature solution that satisfies the restrictions and requirements of the program.

Sketch diagrams: National Library
Riga, Latvia
Medium: Black marker pen on smooth paper
Courtesy of Gunnar Birkerts and Associates, Inc. Architects

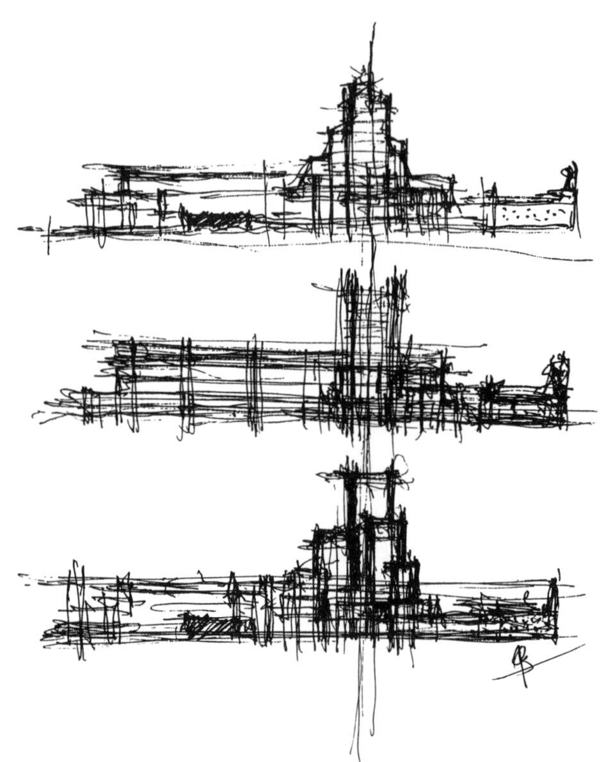

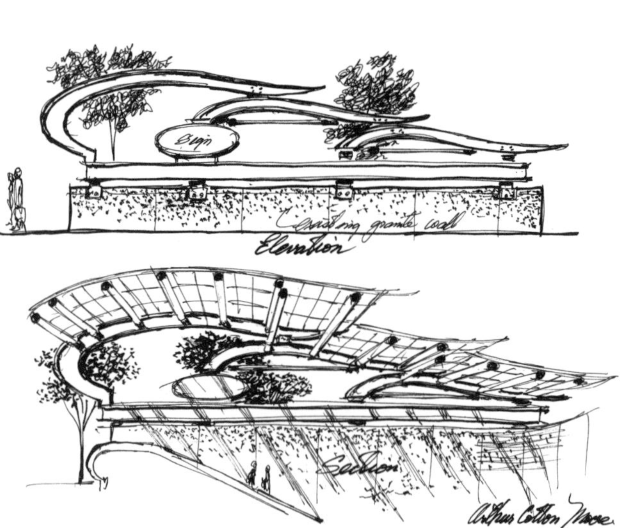

Sketch: Canopies over metro entrances
Washington, D.C.
8.5" × 11" (21.6 × 27.9 cm)
Medium: Ink on vellum
Courtesy of Arthur Cotton Moore/Associates,
Architects • Planners, Washington, D.C. • Royal Oak, Maryland
Drawn by Arthur Cotton Moore, FAIA

Sketch of proposed canopies over the existing metro entrances for metropolitan Washington, D.C., transit system. The curved beams are bent or cut out of stainless steel sheets and are designed to expand or contract laterally in order to adapt to the wide variety of existing entrances. The curved beams support pipe purlin and glass roofs. The canopies are shaped to have natural ventilation and to be evocative of a rapid-transit system. The intent is to provide a light, airy signature structure that will quickly become identified with the system.
[ARCHITECT'S STATEMENT]

Diagrammatic exploration is an evocative way of design sketching. Hand-generated diagrams and computer-modeled diagrams (pp. 452–59) are both forms of conceptual sketching. Likewise, conceptual modeling by fabricating "hands-on" models (study models) using any kind of found material is also a form of conceptual "sketching" in three dimensions.

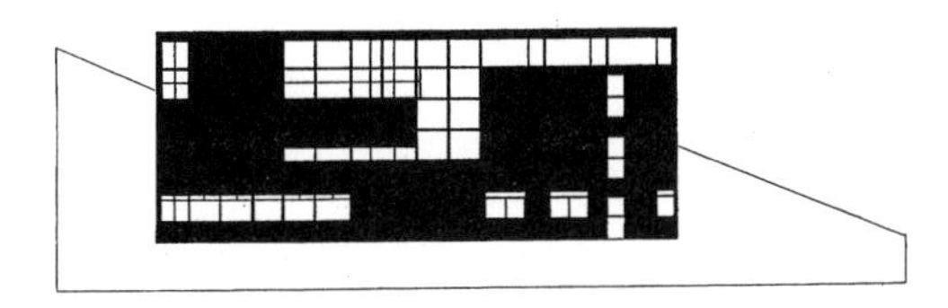

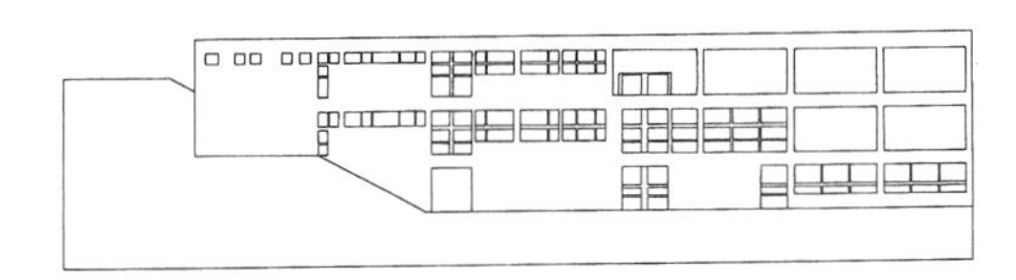

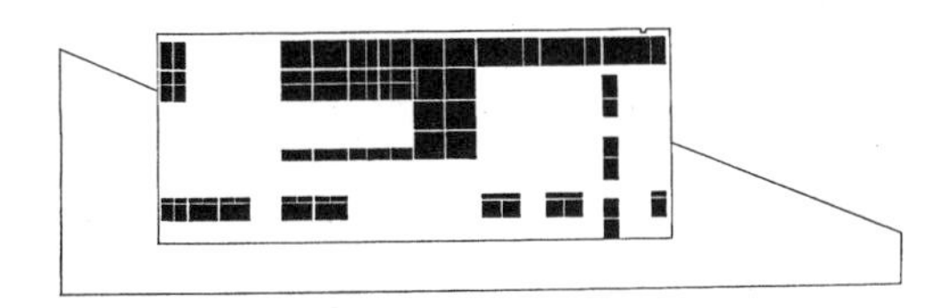

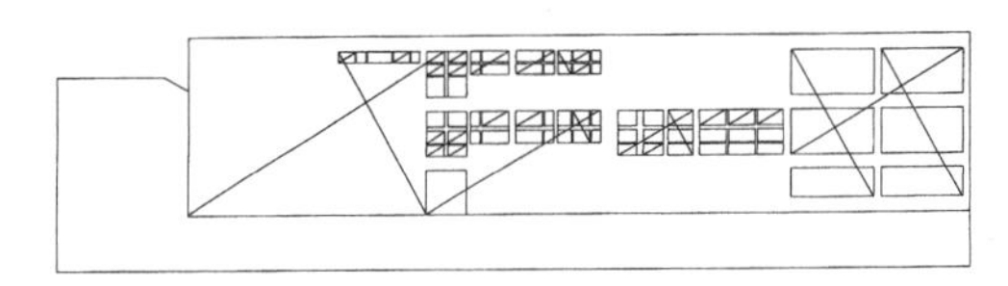

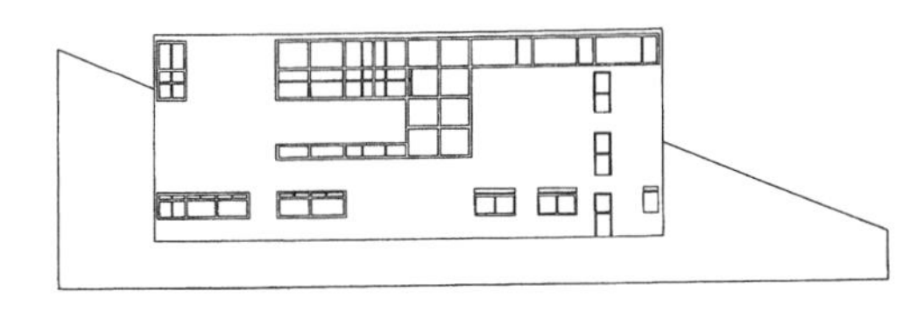

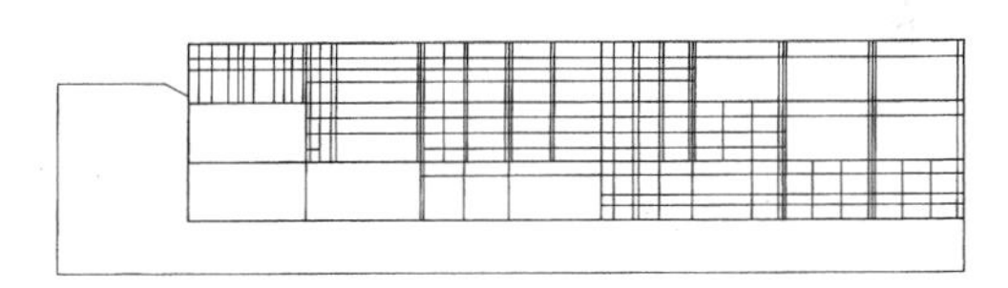

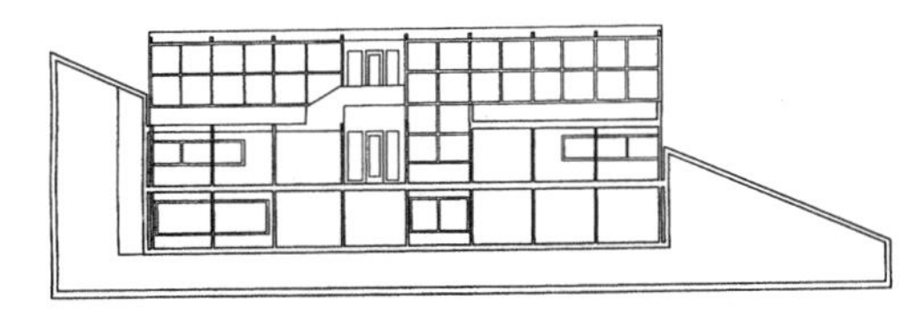

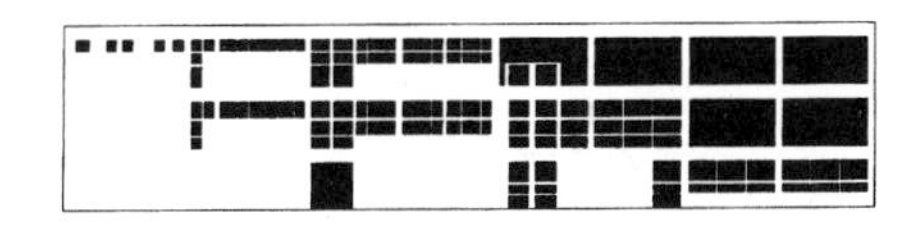

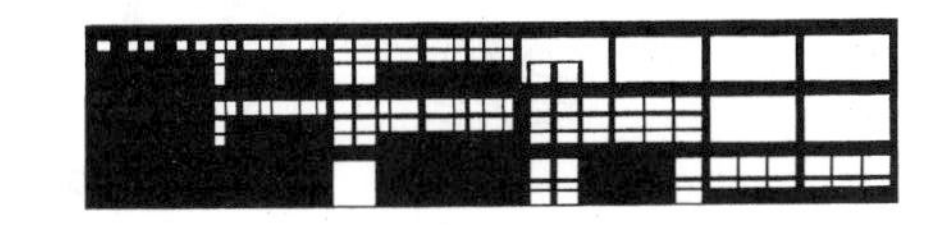

Diagrams: Student projects by Darlene Lawrence (above)
and Karla Armas (right)
Facade studies
Medium: Ink on Mylar
Courtesy of the University of Texas at Arlington
School of Architecture

Formal diagrams, such as the facade studies above, explore aspects of figure–ground relationships, scale and proportion, geometric configuration, and the rhythm and pattern of the elements of enclosure. The elevation diagrams shown display a strong use of figure and ground in the representation of solid (wall) and void (window). These diagrams concentrate on the geometric treatment of the fenestration in a reductive manner. This simplification of the facade prevents the viewer from becoming distracted by other aspects that may appear in an elevation, such as material texture or construction detail.

Diagrams: A study of the Central Glade
University of California at Berkeley
Courtesy of Philip Enquist, Architect

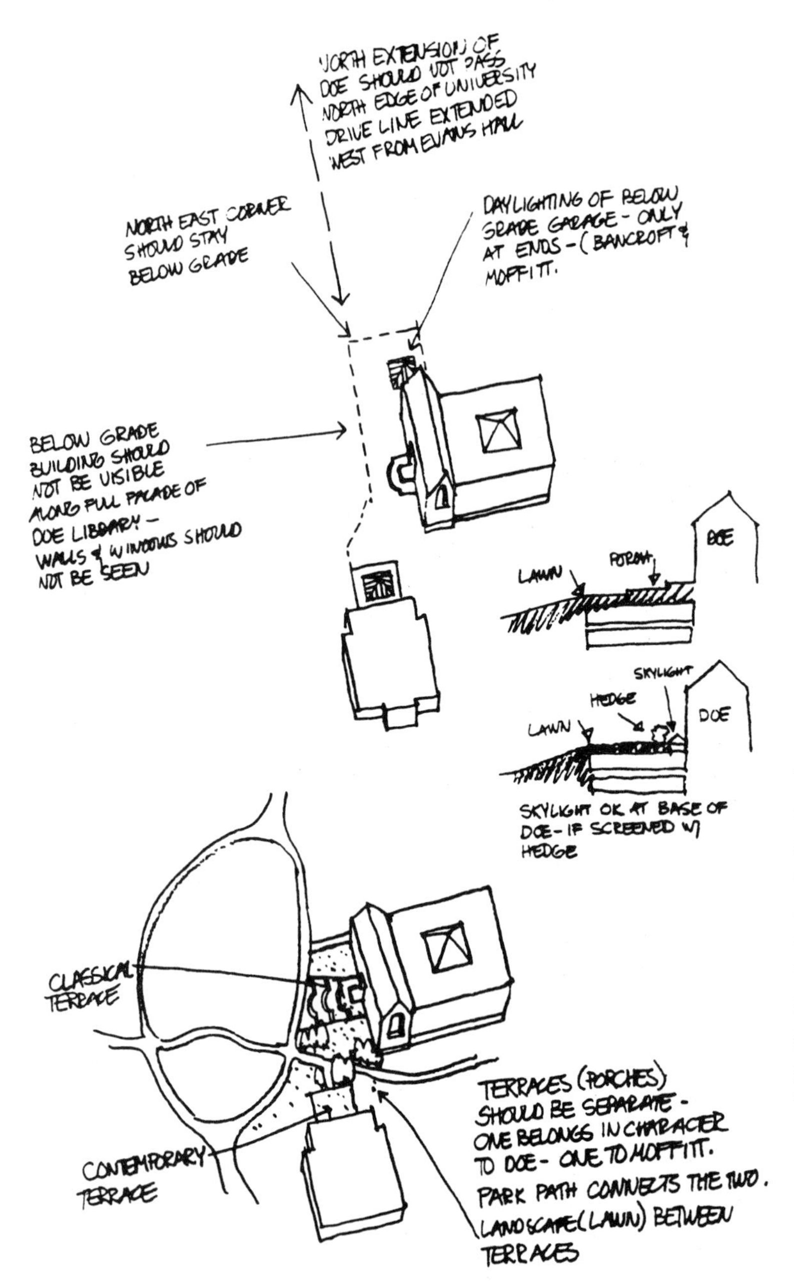
NORTH EXTENSION OF DOE SHOULD NOT PASS NORTH EDGE OF UNIVERSITY DRIVE LINE EXTENDED WEST FROM EVANS HALL
NORTH EAST CORNER SHOULD STAY BELOW GRADE
DAYLIGHTING OF BELOW GRADE GARAGE - ONLY AT ENDS - (BANCROFT & MOFFITT.
BELOW GRADE BUILDING SHOULD NOT BE VISIBLE ALONG FULL FACADE OF DOE LIBRARY - WALLS & WINDOWS SHOULD NOT BE SEEN
DOE
LAWN
PORCH
SKYLIGHT
HEDGE
LAWN
DOE
SKYLIGHT OK AT BASE OF DOE - IF SCREENED W/ HEDGE
CLASSICAL TERRACE
CONTEMPORARY TERRACE
TERRACES (PORCHES) SHOULD BE SEPARATE - ONE BELONGS IN CHARACTER TO DOE - ONE TO MOFFITT.
PARK PATH CONNECTS THE TWO.
LANDSCAPE (LAWN) BETWEEN TERRACES

These quick thumbnail sketch diagrams were done primarily as plan obliques, which can be more easily understood, especially by a layperson, than plan diagrams. Note the additional use of a two-dimensional diagram on this page. Two- and three-dimensional diagrams are frequently used together in analytical studies.

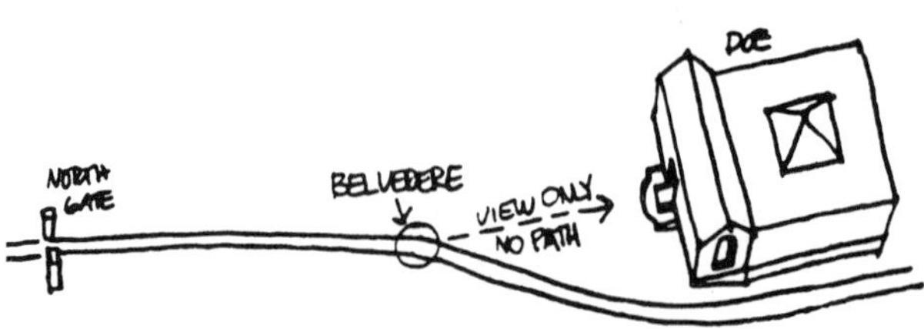
DOE
NORTH GATE
BELVEDERE
VIEW ONLY
NO PATH
NORTH GATE WALK COMES TO GLADE ON AXIS W/ DOE LIBRARY. THE PATH SHOULD CONNECT TO SATHER ROAD - NO PATH SHOULD CROSS GLADE ON FORMAL AXIS WITH DOE'S FRONT DOOR.
Building guidelines - Doe Library

Diagrams: A study of the Central Glade
University of California at Berkeley
Courtesy of Philip Enquist, Architect

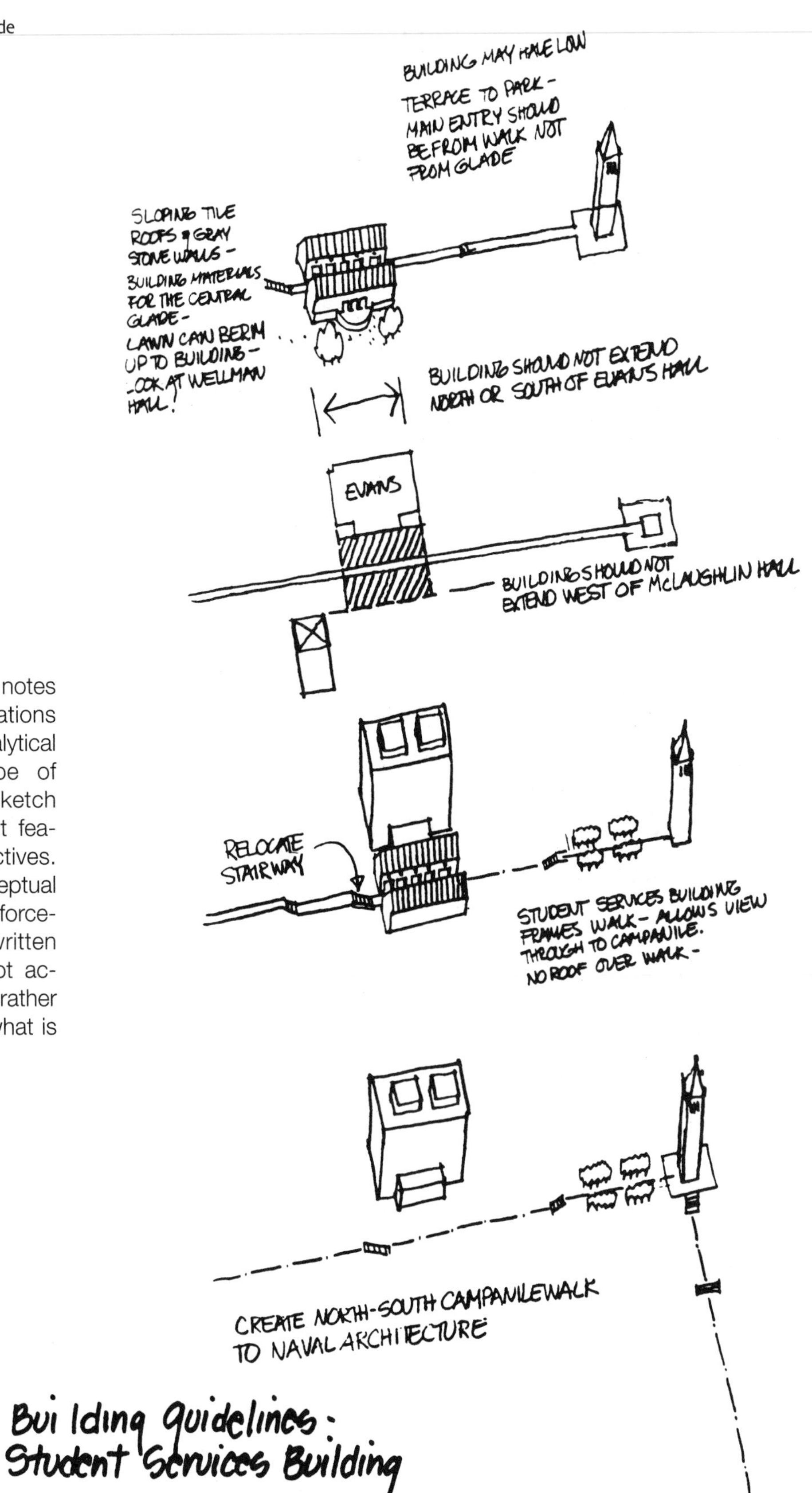
BUILDING MAY HAVE LOW
TERRACE TO PARK -
MAIN ENTRY SHOULD
BE FROM WALK NOT
FROM GLADE
SLOPING TILE
ROOFS & GRAY
STONE WALLS -
BUILDING MATERIALS
FOR THE CENTRAL
GLADE -
LAWN CAN BERM
UP TO BUILDING -
LOOK AT WELLMAN
HALL!
BUILDING SHOULD NOT EXTEND
NORTH OR SOUTH OF EVANS HALL
EVANS
BUILDING SHOULD NOT
EXTEND WEST OF MCLAUGHLIN HALL
RELOCATE
STAIRWAY
STUDENT SERVICES BUILDING
FRAMES WALK - ALLOWS VIEW
THROUGH TO CAMPANILE.
NO ROOF OVER WALK -
CREATE NORTH-SOUTH CAMPANILE WALK
TO NAVAL ARCHITECTURE
Building Guidelines:
Student Services Building

The use of abundant written notes aids in design communications and the design process. Analytical note taking with any type of diagram or conceptual sketch prompts the recall of salient features and important objectives. Think of diagrams and conceptual sketches as visual notes reinforceable by accompanying written notes. These drawings are not accurate representations, but rather a descriptive dissection of what is being observed.

PLAN OBLIQUE SKETCH DIAGRAMS

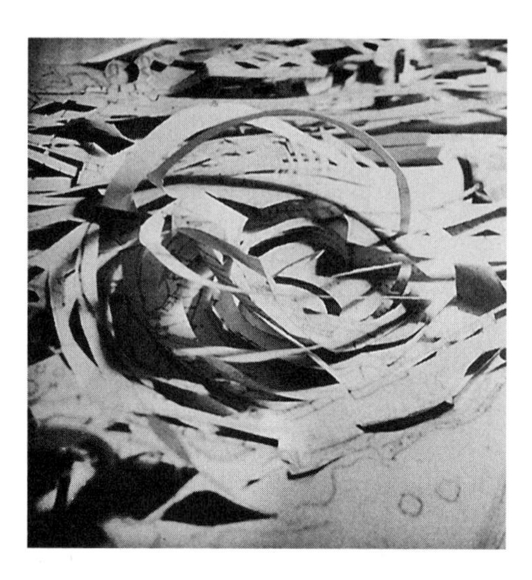

Family® Town 1:5000 master-plan scale model

HomeChurch breakfast scene 1:50 scale model

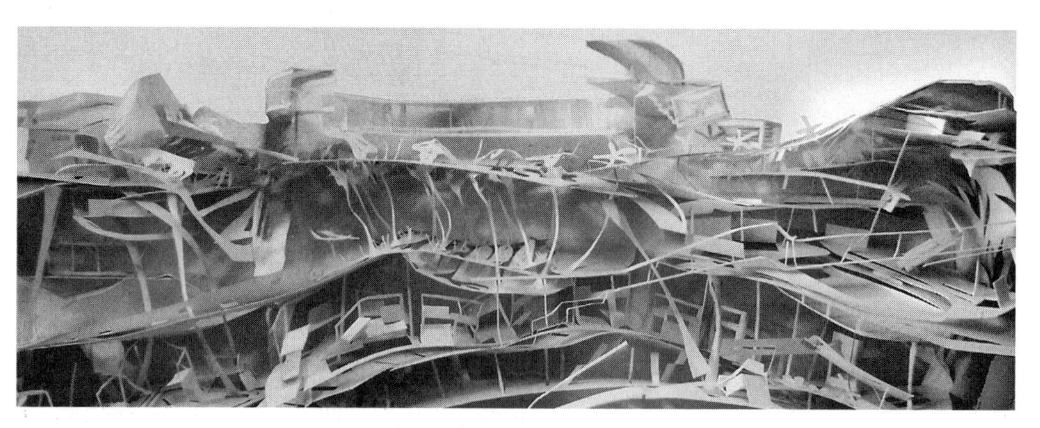

HomeChurch, HomeShop, HomeSchool, and HomePark 1:200 sectional model

Student project by Yu Jordy Fu (this and facing page)
Family® Town London, England, United Kingdom
Medium: For models, lightweight paper; for line drawings, Adobe Illustrator
Department of Architecture
Royal College of Art Kensington Gore, London
Courtesy of Yu Jordy Fu

Conceptual sketching can also be achieved through the use of conceptual sketch models (see Antoine Predock's clay models in Web site Chapter 12). The models above were done manually for an exhibition of work in progress. They were made by using 80 mg and 150 mg normal cartridge paper and UHU glue. This kind of paper is ideal for showing the multiple layers and undulations of the scheme.

My models were cut freehand using a scalpel, without reference to specific drawings. Ten sketch models were made before the final one. The purpose of the model was to express the feeling of spaces and activities, not the form. I wanted the model to look fluent and alive, since it was about people. The architectural strategy focuses on layering, folding, and manipulating solid, void, and light.
[ARCHITECTURE STUDENT'S STATEMENT]

Family® Town
Schedule of phases
(total of 10 phases)

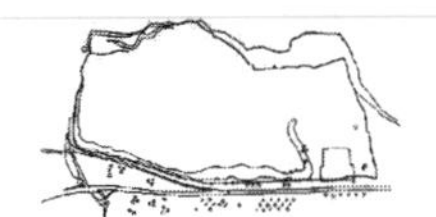

2010 eastern quarry

2012 city hall

2014 town phase 1

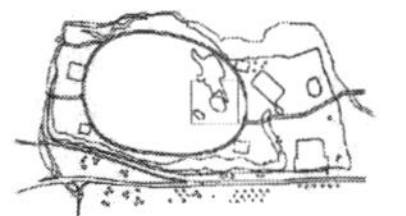

2017 town phase 2

2020 town phase 3

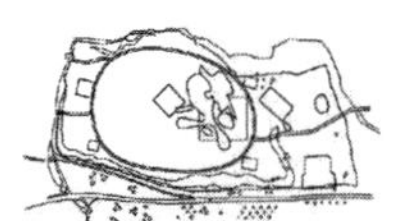

2022 town phase 4

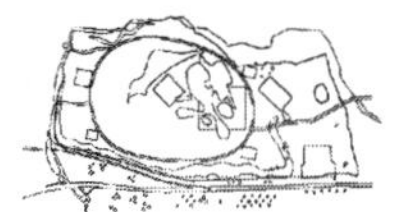

2026 town phase 5

2028 town phase 6

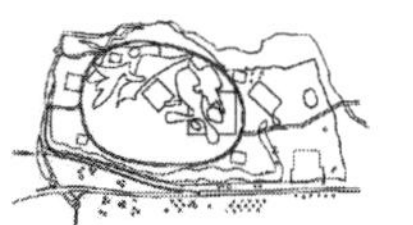

2030 town phase 7

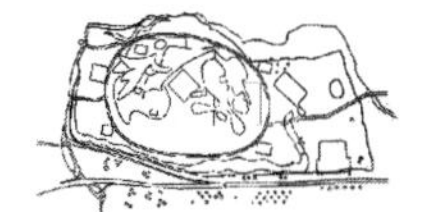

2032 town phase 8

2032 town phase 9

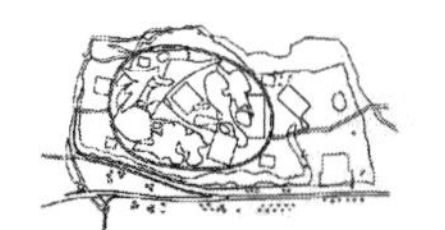

2032 town phase 10

Partial section through site plan (drawn from the sketch model)

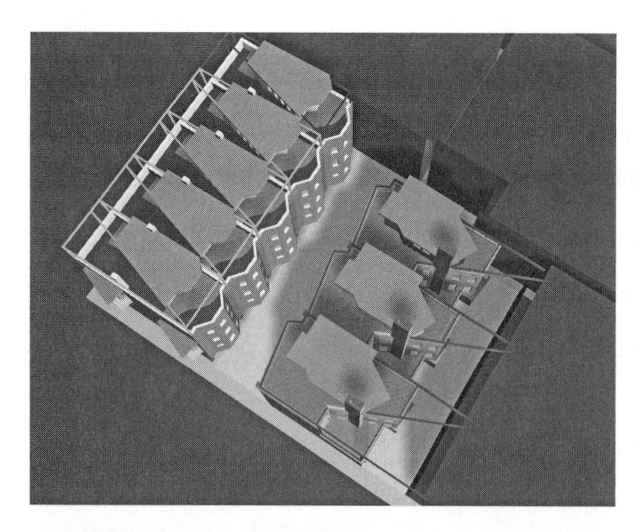

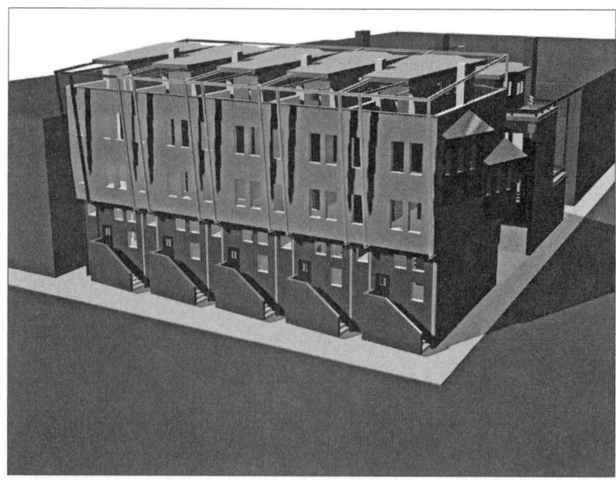

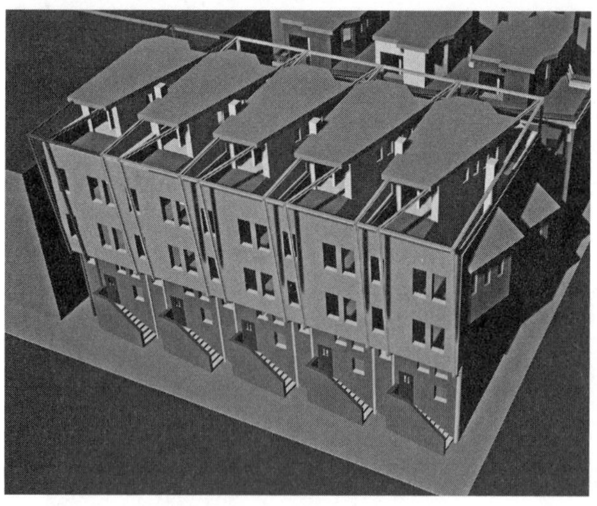

Student project by Robert Reichel (this and facing page)
Baltimore townhouses
Software: IronCAD
Courtesy of studio professor William W. P. Chan
Institute of Architecture and Planning
Morgan State University

The first semester of the first-year graduate program began with simple projects involving problems in descriptive geometry, orthographic drawing, and constructing models with foam board, chipboard, and basswood. The objective is to open up the hand-eye-brain coordination in three-dimensional thinking.

After a survey of a lot of 3-D software, IronCAD was selected because it is user-friendly, and its maneuverability is similar to constructing real models. Shapes and forms are created on screen, positioned, copied, modified, and rotated; it is all done in real time, and it allows the user to work intuitively in designing in three dimensions. The on-screen assemblage can be printed out and sketched over with new ideas. The components can be reconfigured instantly, with no interruption of the creative process. Every model part put into the assemblage is automatically registered and, with a click of the mouse, activated for modification. A small object inside a very tight enclosure can be worked on without disturbing the layers of enclosures, which house the object. Colors, textures, lighting, and materials are available for a more detailed rendition of the scene. It is also possible to move back and forth between 3-D and 2-D drawings. It is ideal for training beginners in architectural design.

[PROFESSOR'S STATEMENT]

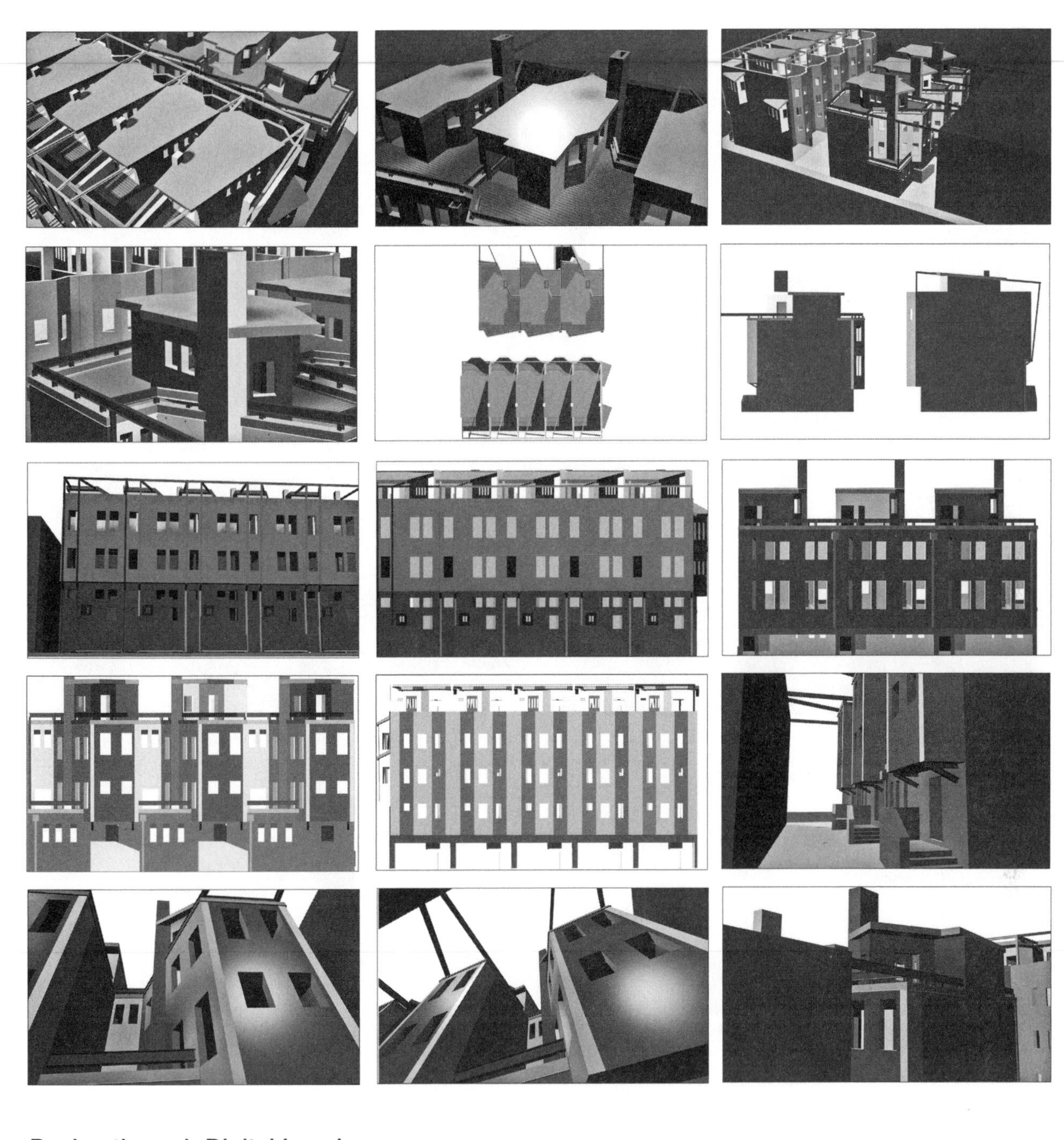

Design through Digital Imaging

With a background in sculpture and furniture design, my visualization and design process has always been three-dimensional. I am used to being able to walk around my work and consider it from any angle. Designing with 3-D modeling software was a natural transition for me. It allows me to mass out buildings using techniques that are conceptually similar to working in wood, metal, or clay. Computer modeling also gives me the opportunity to evaluate my design from any angle or perspective that I want. The program for the townhouses had extreme real-world limitations, such as tightly surrounding existing buildings, limited southern light, and difficult parking requirements. Using IronCAD software allowed me to design by modeling within this space. I then used the program to generate plans, elevations, sections, and drawings based on the model. I could then reassess my design using both the drawings and the model.

[Architecture Student's statement]

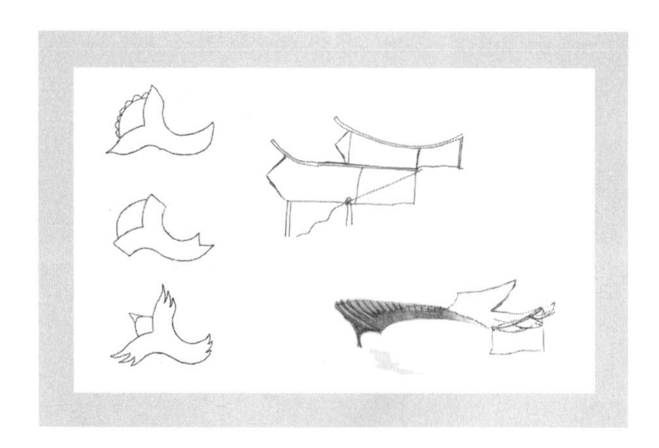

Student project by Matthew Richardson
Herring Run Nature Center
Baltimore, Maryland
Courtesy of Studio Professor William W.P. Chan
Institute of Architecture and Planning
Morgan State University

The design objective was to produce a nature research center in an urban park with diverse topography, allowing access to different research plots on the site. Initially, organic shapes and themes were sketched out on paper. Then, in IronCAD software, a massing was created that rose from a ridgeline in the topography and projected out over the stream valley. The idea was to create a building that looked as if it were taking off in flight as the wind swept up the valley walls. The building would be easily approached from the ridgeline but have a dramatic view over the stream valley. The massing was printed onto paper and sketched over on tracing paper to define the wing shapes and tail of the building. Once these changes were visualized with hand drawing on tracing paper, they were further developed with the 3-D software. The designs of the window facade and promenade railing were altered similarly. Going back and forth between the two media and utilizing the software's ability to view the model from all angles allowed for quick advances in the 3-D design. If relegated to only working with a physical model, there would have been little room for design changes throughout the process; working with a computer model accommodated the design's mutating form more quickly.

[Architecture Student's statement]

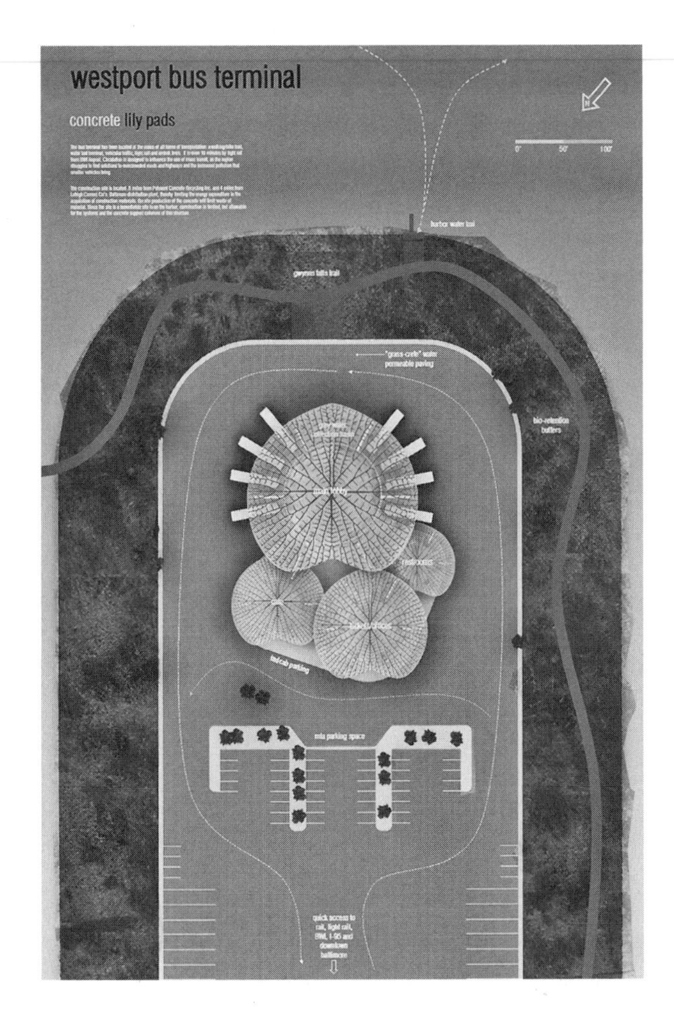

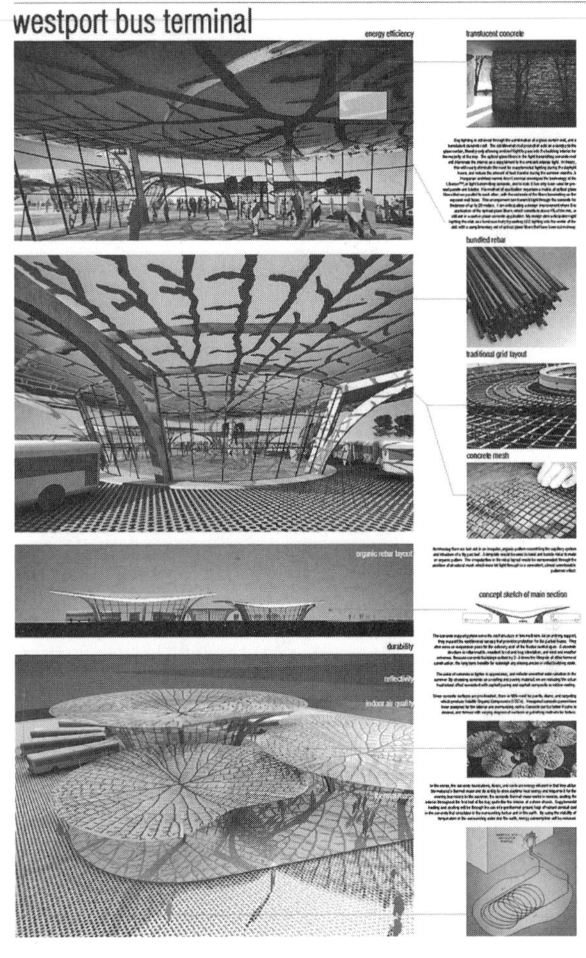

Westport Bus Terminal, Westport, Maryland
Student project by Matthew Richardson (May 2006)
Third place in Association of the Collegiate Schools of Architecture and Portland Cement Association's International Competition: Concrete Thinking for a Sustainable World
Courtesy of Matthew Richardson, Morgan State University, Baltimore, Maryland

Entrants were encouraged to come up with a design that used concrete as a sustainable building material. Students were limited to two, 20" X 30" presentation panels and encouraged to limit the presentations to those aspects of the design that showcased concrete as an innovative structural element. Because sustainable design is clearly evident in the layout of this site, an entire presentation panel was dedicated to the whole site plan, detailing all aspects of the design through a series of leader lines and labels. The second presentation panel displayed section and perspective renderings generated from the 3D Studio Max model, which were subsequently enhanced slightly in Adobe Photoshop. These four renderings were organized at the fullest size that would fit on the presentation panel, leaving room on the right border for details and descriptions of the design. This simple organization process allowed for large renderings while permitting text and details to fully explain the design. The design began as a notebook sketch, and developed through repeated interfacings between computer models and tracing overlays on top of a computer printout. As a nice balance to the beautifully rendered computer images, the initial ink concept sketch was used as one of the details in the right border.

[Architecture Student's statement]

Refer to the section on two-panel presentations in Chapter 10.

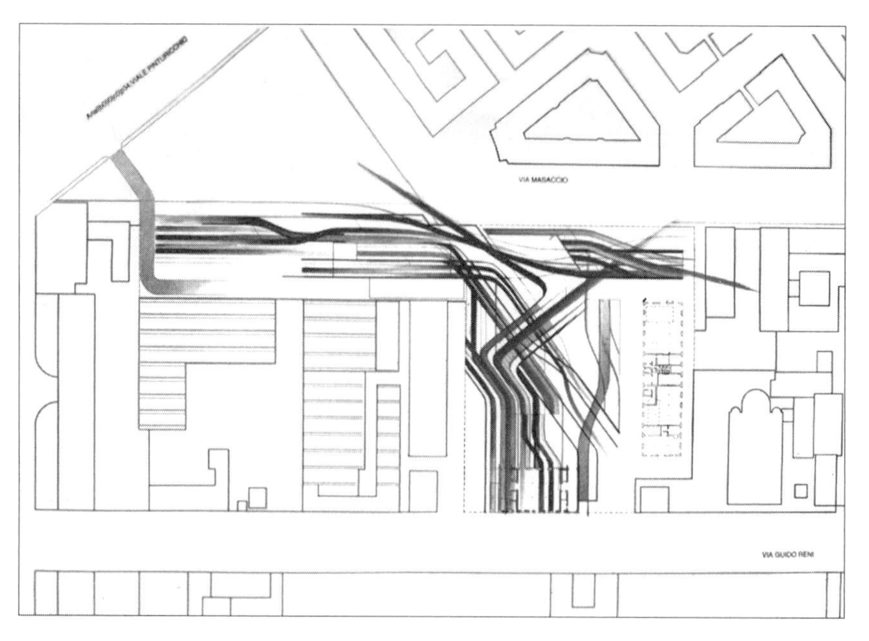

Computer drawing: Contemporary Arts Center, Rome, Italy
Courtesy of Zaha Hadid Architects

A PICT file created by scanning a sketch was then edited in Photoshop. The drawing was then drawn and modified using MiniCAD 7 and VectorWorks.
[ARCHITECT'S STATEMENT]

Computer drawing: Contemporary Arts Center, Rome, Italy
Courtesy of Zaha Hadid Architects

This is a rendering from a computer model that has been enhanced in Photoshop.
[ARCHITECT'S STATEMENT]

Hand sketches are done by Zaha Hadid at the start of most projects. Computer modeling—renderings and drawings—are done simultaneously by the office during each project.
[STATEMENT BY BARBARA KUIT IN THE OFFICE OF ZAHA HADID]

Computer-generated wireframes, like manually executed contour and cross-contour drawings, describe the form of an object. In cross-contour drawings, parallel lines are typically used to traverse the surface of an object. With wireframe drawings, it is possible to visualize the overall shape of a building in a pure sense, without the distractions of nonarchitectural features.

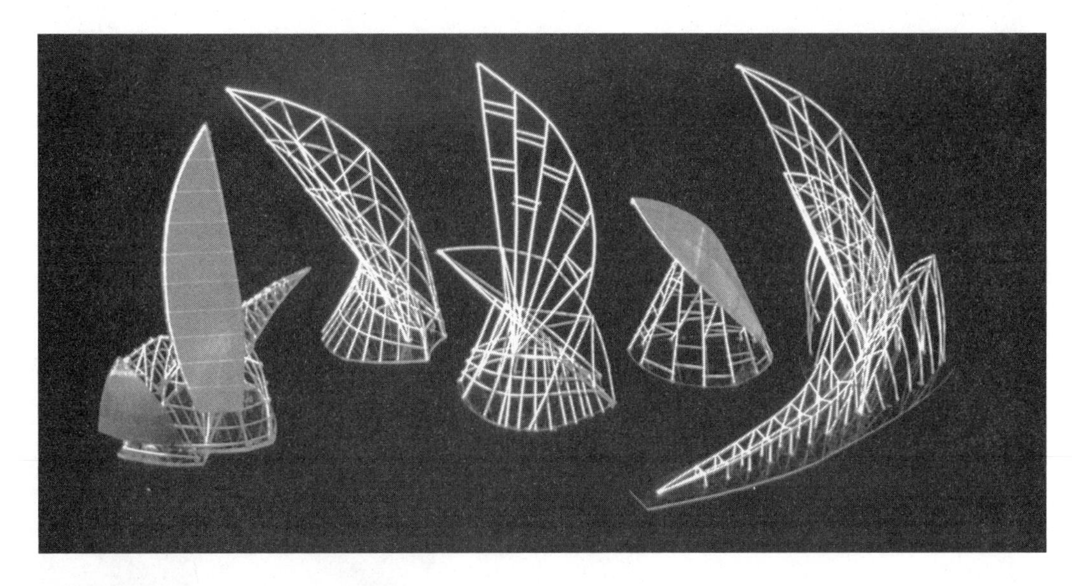

Computer wireframe studies: National Museum of Contemporary Art Osaka, Japan
Courtesy of Cesar Pelli & Associates Architects
Photo credit: M. LaFoe with Cesar Pelli and Associates

Digital photo rendering of aerial view
The National Museum is in the central foreground.
Courtesy of Jun Mitsui Associates

DIGITAL 3-D DIAGRAMS

SEQUENTIAL AERIAL VIEWS

1

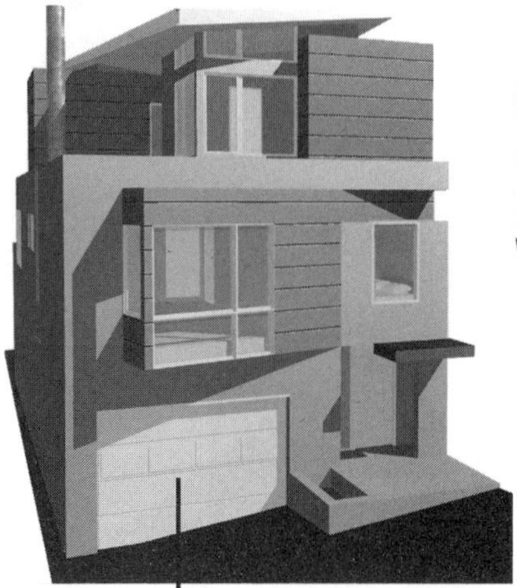

2

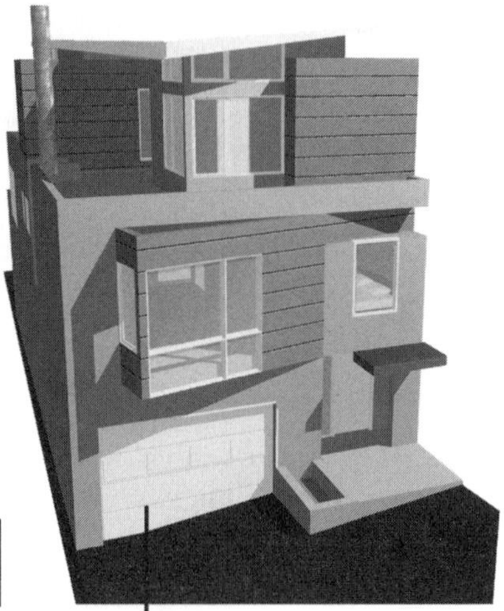

3

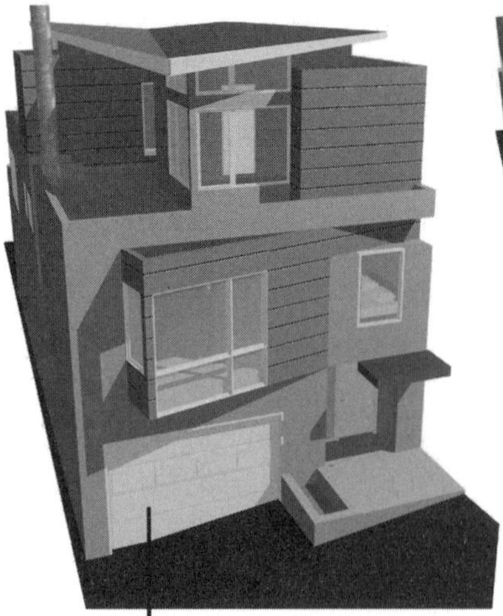

4

5

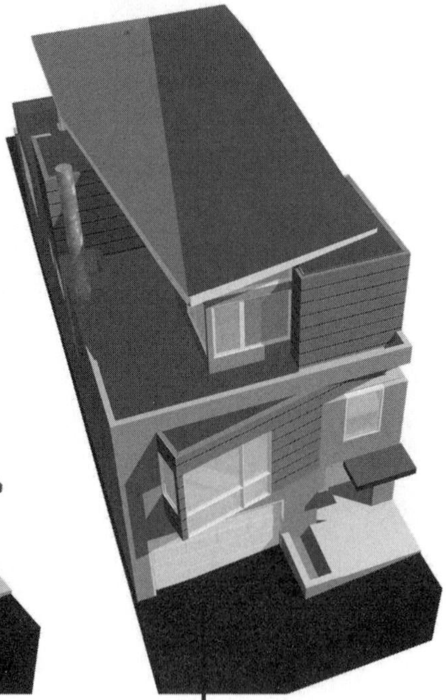

6

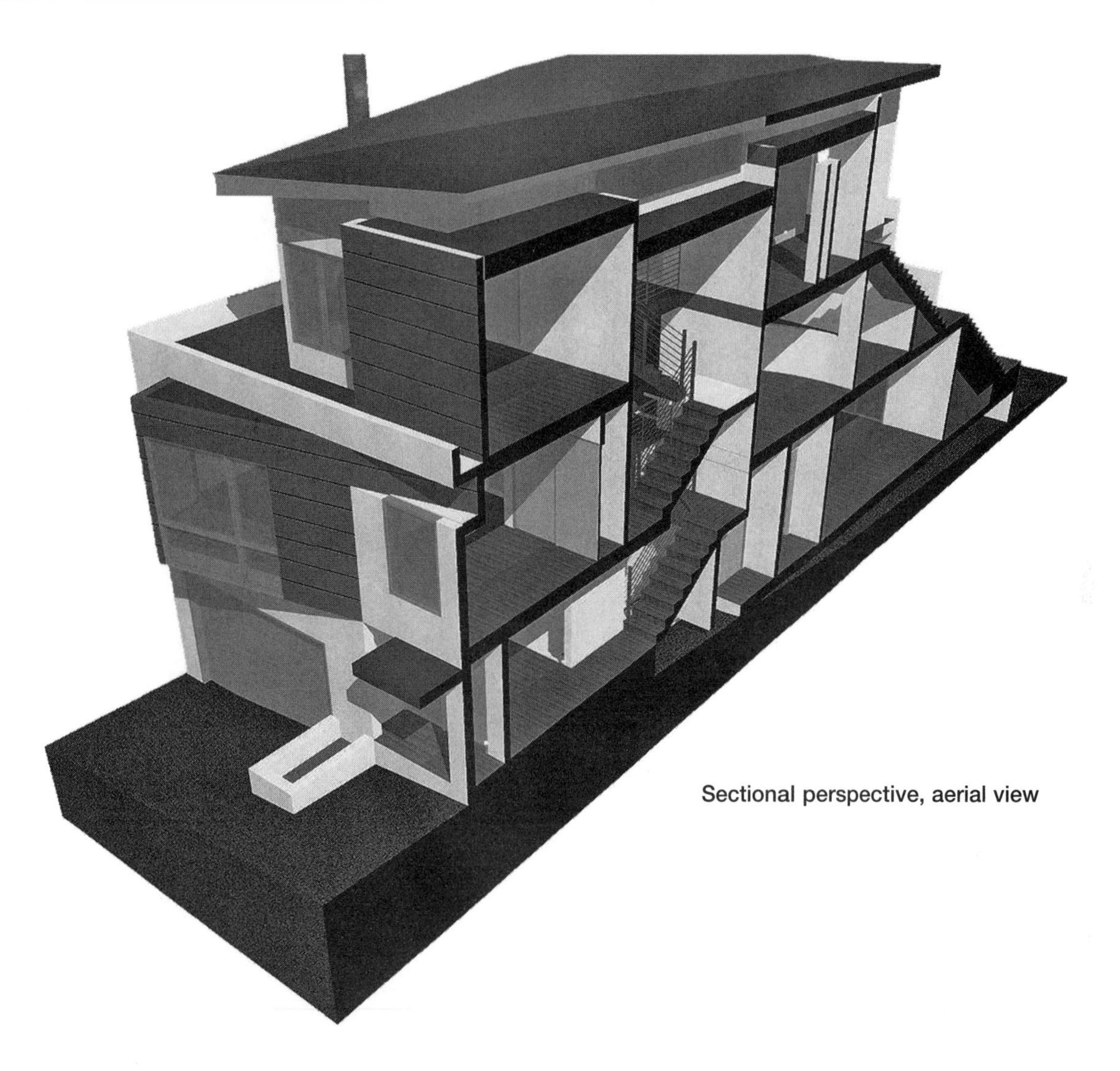

Sectional perspective, aerial view

Images (this and facing page): Douglass Street Residence
San Francisco, California
Medium: ArchiCAD 8 software
Principal in Charge: Mark English
Architectural Illustrations: Masha Barmina
Courtesy of Mark English Architects

The use of a sequence of computer 3-D views helps architects review and explain the relationships among all of the major components in a building at the same time. In this case, the model allowed us to quickly review how changes to any of the roof or facade elements might impact the overall project. The sketches suggested further adjustments to the computer model, which in turn inspired more finished sketches.
[ARCHITECT'S STATEMENT]

Refer to Chapters 12 and 13 in the Web site.

very abstract initial doodle

less abstract

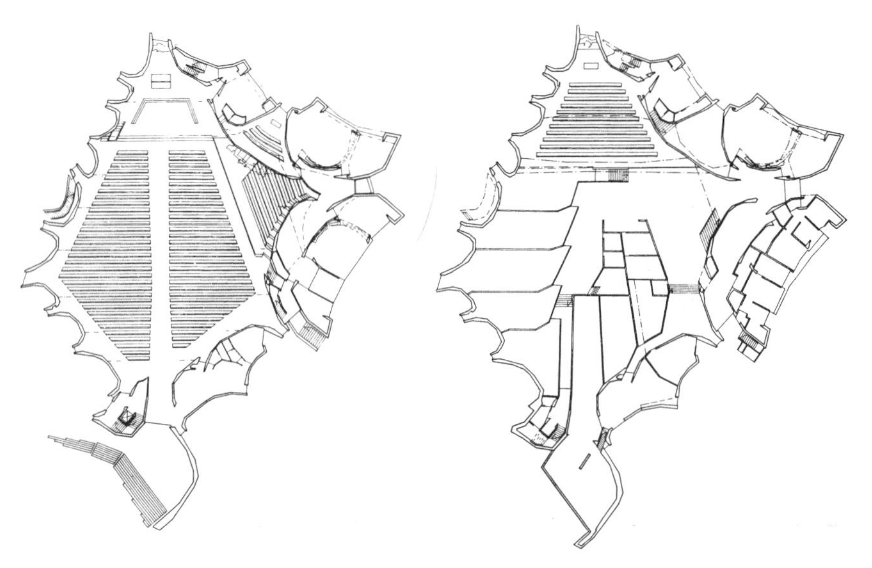

refinement from the abstract

Sketches and drawings: Kaleva Church, Tampere, Finland
Scales: Upper left and bottom 1:50, upper right 1:100
Medium: Charcoal
Courtesy of Raili and Reima Pietilä, Architects

Images in the mind are first visualized (a mental act) and then sketched (a physical act). Sketching ideas on paper helps to evolve other ideas; these concepts are constantly evaluated and reevaluated. The examples here show a progression from creative abstract sketches to more refined drawings.

The ability to formulate mental images comes with practice. Visualizing everyday objects will form the basis for sharpening the conceptual imagination. As ideas occur, they are put on paper. This is an **ideational** drawing. An idea on paper is a visual representation of what something may conceptually look like. Some ideas will be discarded; others will be changed, modified, refined, and expanded.

Reima Pietilä (1923–1993), a world-renowned Finnish architect in the period after Alvar Aalto, stated the following:

Creating architecture is a multimedia process. It involves verbal programming and directing; visualization by sketching floor plans, sections, and elevations; spatialization with the help of a scale model; and materialization by building. Both words and pictures are used to explain architectural form. Neither one nor the other alone is enough to make architecture as a phenomenon sufficiently comprehensible.

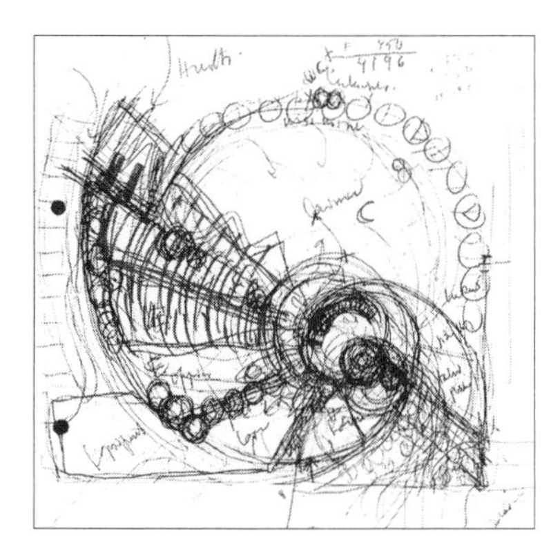

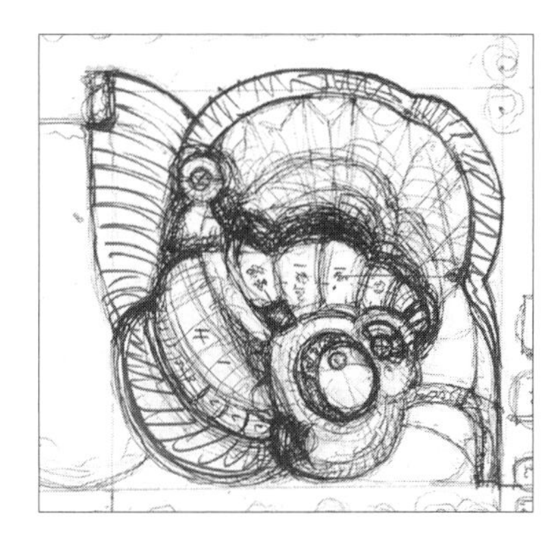

Conceptual sketches and model photo: Tampere Main Library ("Metso"), Tampere City, Finland
Sketches 4" × 4" (10.2 × 10.2 cm), Model scale: 1:200
Courtesy of Raili and Reima Pietilä, Architects

This transparent "silk" (tracing paper) is my miraculous design medium. Almost a nonmaterial, it is cheap and of little value in the artist's permanent works. As my own design tool, this transparent or, more exactly, semitranslucent membrane functions as a catalyst, enabling visions to be fixed. The sketch has no further value after it has delivered its graphic message to the copy machine. Upon construction of the building, perhaps the production drawings go to the archives; but these sketches, though having helped mediate the path towards the form, usually get thrown in the wastepaper basket before too long.

I have thought, however, that these process sketches could be of use in allowing us an insight into how architecture emerges from "scrap," or how architecture emerges almost from that indefinite "anything" that can be behind or beneath the architectural concepts. The pictorial material of this processing design often has very little final form or character: Instead, it possesses more of an artistic multiple message load. Though the sketch is beyond the limited categories of logic and such consequent thinking, the sketch itself is not irrelevant or irrational. The good sketch is a multi-interpretive idea; it can give suitable impulses for feasible alternatives. We must then train ourselves to learn to read them, patiently, allowing much time.

Usually I lay sketch upon sketch, perhaps up to ten times, carefully using the previous one as a basis for the following sketch until I feel "it is there." By then it usually is. My professional visualization opens up its possible routes through such sketch paper procedure. Architectural characteristics, features, traits, etc., are transported, transformed, and transfigured via the sketches. At the end of the process, there are, of course, the final plans, sections, elevations, and details. In the art of architectural graphics, the expressive form follows the implicit function. Its latent message value is much higher than we usually assume, and it is the sketch graphics that generate the spatial vision that will, in turn, become actual architecture.

[Reima Pietilä]

Notes on sketches and the architectural process
Courtesy of Raili and Reima Pietilä, Architects
Reprinted from: *PIETILÄ Intermediate Zones in Modern Architecture* with permission of Raili Pietilä, the Museum of Finnish Architecture, and the Alvar Aalto Museum

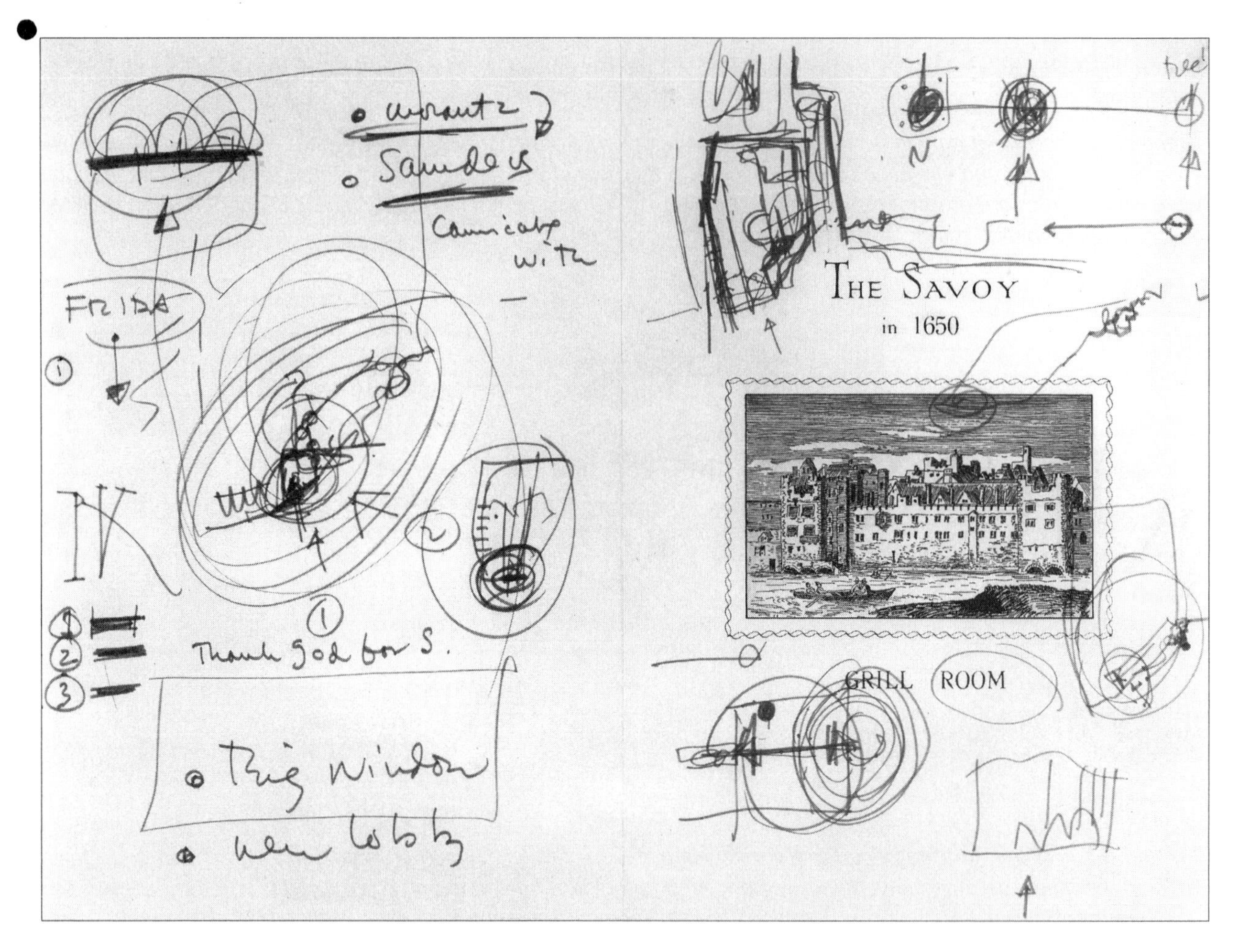

Diagrammatical sketches (both pages): National Gallery, Sainsbury Wing
London, England
Medium: Red felt-tipped pen
Courtesy of Venturi, Scott Brown and Associates, Inc., Architects

For background on the architecture and ideas of Robert Venturi and Denise Scott Brown, see James Venturi's documentary film *Learning from Bob & Denise.*

The ideal sketches are those that evolve from intuition indirectly guiding the hand more than the mind directly guiding the hand. Also, combinations of images and words enrich the process.
[ARCHITECT'S STATEMENT]

These two-dimensional "napkin sketches" (in this case done on a dinner menu) were made by architect Robert Venturi. Designers and architects usually sketch at a minute size as shown above, thus giving us the term **"thumbnail sketches,"** which are about the size of Venturi's small doodles. Sketching at a small scale allows you to explore more ideas and thus consider more possibilities and choices for a design problem. The mind can generate creative thoughts at work, as well as while playing, eating, or answering nature's call. In other words, creative thinking is not altogether controllable, and it is important for the designer to be on alert for creative insights.

Color or black ink is usually a better medium than color or toned pencil values for thumbnail sketches, especially if you plan to do a percentage reduction of the thumbnails to accommodate a certain page or panel size in a presentation.

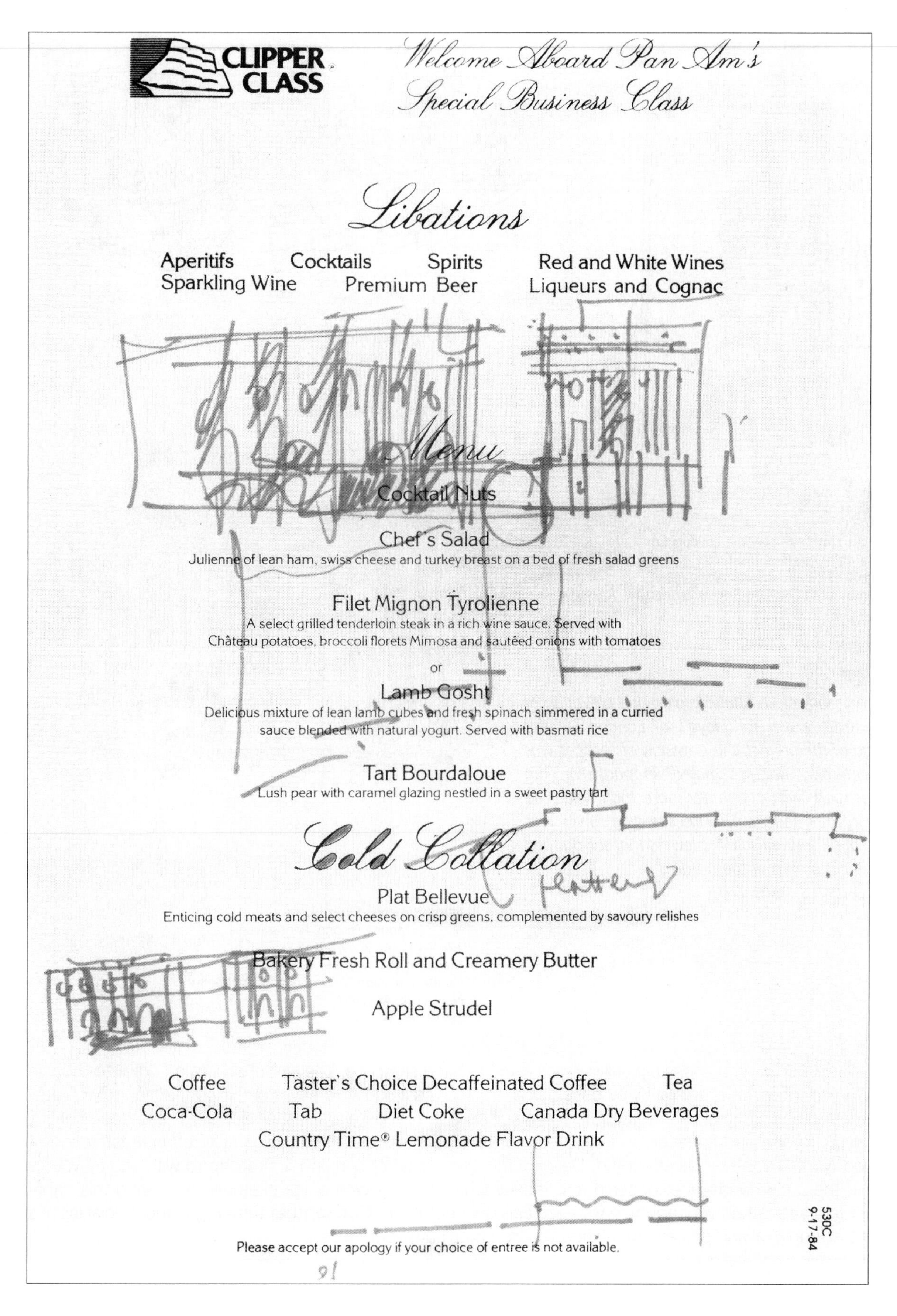

CLIPPER CLASS

Welcome Aboard Pan Am's Special Business Class

Libations

Aperitifs Cocktails Spirits Red and White Wines
Sparkling Wine Premium Beer Liqueurs and Cognac

Menu

Cocktail Nuts

Chef's Salad
Julienne of lean ham, swiss cheese and turkey breast on a bed of fresh salad greens

Filet Mignon Tyrolienne
A select grilled tenderloin steak in a rich wine sauce. Served with Château potatoes, broccoli florets Mimosa and sautéed onions with tomatoes

or

Lamb Gosht
Delicious mixture of lean lamb cubes and fresh spinach simmered in a curried sauce blended with natural yogurt. Served with basmati rice

Tart Bourdaloue
Lush pear with caramel glazing nestled in a sweet pastry tart

Cold Collation

Plat Bellevue
Enticing cold meats and select cheeses on crisp greens, complemented by savoury relishes

Bakery Fresh Roll and Creamery Butter

Apple Strudel

Coffee Taster's Choice Decaffeinated Coffee Tea
Coca-Cola Tab Diet Coke Canada Dry Beverages
Country Time® Lemonade Flavor Drink

Please accept our apology if your choice of entree is not available.

530C
9-17-84

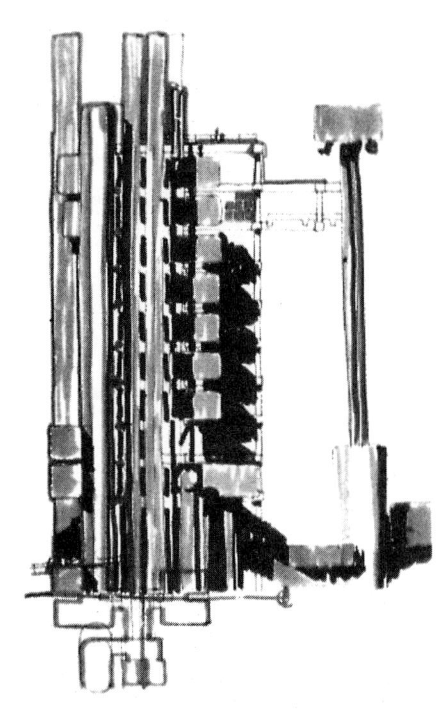

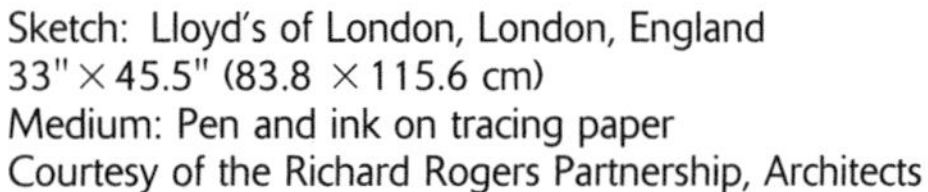

Sketch: Lloyd's of London, London, England
33" × 45.5" (83.8 × 115.6 cm)
Medium: Pen and ink on tracing paper
Courtesy of the Richard Rogers Partnership, Architects

Sketch: University of Toledo's Center for the Visual Arts
Toledo, Ohio
12" × 9" (30.5 × 22.9 cm)
Medium: Ink on paper
Courtesy of Frank O. Gehry, Architect

A very early study showing plan and elevation of a satellite tower for Lloyd's of London. At this stage of the project, the provision of services was considerably underestimated. In particular, the plant room was eventually more than twice the size of that shown. This freestanding tower was one of six servant satellite towers that surrounded the main atrium of the building.
[Architect's statement]

Sketch: Pocono Pines House
Mount Pocono, Pennsylvania
17" × 11" (43.2 × 27.9 cm)
Medium: Pen and ink
Courtesy of Aldo Rossi, Studio di Architettura
New York, Architect

The design-drawing process typically begins with freehand sketches. The sketched design drawings should be artful even though they will rarely be considered art. The artist usually creates permanent artifacts, whereas the designer creates sketches that are referential but do not exist as ends in themselves. These documents give rise to built form and are afterward largely forgotten. The sketches on this page resulted in outstanding completed works by the architects noted. Develop the good habit of carrying a **sketchpad** with you as you travel within the urban landscape; observe and record what you see with quick sketches. Fostering this habit will eventually strengthen your ability to visualize and conceptualize. **Conceptual thinking** is the crucial initial step in the design-drawing process that helps you communicate your ideas.

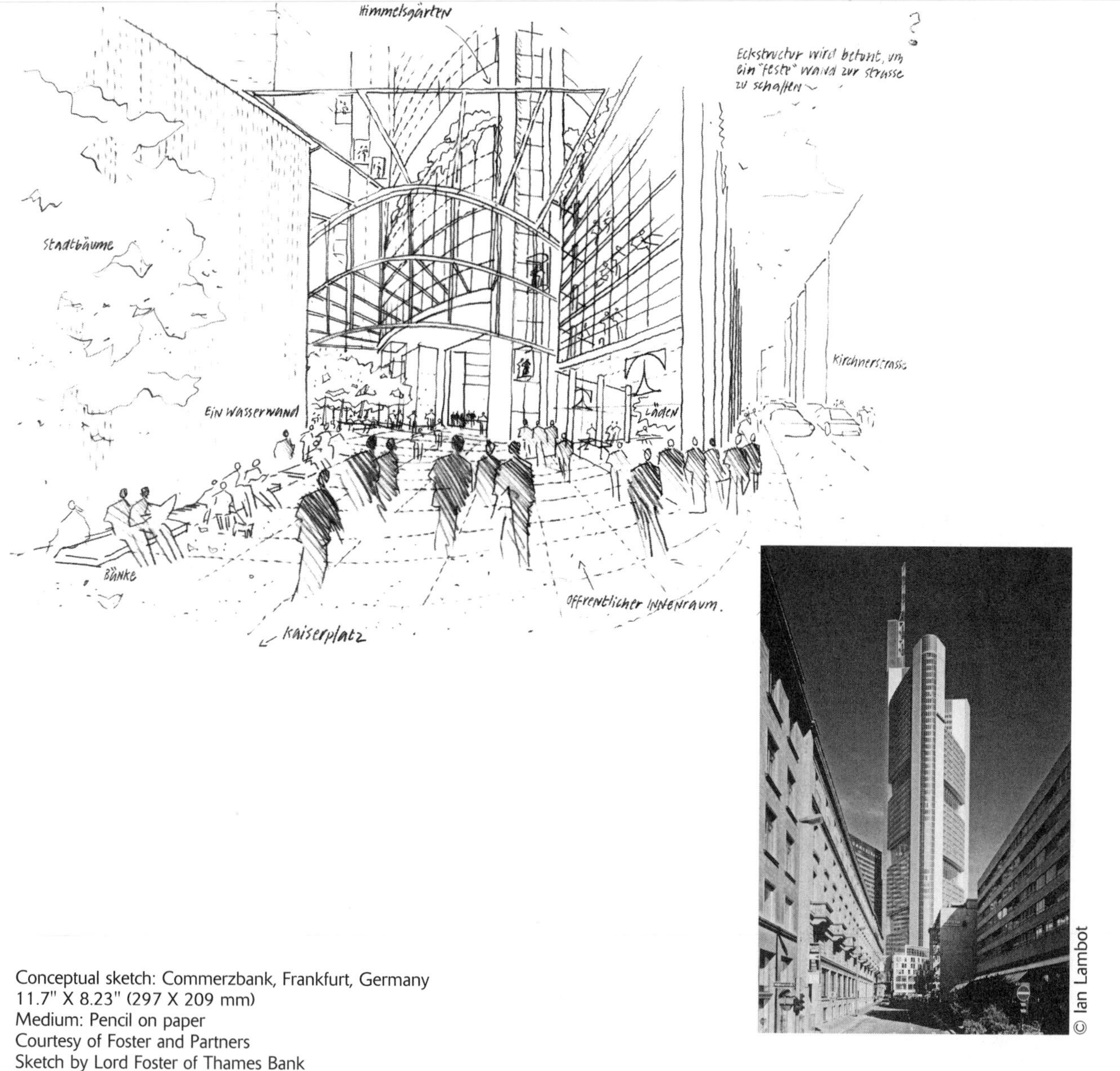

Conceptual sketch: Commerzbank, Frankfurt, Germany
11.7" X 8.23" (297 X 209 mm)
Medium: Pencil on paper
Courtesy of Foster and Partners
Sketch by Lord Foster of Thames Bank

The sketch explores the three-dimensional geometrics that meet at this critical junction—the entrance to the public spaces. It is also mindful of the role that it can play to communicate ideas to others.
[ARCHITECT'S STATEMENT]

Freehand **conceptual sketching** is the most potent means of generating ideas for any type of design. It is unlikely that any medium will fully supplant the immediacy and directness of freehand drawing. In architectural design, recording and evolving ideas as they occur is of utmost importance, and this oldest and most primal method of recording ideas is still essential. The designer should always record exploratory ideas with any accompanying notes (those on the sketch above are in German) on a sketchpad or in a **sketchbook** (logbook) with bond paper that takes any kind of medium. Many architects keep sketchpads or sketchbooks on hand at all times for the express purpose of recording their design ideas. A sketch journal or visual diary can be an invaluable reference source during the design process.

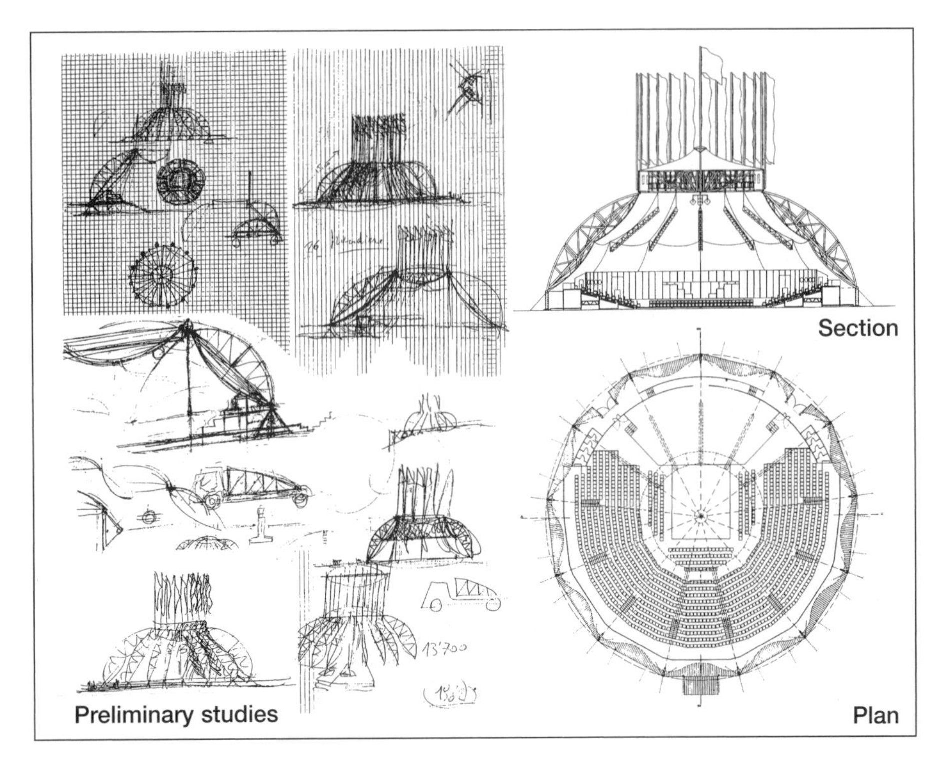

Envisioning and exploring a design concept in the conceptual design stages is a time-consuming, gradual process. Quick freehand doodles and speculative thumbnail sketches are the vital images that make the process work. The preliminary sketch studies in this example typify an analysis and exploratory stage, whereas the hardline drawings typify and represent a synthesis stage.

Design sketches: Tent for the 700th Anniversary of Switzerland
Medium: Pencil
Courtesy of Mario Botta, Architect, Lugano, Switzerland

© Alo Zanetta

Project by Mario Botta, Architect, Lugano, Switzerland
Photographs © Alo Zanetta

Once the human mind has an image, it's very hard to change it. In thinking of the form for a building, it's important to prolong establishing that image for as long as possible, and to do so only after all the information has been gathered.
[ARCHITECT'S STATEMENT]

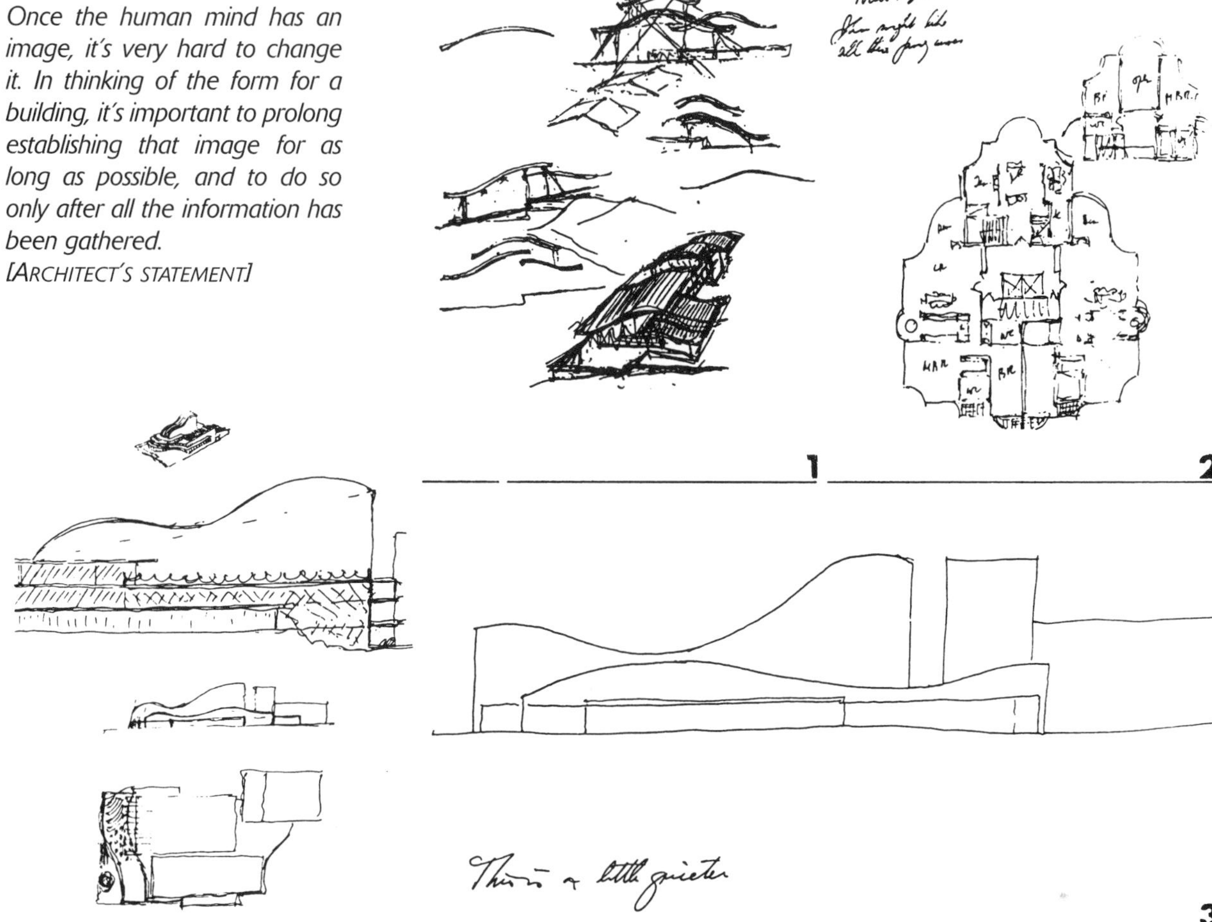

Medium: Black fine-point felt-tipped pen on white trace
Courtesy of Arthur Erickson, FAIA, FRAIC

Sketches: 1. Piney Valley Ranch
Magnus Lindholm
Eagle, Colorado
11" × 14" (27.9 × 35.6 cm)

2. "Nick & Diane, John might like all these fancy curves."
1300 West Pender
Noel Developments
Vancouver, B.C., Canada
11" × 14" (27.9 × 35.6 cm)

3. "This is a little quieter."
Performing Arts Centre
California Polytechnic State University
San Luis Obispo, California
48" × 16" (121.9 × 40.6 cm)

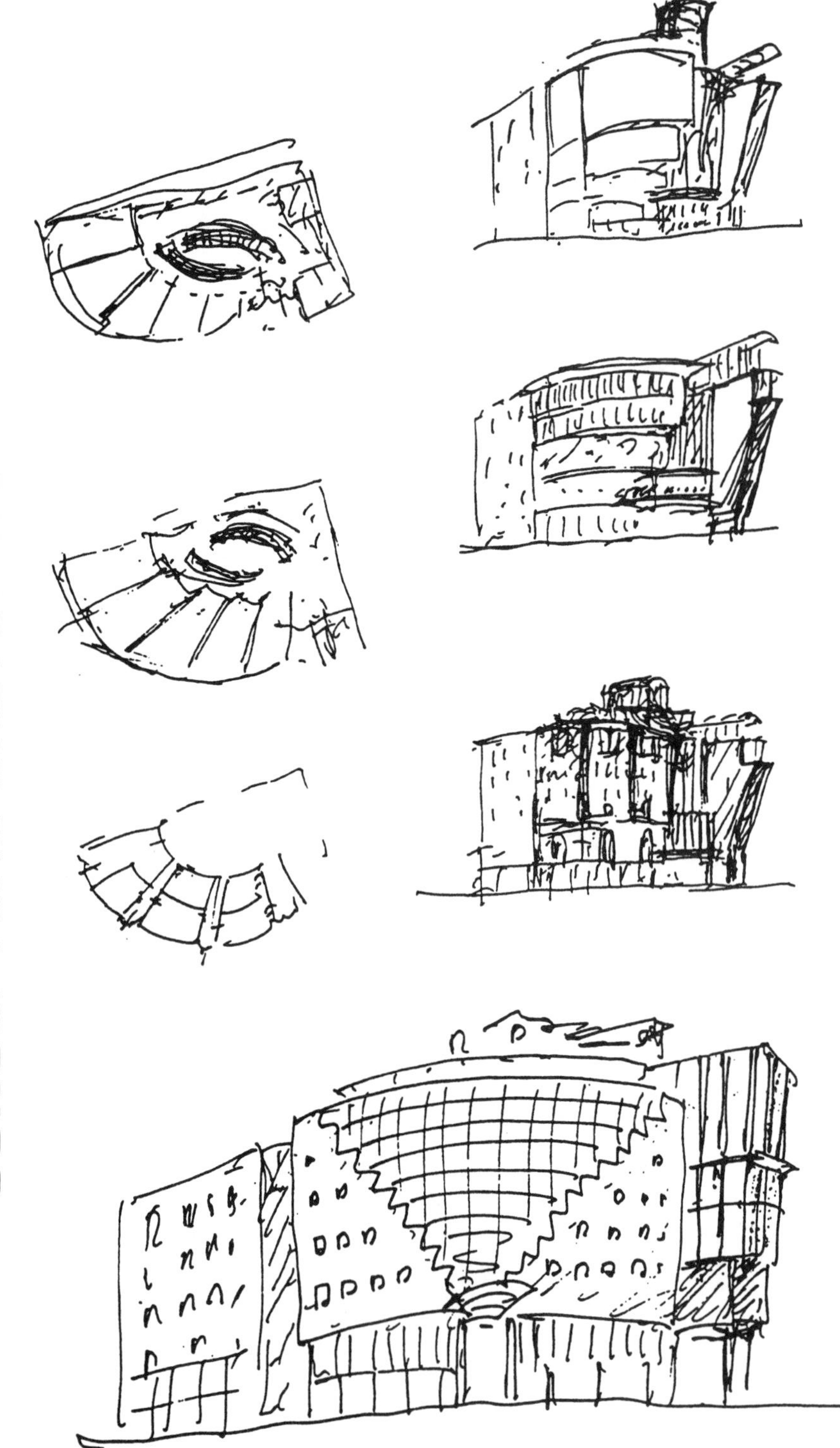

Much like nondirected research in the sciences, sketches can be generated for the purposes of speculation and reflection without any immediate goal in mind. Sometimes these highly imaginative doodles are developed without regard for the pragmatic constraints found in the physical world (e.g., gravity, climate, etc.). Every design professional develops his or her own language in expressing concepts graphically as a way of seeing. Concepts can be approached by thinking in plan, in elevation, in section, in paraline axonometric/oblique images, or in perspective images.

These sketches investigate two different approaches. The top three perspective sketches show stone facades as a veneer and a cantilevering part of the building to separate two urban spaces. The bottom sketch investigates a symmetrical approach with a central entrance, which was not followed up. [ARCHITECT'S STATEMENT]

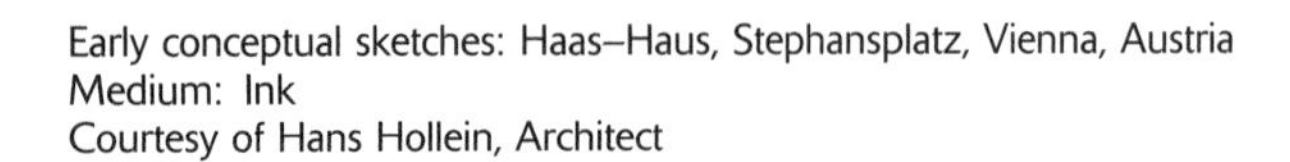

Early conceptual sketches: Haas–Haus, Stephansplatz, Vienna, Austria
Medium: Ink
Courtesy of Hans Hollein, Architect

© Hans Hollein

As you examine the design sketches in this chapter, be aware that different types of media directly affect the feeling of space that is perceived. Architects and design professionals have adopted many traditional artistic media (graphite, ink wash, watercolor, pastel, gouache, etc.) to express their ideas; now they are beginning to exploit the medium of digital technology (see interactive Web site, Chapter 11).

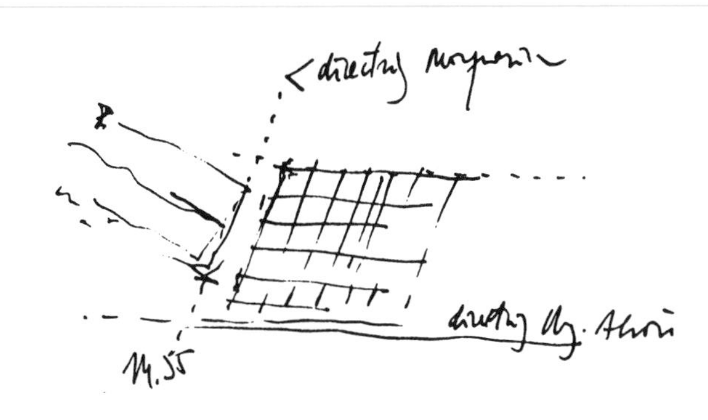

Several sketches of the Atocha Railway Station. One of them speaks about the plan and shows the importance of the existing axes in defining the project. Another two are more related to the description of what a space atmosphere should be: One is related to the lantern, the other to the big hall. The sketch in the middle shows a section. Sketches help to fix the ideas floating in an architect's mind. They often record this early moment when an architect foresees the space to come.
[ARCHITECT'S STATEMENT]

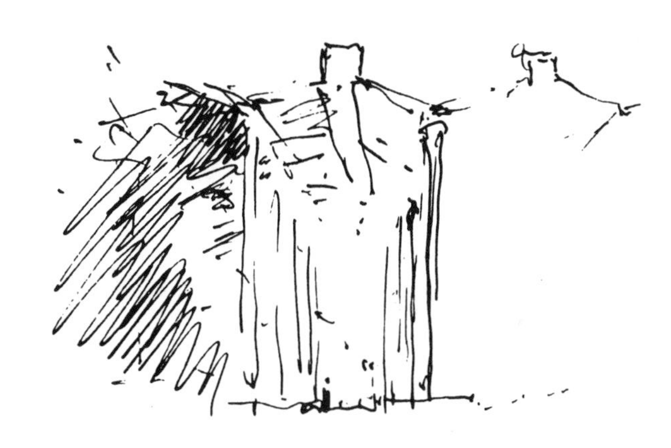

Conceptual sketches: Atocha Station
Madrid, Spain
31.5 × 21.5 cm (12.4" × 8.5")
Medium: Ink
Courtesy of José Rafael Moneo, Architect

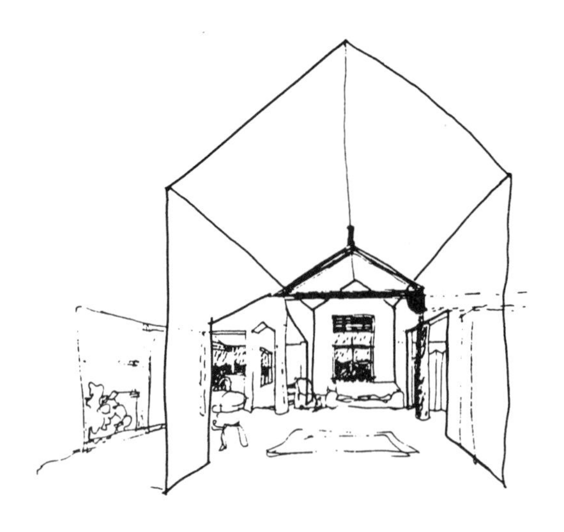

Conceptual design sketches must be done quickly. Speculative sketches should be done freehand so that numerous alternatives can be examined. Conceptual spatial studies are best generated using perspective drawing—especially one-point perspectives. Interior perspectives like those shown here are commonly boxlike (cubic or rectilinear) shapes.

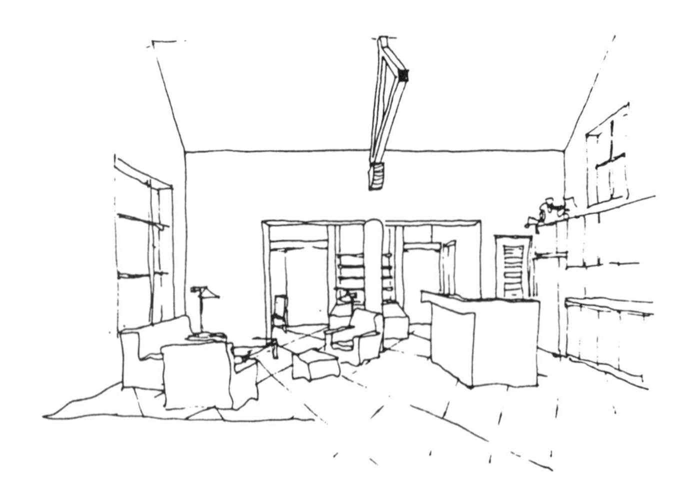

Drawings: Study sketches, Oxley residence, La Jolla, California
Medium: Y&C Stylist pen on trace, 17" X 11" (43.2 X 27.9 cm)
Courtesy of Rob Wellington Quigley, FAIA

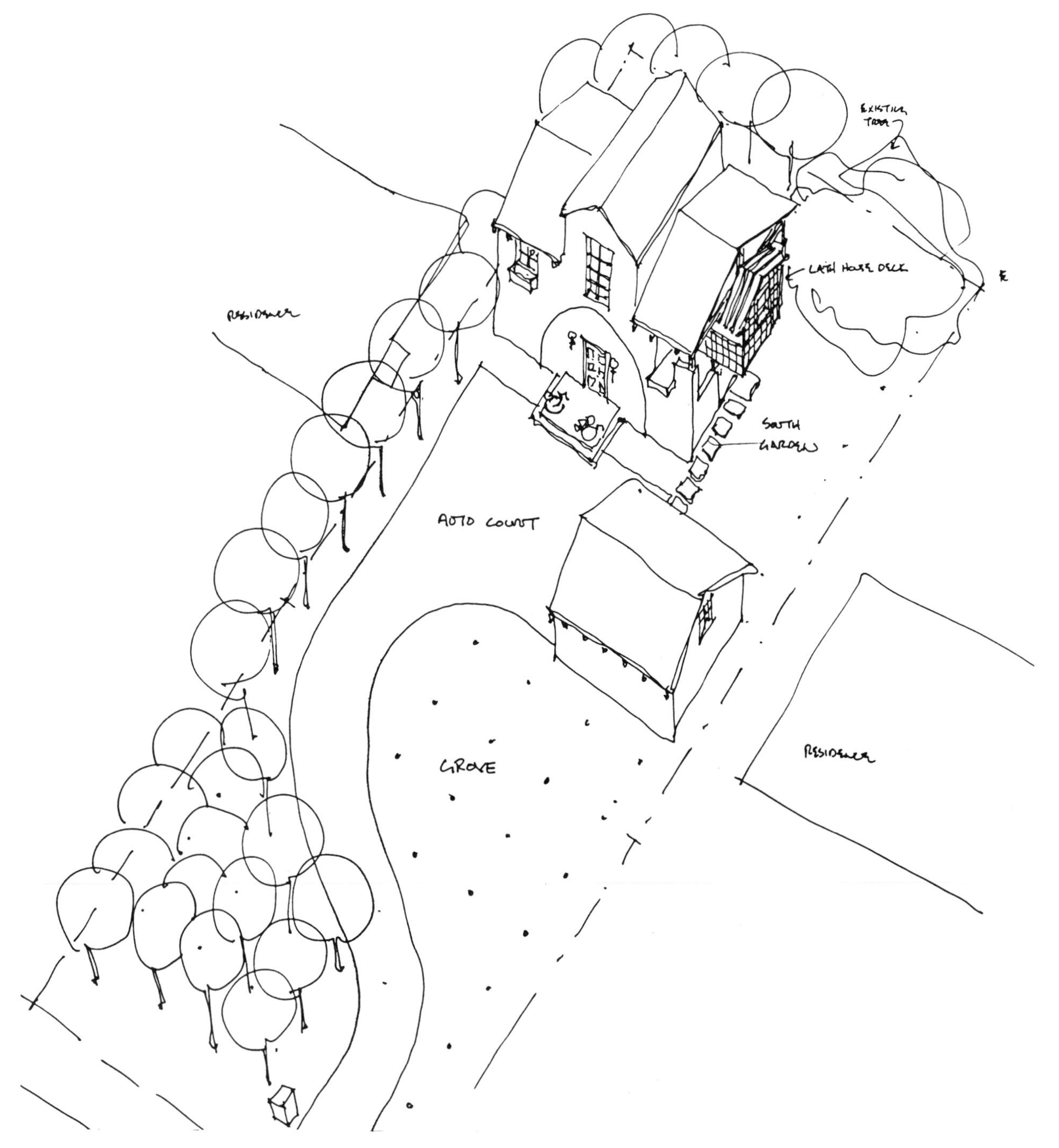

Drawing: Plan oblique sketch for the Oxley residence
La Jolla, California
11" X 17" (27.9 X 43.2 cm)
Medium: Y&C Stylist black fine-tipped pen on trace
Courtesy of Rob Wellington Quigley, FAIA

Pictorial sketches always add an extra dimension to a design concept, especially in the final schematic phases of a project. They help to communicate a design in 3-D to clients, users, and design team members, and reveal spatial concepts not seen in orthographic sketches. This sketch aided in the development of conceiving and confirming ideas prior to the building process.

Sketch: Stairs at entry to New College
University of Virginia, Charlottesville
Medium: Felt-tipped pen on trace, 10" X 8" (25.4 X 20.3 cm)
Courtesy of Tod Williams Billie Tsien Architects

We draw thumbnail perspectives constantly in order to envision space. They help us to bring reality closer to concept.
[ARCHITECT'S STATEMENT]

© Michael Moran, Photographer

Conceptual sketches and model photos: State Archives Centre
Pierrefitte-sur-Seine, France
Courtesy of Massimiliano Fuksas, Architect

These are thumbnail conceptual sketches and model photos of architect Massimiliano Fuksas's competition-winning project for the State Archives Centre in France. Note to what degree the initial hand-sketched ideas contain the essence of the final model. Thumbnails serve as a visual diary, tracing the designer's thought process as the design evolves.

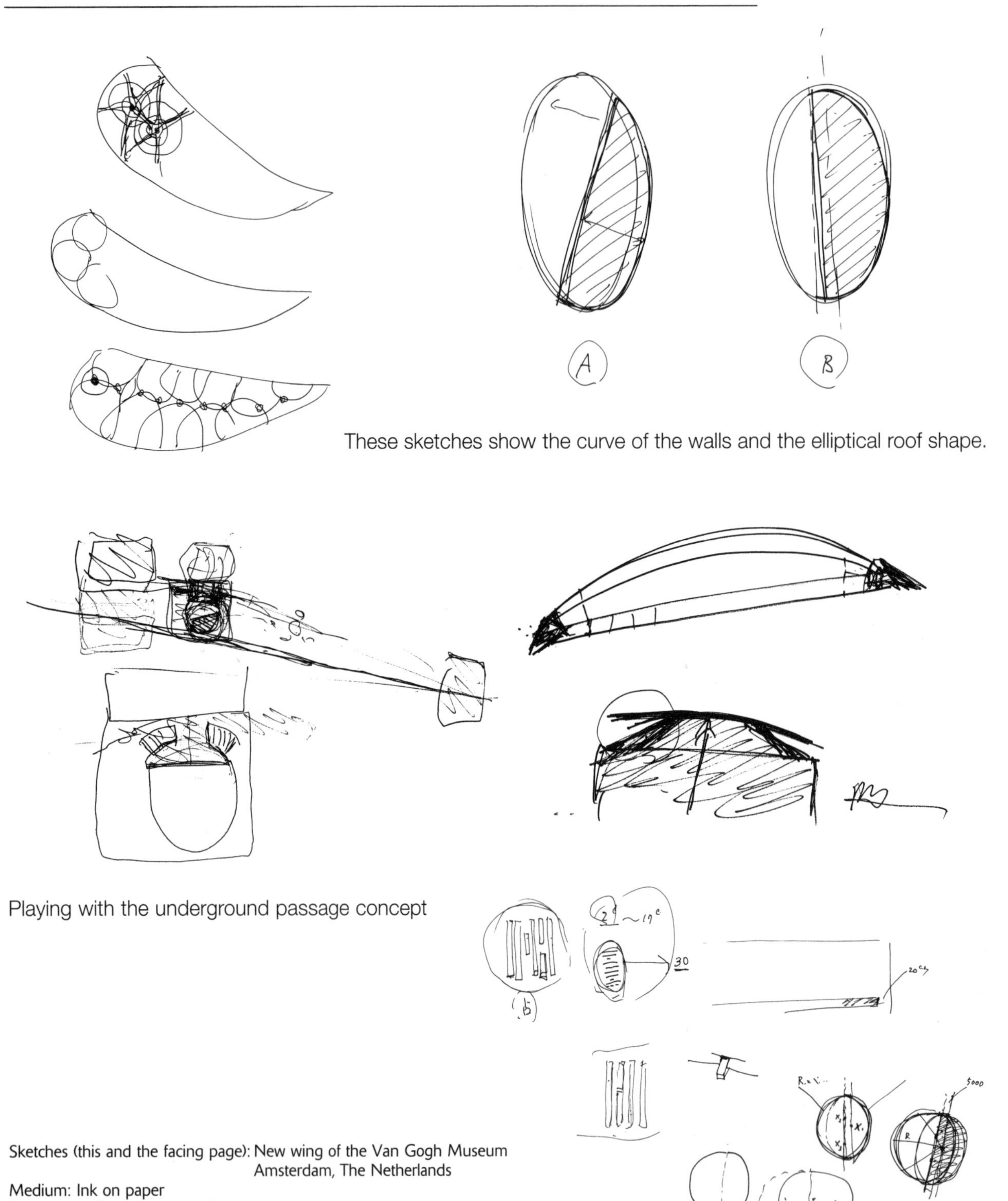

These sketches show the curve of the walls and the elliptical roof shape.

Playing with the underground passage concept

Sketches (this and the facing page): New wing of the Van Gogh Museum
Amsterdam, The Netherlands
Medium: Ink on paper
Courtesy of Kisho Kurokawa Architect

Design concept: The new wing was built in the open space adjacent to the main building of the museum, which was the last work of the Dutch modernist architect Gerrit Rietveld. After considering the whole landscape, 75 percent of the building's area (excluding the main exhibition hall) was constructed underground to minimize the space it would have taken aboveground. The new wing connects to the main building through an underground passage.
[ARCHITECT'S STATEMENT]

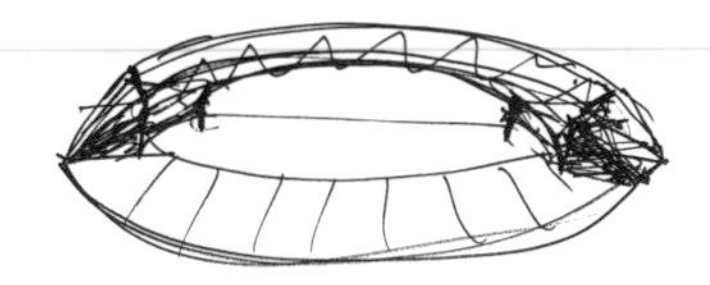

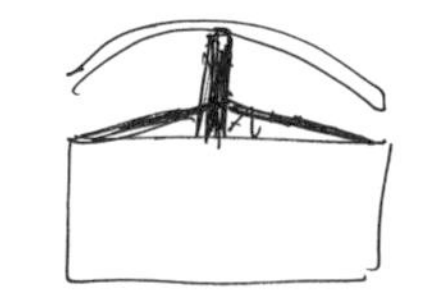

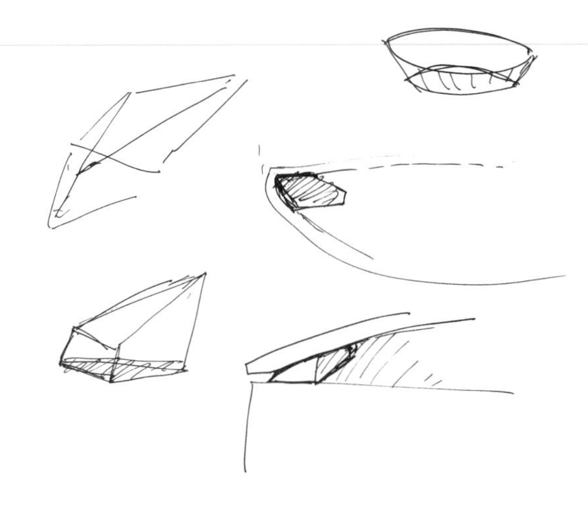

Working on the sunken pool idea

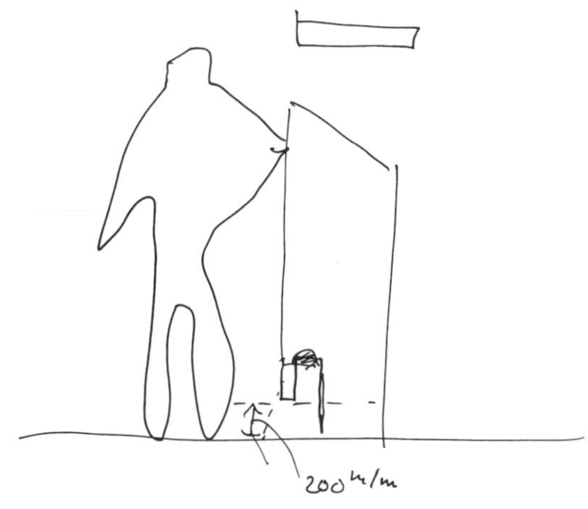

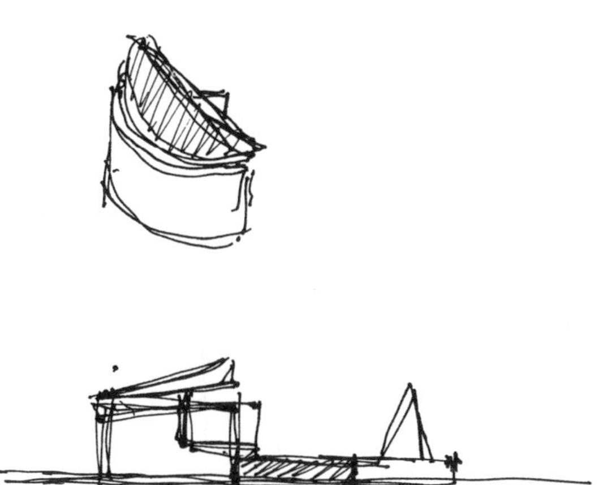

Experimenting with the tilt of the roof

Although Rietveld and Kurokawa share the modernist idea of geometric abstraction, Kurokawa's new wing departs from Rietveld's linear style with curvilinear shapes and lines, employing the traditional Japanese idea of abstraction. One characteristic expressing this idea is the sunken pool, situated between the new wing and the main building. Symbiosis between the new wing and the main building is attained through the open intermediate space created by the pool. The tilt of the elliptical roof and curve of the walls dislocate the center, underscoring the Japanese aesthetic of asymmetry. Through highly abstract simple geometric shapes made complex and, further, through careful manipulation, the abstract symbolism of the new wing strikes a balance between the international and the local.
[Architect's statement]

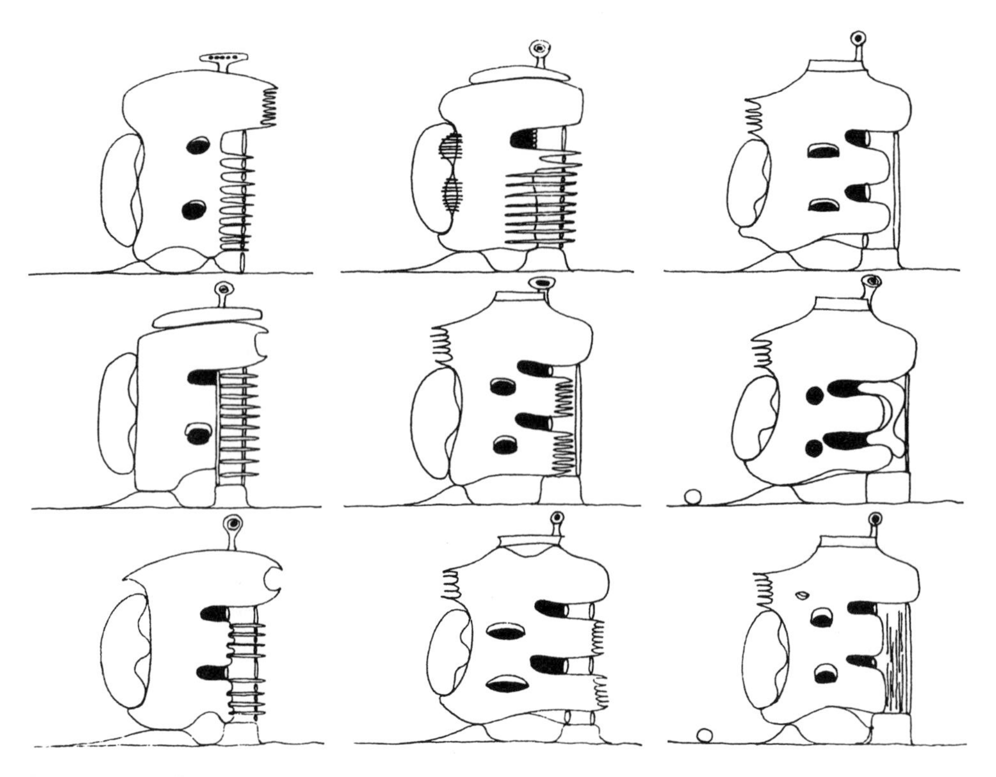

Elevation studies

Sketch diagrams: The Smiling Lion, Mozambique, Africa
Medium: Ink
Courtesy of Amancio Guedes, Architect

Many of my architectural ideas originate in drawings that are common to my painting and sculpture. Others are paraphrases or distorted quotations from other artists' works and ideas. Some originate in other kinds of sights and visions that fascinate and worry me over a span of time or remain always within me. I believe that buildings grow out of each other, that each artist invents his own precursors, that there is an incessant dialogue with many pasts.
[ARCHITECT'S STATEMENT]

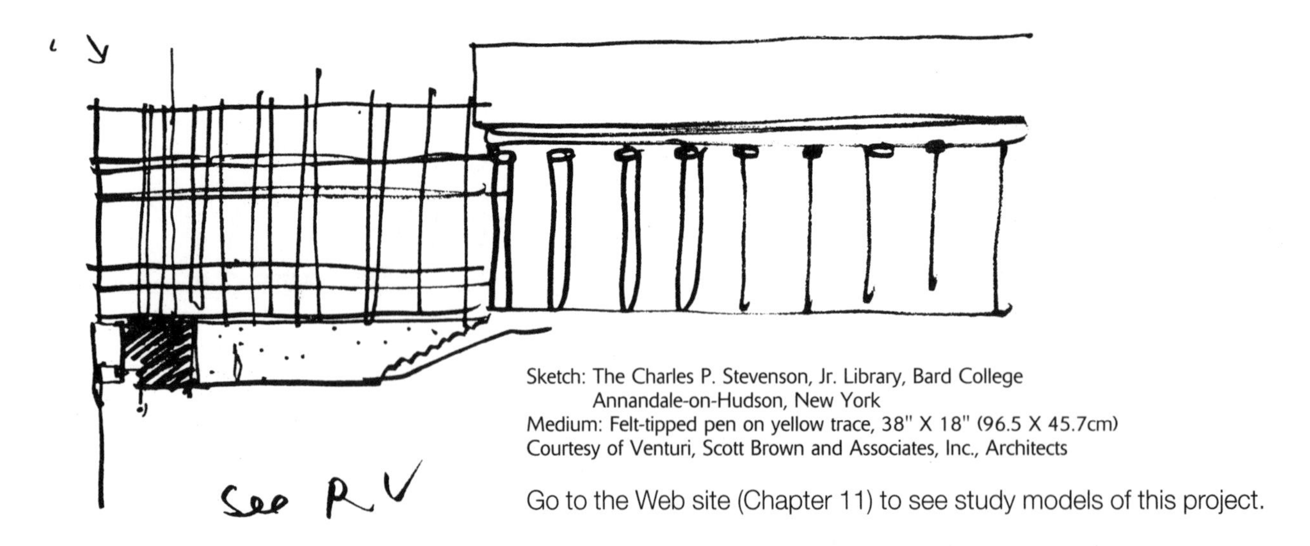

Sketch: The Charles P. Stevenson, Jr. Library, Bard College
Annandale-on-Hudson, New York
Medium: Felt-tipped pen on yellow trace, 38" X 18" (96.5 X 45.7cm)
Courtesy of Venturi, Scott Brown and Associates, Inc., Architects

Go to the Web site (Chapter 11) to see study models of this project.

Sketch studies like this one usually focus on one element of the whole design. This sketch represents the contrasting but evolving rhythms combined within the whole composition of the front facade. The rhythm of the original Classical building is consistent. The new wing inflects toward the old via a crescendo within its metal frame configuration.
[ARCHITECT'S STATEMENT]

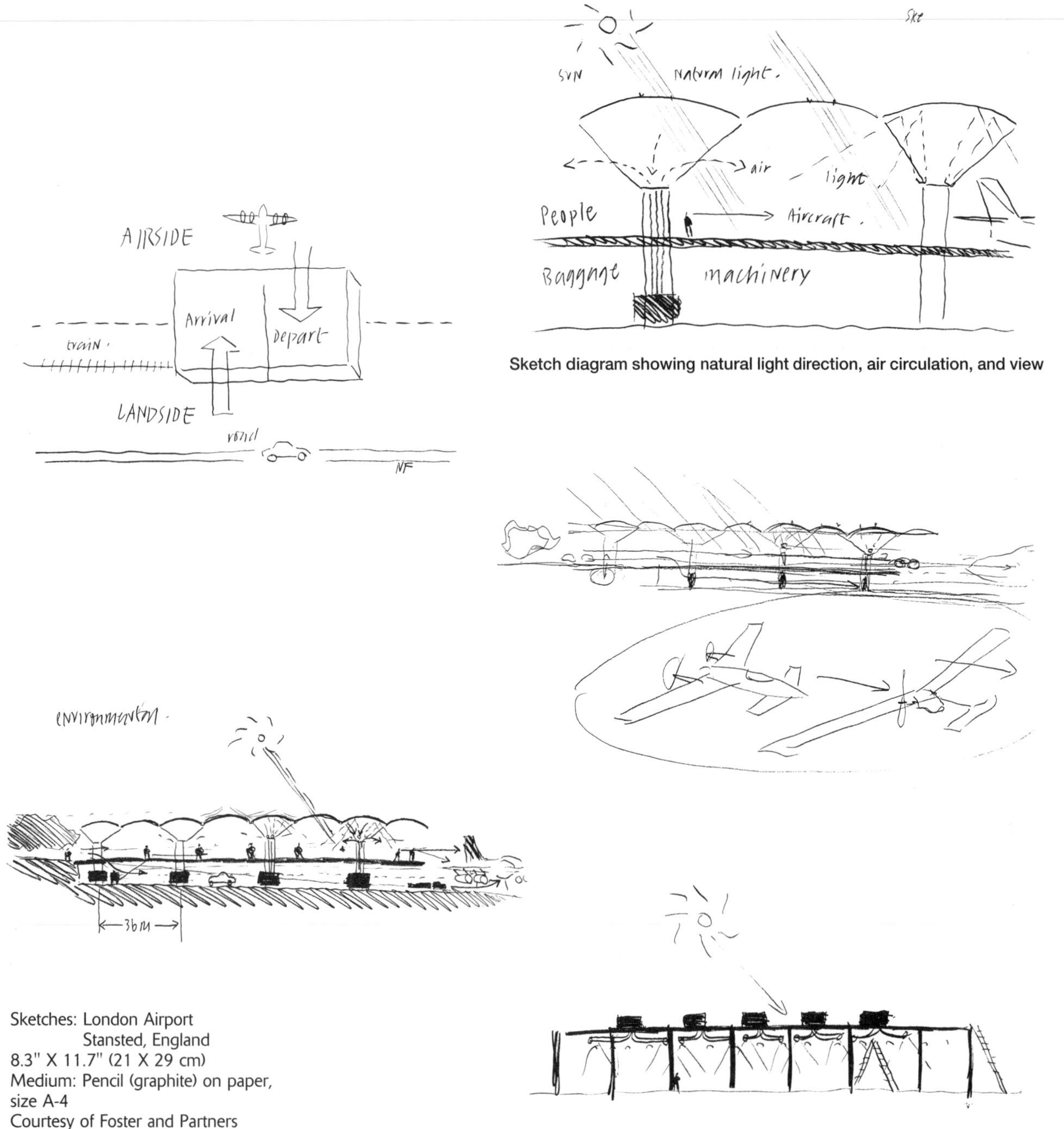

Sketch diagram showing natural light direction, air circulation, and view

Sketches: London Airport
Stansted, England
8.3" X 11.7" (21 X 29 cm)
Medium: Pencil (graphite) on paper, size A-4
Courtesy of Foster and Partners
Drawn by Lord Foster of Thames Bank

With many of the sketches here, I was trying to explain our proposals for the International Terminal at Stansted, London's new third airport. We had drawn inspiration from the early days of flying, when airfields were very simple affairs. There was always a clear airside and landside, so you were never in any doubt about where you were. To depart, you walked toward the aircraft, which was an enjoyable part of the travel experience—there was no need for signs or complex level changes. The arrival sequence was the same straightforward process in reverse.
[ARCHITECT'S STATEMENT]

Lord Foster usually does all of his sketches in an A-4 sketchbook. His conceptual sketches are done by hand, but sometimes computer drawings are used as a guide.

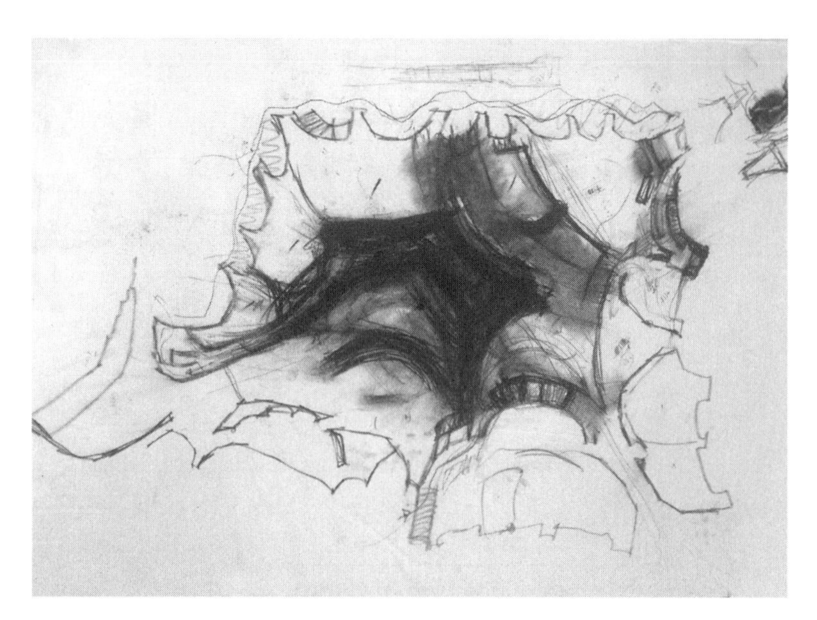

Sketches: Kaleva Church, ground floor
Tampere, Finland
45" × 29" (114.3 × 73.7 cm)
Media: Charcoal and crayon on sketch paper
Sketches by Reima Pietilä
Courtesy of the Pietilä Archive, Helsinki

Photo: Kaleva Church interior, 1966
Courtesy of Raili Pietilä

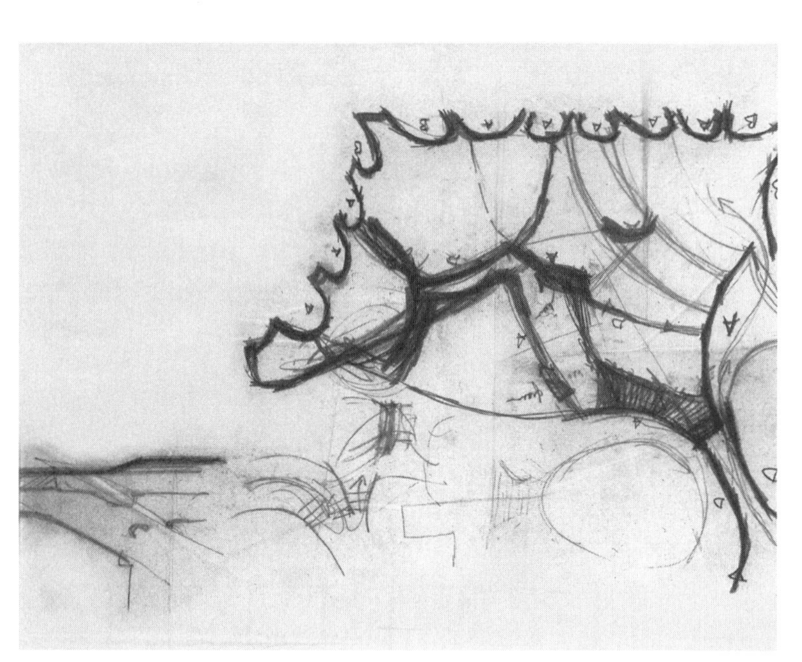

A diagram with a photograph is very telling, because it shows whether the character of the sketch is evident in the actual building (see pp. 478–79).

Perhaps many modernistic designs should be grateful for this thin, unqualified sketch paper. The aesthetic expression of architectural integrity or totality can also be seen to derive from the skillful techniques of transparent designing. These sketches here are merely a sample from hundreds, but it is still possible to note how through these sketches the building grows on the drafting table. These sketches are conceptual tools on the way to becoming objects, and not in themselves detached objects like an artist's graphics. I would advise everyone not to break this vital growth link between these sketches and the actual building they become.
[Architect's statement]

In classic examples of conceptual sketching, such as Erich Mendelsohn's drawing for the Einstein Tower (left) at Potsdam, Germany (ca. 1920) or Ludwig Mies van der Rohe's sketches for the Barcelona Pavilion (ca. 1929), we again see how initial impressions are often precursors to, or contain the essence of, the subsequent, more developed design. The same connection is seen in Frank Gehry's conceptual sketch for his Stata Center at the Massachusetts Institute of Technology and the completed building complex.

In addition to ink-on-paper conceptual sketches, Gehry works extensively with study models. His office is filled with models (each project done at different scales) and looks like a sculptor's studio. Due to the complexity of his designs, the real-space models are quickly digitized so that design modifications can be made on computers.

For background on the architecture and ideas of Frank Gehry, see Sydney Pollack's documentary film *Sketches of Frank Gehry.* Also refer to the Web site (Chapters 12 and 13) on interfacing manual with digital mediums.

© William W. P. Chan

Sketch and photo: The Ray and Maria Stata Center for Computer, Information, and Intelligence Sciences
Cambridge, Massachusetts
Medium: Ink on paper
Sketch by Frank Gehry
Courtesy of Gehry Partners, Architects

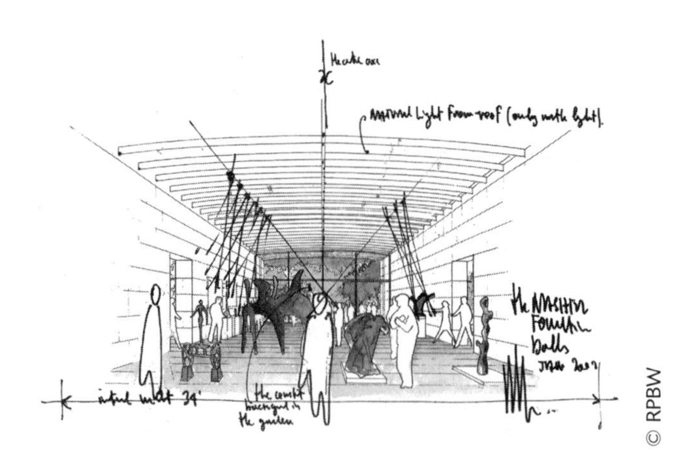

© RPBW

© Dick Davison

© RPBW

© Dick Davison

© Dick Davison

Conceptual perspectives: The Nasher Sculpture Center (1999–2003)
Gallery Pavilion and Gallery Space,
Dallas, Texas
Medium: Watercolor
Courtesy of the Renzo Piano Building Workshop, Architects; E. Baglietto, Partner in Charge
Client: The Nasher Foundation Consultants: Peter Walker & Partners; Ove Arup & Partners; Interloop A/D; Beck Architecture
General Contractor: HCBeck

These quick conceptual sketches were done to convey the spatial quality of the interior of this sculpture center. Quick visualization studies using one-point perspectives are particularly good for capturing the feeling and essence of a space. Handwritten notes were used on the interior sketch to clarify design issues. Note the use of simplified human figures: For rapid visualization studies, details on people are not necessary.

© Christian Richters

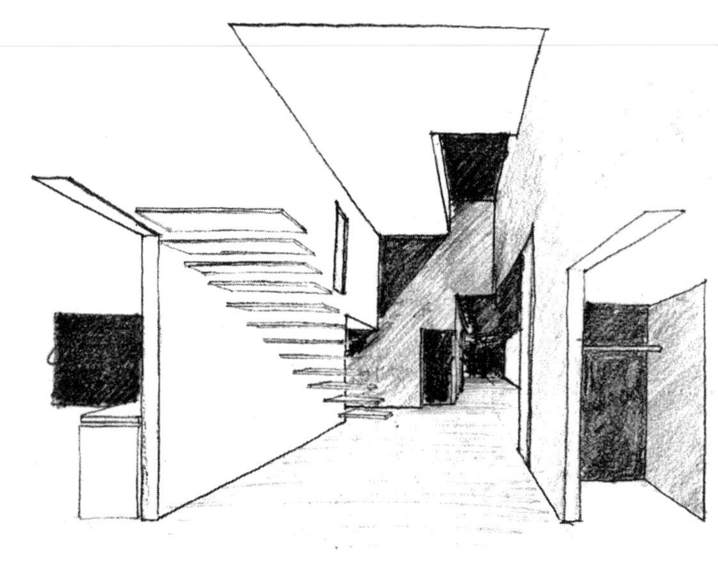
Entrance hall

© Christian Richters

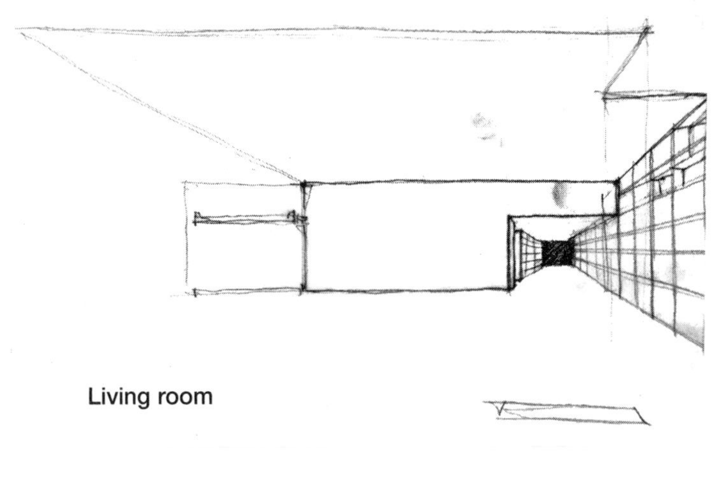
Living room

Conceptual perspectives: Lubbering residence
Herzebrock, Germany
Medium: Pencil with colored pencil
Courtesy of Drewes + Strengearchitekten

© Christian Richters

This quick manual pencil drawing (top right) was accentuated and highlighted with colored pencil. Instead of a rectangular frame, an endless outline was used to show the openness of this porous entrance hall. The space is perforated in all directions in order to keep the space flowing.
[Architect's Statement]

Design sketches of interiors attempt to show the volumetric spatial quality of the conceived form in the most descriptive way. Freehand drawn perspectives (especially frontal, one-point perspectives that emphasize depth of space) are commonly the architect's first choice for speculative representation.

Schematic design study using freehand sketches and computer 3-D models. Design for a dwelling within a bridge. Freehand pen-and-ink and felt-tipped marker drawings. Computer 3-D models with form-Z software.

A freehand sketch provides fluidity of design at the very early stages of idea generation. A computer 3-D model helps to test the schematic idea and develop it into something with more concrete parameters.

[PROFESSOR'S STATEMENT]

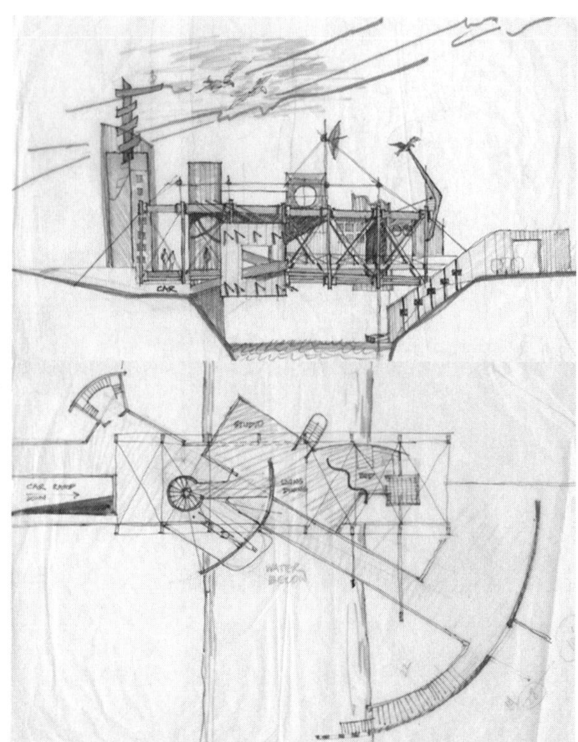

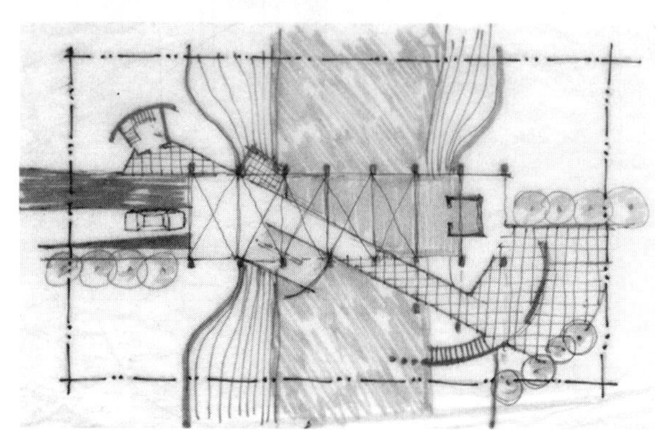

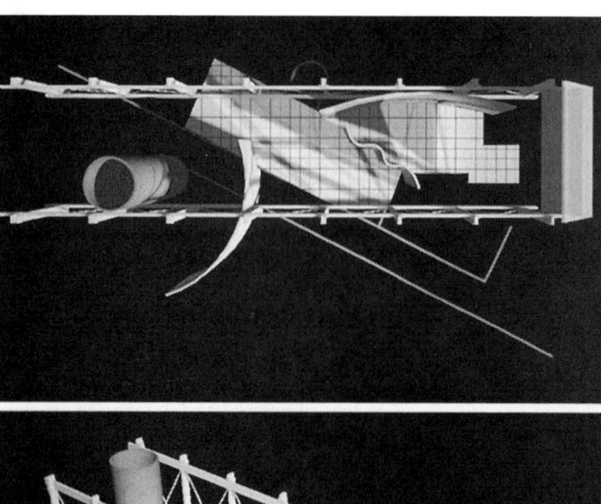

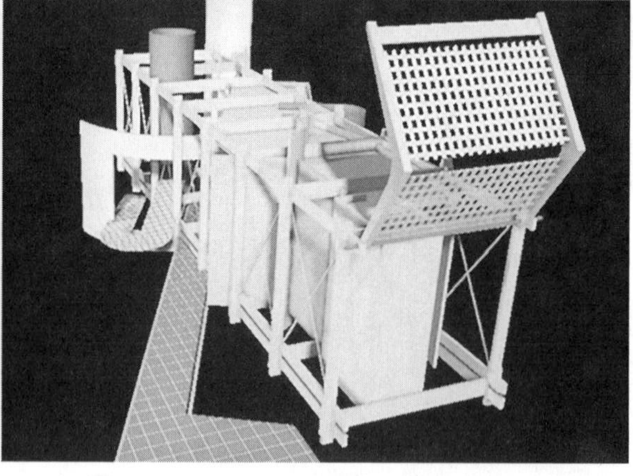

Sketches and conceptual models: Dwelling within a Bridge
Courtesy of Mohammed Saleh Uddin, Ph.D.
Professor, Environmental Design
University of Missouri–Columbia

A photograph of a model can provide a diagrammatic understanding.

Computer modeling allows you to create an infinite number of orientations, as well as to adjust shape and size easily. Digital-modeling programs like form-Z, 3DVIZ, SketchUp, and IronCAD offer three-dimensional features for diagramming that hand drawing alone cannot. For example, variable colorations and transparencies done digitally can add qualities to an image that can't be matched by hand.

These images show computer 3-D study models and photographs of the completed front facade and interior stair details.

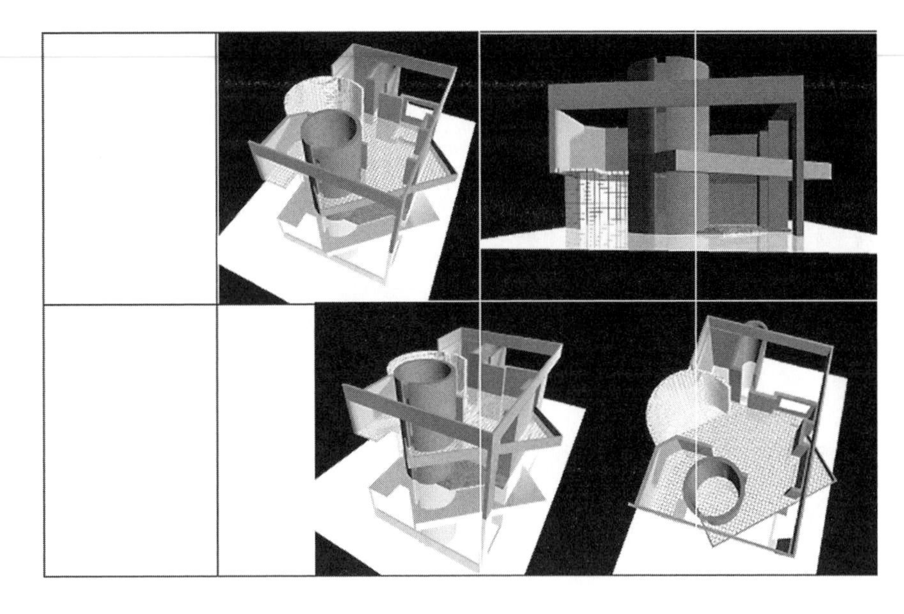

One-family residence with the option of vertical expansion, accommodating privacy of the current design. Restricted site boundaries forced the design to be sculpted from a cubic mass volume. Subtracted mass in the front protects the glazed wall that counterbalances the double-height void in the dining area, sucking air inside the building and facilitating natural airflow year-round. All openings were carefully designed (most openings pushed inward to avoid direct exposure to climatic extremes) to respond to the environmental conditions of the region's hot, humid climate.
[PROFESSOR'S STATEMENT]

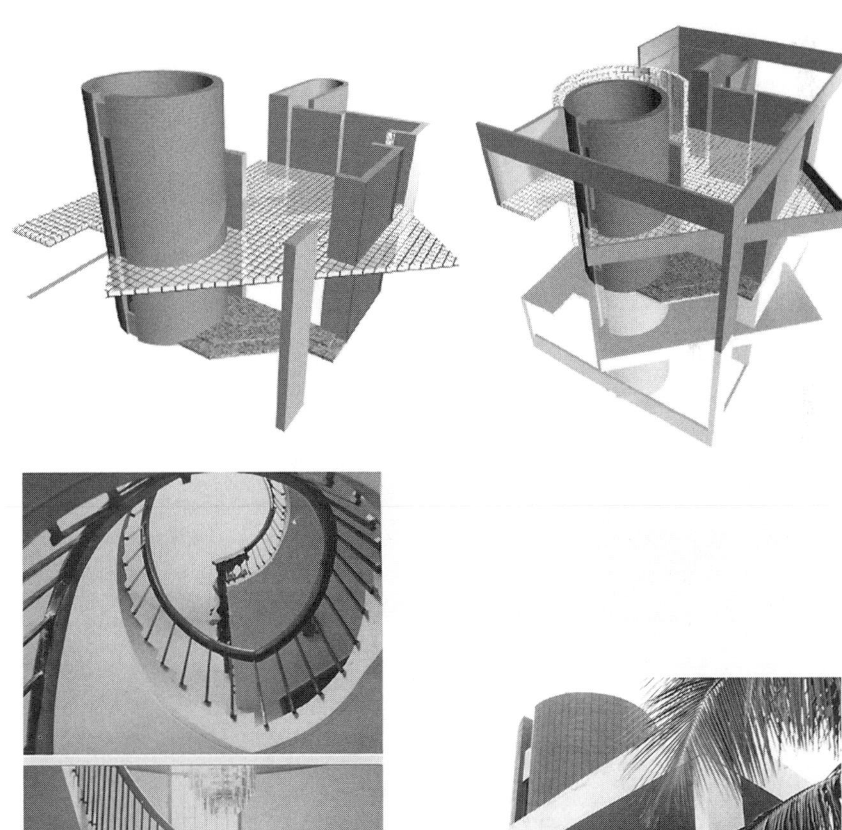

Conceptual models: Rahman residence, Dhaka, Bangladesh
Courtesy of Mohammed Saleh Uddin, Ph.D.
Professor, Environmental Design
University of Missouri–Columbia

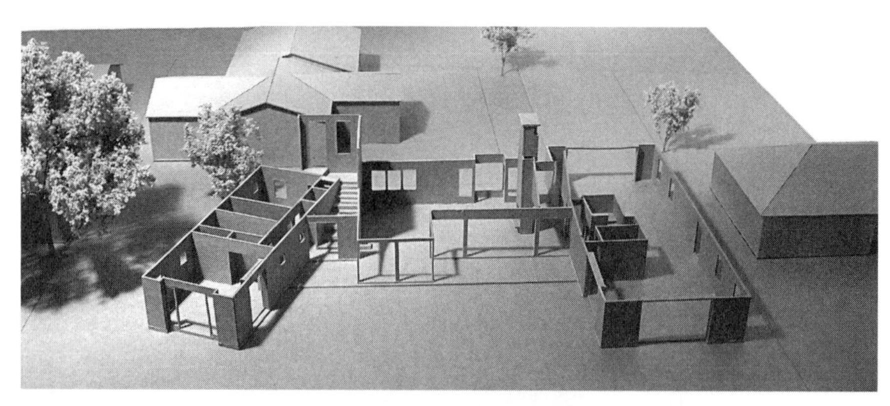

Residence (this and facing page)
Half Moon Bay, California
Cardboard model: Walter Evonuk
Computer illustrations: Walter Evonuk and Masha Barmina
Medium for model materials: Chipboard, wire, and foam
Medium for drawings: Ink on tracing paper
Medium for digital illustrations: ArchiCAD 8
Principal in Charge: Mark English
Courtesy of Mark English Architects

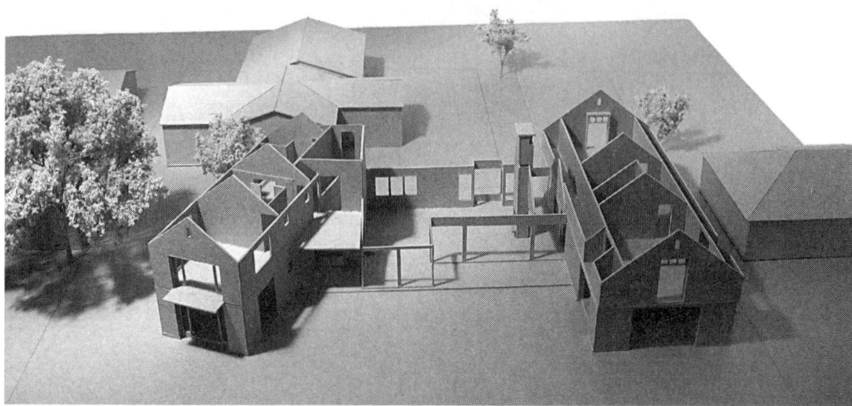

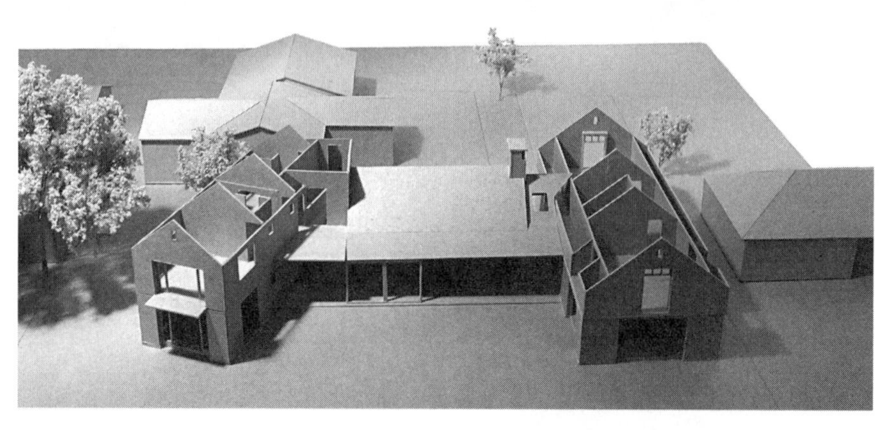

To design and communicate with clients, we often employ several different methods of visual representation. Physical models are helpful in refining the massing and proportion of a building. Their tactile nature often makes them an essential tool when communicating the big picture to our clients. When a model can be dissected to reveal an interior layout, its usefulness is compounded.
[ARCHITECT'S STATEMENT]

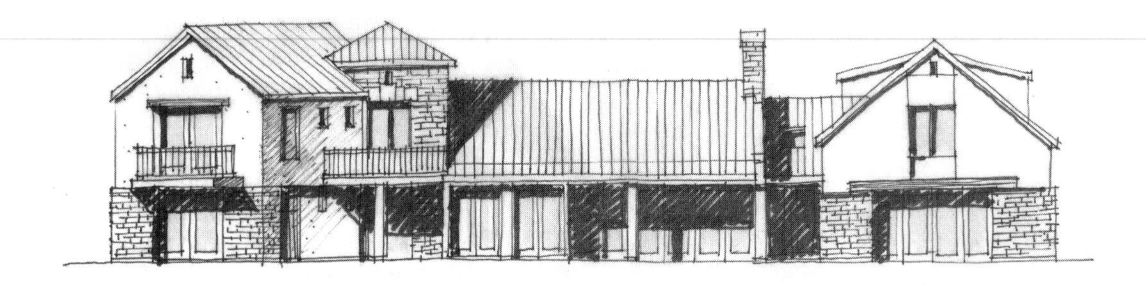

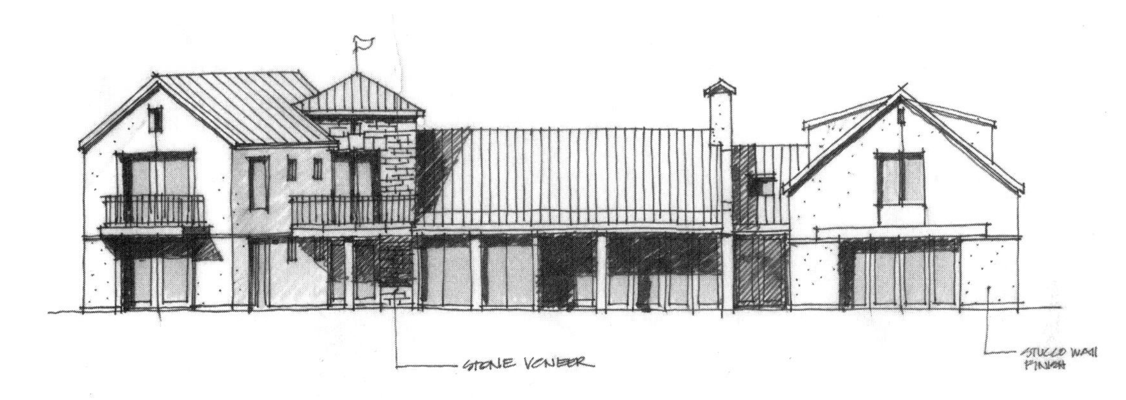

Sketches like these are extremely useful for quick design work. In this case, we were experimenting with various finish materials. Several options were represented while expending relatively few resources in time or materials.
[ARCHITECT'S STATEMENT]

Computer modeling is a vital design tool in our office. These models are useful in the ways physical models are, but can be made much more precise and offer more options for detail, including realistic coloring and textures. While often time-consuming, 3-D modeling can be made affordable by using a program like ArchiCAD 8. Floor plans, sections, and elevations can be extracted from the model and used to speed the production of construction documents.
[ARCHITECT'S STATEMENT]

*The general program requirements were evolved in plan and section initially and continually developed during the course of massing/*partí *study. The sketches below are just a small part of a series done for daily brainstorming sessions to develop the appropriate* partí *to accommodate the technology theme and reconcile the site geometry; in this case, twin curves engaging each other in a high-tech "yin-yang" composition.*

A quick 3-D AutoCAD model was developed for the variations and used as a base for the spontaneous black Prismacolor pencil sketches. Both scaled elevational views and aerial perspectives were used in conjunction with myriad quick foam study models as a basis for discussion and review. The design team was certainly not shy about generating as many options as possible for study and evaluation. Note the series of vignette sketches of how we might engage the sky plane with an appropriate communications/technology gesture.

[DESIGN ILLUSTRATOR'S STATEMENT]

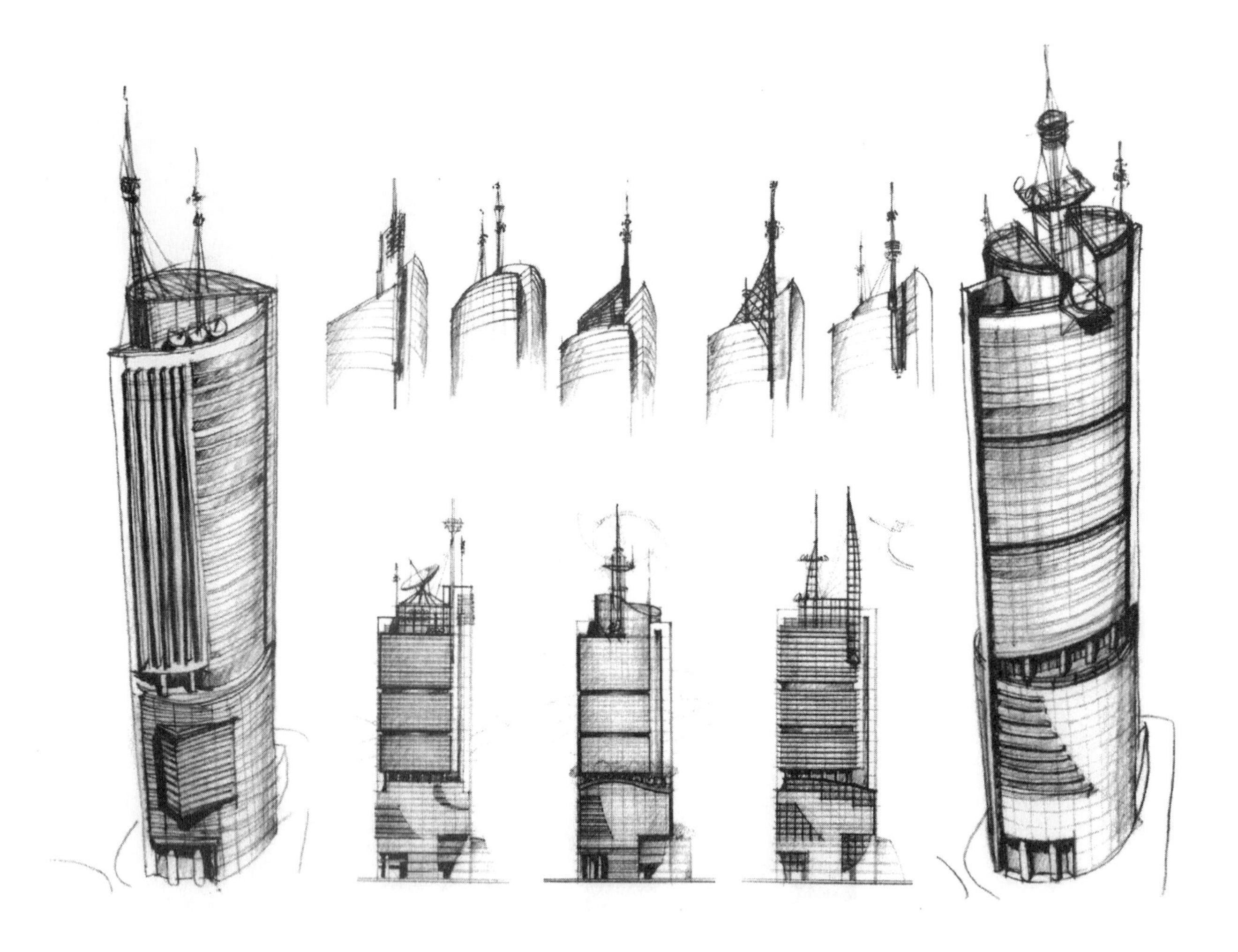

Images: Communications Center Office Tower Competition,
Shanghai, China
Courtesy of KMD, San Francisco: Design Office
Herbert McLaughlin, Design Principal
Lawrence K. Leong, Design Illustrator
Architectural Concept Imaging, San Francisco

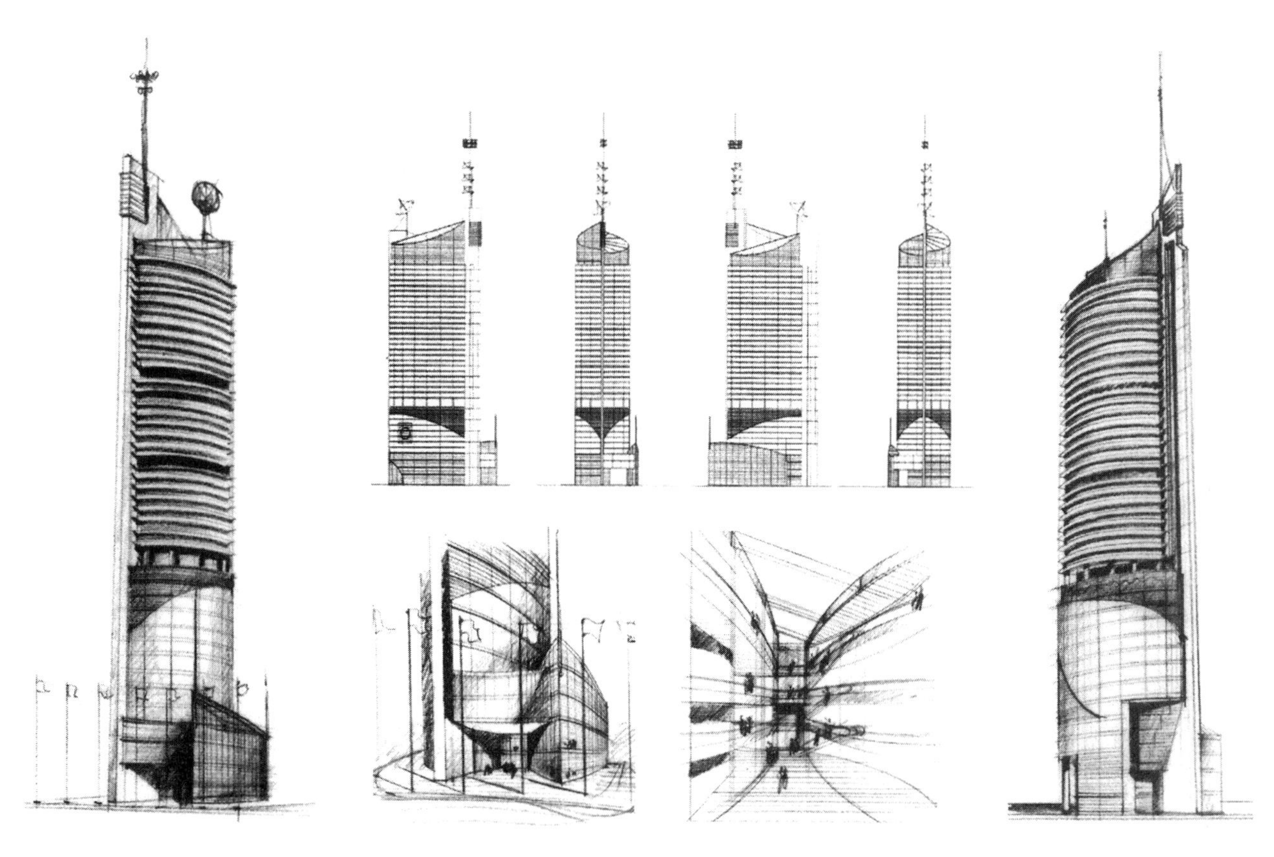

Images: Communications Center Office Tower Competition,
Shanghai, China
Courtesy of KMD, San Francisco: Design Office
Herbert McLaughlin, Design Principal
Lawrence K. Leong, Design Illustrator
Architectural Concept Imaging, San Francisco

Once a partí *direction was decided upon, we refined the black Prismacolor 3-D sketch study vignettes with a concentration on the eye-level experience and viewpoints of key locations. I used AutoCAD elevations to formalize the design conclusions and passed them on to the design team as a base for further refinement and final presentation.*
[DESIGN ILLUSTRATOR'S STATEMENT]

Through the end of the twentieth century and into the beginning of the twenty-first, some have thought that conventional software impedes the creative aspects of visualization in the very early stages of the schematic design process. The inability to replicate the ease and immediacy with which architects and designers have made conceptual hand-drawn sketches for countless design projects has been one of the major barriers in the development of computer technology for architecture. New software applications, such as @Last Software's SketchUp, IronCAD, etc., which can mimic hand-sketched drawings, are now emerging to make design thinking with a computer comparable in its fluidity and spontaneity to freehand conceptual sketching.

10

Presentation Formats

BASICS 491
BASICS APPLIED 502

A fine set of presentation drawings for the purpose of graphic communication is invaluable in architect–client or designer–client relationships. An architectural drawing presentation usually includes conceptual diagrams or sketches, a site plan, floor plans, exterior elevations, site sections, building sections, axonometrics, obliques, and perspectives. The initial stage of the design-drawing process is involved with conceptual diagrams and conceptual drawings. As the design concept evolves, more formal methods of presentation are needed. These presentation formats, whether conventional or avant-garde in approach, must effectively communicate to the targeted audience.

The intent of this chapter is to illustrate various presentation formats with respect to traditional wall presentations. Explore the excellent books listed in the Bibliography for their coverage of other presentation modes (slides, reports, models, etc.).

The following are some of the important terms and concepts you will learn:

Presentation formats	Transparaline	Transobligue
Transmetric	Composite drawings	Competition panels

By viewing a large number of professional competition drawings, you will develop new and fresh ideas on how to handle your own presentations.

Presentation Formats

Topic: Architectural Presentations

Hart 2000.

Miralles 1997.

Topic: Architectural Competition Presentations (Examples)

Competitions magazine

Topic: Portfolios

Mitton 2003.

Linton and Rost 2000.

Chapter Overview

After studying this chapter, you will understand how wall presentations are laid out. You will learn about composite integrated presentations. You will be able to glean ideas for organizing your own single-panel or multipanel presentations. For continued study, refer to Ching's *Architectural Graphics.*

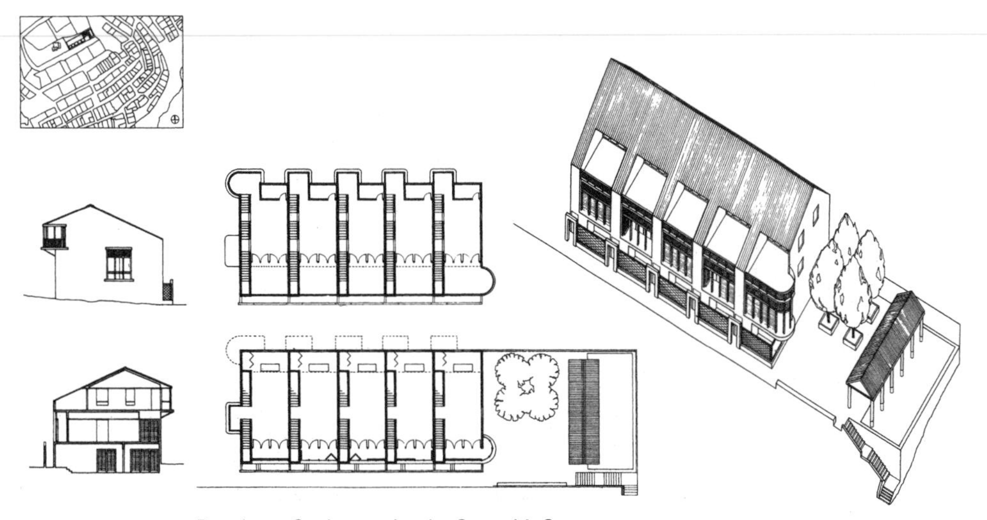

Drawings: Student project by Susan M. Stern
Row housing, Barcelona, Spain
Courtesy of Washington University School of Architecture, St. Louis, Missouri

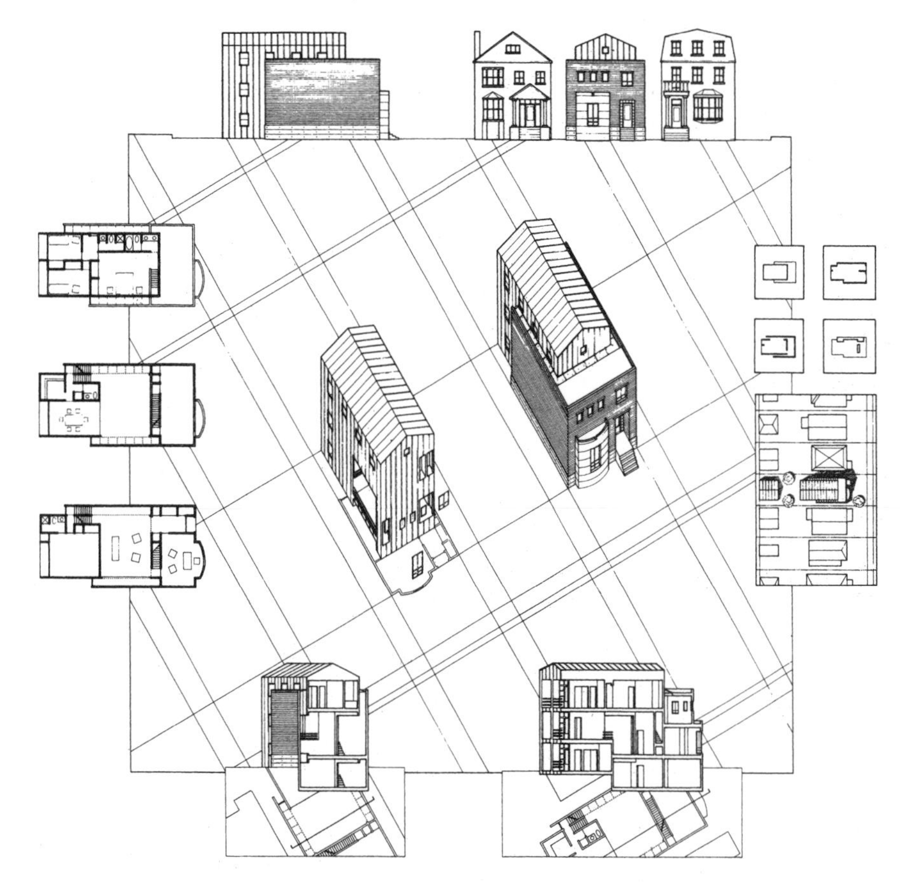

Drawing: Student project by Doug Dolezal
Central West End townhouse
Courtesy of Washington University School of Architecure, St. Louis, Missouri

The primary goal of an architectural presentation is to effectively present design concepts. Implemented design concepts should be drawn and organized in an orderly, structured **format.** Over the years, architects and designers have used many different formats, with the ultimate goal always being the same. This page shows both traditional and more conceptual presentation methods for graphic communications.

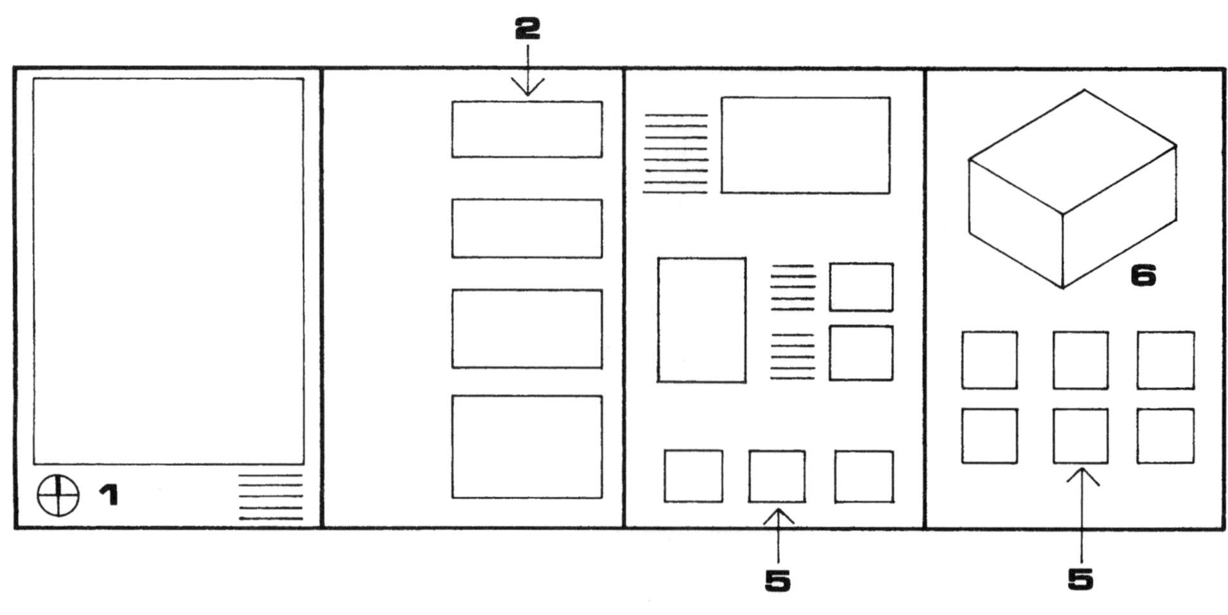

- If possible, orient the site plan with the north arrow up (**1**).
- With adequate vertical space, orient floor plans and elevations to fit in an aligned vertical order (**2**).
- Similarly, floor plans and elevations can relate horizontally if there is adequate horizontal space (**3**).
- Building sections should relate vertically or horizontally to floor plans and elevations in an aligned sequence (**4**).
- Details and notes should be grouped in a visually organized manner (**5**).
- Paralines/perspectives are the cohesive and integrative drawings that help to unify the presentation (**6**).
- The generally accepted order for exhibited drawings is left to right and top to bottom.

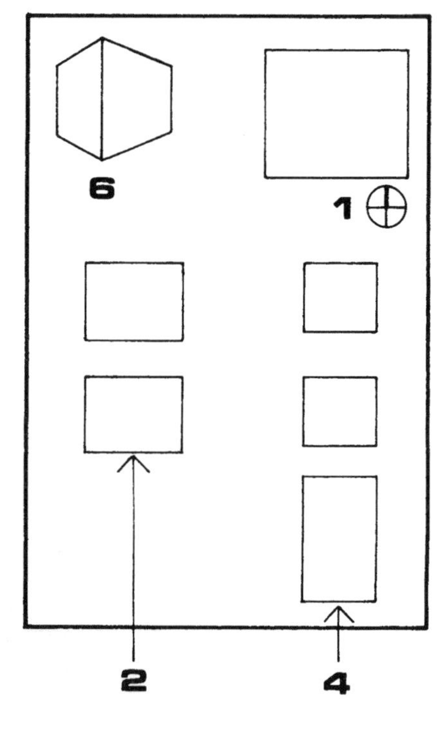

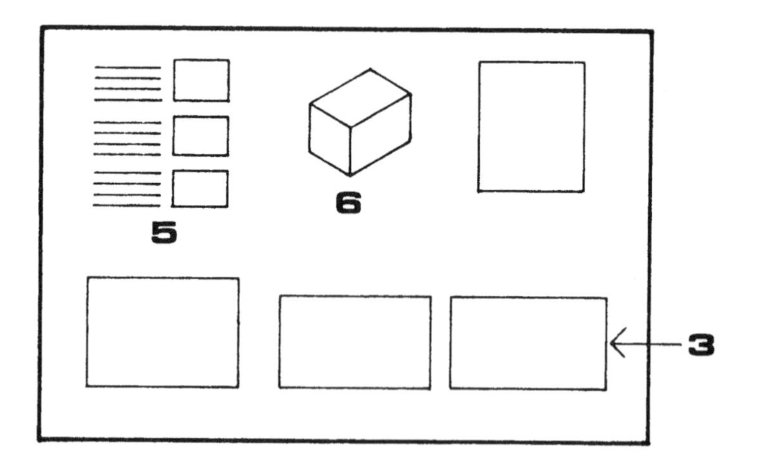

The primary architectural drawings were introduced in the section on conventional orthogonal terminology. By themselves, these drawings have little importance. However, when combined as a totality in a **presentation format,** these drawings become a strong **communicative** tool. Architectural presentations are commonly done on sequential sheets or boards. The organization and composition of drawing elements is flexible as long as there is a thread of continuity and unity, as well as a conceptual focus.

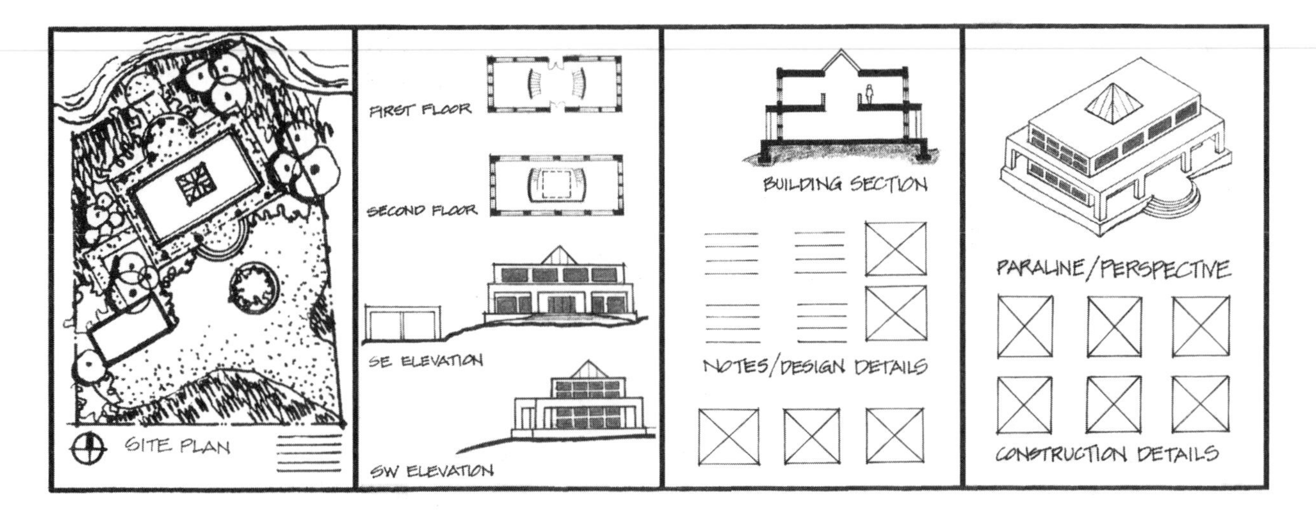

Wall presentations have the advantage of allowing a large audience to view all the drawings in context of one another. The primary components in an architectural presentation are the site plan, floor plans, elevations, sections, and paralines/perspectives. An effective presentation unifying these elements will generally require consistency in scale, orientation, and presentation technique/medium. The size of the audience and the viewing distance are normally the determinants for the choice of scale and the type of medium used.

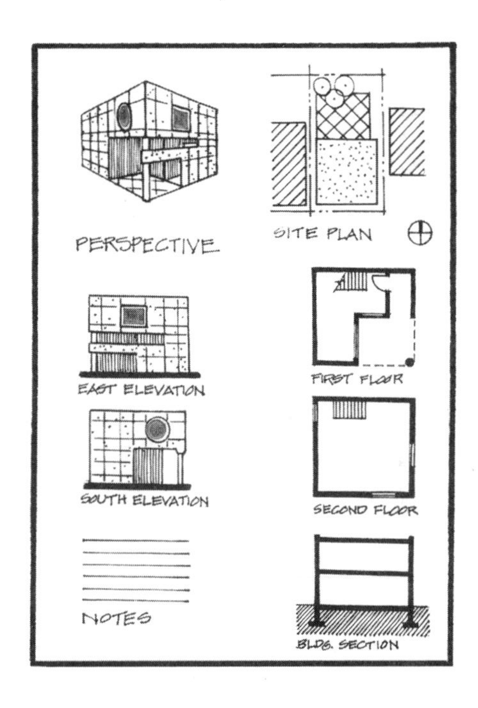

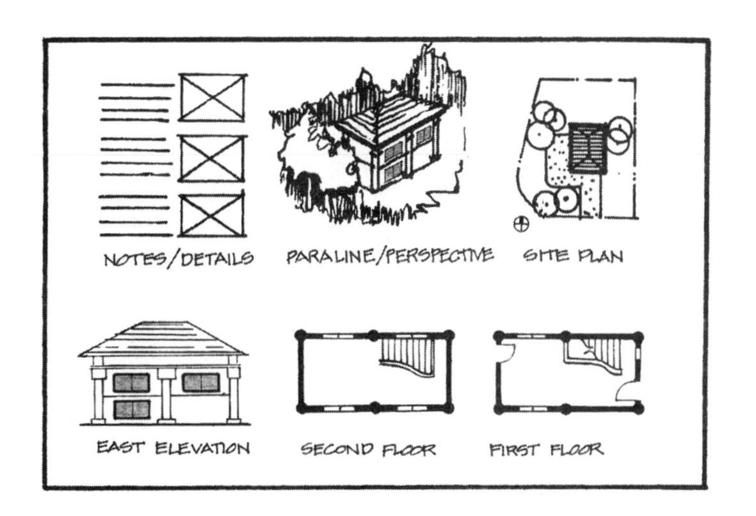

Architectural wall presentation formats are most effective when organized vertically or horizontally. The examples shown are (1) vertically oriented boards or sheets that flow and read horizontally (top row); (2) a horizontally oriented one-board or one-sheet presentation that reads as a total composition (left); and (3) a vertically oriented one-board or one-sheet presentation that reads as a total composition (right). It is often helpful to orient the site plan and floor plans in the same direction. The wall presentation is commonly supplemented with scale models, slides, reports, and the Internet (for schools, private offices, and the lay public).

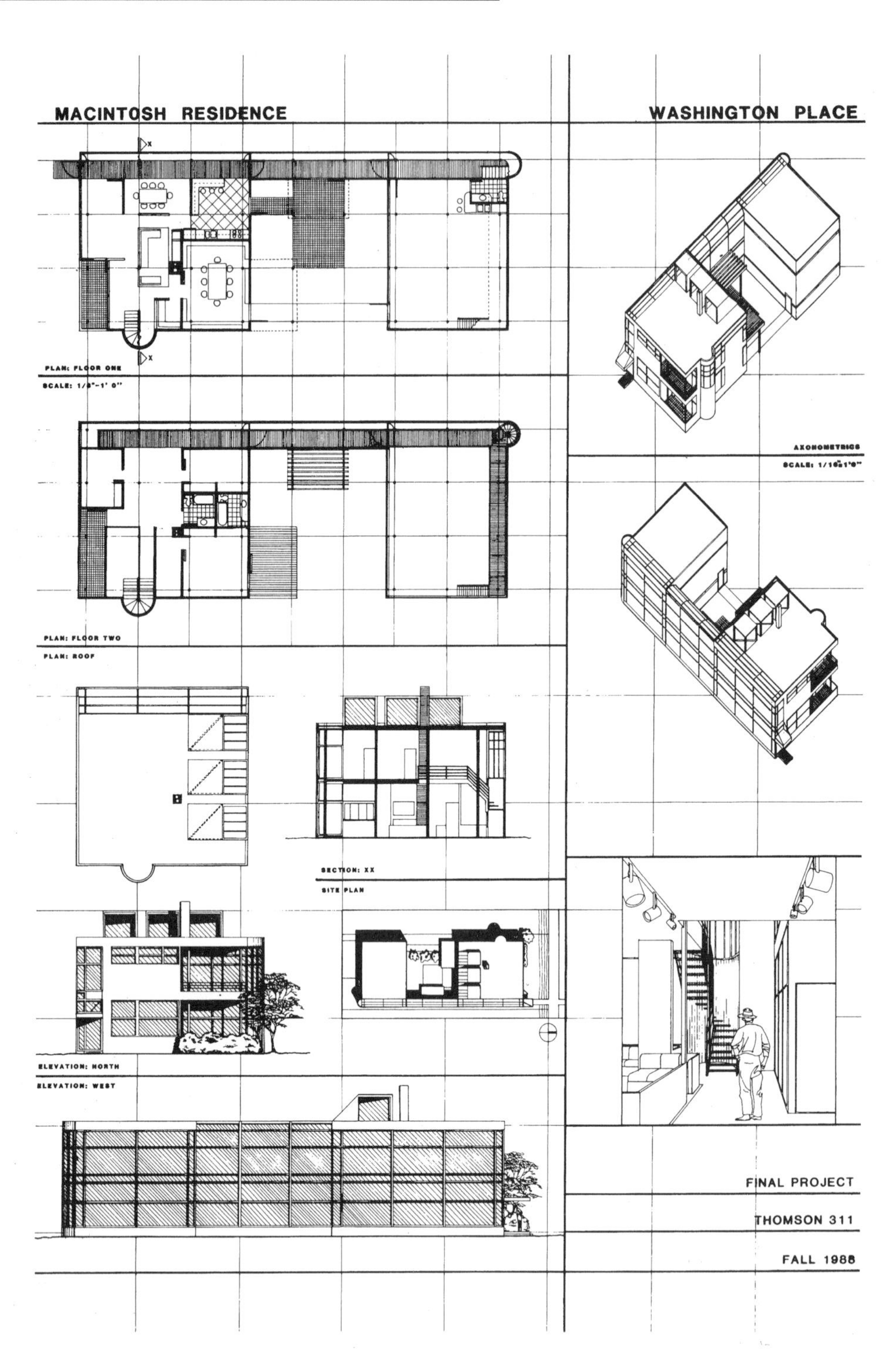

Drawing: Student project by Vaughn Dierks
Macintosh house, St. Louis, Missouri
Courtesy of Washington University School of Architecture, St. Louis, Missouri

This presentation was effectively laid out using a **grid** format. The grid is extremely effective in helping to organize all the drawings and bits of information that go into a comprehensive presentation. The grid should be lightly drawn. The amount of negative space between the drawings is extremely important. Too much space results in drawings that "float"; too little results in a congested layout. As with any artistic composition, the proper figure–background balancing is crucial for all drawings to exist in harmony.

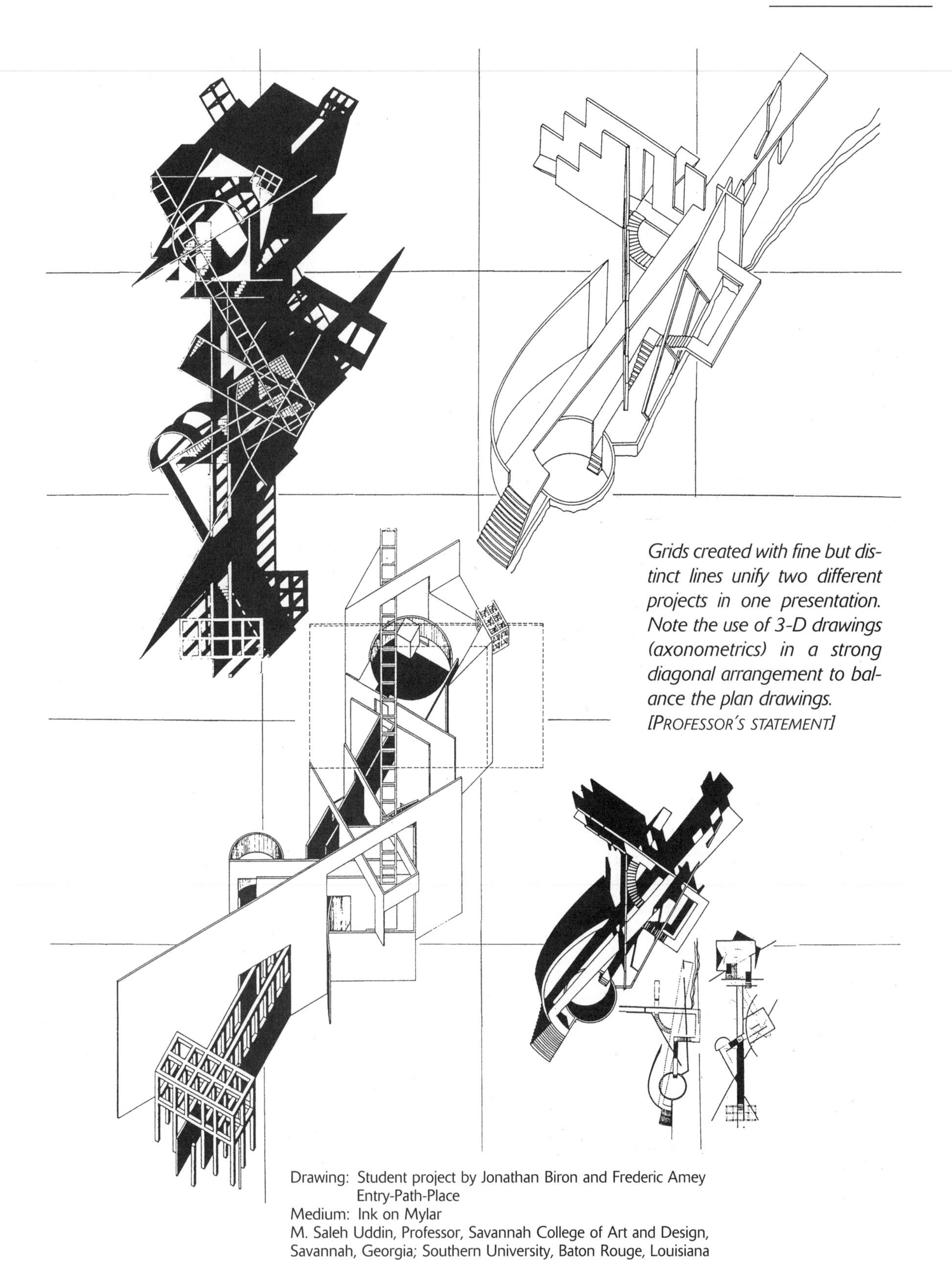

Grids created with fine but distinct lines unify two different projects in one presentation. Note the use of 3-D drawings (axonometrics) in a strong diagonal arrangement to balance the plan drawings. [*PROFESSOR'S STATEMENT*]

Drawing: Student project by Jonathan Biron and Frederic Amey
Entry-Path-Place
Medium: Ink on Mylar
M. Saleh Uddin, Professor, Savannah College of Art and Design, Savannah, Georgia; Southern University, Baton Rouge, Louisiana

Grids give an organized feeling to the multiple images normally used in a presentation. Most grid presentations are set up using squares, but rectangles can also be used. Graphics and text may be placed across or within the grid lines.

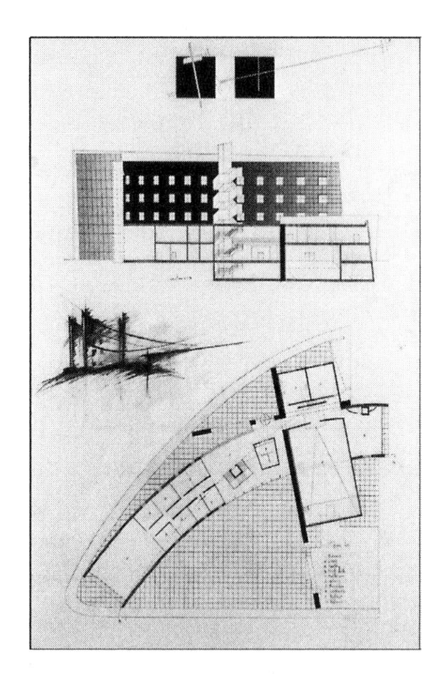

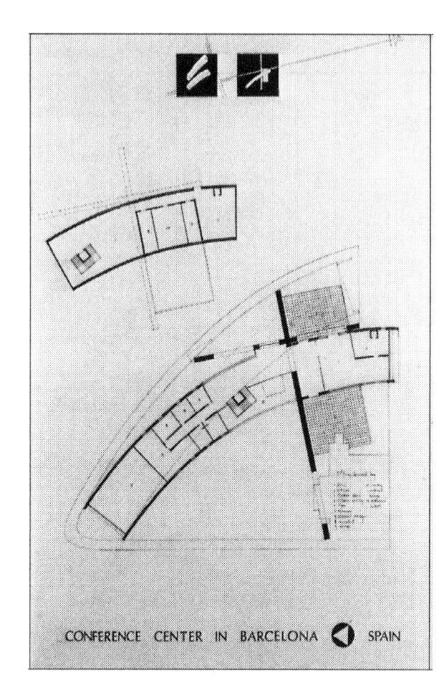

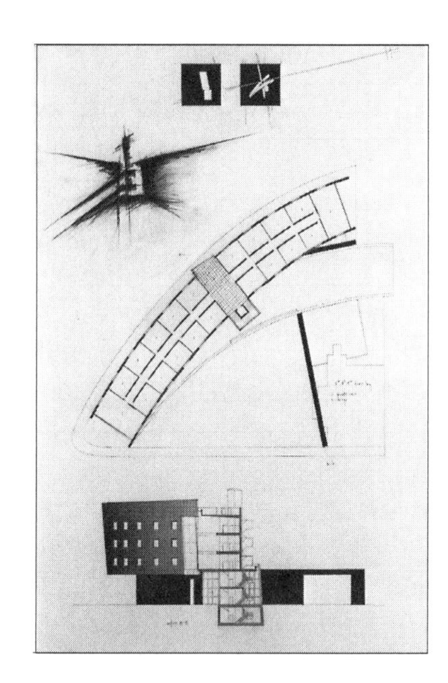

Competition drawings: Student project by Mohd Fadzir Mohd Suhaimi
Barcelona Tile Competition, Barcelona, Spain
Courtesy of Washington University School of Architecture, St. Louis, Missouri

Before the 1980s, a typical set of presentation drawings would display each drawing (plan, elevation, section, etc.) on a separate panel (also termed sheet or board). The eighties saw a movement toward combining several drawing types into one presentation. Since the eighties and into the twenty-first century, design competitions have become more restrictive in their size requirements. This has led many competitors to experiment with and design innovative new formats. When various drawing types are combined on one panel, it is termed a **composite drawing.**

Letter size for titles or labels and any text for architectural presentations depends on how the drawings will be viewed and used. A design jury (a group of teachers, students, or peers that passes judgment on the material being presented) or client responds to the text at different viewing distances, depending on the purpose of the information. A hierarchy of size is clearly shown on the panel on p. 529. The largest letters are in the title: "The Center for Innovative Technology." Second largest are the labels for the drawing: "Ground-Floor Plan, Principal Floor Plan, Regional Site Plan," etc. Third largest are the room labels. And the smallest in size is the text for the concept statement. Ideally, drawings should speak for themselves; the presence of text should be minimized as much as possible. In general, use the smallest lettering size and the simplest style that is legible from the desired distance. In multipanel presentations, try to keep consistency in format, size, shape, orientation, and style of the drawing images. Panel continuity in the medium used can also help unify your presentation. The illustration above shows a student presentation composed of three panels. The latter part of this chapter will show you many professional multipanel competition drawings.

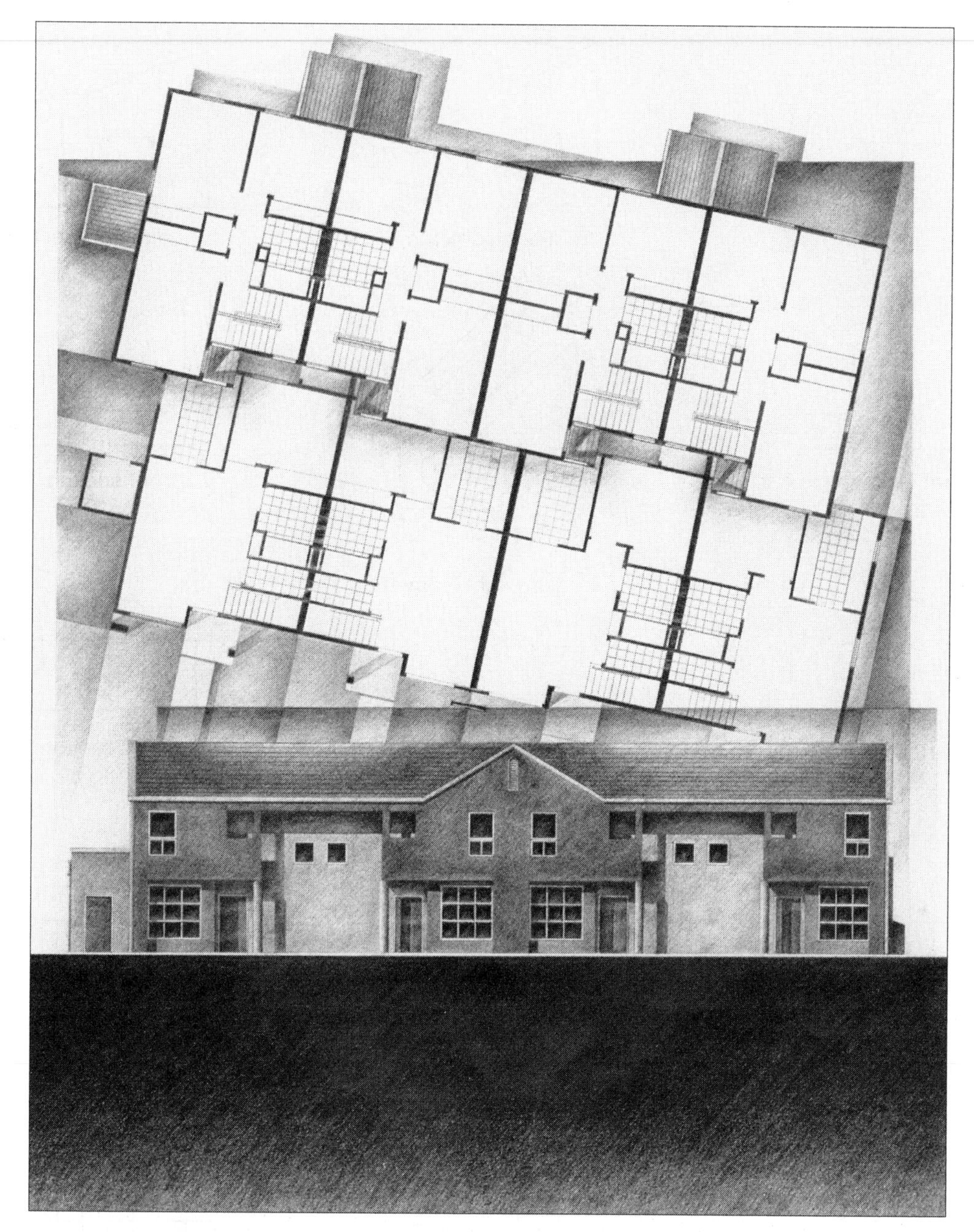

Drawings: Rancho Sespe II, Piru, California
Medium: Pencil
Courtesy of John V. Mutlow, FAIA, Architects

In this composite drawing, the plan and the elevation are composed as one presentation. Care must be taken so that each drawing can be read without losing its clarity. New types of composite drawings using a combination of transparent drawings, superimposed drawings, and hybrid drawings are becoming commonplace in competitions.

The 6B pencil rendition of a two-dimensional elevation with the combination of the dwelling unit floor plans assists in an understanding of the three-dimensional quality of the facade. The design intention is to generate eight different building designs by assembling three unit types to create building identity from unit repetition (the set urban piece). The shade and shadow on the elevation quickly distinguish individual building identity.
[Architect's statement]

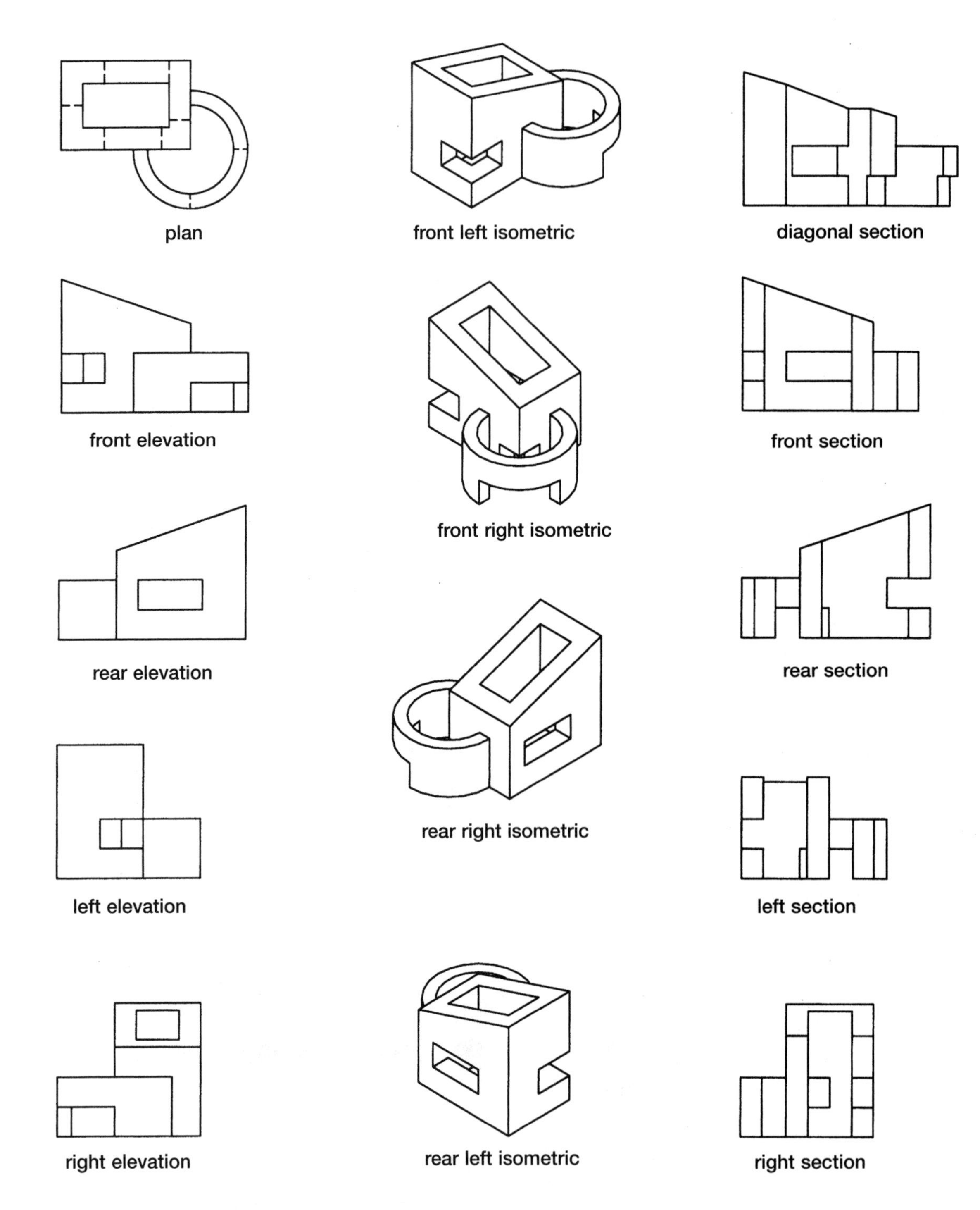

Drawings and subsequent composites designed by Kwok Gorran Tsui,
an architecture graduate of the University of Texas at Austin
Scale: 3/32"=1'0"

Three organizational methods for setting up a composite drawing are shown on the following three pages using the geometric elements on this page. Before designing schematic layouts for a composite drawing, be sure you have accumulated all of the drawing elements and text for the composition. Also determine whether there will be a primary center-of-focus drawing and whether all other drawings will play an equally subordinate role. Examine whether there will be any variation in the scale of the drawings. Think about how to utilize the negative space or background area, as well as how to use framing elements to establish boundaries (real or implied).

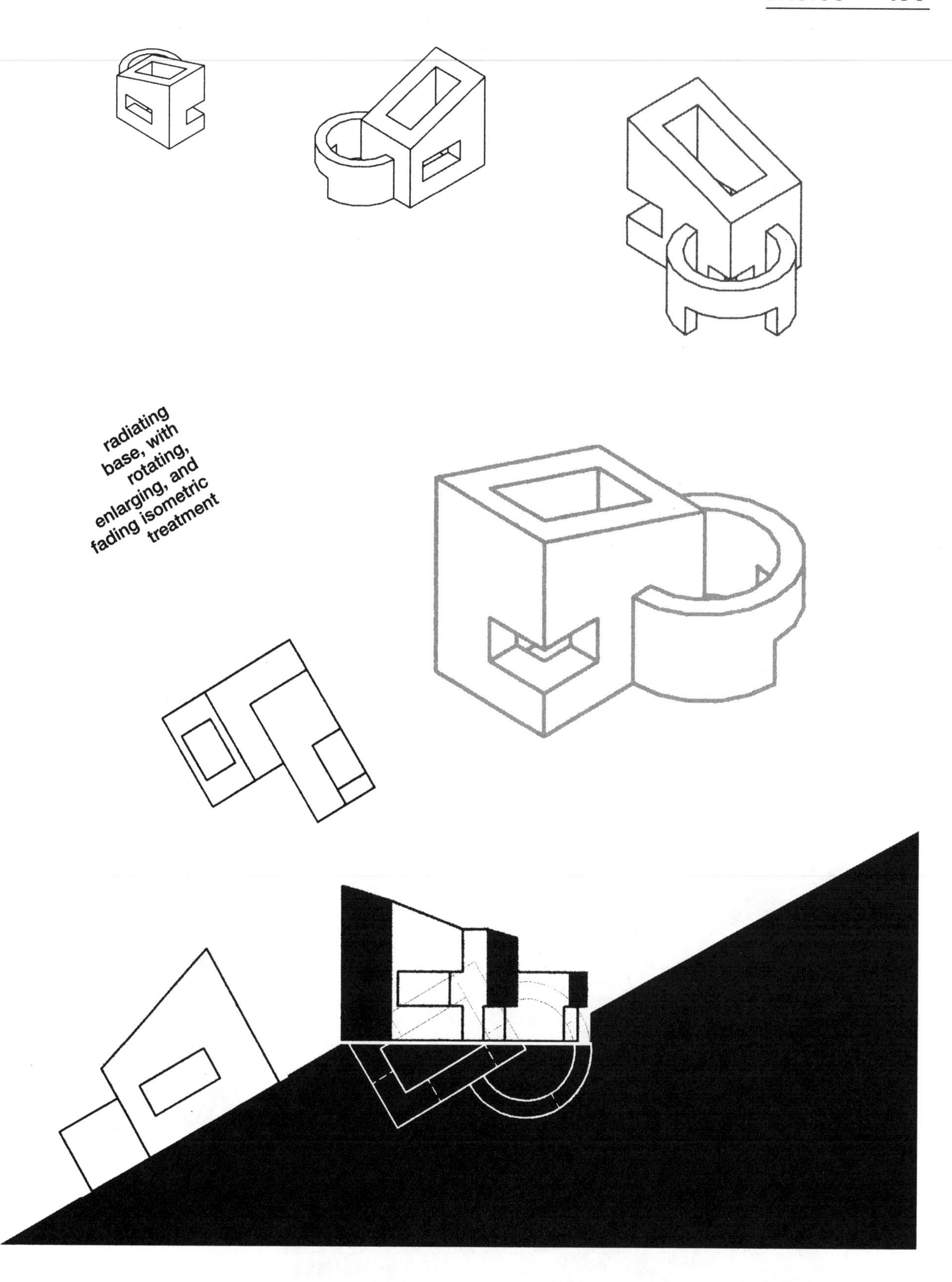

radiating base, with rotating, enlarging, and fading isometric treatment

COMPOSITE DRAWINGS

Paraline drawings like the isometrics shown here are extemely effective in composite integrated presentations. They refer easily to and relate well with orthographic multiview drawings. Perspective drawings can also relate well to multiview drawings, but tend to be more independent (see pp. 538–41).

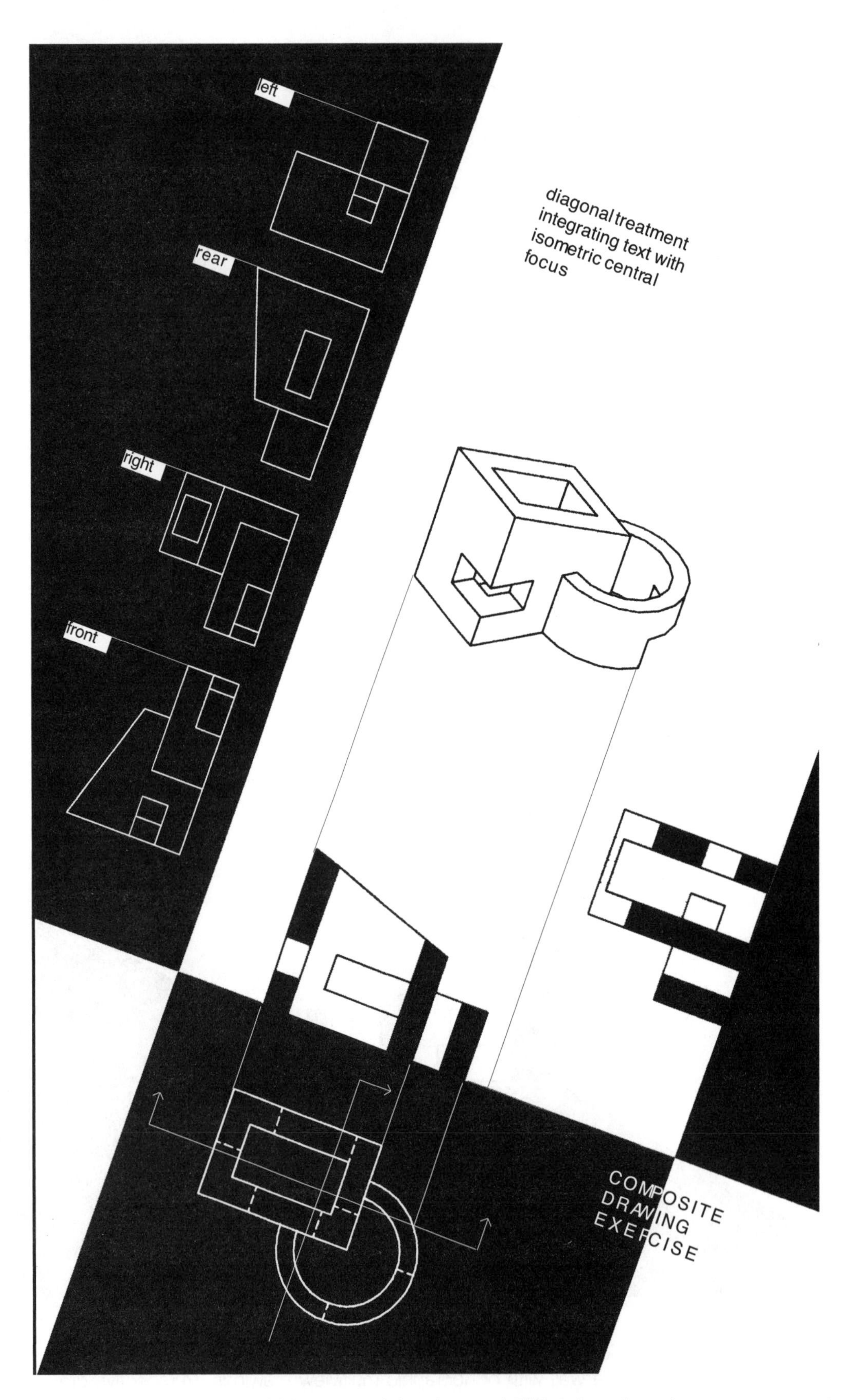

For this example, the wall thicknesses of the abstract building form have been exaggerated.

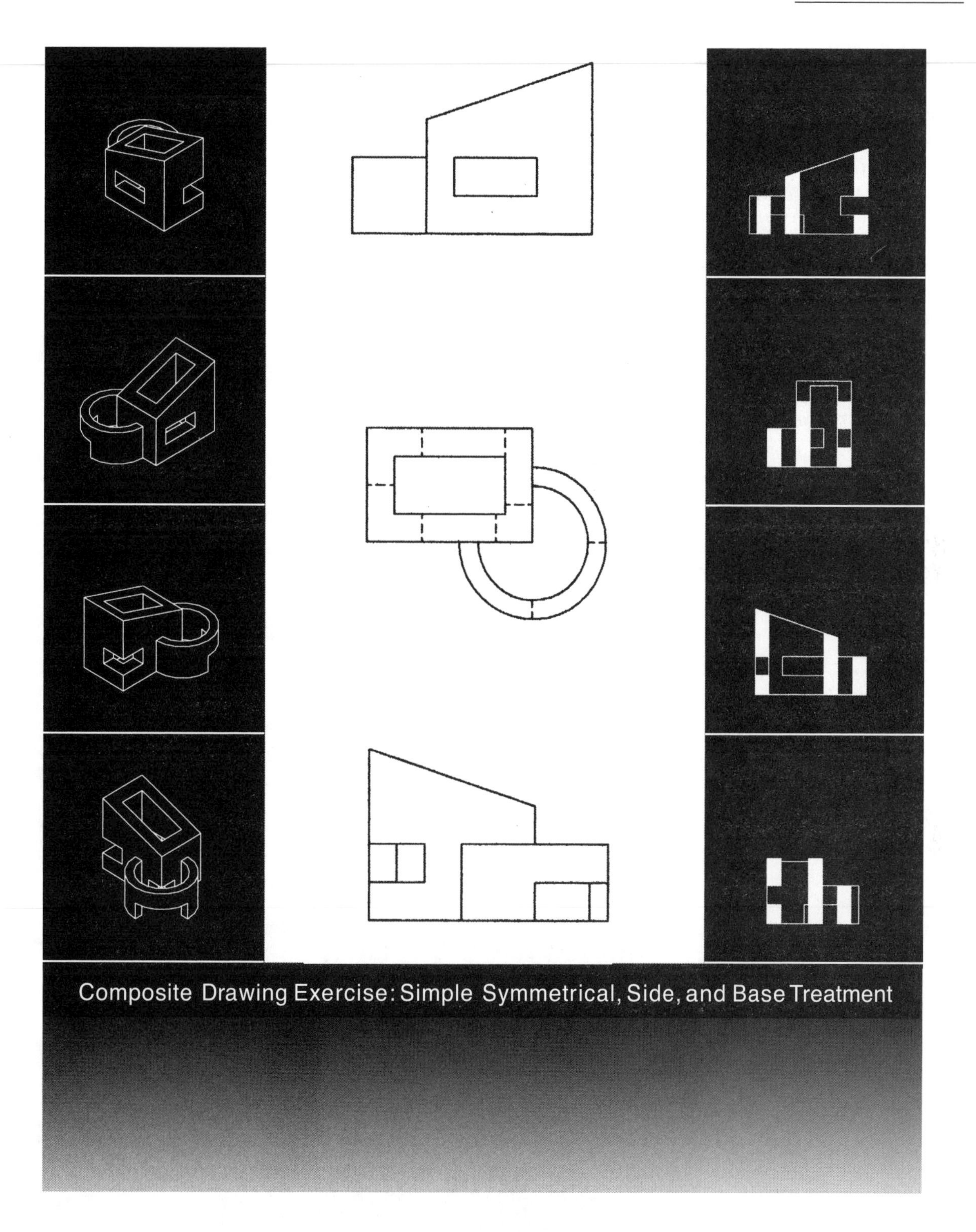

Composite Drawing Exercise: Simple Symmetrical, Side, and Base Treatment

In formulating a composition for a composite drawing layout for any design project, try to be creative in balancing and arranging the elements in the drawing field. The examples on pp. 499–503 and 518 all use a contrasting (in this case dark) field to help organize and unify the seemingly disparate fragments in all of the presentations. A dark or contrasting field with or without a value change can represent the base or ground area where a building sits as an elevation, a section, a perspective, etc. A dark field can also function as a negative space for text or drawing white lines, or as a border to organize specific drawings in their relationship to one another.

This presentation uses a diagonal format, which is achieved by rotating a rectilinear grid format so that it makes an angle with the horizontal and vertical axes. This presentation format refers to the relationship between the new site and the present site of the existing facilities in the historic downtown district of Savannah, Georgia (grid pattern). The presentation is composed of the schematic diagrams on its form-evolution, the site plan, floor plans, elevations, sections, plan obliques, and descriptive text.
[Professor's Statement]

This presentation utilizes reversed printing, in which white lines are drawn on a black background. White on black usually appears more intense than black on white.

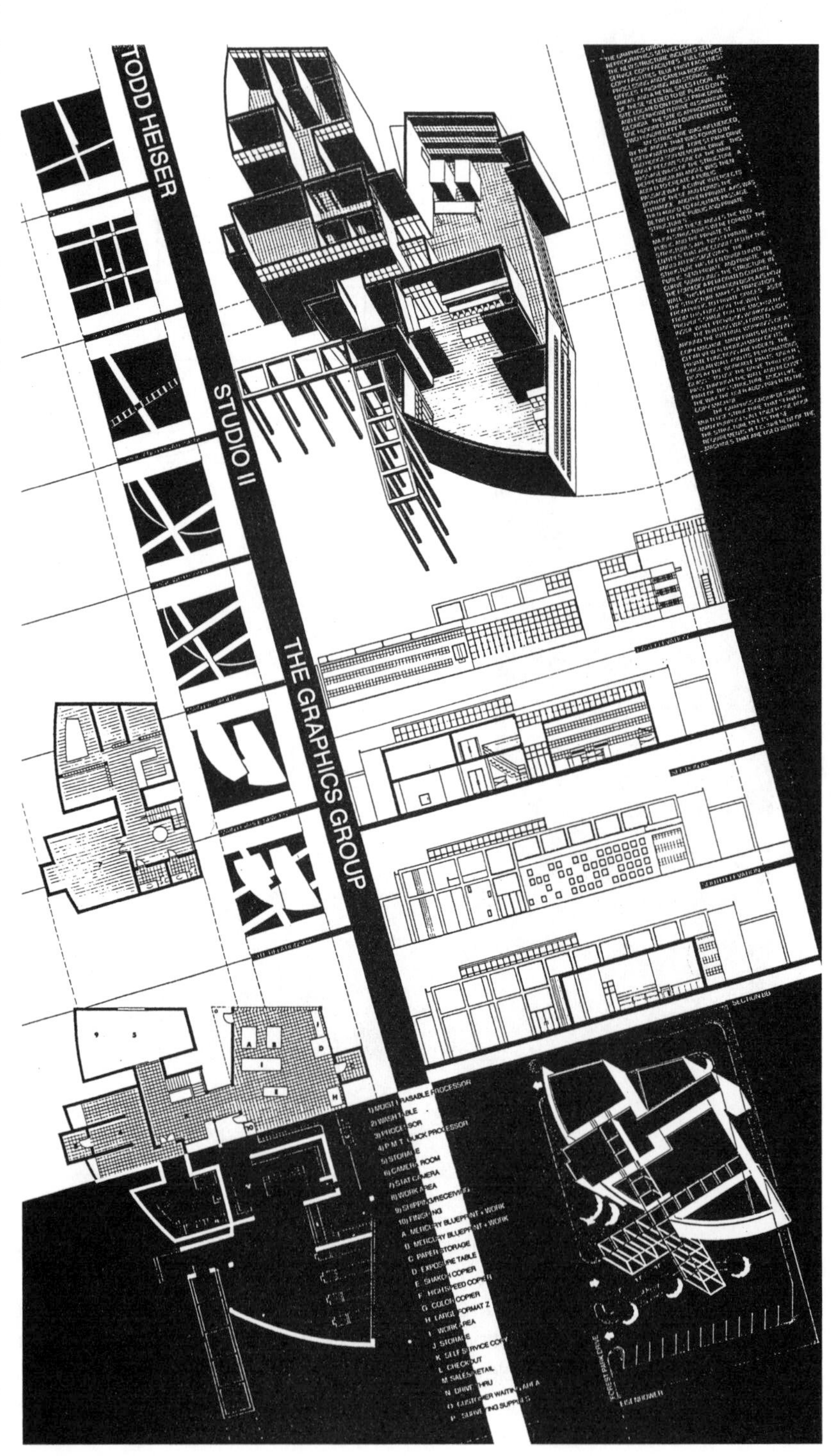

Drawing: Student project by Todd Heiser
Savannah Blue Print and Reprographics
Medium: Ink on Mylar
M. Saleh Uddin, Professor, Savannah College of Art and Design, Savannah, Georgia; Southern University, Baton Rouge, Louisiana

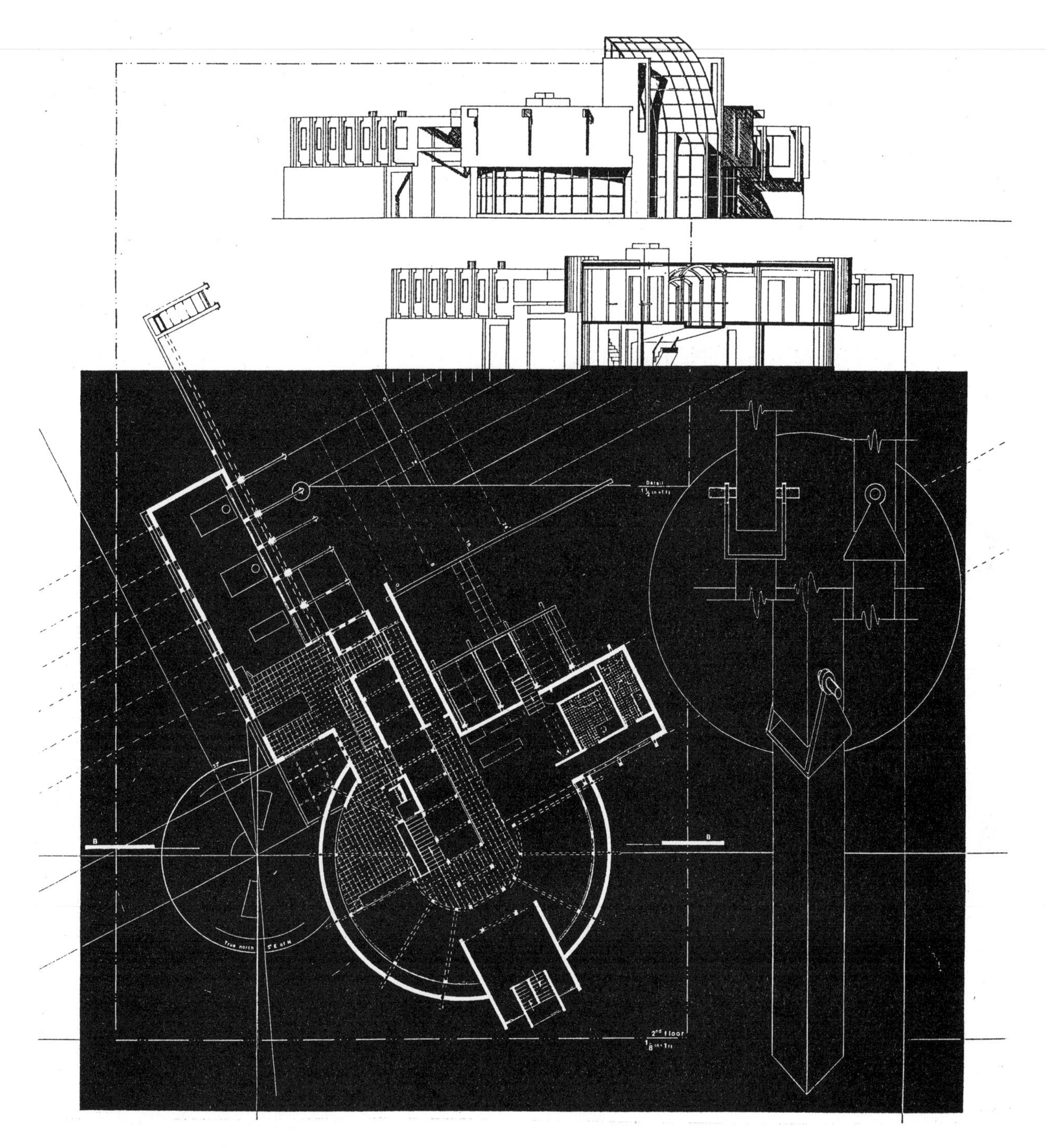

Drawing: Student project by Kevin Schellenbach
Savannah Blue Print and Reprographics
Medium: Ink on vellum
M. Saleh Uddin, Professor, Savannah College of Art and Design, Savannah, Georgia; Southern University, Baton Rouge, Louisiana

This presentation is one sheet of a three-sheet presentation. The composition engages positive and negative images of orthographic drawings. The reverse images of the floor plan and the detail create a baseline for the section drawing. This particular technique effectively separates and highlights section/elevation drawings from floor plans and detail drawings.
[PROFESSOR'S STATEMENT]

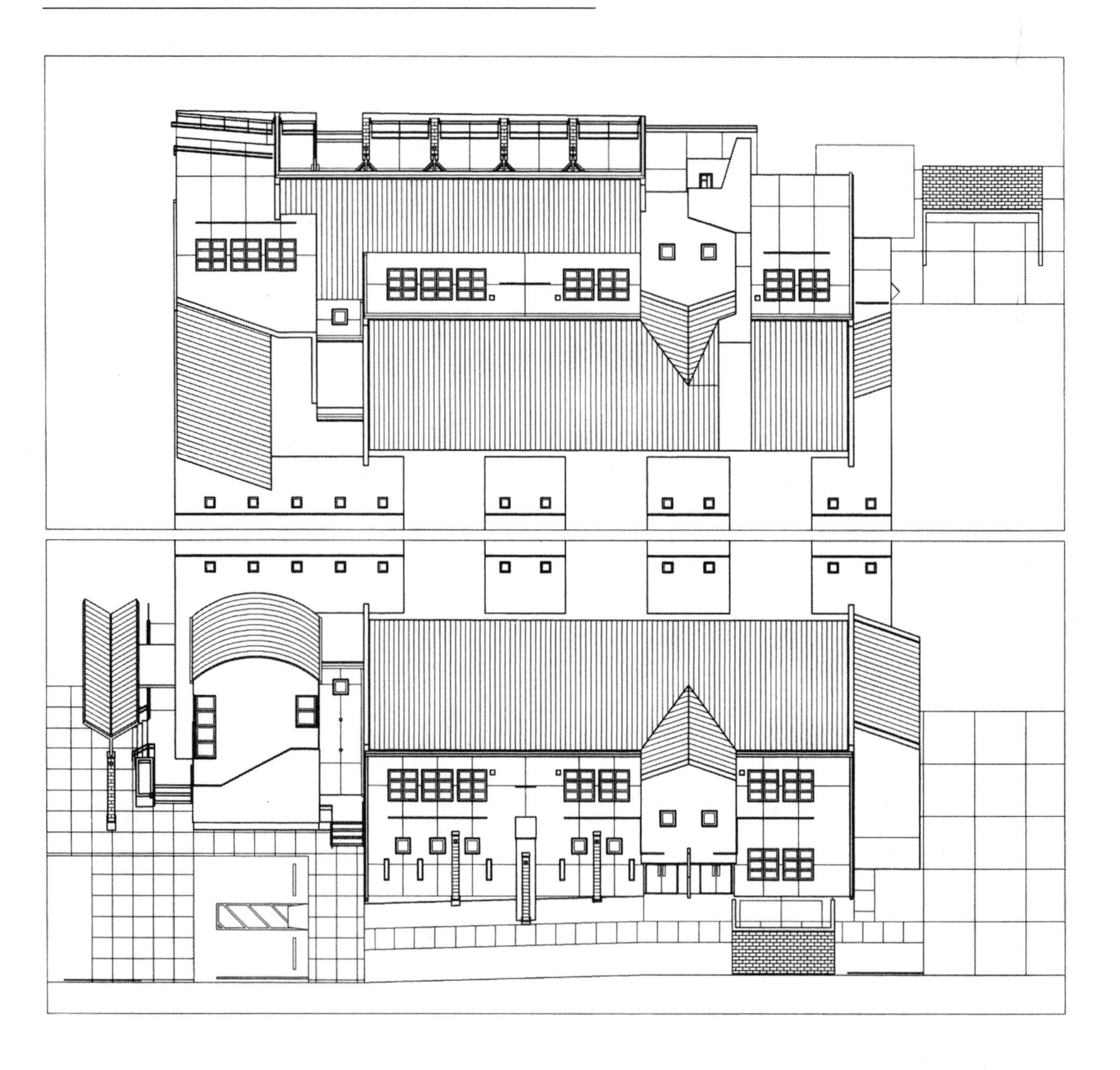

Drawing: Los Angeles Unified School District, Eagle Rock Elementary School
Eagle Rock, California
Drawn by Chilin Huang
Courtesy of Rebecca L. Binder, FAIA, Architecture & Planning

Composite elevations: The combined elevations afford the ability to view both sides of the building simultaneously and to view the corresponding relationships between various parts otherwise hidden from each other. Drawn on AutoCAD Release 12.
[Architect's statement]

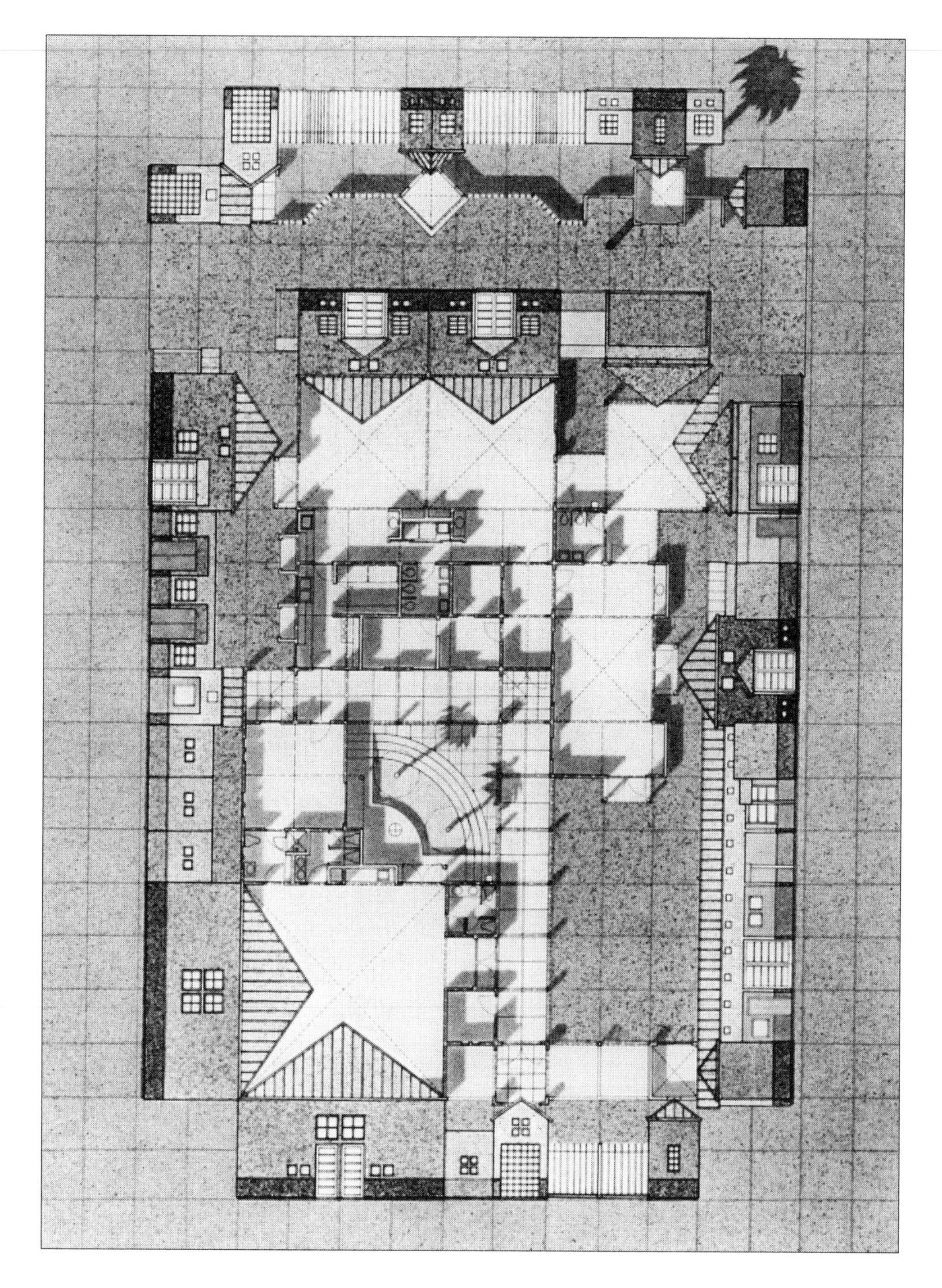

Drawing: Hoover Intergenerational Child Care Center, Los Angeles, California
21" X 26.5" (53.3 X 67.3 cm), Scale: 1/8" = 1'-0"
Medium: ink and color airbrush
Courtesy of John V. Mutlow, FAIA, Architects

Combining floor plan and elevations in one drawing makes the direct relationship between the interior spaces and the elevation easier to understand. The use of airbrush illustrates the color intention of the project and the texture of the materials.
[ARCHITECT'S STATEMENT]

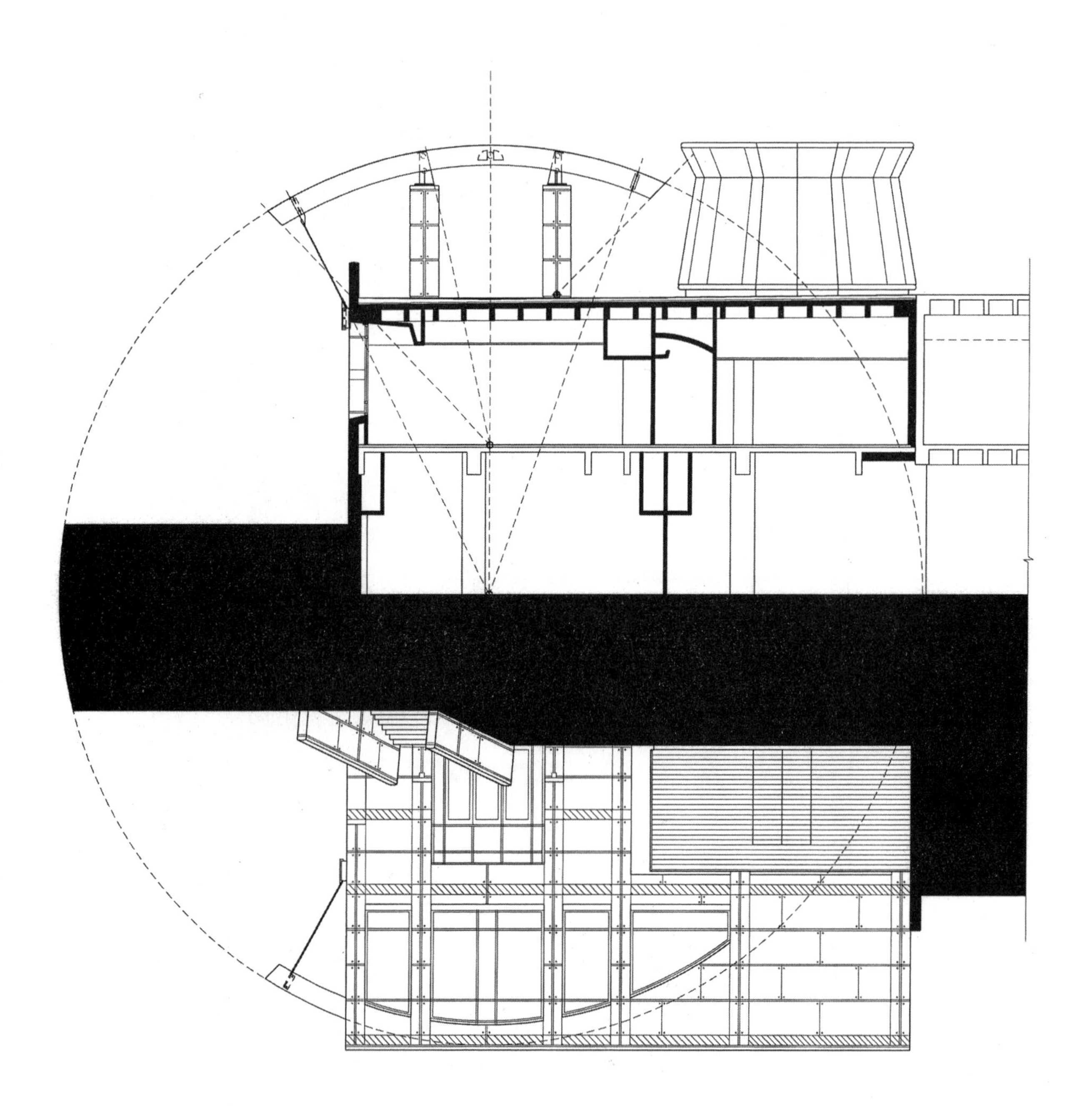

Drawing: University of California–Los Angeles, Ackerman Student Union
Los Angeles, California
Drawn by Chilin Huang
Courtesy of Rebecca L. Binder, FAIA, Architecture & Planning

Composite section, elevation: Through the vehicle of rotation, the drawing conveys the integral connection between the elevation and the section.
[ARCHITECT'S STATEMENT]

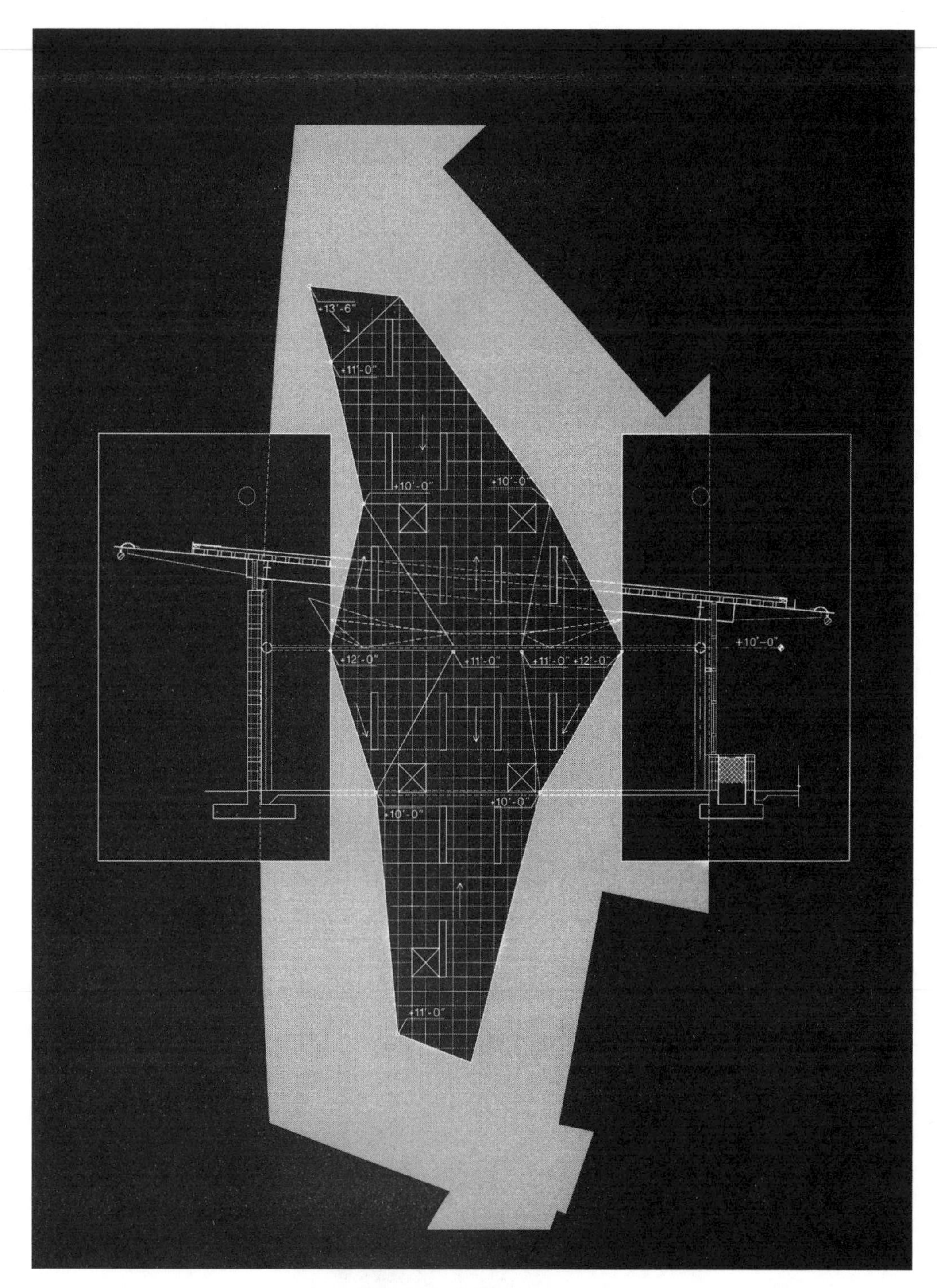

Drawing: University of California at Irvine, Extended Day Care Center
Irvine, California
Drawn by Chilin Huang
Courtesy of Rebecca L. Binder, FAIA, Architecture & Planning

Composite plan, section, reflected ceiling plan: The essence of the design is magnified by the drawing choice, allowing the viewer to understand the reflected ceiling plan [refer to p. 95], overlaid on the floor plan, in juxtaposition to the section that contains it.
[Architect's statement]

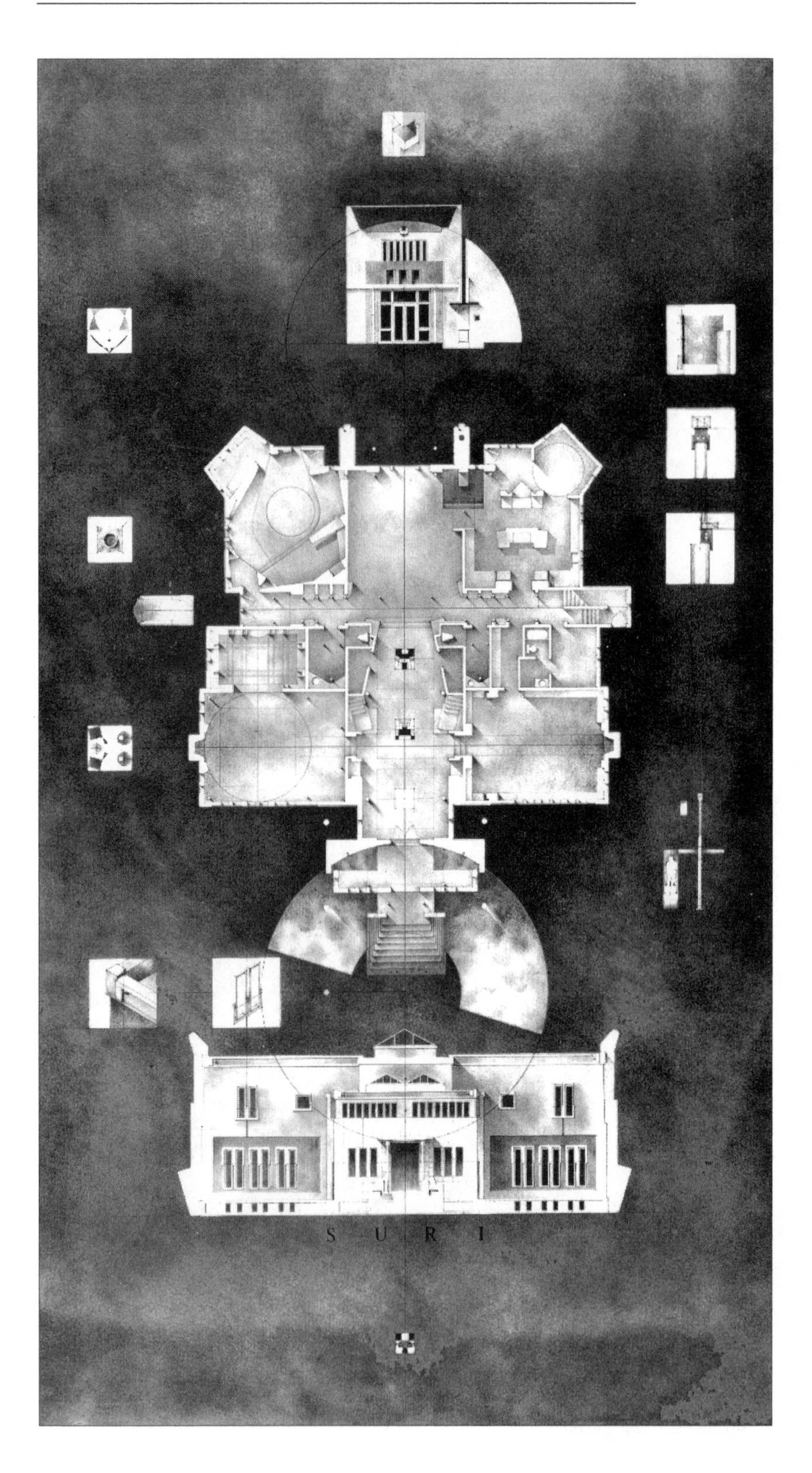

The rendering showcases the character of the building through the representation of several of its defining elements. The plan and front elevation dominate the drawing to express the overall formality of the design. Interior elevations and smaller details ring the edge of the drawing to provide a texture of scale and show off the attention to detail within the actual house. The technique of pencil on vellum, with both hardline and graphite shadowing, is meant to lend a classical and stately air to the overall composition.
[ARCHITECT'S STATEMENT]

Drawing: Suri residence, Los Angeles, California
Plans, elevations, and details composite.
32" × 54" (81.3 × 137 cm), Scale: 3/16"=1'0"
Medium: Pencil and graphite on vellum
Courtesy of House + House Architects, San Francisco
Michael Baushke, Architectural Illustrator

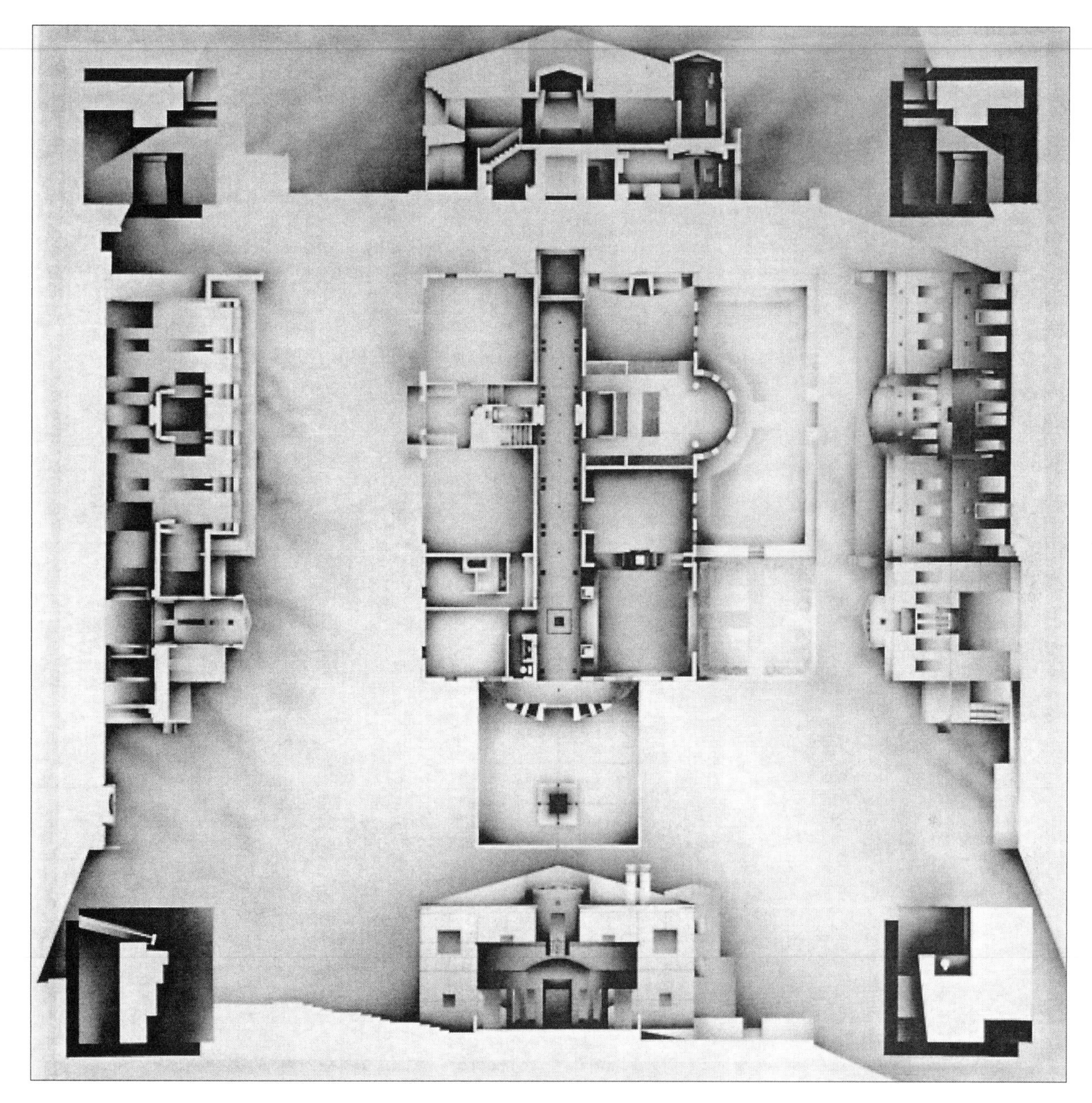

Drawing: Liu residence, Hillsborough, California
Foldout plan, section and elevation composite
40" × 40" (101.6 × 101.6 cm), Scale: 3/16"=1'0"
Medium: Airbrush using acrylic inks on cold-press illustration board
Courtesy of House + House Architects, San Francisco
Mark David English, Architectural Illustrator

The overall composition of the drawing emphasizes the importance of each of the four cardinal directions in the design concept and is statically balanced to reflect harmony. The plan, with white walls and lack of shadowing, illustrates its hieroglyphic nature, which is literally intended to be "read." Elevations, sections, and details are carefully rendered to express the massive quality of the actual building. The four floating detail squares again emphasize the cardinal directions and pictorially bring the details closer to the viewer.
[ARCHITECT'S STATEMENT]

Drawing: Edwards residence, Belize
Foldout sections, oblique elevations and enlarged detail frame composition
40" × 40" (101.6 × 101.6 cm), Scale: 3/16"=1'0"
Medium: Ebony pencil on 1000H vellum
Courtesy of House + House Architects, San Francisco
Mark David English, Architectural Illustrator

The overriding theme of the drawing emphasizes the importance of stage-set design inherent in the building itself. Framing the main image of the drawing with an overscale arch-and-column detail enhances the theatrical nature of the drawing while solidly anchoring the dynamic elements. The drawing is oriented to the cardinal directions where north is the top of the page. The plan reflects its difference from north. As a result, two oblique elevations can show all facades and create a dynamic presentation.
[ARCHITECTURAL ILLUSTRATOR'S STATEMENT]

Transparaline drawings can be either **transmetric** (showing two sides foreshortened) or **transoblique** (showing one side true size and the other either foreshortened or true size). The Edwards residence is transmetric in its elevation views. The Hammonds residence (p. 514) is transoblique (section/elevation is true size) in its elevation view. Also, the Ka Hale Kakuna residence (p. 515) shows both of its elevations in transoblique.

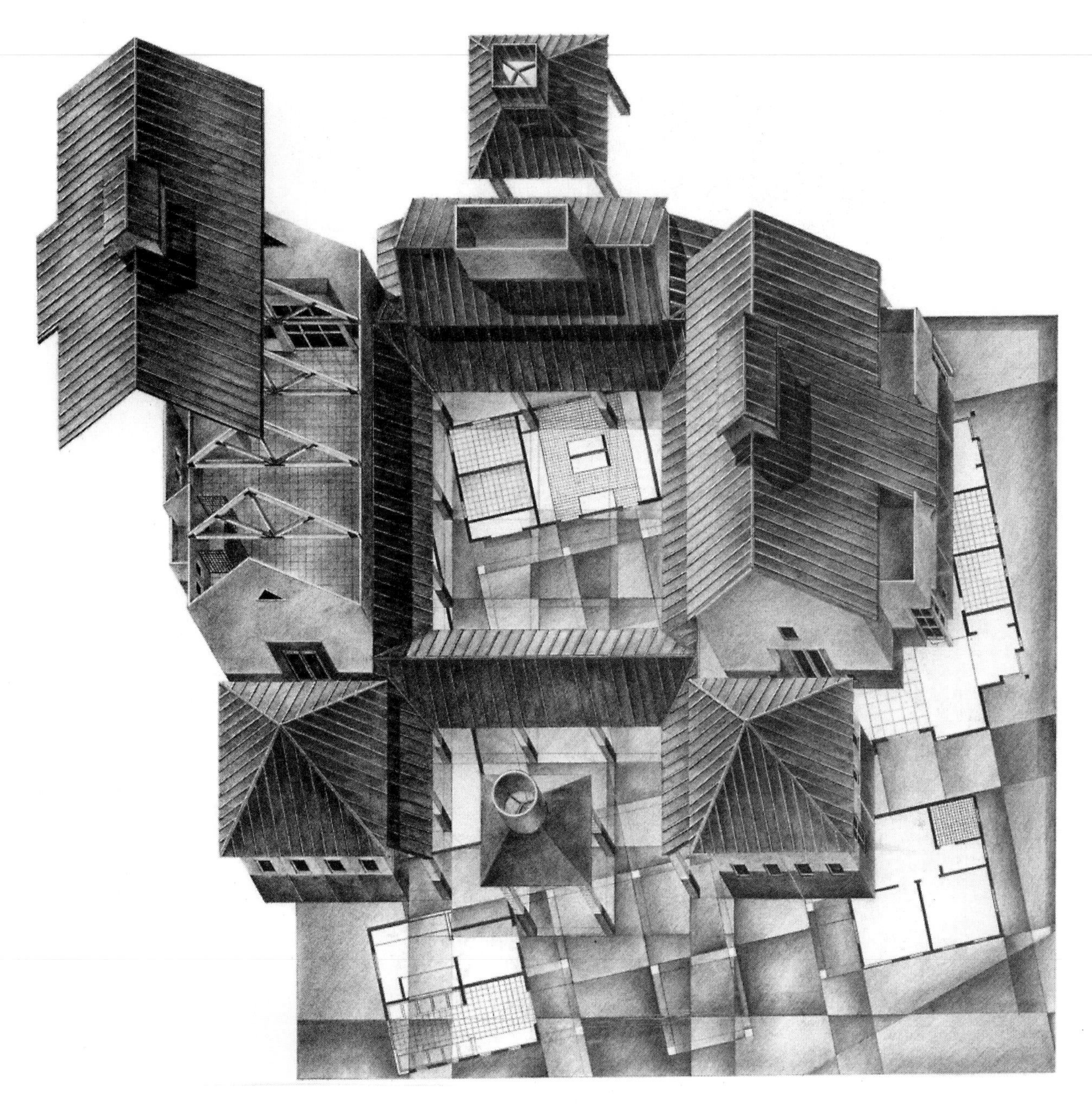

Drawing: Rancho Sespe II, Piru, California
30" × 33" (76.2 × 83.8 cm), Scale: 3/32"=1'0"
Medium: Pencil
Courtesy of John V. Mutlow, FAIA, Architects

This plan oblique drawing of the community center with shadow and shade, rendered in 6B drafting pencil, provides an understanding of the three-dimensional form. The drawing illustrates the roofscape and accentuates the courtyard and its enclosure. The exploded roof and the rendered floor plan as background imply and demonstrate the richness of the spaces and activities.
[ARCHITECT'S STATEMENT]

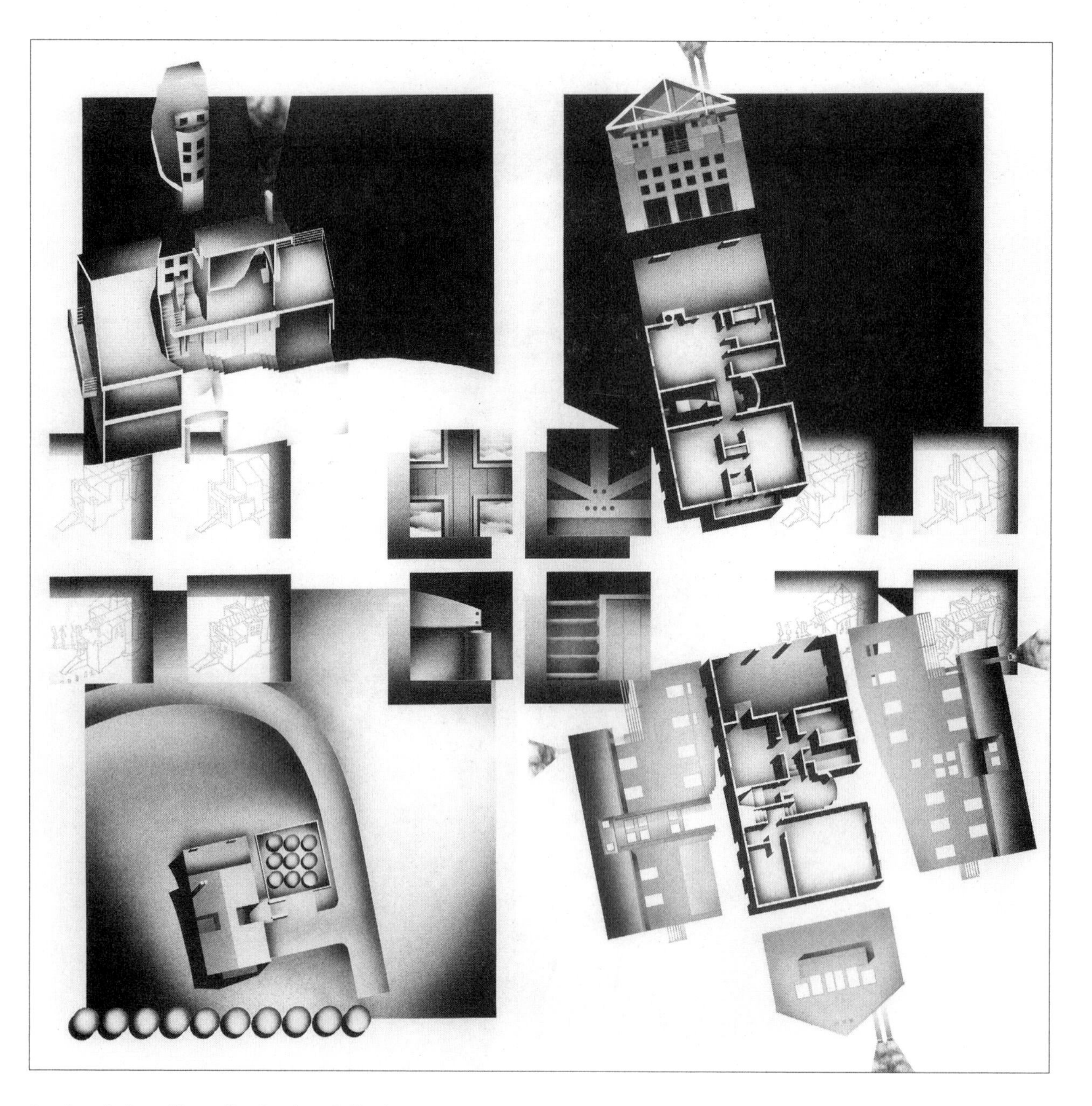

Drawing: Kerby residence, San Anselmo, California
Exploded axonometric with details
30" × 30" (76.2 × 76.2 cm), Scale: ⅛"=1'0"
Medium: Airbrush using acrylic inks on cold-press illustration board; line sketch copier image transfer using mineral spirits
Courtesy of House + House Architects
Mark David English, Architectural Illustrator

The drawing is conceived of as a collage of geometries, scales, and media arranged to represent the interaction between the very graphic building form and the natural setting. The partially exploded axonometric is small in scale to emphasize the overall prototypic "house" form, while the deviation in orientation to the drawing boundary emphasizes the natural setting. The four detail blocks contain the most important architectural "words" and lift off of the picture plane with dropped shadows in an arrangement mirroring a window pattern found as a theme in the house. The concept drawing sketches exhibit their primacy by seemingly receding into the picture plane.
[ARCHITECT'S STATEMENT]

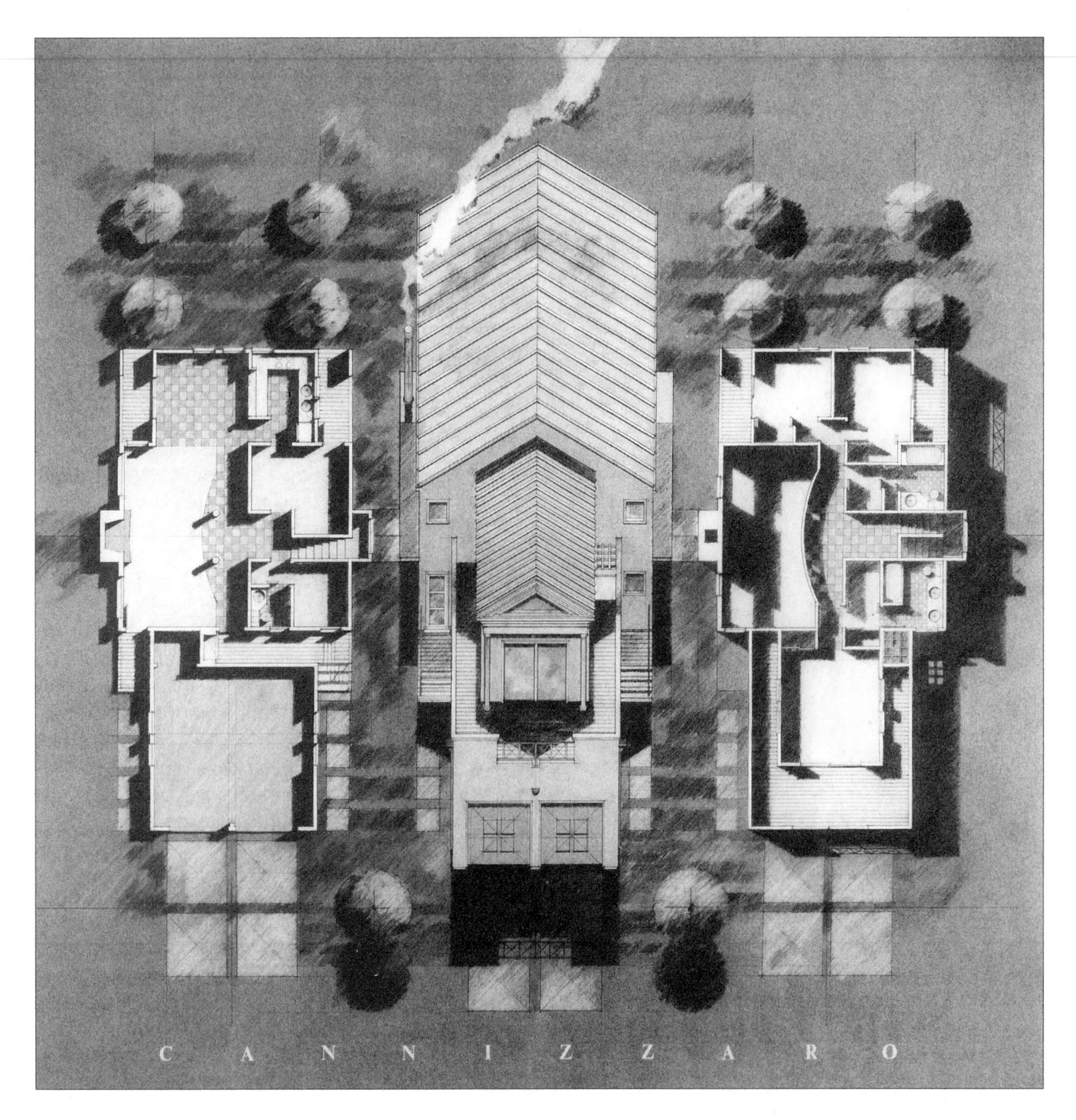

Drawing: Cannizzaro residence, Montara, California
Plan and elevation-oblique composite.
36" × 36" (91.4 × 91.4 cm), Scale: ¼"=1'0"
Medium: Pencil, Prismacolor, and spray paint on vellum
Courtesy of House + House Architects
James Cathcart, Architectural Illustrator

This rendering technique was selected to emphasize the formal layout of the plan and the symmetrical nature of the front elevation. After the basic pencil work was completed, the back of the vellum was spray painted black to provide a gray background. Prismacolor was used on the back and front to create a desired soft pastel effect on the house and also to highlight the landscape elements on the front.
[ARCHITECT'S STATEMENT]

COMPOSITE WITH TRANSOBLIQUE DRAWINGS

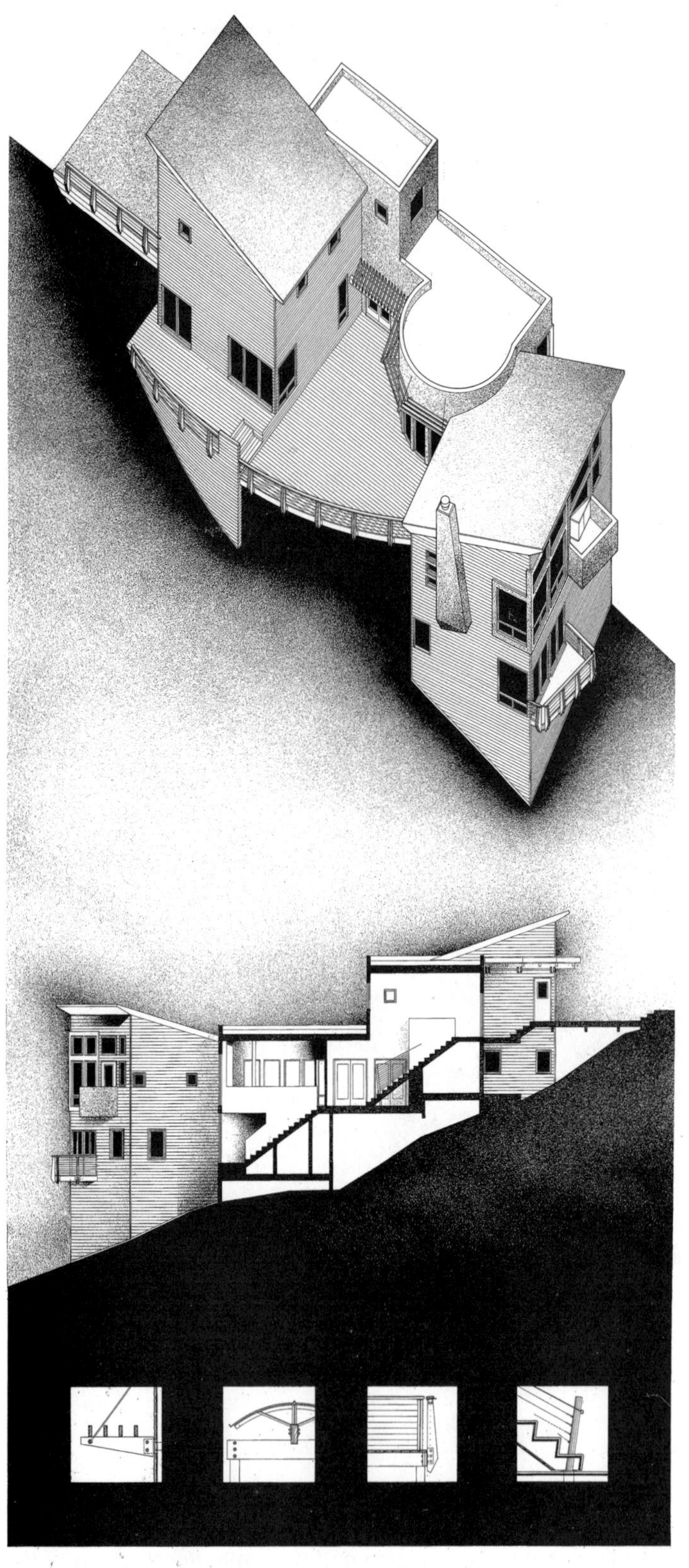

Drawing: Hammonds residence, Berkeley, California
30" × 64" (76.2 × 162.6 cm)
Medium: India ink and airbrush on Mylar
Courtesy of House + House Architects, San Francisco

This house was designed to replace one that was destroyed in Oakland's tragic firestorm in 1992. As in all of our projects, we began the design process by carefully analyzing the site—in this case a steep, narrow, downhill lot. We produced a series of relationship diagrams that studied circulation and spaces in relation to the site. We also built simple three-dimensional study models to investigate the impact of various massing alternatives. This series of plan oblique sketch studies was done concurrently during the early schematic design process to analyze the building's roof shapes, open spaces, massing, fenestration, and scale. These studies were presented to our client along with our plans and models to convey our design process. We found this way of using plan oblique sketching a most valuable design tool.

At the conclusion of the project we decided to produce a formal rendering consisting of three parts: a plan oblique view of the house, a cross-section through the house, and a series of details. Various angles were studied for the plan oblique in order to best convey the building's form. When the overall layout was finalized, the rendering was drawn with ink on Mylar. Airbursh was later applied to provide background tones and building shadows. We feel that this final rendering successfully conveys the building's relationship to the land and its use of form and materials.
[ARCHITECT'S STATEMENT]

The rendering is a composite of drawings graphically laid out around the geometrics of the plan and interrelated through a system of regulating lines. By using multiple images it is possible to understand the building plan and spatial characteristics within the framework of a single drawing. The precision of pen and ink was needed to allow for the finer features to read clearly.

Design: A massive curving wall anchored in lava cliffs encircles and protects a tropical retreat on the island of Maui. By turning its back on the intense south and west sun, the house caters to clients who desired a site-specific home that utilizes the tropical island's unique character and lifestyle. Indoor and outdoor spaces are inseparably linked with disappearing walls that open each room onto outdoor lanais. Intricate screens cast glittering patterns of light and shadow as they trace the sun's path, while tropical vegetation cascades down the lava cliffs and spills inside, tying the feeling in this house to the lush, garden nature of the site. A linking tower offers distant views to the volcano of Haleakala and the Pacific Ocean beyond.
[ARCHITECT'S STATEMENT]

Both elevations shown are **trans-oblique** drawings. Note that in each elevation view, one side is shown true size and the other side is foreshortened (see p. 510).

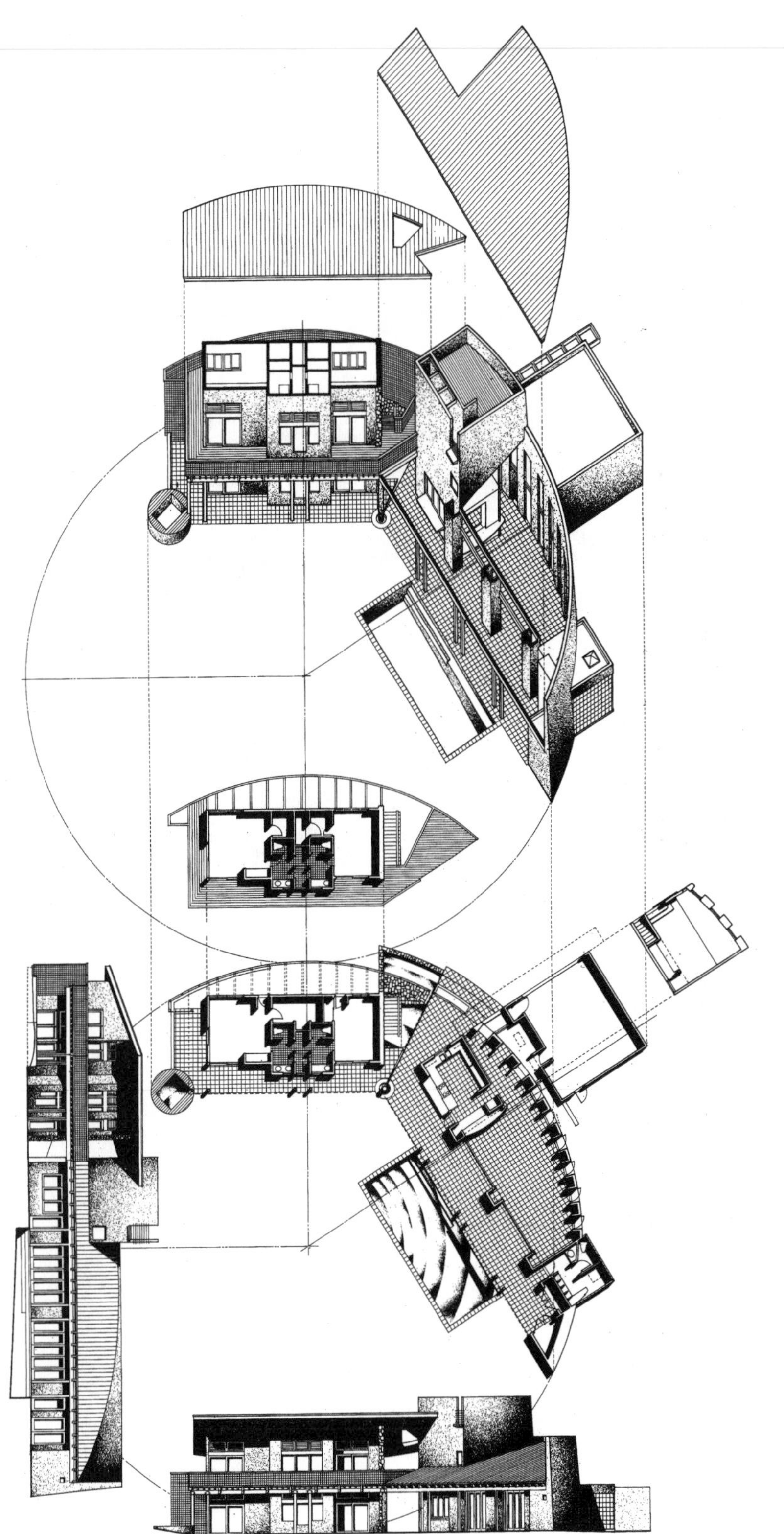

Drawing: Ka Hale Kakuna residence, Maui, Hawaii
Plan oblique, plan, and elevation composite
26" × 48" (66 × 121.9 cm)
Medium: India ink and airbrush on Mylar
Courtesy of House + House Architects, San Francisco; David Haun, Architectural Illustrator

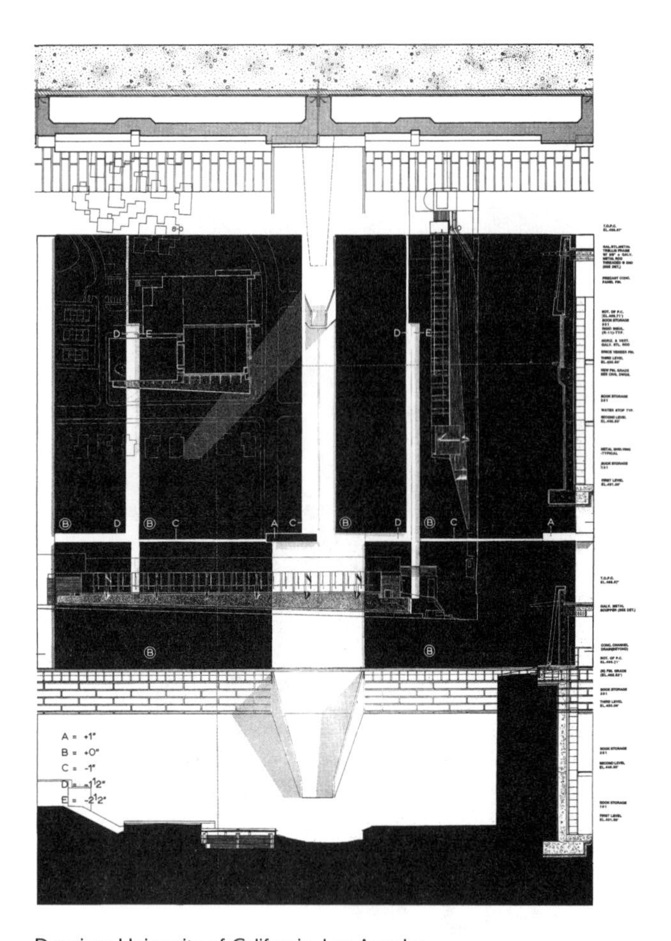

Drawing: University of California–Los Angeles
Southern Regional Library
Los Angeles, California
30" X 40" (76.2 x 101.6 cm), Scale: ⅛" =1'0"
Medium: Ink and reversed printing
Courtesy of Franklin D. Israel Design Associates, Inc., Architects

Superimposing different drawing types allows for the maximization of information in a limited space. Composites can portray a large amount of comprehensive overview information in a single space. They cannot, however, portray conventional drawing information (such as plan, site plan, elevation, section, etc.) in adjacent but separate spaces.

Superimposed composite drawings can have the look of a beautiful abstract artistic composition. Their drawback is that the myriad array of lines and shapes used to compose them can become confusing—sometimes only their originator can understand them. However, when put together with great clarity and little ambiguity, composite hybrids force the viewer to look at the project as one integrated presentation. For example, the fusion and layering of hand-drawn sketches with digital renderings seen in the Sunlaw project (pp. 557–62) results in an effective presentation.

Composites can combine different drawing techniques and types, as well as different media. For example, you can fuse manual with digital techniques (see Chapters 12 and 13 in the Web site). You can even superimpose and combine different ideas.

Drawing: Blades residence, Goleta, California
Medium: Graphite on Mylar
Courtesy of Morphosis and Thom Mayne with Sarah Allan, Architects

Drawing: House in Calderara
Imperia, Italy
Medium: Pencil
Courtesy of Professor George S. Loli
Department of Architecture
University of Louisiana–Lafayette

This ***composite design sketch*** *shows a house in disrepair undergoing a renovation where views and consequently terraces become important design considerations. This drawing documents the client–designer dialogue, which discusses the initial design opportunity.*
[PROFESSOR'S STATEMENT]

Superimposed composites can be refined hardlines or freehand conceptual sketches like the house in Calderara (above). Composites, especially sketched ones, force the viewer to focus more on the interrelationship of all the drawing types. This prevents the tendency, especially among beginners, to think in terms of drawings as individual, isolated pieces of information.

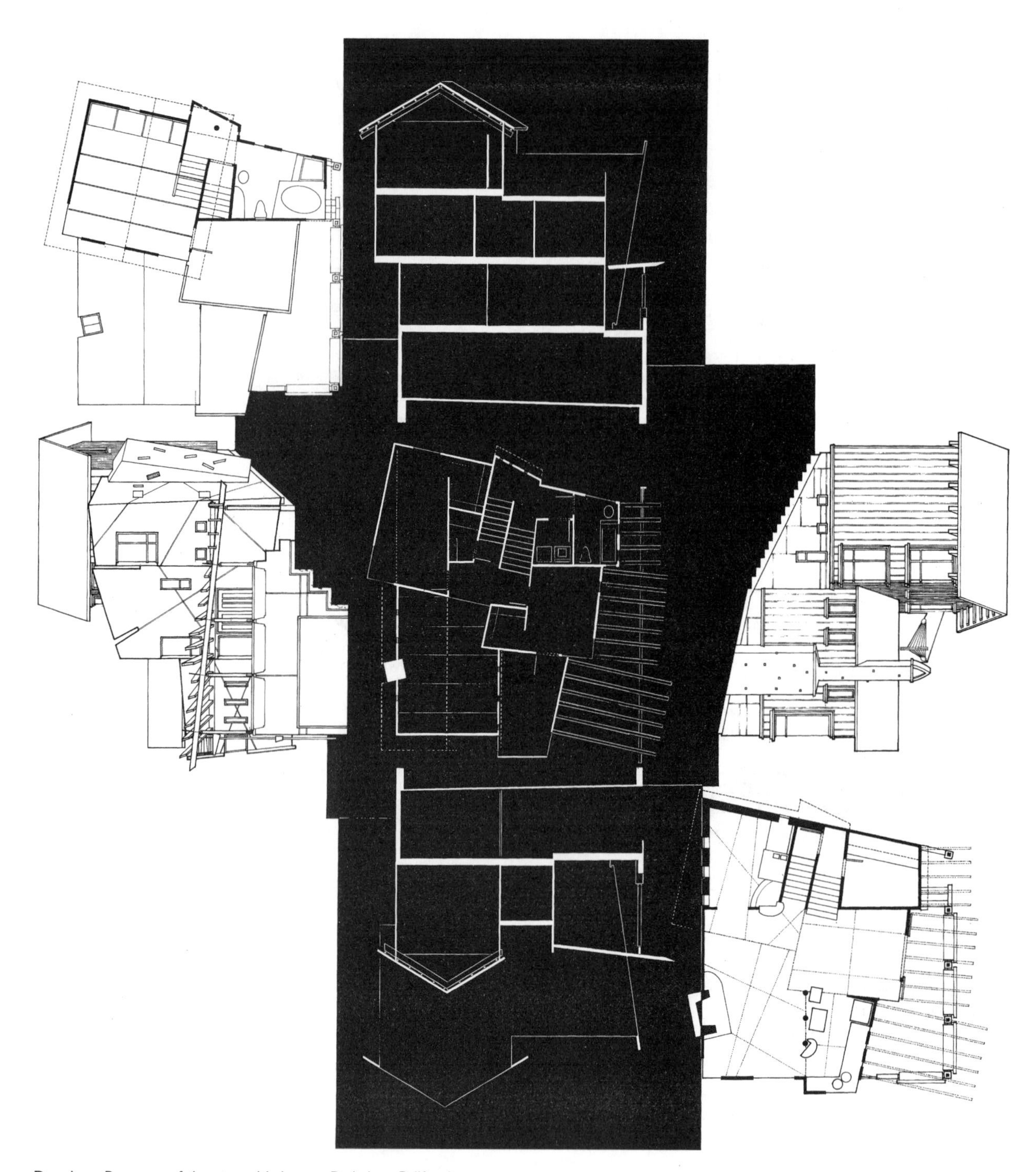

Drawing: Revenge of the stuccoids house, Berkeley, California
24" × 36" (61 × 91.4 cm), Scale: ¼"=1'0"
Medium: Ink on canson paper
Courtesy of David Baker Associates Architects and Nancy Whitcombe

The house represented by this drawing is complex, a collage of discrete ideas and architectural strategies. The complexity of the drawing is compatible with that of the project: simple plans, elevations, and sections alone would not relate the underlying emotional content of the design. The subliminal design intent described intuitively in this composite drawing is greater than the sum of the linear information contained in the separate technical drawings that are its components.
[ARCHITECT'S STATEMENT]

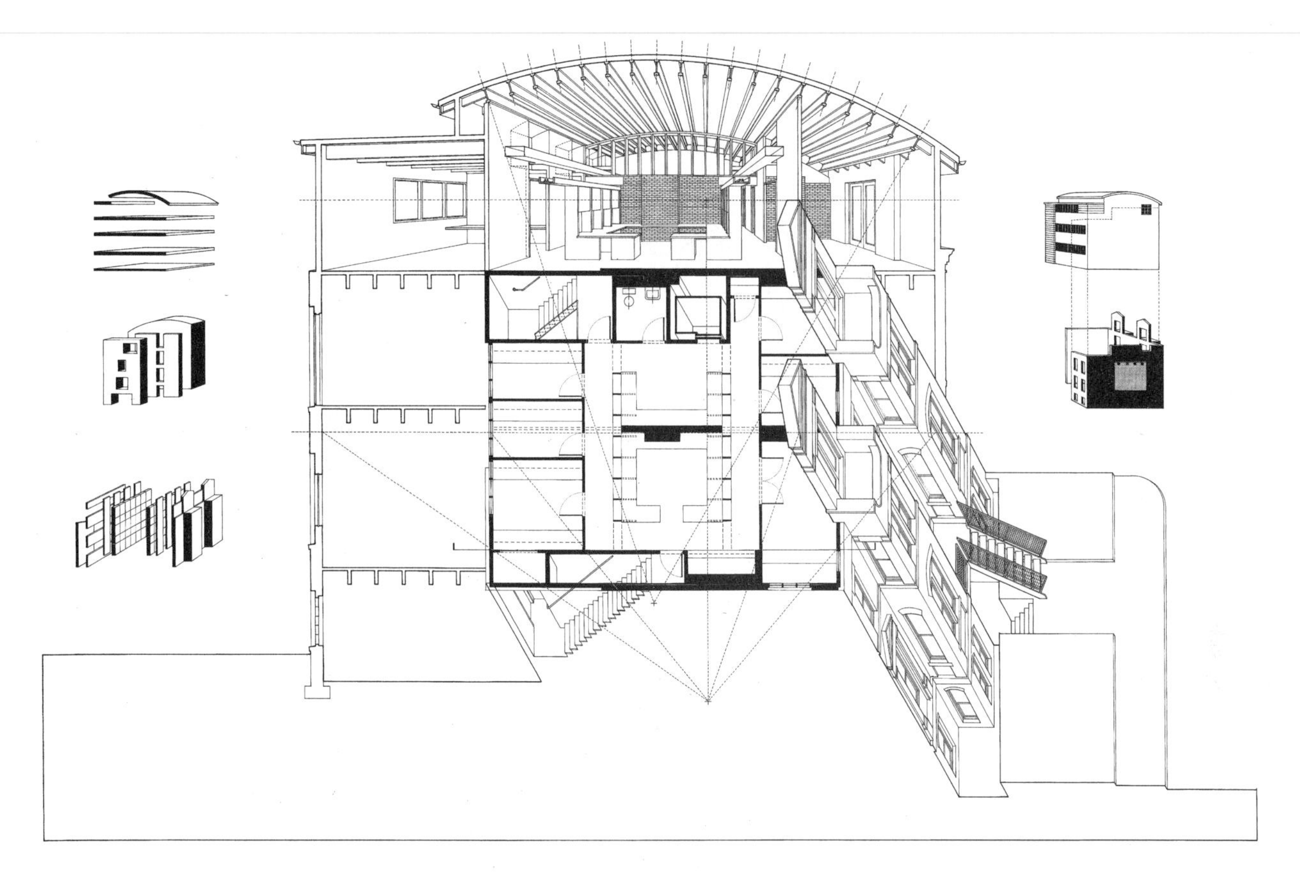

Drawing: National Minority AIDS Council, Washington, D.C.
30" × 42" (76.2 × 106.7 cm), Scale: ¼"=1'0"
Medium: Ink on Mylar
Courtesy of Vyt Gureckas/CORE

The inadequacy of representing a three-dimensional artifact in two dimensions has traditionally been overcome by generating a number of different drawings. However, the act of reconnecting the various drawings or views is left to the mind. Cubism has offered an alternative to this process by presenting simultaneous views on one surface. This drawing is an attempt to take advantage of such a strategy, but whereas cubism relies on transparency and incidental juxtaposition, this drawing employs a more precise set of tangent lines or shared edges to graft one drawing to another. Construction lines are left in place to underscore this process of delineative reconstruction.
[ARCHITECT'S STATEMENT]

The ultimate goal of a composite presentation is to effectively combine the different types of drawing conventions and explanatory text that are being utilized. This will be dependent to a large degree on the restrictions on the size and shape of the presentation panel(s) as well as the organizational method chosen for combining the drawings (grid, toned background, radiation and rotation, central focus, etc.). This **hybrid** presentation combines a perspective section with a plan and a nonvertical z-axis plan oblique. Scan the ingenious and well-thought-out single- and multipanel presentations in the rest of this chapter for hints on how to approach your own presentation format problems.

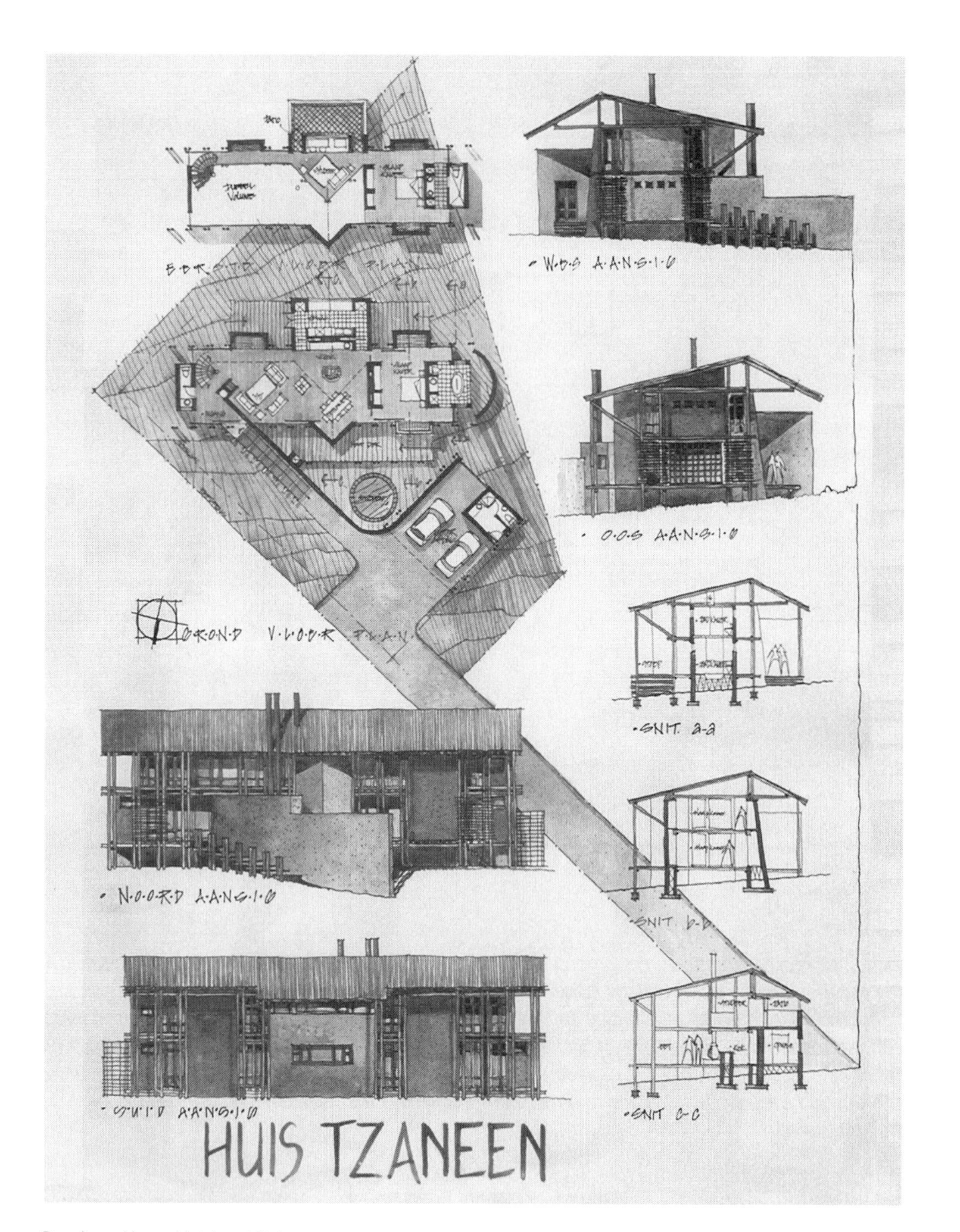

Drawings: House Notnhagel-Deiner
Tzaneen, South Africa
Medium: Watercolor and ink
Design team: 'Ora Joubert and Thomas Gouws
Courtesy of 'Ora Joubert Architects, Pretoria, South Africa

Drawings (facing page): House Bergh
Cape Town, South Africa
Medium: Watercolor and ink
Design team: 'Ora Joubert

In brief, House Notnhagel-Deiner (Tzaneen) is part of a genealogy of projects that attempt a synthesis between Eurocentric theoretical premises and socioeconomic and environmental particularities of southern Africa. To that effect, a concerted effort has been made to appropriate local circumstances through the use of readily available materials, local craft techniques, and sound climatic performance, though respecting the spatial integrity and abstract formalism of orthodox modernism.
[ARCHITECT'S STATEMENT]

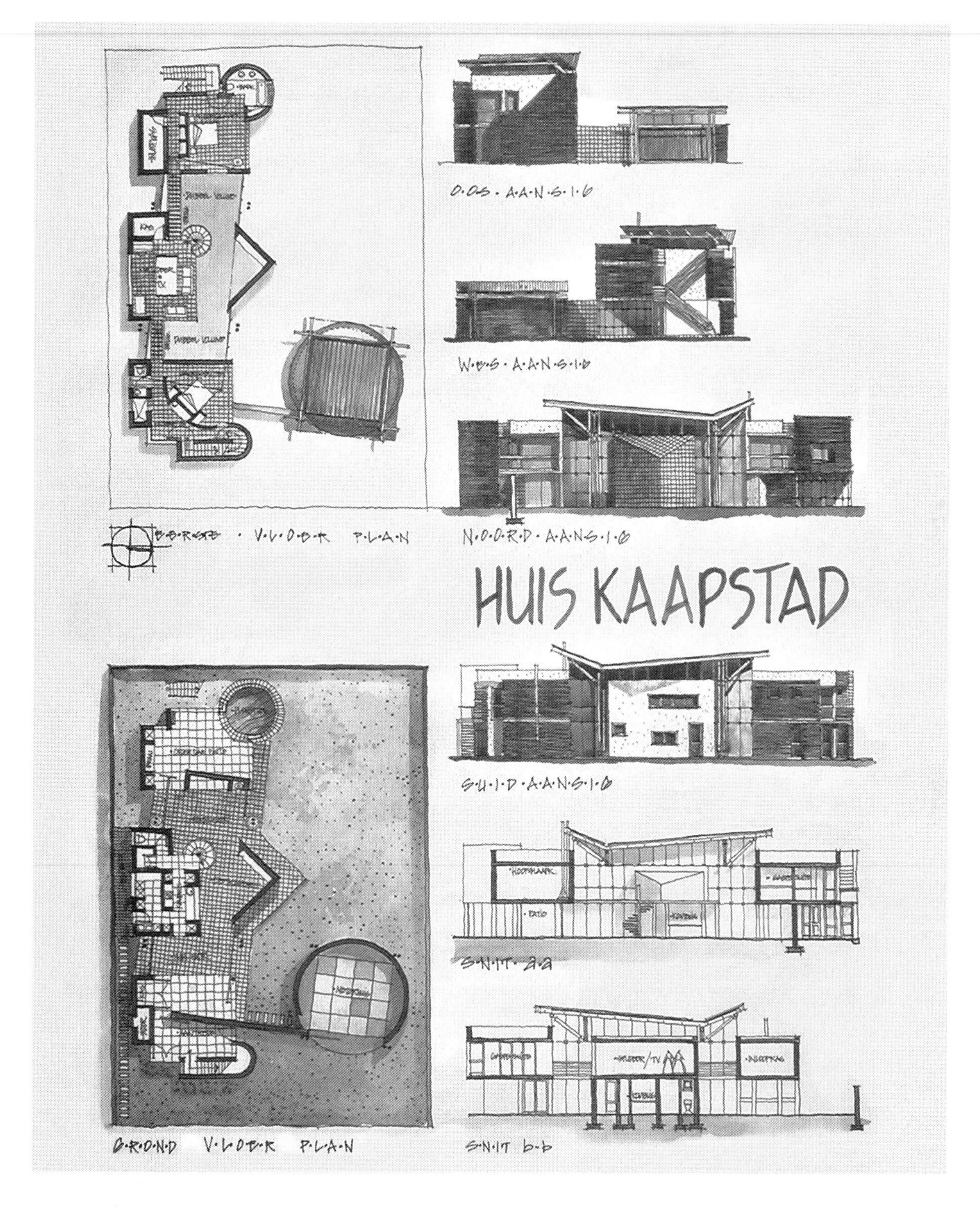

From a conceptual point of view, House Bergh (Cape Town) explores the universal significance of space, combined with a sustained interest in the dynamics generated by colliding geometries. Since the house is situated close to the coast and on a flat, sandy terrain, the slightly lifted floor surface aims at a delicate imprint on the sand. The choice of materials—aluminum roof and ceiling, white bagged walls alternated with flushly jointed plaster brick, and black slate floor and wall tiles—accentuates the integrity of the different formal components within the compositional ensemble. [ARCHITECT'S STATEMENT]

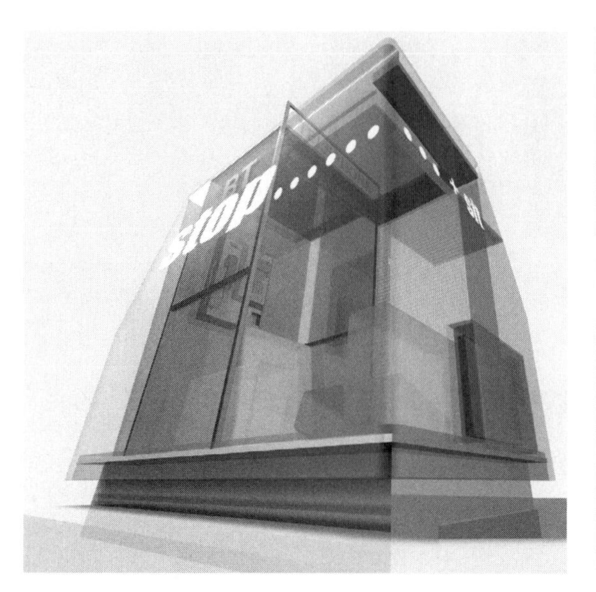

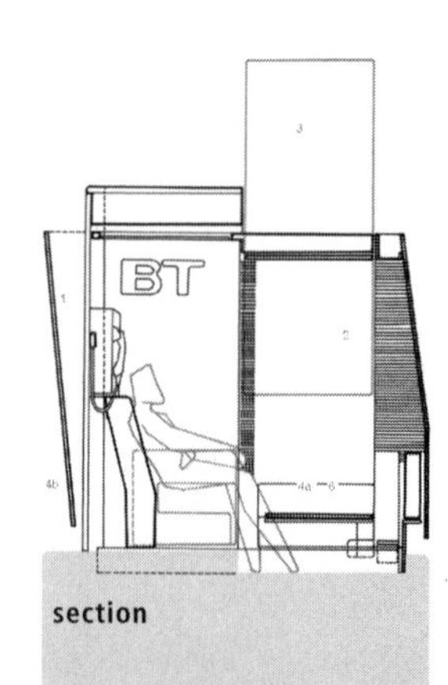

section

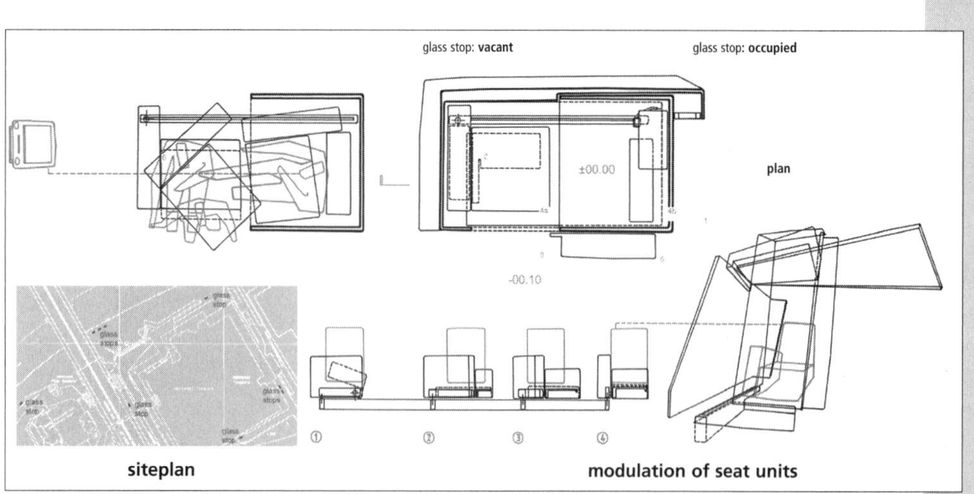

1 **Existing telephone booth**
2 **Vari-focus glazed screen:** creates a boundary of changeable privacy. As the door [3] rotates shut, the electric circuit is closed, completing the lines of liquid crystal running around the perimeter of the booth. The movements of the individual within are now obscured to bystanders and any passers-by.
3 **Closer panel**
4 **Armchair**, consisting of parts **a** + **b**. The two separable units form a complete seat, only when money is inserted and the booth occupied.
5 **Meter:** A unit on the exterior of the booth indicates the amount of time purchased. When the session ends, the door automatically opens out and the armchair disassembles to its default position.
6 **Plasma screen TV** with optional Infra-red headphones

The public telephone has become obsolete with the advent of the mobile telephone. Conversely, the rest area within the city hustle and bustle has almost completely vanished, with street furniture specifically designed to deter loitering.

The **GLASS STOP™** is the solution to these two problems. Making use of the phone power points, a temporary living room is created within the city by wrapping a vari-focus glazed screen around the existing units. Fitted with an armchair and a television, it provides a place for people to rest between shopping, or before an evening rendezvous, without having to purchase a coffee or beer.

Panel image: Central Glass Co. Japan: Public Space: Glass Booth Competition
Courtesy of Studio 8 Architects: cj Lim with Ed Liu and Michael Kong

glass stop

The composition attempts to illustrate the social and cultural significance of the telephone booth, now and into the future. It shows the design in a variety of inhabited and empty conditions, suggesting possibilities of social inhabitation and choreography. The drawings were hand drawn, allowing degrees of imperfection, while the computer rendering shows the contrasting nature between the existing booth and its new shell.
[ARCHITECT'S STATEMENT]

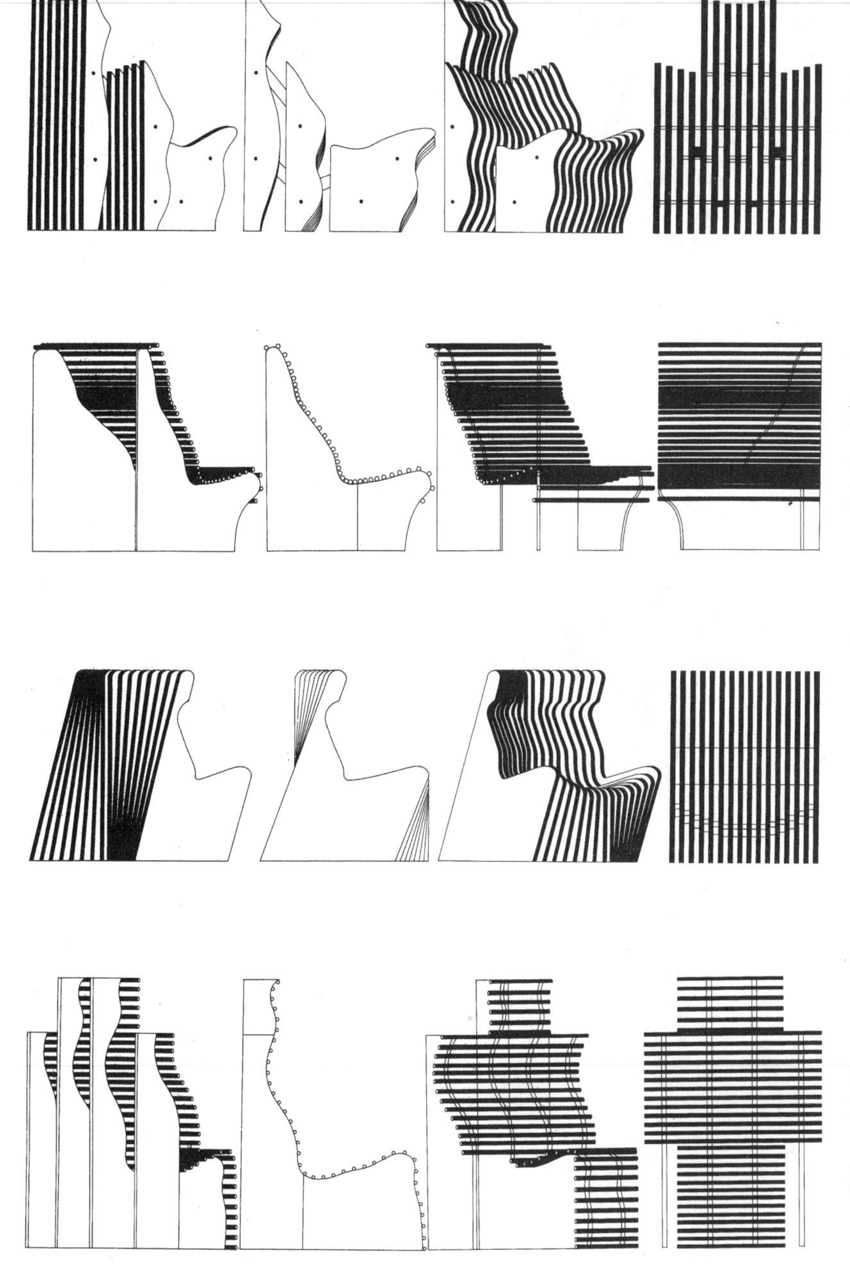

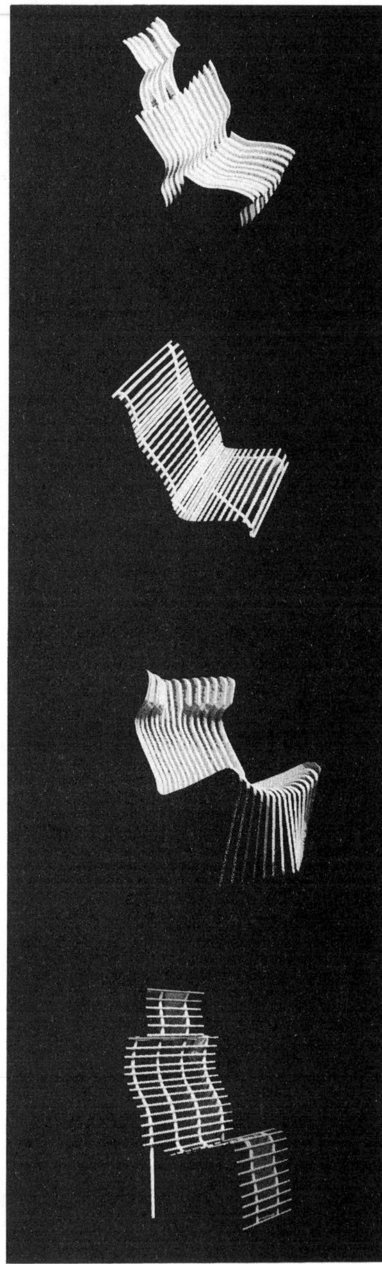

ONE-PANEL PRESENTATION

Drawings: Student project by Scott Benner, Mark Honderick, Jeff Hoeft, and Juan Lopez
Rhythms to Sit On
Medium: Ink on Mylar and photography
Courtesy of the University of Texas at Arlington, School of Architecture

Presentation formats for projects smaller than buildings normally do not require all of the primary architectural drawings (plan, elevation, section, etc.). This example utilizes only elevation drawings and model photographs to completely illustrate the design. Note that the projects could involve full-size mock-up models large enough to allow the designer to interact with the design.

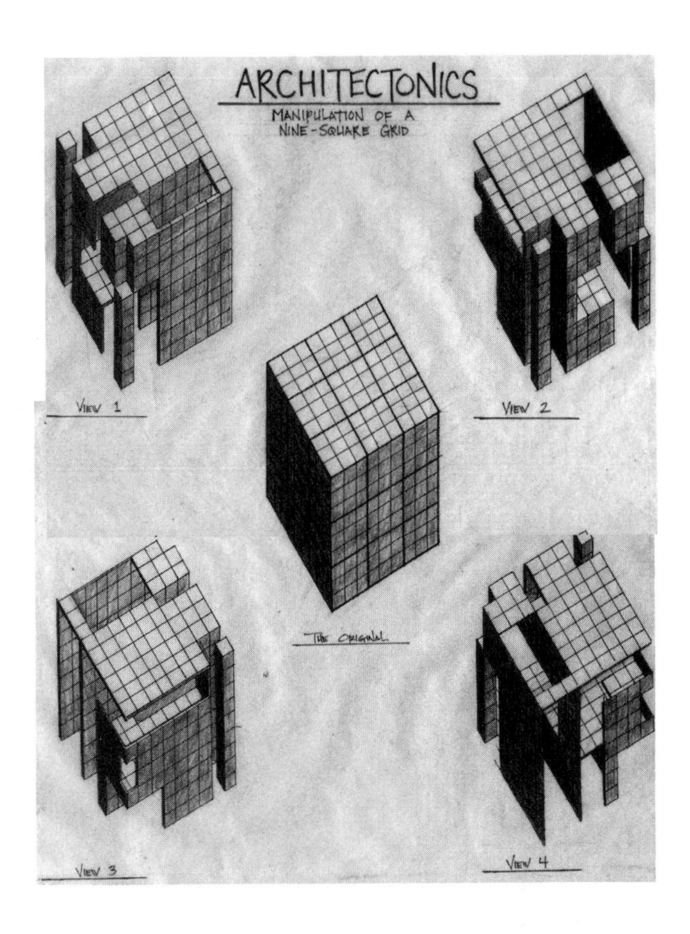

Assignment: Starting with a nine-square grid, develop a series of studies that explore figure and ground, solid and void, shade and shadow, and transparency. Project the grid into three-dimensional form.

Format: Using ink and pencil on two sheets of tracing paper (20" X 20"), present your findings using sketches and drawings.
[PROFESSOR'S STATEMENT]

Student project by Tommy Solomon
Courtesy of Studio Professor Michael Hagge
Architecture Program
University of Memphis

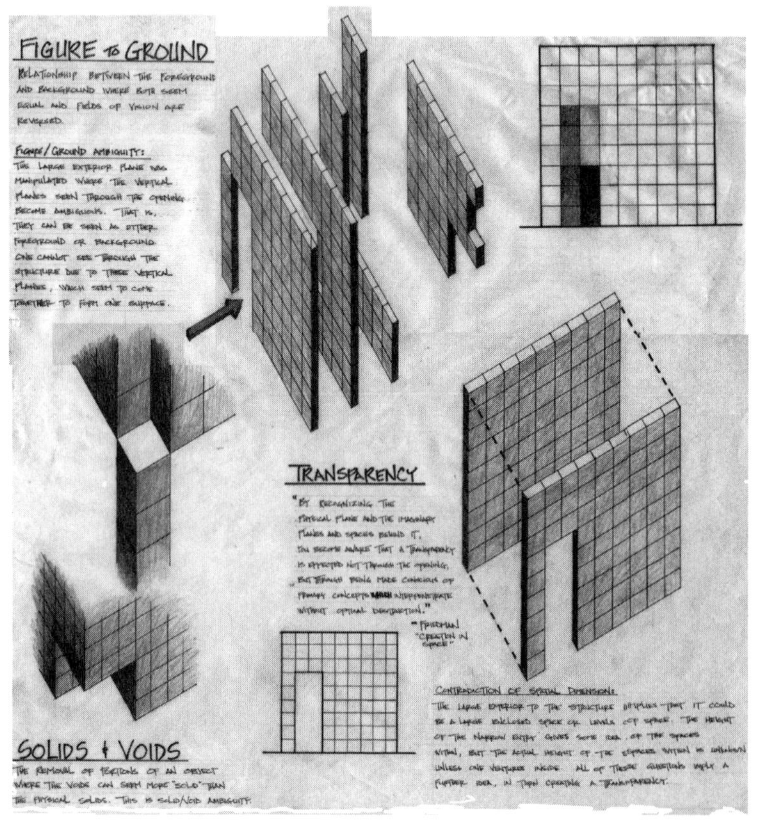

Problem courtesy of Professor Michael Hagge
Architecture Program
University of Memphis

A Study of Architecture: Residential (Grotta House by Richard Meier)

Assignment: Select a residential structure and receive approval from the faculty. Then prepare an analysis of the building. Consider geometry, scale, proportions, mass, hierarchy, texture, materials, and more. Look beyond the representation in the books and periodicals. Make decisions. Make assumptions. Put yourself into the built world. Put yourself into the place.

Format: This assignment must be developed using sketches and drawings. These must be presented on two 20" X 20" boards. Consider the composition of the boards (hint: use one for analyses and one for supporting information). All work must be drawn (no photocopies!). Submit a written analysis and include appropriate graphics. The written element must be typed; the graphics should be able to stand separately from the presentation boards.

[PROFESSOR'S STATEMENT]

Problem courtesy of Professor Michael Hagge
Architecture Program
University of Memphis

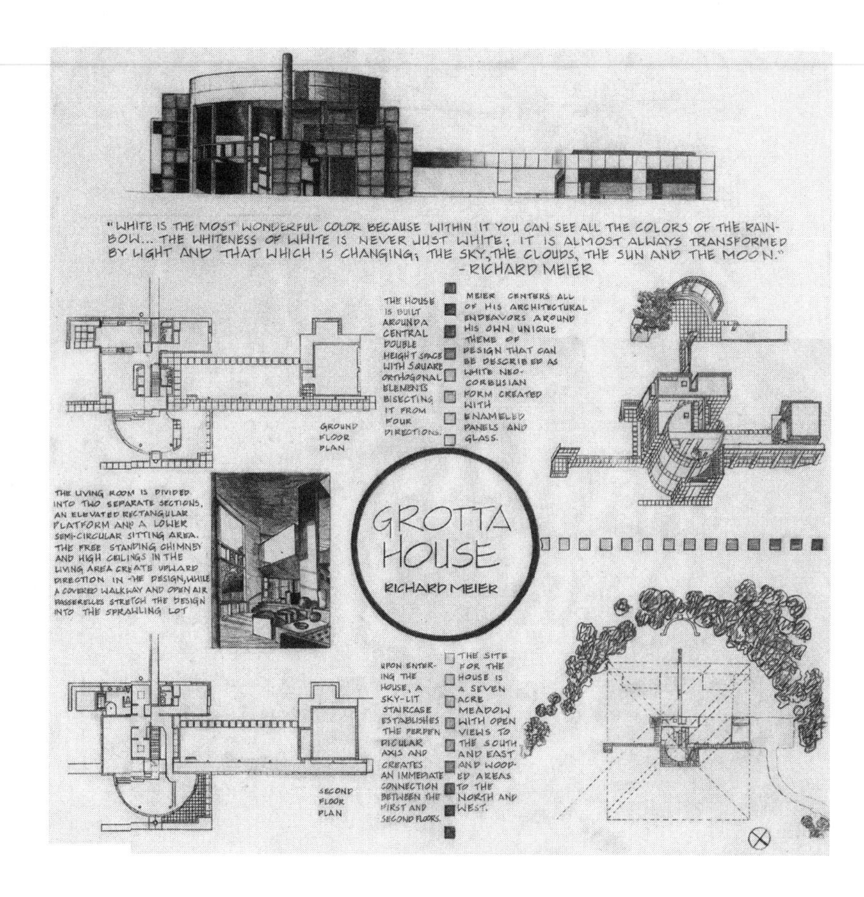

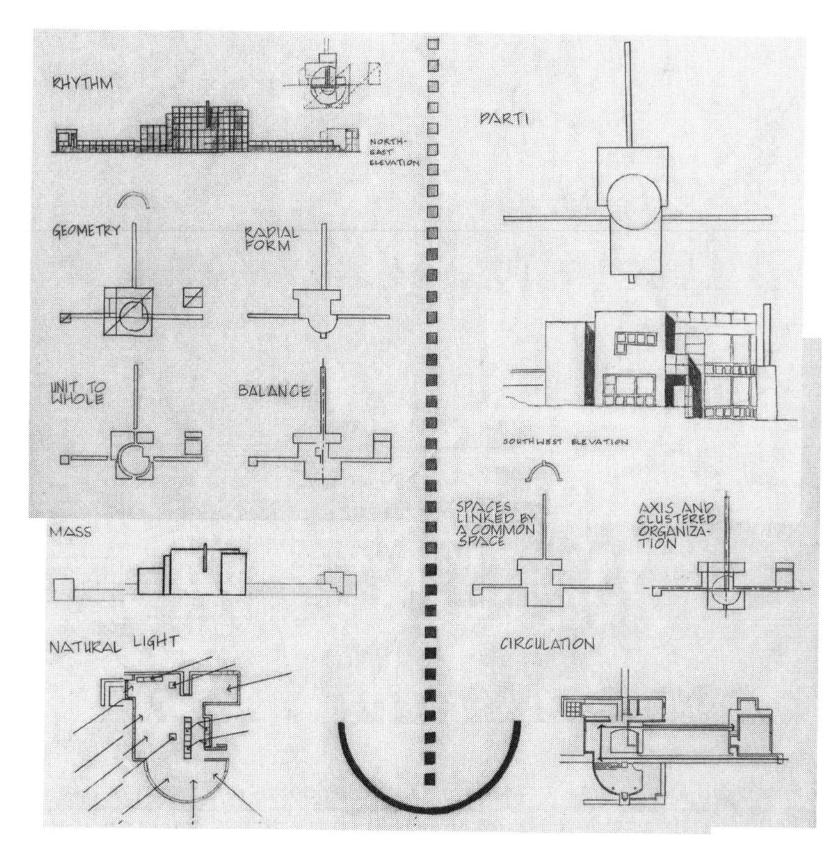

Student project by Amy Clyce
Medium: Graphite on vellum
Courtesy of Studio Professor Michael Hagge
Architecture Program
University of Memphis

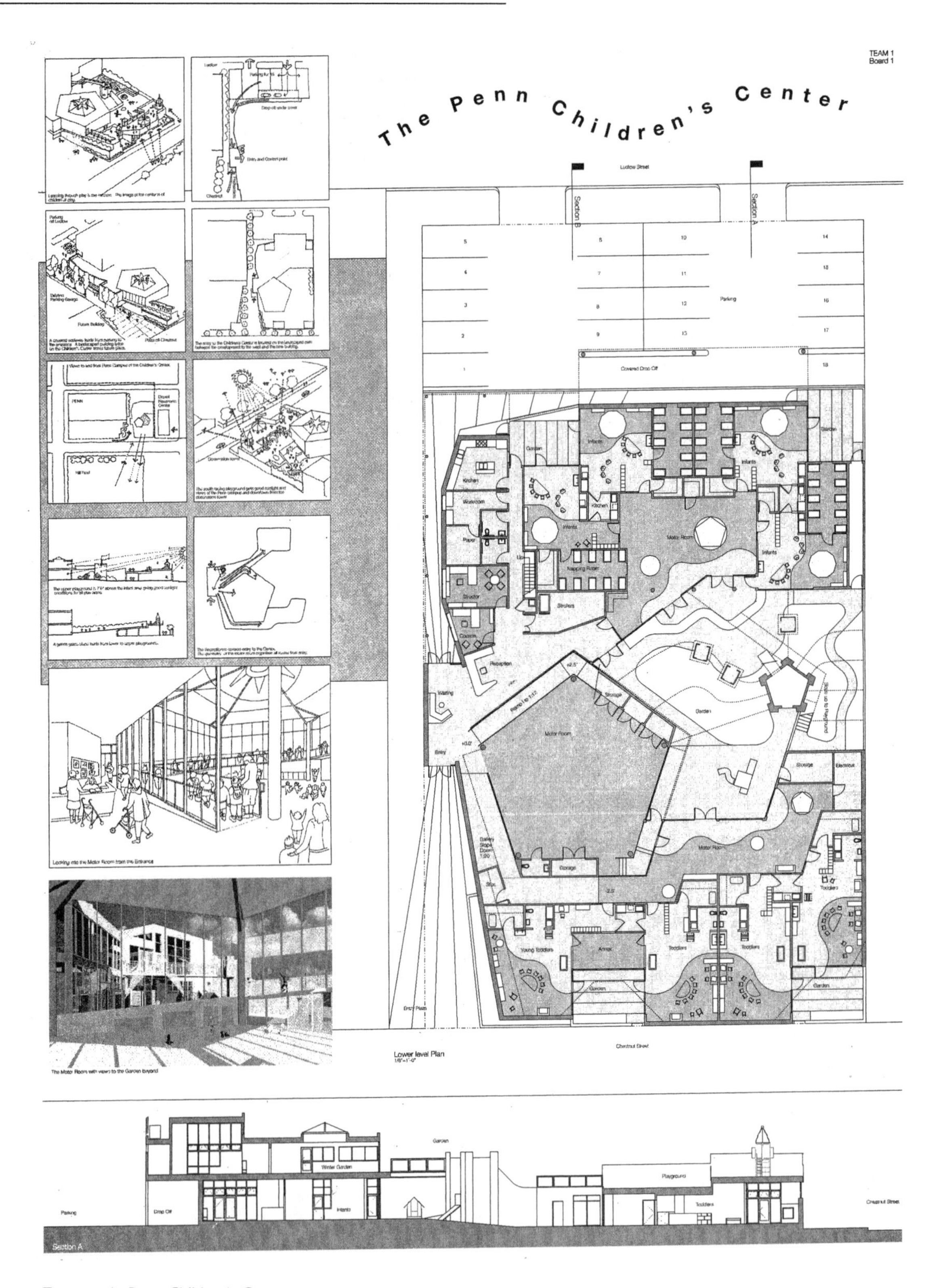

Two panels: Penn Children's Center
Courtesy of Adèle Naudé Santos and Associates

The sections form a base for the layout, while diagrams and vignettes are arranged to tell a story about the scheme. A large number of required drawings had to be accommodated on two boards.
[ARCHITECT'S STATEMENT]

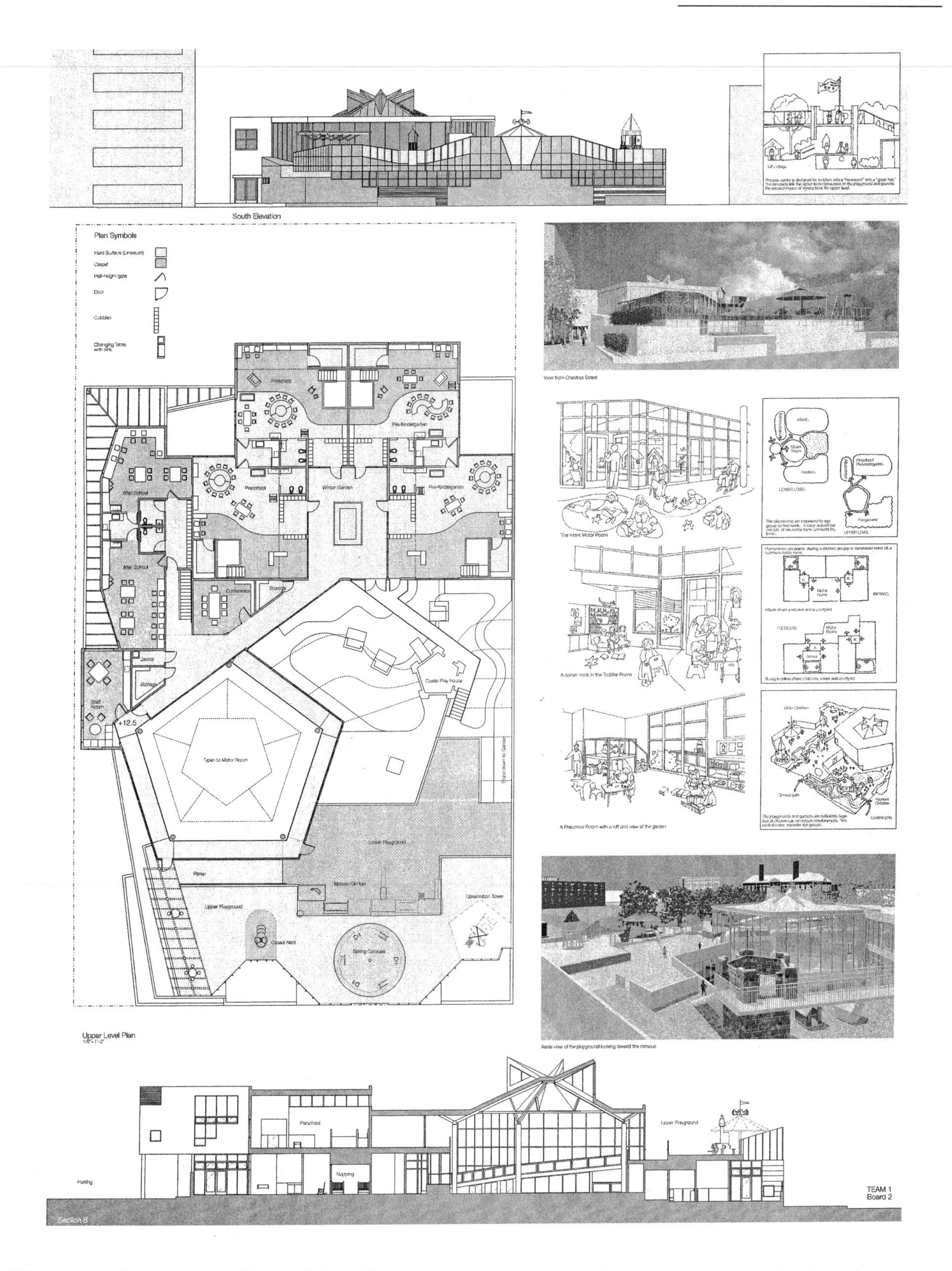

When more than one panel is used, how the panels relate to one another must be assessed. Here the visually balanced presentation uses building sections on a heavy ground line to tie the two panels together horizontally. See this same method employed using elevations and sections in the four-panel presentation on pp. 538–41. Note also the similar juxtaposition of diagrams and vignettes with orthographic drawings.

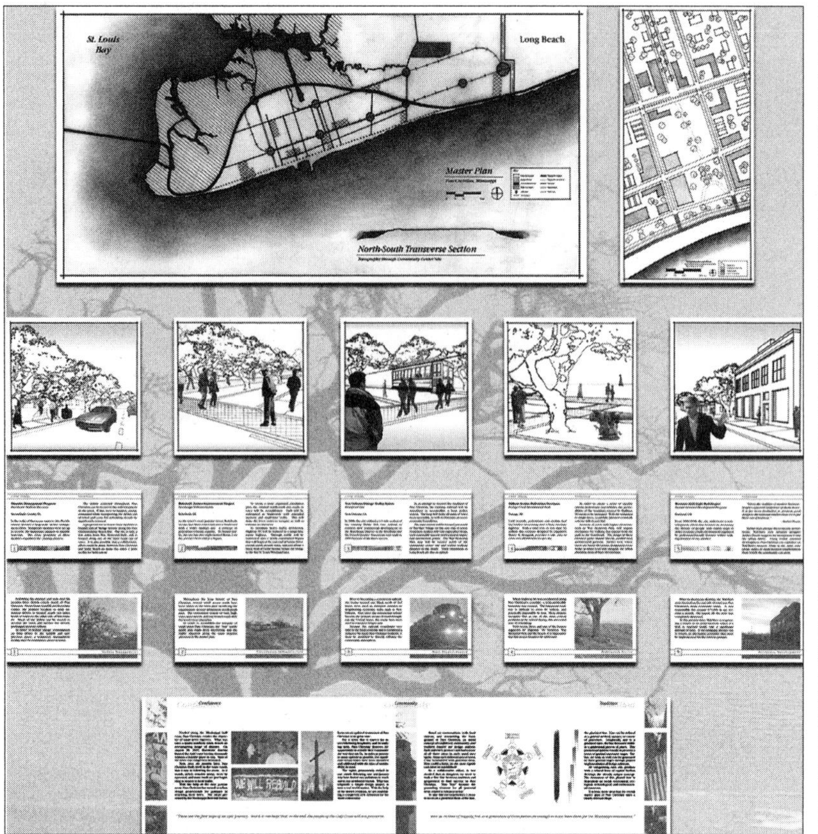

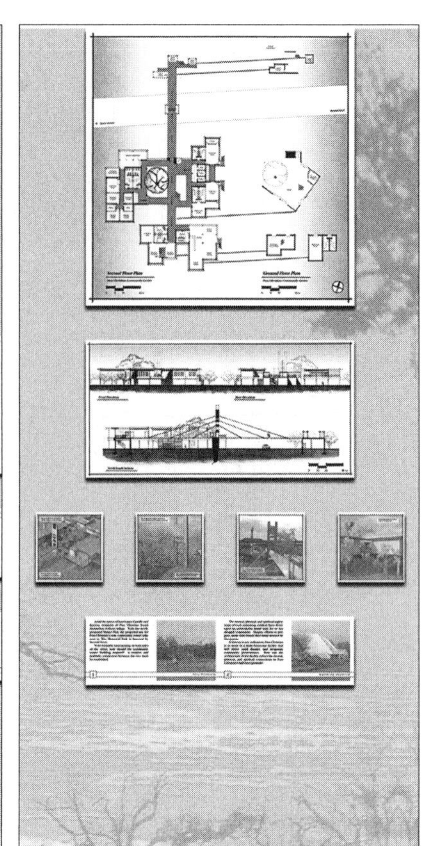

Composite presentation using a square grid system
Student project by Jason Hearn
Pass Christian Community Center, Pass Christian, Mississippi
Medium: Laser prints mounted on black foam core
Courtesy of Professor LaRaine Papa Montgomery, Savannah College of Art and Design

The course of study for which these boards were created was divided into two ten-week sessions. During the trip, the studio discovered that the wrath of Hurricane Katrina left very little, if any, site characteristics on which to base the community center designs. The focus quickly switched to community planning as a means of creating site, while the community center project was put on hold. For this reason, the boards were created ten weeks apart. A 4 X 4 square was used as the key proportioning unit. Each element on the boards is proportional to every other element.

Using the photograph of the surviving oak tree, the concept, problem, and solution were organized in a way that promoted the design process. The dense initial concept and background information that consistently influenced the entire twenty-week study is placed at the base of the tree trunk in rich color. Directly above the concept panel, the problem panels are placed in a horizontal band. Symbolically, this lower band of problems establishes the oldest and largest branches of the tree. Next, a horizontal band of solution panels addresses the issues introduced below, further growing and developing. Five photomontage perspectives take the information presented in the problem panels, and visually explain the information proposed in the solution panels. It is from here that the community master and neighborhood plans are finalized. Because these drawings are the final product, they are presented at a large scale, and centered at the top of the board, creating the pinnacle of the live oak. The tip of a lower branch extends horizontally from the master-plan board to the new community center board. Here, the immediate site and building issues for the center are presented. Compositionally, this keeps all problem panels in line, while giving the building design room to grow. Photographs of the physical depict structural aspects of the building that reflect the concepts of the designer, as well as those associated with sustainability. Again, photomontage is utilized in the elevation and section drawings to further the design visually. At the apex, drawn at a larger scale for emphasis, is the final master floor plan of the building. It is in this drawing that all aspects of the design are depicted: concept, program, form. Because the plan drawings run horizontally across the top, the viewer can create a clear distinction through scales, from community to neighborhood to building. When placed together, the dimensioning of both boards encompasses the initial proportioning units established from the beginning.
[ARCHITECTURE STUDENT'S STATEMENT]

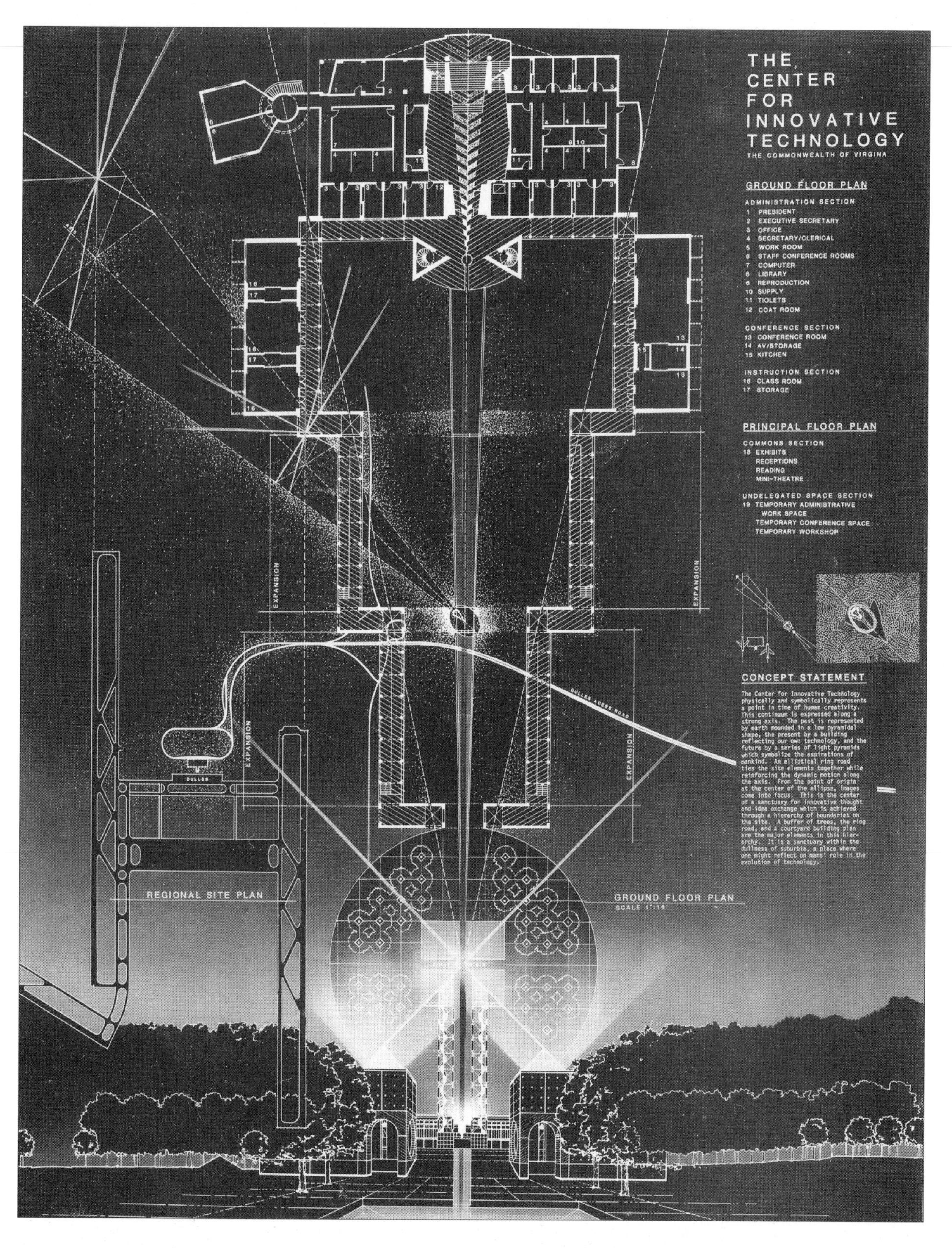

THE CENTER FOR INNOVATIVE TECHNOLOGY
THE COMMONWEALTH OF VIRGINA
GROUND FLOOR PLAN
ADMINISTRATION SECTION
1 PRESIDENT
2 EXECUTIVE SECRETARY
3 OFFICE
4 SECRETARY/CLERICAL
5 WORK ROOM
6 STAFF CONFERENCE ROOMS
7 COMPUTER
8 LIBRARY
9 REPRODUCTION
10 SUPPLY
11 TIOLETS
12 COAT ROOM
CONFERENCE SECTION
13 CONFERENCE ROOM
14 AV/STORAGE
15 KITCHEN
INSTRUCTION SECTION
16 CLASS ROOM
17 STORAGE
PRINCIPAL FLOOR PLAN
COMMONS SECTION
18 EXHIBITS
RECEPTIONS
READING
MINI-THEATRE
UNDELEGATED SPACE SECTION
19 TEMPORARY ADMINISTRATIVE WORK SPACE
TEMPORARY CONFERENCE SPACE
TEMPORARY WORKSHOP
CONCEPT STATEMENT
The Center for Innovative Technology physically and symbolically represents a point in time of human creativity. This continuum is expressed along a strong axis. The past is represented by earth mounded in a low pyramidal shape, the present by a building reflecting our own technology, and the future by a series of light pyramids which symbolize the aspirations of mankind. An elliptical ring road ties the site elements together while reinforcing the dynamic motion along the axis. From the point of origin at the center of the ellipse, images come into focus. This is the center of a sanctuary for innovative thought and idea exchange which is achieved through a hierarchy of boundaries on the site. A buffer of trees, the ring road, and a courtyard building plan are the major elements in this hierarchy. It is a sanctuary within the dullness of suburbia, a place where one might reflect on mans' role in the evolution of technology.
EXPANSION
EXPANSION
EXPANSION
EXPANSION
DULLES ACCESS ROAD
REGIONAL SITE PLAN
GROUND FLOOR PLAN

Three panels: The Center for Innovative Technology Competition, Reston, Virginia, first place
All three competition drawings: 24" × 30" (61 × 76.2 cm)
Competition team architects: William W.P. Chan, Peter Fillat, Rod Henderer, Tim Pellowski, and Mark Tuttle
Courtesy of William W.P. Chan, Architect

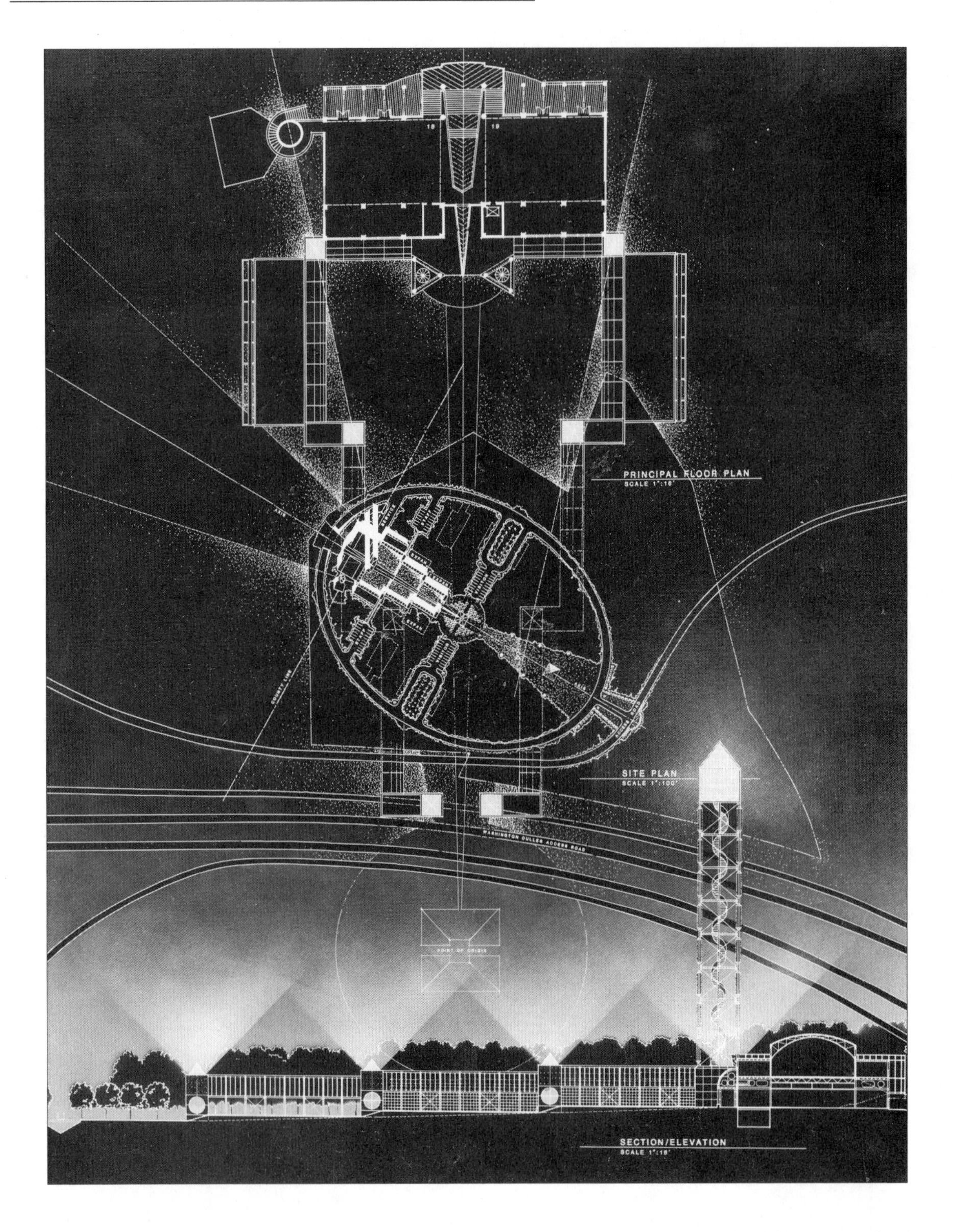

An objective of competition drawings is to achieve clarity of presentation while maintaining strong visual interest and complexity. Since the site plan, elevations, sections, plan obliques (axonometrics), and perspectives depict a specific aspect of the designed environment, we wanted to fuse them together into a graphic whole. Hence, we decided on a black background to unify these disparate elements. White lines on a pure black background appear too cold and lack a three-dimensional quality. A warm glow of airbrush yellow and orange was selectively sprayed onto the print to enhance the effect.
[Architect's statement]

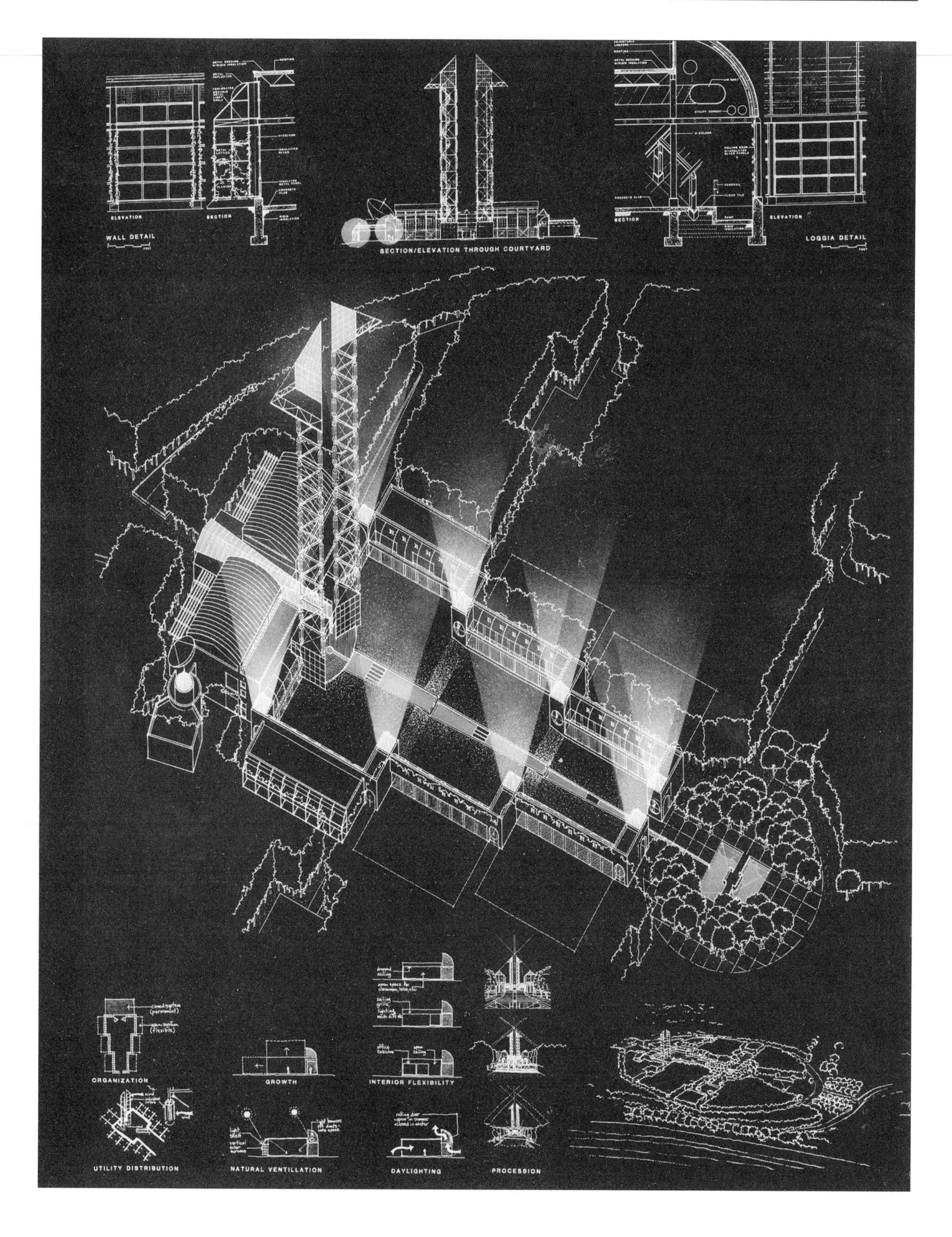
ELEVATION
SECTION
WALL DETAIL
SECTION/ELEVATION THROUGH COURTYARD
SECTION
ELEVATION
LOGGIA DETAIL
ORGANIZATION
GROWTH
INTERIOR FLEXIBILITY
UTILITY DISTRIBUTION
NATURAL VENTILLATION
DAYLIGHTING
PROCESSION

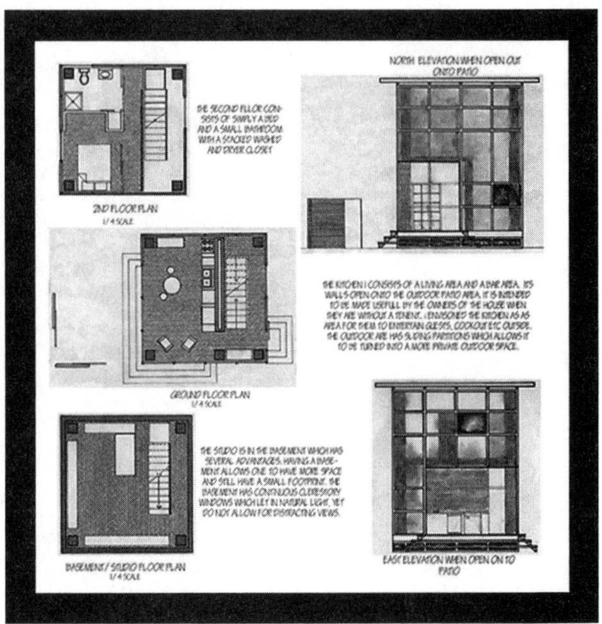

Student project by Anthea Selkirk
Courtesy of Studio Professor Michael Hagge
Architecture Program
University of Memphis

Problem courtesy of Professor Michael Hagge
Architecture Program
University of Memphis

Multifunction Building in a Historic Neighborhood

Design a two-story multifunction building consisting of a studio and a living space. The final presentation should include a site plan, floor plans, elevations, a section, a wall detail, an interior cutaway perspective, and exterior perspectives. Present the work on a unified set of four 20" X 20" boards containing all relevant information to enable the project to be understood without verbal communication.

Use ink on vellum and Photoshop as the media.
[PROFESSOR'S STATEMENT]

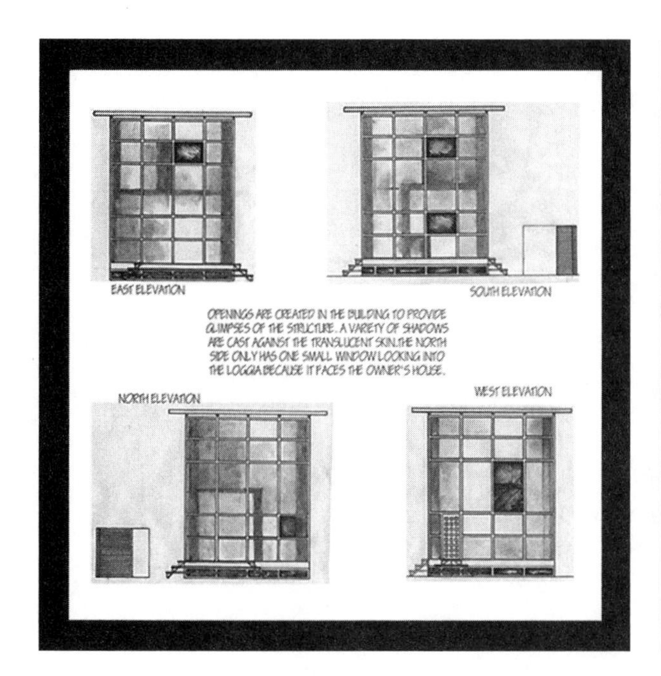
EAST ELEVATION
SOUTH ELEVATION
OPENINGS ARE CREATED IN THE BUILDING TO PROVIDE GLIMPSES OF THE STRUCTURE. A VARIETY OF SHADOWS ARE CAST AGAINST THE TRANSLUCENT SKIN.THE NORTH SIDE ONLY HAS ONE SMALL WINDOW LOOKING INTO THE LOGGIA BECAUSE IT FACES THE OWNER'S HOUSE.
NORTH ELEVATION
WEST ELEVATION

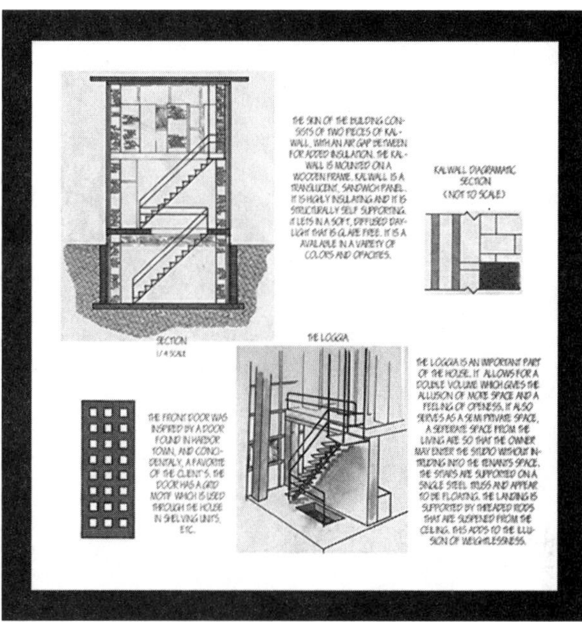
THE SKIN OF THE BUILDING CONSISTS OF TWO PIECES OF KALWALL, WITH AN AIR GAP BETWEEN FOR ADDED INSULATION. THE KALWALL IS MOUNTED ON A WOODEN FRAME. KALWALL IS A TRANSLUCENT, SANDWICH PANEL. IT IS HIGHLY INSULATING AND IT IS STRUCTURALLY SELF SUPPORTING. IT LETS IN A SOFT, DIFFUSED DAYLIGHT THAT IS GLARE FREE. IT IS AVAILABLE IN A VARIETY OF COLORS AND OPACITIES.
KALWALL DIAGRAMATIC SECTION (NOT TO SCALE)
SECTION
1/4 SCALE
THE LOGGIA
THE FRONT DOOR WAS INSPIRED BY A DOOR FOUND IN HARBOR TOWN, AND COINCIDENTALY, A FAVORITE OF THE CLIENT'S. THE DOOR HAS A GRID MOTIF WHICH IS USED THROUGH THE HOUSE IN SHELVING UNITS, ETC.
THE LOGGIA IS AN IMPORTANT PART OF THE HOUSE. IT ALLOWS FOR A DOUBLE VOLUME WHICH GIVES THE ALLUSION OF MORE SPACE AND A FEELING OF OPENESS. IT ALSO SERVES AS A SEMI PRIVATE SPACE, A SEPERATE SPACE FROM THE LIVING ARE SO THAT THE OWNER MAY ENTER THE STUDIO WITHOUT INTRUDING INTO THE TENANTS SPACE. THE STAIRS ARE SUPPORTED ON A SINGLE STEEL TRUSS AND APPEAR TO BE FLOATING. THE LANDING IS SUPPORTED BY THREADED RODS THAT ARE SUSPENDED FROM THE CEILING. THIS ADDS TO THE ILLUSION OF WEIGHTLESSNESS.

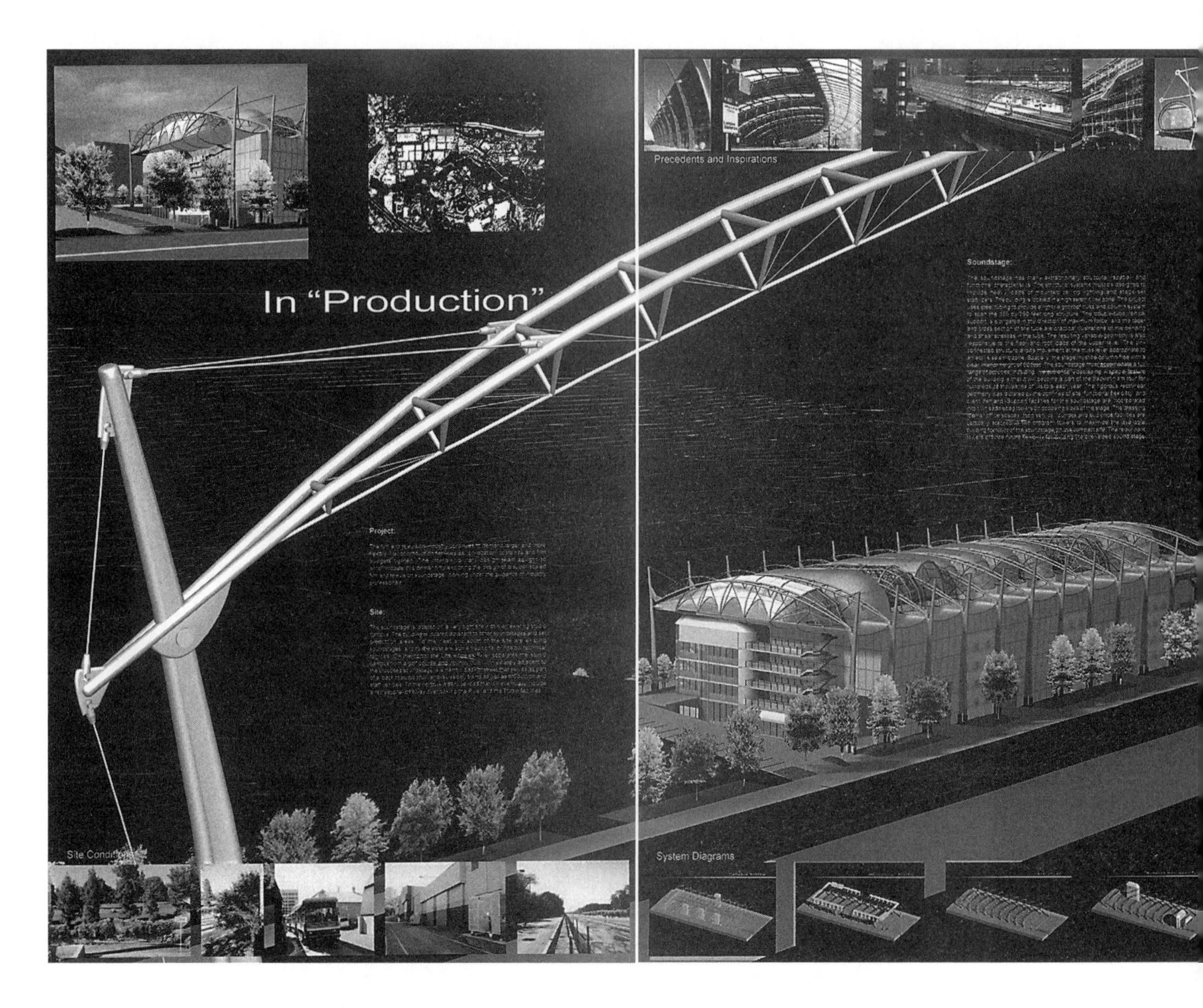

Drawing: Four-board presentation for a student competition
Student project by Theresia Kurnadi, with help from Melissa Hsu
Media: Hand sketches; Software: form-Z, Photoshop, PageMaker
Courtesy of Professors Douglas Noble and Karen Kensek
University of Southern California, School of Architecture

A horizontal band of drawn or photographic elements (see also pp. 557–62), in addition to a strong ground line (see pp. 526–27), is used to unify the panels.

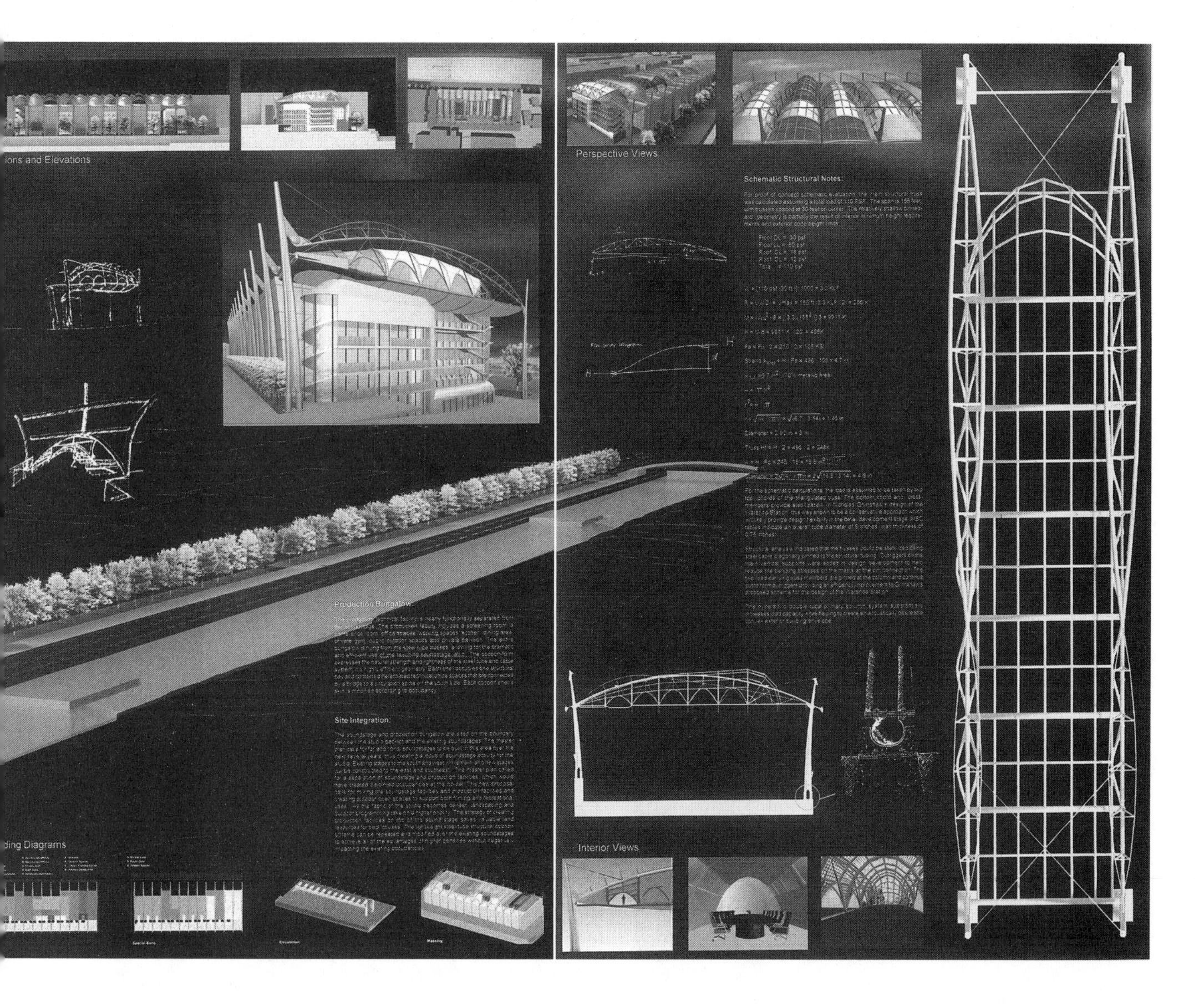

This project for an undergraduate design studio competition includes a large film and TV sound stage with a penthouse production facility. After initial sketches, the project was developed entirely on the computer in three dimensions by Theresia Kurnadi. Melissa Hsu assisted in the creation of the four presentation boards.

The presentation boards include hand sketches, site-analysis photographs, narrative programmatic and philosophy statements, three-dimensional diagrams, structural analysis, and details. Many of the images were manipulated and composited in Photoshop and then assembled in PageMaker for the final board layout.

[Professors' statement]

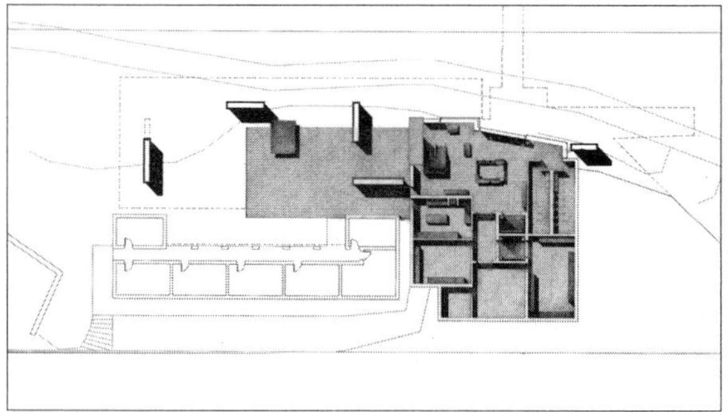

Level new building

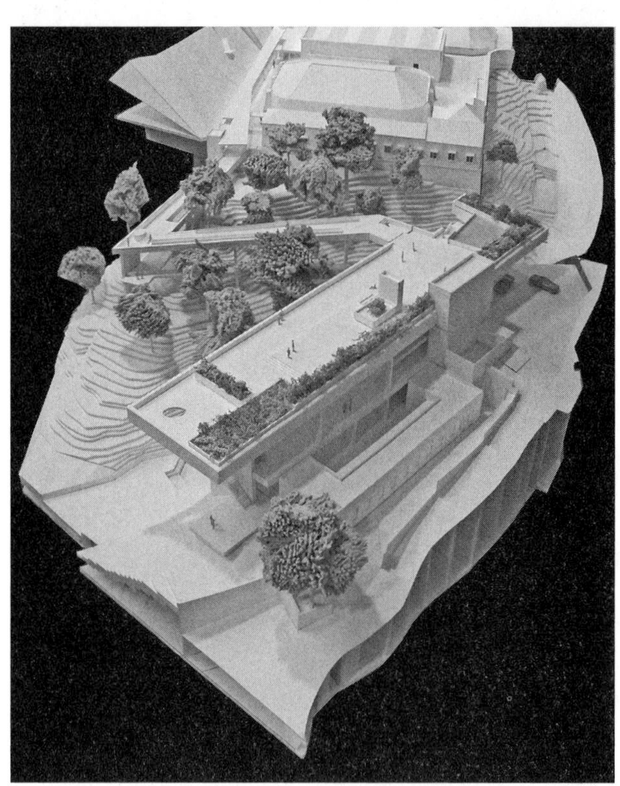

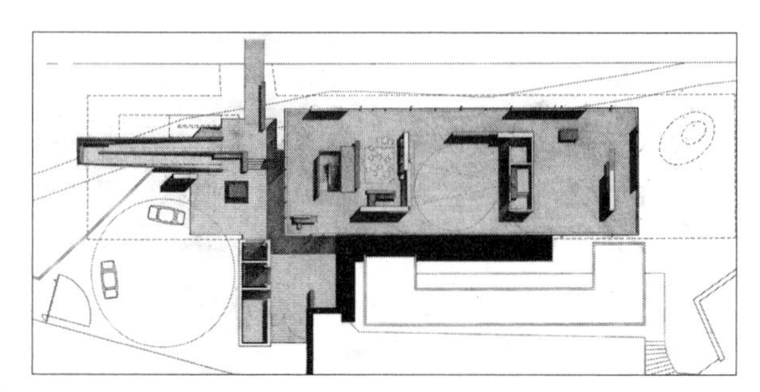

Level new building

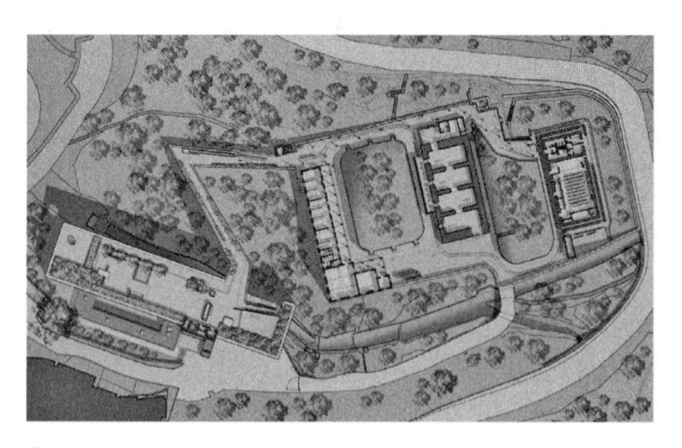

Site plan

Competition drawings: Asia Society Hong Kong Center
Hong Kong, China
Medium: First drawn as line drawings in AutoCAD, then rendered by hand with graphite and colored pencil
Model: Foam core; Perspective: Watercolor
Courtesy of Tod Williams Billie Tsien Architects

Sometimes competition requirements for a design concept presentation are somewhat loose. This project—a complex in Hong Kong for lectures, conferences, art exhibitions, performances, and film sponsored and organized by the Asia Society—is one such example. No specific number of panels was required, and the actual technique of the presentation was left to the discretion of each participating firm. Basic requirements included a 1:200 model (the base model for all competitors provided), 1:50 floor plans, a building section, a 1:20 partial elevation, and a perspective.

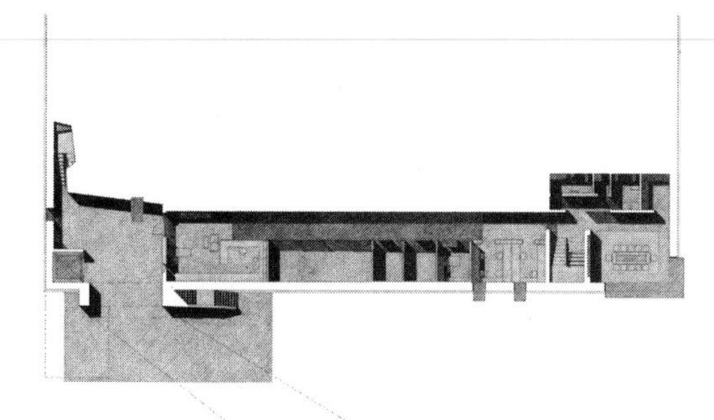

Lab plan

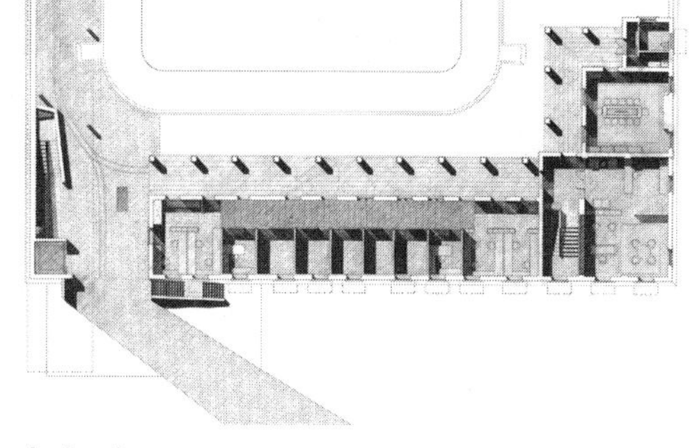

Lab plan

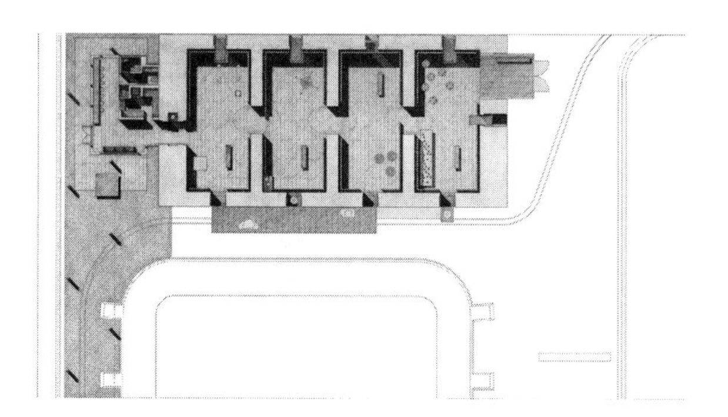

Magazine A plan

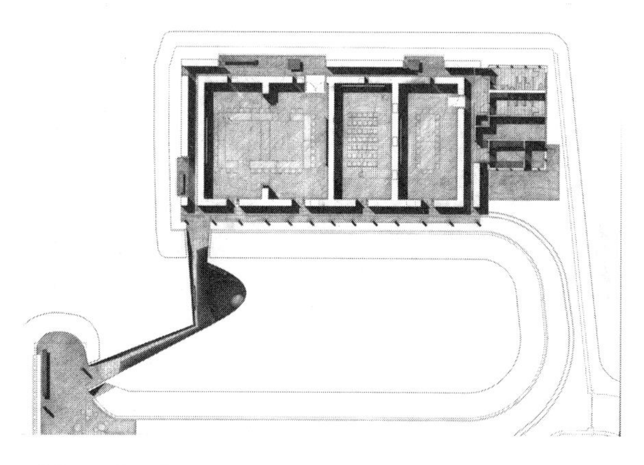

Magazine B plan

Magazine A section/partial elevation

The panels are so informal because all three competitors presented their projects in person, right after pinning up their boards. A winner was then chosen immediately after all the presentations.
[ARCHITECT'S STATEMENT]

Competition Drawings: Asia Society Hong Kong Center
Hong Kong, China
Medium: First drawn as line drawings in AutoCAD, then rendered by hand with graphite and colored pencil
Courtesy of Tod Williams Billie Tsien Architects

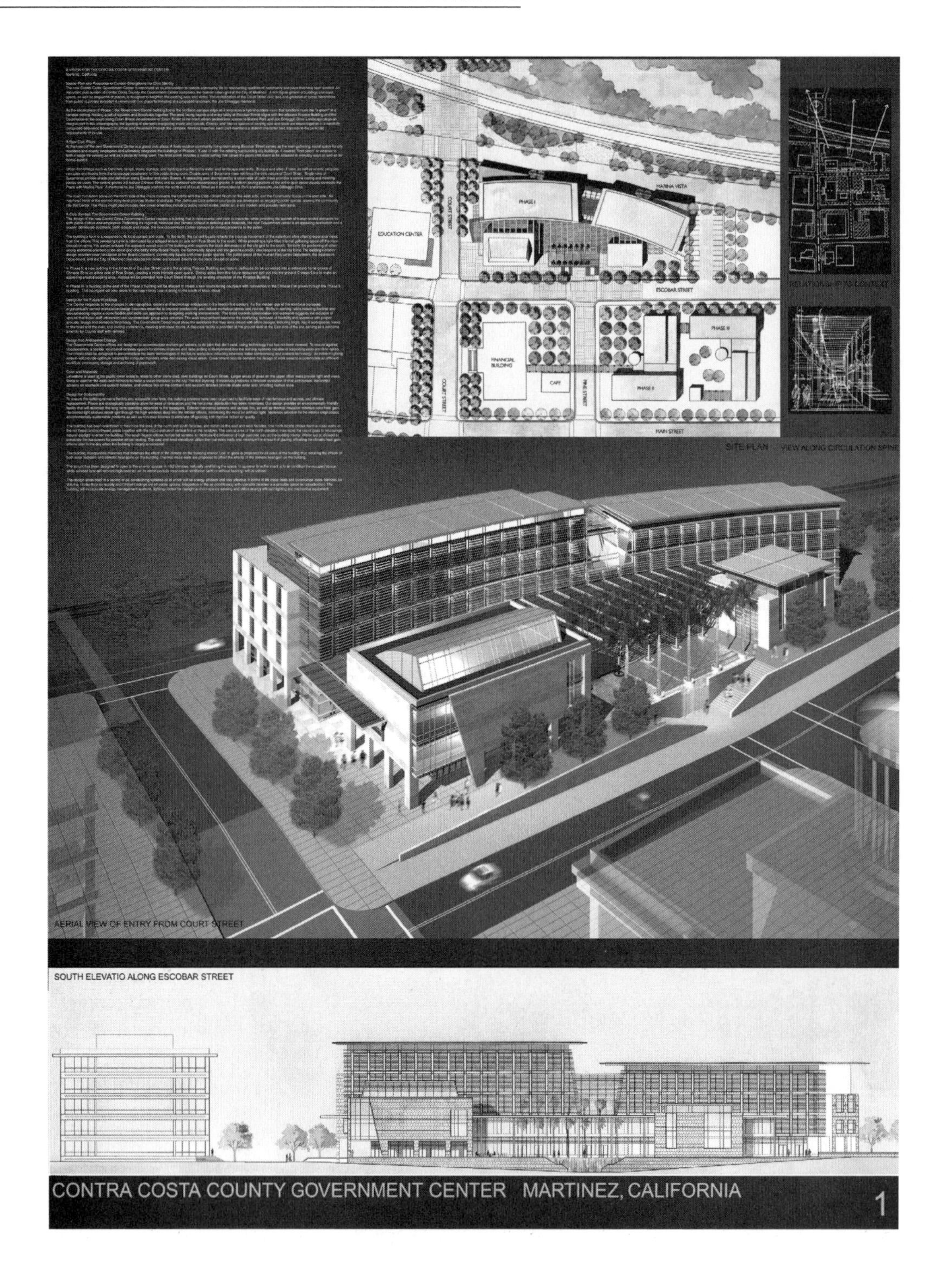

Four panels: Contra Costa Government Competition, Martinez, California
Courtesy of design architect: Moore Ruble Yudell
Principal-in-charge, principal architect: John Ruble
Principal architect: Buzz Yudell
Associate-in-charge/project architect: James Mary O'Connor
Project team: Lisa Belian, Tony Tran, Ed Diamante, Kaoru Orime, Roger Lopez, Ross Morishige, Janet Sager
Digital rendering: Craig Shimahara
Models: Mark Grand, Donald Hornbeck, Joshua Lunn
Associate architect: Fisher-Friedman Associates: Rodney Freidman, Dan Howard, Robert J. Geering
Interior design: Marcy Li Wong Architects
Owner: Contra Costa County
Project management: O'Brien Kreitzberg
Principal: Mark Tortorich

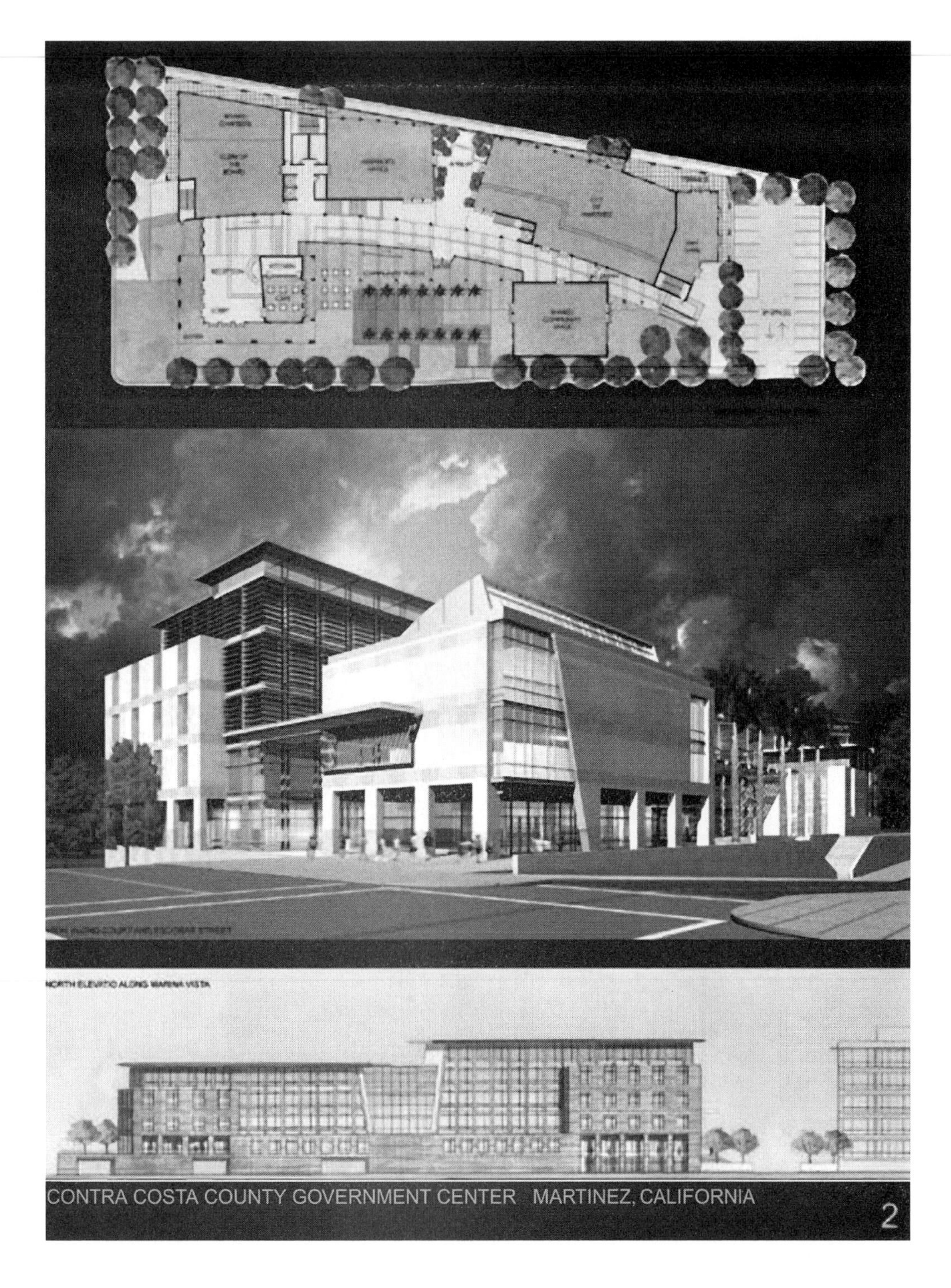

The four competition boards were presented using a clear organizing principle—a tripartite composition that would read as three horizontal bands when the four boards are put together side by side. The size of each board is 30″ wide by 40″ high.

The central and largest band contains the digital three-dimensional renderings of the exterior of the building, one rendering on each board. Maximized in proportion, this band is intended to effectively draw the viewer's attention into the deisgn of the architecture. The band at the bottom is composed of elevations and sections, providing a linear base for the boards. The band at the top contains floor plans and a site plan, with the ground-floor plan and second-floor plan at a larger scale than the others.

It was important to create this simple and clear composition because in a competition forum there is little time to present your design idea to the jury. The simple and uncluttered organization of images helps the jury visualize and understand the design idea in the quickest and easiest way possible.

[ARCHITECT'S STATEMENT]

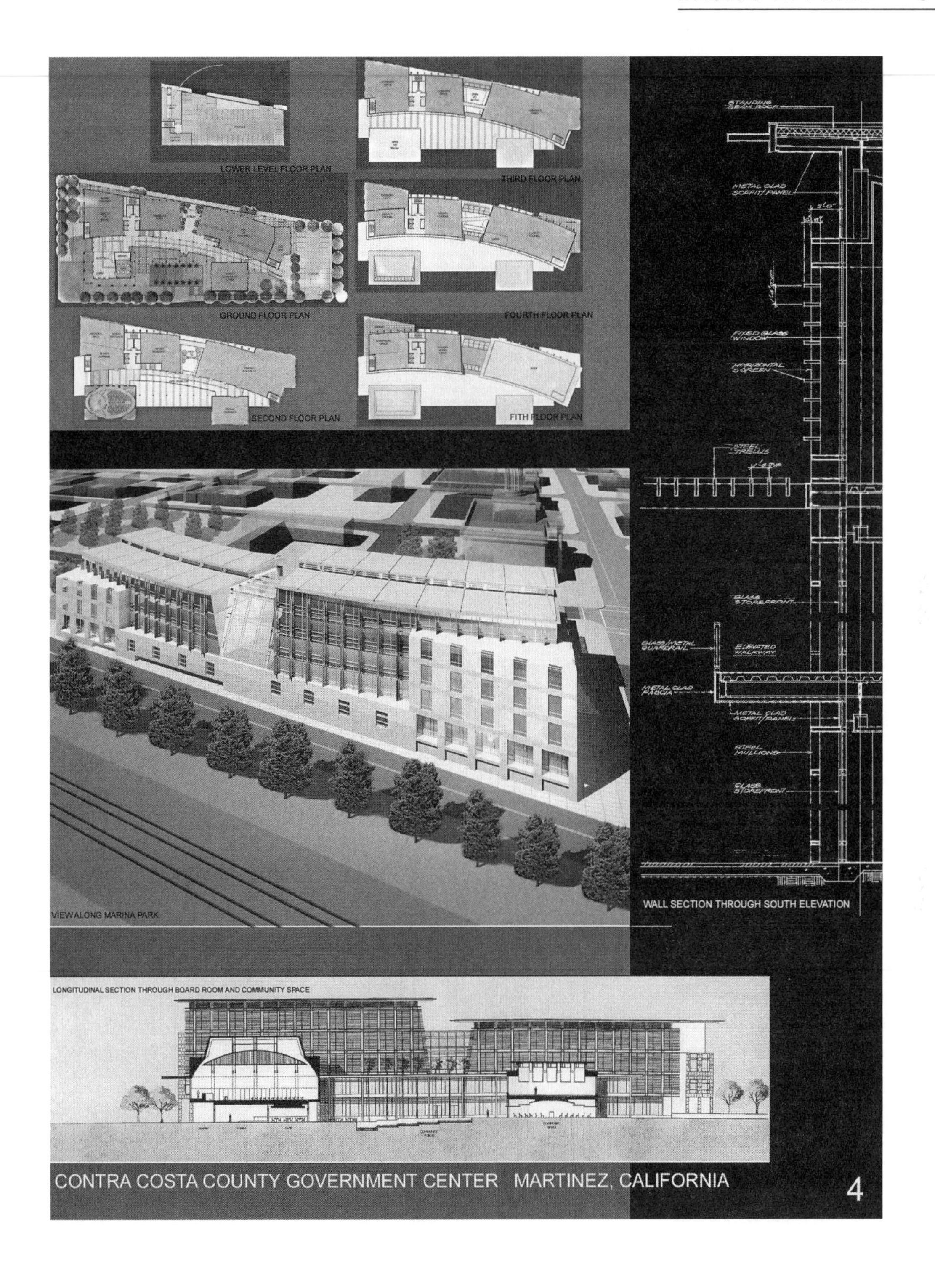
LOWER LEVEL FLOOR PLAN
THIRD FLOOR PLAN
GROUND FLOOR PLAN
FOURTH FLOOR PLAN
SECOND FLOOR PLAN
FITH FLOOR PLAN
STANDING SEAM ROOF
METAL CLAD SOFFIT/PANEL
FIXED GLASS WINDOW
HORIZONTAL SCREEN
STEEL TRELLIS
GLASS STOREFRONT
GLASS/METAL GUARDRAIL
ELEVATED WALKWAY
METAL CLAD FASCIA
METAL CLAD SOFFIT/PANEL
STEEL MULLIONS
GLASS STOREFRONT
VIEWALONG MARINA PARK
WALL SECTION THROUGH SOUTH ELEVATION
LONGITUDINAL SECTION THROUGH BOARD ROOM AND COMMUNITY SPACE
CONTRA COSTA COUNTY GOVERNMENT CENTER MARTINEZ, CALIFORNIA
4

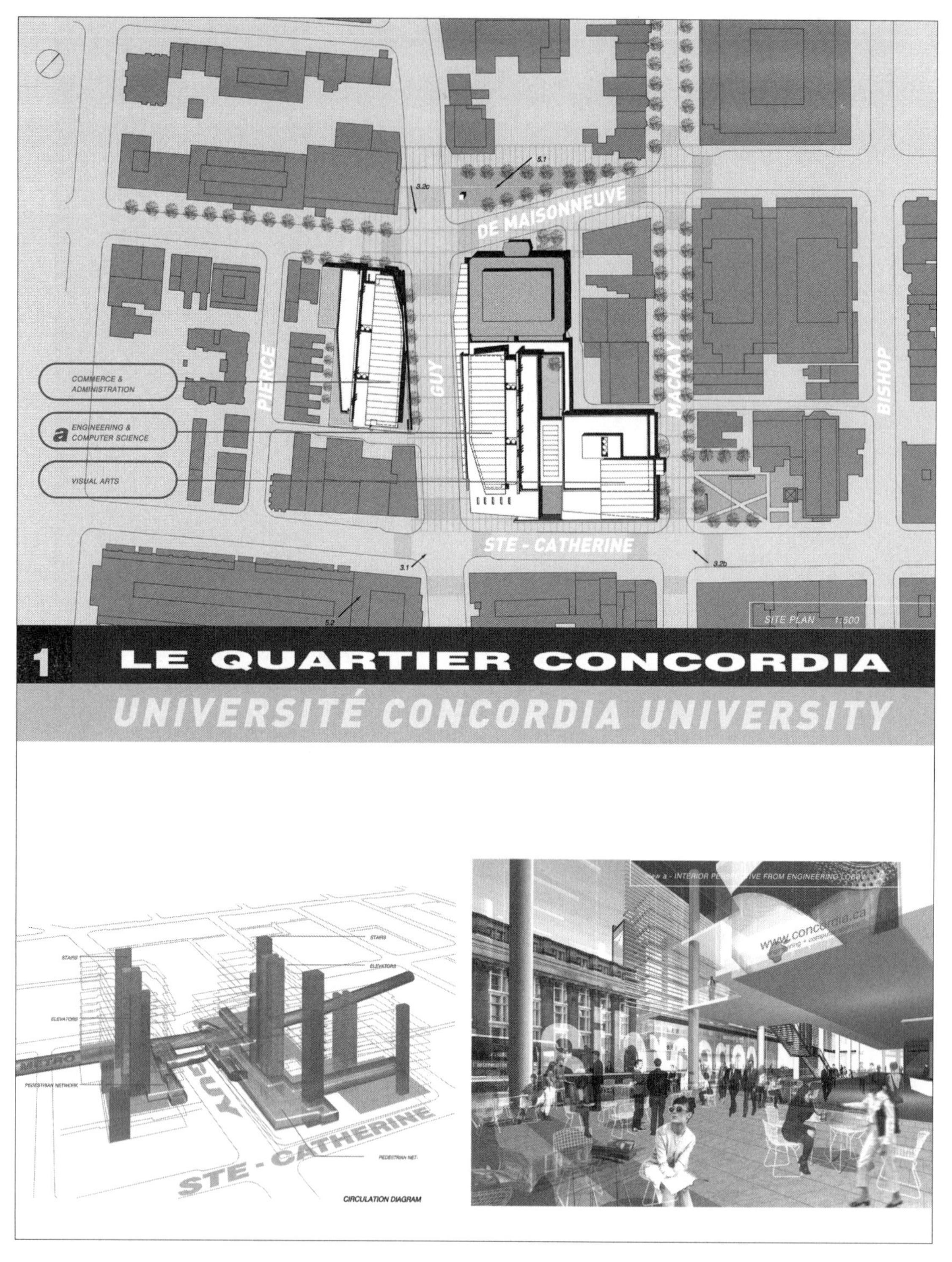

Five panels: New Integrated Complex, Concordia University, Montreal, Quebec, Canada
Courtesy of Kuwabara Payne McKenna Blumberg Architects and Fichten Soiferman Architects, in joint venture

This series of five panels, each 33″ × 47″, illustrates the winning entry prepared by Kuwabara Payne McKenna Blumberg Architects for an invited competition for the new $160 million complex of buildings for the downtown campus of Concordia University in Montreal, Quebec. The architects chose to use bilingual captions on all the panels to acknowledge the roles of both English and French on the Concordia campus in this densely built-up area of downtown Montreal. To unify all five panels, the architects employed a horizontal red band running through the middle of each panel. The red color was derived from the university crest and coat of arms.

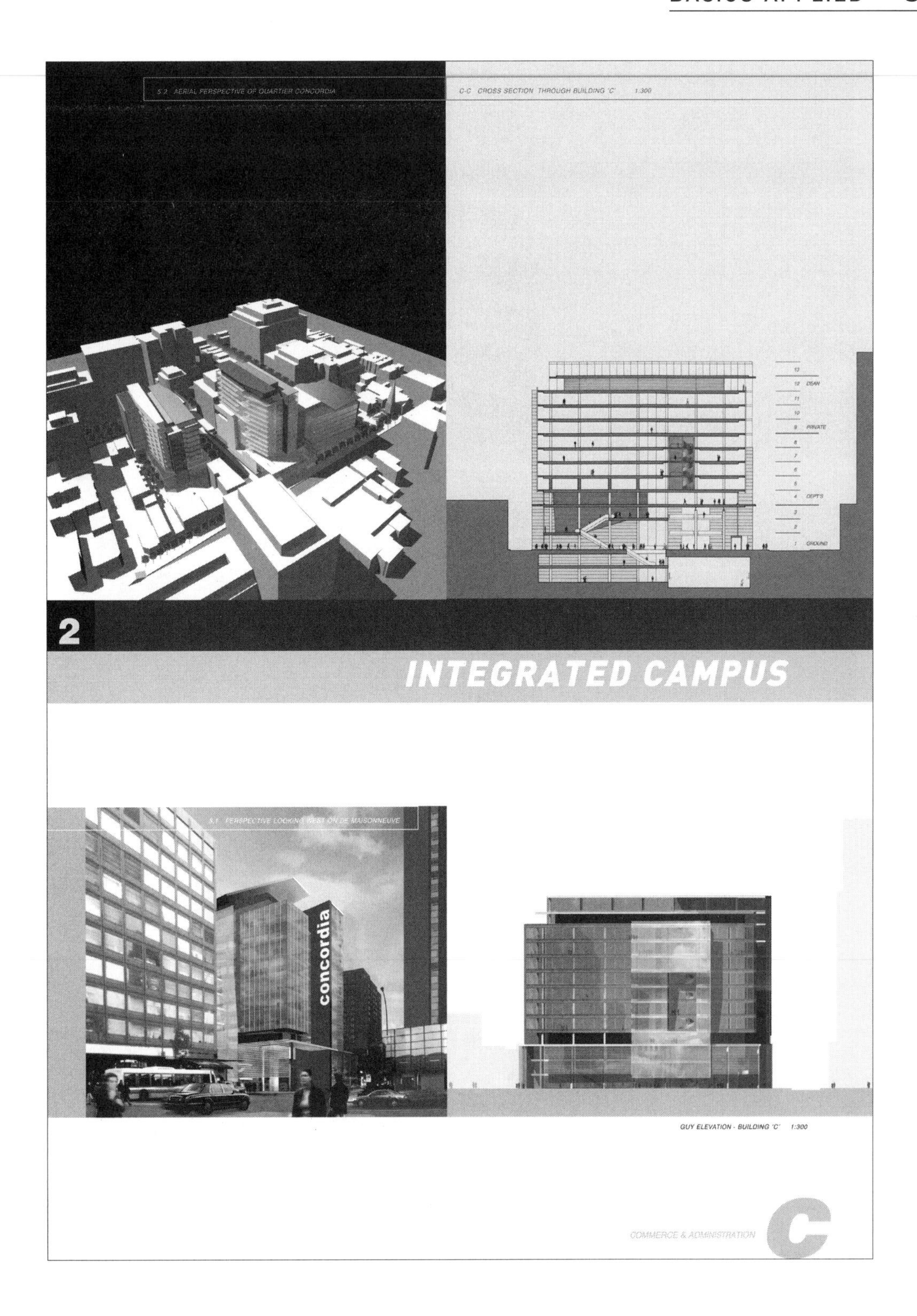

The exterior perspectives on panels 2, 3, and 4 were a mandatory requirement, and are drawn from fixed vantage points on the streets adjacent, as specified in the competition conditions. This enabled the jury members to compare the competitors' designs all viewed from the same perspective. To convey the importance of student life and culture in the three new buildings, we chose to show the buildings in both daytime and nighttime perspectives. This idea of "studio culture," of open and accessible buildings used twenty-four hours a day, is further expressed in the "24-7" logo on panel 1.

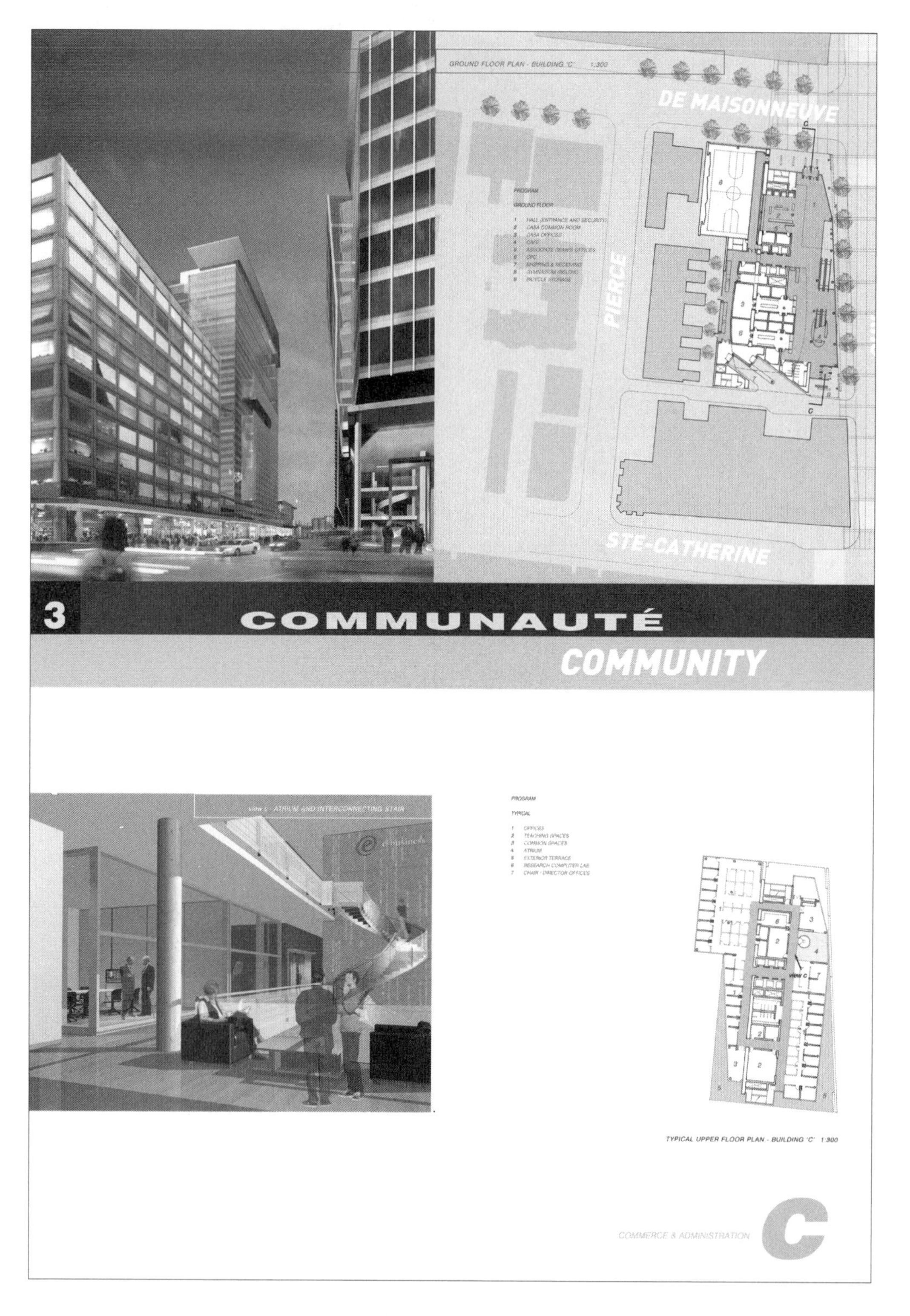

The perspective diagram in panel 1 and the axonometric drawing in panel 4 were also mandatory. We chose to render them as transparent volumes to allow the jury to comprehend the complex layering of streets, sidewalks, subways, vertical core circulation, and circulation at grade throughout the buildings. Green was used on ground-floor plans to denote public space and how it can extend the public realm from sidewalks into and through the new buildings. Gray, another pervasive color found throughout Montreal in the gray stone buildings, was used on plans and in one monochromatic perspective on panel 3.

[Architects' statement]

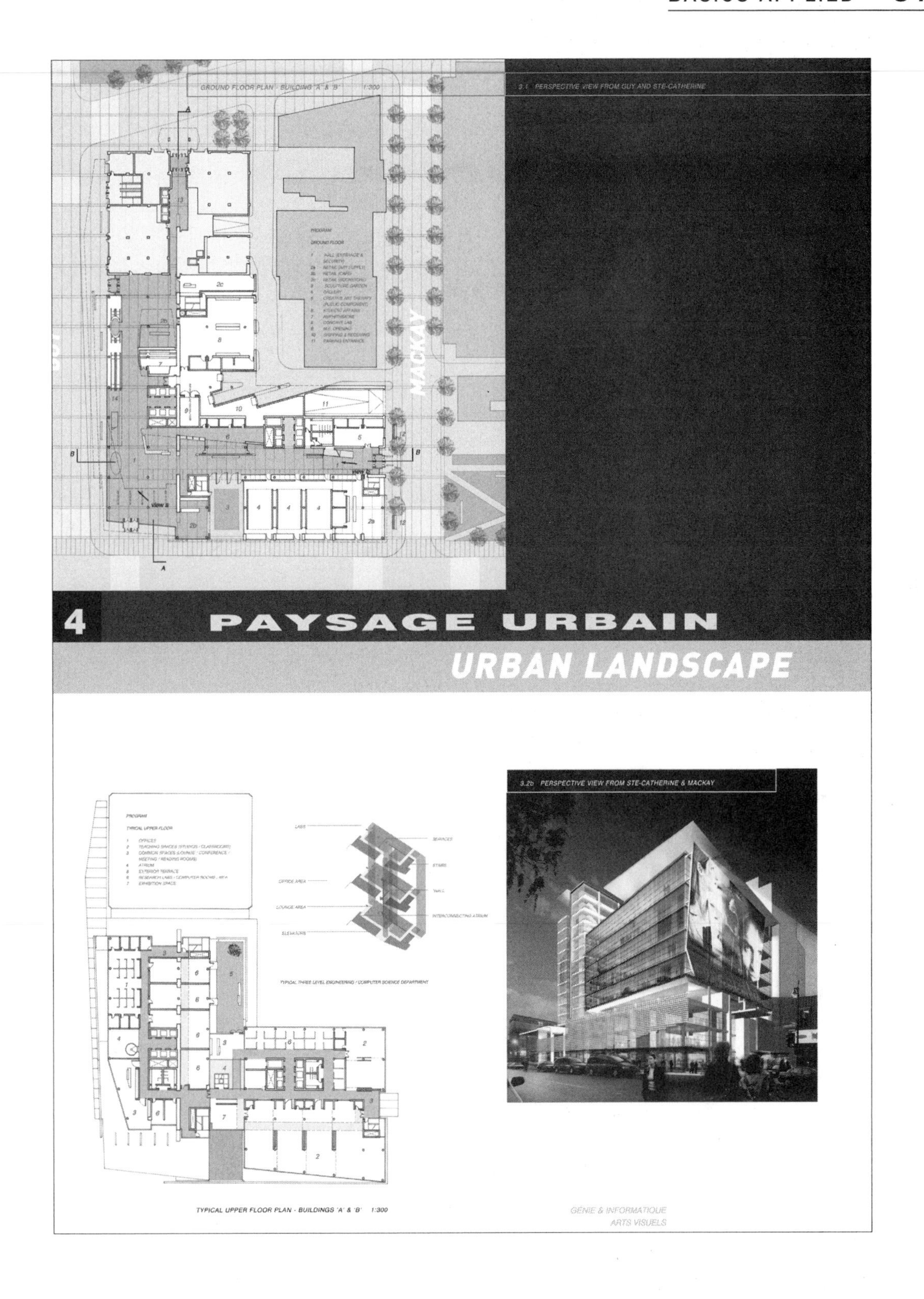
GROUND FLOOR PLAN - BUILDING 'A' & 'B' 1:300
3.1 PERSPECTIVE VIEW FROM GUY AND STE-CATHERINE
MACKAY
4
PAYSAGE URBAIN
URBAN LANDSCAPE
3.2b PERSPECTIVE VIEW FROM STE-CATHERINE & MACKAY
TYPICAL UPPER FLOOR PLAN - BUILDINGS 'A' & 'B' 1:300
GÉNIE & INFORMATIQUE
ARTS VISUELS

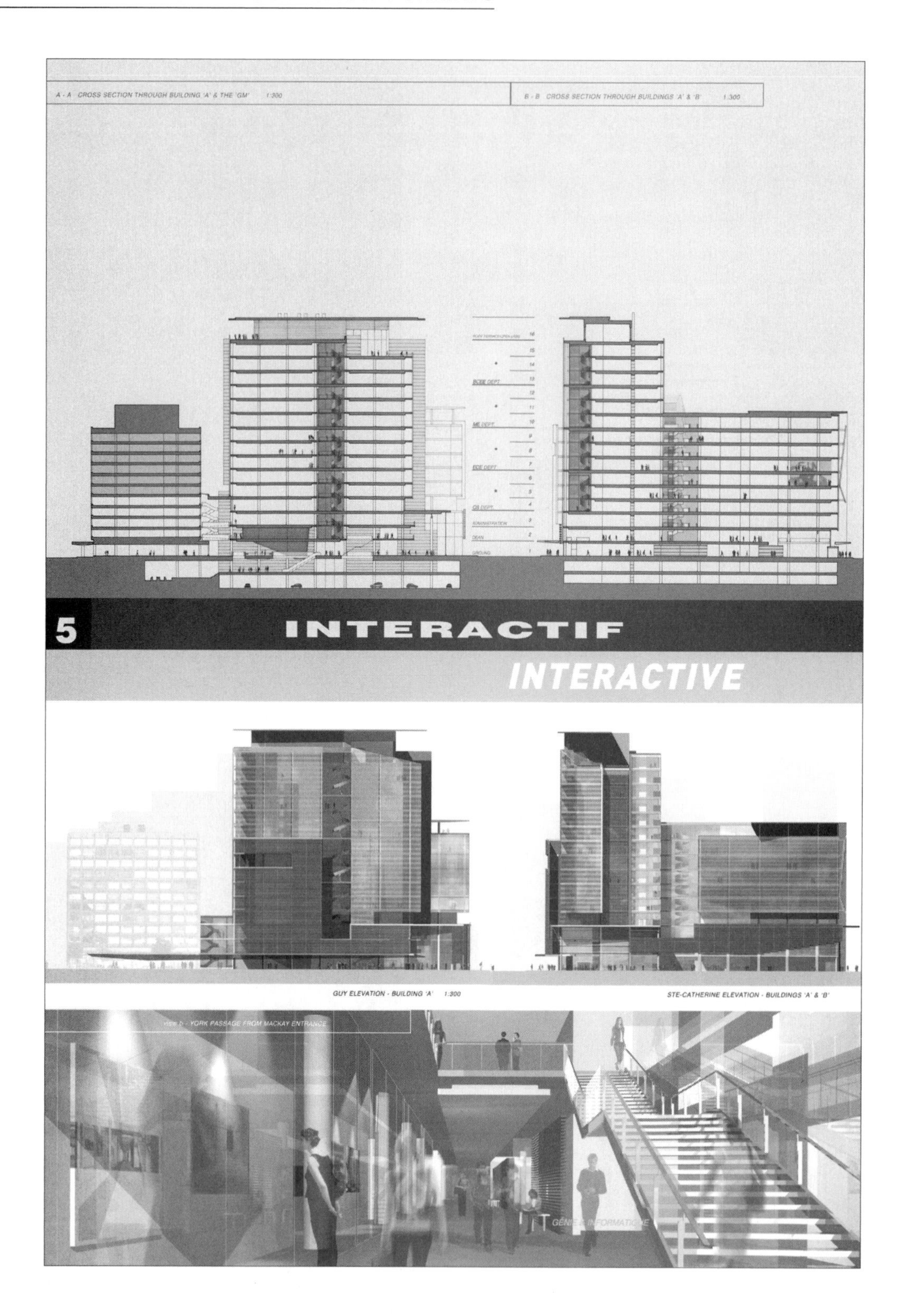
A - A CROSS SECTION THROUGH BUILDING 'A' & THE 'GM' 1:300
B - B CROSS SECTION THROUGH BUILDINGS 'A' & 'B' 1:300
5
INTERACTIF
INTERACTIVE
GUY ELEVATION - BUILDING 'A' 1:300
STE-CATHERINE ELEVATION - BUILDINGS 'A' & 'B'
YORK PASSAGE FROM MACKAY ENTRANCE

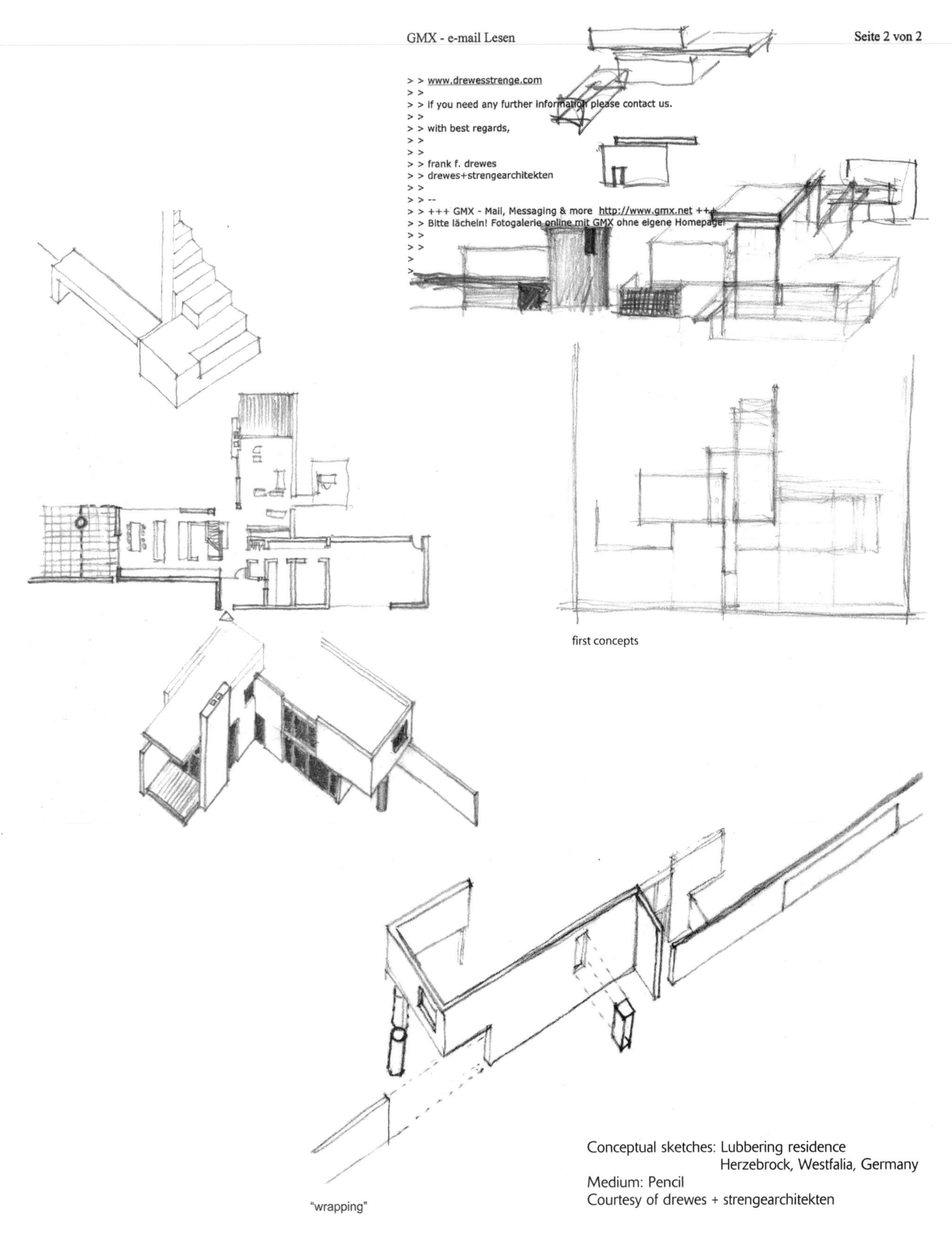

first concepts

"wrapping"

Conceptual sketches: Lubbering residence
Herzebrock, Westfalia, Germany
Medium: Pencil
Courtesy of drewes + strengearchitekten

The concept sketch (upper right) was drawn on an e-mail that had been printed. This is a good example of a conceptual sketch: ideas are placed on any kind of paper—blank or not.

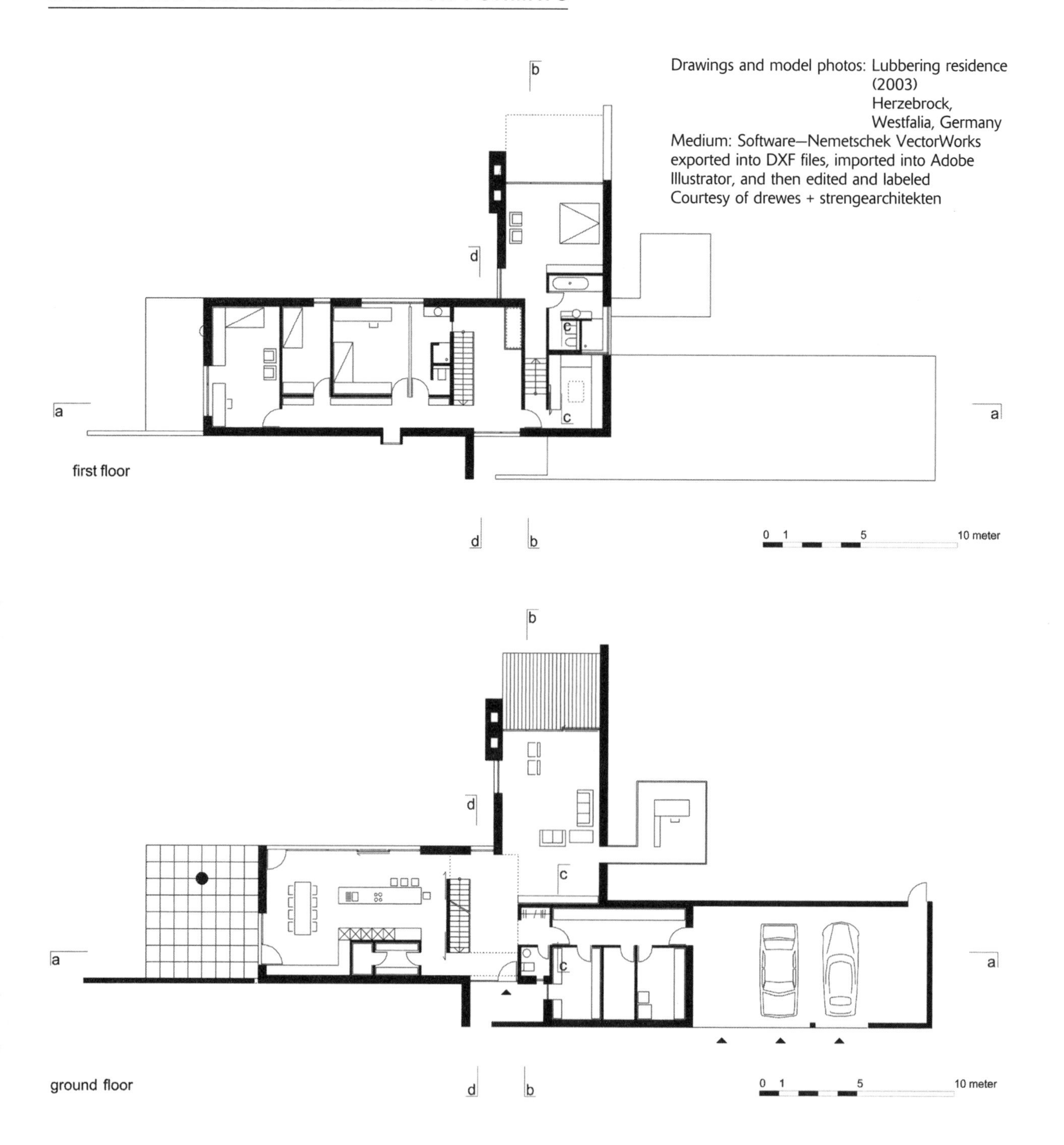

Drawings and model photos: Lubbering residence (2003)
Herzebrock, Westfalia, Germany
Medium: Software—Nemetschek VectorWorks exported into DXF files, imported into Adobe Illustrator, and then edited and labeled
Courtesy of drewes + strengearchitekten

The Lubbering residence (2,717 sq. ft.) was designed for a large lot in a light industrial area, next to a recently built factory with magnificent views of the landscape. The clients, a young family, required a house that would accommodate both their public and private lives.

Program requirements are divided between the two angles and the two floors of the residence. The access level consists of the spacious kitchen–dining area and the living room, which are linked via a two-story atrium space. The satellite study is a remote appendix with glass walls, accessed via a glass tunnel. The upper level contains the private spaces (bedrooms, bathrooms, and guest room). The services and garage define a long, one-story public facade without any windows or openings. The tall, narrow entrance slot and a colored window on the second floor are the only hints of habitation.

[ARCHITECTS' STATEMENT]

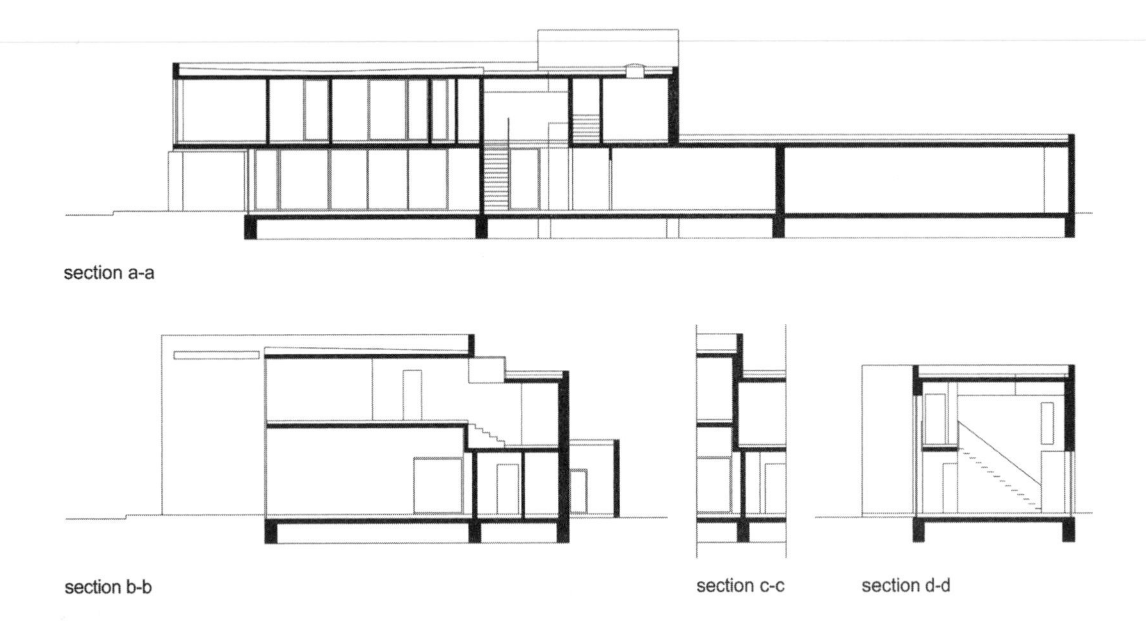

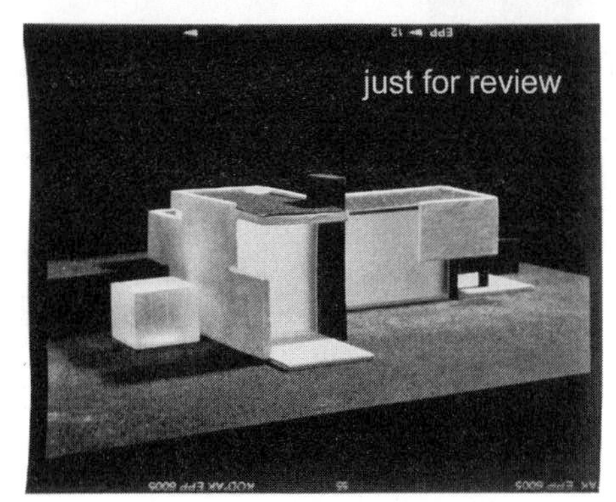

The abstract composition is intended to evoke curiosity and to formally link the residence and the factory. The different materials (stucco, steel, wood) and facade textures clarify the distinct yet interrelated components of the building. [ARCHITECTS' STATEMENT]

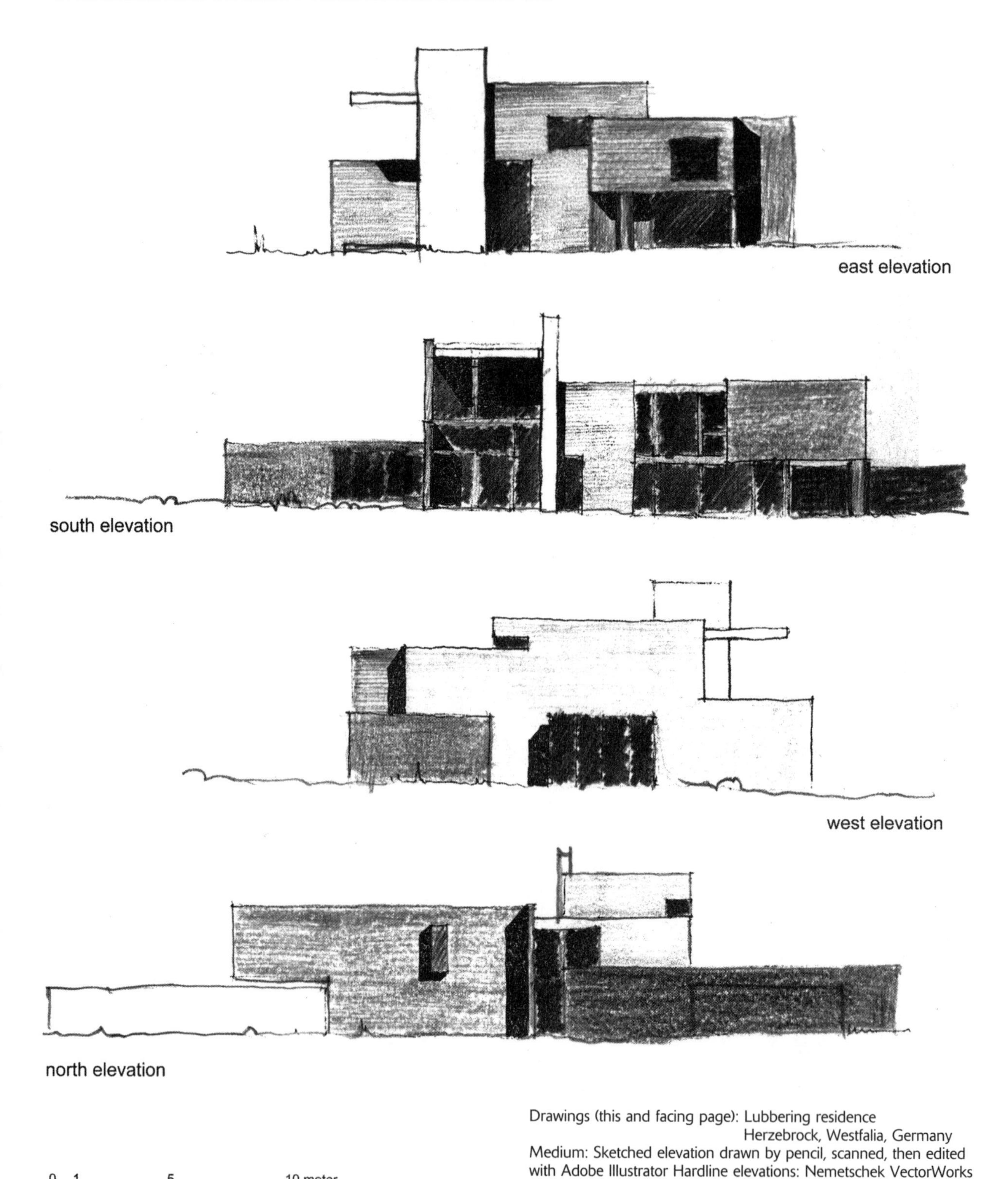

Drawings (this and facing page): Lubbering residence
Herzebrock, Westfalia, Germany
Medium: Sketched elevation drawn by pencil, scanned, then edited with Adobe Illustrator Hardline elevations: Nemetschek VectorWorks
Courtesy of drewes + strengearchitekten

The project was a direct private commission for a commercial client of ours. We did not have to do a formal presentation because the client trusts us. The entire presentation was done on a sketch basis. However, a formal presentation and model was done for inclusion as a Global Architecture (GA) project in 2004.
[ARCHITECTS' STATEMENT]

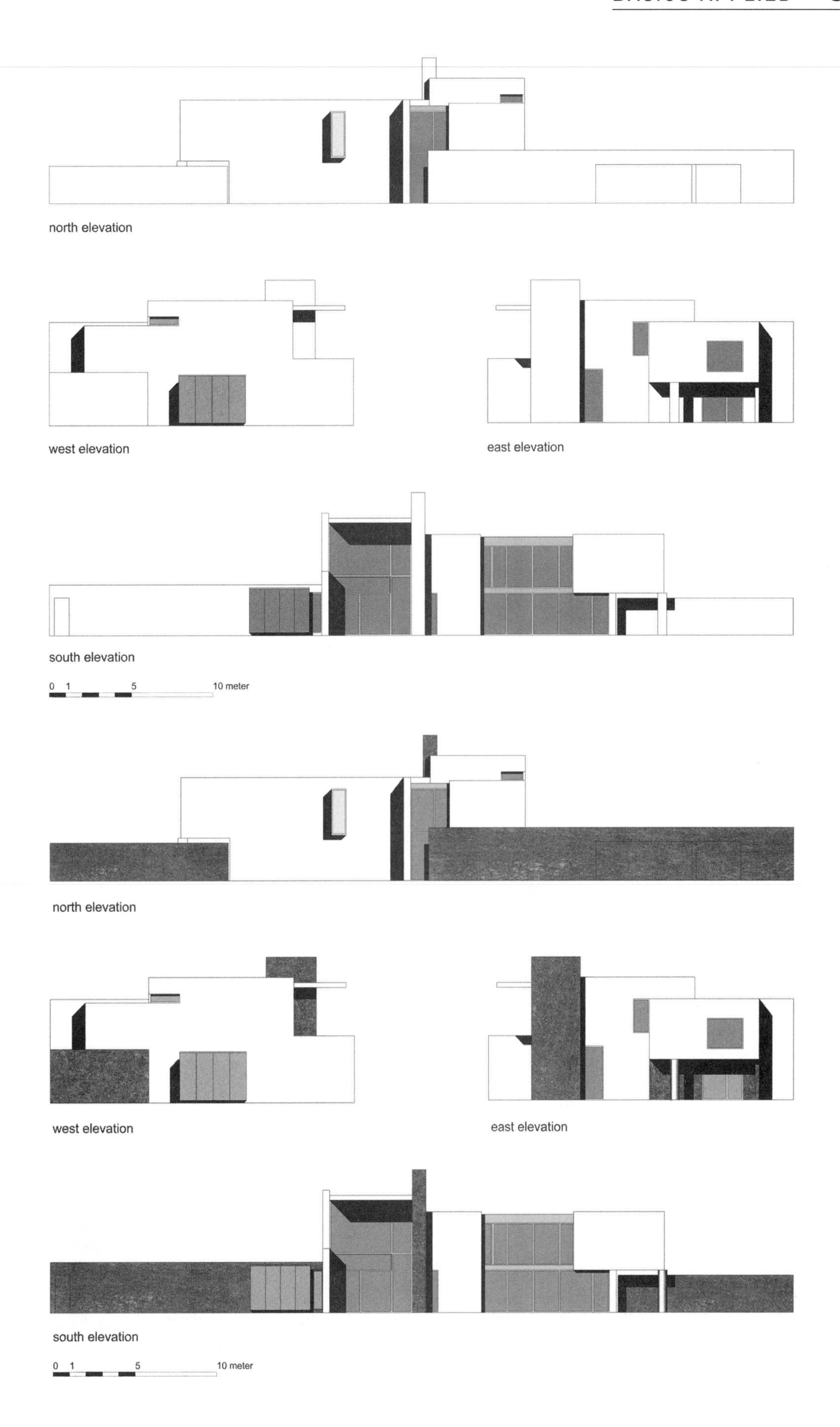

FLEXIBLE PANEL PRESENTATION

FIVE-PANEL PRESENTATION

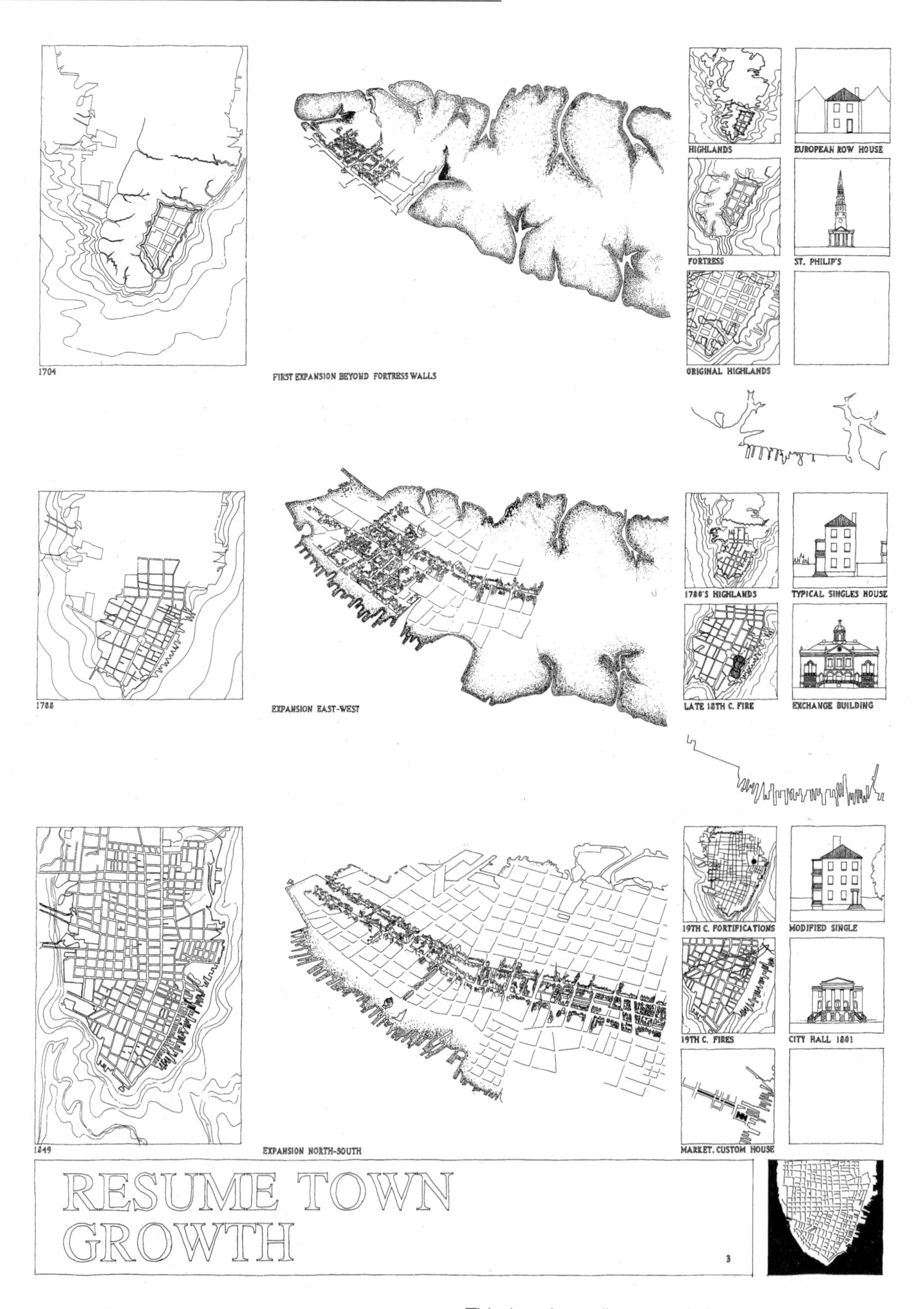

Drawings: Student projects, Charleston, South Carolina
Studio Instructors: George J. Martin and Stanley I. Hallet
Courtesy of the Catholic University of America
School of Architecture and Planning, Washington, D.C.

This is a long, linear analytic documentation of many student projects that uses a simple grid layout format. The pages connect sequentially.

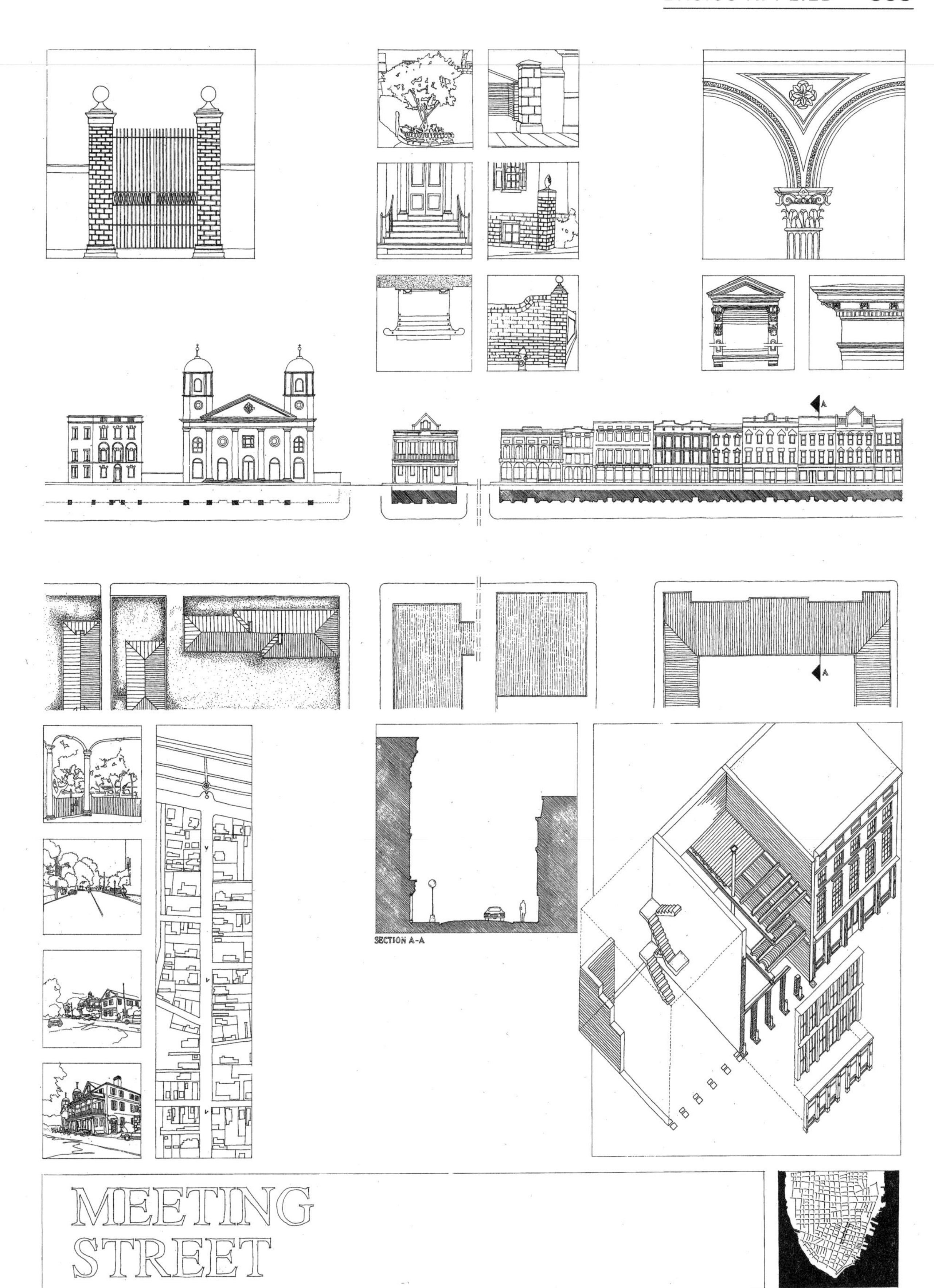

FIVE-PANEL PRESENTATION

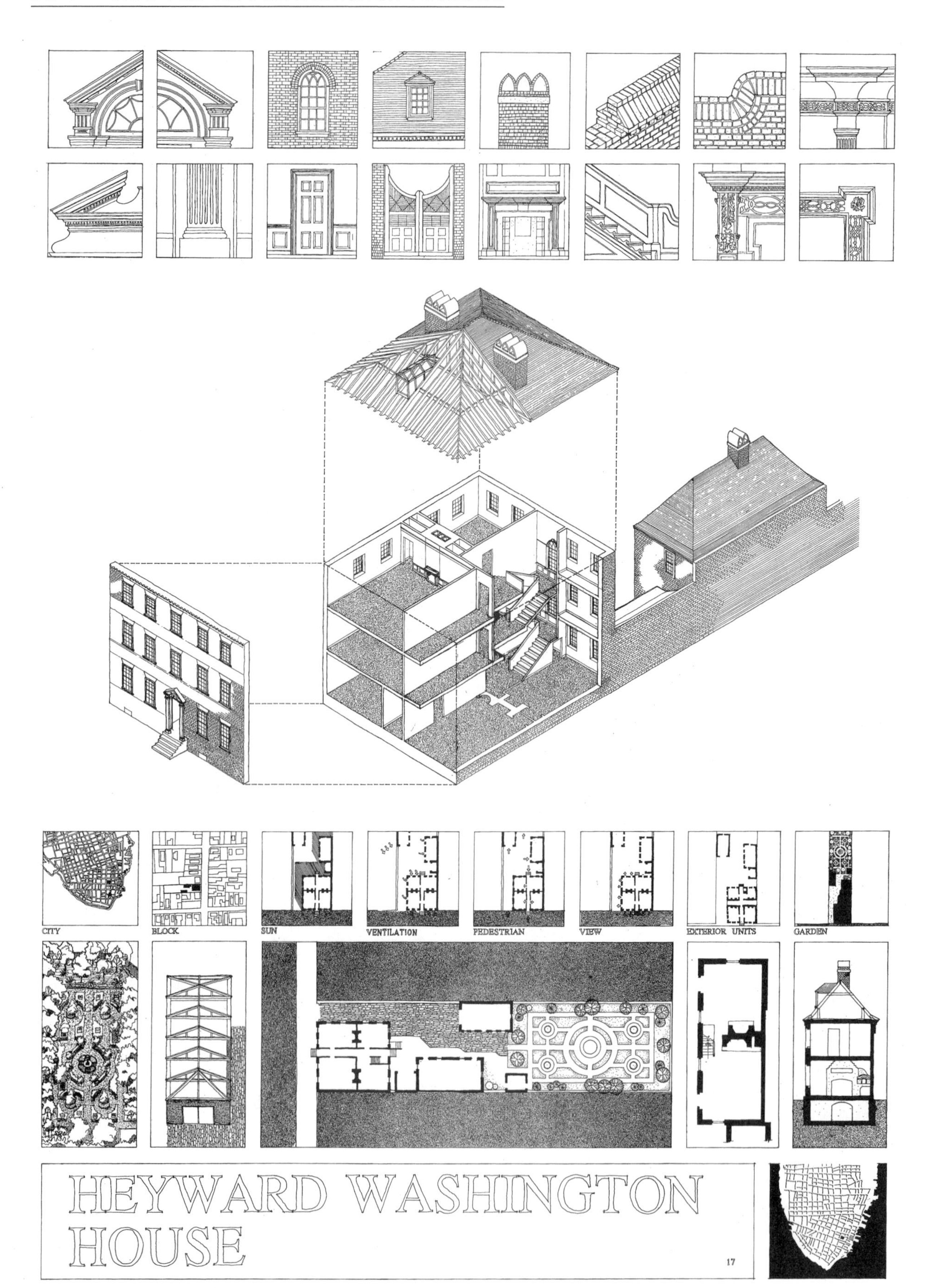
CITY
BLOCK
SUN
VENTILATION
PEDESTRIAN
VIEW
EXTERIOR UNITS
GARDEN
HEYWARD WASHINGTON HOUSE
17

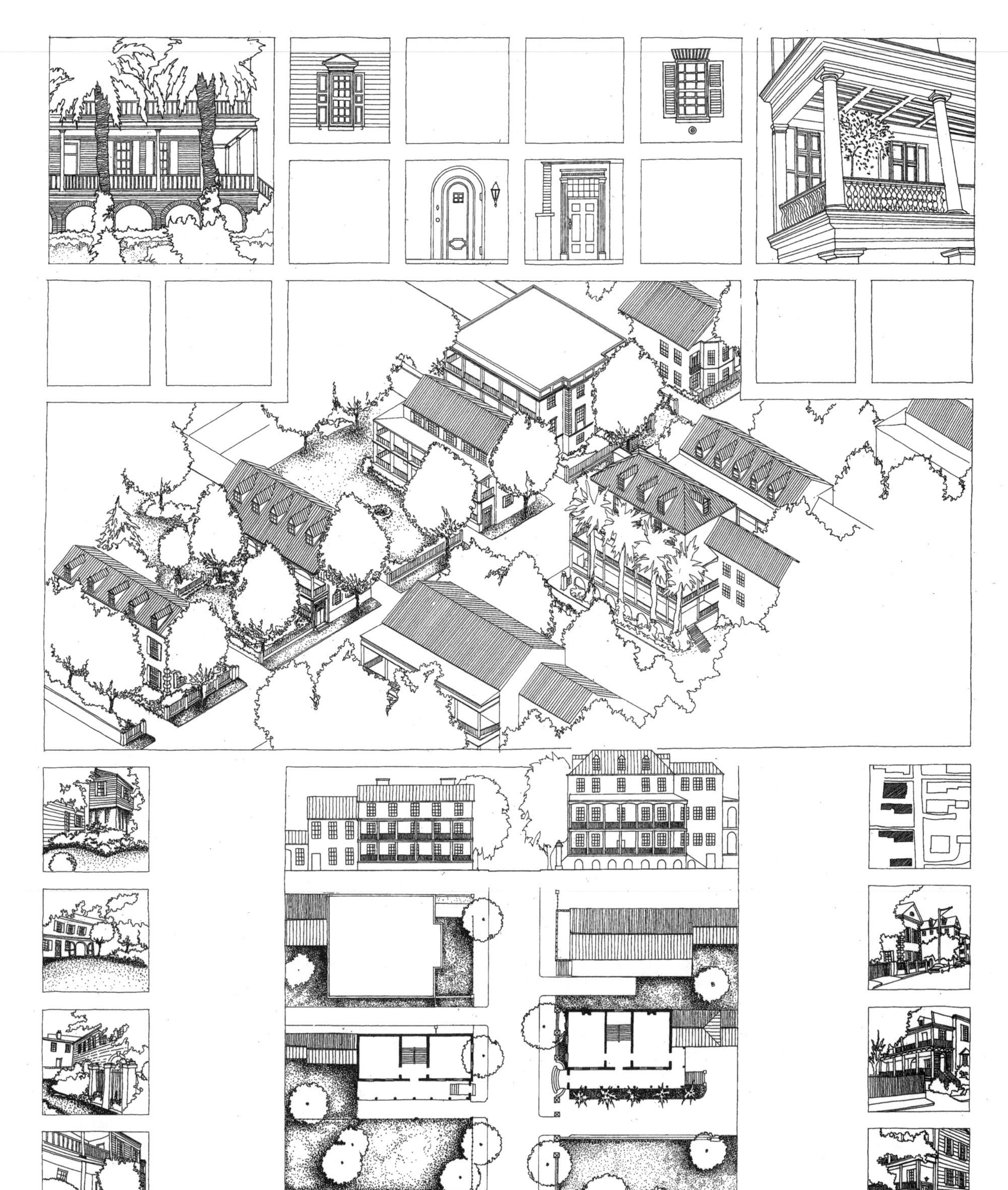

LEGARE
STREET

14

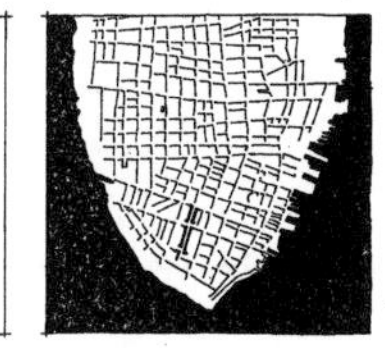

FIVE-PANEL PRESENTATION

FIVE-PANEL PRESENTATION

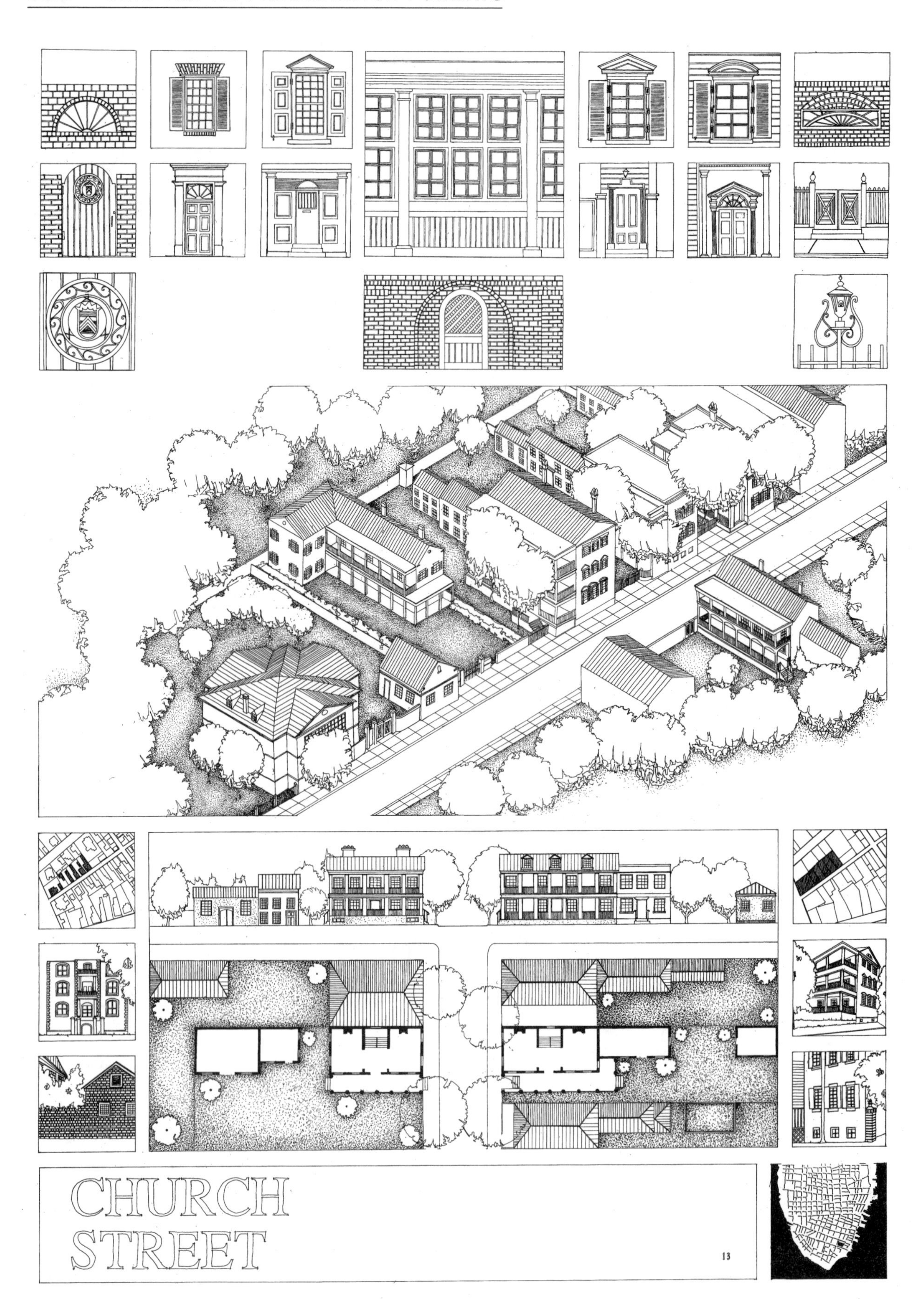

To present the design process of the Sunlaw Project, we used layers of information across each board. The inspiration came from Hollywood and the metaphor of the film strip. We used a diverse combination of media, from hand drawn sketches and construction documents to digital images. These were scanned and then assembled to convey the metaphor of the movies.

The movie metaphor is most obvious in a continuous running band, similar to a film strip, at the bottom of each page. This band contains images that display various aspects of the project, such as its site, context, and the historical precedents of tower design.

We used a dark blue background on each board as a framing device for the images. This background also contains screened construction drawings of the existing power plant machinery to evoke the context. Superimposed on this background are hand-drawn sketches or computer renderings of the new canopy and enclosure. The layering of the existing machine imagery and the dynamic renderings of the new canopy design create a rich and striking contrast.

We used two formats for this presentation: 20″ × 20″ boards and a booklet of 11″ × 17″ heavy sheets.

[Architect's statement]

Six panels: Sunlaw Power Plant Canopy & Enclosure,
Los Angeles, California
Courtesy of design architect: Moore Ruble Yudell
Principal-in-charge, principal architect: John Ruble
Principal architect: Buzz Yudell
Associate-in-charge/project architect: James Mary O'Connor
Project team: Ross Morishige, Lisa Belian
Digital renderings: Ross Morishige
Graphic design: Janet Sager
Owner: Sunlaw Energy Corporation
Chairman: Robert N. Danziger
President: Michael A. Levin
Project manager: Timothy G. Smith

SIX-PANEL PRESENTATION

SIX-PANEL PRESENTATION

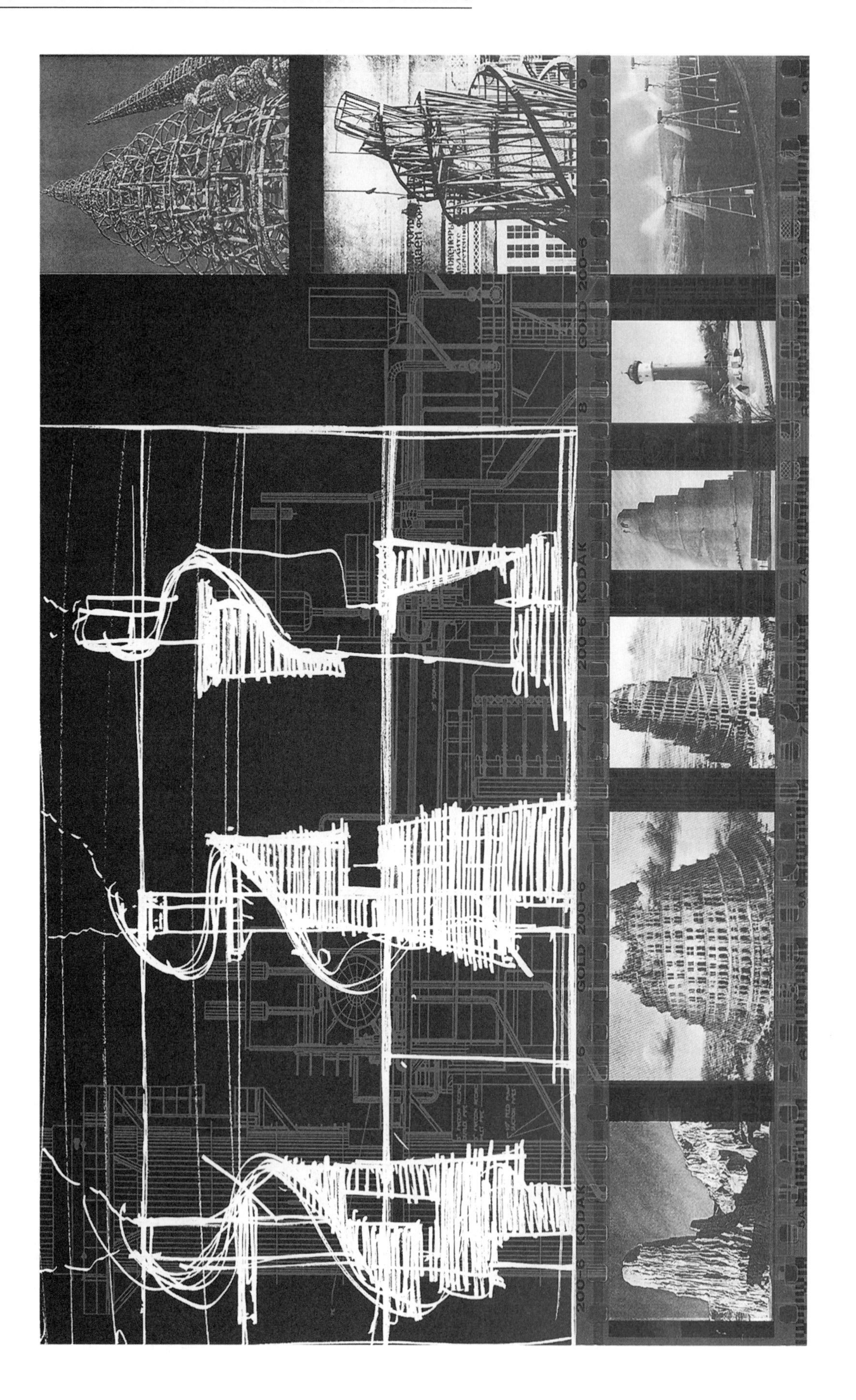

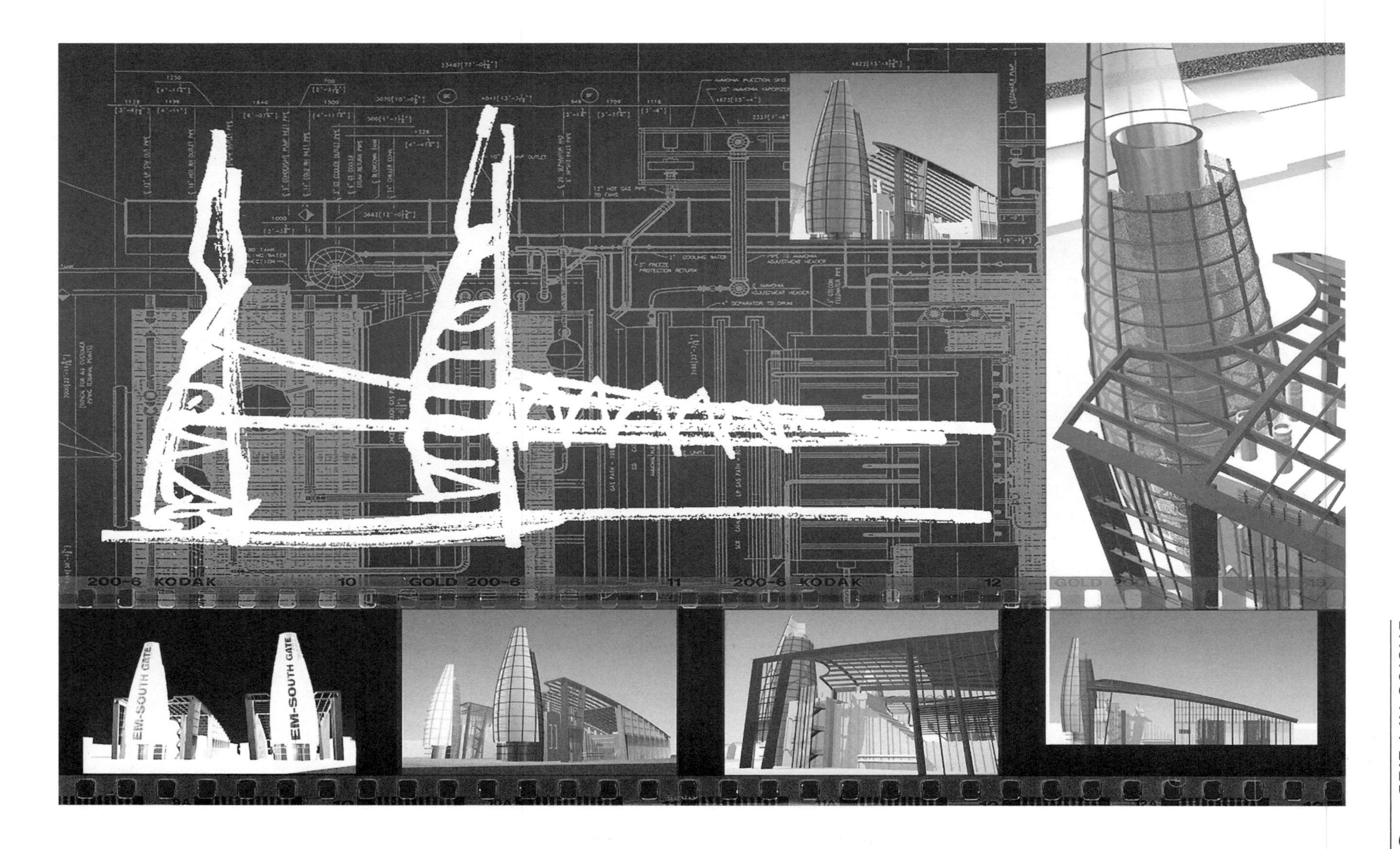

SIX-PANEL PRESENTATION

SIX-PANEL PRESENTATION

SIX-PANEL PRESENTATION

SIX-PANEL PRESENTATION

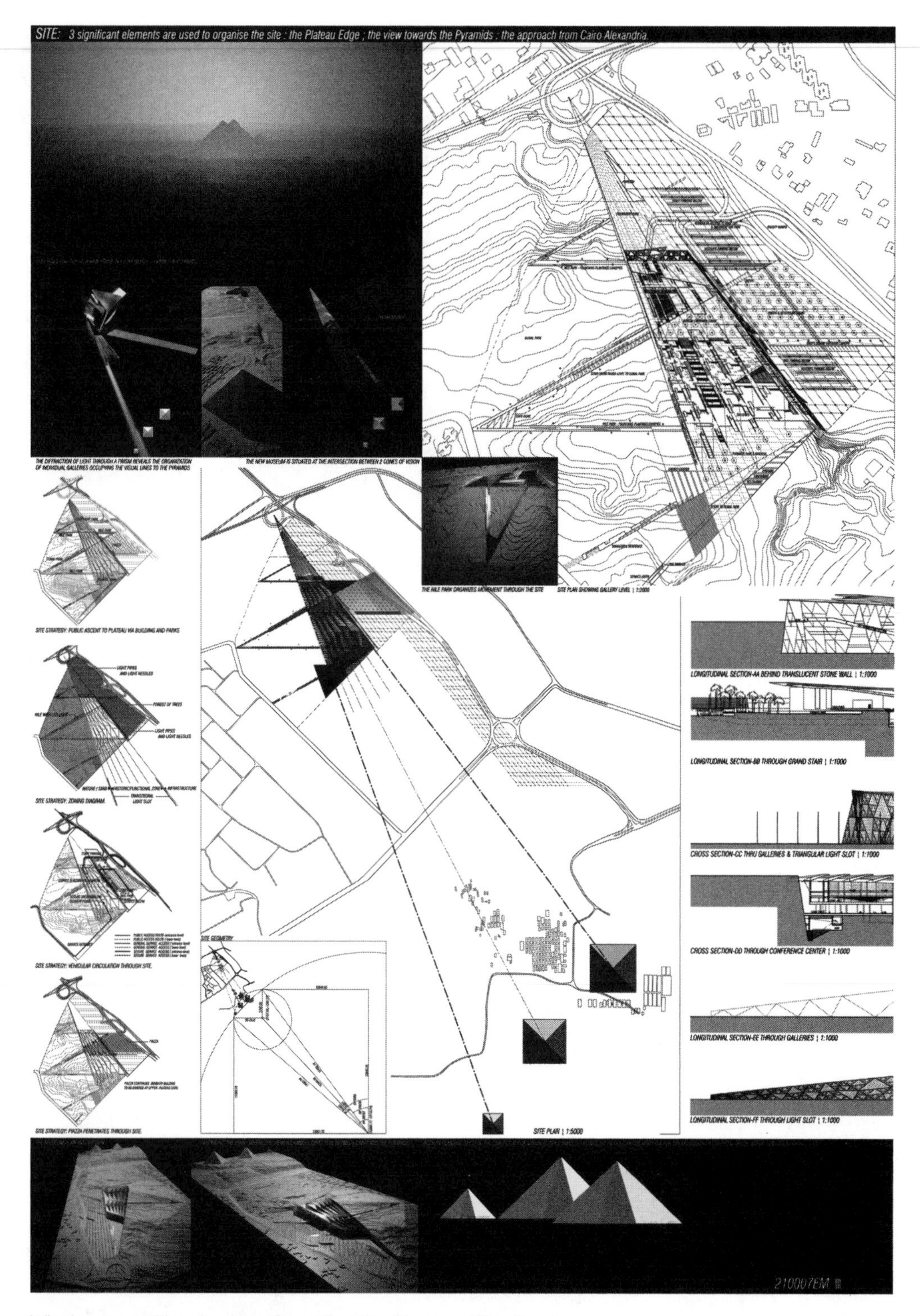

Winning competition drawings: Grand Egyptian Museum, Giza, Egypt
Medium: The drawings were done in AutoCAD. The images were done in 3D Studio Max, finished in Photoshop, and then reimported into AutoCAD for printing.
Model by Kandor Modelmakers, London, England
Model photos by Richard Davies, Photographer, London, England
Courtesy of heneghan.peng.architects

As you peruse the six panels of this beautiful set of winning competition drawings, try to find the elements that tie the panels together, making it a unified presentation. With over 1,500 submittals, this $335 million project was one of the largest competitions ever.

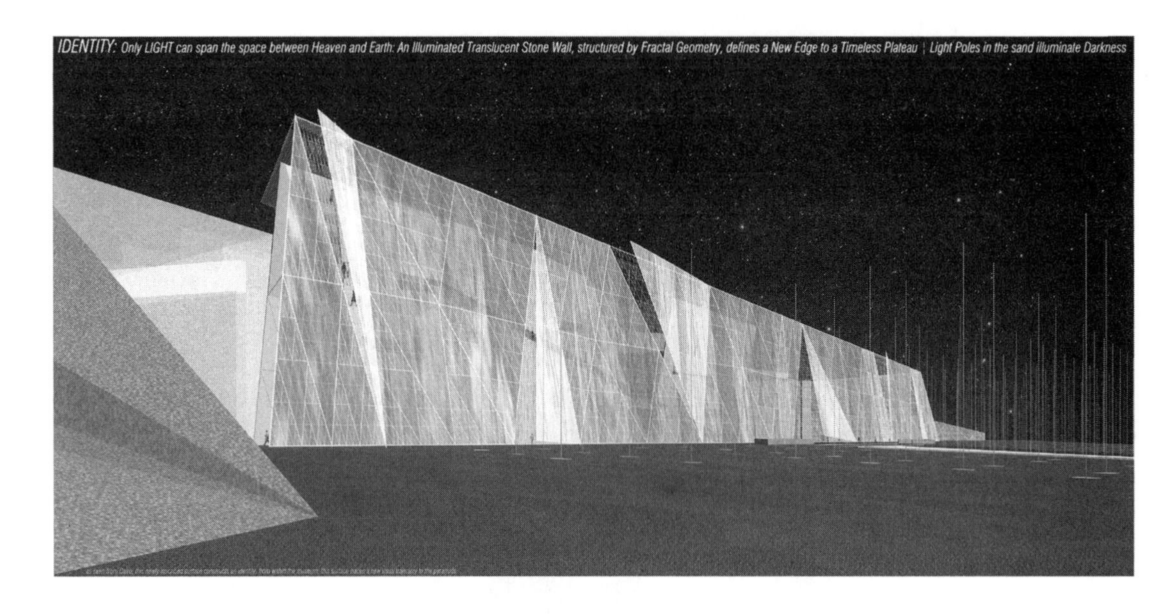

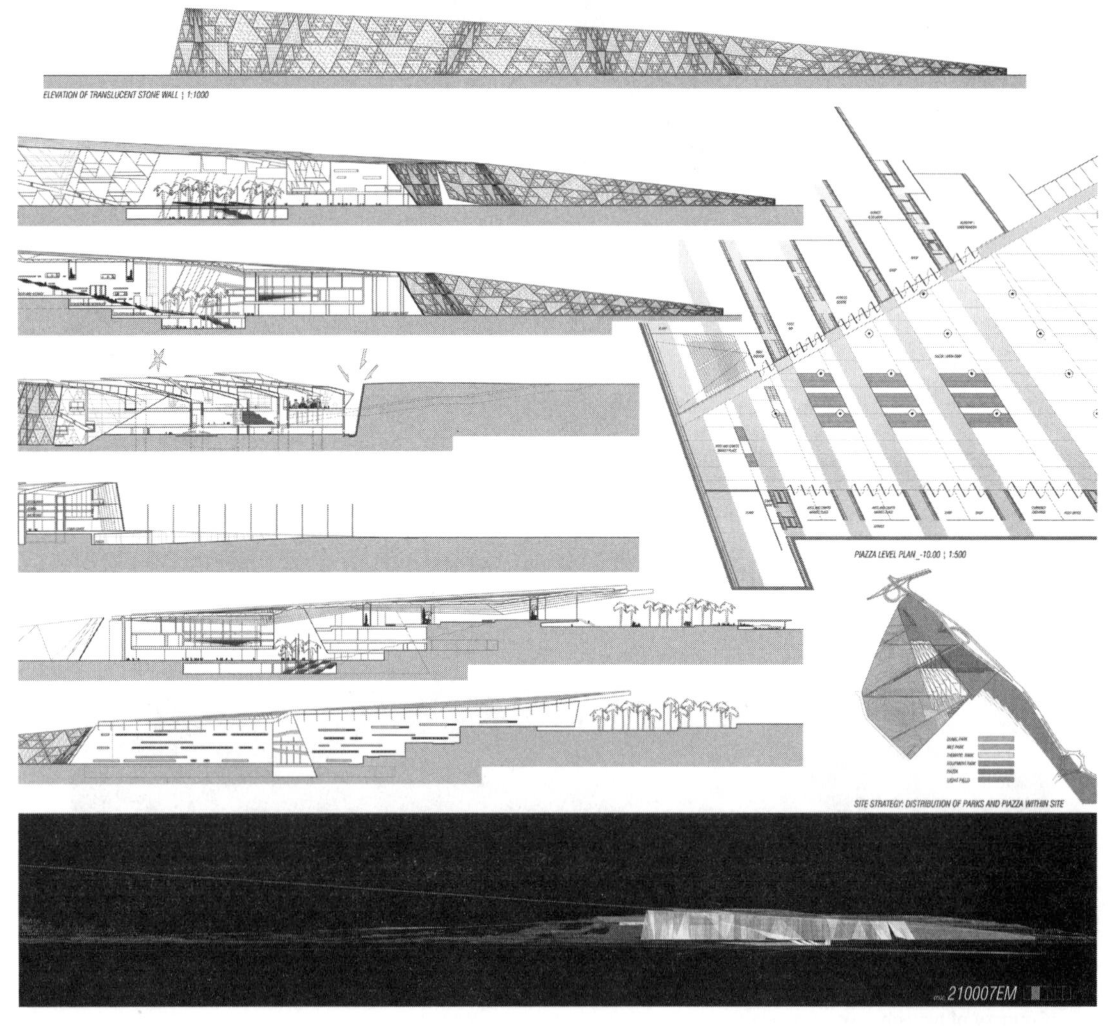

Design **competitions** in architecture have been popular historically. Globally, there has been an increase in commissions awarded on the basis of the results of design competitions. Upon closer scrutiny, architectural competitions do have their drawbacks. One major drawback is that the competitors have absolutely no

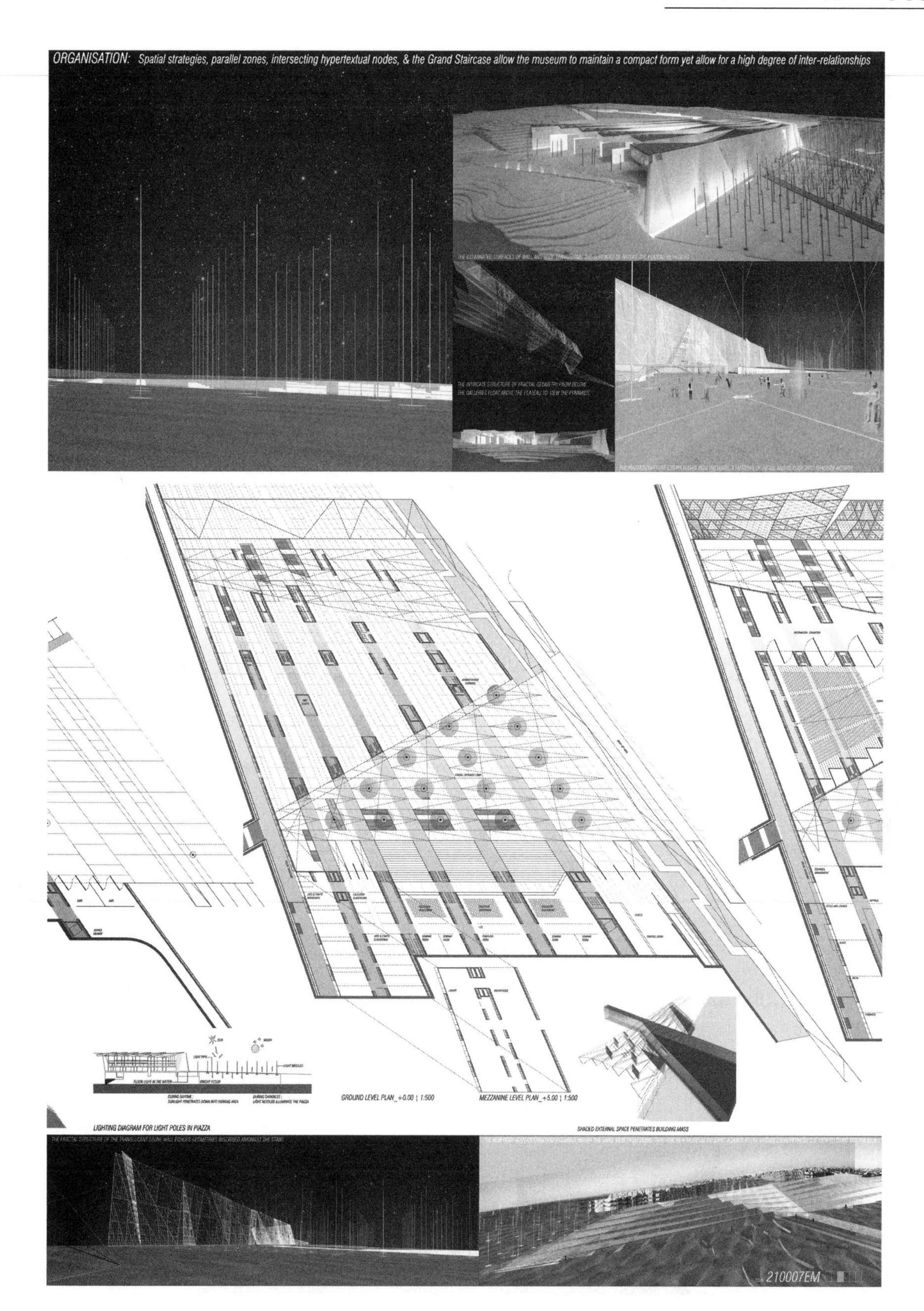
ORGANISATION: Spatial strategies, parallel zones, intersecting hypertextual nodes, & the Grand Staircase allow the museum to maintain a compact form yet allow for a high degree of inter-relationships
GROUND LEVEL PLAN_+0.00 | 1:500
MEZZANINE LEVEL PLAN_+5.00 | 1:500
LIGHTING DIAGRAM FOR LIGHT POLES IN PIAZZA
SHADED EXTERNAL SPACE PENETRATES BUILDING MASS
210007EM

contact with the users, and therefore no opportunity to discuss the program and the budget with the client directly. This leaves them without a complete understanding of the design goals and objectives. Competitions also tend to be very restrictive in their requirements, and in the early stages, the competitors

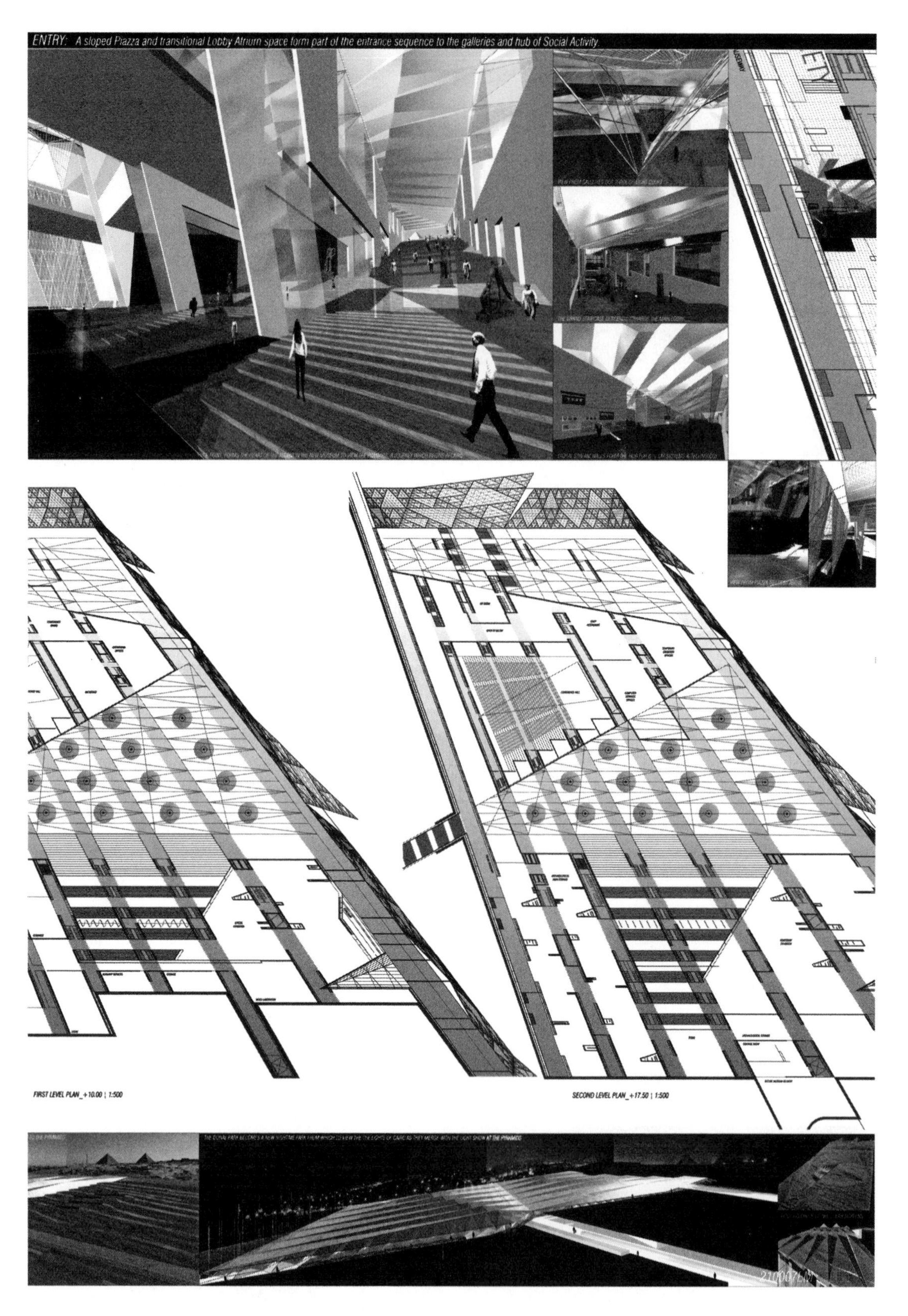
ENTRY: A sloped Piazza and transitional Lobby Atrium space form part of the entrance sequence to the galleries and hub of Social Activity
FIRST LEVEL PLAN_+10.00 | 1:500
SECOND LEVEL PLAN_+17.50 | 1:500

are not there to present their designs. Most competitions are judged anonymously. On the positive side, competitions can be a venue to start or launch successful careers for young architects. They are also a good creative outlet for individuals who are involved in the more mundane aspects of architectural practice.

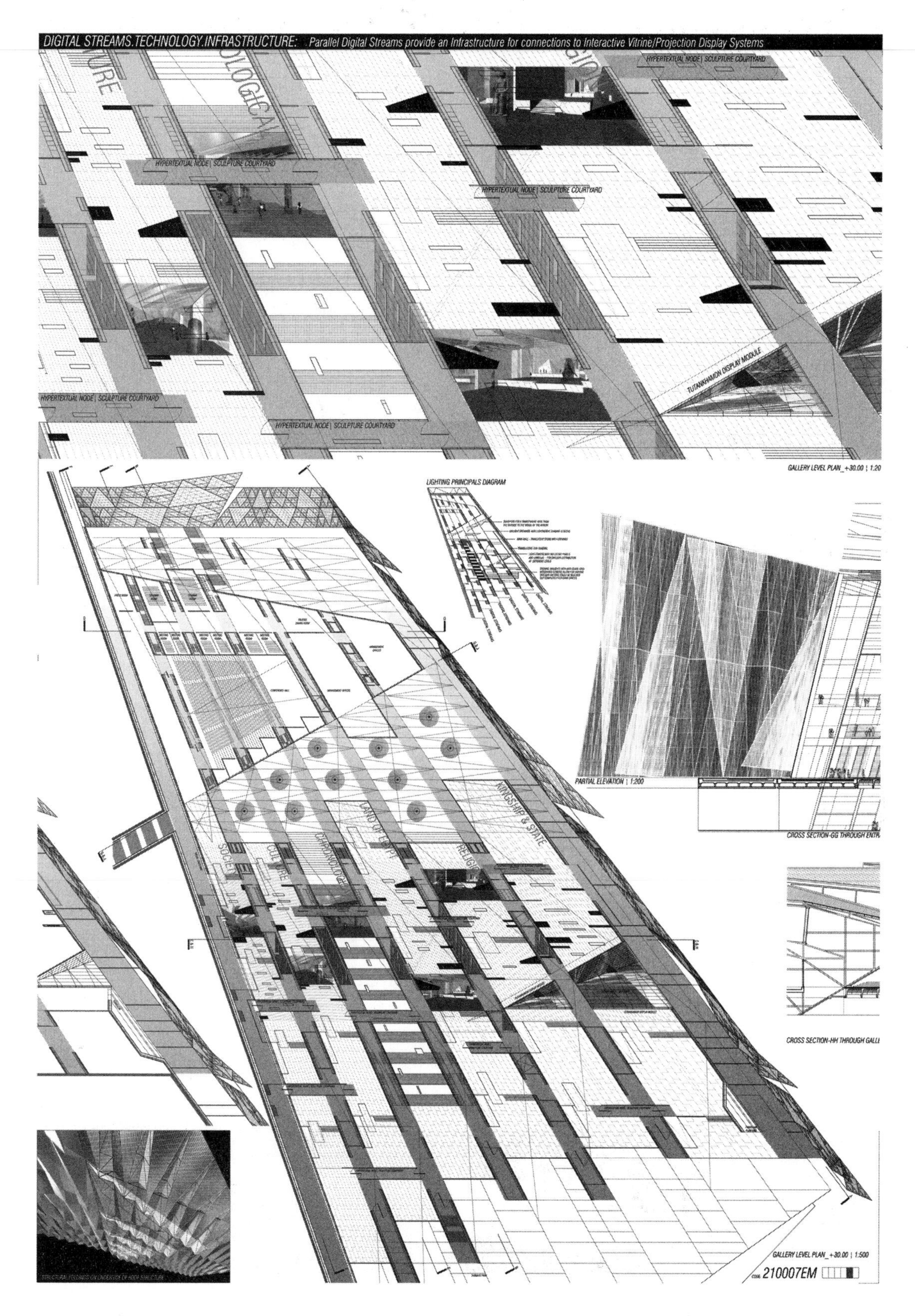

A variety of media and every kind of drawing type are used in competition drawings for expressing and communicating design intentions to juries. This presentation used digital media as well as model photographs.

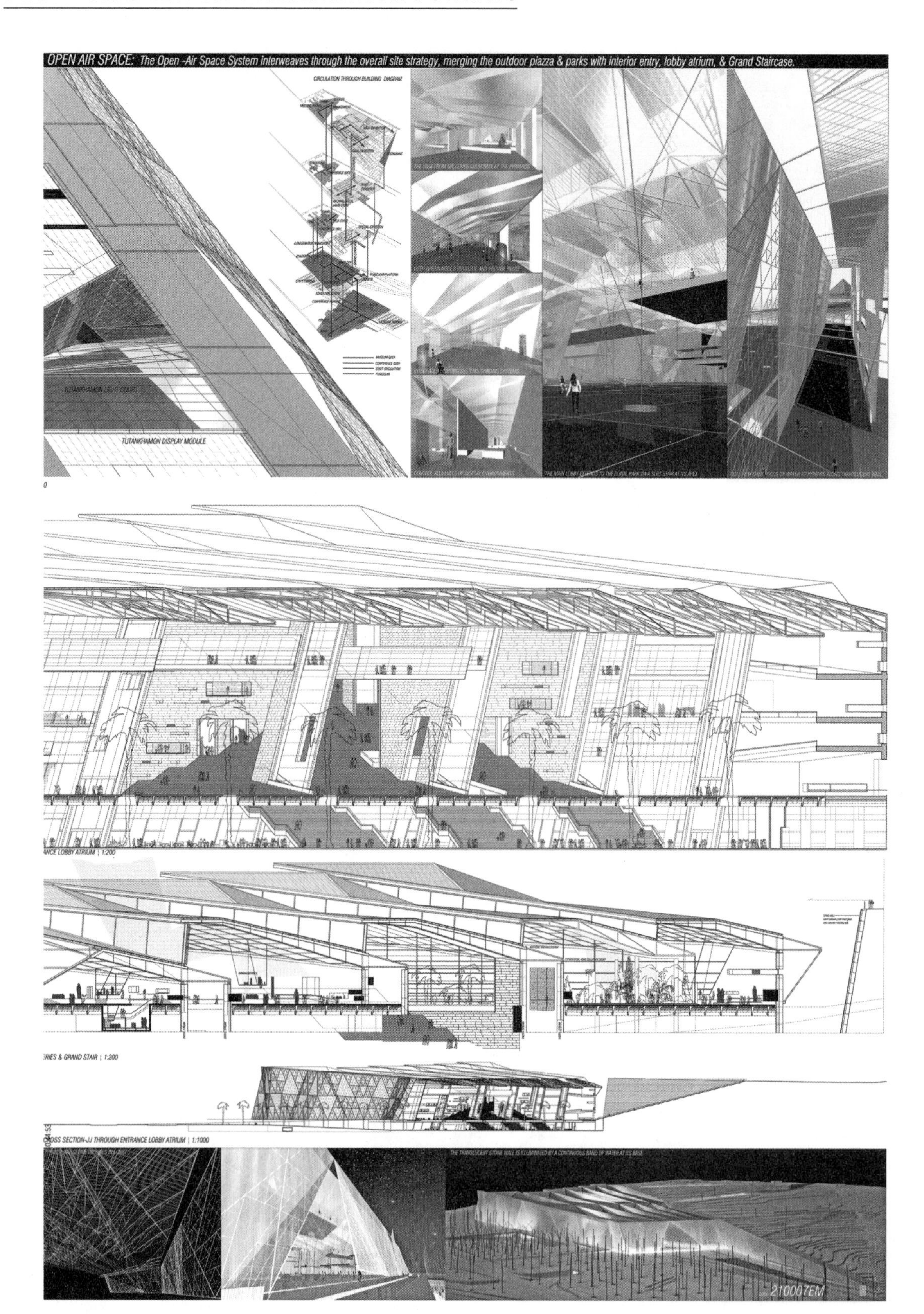

Keep in mind that the most sophisticated design idea will not win if it is not presented well or clearly. A concept must be presented imaginatively and simply so that it is readily understood by the judges.

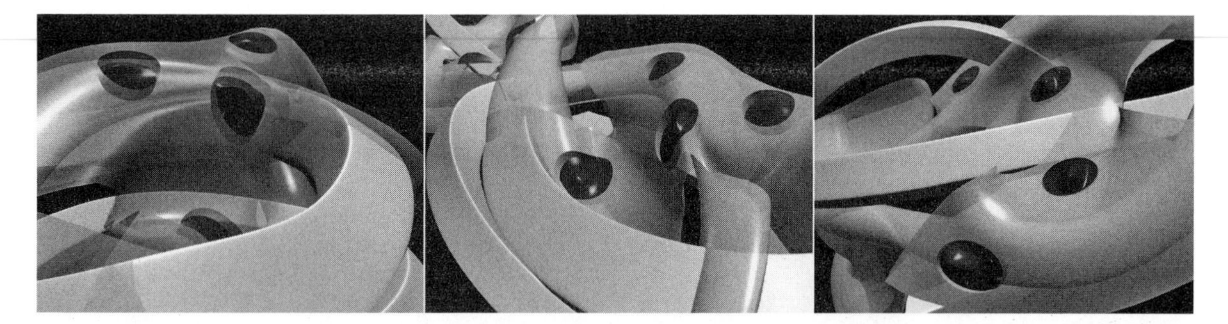

Images: Guggenheim Virtual Museum, New York, New York
Medium: Software—Alias, Maya, Cosmo Worlds VRML, Adobe Photoshop, Adobe Premiere, Macromedia Flash
Courtesy of Hani Rashid and Lise Ann Couture, Asymptote
Project team: John Cleater, Noboru Ota, David Serero, Florian Pfeifer, Ruth Ron, Birgit Schoenbrodt

When speaking of an architecture for the next millennium, one must consider two conditions: that the physical space of architecture as we have always known it (enclosure, form, and permanence) will without a doubt persevere, and that it will exist alongside the virtual architecture, surfacing in the digital domain of the Internet. Buildings, institutions, spaces, and objects are now being constructed, navigated, experienced, comprehended, and altered in their virtual states by countless people across global networks. This new architecture of liquidity, flux, and mutability is predicated on technological advances and fueled by a basic human desire to probe the unknown. The path that both architectures, the real and the virtual, inevitably take will be one of convergence. Historically, architecture has struggled with the dialectic of the real and the virtual: Architecture's stability and actuality have always been tempered by the metaphysical and the poetic.
[ARCHITECT'S STATEMENT]

EXPLODED VIEW

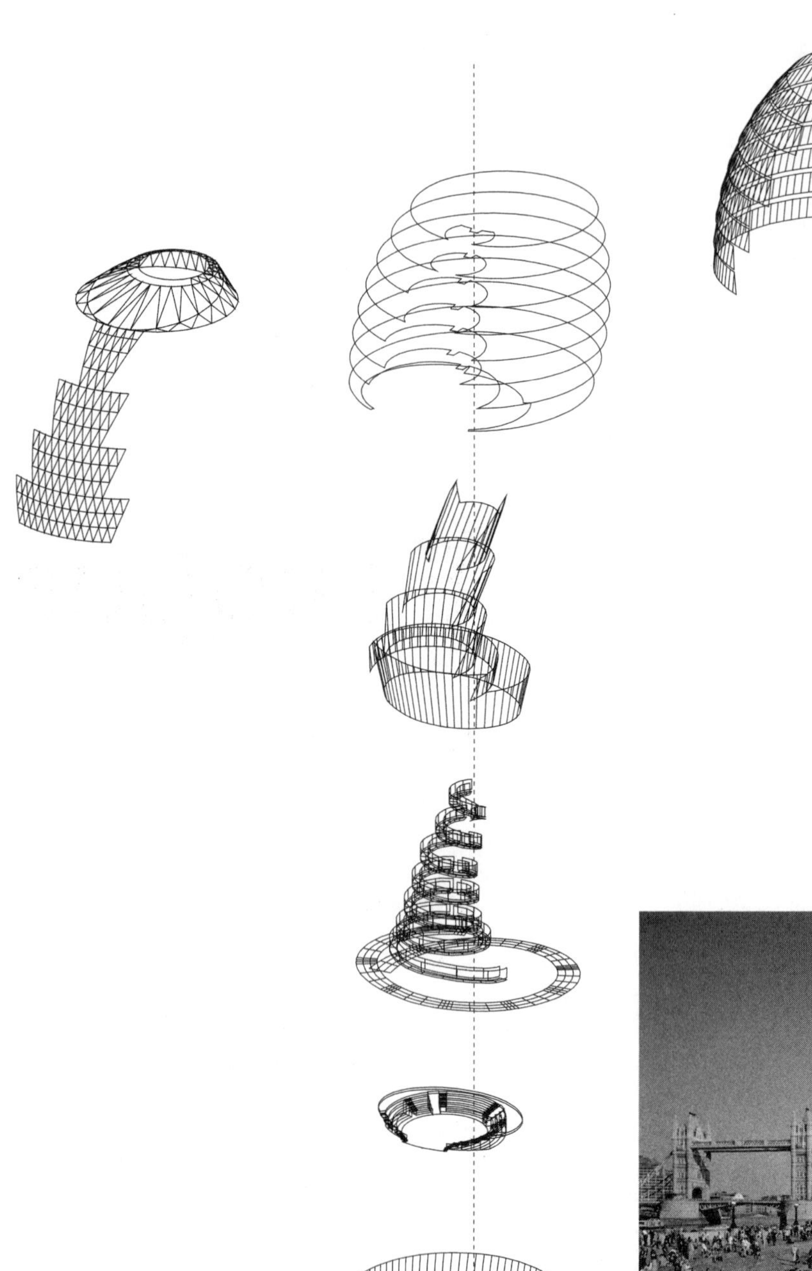

© Nigel Young/Foster and Partners

Exploded View

Drawing: Greater London Authority Headquarters
London, England
Medium: Software–Microstation
Courtesy of Foster and Partners

Epilogue

The primary intent of this book is to provide students and design professionals with graphic tools essential to visual communication. Architectural graphics skills are a powerful tool for conceptualizing, documenting, and expressing architectural ideas. The variety of drawing types and methods demonstrates that a wide range of graphic tools and techniques are available for conveying architectural ideas in the design process. This primer introduces the various media currently being used, so that the reader may have a sense of the range of visualizing possibilities in the field.

Designers must express, develop, and communicate architectural ideas. To do so, all designers—students and professionals alike—eventually settle on the tools and techniques best suited to them, whether these are freehand conceptual sketches or hardline representational drawings. Some architects and designers enjoy the feeling of a soft lead pencil on heavy white tracing paper. The softness of graphite can create a suggestive atmospheric character, especially in perspective images. Others become prolific in their expression of ideas when they use a felt-tipped pen or colored pencil on yellow tracing paper. Prismacolor pencils give a soft impressionistic feeling to architectural sketches. And still others prefer the precise feeling of ink on Mylar, especially with paraline drawings. Every medium affects the quality of not only spatial perception but also design ideas, especially at the design-drawing stage. For example, charcoal almost automatically evokes light and shadow, whereas a fine-point pen may cause you to delineate more and to think in terms of contours, connections, and details.

Because the computer and computer-generated drawings have become commonplace in design education and practice, it is all the more important to maintain a strong relationship with traditional drawing media and methods such as freehand sketching. Because of the intimate and immediate reciprocity between the human imagination and drawing, this most ancient form of expression will always remain a powerful and effective way to generate and communicate ideas.

The reader should explore the many books listed in the Bibliography that elaborate on architectural drawing as technique and/or process. Such exploration, along with a careful study of this volume and its related Web site, should enrich his or her knowledge of architectural drawing.

Drawing Exercises

A textbook or reference on architectural drawing would not be complete without suggestions for how to apply some of the more important techniques covered. The goal of this section on drawing exercises is to show a variety of problem/project approaches, as well as a diversity of applications. The intent is to allow architecture educators to glean information from these exercises so that they can formulate creative problems that suit their own classes and educational objectives.

Organization of the Drawing Exercises

The problems and projects in this section have been divided into two levels. Level One consists of very basic problems that are abstract in design and simple in geometric configuration. To pass a beginning course in architectural drawing/graphics, students should demonstrate overall understanding of, and skill in, solving these exercises. Students should also be encouraged to do freehand sketches to explore possible solutions for each problem.

Level Two problems are more complex than those in Level One, and, in some cases, are more purely architectural in character. They usually involve design as well as drawing and are suitable for more experienced beginners or for classes in which students work at their own pace. Students with a strong background in high school mechanical drawing or college engineering drawing, or those with experience in the design professions other than architecture (e.g., graphic design, industrial and product design, etc.) should concentrate on Level Two problems. As in Level One, the resolution of Level Two problem solutions should stress the incorporation of freehand sketching skills.

Sketches Demonstrating Light and Shade

To work on the following exercise, you may need to bring to class a small item suitable for a still-life painting. I suggest a simple shape—a piece of fruit, vegetable, etc. You may also wish to bring a plate or cloth on which to put the item.

In this exercise you may experiment with a variety of mixed-media techniques, such as pencil sketch with watercolor, felt pen or ink line with watercolor, pencil, etc.

The intent of this exercise is to demonstrate how the use of light and shade can give an object form—a three-dimensional quality. Choose a simple object and sketch and/or paint in color four postcard-size sketches. You may use an object more than once by changing the light source (i.e., by changing the direction or strength of the light source). Alternatively, you may wish to go outside and sketch (or paint) a simple architectural or landscape subject.

Hint: Choose objects that have a simple basic form—a cube, cylinder, sphere, cone, etc.—and have one strong, directional light source. Tonal studies in pencil or monochromatic watercolor may help define light, shade, and composition.

Please include any preliminary studies with your assignment.

You will be assessed on the following criteria:

- Use of light and shade
- Technique (watercolor, mixed media, etc.)
- Use of color
- Composition

Courtesy of Professor Jane Grealy
Department of Architecture
Queensland University of Technology
Brisbane, Australia

REFER TO CHAPTER 3

Student project by Daniella Lancuba
Medium: Watercolor
Department of Architecture
Queensland University of Technology
Brisbane, Australia

Drawing Positive and Negative

Perceiving forms and shapes is a major step in learning to draw. Everyday objects (such as forks, spoons, chairs, and lamps) make good subjects for learning to draw negative space. Beginning to understand the difference between drawing negative space (the area around the object) and positive space (the object being drawn) perceptually can alter your approach to drawing.

Drawing negative space is drawing the object of our focus by defining the space around the object. The tendency for beginning students is to want to draw the object. In this case, students must overcome preconceived notions of what they are seeing and are compelled to recognize that the negative space is just as informative about the object being drawn. Issues of foreshortening and perspective become less of a perceptual hindrance because the focus is on shape, not depth.

Charcoal is the best medium to use for this project; it makes the student focus on the importance of negative space. Observe the object from different viewpoints, looking for negative shapes. Capture the shapes of the object first as contours, being careful to capture all the nuances of the object. Once they are delineated, fill these areas with the charcoal.

This assignment makes the complex object simple. It simplifies all the intricate relationships of the object so the student can understand and draw it. Once the basic understanding of positive and negative has been achieved, students may proceed to more complex objects, such as landscape or architecture. The examples presented in this exercise demonstrate drawing positive and negative with motorcycles. Notice handlebars, mirrors, wheels, spokes, and fenders defined by the delineation of the dark negative shapes. You can even read the reclining nature of the handlebars of the motorcycle.

Project: Courtesy of Professor Fernando Magallanes
Design Fundamentals Studio—Fall 2000
College of Design
North Carolina State University

REFER TO CHAPTER 3

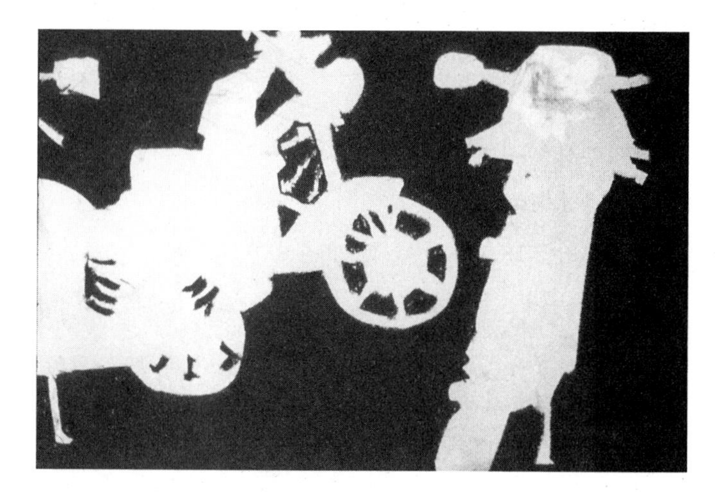

The student example is from the Design Fundamentals Studio—Fall 2000
North Carolina State University
Medium: Charcoal on $8\frac{1}{2}" \times 11"$ sketch paper

Drawing: Student project by John Rubins
Head and face study
Medium: Ink
Courtesy of Washington University
School of Architecture, St. Louis, Missouri

Cognizance of Negative Space

One excellent exercise is to reverse the positive and negative (figure and ground) spaces, as shown in the face study (left). Always try to draw the significant negative space by delineating the common boundary line that defines the form. It takes a keen, educated eye to recognize negative shapes because we have been conditioned to see positive shapes. Also notice that you can only make sense of the black negative areas when viewing them right side up.

REFER TO CHAPTER 3

Freehand Drawing: Multiple Sketches

Break into groups and, using ink pens of varying thickness, sketch the visual images that you see displayed around the studio. We will begin with 30-second, 60-second, 1.5-minute, and 3-minute sketches. A final sketch of 5 minutes in duration will complete the exercise. The sketches will range in complexity and graphic expression. Pay close attention to the proportion of the image on the page and the style of sketch being used in the examples. Relax.... Sketch freely and quickly. Place a 5-minute sketch, 3-minute sketch, a 1.5-minute sketch, a 1-minute sketch, and a 30-second sketch on the page, as shown below.

Problem courtesy of Assistant Professor Daniel K. Mullin, AIA, NCARB
Graphic Communication course
Department of Architecture
University of Idaho–Moscow

REFER TO CHAPTER 3

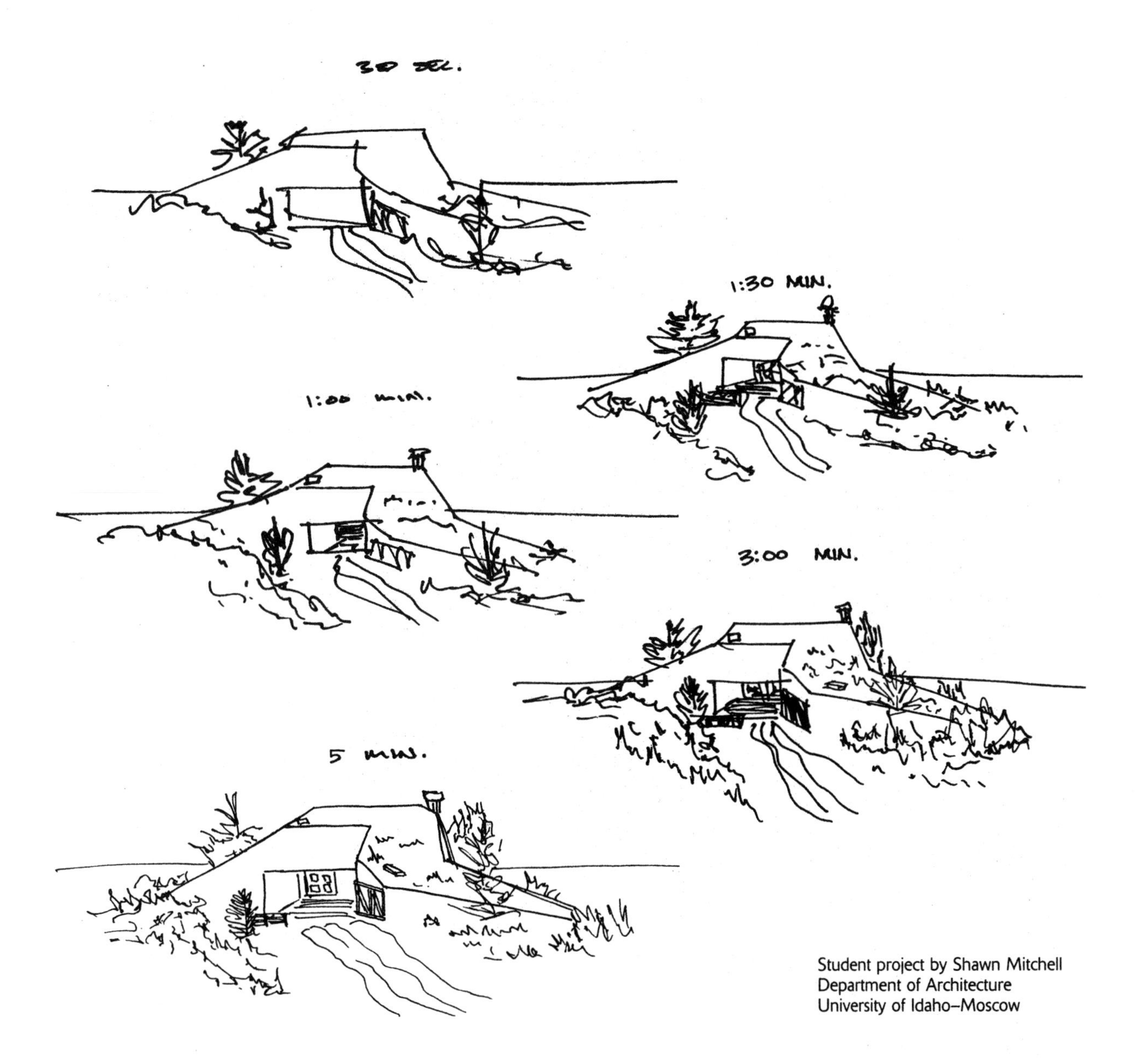

Student project by Shawn Mitchell
Department of Architecture
University of Idaho–Moscow

Human Body and Proportion

Time frame: 3 weeks

(**1**). On large paper, measure and outline your body's length, width, and circumference at full scale. Create a notational system to record your measurements. Note any kinds of relationships that develop between the numbers as you measure. (**2**). Explore the concept of module—a unit of measure for expressing proportional relationships. Draw the different parts of the body that you could use to divide it. Test out different parts of your body and determine if they are more easily divisible by one part than by another part. Make a proposal for a module using either parts of the body, measurements of the body, or numerical distances, articulating the relationship between part and whole. (**3**). Devise a proportional system for the body using your modules. Make a drawing of that system at a 1:1 scale. Contextualize the body within a larger whole. Make two or three large-scale drawings to investigate these three points.

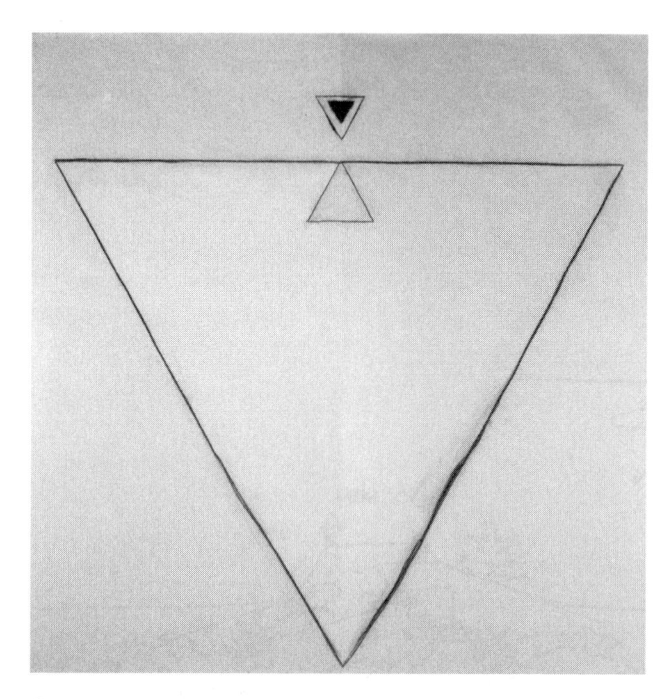

Student project by Reid Cigolle
Medium: Charcoal on bond paper
6' X 6' (15.2 X 15.2 cm) and 3' X 6' (7.6 X 15.2 cm)
Course: Freehand Drawing
Courtesy of Professors Joan Waltemath and Andrew Tripp
Irwin S. Chanin School of Architecture of The Cooper Union

For the first part of the assignment I began by measuring distances between different points in the body. Once I found these numbers, I looked for proportional similarities between the different relationships in the body. I decided to focus on the equilateral triangles that I was able to extract from my measurements. Using four triangles—the outstretched arms to the feet, the ears to the chin, the eyes to the mouth, and the nipples to the base of the neck—I set out to create a drawing that would emphasize these relationships in an obvious way without losing their connection to the human body. The simple clarity of the triangles does not eliminate their humanness due to the drawing's scale and the way the top two triangles echo the construction of the face with an outline of the head to an outline of the face.
[*ARCHITECTURE STUDENT'S STATEMENT FOR POINTS 1 AND 2*]

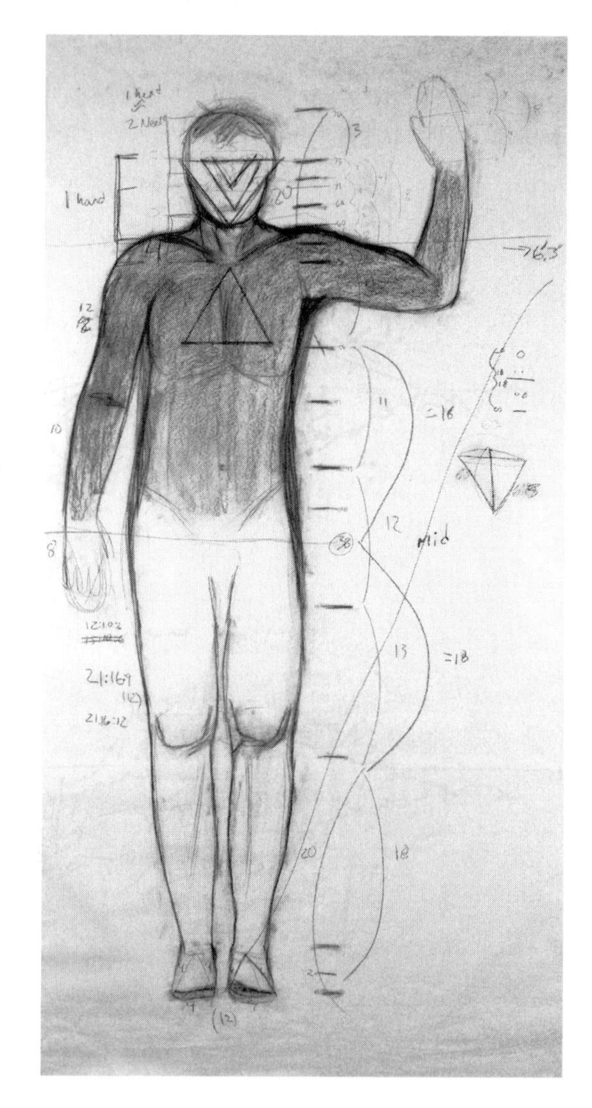

REFER TO CHAPTER 3

Still Life: Tone and Texture Exercise

TASK
Assemble and arrange a still life composed of various objects on a surface (such as household objects, food, office supplies, tools, kitchen implements, fabric, etc.). Cast a strong light source from a single lamp in a darkened room.

ASSIGNMENT
Render the forms of the composition with black pen on white paper. You may use light pencil to construct lines. Study the composition to determine which values of the observed shapes receive little or no tone (represented by light surfaces), and which receive medium or dark tones, for deep shade or shadows. Pay attention to surface quality and texture (shiny, dull, patterned, etc.), and be conscious of line weight and stroke direction in rendering various textures.

OBJECTIVES
This exercise provides practice in the observation of light sources, rendering techniques (hatching, stippling, solid tone), and making decisions on defining shape and contrast within the visual field.

MEDIA
Heavy white paper
Black permanent marking pens (assorted weights)

OPTIONS
Try the study without light pencil for bolder decision making.
Try different shading techniques and hatches.
Use an architectural model of a neighborhood.

SOURCES
1. The work of Giorgio Morandi
2. Guptill, Arthur L. 1976. *Rendering in Pen and Ink.* New York: Watson-Guptill.

Still Life: Value Exercise

TASK
Assemble and arrange a still life composed of various objects (such as household objects, food, office supplies, tools, kitchen implements, fabric, etc.) on a horizontal surface. Cast a strong light source from a single lamp in a darkened room.

ASSIGNMENT
Render the forms of the composition on a medium-value gray paper using a white and dark rendering media. Study the composition to determine which values of the given shapes receive darker saturation for deep shade or shadows, little or no treatment for medium values, and white saturation for surfaces reflecting light.

OBJECTIVES
This exercise encourages the observation of light source, treatment of light as a material object through media rendering, and new thinking about drawing with a dark medium on a light surface.

MEDIA
Gray charcoal or pastel paper (40–60%)
Charcoal, or black Conté crayon, pastel, or Prismacolor
White chalk, Conté, pastel, or Prismacolor pencil

OPTIONS
Use black paper and only white rendering media.
Experiment with various combinations of media on gray paper.
Try a black ink wash with a white medium on gray paper.
Use an architectural model of a neighborhood.

Courtesy of Jonathan Brandt,
Visiting Professor
College of Architecture
Texas A&M University

REFER TO CHAPTER 3

Panoramic Fantasy

TASK
Select several of your favorite sketches and photocopy them at various sizes and dimensions.

ASSIGNMENT
Assemble your sketches into a collage and tape them together. Try to establish interesting or ambiguous relationships among objects in terms of perspective, juxtaposition of scale, and illusion of depth. Trace off a contour drawing.

OBJECTIVE
To expand the imagination by recognizing new relationships between juxtaposed images.

MEDIA
Photocopies of sketches
Pen and pencil
Tracing paper

OPTIONS
Try rendering your fantastic contour image in the media of your choice. You may want to make a transfer onto heavier paper.

Field Study: Panorama

TASK
Select a high or commanding vantage point over a city or distinctive site.

ASSIGNMENT
Study a wide-open panoramic view (180° or more) and record selected objects concisely and abstractly in a contour drawing. Record notable buildings, landmarks, natural features, etc. Take notes by labeling or naming them. By doing this, you are enlarging your awareness of the visual field despite recording it in a fixed position. You will also develop keener observation skills.

OBJECTIVE
To develop observation and abstraction skills while learning names and places.

MEDIA
Horizontal-format sketchbook or long sketch paper
Pen and pencil
Map of what you see

OPTIONS
Try selectively rendering what you see as time permits.

Courtesy of Jonathan Brandt, Visiting Professor
College of Architecture
Texas A&M University

REFER TO CHAPTER 3

Field Study: Building Context

TASK
Select a building or ensemble of buildings forming a distinctive space.

ASSIGNMENT
Render the forms of the composition on a medium-value paper using ink wash and white rendering media. Record from observation by setting up a freehand pencil-line perspective. Study the composition to determine which values of the architectural or natural shapes and voids receive dark saturation for deep shade or shadows, little or no treatment for medium values, and white saturation for the surfaces reflecting light.

OBJECTIVES
To encourage the observation of light source, treatment of light as a material object through media rendering, and the revision of typical thinking about drawing with a dark medium on a light surface.

MEDIA
Medium-value charcoal or pastel paper (30–50%)
Ink and painted wash
White Prismacolor pencil
No. 2 pencil

OPTIONS
Try various medium-value colored papers with colored inks.

Field Study: Plan, Perspective, Detail

TASK
Select a distinctive space bounded by architectural walls.

ASSIGNMENT
Record the plan in space. Select several salient details and record them also, doing quick, analytical contour drawings. Then find two or three views that you feel best describe the space visually, and record them on the plan. Select at least one approach view to give a sense of time in a series of contour drawings with framed views. Arrange your sketches on the page. Also, jot down any verbal notes about anything remarkable you see.

OBJECTIVES
To study an architectural space from observation by recording a range of scales in drawing vignettes, including close-up details and more general sketches from a distance. By doing this, you will develop keener observation skills for proportion and scale while learning names and places.

MEDIA
Sketchbook or sketchpad
Pen and pencil
Guidebook and/or plan of what you see

OPTIONS
Try selectively rendering what you see as time permits.

Courtesy of Jonathan Brandt, Visiting Professor
Texas A&M University
College of Architecture

REFER TO CHAPTER 3

The Architectural Journey

The objectives in this program—Architectural Drawing I—were to encourage students to investigate their environment through the eyes of architects in order to become proficient in a range of techniques and media, and to encourage students to explore and experiment with the design process through mark-making.

Students come to architecture school from a variety of arts backgrounds and with a wide range of skills, including graphics and technical drawing. But they do not have the flexibility to move across a wide range of media, techniques, and conventions that would allow them to focus on the chosen extent of their subjects. Along with the techniques of plan, section, elevation, axonometric, and perspective, I chose to further their experience to incorporate shadow, texture veil, transparency, and reflection. This creates a larger framework, through which they can critique and evaluate the limits of conventional techniques in order to enrich their way of seeing and designing. I encouraged students to develop their own techniques through experimentation—to consider what drawing is. I believe that knowledge of the subject—be it the human figure or architecture—comes from direct observation and experience.

Elements of mark-making can bring attention to aspects and dimensions of the subject under consideration. The drawing process then becomes a kind of shorthand that evokes the actual subject from a mere representation. These processes are considered through sketches, thumbnails, different media, and the inclusion and exclusion of some information. Investigations of textures, outlines, and light values are all brought to bear on the more familiar conventions of plan, section, elevation, and perspective.

Through journeys through the city, students were encouraged to broaden their experience of buildings. The word "voyage" names both a journey of exploration and the record of that journey and its discoveries. The voyage concept was invoked to create an appreciation of drawing as a means of making and marking architectural discoveries. In this respect, architectural drawing was considered not as a neutral tool for picturing a scene, but rather as a means of analysis and critical enquiry, a means of looking to learn and discover. Therefore, the student can see the rules of perspective, such as vanishing points and planes of vision, all relative to the actual experience. Given a base in direct observation, the student has the ability to make renderings of light that are about light rather than shadow projections, perspectives that are about space rather than perspective construction, and plans that are about building experience.

My notion of drawing is founded on observation and experience: to practice seeing, practice drawing, and investigate buildings—to study reality and the experience of the building and make comparisons between the drawing and the reality of the building experienced. To practice drawing conventions and to determine how effective they are at communicating experience and space, and to encourage students to develop an understanding of their environment with all their senses so these investigations will inform a drawing and the ability to construct understanding through drawing.

The key to drawing is to draw constantly; to keep the drawing and design processes open is to master the ideas of drawing for communication. Those drawings that are based on technique and convention, and those drawings used to see, perhaps do not have to be legible, but should rather increase observational and exploration skills.

REFER TO CHAPTERS 3 AND 6

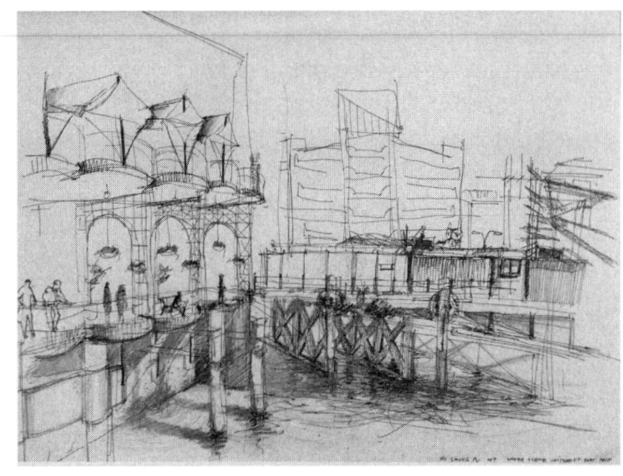

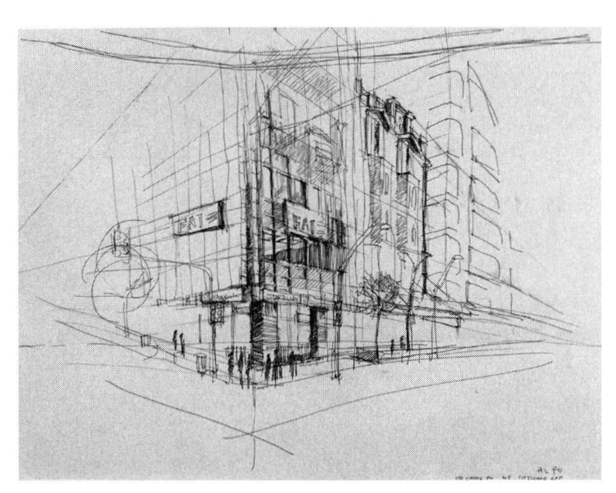

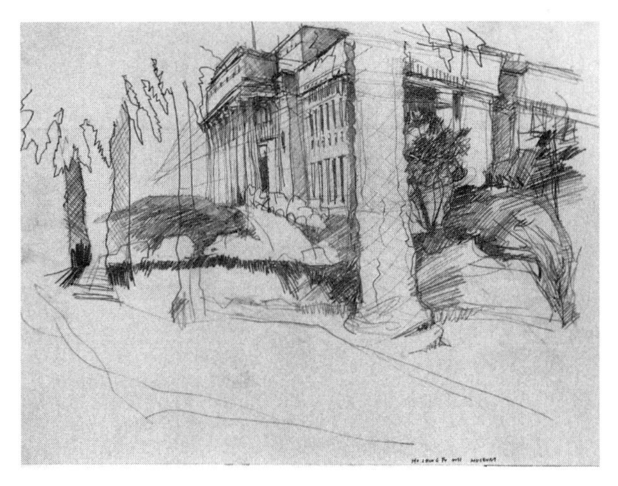

Problem: Courtesy of Susan Hedges, CAS Support Manager
School of Architecture
National Institute of Creative Arts and Industries
University of Auckland, New Zealand

Student project by Ho Ching Fu (Architectural Drawing I)
Courtesy of Studio Supervisor Susan Hedges
School of Architecture, National Institute of Creative Arts and Industries
University of Auckland, New Zealand

Drawing Eggs

It is essential for the beginning student to develop sensitivity to light falling on an object and an ability to draw the light qualities on a two-dimensional surface. The observation of light and the creation of shadows and tones are what the student must capture on paper. The students are asked to bring half a dozen (preferably white) eggs to drawing class. The media for this exercise can be pencil, ink, charcoal, and gray marker. The students will make three drawings, each using only one medium to allow students to learn the individual strengths and weaknesses of each medium used. One hour is spent on each drawing on 14" × 17" sketchbook paper. Various ways of creating value may be explored: line, smudging, layering, stippling, or random marks.

Set the eggs in different types of light. Draw first in filtered light with minor light variation. Later move the eggs to a place of intense light using full sun or a strong lamp. Place the eggs on a clean white surface, like a sheet of white sketch paper.

This exercise will introduce students to various types of light (highlight, shadow, reflective light, and shade) that become apparent in studying the light falling on the eggs. In a one-hour period the light will change, so it is important that the students make an overall still-life sketch of the eggs to work on later outside of class.

Project: Courtesy of Professor Fernando Magallanes
Design Fundamentals Studio—Fall 2000
College of Design
North Carolina State University

REFER TO CHAPTERS 3 AND 9

Student project by Rebecca Pezdek
Medium: Pencil on 81/2" × 11" sketch paper
Design Fundamentals Studio—Fall 2000
North Carolina State University

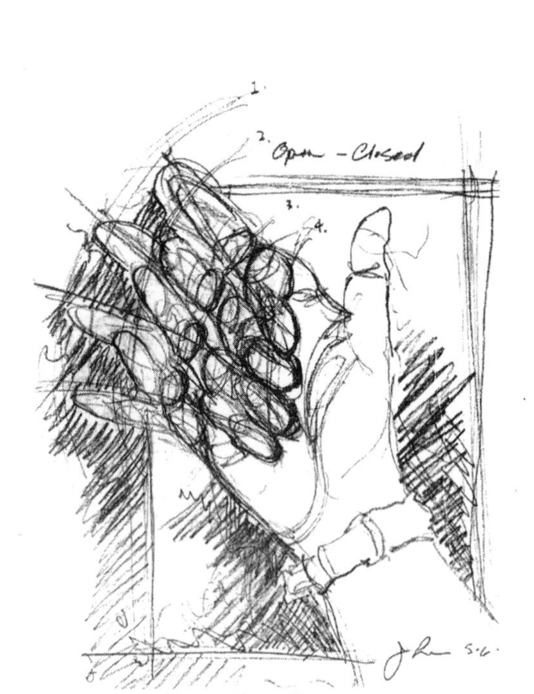

Drawing: Open and closed hand
Medium: Ink on trace 7.5" X 7.5" (19.1 X 19.1 cm)
Courtesy of Professor Jerry W. Lum
City College of San Francisco
Department of Architecture

Drawing Hands in Action

In this exercise, you will draw either the hand opposite your drawing hand or your drawing hand by using a mirror. The hand, with its wide range of possible positions, is probably the most challenging part of the human anatomy to draw. Remember that a hand's length is approximately double its width. Start sketching with frozen, still positions and progress to showing the open and closed hand in intermediate positions (simulating the hand in motion).

REFER TO CHAPTER 3

The Architect's Scale

Using the engineer's scale indicated on the left, measure and draw the stipulated lengths indicated above each group. Proper order of sequence corresponds left to right with top to bottom.
3" means 3" = 1'-0".

REFER TO CHAPTER 1

4", 3¾", 5½"

Full Scale — — —

40'-0", 28'-6", 64'-0"

3/32" — — —

36'-0", 25'-0", 41'-6"

1/8" — — —

6'-0", 27'-6", 18'-6"

3/16" — — —

10'-0", 5'-6", 22'-0"

1/4" — — —

7'-0", 4'-6", 13'-8"

3/8" — — —

9'-9", 7'-6", 4'-3"

1/2" — — —

4'-3", 6'-6", 7'-0"

3/4" — — —

3'-6", 5'-0", 5'-9"

1" — — —

2'-0", 3'-4", 4'-0"

1½" — — —

1'-0", 1'-6", 2'-1"

3" — — —

The Engineer's Scale and the Metric Scale

Using the engineer's scale indicated on the left, measure and draw the stipulated lengths indicated above each group. Proper order of sequence corresponds left to right with top to bottom.
4 means 1" = 4'-0"; 30 means 1" = 30'-0".

For the bottom two groups: Using the metric scale, measure either millimeters (mm) or centimeters (cm) to the stipulated lengths indicated above each group.

REFER TO CHAPTER 1

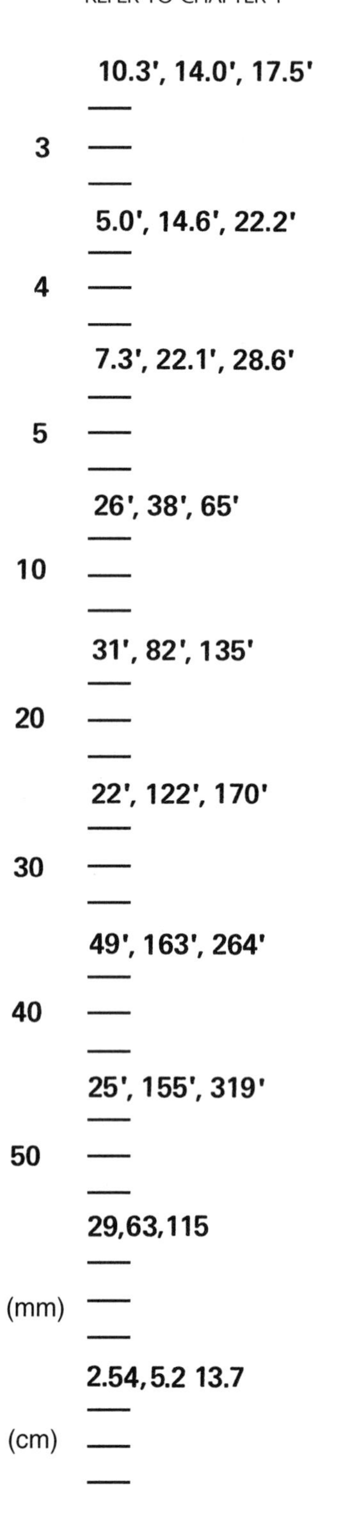

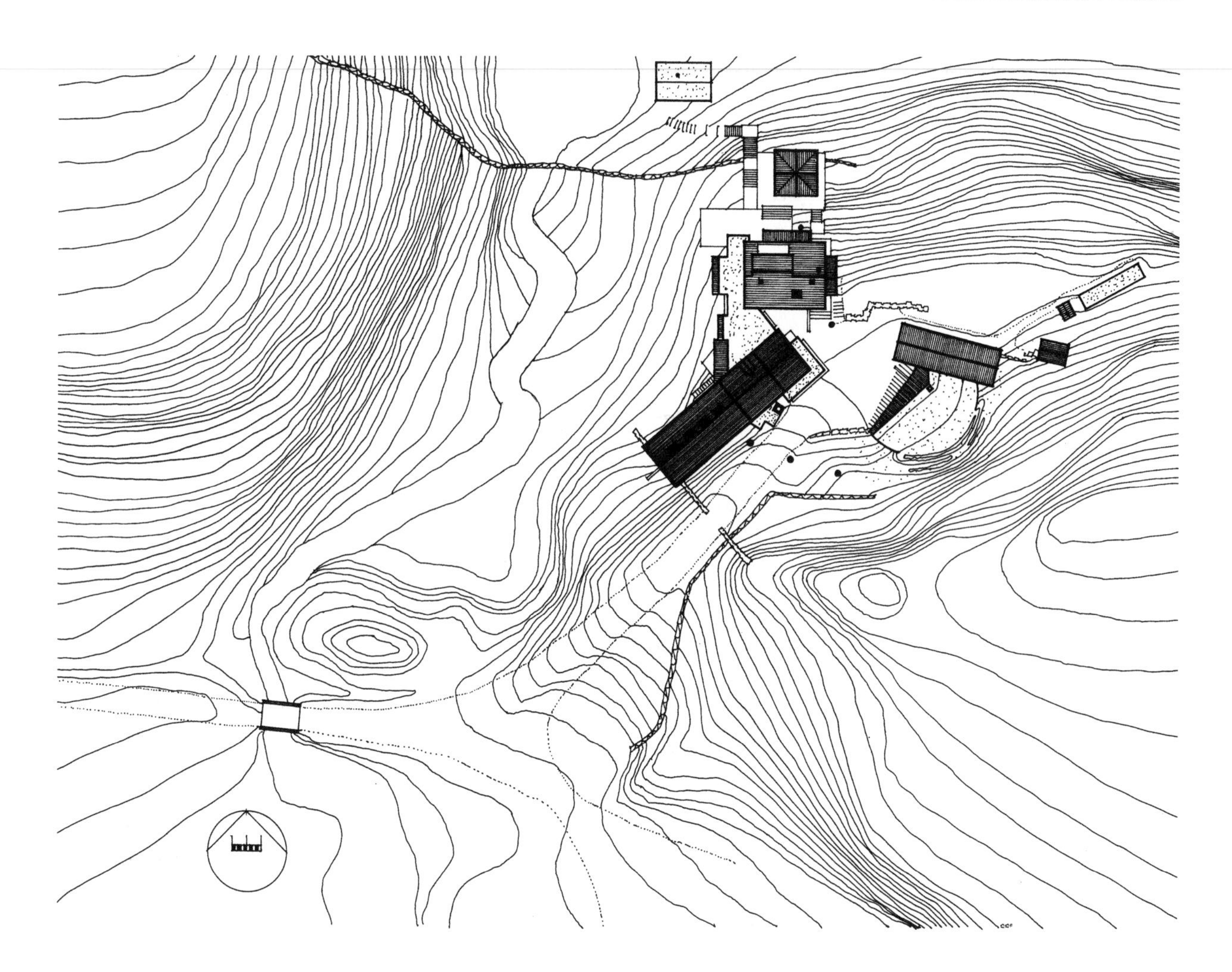

Drawing: Brandenburg's Ravenwood Studio, Ely, Minnesota
22" × 34" (55.9 × 86.4 cm)
Medium: Ink on Mylar
Courtesy of Salmela Architect

Contour Drawing

Answer the following questions about the above contour drawing. (As an optional exercise, do the same for the site plans on pp. 382 and 386.)

1. Do any of the contour lines cross each other?
2. Circle and label areas where you think there is, for the most part, a constant slope.
3. Circle and label areas where you think there is, for the most part, a steep slope.
4. Circle and label areas where you think there is, for the most part, a gentle slope.
5. Circle and identify the tops of hills.

REFER TO CHAPTER 1

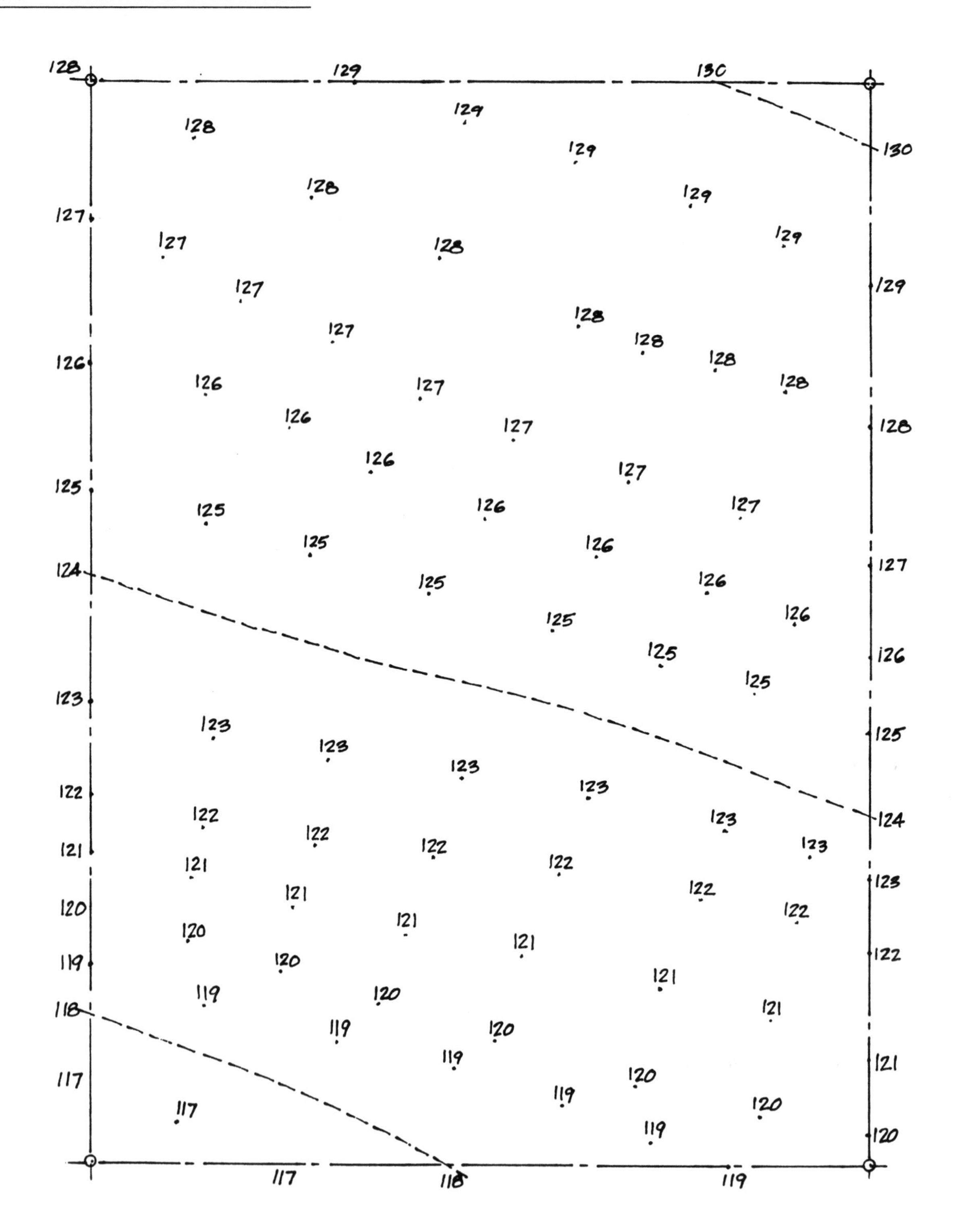

Given: a partially completed **contour** map of a building site

Required: Using a flexible curve, a french curve, or your own freehand technique, carefully connect contour lines of constant elevation. You can draw the contour lines either as continuous solid lines, a series of small dashed lines (see p. 386), or a series of small dots (see p. 369). Cut a small line segment through the contour lines and try to interpolate the correct profile. Do the same for p. 386.

REFER TO CHAPTER 1

Hand Lettering: Freehand, Using Capitals

Tell me something about yourself (with a sharpened soft pencil) and why you are pursuing the path of an architect or interior designer. What do you hope to get out of this class? Tell me a story, anything—just fill this page with writing.

Draw *light*, ⅛"-wide guidelines with a 2H lead. Allow for 1⁄16" space between the guidelines. Start 1" in from the sides of this typewritten text and 1" from the bottom of this text and end up 1" from the bottom of this page. Relax and write using all capitals.

Problem: Courtesy of Assistant Professor Daniel K. Mullin, AIA, NCARB
Graphic Communication course
Department of Architecture
University of Idaho–Moscow

REFER TO CHAPTER 2

Hand Lettering: Freehand, Using Capitals

Using a lettering height and layout as stipulated by your instructor and simple vertical block capitals, carefully letter the following statement by architect James Wines of SITE.

The range of drawing techniques—from Beaux Arts watercolors to digital simulation—has become the basis of lively debate, and, sometimes, a philosophical battleground. There is still a classically based group that regards all computerization as anathema and clings to the sanctity of eye and hand as the only means of describing the spirit of flux and change in nature. At the opposite pole, there are CAD cadets who have never touched paper with pencil and look on manual rendering as hopelessly out of touch with a cybernetic future. I find myself in the middle zone and look at the ultimate value of any drawing in terms of the quality of the idea it is describing. Thus the computer printout is no different than the pencil sketch, since both can function as evidence of either processed garbage or harvested creativity.
[ARCHITECT'S STATEMENT]

REFER TO CHAPTER 2

Drawing Skills/Line Weights

With this project you will continue to learn how to use the drafting tools in which you have made a significant investment. You will be required to draw with your parallel bar or T-square, 30°–60° triangle, 45°–45° triangle, and compass.

Draw the figures shown below (enlarged 60%) using a graphite lead and a leadholder. Construct the figures and shapes from the data given. Three different line weights are shown in the reference drawing but are exaggerated for clarity. All information necessary to complete these drawings is shown. Remember that squares, circles, and triangles have inherent relational geometries. Give special attention to line quality and the accuracy and consistency of the scaled drawing. Draw all lines with the aid of drafting tools. *Use no freehand lines.*

Format: On a 12" × 18" sheet of vellum oriented horizontally, begin by drawing a borderline ½" from the edge of the sheet on all sides. Construct the drawing fields as large as possible, 2" from the top and side border lines. Lay out the overall information first, then draw in the figures as indicated by the specific dimensional instructions. The scale is full-size.

Draw a line ¾" from the bottom border line for a title block. Lettering a title block is required. Letters should be ½" high on one line of guidelines within the center of the title block. Center the lettering. Give your name, the date, and the assignment number.

Some points about drafting to keep in mind:

1. Good line quality requires sharpness, blackness, and proper line weight.
2. You are working with scaled drawings. Scaled drawings are reductions in which all dimensions remain proportional. Construction of drawings is always preferable to measuring and scaling the graphic images. *Never scale the drawings,* unless no other means exists.
3. Construct object outlines lightly at first, then "heavy" them up to achieve proper line weight.
4. Practice before beginning the final drawing. Do not expect to draw this only once.

Grading criteria will include line quality, line weight, accuracy, and graphic presentation.

Project: Courtesy of Professor Steve Temple
School of Architecture
University of Texas San Antonio

REFER TO CHAPTER 2

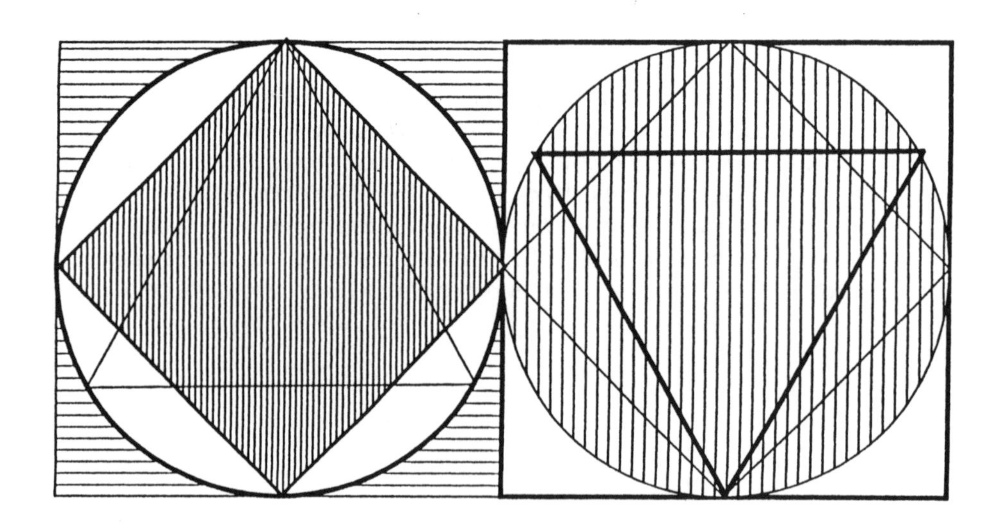

Longitudinal and Transverse Sections

This assignment emphasizes the relationship between a found object and drawings developed from that object. The drawings in this exercise will be based on a drawing type termed a "section."

Begin by doing some experimental research on objects. For example, go to the grocery store and buy different fruits and vegetables. Slice them in different directions and notice how the sectional configuration changes or remains similar. Compare cross-sectional cuts on a string bean, a watermelon, and a green bell pepper. The string bean and even the watermelon have similar geometric shapes at different sliced locations, but the bell pepper changes dramatically.

Examine biology and botany books showing sections through the human body and tree trunks or tree branches. In medicine, radiologists can cut through an infinite number of locations on the human body with X-rays. As the X-ray slice through the human body varies, each image will differ in varying degrees from the previous image.

The section drawing is a way of understanding the contour, volume, edges, and insides of an object in space. It reveals the inner workings of an object and its inner space.

Required: Obtain three objects that possess interesting sectional characteristics. The objects cannot be transparent. It is best if the sections are not similar or identical as you cut different locations. Your objective is to explain through drawing the inner details of the object. For this assignment, you will develop an elevation and one longitudinal section. You will also be required to develop four transverse sections based on observation, deduction, and scaled measurement. Draw on tracing paper first. Do numerous freehand sections to determine what explains the object best. The final drawing will be pencil on 18" × 24" smooth white Bristol board. All areas of concern, such as placement, composition, and sequence of drawings, should be addressed during class and before you begin the final drawings. For one of the section drawings, you will be required to depict the object as it casts shadows on a background.

Problem: Courtesy of the California College of Art and Crafts
School of Architectural Studies
Studio Professors: Hank Dunlop and Mark Jensen

REFER TO CHAPTERS 4 AND 7

Orthographic Projection: Hardline

Time frame: One week

Objectives

This assignment is a test of your abilities to resolve a complex abstract object into the three-view orthographic format, as well as to accurately measure and draw to scale. It also provides continued practice in layout and drawing technique.

Project

Draw the top, front, and side views of one of the following, in orthographic projection. Draw in hardline (not freehand) and use graphite.

1. Draw one **auto part** in full scale (actual size), or
2. Draw two different pieces of **Styrofoam** in half-scale.

Format

Use a sheet of vellum measuring 18" × 24" oriented horizontally. Draw a borderline ½" from the edge of the sheet. Provide ¾" high guidelines at the bottom of the sheet located ½" from the bottom borderline. Letter your name, project number, and the date.

Lay out the three-view format of each object side by side (three views for the auto parts; two separate three-view sets for the Styrofoam objects). Spacing between views must be equal. Spacing between sets of views is up to you.

Rules

Large curves in the objects must be drawn on your elevation views. Small radii (less than ¼") can be shown as a corner.

Elements of each view must *project* and *align* from view to view. *No freehand drawing.* Your drawings must be *constructed.* All lines must be drawn with instruments. Construction guidelines, if drawn *lightly,* are acceptable on the finished drawing.

Drawing Tips

Prior to beginning your final drawing, make a series of sketches of the objects to explore the relationships of the parts of the objects. Also in sketches, explore the actual size of the drawings that will need to be laid out on your sheet prior to attempting your final drawing.

Project: Courtesy of Professor Steve Temple
School of Architecture
University of Texas–San Antonio

REFER TO CHAPTER 4

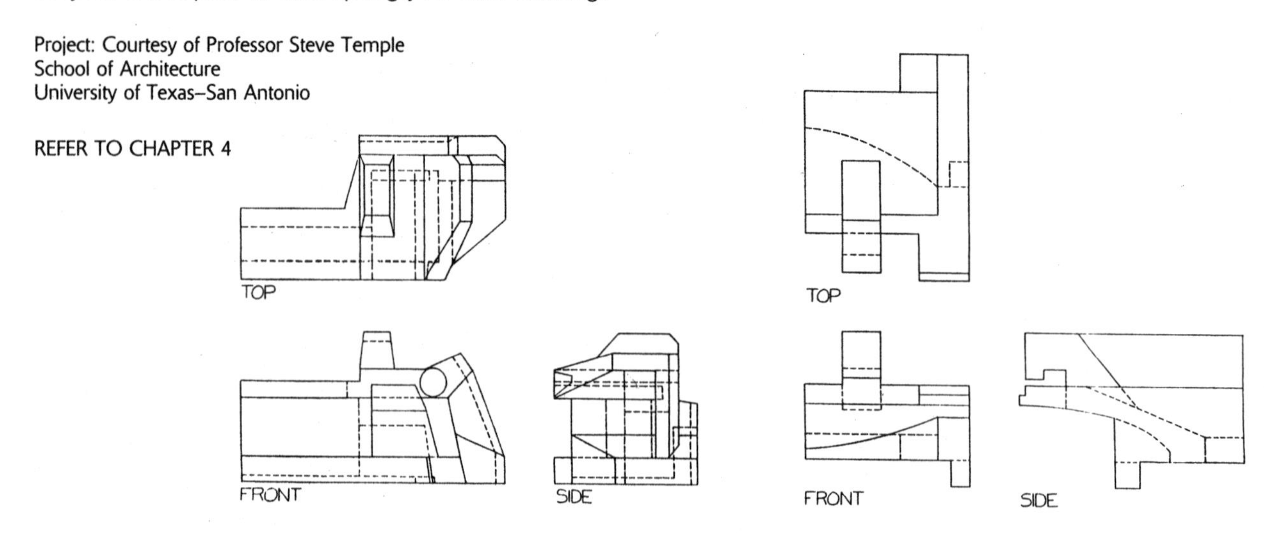

Drawing: Student project by Bethany Biddle
Department of Interior Design
University of North Carolina–Greensboro

Plan and Elevation Graphic Conventions

Time frame: One week
Required materials: A 25' measuring tape

1. Assemble into groups of three (use a sign-up sheet). Measure together — draw your final drawing separately.
2. Locate a classroom with windows seating at least twenty somewhere on campus. Measure the room. On a rough sketch of the floor plan and interior elevations, add the measurements. This will be used as a reference to draw an accurate, scaled drawing of the floor plan and interior elevations. Assume a horizontal section is cut at 4'0" above the floor. Include all furniture in both the plan and elevations.
3. Individually, each student will then draw the plan and interior elevations from the measurements in ⅜" = 1'0" scale on a single sheet of 24" × 36" vellum in graphite, according to the following format:

   The plan should be located in the center of the sheet with north at the top of the sheet. The respective interior elevations should then be drawn as projections around the plan: the elevation you see when facing north to the top, the elevation you see when facing east to the right side, and so on.
4. Draw all furniture and built-in cabinets. Draw all wall elements. Show three-dimensional ceiling elements on the plan using the dashed-line convention. The use of templates is permitted.
5. Title block at bottom of sheet: Letter on two lines at ½" high with a ¼" space between lines, as follows:

   Top line (containing the title): as-built drawings, name of campus building, room number

   Bottom line: your name, the date, the scale used

Project: Courtesy of Professor Steve Temple
School of Architecture
University of Texas–San Antonio

REFER TO CHAPTER 4

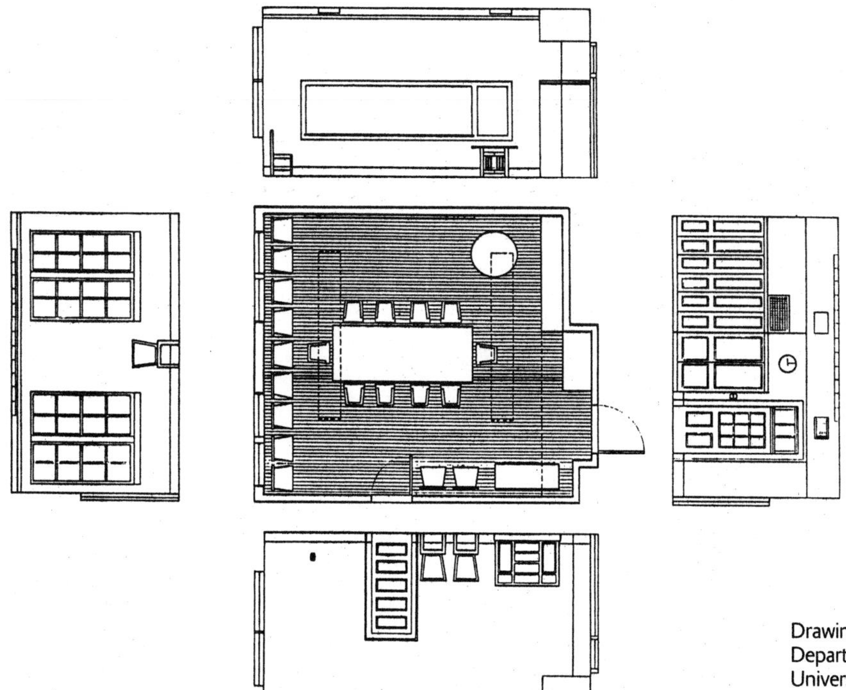

Drawing: Student project by Christine Bottom
Department of Interior Design
University of North Carolina–Greensboro

Section: Graphic Conventions

Time frame: Ten days to two weeks

This assignment will introduce you to the graphics of **building sections** by projecting a building section from a plan and another cross section.

- Choose one of the buildings presented in class.
- Each building is limited to three students.
- A sign-up sheet will be posted for each.

In graphite on a sheet of 24" x 36" vellum, lay out and draw (trace) the floor plan and one section in a projected format, with the plan in correct orientation projected below the section. It will be necessary to enlarge the drawings on a photocopier to fit on the sheet in as large a scale as possible, preferably in a common scale found on an architect's or engineer's scale. Draw a graphic scale on the finished drawing.

Then, **construct** the opposing cross section that is not given, using **projection lines** as an aid to complete any missing data. Elements of the two building sections must be consistent with each other and must be drawn using a method of projecting construction lines.

In order to complete the missing cross section, it may be necessary to develop a strategy for completing missing information by either using your knowledge of design or researching the particular building.

Provide a lettered title block at least ½" high at the top of the sheet, including your name, assignment number, the name of the building, and the date of the building.

This is a drawing exercise — you are expected to produce a sophisticated drawing using various line weights, good line quality, a well-composed layout, and quality lettering.

Project: Courtesy of Professor Steve Temple
School of Architecture
University of Texas–San Antonio

REFER TO CHAPTER 4

Identifying Surfaces, Isometric Views, and Missing Views

In the first group of three, identify the surfaces in the orthographic views. Note the example at left. In the next group of three, sketch the isometric of each below in the spaces provided. In the final two boxes, sketch the three missing orthographic views from the given isometric drawing.

Evaluation of similar problems will be based on: drawing accuracy and comprehension, composed sheet layout-borders, lettering, etc. (if applicable), and line quality.

REFER TO CHAPTER 5

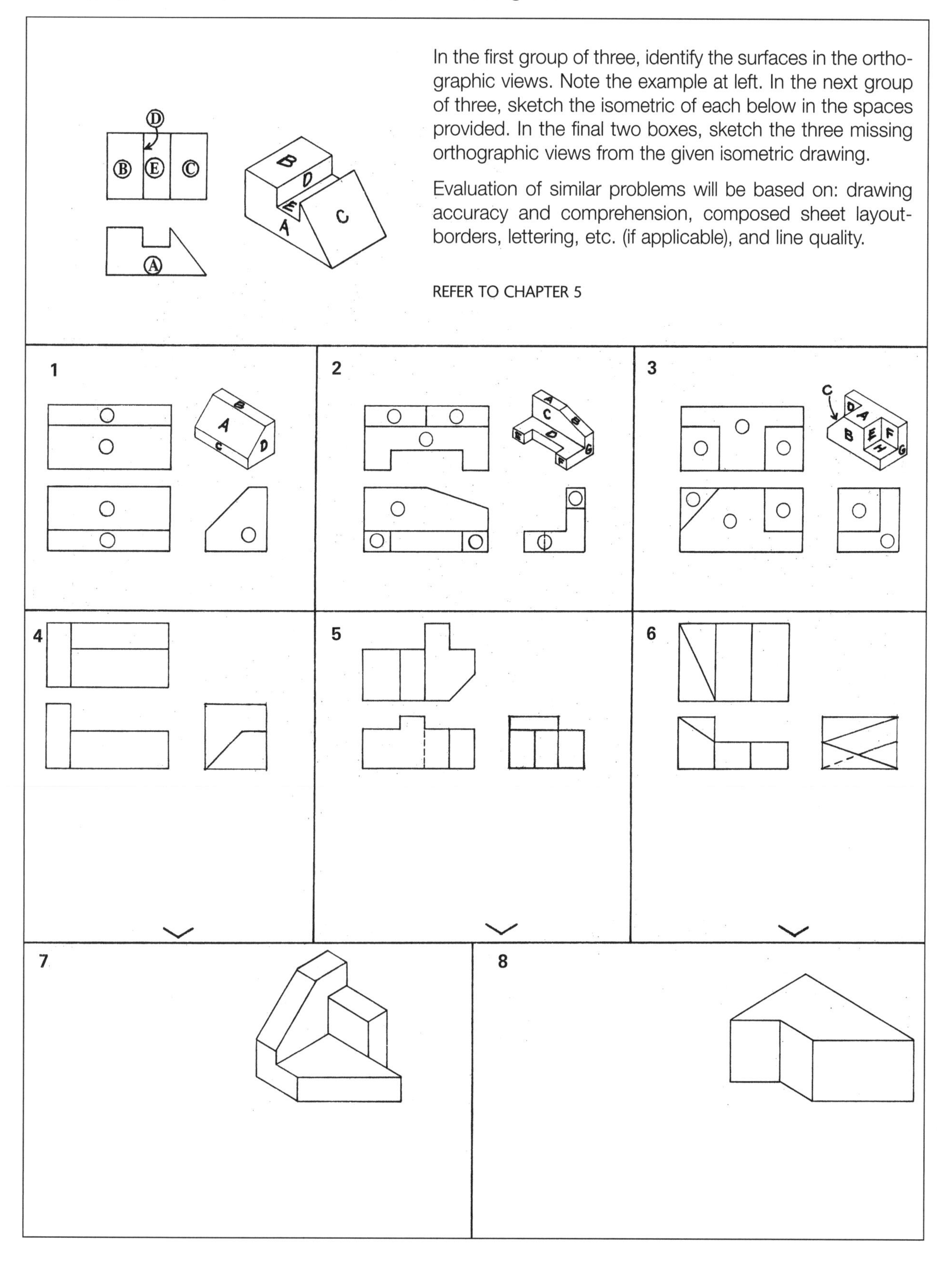

Missing Views

From the given views of the object, construct the left side, back, and bottom views.

Scale: $\frac{1}{8}$"=1'0"

Note: Folding plane lines in these two exercises are mainly for instructional purposes. Delete them in photocopies if your instructor so desires.

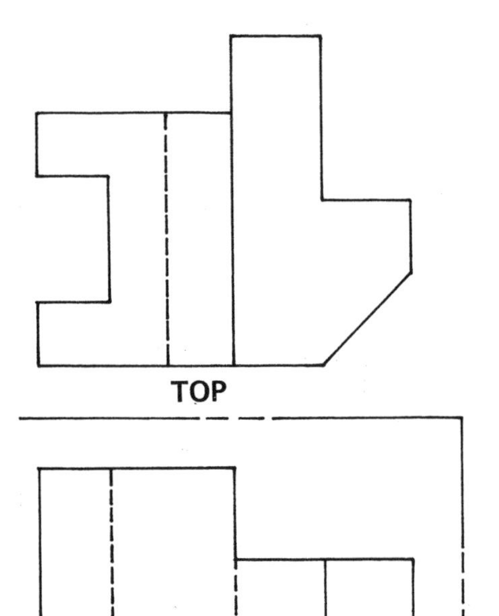

FRONT

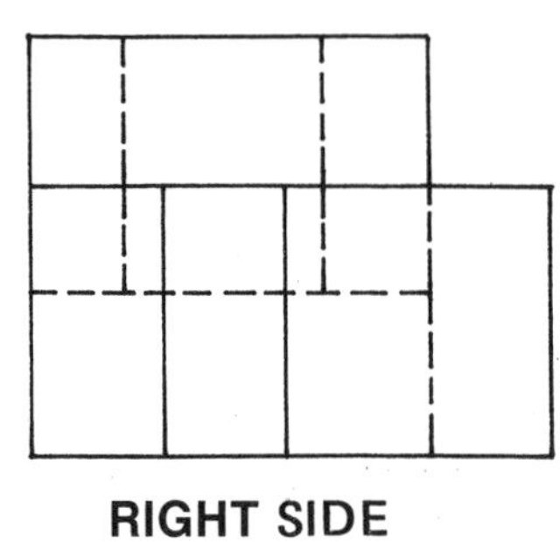

RIGHT SIDE

Missing Views

From the given views of the object, construct the right side, bottom, and back views.

Scale: $\frac{3}{8}$"=1'0"

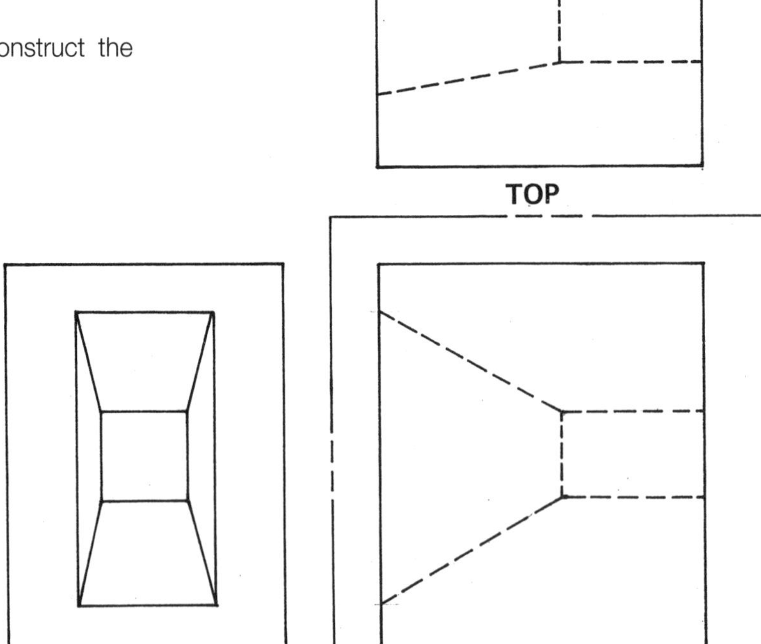

LEFT SIDE FRONT

In resolving multiview problems, always try to visualize with sketches the three-dimensional construct.

REFER TO CHAPTER 5

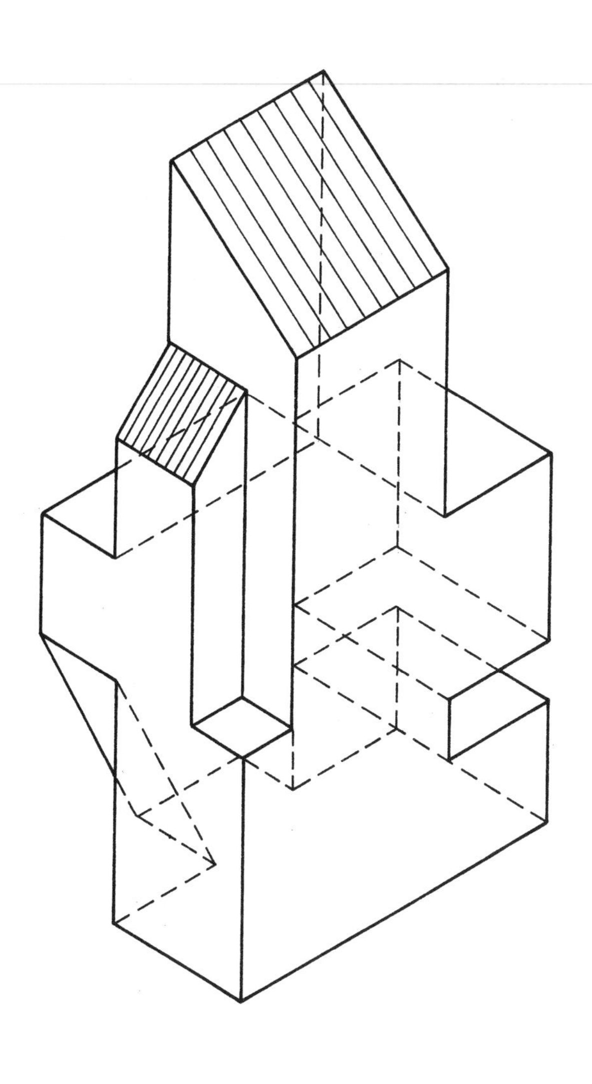

Six Orthographic Views

Shown at left is an isometric drawing with hidden lines to help you visualize the form. Construct six orthographic views. Draw them first with hidden lines and then without hidden lines, as would be seen in architectural plans and elevations.

Student project by Ellen W. Ng
Courtesy of the Department of Architecture
City College of San Francisco

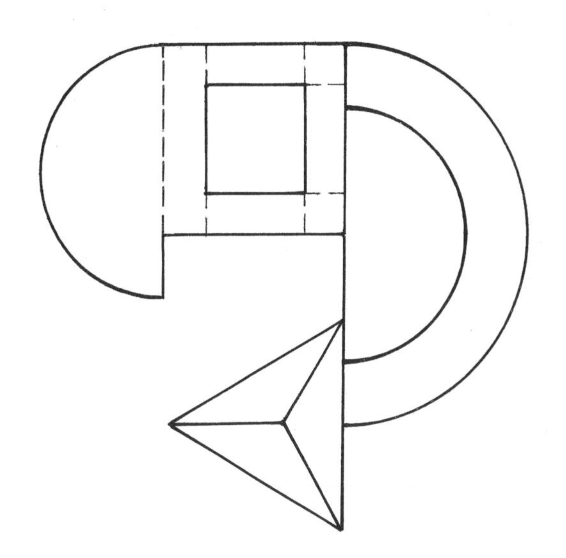

Student project by Erna Egli and Joanna Hostetler
Courtesy of the Department of Architecture
City College of San Francisco

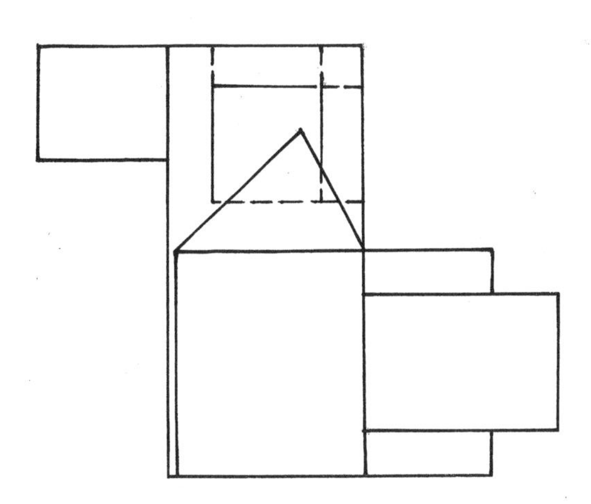

Missing View / Isometric / Plan Oblique

Construct the missing right-side elevation from the given plan and elevation views. Then construct an isometric drawing and a plan oblique drawing at 45°–45°.

REFER TO CHAPTER 5

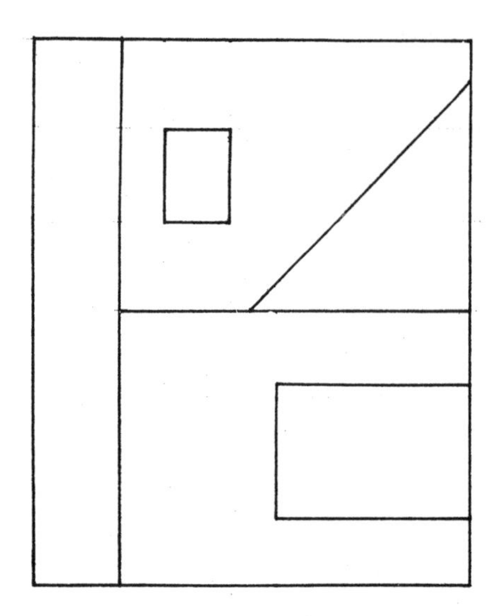

Isometric Views/Dimetric View

From the plan and two elevations of a simple block form, visualize and sketch what you think the four isometric views from the four different corners will look like. Then accurately construct the four isometric drawings. As an optional additional exercise, construct a dimetric view from a vantage point of your choice, emphasizing one or two of the principal planes.

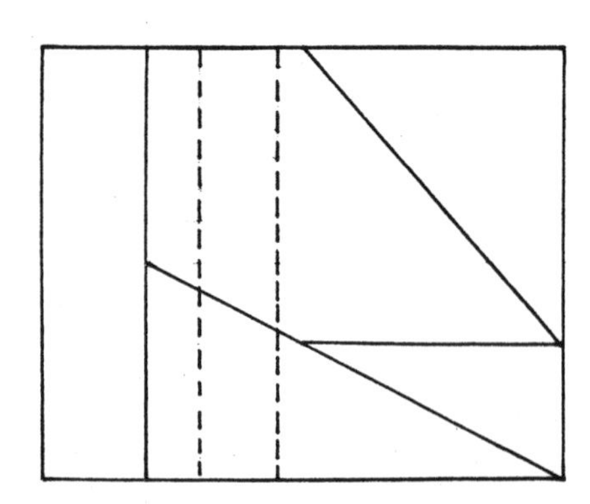

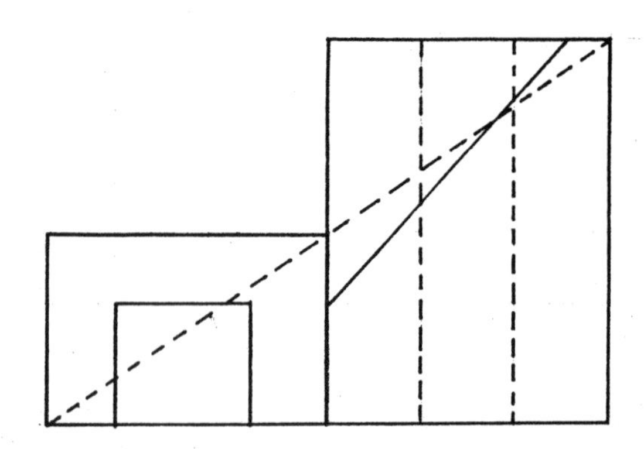

LEVEL ONE

Student project by Linda Gigli
Courtesy of the Department of Architecture
City College of San Francisco

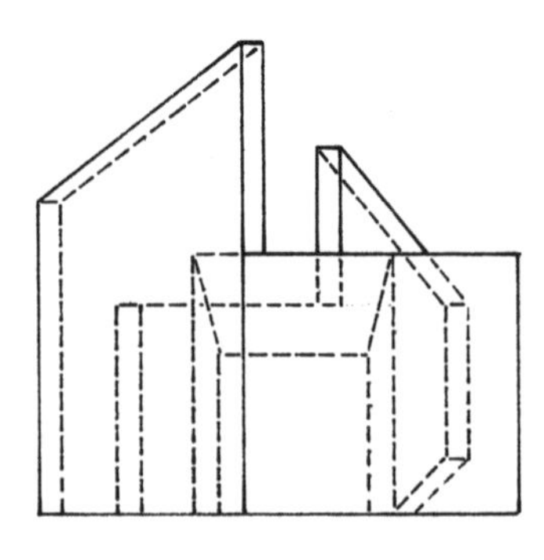

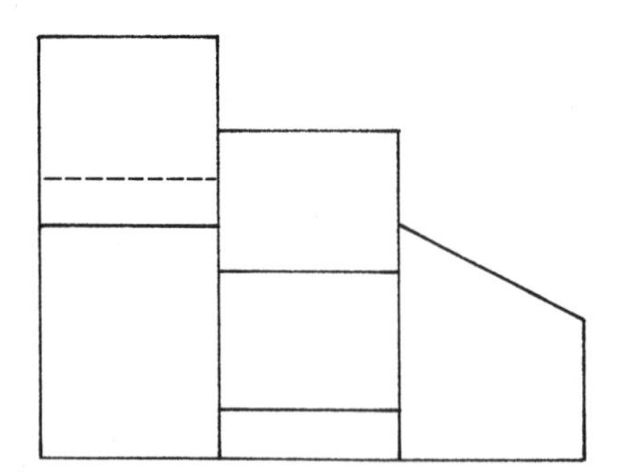

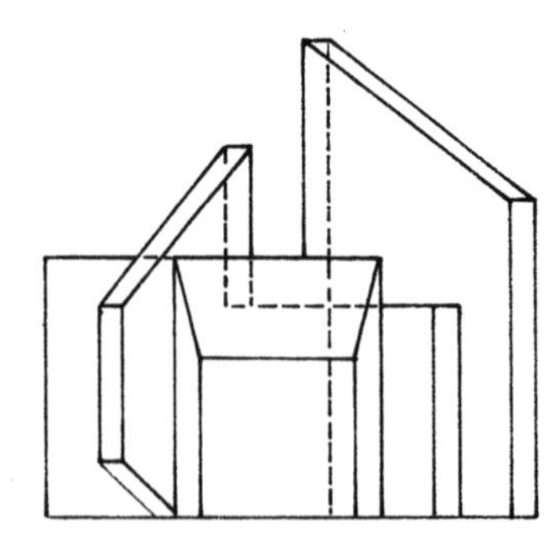

Missing Views

From the three elevation views of this fairly complex form, visualize and sketch what you think the plan view and rear elevation will look like. Then accurately construct these views. Show hidden lines.

REFER TO CHAPTER 5

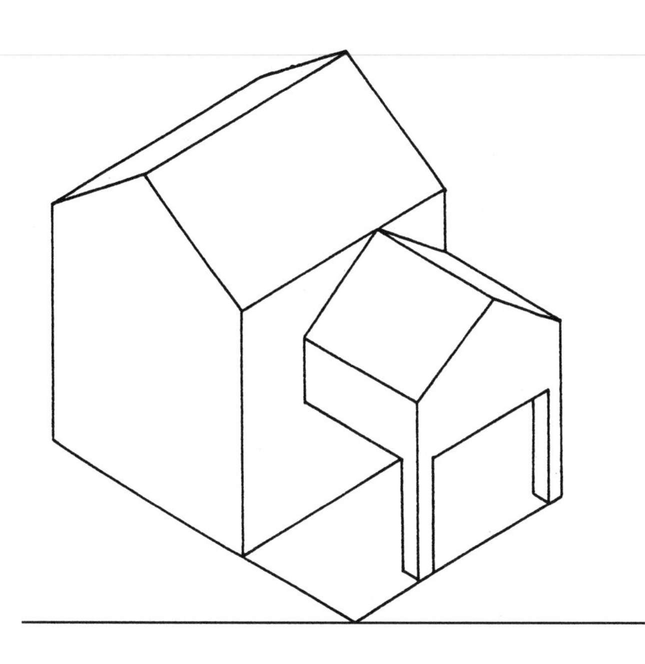

Comprehensive Paraline Problem

1. Construct the roof plan, the front elevation, and the side elevation views.
2. Construct two plan obliques: one at 45°–45° and one at 60°–30°.
3. Using the plan configuration, construct a plan oblique with a nonvertical z-axis that is 60° from the horizontal.
4. Using the side elevation, construct an elevation oblique, using 45°–1:½:1.
5. Using the side elevation, construct a frontal elevation oblique 0°–1:1.
6. Construct a worm's-eye plan oblique.

Scale: 1⁄16"=1'0"

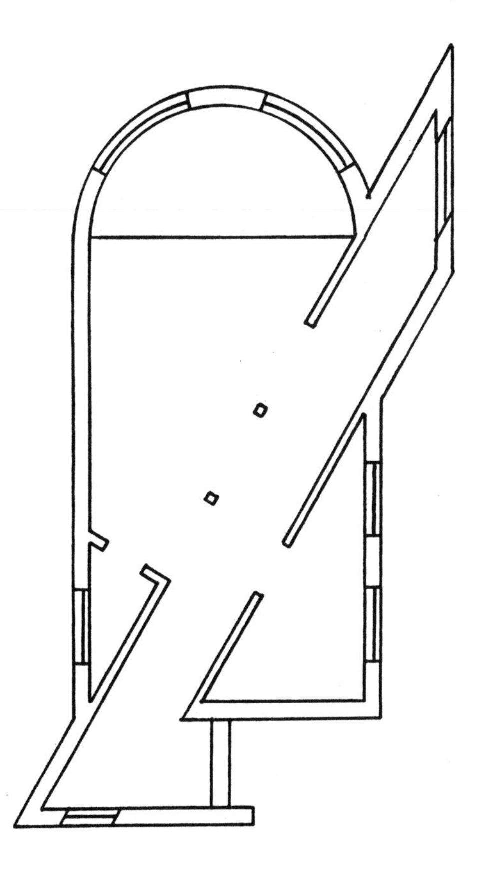

Plan Oblique

Rotate this plan view of a small building 30° from the horizontal so that you can construct a 30°–60° plan oblique view. Make the elevation of the plan cut 4' above the exterior ground level.

Scale: 3⁄32"=1'0"

Courtesy of Kwok Gorran Tsui, an architecture graduate of the University of Texas at Austin

REFER TO CHAPTER 5

Plan Oblique

TIME FRAME: One week

Instructors should develop their own plan and interior elevations and give them to their students. From the plan and interior elevations on p. 601, construct a plan oblique view in ½" = 1'-0" scale in graphite on an 18" × 24" vellum oriented horizontally. Use corner A for the front corner of the plan oblique. Remove walls AB and AD for a better view of the space.

Format: Draw a borderline ½" from the edge and include a 1" high title block at the bottom. In the center of the title block, in ¾" high lettering guidelines, letter your name, project number, and the date. The orthographic drawings should be in ¼" scale.

Turn in a blueprint for evaluation.

Give thought to the layout on your sheet so as to produce an aesthetically pleasing overall drawing effect. Line weights should be varied to aid in the perception of depth.

ADDITIONAL

1. Draw the grid on the floor only. (The grid may remain on the walls as light guidelines, which will not show on a blueprint).
2. Design and draw a different lamp with a round lamp shade on each of the two side tables.
3. Draw four platonic objects sitting on the fireplace mantle.
4. Draw two 18" × 28" paintings in frames on two of the walls.
5. Draw a six-panel door in the doorway of wall CD.
6. Draw a 24" × 42" casement window in wall CD above the plant. The case molding frame should be rectangular.

PLAN OBLIQUE (according to name)

Last name A–E: 45° plan projection
Last name F–J: 30° left–60° right plan oblique
Last name K–Q: 30° isometric
Last name R–Z: 30° right–60° left plan oblique

Project: Courtesy of Professor Steve Temple
School of Architecture
University of Texas–San Antonio

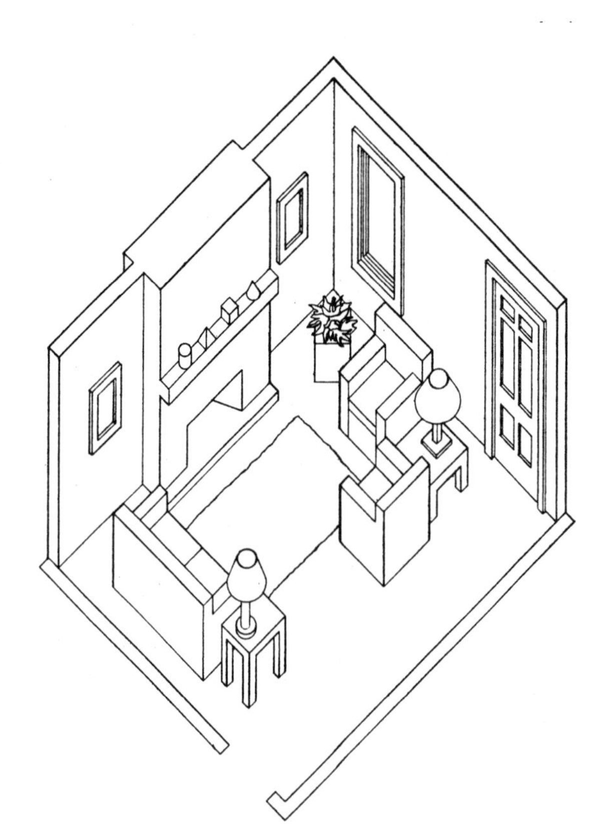

Student project by Christine Bottom
Department of Interior Design
University of North Carolina–Greensboro

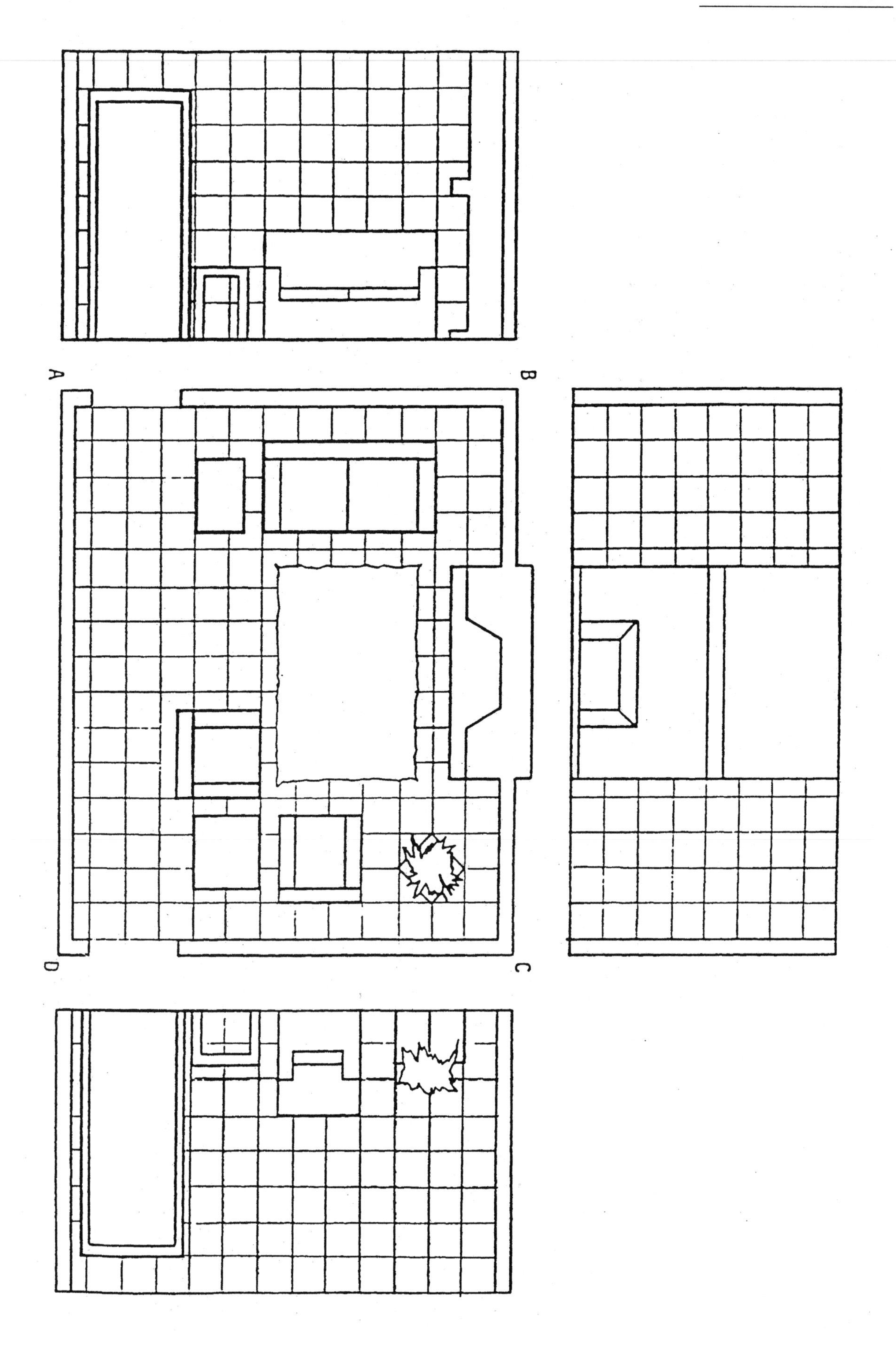
A
B
C
D

Given: A plan view and one elevation of an L-shaped seating area.

Required: Select a horizon line and station point and construct a **two-point perspective.** Also draw to scale two **human figures** in conversation, one sitting and one standing.

Scale: ¼"=1'0"

Student project by Amy Man
Courtesy of the Department of Architecture
City College of San Francisco

REFER TO CHAPTERS 6 and 9

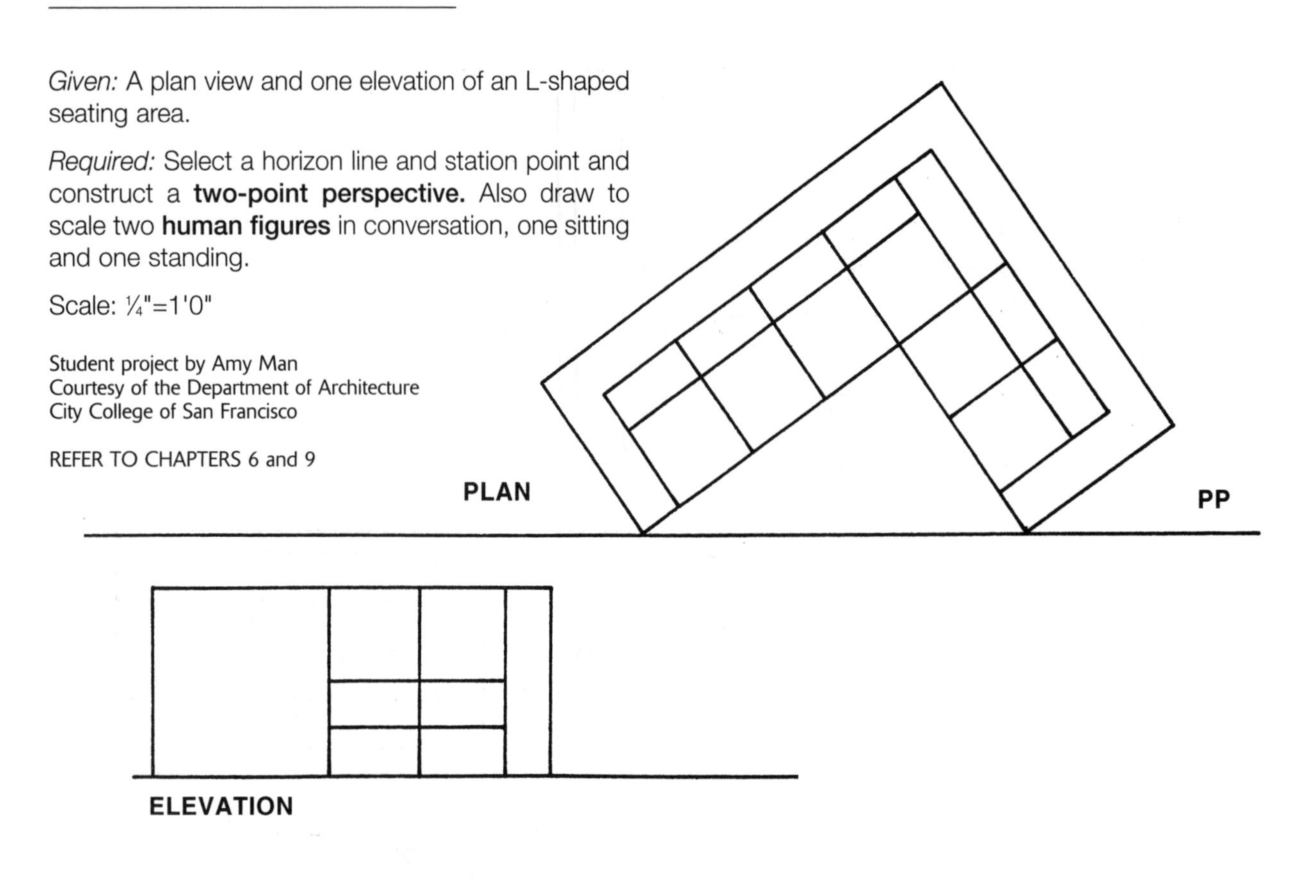

Given: A plan view and one elevation of a building form.

Required: Construct a **two-point perspective.** The elevation view is looking directly perpendicular to the picture plane. For these two problems, choose a station point that has an angle of about 30° from the station point to the viewed extremes of the object. As an optional additional exercise, add exterior **vegetation** and landscaping.

Scale: $\frac{1}{16}$"=1'0"

REFER TO CHAPTERS 6 AND 8

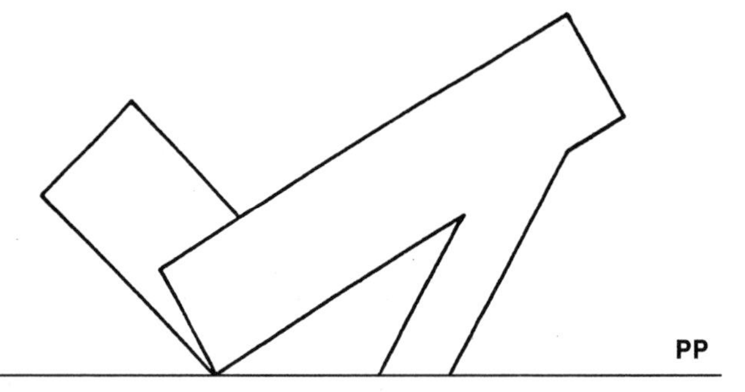

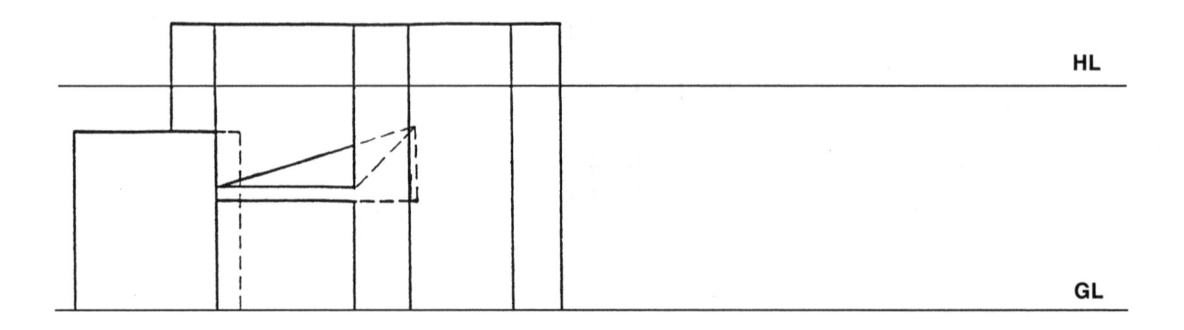

Two-Point Perspective

THE AIM

An exercise in three-dimensional representation utilizing the method of constructing two-point architectural perspective to create a realistic or lifelike image of form and space.

THE TASK

Present a two-point perspective of the family house at Riva San Vitale by Mario Botta. Select a viewpoint showing the main terrace (e.g., looking at the building from the southeast corner). Position the station point and picture plane appropriately to achieve a realistic view. You may show the setup grid and construction lines in the final presentation, using a fine pen (0.1 or 0.2) with red or blue ink. Drawings must be done in black ink, drafted either with technical or felt-tipped pens (Uni Pin fine-line pens are good).

Re-present the elevations of the building with shadows, using the shading techniques described in the lectures. Note that the elevations to be shaded are separate drawings from the perspective drawing. You can cut and paste the elevations (then photocopy the whole sheet) or redraw them (for better line quality) onto your final presentation sheet. When placing the drawings, think about the layout of the sheet for readability and coherence. Pay attention to the techniques introduced in the previous lectures, including line quality and use of drafting equipment.

REQUIREMENTS

1. In class you will be required to practice setting up two-point perspectives. Bring your drawing tools.
2. The final presentation will be a perspective view and three elevations on one A3 sheet of paper, in vertical (portrait) format, with the logo in the bottom right corner. The drawing must be in ink.

ASSESSMENT CRITERIA

Students will be assessed on:

- Accuracy and coherence of perspective
- Selection of viewpoint
- Line quality and rendering
- Sheet layout and perspective setup
- Neatness of presentation

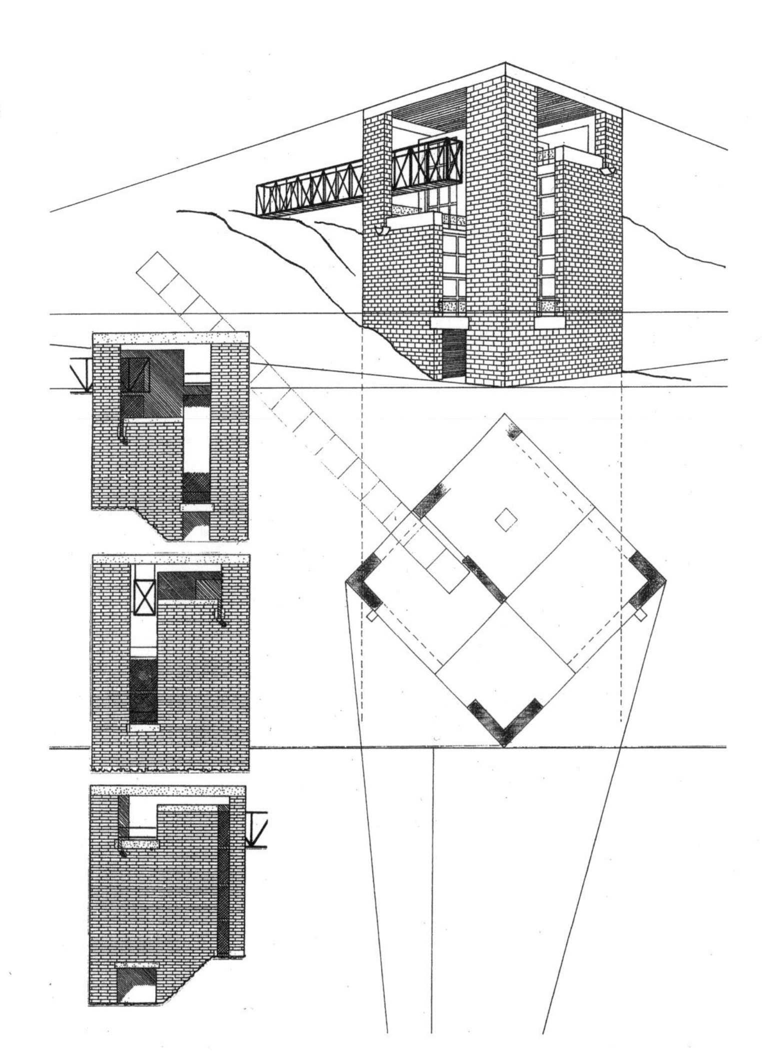

Courtesy of Dr. Samer Akkach
Drawing Architecture & Landscape I
School of Architecture, Landscape Architecture and Urban Design
Adelaide University, South Australia

REFER TO CHAPTERS 6 AND 7

Drawing: Student project by Sue Fletcher
Courtesy of the School of Architecture,. Landscape Architecture and Urban Design
Adelaide University, South Australia

Perspective Reflections

Given: A roof plan view and right side elevation of a schematic block form for a house boat with the HL, PP, GL, and SP, as noted.
Scale: 1/16" = 1'-0"

Required: Construct a perspective of the house boat and a perspective of its reflection in the water. Label all vanishing points.

REFER TO CHAPTERS 6 AND 8

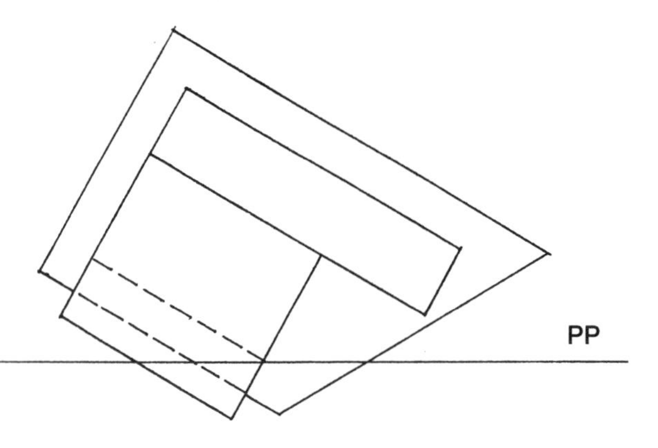

PP

+ SP

HL

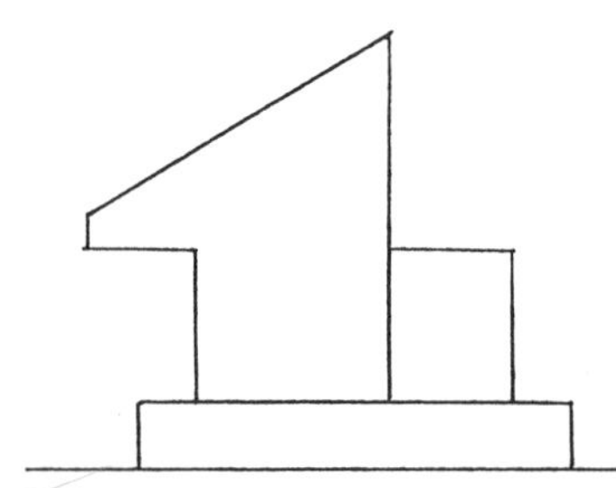

GL or water line

© Mark Dziewulski

Photo: Lakeside Studio
Carmichael, California
Courtesy of Mark Dziewulski, Architect
www.dzarchitect.com

Photo by Keith Cronin

The selected HL for this exercise is considerably above normal eye level. Move the HL to roughly normal human eye level and generate another perspective. The resulting angle above the ground plane will be similar to the reflection seen in the photo of the house. This photo is an excellent example of a complete reflection of a structure in still water.

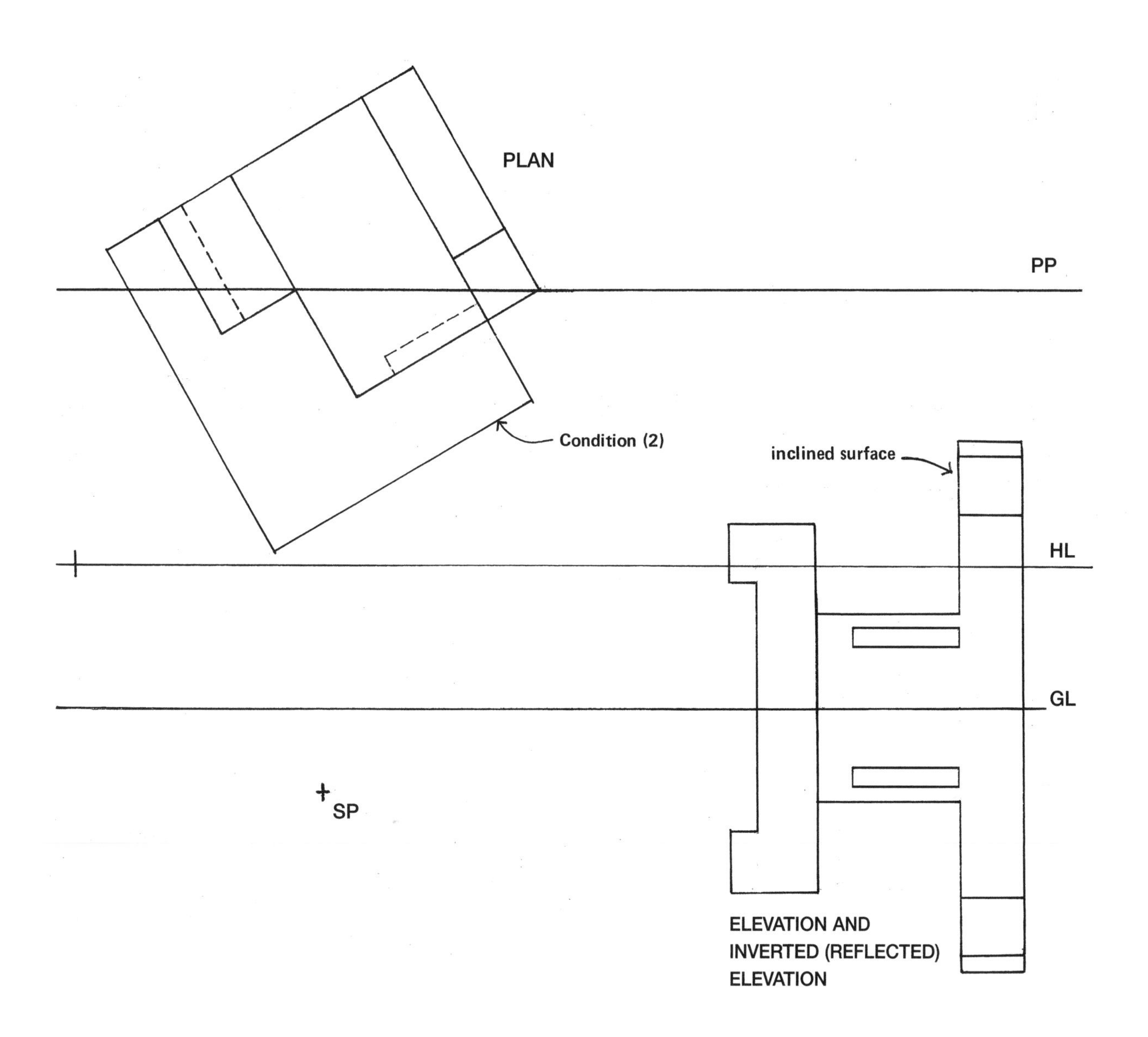

Perspective Reflections

Given: The plan, elevation, and inverted elevation of a building touching a **reflecting surface.**

Required: Draw a two-point perspective of the building and show its exact reflection. Scale: $\frac{1}{16}$" = 1'0"

Condition (2): Draw this edge of a reflecting pool. Notice how this results in a partial reflected image. As an optional additional exercise, render the reflection in the pool.

REFER TO CHAPTERS 6 AND 8

Perspective Cutaways and Section Perspectives

Perspective cutaway views and two-point section perspectives are excellent ways of showing the interior of a design concept. This exercise encourages the use of these methods for viewing the inside of any building project.

One-Point Perspective

THE AIM
An exercise in three-dimensional representation that uses one-point architectural perspective to create a realistic, lifelike image of form and space.

THE TASK
You are required to present a one-point perspective of your kitchen (or a friend's kitchen, if you do not have one). Try not to use a photograph. Select a viewpoint that gives a representation close to the visual perception of the space. Pay attention to the techniques introduced in the previous lectures, such as line quality, use of drafting equipment, etc. Use this exercise to communicate a spatial experience as well, exploring form, order, texture, shape, and proportion.

REQUIREMENTS
1. Bring in an accurate, scaled sketch plan and sketch elevation(s) of your kitchen.
2. Bring in an appropriate grid and a draft setup of the one-point perspective of your kitchen.
3. The final presentation should be the perspective view on one A3 sheet of paper, in vertical (portrait) format, with the logo in the bottom right corner. The drawing may be in pencil or ink.

ASSESSMENT CRITERIA
Students will be assessed on:

- Accuracy and coherence of perspective
- Selection of viewpoint and perspective setup
- Line quality and rendering
- Sheet layout and neatness of presentation

Courtesy of Dr. Samer Akkach
Drawing Architecture & Landscape I
School of Architecture, Landscape Architecture and Urban Design
Adelaide University, South Australia

REFER TO CHAPTERS 6 AND 8

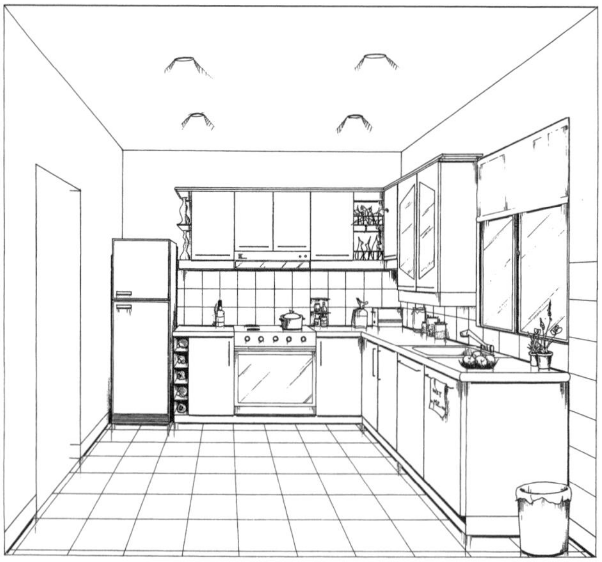

Student project by Sin Jee Lai
One-point perspective
Original size A3, 29.7 X 42 cm
School of Architecture, Landscape Architecture and Urban Design
University of Adelaide, South Australia

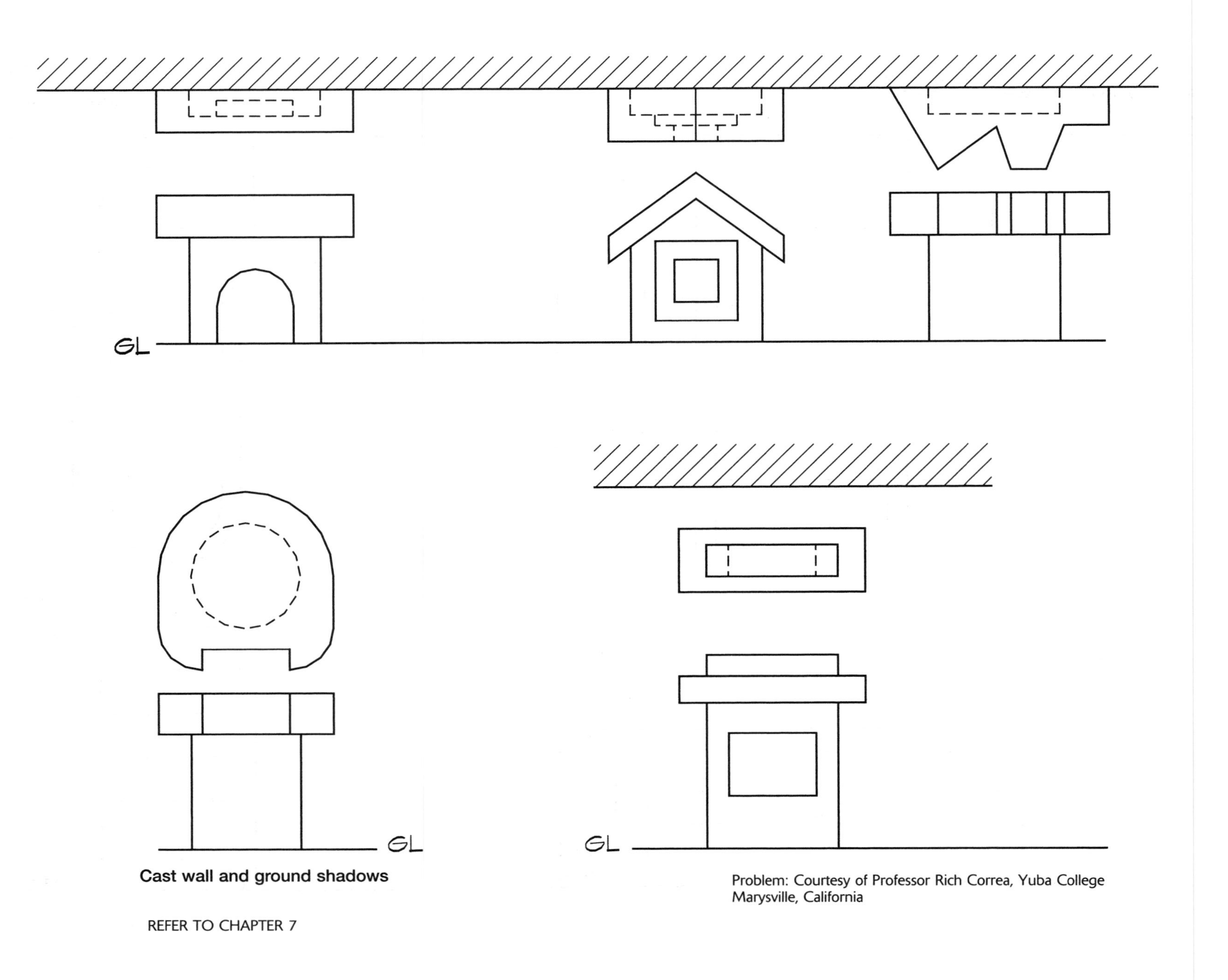

Cast wall and ground shadows

REFER TO CHAPTER 7

Problem: Courtesy of Professor Rich Correa, Yuba College
Marysville, California

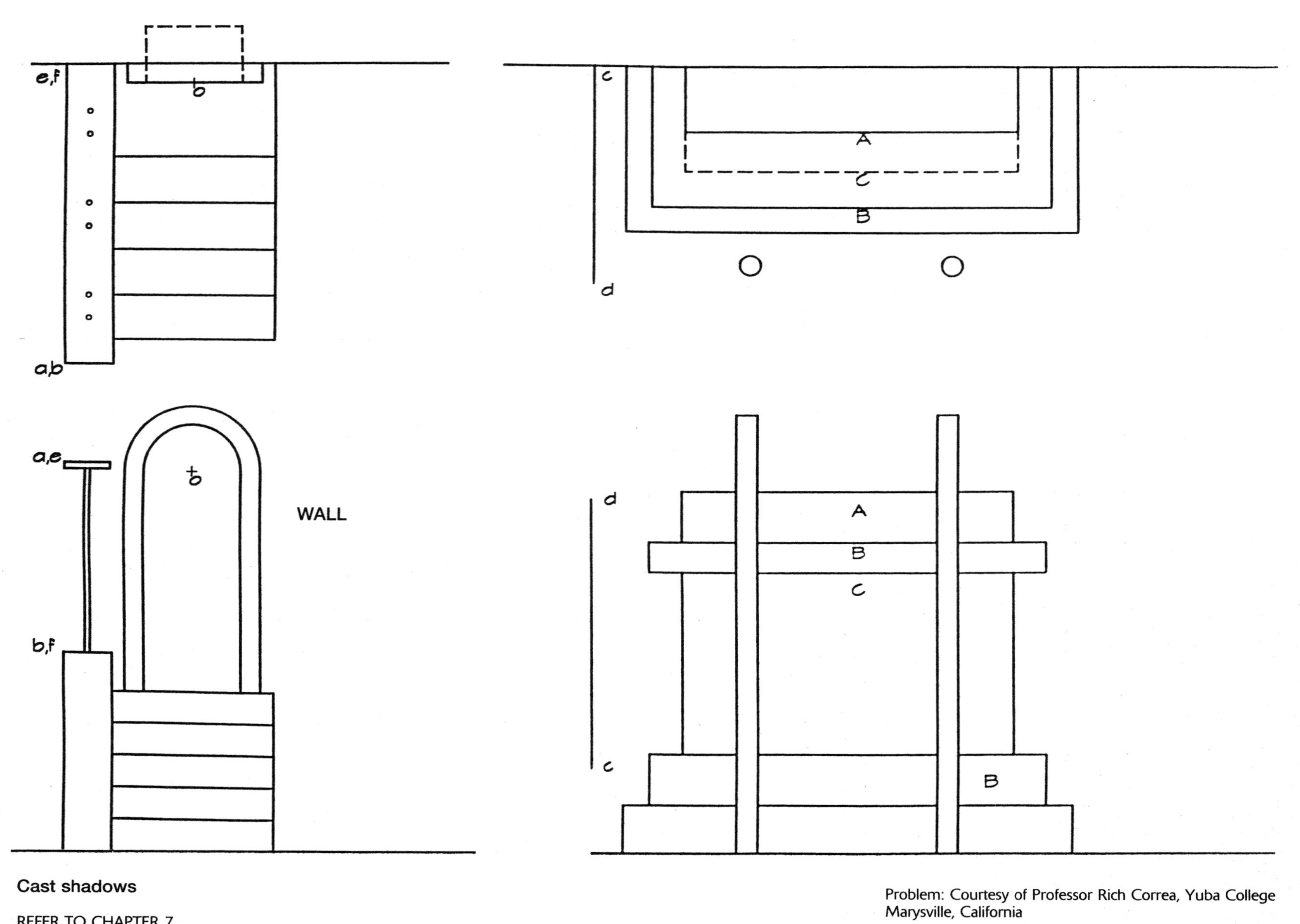

Cast shadows

REFER TO CHAPTER 7

Problem: Courtesy of Professor Rich Correa, Yuba College
Marysville, California

Comprehensive Problem: Paralines, Perspectives, Shadows, and Rendering

1. Draw both isometric and plan oblique sketches of how you think the stair element should appear.
2. Draw two different accurate isometric drawings.
3. Choose perspective variables and draw two, two-point perspectives (¼"=1'0").
4. Add shadows and shades to each of the above.
5. Add two human figures, one each at two different levels, drawn to scale.

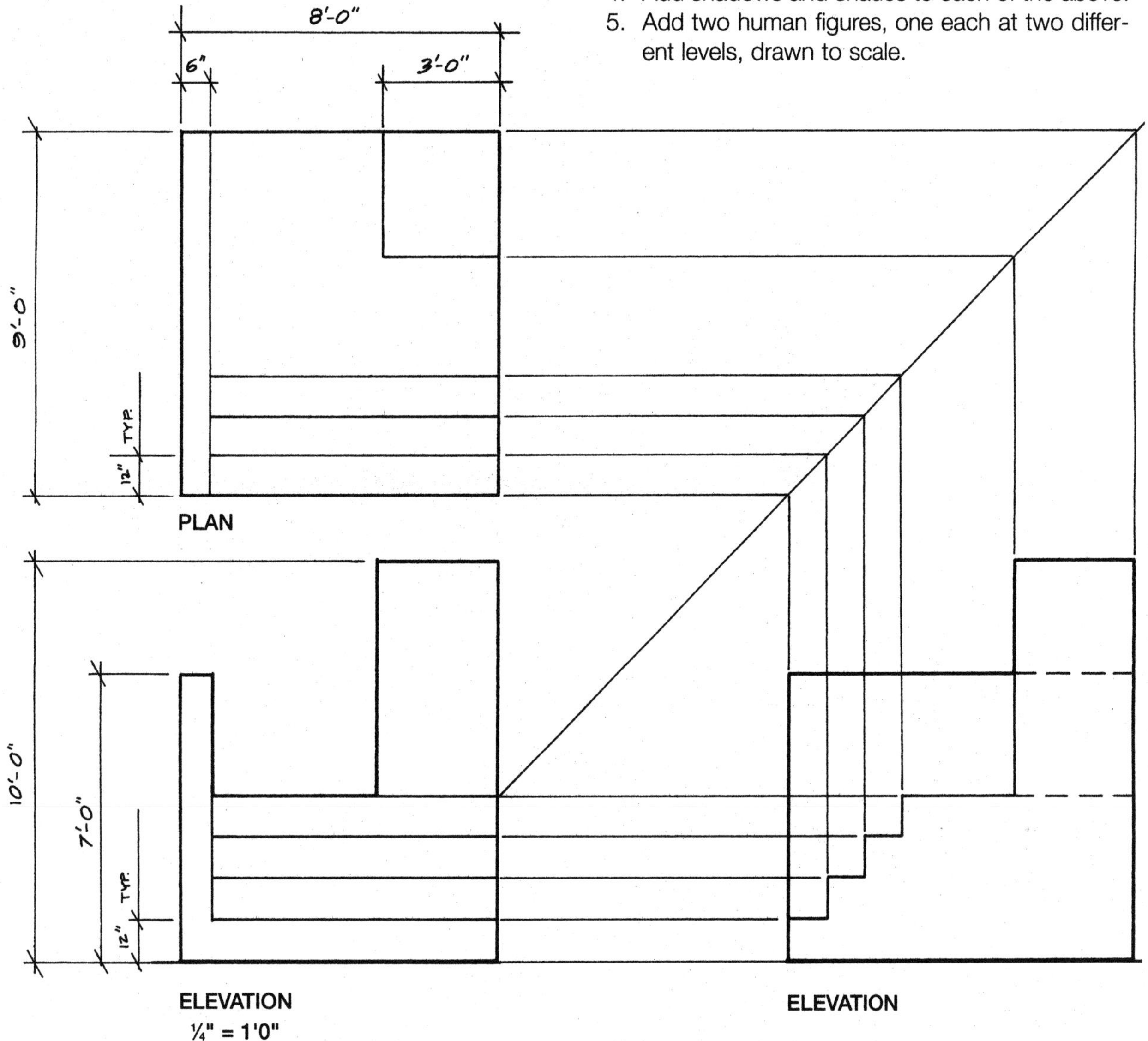

Problem: Courtesy of Professor Thomas L. Turman,
Department of Architecture
Laney College
Oakland, California

REFER TO CHAPTERS 5, 6, 7, AND 8

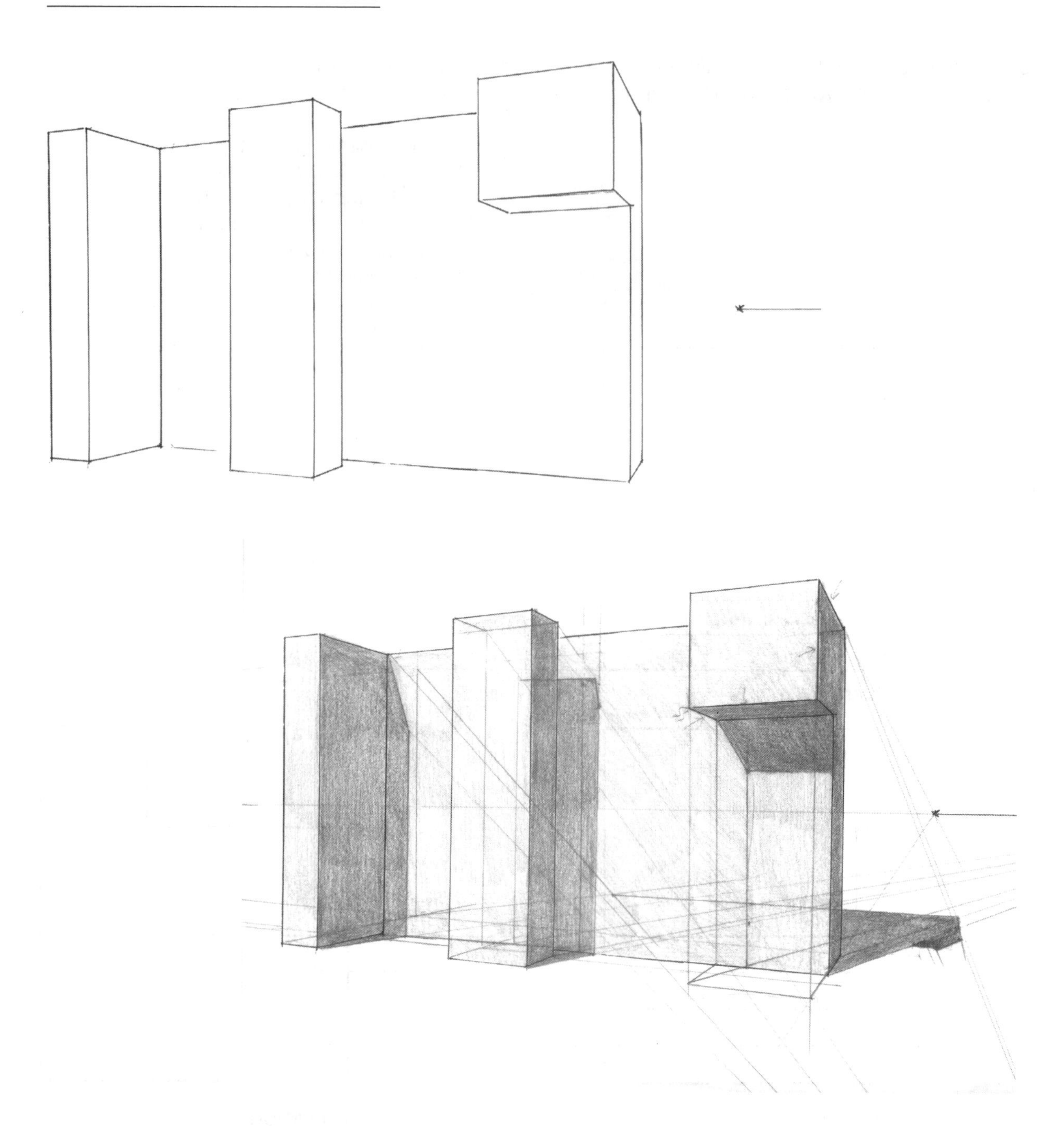

Shadow Construction (Two-Vanishing-Point Method)

In this exercise, the students are given a handout upon which is a shadow-casting model. The models are designed to create specific shadow shapes that can be constructed using the two-vanishing-point method. The advantage of this method is that shadows can be constructed in perspective: orthographics are not necessary. The first shadow point is given (i.e., casting point A projects a shadow to shadow point A). From there, the shadow VP can be extended, then the sun VP and the shadow can be constructed (see example).

Problem: Courtesy of Professor Dick Davison
College of Architecture
Texas A&M University

REFER TO CHAPTER 7

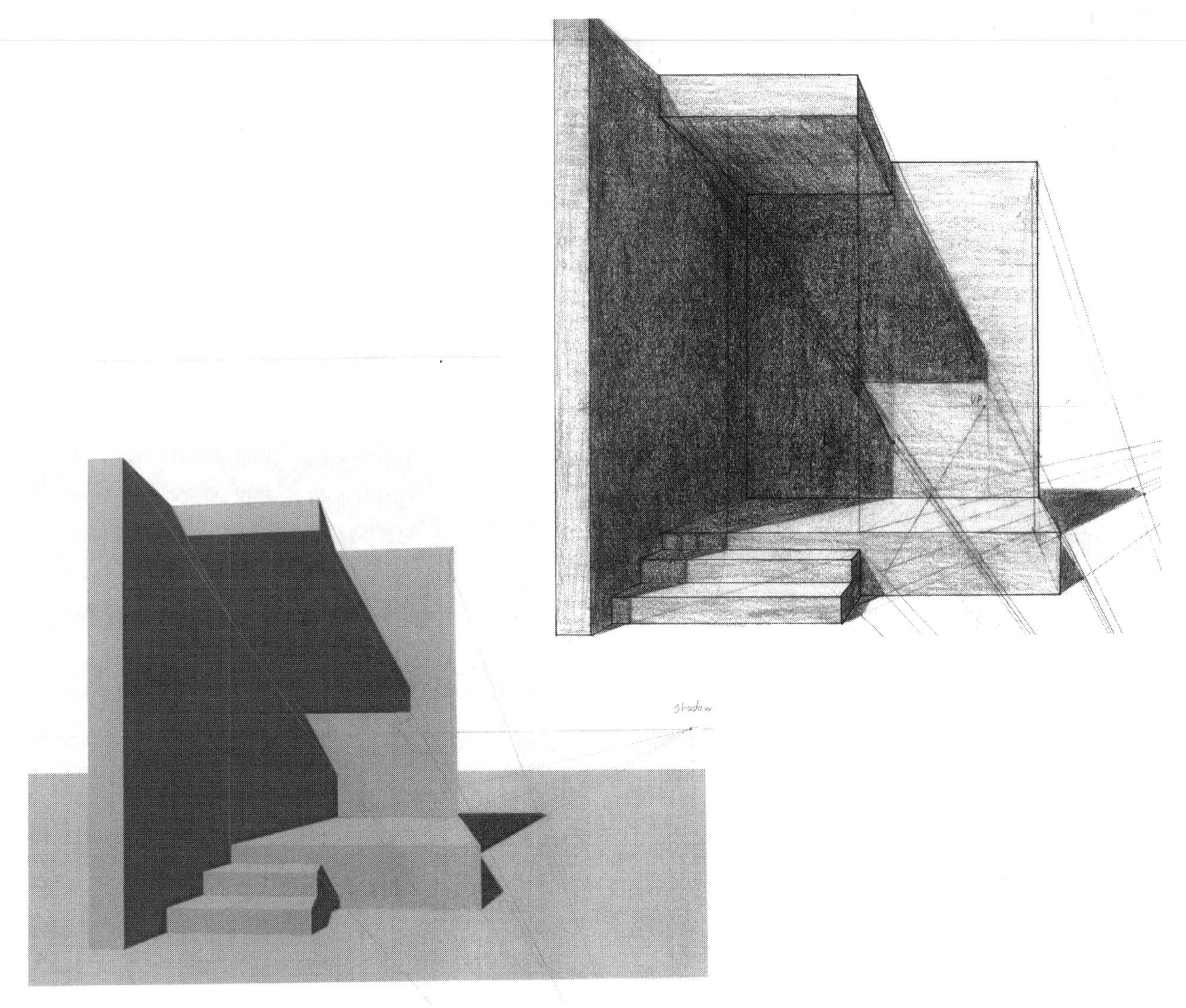

Shadow Construction (2 VP Method)

Shadow Model Design (Using 3D Studio Viz)

The students are asked to design and draw a model and then construct shadows using the 2 VP method. Requirements for the models are as follows:

- The model should have two vertical walls.
- The model should have a flat "roof."
- There should be a level change with at least one step between levels.

After the model is designed and drawn in perspective and the shadows are constructed, the students use 3D Studio Viz to reproduce the model with the same light direction as a check for the hand drawing. Two drawings are turned in: The first is designed and drawn by hand; the second is a computer-generated "copy" of the first.

Drawing: Student project by Rebecca Flannery
Problem: Courtesy of Professor Dick Davison
College of Architecture
Texas A&M University

REFER TO CHAPTER 7

Rendering Techniques

Design an abstract composition of geometric forms and draw it in axonometric or plan oblique. Render the composition with the following six techniques: (1) dots, (2) parallel lines, (3) multidirectional lines, (4) scribbles, (5) contrast black-and-white, and (6) tonal value in lead pencil.

Student project by Christopher Wilson
Studio Professor: M. Saleh Uddin
Courtesy of the Department of Environmental Design
University of Missouri–Columbia

REFER TO CHAPTERS 5 AND 8

Student project by Roberto Vega
Size: 8" X 12" (20.3 X 30.5 cm)
Media: (Clockwise from upper left) Charcoal, pastel, wash, fine-point technical ink pen, felt-tipped pen, and pencil (graphite)
Studio Professor: LaRaine Papa Montgomery
Courtesy of Savannah College of Art and Design

Rendering by Exploring Different Media

Choose a building and zoom in on an architectural detail. Compose the detail and create a series of renderings exploring the variety of effects with different media.

Objective: To sharpen the student's eye by looking at the environment and analyzing and communicating what he or she sees.

REFER TO CHAPTERS 3 AND 8 AND WEB SITE CHAPTER 11

The axonometric below, although an unrealistic view, was utilized to help my client understand the massing, proportions, and relationships of the building components, whereas the perspective at right portrays a humanistic view and expresses the impact of the receding facade. Soft pencil allows a varied expression of line and tone weight within a single stroke, giving an informal quality to the sketches.

This is a conceptual massing study of a hillside residence in the area of Oakland, California. Blended within a hillside setting, it utilizes the advantages of light and view while borrowing the massing style of Tuscany.
[ARCHITECT'S STATEMENT]

Sketches: Woo residence, Oakland, California
Perspective: 12" × 12" (30.5 × 30.5 cm)
Axonometric: 18" × 18" (45.7 × 45.7 cm)
Scale: ⅛"=1'0"
Medium: HB pencil
Courtesy of Kenzo Handa, Architect

Conceptual Massing Studies

For your design studio project, do conceptual massing studies utilizing paraline and/or perspective concept sketches. Choose a medium you are comfortable with. This professional example was done with graphite; the axonometric form was accentuated with soft shadows. Lightly shaded tones were used to express texture. During any massing study, focus on the desired vantage point, the values of the surrounding landscape, and the sculptural three-dimensionality of the desired form.

REFER TO CHAPTERS 5, 6, AND 9

"Plan Oblique" A Mixed-Media Drawing
Media: Pastel, graphite, and color pencil
Courtesy of Professor Dick Davison
College of Architecture
Texas A&M University

In this drawing, several media are used simultaneously.

1. *I begin with an underlayment of pastel—several colors, but predominantly yellow in this case. Into this base, the original plan is drawn in graphite. I do not yet fix the pastel because it is possible to create tonal variations and light effects by erasing into one area or another.*
2. *As the verticals are brought up I develop tones and textures with a mix of color pencil (usually Derwent) and graphite. The pastel acts as a ground to respond to, not unlike the way a marker ground can be drawn over with finer instruments to create sharpness and detail.*
3. *Portions of the building are emphasized and refined more than others. This creates a kind of "optical" quality that contrasts with the uniform scale of the oblique view.*

[PROFESSOR'S STATEMENT]

Project for a mixed-media drawing

Study the tips on handling mixed media on the book's Web site. Then study the techniques in the example above, titled "Plan Oblique." Using the theme of a utopian building, develop an image using mixed media. Experiment with the following media to create your solution: a graphite drawing, a laser copy of this drawing, colored pencil, and acrylic paint (see the professor's creation using this theme on the Web site).

Courtesy of Professor Dick Davison
College of Architecture
Texas A&M University

REFER TO CHAPTERS 3, 9, and WEB SITE CHAPTER 11

The Hourglass

This exercise is so named because the students, using drawing to parallel the design process, gather (draw) large amounts of often random information (the top of the hourglass), come to understand it well enough to reduce it to its core (the center of the hourglass), and then reorganize and re-present it as coherent architectural ideas and forms (the bottom of the hourglass).

The general goals of this drawing exercise (and the five weeks that were devoted to this same issue) are (1) to gain an ability to use drawing to develop ideas rather than merely illustrate them, and (2) to understand how various forms of drawing can look at different aspects of an idea, from the most essential and gestural to more "embellished" drawing, and how the different forms of drawing build on and influence one another and the overall idea.

The students look at early conceptual drawings by Maya Lin, Le Corbusier, and Tadao Ando, making particular connection between Ando's drawing and written language — drawings that isolate or carry the seeds for the entire idea. This type of drawing looks at the whole by, essentially, leaving out the parts. The students also look at Picasso's one-liners as another model of how to resolve disparate pieces into a fluid whole; in this case, however, the parts are included but are conceived of as part of a single, fluid whole.

The students used these various forms of drawing (1) to look at existing buildings and reverse this process, cooking them down to their essentials, and then (2) to begin to conceive of their own not-yet-existing projects going in the other direction, from essential summaries to more fully detailed ideas. Those students who were in a concurrent studio were required to use these ideas in their studio projects and to illustrate, in a single image and without words, the connection of these ideas to their studio process. A number of the students were in studios that dealt with a degree of metaphor in the early stages, hence the images that occur in some of their pieces. They initially had to present their ideas on a 2' × 3' board; then they had to reduce the content and the scale down to an 8½" × 11" image.

Project: Courtesy of Professor Bob Hansman
School of Architecture
Washington University, St. Louis, Missouri

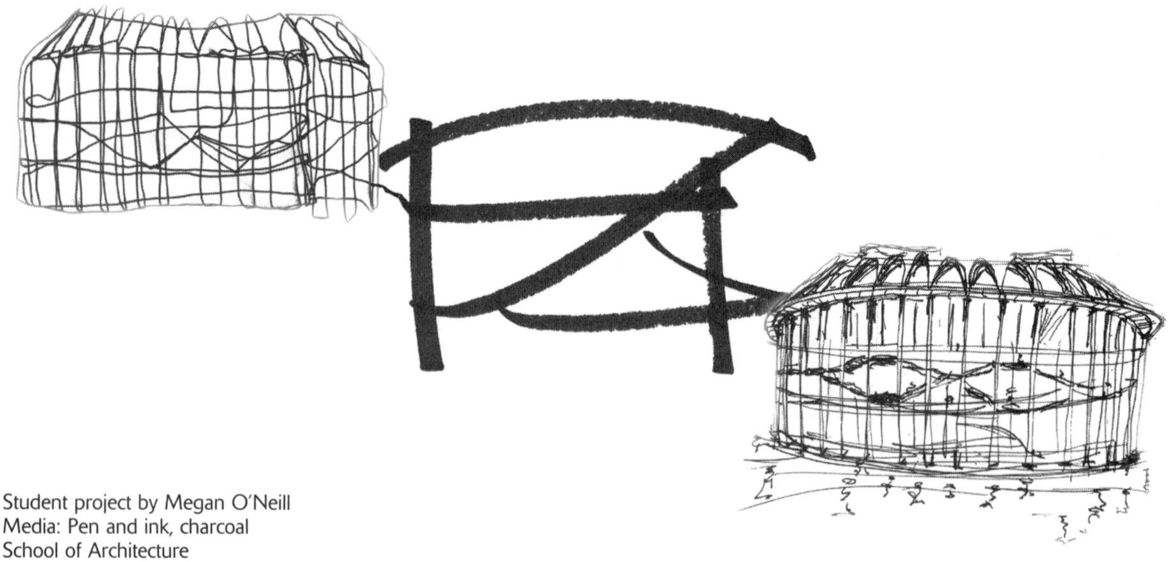

Student project by Megan O'Neill
Media: Pen and ink, charcoal
School of Architecture
Washington University, St. Louis, Missouri

REFER TO CHAPTER 9

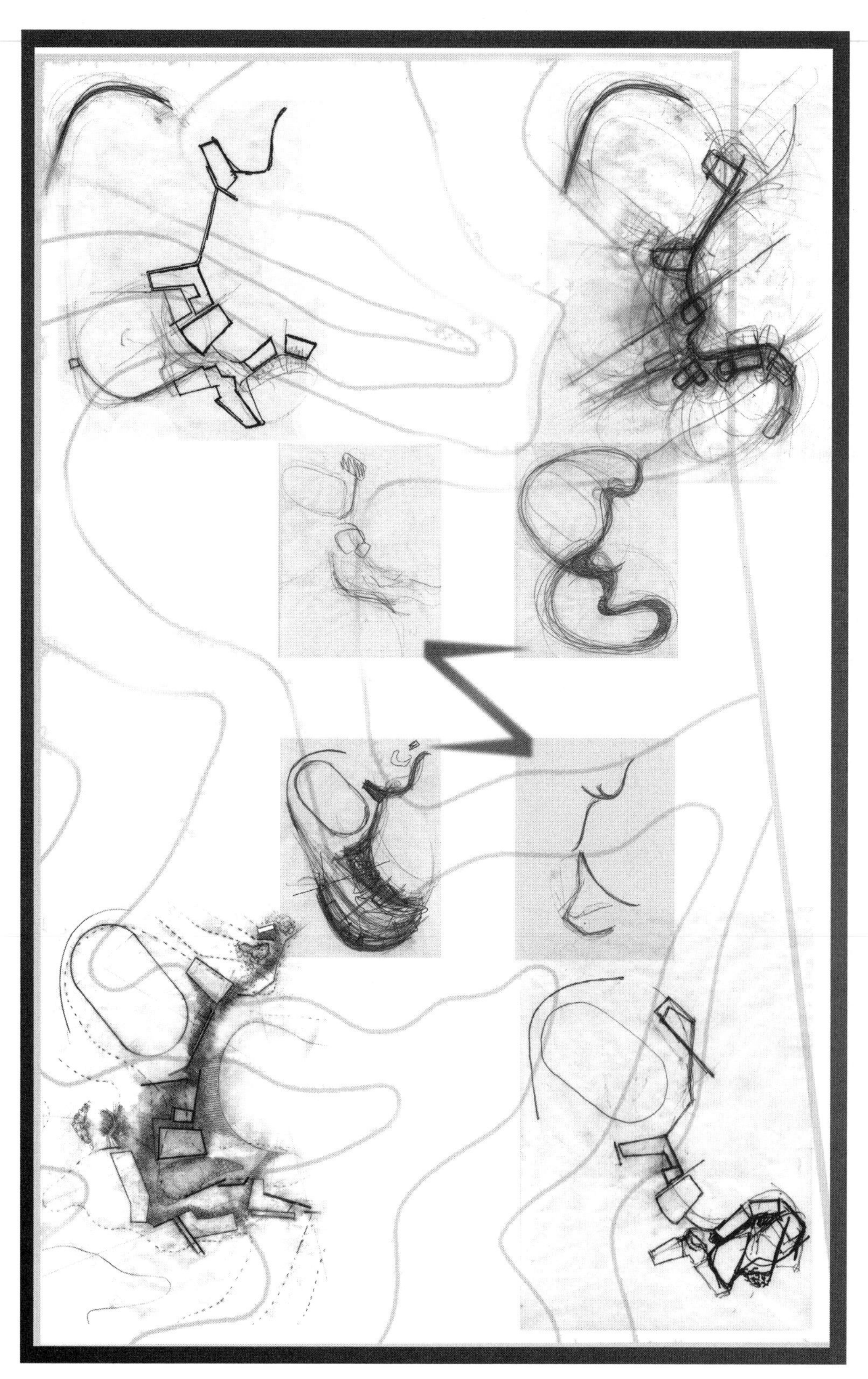

Student project by Jonah Chiarenza
Medium: Pencil and computer touch-up
School of Architecture
Washington University, St. Louis, Missouri

Vocabulary and Diagramming

Developing an architectural vocabulary is an important part of architectural communication and design. On the following page is a vocabulary list used in communicating architectural design principles. It is important that you understand these terms and are able to apply them. You will be expected to use these terms in the review of your own work and others'. Be prepared to verbally and graphically define these terms at a moment's notice.

OBJECTIVES
- Develop a graphic and verbal language for describing concepts, form, and organization principles of design.
- Develop a methodology for diagramming.
- Enhance spatial understanding.
- Develop representation skills for the communication of ideas.

PROCESS
- Define each term on the following page in written (architectural lettering) and graphic form (freehand with black felt-tip pen).
- Use your own words for the written definition based on the supporting examples throughout the chapters.
- Create your own diagrams based on the supporting examples throughout the chapters.
- Make a photocopy of the assignment to turn in.

READING
- Ching, 2007

NOTES
Bring the following materials to class:

- Chipboard — three thicknesses
- Adhesives
- Cutting tools
- Various other modeling supplies, such as Plexiglas, wire, aluminum tubing, basswood, metal screen/mesh, etc.

Project: Courtesy of Professor Steve Temple
School of Architecture
University of Texas–San Antonio, and
Professor Edward K. Fabian
Hammons School of Architecture
Drury University
Springfield, Missouri

REFER TO CHAPTER 9

Axis:

Symmetry:

Asymmetry:

Continue to lay out rectangles approximately 2" × 1½" in which to illustrate the following terms:

Hierarchy	Rhythm	Datum	Linear form
Radial form	Clustered form	Grid form	Centralized organization
Linear organization	Radial organization	Clustered organization	Grid organization
Spatial tension	Edge-to-edge contact	Face-to-face contact	Interlocking volumes
Transformation	Dimensional transformation	Subtractive transformation	Additive transformation

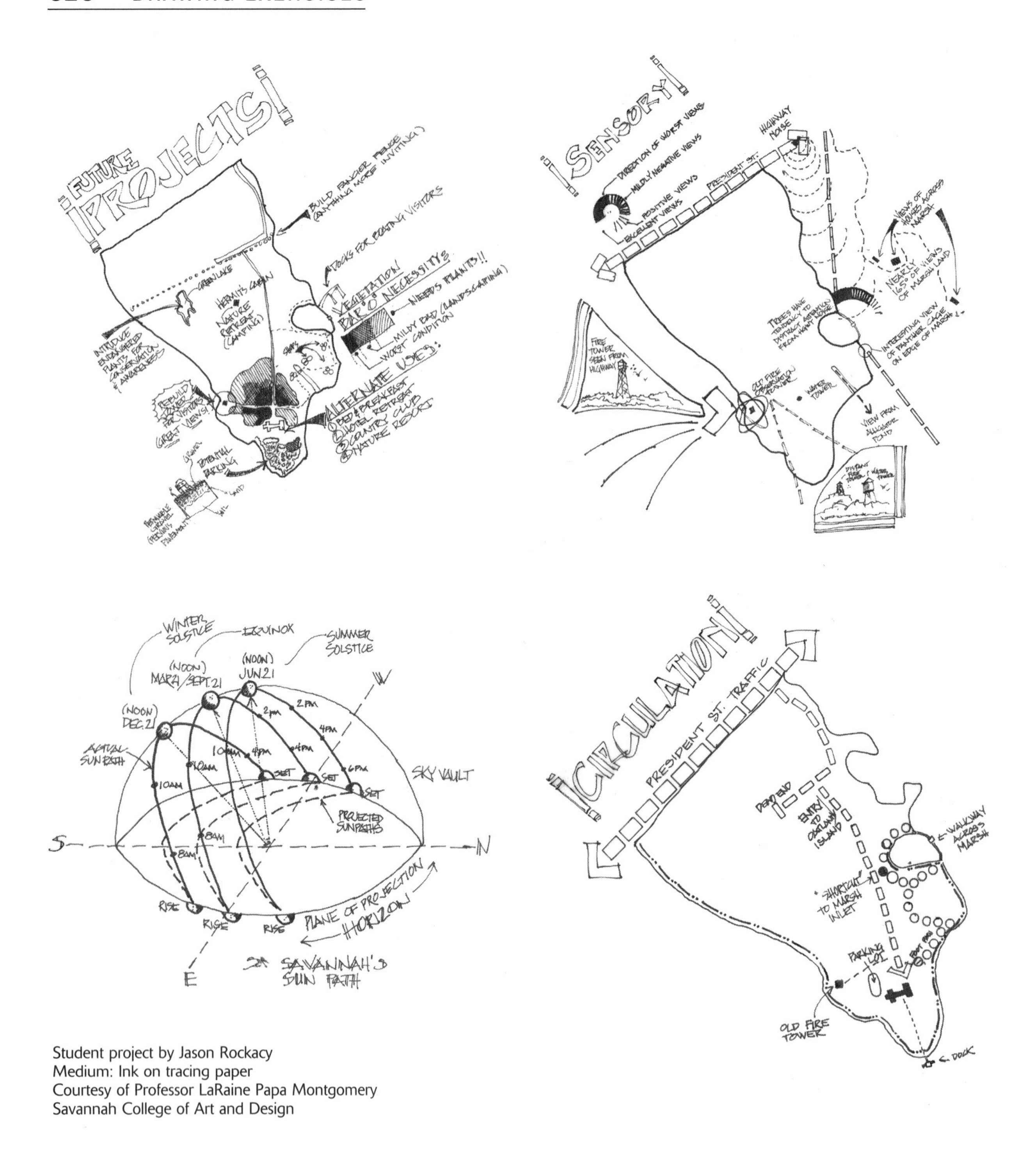

Student project by Jason Rockacy
Medium: Ink on tracing paper
Courtesy of Professor LaRaine Papa Montgomery
Savannah College of Art and Design

Site Analysis Diagrams

Assignment: Architecture students and elementary school students work together on the design of a children's discovery center dedicated to learning about the natural environment. As the teams develop building design concepts, a clear graphic diagramming language is used to communicate site forces, such as solar angles, sun and shade patterns, conservation land-use planning, and sensitive circulation through the marsh and maritime forest. Diagrams quickly illustrate complex, interrelated issues that lead to architectural decisions.

REFER TO CHAPTER 9

Student project by Katarzyna Zycinska-White, who interviewed second-year student Alzbeta Bowden
Medium: Ink, Sharpie, brown and green Prismacolors, and photos altered in Photoshop on buff posterboard
Courtesy of Studio Professor Michael Hagge
Architecture Program
University of Memphis

An Interview with an Architecture Student

Assignment: Select one architecture student from another studio. Set up an appointment and interview the student you select about his or her work, focusing on either current or past projects. Look at drawings, sketches, study models, final models, notations, etc. Learn about how he or she goes about the work, as well as the work itself.

Format: This assignment must be developed using sketches and drawings in a composite layout. The drawing must be presented on one 20" X 20" board.

Problem: Courtesy of Professor Michael Hagge
Architecture Program
University of Memphis

REFER TO CHAPTER 10

Composite Presentation Boards

Design and create a presentation board communicating the concept and architectural intent of your proposal for your final design studio project, "A Place for Rejuvenation."

Hang your work on the wall outside your studio space.

The board will consist of eight 10" × 16" boards (to fit on the scanner bed), arranged into a single 40" × 32" composition. The material of the boards may be foam core, poster board, museum board, or any other stiff sheet material that supports your graphic concept(s).

The scale of your drawings and models may change as necessary to fit onto the boards.

Example:

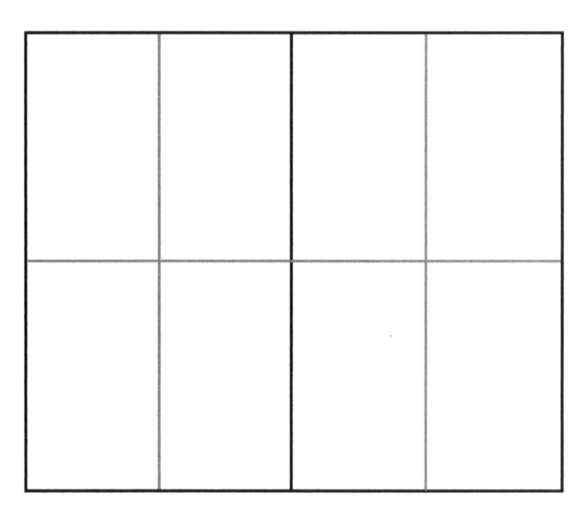

Include the following information (at minimum) on your presentation boards:

Site context: typed statements, graphics, and photographs

Concept statement: typed

Site plan with site section

Final model of building with local site circumstances: Photograph the model, including shadows and a uniform and nondistracting background.

Local context model: Photograph the site model, including shadows and a uniform and nondistracting background. Also include photographs of the actual site, if possible.

Floor plan(s)

Building sections: two, one in each direction, showing site section

Perspective Views: interior and exterior

Project: Courtesy of Professor Steve Temple
School of Architecture
University of Texas–San Antonio

REFER TO CHAPTER 10

Three-Dimensional Electronic Modeling and Visualization

To practice composing and superimposing three-dimensional models using digital and manual techniques, students visualized and drew a plan in three dimensions both by hand and using electronic modeling. They also hand constructed a model in scale to comprehend the total three-dimensionality of the visualized structure. The 3-D electronic model with surface texture and lighting was created using form-Z software. Selected views, ranging from two-dimensional plan or elevation to three-dimensional perspective views with varying camera lenses, were saved to compose one integrated presentation. Images were brought into Photoshop to compose, to change scale, and to add filter effects. Final presentation size ranged between 17" × 22" and 24" × 36".

Student: Corey Sengstacken
Professor: M. Saleh Uddin
Course: Design Communications I
Department of Environmental Design
University of Missouri–Columbia

Student: Kelly Parker
Professor: M. Saleh Uddin
Course: Design Communications I
Department of Environmental Design
University of Missouri–Columbia

REFER TO CHAPTERS 3, 4, 6, 10, and WEB SITE CHAPTER 11

Observing and Detailing

THE AIM
This is a defamiliarization exercise to enhance your visual perception and drawing skills. It is an exercise in observation, measurement, and detailing using basic projection principles and drafting techniques.

THE TASK
You are required to select and photograph five openings, and to graphically describe three of them. You may choose openings that you are familiar with or ones that challenge your familiarity. The most obvious example of an opening is a window, but you may use other examples. Discuss your selection with the tutors. The opening should have a sill and a head, and may be in a glass, masonry, timber, or steel wall. Window details vary in complexity, and your attempt to deal with difficult examples will be considered in the assessment.

REQUIREMENTS
1. For the tutorial meeting, bring in your photos of the five openings and sketch detailing of at least three for feedback.
2. For the final presentation, graphically describe an elevation or part-elevation at a scale of 1:20; two sections at the same scale, one through the head and sill and one through the jambs; and a paraline projection of a vertical (head/sill) section for each of the three openings you selected.

ASSESSMENT CRITERIA
Students will be assessed on:

- Accuracy of scale and neatness of drafting
- Appropriateness of line type
- Sheet layout and clarity of graphic expressions
- Complexity of detailing selected
- Dimension, lettering, and annotation

Courtesy of Dr. Samer Akkach
Drawing Architecture & Landscape I
School of Architecture, Landscape Architecture and Urban Design
Adelaide University, South Australia

REFER TO CHAPTERS 4 AND 5

Presentation Format Based on a Rectangular Grid System

For a design solution of a small or medium-size building that you may come up with in your design studio, try to use a rectangular grid system to organize the presentation layout of your site plan, plans, elevations, sections, paralines, perspectives, diagrams, and sketches. Scale: ⅛" = 1'0". See a well-organized layout in the Web site drawing exercises solutions section.

REFER TO CHAPTER 10

Given: An isometric drawing of a building complex

Required: Construct a roof plan and two elevations of the visible sides.

Scale: $\frac{3}{32}$" = 1'0"

REFER TO CHAPTER 5

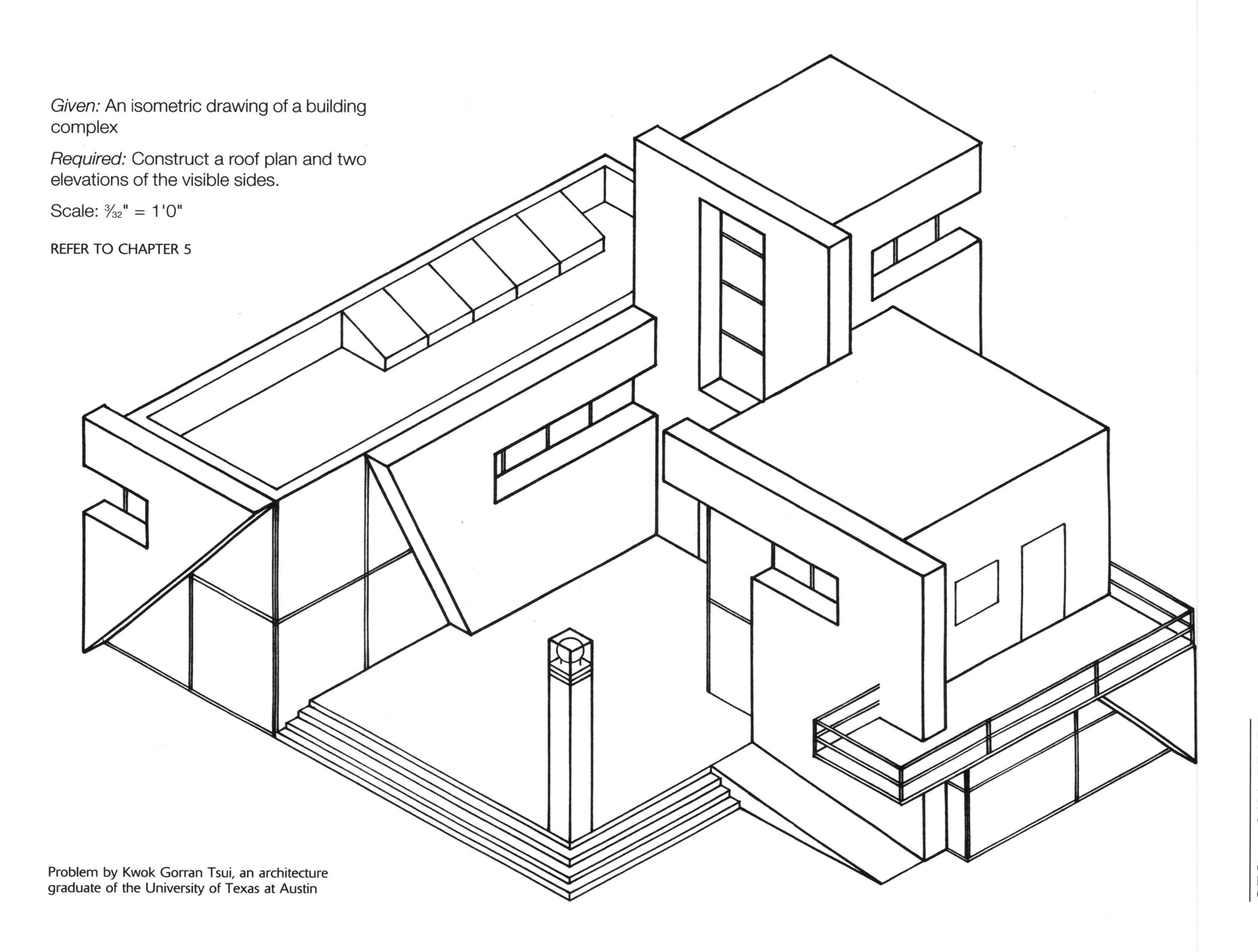

Problem by Kwok Gorran Tsui, an architecture graduate of the University of Texas at Austin

Plan–Section–Elevation Graphics

Time frame: One week

Locate a piece of furniture that has at least one drawer and another mechanism of movement, such as the leaf of a drop-leaf table. Make sketch drawings of the piece with measurements to use in making the drawings listed below.

Draw the **top, front, side(s), plan, section(s),** and **detail** views in a projected layout. Draw all except the detail drawings in 1" = 1'0" scale. Draw at least two different details at 3" = 1'0" scale. Give each drawing a title and reference number, and key the drawing to the original source (for example, show and label cutting plane lines).

Include overall dimensions of your drawings.

FORMAT
Draw in graphite on one sheet of 24" × 36" vellum oriented horizontally or vertically. All drawings should fit on one sheet of drawing paper. The overall layout is up to you. Draw a border and a title block on the sheet; letter your name, the name of the furniture, project number, and the date ¾" high.

Project: Courtesy of Professor Steve Temple
School of Architecture
University of Texas–San Antonio

REFER TO CHAPTER 4

Exploded Isometric

From a project in your design studio related to a small object with components or to a small building with component parts, construct an isometric drawing. Then, next to the isometric drawing, construct an exploded isometric showing the overlap of the component parts. Choose an appropriate scale.

REFER TO CHAPTER 5

Plan and Paraline Shadows for a Structure

Slightly modify the design of the object shown on pp. 360–61 (i.e., change the shape and size of the wall openings, etc.). Using the plan and elevation views, manually cast the shadow using the point-by-point method discussed on pp. 344–45. Construct a 45°–45° plan oblique of this object and cast shadows with the light ray parallel to the picture plane (see pp. 324–25).

Combining Horizontal and Vertical Section Cuts

With a design project from one of your design studies, utilize a combination of horizontal and vertical section cuts to reveal the interior of your building.

REFER TO CHAPTER 7

Enlarge 20% to use at scales specified.

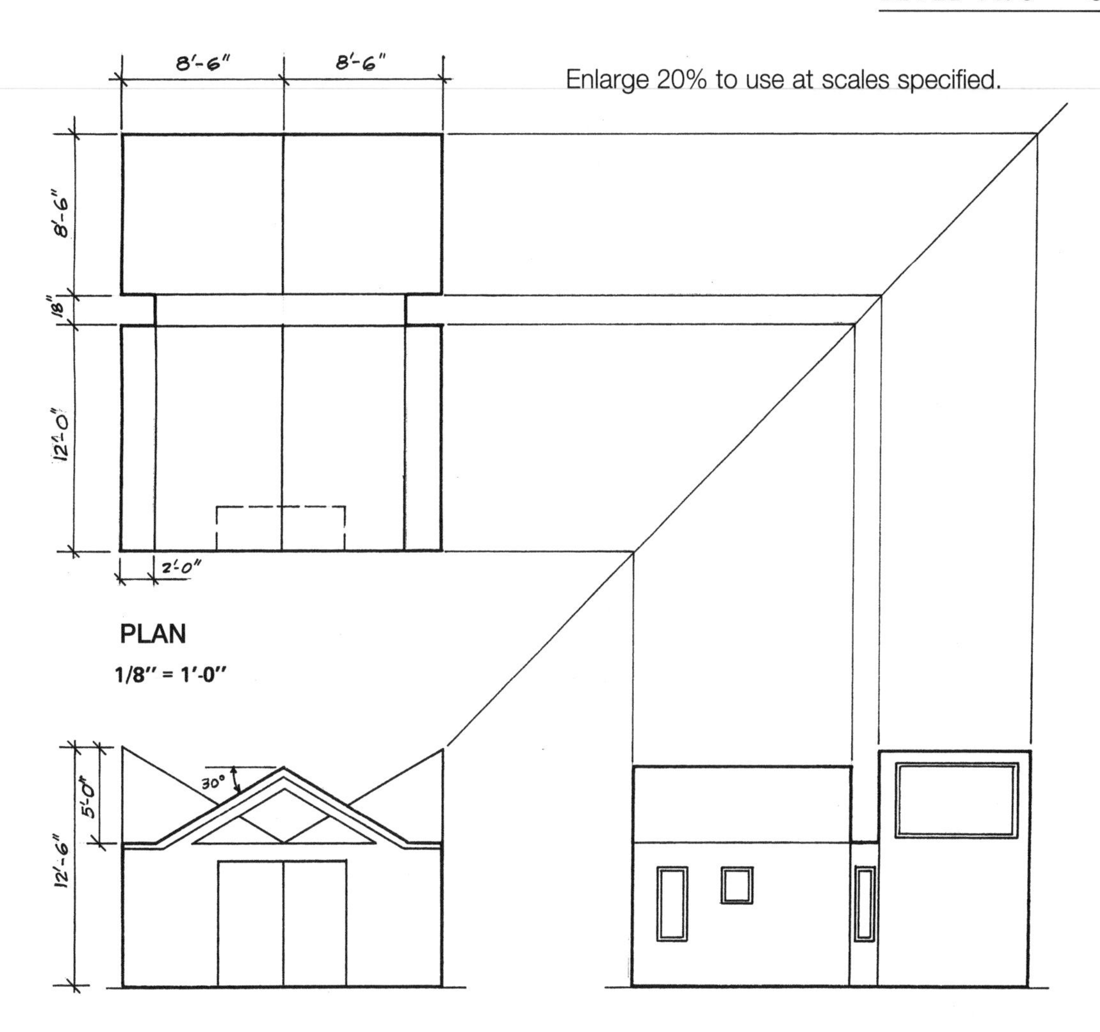

Given: Two elevations and a roof plan of a building form

Required: Construct a 60°–30° plan oblique. Cast shadows with the light rays parallel to the picture plane. Construct a two-point perspective bird's-eye view. Cast shadows with the same condition as above.

Courtesy of Professor Thomas L. Turman
Laney College, Oakland, California

REFER TO CHAPTERS 5, 6, and 7

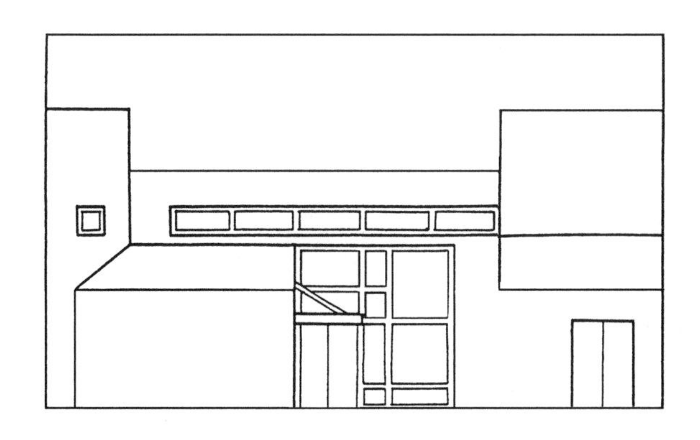

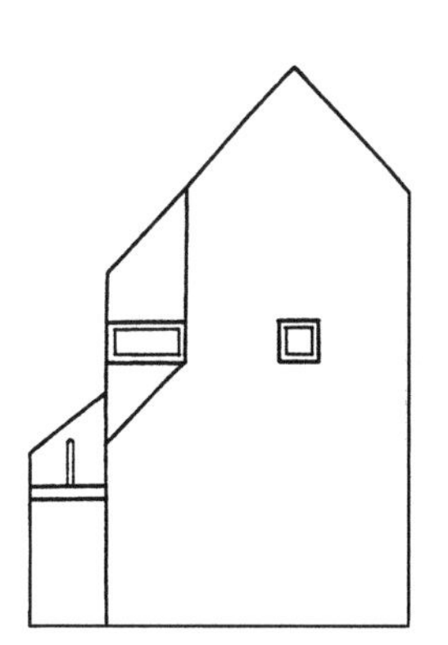

Given: Two elevations of a building form

Required: 1. Construct the missing roof plan.
2. Construct a 30°–30° isometric drawing.

Scale: 1/16"=1'0"

REFER TO CHAPTER 5

Revealing Perspective View

The purpose of this project is to create a single drawing that communicates several kinds of information at once. You have before you information about a building you chose from several options. You will use the information that the orthographic drawings and/or photographs reveal and apply that information to a perspective view that not only shows your building in perspective, but also locates the plan and sectional views in the perspective view.

MAKING THE DRAWING

Use the plan you have, or redraw it, and make a projection in perspective (plan projection) onto a large format such that the resulting view shows as much of your building as possible while allowing you to locate, *in the perspective view,* the section and plan. The drawing of the building should reveal as much as possible about the building's spaces. You may want to make parts of the building, or the entire building, transparent.

RESULT

The more you can show about the building and, in particular, the building space, the better. Therefore, it will be crucial to pay attention to those qualities that create clarity in an otherwise complex image, such as line weight, degrees of contrast, correct foreshortening, and color contrasts. The result should be a complex but clear drawing that reveals the building's essential shape (interior and exterior), as well as the locations of your orthographic cuts.

Projection drawing size: 24" × 36"
Media are negotiable
Color is required but negotiable

Courtesy of Professor Dick Davison
College of Architecture
Texas A&M University

REFER TO CHAPTERS 5 and 6

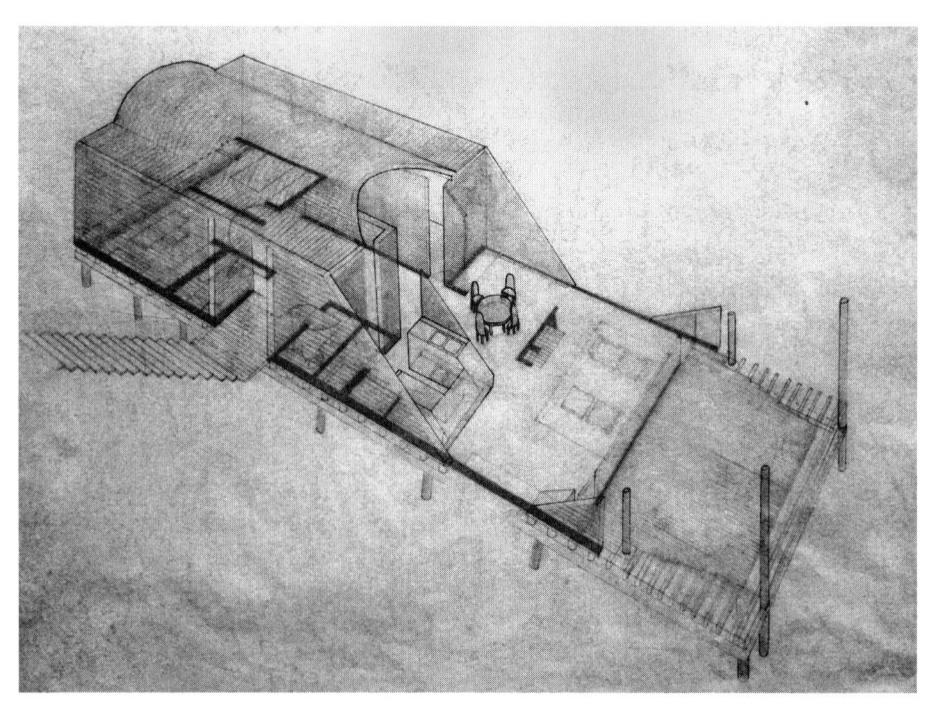

Drawing: Student project by Daniel Clarke
Based on the Gallery House by Architect Glenn Murcutt

Analytical Diagramming and Presentation Formats

Assignment: Study the Calhoun Ward in Savannah, Georgia's Historic District. Develop a presentation comprised of diagrams reflecting both the macro and the micro scales of this site context. For the macro scale, develop figure–ground drawings of the district from Park Street to the Savannah River and a figure–ground building footprint of a single ward. Then study the micro scale of the open square in the center of each ward and create a corresponding section diagram that studies the height–width proportional relationship in the square and the surrounding buildings. Each diagram should have overlays addressing various issues, including circulation.

Student project by Cameron Carver (pp. 629–32)
Savannah's Calhoun Ward
Savannah, Georgia
Medium: Ink on vellum
Courtesy of Professor LaRaine Papa Montgomery
Savannah College of Art and Design

REFER TO CHAPTERS 9 and 10

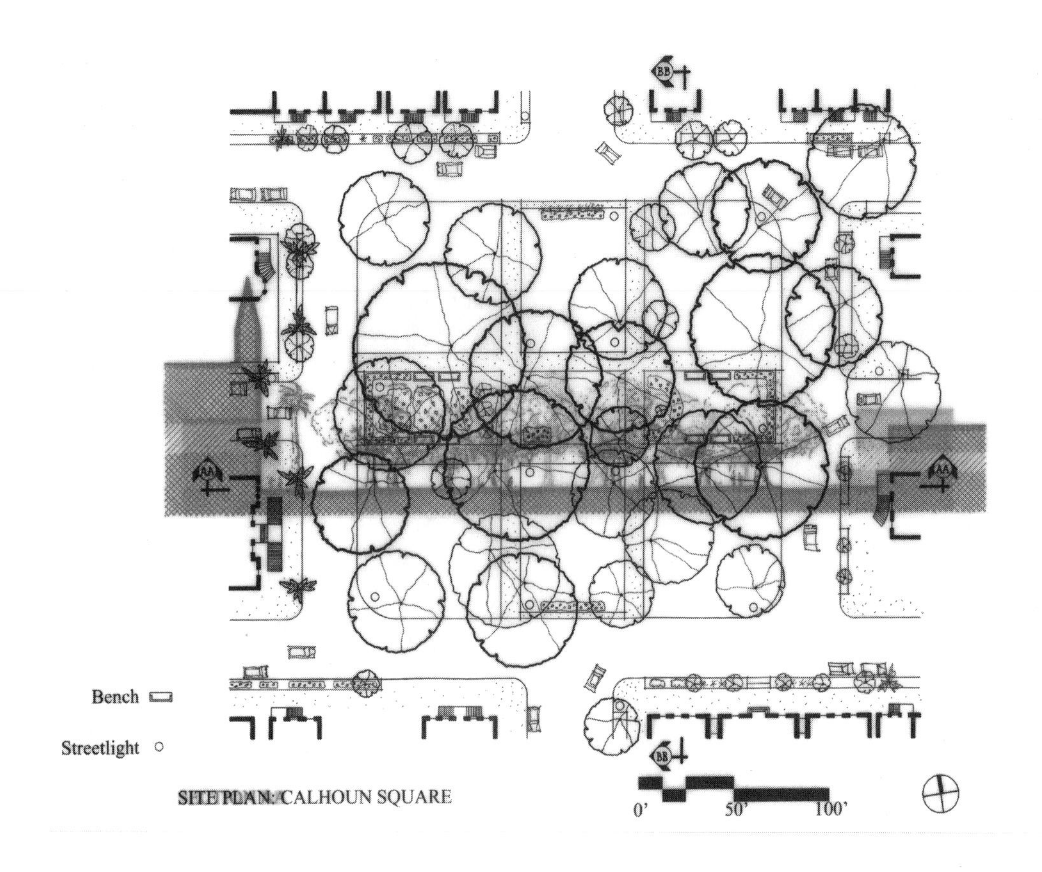

SITE PLAN: CALHOUN SQUARE

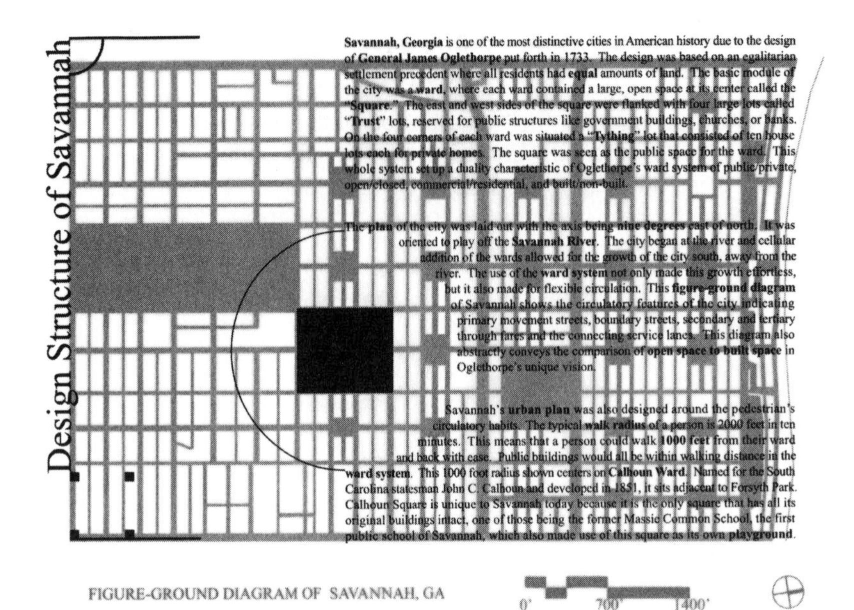
Design Structure of Savannah
Savannah, Georgia is one of the most distinctive cities in American history due to the design of General James Oglethorpe put forth in 1733. The design was based on an egalitarian settlement precedent where all residents had equal amounts of land. The basic module of the city was a ward, where each ward contained a large, open space at its center called the "Square." The east and west sides of the square were flanked with four large lots called "Trust" lots, reserved for public structures like government buildings, churches, or banks. On the four corners of each ward was situated a "Tything" lot that consisted of ten house lots each for private homes. The square was seen as the public space for the ward. This whole system set up a duality characteristic of Oglethorpe's ward system of public/private, open/closed, commercial/residential, and built/non-built.
The plan of the city was laid out with the axis being nine degrees east of north. It was oriented to play off the Savannah River. The city began at the river and cellular addition of the wards allowed for the growth of the city south, away from the river. The use of the ward system not only made this growth effortless, but it also made for flexible circulation. This figure-ground diagram of Savannah shows the circulatory features of the city indicating primary movement streets, boundary streets, secondary and tertiary through fares and the connecting service lanes. This diagram also abstractly conveys the comparison of open space to built space in Oglethorpe's unique vision.
Savannah's urban plan was also designed around the pedestrian's circulatory habits. The typical walk radius of a person is 2000 feet in ten minutes. This means that a person could walk 1000 feet from their ward and back with ease. Public buildings would all be within walking distance in the ward system. This 1000 foot radius shown centers on Calhoun Ward. Named for the South Carolina statesman John C. Calhoun and developed in 1851, it sits adjacent to Forsyth Park. Calhoun Square is unique to Savannah today because it is the only square that has all its original buildings intact, one of those being the former Massie Common School, the first public school of Savannah, which also made use of this square as its own playground.

FIGURE-GROUND DIAGRAM OF SAVANNAH, GA

0' 700' 1400'

3

William Rogers House
Side garden with a view through a cast iron gate; flower beds oulined with up-ended ale bottles from the brewery of the first owner, William Rogers.

2

Wesley Monumental United Methodist Church
This Gothic Revival Style church stands in honor of brothers Charles and John Wesley, the founders of the Methodist religion. Spires and Gothic arches make it easily seen above the very residential Calhoun Ward.

1

Massie Heritage Interpretation Center
The former Massie Common School was the first city-operated elementary school in Savannah. Calhoun Square became the playground for the children until 1974, when the school closed after 118 years.

VIEWS

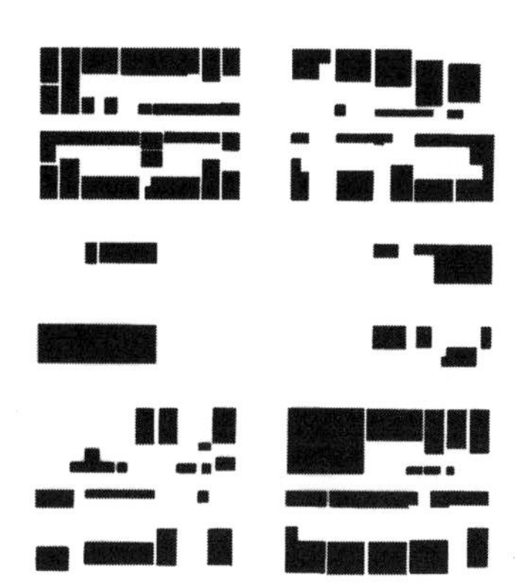

CALHOUN WARD BUILDING FOOTPRINTS

Primary

Secondary

Residential

Mixed Use

Wesley Monumental United Methodist Church
This Gothic Revival Style church stands in honor of brothers Charles and John Wesley, the founders of the Methodist religion. Spires and Gothic arches make it easily seen above the very residential Calhoun Ward.

William Rogers House
Side garden with a view through a cast iron gate; flower beds oulined with up-ended ale bottles from the brewery of the first owner, William Rogers.

Massie Heritage Interpretation Center
The former Massie Common School was the first city-operated elementary school in Savannah. Calhoun Square became the playground for the children until 1974 ... after 118 years.

CALHOUN WARD BUILDING FOOTPRINTS

0' 200' 400'

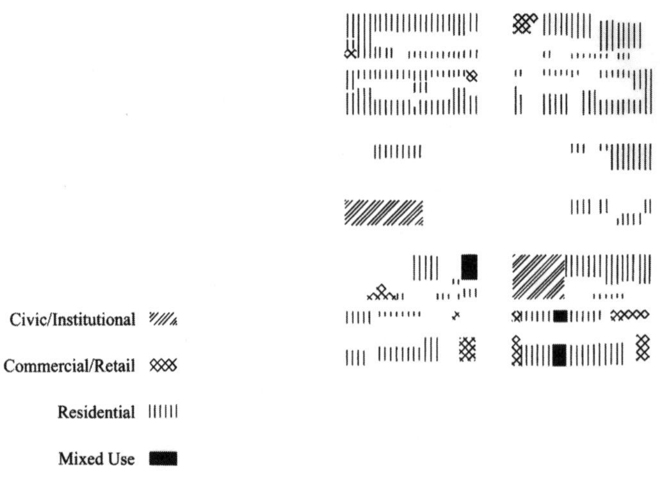

ZONING IN CALHOUN WARD

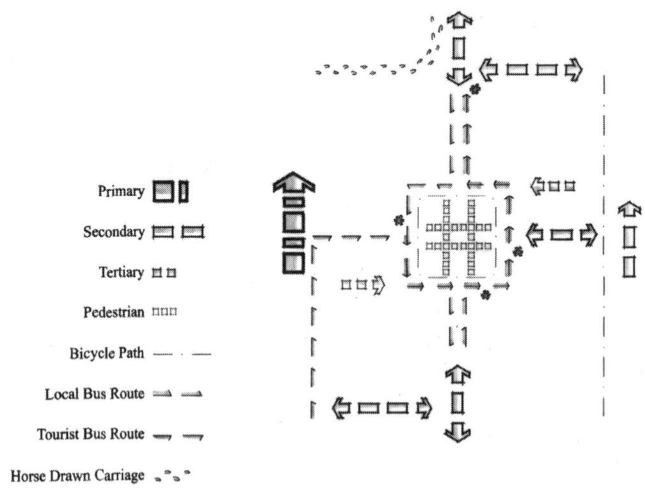

CIRCULATION: VEHICULAR AND PEDESTRIAN

Paraline Drawings: Isometric/Oblique and Section Perspective

Using leadholders with soft and hard leads, draw the 30°–30° isometric, plan oblique, and elevation oblique for the building indicated below. Drawings should be at ⅛"=1'0" scale. The layout lines should be lightly drawn with a 2H lead and the remaining lines with a softer F or HB lead. Focus on crisp, clear lines. Use 8.5" × 11" 1000H vellum for the final drawing and trace for initial layout. Label and date all drawings.

As an additional optional exercise, cut a section through the building just behind the wall of the East Elevation but slicing the window area. Using a measuring point (diagonal vanishing point), construct a one-point section perspective of the interior space (see pp. 215, 216, 224, and 225). Construct a plan grid on the floor plane and draw two human figures at different distances in order to give scale.

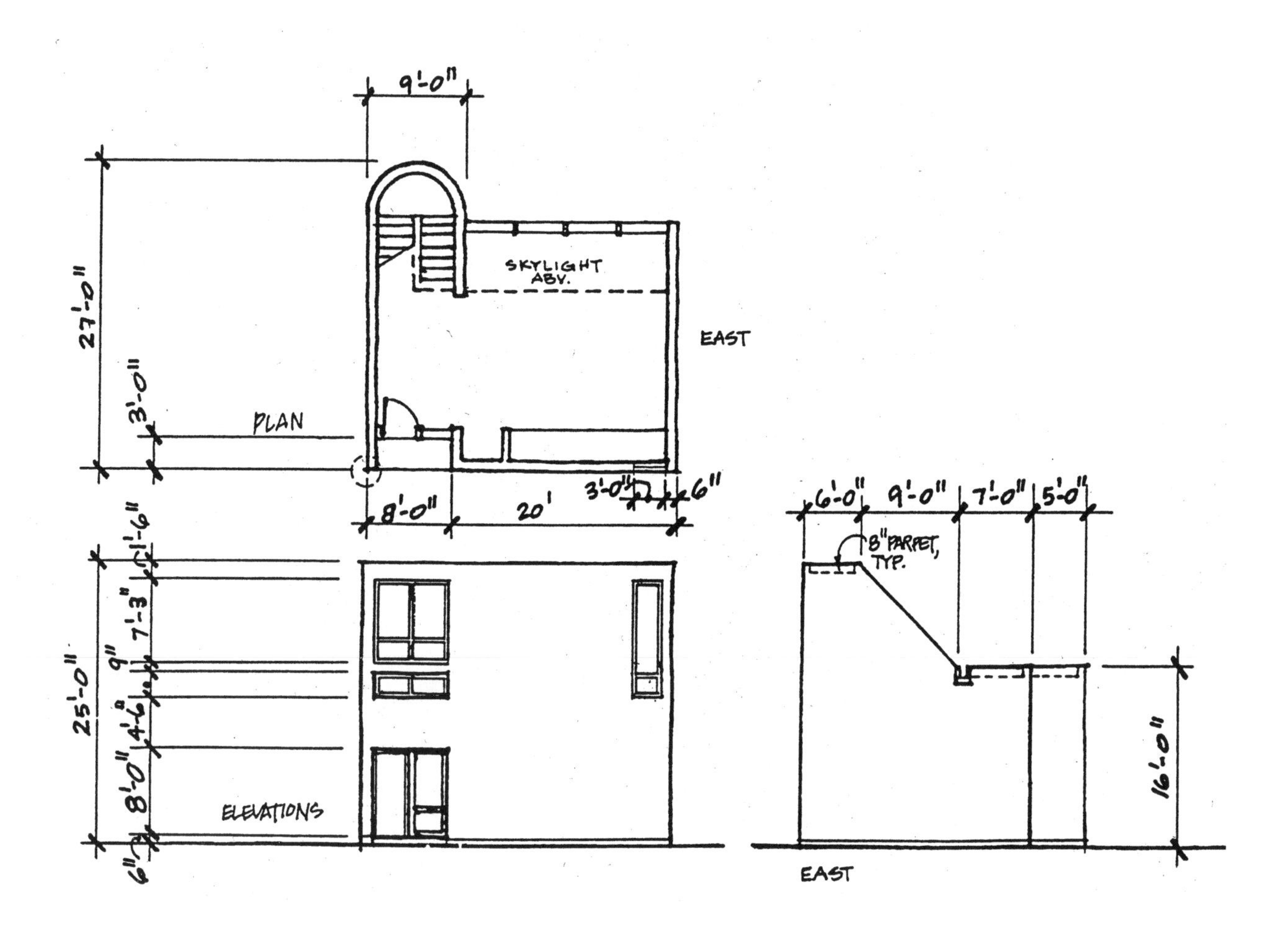

Problem: Courtesy of Instructor Daniel K. Mullin, AIA, NCARB
Graphic Communication course
Department of Architecture
University of Idaho–Moscow

REFER TO CHAPTERS 4, 5, 6, and 8

Axonometric Drawing

Lay out the Cutler house as an isometric or plan oblique drawing with 2H lead on trace. Use ⅛" scale. Show all windows, steps, roof planes, decks, etc., that come into view. Each student may decide which view to illustrate. After completing the trace drawing, transfer it to 8½" × 11" vellum for the final drawing.

Problem: Courtesy of Instructor Daniel K. Mullin, AIA, NCARB
Graphic Communication course
Department of Architecture
University of Idaho–Moscow

Drawings and Model from an Architectural Detail

OBJECTIVE

The goal of this project is to have students do research on looking for interesting architectural details. From the available options, he or she will select a detail/section, make a model of this detail, and do drawings of this detail.

PART ONE

Build a model of a slice of the detail.

- Show as many details/layers as reasonable.
- Try to approximate the actual materials in quality and look.
- Select scale as needed.
- As a guideline, the size of the model should be approximately 16" high × 4" wide × 4" deep.
- The base should be 6" × 12" × ¾".

PART TWO

Draw an "assembly" oblique or isometric of the model that you built. Show parts separated as they are built up together. Work on vellum with graphite. The scale varies with each project. After obtaining instructor approval, trace the "assembly" drawing onto a Mylar sheet using technical pens of two different line weights (one for section lines and one for visible lines.) Render according to the instructor's requirements and demonstrations if necessary.

REFERENCES

Ford 1990.
Details in architectural books and magazines

Courtesy of Studio Professor Arpad D. Ronaszegi
Division of Architecture
Andrews University
Battle Creek, Michigan

REFER TO CHAPTER 5

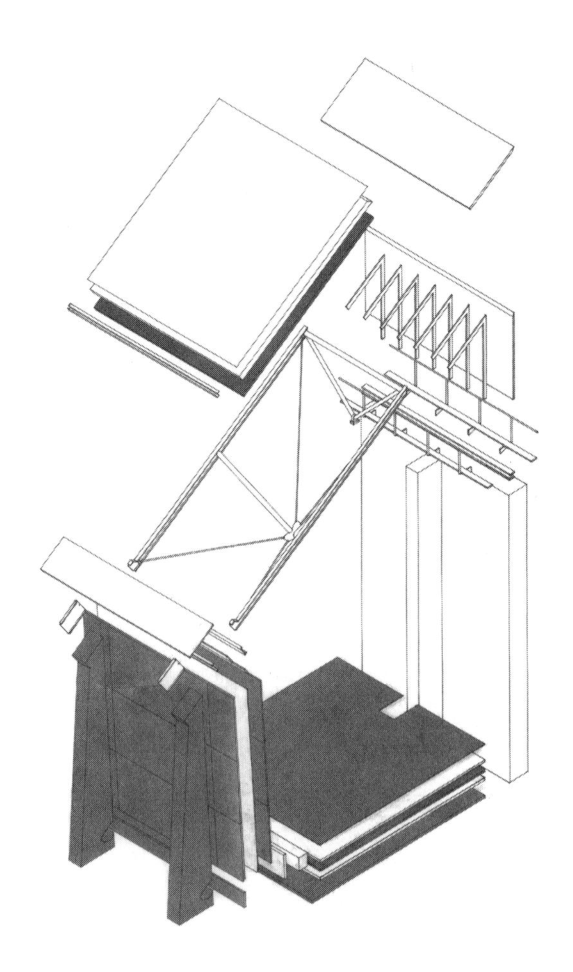

Drawing: Student project by Stephen Zerne
Division of Architecture
Andrews University

Comprehensive Project: Isometric and Exploded View

Time frame: Three weeks

PART ONE

Locate a piece of furniture that has at least one drawer and another mechanism of movement, such as the leaf of a drop-leaf table. Make sketch drawings of the piece with measurements to use in making the drawings listed below.

Draw the **top, front, side(s), plan, section(s),** and **vertical section(s)** in a projected layout. In addition, draw two details as scaled enlargements of section drawings. (Details may *not* be drawn as axonometric drawings.) Draw all except the detail drawings in 1½" = 1'0" scale. Draw at least two different vertical section details at 3" = 1'0" scale.

Show and label *all* section cutting plane lines. Give each independent drawing a title and reference number and key the drawing to the original source.

Include overall dimensions of your drawings.

PART TWO

Using the piece of furniture for which you constructed orthographic drawings in a previous assignment, construct additional drawings of the piece as follows:

1. An **isometric** at 1½" scale
2. An **exploded isometric** at 1½" scale

FORMAT

Draw in graphite on one sheet of 24" × 36" vellum oriented horizontally or vertically. All drawings should fit on one sheet of drawing paper. The overall layout is up to you. Draw a border on the sheet and a title block on the bottom of the sheet with ¾"-high lettering. Include in the title block:

1. Your name and the date
2. Title: FINAL PROJECT

Project: Courtesy of Professor Steve Temple
School of Architecture
University of Texas–San Antonio

REFER TO CHAPTER 5

STRUCTURAL FRAME/DRAWINGS AND MODEL

Design a structural frame using any kind of cardboard (corrugated, matte, pebble, illustration, etc.) without the use of glue or hinging mechanisms. The frame must span at least 3' and be capable of supporting 30 lbs of textbooks.

PRESENTATION REQUIREMENTS

1. Conceptual sketches of your idea
2. Orthographic, isometric, and plan oblique drawings of the solution
3. Exploded axonometric or exploded perspective to show how component parts go together
4. Model of the design solution

Courtesy of the Department of Architecture
City College of San Francisco

REFER TO CHAPTERS 4, 5, 6, and 9

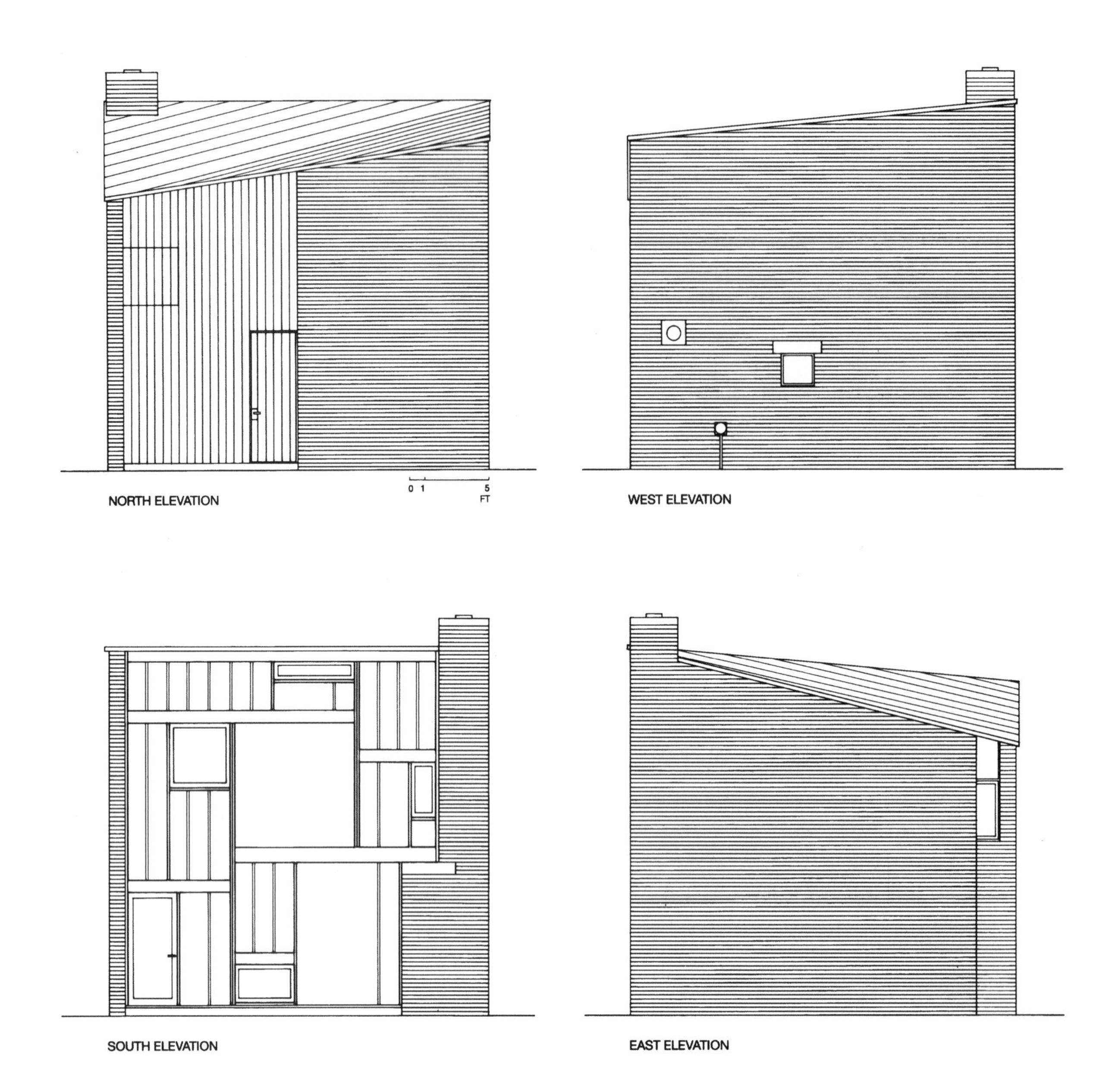

Drawings: Marking house, Catskill Mountains, New York
Design: 1992–1993
Courtesy of the Architecture Research Office, Adam Yarinsky, partner

Floor Plans, Roof Plan, Section, Elevations, Perspective, Section Perspective: Hardline

On this and the facing page are drawings for the Marking house. As an exercise in hand hardline drawing, use a scale stipulated by your instructor and redraw them on 12" × 18" 1000H vellum. Then, using the south and west elevations along with the three plan views oriented 30° from the horizontal, construct a perspective view with the station point 30' above the ground line. As an additional visualization exercise, try to sketch what you think the interior space would look like if you were standing on the stairway platform looking toward the opposite corner of the room (front entrance area).

REFER TO CHAPTERS 3, 4, 6, AND 8

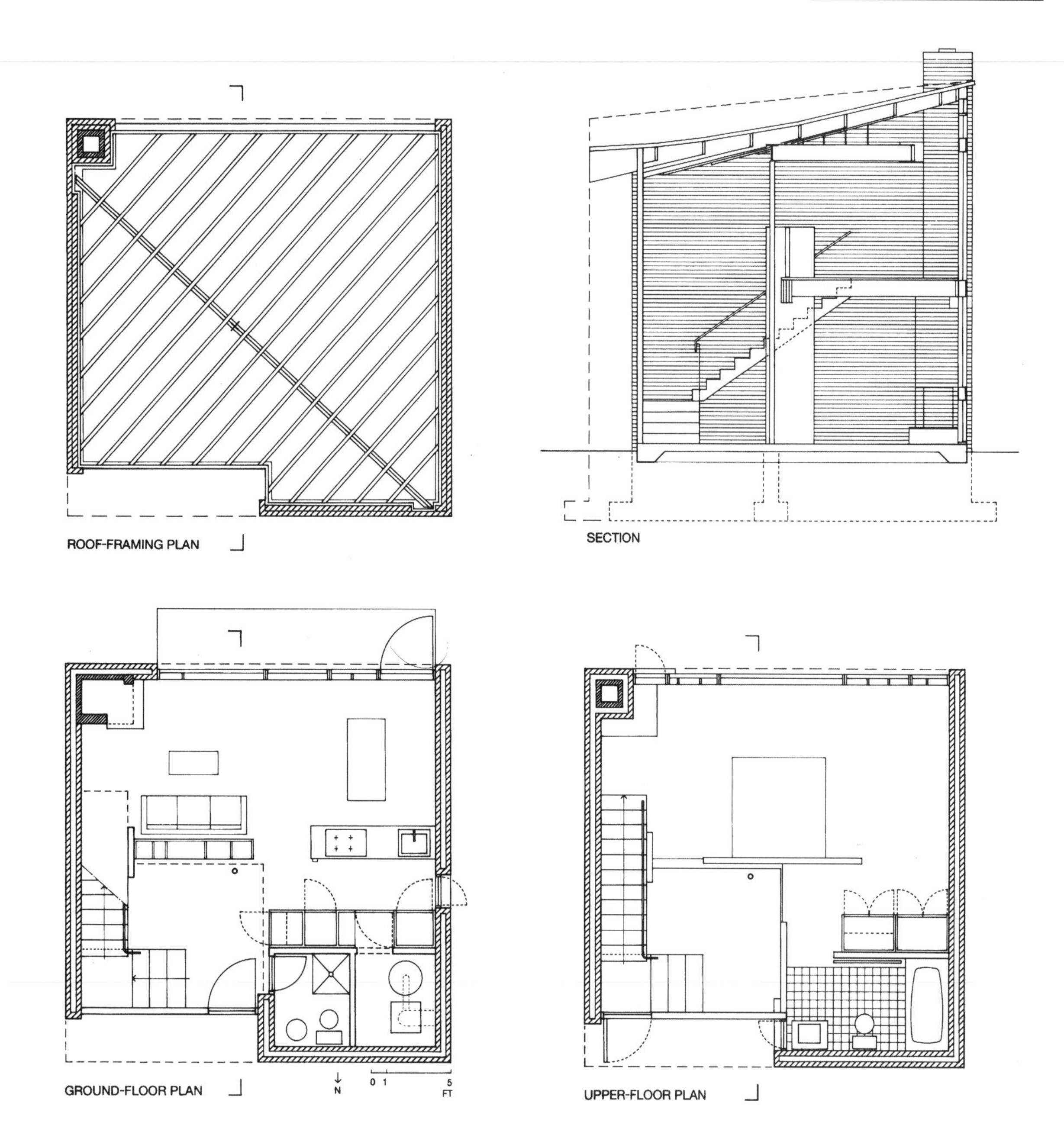

Drawings: Marking house, Catskill Mountains, New York
Design: 1992–1993
Courtesy of the Architecture Research Office, Adam Yarinsky, partner

Use the ground- and upper-floor plans and place them in the same position (30° from the horizontal) as the roof-framing plan to complete the entire perspective view with the fenestration.

Scale: 3/32"=1'0"

As an additional optional exercise, use a measuring point (diagonal vanishing point) and construct a one-point **section perspective** (note the shallow depth of field) with the given section looking in the direction indicated. Construct a plan grid on the floor plane and draw two human figures in the interior space.

Revealing an Expanded, Exploded, or Cutaway View

Find a familiar object (for example, a clock, lamp, piece of furniture, bicycle, etc.) or a set (like a LEGO set) that contains between 15 and 30 parts.

Consider how this object (or group) is assembled and how it would be disassembled.

Your goal is to make a single drawing that shows all parts of your object or group, and suggest how it is put together.

Construct either a paraline or perspective drawing in an expanded, exploded, or cutaway view. It may be partially expanded or exploded, and it may have transparency. Convey as much as possible in a single view while still maintaining a high degree of clarity. The medium should be graphite or ink (color is optional).

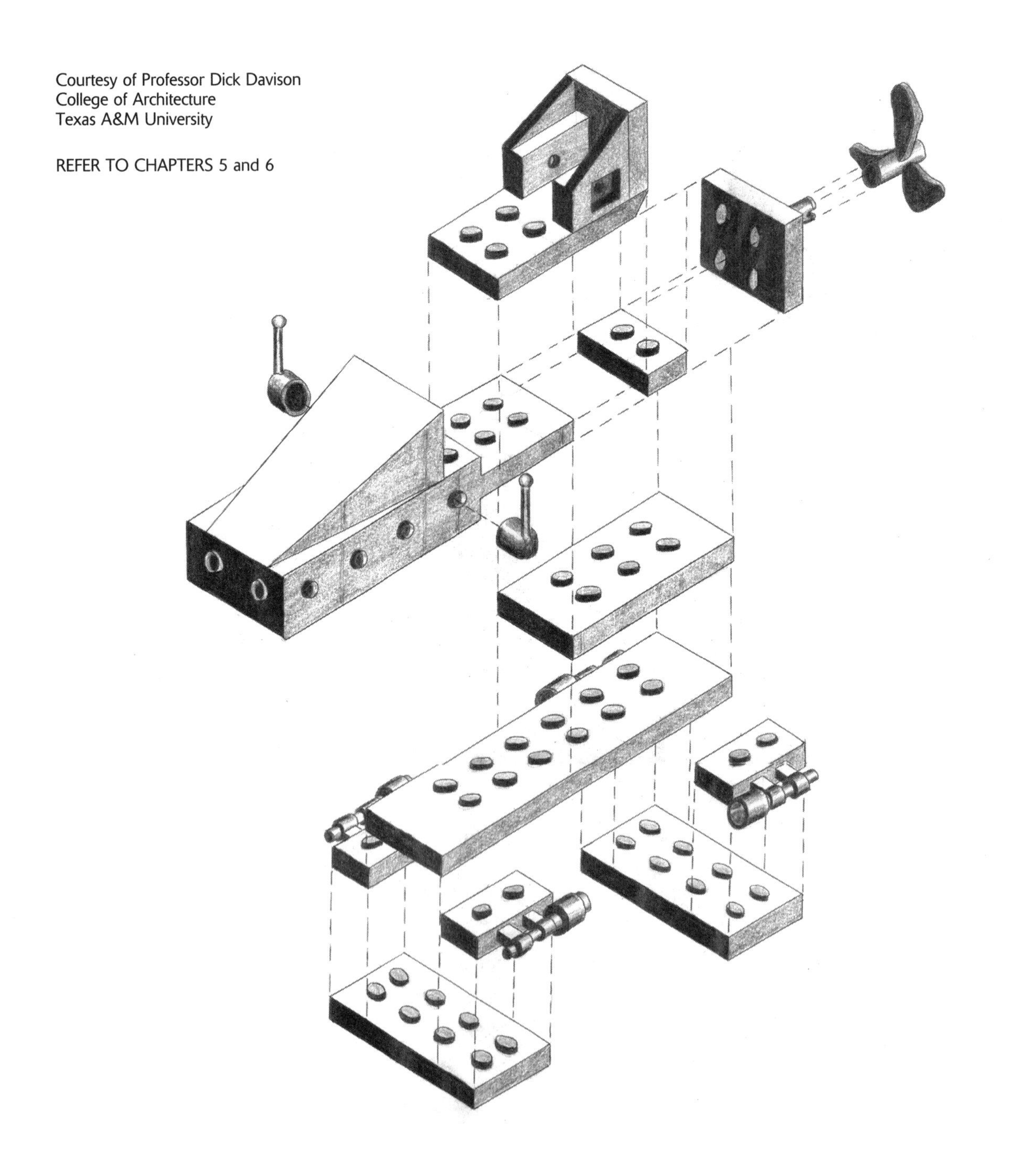

Courtesy of Professor Dick Davison
College of Architecture
Texas A&M University

REFER TO CHAPTERS 5 and 6

Dot and Line Rendering Techniques

Graphic exercises can introduce dynamic methods of portraying elements of a design. Dot and line compositions create an abstract representation of a form or space with a focus on one or two significant characteristics. The line and dot renderings illustrated here are of a San Francisco residence. (**1**) For the interior, address line density and spacing to emphasize the geometry and verticality of the entrance foyer. Also focus on stippled dot concentration for tonal value to express the quality of an interior space. (**2**) For the exterior, use stippled dot concentration for tonal value.

REFER TO CHAPTER 8

(2)

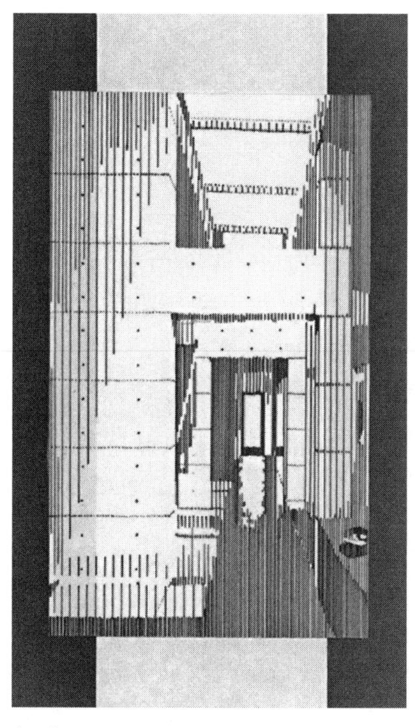

(1)

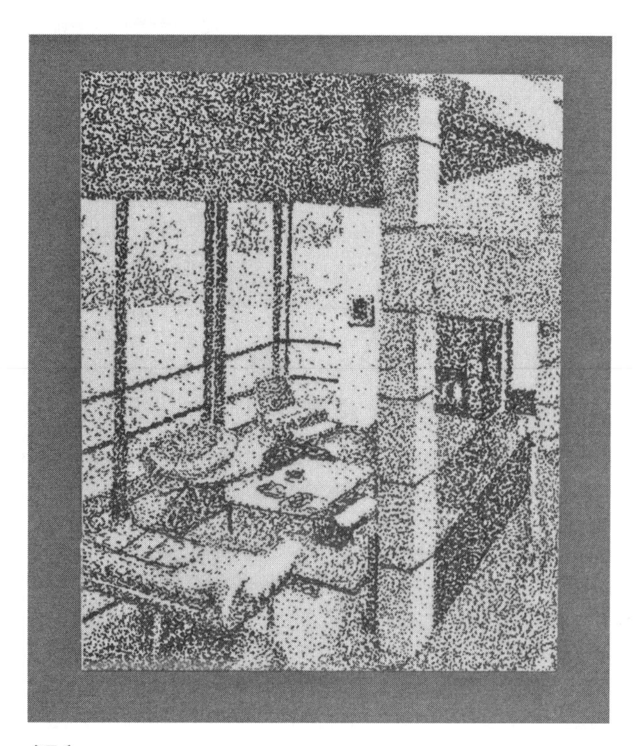

(1)

Kohavi house, San Francisco, California
Renderings: Student project by Jason Hearn
Medium: Ink on vellum
11" X 17" (27.9 X 43.2 cm)
Courtesy of La Raine Papa Montgomery
Savannah College of Art and Design

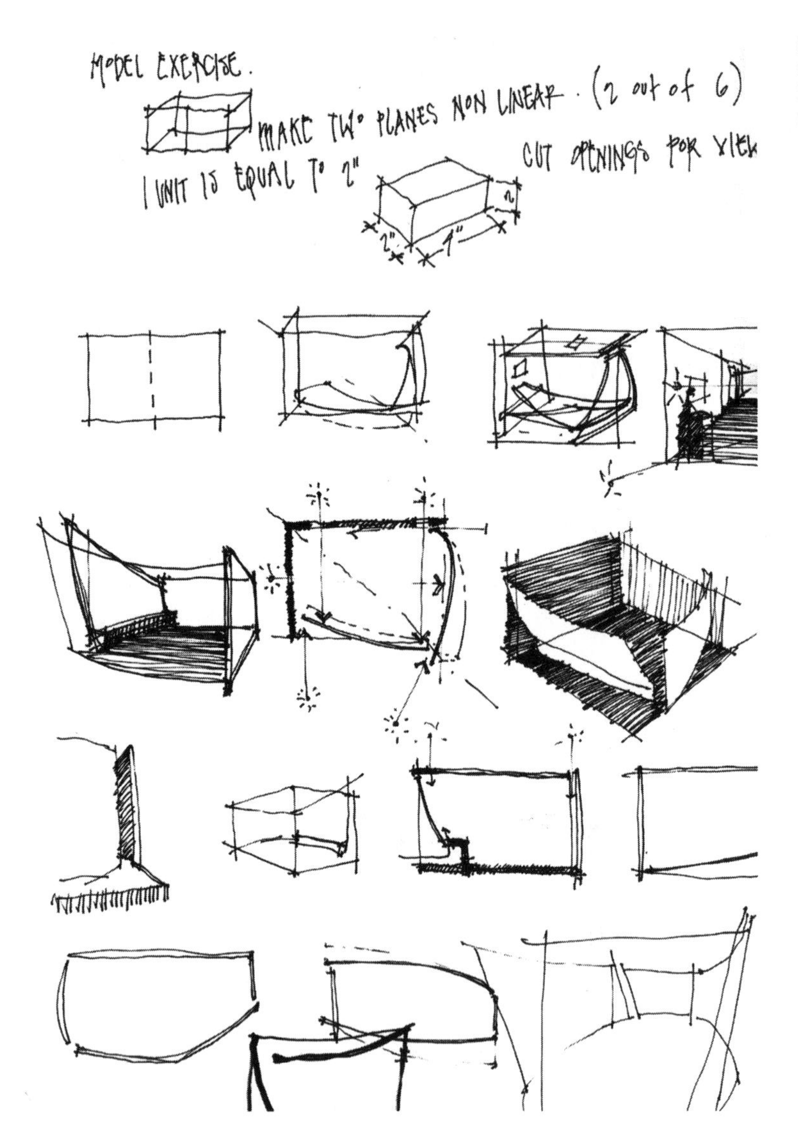

Sketches: Student project by Charles Roberts
Courtesy of Studio Professor William W.P. Chan
Institute of Architecture and Planning
Morgan State University

Black and White 2" X 2" X 4"

Problem Statement: Starting with a given volume measuring 2" x 2" x 4", manipulate two planes. Create a duplicate of the final design and study the relationship between the two forms when placed in multiple positions.

Media: Ink pen, sketchbook, Bristol board, Photoshop, and PageMaker

This design-drawing exercise began by simply bending two planes into simple curves, working back and forth between rough paper models and sketches. Next, the two planes were expressed in more complex form, such that the experience of a person either inside or outside this form would be more dynamic than if the planes were expressed merely by simple planar curves. The complex curved form was explored again through a series of sketches and sketch models until a final form was settled on. The way the final solution was expressed may make it seem that more than two planes were modified; however, four flat sides still remain. Next, the shape was duplicated. Through basic digital photography and lighting, the two models were photographed in different combinations and set adjacent to a regular geometric form—the sphere in this case. Each scene was analyzed for its positive and negative aspects. For example, the residual spaces became places and changed within each scene. The positive volumes also took on new form when exhibited together in different positions.
[ARCHITECTURE STUDENT'S STATEMENT]

Sketches and photos: Student project by Charles Roberts
Courtesy of Professor William W.P. Chan
Institute of Architecture and Planning
Morgan State University

REFER TO CHAPTER 9

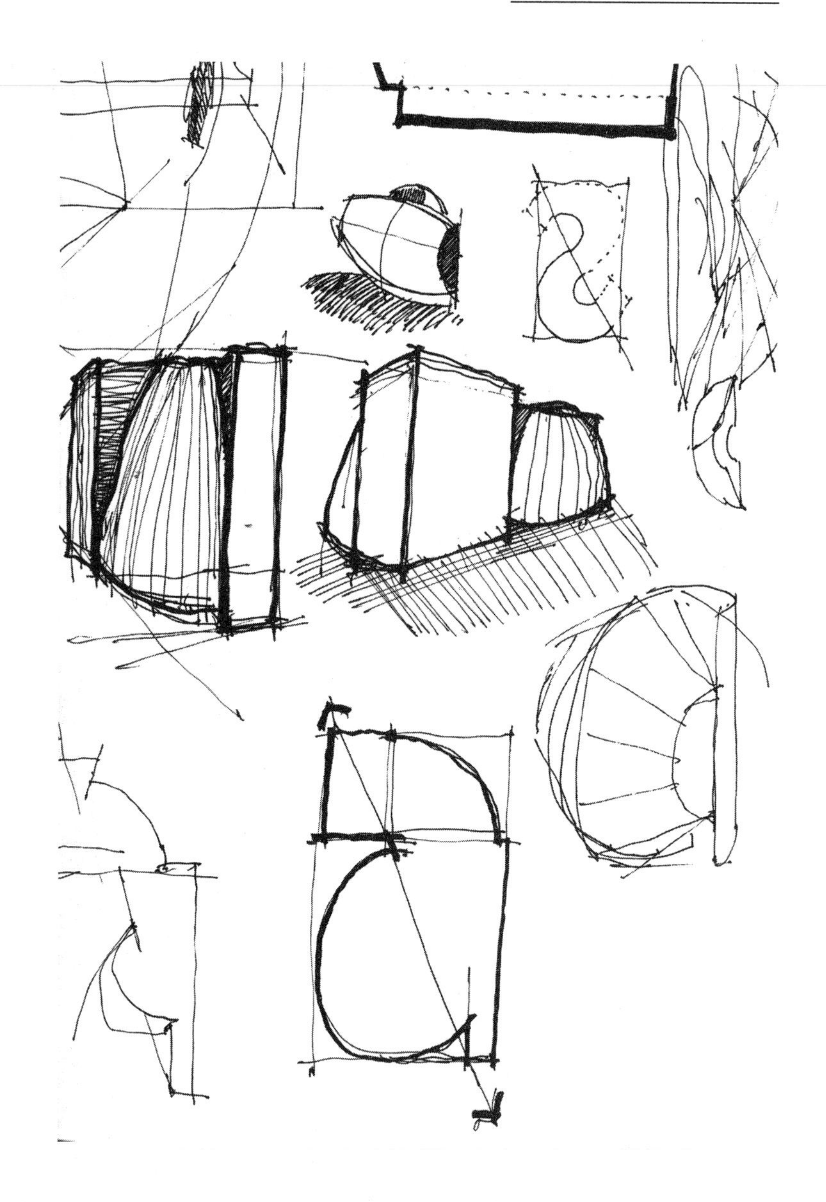

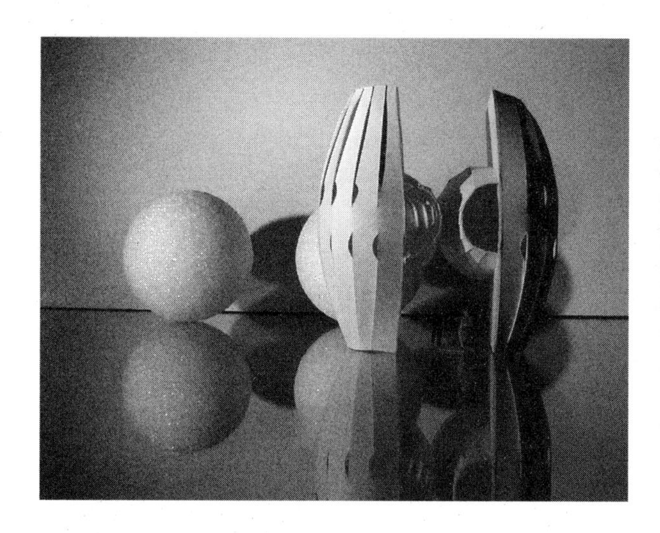

Geometric Refinement and Construction

This is the first project given to first-semester freshmen in the undergraduate program in architecture at the University of Buffalo—State University of New York. Instructor: Associate Professor Beth Tauke.

INTRODUCTION

As geometers, equipped only with compasses and straightedges, we enter the two-dimensional world of the representation of form. A link is forged between the most concrete (form and measure) and the most abstract realms of thought. By seeking the invariable relationships by which forms are governed and interconnected, we bring ourselves into resonance with universal order.
[ROBERT LAWLER]

DEFINITIONS

Geometric refinement is the superimposition of a grid system on the predetermined outline of a space and/or form and the subsequent geometric adjustment of the outline to adhere to the limitations imposed by the grid.

Geometric construction is different from refinement in that a form is developed by starting with two points (line) that grow in an order dictated by the rules of geometry and proportion coupled with the maker's thought processes. Unlike refinement, which involves a constant modular order and an external imposition of a grid on a shape, construction involves an organic order and an internal system of growth.

OBJECTIVES

- To study the geometric characteristics and constructs of space
- To compare numeric and geometric systems of measure
- To experience the differences between geometric refinement and construction
- To use various systems as tools to both analyze and develop forms
- To understand the concepts of growth and mapping systems
- To discover the impact that systems can have on the forms within them and vice versa
- To study the principles, purposes, and consequences of perspective projection

PROCESS

A. Select an object with the following characteristics: a) interior cavities, b) asymmetry on at least one axis, c) recognizable silhouette, d) less than one cubic foot in size. Document the object with section drawings of all three axes.
B. Using a 45° grid system, a set of limitations, and drafting tools as guides, develop geometric refinements of the interior space of the object on all three axes.
C. Using geometric principles and drafting tools as guides, develop geometric constructions of the interior space of the object on all three axes.
D. Develop a constructed perspective representation of the triaxial geometries of the object's interior space.
E. Develop a drawing that uses, adapts, or alters a perspective projection system to suggest movement in the object's interior space.

REQUIREMENTS AND SUGGESTED METHODS

1. Carefully examine the object to determine the sections that will most fully communicate its space and form.
2. Cut and measure the object and its interior space on the primary axis. Take enough measurements to accurately reproduce the section. Reconnect the sections. Then cut the object on its secondary axis. Again, measure the object and its interior space to accurately reproduce the section. Reconnect these sections. Finally, cut the mold on its tertiary axis and repeat the process.
3. Use geometric tools (triangles, T-square or parallel rule, and compass only) for the development of the drawings.
4. Use the layout of the sections to communicate the relationship that the drawings have to one another.
5. Use line weight to differentiate form from space.
6. The final section drawings should be in graphite on drawing paper specified by your instructor.

7. Preliminary refinements and constructions should be drawn in pencil on trace. All points on the preliminary refinements should be marked with small x's or dots.
8. Refinement prescripts include the following:
   - All lines begin and end on grid points. (Grid points are the places where two or more lines intersect.)
   - The center of every circle or partial circle (curve) should be positioned on grid points.
   - The endpoints of the beginning and ending radii of every curve should be positioned on grid points.
9. Use the object itself to determine either the width or length of the grid. Consider the grid relationship between each section. Do they correspond with one another?
10. When analyzing the underlying structure of the interior space of the object for the purposes of construction, begin by searching for primary geometric relationships and systems. Locate a line that appears to be central to the development of the form. Using geometric tools, develop from that line a sequence of geometric moves that are logical and related to one another. (No numeric measurements are needed and no arbitrary moves should be made in this process.) Consider the geometric relationship between each section. Do they correspond with one another?
11. Although it is painstaking, number and write, on a separate overlay, a description of each move in the development of the construction. This extra step assists in maintaining a geometric sequence devoid of arbitrary moves, and helps in the communication of your process.
12. For Statement D, one-, two-, or three-point perspective may be used. All construction lines should remain in the drawings.
13. For Statement E, consider the introduction of multiple points of view, interlocking spaces, and/or multiple projection systems (paraline and perspective). Carefully consider your specific intentions for this drawing: What kind of movement and/or movement conditions are you attempting to represent?
14. Final refinements, constructions, and perspectives should be inked. The drawing surface should be double-sided Mylar. Eliminate x's and numbers on final drawings.
15. At least two line weights should be used on the final drawings—heavier lines for the outline of the interior space and object silhouette, and lighter lines for grids and geometric structure. Carefully consider the proportions of the line weights.

REFERENCES

Henderson 1983.
Tauke, Beth. "Geometric Definitions and Formulas."

SUBMISSION

Object, section drawings, preliminary traces, final refinement(s) and construction(s), written explanation of construction process, perspective drawing, perspective movement drawing

EVALUATION CRITERIA

- Object selection
- Comprehension/accuracy of selection
- Comprehension of refinement/construction concepts
- Logic of construction description
- Comprehension of constructed perspective
- Efficiency/complexity of drawings
- Proportion
- Precision/technique

CRITIQUE ISSUES

1. How did you determine the sections?
2. How has the structure within which you are working affected the shape of the interior space of the object?
3. How has the space/shape with which you are working affected the structure/system?
4. How do the systems of geometric refinement and construction vary? Use your drawings to show examples of your main points.
5. How have the geometric systems you are using described three-dimensional space? How are the descriptions different from "actual" three-dimensional space?
6. These geometric systems are often used by designers and architects in the development and production of ideas. Discuss the appropriateness/inappropriateness of these systems under various conditions.
7. Discuss other entities that are affected by the systems in which they exist.
8. Discuss other systems that are affected by the entities existing in them.

Geometric Refinement and Construction

Courtesy of Associate Professor Beth Tauke
Department of Architecture, School of Architecture and Planning
University of Buffalo–State University of New York
Student project by Alberto Rios (pp. 644–45)

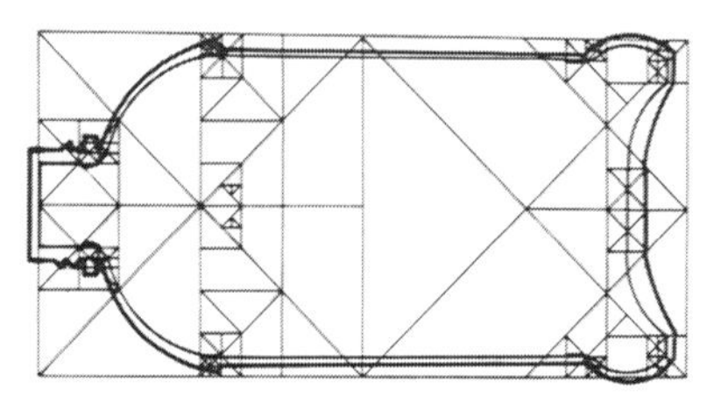

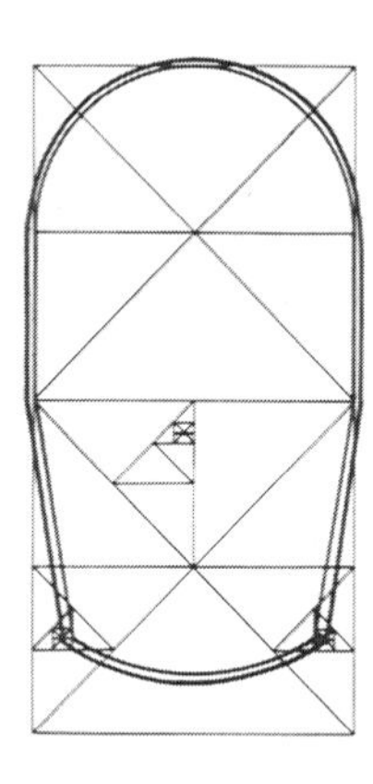

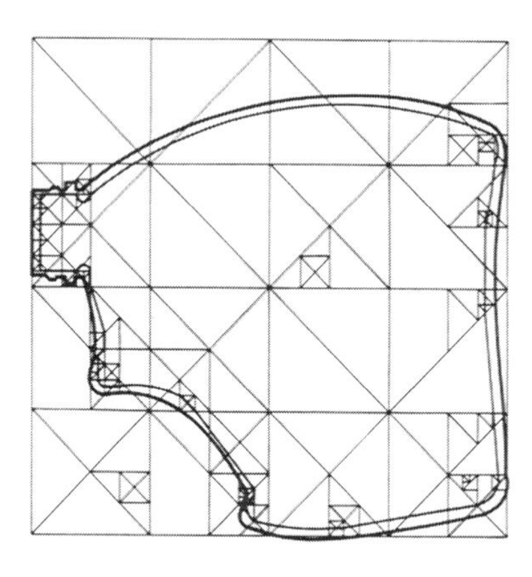

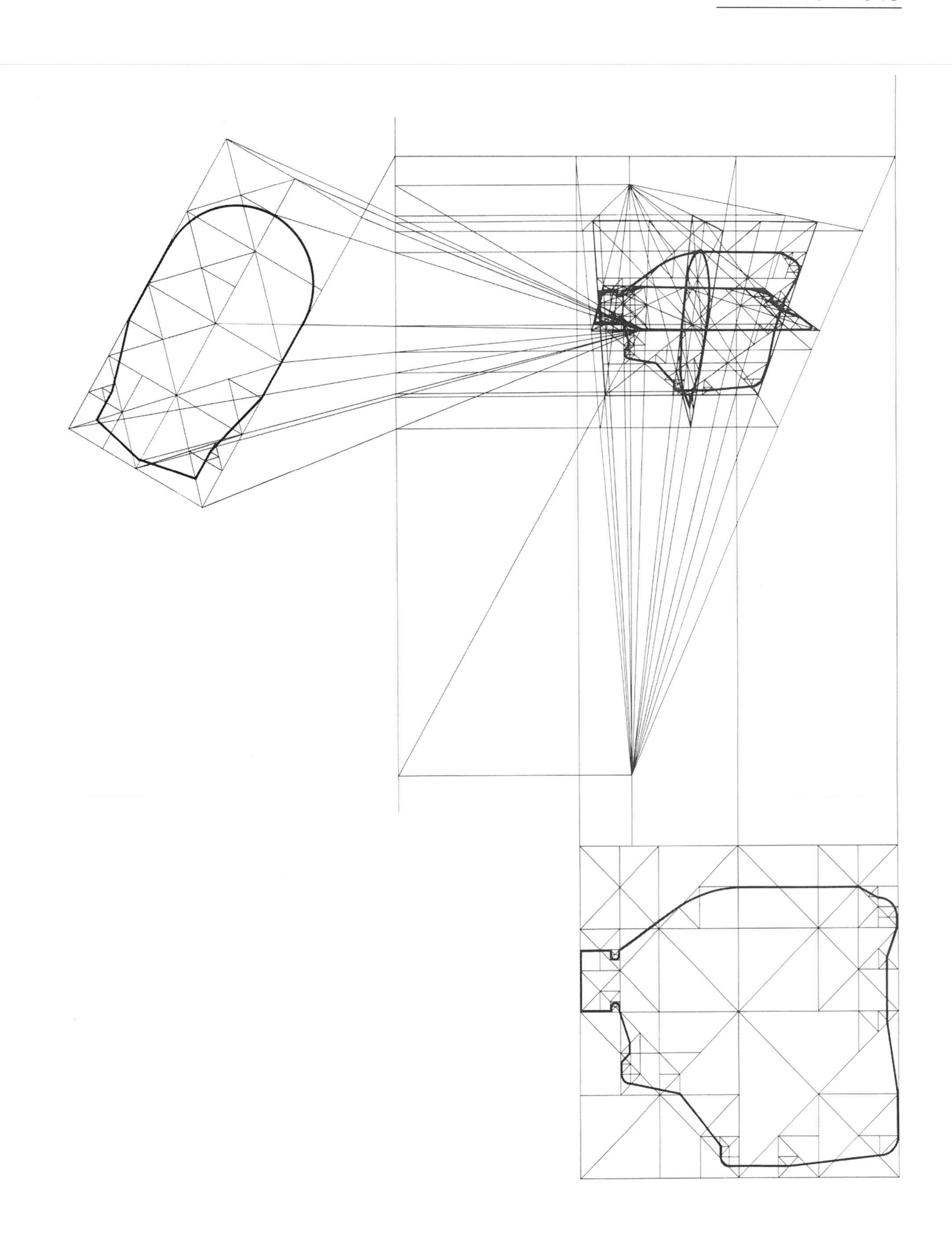

Architectural Analysis and Abstraction

DURATION
A five-week project with a site visit on the third day. Parts one and two are completed in two weeks; part three in the third week. Meet at the site with a camera, sketchbook, and tape measure.

SPECULATIONS
(**A**) How can previously introduced techniques of abstraction and communication be utilized to explore the relationship between the formal construction of a space and a resultant experience? (**B**) How can a project-specific attitude toward the application of architectural graphic conventions (i.e., plan, section/elevation, etc.) foster greater conviction in the crafting of a drawing? (**C**) How can architectural drawing be more than the terminal product of a design process? Can it be continued as a method to explore the mechanics of architectural experience, and as an eventual means to an end?

Through the exercises in this course, students have begun to develop the ability to analyze and communicate their perceptions of events, places, and formal compositions via various drawing and diagramming techniques. They have been taught that the mechanics of form and experience are interdependent—that one works as the mechanics for the other. Architecture, as a cultural construct that manipulates form, time, and space within the bounds of specific intents, is no different. When considering built form or space, the same analytical process may be applied to understand how experiences are created, how those experiences influence human interaction, and how they may transform over a period of time.

In this final exploration for the course, students will be required to thoroughly examine a built environment. The project will begin with the employment of previously utilized techniques of observation and analysis, transitioning via methods of abstraction and representation. The project will culminate with the construction of a composition that clearly and accurately communicates an understanding of the spatial mechanics at work.

METHODOLOGY PART I

Qualitative/Experiential Survey
Students are to visit a specific space, assigned by the instructor, and develop a series of clear, complete notations and a minimum of five diagrams that fully capture the qualities of the overall experience of the space as defined by each individual. Students are required to explore the space extensively, spending enough time to recognize patterns specific to it, and take note of any and all of its qualities. These may include, but are not limited to:

Connection to the space's exterior (required)
Directionality
Organizational principles
Magnitude and hierarchy
Movements in and through the space
Transitional/static space
Vertical spaces/Horizontal spaces
Scale
Enclosed spaces/Open spaces
Materiality of edges
Reflectivity of surfaces
Patterns and textures
Quality/directionality of light
Quality of sound
Quality of the space's edges/boundaries (don't forget the edges that define vertical limits!)

Diagrams should be drawn proportionally correct, with the proportions relative to the building's specific forms. The survey should begin to include measured drawings (such as a measured plan) to assist in the proportional accuracy of the diagrams. Final diagrams are to be ink, lead, and/or collage on 12" X 12" vellum.

Students must also take at least three, five-image photomontages. These are all to include both the horizontal *and* vertical dimensions.

Quantitative/Formal Survey
Once an understanding of the experiential qualities and their extents has been established, students are to return to the space and conduct a full measured survey of the formal aspects of those areas. Each student will be required to generate a minimum of one plan, three section/elevations, and one accurate freehand perspective, but additional drawings may be necessary to fully describe the overall space.

Using surveying techniques to be reviewed in the studio, students will record all dimensions and data on-site, in their sketchbooks. This data will be the basis for the development of the hardline drawings, although additional site visits are recommended, as required. The extent of each student's survey should be established by the limits of the experiences noted during the qualitative survey, and should include all forms that contributed to those experiences.

NOTE: The edges of the space may not necessarily line up with the formal edges of the space.

The drawings are to be to scale in lead and/or ink on 18" × 24" vellum. Lay out the drawings first, using construction lines to determine composition and scale. All drawings are to be drawn to the same scale, and should fill the sheet—therefore, the largest drawing will set the scale. Excellent drafting quality is expected; freehand lines are not acceptable (except in the perspective).

METHODOLOGY PART II

Analytic Composition
Referencing all of the information gathered to this point and using all of the individual drawings developed, construct a composition that communicates the relationship between the information gathered during the two surveys. This drawing will merge information derived from the experiences of the space and the building's physical qualities and should be an investigation into the relationships between them. Draw from the diagrams, measured drawings, sketches, notes, and photomontages that were created over the course of the project as material for the composition. The overall composition should convey a clear understanding of the specific space/experience. The final composition is to be on a 30" X 42" sheet of vellum or Mylar. Media may include pencil, ink, photographic reproduction, and collage techniques, etc. Along with the final drawing composition, each student must develop a concise, typewritten objective and rich narrative describing the nature of his or her experiences using descriptive spatial terms introduced in this course. Describe the organizational elements, dynamic qualities, material qualities, effect of light, and any other factors that influenced the experience.

Materials
Sketchbook, tracing paper, vellum, lead/leadholder, ink pens, various sketching pencils (2H, HB, 2B, 4B), camera and film; other materials assigned for the final composition

Project courtesy of Professor Richard H. Shiga
Department of Architecture
Portland State University

REFER TO CHAPTERS 1, 3, 4, AND 9

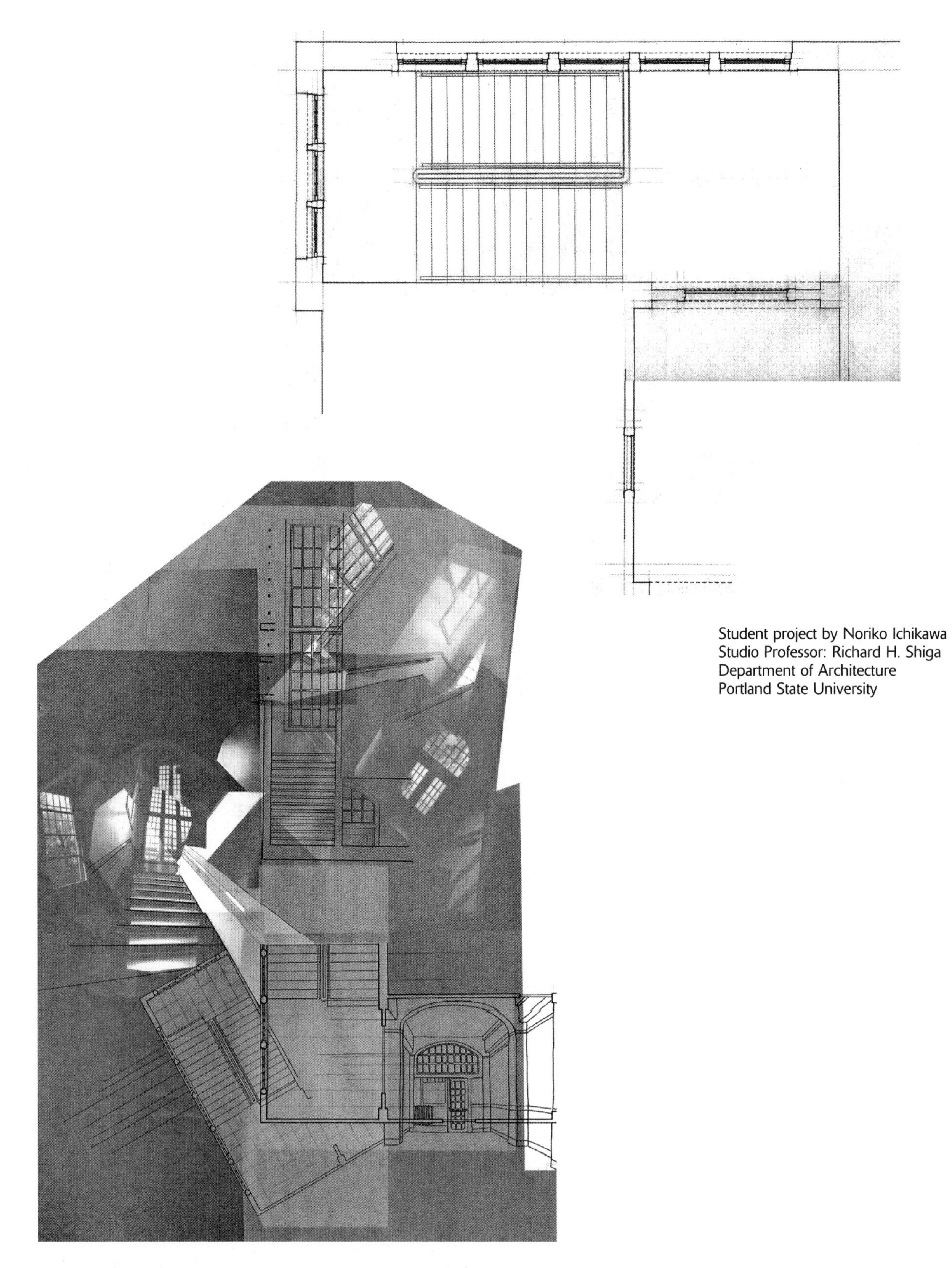

Student project by Noriko Ichikawa
Studio Professor: Richard H. Shiga
Department of Architecture
Portland State University

Student project by Sonia Smythe
Studio Professor: Richard H. Shiga
Department of Architecture
Portland State University

Student project by Sarah Royalty
Studio Professor: Richard H. Shiga
Department of Architecture
Portland State University

Student project by Suzanne Berekoff
Studio Professor: Richard H. Shiga
Department of Architecture
Portland State University

Dwellings for Inhabitants with Exaggerated Personalities

TIME FRAME: Four weeks, working individually

Assignment: Each student is assigned and interviews a person with a personality disorder one to one. The interviewees may have disordered personalities that show instability, introversion, or extroversion. They are analyzed in terms of important basic concept values that determine how they might like a house designed for them.

Goals and Methodology: To design quality spaces based on the functional requirements of the people with disordered personalities. After initial hand-drawn conceptual ideas are formulated and study models are made, use 3-D modeling software very early in the design process to explore spatial solutions as a complement to the traditional design process.

Comments: Through the use of 3-D modeling software early in the process, students have a greater capacity for handling multiple interfacing variables.

REFER TO CHAPTER 9 AND WEB SITE CHAPTER 11

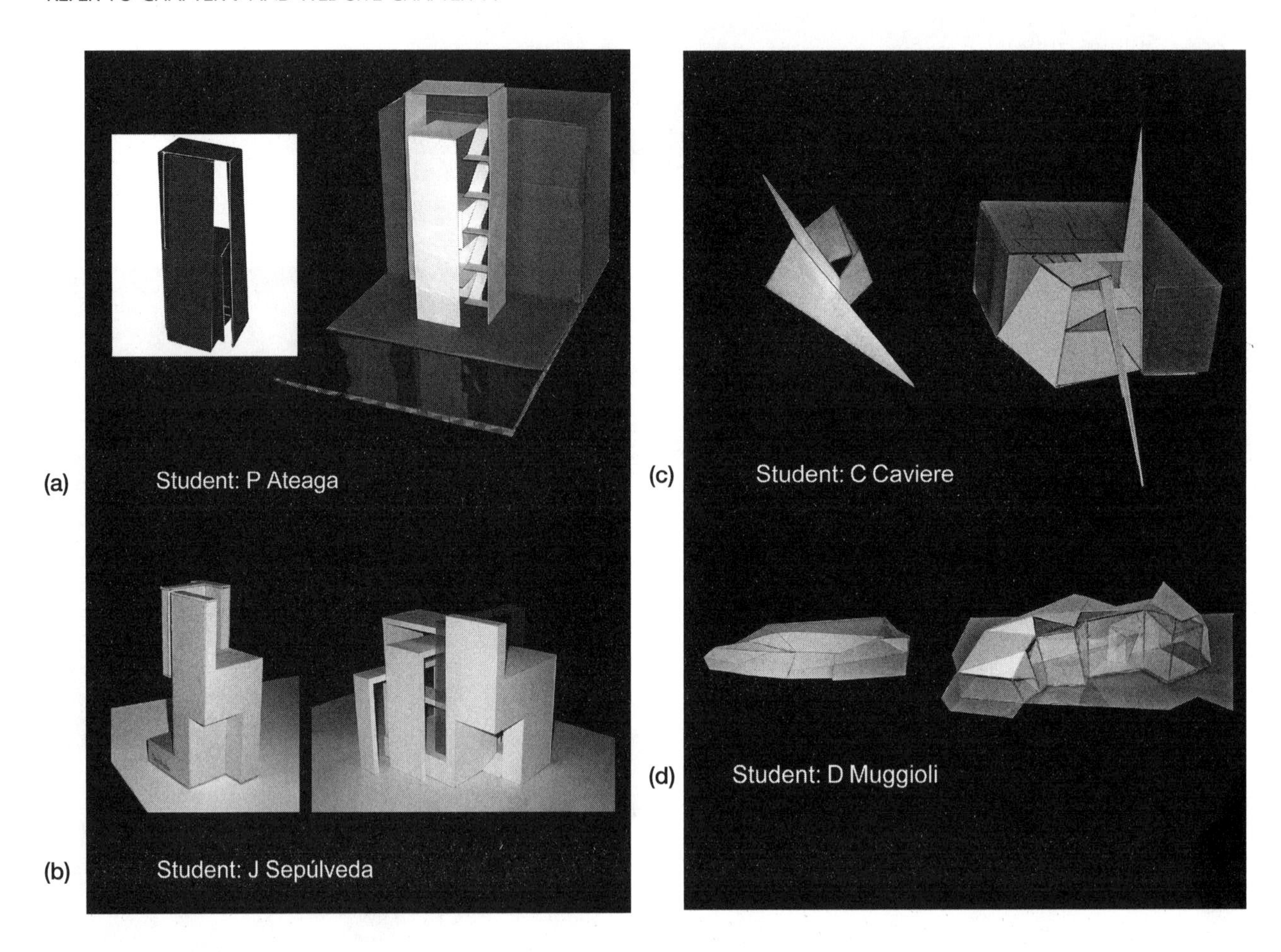

Student projects by (a) P. Ateaga (b) J. Sepulveda (c) C. Cavieres (d) D. Muggioli
(Also see facing page)
Medium: Computer 3-D models with form-Z software
Courtesy of Studio Professor Marcela Pizzi
Associate Team: Jose Saavedra, Mariana Donoso, Andres Caviedes, Tomas Villalon
Faculty of Architecture and Urbanism
University of Chile at Santiago

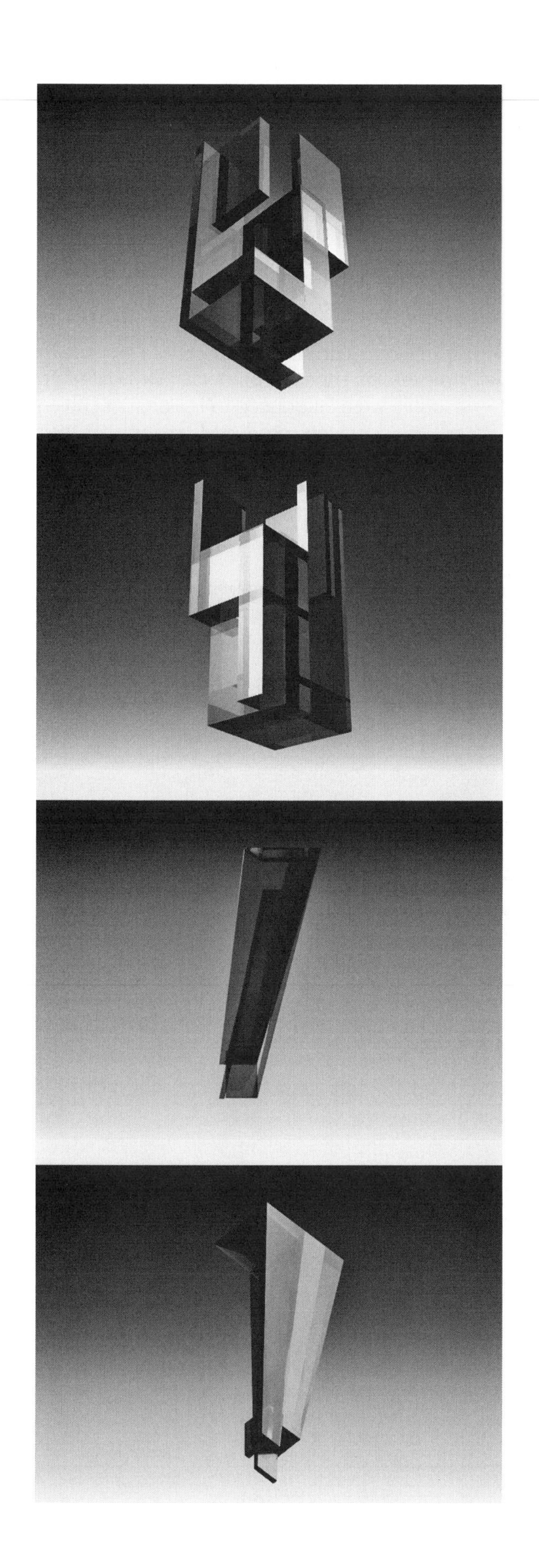

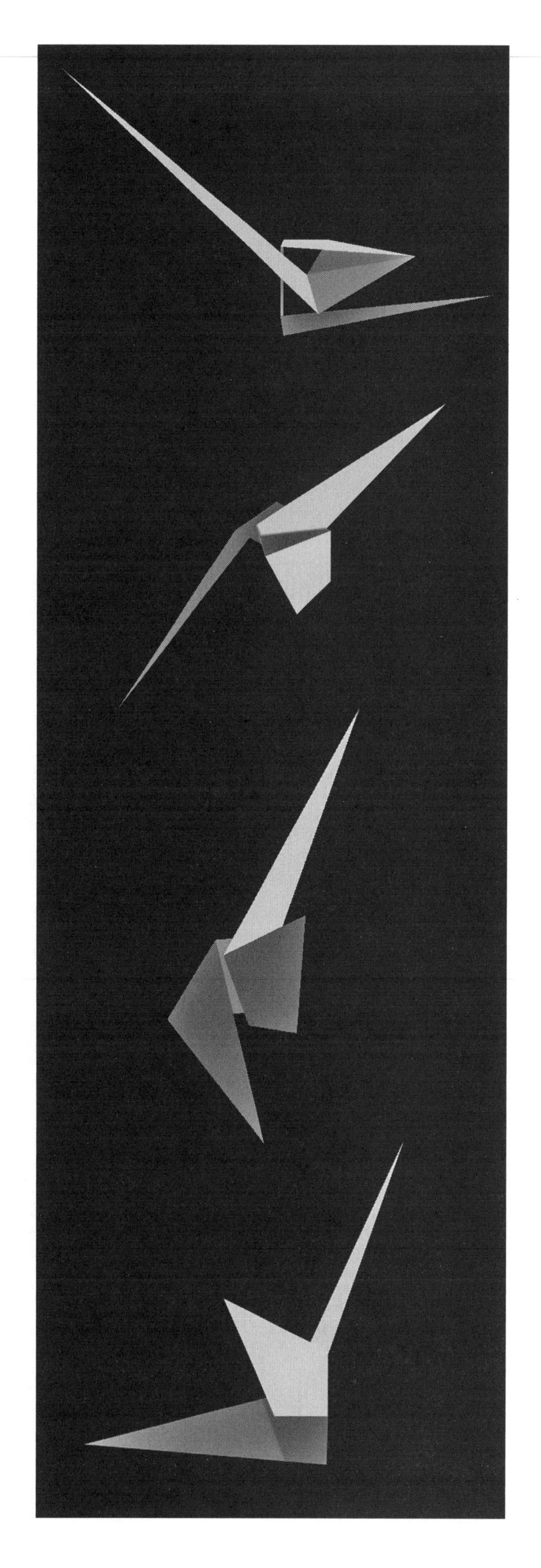

Origamic Architecture, Visualization, and 3-D Modeling in Real Space

TIME FRAME: Two weeks

Background: Origamic architecture (developed by Japanese architect Masahiro Chatani) is the art of making pop-up cards by cutting and folding from a single sheet of paper. They can be folded flat for storage or mailing in conventional envelopes, but when unfolded, magic happens—the cards pop up into an amazing and delightful three-dimensional structure. Origamic architecture transforms three-dimensional objects into two-dimensional patterns and back to three-dimensional objects again. More than cutting and folding, origamic architecture sharpens logical thinking and the ability to discern the essence of beauty in things.

Assignment: In this exercise, students were required to develop models of landmark buildings in Kuwait using the techniques of origamic architecture. During the first week, students were introduced to the craft of cutting and folding papers using simple exercises. At the end of week one, students produced pop-ups of their names. During the second week, each student selected and visited a landmark building in Kuwait. Each student studied drawings and photos of the building as well as its overall form. Finally, students had to figure out how to develop a pop-up for their buildings. Some of the projects were more difficult than others, but all of them achieved the goal of helping the student to visualize and think in three dimensions.

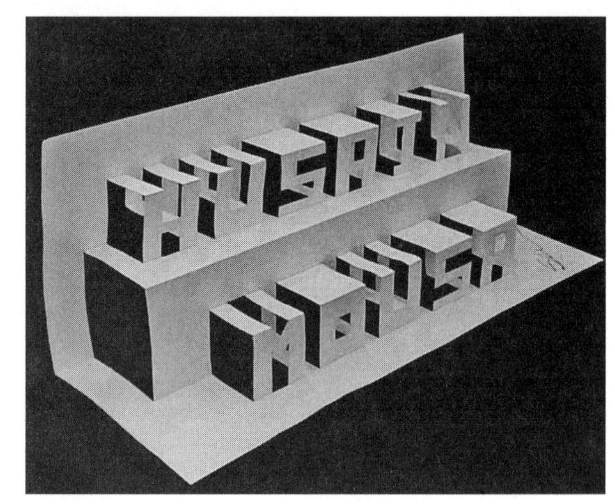

Student project by Hussain Mussa
Department of Architecture
Kuwait University
Courtesy of Studio Professor Yasser Mahgoub

REFER TO CHAPTER 9

Drawing project based on a sketch by architect Lebbeus Woods
Student project by Melanie Beisswenger
Software: 3D Studio MAX, Premiere
Courtesy of Professors Karen Kensek and Douglas Noble
School of Architecture
University of Southern California

Digital Drawing Based on a Sketch

This project was inspired by a Lebbeus Woods sketch titled Houses in Tension (reconstruction of the air-space). *Melanie Beisswenger modeled and rendered the indeterminate form and then used it as a basis for a kinetic transformation of her own design. She started by digitally reconstructing the architecture from the incomplete drawings that were available. Many different materials were scanned and edited to achieve the textures she desired. Near the end of the semester, she remodeled the "flying creature" using NURBS (nonuniform rational B-splines) to achieve more fluid contours and shapes. Shown is a single rendered image and fifteen frames from the Premiere animation. [PROFESSORS' STATEMENT]*

REFER TO CHAPTER 10 AND WEB SITE CHAPTER 11

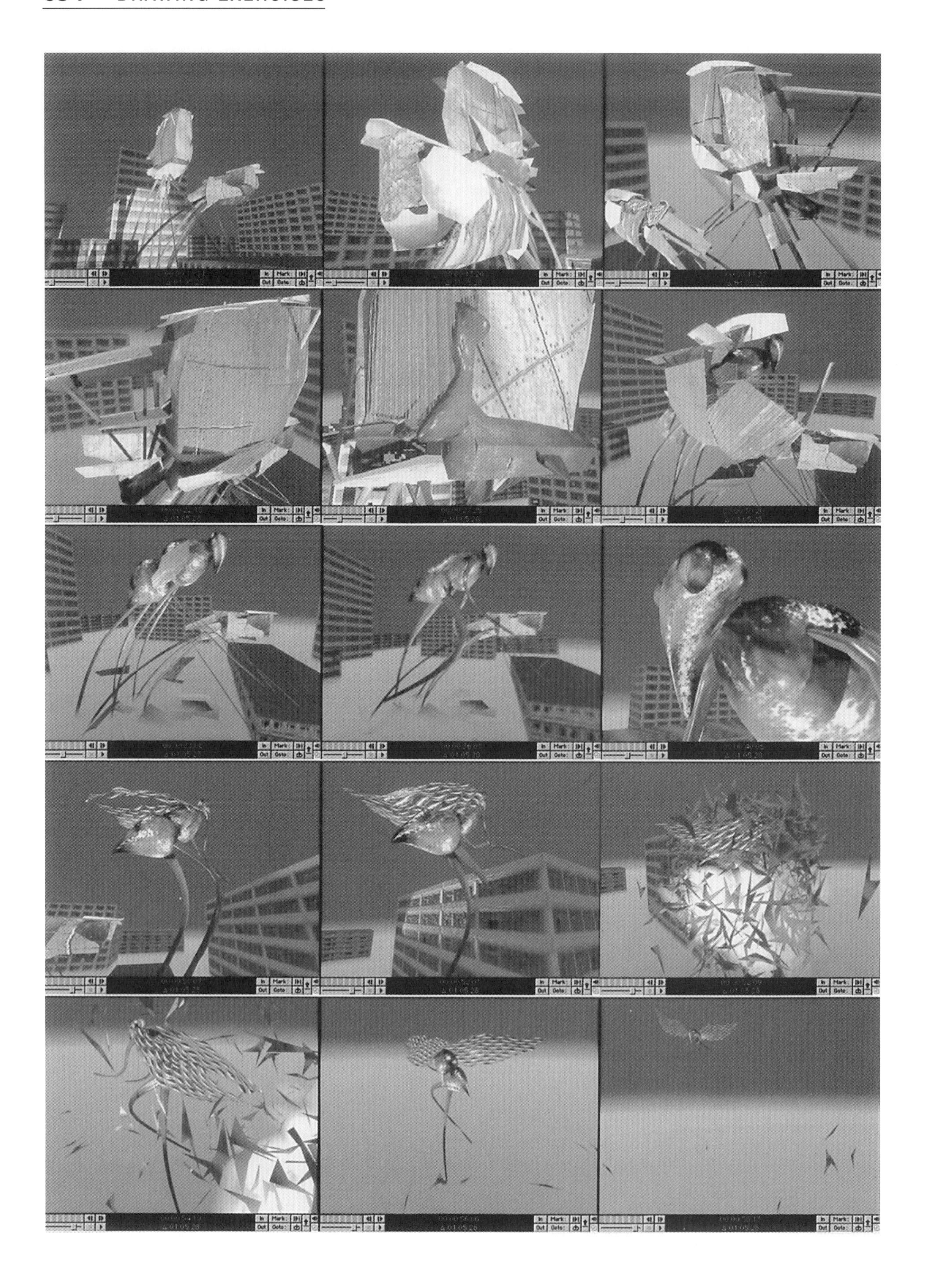

Bibliography

Adler, D. 2000. *Metric Handbook: Planning and Design Data.* Architectural Press.

Ambroziak, B. M. 2005. *Michael Graves Images of a Grand Tour.* Princeton Architectural Press

Bahamon, A. 2007. *Sketch: Houses: How Architects Conceive Residential Architecture.* Loft Publi-cations.

Bleck, B. (Ed.). 1994. *Alvaro Siza City Sketches.* Birkhäuser.

Bridgman, G. 2001. *Bridgman's Complete Guide to Drawing from Life.* Sterling.

Brooks, H. A. 1997. *Le Corbusier's Formative Years.* University of Chicago Press.

Buckles, G. M. 1995. *Building Architectural & Interior Models Fast!* Belpine.

Cappellato, G. 2003. *Mario Botta: Light and Gravity.* Prestel.

Carter, R., B. Day, & P. Meggs. 2007. *Typographic Design: Form and Communication.* 4th ed. Wiley.

Chen, J., & W. T. Cooper. 1996. *Architectural Perspective Grids.* McGraw-Hill.

Ching, F. D. K. 1990. *Drawing: A Creative Process.* Wiley.

———. 2007. *Architecture: Form, Space, and Order.* 3rd ed. Wiley.

———. 1998. *Design Drawing.* Wiley.

———. 2003. *Architectural Graphics.* 4th ed. Wiley.

Clark, R., & M. Pause. 2005. *Precedents in Architecture.* Wiley.

Collyer, G. S. 2004. *Competing Globally in Architecture Competitions.* Academy Press.

Cooper, D. 2000. *Drawing and Perceiving.* Wiley.

Craig, J. 1990. *Basic Typography: A Design Manual.* Watson-Guptill.

Crowe, N., & P. Laseau. 1997. *Visual Notes.* Wiley.

Crowe, P. 1996. *Architectural Rendering.* McGraw-Hill.

Dal Co, F. & G. Massariol. 2002. *Carlo Scarpa: The Complete Works.* Rizzoli.

D'Amelio, J. 2004. *Perspective Drawing Handbook.* Dover.

Dodson, B. 1990. *Keys to Drawing.* North Light.

Dombek, G., & T. Porter. 2003. *Airbrush Illustration for Architecture.* W. W. Norton.

Doyle, M. E. 1999. *Color Drawing.* Wiley.

Edwards, B. 1999. *The New Drawing on the Right Side of the Brain.* Tarcher.

Elam, K. 2001. *Geometry of Design.* Princeton Architectural Press.

Eisenmann, P. 1999. *Diagram Diaries.* Universe Publishing.

Evans, R. 2000. *The Projective Cast: Architecture and Its Three Geometries.* MIT Press.

Ferriss, H. 1986. *The Metropolis of Tomorrow.* Princeton Architectural Press.

———. 1998. *Power in Buildings: An Artist's View of Contemporary Architecture.* H & I.

Ford, E. 1990. *Details of Modern Architecture.* MIT Press.

Forseth, K. 1980. *Graphics for Architecture.* Wiley.

Fraser, I., & R. Henmi. 1997. *Envisioning Architecture: An Analysis for Drawing.* Wiley

Friedman, J. 2000. *Creation in Space.* Kendall Hunt.

Futagawa, Y. 1981. *Paul Rudolph: Architectural Drawings.* Architectural Book Publishing Company.

Gill, R. W. 1980. *Basic Perspective.* Thames and Hudson.

Goldstein, N. 1997. *Design and Composition.* Prentice Hall.

Hadid, Z. 2001. *Zaha Hadid 1996–2001.* El Croquis.

Hanks, K., & L. Belliston. 1977. *Draw.* William Kaufmann.

———. 1992. *Rapid Viz.* Crisp Publications.

Hart, R. 2000. *Photographing Your Artwork.* Amherst Media.

Henderson, L. Dalrymple. 1983. *The Fourth Dimension and Non-Euclidean Geometry in Modern Art.* Princeton University Press.

Herbert, D. M. 1993. *Architecture Study Drawings: Their Characteristics and Their Properties as a Graphic Medium for Thinking in Design.* Wiley.

Holl, S., & L. Muller. 2002. *Steven Holl Written in Water.* Lars Muller Verlag.

Jeanneret-Gris, C. 1981. *Le Corbusier Sketchbooks, 1914–1948.* MIT Press.

Johnson, E., & M. Lewis. 1999. *Drawn from the Source: The Travel Sketches of Louis I. Kahn.* MIT Press.

Kahn, N. 2003. *My Architect.* [Film documentary].

Kasprisin, R. J. 1991. *Watercolor in Architectural Design.* Wiley.

———. 1999. *Design Media.* Wiley.

Kasprisin, R. J., & J. Pettinari. 1990. *Visual Thinking for Architects and Designers: Visualizing Context in Design.* Wiley.

Khemlani, L. 1999. *Into 3D with Form-Z: Modeling, Rendering, Animation.* McGraw-Hall.

Kliment, S. 1984. *Architectural Sketching and Rendering.* Whitney.

Knoll, W., & M. Hechinger. 1992. *Architectural Models: Construction Techniques.* McGraw-Hill.

Laseau, P. 2000. *Graphic Thinking for Architects and Designers.* Wiley.

Lawson, P. 1978. *Lawson Perspective Charts with English or Metric Units.* Wiley.

Leich, J. F. 1980. *Architectural Visions: The Drawings of Hugh Ferriss.* Whitney.

Lin, M. W. 1993. *Drawing and Designing With Confidence: A Step By Step Guide.* Wiley.

———. 2000. *Boundaries.* Simon & Schuster.

Linton, H., & S. Rost. 2000. *Portfolio Design.* 2nd ed. W. W. Norton.

Lockard, W. K. 1993. *Freehand Perspective for Designers: Including Shadowcasting and Entourage.* Crisp Publications.

———. 1994. *Drawing as a Means to Architecture.* William Kaufmann.

———. 1994. *Drawing Techniques for Designers: Advocating Line and Tone Drawing.* Crisp Publications.

———. 2001. *Design Drawing.* W. W. Norton.

———. 2001. *Design Drawing Experiences.* W. W. Norton.

Mann, T. 2004. *Time Management for Architects & Designers: Challenges and Remedies.* W. W. Norton.

Mendolwitz, D., & D. Wakeham. 1993. *Guide to Drawing.* International Thomson.

Mills, C. B. 2000. *Designing with Models.* Wiley.

Miralles, E. 1997. *Enric Miralles: Works and Projects, 1975–1995.* Monacelli.

Mitton, M. 2003. *Interior Design Visual Presentation.* Wiley.

Nerdinger, W. (Ed.). 2004. *Dinner for Architects: A Collection of Napkin Sketches.* W. W. Norton.

Novitski, B. J. 1999. *Rendering Real and Imagined Buildings.* Rockport.

Orr, F. 1995. *Scale in Architecture.* New York: Van Nostrand Reinhold.

Paulo dos Santos, J. 1994. *Alvaro Siza Works & Projects: 1954–1992.* Gustavo Gili.

Pelli, C. 1991. *Cesar Pelli: Buildings and Projects: 1965–1990.* Rizzoli.

Pérez-Gomez, A., & L. Pelletier. 2000. *Architectural Representation and the Perspective Hinge.* MIT Press.

Pfeiffer, B. B. 1996. *Frank Lloyd Wright Drawings.* Abradale Press.

Pollack, S. 2006. *Sketches of Frank Gehry.* [Film documentary].

Porter, T., & S. Goodman. 1985. *Manual of Graphic Techniques 4.* MacMillan General Reference.

Portoghesi, P. 2000. *Aldo Rossi: The Sketchbooks 1990–1997.* Thames and Hudson.

Predock, A. 1995. *Architectural Journeys: Antoine Predock.* St. Martin's Press.

Rappolt, M., & R. Violette. 2004. *Gehry Draws.* The MIT Press.

Ray, K. R., L. Lokko, & I. Marjanovic. 2003. *The Portfolio: An Architectural Student's Handbook.* Elsevier Ltd.

Robbins, E. 1997. *Why Architects Draw.* The MIT Press.

Ruskin. J. 1971. *The Elements of Drawing.* Dover.

Sasin, F. 2004. *Michael Graves: Buildings and Projects: 1995–2003.* Rizzoli.

Soleri, P. 1971. *The Sketchbooks of Paolo Soleri.* MIT Press.

Sutherland, M. 1989. *Lettering for Architects and Designers.* Wiley.

Uddin, M. S. 1996. *Axonometric and Oblique Drawing.* McGraw-Hill.

———. 1997. *Composite Drawing.*

———. 1999. *Digital Architecture.* McGraw-Hill.

Venturi, J. 2007. *Learning from Bob and Denise.* [Film documentary].

Vrooman, D. 1997. *Architecture, Perspective, Shadows, Reflections.* Wiley.

Walker, T. D., & D. Davis. 1999. *Plan Graphics.* Wiley.

Wallschlaeger, C., & C. Busic-Snyder. 1992. *Basic Visual Concepts and Principles.* McGraw-Hill.

Wang, T. C. 1993. *Sketching With Markers.* Wiley.

———. 1997. *Plan and Section Drawing.* Wiley.

———. 2002. *Pencil Sketching.* 2nd ed. Wiley.

Watson, E. W. 1985. *The Art of Pencil Drawing.* Watson-Guptill.

White, E. T. 1972. *Graphics Vocabulary for Architectural Presentation.* Architectural Media.

Wright, F. L. 1984. *Drawings and Plans of Frank Lloyd Wright: The Early Period (1893–1909).* Dover.

Wu, K. 1990. *Freehand Sketching in the Architectural Environment.* Wiley.

Zardini, M. (Ed.). 1996. *Santiago Calatrava Secret Sketchbook.* Monacelli.

Zevi, B. 1999. *Erich Mendelsohn: Complete Works.* Basel.

About the Author

Rendow Yee, Professor Emeritus, received his education at the University of California at Berkeley and at Washington University in Saint Louis, where he received his master of architecture degree. He was involved with architectural education for more than twenty years at the City College of San Francisco and served as chair of the architecture department there from 1982 to 1990. Professional organizations with which he has been affiliated include the American Society of Civil Engineers, the American Society for Engineering Education, the American Institute of Architects, and the California Council of Architectural Education.

Subject Index

adhesives, model-making, 17
aerial view. *See* bird's-eye perspective
altitude, solar angle, 310
anthropometrics, representational sketching, 62–63
arcade shadows, 336–337
architect's scale, 18–19, 585
architectural journey, drawing exercises (level one), 582–583
architectural observation sketching, line types, 56
architectural templates, 13
arrowed line, two-dimensional diagrams, 434–435
artificial lighting, delineation and rendering (interiors), 418
assembly drawing, linear perspective drawing, 281
automobiles. *See* cars
axes addition, orthographic and paraline drawing, 147
axial lines, non-axial lines and, orthographic and paraline drawing, 146
axonometric drawing
    compared, orthographic and paraline drawing, 127
    defined, 115
    drawing exercises (level two), 634
    isometric drawing construction, 136–137
    oblique drawings compared, 130
axonometric projection system, orthographic and paraline drawing compared, 126
azimuth, solar angle, 310

background, travel sketching, 79
ballpoint pens, representational sketching, 45
bearing, solar angle, 310
bevel scale, 18
bird's-eye perspective
    downhill and uphill views, linear perspective drawing, 208–209
    linear perspective drawing, 202–203, 266–269
        building examples, 267
        cityscapes, 268
        plan oblique, 269
    one-point perspective from above, linear perspective drawing, 204–205
blind contour drawing, representational sketching, 64–65
blocking out, representational sketching, 48–49
block visualization sketches, orthographic and paraline drawing, 121–123
bubble diagram, relationship diagrams, 440
building design section. *See* design section
buildings, representational sketching, 70–73
building section, orthogonal terminology, 91. *See also* section
building theme, presentation formats, composite drawings, 512

canopy shadows, 336
cars
    delineation and rendering, 396–397
        perspective, 397
        plan and elevation, 396
    representational sketching, 68–69
ceiling plan, reflected, composite plan, section and, presentation formats, 507
center of vision, midpoint and perspective field of view, 255
charcoal, travel sketching, 75
chipboard illustration board, 16
circle construction
    isometric, orthographic and paraline drawing, 142
    linear perspective drawing, 210–211
    paraline, orthographic and paraline drawing, 143
    plan oblique horizontal, orthographic and paraline drawing, 144–145
circulation, graphic diagram, 430–431
cityscapes, bird's-eye perspective, 268
cleaning aids, tools, 7
cluster plan, orthogonal terminology, 87
clutch pencils, 4
colonnade shadows, 336–337
color, value language, 374
compass
    described, 10
    use of, 12–13
composite design sketch, 517
composite drawings. *See also* presentation formats
    building theme, presentation formats, 512
    design sketch, presentation formats, 516–517
    drawing exercises (level one), 622
    orthographic and paraline drawing, 153
    plan, section, and reflected ceiling plan, presentation formats, 507
    plan and elevation oblique, presentation formats, 513
    plan/elevation/details, presentation formats, 508
    plan/section/elevation/details, presentation formats, 509
    presentation formats
        generally, 496–503
        nonvertical z-axis drawing, 511
    section and elevation, presentation formats, 506
    superimposed, presentation formats, 516–517
    transmetric drawings, presentation formats, 510
    transoblique drawings, presentation formats, 514–515
    transverse section, orthogonal terminology, 105, 106–107
    unfolded elevations, presentation formats, 504
    unfolded plan/elevation, presentation formats, 505
computer-generated lettering, 29
computer imaging. *See also* specific computer applications
    manually casted shadow compared, 360–361
    perspective shadows, 362–363
conceptual diagramming and sketching, 427–487
    alternative diagrams, 436–437
    design process, 442
    drawing exercises (level one), 584, 614–615, 618–620
    drawing exercises (level two), 629–632, 635, 640–641, 646–649, 650–651
    elevation and section diagrams (sketched), 446
    elevation diagram (hardline), 447
    formal/spatial diagrams, 441
    ideational drawing, 460–461
    modeling, 482–487
    modeling and sketching, 482
    overview, 427–429
    phase diagram, 451
    plan diagram, 444–445
    plan oblique sketch diagram, 448–449
    relationship diagrams, 440
    representational sketching, 81
    site diagrams, 438–439
    sketching, 464–481
    sketching and modeling, 482
    symbols, 430–436
        generally, 430–431

conceptual diagramming and sketching (cont'd)
three-dimensional diagrams, 435
two-dimensional diagrams, 433–434
usage, 432
3-D diagrams, digital, 452–459
3-D sketch models, in real space, 450
thumbnail sketches, 462–463
vertical section diagrams, 443
conceptual rendering, mixed media, 422–423
cone of vision, linear perspective drawing, 188, 189
configuration (shape), still lifes, representational sketching, 61
construction lines, representational sketching, 48–49
construction section, orthogonal terminology, 92
context, representational sketching, buildings, 72
contextual environment, orthogonal terminology, 92
continuous value, defined, 370
contour drawing
drawing exercises (level one), 587–588
French curves, 9
representational sketching, 63, 64
contour language, delineation and rendering, 372–373
contour lines, still lifes, representational sketching, 61
contrast, delineation and rendering, 369
conventional orthogonal terminology. *See* orthogonal terminology
convergence
distortion, linear perspective drawing, 197
foreshortening and, linear perspective drawing, 185
two-point perspective, plan/elevation (office method), 231
converging lines, three-point perspective, 277
corresponding points, projection using, light, shade, and shadow, 344
cube-judgment system, three-point perspective, 276
cues, linear perspective drawing, 186
curvilinear forms and surfaces, light, shade, and shadow, 315, 349
cutaways
drawing exercises (level one), 606–609
drawing exercises (level two), 638
45 degree diagonal line, plan obliques, 148
cuts, design section, orthogonal terminology, 102
cutters, model-making, 17
cylindrical forms, light, shade, and shadow, 342

dashed line
drawing of, 34, 35
45 degree diagonal line, plan obliques, 148
delineation and rendering, 367–425. *See also* rendering
cars, 396–397
perspective, 397
plan and elevation, 396
contour language, 372–373
digital rendering, 424–425
drawing exercises (level one), 602, 605, 606–609, 613
drawing exercises (level two), 633, 636–637, 639
elevation material symbols, 390–391
floorscape, 384
floor surface material indications, 385
furniture, 394–395
ground surface indications, 386–387
hard surfaces, 383
human figures
generally, 392–393
horizon line, 410–411
lighting (interior), 418–419
artificial, 418
natural, 419
materials symbols, 402–403
mixed media conceptual rendering, 422–423
overview, 367–369
pen and ink rendering, 420–421
plan oblique accessories, 412–413
furniture and human figures, 412
trees, 413
reflections, 398–401
glass, 400–401, 414–415
polished surfaces, 416–417
water, 398–399
soft surfaces, 382
trees, 388
foreground, 404
middleground, 405
in perspective, 389
in plan, 380–381
value language, 374–377
generally, 374–375
sun, shade, and shadow, 376–377
value scales
toning techniques, 378–379
value grading techniques, 371
value types, 370
vegetation
exterior, 407–409
interior, 406–407
depth, contour and, delineation and rendering, 372
descriptive geometry
defined, 116
true-length and foreshortened lines, 116
design drawing, importance of, 436
design process, conceptual diagramming and sketching, 442
design section, orthogonal terminology, 92, 102–103
detail(s)
composite drawings, presentation formats, 508, 509
drawing exercises (level one), 581
drawing exercises (level two), 634
diagonal vanishing points
linear perspective drawing, 254
one-point grid, 214–216
diagram
abstraction, 460
defined, 432
diagramming. *See* conceptual diagramming and sketching
digital rendering, delineation and rendering, 424–425
digital shadows, manually casted shadow compared, 360–361
digital 3-D diagrams, conceptual diagramming and sketching, 452–459
dimetric drawing
defined, 115
drawing exercises (level one), 598
multiview and single-view drawings, 128–129
types of, compared, 127
diminution, overlapping and, linear perspective drawing, 184
direct measurement, multiplying, dividing, and transferring, 243
distance
contour and, delineation and rendering, 372
value language, 375
distortion, linear perspective drawing, 188, 196–197
divider
described, 10
use of, 12–13
dividing
with diagonal, linear perspective drawing, 251
linear perspective drawing, 242–245
by measuring, linear perspective drawing, 243
doors, orthogonal terminology, 111
dormers, perspective shadows, 358–359
double bevel scale, 18
downhill and uphill views, linear perspective drawing, 208–209
downward convergence, looking up, 275
drawing boards, types of, 3
drawing exercises (level one), 575–623
architectural journey, 582–583
composite presentation boards, 622
conceptual massing studies, 614–615
contour drawing, 587–588
eggs, 584
field studies, 581
freehand drawing, 577
graphic conventions, 593–594
hand lettering, 589
hourglass exercise, 616–617
human body and proportion, 578
interview with a student, 621
isometric/dimetric views, 598
light and shade, 575
line types, 590
missing views, 595–596, 597, 598
mixed-media drawing, 615
orthographic projection, 592
orthographic views, 597
panorama, 580
paraline drawing, 599
perspective cutaways and section perspectives, 606–609
perspective reflections, 604–605
plan oblique, 599, 600–602
positive and negative space, 576
rendering techniques, 612–614
scales, 585–586
section drawing, 591
shadow construction, 610–611
site analysis diagrams, 620

surface identification, isometric views, and missing views, 595
3-D modeling, 623
tone and texture, 579
two-point perspective, 602–603
vocabulary and diagramming, 618–619
drawing exercises (level two), 624–659
analytical diagramming and presentation formats, 629–632
architectural analysis and abstraction, 646–649
axonometric drawing, 634
black and white 2" X 2" X 4," 640–641
comprehensive project (isometric and exploded view), 635
details, 634
digital drawing based on sketch, 653–654
dot and line rendering techniques, 639
dwellings for exaggerated personality, 650–651
expanded, exploded, or cutaway view, 638
exploded isometric, 626
geometric refinement and construction, 642–645
hardline drawing, 636–637
observing and detailing, 624
origamic architecture, visualization, and 3-D modeling, 652
orthographic and paraline drawing, 625
paraline drawings, 633
perspective view, 628
plan and paraline shadows, 626
plan/section/elevation graphics, 626
section cuts (horizontal and vertical) combined, 626–627
drawing table
types of, 3
workstation setup, 15
drawing types, compared, orthographic and paraline drawing, 127
dual-axes angles, tri-axes angles and, orthographic and paraline drawing, 151
duster, cleaning aids, 7

edges, value language, 377
edge view, orthographic and paraline drawing, 117
eggs, drawing exercises (level one), 584
eight-point perspective, vertical circles, 285
element axonometric
expanded view, orthographic and paraline drawing, 170
exploded view, orthographic and paraline drawing, 171
orthographic and paraline drawing, 169–171
elevation(s)
cars, delineation and rendering, 396
composite drawings, presentation formats, 508, 509
composite section and elevation, presentation formats, 506
drawing exercises (level one), 593
labeling, 104
multiview and single-view drawings, 128–129
orthogonal terminology, 90
shadow, 345, 350–351
true-length and foreshortened lines, 116
two-point perspective, linear perspective drawing, 230–232
unfolded composite elevations, presentation formats, 504
unfolded plan/elevation, presentation formats, 505
elevation diagram
hardline, conceptual diagramming and sketching, 447
sketched, conceptual diagramming and sketching, 446
elevation lines, design section, orthogonal terminology, 103
elevation material, symbols, delineation and rendering, 390–391
elevation oblique(s)
building examples, orthographic and paraline drawing, 160–161
compared, orthographic and paraline drawing, 132–133
composite drawings, presentation formats, 513
drawing types compared, orthographic and paraline drawing, 127
expanded, orthographic and paraline drawing, 172–173
use of, orthographic and paraline drawing, 162–163
elevation view
orthogonal terminology, 92
shadows, 316
ellipses, perspective circles, 210–211
emphasis, line types, 37
engineer's scale, 18, 20, 586
entourage. *See* delineation and rendering
erasing aids, tools, 7
expanded elevation obliques, orthographic and paraline drawing, 172–173
expanded view
drawing exercises (level two), 638
element axonometric, orthographic and paraline drawing, 170
orthographic and paraline drawing, 167
exploded view(s)
assembly drawing, linear perspective drawing, 281
drawing exercises (level two), 635, 638
element axonometric, orthographic and paraline drawing, 171
isometric
drawing exercises (level two), 626
orthographic and paraline drawing, 168
oblique view, simultaneous, orthographic and paraline drawing, 179
orthographic and paraline drawing, 166
perspective, linear perspective drawing, 280
presentation formats, 570
expression, value language, 376
exterior grid example, one-point perspective, linear perspective drawing, 222–223
exteriors, isometric and plan oblique drawings, 131
exterior vegetation, delineation and rendering, 407–409
eye-level line, defined, 187
eye-level view, linear perspective drawing, 202–203

false horizon, downhill and uphill views, 209
felt-tipped markers, representational sketching, 45
field studies, drawing exercises (level one), 581
fine-line leadholder, 4
finished rendering, linear perspective drawing, 303
five-panel presentation formats, 542–546, 552–556
flat bevel scale, 18
flexible curve rule, described, 8
flexible panel presentation formats, 536–537, 547–551
floor plan. *See also* plan
alignment indications, 99
drawing steps, 96–97
orthogonal terminology, 90, 92
wall indications, 98
floorscape
floor plan alignment indications, 99
rendering, 384
floor surface material, delineation and rendering, 385
foam core board, illustration board, 16
focal point, representational sketching, 72
folding plane line, orthogonal view, 89
foreground, travel sketching, 79
foreground trees, delineation and rendering, 404
foreshortened lines, orthographic and paraline drawing, 116
foreshortening
convergence and, linear perspective drawing, 185
orthogonal terminology, 90
form, value language, 374
formal/spatial diagrams, conceptual diagramming and sketching, 441
formats. *See* presentation formats
45 degree diagonal line
orthogonal view, 89
plan obliques, orthographic and paraline drawing, 148
station point placement and, one-point perspective, linear perspective drawing, 224
four-panel presentation formats, 532–535, 538–541
four-point perspective, vertical circles, 284
freehand drawing, drawing exercises (level one), 577
French curves, 8–9
frontal elevation plane, orthogonal terminology, 88
front elevation, orthogonal terminology, 87
furniture
delineation and rendering, 394–395
plan oblique accessories, delineation and rendering, 412

geometric shapes
descriptive geometry, 116
representational sketching, 39, 70

geometric shapes *(cont'd)*
tool drawing of, 12–13
gesture drawing
drawing exercises (level two), 642–645
representational sketching, 62
glass
reflections
delineation and rendering, 414–415
glass box, orthogonal terminology, 88
glass reflection, delineation and rendering, 400–401, 414–415
glue guns, model-making, 17
glues, model-making, 17
graphic communications, presentation formats, 492
graphic conventions, drawing exercises (level one), 593–594
graphic diagram, 430
graphic scales, orthogonal terminology, 100
graphite pencils. *See* pencils
grid charts, linear perspective drawing, 246–247
grid format, presentation formats, 494–495
grids, one-point perspective, linear perspective drawing, 214–216
ground line
defined, 187
linear perspective drawing, 189
ground surface, delineation and rendering, 386–387

hand lettering
described, 28, 30–31
drawing exercises (level one), 589
overview, 25
hard surfaces, delineation and rendering, 383
hatching
delineation and rendering, glass reflection, 415
value scales and toning techniques, 378
hidden line, drawing of, 34, 35
historic neighborhood
drawing exercises (level two), 629–632
four-panel presentation formats, 532
horizon line
defined, 187
station point and, pictorial effect, 192
horizontal circles
linear perspective drawing, 287
perspective circles, 210–211
plan oblique, orthographic and paraline drawing, 144–145
horizontal measuring line, defined, 187
horizontal plan plane, orthogonal terminology, 88
human figures and form
delineation and rendering, 392–393
horizon line, 410–411
plan oblique accessories, 412
drawing exercises (level one), 578, 584, 602
representational sketching, 62–63
hybrid drawings, linear perspective drawing, 282–283

ideational drawing, 460–461
illustration board, described, 16
image, orthogonal terminology, 88
image quality, representational sketching, 81
inclined surfaces, shadow, 346–348
incremental growth, plan obliques, 154–155
inks, technical pens, 6
interiors
isometric and plan oblique drawings, 131
isometric drawing construction, 137
office method
one-point perspective, linear perspective drawing, 213
two-point perspective, linear perspective drawing, 262–265
interior vegetation, delineation and rendering, 406–407
intersecting surfaces, perspective shadows, 327
invisible line, drawing of, 34, 35
isometric circle construction, orthographic and paraline drawing, 142
isometric drawings
defined, 115
drawing exercises (level one), 595, 597, 598
drawing exercises (level two), 633, 635
multiview and single-view drawings, 128–129
orthographic and paraline drawing, 136–137
plan oblique drawings compared, 131
types of, compared, orthographic and paraline drawing, 127
isometric paraline shadows, light, shade, and shadow, 322–323
isometric projection system, compared, orthographic and paraline drawing, 126

knives, model-making, 17

labeling, orthogonal terminology, 104–105
latitude, solar angle, 310
Lawson Perspective Charts, 246–247
leads. *See also* pencils
line type and line weight, 32
representational sketching, 50, 52–55
sketching, 42–43
lettering, 23–31. *See also* line types
computer-generated, 29
drawing exercises (level one), 589
hand lettering, 28, 30–31
overview, 25
typefaces, 26–27
light, shade, and shadow, 305–365. *See also* shadow
canopy, colonnade, and arcade shadows, 336–337
concepts in, 309
curvilinear forms, 315
curvilinear surfaces, 349
cylindrical forms and niches, 342
drawing exercises (level one), 575, 584, 591, 610–611
drawing exercises (level two), 626, 627
elevation, 345, 350–351
elevation view shadows, 316
historical significance, 308
inclined surfaces, 346–348
isometric paraline shadows, 322–323
manually casted and digital shadows, 360–361
niches, 342–343
nonoverlapping shadows, 338
overhang shadows
perforated, 335
solid, 334
overlapping shadows, 339
overview, 305–307
paraline shadows, 356–357
perspective shadows
computer imaging, 362–363
of dormers and overhangs, 358–359
intersecting surfaces, 327
perspective shades and, 328–331
on surfaces, 332–333
vanishing points, 326
plan and elevation, 345
plan oblique paraline shadows, 324–325
plan view, 317, 354
projection, using corresponding points, 344
recessions and protrusions, 343
rectilinear forms, 314
section, 355
shadow intensity, on receding surfaces, 321
shadow principles, 312–313
site plans and roofs, 352–353
sketches and renderings, 364–365
solar angle diagrams, 310–311
stairway shadows, 340–341
still lifes, 61
lighting (delineation and rendering), 418–419
artificial, 418
natural, 419
light rays, defined, 309
light source, shadow, 309
light studies, design section, 102
linear perspective drawing, 181–303
assembly drawing, 281
bird's-eye perspective, 202–203, 266–269
building examples, 267
cityscapes, 268
plan oblique, 269
underside view and, 271
circles, 210–211
horizontal, 287
vertical, 284–286
cone of vision, 188, 189
convergence and foreshortening, 185
cues, 186
diagonal vanishing points, 254
diminution and overlapping, 184
distortion, 188, 196–197
downhill and uphill views, 208–209
drawing exercises (level one), 581, 602–609, 614–615, 623
drawing exercises (level two), 627–628, 633, 635, 636–637, 638
exploded perspective, 280
eye-level view, 202–203
finished rendering, 303
glossary, 187
grid charts, 246–247

hybrid drawings, 282–283
looking down, 275
looking up, 274
looking up and looking down, 272–273
measuring points and oblique lines, 256–257
midpoint and perspective field of view, 255
multiple vanishing points (office method), 234–235
multiplying, dividing, and transferring, 242–245
direct measurement, 243
dividing with diagonal, 251
multiplying by measuring, 245
multiplying by measuring plus diagonal, 249
multiplying with diagonal, 250
parallel transfer, 244
projected depth using diagonals, 252–253
transferring with diagonal, 248
noncircular curvilinear forms, 288–289
object/picture plane relationship (office method), 236–237
oblique vanishing points, 238–241
one-point perspective, 198, 200–201
from above, 204–205
from below, 206–207
exterior grid example, 222–223
grids, 214–216
interiors (office method), 213
plan/elevation (office method), 212
plan perspective, 220–221
section views, 217–219
simplified one-point, 226–229
station point placement and 45 degree diagonal lines, 224
station point variability, 225
overview, 181–183
perspective field, 188, 189
pictorial effect, 192–195
orientation change, 193
picture plane, 194
station point, 195
station point and horizon line, 192
picture plane, 189, 190–191
reflections, 290–297
drawing exercises (level one), 604–605
physics of, 290
vertical reflecting surfaces, 295
water, 293, 297
wet pavement, 296
three-point perspective, 276–279
two-point perspective, 199–201
application, 233
interiors (office method), 262–265
plan/elevation (office method), 230–232, 262
scale establishment in, 258–261
underside view, 270–271
view development, 298–302
worm's-eye view, 202–203
line of sight
defined, 187
linear perspective drawing, 189
line quality, line types and, 36
line types, 23, 32–37. *See also* lettering
architectural observation sketching, 56
drawing exercises (level one), 590
emphasis, 37
line quality and, 36
line weight and, 32, 36
representational sketching, 52–55
use of, 33–35
value language, 377
line weight, line type and, 32
location plan, orthogonal terminology, 101
longitude, solar angle, 310
longitudinal section
drawing exercises (level one), 591
orthogonal terminology, 90, 103

manually casted shadow, digital shadows compared, 360–361
markers, representational sketching, 44–45
materials symbols
delineation and rendering, 402–403
elevation material, delineation and rendering, 390–391
measuring point
oblique lines and, linear perspective drawing, 256–257
one-point grid, 214–216
mechanical leadholder (clutch pencil), 4
medium, representational sketching, 57
metric scale, 21, 586
middle ground, travel sketching, 79
middleground trees, delineation and rendering, 405
midpoint
defined, 187
perspective field of view and, linear perspective drawing, 255
mixed-media conceptual rendering, 422–423
mixed-media drawing, drawing exercises (level one), 615
model-making tools, 17
multioblique combinations, orthographic and paraline drawing, 164–165
multiple vanishing points, linear perspective drawing, 234–235
multiplying
with diagonal, linear perspective drawing, 250
linear perspective drawing, 242–245
by measuring, multiplying, dividing, and transferring, linear perspective drawing, 245
by measuring plus diagonal, linear perspective drawing, 249
multiview drawings, single-view drawings and, 128–129. *See also* orthographic drawing

natural lighting, delineation and rendering (interiors), 419
negative space, drawing exercises (level one), 576
niches, light, shade, and shadow, 342–343
nodes, graphic diagram, 430–431
non-axial lines, axial lines and, orthographic and paraline drawing, 146
noncircular curvilinear forms, linear perspective drawing, 288–289
nonlinear forms, axial and non-axial lines, orthographic and paraline drawing, 146
nonoverlapping shadows, 338
nonvertical z-axis
plan obliques, orthographic and paraline drawing, 156–158
presentation formats, composite drawings, 511
stepped plan, plan obliques, orthographic and paraline drawing, 159
north arrows, orthogonal terminology, 100

object/picture plane relationship, linear perspective drawing, 236–237
oblique drawing(s)
axonometric drawings compared, 130
defined, 115
drawing exercises (level two), 633
measuring points and, linear perspective drawing, 256–257
multiview and single-view drawings, 128–129
orthographic and paraline drawing, 141
paraline, compared, orthographic and paraline drawing, 127
oblique projection system, compared, orthographic and paraline drawing, 126
oblique vanishing points, linear perspective drawing, 238–241
Olfa knife, model-making, 17
one-panel presentation formats, 520–523
one-point perspective
from above, linear perspective drawing, 204–205
from below, linear perspective drawing, 206–207
drawing exercises (level one), 606–609
exterior grid example, linear perspective drawing, 222–223
grids, linear perspective drawing, 214–216
linear perspective drawing, 198, 200–201
interiors (office method), 213
plan/elevation (office method), 212
plan perspective, linear perspective drawing, 220–221
section views, linear perspective drawing, 217–219
simplified one-point, linear perspective drawing, 226–229
station point placement and 45 degree diagonal lines, linear perspective drawing, 224
station point variability, linear perspective drawing, 225
opposite bevel scale, 18
orientation
north arrows, orthogonal terminology, 100
value language, 375, 376
orientation change, pictorial effect, 193
origamic architecture, drawing exercises (level two), 652
orthogonal, defined, 87
orthogonal projection, drawing exercises (level one), 592

orthogonal terminology, 85–111
  building section, 91
  composite sections, 105, 106–107
  design section, 102–103
  doors, 111
  drawing exercises (level one), 591–594, 614–615, 623
  drawing exercises (level two), 626, 633, 635, 636–637, 646–649
  elevation, 90
  elevation views, 92
  floorscape/floor plan alignment, 99
  labeling, 104–105
  north arrows and graphic scales, 100
  overview, 85–87
  plan, 90
  plan drawing steps, 96–97
  planes of projection, 88
  plan types, 92
  plan wall indications, 98
  reflected ceiling plan, 92, 95
  roof plan, 92, 94
  section, 90
  section types, 92
  site plan, 101
  stairways, 108–109
  views, 89
  windows, 110
orthographic drawing, defined, 115
orthographic and paraline drawing, 113–179, 125
  axes addition, 147
  axial and non-axial lines, 146
  axonometric and obliques compared, 130
  block visualization sketches, 121–123
  composite drawings, 153, 499
  definitions, 115
  drawing exercises (level one), 595–599
  drawing exercises (level two), 625, 626, 627–628, 633, 634, 635, 636–637, 638
  drawing types compared, 127
  dual-axes and tri-axes angles, 151
  element axonometric, 169–171
    expanded view, 170
    exploded view, 171
  elevation obliques
    building examples, 160–161
    compared, 132–133
    expanded, 172–173
    use of, 162–163
  expanded view, 167
  exploded isometric, 168
  exploded views
    generally, 166
    oblique simultaneous, 179
  frontal elevation oblique, 134–135
  isometric and plan oblique drawings, 131
  isometric circle construction, 142
  isometric drawing construction, 136–137
  multioblique combinations, 164–165
  multiview and single-view drawings, 128–129
  oblique construction, 141
  orthographic views, 125
  overview, 113–114
  paraline circle construction, 143
  plan obliques, 148–150
    construction, 139–140
    horizontal circle construction, 144–145
    incremental growth, 154–155
    measurements, 138
    nonvertical z-axis, 156–158
    nonvertical z-axis stepped plan, 159
  point view, edge view, and true shape, 117
  projection systems compared, 126
  section cuts, combining of, 152
  six-view drawings, 124
  six-view visualization sketches, 118–119
  true-length and foreshortened lines, 116
  up and down views (simultaneous), 175, 177–178
  upviews, 173–174
  upviews as dimetrics and isometrics, 176
  visualization sketches, 120
orthographic perspective cues, 186
orthographic projection
  defined, 88
  systems compared, orthographic and paraline drawing, 126
overhang shadows
  perforated, 335
  perspective shadows, 358–359
  solid, 334
overlapping, diminution and, linear perspective drawing, 184
overlapping shadows, 339
overlays, described, 13

panorama, drawing exercises (level one), 580
paraline drawing(s). *See also* orthographic and paraline drawing
  axonometric, compared, 127
  circle construction, 143
  defined, 115
  drawing exercises (level one), 599
  drawing exercises (level two), 633
  oblique, compared, 127
paraline perspective cues, 186
paraline shadows, 356–357
  isometric, light, shade, and shadow, 322–323
  plan oblique, light, shade, and shadow, 324–325
parallel roller rule, described, 14
parallel shadow lines, inclined surfaces, 348
parallel transfer, multiplying, dividing, and transferring, linear perspective drawing, 244
partì diagram, conceptual diagramming and sketching, 445
pastels, representational sketching, 59
pencils, 4–5. *See also* leads
  graphite, 4
  line type and line weight, 32
  representational sketching, 42–43
  sharpening and use of, 5
  use of, 11
pencil strokes, representational sketching, 50
pen and ink rendering, 420–421
pens, representational sketching, 44–45
pen strokes, representational sketching, 51, 52
perpendicular lines, orthogonal terminology, 88
perspective(s)
  cars, delineation and rendering, 397
  defined, 183
  drawing types compared, orthographic and paraline drawing, 127
perspective drawing. *See* linear perspective drawing
perspective field
  linear perspective drawing, 188, 189
  midpoint and, linear perspective drawing, 255
perspective projection system, compared, orthographic and paraline drawing, 126
perspective sections
  drawing exercises (level one), 606–609
  interiors, one-point perspective, 213, 217–219
perspective shades, perspective shadows and, 328–331
perspective shadows
  computer imaging, 362–363
  of dormers and overhangs, 358–359
  intersecting surfaces, 327
  perspective shades and, 328–331
  on surfaces, 332–333
  vanishing points, 326
phase diagram, conceptual diagramming and sketching, 451
pictorial effect, 192–195
  composite sections, orthogonal terminology, 107
  orientation change, 193
  picture plane, 194
  station point, 195
  station point and horizon line, 192
pictorial symbols, site diagrams, 438
picture plane
  defined, 187
  linear perspective drawing, 189, 190–191
  object/picture plane relationship (office method), linear perspective drawing, 236–237
  orthogonal terminology, 88
  perspective shadows and shades, 328
  pictorial effect, 194
plan
  alignment indications, 99
  cars, delineation and rendering, 396
  composite drawings, presentation formats, 508, 509
  defined, 90
  drawing exercises (level one), 593
  drawing steps, orthogonal terminology, 96–97
  shadow, 345
  two-point perspective, linear perspective drawing, 230–232
  types of, orthogonal terminology, 92
  unfolded plan/elevation, presentation formats, 505
plan diagram, conceptual diagramming and sketching, 444–445
planes of projection, orthogonal terminology, 88

plan oblique
accessories (delineation and rendering), 412–413
furniture and human figures, 412
trees, 413
axonometric and obliques compared, 130
bird's-eye perspective, linear perspective drawing, 269
composite drawings, presentation formats, 513
drawing exercises (level one), 597, 599, 600–602, 615
horizontal circle construction, orthographic and paraline drawing, 144–145
incremental growth, orthographic and paraline drawing, 154–155
isometric drawings compared, 131
measurements, orthographic and paraline drawing, 138
nonvertical z-axis, orthographic and paraline drawing, 156–158
nonvertical z-axis stepped plan, orthographic and paraline drawing, 159
orthographic and paraline drawing, 139–140, 148–150
paraline shadows, light, shade, and shadow, 324–325
sketch diagram, conceptual diagramming and sketching, 448–449
plan perspective
interiors, one-point perspective, 213
one-point perspective, linear perspective drawing, 220–221
plan view
shadows, 317
shadow within, 354
plan wall indications, orthogonal terminology, 98
plastic film, tracing paper, 16
point convergence, drawing types compared, orthographic and paraline drawing, 127
point view, orthographic and paraline drawing, 117
polished surfaces, reflections, delineation and rendering, 416–417
positive space, drawing exercises (level one), 576
presentation formats, 489–570
composite drawings, 496–519
building theme, 512
nonvertical z-axis drawing, 511
plan, section, and reflected ceiling plan, 507
plan and elevation oblique, 513
plan/elevation/details, 508
plan/section/elevation/details, 509
section and elevation, 506
superimposed, 516–517
transmetric drawings, 510
transoblique drawings, 514–515
unfolded composite elevations, 504
unfolded plan/elevation, 505
drawing exercises (level one), 621–623
drawing exercises (level two), 624, 629–632, 653–654
exploded view, 570
five-panel, 542–546, 552–556
flexible panel, 536–537, 547–551
four-panel, 532–535, 538–541
graphic communications, 492
grid format, 494–495
one-panel, 520–523
overview, 489–491
six-panel, 557–568
three-panel, 529–531
two-panel, 524–528
virtual buildings, 569
wall presentations, 493
presentation typography, lettering, 27
pressure transfer lettering, 26
primary contour, delineation and rendering, 372
profile elevation plane, orthogonal terminology, 88
profiling, value language, 377
projected depth, using diagonals, linear perspective drawing, 252–253
projection, using corresponding points, light, shade, and shadow, 344
projection systems, compared, orthographic and paraline drawing, 126
projector ray, defined, 88
proportion, sighting, 41
protractor, described, 8
protrusions, light, shade, and shadow, 343

rapid rule scale, 18
razor saw, model-making, 17
receding surfaces, shadow intensity on, 321
recessions, light, shade, and shadow, 343
rectilinear forms, light, shade, and shadow, 314
reflected ceiling plan
composite plan, section and, presentation formats, 507
orthogonal terminology, 92, 95
reflections
delineation and rendering, 398–401
glass, 400–401, 414–415
polished surfaces, 416–417
water, 398–399
linear perspective drawing, 290–297
drawing exercises (level one), 604–605
physics of, 290
vertical reflecting surfaces, 295
water, 293, 297
wet pavement, 296
relationship diagrams, 440
rendering. *See also* delineation and rendering
defined, 369
drawing exercises (level one), 612–614
shadows in, 364–365
representational sketching, 39–83
architectural observation sketching, 56
ballpoint pens and felt-tipped markers, 45
blind contour drawing, 64–65
blocking out and construction lines, 48–49
buildings, 70–73
cars, 68–69
conceptual sketches, 81
contour drawing, 63
drawing exercises (level one), 575–581, 584
drawing exercises (level two), 636–637, 646–649
finished sketches, 58
gesture drawing, 62
medium, 57
overview, 39–41
pencils, 42–43
pencil strokes, 50
pens and markers, 44–45
pen strokes, 51
sighting, 46–47
still lifes, 60–61
stroke character, 52–55, 59
study sketches, 82–83
travel sketching, 72, 74–80, 82, 83
trees, 66–67
roof(s), site plans and, shadow, 352–353
roof plan
multiview and single-view drawings, 129
orthogonal terminology, 92, 94
rubber cement, model-making, 17

sandpaper block, 5
sans serif type, 26
scale
establishment of, two-point perspective drawing, 258–261
graphic, orthogonal terminology, 100
scales, 18–21, 585–586
sciagraphy, 308–309
scribbing, 378–379
secondary contour, delineation and rendering, 372
section
composite drawings, presentation formats, 509
composite plan, section, and reflected ceiling plan, presentation formats, 507
composite section and elevation, presentation formats, 506
diagrams, sketched, conceptual diagramming and sketching, 446
drawing exercises (level two), 633
labeling, 104–105
orthogonal terminology, 87, 90
perspective
drawing exercises (level one), 606–609
interiors, one-point perspective, 213, 217–219
one-point perspective, linear perspective drawing, 217–219
shadow within, 355
types of, orthogonal terminology, 92
sectional elevation, design section, orthogonal terminology, 103
section arrows, orthogonal terminology, 92
section cuts, combining of, orthographic and paraline drawing, 152
serif type, 26
shade, defined, 309. *See also* light, shade, and shadow
shade line, curvilinear forms, 315
shadow. *See also* light, shade, and shadow
canopy, colonnade, and arcade shadows, 336–337

shadow *(cont'd)*
concepts in, 309
curvilinear surfaces, 349
defined, 309
drawing exercises (level one), 610–611
elevation, 345, 350–351
inclined surfaces, 346–348
intensity of, on receding surfaces, 321
manually casted and digital shadows, 360–361
nonoverlapping, 338
overlapping, 339
paraline shadows, 356–357
perforated overhang, 335
perspective shadows
computer imaging, 362–363
of dormers and overhangs, 358–359
intersecting surfaces, 327
on surfaces, 332–333
vanishing points, 326
plan and elevation, 345
plan view, 354
principles, 312–313
section, 355
site plans and roofs, 352–353
sketches and renderings, 364–365
solid overhang, 334
stairway, 340–341
value language, 375
shadow line
curvilinear forms, 315
defined, 309
shape (configuration), still lifes, representational sketching, 61
sharpening, graphite pencils, 5
side elevation, orthogonal terminology, 87
sighting
proportion, 41
representational sketching, 46–47
simplified one-point perspective, linear perspective drawing, 226–229
simultaneous oblique exploded views, 179
simultaneous up and down views, 175, 177–178
single-view drawings, multiview drawings and, 128–129. *See also* paraline drawing(s)
singular forms combined, light, shade, and shadow, 317–320
site analysis diagrams, drawing exercises (level one), 620
site diagrams, conceptual diagramming and sketching, 438–439
site plan
multiview and single-view drawings, 129
orthogonal terminology, 101
roofs and, shadow, 352–353
site section, orthogonal terminology, 92
site topography, contour drawing, 9
six-panel presentation formats, 557–568
60 degree axes angles, plan obliques, orthographic and paraline drawing, 149–150
six-view drawings, 124
six-view visualization sketches, 118–119
sketchbook, 465
sketches, renderings and, shadow, 364–365
sketching. *See* conceptual diagramming and sketching; representational sketching
sketching pencils and papers, 42–43
sketchpad, 464
soft surfaces, delineation and rendering, 382
solar angle diagrams, 310–311
solstice, defined, 310
space usage, graphic diagram, 430–431
spatial profiling, delineation and rendering, 373
stairway, orthogonal terminology, 108–109
stairway shadows, 340–341
station point
defined, 187
horizon line and, pictorial effect, 192
linear perspective drawing, 189, 191
pictorial effect, 195
variability
45 degree diagonal lines and, one-point perspective, 224
one-point perspective, linear perspective drawing, 225
stenciled lettering, 25
stepped plan nonvertical z-axis, plan obliques, orthographic and paraline drawing, 159
still lifes
drawing exercises (level one), 579
representational sketching, 60–61
stippling, 378
stroke character, 52–55, 59
study sketches, 82–83
sun, shade, and shadow, value language, 376–377
superimposed composite drawings, presentation formats, 516–517
surfaces
drawing exercises (level one), 595
hard, delineation and rendering, 383
polished, reflections, delineation and rendering, 416–417
soft, delineation and rendering, 382
symbol(s)
conceptual diagramming and sketching, 430–436
generally, 430–431
three-dimensional diagrams, 435
two-dimensional diagrams, 433–434
usage, 432
defined, 431
elevation material, delineation and rendering, 390–391
materials, delineation and rendering, 402–403
symbolic language, defined, 431

tangent arc, 13
technical pens, 6
templates, 13
tertiary contour, delineation and rendering, 372
texture
drawing exercises (level one), 579
value language, 374
30 degree/60 degree axes angles, plan obliques, 149–150
30 degree/60 degree shortcut
oblique lines, measuring points and, linear perspective drawing, 257
two-point perspective, scale establishment in, 260
3-D diagrams
digital, conceptual diagramming and sketching, 452–459
symbols, 435
3-D modeling
conceptual diagramming and sketching, 482–487
drawing exercises (level one), 623
drawing exercises (level two), 650–651, 652
sketch models in real space, 450, 484
three-panel presentation formats, 529–531
three-point perspective, 276–279
thumbnail sketches, 462–463
tilted circle, perspective circles, 211
tone, drawing exercises (level one), 579
toning techniques, value scales, 378–379
tools, 1–21
care of, 1
cleaning and erasing aids, 7
compass, 10
divider, 10
drawing boards, 3
drawing exercises (level one), 585–588
drawing exercises (level two), 646–649
drawing table, 3
illustration board, 16
model-making, 17
parallel roller rule, 14
pencils, 4–5, 32, 42–43
pens and markers, 44–45
scales, 18–21
sketchpad, 464
technical pens, 6
templates, 13
tracing paper, 16
triangles, T-squares, and French curves, 8, 9
use of, 11–13
workstation setup, 15
tracing boards, described, 16
tracing paper
described, 16
sketching, 42
transferring
with diagonal, linear perspective drawing, 248
linear perspective drawing, 242–245
parallel transfer, linear perspective drawing, 244
transformative understanding, 429
transmetric drawings, presentation formats, composite drawings, 510
transoblique drawings, presentation formats, composite drawings, 510, 514–515
transparaline drawing
multiview and single-view drawings, 128–129
presentation formats, composite drawings, 510
travel sketching, 72, 74–80, 82, 83
trees, 388. *See also* vegetation
foreground, 404
middleground, 405
perspective drawing, 389
in plan, 380–381

plan oblique accessories, 413
representational sketching, 66–67
triangle
described, 8
use of, 11–12
triangular scale, 18
tri-axes angles, dual-axes angles and, 151
trimetric drawings
defined, 115
types of, compared, orthographic and paraline drawing, 127
true height, linear perspective drawing, 191, 195
true-length lines, orthographic and paraline drawing, 116
true shape
axonometric and obliques compared, 130
elevation obliques compared, 132–133
orthogonal terminology, 90
orthographic and paraline drawing, 117
true shape plan obliques, isometric and plan oblique drawings, 131
true size
axonometric and obliques compared, 130
elevation obliques compared, 132–133
T-square
described, 8
use of, 11–12
twelve-point perspective
horizontal circles, 287
vertical circles, 286
two-dimensional diagrams, symbols, 433–434
two-panel presentation formats, 524–528
two-point perspective
application, linear perspective drawing, 233
drawing exercises (level one), 602–603
linear perspective drawing, 199–201
plan/elevation (office method), linear perspective drawing, 230–232
scale establishment in, linear perspective drawing, 258–261
typefaces, lettering, 26–27
typography, lettering, 25
underlays, described, 13
underside view, linear perspective drawing, 270–271
unfolded composite elevations, presentation formats, 504
unfolded plan/elevation, presentation formats, 505
up and down views (simultaneous), orthographic and paraline drawing, 175, 177–178
uphill and downhill views, linear perspective drawing, 208–209
upviews. *See also* worm's-eye view
as dimetrics and isometrics, orthographic and paraline drawing, 176
orthographic and paraline drawing, 173–174
upward convergence, looking up, 274, 276
utility knives, model-making, 17

value grading techniques
drawing exercises (level one), 579
value scales, delineation and rendering, 371
value language
generally, 374–377
sun, shade, and shadow, 376–377
value of lines, defined, 370
value scales
toning techniques, 378–379
value grading techniques, 371
value study, representational sketching, 59
value types, delineation and rendering, 370
vanishing point(s)
defined, 187
drawing exercises (level one), 610–611
perspective shadows, 326
variable station point, two-point perspective, 263
vegetation. *See also* trees
drawing exercises (level one), 602
exterior, delineation and rendering, 407–409
interior, delineation and rendering, 406–407
vehicles. *See* cars
vellums, tracing paper, 16
vertical circle
linear perspective drawing, 284–286
perspective circles, 210–211
vertical measuring line
defined, 187
object/picture plane relationship, 236–237
vertical reflecting surface, 295
vertical section diagram, 443
vertical vanishing point, 274
view, orthogonal terminology, 89
view development, linear perspective drawing, 298–302
vignette, sketching, 53
virtual buildings, presentation formats, 569
visible line, drawing of, 34, 35
visualization, 429
visualization sketches
orthographic and paraline drawing, 120
six-view, orthographic and paraline drawing, 118–119
visual rays, defined, 126
visual thinking, 429

wall presentations, presentation formats, 493
water reflection
delineation and rendering, 398–399
linear perspective drawing, 293, 297
wet pavement reflection, linear perspective drawing, 296
windows
design section, orthogonal terminology, 102
orthogonal terminology, 110
woodcase graphite drawing pencils, 4
workstation setup, 15
worm's-eye view. *See also* upviews
downhill and uphill views, linear perspective drawing, 208–209
linear perspective drawing, 202–203
one-point perspective from below, linear perspective drawing, 206–207
plan, multiview and single-view drawings, 128–129
plan perspectives, interiors, one-point perspective, 213

X-Acto knife, model-making, 17

zoning, graphic diagram, 430–431

Contributor Index

Aalto, Alvar, 288, 461
Abacus Architects & Planners, 166
Abbott, Laurie, 44
Adams, William, 324, 350
Adelaide University, South Australia, 603, 606
Adèle Naudé Santos and Associates, Architects, 434, 435, 526
A. Epstein & Sons, Architects, 252
Agrest, Diana, 341
Aguila, Ron, 152
Akkach, Samer, 603
Alianza Architectos/An Architect's Alliance, 356
Allan, Sarah, 516
Allen, Gerald, 359
Allen, Harbinson & Associates, 353
Allen, Keith, 176
American Museum of Natural History, 200
Ames, Anthony, 99, 135, 219, 345
Amey, Frederic, 495
Ando, Tadao, 190, 355, 616
Andrews University, 634
Arata Isozaki & Associates, Architects, 292, 307
The Architects Collaborative (TAC), 268
Architectural Network, 58, 432, 433, 486
Architectural Research Office, 636–637
Architekturb¸ro Bolles-Wilson + Partner, 162, 171
ARC-ID Corporation, 293
Armas, Karla, 447
Arp, Jim, 268
Arquitectonica International Corporation, 160, 352
Arthur Cotton Moore/Associates, 446
Arup, Ove, 211, 336
Ateaga, P., 650
Atelier Henri Gaudin, 288
Audrain, Paul, 277
Aukland, University of, New Zealand, 583
Aulenti, Gaetana, 394, 395
Avila, Manuel, 265, 301, 302, 405

Bacino, Richard, 213
Backen Arrigoni & Ross, Inc, 25, 285, 389, 395
Baglietto, E., 480
Baker, David, 144, 199, 272, 334, 391, 518
Barcelon & Jang, 66
Barmina, Masha, 459, 484
Barney Davidge Associates, 388
Barton Myers Associates, Architects, 392
Baushke, Michael, 165, 508
Beissenger, Melanie, 653
Belian, Lisa, 538, 557
Benedict, William R., 186, 188, 242, 244, 248, 251, 254, 257, 258, 260, 286, 370, 372, 374, 376
Benner, Scott, 523
Berekoff, Suzanne, 649
Betts, Hobart D., 144
B FIVE STUDIO, 383
Biddle, Bethany, 592
Binder, Rebecca L., 167, 179, 205, 206, 504, 506, 507
Birkets, Gunnar, 102, 434
Biron, Jonathan, 495
Blanchard, Brian, 64
Bohigas, Oriol, 157
Bohlin Cywinski Jackson Architects, 173, 218
Bonar, James, 326
Botta, Mario, 104, 155, 466
Bottom, Christine, 593, 600
Bowman, Obie G., 380
Brandt, Jonathan, 61, 579, 580, 581
Brian Healy Architects, 164, 307
Brown, Terry, 149
Bruckner & Partner, 233
Bulaj, Marek, 346, 347
Bull Stockwell & Allen Architects, 214

Cagri, Behan, 74
Calatrava, Santiago, 116
California, University of, at Berkeley, 448, 449
California College of Arts and Crafts, 591
California Polytechnic State University School of Architecture, San Luis Obispo, California, 37, 186, 188, 242, 244, 248, 251, 254, 257, 258, 260, 286, 370, 372, 374, 376
Cappleman, Owen, 63
Carlos Diniz Associates, 415
Carver, Cameron, 629
Castro, Noé, 339
Cathcart, James, 513
Catholic University of America School of Architecture & Planning, Washington, D. C., 342, 552
Caviedes, Andres, 650
Cavieres, C., 650
Cederna, Ann, 342
Cesar Pelli & Associates, 58, 59, 67, 272, 457
Chan, William W. P., 441, 452, 454, 479, 529, 640, 641
Chang, Leopoldo, 199
Chaw, Marcus, 205, 206, 208, 244, 284
Chen, Wenjie, 68, 69, 397
Chiang, Robin, 412
Chiarenza, Jonah, 617
Chile, University of, at Santiago, 650
Christ, Alan, 238
Chu, Ebby, 65
Chun/Ishimaru & Associates, 214, 295, 392, 417
Cigolle, Reid, 578
City College of San Francisco, 31, 51, 64, 65, 75, 119, 124, 146, 209, 336, 339, 438, 584, 597, 598, 602, 635
Clarke, Daniel, 628
Clark & Menefee, Architects, 99
Cleater, John, 569
Clyce, Amy, 525
Collins, Ryan, 60, 61
Columbia School of Architecture Planning and Preservation (CSAAP), 199, 202, 238, 262, 277
Compton, Christopher, 282
Concordia Architects, 149
Coolidge, Robert T., 167
The Cooper Union, 578
COOP HIMMELB(L)AU Architects, 206, 424, 425
CORE, 519
Couture, Lise Ann, 569
Cox Richardson Architects and Planners, 211
Cronin, Keith, 604
Croxton Collaborative Architects, 256
Crump, John, 145
Cuevas, Herbert, 388
Cullen, Gordon, 409
Cummins, Margaret, 247

David A. Harris, DHT^2 Architects & Planners, 143
David Baker Associates Architects, 144, 199, 272, 334, 391, 518
Davidge, Barney, 388
David Rockwood Architects & Associates, 197
Davies, Richard, 563
Davison, Dick, 480, 610, 611, 615, 628, 638
DeStefano & Partners, Architects, 302
DHT^2 Architects & Planners, 143
Diamante, Ed, 538
Diamond, A. J., 170, 176
Dierks, Vaughn, 494
Diniz, Carlos, 415
Dinkeloo, John, 290
Do, Thanh, 209

Dolezal, Doug, 491
Donoso, Mariana, 650
Doshi, B. V., 156
Dougherty & Doughterty, 157
Drewes + Strengearchitekten, 481, 547, 548, 550
Drury University, Springfield, Missouri, 618
Dunlop, Hank, 591
Dunnette, Lee, 194
Dziewulski, Mark, 604

Eames, Charles, 394
EDAW, 169
Edgeley, Peter, 275
ED2 International Architects, 380, 406
Egli, Erna, 146
Eisenman, Peter D., 265
Ellerbe-Becket, Inc., 137, 418
English, Mark David, 98, 150, 220, 221, 354, 459, 484, 509, 510, 512
Enquist, Philip, 448, 449
Erickson, Arthur, 467
Ernst, Chris, 119
Esfandiary, Iraj Yamin, 312
Evanusa, Stephen S., 378, 420
Evonuk, Walter, 484

Fabian, Edward K., 618
Farrell, Terry, 120, 321
Fehlman LaBarre Architects, 300, 411
Fernandez, Olallo L., 195
Ferriss, Hugh, 59
Fichten Soiferman Architects, 542
Fieldman, Michael, 108, 177, 322, 372
Figureras, Rosalino, 52
Fillat, Peter, 529
Fineman, Howard, 224
Finnen, D., 200
Fisher, Frederick, 164
Fisher-Friedman Associates, 46–47, 538
Fletcher, Sue, 603
Forster, Al, 69, 235, 298, 299, 300, 393, 410, 411
Foster and Partners, 137, 465, 477, 570
Fox Fowle Architects, 273
Frank Gehry Bentwood Collection, 394
Franklin D. Israel Design Associates, Inc., Architects, 516
Friedman, Rodney, 538
FTL Architects, 52
Fu, Ho Ching, 583
Fuksas, Massimiliano, 473
Fumihiko Maki and Associates, 156
Funk & Schr˚der Architekten, 240, 241

Gabellini Associates, 109
Gambrel, Steve, 197
Garofalo, Giancarlo, 154
Gaudi, Antonio, 52
Gaudin, Henri, 288
GBQC Architects, 218
Geering, Robert J., 538
Gehry, Frank O., 352, 394, 418, 464, 479
GGLO Architecture and Interior Design, 103
Gigli, Linda, 598
Gillam, Jim, 395
Gomez-Pimienta, Bernardo, 280
Goosen & Associates, Architects, 295
Gouws, Thomas, 520
Grand, Mark, 538

Graves, Michael, 291, 346, 347
Grealy, Jane, 409, 575
Group Four Architecture, 412
Grubbs, Christopher, 398, 399
Guedes, Amancio, 476
Gund, Graham, 260
Gunnar Birkerts and Associates, Inc., Architects, 102, 434
Gureckas, Vyt/CORE, 519
Gwathmey Siegel & Associates, Architects, 99, 145, 149, 307

Hadid, Zaha M., 271, 394, 456
Hadley, Marcia Gamble, 101
Hagge, Michael, 524, 525, 532, 621
Haggerton, Alysha, 60, 61
Hallet, Stanley I., 552
Halprin, Lawrence, 75, 76
Hamilton, Robert L., 51
Hamilton, Tod, 136, 137
Hamzah, Tengku Robert, 442
Handa, Kenzo, 440, 614
Hansman, Bob, 616
Harbinson, Jeffrey, 359
Hardy, Hugh, 56
Hariri & Hariri, Architects, 98, 166, 168, 396
Harris, David A., 143
Harris, Steven, 382, 392
Haskell, Kim, 160
Hasselman, Peter, 169
Haun, David, 515
Heald, David, 183
Healy, Brian, 164, 307
Hearn, Jason, 639
Hedges, Susan, 583
Heery International, Inc., 148
Heino Stamm Planungsb¸ro, 233
Heiser, Todd, 502
Heller & Manus Architects, 333
Hellmuth, Obata, and Kassalbuam, Architects, 150, 419
Henderer, Rod, 529
heneghan.peng.architects, 563
Hertzberger, Herman, 217
Hess, Armin, 424, 425
Hill, Donovan, 409
Hodgetts + Fung Design Associates, 436, 437
Hoeft, Jeff, 523
Hoffpauir, Stephan, 296, 297
Holl, Steven, 160, 317
Hollein, Hans, 105, 222, 468
Holt Hinshaw Pfau Jones Architecture, 343, 351
Honderick, Mark, 523
Horn, Richard, 406
Hornbeck, Donald, 538
Hostetler, Joanna, 146
House, Steven, 45, 76, 77, 83, 356
House + House, Architects, 150, 165, 354, 508, 509, 510, 512, 513, 514, 515
Howard, Dan, 538
Hsu, Melissa, 534, 535
Huang, Chilin, 504, 506, 507

Ichikawa, Noriko, 648
Idaho, University of, Moscow, 577, 589, 633, 634
Iida Archiship Studio, 232

I. M. Pei & Partners, 330
Inglese Architecture, 98, 220, 221, 363
Interface Architects, 400, 416
Ishimoto, Yasuhiro, 291, 307
Isozaki, Arata, 292, 307
Israel, Franklin D., 516

Jacobsen, Hugh Newell, 378, 383, 420
James Stirling Wilford and Associates, 101
James Wines/SITE, 254, 257, 589
Jennings, Jim, 283
Jennings, Maurcie, 198, 383, 388
Jennings, Star, 220, 221, 363
Jennings + Stout, Architects, 283
Jensen, Mark, 591
Jensen + Macy Architects, 172
Jones, Fay, 198, 383, 388
Jones, Partners, 281, 329, 331
Joubert, Ora, 151, 520
The J. Paul Getty Trust, 443
Jun Mitsui Associates, 457

Kandor Modelmakers, London, England, 563
Kanner, Stephen, 71, 81, 203, 210
Kanner Architects, 149, 203, 210
Ke, James, 75
Kellen, David, 383
Kennethpark Architecture, 263
Kensek, Karen, 534, 653
Kessler, William, 382
King, Jerome, 388
Kinkead, Jennifer, 238
Klein, Richard, 95
KMD, 486, 487
KMD/PD Architects in joint venture with the Architectural Network, 58, 432, 433, 486
Knight Architects Engineers Planners Inc., 301
Knoll, 125, 394
Koetter Kim & Associates, Inc, 218, 252, 393, 430
Kohn Pedersen Fox Associates, 21
Kong, Michael, 522
Korn, Kathryn, 52
Korth Sunseri Architects, 296
Kotas, Jeremy, 314, 315
Krueck & Sexton, Architects, 355
Kucher/Rutherford, Inc, 101
Kuit, Barbara, 456
Kurnadi, Theresia, 534, 535
Kurokawa, Kisho, 474, 475
Kuwabara Payne McKenna Blumberg Architects, 542
Kuwait University, 652

LaFoe, M., 457
Lai, Sin Jee, 606
Lam, Amaza Lai Cheng, 64
Lancuba, Daniella, 575
Laney College, Oakland, California, 310, 609, 627
Lawrence, Darlene, 447
Leary, James A., 261
Le Corbusier, 616
Leddy, Tanner, 337
Lee, Albert, 184, 348
Legoretta, Ricardo, 339, 439
Legoretta, Victor, 339, 439
Legoretta Arquitectos, 339, 439

Lenz, Eberhard, 308
Leong, Lawrence Ko, 67, 71, 75, 76, 78, 209, 422, 423, 487
Leong, Winnie T., 209
Lew, Ellen, 124
Lewis, Diane, 282
Liefhebber, Martin, 392
Lim, cj, 522
Lin, Maya, 616
Lin, Pershing C., 339
Lincer, Doug, 353
Liu, Ed, 522
Loli, George S., 72, 517
Lopez, Juan, 523
Lopez, Roger, 538
Los Angeles Community Design Center, 326
Louisiana, University of, Lafayette, 517
Lowing, Tom, 325
Lui, Marcus, 404, 406, 407, 421
Lum, Jerry W., 584
Lunn, Joshua, 538
Lupo, Frank, 101

Machado, Rudolfo, 219, 255
Mack, Mark, 164, 233
MacKay, David7, 157
Magallanes, Fernando, 576, 584
Mahgoub, Yasser, 652
Maki and Associates, 21
Man, Amy, 602
Marcus Lui & Associates, 404, 406, 407, 421
Martin, Dennis, 64, 65
Martin, George J., 552
Martinez/Wong Associates, 210
Martorell, Josep, 157
Maryland, University of, School of Architecture, 74
Matei, Corvin, 53, 55, 190, 401
Mayne, Thom, 516
MBM Arquitectes, 157
McGee, Mel, 204
McGinnis, Lois, 198
McGrath, Norman, 293
McLarand Vasquez Emsiek & Partners, 69
McLaughlin, Herbert, 487
McNeill, Barry, 198
Meier, Richard, 289, 338, 394, 402, 443, 525
Memphis, University of, 524, 525, 532, 621
Mendelsohn, Erich, 479
Mesiniaga, Menara, 442
Metz, Dan, 139, 143
Meyer, Richard Conway, 160
Michael Blakemore/Sandy & Babcock, Inc., 25
Michael Fieldman & Partners, 108, 177, 322, 372
Michelangelo, 206
Mickle, Peter, 282
Mies van der Rohe, Ludwig, 252, 355, 479
Miller, Kenneth E., 419
Miralles, Enric, 239
Missouri, University of, Columbia, 360, 361, 482, 483, 612, 623
Mitchell, Shawn, 577
Mitsui, Jun, 457
Moneo, José Rafael, 469
Montgomery, LaRaine Papa, 528, 613, 620, 629, 639
Moore, Arthur Cotton, 446
Moore, Charles, 44, 54, 67, 332
Moorehead, Gerald, 327
Moore Ruble Yudell, Architects, 298, 538, 557
Moran, Michael, 472
Morgan, Cort, 289
Morgan, William, 382
Morgan State University, 441, 452, 454, 455, 640, 641
Morishige, Ross, 538, 557
Moshe Safdie and Associates, Inc., 102
Moss, Eric Owen, 174, 207, 217
Muggioli, D., 650
Mujica, Jacquelyn, 119
Mullin, Daniel K., 577, 589, 633, 634
Murphy/Jahn Architects, 210, 252
Mussa, Hussain, 652
Mutlow, John V., 159, 169, 170, 178, 312, 357, 384, 497, 505, 511
Myers, Barton, 392

Nadine, Markova, 339
Nalley, Brigette, 388
Ng, Ellen W., 597
Niles, Edward R., 103
Nishimoto, Taeg, 239
Noble, Douglas, 534, 653
NORR Partnership LTD./NORR Health Care Design Group, 205
Norten, Enrique, 280
North Carolina, University of, Greensboro, 592, 593, 600
North Carolina State University, 576, 584
Nota, Dean, 104, 106, 129

O'Connor, James Mary, 538, 557
Office for Metropolitan Architecture (OMA), 160
Oles, Paul Stevenson, 256, 393, 400, 416
O'Neill, Megan, 616
OrdoÒez, Carlos, 280
Orime, Kaoru, 538
Orona, Daniel, 339
Ota, Noboru, 569
Othman, Wan, 43
Owen, Christopher H. L., 293

Pappageorge Haymes Ltd., 139
Parker, Kelly, 623
Parker, Stephen W., 78, 80
Parnass, Jordan, 202
Patkau Architects, 105, 335
Pei, I. M., 194, 330
Pei Cobb Freed & Partners / Michael Macary Architects, 194, 393
Pelli, Cesar, 58, 59, 67, 272, 457
Pellowski, Tim, 529
Perkins & Will Architects, 201, 242, 243, 261, 265, 350, 370
Perry, Dean, Rogers, and Partners: Architects, 139
Peters, Robert W., 356
Pezdek, Rebecca, 584
Pfeifer, Florian, 569
Piano, Renzo, 336, 480
Pietilä, Raili, 460, 461, 478
Pietilä, Reima, 460, 461
PinÛs, Carme, 239
Poey, J., 414
Pollack, Sydney, 479
Polshek Partnership Architects, 200
Portland State University, 647, 648, 649
Predock, Antoine, 264, 413
Prix, Wolf D., 206
Projects International, 398

Queensland University of Technology, Brisbane, Australia, 575
Quigley, Rob Wellington, 164, 205, 470, 471

Rafael ViÒoly Architects, 57, 70
Ragle, Ben, 37
Raili and Reima Pietilä, Architects, 460, 461
Raney, Vincent, 407
Rantonnen, Johanna, 41
Rashid, Hani, 569
Rawn, William, 175
Ream, James, 381
Refuerzo, Ben J., 429
Reichel, Robert, 452
Reynolds, Robert J., 293
Richard Meier & Partners, Architects, 289, 338, 394, 402, 443, 525
Richard Rogers Partnership, Architects, 142, 464
Richardson, Matthew, 454, 455
Richters, Christian, 481
Rico, G. Nino, 154
Rietveld, R., 217, 475
Riken Yamamoto & Field Shop, Architects, 349
Rios, Alberto, 644
Roberts, Charles, 15, 441, 640, 641
Roberts, Stephen, 353
Robinson Mills & Williams, Architects, 69, 299
Roche, Kevin, 290
Rockacy, Jason, 620
Rockwood, David, 197
Rogers, Richard, 142, 464
Ron, Ruth, 569
Ronaszegi, Arpad Daniel, 226, 228, 278, 279, 325, 634
Rosenthal, Steve, 330
Rossi, Aldo, 316, 433, 464
Rowen, Daniel, 101
Royal College of Art, Kensington Gore, London, England, 450
Royalty, Sarah, 649
R-2 ARCH Designers/Researchers, 429
Rubins, John, 576
Ruble, John, 538, 557
Rudolph, Paul, 198

Saavedra, Jose, 650
Saber, G. Lawrence, 407
Sager, Janet, 538, 557
Sanaksenaho, Matti, 385
Sanders, Roosevelt, 379
Sandy & Babcock, Inc., 78, 369, 386
San Francisco, City College of, 31, 51, 64, 65, 75, 119, 124, 146, 209, 336, 339, 438, 584, 597, 598, 602, 635
Santos, Adèle Naudé, 434, 435, 526
Savannah College of Art and Design, Georgia, 145, 226, 228, 379, 495, 502, 503, 528, 620, 629, 639

Schaller, Thomas Wells, 236
Schellenbach, Kevin, 503
Schiffhauer, Robert, 62
Schmitt, Donald, 170, 176
Schoenbrodt, Birgit, 569
Schreier, John, 266
Schwartz, David M., 337
Selkirk, Anthea, 532
Sengstacken, Corey, 623
Seow, Timothy, 394
Sepulveda, J., 650
Serero, David, 277, 569
Shanley, Monica, 349
Shay, James, 158, 203, 267, 378
Shelby, Michael Patrick, 198
Shen, Lily, 438
Shepley, Rutan and Coolidge, Archtects, 185
Shiga, Richard H., 647, 649
Shigeru Ban Architects, 313
Shimahara, Craig, 538
Silvetti, Jorge, 219, 255
Simon, Mark, 332
Simon Martin-Vegue Winkelstein Moris, Interior Design, 152, 153, 407
Simpson Gumpertz & Heger, Inc., 404
Skidmore, Owings & Merrill, 333, 399
Smythe, Sonia, 648
Sobieraj, Jennifer, 65
Solomon, Daniel, 381
Solomon, Tommy, 524
Solomon & Bauer Architects, Inc., 148
Southern California, University of, 534, 653
Southern University, Baton Rouge, Louisiana, 145
Stackel, Greg, 262
Stacy, Maytum, 337
Stanton, Margaret, 74
State University of New York - Buffalo, 644
Stegeman, Mark, 361
Stern, Robert A. M., 300, 390
Steven Harris & Associates, 382, 392
Steven Holl Architects, 160, 317
Stringer, Leigh, 70
Studio 8 Architects, 522
Suhaimi, Mohd Fadzir Mohd, 496
Sverdrup Facilities, 218
The SWA Group, 328, 330, 380, 387
Swiczinsky, Helmut, 206
Szasz, Peter, 285, 389

Takamatsu, Shin, 342
Takenaka Corporation, 67
Tamano & Chaw Residential Design, 94
Tanner Leddy Maytum Stacy Architects, 403
Tapley/Lunow Architects, 327
Tauke, Beth, 644
Tchoban, Sergei, 364, 365
Temple, Steve, 590, 592, 593, 594, 600, 618, 622, 626, 635
TEN Arquitectos, 280
Terry Farrell & Partners, Architects, 120, 321
Texas, University of, at Arlington, 53, 55, 190, 198, 289, 353, 401, 447, 523
Texas, University of, at Austin, 63, 119, 147, 498, 599, 625
Texas, University of, at San Antonio, 590, 592, 593, 594, 600, 618, 622, 626, 635
Texas A&M University, 48–49, 50, 61, 62, 64, 65, 73, 79, 276, 308, 579, 580, 581, 610, 611, 615, 628, 638
Thirteenth Street Architects, Inc., 320
Thistlethwaite, David R., 438
Thompson, Ian, 151
Tigerman, Stanley, 82, 444
Tigerman McCurry Architects, 87, 429
Tishman Realty & Construction Company, 291
Tod Williams Billie Tsien Architects, 422, 423, 472, 536, 537
Toy, Steven, 321
Tran, Tony, 538
Tremain, Dale, 137
T. R. Hamzah & Yeang, Architects, 311, 442
Tripp, Andrew, 578
Troughton McAslan Architects, 134
Tsai, Richard, 379
Tsao & McKown Architects, 384
Tsien, Billie, 422, 423, 472, 536, 537
Tsui, Kwok Gorran, 147, 245, 336, 498, 599, 625
Turman, Thomas L., 310, 609, 627
Turnbull, William, 392
Tuttle, Mark, 529

Uddin, Mohammed Saleh, 145, 379, 482, 483, 495, 502, 503, 612, 623
Ungers, Oswald Mathias, 267
University of Aukland, New Zealand, 583
University of California at Berkeley, 448, 449
University of Chile at Santiago, 650
University of Idaho - Moscow, 577, 589, 633, 634
University of Louisiana - Lafayette, 517
University of Maryland School of Architecture, 74
University of Memphis, 524, 525, 532, 621
University of Missouri - Columbia, 360, 361, 482, 483, 612, 623
University of North Carolina - Greensboro, 592, 593, 600
University of Southern California School of Architecture, 534, 653
University of Texas at Arlington School of Architecture, 53, 55, 190, 198, 289, 353, 401, 447, 523
University of Texas at Austin School of Architecture, 63, 119, 147, 498, 599, 625
University of Texas at San Antonio, 590, 592, 593, 594, 600, 618, 622, 626, 635
University of Virginia School of Architecture, 41, 74, 197
Vega, Roberto, 613
Venturi, Robert, 29
Venturi, Scott Brown and Associates, Inc., 27, 32, 83, 89, 208, 462, 476
Verderber, Stephen F., 429
Villalon, Tomas, 650
ViÒoly, Rafael, 70, 225
Virginia, University of, School of Architecture, 41, 74, 197
Vitols Associates, 236
Von Mauer, Andrew, 325
Voorsanger, Bartholomew, 134
Vrooman, Dik, 276

Waltemath, Joan, 578
Ware Malcomb, 68
Waronska, Monika, 275
Washington University School of Architecture, St. Louis, Missouri, 43, 52, 70, 137, 174, 208, 213, 224, 237, 238, 286, 308, 379, 491, 494, 496, 576, 616, 617
Wei, Wesley, 223
Wenger, Stacey, 208
Wenjie Studio, 68, 69, 276
Whitcombe, Nancy, 518
Whitehurst, Bill, 291
Wight & Company/Fitch-Fitzgerald, Inc., 95
Wilford, Duke, 286
Wilford, James Stirling, 101
William Kessler and Associates, 382
William Rawn Associates, Architects, Inc., 175
Williams, Tod, 422, 423, 472, 536, 537
William Turnbull Associates, 382
Willis, Beverly, 414
Wilson, Christopher, 612
Wines, James, 254, 257, 589
Winkeljohn, Bradford, 202
Wong, John L., 387
Wong, Kam, 31
Wong, Marci Li, 538
Woo, George C. T., 353
Woo, Kyu Sung, 148
Woodcock, David G., 50, 73, 79
Woods, Lebbeus, 653
Wright, Frank Lloyd, 81, 183, 406

Xie, William, 339

Yarinsky, Adam, 636–637
Yeang, Kenneth, 442
Yee, Rendow, 116, 185, 228, 290, 309, 467
Yeomans, Ed, 308
Yim, Charles, 343, 413
Yu, Fu Jordy, 450
Yudell, Buzz, 538, 557

Zaha Hadid Architects, 271, 394, 456
Zainul, A. Zainie, 237
Zanetta, Alo, 466
Zendarski, Art, 418
Zycinska-White, Katarzyna, 621

Web Site Contributor Index

Almazyed, S. 15-18
Al Saqali 15-18
Avila, Manuel 11-9, 11-11
11-12, 11-13
Aziz, Michael 14-10, 14-11
Baker, Shane 11-62
Beesley, Philip 11-62
Bekerman, G. 11-69
Benedict, William R. A8 to A15
Binder, Rebecca L. 11-65
Bligh Voller Neild 11-6
Chan, William W.P 11-63, 14-12, 14-13,
15-31
Chen, Wenjie 11-23
Cheng, Jia Huan A1
Cleater, John 11-67
Corbusier, le 11-69
Couture, Lise Ann 11-67
Cutler, James 15-25 to 15-29
Davies, Richard 11-56
Davison, Dick 11-46
Dharmadhikari, Kirti 11-47
Duncan, Don 15-31
Dunlop, Hank 15-12
Edgeley, Peter 11-2, 11-8, 11-10,
11-42, 11-44
English, Mark 11-57, 11-58, 11-59
Feiss, Eric 14-86 to 14-106
Fuksas, Massimiliano 12-2 to 12-9
Gagosian Gallery 11-17
Graves, Michael & Associates 11-19, 11-20
Grealy, Jane 11-4, 11-5, 11-6
11-7, 11-26, 11-40
15-15, 15-16
Gribou, Julius M. 11-47
Guymer, Bailey 11-7
Hadid, Zaha 12-28 to 12-32
Hallberg, Amanda 15-29
Heilbronn and Partners 11-4
heneghan. peng 11-56
Holl, Steven 11-35, 11-36, 11-70
Houlihan, Patrick 15-32
Huot, Kieth 15-24
Huang, Chang Shan 11-24, 11-25
11-38
Inglese Architecture 11-57, 11-58
11-59
Jennings, Star 11-57, 11-58
11-59
Jensen, Mark 15-12
Jonsson, Gudmundur 11-18, 11-39
11-66
Jules, Chris A1
Kandor Modelmakers 11-56
Kahn, Louis 11-67
Langendorf, Nancy 15-32
Leiou, Manipay 11-49
Linehan, Nicholas 15-31
Loli, George S. 11-14, 11-15
11-30, 15-18, 15-20
Lucien La Grange & Associates 11-9
Luescher, Andreas 14-4
Mahgoub, Yasser 15-22, 15-23
Maffei, Jerry 11-48
Manley II, Eugene 14-15 to 14-45
Marshall, Peter 11-62
Martinez, Regina 11-63
Maya Lin Studio 11-17
Meier, Richard 11-69
Miranda, Valerian 11-3, 11-47, 11-48
11-49, 11-51
Mullin, Daniel K. 15-25 to 15-29
Munsell, Albert H. 11-70
Neiman, Bennett Robert 11-63, 11-64
OMA & Koolhaas, Rem 11-52, 11-53
Ota, Noboru 11-67
Palushock, Jr., Edward P. 15-24
Pei, I.M. 11-30, 11-69
Pelli, Cesar 11-18, 11-69
11-68
Pfeifer, Florian 11-67
Predock, Antoine Chapter 13
Rashid, Hani 11-67
Ratner, Barbara Worth 11-28, 11-37
Rice, Chris 15-31
Rogers-Varland, Julie 14-3
Ron, Ruth 11-67
Ronaszegi, Arpad 14-3
Rossi, Aldo 11-34
Saarinen, Eero 11-69
Safdie, Moshe 11-21, 11-22
11-23
Sakairi, Mitsuru 11-51
Schoenbrodt, Birgit 11-67
Seebohm, Thomas 11-62
Serero, David 11-67
Shanghai Modern Architectural Design Co. Ltd. A1
Sight Corporation 11-68
Temple, Steve 15-30
Solomon, Daniel 11-55
Thayer, Tim 11-17
Total Project Group 11-5
Tsui, Kwok Gorran 15-15
Venturi Scott Brown 11-54
Vinoly, Rafael 12-10 to 12-27
Ware, Stanton 11-48
Watkins, Cliff 14-46 to 14-85
Wenjie Studio 11-23
White, Kenneth 11-47
Wildman, Heather Figley 14-5 to 14-9
Wojtyra, Magda 11-62
Wright, Frank Lloyd 11-69
Yim, Charles A1